The Blue Helmets

A Review of United Nations Peace-keeping

Third edition

The Blue Helmets

A Review of United Nations Peace-keeping

Third edition

Published by the United Nations
Department of Public Information
New York, NY 10017

Editor's note

This third edition of *The Blue Helmets* is based on publicly available United Nations documents and information materials. The footnotes refer the reader to these documents and materials, which may be consulted at libraries around the world designated as depository libraries for United Nations documents. Many of the documents may also be accessed through the United Nations home page on the World Wide Web at "http://www.un.org". The symbol S/.... refers to documents of the Security Council; A/.... to documents of the General Assembly. Most other symbols, for example SG/SM/.... or REF/..., refer to press releases issued by the Department of Public Information.

Please note that the names of countries used in this book are, in most cases, those in use at the time the event occurred. References to "the Secretary-General" should be read in the context of the time-period under review and the terms of office of the respective Secretaries-General: Trygve Lie (from February 1946); Dag Hammarskjöld (from April 1953); U Thant (from November 1961); Kurt Waldheim (from January 1972); Javier Pérez de Cuéllar (from January 1982); Boutros Boutros-Ghali (from January 1992).

Copyright © 1996 United Nations
The Blue Helmets
A Review of United Nations Peace-keeping
ISBN 92-1-100611-2
United Nations publication
Sales No. E.96.I.14
Printed on recycled paper by the United Nations Reproduction Section,
 New York

Peace-keeping operations past and present

1. UNTSO
United Nations Truce Supervision Organization
June 1948–

2. UNMOGIP
United Nations Military Observer Group in India and Pakistan
January 1949–

3. UNEF I
First United Nations Emergency Force
November 1956–June 1967

4. UNOGIL
United Nations Observation Group in Lebanon
June 1958–December 1958

5. ONUC
United Nations Operation in the Congo
July 1960–June 1964

6. UNSF
United Nations Security Force in West New Guinea (West Irian)
October 1962–April 1963

7. UNYOM
United Nations Yemen Observation Mission
July 1963–September 1964

8. UNFICYP
United Nations Peace-keeping Force in Cyprus
March 1964–

9. DOMREP
Mission of the Representative of the Secretary-General in the Dominican Republic
May 1965–October 1966

10. UNIPOM
United Nations India-Pakistan Observation Mission
September 1965–March 1966

11. UNEF II
Second United Nations Emergency Force
October 1973–July 1979

12. UNDOF
United Nations Disengagement Observer Force
June 1974–

13. UNIFIL
United Nations Interim Force in Lebanon
March 1978—

14. UNGOMAP
United Nations Good Offices Mission in Afghanistan and Pakistan
May 1988–March 1990

15. UNIIMOG
United Nations Iran-Iraq Military Observer Group
August 1988–February 1991

16. UNAVEM I
United Nations Angola Verification Mission I
January 1989–May 1991

17. UNTAG
United Nations Transition Assistance Group
April 1989–March 1990

18. ONUCA
United Nations Observer Group in Central America
November 1989–January 1992

19. UNIKOM
United Nations Iraq-Kuwait Observation Mission
April 1991—

20. UNAVEM II
United Nations Angola Verification Mission II
May 1991–February 1995

21. ONUSAL
United Nations Observer Mission in El Salvador
July 1991–April 1995

22. MINURSO
United Nations Mission for the Referendum in Western Sahara
April 1991—

23. UNAMIC
United Nations Advance Mission in Cambodia
October 1991–March 1992

24. UNPROFOR
United Nations Protection Force
March 1992–December 1995

25. UNTAC
United Nations Transitional Authority in Cambodia
March 1992–September 1993

26. UNOSOM I
United Nations Operation in Somalia I
April 1992–March 1993

27. ONUMOZ
United Nations Operation in Mozambique
December 1992–December 1994

28. UNOSOM II
United Nations Operation in Somalia II
March 1993–March 1995

29. UNOMUR
United Nations Observer Mission Uganda-Rwanda
June 1993–September 1994

30. UNOMIG
United Nations Observer Mission in Georgia
August 1993–

31. UNOMIL
United Nations Observer Mission in Liberia
September 1993–

32. UNMIH
United Nations Mission in Haiti
September 1993–June 1996

33. UNAMIR
United Nations Assistance Mission for Rwanda
October 1993–March 1996

34. UNASOG
United Nations Aouzou Strip Observer Group
May 1994–June 1994

35. UNMOT
United Nations Mission of Observers in Tajikistan
December 1994–

36. UNAVEM III
United Nations Angola Verification Mission III
February 1995–

37. UNCRO
United Nations Confidence Restoration Operation in Croatia
March 1995–January 1996

38. UNPREDEP
United Nations Preventive Deployment Force
March 1995–

39. UNMIBH
United Nations Mission in Bosnia and Herzegovina
December 1995–

40. UNTAES
United Nations Transitional Administration for Eastern Slavonia,
Baranja and Western Sirmium
January 1996–

41. UNMOP
United Nations Mission of Observers in Prevlaka
January 1996–

United Nations peace-keeping operations as of June 1996

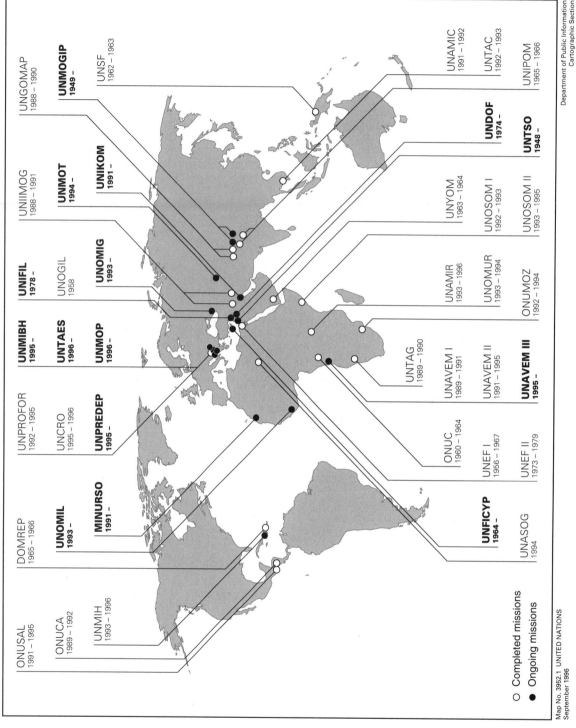

ONUSAL
1991 – 1995

ONUCA
1989 – 1992

UNMIH
1993 – 1996

DOMREP
1965 – 1966

UNOMIL
1993 –

MINURSO
1991 –

UNPROFOR
1992 – 1995

UNCRO
1995 – 1996

UNPREDEP
1995 –

UNMIBH
1995 –

UNTAES
1996 –

UNMOP
1996 –

UNIIMOG
1988 – 1991

UNMOT
1994 –

UNIKOM
1991 –

UNIFIL
1978 –

UNOGIL
1958

UNOMIG
1993 –

UNGOMAP
1988 – 1990

UNMOGIP
1949 –

UNSF
1962 – 1963

UNAMIC
1991 – 1992

UNTAC
1992 – 1993

UNIPOM
1965 – 1966

UNDOF
1974 –

UNTSO
1948 –

UNYOM
1963 – 1964

UNOSOM I
1992 – 1993

UNOSOM II
1993 – 1995

UNAMIR
1993 – 1996

UNOMUR
1993 – 1994

ONUMOZ
1992 – 1994

UNTAG
1989 – 1990

UNAVEM I
1989 – 1991

UNAVEM II
1991 – 1995

UNAVEM III
1995 –

ONUC
1960 – 1964

UNEF I
1956 – 1967

UNEF II
1973 – 1979

UNFICYP
1964 –

UNASOG
1994

○ Completed missions
● Ongoing missions

Department of Public Information
Cartographic Section

Map No. 3952.1 UNITED NATIONS
September 1996

Contents

List of maps and charts

List of acronyms

ADL	Armistice Demarcation Line
AFL	Armed Forces of Liberia
AHT	Advance Humanitarian Team
ANC	Armée nationale congolaise
ANKI	National Army of Independent Kampuchea
ARENA	Alianza Republicana Nacionalista
ARSK	Krajina Serb army
ASEAN	Association of South East Asian Nations
BLDP	Buddhist Liberal Democratic Party
CBM	confidence-building measure
CCF	Cease-fire Commission
CCFADM	Joint Commission for the Formation of the Mozambican Defence Force
CD	Convergencia Democrática
CIAV	International Support and Verification Commission
CIS	Commonwealth of Independent States
CIVPOL	United Nations Civilian Police (component)
CIVS	International Verification and Follow-up Commission
CMAC	Cambodian Mine Action Centre
CMLO	Chief Military Liaison Officer
CMO	Chief Military Observer
COMPOL	Police Commission
COPAZ	National Commission for the Consolidation of Peace
CORE	Reintegration Commission
CPAF	Cambodian People's Armed Forces
CPP	Cambodian People's Party
CRC	Central Revolutionary Council
CSC	Supervisory and Monitoring Commission
CSCE	Conference on Security and Cooperation in Europe
DMZ	demilitarized zone
DOMREP	Mission of the Representative of the Secretary-General in the Dominican Republic
DTA	Democratic Turnhalle Alliance
ECE	Economic Commission for Europe
ECO	Economic Cooperation Organization
ECOMOG	ECOWAS Monitoring Group
ECOWAS	Economic Community of West African States
EIMAC	Egypt-Israel Mixed Armistice Commission
EOM	Electoral Observation Mission
EST	Eastern Standard Time
FAA	Angolan Armed Forces
FADH	Haitian Armed Forces
FADM	Mozambican Defence Force
FALA	Forças Armadas de Libertação de Angola
FAO	Food and Agriculture Organization
FAPLA	Forças Armadas Populares de Libertação de Angola
FLEC/FAC	Frente de Libertação do Enclave de Cabinda/Forças Armadas de Cabinda
FMLN	Frente Farabundo Martí para la Liberación Nacional
FNLA	Frente Nacional de Libertação de Angola
FRAPH	Front révolutionnaire pour l'avancement et le progrès en Haiti
FRELIMO	Frente da Libertação de Moçambique
Frente POLISARIO	Popular Front for the Liberation of Saguia el-Hamra and Rio de Oro

FUNCINPEC	United National Front for an Independent, Neutral, Peaceful and Cooperative Cambodia
GNPC	Interim Joint Administration
HABITAT	United Nations Centre for Human Settlement
HRFOR	Human Rights Field Operation in Rwanda
HV	Croatian Army
HVO	Croat Defence Council
IAEA	International Atomic Energy Agency
IAPF	Inter-American Peace Force
IASC	Inter-Agency Standing Committee
ICA	Israeli-controlled area
ICFY	International Conference on the Former Yugoslavia
ICITAP	International Criminal Investigative Training Assistance Programme
ICJ	International Court of Justice
ICORC	International Committee on the Reconstruction of Cambodia
ICRC	International Committee of the Red Cross
IDF	Israel Defence Forces
IFOR	Implementation Force
IGNU	Interim Government of National Unity
ILMAC	Israel-Lebanon Mixed Armistice Commission
IMF	International Monetary Fund
IOM	International Organization for Migration
IPTF	United Nations International Police Task Force
ISMAC	Israel-Syria Mixed Armistice Commission
JMC	Joint Monitoring Commission
JNA	Yugoslav People's Army
JPMC	Joint Political-Military Commission
JVMC	Joint Verification and Monitoring Commission
KPNLAF	Khmer People's National Liberation Armed Forces
KPNLF	Khmer People's Liberation Front
LAS	League of Arab States
LCY	League of Communists of Yugoslavia
LDF	Lofa Defence Force
LNC	Liberian National Conference
LNM	Lebanese National Movement
LPC	Liberian Peace Council
MAC	Mixed Armistice Commission
MAC	Movimiento Auténtico Cristiano
MCTU	Mine Clearance Training Unit
MFO	Multinational Force and Observers
MICIVIH	International Civilian Mission in Haiti
MINUGUA	United Nations Mission for the Verification of Human Rights in Guatemala
MINURSO	United Nations Mission for the Referendum in Western Sahara
MINUSAL	United Nations Mission in El Salvador
MMWG	mixed military working group
MNF	multinational force
MNR	Movimiento Nacional Revolucionaria
MPLA	Movimento Popular de Libertação de Angola
MSN	Movimiento de Solidaridad Nacional
NAC	North Atlantic Council
NADK	National Army of Democratic Kampuchea
NATO	North Atlantic Treaty Organization
NEC	National Electoral Council
NGO	non-governmental organization
NMOG	Neutral Military Observer Group

NPFL	National Patriotic Front of Liberia
OAS	Organization of American States
OAU	Organization of African Unity
ODD	Observer Detachment Damascus
OGB	Observer Group Beirut
OGE	Observer Group Egypt
OGG	Observer Group Golan
OGL	Observer Group Lebanon
OIC	Organization of the Islamic Conference
ONUC	United Nations Operation in the Congo
ONUCA	United Nations Observer Group in Central America
ONUMOZ	United Nations Operation in Mozambique
ONUSAL	United Nations Observer Mission in El Salvador
ONUVEH	United Nations Observer Group for the Verification of the Elections in Haiti
ONUVEN	United Nations Observer Mission to verify the electoral process in Nicaragua
OSCE	Organization for Security and Cooperation in Europe
OSGA	Office of the Secretary-General in Afghanistan
OSGAP	Office of the Secretary-General in Afghanistan and Pakistan
PAHO	Pan American Health Organization
PANALU	Parti national lumumbiste
PAT	Auxiliary Transitory Police
PCN	Partido Conciliación Nacional
PDC	Partido Demócrata Cristiano
PDK	Party of Democratic Kampuchea
PLO	Palestine Liberation Organization
PMU	Partido Movimiento de Unidad
PNC	National Civil Police
RENAMO	Resistência Nacional Moçambicana
RGF	Rwandese Government Forces
RPA	Rwandese Patriotic Army
RPF	Rwandese Patriotic Front
RRF	rapid reaction force
SACB	Somali Aid Coordination Body
SADF	South Africa Defence Force
SADR	"Saharan Arab Democratic Republic"
SAMO	Somali Africans Muki Organization
SDA	Somali Democratic Alliance
SDF	Self-Defence Forces
SDM	Somali Democratic Movement
SLA	"South Lebanon Army"
SNA	Somali National Alliance
SNC	Supreme National Council
SNDU	Somali National Democratic Union
SNF	Somali National Front
SNM	Somali National Movement
SNU	Somali National Union
SOC	State of Cambodia
SOFA	Status of Forces Agreement
SPM	Somali Patriotic Movement
SSA	Somali Salvation Alliance
SSDF	Somali Salvation Democratic Front
SSNM	Southern Somali National Movement
SWAPO	South West Africa People's Organization
SWAPOL	South West Africa Police
SWATF	South West Africa Territorial Force

TNC	Transitional National Council
UCAH	United Nations Humanitarian Assistance Coordination Unit
UD	União Democrática
ULIMO	United Liberation Movement of Liberia for Democracy
UNAMIC	United Nations Advance Mission in Cambodia
UNAMIR	United Nations Assistance Mission for Rwanda
UNASOG	United Nations Aouzou Strip Observer Group
UNAVEM I	United Nations Angola Verification Mission I
UNAVEM II	United Nations Angola Verification Mission II
UNAVEM III	United Nations Angola Verification Mission III
UNCIP	United Nations Commission for India and Pakistan
UNCIVPOL	United Nations Civilian Police
UNCRO	United Nations Confidence Restoration Operation in Croatia
UNCTAD	United Nations Conference on Trade and Development
UNDOF	United Nations Disengagement Observer Force
UNDP	United Nations Development Programme
UNEF I	First United Nations Emergency Force
UNEF II	Second United Nations Emergency Force
UNESCO	United Nations Educational, Scientific and Cultural Organization
UNFICYP	United Nations Peace-keeping Force in Cyprus
UNFPA	United Nations Population Fund
UNGOMAP	United Nations Good Offices Mission in Afghanistan and Pakistan
UNHCR	Office of the United Nations High Commissioner for Refugees
UNICEF	United Nations Children's Fund
UNIDO	United Nations Industrial Development Organization
UNIFIL	United Nations Interim Force in Lebanon
UNIIMOG	United Nations Iran-Iraq Military Observer Group
UNIKOM	United Nations Iraq-Kuwait Observation Mission
UNIPOM	United Nations India-Pakistan Observation Mission
UNITA	União Nacional para a Independência Total de Angola
UNITAF	Unified Task Force
UNLOB	United Nations Liaison Office in Beirut
UNMIBH	United Nations Mission in Bosnia and Herzegovina
UNMIH	United Nations Mission in Haiti
UNMO	United Nations military observer
UNMOGIP	United Nations Military Observer Group in India and Pakistan
UNMOP	United Nations Mission of Observers in Prevlaka
UNMOT	United Nations Mission of Observers in Tajikistan
UNOCHA	United Nations Office for the Coordination of Humanitarian Assistance to Afghanistan
UNOGIL	United Nations Observation Group in Lebanon
UNOHAC	United Nations Office for Humanitarian Assistance Coordination
UNOMIG	United Nations Observer Mission in Georgia
UNOMIL	United Nations Observer Mission in Liberia
UNOMUR	United Nations Observer Mission Uganda-Rwanda
UNOSOM I	United Nations Operation in Somalia I
UNOSOM II	United Nations Operation in Somalia II
UNPA	United Nations Protected Area
UNPF-HQ	United Nations Peace Forces headquarters
UNPF	United Nations Peace Forces
UNPREDEP	United Nations Preventive Deployment Force
UNPROFOR	United Nations Protection Force
UNREO	United Nations Rwanda Emergency Office
UNRWA	United Nations Relief and Works Agency for Palestine Refugees in the Near East

UNSCOL	United Nations Special Coordinator's Office
UNSF	United Nations Security Force in West New Guinea (West Irian)
UNTAC	United Nations Transitional Authority in Cambodia
UNTAES	United Nations Transitional Administration for Eastern Slavonia, Baranja and Western Sirmium
UNTAG	United Nations Transition Assistance Group
UNTEA	United Nations Temporary Executive Authority
UNTSO	United Nations Truce Supervision Organization
UNV	United Nations Volunteer
UNYOM	United Nations Yemen Observation Mission
USC	United Somali Congress
USF	United Somali Front
USP	United Somali Party
UTU	United Tajik Opposition
VOA	Voice of America
WFP	World Food Programme
WHO	World Health Organization

Part I
Introduction

Introduction

The concept of peace-keeping

The concept of peace-keeping evolved soon after the United Nations was founded, born of necessity as a largely improvised response to the times. Serving under the United Nations flag, military personnel from many countries have carried out tasks which range from monitoring cease-fire arrangements while peace agreements were being hammered out to assisting troop withdrawals, providing buffer zones between opposing forces and helping implement final settlements to conflicts. With the end of the cold war, peace-keeping operations have grown in number and complexity.

As of June 1996, the United Nations has mounted 41 peace-keeping operations. Fifteen were established in the 40 years between 1948 and 1988; the other 26 have all been set up since 1989. More than 750,000 military and civilian personnel have taken part. Whatever the requirements reflected in a specific mandate, peace-keeping operations are always dynamic and demanding. Peace-keepers have been deployed in both favourable and unfavourable conditions: in circumstances where political good will exists and relative stability has been achieved after the parties have entered into negotiated settlements, and in situations where the climate is one of continued hostility, obstruction and danger.

Most early peace-keeping operations responded to inter-State conflict. In recent years, however, peace-keeping has more often addressed conflicts within States, sometimes where Governments no longer function. Soldiers serving under United Nations command as peace-keeping observers or troops, wearing their familiar blue berets or blue helmets, are being joined by increasing numbers of civilians. Together, they have been given ever more challenging mandates. They have helped promote national reconciliation and respect for human rights, and organized and monitored elections. Humanitarian tasks have been brought within the purview of peace-keeping. Peace-keepers have even participated in the reconstruction of State institutions. As peace-keeping has evolved, the international community has had to confront the issue of State sovereignty and to rethink the United Nations role in securing peace in what has come to be known as the "failed State".

This third edition of *The Blue Helmets* includes a comprehensive account of this new type, or "second generation", of peace-keeping. Along with "classical" peace-keeping activities such as those in Cyprus, the Middle East and South Asia, this edition covers a range of United Nations efforts in the field, from helping to negotiate and implement a complex peace agreement in Angola to protecting the delivery of humanitarian assistance in Bosnia and Herzegovina and in Somalia; from preparing and conducting elections in Cambodia to maintaining a secure and stable environment for a return to democracy in Haiti.

The price of keeping the peace has, at times, been very high. The United Nations and the entire international community owe a debt of gratitude to peace-keeping personnel, military and civilian, for their courage and sacrifice in confronting challenges to peace and security. More than 1,400 peace-keepers have died while serving under the United Nations flag, more than half in the last four years. The United Nations is proud of what they have achieved. Their sacrifices have brought new hope to many millions of people as conflict-ridden societies have made the difficult transition to peace.

Peace-keeping has done enormous good, but peace-keeping missions have not always achieved all their goals. Lessons have been learned — sometimes the hard way. When United Nations operations have been assigned peace-keeping and peace-enforcement roles without receiving military resources, equipment and logistic support commensurate to these tasks, peace-keepers have suffered heavy strains and pressures and the United Nations itself has come under attack. When mandates have been unclear or when necessary political and material support has been lacking, United Nations operations have found themselves hamstrung. Member States, United Nations bodies, the Secretariat's Department of Peace-keeping Operations and various multilateral organizations are intensifying their efforts to define more clearly the principles of peace-keeping, including guidelines on how and when to act. I encourage these contributions as a means of developing greater international cooperation and of improving the capability of the Organization for a quick and decisive response to threats to the peace. We must apply the lessons learned from setbacks and build upon our successes in order to deal more effectively with, and strive to prevent, the outbreak of conflict. The United Nations will then be in a better position to direct its full attention to long-term assistance aimed at development and democratization.

Peace-keeping in the cold-war years

The first purpose of the United Nations enunciated in the Charter is to maintain international peace and security. The term "peace-keeping", however, does not appear in that document, and the very concept — non-violent use of military force to preserve peace — differs fundamentally from the enforcement action described in the Charter. The organ to which the Charter assigns primary responsibility for maintaining international peace and security is the Security Council. Implementation of the Charter's relevant provisions relies largely on the unanimous consent of the Council's permanent members — China, France, the Russian Federation (originally the Soviet Union), the United Kingdom and the United States. Until the end of the cold war, the frequent lack of unanimity among them meant that these provisions were never fully given effect. The Council therefore resorted to other measures to promote and preserve peace, such as the good offices of the Secretary-General, conciliation, mediation — and peace-keeping.

The first observer operation, the United Nations Truce Supervision Organization (UNTSO), was set up by the Security Council in the Middle East in 1948. The unarmed observers of UNTSO continue to this day to help stabilize the region.

Peace-keeping operations have also been authorized by the General Assembly. In 1956, paralysis in the Security Council led the General Assembly to set up the first United Nations peace-keeping force, the United Nations Emergency Force (UNEF I). UNEF provided the model for classical peace-keeping, which requires the consent of the protagonists, impartiality on the part of United Nations forces, and resort to arms only in self-defence. The immediate objective of this classical form of peace-keeping is to facilitate conditions for a more comprehensive peace agreement. It offers combatants an opportunity to stop fighting and to explore fresh avenues towards peace, and allows time for the Secretary-General or other ne-gotiators to do their work. Peace-keeping is not a perfect instrument, but it has repeatedly proved its utility as a means for securing peace, as recognized by the award of the Nobel Peace Prize in 1988 to United Nations peace-keepers.

New dilemmas

The easing of the East-West confrontation enhanced cooperation in the Security Council and provided opportunities to resolve long-standing conflicts. But the end of the cold war also saw other conflicts erupt, giving rise to fierce claims of sub-national identity based on ethnicity, religion, culture and language, which often resulted in armed conflict. Responding to the new political landscape, the international community turned to peace-keeping, which grew rapidly in size and scope. In January 1988, 11,121 military, police and civilian personnel were deployed in United Nations peace-keeping operations, and the annual budget for peace-keeping was $230.4 million. In December 1994, 77,783 personnel were deployed — the highest number to date — and annual United Nations peace-keeping expenditures reached $3.6 billion.

As numbers grew, so did the complexity of the situations confronting the Blue Helmets and the United Nations. Most difficult and arduous among them were challenges presented by "failed States" where governmental functions were suspended, the police and judiciary had collapsed, infrastructure destroyed and populations up-rooted. The breakdown of a supervening political authority in Rwanda, Somalia, Liberia and the former Yugoslavia, for example, led to crimes against humanity, mass killings, massive displacement of populations, general banditry and chaos. In the case of Rwanda, the result was genocide. In current conflicts, many combatants are not soldiers of regular armies but militias or groups of armed civilians — sometimes children — with little discipline and an ill-defined command structure. Civilians are the main targets, constituting some 90 per cent of casualties; about half of these, too, are children. In 1995, some 27.4 million people worldwide — including 14.5 million refugees, as well as internally displaced persons, returnees and others predominantly affected by conflict — were of direct concern to the United Nations High Commissioner for Refugees. At the end of 1995, the total number of internally displaced persons worldwide was estimated at between 35 million and 40 million.

The second generation

Second-generation peace-keeping operations are multifunctional, with political, humanitarian, social and economic components requiring civilian experts and relief specialists to work in parallel with soldiers. Objectives include helping the warring parties move from violent conflict towards political reconciliation, democratic consolidation and reconstruction. In Mozambique and El Salvador, the Blue Helmets and their civilian colleagues have, among other tasks, helped to regroup and demobilize combatants, destroy weapons, coordinate massive humanitarian assistance programmes and monitor human rights. Missions in Haiti, Somalia and Cambodia have been tasked with contributing to rebuilding a society's capacity to govern itself. Peace-keepers have trained new police, worked to reinstate judicial systems, overseen existing administrative structures; designed and supervised constitutional reforms; and organized, supervised or observed elections.

The United Nations, as a neutral intervening force and honest broker, remains an important factor in peace-keeping and confidence building. Maintaining neutrality, however, can present peace-keepers with a dilemma, especially when they confront situations in which civilians are victimized, or when the Blue Helmets themselves are attacked or killed. Combatants may attempt to play the United Nations off against opponents in order to gain advantage, or deny relief workers access to populations and confiscate relief supplies and equipment. Where governmental authority has broken down, there is a limit to United Nations action. Member States are reluctant to assume responsibility for maintaining law and order in another State, and the United Nations cannot impose a new political structure or new State institution. It is imperative that the United Nations and the international community integrate the relevant dimensions of these problems when developing a coherent vision, strategy and plan of action for responding to such situations.

An Agenda for Peace

On 31 January 1992, the Security Council met for the first time at the level of heads of State or Government to consider the new opportunities for international peace and security. At that meeting, the Council asked me for an "analysis and recommendations on ways of strengthening and making more efficient within the framework and provisions of the Charter the capacity of the United Nations for preventive diplomacy, for peacemaking and for peace-keeping".

In response, I submitted a report on 17 June 1992 entitled *An Agenda for Peace*,[1] followed by a supplement[2] to the report on 3 January 1995, which considered the vital role of the United Nations in pursuing and preserving peace. A central theme of this report is that the role of the United Nations must be to assist in a progression from conflict prevention, resolution and emergency assistance to reconstruction and rehabilitation, and then to economic and social development. Peace-keeping should be part of an integrated approach to peace-building, encompassing political, social, economic, humanitarian and human rights aspects. Peace-keeping must also be understood as one of many means available to the United Nations for the maintenance of international peace and security. Attention should be paid to developing and refining all the instruments for resolving disputes, for preventing disputes from escalating into conflicts, and for limiting the spread of conflicts once they occur.

Early warning mechanisms are among the instruments available to the United Nations in its efforts to prevent conflict. The United Nations Secretariat has significantly strengthened its capacity to monitor, analyse and assess political developments throughout the world and to detect impending crises. Its early-warning network takes account not only of threats of armed conflict but also of environmental hazards, the risk of nuclear accident, natural disasters, mass population movements, the threat of famine and the spread of disease.

Peacemaking instruments such as quiet diplomacy and preventive troop deployments can be used to build trust and constructive interaction among former enemies, and to shore up fragile peace. Disarmament, and increasingly "micro-disarmament" — which pertains to light weapons and millions of landmines, the chief killers in conflicts today — can be implemented in conjunction with almost all other United Nations peace activities, either on an agreed basis or in the context of coercive action.

Sanctions, including arms embargoes, can also be effective instruments to bring peace. Their purpose, however, must be to modify the behaviour of parties, not to punish them or to exact retribution. Sanctions, and particularly economic

---

[1]A/47/277-S/24111. See also *An Agenda for Peace*, Second Edition, Sales No.E.95.I.15. [2]A/50/60-S/1995/1. See also *An Agenda for Peace*, Second Edition, Sales No.E.95.I.15.

sanctions, are a blunt instrument that must be used with caution. They are often difficult to monitor and can have unintended effects. They also risk inflicting suffering on vulnerable populations without significantly affecting the behaviour of the political leaders they are intended to influence.

The United Nations capability to enforce peace remains largely undeveloped, despite Charter provisions to that effect. The United Nations has no standing army or forces of its own. The Security Council's Military Staff Committee has never undertaken the strategic direction of forces put at the disposal of the Council, as foreseen under the Charter. The Security Council has, nevertheless, authorized States to undertake enforcement action. Action of this type, such as that taken in the Korean peninsula in 1950 and against Iraq in 1991, while authorized by the United Nations, was not under United Nations command. The Security Council has also authorized Member States to use all necessary means to achieve specific goals in operations in Somalia, Rwanda and Haiti, separate from United Nations peace-keeping missions. In Bosnia and Herzegovina, the Security Council authorized Member States to act through a regional arrangement (the North Atlantic Treaty Organization) in support of United Nations peace-keepers.

Enforcement action, duly authorized by the Security Council, is greatly preferable to the unilateral use of force. Such action is, however, a double-edged sword. It offers the Organization a capacity not otherwise available but carries with it the risk of potential damage to the credibility and stature of the United Nations. Once the Security Council authorizes such interventions, States may claim international legitimacy and approval for measures not initially envisaged by the Council.

Peace-keeping and peace enforcement are distinct undertakings. Each can be effective in the appropriate circumstances. However, neither peace enforcement nor peace-keeping can eliminate the sources of conflict. Nations and communities themselves bear the responsibility for learning the arts of coexistence and appreciating the richness of diversity. They must devote sustained effort to promoting respect for fundamental principles of human rights and to developing national institutions capable of ensuring the economic and social welfare of all citizens. This process takes time and resources, but will ultimately help eradicate the root causes of war.

Successes and setbacks

To build peace systemically, United Nations peace-keepers have undertaken activities that address the needs of entire societies in crisis. United Nations operations have aided transitions to peace in Cambodia, El Salvador, Haiti, Mozambique and other countries, offering their people the possibility of development and stability. International assistance, supported by United Nations peace-keepers, defeated famine in Somalia. In the former Yugoslavia, the Blue Helmets helped save countless lives and, working with the humanitarian agencies of the United Nations system and non-governmental organizations, eased the suffering of millions.

There have also been setbacks, however. In Somalia, national reconciliation was not achieved. Faced with the refusal of the parties to resolve their differences peacefully, the international community concluded that the cost and burden of maintaining the United Nations Operation in Somalia could no longer be justified and withdrew the peace-keepers. In the former Yugoslavia, unceasing conflict, entrenched hostility, lack of commitment and an absence of good faith among the parties characterized the crisis. The vulnerability of lightly armed, widely dispersed peace-keepers was dramatically illustrated in Bosnia and Herzegovina, where Governments assigned to the United Nations the impossible task of serving as peace-keeper in the midst of war.

Peace-keeping operations are inherently risky, even when a cease-fire is in place and the parties to a conflict cooperate and have consented to the deployment. Cease-fire agreements have been broken. Combatants have failed to respect the international status of United Nations military and civilian personnel. In March 1993,[3] the Security Council demanded that States and other parties to conflicts take all possible steps to ensure the safety and security of United Nations forces and personnel. In particular, the Council said that in the absence of State authority it would consider measures appropriate to the circumstances to ensure that persons responsible for attacks and other acts of violence against United Nations forces and personnel were held accountable.

[3]S/25493.

Learning the limits

The United Nations cannot keep peace when there is no peace to keep. When fighting re-erupted in Angola in October 1992, the observation mission there had to be scaled back until diplomatic efforts by my Special Representative and other negotiators brought the peace process back on course. In Haiti, the United Nations peace-keeping mission was suspended until a separate, multinational enforcement operation authorized by the Security Council established a secure and stable environment. In Somalia, much more would have been accomplished had the leaders and factions committed themselves to ending their armed conflicts and pursuing political reconciliation. The United Nations can serve as catalyst, framework and support mechanism for parties to seek peace and can help when hostile factions are prepared to work towards this common goal. But viable political structures or institutions cannot be imposed from the outside. Ultimately, no instrument can bring about peace without the will of the parties to the conflict to achieve peace.

A decision to withdraw the Blue Helmets in the midst of a conflict is never an easy one. It is, however, an issue that has confronted the Organization with increasing frequency in recent years and demands further reflection. In the absence of a solution to intractable conflicts, and without ready alternatives to peace-keeping, the question remains: In time of conflict, can the United Nations and the international community abandon afflicted populations to their fate?

Towards a better peace-keeping

Effective United Nations peace-keeping requires the full consent and cooperation of the parties; United Nations peace-keepers must maintain their neutrality; they must have a clear and practicable mandate; and Member States must support them with the necessary human and financial resources. Fundamental questions must be addressed if peace-keepers are to be deployed in the service of the international community: What is the proper role of the United Nations in conflict situations? Is the Organization adequately equipped for the tasks assigned to it? Are Governments willing to maintain their support in the face of difficulties? The point of departure in the search for answers must be the recognition that the United Nations is only as effective as the Member States allow it to be.

There are encouraging signs that States are working towards a more unified approach to future peace-keeping. On 3 May 1994, the President of the Security Council issued a statement,[4] on behalf of Council, which focused on defining clearer guidelines and principles for peace-keeping. Some have interpreted this as a step back from the activist approach of the immediate post-cold-war period. I believe, however, that it should be seen as a step forward.

The statement incorporates many elements consistent with earlier guidelines. They include a determination: that the conflict is likely to constitute a threat to international peace and security; that the safety and security of United Nations personnel can be ensured; that a cease-fire exists, and that the parties have committed themselves to the peace process; and that a clear political goal can be reflected in a peace-keeping mandate. Recognizing the growth in size and complexity of peace-keeping operations, the Council acknowledged that closer consultation was required among its members, troop contributors and the United Nations Secretariat, as well as closer coordination with regional or subregional organizations and arrangements.

The Council also encouraged my own efforts to finalize stand-by arrangements to reduce the time required to mount peace-keeping operations. The stand-by system is based on conditional offers by Member States which specify what resources — military and civilian personnel, specialized services and equipment — they can make available for possible United Nations use, along with response times. The stand-by system has already proved helpful in the planning for the United Nations Angola Verification Mission III and the United Nations Mission in Haiti.

These stand-by resources are not peace-enforcement units. They are designated for use in United Nations peace-keeping operations mandated by the Security Council. Stand-by troops remain in their home country, training for specific tasks or functions in accordance with United Nations guidelines. Central to the success of these arrangements is the exchange of detailed information to facilitate planning and preparation both for the troop-contributing country and for the United Nations. This information is stored by the United Nations in a confidential database and updated annually. The number of States entering into

---

[4]S/PRST/1994/22.

such arrangements is growing. As of 31 October 1995, a total of 55,000 personnel from 47 Member States were included in the database.

The stand-by system permits planners to know well in advance what provisions need to be made and where deficiencies exist. This initiative aims at streamlining the laborious process of identifying and securing the financial, material and personnel resources needed for each mission. In the past, delays in this process have hindered timely deployment of United Nations peace-keepers, increasing the risk that carefully negotiated agreements would unravel. The Organization has also repeatedly been called upon to mount operations rapidly despite inadequate and dwindling resources: too few available specialized units; critical equipment shortages; lack of logistical support; and too few personnel readily available to serve as military observers, civilian police, other civilian experts and trainers.

On 22 February 1995,[5] the Council expressed its belief that enhancing stand-by arrangements should be the first priority in improving the capacity for rapid deployment. The Secretariat aims to improve and expand the database with more detailed information on response times for individual units, political or material preconditions and transport specifications.

Closer coordination

The multifunctional nature of peace-keeping and peace-building places new demands on the United Nations system. To avert or mitigate the destructive effects of complex crises, it is essential that the United Nations Secretariat and United Nations agencies share a common view of the nature of a problem and the options for action. Within the Secretariat, a new framework for coordination is being developed by the Departments of Humanitarian Affairs, Political Affairs and Peace-keeping Operations. The framework expands as necessary to include other departments or agencies of the United Nations system in routine monitoring and early-warning analysis, assessment of options, fact-finding and the planning and implementation of field operations.

The United Nations Charter assigns primary responsibility for maintaining international peace and security to the Security Council, but it also encourages the settlement of local disputes through regional arrangements and provides, in Chapter VIII, for United Nations cooperation with regional arrangements in the maintenance of international peace and security. Such cooperation includes consultation, diplomatic and operational support, co-deployment of personnel and joint operations. United Nations observers are, for example, currently co-deployed in Liberia with a military mission from the Economic Community of West African States, and in Georgia and Tajikistan with missions from the Commonwealth of Independent States. In Somalia, the efforts of three different regional groups — the Organization of African Unity, the League of Arab States and the Organization of the Islamic Conference — complemented the efforts of the United Nations. The Association of South-East Asian Nations and individual States from several regions met together with the parties to the conflict in Cambodia at an international conference to work with the United Nations towards a transition to peace in that country.

Combined efforts of this kind permit the United Nations to benefit from the influence and expertise of regional organizations, while easing the material and financial burdens on the United Nations. Delegation of authority to concerned States or organizations can also strengthen the legitimacy of international involvement in the settlement of conflicts, while democratizing the international system. The potential initiatives and procedures along these lines are wide-ranging and varied, and lend themselves to adaptation to the realities of each case.

Operations in the field are only the most visible part of a larger, complex set of international political efforts. It is self-evident that in addition to the full support of the Security Council and the support and cooperation of regional organizations, peace-keeping operations require the support of troop-contributing countries. Countries which volunteer personnel for service with the United Nations are understandably anxious about the safety and the well-being of their soldiers. I have endeavoured to meet their concerns by providing troop contributors with regular briefings and by engaging them in dialogue on the conduct of these missions. The Security Council also now meets, as a matter of course, with troop contributors as it considers decisions relating to peace-keeping operations.

Evolving practice in this area must not, however, blur the three distinct levels of authority over United Nations peace-keeping. The Security Council must have overall political direction; the Secretary-General has the responsibility for executive direction and command; and the chief of mis-

[5]S/PRST/1995/9.

sion commands on the ground. The appropriate locus for resolving questions concerning overall policy, command and control of these operations is United Nations Headquarters in New York.

*

* *

The cold war is already history. Barriers that long divided countries and people have fallen. There is new potential for the United Nations to advance a vision of a world without war and of shared prosperity and peace.

At the same time, these are days of uncertainty and change. Commerce, communications and environmental concerns transcend the administrative borders of States. Demands of subnational groups, based on narrow claims, raise the danger of endless fragmentation in world affairs. Peace, security and economic well-being remain distant but legitimate goals. Today's leaders face the multiple tasks of understanding and coping with rapid change and competing claims, while finding a balance between the needs of good internal governance and the requirements of an increasingly interdependent world.

The United Nations remains a key instrument for coping with new situations facing the international community and for trying to prevent and resolve the new breed of conflicts. But even as the United Nations as an institution attempts to adapt and adjust to meet these new challenges, it stands in 1996 in the midst of a financial crisis. Many Member States have failed to meet their Charter obligation to pay, in full and on time, their share of the costs of activities they themselves have authorized. Peace-keeping has been among the most visible and successful of these activities.

United Nations peace-keeping stands out as one of the Organization's most original and ambitious undertakings in its efforts to control conflict and promote peace. It was an inspired innovation. The Blue Helmets will continue to break new ground as the United Nations is called upon not only to contain conflicts and alleviate the suffering they cause, but also to prevent the outbreak of war among nations and to build towards enduring peace.

Boutros Boutros-Ghali

Part II
The Middle East

Chapter 1
General review

The United Nations has been concerned with the situation in the Middle East from its earliest days. It is an issue which has claimed a great deal of the Organization's time and attention. Over five decades, in response to the various conflicts there, the Organization has formulated principles for a peaceful settlement and established a number of peace-keeping operations. In fact, it is the issue out of which the concept of United Nations peace-keeping evolved. The first such operation, an observer mission, was created in the Middle East in 1948; the first of the United Nations peace-keeping forces was also created in the Middle East, in 1956.

At the core of the situation in the Middle East is the Arab-Israeli conflict, which has its origin in the problem of Palestine. This arose from the conflicting claims of the Arab and Jewish communities over the future status of that territory. In 1947, Palestine was a Territory administered by the United Kingdom under a Mandate from the League of Nations. Its population was about 2 million, two thirds of whom were Arabs and one third Jews. Both communities laid claims to the control of the entire Territory after the United Kingdom Mandate ended. Unable to find a solution acceptable to both communities, the British Government brought the matter before the General Assembly in April 1947. A Special Committee appointed by the Assembly to make recommendations for the future status of Palestine proposed in a majority plan the partition of the Territory into an Arab State and a Jewish State, with an international regime for Jerusalem. The partition plan was adopted by the Assembly in November. A United Nations Palestine Commission was to carry out its recommendations, with the assistance of the Security Council. The plan was not accepted by the Palestinian Arabs and Arab States, and the Commission's efforts were inconclusive.

As the impasse continued, violent fighting broke out in Palestine, and the Security Council on 23 April 1948 established a Truce Commission for Palestine, composed of the consular representatives of Belgium, France and the United States, to supervise a cease-fire the Council had called for. The Assembly on 14 May decided to appoint a United Nations Mediator for Palestine who would promote a peaceful adjustment of the future situation of Palestine. On the same day, the United Kingdom relinquished its Mandate over Palestine, and the Jewish Agency proclaimed the State of Israel (which became a United Nations Member a year later, on 11 May 1949) on the territory allotted under the partition plan. The next day, the Palestinian Arabs, assisted by Arab States, opened hostilities against Israel. The war ended with a truce, called for by the Security Council, which was to be supervised by the United Nations Mediator with the assistance of military observers. The first United Nations peace-keeping operation, the United Nations Truce Supervision Organization (UNTSO), came into being as a consequence.

Since 1948, there have been five full-fledged wars directly connected with the Arab-Israeli conflict. Of the United Nations peace-keeping operations established in the region, three are still active — the UNTSO operation, an observer force on the Golan Heights and a peace-keeping force in southern Lebanon. Two other operations, now discontinued, were the first and second United Nations Emergency Forces, both in the Egypt-Israel sector.

Many efforts have been made over the years to arrive at a peaceful settlement, but success appeared elusive. The visit in November 1977 of Egyptian President Anwar Sadat to Jerusalem introduced a new dynamic in the Middle East. Direct negotiations between Egypt and Israel led in September 1978 to two agreements known as the Camp David accords, one on a framework for peace in the Middle East, and the other on a framework for concluding a peace treaty between Egypt and Israel, which was signed in March 1979. Under the peace treaty, Israel withdrew from the Sinai, over which Egypt then took control.

In October 1991, a Peace Conference on the Middle East opened in Madrid, co-sponsored by the Soviet Union and the United States. One year later, the co-sponsors invited the United

Nations to attend as a full participant in the multilateral negotiations. By September 1993, following several months of secret negotiations, Israel and the Palestine Liberation Organization (PLO) were able to exchange letters of mutual recognition. The PLO recognized Israel's right to exist, and Israel recognized the PLO as the representative of the Palestinian people. Three days later, at a ceremony in Washington, D.C., Israel and the PLO signed the Declaration of Principles on Interim Self-Government Arrangements. The historic agreement opened the way to Palestinian self-rule. The parties subsequently agreed to the transfer of powers from Israel to the Palestinian Authority, to the withdrawal of Israeli forces from major West Bank towns and to the holding of elections for the Palestinian Council.

The state of war between Israel and Jordan was ended on 26 October 1994 when the two countries concluded the Treaty of Peace. This leaves two sectors where progress has yet to be made: the Israel-Lebanon and the Israel-Syria sectors. Along the Israeli-Lebanese border, the situation continues to be tense and volatile. Israel maintains its occupation of parts of Lebanon, where its forces continue to be attacked by armed elements who have proclaimed their resistance against the occupation. At times, these hostilities escalate to high levels and include attacks against civilian targets on both sides. By contrast, the situation in the Israel-Syria sector has been calm. However, as of early 1996, direct negotiations between the parties have yielded no tangible results.

Chapter 2
United Nations Truce Supervision Organization (UNTSO)

Chapter 2

United Nations Truce Supervision Organization (UNTSO)

A. Introduction

The first peace-keeping operation in the Middle East was the United Nations Truce Supervision Organization (UNTSO), which continues to operate in the Middle East. UNTSO initially came into being during the Arab-Israeli war of 1948 to supervise the truce called for in Palestine by the Security Council. In 1949, its military observers (UNMOs) remained to supervise the Armistice Agreements between Israel and its Arab neighbours, which were for many years the main basis of the uneasy truce in the whole area. UNTSO's activities have been and still are spread over territory within five States, and therefore it has relations with five host countries (Egypt, Israel, Jordan, Lebanon, Syrian Arab Republic).

Following the wars of 1956, 1967 and 1973, the functions of the observers changed in the light of changing circumstances, but they remained in the area, acting as go-betweens for the hostile parties and as the means by which isolated incidents could be contained and prevented from escalating into major conflicts.

UNTSO personnel have also been available at short notice to form the nucleus of other peace-keeping operations and have remained to assist those operations. The availability of the UNMOs for almost immediate deployment after the Security Council had acted to create a new operation has been an enormous contributory factor to the success of those operations. Rapid deployment of United Nations peace-keepers has been essential to the success of many operations, since their actual presence has been the initial deterrent to renewed fighting.

In the Middle East, groups of UNTSO military observers are today attached to the peace-keeping forces in the area: the United Nations Disengagement Observer Force (UNDOF) in the Golan Heights and the United Nations Interim Force in Lebanon (UNIFIL). A group remains in Sinai to maintain a United Nations presence in that peninsula. In addition, UNTSO maintains offices in Beirut and Damascus.

At the present time, the following countries provide military observers to UNTSO: Argentina, Australia, Austria, Belgium, Canada, Chile, China, Denmark, Finland, France, Ireland, Italy, Netherlands, New Zealand, Norway, Russian Federation, Sweden, Switzerland and United States. UNTSO's authorized strength in early 1996 was 178 observers.

B. Supervision of the truce

The first observer group

In early May 1948, the Truce Commission established by the Security Council the previous month brought to the Council's attention the need for control personnel for effective supervision of the cease-fire which the Council had called for when it created the Commission. As the situation worsened, the Commission, on 21 May, formally asked the Council to send military observers to assist it.

On 29 May, the Security Council called for a four-week cessation of all acts of armed force and non-introduction of fighting personnel or war material into Palestine and Arab countries involved in the fighting. The Council decided that

UNTSO deployment as of August 1996

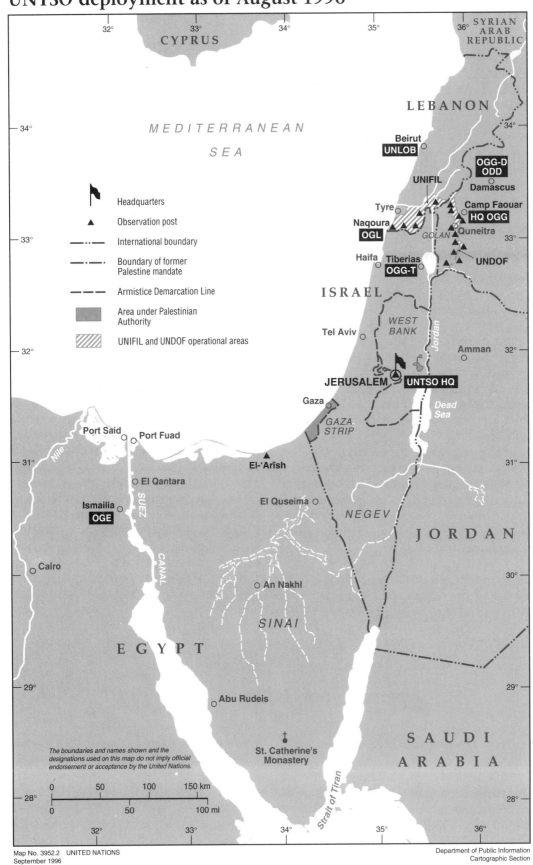

Headquarters

▲ Observation post

International boundary

Boundary of former
Palestine mandate

Armistice Demarcation Line

Area under Palestinian
Authority

UNIFIL and UNDOF operational areas

CYPRUS

MEDITERRANEAN
SEA

SYRIAN
ARAB
REPUBLIC

LEBANON

Beirut
UNLOB

UNIFIL

Tyre

Naqoura
OGL

Haifa

OGG-D
ODD
Damascus

Camp Faouar
HQ OGG
Quneitra
GOLAN
UNDOF

Tiberias
OGG-T

ISRAEL

WEST
BANK

Tel Aviv

Jordan

Amman

JERUSALEM   UNTSO HQ

Dead
Sea

Gaza

GAZA
STRIP

Port Said   Port Fuad

El-'Arîsh

El Qantara

El Quseima

NEGEV

JORDAN

Ismailia
OGE

An Nakhl

SINAI

Cairo

EGYPT

Abu Rudeis

St. Catherine's
Monastery

SAUDI

ARABIA

Strait of Tiran

Nile

SUEZ

CANAL

The boundaries and names shown and the
designations used on this map do not imply official
endorsement or acceptance by the United Nations.

| 0 | 50 | 100 | 150 km |

| 0 | 50 | 100 mi |

Map No. 3952.2   UNITED NATIONS
September 1996

Department of Public Information
Cartographic Section

the Mediator (Count Folke Bernadotte, of Sweden), in concert with the Truce Commission, should supervise the truce and be provided with a sufficient number of military observers for that purpose. Resolution 50 (1948) formed the basis of what would become UNTSO.

After intensive discussions in the area, the Mediator reported a truce agreement, which went into effect on 11 June 1948.[1] Ralph J. Bunche, then Personal Representative of the Secretary-General, was instrumental, with the Mediator, in putting into effect the arrangements for the group of military observers. These arrangements had to be made without previous guidelines and implemented within a period of less than two weeks between the adoption of the Council's resolution and the effective truce.

The question of the nationality of the observers was resolved by the Mediator's requesting 21 observers each from the States members of the Truce Commission (Belgium, France and the United States), with a further five senior staff officers coming from his own country (Sweden), to act as his personal representatives in supervising the truce. The Mediator appointed one of them, Lieutenant-General Count Thord Bonde, as his Chief of Staff. The United States supplied 10 auxiliary technical personnel such as aircraft pilots and radio operators. The Secretary-General made available 51 guards, recruited from the Secretariat's security force at Headquarters, to assist the military observers.

While these arrangements were being made, the beginnings of what were to become different positions on the question of authority became discernible. The Soviet Union made known its view that the selection of military observers should be decided by the Security Council, and expressed the hope that Soviet observers would be appointed. This view was not supported by the Council.

Administratively, the observers remained under their respective army establishments, receiving their normal remunerations from their Governments but getting a daily subsistence allowance from the United Nations, which also met extra expenses resulting from the mission. National uniforms were worn with a United Nations armband. (The distinctive blue beret with United Nations badge was not used until November 1956.) During their assignments with the Organization, the observers were to take orders only from the United Nations authorities. The parties to the conflict were required to cooperate with the observers, to whom the Convention on the Privileges and Immunities of the United Nations applied, and ensure their safety and freedom of movement.

The first group of 36 observers arrived in Cairo between 11 and 14 June and were immediately deployed in Palestine and some of the Arab countries. The number of observers was subsequently increased to 93 — 31 from each of the States members of the Truce Commission. Their activities, under the general control of the Secretary-General, were directed in the field by the Chief of Staff on behalf of the Mediator. For political and practical reasons, the Mediator clearly separated the truce operation from his mediation mission, with Haifa becoming the temporary headquarters for the former and the island of Rhodes remaining the base for the latter. Close liaison was maintained between the Commission, which supervised the truce in Jerusalem, and the Mediator, who supervised the remainder of the operations area. The functions of the observers and the operating procedures were laid down by the Mediator in consultation with the Secretary-General.

Method of operation

These observers were, and remain today, unarmed. They operated then, as they still do, with the consent of the parties and were dependent on the cooperation of the parties for their effectiveness. Thus they had no power to prevent a violation of the truce or to enforce any decisions. There was no element of enforcement in their functioning, although their very presence was something of a deterrent to violations of the truce and, acting on the basis of United Nations resolutions, they exercised a degree of moral suasion. In the case of any complaint or incident where they could not achieve a settlement between the parties on the spot, their only recourse was to report the matter to their supervisors and ultimately to the Mediator; in turn, at his discretion, he could report to the Secretary-General and, through him, to the Security Council. Complaints from local civilians or from troops of the parties concerned were dealt with by observers on the spot, those from military commanders by an area commander or the Chief of Staff, and those from Governments by the Mediator himself. In cases requiring investigation, the inquiries were carried out by observers at the scene whenever possible.

The four-week truce expired on 9 July 1948. While the provisional Government of Israel accepted the Mediator's proposal for an extension,

[1] A/648, S/829.

the Arab Governments did not. As soon as the truce expired, large-scale fighting erupted again between Arab and Israeli forces. On 15 July, in response to an appeal by the Mediator, the Security Council ordered a cease-fire, with a clear threat of applying the enforcement procedures of Chapter VII of the United Nations Charter if necessary (resolution 54 (1948)). The Mediator set the time for commencement of the cease-fire at 1500 GMT on 18 July. Both parties complied with the Council's cease-fire order and all fighting stopped by the appointed time.

The second group

Since the new truce was of indefinite duration and was to remain in force until a peaceful adjustment of the situation in Palestine was reached, a more elaborate system of truce supervision was required. As the observers for the first truce and their equipment had already left the area, the new operation had to be created and equipped from scratch. However, profiting from the experience gained earlier, the Mediator was able to set up a larger and more effective operation in a relatively short time.

The Mediator requested the Governments of Belgium, France and the United States each to place at his disposal 100 observers for the supervision of the truce. By 1 August 1948, 137 of those observers had arrived in the mission area. Subsequently, a total of 682 observers and auxiliary technical personnel was requested by the Mediator, of which 572 were actually provided. Major-General Aage Lundström of the Swedish Air Force was appointed Chief of Staff, and he and nine other Swedish officers formed the Mediator's personal staff. The headquarters of the operation remained in Haifa and the general principles and rules devised for the first truce continued to apply. However, the deployment of observers underwent important changes. Observers were now divided into a number of groups assigned to each Arab army and each Israeli army group. One group was assigned to Jerusalem, one to cover the coast and ports of the truce area, one to control convoys between Tel Aviv and Jerusalem and, later, an additional group was set up to cover airports in the truce area. The Chief of Staff was assisted by a Central Truce Supervision Board, presided over by him and consisting of a senior officer from each member of the Truce Commission, together with the Chief of Staff's political adviser, who was a member of the United Nations Secretariat.

On 17 September 1948, the Mediator was assassinated in Jerusalem by Jewish terrorists belonging to the Lehi Organization, also known as the Stern Gang. Ralph Bunche took over the Mediator's duties and was appointed Acting Mediator. Increased tension led to renewed fighting in October in Jerusalem, the Negev and, to a lesser extent, the Lebanese sector. The Security Council adopted a series of decisions and resolutions to restore the cease-fire and strengthen the observation operation.

The decisions and resolutions of the Security Council between October and December 1948 were the following: on 19 October, a call for an immediate and effective cease-fire in the Negev, to be followed by negotiations through United Nations intermediaries to settle outstanding problems in the area; also on 19 October, a call to the Governments and authorities concerned to grant United Nations observers freedom of movement and access in their areas of operation, to ensure their safety and to cooperate fully with them in their conduct of investigations into incidents; on 4 November, a call to Governments concerned to withdraw their troops to the positions they had occupied on 14 October and to establish truce lines and such neutral or demilitarized zones as desirable; and, on 16 November, a request to the parties to seek agreement directly or through the Acting Mediator with a view to the immediate establishment of an armistice.

Acting Mediator's efforts

With the full support of the Security Council and the General Assembly, the Acting Mediator resumed his mediating efforts, concentrating first on arranging indirect negotiations between Egypt and Israel. But his efforts were momentarily interrupted in late December, when hostilities erupted again between Egyptian and Israeli forces in southern Palestine.

Upon receipt of the Acting Mediator's report on this subject, the Security Council adopted another resolution on 29 December,[2] by which it called upon the Governments concerned to order an immediate cease-fire and to facilitate the complete supervision of the truce by United Nations observers. An effective cease-fire was established by the Acting Mediator soon afterwards.

[2]S/RES/66 (1948).

C. General Armistice Agreements

Four General Armistice Agreements

The Acting Mediator's efforts led to the conclusion of four General Armistice Agreements between Israel and the four neighbouring Arab States — Egypt, Jordan, Lebanon and Syria — in early 1949. On 11 August 1949, the Security Council assigned new functions to UNTSO in line with these Agreements.[3] The role of Mediator was ended. While the resolution made no reference to the Truce Commission, this body had become inactive since the armistice and had in fact been abolished, although the Council took no formal decision to that effect.

With the termination of the role of the Mediator, UNTSO became an autonomous operation, officially a subsidiary organ of the Council, with the Chief of Staff assuming command. Its method of operation was radically altered, since its main responsibility now was to assist the parties in supervising the application and observance of the General Armistice Agreements.

UNTSO's main responsibilities related to the work of the Mixed Armistice Commissions (MACs) set up by the Armistice Agreements. The Egypt-Israel General Armistice Agreement provided for a MAC of seven members, three from each side and the Chief of Staff (or a senior officer designated by him) as Chairman. The Commission was empowered to employ observers who, if they were to be United Nations military observers, would remain under UNTSO command. The other General Armistice Agreements were similar, except that the respective MACs were composed of five members, two from each party and the Chairman.

Structural changes

The Chief of Staff, as commander of the operation, reported to the Secretary-General and was responsible to him. Although the title of Chief of Staff was no longer fully suitable, it was maintained since it was specifically mentioned in the Armistice Agreements and also in Security Council resolution 73 (1949). Until 1951, the Chief of Staff had, administratively, the same status as the observers. This was changed in that year when he was given an appointment as a senior official of the United Nations Secretariat with the grade of Principal Director (later Assistant Secretary-General).

This arrangement, which greatly strengthened the control of the Secretary-General over UNTSO, was applied to the heads of subsequent peace-keeping operations.

Demilitarized zones

In two cases, armistice arrangements included the establishment of demilitarized zones. One of these zones was established in the El Auja area on the Israeli side of the Armistice Demarcation Line between Egypt and Israel. The Egypt-Israel General Armistice Agreement provided that both Egyptian and Israeli armed forces should be totally excluded from the demilitarized zone and that the Chairman of the Egypt-Israel Mixed Armistice Commission and the observers attached to the Commission should be responsible for ensuring the full implementation of this provision. The Israel-Syria Armistice Agreement contained similar provisions concerning the demilitarized zone established near Lake Tiberias. In this case, the Chairman of the Israel-Syria Mixed Armistice Commission was also empowered to authorize the return of civilians to villages and settlements in the demilitarized zone and the employment of limited numbers of locally recruited civilian police in the zone for internal security purposes.

Mixed Armistice Commissions

The main task of the Commissions was the investigation and examination of the claims or complaints presented by the parties relating to the application and observance of the Armistice Agreements. These claims or complaints concerned, mainly, firing across the Armistice Demarcation Line, crossing of the Line by persons or animals, overflights on the wrong side of the Line, the presence of troops or equipment in demilitarized zones or defensive areas and illegal cultivation contrary to agreements. Occasionally, the Commissions also gave attention to special problems of common interest to the parties.

The observers assigned to each Commission carried out the investigations of complaints submitted to the Commission. They assisted in the handing over of people who had crossed the Armistice Demarcation Line, as well as the handing

[3]S/RES/73 (1949).

over of animals and property, and they witnessed the work done by the parties under anti-malaria, anti-rabies and anti-locust agreements. They also participated in rescue and search missions when such missions were undertaken by UNTSO at the request of one of the parties. The Chief of Staff was given special responsibilities for the protection of Mount Scopus, in Jerusalem.

Cease-fire supervision

In addition to its functions relating to the General Armistice Agreements, UNTSO had the responsibility of observing and maintaining the cease-fire, ordered by the Security Council in its resolution 54 (1948), which continued to be in force. When an outbreak of violence threatened, the Chief of Staff of UNTSO would, on his own initiative, seek to prevent it by appealing to the parties for restraint, and when a firing incident actually occurred, he would arrange for an immediate cease-fire. In serious cases, the Chief of Staff could bring the matter to the attention of the Security Council through the Secretary-General.

Government House, UNTSO headquarters

On 25 May 1949, the headquarters of UNTSO was transferred from Haifa to Government House in Jerusalem. Government House had been the seat of the British Mandatory Administration during the Mandate period. On the departure of the British authorities from Palestine, and at their request, the International Committee of the Red Cross took over Government House in trust for any successor administration and, during the early fighting in Jerusalem, it established a neutral zone in the area where the building and its grounds were located. On 7 October 1948, following renewed fighting, during which the status of the neutral zone was violated by both Israeli and Jordanian forces, the International Committee transferred Government House and the surrounding grounds to United Nations protection. Both States parties were informed of these arrangements and did not raise any objections.

The cease-fire agreement of 30 November 1948 for the Jerusalem area left intact Government House and the neutral zone. The General Armistice Agreement concluded between Israel and Jordan on 3 April 1949 provided that in the Jerusalem sector the Armistice Demarcation Lines should correspond to the lines defined in the cease-fire agreement of 30 November 1948, and therefore the

status of the Government House area and the neutral zone remained unaltered. Shortly after the conclusion of the Armistice Agreement, Government House became the headquarters of the United Nations Truce Supervision Organization.

On 5 June 1967, after fighting broke out in Jerusalem, Israeli forces occupied Government House and escorted UNTSO staff out of its premises. The Secretary-General at United Nations Headquarters and the Chief of Staff in Jerusalem repeatedly pressed the Israeli authorities for the return of Government House to UNTSO. After lengthy negotiations, the Israeli Government agreed on 22 August 1967 to return Government House and most of its surrounding grounds.[4] The headquarters of UNTSO was immediately re-established at Government House and has remained there until today.

Commission headquarters

The reorganization of UNTSO after August 1949 was geared to the activities of the four Mixed Armistice Commissions. Each Commission had a headquarters and such ancillary installations as it decided to establish. The headquarters of the Israel-Jordan Mixed Armistice Commission was set up in the neutral zone in Jerusalem. The Israel-Lebanon Mixed Armistice Commission (ILMAC) was headquartered in Beirut with a substation located at Naqoura near the Armistice Demarcation Line. The Israel-Syria Mixed Armistice Commission (ISMAC) was established in Damascus with a control centre at Tiberias on the Israeli side of the Armistice Demarcation Line. Finally, the Egypt-Israel Mixed Armistice Commission (EIMAC) was established in the demilitarized zone of El Auja and was later transferred to Gaza.

Implementation of the Armistice Agreements

The 1949 General Armistice Agreements were meant to be temporary arrangements to be followed by the conclusion of peace treaties. But that was not to be. Two major obstacles appeared soon after the signing of the Armistice Agreements. Israel, for security reasons, refused to let the many Palestinian Arab refugees who had fled their homes during the hostilities return to the areas it controlled, and the Arabs continued to refuse to recognize the existence of Israel and to enter into

[4]S/7930/Add.29.

peace negotiations with it. Thus, the basic issues remained unresolved.

Because of constant disagreement between the parties, the Chief of Staff and the UNTSO observers assigned to the Commissions came to play an increasingly important role. In each Commission, sensitive issues were often deadlocked and resolutions had to be decided by the casting vote of the Chairman. Most investigations into incidents and violations of the Armistice Agreements were carried out by UNTSO observers alone, since the military representatives of the parties could not work with each other. To smooth over difficulties and avert incidents, UNTSO personnel often had to exercise good offices or act as mediators. But, however active and important their functions were, the ultimate responsibility for the observance and application of the provisions of the Armistice Agreements rested with the parties themselves, and without their cooperation and goodwill the Agreements steadily eroded.

Egypt-Israel Mixed Armistice Commission

The difficulties encountered in the implementation of the General Armistice Agreements and the relationships between the parties varied from one Mixed Armistice Commission to another. The most difficult Commission was the Egypt-Israel Mixed Armistice Commission. From the start, Egypt strongly protested against Israel's expulsion of thousands of Palestinians to the Gaza Strip. The matter was brought before the Security Council, which, in its resolution 89 (1950) of 17 November 1950, requested EIMAC to give urgent attention to the Egyptian complaint and reminded both Egypt and Israel, as Member States of the United Nations, of their obligations under the Charter to settle their outstanding differences. But despite the Council's decision, the problem remained unresolved. In 1951 Egypt decided to impose restrictions on the passage of international commercial shipping and goods destined for Israel through the Suez Canal. Despite the request contained in Security Council resolution 95 (1951) of 1 September 1951, Egypt maintained these restrictions, and indeed extended them to the Strait of Tiran in 1953. By early 1955, Palestinian *fedayeen* undertook, with increasing frequency, commando raids into Israeli territory, which were followed by harsh retaliation from Israel. In reaction to the establishment of Egyptian military positions in the El Quseim–Abu Aweigila area, near the border, the Israeli forces occupied the demilitarized zone of

El Auja on 21 September 1956 and, shortly thereafter, the Commission became paralysed as Israel prevented the Egyptian delegates to the Commission from entering the area.

Following the outbreak of the October 1956 war, Israel denounced the Armistice Agreement with Egypt. After that, the Israeli Government refused to take part in EIMAC. The Secretary-General did not accept this unilateral denunciation as valid, and consequently UNTSO continued to maintain the machinery of the Mixed Armistice Commission. The Commission's headquarters was transferred from El Auja to the town of Gaza in Egyptian-controlled territory. The Commission continued to examine complaints submitted by Egypt, and UNTSO observers continued to conduct patrols on the Egyptian side of the Armistice Demarcation Line. But without Israel's cooperation, these activities were largely symbolic and the real peace-keeping functions were carried out by the United Nations Emergency Force (UNEF I), which was established in the wake of the war and with which UNTSO cooperated closely.

Eleven years later, when UNEF I was withdrawn at the request of the Egyptian Government, the Secretary-General pointed out in his report[5] of 19 May 1967 to the Security Council that EIMAC remained in existence and could, as it had done prior to the establishment of UNEF, provide a limited form of United Nations presence in the area. With this in view, the number of observers assigned to the Commission was brought up from 6 to 20 towards the end of May and their patrol activities along the Armistice Demarcation Line were markedly increased. The Government of Israel, while maintaining its position on the Armistice Agreement, raised no objection to this action, and the additional observers sent from Jerusalem to Gaza passed through the Israeli checkpoint on the coastal road without difficulty. But this emergency measure was not enough and, soon after the withdrawal of UNEF, war erupted again between Israel and Arab States.

Israel-Syria Mixed Armistice Commission

Great difficulties were also experienced by the Israel-Syria Mixed Armistice Commission. Two of the most frequent disputes concerned the cultivation by Israeli farmers of disputed lands in the demilitarized zone and the activities of Israeli patrols and fishermen on the eastern side of Lake

[5] S/7896.

Tiberias next to the Armistice Demarcation Line. These Israeli activities were considered to be illegal by the Syrians and often led to intense exchanges of fire between Israeli and Syrian forces. In addition, there was the unending cycle of violence marked by Palestinian commando raids and Israeli reprisals in the border areas.

In order to ease the situation, the Chief of Staff of UNTSO decided, with the agreement of the parties, to establish in the 1950s a number of observation posts along the Armistice Demarcation Line. These served to reduce tension to some extent in the sensitive areas, but incidents nevertheless continued to occur frequently. On 19 January 1956, after a particularly violent Israeli attack against Syrian forces, the Security Council adopted resolution 111 (1956), by which it condemned the attack and called once again on the parties to implement the General Armistice Agreement and to respect the Armistice Demarcation Line and the demilitarized zone. But, despite the call of the Security Council, the situation was not improved. As of 14 October 1966, there were 35,485 Israeli complaints and 30,600 Syrian complaints pending before the Commission. The Commission was completely paralysed by the large number of complaints and constant disputes between the parties. It held its last regular meeting in 1951 and its last emergency meeting in February 1960. From 1966 onwards, relations between Israel and Syria deteriorated sharply. At the beginning of 1967, the Secretary-General succeeded in arranging a series of "extraordinary emergency meetings" of the Commission in order to discuss the cultivation problem in the demilitarized zone which at the time had led to many incidents. But these meetings ended in failure, and on 7 April a serious incident occurred during which Israeli aircraft attacked Damascus itself and shot down six Syrian aircraft. This incident marked the beginning of a new escalation which eventually led to the June 1967 war.

Israel-Jordan Mixed Armistice Commission

The Israel-Jordan Armistice Agreement was subject to different pressures. The West Bank and the Old City of Jerusalem formed part of the Holy Land and were of special importance. They contained large numbers of Palestinian Arabs, many of whom were uprooted and displaced from the area held by Israel. A narrow strip of neutral zone supervised by the United Nations separated the Israeli and Jordanian sectors of the Holy City. The Armistice Agreement created two enclaves: an Israeli enclave on Mount Scopus in Jerusalem and a Jordanian enclave in Latrun on the road from Jerusalem to Tel Aviv. The West Bank was a staging area for the activities of Palestinian *fedayeen*. These factors led to many disputes and problems, which often resulted in exchanges of fire across the Line between the two opposing armies. Despite the difficulties, the Commission continued to meet in emergency sessions until June 1967, and subcommittee meetings were held regularly, on a weekly basis, in an effort to resolve outstanding problems.

Israel-Lebanon Mixed Armistice Commission

Unlike the other Commissions, that for Israel-Lebanon functioned smoothly and often effectively from 1949 until 1967. The main difficulties arose in connection with the activities of Palestinian commandos. However, the Lebanese authorities acted firmly to stop or contain those activities and there were few incidents along the Armistice Demarcation Line. Problems of common concern were discussed and resolved in regular meetings of the Commission, which functioned until the June 1967 war, when Israel denounced the Armistice Agreement with Lebanon as it did the others, although no hostilities took place along the Israel-Lebanon Armistice Demarcation Line.

Observer strength

As for the personnel involved, in 1948 there were 572 observers and auxiliary technical personnel, but with the entry into force of the General Armistice Agreements, UNTSO's observer strength was reduced to between 30 and 140 according to prevailing circumstances. It had 128 observers at the outbreak of the June 1967 war.

D. Cease-fire observation operations, 1967–1973

Background

UNTSO played a crucial role in helping to bring the June 1967 war to an end.

The war started in the early morning of 5 June between Israeli and Egyptian forces and quickly spread to the Jordanian and Syrian fronts. On 6 June, the Security Council adopted resolution 233 (1967), calling upon the Governments concerned to take forthwith, as a first step, all measures for an immediate cease-fire. As hostilities continued, the Council met again on 7 June and, by resolution 234 (1967), demanded that the Governments concerned should discontinue all military activities at 2000 hours GMT on the same day. Fighting stopped on the Egyptian and Jordanian fronts on 8 June, but it went on unabated between the Israeli and Syrian forces on the Golan Heights. On 9 June, the Security Council adopted resolution 235 (1967), by which it confirmed its previous resolutions for an immediate cease-fire, demanded that hostilities should cease forthwith and requested the Secretary-General "to make immediate contacts with the Governments of Israel and Syria to arrange immediate compliance with the above-mentioned resolutions, and to report to the Security Council not later than two hours from now".

On instructions from the Secretary-General, the Chief of Staff of UNTSO, Lieutenant-General Odd Bull of Norway, contacted the Israeli and Syrian authorities on 10 June and proposed to them, as a practical arrangement for implementing the cease-fire demanded by the Security Council, that both sides cease all firing and movement forward at 1630 hours GMT on the same day. He also proposed that the observers, accompanied by liaison officers of each side, be deployed along the front lines as soon as possible in order to observe the implementation of the cease-fire. Those proposals were accepted by both sides and the UNMOs were deployed accordingly in the combat area in the early morning of 11 June.

Israel-Syria sector

On the following days, UNTSO observers demarcated the cease-fire lines on each side. The two cease-fire lines, which included a buffer zone approximately one to three miles wide, were agreed to by the two sides in indirect negotiations conducted by the observers. In signing the map demarcating the cease-fire lines, the Syrian representative stressed that the lines were a purely practical arrangement for the specific purpose of facilitating the observation of the cease-fire by the United Nations and should not affect or prejudice the claims and positions of the Syrian Government.

With the demarcation of the cease-fire lines, UNTSO set up a number of observation posts on each side of the buffer zone. There were, by the end of 1967, seven observation posts on the Israeli side and nine on the Syrian side. Those on the Syrian side were under the control of the headquarters of ISMAC in Damascus and those on the Israeli side reported to the Control Centre at Tiberias. General direction was assumed by the Chief of Staff of UNTSO. The observers, all of whom were drawn from the existing establishment of UNTSO, performed their duties by manning the observation posts and by conducting patrols along the lines as necessary. The two parties were notified by the Chief of Staff of UNTSO that all firings, movements forward of the cease-fire line on each side and overflights would be considered as breaches of the cease-fire.

Arrangements made by the Chief of Staff were endorsed by the Security Council, which, in resolution 236 (1967) of 11 June 1967 affirmed that its demand for a cease-fire and discontinuance of all military activities included a prohibition of any forward military movements subsequent to the cease-fire; called for the prompt return to the cease-fire positions of any troops which might have moved forward subsequent to 1630 hours GMT on 10 June 1967; and called for "full co-operation with the Chief of Staff of the United Nations Truce Supervision Organization and the observers in implementing the cease-fire, including freedom of movement and adequate communications facilities".

After the adoption of the resolution, the observers submitted regularly to the Security Council, through the Secretary-General, reports on the cease-fire situation in the Israel-Syria sector. These arrangements continued until the October 1973 war.

Suez Canal area

When the cease-fire went into effect in the Egypt-Israel sector on 8 June 1967, no observation machinery was set up in that area. At that time, the Israeli forces had reached the eastern bank of the Suez Canal, except for a small area around Port Fuad on the northern tip of the Canal. The situation in the Suez Canal sector was generally quiet during the last part of June but, from early July on, tension began to rise. On 8 July, heavy fighting broke out between Egyptian and Israeli forces at various locations along the Canal, with each side accusing the other of violations of the cease-fire. When the Security Council met on that day, the Secretary-General expressed regret that he was unable to provide the Council with information about the new outbreak of fighting since no United Nations observers were stationed in the area. In this connection, he indicated that as early as 4 July he had decided to take the initiative towards a possible alleviation of this situation and had undertaken exploratory talks with the representatives of Egypt and Israel about the stationing of United Nations military observers in the Canal sector.

On 9 July, the Security Council approved a consensus statement in accordance with which the Secretary-General requested the Chief of Staff of UNTSO to work out with the Governments of Egypt[6] and Israel, as speedily as possible, the necessary arrangements to station observers in the Suez Canal sector. Two days later, having received the agreement of both parties, the Secretary-General instructed the Chief of Staff to work out with the local authorities of both sides a plan for the actual stationing of military observers.

The Chief of Staff proceeded in much the same way as for the observation operation on the Golan Heights. The problem of demarcation of the cease-fire lines was much simpler in this case, since, except for the Port Fuad area, the Suez Canal itself constituted a natural buffer zone. The observers made an attempt to demarcate a line of separation in the Port Fuad area, but no agreement could be reached. This question, therefore, remained a subject of controversy, but because of the marshy terrain in the area there were few incidents.

The observation operation began on 17 July when seven observation posts were established along the Canal. This number was eventually increased to 15: eight on the eastern side of the Canal under the Control Centre at Qantara and seven on the western side under the Control Centre at Ismailia. At the beginning, military observers drawn from the existing UNTSO establishment were assigned to the Suez Canal. However, the nationalities of the observers gave rise to some difficulty, as certain countries were not acceptable to Israel, and others not acceptable to Egypt. Fi-

nally, after lengthy discussions, agreements were reached on six countries from which observers might be drawn: Austria, Burma, Chile, Finland, France and Sweden. The original observers were then replaced by 90 new observers from those six countries.

The main task of the observers was to observe and report on breaches of the cease-fire, including firings, overflights and movements forward, which, in this case, meant movement of boats and craft in the Canal. An understanding was reached on 27 July whereby the two parties agreed to stop all military activities in the Suez Canal, including the movement in or into the Canal of boats or craft for one month, it being understood that the Canal authorities would continue to re-victual and secure the safety of the 15 ships stranded in the Canal. This agreement was later extended indefinitely.[7]

With these arrangements, the situation in the Suez Canal sector became stabilized and, although there were occasional exchanges of fire, the cease-fire generally held. This lull lasted until early 1969, when fighting suddenly broke out again. From that time until August 1970, there were intense exchanges of artillery fire across the Canal between the Egyptian and Israeli positions every day, with occasional air strikes by one side or the other. This period of fighting, which lasted nearly 20 months, was known as the "war of attrition". It was full-fledged warfare except that the positions of the opposing armies did not move forward. During the entire period of hostilities, the Secretary-General reported in detail to the Security Council on all the developments monitored by the observers, and appealed on several occasions for an end to the hostilities, but his efforts were inconclusive. Egypt stated that it refused to continue to observe the cease-fire, which it regarded as in effect perpetuating the Israeli occupation of its sovereign territory, while Israel asserted that it would observe the cease-fire only if the other side were willing to do so. Neither side brought the matter before the Security Council and, largely because of the opposing positions taken by two of the permanent members, the Council did not attempt to take it up.

---

[6]Documents of these years refer to Egypt as the United Arab Republic. Egypt and Syria, separate Members of the United Nations since 1945, joined together in February 1958 to form the United Arab Republic. In September 1961, the Syrian Arab Republic resumed its status as an independent State and its separate membership in the United Nations. Egypt retained the title of the United Arab Republic, reverting to the name of Egypt, or Arab Republic of Egypt, in 1971. For convenience, the title of Egypt is used in this book wherever possible. [7]S/8053/Add.1,2.

The fighting came to an end on 7 August 1970 under a proposal initiated by the United States Government. Under the proposal, Egypt, Israel and Jordan agreed to designate representatives to discussions to be held under the auspices of the Special Representative of the Secretary-General for the Middle East, Ambassador Gunnar V. Jarring, of Sweden.[8] In order to facilitate the Special Representative's task of promoting agreement in accordance with Security Council resolution 242 (1967) of 22 November 1967 (containing general principles for a Middle East settlement), they undertook strictly to observe the cease-fire resolutions of the Security Council as from 7 August. On that day, fighting stopped in the Suez Canal sector and the situation there remained quiet until 6 October 1973, when hostilities once again broke out between Egyptian and Israeli forces.

Israel-Jordan sector

No cease-fire observation was established in the Israel-Jordan sector. At the end of the June 1967 war, Israeli forces had occupied the entire West Bank up to the Jordan River. The situation in that sector was generally quiet until the end of 1967 but there was increasing tension in 1968 and 1969, mainly because of the activities of Palestinian commandos operating from the east side of the Jordan Valley and retaliatory action by the Israeli forces. The Secretary-General sounded out the Israeli and Jordanian authorities about the possibility of stationing United Nations observers in the Jordan Valley but could not secure an agreement. On several occasions, the Security Council met to consider serious incidents in the Israel-Jordan sector, and the Secretary-General drew attention to the fact that in the absence of agreements from the parties or of a decision by the Security Council, it was not possible to establish a machinery for the observation of the cease-fire in the sector.

The situation in the Israel-Jordan sector, however, became much quieter after September 1970, when the bulk of the Palestinian armed elements moved to Lebanon.

Israel-Lebanon sector

During the June 1967 war, no fighting took place between Israel and Lebanon, and the Armistice Demarcation Line between the two countries remained intact. Nevertheless, the Israeli Government denounced the Armistice Agreement with Lebanon after the war, as it did the other Armistice Agreements, on the grounds that during the hostilities Lebanese authorities had claimed that they were at war with Israel. The Lebanese Government, however, denied this and insisted on the continued validity of the Agreement. Since the Secretary-General held the view that the Armistice Agreement could not be denounced unilaterally, UNTSO continued to maintain the headquarters of ILMAC at Beirut, as well as a substation at Naqoura in southern Lebanon. But the Commission had few activities and the number of observers assigned to it was considerably reduced.

Following the 1967 war, the Palestinian population in Lebanon markedly increased with the influx of a sizeable number of displaced persons from the occupied West Bank and Gaza, and the Palestine Liberation Army stepped up its training activities in the country, especially in the south. As a result, anti-Israeli raids by Palestinian commandos from Lebanon and reprisals by Israeli forces became more frequent. The situation deteriorated further following the departure of Palestinian armed elements in 1970 from Jordan to Lebanon.

In early 1972, tension heightened in the Israel-Lebanon sector as a result of increasing activities by Palestinian commandos based in southern Lebanon and severe reprisal attacks by Israeli forces. On 29 March, the Permanent Representative of Lebanon to the United Nations submitted the following request to the Security Council:

> "The Lebanese Government, because of repeated Israeli aggression against Lebanon and because the work of the Lebanon-Israel Mixed Armistice Commission has been paralysed since 1967, wishes the Security Council to take necessary action to strengthen the United Nations machinery in the Lebanese-Israeli sector by increasing the number of observers, on the basis of the Armistice Agreement of 1949." [9]

On 30 March, the members of the Security Council decided that the request of the Lebanese Government should be met, and asked the Secretary-General to make the necessary arrangements to this effect. In a memorandum dated 4 April,[10] the Secretary-General informed the Council that, following consultations with the Lebanese authorities, the Chief of Staff of UNTSO had

[8] S/9902. [9] S/10611, annex. [10] Ibid.

recommended the establishment of three observation posts on the Lebanese side of the Armistice Demarcation Line, together with an increase in the number of observers assigned to the Armistice Commission from the existing seven to 21. On 19 April 1972, the members of the Security Council, in informal consultations, agreed with the proposed plans.

The cease-fire observation operation in the Israel-Lebanon sector commenced on 24 April 1972 with the establishment of the three proposed observation posts, all on Lebanese territory. Two additional observation posts were later set up and the total observer strength was increased to 34. Those observers, who were all drawn from the existing establishment of UNTSO, manned the five observation posts and conducted patrols along the Armistice Demarcation Line as necessary. Their responsibility was to observe and report on violations of the Demarcation Line.

Unlike the previous cease-fire observer operations, the one in Lebanon was established without the agreement of Israel. However, Israel did not seek to obstruct the operation, and the additional observers and their equipment which were transferred from Jerusalem to southern Lebanon passed through the Israeli border checkpoint without hindrance.

From April 1972 until the Israeli invasion of Lebanon in March 1978, the observers assigned to the Israel-Lebanon sector reported regularly to the Security Council, through the Secretary-General, on the situation along the Armistice Demarcation Line. These reports dealt mainly with violations of the Line by the Israeli forces, since no such violations were committed by the Lebanese forces. The Israeli violations included firings across the Line, overflights and the establishment of some six positions on the Lebanese side of the Line.

Maintenance of the armistice supervision machinery

Having already denounced the Armistice Agreement with Egypt in 1956, Israel denounced the other three agreements after the war of 1967. The Secretary-General did not accept this act as valid for reasons that he explained in the introduction to his annual report to the General Assembly as follows:

"...there has been no indication either in the General Assembly or in the Security Council that the validity and applicability of the Armistice Agreements have been changed as a result of the recent hostilities or of the war of 1956; each Agreement, in fact, contains a provision that it will remain in force 'until a peaceful settlement between the parties is achieved'. Nor has the Security Council or the General Assembly taken any steps to change the pertinent resolutions of either organ relating to the Armistice Agreements or to the earlier cease-fire demands. The Agreements provide that by mutual consent the signatories can revise or suspend them. There is no provision in them for unilateral termination of their application. This has been the United Nations position all along and will continue to be the position until a competent organ decides otherwise."[11]

Accordingly, the machinery for the supervision of the Armistice Agreements has been maintained in those sectors where no peaceful settlement has been achieved. The Chiefs of the UNTSO observers in Beirut and Damascus are the nominal Chairmen of the Israel-Lebanon and Israel-Syria Mixed Armistice Commissions, respectively.

E. Activities since 1973

Egypt-Israel sector

Cease-fire observation in the Suez Canal sector was terminated shortly after the outbreak of the October 1973 war, at the request of the Egyptian Government. On 6 October, in a surprise attack, Egyptian forces crossed the Canal and soon advanced beyond the UNTSO observation posts on the eastern bank of the Canal, while, in a coordinated move, Syrian troops simultaneously attacked the Israeli positions on the Golan Heights. The first days of the war were marked by heavy air

[11]A/6701/Add.1.

and ground activity, which was fully reported to the Security Council by the Secretary-General on the basis of information received from the observers. In the course of the hostilities, two United Nations observers were killed.

On 8 October, the Egyptian Permanent Representative informed the Secretary-General that, since the United Nations observers were now behind the Egyptian lines, which put them in physical danger and made their presence unnecessary, the Government of Egypt requested the Secretary-General to take measures for their transfer to Cairo for their security. The Secretary-General immediately brought this request to the attention of the Security Council, which agreed that it should be acceded to. By 9 October, all the United Nations observation posts on both sides of the Canal were closed and the observers were withdrawn to the Cairo area.

Following the closure of the observation posts, the United Nations no longer had direct information on the hostilities between Egypt and Israel which were raging in the western part of the Sinai.

Assistance to UNEF II

The October 1973 war and its aftermath are described in greater detail in the chapter below on the Second United Nations Emergency Force (UNEF II). As far as UNTSO is concerned, Security Council resolution 340 (1973) of 25 October 1973 provided for an increase in the number of UNTSO observers in the Egypt-Israel sector and gave them the task of assisting and cooperating with UNEF II in the fulfilment of that Force's mandate. During the initial phase, the observers manned certain checkpoints and observation posts in the area controlled by UNEF II. They also assisted in exchanges of prisoners of war and undertook searches for bodies of soldiers killed during the hostilities. In addition, some observers were assigned as staff officers at UNEF II headquarters. After the conclusion of the disengagement agreement of January 1974, they conducted patrols in the buffer zone established in the Sinai and carried out inspections of the area of limitation of forces and armament on both sides of the buffer zone. While the observers remained administratively attached to UNTSO, they were placed under the operational control of the Commander of UNEF II.

At the end of October 1973, additional observers (3 from Sweden and 10 from Finland), were provided at the request of the Secretary-General to strengthen the observer group in the Egypt-Israel sector. Thus the total strength of UNTSO was increased to 225 observers, from 16 countries. In November 1973, the Governments of the United States and of the Soviet Union, in a joint approach to the Secretary-General, offered to make available observers from their countries for service with UNTSO. The Soviet Union would provide 36 observers and the United States 28 — who, with the 8 Americans already assigned to the mission, would bring the number of United States observers also to 36. The Secretary-General accepted these offers with the informal concurrence of the Security Council.

Observer Group Egypt

In July 1979, the mandate of UNEF II lapsed. On 24 July 1979, the Secretary-General, after consultations held by the Security Council, issued a statement in which he indicated that, in view of the fact that the withdrawal of UNEF was without prejudice to the continued presence of the UNTSO observers in the area, he intended to make, in accordance with existing decisions of the Security Council, the necessary arrangements to ensure the further functioning of UNTSO. The peace treaty concluded in 1979 between Egypt and Israel superseded the 1949 Armistice Agreement in that sector and thus terminated the Egypt-Israel Mixed Armistice Commission.

In accordance with the statement referred to above and at the request of the Egyptian Government, UNTSO has continued to maintain a presence in the area. Its observers in the Egypt-Israel sector are organized as Observer Group Egypt (OGE), with a strength in early 1996 of some 14 military observers. At first, OGE operated six outposts in the Sinai and an outpost at Ismailia and conducted patrols in most parts of the Sinai, except for an area under the Multinational Force and Observers (MFO). This operation was set up outside the United Nations in 1982 to supervise the implementation of the peace treaty between Egypt and Israel concluded in 1979. OGE headquarters in Cairo maintained liaison for UNTSO with the Egyptian authorities. The number of outposts has been reduced in subsequent streamlining exercises; its headquarters has been moved to Ismailia. In 1995, OGE operated one outpost in El Arish and the frequency of patrols has been reduced accordingly. UNTSO also maintained a liaison office in Gaza, which was closed in April 1996.

Israel-Syria sector

During the October 1973 war, the central part of the buffer zone established by UNTSO on the Golan Heights was the scene of fierce fighting. In the first days of the war, Syrian forces attacked and overran several Israeli positions along the cease-fire lines. However, by 11 October, the Israeli troops had counter-attacked and in turn crossed over to the eastern side of the buffer zone on either side of the Quneitra-Damascus road. As the battle developed, some of the United Nations observation posts had to be evacuated, but others continued to operate.

When the cease-fire called for by the Security Council took effect on 25 October 1973, Israeli forces had occupied a pocket around the village of Saassa on the eastern side of the buffer zone, some 40 kilometres west of Damascus. The United Nations observers set up temporary observation posts around that pocket, and with these changes, the cease-fire observation operation was resumed.

Assistance to UNDOF

UNTSO's cease-fire observation in the Israel-Syria sector was discontinued on 31 May 1974 when the United Nations Disengagement Observer Force was established and the 90 United Nations observers assigned to the Israel-Syria sector were detailed to UNDOF as an integral part of the Force. Operating out of Tiberias and Damascus, they manned observation posts located near the area of operation and in the vicinity of the lines on both sides, and they conducted the fortnightly inspections of the areas of limitation in armaments and forces provided for under the disengagement agreement of 1974. In 1979, the observers detailed to assist UNDOF were formed into Observer Group Golan (OGG), which has continued to carry out the tasks described above, under the supervision and operational control of the UNDOF commander.

Under the terms of the protocol to the disengagement agreement, the personnel of UNDOF must come from Members of the United Nations that are not permanent members of the Security Council. Observers from those countries assigned to the Israel-Syria sector are not therefore involved in the supervision of the disengagement agreement. They form a separate unit, the Observer Detachment Damascus (ODD), which performs liaison and support functions for OGG.

The UNTSO establishment in the Israel-Syria sector is, in early 1996, the largest in the mission area. It comprises altogether some 85 military observers.

Israel-Jordan sector

During the war of 1973, the Israel-Jordan sector remained quiet. UNTSO continued to maintain a small liaison office in Amman, which was staffed by two military observers. The chief of the office was also the designated chairman of the Israel–Hashemite Kingdom of Jordan Mixed Armistice Commission. In 1994, Israel and Jordan concluded a peace treaty, and the UNTSO office in Amman was closed the following year. Since then, liaison with the Jordanian authorities has been handled by UNTSO headquarters in Jerusalem.

Israel-Lebanon sector

The UNTSO operation in the Israel-Lebanon sector experienced severe difficulties following the outbreak of civil war in Lebanon in 1975. Since the UNTSO observers were not armed, their security had to be ensured by the host Government. When the five observation posts were set up along the Armistice Demarcation Line in 1972, the Lebanese army established a checkpoint next to each of them. At the beginning of the civil war, the Lebanese army disintegrated and the United Nations observers manning the posts were left on their own in an increasingly dangerous situation. The Secretary-General had three choices at the time: suspend the operation, arm the observers for their protection, or ask them to continue to operate as before in spite of the changed conditions. After careful consideration and consultation with the contributing countries, the last-mentioned solution was adopted. On a number of occasions, observers' vehicles were hijacked and their observation posts broken into by one faction or another. But there were few serious incidents and, on the whole, the fighting factions respected the status of the United Nations observers.

Assistance to UNIFIL

When the Security Council established the United Nations Interim Force in Lebanon in March 1978, UNTSO's cease-fire observation in the Israel-Lebanon sector was discontinued and the observers were assigned to assist UNIFIL in the fulfilment of its tasks. It was stipulated, however, that the military observers of UNTSO would continue to function on the Armistice Demarcation Line after the termination of the mandate of UNIFIL.[12]

The observers assigned to assist UNIFIL were formed into Observer Group Lebanon (OGL) and were placed under the operational control of the commander of UNIFIL. They manned observation posts, conducted patrols and carried out liaison duties with parties active in and around the UNIFIL area of operation. They also performed staff duties at UNIFIL headquarters, especially in the early days of the Force. The headquarters of ILMAC in Beirut did not become part of OGL, but it functioned as a liaison office for UNIFIL until that Force established its own liaison office in Beirut.

In early 1996, OGL comprises some 54 military observers. They continue to man the five observation posts along the Lebanese side of the Armistice Demarcation Line and operate four mobile teams in parts of the UNIFIL area of operation, including those that are under Israeli control and where UNIFIL units are not deployed.

Despite UNIFIL's presence, southern Lebanon has remained the most hazardous assignment for the UNTSO observers. They have often been caught in cross-fire and one died as a result of a mine explosion in January 1988. While the various parties and groups have generally continued to respect the international status of the unarmed observers, some of them have been threatened on account of their nationality. On 17 February 1988, the Chief of OGL, Lieutenant Colonel William R. Higgins (United States), was kidnapped south of Tyre by unknown persons. Strenuous efforts were made to establish his whereabouts and obtain his release, but on 31 July 1989, the group which claimed to be holding him announced that they had killed him. His remains were recovered on 23 December 1991 and brought to the United States.

Observer Group Beirut

In June 1982, Israeli forces invaded Lebanon again and soon reached Beirut, where the Palestine Liberation Organization (PLO) had its headquarters and where many PLO fighters had concentrated. The PLO called for the deployment of UNIFIL in the Beirut area, but this was strongly opposed by Israel. Various proposals for the establishment of a United Nations military observer group in and around Beirut were examined by the Security Council in June and July, but no agreement could be reached. On 1 August, after Israel's forces had entered West Beirut, the Security Council authorized the Secretary-General to deploy im-

mediately, on the request of the Government of Lebanon, United Nations observers to monitor the situation in and around Beirut. The Secretary-General instructed UNTSO to make the necessary arrangements in consultation with the parties concerned. When the Israeli reply was delayed, the Secretary-General immediately set up observation machinery in the Beirut area in territory controlled by the Lebanese Government. The 10 observers assigned to ILMAC were constituted as the Observer Group Beirut (OGB) and took up their new duties on 3 August. The same day, the Israeli forces resumed their advance on West Beirut. Their unwillingness to cooperate with UNTSO prevented the reinforcement of OGB, as the observers could not reach Beirut without passing through Israeli checkpoints.

In the mean time, the United States worked out arrangements for the evacuation of the PLO fighters under the supervision of a multinational force (MNF), not connected with the United Nations. This operation was completed on 1 September and the MNF was withdrawn.

On 14 September, Bashir Gemayel, the President-elect of Lebanon, was assassinated. The next morning the Israeli forces returned in strength to West Beirut. On the afternoon of 17 September, units of the Christian militia of which Gemayel had been the leader entered the Sabra and Shatila refugee camps in the southern suburbs of Beirut and killed a large number of Palestinian refugees. In the early hours of 19 September, by resolution 521 (1982), the Security Council condemned the massacre and authorized the Secretary-General to increase the number of observers in and around Beirut from 10 to 50. The Council also requested the Secretary-General to initiate urgent consultations on additional steps which the Council might take, including the possible deployment of United Nations forces.

On 20 September, the Secretary-General was able to inform the Security Council that the additional observers were on their way to Beirut. He also reported that about 2,000 men from UNIFIL could be sent to Beirut, if required.[13] However, on 24 September, the MNF returned to Beirut. It remained there until 1984.

The UNTSO observers in Beirut performed their duties by means of observation posts and mobile patrols. Their task was to monitor the situation in and around Beirut, with emphasis on developments involving Israelis and Palestinians. Following the withdrawal of the Israeli forces from

[12]S/12611. [13]S/15408.

the Beirut area in September 1983, the tasks of the Observer Group were reduced. In mid-1992, OGB was converted to the United Nations Liaison Office in Beirut (UNLOB). This office performs liaison functions for UNTSO. The chief of UNLOB is also the designated chairman of ILMAC.

Financial aspects

Since its establishment in 1948, UNTSO has been financed from the regular budget of the United Nations. Its costs are therefore assessed as part of each biennial programme budget. The financial situation of the Organization provided the impetus for a number of consecutive streamlining exercises, which brought the number of military observers down from 298 in 1990 to 178 in 1996. At the end of 1995, UNTSO's total expenditures since its inception amounted to some $463,667,258.

Assistance to other operations

Throughout UNTSO's history, the military officers assigned as United Nations observers to UNTSO have frequently been drawn on as a reserve of experienced personnel, especially in setting up new peace-keeping operations. Able to move at extremely short notice, they have given valuable service in the initial phases of all the peace-keeping operations in the Middle East, and in other operations. UNTSO's military observers and its communications system were invaluable in setting up the First United Nations Emergency Force (UNEF I) at short notice during the time of the Suez crisis, as well as for the United Nations Operation in the Congo (ONUC) in 1960, the United Nations Observation Group in Lebanon (UNOGIL) during the crisis of 1958, the United Nations Yemen Observation Mission (UNYOM) in 1963, the Second United Nations Emergency Force (UNEF II) in Sinai in 1973, the United Nations Disengagement Observer Force (UNDOF) the following year, and the United Nations Interim Force in Lebanon (UNIFIL) in 1978.

UNTSO observers were also deployed to the United Nations Good Offices Mission in Afghanistan and Pakistan (UNGOMAP) and the United Nations Iran-Iraq Military Observer Group (UNIIMOG) in 1988, the United Nations Angola Verification Mission (UNAVEM) and the United Nations Observer Group in Central America (ONUCA) in 1989, the United Nations Observer Group for the Verification of the Elections in Haiti (ONUVEH) in 1990, the United Nations Iraq-Kuwait Observation Mission (UNIKOM) in 1991, the United Nations Protection Force (UNPROFOR) in 1992 and the United Nations Operation in Mozambique (ONUMOZ) also in 1992.

In addition, UNTSO contributed observers to two small military observer teams which were stationed in Tehran and Baghdad from 1984 to 1988 to monitor the moratorium arranged by the Secretary-General on military attacks against civilian centres during the conflict between Iran and Iraq.[14]

[14] S/16627.

Chapter 3
First United Nations Emergency Force (UNEF I)

A. Creation
Background
General Assembly's first emergency special session
Enabling resolutions of the United Nations Force
Concept and guiding principles
Advisory Committee
Further General Assembly resolutions
Initial stages of UNEF
Negotiations with the Egyptian Government
The good faith agreement
Other memoranda and agreements
Status of the Force agreement
Negotiations with the participating countries
UNEF's composition
UNEF's organization

B. Cease-fire and withdrawal of foreign forces
Establishment of the cease-fire
Withdrawal of the Anglo-French force
Initial withdrawal of the Israeli forces: November 1956–mid-January 1957
Sharm el Sheikh and the Gaza Strip
Second withdrawal of Israeli forces: February 1957
Final withdrawal of Israeli forces: March 1957

C. UNEF deployment
Deployment along the Armistice Demarcation Line
Phases of deployment and activities
First phase: Suez Canal area (November–December 1956)
Second phase: Sinai peninsula (December 1956–March 1957)
Third phase: Gaza Strip and Sharm el Sheikh (March 1957)
Final phase: deployment along the borders (March 1957–May 1967)
UNEF withdrawal, 1967

Chapter 3

First United Nations
Emergency Force (UNEF I)

A. Creation

Background

In October 1956, the United Nations faced a major crisis. The 1949 General Armistice Agreement between Egypt and Israel — concluded under the auspices of and supervised by the United Nations — collapsed when Israel and two major Powers occupied large portions of Egyptian territory. The Organization reacted to the crisis with speed and firmness and, to overcome it, conceived a new form of peace-keeping and set up its first peace-keeping force. This historic development was made possible mainly through the vision, resourcefulness and determination of Secretary-General Dag Hammarskjöld and Mr. Lester Pearson, who was at the time Secretary for External Affairs of Canada.

Since the summer of 1955, relations between Egypt and Israel had been steadily deteriorating, despite the efforts of the Chief of Staff of UNTSO and the Secretary-General himself. Palestinian *fedayeen*, with the support of the Egyptian Government, had been launching frequent raids against Israel from their bases in Gaza, and these had been followed by increasingly strong reprisal attacks by Israeli armed forces. The decision taken by Egypt in the early 1950s to restrict Israeli shipping through the Suez Canal and the Strait of Tiran at the entrance to the Gulf of Aqaba, in contravention of a decision of the Security Council, remained a controversial and destabilizing issue. In the heightening tension, the control of armaments — which the Tripartite Declaration of France, the United Kingdom and the United States, of May 1950, had sought to achieve in the Middle East — had broken down, and Egypt and Israel were engaging in an intense arms race, with the East and the West supplying sophisticated weapons and equipment to the opposing sides.

On 19 July 1956, the United States Government decided to withdraw its financial aid for the Aswan Dam project on the Nile River. President Gamal Abdel Nasser announced the nationaliza-tion of the Suez Canal Company a week later and declared that Canal dues would be used to finance the Aswan project.

On 23 September 1956, the Governments of France and the United Kingdom requested[1] the President of the Security Council to convene the Council to consider the "situation created by the unilateral action of the Egyptian Government in bringing to an end the system of international operation of the Suez Canal, which was confirmed and completed by the Suez Canal Convention of 1888". On the following day, Egypt countered with a request[2] that the Security Council consider "actions against Egypt by some Powers, particularly France and the United Kingdom, which constitute a danger to international peace and security and are serious violations of the Charter of the United Nations".

The Security Council first met on 26 September to consider both items. At the same time, private negotiations were being carried out between the Foreign Ministers of the three countries with the good offices of the Secretary-General. By 12 October, the Secretary-General was able to work out six principles on which there seemed to be general agreement. These principles were incorporated in a draft resolution which the Security Council unanimously adopted on the next day. This became resolution 118 (1956), by which the Security Council "agrees that any settlement of the Suez question should meet the following requirements:

"(1) There should be free and open transit through the Canal without discrimination, overt or covert — this covers both political and technical aspects;

[1]S/3654. [2]S/3656.

"(2) The sovereignty of Egypt should be respected;

"(3) The operation of the Canal should be insulated from the politics of any country;

"(4) The manner of fixing tolls and charges should be decided by agreement between Egypt and the users;

"(5) A fair proportion of the dues should be allotted to development;

"(6) In case of disputes, unresolved affairs between the Suez Canal Company and the Egyptian Government should be settled by arbitration with suitable terms of reference and suitable provisions for the payment of sums found to be due."

Following the adoption of this resolution, the Secretary-General announced that he would pursue his efforts to promote an agreement based on the principles laid down by the Security Council. However, a new situation developed in late October 1956, when Israel, in cooperation with the British and French Governments, launched an all-out attack on Egypt.

The Israeli forces crossed the border on the morning of 29 October, advancing in three columns towards El Arish, Ismailia and the Mitla Pass. In the early hours of 30 October, the Chief of Staff of UNTSO, Major-General E.L.M. Burns (Canada), called for a cease-fire and requested Israel to pull its forces back to its side of the border. In the afternoon of the same day, the British and French Governments addressed a joint ultimatum to Egypt and Israel calling on both sides to cease hostilities within 12 hours and to withdraw their forces to a distance of 10 miles on each side of the Suez Canal. They also requested Egypt to allow Anglo-French forces to be stationed temporarily on the Canal at Port Said, Ismailia and Suez for the purpose of separating the belligerents and ensuring the safety of shipping. The ultimatum was accepted by Israel whose troops in any case were still far from the Suez Canal, but it was rejected by Egypt. On 31 October, France and the United Kingdom launched an air attack against targets in Egypt, which was followed shortly by a landing of their troops near Port Said at the northern end of the Canal.

General Assembly's first emergency special session

The Security Council held a meeting on 30 October at the request of the United States, which submitted a draft resolution[3] calling upon Israel immediately to withdraw its armed forces behind the established armistice lines. It was not adopted because of British and French vetoes. A similar draft resolution[4] sponsored by the Soviet Union was also rejected. The matter was then transferred to the General Assembly, on a proposal by Yugoslavia, in accordance with the procedure provided by Assembly resolution 377 (V) of 3 November 1950 entitled "Uniting for peace". Thus, the first emergency special session of the General Assembly called under that resolution was convened on 1 November 1956.

In the early hours of the next day, the General Assembly adopted, on the proposal of the United States, resolution 997 (ES-I), calling for an immediate cease-fire, the withdrawal of all forces behind the armistice lines and the reopening of the Canal. The Secretary-General was requested to observe and report promptly on compliance to the Security Council and to the General Assembly, for such further action as those bodies might deem appropriate in accordance with the United Nations Charter.

The resolution was adopted by 64 votes to 5, with 6 abstentions. The dissenters were Australia and New Zealand, in addition to France, Israel and the United Kingdom. In explaining Canada's abstention, Lester Pearson stated that the resolution did not provide for, along with the cease-fire and a withdrawal of troops, any steps to be taken by the United Nations for a peace settlement, without which a cease-fire would be only of a temporary nature at best.

Before the session, Mr. Pearson had had extensive discussions with the Secretary-General and he felt that it might be necessary to establish some sort of United Nations police force to help resolve the crisis. Mr. Pearson submitted to the General Assembly, when it reconvened the next morning, a draft resolution on the establishment of an emergency international United Nations force.

[3]S/3710. [4]S/3713/Rev.1.

Enabling resolutions of the United Nations Force

The Canadian proposal was adopted by the General Assembly on the same morning and became resolution 998 (ES-I) of 4 November 1956, by which the Assembly:

"Requests, as a matter of priority, the Secretary-General to submit to it within forty-eight hours a plan for the setting up, with the consent of the nations concerned, of an emergency international United Nations Force to secure and supervise the cessation of hostilities in accordance with all the terms of the aforementioned resolution 997 (ES-I);."

The voting was 57 to none, with 19 abstentions. Egypt, France, Israel, the United Kingdom and the Soviet Union and Eastern European States were among the abstainers.

At the same meeting, the General Assembly also adopted resolution 999 (ES-I), by which it reaffirmed resolution 997 (ES-I) and authorized the Secretary-General immediately to arrange with the parties concerned for the implementation of the cease-fire and the halting of the movement of military forces and arms into the area.

On the same day, the Secretary-General submitted his first report[5] on the plan for an emergency international United Nations Force, in which he recommended certain preliminary steps, including the immediate setting up of a United Nations Command. All his recommendations were endorsed by the General Assembly and included in resolution 1000 (ES-I) adopted on 5 November 1956, by which the Assembly:

■ Established a United Nations Command for an emergency international Force to secure and supervise the cessation of hostilities in accordance with all the terms of General Assembly resolution 997 (ES-I) of 2 November 1956;

■ Appointed, on an emergency basis, the Chief of Staff of UNTSO, Major-General (later Lieutenant-General) E.L.M. Burns, as Chief of the Command;

■ Authorized the Chief of the Command immediately to recruit, from the observer corps of UNTSO, a limited number of officers who were to be nationals of countries other than those having permanent membership in the Security Council, and further authorized him, in consultation with the Secretary-General, to undertake the recruitment directly, from various Member States other than the permanent members of the Security Council, of the additional number of officers needed;

■ Invited the Secretary-General to take such administrative measures as might be necessary for prompt execution of the actions envisaged.

The resolution was adopted by 57 votes to none, with 19 abstentions. As with resolution 998 (ES-I), Egypt, France, Israel, the United Kingdom, the Soviet Union and Eastern European States abstained.

Concept and guiding principles

On 6 November, the Secretary-General submitted to the General Assembly his second and final report[6] on the plan for an emergency United Nations Force. In this report, he defined the concept of the new Force and certain guiding principles for its organization and functioning. The main points:

(a) At the outset, an emergency international United Nations Force could be developed on the basis of three concepts. In the first place, it could be set up on the basis of principles reflected in the constitution of the United Nations itself. This would mean that its chief responsible officer should be appointed by the United Nations itself and in his functions should be responsible ultimately to the General Assembly and/or the Security Council. His authority should be so defined as to make him fully independent of the policies of any one nation and his relations to the Secretary-General should correspond to those of the Chief of Staff of UNTSO. A second possibility would be for the United Nations to charge a country, or a group of countries, with the responsibility to provide independently for an international Force serving for the purposes determined by the United Nations. In this approach, which was followed in the case of the Unified Command in Korea, it would obviously be impossible to achieve the same independence in relation to national policies as would be established through the first

[5]A/3289. [6]A/3302.

concept. Finally, as a third possibility, an international Force might be set up in agreement among a group of nations, later to be brought into an appropriate relationship to the United Nations. This approach was open to the same reservation as the second concept and possibly others. The Secretary-General noted that in deciding on 5 November 1956 to establish a United Nations Command, on an emergency basis, the General Assembly had chosen the first type of international force.

(b) The Secretary-General set out certain guiding principles for the organization and functioning of the Force:

- The decision taken by the General Assembly on the United Nations Command recognized the independence of the Chief of Command and established the principle that the Force should be recruited from Member States other than the permanent members of the Security Council. In this context, the Secretary-General observed that the question of the composition of the staff and contingents should not be subject to agreement by the parties involved since such a requirement would be difficult to reconcile with the development of the international Force along the course already being followed by the General Assembly.

- The terms of reference of the Force were to secure and supervise the cessation of hostilities in accordance with all the terms of the General Assembly's resolution 997 (ES-I) of 2 November 1956. It followed from its terms of reference that there was no intent in the establishment of the Force to influence the military balance in the current conflict, and thereby the political balance affecting efforts to settle the conflict. The Force should be of a temporary nature, the length of its assignment being determined by the needs arising out of the current conflict.

(c) Guidelines on the functions to be performed were outlined:

- The General Assembly's resolution of 2 November 1956 urged that "all parties now involved in hostilities in the area agree to an immediate cease-fire and, as part thereof, halt the movement of military forces and arms into the area", and further urged the parties to the Armistice Agreements promptly to withdraw all forces behind the armistice lines, to desist from raids against those lines into neighbouring territories and to observe scrupulously the provisions of the Agreements. These two provisions combined indicated that the functions of the United Nations Force would be, when a cease-fire was established, to enter Egyptian territory with the consent of the Egyptian Government, in order to help maintain quiet during and after the withdrawal of non-Egyptian forces and to secure compliance with the other terms established in the resolution.

- The Force obviously should have no rights other than those necessary for the execution of its functions, in cooperation with local authorities. It would be more than an observer corps, but in no way a military force temporarily controlling the territory in which it was stationed; nor should the Force have functions exceeding those necessary to secure peaceful conditions, on the assumption that the parties to the conflict would take all necessary steps for compliance with the recommendations of the General Assembly. Its functions could, on this basis, be assumed to cover an area extending roughly from the Suez Canal to the Armistice Demarcation Lines established in the Armistice Agreement between Egypt and Israel.

(d) The Secretary-General indicated that the question as to how the Force should be financed required further study. A basic rule, which could be applied provisionally, would be that a State providing a unit would be responsible for all costs of equipment and salaries, while all other costs should be financed by the United Nations outside its normal budget. It was obviously impossible to make any estimate of the costs without knowledge of the size of the Force and the length of its assignment. The only practical course therefore would be for the General Assembly to vote on a general authorization for those costs on the basis of general principles such as those suggested in the report.

(e) The Secretary-General stated that, because of the time factor, he could discuss the question of participation in the Force with only a limited number of Member Governments. The reaction so far led him to believe that it should be possible to meet quickly at least the most basic need for personnel. It was his hope that broader participation would be possible as soon as a plan was approved so that a more definite judgement might be possible concerning the implications of participation. Noting that several matters had to be left open because of the lack of time and the need for further study, the Secretary-General suggested that those matters be submitted to exploration by a small committee of the General Assembly. Such a committee might also serve as an advisory committee to the Secretary-General for questions relating to the operation.

Advisory Committee

After considering the report of the Secretary-General, the General Assembly adopted, on 7 November, resolution 1001 (ES-I) approving the guiding principles for the organization and functioning of the emergency international United Nations Force as expounded in the Secretary-General's report; concurring in the definition of the functions of the Force in the report; and approving provisionally the basic rule concerning the financing of the Force laid down in that report. The Assembly established an Advisory Committee composed of Brazil, Canada, Ceylon, Colombia, India, Norway and Pakistan. It requested the Committee, whose Chairman was the Secretary-General, to undertake the development of those aspects of the planning for the Force and its operation not already dealt with by the General Assembly and which did not fall within the area of the direct responsibility of the Chief of Command. It authorized the Secretary-General to issue all regulations and instructions essential to the effective functioning of the Force, following consultation with the Committee, and to take all other necessary administrative and executive action. The Committee was to continue to assist the Secretary-General in his responsibilities, and it could request the convening of the General Assembly if necessary. Finally, the Assembly requested all Member States to afford assistance as necessary to the United Nations Command in the performance of its functions, including arrangements for passage to and from the area involved.

This resolution, which, with resolution 998 (ES-I) of 4 November, formed the basis for the establishment of the United Nations Emergency Force, was adopted by 64 votes to none, with 12 abstentions. France and the United Kingdom voted this time with the majority. Egypt and Israel remained with the abstainers, together with South Africa and the Soviet Union and Eastern European States. The representatives of France and the United Kingdom indicated that the resolution was acceptable to their Governments because it provided, as they had urged, for an effective international Force in the area. In explaining his abstention, the representative of the Soviet Union stated that the establishment of the Force under General Assembly resolution 1000 (ES-I) and the plan for its implementation in resolution 1001 (ES-I) were contrary to the Charter, and that the only reason for abstaining rather than voting against the proposal lay in the hope of preventing any further extension of the aggression against Egypt.

Further General Assembly resolutions

On the same day, 7 November, the General Assembly also adopted resolution 1002 (ES-I), by which it called once again upon Israel immediately to withdraw all its forces behind the armistice lines, and upon France and the United Kingdom immediately to withdraw all their forces from Egyptian territory.

The voting was 65 to 1, with 10 abstentions. Israel cast the lone negative vote. France and the United Kingdom abstained, together with Australia, Belgium, Laos, Luxembourg, the Netherlands, New Zealand, Portugal and South Africa. The representatives of France and the United Kingdom indicated that an immediate withdrawal of their forces could lead to a power vacuum between Egyptian and Israeli forces and that withdrawal could only be effected subsequent to proof of the effective operation of UNEF.

The first emergency special session of the General Assembly ended on 10 November 1956. Before closing the session, the Assembly adopted resolution 1003 (ES-I), by which it decided to refer the matter to its eleventh regular session which was then about to convene.

During the first emergency special session, the General Assembly had adopted a total of seven resolutions. By these resolutions, the Assembly gave the Secretary-General the authority and support he required to bring about the cessation of hostilities in Egypt and the withdrawal of foreign troops from Egyptian territory with the assistance of a new type of peace-keeping machinery, the United Nations peace-keeping force. The idea of such a force, which was to have such an impact on the work of the United Nations for the maintenance of international peace and security, came initially from Mr. Lester Pearson. Secretary-General Dag Hammarskjöld made it a practical reality.

Initial stages of UNEF

The United Nations Emergency Force was the key element in the United Nations efforts to resolve the crisis arising from the military action of the Israeli and Anglo-French forces against Egypt. It was a pre-condition for securing the cease-fire and a pre-condition for bringing about the withdrawal of the invading forces. Therefore, a priority objective of the Secretary-General, after the adoption of the enabling resolutions, was to assemble a usable Force and land it in Egypt as rapidly as possible.

The establishment of this first peace-keeping Force in United Nations history was a task of great complexity. The concept had no real precedent. The nearest parallel was UNTSO, which also had peace-keeping functions but was a much simpler operation and did not provide much help as regards the many organizational and operational problems involved.

Immediately after the Assembly authorized the Force, the Chief of Command, General Burns, who was in Jerusalem at the time, selected a group of UNTSO observers who began planning the organization of the new Force. The Secretary-General approached the Governments of the potential participating countries to obtain the required military personnel. He also initiated negotiations with the Egyptian Government to secure its agreement as the host country for the entry and stationing of the Force in Egypt.

Negotiations with the Egyptian Government

A key principle governing the stationing and functioning of UNEF, and later of all other peace-keeping forces, was the consent of the host Government. Since it was not an enforcement action under Chapter VII of the Charter, UNEF could enter and operate in Egypt only with the consent of the Egyptian Government. This principle was clearly stated by the General Assembly in adopting resolution 1001 (ES-I) of 7 November 1956 concerning the establishment of UNEF.

Immediately after the adoption of that resolution, the Secretary-General instructed General Burns to approach the Egyptian authorities in Cairo in order to prepare the ground for the prompt implementation of the resolution. The Government of Egypt had already accepted the terms of resolution 1000 (ES-I) on the establishment of a United Nations Command, and this was considered by the Secretary-General as an acceptance in principle of the Force itself.

However, before consenting to the arrival of the Force on its territory, Egypt wished to have certain points in the Assembly resolution clarified. In particular, it wanted to know in clearer terms the functions of the Force, especially in regard to whether, when the Force reached the Armistice Demarcation Line, the Governments concerned would agree to the areas to be occupied by it, how long the Force would stay, whether it was supposed to have functions in the Suez Canal area apart from observing the withdrawal of the Anglo-French forces and whether it would stay in the Canal area after the Anglo-French withdrawal.

Firm assurance was given to the Egyptian authorities that cooperation with the United Nations would not infringe Egyptian sovereignty, detract from Egypt's power freely to negotiate a settlement on the Suez Canal or submit Egypt to any control from the outside. The Secretary-General impressed upon those authorities that the Force provided a guarantee for the withdrawal of foreign forces from Egypt and that, since it would come only with Egypt's consent, it could not stay or operate in Egypt if that consent were withdrawn.

On the basis of the General Assembly's resolutions as interpreted by the Secretary-General, the Government of Egypt gave its consent on 14 November to the arrival of UNEF in Egypt, and the first transport of UNEF troops took place on the next day.

While the exchange of views that had taken place was considered sufficient as a basis for the sending of the first units of UNEF to Egypt, the Secretary-General felt that a firmer foundation had to be laid for the presence and functioning of the Force in Egypt and for the continued cooperation with the Egyptian authorities. He also considered it essential to discuss personally with the Egyptian authorities, at the highest level, various questions which flowed from the decision to send the Force to Egypt, including the selection of national contingents.

The Secretary-General therefore visited Cairo from 16 to 18 November. During this visit, he reached agreement with the Egyptian Government on the composition of the Force. President Nasser had first opposed the inclusion of the Canadian, Danish and Norwegian units because they belonged to the North Atlantic Treaty Organization (NATO) and because, in his view, Canada and the United Kingdom were too congeneric. But on the insistence of the Secretary-General, this opposition was withdrawn. The basic discussions centred on the stationing and functioning of the Force.

The good faith agreement

On this essential matter, a "good faith agreement" was worked out and included in an aide-memoire[7] which served as the basis for the stationing of UNEF in Egypt. It noted that the Assembly, by resolution 1001 (ES-I), had approved the principle that the Force could not be requested "to be stationed or operate on the territory of a given country without the consent of the Government of that country". It then went on to say:

> The Government of Egypt and the Secretary-General of the United Nations have stated their understanding on the basic points for the presence and functioning of UNEF as follows:
>
> 1. The Government of Egypt declares that, when exercising its sovereign rights on any matter concerning the presence and functioning of UNEF, it will be guided, in good faith, by its acceptance of General Assembly resolution 1000 (ES-I) of 5 November 1956.
>
> 2. The United Nations takes note of this declaration of the Government of Egypt and declares that the activities of UNEF will be guided, in good faith, by the task established for the Force in the aforementioned resolutions; in particular, the United Nations, understanding this to correspond to the wishes of the Government of Egypt, reaffirms its willingness to maintain UNEF until its task is completed.
>
> 3. The Government of Egypt and the Secretary-General declare that it is their intention to proceed forthwith, in the light of points 1 and 2 above, to explore jointly concrete aspects of the functioning of UNEF, including its stationing

and the question of its lines of communication and supply; the Government of Egypt, confirming its intention to facilitate the functioning of UNEF, and the United Nations are agreed to expedite in cooperation the implementation of guiding principles arrived at as a result of that joint exploration on the basis of the resolutions of the General Assembly.[8]

The Secretary-General brought this aide-memoire to the attention of the General Assembly in a report[9] of 20 November 1956. In so doing, he stated that "...The aide-memoire, if noted with approval by the General Assembly, with the concurrence of Egypt, would establish an understanding between the United Nations and Egypt on which the cooperation could be developed and necessary agreements on various details be elaborated." No objection was raised by the Assembly in this connection.

Other memoranda and agreements

In addition to the good faith agreement, two other memoranda were agreed upon between the Secretary-General and President Nasser. One of them set out the understanding that the area to be occupied by UNEF after the Israeli withdrawal would be subject to agreement and that the Force would have no function in the Port Said and the Suez Canal areas after the withdrawal of the Anglo-French troops. UNEF could not stay or operate in Egypt unless Egypt continued its consent. The other memorandum specifically separated the question of the reopening of the Suez Canal from the functions of UNEF. The Secretary-General brought these memoranda to the attention of the Advisory Committee.

With these agreements, UNEF was set up. Subsequent discussions were continued between the Secretariat and the Egyptian authorities to work out more detailed and comprehensive arrangements on the status of the Force in Egypt. These arrangements were set out in a letter dated 8 February 1957 from the Secretary-General to the Minister for Foreign Affairs of Egypt and were accepted by the latter in his reply of the same date to the Secretary-General.[10] This exchange of letters constituted the agreement on the status of the United Nations Emergency Force in Egypt which

[7]Ibid. [8]A/3375, annex. [9]A/3375. [10]A/3526.

the General Assembly noted with approval in its resolution 1126 (XI) of 22 February 1957.

Status of the Force agreement

The status of the Force agreement covered a wide range of problems, including the premises of the Force and the use of the United Nations flag, freedom of movement, privileges and immunities of the Force, civil and criminal jurisdiction and settlement of disputes or claims. Two of the key provisions concerned freedom of movement and criminal jurisdiction. Members of the Force were to enjoy full freedom of movement in the performance of their duties. They were to be subject to the exclusive jurisdiction of their respective national Governments in respect of any criminal offences which they might commit in Egypt.

The agreement on the status of UNEF was the first document of this kind. It provided a pattern which was followed for the subsequent peace-keeping forces in the Congo and Cyprus and was used as a precedent to deal with various problems arising from the operations of UNEF II, UNDOF and UNIFIL.

Negotiations with the participating countries

The principles of consent applied not only to the host Government but also to the participating countries. In accordance with the principles approved by the General Assembly, the Force was to be composed of national contingents accepted for service by the Secretary-General from among those voluntarily offered by Member States. Troops from the permanent members of the Security Council or from any country which, for geographical and other reasons, might have a special interest in the conflict would be excluded. In selecting the contingents, the Secretary-General had to take due account of the views of the host Government and such other factors as their suitability in terms of the needs of the Force, their size and availability, the extent to which they would be self-contained, the undesirability of too great a variation in ordnance and basic equipment, the problem of transportation and the goal of balanced composition.

The size of the Force was to be determined by the Commander in consultation with the Secretary-General and in the light of the functions to be performed. The original estimate by the Force Commander of the manpower needs to perform those tasks was the equivalent of two combat brigades, or about 6,000 men. It was decided that the national contingents should be sufficiently large to be relatively self-contained and that the Force should have adequate support units, including a light air-unit. From the point of view of balance, it was desirable that the differences in the size of the units should not be so great as to lead to excessive dependence on any one State.

The Secretary-General sought certain assurances from the participating countries. He pointed out that the effective functioning of UNEF required that some continuity of service of the participating units should be assured in order to enable the Force Commander to plan his operations. He also insisted that the Commander of each national contingent should take orders exclusively from the Force Commander and should be in a position to exercise the necessary disciplinary authority with the members of his contingent.

The arrangements between the United Nations and the contributing countries were expanded and set out in formal agreements in the form of an exchange of letters between the Secretary-General and the respective participating Governments.

By 5 November 1956, Canada, Colombia, Denmark, Finland, Norway, Pakistan and Sweden had replied affirmatively. In the following days, Afghanistan, Brazil, Burma, Ceylon, Chile, Czechoslovakia, Ecuador, Ethiopia, India, Indonesia, Iran, Laos, New Zealand, Peru, the Philippines, Romania and Yugoslavia also offered to provide contingents. In addition, the United States Government informed the Secretary-General that it was prepared to help as regards airlifts, shipping, transport and supplies. Italy agreed to place at the disposal of the United Nations the facilities of Capodichino Airport at Naples for the assembly and transit of UNEF personnel and equipment and to help in the airlift of personnel and equipment from Italy to Egypt. The Swiss Government, a non-member State, offered to defray part of the cost of Swissair charter planes.

UNEF's composition

In consultation with the Force Commander and after discussions with the Government of Egypt, the Secretary-General accepted contingents from 10 countries: Brazil, Canada, Colombia, Denmark, Finland, India, Indonesia, Norway, Sweden and Yugoslavia. The offers of assistance from the United States, Italy and Switzerland were also accepted. With the agreement of

Egypt, an air base at Abu Suweir near Ismailia was used as the central depot for the early contingents.

The extent of the area to be covered by UNEF called for highly mobile reconnaissance. This need was met by Yugoslavia, which provided a complete reconnaissance battalion. Canada later supplied a fully equipped, light-armoured squadron. Supporting units were obtained and assigned with the same urgency as those engaged in patrolling. The Indian contingent was given responsibility for the supply depot and the service institute; Canada and India provided units for transport, the Provost Marshal and signals; Norway and Canada covered the medical needs. The Canadian contingent was also made responsible for the ordnance depot and workshop, the base post office, engineering, the dental unit, movement control and air support.

General Burns and his group of UNTSO military observers arrived in Cairo on 12 November 1956 and set up a temporary headquarters there. The first UNEF units, composed of Colombians, Danes and Norwegians, flew to Egypt on 15 and 16 November. They were followed by other contingents. The target strength of about 6,000 men was reached in February 1957 after the Brazilian battalion had arrived at Port Said by sea. With the appointment of staff officers selected from the participating countries, the UNTSO military observers returned to their normal duties in Jerusalem.

The Governments of Indonesia and Finland, which had agreed to participate in the Force only for a limited period, withdrew their contingents in September and December 1957, respectively. The Colombian Government withdrew its contingent in December 1958. The other contingents continued to serve with UNEF until the withdrawal of the Force in 1967. The deployment and assignment of the contingents were changed from time to time according to the requirements of the operation.

The strength of the Force remained at the authorized level of about 6,000 until the end of 1957. In the following years, it was gradually reduced because the situation in the area of operation remained quiet and also because of financial difficulties. There were 5,341 all ranks with the Force in 1960, 5,102 in 1963, 4,581 in 1965 and 3,959 in 1966. In November 1965, a survey team was sent to the area to examine the possibility of further reductions. In accordance with its recommendations, the strength was further brought down to 3,378 at the time the Force began its withdrawal in May 1967.

UNEF's organization

The United Nations Emergency Force, established by the General Assembly, was a subsidiary organ of the Assembly under Article 22 of the Charter. It was directed by the Secretary-General under the general authority of the General Assembly.

The Secretary-General was authorized to issue all regulations and instructions which might be essential to the effective functioning of the Force and to take all other necessary administrative and executive actions. To assist him in these matters, he set up an informal military group at Headquarters composed of military representatives of participating countries and headed by his military adviser — Major-General I.A.E. Martola (Finland), during the formative period. The Secretary-General was also assisted by the Advisory Committee established under Assembly resolution 1001 (ES-I).

The command of the Force was assumed in the field by the Force Commander (originally designated as the Chief of Command), who was appointed by the General Assembly on the recommendation of the Secretary-General. The Commander was operationally responsible for the performance of all functions assigned to the Force by the United Nations and for the deployment and assignment of the troops placed at the disposal of the Force. He had direct authority for the operation of the Force and also was responsible for the provision of facilities, supplies and auxiliary services. He reported to the Secretary-General and was responsible to him. He was normally a general officer seconded by a Member State at the request of the Secretary-General, and during his assignment with the United Nations received an appointment as a senior official of the United Nations Secretariat with the rank of Assistant Secretary-General (Under-Secretary during Dag Hammarskjöld's time).

The Force Commander was authorized to appoint the officers of his command in consultation with the Secretary-General. In selecting the officers, the Commander was required to give due consideration to the goal of a balanced composition and to the importance of contributions made by the participating countries. The national contingents were under the command of the contingent commanders, who were appointed by their respective Governments. These contingents remained part of their respective national armed forces but, during their assignment to UNEF, they owed international allegiance and were placed under the operational control of the United Nations. This control was exercised through the contingent commanders, who received their instructions from the Force Commander. Changes in contingent commanders were made by the Governments of participating countries in consultation with the Force Commander.

The officers and soldiers of each contingent continued to wear their national uniforms but with United Nations insignia. The blue beret and helmet were created by Secretary-General Hammarskjöld during the formative days of UNEF.

Responsibility for disciplinary action in national contingents rested with the contingent commanders. Reports concerning disciplinary ac-

tion were communicated to the Force Commander, who might consult with the contingent commanders and, if necessary, with the authorities of the participating Governments concerned.

Military police were provided by the Force Commander for all camps, establishments and other premises occupied by the Force and for such areas where the Force was deployed in the performance of its functions. Elsewhere, UNEF military police might be employed in so far as such employment was necessary to maintain discipline and order among members of the Force, subject to arrangements with the authorities of the host country and in liaison with those authorities.

B. Cease-fire and withdrawal of foreign forces

Establishment of the cease-fire

The first objective of Secretary-General Hammarskjöld was to secure a cease-fire in accordance with the call of the General Assembly contained in resolution 997 (ES-I) of 2 November 1956.

During the meeting at which this resolution was adopted, the representative of Israel stated that his Government agreed to an immediate cease-fire, provided that a similar answer was forthcoming from Egypt. On the same day, the Egyptian Government informed the Secretary-General that it would accept the call for a cease-fire on the condition that military actions against Egypt were stopped. The Secretary-General immediately notified Israel, France and the United Kingdom of Egypt's position and called[11] upon all four parties to bring hostilities to an end.

On 4 November, the Secretary-General requested all four parties concerned to bring to a halt all hostile military action by 2400 hours GMT on the same day. In identical messages[12] addressed to the Governments of France and the United Kingdom, he pointed out that in the light of the replies received from Egypt and Israel, it was obvious that the positions of France and the United Kingdom would determine whether or not it would be possible to achieve a cease-fire between Egypt and Israel. He urged the two Governments to give him a definitive acceptance on his cease-fire call at the earliest possible moment. On 5 November, France and the United Kingdom informed[13] the Secretary-General that as soon as the Governments of Egypt

and Israel signified acceptance of, and the United Nations endorsed a plan for, an international Force with the prescribed functions, they would cease all military action.

Later in the day, the British representative announced that a cease-fire had been ordered at Port Said. Orders had also been given to cease all bombing forthwith throughout Egypt, and other forms of air action would be limited to the support of any necessary operation in the Canal area. Also on the same day, Egypt accepted the Secretary-General's request for a cease-fire without any attached conditions and Israel informed the Secretary-General that in the light of Egypt's declaration, it confirmed its readiness to agree to a cease-fire.

In an aide-mémoire[14] dated 5 November, the Secretary-General informed France and the United Kingdom that, since on that date the General Assembly had taken a decisive step towards setting up the international Force by establishing a United Nations Command, and since Egypt and Israel had agreed, without conditions, to a cease-fire, the conditions for a general cease-fire would seem to be established.

In their replies[15] of 6 November, the two Governments announced that their forces were being ordered to cease fire at midnight GMT on the same day, pending confirmation that Egypt and Israel had accepted an unconditional cease-fire and that there would be a United Nations Force

---

[11]A/3287. [12]Ibid. [13]A/3294 and A/3293. [14]A/3310. [15]A/3306 and A/3307.

competent to secure and supervise the attainment of the objectives of resolution 997 (ES-I). The Secretary-General promptly informed Egypt and Israel that the cease-fire would become effective at midnight. He noted that the Assembly had not made the cease-fire dependent on the creation or the functioning of UNEF, since its call for a cease-fire and its decision to establish the Force were in separate resolutions.

The cease-fire was established at midnight GMT on 7/8 November and, except for isolated incidents, generally held.

Withdrawal of the Anglo-French force

At the same time as the Secretary-General was taking urgent steps to set up the new Force, he was pressing France and the United Kingdom for an early withdrawal of their forces from the Port Said area.

The two Governments told him that their troops would be withdrawn as soon as the proposed United Nations Force was in a position to assume effectively the tasks assigned to it and, in particular, to ensure that hostilities would not be resumed in the area.

The Secretary-General therefore endeavoured to move the first units of UNEF to Egypt and build up its strength as rapidly as he could. But the establishment of this first United Nations peace-keeping force was not an easy job, and it took time to obtain the required units from the various contributing countries, transport them to the area of operations and make them fully operational. The first units from the Colombian, Danish and Norwegian contingents arrived in the area on 15 and 16 November and were immediately deployed in the Suez Canal area.

On 24 November, the General Assembly adopted resolution 1120 (XI), by which it noted with regret that two thirds of the French forces and all of the British forces remained in Egypt, and it reiterated its call to the British and French Governments for the immediate withdrawal of their forces.

In messages[16] dated 3 December, the British and French Governments noted that an effective United Nations Force was currently arriving in Egypt, that the Secretary-General had accepted the responsibility for organizing the task of clearing the Suez Canal as expeditiously as possible, that free and secure transit would be re-established through the Canal when it was cleared and that the Secretary-General would promote as quickly as possible negotiations with regard to the future regime of the Canal on the basis of the six requirements set out in the Security Council's resolution 118 (1956) of 13 October 1956. The two Governments confirmed their decision to continue the withdrawal of their forces from the Port Said area without delay.

The Secretary-General immediately instructed[17] General Burns to get in touch with the Anglo-French Commander and work out with him arrangements for the complete withdrawal of the Anglo-French forces without delay, ensuring that UNEF would be in a position to assume its responsibilities in the Port Said area by the middle of December.

On 22 December, the withdrawal of the Anglo-French forces was completed and UNEF took over the Port Said area.

Initial withdrawal of the Israeli forces: November 1956– mid-January 1957

The negotiations undertaken by the Secretary-General to achieve the withdrawal of the Anglo-French forces required nearly two months; those regarding the withdrawal of Israeli forces took much longer. By resolution 997 (ES-I) of 2 November 1956, the General Assembly had urged the parties to the Armistice Agreements promptly to withdraw all forces behind the armistice lines, to desist from raids across those lines into neighbouring territory and to observe scrupulously the Armistice Agreements. In resolution 1002 (ES-I) of 7 November, the Assembly, after noting its decision to establish a United Nations Command for an international force, called once again upon Israel immediately to withdraw its forces behind the armistice lines.

On 7 November, the Prime Minister of Israel, Mr. David Ben Gurion, in a statement to the Israeli Knesset (Parliament), stated that the armistice lines between Egypt and Israel had no validity and that "on no account will Israel agree to the stationing of a foreign force, no matter how called, in her territory, or in any of the areas occupied by her". On hearing of this statement, the Secretary-General immediately wrote to the Minister for Foreign Affairs of Israel, Mrs. Golda Meir, to inform her that this position was in violation of the resolutions of the General Assembly and, if maintained, would seriously complicate the task of giving effect to those resolutions.

---

[16]A/3415. [17]Ibid.

On 21 November, in reply to queries by the Secretary-General, the Government of Israel stated[18] that there had already been a withdrawal of its forces for varying distances along the entire Egyptian frontier. It reiterated its position regarding the withdrawal of the Israeli forces and indicated that the satisfactory arrangements it sought were such as would ensure Israel's security against the recurrence of the threat or danger of attack and against acts of belligerency by land or sea. Noting that it had not yet had an opportunity to discuss the question of satisfactory arrangements to be made with the United Nations in connection with UNEF, it stated that it was awaiting information on the proposed size, location and stationing arrangements of the Force and on the methods proposed for the discharge of its functions as laid down in the General Assembly's resolutions of 2, 5 and 7 November. It was also awaiting a clarification by Egypt on its policy and intention with respect to belligerency or peace with Israel which must influence Israel's dispositions on matters affecting its security.

At a meeting held on 24 November, the General Assembly adopted resolution 1120 (XI) by which, after noting that the Israeli forces had not yet been withdrawn behind the armistice lines, reiterated its call to Israel to comply forthwith with its resolution. On the same day, the representative of Israel informed[19] the Secretary-General that the equivalent of two infantry brigades had been withdrawn from Egyptian territory into Israel.

In a letter[20] dated 1 December, the representative of Israel advised the Secretary-General that on the morning of 3 December, Israeli forces would be removed from a wide belt of territory (about 50 kilometres) in proximity to the Suez Canal along its entire length. Elements of UNEF immediately entered the evacuated area, although progress in this process was slowed down because of minefields and destroyed roads. On 11 December, Israel announced that it was ready to effect further withdrawal of troops in the Sinai peninsula in order to enable UNEF to extend its occupation eastward.

General Burns met with General Moshe Dayan, the Israeli Commander, on the morning of 16 December. They agreed on specific arrangements for a first phase of withdrawal, and UNEF troops moved forward to within five kilometres of new Israeli positions.

Regarding further withdrawals, General Dayan informed the UNEF Commander that, according to his instructions, the Israeli forces were to withdraw from the remainder of the Sinai at an approximate rate of 25 kilometres each week dur-

ing the next four weeks. This plan was considered by General Burns to be inadequate. Consequently, at his request, a new withdrawal proposal was submitted by the Israeli Government on 21 December. The new proposal envisaged that the remaining Israeli withdrawal would take place in two phases. The second phase would involve a full Israeli withdrawal behind the armistice lines at an unstated date.

In accordance with this proposal, a further withdrawal of Israeli forces took place on 7 and 8 January 1957 to a north-south line roughly following meridian 33 degrees, 44 minutes, leaving no Israeli forces west of El Arish. On 15 January, the Israeli forces withdrew eastward another 25 to 30 kilometres, except in the area of Sharm el Sheikh. This phase involved the entry into El Arish and St. Catherine's Monastery of the United Nations Emergency Force, which had closely followed the withdrawing Israeli troops.

Sharm el Sheikh and the Gaza Strip

A day earlier, on 14 January, the Government of Israel had informed the Secretary-General that by 22 January the Sinai Desert would be entirely evacuated by Israeli forces with the exception of the Sharm el Sheikh area, that is "the strip on the western coast of the Gulf of Aqaba which at present ensures freedom of navigation in the Strait of Tiran and in the Gulf". Reporting[21] on this matter to the General Assembly, the Secretary-General stated that under the terms of the Assembly's resolution, the Israeli forces should be withdrawn also from that area.

In this connection, he observed that the international significance of the Gulf of Aqaba might be considered to justify the right of innocent passage through the Strait of Tiran and the Gulf in accordance with recognized rules of international law. He did not consider that a discussion of the various aspects of this matter and its possible relation to the action requested in the General Assembly on the Middle East crisis fell within the mandate established for him in resolution 999 (ES-I) of 4 November. Like the cease-fire, withdrawal was a preliminary and essential phase in the process through which a viable basis might be laid for peaceful conditions in the area. The General Assembly, in giving high priority to the cease-fire and withdrawal, in no way disregarded all the other aims which must be achieved in order to create

[18]A/3384, annex 2. [19]A/3389/Add.1. [20]A/3410. [21]A/3500.

more satisfactory conditions than those prevailing during the period preceding the crisis. The basic function of UNEF, which was to help maintain quiet, gave the Force great value as a background for efforts towards resolving such pending problems, although it was not in itself a means to that end.

On 19 January 1957, the General Assembly adopted resolution 1123 (XI) by which, after recalling its resolutions of 2, 4, 7 and 24 November 1956, requested the Secretary-General "to continue his efforts for securing the complete withdrawal of Israel in pursuance of the above-mentioned resolutions, and to report on such completion to the General Assembly, within five days".

In pursuance of that resolution, the Secretary-General held further discussions with Israeli representatives on 20 and 23 January. On 23 January, Israel presented[22] its views in an aide-memoire on the Israeli position on the Sharm el Sheikh area and the Gaza Strip. Its position on each of the two areas was:

(a) For the Sharm el Sheikh area, Israel's aim was the simultaneous reconciliation of two objectives: the withdrawal of Israeli forces from that area and the guaranteeing of permanent freedom of navigation by the prevention of belligerence. In this matter, Egyptian compliance with the decision of the Security Council — resolution 95 (1951) of 1 September 1951 — had a legal and chronological priority over Israel's duty to fulfil recommendations in which Egypt had an interest. Accordingly, Israel formally requested the Secretary-General to ascertain Egypt's intentions with respect to the Council's 1951 resolution concerning the Suez Canal.

(b) For the Gaza Strip, Israel, after questioning the legality of the Egyptian occupation of Gaza from 1948 to 1956 and criticizing its actions during this period, proposed a plan under which the Israeli military forces would be withdrawn but an Israeli civilian administration would remain to deal with security and administrative matters; the United Nations Emergency Force would not enter and be deployed in the Gaza area, but Israel would cooperate with the United Nations Relief and Works Agency for Palestine Refugees in the Near East (UNRWA) regarding the care and maintenance of the refugees in the area. In this connection, Israel was ready to work out with the United Nations a suitable relationship with respect to the Gaza Strip.

The position of the Secretary-General was set out in his report[23] of 24 January 1957:

▪ In connection with the question of Israeli withdrawal from the Sharm el Sheikh area, attention had been directed to the situation in the Strait of Tiran and the Gulf of Aqaba. This problem was of longer duration and was not directly related to the current crisis. It followed from principles guiding the United Nations that the Israeli military action and its consequences should not be elements influencing the solution of this problem. The Secretary-General concluded that upon the withdrawal of the Israeli forces, UNEF would have to follow them in the same way as it had in other parts of the Sinai, its movements being determined by its duties in respect of the cease-fire and the withdrawal. In accordance with the general legal principles recognized as decisive for the deployment of the Force, UNEF should not be used in such a way as to prejudice the solution of the controversial questions involved.

▪ Regarding the status of Gaza, the United Nations could not recognize a change of the de facto situation created under the Armistice Agreement, by which the administration and security in the Strip were left in the hands of Egypt, unless the change was brought about through settlement between the parties. Nor could it lend its assistance to the maintenance of a de facto situation contrary to the one created by the Agreement. These considerations excluded the United Nations from accepting Israeli control over the area even if it were of a non-military character. Deployment of UNEF in Gaza under the resolutions of the General Assembly would have to be on the same basis as its deployment along the Armistice Demarcation Line and in the Sinai peninsula. Any broader function for it in that area, in view of the terms of the Armistice Agreement and a recognized principle of international law, would require the consent of Egypt.

[22] A/3511. [23] A/3512.

Second withdrawal of Israeli forces: February 1957

On 2 February 1957, the General Assembly, after receiving the Secretary-General's report, adopted two resolutions.

By resolution 1124 (XI), it deplored the failure of Israel to complete its withdrawal behind the Armistice Demarcation Line and called upon it to do so without delay. By resolution 1125 (XI), the Assembly, recognizing that withdrawal by Israel must be followed by action which would assure progress towards the creation of peaceful conditions, called upon Egypt and Israel scrupulously to observe the provisions of the 1949 General Armistice Agreement and considered that "after full withdrawal of Israel from the Sharm el Sheikh and the Gaza areas, the scrupulous maintenance of the Armistice Agreement requires the placing of the United Nations Emergency Force on the Egyptian-Israel Armistice Demarcation Line and the implementation of other measures as proposed in the Secretary-General's report, with due regard to the considerations set out therein with a view to assist in achieving situations conducive to the maintenance of peaceful conditions in the area". The General Assembly further requested the Secretary-General, in consultation with the parties concerned, to take steps to carry out these measures and to report to it as appropriate.

On 4 February, the Secretary-General met with the representative of Israel to discuss implementation of the Assembly's resolutions. Israel presented to him an aide-memoire[24] in which it raised two points. First, it requested the Secretary-General to ask the Government of Egypt whether Egypt agreed "to the mutual and full abstention from belligerent acts, by land, air and sea, on withdrawal of Israeli troops". Secondly, Israel sought clarification as to whether "immediately on the withdrawal of Israeli forces from the Sharm el Sheikh area, units of the United Nations Emergency Force will be stationed along the western shore of the Gulf of Aqaba in order to act as a restraint against hostile acts, and will remain so deployed until another effective means is agreed upon between the parties concerned for ensuring permanent freedom of navigation and the absence of belligerent acts in the Strait of Tiran and the Gulf of Aqaba".

During the same meeting, the Secretary-General asked whether, with regard to Gaza, it was understood by the Government of Israel that the withdrawal had to cover elements of civilian administration as well as military troops. He consid-

ered a clarification on this point to be a prerequisite to further consideration of the Israeli aide-memoire. There was, in his view, an unavoidable connection between Israel's willingness to comply fully with General Assembly resolution 1124 (XI) as concerned the Gaza Strip and what might be done towards maintaining quiet in the Sharm el Sheikh area, and it was unrealistic to assume that the latter question could be solved while Israel remained in Gaza.

With regard to the second point raised by Israel, the Secretary-General noted that the debate in the General Assembly and the report on which it was based made it clear that the stationing of the United Nations Emergency Force at Sharm el Sheikh would require Egyptian consent. In the light of this implication of Israel's question, the Secretary-General considered it important, as a basis for his consideration of the aide-memoire, to learn whether Israel itself consented in principle to the stationing of UNEF units on its territory in implementation of the functions established for the Force by the Assembly's resolutions and, in particular, its resolution 1125 (XI) where it was indicated that the Force should be placed on the Egyptian-Israeli Armistice Demarcation Line.

This meeting was followed by an exchange of communications between the Secretary-General and the representative of Israel, and a meeting between them was held on 10 February. But these were all inconclusive, as each side wanted to receive the clarifications it had sought before replying to the questions addressed to it. In this connection, the Secretary-General stated that the fact that Israel had not found it possible to clarify elements decisive for the consideration of its requests had complicated the efforts to achieve implementation of the Assembly's resolutions.

In reporting[25] on this matter to the General Assembly on 11 February, the Secretary-General commented that the relationship between resolution 1124 (XI) on withdrawal and resolution 1125 (XI) on measures to be carried out after withdrawal afforded the possibility of informal explorations of the whole field covered by these two resolutions, preparatory to negotiations. Later, the results of such explorations might be used in the negotiations through a constructive combination of measures, representing for the two countries parallel progress towards the peaceful conditions sought. However, such explorations could not be permitted to invert the sequence between withdrawal and other measures, nor to disrupt the

[24]A/3527, annex I. [25]A/3527.

evolution of negotiations towards their goal. Progress towards peaceful conditions, following the general policy suggested in the last report of the Secretary-General, on which General Assembly resolution 1125 (XI) was based, had to be achieved gradually.

Final withdrawal of Israeli forces: March 1957

In concluding his report, the Secretary-General stated that, in the situation now facing the United Nations, the General Assembly, as a matter of priority, might wish to indicate how it wished him to proceed with further steps to carry out its decisions.

The Assembly did not adopt any further resolution on this matter after the Secretary-General's report, but the Israeli Government eventually softened its position on the withdrawal from the Gaza Strip, although it maintained its denunciation of the 1949 General Armistice Agreement with Egypt and continued to oppose the stationing of the United Nations Emergency Force on its side of the Armistice Demarcation Line.

On 1 March, the Foreign Minister of Israel announced in the General Assembly the decision of her Government to act in compliance with the request contained in Assembly resolution 1124 (XI) to withdraw behind the Armistice Demarcation Line.

The same day, the Secretary-General instructed the Commander of UNEF as a matter of utmost urgency to arrange for a meeting with the Commander-in-Chief of the Israeli forces in order to agree with him on arrangements for the complete and unconditional withdrawal of Israel in accordance with the Assembly's decision.

On 4 March, the declaration of 1 March was confirmed by the Israeli Government. The same day, General Burns met at Lydda with General Dayan. Technical arrangements were agreed upon for the withdrawal of the Israeli forces and the entry of UNEF troops into the Gaza Strip during the hours of curfew on the night of 6/7 March. Agreement was also reached for a similar takeover of the Sharm el Sheikh area on 8 March.

On 6 March, General Burns reported that UNEF troops were in position in all camps and centres of population in the Gaza Strip. The operation was carried out according to plan and without incident. By 0400 hours GMT, all Israelis had withdrawn from the Strip with the exception of an Israeli troop unit at Rafah Camp. By agreement, that last Israeli element was to be withdrawn at 1600 hours GMT on 8 March and full withdrawal from the Sharm el Sheikh area would be effected at the same time. These withdrawals took place as agreed and thus the Secretary-General was able to report to the General Assembly on 8 March 1957 full compliance with its resolution 1124 (XI) of 2 February 1957.

C. UNEF deployment

Deployment along the Armistice Demarcation Line

In its resolution 1125 (XI), on measures to be taken after the withdrawal of the Israeli forces from Egyptian territory, the General Assembly called upon the Governments of Egypt and Israel to observe scrupulously the provisions of the 1949 General Armistice Agreement and considered that, after full withdrawal of Israel from the Sharm el Sheikh and Gaza areas, "the scrupulous maintenance of the Armistice Agreement requires the placing of the United Nations Emergency Force on the Egyptian-Israel Armistice Demarcation Line".

On 11 February 1957, the Secretary-General reported[26] to the Assembly that Egypt had reaffirmed its intent to observe fully the provisions of the Armistice Agreement to which it was a party, on the assumption that observance would be reciprocal. The Secretary-General drew attention to the desire expressed by Egypt to see an end to all raids and incursions across the Armistice Line in both directions, with effective assistance from United Nations auxiliary organs to that effect.

Israel maintained its denunciation of the Armistice Agreement. In a letter[27] of 25 January, the representative of Israel had stated that "Israel does not claim that the absence of an armistice agreement means the existence of a state of war with Egypt, even though Egypt insisted on the existence of a state of war even when the Agree-

---

[26]Ibid. [27]A/3527, annex V.

ment was in existence. Israel is prepared to confirm its position on this by signing immediately with Egypt an agreement of non-belligerency and mutual non-aggression, but the Agreement, violated and broken, is beyond repair".

The Secretary-General did not accept Israel's denunciation as valid, as there was no provision in the 1949 Agreement for unilateral termination of its application. Consequently, the machinery for the supervision of the Armistice Agreement was maintained by UNTSO.

In his report[28] of 8 March 1957, the Secretary-General informed the General Assembly that arrangements would be made through which, without any change in the legal structure or status of UNTSO, its functions in the Gaza area would be placed under the operational control of UNEF. Close cooperation between the two United Nations peace-keeping operations was maintained.

Regarding the placing of UNEF along the Armistice Demarcation Line, the Secretary-General interpreted this as requiring the deployment of the Force on both sides of the Line. The Egyptian Government had consented to the deployment of UNEF on its territory along the Line as well as in the Sharm el Sheikh area on the basis of the "good faith agreement" set out in the aide-memoire of November 1956. At the beginning of February 1957, the Secretary-General had sought clarification from Israel as to whether, as a question of principle, it agreed to the stationing of UNEF units on its side of the Armistice Demarcation Line. No clarification was obtained and, in a letter[29] dated 6 February to the representative of Israel, the Secretary-General said he assumed that, at least for the present, Israel's reply to this question was essentially negative. In view of the Israeli position, UNEF could be deployed only on the Egyptian side.

As of 8 March 1957, UNEF was deployed along the western side of the Armistice Demarcation Line along the Gaza Strip, along the international frontier between the Sinai and Israel, as well as in the Sharm el Sheikh area.

Phases of deployment and activities

UNEF began operating in Egypt on 12 November 1956, when the Force Commander and a group of military observers detached from UNTSO set up a temporary headquarters in Cairo. It was withdrawn ten-and-a-half years later, on 18 May 1967, at the request of the Egyptian Government. The operation of the Force during this period may be divided into four phases: the first phase, which

extended from mid-November to late December 1956, was centred on the withdrawal of the Anglo-French forces from the Port Said area. The second, from that time to early March 1957, concerned the withdrawal of the Israeli forces from the Sinai peninsula, except the Gaza Strip and the Sharm el Sheikh area. The third, in March, related to those areas. The fourth and last phase, which began with the deployment of UNEF along the borders between Egypt and Israel, covered a period of more than 10 years from March 1957 until May 1967, during which time the Force effectively maintained peace in those sensitive areas.

First phase: Suez Canal area (November–December 1956)

When UNEF became operational in mid-November 1956, the cease-fire had been achieved and was generally holding. The Anglo-French forces were occupying the Port Said area including Port Fuad in the northern end of the Suez Canal. The Israeli forces were deployed east of the Canal about 10 kilometres from it. The Secretary-General was actively negotiating with the three Governments concerned and pressing for the early withdrawal of their forces from Egyptian soil.

The objectives of UNEF were to supervise the cessation of hostilities and to assist in the withdrawal process once agreement was reached on this matter. Shortly after its arrival in Egypt, UNEF was interposed between the Anglo-French and the Egyptian forces, occupying a buffer zone. All incidents involving the cease-fire were reported to the proper authorities, who were urged to prevent recurrences. No provisions had been made for the establishment of joint machinery whereby incidents could be examined and discussed. UNEF's role was limited to investigating, reporting and, if warranted, protesting to the relevant authorities.

By arrangements with the Anglo-French forces, units of UNEF entered Port Said and Port Fuad and took responsibility for maintaining law and order in certain areas, in cooperation with the local authorities. The Force also undertook guard duty of some vulnerable installations and other points.

In the period of transition, when the Anglo-French forces were preparing to leave and during the withdrawal process, UNEF undertook certain essential administrative functions such as security and the protection of public and private

[28]A/3568. [29]A/3527, annex III.

property, with the cooperation of the Governor and the Police Inspector in Port Said. With the sanction of the local authorities, UNEF personnel also performed administrative functions with respect to public services, utilities and arrangements for the provisioning of the local population with foodstuffs, and exercised limited powers of detention. All administrative and policing responsibilities were turned over to the Egyptian authorities the day following the Anglo-French evacuation.

Other tasks of the Force included clearing minefields in the Suez Canal area and arranging for exchanges of prisoners and detainees between the Egyptian Government and the Anglo-French command. In the last stage of the withdrawal of the Anglo-French troops from Port Said and Port Fuad, UNEF units were stationed around the final perimeter of the zone occupied by the withdrawing forces, thus preventing clashes between them and the Egyptian troops.

Second phase: Sinai peninsula (December 1956–March 1957)

After the withdrawal of the Anglo-French forces, UNEF concentrated its efforts on maintaining the cease-fire between the Egyptian and Israeli forces and on arranging for Israeli withdrawal from Egyptian territory.

The Israeli forces withdrew from the Sinai peninsula, with the exception of the Gaza and the Sharm el Sheikh areas, in three stages: on 3 December 1956, on 7 and 8 January 1957 and from 15 to 22 January 1957.

On the whole, the functions performed by UNEF in the Sinai were similar to those undertaken in the Canal area. The Force was interposed between the Egyptian and Israeli forces in a temporary buffer zone from 3 December onwards, moving eastbound as the Israeli forces withdrew, and in accordance with pre-arranged procedures.

During the successive stages of the Israeli withdrawal, UNEF temporarily undertook some local civic responsibilities, including security functions in a few inhabited areas, handing over such responsibilities to the Egyptian civilian authorities as soon as they returned to their posts. The Force also arranged and carried out exchanges of prisoners of war between Egypt and Israel and discharged certain investigatory functions. It cleared minefields in the Sinai and repaired portions of damaged roads and tracks crossing the peninsula.

Third phase: Gaza Strip and Sharm el Sheikh (March 1957)

After 22 January 1957, Israel held on to the last two areas it still occupied. The persistent negotiations to ensure withdrawal are described above. The withdrawal from the Gaza Strip took place on 6 and 7 March 1957 and that from the Sharm el Sheikh area from 8 to 12 March.

In accordance with the arrangements agreed to by the Egyptian Government, a UNEF detachment was stationed in Sharm el Sheikh following the withdrawal of the Israeli forces. This detachment maintained an observation post and kept the Strait of Tiran under constant watch.

In the Gaza Strip, two local conditions were of special concern to UNEF as it moved into the area. It was across the Armistice Demarcation Line along the Strip that the greatest number of infiltrations and raids had occurred during past years and there were in the area a large number of Palestinian Arab refugees, who were being assisted by UNRWA.

UNEF units entered the Gaza Strip on 6 March as the withdrawal of Israeli forces began. As a first step, arrangements were made between the Force Commander and the Israeli authorities for the United Nations to assume its responsibilities in the Strip as the Israeli troops and civil administrators withdrew.

On 7 March, General Burns notified the population of Gaza that UNEF, acting in fulfilment of its functions as determined by the General Assembly and with the consent of the Government of Egypt, was being deployed in the area for the purpose of maintaining quiet during and after the withdrawal of the Israeli forces. He also announced that until further arrangements were made, UNEF had assumed responsibility for civil affairs in the area and that UNRWA would continue to provide food and other services as in the past.

The involvement of UNEF in civil administration was of a purely temporary nature, pending the re-establishment of local civilian authority. In this connection, UNEF cooperated closely with UNRWA in meeting the needs of the local population. The operation of the Force during this initial period was greatly facilitated by the presence in Gaza of an important branch of UNRWA and by the fact that the Egypt-Israel Mixed Armistice Commission had its headquarters in Gaza and made available to the Force its personnel and its communications facilities.

UNEF I deployment as of August 1957

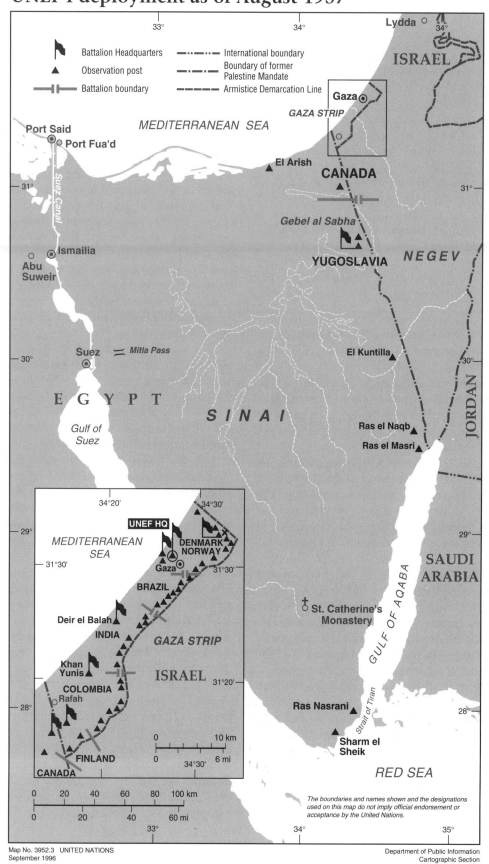

Legend:
- Battalion Headquarters
- Observation post
- Battalion boundary
- International boundary
- Boundary of former Palestine Mandate
- Armistice Demarcation Line

MEDITERRANEAN SEA

ISRAEL

Lydda

Gaza

GAZA STRIP

Port Said
Port Fua'd

El Arish

CANADA

Suez Canal

Gebel al Sabha

YUGOSLAVIA

NEGEV

Ismailia

Abu Suweir

Suez

Mitla Pass

El Kuntilla

EGYPT

SINAI

Gulf of Suez

JORDAN

Ras el Naqb

Ras el Masri

SAUDI ARABIA

GULF OF AQABA

St. Catherine's Monastery

Strait of Tiran

Ras Nasrani

Sharm el Sheik

RED SEA

Inset map (Gaza Strip)

MEDITERRANEAN SEA

UNEF HQ

DENMARK NORWAY

Gaza

BRAZIL

Deir el Balah

INDIA

GAZA STRIP

ISRAEL

Khan Yunis

COLOMBIA
Rafah

FINLAND

CANADA

0   10 km
0   6 mi

0   20   40   60   80   100 km
0   20   40   60 mi

The boundaries and names shown and the designations used on this map do not imply official endorsement or acceptance by the United Nations.

Map No. 3952.3   UNITED NATIONS
September 1996

Department of Public Information
Cartographic Section

Final phase: deployment along the borders (March 1957– May 1967)

After the completion of the withdrawal of all foreign forces from Egyptian territory, the main objective of UNEF was to supervise the cessation of hostilities between Egypt and Israel. Its basic functions were to act as an informal buffer between the Egyptian and Israeli forces along the Armistice Demarcation Line (ADL) and the international frontier in order to avoid incidents, prevent illegal crossings of the Line by civilians of either side for whatever purposes, and to observe and report on all violations of the Line whether on land, sea or in the air.

To perform these functions, UNEF troops were deployed on the western side of the ADL and the international frontier, covering a distance of 273 kilometres. The Sinai coast from the northern end of the Gulf of Aqaba to the Strait of Tiran, a further distance of 187 kilometres, was kept under observation by UNEF air reconnaissance. As indicated earlier, a UNEF detachment was stationed at Sharm el Sheikh near the Strait of Tiran.

By day, the entire length of the ADL (about 59 kilometres) was kept under observation by some 72 intervisible observation posts. Each post was manned during daylight hours; by night, the sentries were withdrawn and replaced by patrols of five to seven men each. The patrols moved on foot, covering the length of the ADL on an average of three rounds each night and giving particular attention to roads likely to be used by infiltrators. Platoon camps were set up to the rear of the posts, each holding a reserve detachment available to go to the aid of an observation post or patrol should the need arise. Telephone communications by day and a system of flare signals, supplemented by wireless, at night ensured a speedy response to calls for help.

Along the international frontier, rough terrain and scattered minefields restricted the access roads for potential infiltrators, who tended to confine their activities to certain areas. These sensitive areas were covered by a system of patrols. Eight outposts were established along the frontier. Motor patrols from these outposts covered the areas between the outposts and certain tracks. In addition to ground observers, the entire length of the international frontier was also patrolled by air reconnaissance planes on a daily basis, later reduced to three times a week. Any suspicious activity seen from the air could be checked by ground patrols dispatched from the outposts.

To prevent infiltration and incidents, UNEF secured the cooperation of the Egyptian authorities. The inhabitants of Gaza were officially informed that the Government of Egypt, as a matter of policy, was opposed to infiltration across the Armistice Demarcation Line. They were notified that they were forbidden to approach the ADL within 50 to 100 metres by day and 500 metres by night. The police in Gaza were instructed to take effective measures to find persons responsible for laying mines and for other incidents and to prevent recurrences. The local Palestinian police also cooperated with UNEF in preventing infiltrations. UNEF was authorized to apprehend infiltrators and persons approaching the ADL in suspicious circumstances. In practice, this applied to a zone extending up to 500 metres from the line. The persons so apprehended were interrogated by UNEF and then were handed over to the local police.

In the performance of their duties, UNEF soldiers were not authorized to use force except in self-defence. They were never to take the initiative in the use of force, but could respond with fire to an armed attack upon them, even though this might result from a refusal on their part to obey an order from the attacking party not to resist. UNEF maintained close liaison with the two parties, particularly with the Egyptian authorities as representatives of the host Government.

UNEF enjoyed full freedom of movement in the Gaza Strip and between the Sinai posts, UNEF headquarters and the units deployed along the Armistice Demarcation Line. This included freedom of flight over the Sinai peninsula and the Gaza Strip for UNEF aircraft, as well as the manning of the Gaza airport by UNEF.

The deployment of UNEF along the ADL raised a question of the respective responsibilities of the Force and UNTSO. As indicated earlier, Israel denounced the General Armistice Agreement with Egypt in early November 1956, but the United Nations did not accept this unilateral action. Therefore, the Chairman of the Egypt-Israel Mixed Armistice Commission and the UNTSO military observers had remained at their posts throughout the Israeli occupation of the Gaza Strip and afterwards. Upon the withdrawal of the Israeli forces, the Secretary-General, as a practical arrangement and without any change in the legal status of the Mixed Armistice Commission, placed the UNTSO personnel assigned to EIMAC under the operational control of the Commander of UNEF. In view of its position with respect to the General Armistice Agreement, the Government of Israel lodged its complaints of violations of the ADL only with UNEF, but the Force maintained that official investigations of incidents should be carried out through the Armistice Commission. In practice, problems arising between Israel and the United Nations relating to matters covered by the General Armistice Agreement were resolved in a practical way, with UNEF taking over some of the duties previously performed by UNTSO.

The activities carried out by UNEF following its deployment along the Armistice Demarcation Line and the international frontier, and the methods followed in this connection, remained virtually unchanged until the withdrawal of the Force in May 1967. Its area of operations, which had been one of the most disturbed areas in the Middle East, became remarkably quiet. Incidents, such as crossings of the ADL/international frontier, firing across the Line and air violations, naturally continued to occur, but they were relatively infrequent and generally of a minor nature. Virtually uninterrupted peace prevailed in the area, thanks to the presence and activities of UNEF.

UNEF withdrawal, 1967

While quiet prevailed along the Egyptian-Israeli borders after November 1956, there was continued tension in other sectors of the Middle East, particularly on the Israel-Jordan and Israel-Syria fronts. After the creation, in 1964, of the Palestine Liberation Organization and its main group, El Fatah, there appeared to be a new level of organization and training of Palestinian commandos. Palestinian raids against Israel, conducted mainly from Jordanian and Syrian territory, became a regular occurrence, and the Israeli forces reacted with increasingly violent retaliation. There was a marked contrast between the quiet along the Egyptian border and the confrontation situation in other sectors.

In early 1967, tension between Israel and Syria again reached a critical level, mainly because of disputes over cultivation rights in the demilitarized zone near Lake Tiberias. For years, Syria complained that Israelis were illegally seizing lands belonging to Arab Palestinians in the demilitarized zone, and the cultivation of disputed land had led to frequent firing incidents between Israeli and Syrian forces. Efforts within the Mixed Armistice Commission failed. On 7 April 1967, an exchange of fire across disputed farmland led to heavy shelling of Israeli villages by Syrian artillery and intensive air attacks by Israel against Syrian targets — the most serious clash since 1956. The incidents

of 7 April were followed by a heightening of tension in the entire region, despite appeals by Secretary-General U Thant for restraint, and the moderating efforts of UNTSO.

In the evening of 16 May, the UNEF Commander received a request[30] from the Egyptian Commander-in-Chief of the armed forces for withdrawal of "all UN troops which installed OP's [observation posts] along our borders". The General who handed the message to the Force Commander told him that UNEF must order immediate withdrawal from El Sabha and Sharm el Sheikh, commanding the Strait of Tiran and therefore access to the Red Sea and southern Israel. The UNEF Commander replied that he did not have authority to do that. The Secretary-General, on being informed, gave instructions to the Commander to "be firm in maintaining UNEF positions while being as understanding and as diplomatic as possible in your relations with local UAR [United Arab Republic] officials". While the Secretary-General sought clarifications from Cairo, Egyptian troops moved onto UNEF's line, occupying some United Nations posts.

The Secretary-General met with members of the UNEF Advisory Committee and told them of the events in the field, making it known that if a formal request for UNEF's withdrawal came from the Egyptian Government he would have to comply. He pointed out that the Force was on Egyptian territory only with the consent of the Government and could not remain there without it. He also consulted members of the Security Council. The various meetings held by the Secretary-General showed that within the United Nations there was a deep division among the membership of the Advisory Committee and the Security Council on the course of action to be followed. After consulting the Advisory Committee, the Secretary-General informed the representative of Egypt that while he did not question in any sense Egypt's authority to deploy its troops as it saw fit on its own territory, the deployment of Egyptian troops in areas where UNEF troops were stationed might have very serious implications for UNEF and its continued presence in the area.

In the meantime, the Egyptian Foreign Minister in Cairo summoned representatives of nations with troops in UNEF to inform them that UNEF had terminated its tasks in Egypt and the Gaza Strip and must depart forthwith. The Governments of India and Yugoslavia decided that, whatever the decision of the Secretary-General,

[30]A/6669 and A/6730.

they would withdraw their contingents from UNEF. The same day, 18 May, Egyptian soldiers prevented UNEF troops from entering their posts.

While these activities were taking place, the Secretary-General raised with the Israeli Government the question of stationing UNEF on the Israeli side of the Line, thus maintaining the buffer, but this was declared entirely unacceptable to Israel. Shortly thereafter, the Permanent Representative of Egypt delivered a message to the Secretary-General stating his Government's decision to terminate UNEF's presence in the territory of Egypt and the Gaza Strip and requesting steps for withdrawal as soon as possible. The Secretary-General informed contributing countries he would report to the General Assembly and the Security Council about the events, stating it was up to Member countries to decide whether the competent organs should or could take up the matter and pursue it accordingly. He then informed Egypt that the request would be complied with, while indicating his serious misgivings. UNEF's Commander was instructed to take the necessary action for withdrawal to begin on 19 May and end in the last days of June.

During two tense days from 16 to 18 May 1967, the Secretary-General did all he could to persuade Egypt not to request the withdrawal of UNEF and to persuade Israel to accept the Force on its side of the border. But neither Government agreed to cooperate. In such circumstances, the Secretary-General could have brought the matter before the Security Council by invoking Article 99 of the Charter, but he chose not to do so because he knew that with the United States and the Soviet Union firmly on opposing sides of the question, no action could be taken by the Council.

The fundamental fact is that United Nations peace-keeping operations are based on the principle of consent. To maintain UNEF in Egypt against the will of the Egyptian Government, even if it had been possible to do so, which was not the case, would have created a dangerous precedent which would have deterred potential host Governments from accepting future United Nations peace-keeping operations on their soil.

In the case of UNEF, its withdrawal would not have, in itself, necessarily led to war in the area. Following an appeal by the Secretary-General, the Government of Israel made it known to U Thant that it would exercise restraint but would consider a resumption of terrorist activities along the borders, or the closure of the Strait of Tiran to Israeli shipping, as *casus belli*. Immediately after the withdrawal of UNEF, the Secretary-General increased the number of UNTSO observers of the Egypt-Israel Mixed Armistice Commission to provide a United Nations presence along the Armistice Demarcation Line, and he arranged to visit Cairo on 22 May to discuss with the Egyptian Government possible security arrangements along the Egyptian-Israeli borders. However, just before he arrived in Cairo, President Nasser announced the closure of the Strait of Tiran. With this decision the die was cast, and, on 5 June, full-fledged war erupted.

Some UNEF units which were awaiting repatriation were caught up in the fighting in Gaza, and 15 United Nations troops were killed. All military personnel had gone by 13 June, except for the Force Commander and a small group of staff officers who left on 17 June.

UNEF is a telling example of the importance of United Nations peace-keeping forces and their limitations. Its establishment in October 1956 put an end to a destructive war and, for more than 10 years, it effectively maintained peace in one of the most sensitive areas of the Middle East. But in the absence of a complementary peacemaking effort, the root cause of the conflict between Egypt and Israel remained unresolved. Moreover, because Israel refused to accept UNEF on its territory, the Force had to be deployed only on the Egyptian side of the border, and thus its functioning was entirely contingent upon the consent of Egypt as the host country. Once that consent was withdrawn, its operation could no longer be maintained.

Chapter 4

Second United Nations Emergency Force (UNEF II)

Chapter 4
Second United Nations Emergency Force (UNEF II)

A. Background

The situation in the Suez Canal sector and on the Golan Heights from June 1967 until October 1973 is described in the chapter on UNTSO, which had set up cease-fire observation operations in those areas.

On 6 October 1973, in a surprise move, Egyptian forces crossed the Canal and soon advanced beyond the UNTSO observation posts on its eastern bank, while, in a coordinated move, Syrian troops simultaneously attacked the Israeli positions on the Golan Heights. By 9 October, following a request by Egypt acceded to by the Security Council, United Nations observation posts on both sides of the Canal were closed and the observers withdrawn.

The Security Council met from 8 to 12 October to consider the conflict and the overall situation, but, because of the opposing positions of the major Powers, could not reach a decision. Meanwhile war raged on. By 21 October, the situation had become critical; an Israeli armoured column had crossed the Canal where it was engaging Egyptian forces, and the Egyptian Third Army on the east bank was about to be cut off. The Soviet Union and the United States jointly requested an urgent meeting of the Security Council. On 22 October, the Council, on a proposal submitted jointly by the two major Powers, adopted resolution 338 (1973) which called for a cease-fire and a start to implementing resolution 242 (1967). The cease-fire call was confirmed in resolution 339 (1973) of 23 October, and the Secretary-General was requested to dispatch United Nations observers immediately.

Fighting continued, however, and President Anwar Sadat of Egypt issued direct appeals to the Soviet Union and the United States, requesting them to send American and Soviet troops to the area to enforce the cease-fire. The United States Government was opposed to the request, but the Soviet Union agreed. The two major Powers, in disagreement after their joint cease-fire initiative, were suddenly on a collision course, each threatening military action. It was probably the most dangerous situation confronting the world since the Cuban missile crisis of October 1962.

At the request of Egypt, the Security Council was convened again on 24 October. The non-aligned members of the Council, in close cooperation with the Secretary-General, worked out a resolution calling for an increase in UNTSO observers in the area and the establishment of a new United Nations peace-keeping force, which became the second United Nations Emergency Force (UNEF II). The establishment and dispatch of the new peace-keeping operation effectively brought the crisis to an end.

Establishment

On 25 October 1973, on a proposal by Guinea, India, Indonesia, Kenya, Panama, Peru, the Sudan and Yugoslavia, the Security Council adopted resolution 340 (1973), by which it demanded that an immediate and complete cease-fire be observed and that the parties return to the positions occupied by them at 1650 hours GMT on 22 October 1973. The Council also requested the Secretary-General, as an immediate step, to increase the number of United Nations military observers on both sides, and decided to set up immediately under its authority a United Nations Emergency Force to be composed of personnel drawn from United Nations Member States except the permanent members of the Security Council. It requested the Secretary-General to report within 24 hours on the steps taken to that effect.

Immediately after the adoption of the resolution, the Secretary-General addressed a letter[1] to the President of the Security Council, indi-

---

[1] S/11049.

cating that he would deliver the requested report within the time-limit set by the Council. In the meantime, as an urgent measure and in order that the Emergency Force might reach the area of conflict as soon as possible, he proposed to arrange for units of the Austrian, Finnish and Swedish contingents serving with the United Nations Peace-keeping Force in Cyprus (UNFICYP) to proceed immediately to Egypt. He also proposed to appoint Major-General (later Lieutenant-General) Ensio P. H. Siilasvuo (Finland), the Chief of Staff of UNTSO, as interim Commander of the new Force and to ask him to set up a provisional headquarters in Cairo with personnel from UNTSO.

The Secretary-General requested the Council President to let him know urgently whether the proposal was acceptable to the members of the Council, adding that the proposed steps would be without prejudice to the more detailed and comprehensive report on the Emergency Force which he would submit to the Council on the next day. The President, after informally consulting the members of the Council, conveyed the Council's agreement to the Secretary-General on the same evening. This procedure would henceforth be used frequently by the Secretary-General to get the Security Council's consent when measures needed to be taken.

Guidelines for UNEF II

The Secretary-General's report[2] requested by the Council set forth proposals regarding the guidelines for the functioning of the Force as well as a plan of action for the initial stages of the operation.

The proposed principles and guidelines for the Emergency Force were as follows:

(a) Three essential conditions must be met for the Force to be effective. First, it must have at all times the full confidence and backing of the Security Council. Secondly, it must operate with the full cooperation of the parties concerned. Thirdly, it must be able to function as an integrated and efficient military unit.

(b) The Force would be under the command of the United Nations, vested in the Secretary-General, under the authority of the Security Council. The command in the field would be exercised by a Force Commander appointed by the Secretary-General with the Council's consent. The Commander would be responsible to the Secretary-General. The Secretary-General would keep the Security Council fully informed of developments relating to the functioning of the Force. All matters

which could affect the nature or the continued effective functioning of the Force would be referred to the Council for its decision.

(c) The Force must enjoy the freedom of movement and communication and other facilities necessary for the performance of its tasks. The Force and its personnel should be granted all relevant privileges and immunities provided for by the Convention on the Privileges and Immunities of the United Nations. The Force should operate at all times separately from the armed forces of the parties concerned. Consequently, separate quarters and, wherever desirable and feasible, buffer zones would have to be arranged with the cooperation of the parties. Appropriate agreements on the status of the Force would also have to be concluded with the parties.

(d) The Force would be composed of a number of contingents to be provided by selected countries, upon the request of the Secretary-General. The contingents would be selected in consultation with the Security Council and with the parties concerned, bearing in mind the accepted principle of equitable geographical representation.

(e) The Force would be provided with weapons of a defensive character only. It would not use force except in self-defence. Self-defence would include resistance to attempts by forceful means to prevent it from discharging its duties under the Security Council's mandate. The Force would proceed on the assumption that the parties to the conflict would take all the necessary steps for compliance with the Council's decisions.

(f) In performing its functions, the Force would act with complete impartiality and would avoid actions which could prejudice the rights, claims or positions of the parties concerned.

(g) The costs of the Force would be considered as expenses of the Organization to be borne by the Members, as apportioned by the General Assembly.

In the same report, the Secretary-General set forth certain urgent steps to be taken. In order that UNEF II might fulfil the responsibilities entrusted to it, it was considered necessary that the Force should have a total strength in the order of 7,000. The Force would initially be stationed in the area for a period of six months, subject to extension.

The Secretary-General engaged in the necessary consultations with a number of Governments, in addition to Austria, Finland and Sweden, regarding provision of contingents of suitable size

[2]S/11052/Rev.1.

for the Force at the earliest possible time. In addition to his requests to countries to provide contingents for the Force, the Secretary-General proposed to seek logistic support as necessary from a number of other countries, which might include the permanent members of the Security Council.

Finally, the Secretary-General stated that, while there were many unknown factors, the best possible preliminary estimate of cost, based upon past experience and practice, was approximately $30 million for the Force for a six-month period.

This report was approved by the Security Council on 27 October by its resolution 341 (1973). In accordance with the Secretary-General's recommendations, the Council set up the new Force — for an initial period of six months, subject to extension.

Composition and strength of the Force

UNEF II had already begun its operations on the basis of interim arrangements approved by the Security Council. On the morning of 26 October, General Siilasvuo and his group of UNTSO military observers set up temporary headquarters in Cairo using UNTSO's liaison office. During the same afternoon, advance elements of Austrian, Finnish and Swedish troops arrived from Cyprus and were immediately deployed along the front line. They were joined a few days later by an Irish company. The four contingents were quickly reinforced, and their presence and activities effectively defused a highly explosive situation.

Having taken these emergency measures, the Secretary-General had now to secure other contingents and build up the Force to its authorized level of 7,000 all ranks. In accordance with the guidelines approved by the Security Council, the Force was to be composed of contingents from countries selected by the Secretary-General, in consultation with the parties and the Security Council, bearing in mind the principle of equitable geographical representation.

The question of the composition of the Force gave rise to some difficulties during the consultations with the Security Council. In view of the need to set up a working force without delay, the Secretary-General wanted to secure contingents from countries that could provide the required troops at short notice. In particular, he had planned to ask Canada to supply the logistics component, since it was, aside from the major Powers, one of the few countries which could readily do so. But the Soviet Union insisted that a Warsaw

Pact country should be included in the new Force if a North Atlantic Treaty Organization member was. After a lengthy debate held in closed session, the Security Council decided that the Secretary-General should consult with Ghana (African regional group), Indonesia and Nepal (Asian regional group), Panama and Peru (Latin American regional group), Poland (Eastern European regional group) and Canada (Western European and other States group) — the two last-mentioned having particular responsibility for logistic support.

In accordance with this decision, the Secretary-General held urgent consultations with the various Governments concerned with a view to obtaining the required personnel and equipment and working out acceptable administrative and financial arrangements. As a result of these contacts, in addition to Austria, Finland, Ireland and Sweden, whose troops had already arrived, Canada, Ghana, Indonesia, Nepal, Panama, Peru, Poland and Senegal were asked to provide contingents.

The Secretary-General had planned to set a ceiling of 600 for each contingent. However, in view of the complexity of the logistical problems and the decision of the Security Council to divide responsibilities in this regard between Canada and Poland, whose respective military establishments were differently organized and had different equipment and weapons, the strength of the logistical support elements had to be considerably increased.

The strength of the Canadian and Polish logistics components and the division of responsibilities between them were the subject of lengthy negotiations between the military representatives of those two countries and experts from the Secretariat. After more than two weeks of such discussions, an understanding was reached.[3] The logistics support system was to be composed of a Polish road transport unit including a maintenance element, and a Canadian service unit consisting of a supply company, a maintenance company, a movement control unit and a postal detachment. In addition, Canada would provide an aviation unit and Poland a medical unit subject to the availability of a suitable building. The Canadian contingent would have a total strength of about 1,000 and the Polish contingent about 800.

While these negotiations were going on, General Siilasvuo was pressing for the early arrival of the logistics units. He indicated that because of the difficulty of getting local supplies, it was important that the logistics facilities be set up before

[3]S/11056/Add.6, annex.

the arrival of additional contingents. In the light of this recommendation, it was decided that the Austrian, Finnish, Irish and Swedish units which had arrived in the area at the beginning of the operation should be brought up to battalion strength as soon as possible, and operate with vehicles, stores and equipment borrowed from UNFICYP and from UNTSO.

By mid-November, advance parties of the Canadian and Polish contingents had arrived in the area and they were soon followed by the main bodies of those contingents. By the end of November, the logistics components were well established and the other contingents of UNEF II began to arrive in the area at a steady rate. By 20 February 1974, the strength of UNEF II had reached the authorized level of 7,000 (actually, 6,973). It included contingents from 12 countries: Austria (604), Canada (1,097), Finland (637), Ghana (499), Indonesia (550), Ireland (271), Nepal (571), Panama (406), Peru (497), Poland (822), Senegal (399), Sweden (620).

From February until May 1974, the strength of UNEF II was slightly decreased (to 6,645), mainly because of some reduction of the Finnish, Peruvian and Swedish contingents. In May, the Irish contingent was withdrawn at the request of its Government. Following the adoption of Security Council resolution 350 (1974) of 31 May 1974 on the establishment of the United Nations Disengagement Observer Force (UNDOF), and the approval by the Council of interim arrangements proposed by the Secretary-General to give effect to that resolution, the Austrian and Peruvian contingents and elements of the Canadian and Polish logistics contingents (approximately 1,050 troops in all) were transferred from UNEF II to UNDOF in Syria. As a result, the total strength of UNEF II decreased to 5,079 in June 1974. It was brought up to 5,527 at the end of July with the arrival of additional Canadian and Polish personnel.

The Nepalese contingent was withdrawn beginning in August 1974 and the Panamanian contingent in November 1974. The total strength of UNEF II, with contingents from seven countries, was progressively reduced to 3,987 by October 1975.

On 17 October 1975, the Secretary-General reported[4] to the Security Council that, owing to the more extensive responsibilities entrusted to UNEF II under an Agreement between Egypt and Israel signed at Geneva on 4 September 1975 and the large increase in the areas of operation, additional military personnel would be needed to en-

able the Force to execute its new functions adequately. He proposed accordingly to reinforce each non-logistic contingent by one company (an increase of some 750 all ranks) and the Polish and Canadian logistics contingents by 50 and 36 men, respectively. He also proposed to reinforce the air unit by additional aircraft and helicopters. In accordance with the Secretary-General's request, Finland, Ghana, Indonesia and Sweden each agreed to supply an additional rifle company while Canada and Poland provided additional personnel for logistic support. After consulting[5] the Security Council in May 1976, the Secretary-General accepted the offer of the Government of Australia to supply four helicopters with their crews and support personnel (45 men) to UNEF II.

The Senegalese contingent was withdrawn in May and June 1976. In a report[6] of 18 October 1976, the Secretary-General noted that in view of the satisfactory results in operational arrangements in the current circumstances, and in the interest of economy, there was for the time being no intention to provide for the replacement of the Senegalese contingent unless a change in the situation should make it necessary. Upon the withdrawal of the Senegalese contingent, the total strength of UNEF II was reduced to 4,174. It remained more or less at that level during the next three years. At the time of its withdrawal in July 1979, UNEF II had 4,031 personnel, and its various contingents were: Australia (46), Canada (844), Finland (522), Ghana (595), Indonesia (510), Poland (923), Sweden (591). Of this total, 99 all ranks were assigned to UNEF II headquarters. The international civilian supporting staff of that headquarters numbered 160. In addition to the above, UNEF II was assisted by 120 military observers from UNTSO.

Mandate renewals

The mandate of UNEF II which was originally approved for six months, until 24 April 1974, was subsequently renewed eight times. Each time, as the date of expiry of the mandate approached, the Secretary-General submitted a report to the Security Council on the activities of the Force during the period of the mandate. In each of those reports, the Secretary-General expressed the view that the continued presence of UNEF II in the area was essential, and he recommended, after consultations with the parties, that its mandate be extended for a further period. In each case, the

---

[4]S/11849. [5]S/12089. [6]S/12212.

Council took note of the Secretary-General's report and decided to extend the mandate of the Force accordingly. Thus the mandate of UNEF II was extended for six months in April 1974 (resolution 346 (1974)); for another six months in October (resolution 362 (1974)); for three months in April 1975 (resolution 368 (1975)); another three months in July (resolution 371 (1975)); and for one year in October 1975 (resolution 378 (1975)), in October 1976 (resolution 396 (1976)) and again in October 1977 (resolution 416 (1977)). In October 1978, the mandate of UNEF II was extended a last time for nine months, until 24 July 1979 (resolution 438 (1978)).

The discussions and decisions of the Security Council on the extension of the mandate naturally reflected the situation on the ground and the status of the negotiations undertaken for the disengagement of the forces in the area. Following the conclusion of the first disengagement agreement, in January 1974, both sides readily agreed to have the mandate extended for a further period of six months beyond 24 April 1974. But in April and July 1975, when negotiations aimed at the second disengagement of forces were deadlocked, Egypt declined to extend the mandate of the Force for more than three months and, in fact, consented to the extension in July 1975 only after a special appeal by the Security Council. In contrast, when the September 1975 disengagement agreement was finally concluded, both parties wanted the period of extension to be expanded to one year, and the Security Council so agreed. In October 1978, the Soviet Union, which was opposed to the Camp David accords concluded earlier that year, opposed a further extension for one year, and the Security Council finally settled for an extension period of nine months. In July 1979, after the signing of the peace treaty between Egypt and Israel, which had entered into force on 25 April 1979, the Council was unable to extend the mandate of UNEF II and decided to let it lapse.

In this connection, in his report[7] to the Security Council of 19 July 1979, the Secretary-General noted that the original context in which UNEF II had been created and in which it had previously functioned had basically changed during the past nine months. While the Governments of Egypt and Israel had both expressed themselves in favour of an extension of the mandate of UNEF II, the Soviet Union had expressed opposition to such a course. In this regard, the Secretary-General recalled that, according to the guidelines approved by the Security Council in October 1973, all matters which might affect the nature or the continued effective functioning of the Force would be referred to the Council for its decision. The Secretary-General added that whatever decisions the Council might reach, he would be ready to make the necessary arrangements.

The Security Council did not extend the mandate of UNEF II, which lapsed on 24 July 1979.

UNEF command

General Siilasvuo, who had commanded UNEF II on an interim basis during its initial period, was appointed UNEF Commander on 12 November 1973 by the Secretary-General, with the consent of the Security Council. In August 1975, he was assigned to the new post of Chief Coordinator of the United Nations Peace-keeping Missions in the Middle East and was replaced as UNEF Commander by Major-General (later Lieutenant-General) Bengt Liljestrand (Sweden), who held the post until 1 December 1976. Major-General Rais Abin (Indonesia), who became Acting Force Commander on that date, was appointed UNEF Commander on 1 January 1977 and held the post until the withdrawal of the Force in 1979.

Status of the Force

In accordance with established practice, the United Nations sought to work out an agreement on the status of the Force with Egypt as the host country and also with Israel as the other party concerned. The Office of Legal Affairs of the Secretariat engaged in negotiations to this end with both countries' Permanent Missions to the United Nations.

While no special agreement could be drawn up, it was agreed that as a practical arrangement the parties would be guided by the provision of the status of the Force agreement for UNEF I as well as by the Convention on the Privileges and Immunities of the United Nations.

With this understanding, the Force functioned smoothly and effectively. There were, of course, a number of organizational, operational and administrative problems. One of the main difficulties concerned the question of freedom of movement. The Israeli Government had opposed the inclusion in UNEF II of contingents from Ghana, Indonesia, Poland and Senegal on the grounds that these countries had no diplomatic relations with Israel, and it refused to extend to

[7] S/13460.

the personnel of their contingents freedom of movement in the areas it controlled.

The Secretary-General strongly protested against these restrictions for practical reasons and as a matter of principle. He took the position that UNEF II must function as an integrated and efficient military unit and that no differentiation should be made regarding the United Nations status of the various contingents. But despite his efforts and those of the Force Commander, the Israeli authorities maintained the restrictions, and the contingents affected had to be deployed within the United Nations buffer zones or in the Egyptian-controlled areas. The restrictions on the freedom of movement were also applied to Soviet observers attached to UNEF II.

B. Activities of the Force

The terms of reference of UNEF II were to supervise the implementation of Security Council resolution 340 (1973), which demanded that an immediate and complete cease-fire be observed and that the parties return to the positions they had occupied at 1650 hours GMT on 22 October 1973. The Force would use its best efforts to prevent a recurrence of the fighting, and in the fulfilment of its tasks it would have the cooperation of the military observers of UNTSO. UNEF II was also to cooperate with the International Committee of the Red Cross in its humanitarian endeavours in the area.

These terms of reference, which were approved[8] by the Security Council on 27 October, remained unchanged during UNEF's entire mandate, but within this general framework the activities of the Force varied considerably over the years in the light of prevailing circumstances and of the agreements reached between the parties.

In the light of changing developments, the activities of UNEF II may be divided into four main phases.

First phase: October 1973– January 1974

Following the establishment of UNEF II, its immediate objective was to stop the fighting and prevent all movement forward of the troops on both sides. Urgent measures also had to be taken to provide Suez city and the Egyptian Third Army trapped on the east bank of the Canal with non-military supplies.

Troops from Austria, Finland, Sweden and, later, Ireland were dispatched to the front line as soon as they arrived. They interposed themselves whenever possible between the forward positions of the opposing forces. Observation posts and checkpoints were set up and patrols undertaken, with the assistance of UNTSO observers, in sensitive areas. These activities were carried out in close liaison with the parties concerned. With these measures, the situation was stabilized, the cease-fire was generally observed, and there were only a few incidents, which were resolved with the assistance of UNEF II.

A meeting between high-level military representatives of Egypt and Israel took place in the presence of UNEF representatives on 27 October 1973 at kilometre-marker 109 on the Cairo-Suez road to discuss the observance of the cease-fire demanded by the Security Council, as well as various humanitarian questions. At this meeting, preliminary arrangements were also agreed upon for the dispatch of non-military supplies to the town of Suez and the Egyptian Third Army. In accordance with these arrangements, convoys of lorries driven by UNEF II personnel were organized under the supervision of the Force and the International Committee of the Red Cross (ICRC) to bring supplies of a non-military nature through Israeli-held territory to Suez, and then to the Egyptian Third Army across the Canal.

These priority tasks having been met, UNEF II turned to the Security Council's demand for the return of the forces of both parties to the positions they had occupied on 22 October 1973. More meetings were held at kilometre-marker 109 to discuss this matter, together with possible mutual disengagement and the establishment of buffer zones to be manned by UNEF II.

In the meantime, the United States Secretary of State, Mr. Henry A. Kissinger, during visits to Egypt and Israel, succeeded in working out a preliminary agreement between the two countries

[8]S/11052/Rev.1.

for the implementation of Council resolutions 338 (1973) and 339 (1973). He transmitted[9] it on 9 November to Secretary-General Kurt Waldheim, who immediately instructed General Siilasvuo to take the necessary measures and to make available his good offices, as appropriate, for carrying out the terms of that agreement. On 11 November, at kilometre-marker 101 on the Cairo-Suez road, the new site for meetings, the agreement was signed by Major-General Mohamed El-Gamasy for Egypt and by Major-General Aharon Yaariv for Israel. It was also signed by General Siilasvuo on behalf of the United Nations.

The agreement, which was to enter into force immediately, contained the following six points: (1) Egypt and Israel agreed to observe scrupulously the cease-fire called for by the Security Council; (2) Both sides agreed that discussions between them would begin immediately to settle the question of the return to the 22 October positions; (3) The town of Suez would receive daily supplies of food, water and medicine and all wounded civilians in the town would be evacuated; (4) There would be no impediment to the movement of non-military supplies to the east bank; (5) The Israeli checkpoints on the Cairo-Suez road would be replaced by United Nations checkpoints; and (6) As soon as the United Nations checkpoints were established on that road, there would be an exchange of all prisoners of war, including wounded.

Immediately after the signing of this agreement, the parties started discussions under the auspices of General Siilasvuo on the modalities of its implementation. These discussions continued sporadically until January 1974.

Except for the provision on the return to the 22 October positions, the agreement was implemented without much difficulty.

On the morning of 15 November, the Israeli personnel at the checkpoints on the Cairo-Suez road were replaced by UNEF II personnel. Convoys of non-military supplies plied smoothly to and from Suez. As these convoys had to be driven by UNEF II personnel, some 100 military drivers were supplied by the Governments of Austria, Finland and Sweden at very short notice at the request of the Secretary-General. The exchange of prisoners of war took place in mid-November with aircraft made available without cost by the Swiss Government to the International Committee of the Red Cross.

But the most important clause, which concerned the return to the 22 October positions and the separation of the opposing forces under United Nations auspices, remained unresolved despite General Siilasvuo's efforts. On 29 November, Egypt broke off the negotiations, a decision which inevitably created a heightening of tension in the area. However, thanks to the presence of UNEF II, the cease-fire continued to hold.

Until mid-November, the operations were carried out by the Austrian, Finnish, Irish and Swedish battalions. After that date, the Canadian and Polish logistics components started to arrive. These were followed by other contingents. By mid-January 1974, 10 contingents were at hand. These contingents were deployed[10] as follows:

- The Swedish battalion had established its headquarters in Ismailia and was deployed in the northern sector, both east and west of the Suez Canal, north of the town. The battalion provided the Force Reserve and drivers for the UNEF II convoys carrying non-military supplies to the Egyptian troops on the east bank of the Canal.

- The Austrian battalion had its headquarters in Ismailia and was deployed south of that town, west of the Canal. The battalion also provided drivers for the UNEF II convoys.

- The Finnish battalion had its headquarters in Suez city, and was deployed south of the Cairo-Suez road, including the Suez city and Adabiya areas. The battalion supervised the UNEF II convoys, as well as the supply convoys for Suez city.

- The Irish battalion, with headquarters in Rabah, was deployed in the northern sector east of the Suez Canal in the Qantara area.

- The Peruvian battalion, with headquarters in Rabah, was carrying out reconnaissance of its future positions, which would be located in the central sector east of the Suez Canal, south of the Irish battalion's area of responsibility.

- The Panamanian battalion, also with headquarters in Rabah, was carrying out reconnaissance of its future positions, which would be located in the southern sector east of the Suez Canal, south of

[9]S/11091 and S/11056/Add.3, annex. [10]S/11056/Add.7.

the Peruvian battalion's area of responsibility.

■ The Indonesian battalion was to be deployed west of the Canal with base camp at Ismailia.

■ The Senegalese battalion had not yet arrived except for an advance party which was carrying out reconnaissance for future operational assignment.

■ The Canadian logistic support unit, with base camp in Cairo, provided supply, maintenance, communications and postal services throughout the mission area.

■ The Polish logistic support unit, with base camp in Cairo, provided drivers for UNEF II transport and was carrying out reconnaissance in preparation for the establishment of the UNEF II field hospital.

The headquarters of UNEF II, with an international staff on which the various contributing countries were represented, remained in Cairo.

Second phase: January 1974–October 1975

While the negotiations at kilometre-marker 101 for the return to the 22 October positions were dragging on, the United States and the Soviet Union initiated a joint effort to promote the implementation of Security Council resolution 338 (1973), which called for negotiations to start between the parties concerned under appropriate auspices aimed at establishing a just and durable peace in the Middle East. This effort resulted in the convening of the Peace Conference on the Middle East at Geneva on 21 December 1973 under the auspices of the United Nations and the co-chairmanship of the two Powers. The Secretary-General was asked to serve as the convener of the Conference and to preside at the opening phase which would be held at the Foreign Minister level. The Governments of Egypt, Israel and Jordan accepted to attend, but Syria refused and the Palestine Liberation Organization (PLO) was not invited.

The Conference, which discussed the disengagement of forces in the Egypt-Israel sector, as well as a comprehensive settlement of the Middle East problem, was inconclusive and adjourned on 22 December 1973 after three meetings. Before

adjourning, it decided to continue to work through the setting up of a Military Working Group, which would start discussing forthwith the question of disengagement of forces. The Working Group was composed of the military representatives of Egypt and Israel and the Commander of UNEF II as Chairman.

During the first half of January 1974, the United States Secretary of State undertook a new mediation effort. In negotiating separately with the Governments of Egypt and Israel, in what was known as his "shuttle diplomacy", he worked out an agreement on the disengagement and separation of their military forces. This agreement was signed on 18 January 1974 by the military representatives of Egypt and Israel, and by General Siilasvuo as witness, within the framework of the Military Working Group of the Geneva Peace Conference at a meeting held at kilometre-marker 101 on the Cairo-Suez road. The agreement provided for the deployment of Egyptian forces on the eastern side of the Canal, west of a line designated on the map annexed to the agreement (the line ran parallel to the Canal, about 10 kilometres east of it), the deployment of Israeli forces east of another line, the establishment of a zone of disengagement manned by UNEF II, and areas of limited forces and armament on both sides of that zone.

In subsequent meetings held at kilometre-marker 101 under the chairmanship of General Siilasvuo, the military representatives of Egypt and Israel worked out a detailed procedure for the implementation of the agreement.

In accordance with this procedure, the disengagement operation began on 25 January. The operation proceeded by phases. At each phase, Israeli forces withdrew from a designated area after handing it over to UNEF II, and UNEF II held that area for a few hours before turning it over to the Egyptian forces. During the entire disengagement process, UNEF II interposed between the forces of the two sides by establishing temporary buffer zones. UNEF II was also responsible for the survey and marking of the lines of disengagement, which was carried out by UNTSO military observers under UNEF II supervision, with the assistance of Egyptian and Israeli army surveyors for their respective sides. The whole operation was carried out smoothly according to plan and was completed[11] by 4 March 1974.

After the completion of the operation, most non-logistic contingents were deployed in or near the newly established zone of disengagement.

[11] S/11056/Add.13.

By mid-March, UNEF II had a total strength of 6,814 all ranks. The various contingents were deployed[12] as follows:

- The Irish battalion had its base camp at Rabah. It manned eight outposts in the zone of disengagement from the Mediterranean Sea to a line immediately south of Qantara.

- The Peruvian battalion had its base camp at Rabah. It manned 10 outposts in the zone of disengagement, in a sector from the southern limit of the Irish battalion to a line directly east of Ismailia.

- The Swedish battalion had its base camp at Ismailia. It manned 14 outposts in the zone of disengagement, in a sector from the southern limit of the Peruvian battalion to a line east of Deversoir.

- The Indonesian battalion had its base camp at Ismailia. It manned 14 outposts in the zone of disengagement, in a sector from the southern limit of the Swedish battalion to a line east of Kabrit.

- The Senegalese battalion had its base camp at Suez city. It manned 12 outposts in the zone of disengagement, in a sector from the southern limit of the Indonesian battalion to a line east of a point 10 kilometres north of Suez.

- The Finnish battalion had its base camp at Suez city. It manned 15 outposts in the zone of disengagement, in a sector from the southern limit of the Senegalese battalion to the Gulf of Suez.

The headquarters of UNEF II was moved to Ismailia in August 1974.

As a result of this disengagement, the situation in the Egypt-Israel sector became much more stable. The main task of UNEF II was the manning and control of the zone of disengagement and, to do this, it established static checkpoints and observation posts and conducted mobile patrols. It also carried out, with the assistance of UNTSO observers, weekly and later bi-weekly inspections of the areas of limited forces and armament (30 kilometre zone), as well as inspections of other areas agreed by the parties. The Force Commander continued the practice of separate meetings with the military authorities of Egypt and Israel concerning the implementation of the Force's terms of reference and the inspections carried out by UNEF II, and he continued to lend his assistance and good offices in cases where one of the parties raised questions concerning the observance of the agreed limitations of forces and armament.

In addition, UNEF II continued to cooperate with the International Committee of the Red Cross on humanitarian matters. It played an important part in assisting in exchanges of prisoners of war and the transfer of civilians from one side to the other. UNEF II also undertook an operation, which was completed in July 1974, for the search for the remains of soldiers killed during the October 1973 war.

In view of the quiet that prevailed in the area, it was possible to reduce gradually the strength of UNEF II. The Irish Government decided to withdraw its troops in May 1974. In June, following the establishment of the United Nations Disengagement Observer Force on the Golan Heights, the Security Council decided, upon the recommendation of the Secretary-General, to transfer the Austrian and Peruvian contingents and elements of the Canadian and Polish logistics components to the new UNDOF. The Nepalese contingent, which had been made available to the United Nations for six months only, was repatriated in August and September 1974. Finally, the Panamanian contingent was withdrawn in November 1974. As a result of these and later developments, the total strength of UNEF II decreased to 5,079 in June 1974, 4,029 in April 1975 and 3,987 in October 1975.

Third phase: November 1975–May 1979

In September 1975, the United States Secretary of State, through further indirect negotiations, succeeded in obtaining the agreement of Egypt and Israel for a second disengagement of their forces in the Sinai. The new agreement[13] provided for the redeployment of Israeli forces east of lines designated in a map annexed to the agreement, the redeployment of the Egyptian forces westwards and the establishment of buffer zones controlled by UNEF II. It also provided that there would be no military forces in the southern areas of Ras Sudr and Abu Rudais. On both sides of the buffer zones, two areas of limited forces and armament were to be set up where the number of military personnel should be limited to 8,000 and

[12]S/11056/Add.14. [13]S/11818/Add.1.

the armament to 75 tanks and 72 artillery pieces, including heavy mortars.

Finally, the agreement set up a joint commission, under the aegis of the United Nations Chief Coordinator of the United Nations Peacekeeping Missions in the Middle East, to consider any problems arising from the agreement and to assist UNEF II in the execution of its mandate. Attached to the agreement was a United States plan to establish an early warning system in the area of the Giddi and Mitla Passes, consisting of three watch stations set up by the United States and of two surveillance stations, one operated by Egyptian personnel and the other by Israeli personnel.

The Secretary-General submitted[14] reports to the Security Council on this matter in September 1975. He advised the Council that the new agreement between Egypt and Israel had been initialled by the parties on 1 September and would be signed by them at Geneva on 4 September. Following the signing, the representatives of Egypt and Israel were, within five days, to begin preparation of a detailed protocol for the implementation of the basic agreement in the Military Working Group of the Geneva Peace Conference on the Middle East. In accordance with previous practice, the Secretary-General instructed General Siilasvuo, the Chief Coordinator, who had presided at the previous meetings of the Military Working Group, to proceed to Geneva so as to be available in the same capacity for the forthcoming meetings of the Working Group.

The Working Group, meeting under the chairmanship of General Siilasvuo, reached agreement on the protocol of the agreement, which was signed on 22 September by the representatives of the two parties and by General Siilasvuo as witness. The protocol set out a detailed procedure for the implementation of the agreement.

The responsibilities entrusted to UNEF II under the agreement of 4 September and its protocol were much more extensive than those it had had previously, and its area of operations was much larger. The Force's first task was to mark on the ground the new lines of disengagement. To carry out this work, a group of surveyors was supplied by Sweden, at the request of the Secretary-General. Work began in October 1975 and was completed in January 1976, in accordance with the timetable set out in the protocol.

In November 1975, UNEF II began its assistance to the parties for the redeployment of their forces. The first phase of the redeployment took place in the southern area and was completed on 1 December 1975. During that period, UNEF II, through the Chief Coordinator, supervised the transfer of the oilfields and installations in the area. The second phase of the redeployment, which took place in the northern area, began on 12 January 1976 and was completed on 22 February. The Force monitored the redeployment of the forces of the two parties by providing buffer times for the transfer of evacuated areas to Egyptian control, occupying temporary buffer zones and manning temporary observation posts. The Force acted as a secure channel of communication and contact between the parties throughout the redeployment process.

After the completion of the redeployment operation, UNEF II carried out the long-term functions specified in the protocol. In the southern area, its task was to assure that no military or paramilitary forces of any kind, military fortifications or military installations were in the area. To perform that task, it established checkpoints and observation posts in accordance with the protocol and conducted patrols throughout the area, including air patrols. It also ensured the control of buffer zones in the southern area and, to this effect, it maintained permanent checkpoints along the buffer-zone lines. It also supervised the use of common road sections by the parties in accordance with arrangements agreed to by them and it provided escorts in those sections when necessary.

The functions of UNEF II in the buffer zone in the northern area were carried out by means of a system of checkpoints, observation posts and patrols by land. In the early-warning-system area, which was located in the buffer zone, UNEF II provided escorts, as required, to and from the United States watch stations and the Egyptian and Israeli surveillance stations. The Force was also entrusted with the task of ensuring the maintenance of the agreed limitations of forces and armament within the areas specified in the agreement and, to this effect, it conducted bi-weekly inspections. Those inspections were carried out by UNTSO military observers under UNEF supervision, accompanied by liaison officers of the respective parties.

The joint commission established by the disengagement agreement met in the buffer zone under the chairmanship of the United Nations Chief Coordinator as occasion required. The Force received a number of complaints from both parties alleging violations by the other side. Those complaints were taken up with the party concerned by the Force Commander or the Chief Coordinator

[14]S/11818 and Add.1-4.

UNEF II deployment as of July 1979

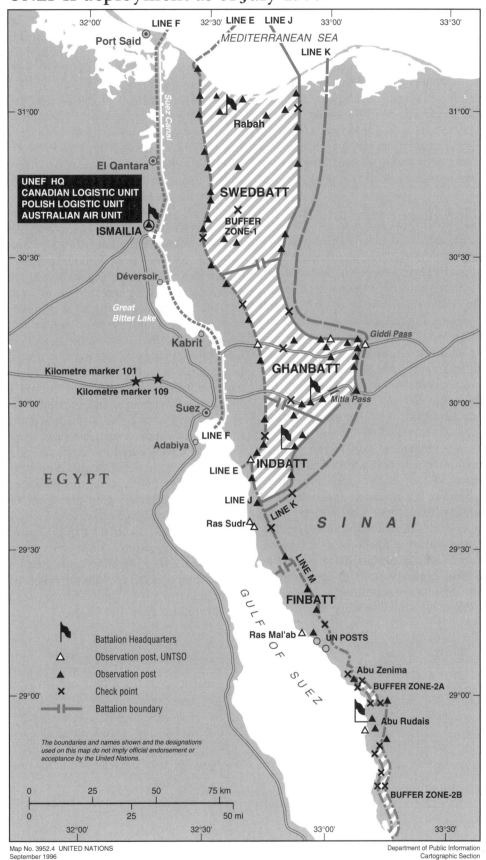

and, in some instances, were referred to the joint commission.

The Force maintained close contact with representatives of the International Committee of the Red Cross in its humanitarian endeavours and extended its assistance in providing facilities for family reunions and student exchanges, which took place at an agreed site in the buffer zone.

All these tasks were carried out efficiently. There were few incidents and problems and, whenever they occurred, they were resolved without difficulty with the cooperation of the parties concerned.

Fourth phase: May–July 1979

The peace treaty concluded in March 1979 between Egypt and Israel as a result of negotiations conducted under the auspices of the United States, and which entered into force on 25 April, had a direct bearing on the termination of UNEF II and affected its activities during the final period.

The treaty provided that, upon completion of a phased Israeli withdrawal over three years, security arrangements on both sides of the Egyptian-Israeli border would be made with the assistance of United Nations forces and observers. Article VI stipulated that "the parties will request the United Nations to provide forces and observers to supervise the implementation of the security arrangements". The United Nations forces and observers would have been asked to perform a variety of duties, including the operation of checkpoints, reconnaissance patrols and observation posts along the boundaries of and within the demilitarized zone, and ensuring freedom of navigation through the Strait of Tiran. United Nations forces would also have been stationed in certain areas adjoining the demilitarized zone on the Egyptian side, and United Nations observers would have

patrolled a specified area on the Israeli side of the international boundary. In an annex to the treaty, the United States undertook to organize a multinational force of equivalent strength if the United Nations were unable to monitor the forces as envisaged by the treaty.

The intention of the parties was to have UNEF II perform these tasks. However, there was strong opposition to the treaty from the PLO and many Arab States, and opposition by the Soviet Union in the Security Council. As previously stated, the Security Council decided to allow the mandate of the Force to lapse on 24 July 1979.

On 25 May 1979, in pursuance of the relevant provisions of the peace treaty, the Israeli forces withdrew from the northern Sinai to the east of El Arish and the Egyptians took over control of that area. UNEF II was not involved in this move except by permitting access of Egyptian personnel to the buffer zone and the areas of limited forces and armament and by providing escorts to the parties within these areas as the Israeli withdrawal was being carried out. During this process, UNEF II withdrew from the northern part of the buffer zone, which was handed over to the Egyptian authorities. Except in areas of the Sinai controlled by Egyptian forces, UNEF II continued to function as previously. In particular, it continued to provide a physical separation of the areas of limited forces and armament. It also provided escorts to authorized non-United Nations visitors and to personnel of the parties travelling to and from the early-warning-system stations.

After the mandate of UNEF II lapsed in July 1979, the various contingents were rapidly repatriated, except for a Swedish guard unit and limited groups of the Canadian and Polish logistics contingents which remained in the area to assist in the winding up of the Force.

Chapter 5
United Nations Disengagement Observer Force (UNDOF)

A. Background and establishment
Background
Agreement on disengagement of forces
Protocol on UNDOF
Establishment of UNDOF
Secretary-General's proposal
Military Working Group
UNDOF beginnings
Extension of the mandate
Organization of UNDOF
UNDOF strength
Financial aspects

B. Activities of UNDOF
Initial deployment
Disengagement operation
Supervision of the Agreement
Humanitarian activities
Incidents and casualties
Current situation

Chapter 5

United Nations Disengagement Observer Force (UNDOF)

A. Background and establishment

Background

At the end of the October 1973 war, while tranquillity was restored on the Egyptian front with the deployment of the second United Nations Emergency Force (UNEF II), no new peace-keeping force was established on the Syrian front in the Golan Heights. There, fighting subsided following the cease-fire call contained in Security Council resolution 338 (1973) of 22 October 1973. By that time, the Israeli forces had crossed the 1967 cease-fire lines and occupied a salient up to and including the village of Saassa on the Quneitra-Damascus road. United Nations military observers set up temporary observation posts around that salient and, with these changes, the cease-fire observation operation in the Israel-Syria sector was resumed.

However, tension remained high in the area. There was a continuous pattern of incidents in and around the buffer zone supervised by the United Nations military observers. These involved artillery, mortar and automatic-weapon fire, and overflights by Israeli and Syrian aircraft. Frequent complaints of cease-fire violations were submitted by the two parties, although cease-fires proposed from time to time by the United Nations observers resulted in temporary cessation of firing. From early March 1974 until the end of May, the situation in the sector became increasingly unstable, and firing — involving use of artillery, tanks and rockets — intensified. Against this background, the United States Secretary of State undertook a diplomatic mission, which resulted in the conclusion of an Agreement on Disengagement between Israeli and Syrian Forces in May 1974.

Agreement on disengagement of forces

The Secretary-General, who was kept informed of these developments, reported[1] to the Security Council on 29 May that the signing of the Agreement would take place on 31 May 1974 in the Egyptian-Israeli Military Working Group of the Geneva Peace Conference on the Middle East. He also informed the Council that he had instructed Lieutenant-General Ensio P. H. Siilasvuo, the Commander of UNEF, to be available for the signing of the Agreement, under the aegis of the United Nations.

On 30 May, the Secretary-General transmitted to the Security Council the text[2] of the Agreement as well as the Protocol to that Agreement which dealt with the establishment of the United Nations Disengagement Observer Force (UNDOF).

Under the terms of the Agreement, Israel and Syria were scrupulously to observe the cease-fire on land, sea and in the air, and refrain from all military actions against each other from the time of the signing of the document, in implementation of Security Council resolution 338 (1973). It further provided that the two military forces would be separated in accordance with agreed principles, which called for the establishment of an area of separation and of two equal areas of limitation of armament and forces on both sides of the area. The detailed plan for the disengagement of forces would be worked out by the military representatives of Israel and Syria in the Military Working Group. They were to begin their work 24 hours after the signing of the Agreement and complete it within five days. Disengagement was to begin within 24 hours thereafter and be completed not later than 20 days after it had begun. The provisions of the Agreement concerning the cease-fire and the separation of forces were to be inspected by UNDOF personnel. All wounded prisoners of war were to be repatriated within 24 hours after signature of the Agreement, and all other prisoners upon completion of the work of

[1]S/11302. [2]S/11302/Add.1, annexes I and II.

the Military Working Group. The bodies of all dead soldiers held by either side would be returned for burial within 10 days. The final paragraph of the Agreement stated that it was not a peace agreement, but that it was a step towards a just and durable peace on the basis of Security Council resolution 338 (1973).

Protocol on UNDOF

According to the Protocol to the Agreement, Israel and Syria agreed that the function of UNDOF would be to maintain the cease-fire, to see that it was strictly observed, and to supervise the Agreement and Protocol with regard to the areas of separation and limitation. In carrying out its mission, the Force was to comply with generally applicable Syrian laws and regulations and not hamper the functioning of local civil administration. It was to enjoy the freedom of movement and communication necessary for its mission and be provided with personal weapons of a defensive character to be used only in self-defence.

The strength of UNDOF was set at 1,250, to be selected by the Secretary-General, in consultation with the parties, from Member States of the United Nations which were not permanent members of the Security Council.

In transmitting the documents, the Secretary-General, noting that the Protocol called for the creation of a United Nations Disengagement Observer Force, indicated that he would take the necessary steps in accordance with the Protocol's provisions, if the Security Council should so decide. He intended that the proposed Force would be drawn, at least initially, from United Nations military personnel already in the area.

Establishment of UNDOF

On 30 May 1974, the representative of the United States requested[3] an urgent meeting of the Security Council to consider the situation in the Middle East, in particular the disengagement of Israeli and Syrian forces. At the meeting, the Secretary-General drew attention to his reports on this matter and said that, were the Council so to decide, he would set up UNDOF on the basis of the same general principles which had governed the establishment of UNEF II.

On 31 May, the Agreement on Disengagement and the Protocol were signed at Geneva by the military representatives of Israel and Syria. Later on the same day, the Security Council adopted resolution 350 (1974) by which it decided

to set up UNDOF immediately, under its authority, and requested the Secretary-General to take the necessary steps.

The Force was established for an initial period of six months, subject to renewal by the Security Council. The Secretary-General was asked to keep the Council fully informed of further developments.

Secretary-General's proposal

After the adoption of the resolution, the Secretary-General presented his proposals for interim arrangements. He suggested that initially UNDOF should comprise the Austrian and Peruvian contingents from UNEF II, supported by logistical elements from Canada and Poland, also to be drawn from UNEF II, and by UNTSO military observers who were already deployed in the area (except those from permanent member countries of the Security Council). The Secretary-General also proposed to appoint, as interim Commander, Brigadier-General Gonzalo Briceño Zevallos of Peru, who was at the time commanding the northern brigade of UNEF II. The interim Commander was to be assisted by staff officers drawn from UNEF and UNTSO. The Security Council agreed to the Secretary-General's proposals.

Military Working Group

The Military Working Group met in Geneva from 31 May until 5 June 1974 under the chairmanship of General Siilasvuo to work out practical arrangements for the disengagement of forces.[4]

Military representatives of the Syrian Arab Republic joined the Group, and the representatives of the Soviet Union and the United States, as co-chairmen of the Geneva Peace Conference, also participated in the meetings.

Full agreement was reached on a disengagement plan, with a timetable for the withdrawal of Israeli forces from the areas east of the 1967 cease-fire line, as well as from Quneitra and Rafid, and the demilitarization of an area west of Quneitra. A map showing the different phases of disengagement was signed at the final meeting on 5 June.

In the negotiations in the Military Working Group, the two parties also agreed that both sides would repatriate all prisoners of war by 6 June, and that they would cooperate with the In-

[3]S/11304. [4]S/11302/Add.2.

ternational Committee of the Red Cross in carrying out its mandate, including the exchange of bodies, which was also to be completed by 6 June. They would make available all information and maps of minefields in their respective areas and the areas to be handed over by them.

UNDOF beginnings

On 3 June 1974, the Secretary-General, having obtained the agreement of the Government of Peru, appointed General Briceño as interim Commander of UNDOF. General Briceño arrived in Damascus from Cairo on the same day and immediately established a provisional headquarters in the premises of the Israel-Syria Mixed Armistice Commission, assuming command over the 90 UNTSO observers detailed to UNDOF.

Later the same day, advance parties of the Austrian and Peruvian contingents arrived in the mission area. They were joined on the following days by the remainder of the two contingents and the Canadian and Polish logistic elements. Some logistic support was given by UNEF.

By 16 June 1974, the strength of UNDOF was brought to 1,218 all ranks, near its authorized level of 1,250.

Extension of the mandate

The initial six-month mandate of UNDOF expired on 30 November 1974. Since then, the mandate has been repeatedly extended by the Security Council upon the recommendation of the Secretary-General and with the agreement of the two parties concerned.

In November 1975, Syria was reluctant to agree to a further extension because no progress had been made in the settlement of the wider Middle East problem. The Secretary-General met with President Hafez Al Assad in Damascus that month and, after extensive discussions, the President gave his agreement for the renewal of the UNDOF mandate for another period of six months, to be combined with a specific provision that the Security Council would convene, in January 1976, to hold a substantive debate on the Middle East problem, including the Palestine question, with the participation of representatives of the Palestine Liberation Organization.[5]

Extending the UNDOF mandate for a further six months, the Security Council, in resolution 381 (1975) of 30 November 1975, decided to reconvene on 12 January 1976 to continue the debate on the Middle East problem, taking into account all relevant United Nations resolutions.

In May 1976, the Secretary-General again had to travel to Damascus to secure the agreement of the Syrian Government for a further extension. However, from November 1976 onwards, the two parties readily gave their agreement for further extensions. On each occasion since that date, the Security Council, in renewing UNDOF's mandate for further six-month periods, called on the parties concerned to implement resolution 338 (1973) and requested the Secretary-General to submit at the end of the extension period a report on the measures taken to implement that resolution. In connection with the adoption of the resolutions on the renewal of the mandate, the President of the Security Council made a complementary statement on each occasion endorsing the view of the Secretary-General that, despite the prevailing quiet in the Israel-Syria sector, the situation in the Middle East as a whole would remain unstable and potentially dangerous unless real progress could be made towards a just and lasting settlement of the Middle East problem in all its aspects.

On 14 December 1981, the Israeli Government decided to apply Israeli law in the occupied Golan Heights. Syria strongly protested against this decision, and both the Security Council and the General Assembly declared that it was null and void. The Israeli decision, however, has not affected the operation of UNDOF in any significant way.

Organization of UNDOF

The organization of UNDOF is similar to that of UNEF II. The Force is under the exclusive command and control of the United Nations at all times. The Force Commander is appointed by the Secretary-General with the consent of the Security Council and is responsible to him. Following General Briceño, who was interim Commander until 15 December 1974, the command of UNDOF was assumed by Colonel (later Major-General) Hannes Philipp, of Austria (December 1974-April 1979); Colonel (later Major-General) Günther G. Greindl, also of Austria (until February 1981); Major-General Erkki R. Kaira, of Finland (until June 1982); Major-General Carl-Gustav Stahl, of Sweden (until May 1985); Major-General Gustav Hägglund, of Finland (until May 1986); Major-General Gustaf Welin, of Sweden (until September 1988); Major-General Adolf Radauer, of Austria (until September

[5]S/11883/Add.1.

1991); Major-General Roman Misztal, of Poland (until November 1994); Colonel Jan Kempara, of Poland (Acting Force Commander until January 1995); Major-General Johannes C. Kosters, of the Netherlands (since January 1995).

UNDOF was originally composed of the Austrian and Peruvian contingents and the Canadian and Polish logistic elements transferred from UNEF II. The Peruvian contingent was withdrawn in July 1975 and replaced by an Iranian contingent in August of that year. This contingent was in turn withdrawn in March 1979 and replaced by a Finnish contingent. In 1993, the Government of Finland decided to withdraw its infantry battalion by the end of that year. It was replaced by an infantry unit from Poland in December 1993. At the same time, the Polish logistic unit was withdrawn and logistic support was consolidated in the hands of the Canadian logistic unit, which was slightly strengthened. Some logistic tasks were assumed by the infantry battalions themselves. UNDOF in early 1996 was composed of infantry battalions from Austria and Poland and a logistic unit from Canada; a transport platoon from Japan joined the logistic unit in February 1996. Four observers, detailed from UNTSO, are included in UNDOF as an integral part of the Force. These observers are not nationals of permanent members of the Security Council. In addition, UNTSO observers assigned to the Israel-Syria Mixed Armistice Commission and organized in Observer Group Golan assist UNDOF under the operational control of the Force Commander of UNDOF.

UNDOF strength

Within two weeks of its establishment, the total strength of UNDOF was brought to near its authorized level of about 1,250. From that time until August 1979 — except for a brief period from March to August 1979 when the strength of the Force was temporarily below the authorized level as a result of the withdrawal of the Iranian battalion — the strength of UNDOF remained around that figure. In August 1979,[6] the Secretary-General informed the Security Council that, as a result of the withdrawal of UNEF II, which had hitherto provided third-line logistic support to UNDOF, it had become necessary to strengthen the existing

Canadian and Polish logistic units. The Security Council agreed to the proposed increase to 1,450. Following consultations with the parties, the strength of UNDOF was gradually brought up to 1,331 in May 1985.

In 1992, with a view to reducing expenditures, UNDOF underwent streamlining, which involved a 15 per cent reduction of each military contingent and of the internationally recruited civilian staff, with attendant savings in transport and accommodations. The reduction affected headquarters and support elements; the number of soldiers on operational duty in the observation posts and on patrol remained the same. In 1993, as a result of the restructuring [see above], the authorized military strength of the Force was further reduced by 88. As of March 1996, UNDOF comprised 1,054 troops from Austria (463), Canada (188), Japan (45) and Poland (358), as well as 4 military observers seconded by UNTSO. In addition, UNDOF was assisted by the 85 UNTSO military observers of the Observer Group Golan (OGG).

Financial aspects

From its inception UNDOF has been financed from the amounts appropriated for UNEF II, for which the establishment of a special account had been authorized by General Assembly resolution 3101 (XXVIII) of 11 December 1973. In accordance with this resolution, the costs of UNEF II were levied upon all Member States. In its resolution 3211 B (XXIX) of 29 November 1974, the General Assembly requested the Secretary-General to continue to maintain the special account, to which appropriations for both Forces were now credited. Following the termination of UNEF II in July 1979, the account remained open for UNDOF. Total expenditures from the inception of UNEF II until liquidation in 1980 and for UNDOF from inception to 31 May 1996 were estimated at $1,089,300,000, of which approximately $446,487,000 represented expenditures for UNEF II and $642,813,000 represented expenditures for UNDOF. In 1996, the annual cost of UNDOF was estimated at approximately $32.0 million.

[6] S/13479.

B. Activities of UNDOF

Initial deployment

Following the signing of the Agreement on Disengagement, all firings ceased in the Israel-Syria sector as of 1109 hours GMT on 31 May 1974. This was confirmed by the United Nations military observers stationed in the sector. These observers, who were later incorporated into UNDOF, continued to man selected observation posts and patrol bases along the cease-fire line while the newly arrived contingents of UNDOF began deployment in the area. The Austrian and Peruvian infantry battalions set up positions between the Israeli and Syrian forces, the former in the Saassa area and the latter from Quneitra south along the cease-fire lines.

Disengagement operation

The disengagement operation began on 14 June and proceeded apace until 27 June. In accordance with the agreed plan, the operation was carried out in four phases.

During the first phase, the Israeli forces handed over to UNDOF an area of some 270 square kilometres (about 28 square kilometres in the Saassa area and about 243 square kilometres east of Lake Tiberias) in the afternoon of 14 June. The next morning, the Syrian forces commenced deploying in that area while UNDOF established a new buffer zone west of the evacuated area.

The same procedure was followed for the second phase, which took place on 18 and 19 June and covered an area of some 374 square kilometres (about 214 square kilometres east of Lake Tiberias and about 160 square kilometres north and northwest of the Saassa area), and for the third phase, which took place on 23 June and involved an area of about 132 square kilometres east and north of Quneitra.

The fourth phase took place on 24 and 25 June. During that phase, the Israeli forces evacuated the area of separation, which was taken over by UNDOF. On 25 June, after UNDOF completed its deployment, Syrian civilian administration was established in the area of separation. On 26 June, UNDOF observers inspected the areas of limited forces and armament (in the 10-kilometre zones) on each side of the area of separation. The next day they proceeded with the inspection of the 20-and 25-kilometre zones, thus completing the implementation of the disengagement operation.

The disengagement process was marred by a serious incident during its last phase. Early on the morning of 25 June, four Austrian soldiers were killed and another wounded when their vehicle ran over a landmine on the slopes of Mount Hermon in the area of separation. From 25 to 27 June, at the request of the Syrian Government and on the basis of an agreement reached with the Israeli authorities through UNDOF headquarters, a body of 500 Syrian soldiers equipped with mine-clearing tanks carried out mine-clearing operations at various locations in the area of separation, under the close supervision of UNDOF observers.

Supervision of the Agreement

Following the completion of the disengagement operation, UNDOF undertook the delineation and marking of the lines bounding the area of separation. This task, which was carried out with the cooperation and assistance of the Israeli and Syrian forces on their respective sides, proceeded smoothly and was completed in early July 1974.

After the delineation of the area of separation, UNDOF set up a series of checkpoints and observation posts within that area. In addition, two base camps were established, one on the east side of the area of separation and the other on the west side. At the same time, UNDOF headquarters, which remained in Damascus, was moved from the office of the Israel-Syria Mixed Armistice Commission to a building made available by the Syrian Government. The Quneitra communication relay station, which had been set up by UNTSO, was placed under the control of UNDOF.

In the second part of 1992, most of the military component of UNDOF headquarters was moved from Damascus to Camp Faouar; some elements were moved to Camp Ziouani. This relocation had a positive effect on command and control. Subsequently, Camp Faouar became the main headquarters of the Force. UNDOF also continues to maintain an office at Damascus, which is now located on the premises of the United Nations Relief and Works Agency for Palestine Refugees in the Near East.

UNDOF headquarters maintains close liaison with both sides through their senior military representatives. At the local level, the commanders of the UNDOF units maintain liaison with one side or the other through liaison officers designated by the parties.

UNDOF is deployed within, and close to, the area of separation with base camps and a logistic unit. The Austrian battalion is deployed in the northern part of the area of separation. At present, it maintains 16 positions and 9 outposts. The Polish battalion is deployed in the southern part of the area. At present, it maintains 14 positions and 8 outposts. Its base camp is Camp Ziouani. Mine-clearing is conducted by both battalions under the operational control of UNDOF headquarters.

The Canadian logistic unit is based in Camp Ziouani, with a detachment in Camp Faouar. It performs the second-line general transport tasks, rotation transport, control and management of goods received by UNDOF and maintenance of heavy equipment.

First-line logistic support is internal to the contingents and includes transport of supplies to the positions. Second-line logistic support, as explained above, is provided by the Canadian logistic unit. Third-line support is provided through normal supply channels by the United Nations. Damascus international airport serves as UNDOF's airhead; Tel Aviv international airport is also used. The seaports of Latakia and Haifa are used for sea shipments.

The main function of UNDOF is to supervise the area of separation to make sure that there are no military forces within it. This is carried out by means of static positions and observation posts which are manned 24 hours a day, and by foot and mobile patrols operating along predetermined routes by day and night. Temporary outposts and additional patrols are set up from time to time as occasion requires.

Under a programme undertaken by the Syrian authorities, civilians have continued to return to the area of separation, the population of which has doubled since the establishment of UNDOF. The Syrian Arab Republic has stationed police in the area of separation in exercise of its administrative responsibility. UNDOF has adjusted its operations accordingly to take account of these developments and to continue to carry out effectively its supervisory tasks under the Agreement on Disengagement.

In accordance with the terms of the Agreement on Disengagement, UNDOF conducts fortnightly inspections of the area of limitation of armament and forces. These inspections, which cover the 10-, 20- and 25-kilometre zones on each side of the area of separation, are carried out by United Nations military observers with the assistance of liaison officers from the parties, who accompany the inspection teams on their respective sides. These inspections have generally proceeded smoothly with the cooperation of the parties concerned, although on both sides restrictions are regularly placed on the movement of the inspection teams in some localities. The findings of the inspection teams are communicated to the two parties but are not made public. So far, no serious problems have arisen in this connection.

Humanitarian activities

In addition to its normal peace-keeping functions, UNDOF has carried out activities of a humanitarian nature as occasion requires. At the request of the parties, UNDOF has from time to time exercised its good offices in arranging for the transfer of released prisoners and the bodies of war dead between Israel and Syria. It has assisted the International Committee of the Red Cross (ICRC) by providing it with facilities for the hand-over of prisoners and bodies, for the exchange of parcels and mail across the area of separation, and for the transit of Druze students from the occupied Golan to attend school in Syria. Of particular note was the assistance extended to ICRC on 28 June 1984 when 297 prisoners of war, 16 civilians and the remains of 77 persons were exchanged between Israel and Syria. In 1976, UNDOF worked out arrangements, with the cooperation of the two parties, for periodic reunions of Druze families living on different sides of the area of separation. Those family reunions took place every fortnight in the village of Majdel Chams in the area of separation, under the supervision of UNDOF, until February 1982, when they had to be discontinued because of the controversy arising from Israel's decision in December 1981 to apply Israeli law to the occupied Golan Heights. Within the means available, UNDOF has also provided medical treatment to the local population.

Incidents and casualties

During the initial period, there were a number of serious incidents. Besides the four Austrian soldiers killed and another wounded in a mine incident on 25 June 1974, another mine explosion occurred on 20 April 1977 in which an Austrian officer was killed and an Iranian officer was wounded. Despite the mine-clearing opera-

UNDOF deployment as of November 1995

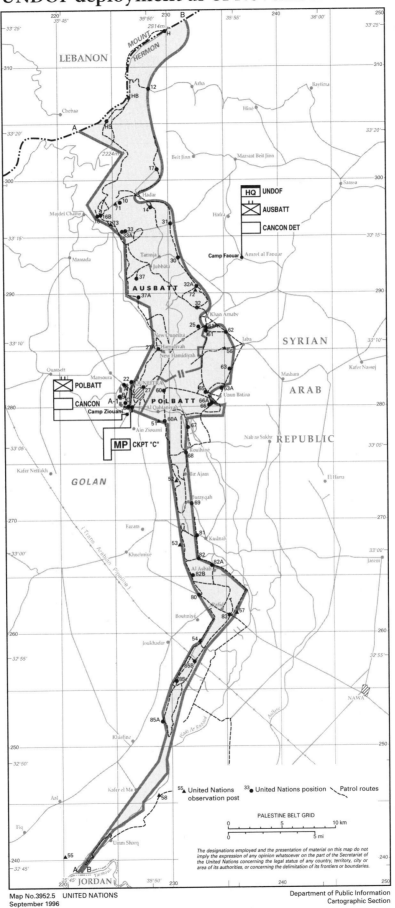

HQ UNDOF

AUSBATT

CANCON DET

55 ▲ United Nations observation post

33 ● United Nations position

Patrol routes

PALESTINE BELT GRID

0   5   10 km

0   5 mi

The designations employed and the presentation of material on this map do not imply the expression of any opinion whatsoever on the part of the Secretariat of the United Nations concerning the legal status of any country, territory, city or area of its authorities, or concerning the delimitation of its frontiers or boundaries.

Map No.3952.5   UNITED NATIONS
September 1996

Department of Public Information
Cartographic Section

tions undertaken by the Syrian forces in 1974, there were still many unexploded mines in and near the area of separation. The engineers of the UNDOF logistic unit continue to search for and defuse unexploded mines, shells and bombs in and near the area.

On 9 August 1974, a United Nations aircraft, flying from Ismailia to Damascus in the established air corridor, crashed as a result of anti-aircraft fire, north-east of the Syrian village of Ad Dimas. All nine Canadians aboard were killed.

In November 1975, there was a shooting incident in which two Syrian shepherds were killed by an Israeli patrol. There were also alleged crossings of the area of separation, resulting in one case in the death of three Israeli citizens. In November 1977, two members of the Iranian battalion came under fire from the Israeli side and both were wounded.

On the night of 22/23 September 1991, fire from an Israel Defence Force position located on the slopes of Mount Hermon killed three armed elements 500 metres east of the cease-fire line, which was within the Syrian administered area. Indications were that they had crossed into Syria from Lebanon. ICRC arranged and conducted the return of the bodies to the families.

In April 1992, a number of firings by Israeli troops at livestock grazing in the area of separation near the line on the Israeli side were a cause of concern for UNDOF and were protested by the Syrian authorities. Following representations by UNDOF to the Israel Defence Forces, this dangerous practice ceased.

In the period between May and September 1994, there were a number of violations by Syrian personnel involving field works and the laying of a minefield in the area of separation. These were removed following representations by the United Nations.

Whenever such incidents occur, UNDOF seeks to resolve the situation by negotiation and appropriate corrective measures. The incidents have not seriously affected the operations of the Force.

Current situation

Since September 1991, there have been no major incidents. The main problems in the area arise from the presence of Syrian shepherds grazing their flocks near the western edge of the area of separation. They sometimes cross the line, either in ignorance or because there are good grazing lands on the other side. A number of shepherds have been killed as a result of detonating mines in the area of separation.

Problems arise for UNDOF as a result of the restrictions placed upon its troops by one party or the other. Because, until 1990, Poland had no diplomatic relations with Israel, the Israeli forces restricted the movement of the Polish unit on the Israeli side of the area of separation. The Force Commander, fully supported by the Secretary-General, protested against these restrictions on the grounds that UNDOF is an integrated unit and all its elements must enjoy freedom of movement on an equal basis. Following the establishment of diplomatic relations between Israel and Poland, this problem was resolved.

As noted above, restrictions are regularly placed by both sides on the movement of the UNDOF inspection teams, which are not allowed to visit certain localities when inspecting the area of limitation of armament and forces. These restrictions are invariably protested by the Force Commander.

On the whole, however, UNDOF encounters no serious difficulties that would affect its smooth functioning. In his periodic reports on the activities of the Force, the Secretary-General has been able to report that the situation in the Israel-Syria sector has remained quiet. In his report submitted to the Security Council in November 1995,[7] the Secretary-General stated that UNDOF had continued to perform its tasks effectively, with the cooperation of the parties. The situation in the Middle East, however, continued to be potentially dangerous and was likely to remain so, unless and until a comprehensive settlement covering all aspects of the Middle East problem could be reached. The Secretary-General believed that, in the prevailing circumstances, the continued presence of the Force in the area was essential and recommended that the Security Council extend the mandate of UNDOF for a further period of six months. Accordingly, the Security Council again renewed the mandate of UNDOF, and called upon the parties concerned to implement its resolution 338 (1973), which had called for a just and durable settlement to the Middle East conflict.[8]

[7]S/1995/952. [8]S/RES/1024 (1995).

Chapter 6
United Nations Interim Force in Lebanon (UNIFIL)

G. Efforts to restore the authority of the Lebanese Government in southern Lebanon

Civilian administration
Army deployment, 1978
Army deployment, 1979
Army deployment, 1980–1981
Efforts to reactivate the General Armistice Agreement

H. Cease-fire: July 1981–April 1982

I. Israeli invasion: 1982–1985

Breakdown of the cease-fire
Israeli invasion, June 1982
UNIFIL's interim tasks

J. Withdrawal of Israeli forces

Naqoura talks (November 1984–January 1985)
Withdrawal of Israeli forces from the Sidon area
Further withdrawals of the Israeli forces

K. Situation from 1985–1995

Israel maintains its occupation
Tensions persist
UNIFIL's functions unchanged
Lebanese Army deployment

L. UNIFIL under fire

Clashes with armed elements
Firing by IDF/SLA
The Norwegian battalion sector
Casualties from mines

M. Continuing importance of UNIFIL

Chapter 6

United Nations Interim Force in Lebanon (UNIFIL)

A. Background and establishment

Background

Although the Lebanese civil war which had broken out in April 1975 officially ended in October 1976 — after the election of President Elias Sarkis, the constitution of a new central Government and the establishment of an Arab Deterrent Force — fighting did not completely stop in southern Lebanon. When Syrian troops of the Deterrent Force deployed towards the south, the Israeli Government threatened to take stern counter-measures if they should advance beyond an imaginary east-west red line, extending south of the Zahrani River. Whether because of this threat or for some other reasons, the Syrian forces stopped short of the red line. The authority of the central Government was not restored in the south. Sporadic fighting continued in that area between the Christian militias, which were assisted by Israel, and the armed elements of the Lebanese National Movement, a loose association of a variety of Moslem and leftist parties, supported by the armed forces of the Palestine Liberation Organization (PLO). The PLO was the dominant force in southern Lebanon at the time and had established many bases in the area. From these it launched commando raids against Israel which were followed by intensive Israeli retaliation.

On 11 March 1978, a commando raid, for which the PLO claimed responsibility, took place in Israel near Tel Aviv and, according to Israeli sources, resulted in 37 deaths and 76 wounded among the Israeli population.[1] In retaliation, Israeli forces invaded Lebanon on the night of 14/15 March, and in a few days occupied the entire region south of the Litani River except for the city of Tyre and its surrounding area.

Establishment of UNIFIL

On 15 March, the Lebanese Government submitted a strong protest[2] to the Security Council against the Israeli invasion. It stated that it was not responsible for the presence of Palestinian bases in southern Lebanon and had no connection with the Palestinian commando operation. It said it had exerted tremendous efforts with the Palestinians and the Arab States in order to keep matters under control, but Israeli objections regarding the entry of the Arab Deterrent Force to the south had prevented the accomplishment of Lebanon's desire to bring the border area under control. The Security Council met on 17 March 1978 and on the following days to consider the Lebanese complaint.

On 19 March, on a proposal by the United States, the Security Council adopted resolution 425 (1978), by which it called for strict respect for the territorial integrity, sovereignty and political independence of Lebanon within its internationally recognized boundaries. It called upon Israel immediately to cease its military action against Lebanese territorial integrity and withdraw forthwith its forces from all Lebanese territory. It also decided, "in the light of the request of the Government of Lebanon, to establish immediately under its authority a United Nations interim force for southern Lebanon for the purpose of confirming the withdrawal of Israeli forces, restoring international peace and security and assisting the Government of Lebanon in ensuring the return of its effective authority in the area, the force to be composed of personnel drawn from Member States". The Council requested the Secretary-General to submit a report to the Council within 24 hours on the implementation of the resolution.

Terms of reference and guidelines

On the same afternoon, the Secretary-General submitted a report[3] to the Security Council in which he set out the terms of reference of

[1]S/12598. [2]S/12600. [3]S/12611.

the new Force, to be called the United Nations Interim Force in Lebanon (UNIFIL), the guidelines for the Force and a plan of action for its speedy establishment.

The Force was to confirm the withdrawal of Israeli forces, restore international peace and security, and assist the Government of Lebanon in ensuring the return of its effective authority in the area. It would establish and maintain itself in an area of operation to be defined in the light of those tasks, and would use its best efforts to prevent the recurrence of fighting and to ensure that its area of operation would not be utilized for hostile activities of any kind. In the fulfilment of its tasks, the Force would have the cooperation of the military observers of the United Nations Truce Supervision Organization (UNTSO), who would continue to function on the Armistice Demarcation Line (ADL) after the termination of UNIFIL's mandate.

In the first stage, the Force would confirm the withdrawal of the Israeli forces from Lebanese territory to the international border. Once this was achieved, it would establish and maintain an area of operation to be defined in consultation with the parties concerned. It would supervise the cessation of hostilities, ensure the peaceful character of the area of operation, control movement and take all measures deemed necessary to assure the effective restoration of Lebanese sovereignty. The Secretary-General also indicated that, with a view to facilitating UNIFIL's tasks, it might be necessary to work out arrangements with Israel and Lebanon as a preliminary measure for the implementation of the Security Council resolution, and it was assumed that both parties would give their full cooperation to UNIFIL in this regard.

Particular emphasis was placed on the principles of non-use of force and non-intervention in the internal affairs of the host country. UNIFIL would not use force except in self-defence, which would include resistance to attempts by forcible means to prevent it from discharging its duties under the Council's mandate. Like any other United Nations peace-keeping operation, UNIFIL could not and should not take on responsibilities which fell under the Government of the country in which it was operating. Those responsibilities should be exercised by the competent Lebanese authorities.

In working out the terms of reference of UNIFIL, the Secretary-General had wanted to define more clearly the area of operation of the Force and its relationship with the PLO. But he could not do so, as the discussions he held with the member States of the Security Council and with other Governments concerned revealed a profound disagreement among them on both subjects. As will be seen later, these two questions weighed heavily on the operations of UNIFIL.

The guidelines proposed by the Secretary-General were essentially the same as those applied to UNEF II and UNDOF. Important decisions on the organization of UNIFIL, such as the appointment of the Force Commander or the selection of contingents, would be taken by the Secretary-General, but he would need to consult the Security Council and obtain its consent. All matters which might affect the nature or the continued effective functioning of the Force would be referred to the Council for its decision.

The Secretary-General said that Lieutenant-General Ensio P. H. Siilasvuo, Chief Coordinator of the United Nations Peace-keeping Missions in the Middle East, would be instructed to contact immediately the Governments of Israel and Lebanon for the purpose of reaching agreement on the modalities of the withdrawal of the Israeli forces and the establishment of a United Nations area of operation. Major-General (later Lieutenant-General) Emmanuel A. Erskine, of Ghana, the Chief of Staff of UNTSO, would be appointed immediately as interim Commander and, pending the arrival of the first contingents of the Force, would perform his tasks with the assistance of a group of UNTSO military observers. At the same time, urgent measures would be taken for the early arrival in the area of contingents of the Force. The Secretary-General proposed that the Force have a total strength of the order of 4,000 and that it be stationed initially in the area for six months. The best possible preliminary cost estimate was approximately $68 million for a Force of 4,000 all ranks for that period. As with UNEF II and UNDOF, the costs of UNIFIL were to be considered as expenses of the Organization to be borne by Member States as apportioned by the General Assembly.

By resolution 426 (1978) of 19 March 1978, the Council approved the Secretary-General's report and decided that UNIFIL should be established for an initial period of six months, subject to extension.

Beginnings of the Force

While the members of the Security Council, in close consultation with the Secretary-General, were discussing the establishment of UNIFIL, the situation in southern Lebanon remained extremely tense and volatile. Israeli forces had occupied most of southern Lebanon up to the Litani River, but the PLO troops regrouped with much of their equipment in the Tyre pocket and in their strongholds north of the Litani, particularly Nabatiyah and Chateau de Beaufort. Intense exchanges of fire continued between the opposing forces.

The Secretary-General's two immediate objectives were to set up the new Force and deploy it along the front lines as soon as possible, and to initiate negotiations on the withdrawal of the Israeli forces.

General Erskine, who had been appointed as interim Commander of UNIFIL on 19 March, immediately set up temporary headquarters at Naqoura in southern Lebanon, in the premises of the UNTSO out-station, with the 45 military observers who were already in the area. These were soon reinforced by 19 additional observers of UNTSO. In order to make UNIFIL operational without delay, the Secretary-General transferred some military personnel from the two existing peacekeeping forces in the Middle East, after obtaining the concurrence of the Governments concerned.

One reinforced company from the Iranian contingent of UNDOF and another from the Swedish contingent of UNEF were temporarily assigned to the new Force, together with a movement control detachment and a signal detachment of the Canadian logistic unit of UNEF.

Meanwhile, urgent action had to be taken to seek and obtain 4,000 troops for the Force. France, Nepal and Norway had already offered to provide contingents. On 21 March, after securing the agreement of the Council, the Secretary-General accepted the offers of the three Governments. Later, in response to an appeal by the Secretary-General, Nigeria and Senegal each agreed to provide an infantry battalion.

The first French troops arrived in Beirut on 23 March; the Norwegian contingent came a week later and the Nepalese by mid-April. With the Canadian, Iranian and Swedish units already in the area, the strength of UNIFIL reached 1,800 all ranks by 8 April, 2,502 by 17 April and 4,016 by the beginning of May.

B. Organizational matters

Strength of the Force

On 1 May 1978, shortly after the Israeli withdrawal began, the Secretary-General recommended[4] that the total strength of the Force should be brought to 6,000. He also indicated that the Governments of Fiji, Iran and Ireland were prepared to make available a battalion each for service with UNIFIL. By resolution 427 (1978) of 3 May 1978, the Security Council approved the Secretary-General's recommendation. The three new battalions arrived in the mission area during the first days of June. The Swedish and Iranian companies that had been temporarily detached from UNEF and UNDOF returned to their parent units.

As of mid-June 1978, the strength of the Force was 6,100. The contingents were: infantry battalions — Fiji (500), France (703), Iran (514), Ireland (665), Nepal (642), Nigeria (669), Norway (723), Senegal (634); logistic units — Canada (102), France (541), Norway (207). In addition, 42 military observers of UNTSO assisted UNIFIL in the performance of its tasks, having been organized on 1 April 1978 as Observer Group Lebanon

(OGL), under the operational control of the Force Commander of UNIFIL.

From June 1978 until June 1981, the strength of UNIFIL varied between 5,750 and 6,100, according to the movements of the various contingents. The Canadian logistic detachments were returned to UNEF in October 1978. At the request of their Governments, the Iranian battalion was withdrawn beginning in January 1979 and the French infantry battalion in March 1979. The last was replaced by a Dutch battalion, which arrived in the mission area by early March; a Ghanaian contingent joined UNIFIL in September 1979.

The strength of UNIFIL was further increased to about 7,000 in early 1982 on the recommendation of the Secretary-General (resolution 501 (1982) of 25 February 1982). In response to a request of the Secretary-General, the French Government agreed to provide a new infantry battalion of about 600 all ranks and the Ghanaian and Irish Governments agreed to increase their battalions.

[4]S/12675.

These changes brought the strength of UNIFIL to 6,945 at the beginning of June 1982. The composition of the Force at that date was: infantry battalions — Fiji (628), France (595), Ghana (557), Ireland (671), Nepal (432), Netherlands (810), Nigeria (696), Norway (660), Senegal (561); headquarters camp command — Ghana (140), Ireland (51); logistic units — France (775), Italy (34), Norway (191), Sweden (144).

Following the second Israeli invasion of Lebanon, in June 1982, the strength and composition of UNIFIL underwent important changes. In September 1982, at the request of the French Government, 482 officers and men of the French infantry battalion were temporarily released from UNIFIL to their national authorities, which incorporated them in the French contingent of the multinational force in Beirut. The Nepalese battalion was withdrawn by 18 November 1982 and replaced by a Finnish battalion. Two companies of the Nigerian battalion were repatriated without replacement in November 1982 and the remainder in January 1983. In October 1983, the Netherlands decided to reduce its contingent from 810 to 150. In February 1984, the French unit withdrawn in 1982 was returned to UNIFIL. In October 1984, the Senegalese contingent was withdrawn and was replaced by a Nepalese battalion which arrived in the area in January–February 1985. In October 1985, the Netherlands contingent was withdrawn, its positions being taken over by the Fijian and Nepalese battalions, the latter increased by an additional infantry company.

In December 1986, the bulk of the infantry and part of the logistic battalions provided by France were withdrawn. The latter was replaced by a Swedish logistic battalion, while the Finnish, Ghanaian and Nepalese contingents were increased and assumed the tasks of the French infantry battalion. The remaining elements of the French logistic battalion and one infantry company formed a French composite battalion, responsible for logistic functions and the protection of the UNIFIL headquarters. Following a substantive redeployment of the Force, the entire French composite battalion was stationed at the Naqoura Camp. At the same time, a composite mechanized company, which would consist of elements of the Fijian, Finnish, Ghanaian, Irish, Nepalese, Norwegian and Swedish battalions, was established as a separate unit called the Force Mobile Reserve. The unit, stationed near the headquarters of the Fijian battalion, is available for quick deployment to trouble spots throughout the UNIFIL area of op-

eration. The Swedish logistic battalion was withdrawn in 1994 and replaced by a Polish unit.

Force Commanders

General Emmanuel A. Erskine of Ghana, who acted as interim commander at the outset of the operation, was appointed Force Commander on 12 April 1978. On 14 February 1981, he was reappointed Chief of Staff of UNTSO and was succeeded at UNIFIL by Lieutenant-General William Callaghan of Ireland (15 February 1981–31 May 1986), who was in turn succeeded by Major-General Gustav Hägglund of Finland (1 June 1986–30 June 1988). General Hägglund was replaced on 1 July 1988 by Lieutenant-General Lars-Eric Wahlgren of Sweden who served until 22 February 1993 when, on 23 February, he was succeeded by Major-General Trond Furuhovde of Norway. Since 1 April 1995, Major-General Stanislaw Franciszek Wozniak of Poland has been the Force Commander of UNIFIL.

During the initial stages of UNIFIL, General Siilasvuo, the Chief Coordinator of the United Nations Peace-keeping Missions in the Middle East, had a leading role in the negotiations with the Israeli authorities concerning the withdrawal of their forces from Lebanon. (After the termination of UNEF II, the post of Chief Coordinator was discontinued in 1979.)

Review and streamlining

On 31 July 1990, the members of the Security Council, during informal consultations, requested the Secretary-General to carry out a review of the scale and deployment of UNIFIL.[5] The review[6] concluded that UNIFIL's scale and deployment were determined by two main factors: the Security Council's commitment to resolution 425 (1978) as the correct solution to the problem of southern Lebanon; and UNIFIL's interim tasks — controlling the level of hostilities in the area of deployment and providing humanitarian support to the civilian population — which were carried out with the Security Council's approval until UNIFIL was enabled to carry out its original mandate.

Prepared in cooperation with the Force Commander, the review took note of the difficulties and dangers faced by the Force in preventing its area from being used for hostile activities when those activities included resistance to an occupation against which the Security Council had re-

[5]S/21833. [6]S/22129/Add.1.

peatedly pronounced itself. It was clear, however, that the solution to this anomaly lay in the withdrawal of Israeli forces from Lebanese territory, as required by resolution 425 (1978), and the progressive assumption by the Lebanese Army of responsibility for security in UNIFIL's area of deployment. UNIFIL could then deploy down to the international border, necessitating in all likelihood an initial increase in the Force's strength.

The review recommended certain measures for streamlining UNIFIL, including reduction in the size of the headquarters and support elements of the six infantry battalions; withdrawal of the heavy mortars with which some of the battalions were equipped; and withdrawal of the armoured escort company deployed at Force headquarters in Naqoura. These measures would produce a saving of some 10 per cent in the Force's strength. The Security Council agreed with most of these recommendations.

The review was carried out at a time when it was particularly difficult to judge the likely course of events in the region. The conclusions were thus short-term. For the medium term, it was hoped that UNIFIL would be able to implement the mandate originally entrusted to it; at that time a new set of options for its scale and deployment would have to be examined. However, since Israel gave no indication of its readiness to withdraw, the short-term conclusions remained valid. The reduction was implemented in the course of 1992 and the number of internationally recruited civilian staff was also reduced by 17 per cent.

Reporting to the Security Council in January 1994,[7] the Secretary-General expressed the hope that the ongoing peace talks would make sufficient progress to justify a further reduction in UNIFIL's strength. In the next report,[8] however, he concluded that no visible progress had been made. Nevertheless, the Secretary-General felt compelled for other reasons to give the most serious consideration to the possibility of a reduction. Despite all appeals to Member States to pay their assessments promptly and to clear their arrears, the funds available in the Force's accounts were barely sufficient to cover three weeks' expenses. This shortfall in assessed contributions was a long-term problem. Since most of the Force's expenditures were directly or indirectly related to personnel, the situation could be improved only by a reduction in strength. This would, in turn, affect the activities of the Force.

Accordingly, the Secretary-General initiated a study to determine how UNIFIL could perform its essential functions in such circumstances.

The Security Council endorsed this initiative in its resolution 974 (1995). Although the study offered no alternative to the existing concept of operations and deployment and did not recommend a reduction in UNIFIL's operational capacity, it identified possibilities for streamlining and achieving economies in the areas of maintenance and logistic support.

Following a further detailed review, undertaken in early 1995, the Force Commander of UNIFIL proposed a slimming-down of his headquarters by 20 per cent, the consolidation of engineer support in one unit, and small reductions of varying size in the infantry battalions. These measures were to result in a reduction in the overall strength of the Force by 10 per cent, representing a direct savings in personnel costs of approximately $10 million per year. The streamlining was expected to be largely completed in the spring of 1996. On the recommendation of the Secretary-General,[9] the Security Council concurred with this proposal.[10]

As at 31 March 1996, the strength of UNIFIL stood at 4,568, composed as follows: Fiji (585), Finland (503), France (285), Ghana (647), Ireland (622), Italy (48), Nepal (599), Norway (745) and Poland (534). In addition, UNIFIL employed approximately 140 international civilian staff and about 190 local Lebanese staff. The Force was assisted by 57 military observers from UNTSO.

Financial aspects

When the Force was set up in March 1978, the Security Council decided that its costs should be considered as expenses of the Organization to be paid by assessed contributions set by the General Assembly. The sum of $2,546.9 million (net) had been appropriated for UNIFIL by the General Assembly for the period from its inception to 31 January 1996. Assessed contributions received during the same period amounted to $2,341.3 million (net). Estimated net expenditure during that period amounted to 2,544.8 million. Because of the serious deficit, which has grown steadily over the years, the United Nations has been forced to cut expenditures and fall further and further behind in reimbursing Governments for the costs they have incurred in contributing troops, equipment and supplies to UNIFIL.

The Secretary-General has repeatedly appealed to all Member States to pay their assessments without delay. Given the importance of

[7]S/1994/62. [8]S/1994/856. [9]S/1995/595. [10]S/RES/1006 (1995).

UNIFIL's mission and the fact that its mandate has repeatedly been renewed by the unanimous vote of the Security Council, the Secretary-General pointed out that it was difficult to understand why such a problem should afflict the Force.

C. UNIFIL activities: March–April 1978

Negotiating problems

UNIFIL has no enforcement power and requires the cooperation of the parties concerned to fulfil its tasks. Resolution 425 (1978) mentioned only Israel and Lebanon. Immediately after the adoption of the resolution, the Secretary-General sought and obtained an undertaking from both of those countries to cooperate with UNIFIL.

To obtain the cooperation of the PLO, the Secretary-General on 27 March issued an appeal to all the parties concerned, including the PLO, for a general cease-fire.[11] This was followed up with a meeting between Mr. Yasser Arafat, Chairman of the Executive Committee of the PLO, and General Erskine, the Force Commander, during which a pledge of cooperation with UNIFIL was secured from the PLO.

Another complication arose from the presence and activities in southern Lebanon of various Lebanese armed elements not controlled by the central Government. UNIFIL could not officially negotiate with these armed elements, although they were very much a part of the problem, some of them having sided with the PLO and others with Israel. The Lebanese National Movement (LNM), a loose association of Lebanese Moslem and leftist parties, allied with the PLO, and the armed elements of the two groups operated under a joint command. When difficulties arose with the armed elements, UNIFIL generally endeavoured to resolve them in negotiations with the PLO leadership.

On the opposite side, UNIFIL had to contend with Lebanese de facto forces, which were composed mainly of Christian militias led by Major Saad Haddad, a renegade officer of the Lebanese National Army. When UNIFIL encountered problems with the de facto forces, it sought the cooperation and assistance of the Israeli authorities, since these forces were armed, trained and supplied by Israel and, by all evidence, closely controlled by it.

Problems concerning the area of operation

A second major difficulty encountered by UNIFIL arose from the lack of a clear definition of its area of operation. Security Council resolution 425 (1978), which was the result of a compromise, was vague on this point. It indicated only that UNIFIL would operate in southern Lebanon and that one of its tasks was to confirm withdrawal of the Israeli forces to the international border. In his report[12] on the implementation of the resolution, which had to take into account the views of the various members of the Security Council, the Secretary-General was unable to propose a clearer definition and merely stated that UNIFIL would set up an area of operation in consultation with the parties. But the parties had very different perceptions of the tasks of UNIFIL and no agreement could be reached on a definition of its area of operation. This difficulty gravely hampered UNIFIL's work from the very start.

First deployment

On 20 March 1978, General Erskine established temporary headquarters in Naqoura. At the same time, General Siilasvuo initiated negotiations with the Israeli authorities in Jerusalem to secure their agreement to withdraw their troops from Lebanon without delay. Pending the withdrawal, plans were made to deploy the UNIFIL troops in a strip of land immediately south of the Litani River and, in particular, to assume control of the Kasmiyah, Akiya and Khardala bridges, which were the three main crossing-points into southern Lebanon.

The Iranian and Swedish companies were instructed to proceed to the Akiya bridge in the central sector and the Khardala bridge in the eastern sector, respectively. Their movement to their destinations was initially delayed by the opposition of the Christian de facto forces which were deployed near those areas. However, this opposi-

[11]S/12620/Add.1. [12]S/12611.

tion was overcome through negotiations with the Israeli authorities, and the proposed deployment took place on 24 March and the following days. The Iranians established a position at the Akiya bridge and expanded their presence around it, while the Swedes were deployed at the Khardala bridge and in the area of Ibil as Saqy farther east. At the end of March, the Norwegian battalion had arrived and was deployed in the eastern sector and the Swedish company redeployed in the central/western sector.

The French battalion was sent to the Tyre region. The initial plan was for the French troops to deploy throughout the Tyre pocket and take control of the Kasmiyah bridge. But this was strongly opposed by the PLO on the grounds that the Israel Defence Forces (IDF) had not in fact occupied either the bridge or the city of Tyre during the fighting, and it became clear that it could not be achieved without heavy fighting and considerable casualties. In New York, the Arab representatives to the United Nations strongly supported the PLO's view that the Tyre pocket should not be included in UNIFIL's area of operation. In these conditions, the Secretary-General decided to delay the proposed deployment, pending negotiations with the PLO; in the event, such deployment was not pressed.

Meanwhile, the French battalion set up its headquarters in former Lebanese army barracks outside the city of Tyre. It established checkpoints around its headquarters and carried out patrolling activities along the front line, on the coastal road from Zahrani to Tyre and in the city of Tyre itself.

The UNTSO observers assigned to UNIFIL, namely Observer Group Lebanon, played an ex- tremely useful role during this formative phase, since they were already familiar with local conditions. They continued to man the five observation posts established by UNTSO in 1972 along the Armistice Demarcation Line. Some observers served as staff officers at the Naqoura headquarters. Teams of two observers each were attached to the various contingents for liaison and other purposes. Other observers provided liaison with the Lebanese authorities, the Israeli forces, the PLO and various other armed groups in southern Lebanon. The office of the Israel-Lebanon Mixed Armistice Commission in Beirut ensured liaison between UNIFIL and the Lebanese Government.

Cease-fire

The situation in southern Lebanon remained volatile during the first days of UNIFIL. As previously mentioned, on 27 March 1978 the Secretary-General had issued an appeal to all the parties concerned to observe a general cease-fire. On 8 April, General Erskine reported[13] that the area had been generally quiet since then. However, considerable tension, with occasional exchanges of fire, continued in the Tyre area and the eastern sector, which was close to the main base of the Christian de facto forces in Marjayoun and the PLO stronghold of Chateau de Beaufort north of the Litani River. UNIFIL troops, which were deployed between the opposing forces in these two sensitive areas, endeavoured to maintain a precarious cease-fire, while the Secretary-General and General Siilasvuo continued to press the Israeli authorities to withdraw their troops from Lebanon without delay.

D. UNIFIL activities: April–June 1978

Initial withdrawal of Israeli forces

On 6 April 1978, the Chief of Staff of the Israel Defence Forces submitted to General Siilas- vuo a plan for an initial withdrawal of the Israeli forces in two phases. In a first phase, to take place on 11 April, the Israeli forces would withdraw from an area west of Marjayoun. The Khardala bridge and a number of villages would be evacuated, but strategic villages such as El Khirba and Dayr Mimas would remain occupied. A second withdrawal would follow on 14 April and would cover a zone extending from a point on the Litani River two kilometres west of the Akiya bridge to a point about one kilometre west of Dayr Mimas. The area to be evacuated during the two first phases would cover about 110 square kilometres, or one tenth of the total occupied territory.

The next day, the Secretary-General indicated that the Israeli plan was not satisfactory since

[13] S/12620/Add.2.

Security Council resolution 425 (1978) called for the withdrawal of Israeli forces without delay from the entire occupied Lebanese territory. The plan, however, was accepted on the understanding that a further withdrawal would be agreed upon at an early date. The proposed withdrawal took place as scheduled without incident. All the positions evacuated by the Israeli forces were handed over to UNIFIL troops.

Further negotiations between General Siilasvuo and the Israeli authorities led to a third phase of the Israeli withdrawal, which took place on 30 April.[14] This withdrawal was more extensive and covered an area of about 550 square kilometres. As in the previous withdrawals, the positions evacuated by the Israeli forces were taken over by UNIFIL troops without incident.

Following the third phase of the Israeli withdrawal, UNIFIL was deployed in two separate zones south of the Litani River within an area of about 650 square kilometres, or approximately 45 per cent of the territory occupied by Israel. The western zone had an area of about 600 square kilometres and the eastern zone about 50 square kilometres. Between the two zones, there was a gap some 15 kilometres wide just south of Chateau de Beaufort. In this gap, UNIFIL was able to maintain only four isolated observation posts, including one at the Khardala bridge.

Pending further withdrawals of the Israeli forces, UNIFIL acted to consolidate its control of the area in which it was deployed. Its main objectives were to supervise and monitor the cease-fire and to ensure that no unauthorized armed personnel entered its area. To this end, observation posts and checkpoints were set up at various points of entry in its area of deployment, and frequent patrols were conducted throughout the area. All unauthorized armed and uniformed personnel were turned back at entry points and, if they were discovered within the area, UNIFIL troops endeavoured to disarm them and escort them out of its area.

Problems after the initial Israeli withdrawal

Following the third phase of the Israeli withdrawal, UNIFIL was faced with two major problems. First, the Israeli Government was reluctant to relinquish the remaining area, and the United Nations efforts to achieve further withdrawal met with increasing resistance. Secondly, PLO armed elements attempted to enter the area evacuated by the Israeli forces on the grounds that they had a legitimate right to do so under the terms of the Cairo agreement of 3 November 1969, concluded between Lebanon and the PLO, under the auspices of President Nasser of Egypt, which dealt with the presence of Palestinians in Lebanon.

The uncooperative attitude of certain PLO armed elements led to some serious clashes during the first days of May in the Tyre area. On 1 May, a group of armed elements attempted to infiltrate a UNIFIL position manned by French soldiers. When challenged, they opened fire on the French guards, who returned the fire in self-defence and killed two infiltrators. In the following days, French troops were ambushed at various locations and, during the ensuing exchanges of fire, three UNIFIL soldiers were killed and 14 wounded, including the Commander of the French battalion.

Negotiations in the area

Strenuous negotiations were undertaken by the Secretary-General and his representatives in the field to prevent infiltration attempts by PLO armed elements and to avoid further incidents. Chairman Arafat confirmed that the PLO would cooperate with UNIFIL and that it would not initiate hostile acts against Israel from southern Lebanon, although it would continue its armed struggle from other areas. While the PLO's presence in southern Lebanon was a matter to be settled between itself and the Lebanese Government, the PLO would facilitate UNIFIL's tasks in response to the Secretary-General's appeal. In particular, the PLO would refrain from infiltrating armed elements into the UNIFIL area of operation. In exchange, Chairman Arafat insisted that the Palestinian armed elements who were already in the UNIFIL area of operation should be allowed to remain there. In order to secure the cooperation of the PLO, UNIFIL agreed to this condition, on the clear understanding that the limited number of armed elements allowed to remain in its area of operation would not be used for military purposes. The agreement involved about 140 armed elements belonging to various groups of the PLO, assembled in six positions.

The Secretary-General reported[15] to the Security Council that for humanitarian reasons, and as an ad hoc arrangement, UNIFIL had agreed to allow the delivery, under UNIFIL control, of certain non-military supplies — food, water and medicine — to limited Palestinian groups still in its area of operation. Strict instructions were given

[14]S/12620/Add.4. [15]S/12620/Add.5.

to the UNIFIL contingents concerned to keep a close watch over the six PLO positions.

Under the pressure of the United Nations, the Israeli Government announced its decision to withdraw its forces from the remaining occupied territory in Lebanon by 13 June 1978. The modalities for the withdrawal were to be determined between the Israeli authorities and Generals Siilasvuo and Erskine.

Following the announcement of this decision, intensive discussions were held between United Nations representatives and the Lebanese Government regarding the deployment of UNIFIL in the area to be evacuated and, in particular, regarding its relationship with the de facto forces under the command of Major Haddad. Pending full establishment of its authority in southern Lebanon, the Lebanese Government announced that it provisionally recognized Major Haddad as de facto commander of the Lebanese armed forces in his present area. The Lebanese army command would issue instructions to Major Haddad to facilitate UNIFIL's mission and deployment.[16]

UNIFIL also engaged in discussions with the Israeli authorities to work out practical arrangements for its deployment in the border area following the Israeli withdrawal. However, no common ground could be reached, and the instructions issued by the Lebanese Government to Major Haddad to facilitate UNIFIL's mission were totally ignored.

On 5 September 1978, Lebanon informed the Secretary-General that the commanders of the so-called "de facto Lebanese forces" were now to be considered as having no further authority whatsoever to act on behalf of the Lebanese Army, to negotiate with the United Nations, or to exercise any legal command in the area.[17]

E. UNIFIL activities: June 1978 – July 1981

Last phase of the Israeli withdrawal

On 13 June 1978, General Erskine reported that the Israeli forces had withdrawn from southern Lebanon. This information was transmitted by the Secretary-General to the Security Council.[18] The manner in which the Israeli forces carried out the last phase of withdrawal, however, created major problems for UNIFIL. In contrast to the procedure followed during the previous three phases, IDF on 13 June turned over most of its positions not to UNIFIL but to the de facto forces of Major Haddad, on the grounds that IDF considered him a legitimate representative of the Lebanese Government. UNIFIL units were able to occupy only five positions evacuated by the Israeli forces on that day, because the de facto forces, which had been strongly armed by the Israelis, threatened to use force to oppose any attempts by UNIFIL to gain wider deployment.

In a letter[19] dated 13 June, Foreign Minister Moshe Dayan informed the Secretary-General that Israel had fulfilled its part in the implementation of Security Council resolution 425 (1978). In his reply,[20] the Secretary-General observed that the difficult task lying ahead for UNIFIL had not been facilitated by the decision of the Israeli Government not to turn over control of the evacuated area to UNIFIL. He added that he was making efforts to deal satisfactorily with the consequences of that development, in cooperation with the Lebanese Government.

Difficulties in deployment

In order to fulfil its mandate, UNIFIL had to be fully deployed in its entire area of operation, including the enclave controlled by the de facto forces of Major Haddad. The first objective of the Force after the events of 13 June 1978 was therefore to expand its deployment in the enclave. Pending realization of this objective, UNIFIL would continue to ensure that the area where it actually was deployed would not be used for hostile activities of any kind. It would endeavour to stop and contain infiltrations by the armed elements of the PLO and the Lebanese National Movement, as well as incursions and encroachments by the de facto forces or the Israeli forces.

It would also endeavour to maintain the cease-fire and prevent a resumption of hostilities in and around its area. At the same time, UNIFIL would exert all possible efforts to assist the Lebanese Government in restoring its authority and

[16]S/12834. [17]S/12620/Add.5. [18]Ibid. [19]S/12736.
[20]S/12738.

promote the return to normalcy in its area of deployment.

In these various fields of activity, UNIFIL encountered serious difficulties. No significant further deployment could be achieved in the enclave and, although hostile actions could, to a large extent, be contained in UNIFIL's area of deployment, there were frequent and destructive exchanges of fire between the opposing forces over and across its area until 24 July 1981, when ceasefire arrangements were worked out through a joint effort by the United States and the United Nations [see below].

The various objectives pursued by the Interim Force were closely interconnected, and setbacks in one inevitably affected the others.

Efforts towards further deployment in the enclave

Immediately after 13 June, the Secretary-General instructed General Siilasvuo and General Erskine to exert every effort, in close cooperation with the Lebanese Government, to achieve progressively wider deployment of UNIFIL in the enclave until the Force would ultimately be in a position effectively to discharge its mandate in its entire area of operation. He made it clear, however, that it remained his intention to utilize peaceful and diplomatic means to achieve this objective.

As a result of renewed efforts, UNIFIL was able to occupy 14 additional positions in the enclave in June and July and another five positions in September 1978. By that date, UNIFIL held a total of 24 positions in the enclave, in addition to its headquarters at Naqoura and the five posts previously established by UNTSO along the Armistice Demarcation Line. But no further deployment could be achieved.

In his report[21] of 13 September 1978 to the Security Council, and in subsequent reports, the Secretary-General pointed to the efforts made by him and his representatives to secure the full deployment of UNIFIL in its area of operation and the lack of progress in this regard. The Council repeatedly reaffirmed its determination to implement its resolutions on UNIFIL in the totality of the area of operation assigned to the Force, and called upon all the parties to extend the necessary cooperation to UNIFIL. The decisions of the Security Council remained unheeded.

This situation prevented UNIFIL from fulfilling an essential part of its mandate and made its other tasks considerably more difficult.

Prevention of infiltration by armed elements

Infiltration attempts resumed and increased soon after 13 June 1978. The inability of UNIFIL to take over the enclave from the pro-Israeli de facto forces undoubtedly contributed to the increase in infiltration attempts. In order to prevent infiltration, UNIFIL, often assisted by Lebanese gendarmes, checked and inspected vehicles and personnel for military equipment and supplies at the checkpoints established at points of entry and along the main and secondary road networks in its area of deployment. Foot and motorized patrols were conducted day and night along key highways, in villages, as well as in remote wadis (ravines), and random night-time listening posts were established at selected localities to detect unauthorized armed movement.

After July 1979, UNIFIL's troops were redeployed in greater density along the perimeter of the UNIFIL area in order better to control infiltration, and a steady effort was made to improve its surveillance and detection capability. In particular, the number of night-vision binoculars and strong searchlights was increased, while the introduction of sophisticated ground surveillance radar provided the Force with an effective early warning system at medium range. Uniformed and armed personnel stopped at the checkpoints or caught by patrols were escorted out of the UNIFIL area.

The Palestinian or Lebanese armed elements stopped at checkpoints generally surrendered their weapons and left the UNIFIL area peacefully. In some cases, however, they reacted by firing at UNIFIL soldiers, who then had to return fire in self-defence. At other times, the infiltrators, after being turned back, would return with reinforcements to attack the UNIFIL position involved. In the most serious instances, armed elements retaliated by laying an ambush against UNIFIL personnel, not only at the scene of the original incident but also against UNIFIL positions or patrols elsewhere. UNIFIL tried to resolve all incidents by negotiation.

Given the difficulty of the terrain, the limited size of UNIFIL and its lack of enforcement power, it was virtually impossible to prevent all infiltration attempts. That difficulty was compounded by the existence of many arms caches in the UNIFIL area. Over the years, the PLO had set up a network of such caches throughout southern Lebanon. UNIFIL found and destroyed many of them, but many others remained.

[21]S/12845.

Since UNIFIL did not want to impede the movement of innocent civilians, persons in civilian clothes could freely enter its area, provided that they had a valid identification card and did not carry weapons. It was relatively easy for PLO personnel and their Lebanese allies to pass through UNIFIL checkpoints unarmed and, once inside the area, get weapons from the caches. Armed elements could also infiltrate into the UNIFIL area with their weapons through uncharted trails and dirt tracks which could not be covered by UNIFIL checkpoints or observation posts. Inside the UNIFIL area, the PLO, and particularly the Lebanese National Movement, still had many sympathizers who voluntarily or under pressure gave the infiltrators shelter or other assistance. Despite its vigilance, UNIFIL could not detect and stop all such infiltrators.

In those conditions, the most effective way of stopping, or at least controlling infiltration was to secure the cooperation of the PLO. The PLO leadership did cooperate with UNIFIL to a significant degree. There were no infiltration attempts on a major scale and, when incidents involving infiltration occurred, the PLO leadership assisted UNIFIL in resolving them. But in a number of cases, the PLO was either unwilling or unable to help, and armed elements succeeded in infiltrating into the UNIFIL area and in setting up some additional positions inside it.

By July 1981, the number of Palestinian armed elements inside the UNIFIL area had increased to about 450, according to UNIFIL estimates, and they had established some 30 positions inside that area. There was, in particular, a concentration of armed element positions in the Jwayya area near the Tyre pocket. UNIFIL tried to have those positions removed by negotiations with the PLO at the highest level, but its efforts were inconclusive.

Nevertheless, UNIFIL did control infiltration by armed elements to an important degree. The number of such elements who succeeded in infiltrating the UNIFIL area was relatively limited, and most of those remained confined to the northern part of the area, well away from the frontier.

UNIFIL's records indicate that after its establishment in March 1978, there was only one major raid into northern Israel by PLO armed elements coming from its area. This happened on 6/7 April 1980, when five armed elements belonging to the Arab Liberation Front crossed the Armistice Demarcation Line and attacked the kibbutz of Misgav Am. To do this, they would have had to cross not only UNIFIL areas but also the enclave

and the border. All five infiltrators and three Israeli civilians were killed.[22]

UNIFIL's attempts at preventing infiltration sometimes led to tense situations at checkpoints and there were several exchanges of fire between armed elements and members of the Force. In one particularly serious incident, on 19 June 1981, armed elements surrounded a Fijian checkpoint after one of them had been refused access, and opened fire. During the ensuing exchange of fire three Fijian soldiers were captured and taken away. While negotiations were in progress, two of the captured soldiers were murdered. The third was able to escape after having been severely mistreated.

Harassment by de facto forces

The activities of the de facto forces under the command of Major Haddad also created serious difficulties for UNIFIL. No precise figures on the strength of those forces were available, but it was generally estimated that they numbered about 1,500 in June 1978. They were formed around a nucleus of some 700 former Christian soldiers of the Lebanese National Army, to which were added smaller groups of Christian phalangists from the north and locally recruited Christian and Shiite villagers. They were financed, trained, armed, uniformed and, by all evidence, controlled by the Israeli authorities.

The measures devised by UNIFIL to prevent infiltrations by the Palestinians and Lebanese leftist armed elements were also applied to the de facto forces, but there were few infiltrators from the enclave, and the main problems the United Nations encountered with these forces concerned their harassment of UNIFIL and the local population, and their attempts to encroach upon the UNIFIL area.

While making clear that full deployment in the enclave remained its main objective, UNIFIL concentrated its immediate efforts on preserving the installations it held there and on securing the freedom of movement it required for this purpose. With the assistance of the Israeli army, a *modus vivendi* was reached with the de facto forces whereby UNIFIL troops would enjoy freedom of movement on the main roads in the enclave five days a week in order to rotate personnel and re-supply its installations. UNIFIL helicopters could fly over the enclave when necessary, but each overflight had to be cleared with Major Haddad's com-

[22]S/13888.

mand on an ad hoc basis. However, even this limited freedom of movement was occasionally denied UNIFIL. When difficulties of one kind or another arose between UNIFIL and the de facto forces, Major Haddad would retaliate by closing the roads in the enclave to United Nations personnel and vehicles. This retaliatory measure would be taken either against UNIFIL as a whole or against specific contingents. During periods of tension, some UNIFIL positions in the enclave, and particularly the five observation posts along the Armistice Demarcation Line, were at times completely isolated, and the United Nations personnel manning them subjected to severe harassment. In some cases, the observation posts were broken into by militiamen, their equipment stolen and the United Nations personnel threatened. On three occasions, the de facto forces attacked the UNIFIL headquarters itself with mortar and artillery fire, causing casualties and considerable material damage.

In October 1978, at about the same time as the PLO intensified its attempts to infiltrate the UNIFIL area, the attitude of the de facto forces hardened further. These forces began to harass the local population in the UNIFIL area in various ways. A number of Shiite villages were subjected to occasional shelling from positions in the enclave, and the villagers were threatened with punitive measures if they continued to cooperate with UNIFIL. In a few instances, the de facto forces sent raiding parties into the UNIFIL area to abduct persons suspected of pro-PLO sentiments or to blow up their houses. This sort of pressure on the local population markedly increased after Major Haddad proclaimed the constitution of the so-called "State of Free Lebanon" in April 1979. UNIFIL strongly protested the harassment with the Israeli authorities. To deter attacks against villages in its area, it established additional positions in their vicinity.

From December 1978 onwards, the de facto forces made several attempts to set up positions within the UNIFIL area. These attempts were carried out by strongly armed groups, sometimes supported by tanks. Whenever this occurred, UNIFIL sent reinforcements to surround the raiding parties and, at the same time, tried by negotiation to have their positions removed, usually with the assistance of the Israeli army. In some cases, the raiding parties were persuaded to leave peacefully, but in others the negotiations were unsuccessful. Thus, five encroachment positions were established by the de facto forces between July 1979 and July 1980, all of which were located in strategic areas commanding views of important access roads.

To remove these positions, UNIFIL would have had to use force against the de facto forces and possibly IDF, and casualties would have been heavy. In the circumstances, it was decided instead to seek a negotiated solution through the Israeli authorities. The Secretary-General raised this matter with the Israeli Government at the highest level but was told that Israel considered those positions important for its security and would not intervene to have them removed.

While, as a matter of principle and policy, UNIFIL sought to contain the actions of the de facto forces by negotiation, its troops were sometimes obliged to resist harassments and to use force in self-defence. Despite the restraint displayed by UNIFIL soldiers, violent incidents occurred in some cases. In one particularly serious incident in April 1980, three soldiers of the Irish battalion were stopped by de facto forces, who shot and badly wounded one soldier and took the other two away. Despite every effort made by UNIFIL to obtain the release of the two captured soldiers, they were murdered.

On 24 April 1980, following an incident in which the de facto forces directed heavy shelling at UNIFIL headquarters, the Security Council adopted resolution 467 (1980), by which it deplored all acts of hostilities against UNIFIL in or through its area of operation and condemned the deliberate shelling of the headquarters.

Israeli activities in and near the enclave

After 13 June 1978, the Israeli Government took the position that its forces had withdrawn from Lebanese territory in accordance with Security Council resolution 425 (1978) and that henceforth it was no longer responsible for what happened in the enclave.

During the initial months, the presence of IDF in the enclave appeared limited, but from November 1979 onwards, IDF activities increased. Israeli soldiers were frequently observed laying mines, manning checkpoints, transporting water and supplies and constructing new positions inside Lebanon in the border areas.

In late 1980, UNIFIL reported an increasing number of encroachments by IDF along the Armistice Demarcation Line.[23] The original border-fence remained intact, but on the Lebanese side of

[23]S/14295.

it IDF established new positions at selected points, laid minefields, fenced in strips of land and built dirt tracks and asphalt roads. At the same time, the presence of IDF inside the enclave was greatly expanded. IDF gun and tank positions were established near Marjayoun, Major Haddad's headquarters, and along the coastal road. IDF personnel were sighted in various locations well inside the enclave. In the course of 1980, IDF openly conducted military exercises near OP Khiam, a United Nations observation post north of the border.

On a number of occasions, IDF carried out incursions into the UNIFIL area in search of PLO armed elements. UNIFIL took all possible measures to stop those incursions, and its efforts led at times to confrontations with IDF personnel, which were generally resolved by negotiation.

In addition to its activities in the enclave, IDF frequently intruded into Lebanese air space and territorial waters. Its aircraft constantly flew over Lebanon for observation purposes and its patrol boats were often observed cruising near the Lebanese coast. The air and sea violations greatly increased after June 1980. During November 1980 alone, UNIFIL observed 312 air violations and 89 sea violations.

F. Hostile actions near the UNIFIL area

The UNIFIL area constituted an imperfect buffer between the opposing forces. As already described, the area was divided into two parts, with a gap of about 15 kilometres between them. In this gap, where the two opposing sides were separated only by the Litani River, UNIFIL was able to set up four positions, including one at the Khardala bridge, to provide at least a limited United Nations presence. But the gun positions of the PLO in its stronghold of Chateau de Beaufort north of the river, and those of the de facto forces in and around Marjayoun, reinforced in 1980 by IDF tanks and artillery, were not far apart. From its positions in the Tyre pocket and Chateau de Beaufort, the PLO's heavy artillery and rockets could easily reach villages and towns in northern Israel, including Nahariyya, Maalot, Metulla and Qiryat Shemona.

From March 1979 onwards, there were frequent exchanges of fire between the PLO and the de facto forces across the gap and over the UNIFIL area. When fighting intensified, IDF would come to the support of the de facto forces and, in retaliation, PLO fighters would direct their heavy artillery and rockets at targets in northern Israel, which would in turn provoke violent reprisals by IDF. Whenever PLO shelling resulted in Israeli casualties, and also after incidents inside Israel or Israeli-occupied territories for which the PLO claimed responsibility, IDF would send its war-planes to launch massive attacks against PLO targets north of the UNIFIL area, sometimes as far as Beirut. In some cases, Israeli commandos were dispatched to destroy PLO installations.

Both the Israeli war-planes and the commandos would, as a rule, avoid the UNIFIL area by flying over the gap or taking the sea route. Since the armed forces engaged in the hostilities were located outside its area, UNIFIL could not take direct action to prevent or stop them. It did, however, endeavour to arrange cease-fires whenever possible, and brought the most serious cases to the attention of the Security Council.

Within one twelve-month period, there were two series of serious hostilities; one in August 1980 and the other in July 1981.

Hostilities of August 1980

During the evening of 18 August 1980, a heavy exchange of fire broke out between the IDF/de facto forces and PLO positions north of the Litani and continued with varying intensity for five days. According to UNIFIL observers,[24] the de facto forces fired approximately 2,460 rounds of artillery, mortar and tank fire, and the PLO armed elements about 300 rounds. On 19 and 20 August, Israeli war-planes attacked various PLO targets in the Chateau de Beaufort and Arnun areas.

On 19 August, while the shelling and bombing were in progress, a group of about 200 IDF troops, transported by helicopter, carried out a commando raid to destroy PLO installations in and around the villages of Arnun and Kafr Tibnit.[25] This operation was preceded by a build-up of IDF personnel and equipment throughout the enclave, where about 50 artillery pieces, 70 assorted vehi-

[24]Ibid. [25]S/14118.

cles and seven heavy helicopters were sighted by UNIFIL. According to Lebanese and Palestinian sources, the attacks resulted in at least 25 killed, including five Lebanese civilians, and 26 wounded, as well as very heavy destruction of houses and other property. The Israeli authorities indicated that the operation was intended to destroy PLO artillery and mortar nests which had shelled Israel's northern settlements and Major Haddad's enclave in southern Lebanon.

Hostilities of July 1981

The fighting which broke out in July 1981 was even more extensive. On 10 July, during an exchange of fire with the IDF/de facto forces' positions, PLO forces shelled the town of Qiryat Shemona in northern Israel with rockets, resulting, according to Israeli authorities,[26] in the wounding of six civilians. On the same day, Israeli warplanes attacked PLO targets in Lebanon north of the UNIFIL area.[27] The air attacks were followed by renewed exchanges of fire between the PLO armed elements' and the IDF and de facto forces' positions.

On 13 and 14 July, widespread Israeli air attacks continued and PLO armed elements again fired rockets into northern Israel, wounding, according to Israeli sources, two Israeli civilians in the coastal town of Nahariyya. The next day, there was a particularly heavy exchange of fire with a total of about 1,000 rounds of artillery, mortar and rockets fired by the two sides.

On 16 and 17 July, exchanges of fire intensified, with Israeli naval vessels joining in, while Israeli aircraft destroyed bridges on the Zahrani and Litani rivers and launched an intense attack on Beirut itself, causing heavy loss of life and damage to property. Exchanges of fire in all sectors, as well as Israeli air strikes and naval bombardments, continued on 18 and 19 July and, on a gradually declining scale, until 24 July.

During the period of intense violence in July, UNIFIL recorded the firing of some 7,500 rounds of artillery, mortar, tank and naval cannons by IDF and the de facto forces, in addition to Israeli

air strikes, and the firing of about 2,500 rounds of artillery, mortar and rockets by PLO armed elements. The total casualties during this period were six dead and 59 wounded on the Israeli side, immeasurably more among the Palestinians and Lebanese.

Security Council action

The Security Council met on 17 July 1981 at the request of the Lebanese Government. On the same day, the Council President issued an urgent appeal to the parties for restraint and an immediate end to all armed attacks. On 21 July, the Council unanimously adopted resolution 490 (1981), by which it called for an immediate cessation of all armed attacks and reaffirmed its commitment to the sovereignty, territorial integrity and independence of Lebanon within its internationally recognized boundaries.

July cease-fire

Following adoption of the resolution, parallel efforts undertaken by the United Nations and the United States Government led to the establishment of a de facto cease-fire on 24 July 1981. On the morning of that day, Ambassador Philip Habib, the personal representative of the President of the United States, issued a statement in Jerusalem to the effect that, as of 1330 hours, 24 July 1981, all hostile military action between Lebanese and Israeli territory in either direction would cease.

The Secretary-General, who had been kept fully informed of the efforts of Ambassador Habib, immediately brought this statement to the attention of the Security Council.[28] He also reported to the Council that the Israeli Government had endorsed the statement, that the Lebanese Government had welcomed it, and that the PLO had assured him that it would observe the cease-fire called for by the Security Council. The Commander of UNIFIL reported on 24 July that, as of 1320 hours local time, the area was quiet.

[26]S/14591. [27]S/14789. [28]S/14613/Add.1.

G. Efforts to restore the authority of the Lebanese Government in southern Lebanon

Civilian administration

After 13 June 1978, when it became apparent that Israeli control would continue in the enclave for an indefinite period, UNIFIL had to alter its original plan. While the Force would continue its efforts to assume control of the enclave through negotiations, it took action to help the Lebanese to deploy as many administrators and elements of the Lebanese army and the internal security forces (gendarmes) as possible in the area controlled by it.

Initially, UNIFIL's attention was focused on getting the Lebanese Government to send civilian administrative and technical personnel and elements of the Lebanese gendarmes to southern Lebanon. By late July 1978,[29] the Lebanese Government was represented south of the Litani River by a civilian administrator residing at Tyre, and by nearly 100 gendarmes based at Tyre and at three centres in the UNIFIL area. The gendarmes worked in close cooperation with UNIFIL. They assisted UNIFIL soldiers in the inspection of personnel and vehicles at checkpoints and, in many instances, served as interpreters and liaison officers with the local population. Civil offences reported to UNIFIL were handed over to the gendarmes for investigation.

UNIFIL carried out various humanitarian activities and rehabilitation programmes in close cooperation with the Lebanese authorities and the Coordinator of United Nations Assistance for the Reconstruction and Development of Lebanon. It took an active part in the execution of projects involving restoration of water, electricity and health services, distribution of supplementary food supplies and the rebuilding and repair of houses, schools and roads. The UNIFIL hospital maintained by the Swedish medical company in the Naqoura Camp and the medical facilities of its contingents were open to the local population, which used those services frequently.

Army deployment, 1978

In the course of July 1978, extensive consultations were held between the Lebanese authorities and UNIFIL regarding the possibility of bringing Lebanese army units to the UNIFIL area of operation. Many obstacles had to be overcome.

The de facto forces and the Israeli authorities were opposed to any move of the Lebanese army to the south. For different reasons, the PLO, which controlled the key coastal road from Sidon to Tyre, also opposed such a move.

The Lebanese National Army was still in the process of reconstruction and reorganization. Despite the difficulties involved, the Government of Lebanon decided to dispatch a task force of the Lebanese army to southern Lebanon on 31 July. This task force, consisting of 700 men and equipment, was to travel to Tibnin through the Bekaa Valley, Kaoukaba, a village on the northern edge of the UNIFIL area, and Marjayoun, the headquarters of the de facto forces. The Secretary-General was informed of this decision on 25 July and an announcement was made by the Lebanese Government on the same day. Following this announcement, UNIFIL contacted the Israeli authorities at various levels and requested their help to ensure that the de facto forces would not oppose the proposed move. The Israeli authorities refused to intervene on the grounds that it was a Lebanese internal affair.

The task force left the Beirut area in the early morning of 31 July and reached Kaoukaba a few hours later. On arrival, it was subjected to intense artillery and mortar fire by the de facto forces. Confronted with this hostile action, the task force stayed in Kaoukaba while the United Nations tried to negotiate agreement for its peaceful transit. But the Secretary-General and his representatives in the field failed to win the support of the Israeli authorities. On the following days, the de facto forces continuously harassed the task force and fired more than 300 artillery rounds at it, killing one Lebanese soldier and wounding nine others. In August, the task force withdrew from Kaoukaba.

Army deployment, 1979

Following this attempt, UNIFIL engaged in new consultations with the Lebanese authorities in an effort to find alternative ways of bringing Lebanese army units into southern Lebanon.

[29] S/12845.

On 22 December 1978,[30] a joint working group of UNIFIL and Lebanese army officials was set up to work out a plan of action. On the proposal of the group, small teams of Lebanese army personnel were flown to southern Lebanon by UNIFIL helicopters and were assigned to various UNIFIL contingents to represent the Lebanese Government in their respective sectors.

In renewing the mandate of UNIFIL for a further period of five months, the Security Council, by resolution 444 (1979) of 19 January 1979, invited the Lebanese Government to draw up, in consultation with the Secretary-General, a phased programme of activities to be carried out over the next three months to promote the restoration of its authority in southern Lebanon. The programme, as worked out by the Lebanese Government with the assistance of UNIFIL, set for its first phase four main objectives: (1) an increase of the Lebanese civilian administrative presence in the south; (2) the introduction of a battalion of the Lebanese National Army in the UNIFIL area; (3) the consolidation of the cease-fire in the area; and (4) further deployment of UNIFIL in the enclave.[31]

Within this programme, a Lebanese army battalion of 500 men was deployed in the UNIFIL area in April 1979. The de facto forces tried to prevent the deployment by subjecting UNIFIL headquarters and some of its positions to intense shelling from 15 to 18 April. These attacks caused casualties and heavy material damage, but UNIFIL stood firm, and the deployment of the Lebanese battalion proceeded as planned and was completed on 17 April. The Lebanese battalion, which was placed under the operational control of the Force Commander, set up its headquarters at Arzun in the Nigerian sector.

Army deployment, 1980–1981

In December 1980, the strength of the Lebanese battalion was increased to 617 men with the addition of some medical and engineering elements. Initially, the Lebanese battalion confined its activities to the immediate vicinity of Arzun, but, from early 1981 on, some of its units were gradually deployed in various UNIFIL sectors.

In June 1981, a second Lebanese battalion was brought to the UNIFIL area, this time without incident, and raised the total strength of the Lebanese army presence in southern Lebanon to 1,350 all ranks.[32] The new battalion included an engineering unit of 130, which assisted in various local projects, and a medical team of 10 assigned to the Tibnin hospital.

Efforts to reactivate the General Armistice Agreement

To promote the restoration of its authority and sovereignty in southern Lebanon, the Lebanese Government sought to reactivate the 1949 General Armistice Agreement between Israel and Lebanon and the Israel-Lebanon Mixed Armistice Commission (ILMAC) established under that Agreement.

In resolution 450 (1979) of 14 June 1979, on a further extension of UNIFIL's mandate, the Security Council reaffirmed the validity of the General Armistice Agreement and called upon the parties to take the necessary steps to reactivate ILMAC. A plan of action, which the Secretary-General worked out in consultation with the Lebanese Government in September 1979,[33] set as the main long-term objective of the Force the restoration of the effective authority of the Lebanese Government in southern Lebanon up to the internationally recognized boundary, and the normalization of the area, including the reactivation of ILMAC in accordance with the 1949 Agreement.

In resolution 467 (1980) of 24 April 1980, the Security Council requested the Secretary-General to convene a meeting of ILMAC, at an appropriate level, to agree on precise recommendations and further to reactivate the General Armistice Agreement conducive to the restoration of the sovereignty of Lebanon over all its territory up to the internationally recognized boundaries.

The Chief of Staff of UNTSO, General Erskine, who had been asked by the Secretary-General to follow up on that resolution, proposed on 18 November 1980 that a meeting preliminary to the convening of ILMAC be held at Naqoura on 1 December.[34] On 25 November, the Lebanese authorities agreed to the proposed meeting and insisted that it be attended by the Chairman of ILMAC. On 26 November, the Israeli authorities replied, stating that the Mixed Armistice Commission was no longer valid and that, as far as they were concerned, the proposed meeting could not be regarded as a preliminary meeting of ILMAC. They added, however, that this should not stand in the way of a meeting between Israeli and Lebanese representatives at the appropriate level, and they agreed to meet with the Lebanese representatives on the date and at the venue suggested by General Erskine.

The meeting took place at UNIFIL headquarters on 1 December 1980, under the chair-

[30]S/13026. [31]S/13258. [32]S/14537. [33]S/13691. [34]S/14295.

manship of the Chief of Staff of UNTSO. Israel and Lebanon were represented by senior military officers. Although the two sides disagreed on the validity of the General Armistice Agreement, they discussed the situation in southern Lebanon, particularly along the border. The Lebanese representative complained about the establishment of IDF positions in southern Lebanon and incursions by IDF personnel into Lebanese territory, while the Israeli representative asserted that Israel had no designs on Lebanon. Following this meeting, the UNTSO Chief of Staff kept in contact with both sides with a view to arranging another meeting in the near future, but no agreement could be reached.

H.   Cease-fire: July 1981– April 1982

The cease-fire arrangements of 24 July 1981 were accepted by all the parties, and on that day all firing stopped [see section F above]. UNIFIL kept close contact with the parties to ensure the maintenance of the cease-fire. Lieutenant-General William Callaghan, Commander of UNIFIL, obtained an undertaking from each of the parties that in the event of a breach of the cease-fire by the opposing side, the other side would exercise maximum restraint and, rather than take retaliatory action, would refer the matter to UNIFIL for resolution.

During the following days, however, the situation remained unstable because a dissident PLO group led by Mr. Ahmed Jebril continued to fire sporadically at targets in the enclave. General Callaghan strongly protested those violations of the cease-fire to the PLO command. Chairman Arafat replied that the firings were due to a misunderstanding and that the PLO was determined to observe strictly the cease-fire. On 27 July, following a meeting with Chairman Arafat, Mr. Jebril announced that his group would respect the cease-fire.

A second problem which threatened the cease-fire during the initial period arose from the continuing overflights of southern Lebanon by Israeli reconnaissance aircraft, which the PLO protested as violations of the cease-fire arrangements. In spite of approaches by the Commander of UNIFIL, Israel refused to stop such overflights on the grounds that they were not covered by the cease-fire arrangements. The Israeli overflights did not, however, provoke retaliatory action by the PLO.

The cease-fire held remarkably well until April 1982. For eight months the situation in southern Lebanon was quiet and there were no firings between the PLO and the IDF/de facto forces in the area.

With the restoration of the cease-fire in July 1981, the general situation in southern Lebanon had become much less tense. However, UNIFIL continued to experience serious difficulties with the armed elements of the PLO and the Lebanese National Movement on the one hand, and with the de facto forces of Major Haddad on the other. The armed elements continued their infiltration attempts after July 1981, though at a lower level. UNIFIL soldiers turned back 175 infiltrators in July 1981, 95 in August, 18 in September, 90 in October, 27 in November, 25 in December, 70 in January 1982, 27 in February, 98 in March, 69 in April and 27 in May. In a more serious development, PLO armed elements established additional positions in the UNIFIL area near the Tyre pocket. The Force immediately placed those positions under close surveillance to ensure that they would not be used for tactical or hostile purposes. At the same time, negotiations were undertaken with the PLO leadership to have them removed, but the talks were inconclusive.

Relations with the de facto forces also remained tense. Those forces continued to impose restrictions on UNIFIL's freedom of movement in the enclave. In the UNIFIL area of deployment, they not only continued to maintain four positions they had established, but set up a new one near the village of At Tiri, in the Irish sector.[35] The Force Commander sought the assistance of the Israeli authorities in this regard, stressing that the position was clearly provocative and might jeopardize the cease-fire. While the negotiations were in progress, the de facto forces harassed the UNIFIL headquarters at Naqoura and some of its positions in the enclave by cutting their supply lines. The harassments were eventually stopped with the help of IDF, but the new position remained.

[35] S/14789.

During this period of relative quiet, UNIFIL had to contend with a new problem in its area. In the later months, Amal, a Shiite political movement with a paramilitary organization, became more active in southern Lebanon, and there was mounting animosity between its followers and members of the pro-Palestinian Lebanese National Movement. Serious clashes broke out between the two groups in January and April 1982 in the Senegalese sector, and UNIFIL had to intervene to help restore law and order.

I. Israeli invasion: 1982 –1985

Breakdown of the cease-fire

In early April 1982, tension markedly increased in southern Lebanon, not because of any violations of the cease-fire in the area but as a consequence of events elsewhere. On 3 April, an Israeli diplomat was assassinated in Paris and the Israeli Government held the PLO responsible, although responsibility was denied by that organization. On 13 April, the Permanent Representative of Israel to the United Nations complained[36] to the Security Council that, on the previous night, two PLO terrorists with large quantities of explosives had attempted to infiltrate into Israel from Jordanian territory. On 21 April, Israel launched massive air attacks against PLO targets in southern Lebanon. The PLO took no retaliatory action.

On the same day, the Secretary-General appealed for an immediate cessation of all hostile acts and urged all parties to exercise maximum restraint so that the cease-fire could be fully restored and maintained. On 22 April, the President of the Security Council issued a statement on behalf of the members of the Council in which he demanded an end to all armed attacks and warned against any recurrence of violations of the cease-fire, in accordance with Security Council resolution 490 (1981) of 21 July 1981.

On 9 May 1982, Israeli aircraft again attacked PLO targets in several localities in Lebanon, causing many casualties. Following these attacks, PLO positions in the Tyre pocket fired rockets into northern Israel, for the first time since July 1981. The next day, the Lebanese Government strongly protested the Israeli air attacks as an act of aggression against Lebanon.[37] The Permanent Representative of Israel also addressed a letter[38] to the President of the Council on that day in which he drew attention to recent terrorist attacks against civilians in Israel, for which Israel held the PLO responsible. Intense efforts were made by the United Nations, both at its New York Headquarters and in the field, to restore the cease-fire. There were no further incidents in the area in May, but the situation remained extremely volatile.

On the night of 3 June, the Israeli Ambassador to the United Kingdom was seriously wounded in London in a terrorist attack. Although the PLO disclaimed any responsibility for this assassination attempt, Israel launched on 4 June massive bombing raids against PLO targets in and around Beirut, causing heavy loss of life and destruction. Shortly after those attacks, intense exchanges of fire broke out between the PLO and the IDF/de facto forces' positions in southern Lebanon, over the UNIFIL area. The Israeli towns of Nahariyya, Qiryat Shemona and Metulla came under PLO artillery and rocket fire.

On the same afternoon, the Secretary-General urgently appealed to all concerned to desist from all hostile acts and to make every effort to restore the cease-fire. Later that day, the President of the Security Council made a similar appeal on behalf of the members of the Council. Nevertheless, the exchanges of artillery fire continued unabated on 5 June in the same general areas. There were also intense Israeli air strikes in the vicinity of Beirut and Damur, and shelling by Israeli naval vessels in the Tyre area.

The Secretary-General, who was in continuous touch with the parties concerned, again made an urgent appeal on 5 June for a simultaneous cessation of hostilities at the earliest possible time. Later the same day, the Security Council met and unanimously adopted resolution 508 (1982), by which it called upon all the parties to the conflict to cease immediately and simultaneously all military activities within Lebanon and across the Israeli-Lebanese border no later than 0600 hours local time on Sunday, 6 June.

[36]S/14972. [37]S/15064. [38]S/15066.

Immediately after the adoption of that resolution, the Secretary-General instructed the Commander of UNIFIL to utilize every possibility of following up on the Council's resolution.[39] On the same evening, the PLO reaffirmed its commitment to stop all military operations across the Lebanese border, while reserving the right to respond to Israeli attacks. The Permanent Representative of Israel to the United Nations informed the Secretary-General that, while Israeli actions were taken in the exercise of its right of self-defence, the Council's resolution would be brought before the Israeli Cabinet. From 2300 hours local time on 5 June until 0600 hours the next morning, there were intermittent and relatively light exchanges of fire between the opposing sides, but shortly after 0600 hours, which was the cease-fire time set by the Security Council, Israeli forces launched intensive air attacks against various PLO targets in southern Lebanon.

Israeli invasion, June 1982

At 1030 hours local time on the morning of 6 June, General Callaghan met with Lieutenant-General Rafael Eitan, the Chief of Staff of IDF, at Metulla in northern Israel. General Callaghan's purpose was to discuss the implementation of Security Council resolution 508 (1982), but instead he was told by General Eitan that IDF planned to launch a military operation into Lebanon within half an hour, at 1100 hours local time. General Eitan also intimated that the Israeli forces would pass through or near UNIFIL positions and that he expected that UNIFIL would raise no physical difficulty to the advancing troops. General Callaghan protested in the strongest terms at this totally unacceptable course of action.

Immediately after the meeting, General Callaghan issued instructions to all UNIFIL units, in case of attack by one of the parties, to block advancing forces, take defensive measures and stay in their positions unless their safety was "seriously imperilled".

At 1100 hours local time, about two IDF mechanized divisions, with full air and naval support, crossed the border and entered the UNIFIL area. They advanced along three main axes: in the western sector, along the coastal road; in the central sector, towards At Tayyibah and the Akiya bridge; and in the eastern sector, through the Chouba-Chebaa area.

In accordance with their general instructions, UNIFIL troops took various measures to stop, or at least delay, the advance of the Israeli forces.

On the coastal road leading to Tyre, Dutch soldiers planted obstacles before an advancing Israeli tank column and damaged one tank. During the encounter, Israeli tank barrels were trained on the Dutch soldiers while Israeli troops pushed aside the obstacles. Other UNIFIL battalions also put up obstacles of various kinds, which were forcibly removed or bulldozed. A small Nepalese position guarding the Khardala bridge stood its ground for two days despite continued harassments and threats. Only after two days, on the morning of 8 June, could the Israeli tanks cross the bridge after partially destroying the Nepalese position.

Despite these efforts, the UNIFIL soldiers with their light defensive weapons could not withstand the massive Israeli invading forces, and the UNIFIL positions in the line of the invasion were bypassed or overrun within 24 hours. One Norwegian soldier was killed by shrapnel on 6 June.

On the morning of 6 June, the Security Council met again and unanimously adopted resolution 509 (1982), by which it demanded that Israel withdraw all its military forces forthwith and unconditionally to the internationally recognized boundaries of Lebanon, and that all parties strictly observe the cease-fire.

On the evening of 7 June, Chairman Arafat informed the Secretary-General that the Lebanese-Palestinian joint command had decided to abide by the Security Council's resolution. The Permanent Representative of Israel replied on behalf of his Government that the "Peace for Galilee" operation had been ordered because of the intolerable situation created by the presence in Lebanon of a large number of "terrorists" operating from that country and threatening the lives of the civilians of Galilee, and that any withdrawal of Israeli forces prior to the conclusion of concrete arrangements which would permanently and reliably preclude hostile action against Israel's citizens was inconceivable.[40]

UNIFIL's interim tasks

In commenting on the invasion in his report[41] of 14 June 1982 to the Security Council, the Secretary-General stated that UNIFIL, like all other United Nations peace-keeping operations, was based on certain fundamental principles, foremost of which was the non-use of force, except in self-defence. The Force was not meant to engage in combat to attain its goals; it had a strictly limited

---

[39]S/15194/Add.1. [40]S/15178. [41]S/15194/Add.2.

strength, armed only with light defensive weapons. It was for these reasons that certain essential conditions had been laid down at the time of the establishment of the Force. Those included, first, that it must function with the full cooperation of the parties concerned and, second, that it must have at all times the full confidence and backing of the Security Council. In this connection, it was a fundamental assumption that the parties would fully abide by the Council's decisions and that, in the event of non-compliance, the Council itself and those Member States in a position to bring their influence to bear would be able to act decisively to ensure respect for those decisions.

In the case of UNIFIL, those conditions were not met. Instead, UNIFIL had been faced with inadequate cooperation throughout its existence, culminating in an overwhelming use of force. Once the Israeli action commenced, it was evident that UNIFIL troops could, at best, maintain their positions and take defensive measures, seeking to impede and protest the advance.

The Israeli invasion of June 1982 radically altered the circumstances in which UNIFIL had been set up and under which it had functioned since March 1978. By 8 June, the UNIFIL area of operation had fallen under Israeli control and the Force had to operate behind the Israeli lines. Under those conditions, UNIFIL could no longer fulfil the tasks entrusted to it by the Security Council. Pending a Council decision on the Force's mandate, which was due to expire on 19 June 1982, the Secretary-General instructed General Callaghan, as an interim measure, to ensure that all UNIFIL troops and the UNTSO military observers attached to it continued to man their positions unless their safety was seriously imperilled, and to provide protection and humanitarian assistance to the local population to the extent possible.[42]

These interim tasks were endorsed by the Security Council on 18 June, when it decided, by resolution 511 (1982), to extend the mandate of UNIFIL for an interim period of two months. At the same time, the Council made clear that the Force's original terms of reference remained valid, and reaffirmed its call for the complete withdrawal of the Israeli forces from Lebanese territory.

In accordance with the instructions of the Secretary-General, UNIFIL remained deployed in its area of operation with only minor adjustments. Some positions considered as non-essential in the changed circumstances were closed down, while others were reinforced. UNTSO observers continued to man the five observation positions along the Armistice Demarcation Line and to maintain

three teams outside the UNIFIL area — at Tyre, at Metulla in northern Israel and at Chateau de Beaufort north of the Litani River.

Much in the same way as they had done before the invasion, UNIFIL troops operated observation posts and checkpoints and conducted patrols in sensitive areas in order to prevent hostile actions and to do what they could to ensure the security and safety of the local population. They continued to prevent infiltrations and incursions into the UNIFIL area by armed irregulars. But they could not control the movement and actions of the Israeli forces or of the irregulars when they acted with those forces' direct support. In such cases, UNIFIL could only monitor their activities and report to the Secretary-General. In carrying out their functions, the UNIFIL troops cooperated closely with the local authorities and with the Lebanese gendarmes when they were available.

In addition, UNIFIL's efforts were devoted to humanitarian assistance. In cooperation with the United Nations Children's Fund (UNICEF) and the International Committee of the Red Cross (ICRC), UNIFIL humanitarian teams distributed to needy local inhabitants food and water and other essential supplies. The UNIFIL hospital at Naqoura and the medical teams of the various national contingents dispensed medical care to the local population, including vaccination campaigns for Lebanese children. UNIFIL also assisted the local authorities with various community projects and with the repair of public buildings such as schools and local dispensaries. A French engineering unit did much to clear the area of mines, shells and explosive devices, which were a constant danger to the population. In many cases, the officers and soldiers of the various contingents made voluntary contributions to help villages in their sectors. Further, Governments of troop-contributing countries provided assistance in the form of new schools or medical centres in their battalions' sectors.

Soon after the invasion, the Israeli forces' presence in the UNIFIL area of deployment was reduced to approximately battalion strength. However, in mid-1983 the activities of a Shiite resistance movement against the Israeli occupation, which became increasingly active in the northern part of the occupied territory, began to spill over into the UNIFIL area. Although the area remained relatively quiet until February 1985, there were occasional attacks against the Israeli forces by resistance groups, particularly in the form of roadside bombs, and counter-measures by the Israeli

[42] S/15194/Add.1.

forces, mainly in the form of cordon-and-search operations in the Shiite villages. UNIFIL could not prevent counter-measures by the Israeli forces, but endeavoured, by pressure and persuasion, to mitigate violence, and protect the civilian population as much as possible. It also provided medical care and humanitarian assistance to the affected population.

In April 1984, three months after the death of Major Haddad, Major-General Antoine Lahad, also a former officer of the Lebanese National Army, took over the command of the de facto forces, which were by then calling themselves the "South Lebanon Army" (SLA). The strength of SLA had been increased to approximately 2,100 as of October 1984. Although Israel gave SLA an expanded role in the northern part of the occupied territory, it did not make any determined attempt to increase its activities in the UNIFIL area.

More serious problems were encountered by UNIFIL when new local militias, armed and uniformed by Israel, began to appear in its area towards the end of June 1982.[43] Like SLA, these militias were not recognized by the Lebanese Government or by the established local authorities. Acting with the assistance of IDF and under its control, they attempted to set up checkpoints and conduct patrols in the villages. They were generally ill-disciplined and their actions were deeply resented by the local inhabitants and often led to friction with them. UNIFIL was under standing instructions to disarm the local militias and to contain their activities whenever they were not accompanied and directly protected by the Israeli forces. A number of incidents occurred at UNIFIL checkpoints when militiamen refused to submit to having their vehicles searched or to surrender their weapons.

Until February 1985, the incidents outlined above were exceptions rather than the rule, and the situation in the UNIFIL area was generally quiet — much quieter than in other parts of Lebanon during those years of turmoil. This was widely recognized by the Lebanese Government and the local population. Each time the mandate of UNIFIL neared its expiration, many *mukhtars* (village mayors) would write to the Secretary-General to beseech him not to withdraw the Force, and the Lebanese Government would request its extension in insistent terms.

The Secretary-General repeatedly recommended the extension of UNIFIL's mandate in accordance with the requests of the Lebanese Government. In support of his recommendation, he pointed out that despite the difficulties confronted by it, UNIFIL remained an important element of stability in southern Lebanon. Its presence represented the commitment of the United Nations to support the independence, sovereignty and territorial integrity of Lebanon and to help bring about the withdrawal of the Israeli forces from Lebanese territory, in accordance with Security Council resolutions 425 (1978) and 509 (1982). A withdrawal of the Force before the Lebanese Government was in a position to assume effective control of the area with its national army and its internal security forces would unquestionably be a serious blow to the prospect of restoring the authority of that Government in southern Lebanon, as well as to the security and welfare of the local population.[44]

J. Withdrawal of Israeli forces

In the meantime, efforts had continued to achieve the withdrawal of the Israeli forces from Lebanon. In the autumn of 1982, the United States had undertaken a diplomatic initiative which led to the signing, on 17 May 1983, of an agreement between Israel and Lebanon. In essence, it provided for the withdrawal of the Israeli and other non-Lebanese forces from Lebanon and for joint security arrangements in southern Lebanon. However, the agreement never came into effect and was eventually abrogated by the Government of Lebanon.

In early September 1983, the Israeli forces, which had been frequently attacked by Lebanese Moslem guerrilla groups, redeployed from the Shuf mountains to south of the Awali River.

In his report[45] of 9 October 1984 to the Security Council, the Secretary-General noted that there was general agreement that an expanded

[43]S/15357. [44]S/16036. [45]S/16776.

mandate for UNIFIL and a widening of its area of operation would be key elements in future arrangements for bringing about the withdrawal of Israeli forces from southern Lebanon and ensuring peace and security in the region and the restoration of Lebanese authority and sovereignty. In extending the mandate of UNIFIL on 12 October, the Security Council requested the Secretary-General to continue consultations with the Government of Lebanon and other parties directly concerned.

Naqoura talks
(November 1984 – January 1985)

Following the adoption of the Security Council's resolution, the Secretary-General approached the Governments of Israel and Lebanon and suggested that they begin negotiations as soon as possible on the withdrawal of Israeli forces from Lebanese territory and related security arrangements in southern Lebanon. After consultations with those Governments, he convoked a conference of military representatives of the two countries at UNIFIL headquarters in Naqoura to discuss those topics. The conference began on 8 November 1984 and met intermittently until 24 January 1985.[46]

From the outset of the conference, the Lebanese representative insisted on the full withdrawal of Israeli forces from Lebanese territory and the subsequent deployment of the Lebanese army together with UNIFIL down to the international boundary, in accordance with Security Council resolution 425 (1978). The Israeli representative took the position that UNIFIL should be deployed in the entire area to be evacuated by the Israeli forces, with its main strength being deployed between the Zahrani and the Awali rivers and eastward to the border between Lebanon and Syria. While Israel would accept a limited UNIFIL presence further south, the Israeli representative maintained that local forces should be responsible for security arrangements in the southernmost part of Lebanon. There was little change in these basic positions as the conference progressed.

On 14 January 1985, the Israeli Government announced a plan for the unilateral redeployment of the Israeli forces in three phases, which was formally presented to the Naqoura conference on 22 January. In the first phase, relating to the western sector, the Israel Defence Forces would evacuate the Sidon area and deploy in the Litani-Nabatiyah region. In the second phase, relating to the eastern sector, IDF would deploy in the Hasbayya area. In the third phase, it would deploy along the Israel-Lebanon international border, while maintaining a security zone in southern Lebanon where local forces (the so-called "South Lebanon Army") would function with IDF backing.

The first phase would be carried out within five weeks. Notification of the timing would be given to the Lebanese Government and the United Nations Secretariat in order to allow them to make arrangements and deploy forces in the areas to be evacuated by IDF. The timing of each subsequent phase would be decided by the Government. Israeli officials indicated subsequently that the second and third phases of the redeployment were tentatively scheduled to be completed in the spring and summer of 1985.

On 24 January 1985, the Lebanese representative announced at the conference that the Israeli redeployment plan did not satisfy his Government's demand for a detailed plan and timetable for the complete withdrawal of Israeli forces from Lebanese territory. While reiterating his Government's willingness to cooperate with the United Nations with a view to expediting the withdrawal of those forces, he maintained that the role of the United Nations could not be discussed before the presentation of such a detailed plan and timetable by Israel.

At the end of the fourteenth meeting, on that date, the Naqoura conference was adjourned *sine die*.

Withdrawal of Israeli forces from the Sidon area

On 16 February, the Israeli forces proceeded with the first phase of the redeployment plan and withdrew from the Sidon area. Early that morning, the Commander of UNIFIL was informed of the withdrawal and immediately communicated it to the Lebanese army authorities. Those authorities advised General Callaghan the next day that the Lebanese army had taken over the evacuated area without incident.

From early February onwards, and particularly after the withdrawal from Sidon, there was an intensification of guerrilla attacks against the Israeli forces by Shiite resistance groups and of Israeli cordon-and-search operations against Shiite villages. An increasing number of these operations occurred in the UNIFIL area. In a statement[47] made on 27 February, the Secretary-General outlined the dilemma faced by UNIFIL. He stated that for obvious reasons the Force had no right to impede

[46]S/17093. [47]Ibid.

Lebanese acts of resistance against the occupying forces, nor did it have the mandate and the means to prevent Israeli countermeasures. In the circumstances, UNIFIL personnel had done their utmost to mitigate violence, protect the civilian population and reduce acts of reprisal to the minimum.

At the request of Lebanon, the Security Council held four meetings from 28 February to 12 March to consider the situation. On 12 March, the Security Council voted on a draft resolution submitted by Lebanon, but did not adopt it, owing to the negative vote of the United States.

Further withdrawals of the Israeli forces

The Israeli forces carried out the second phase of their redeployment in the course of March and April 1985.[48] At the end of the second phase, they were redeployed in a strip of land north of the international border extending from the Mediterranean Sea to the Hasbayya area, with a depth vary-ing between about two kilometres at its narrowest point and about 20 kilometres at its widest.

Following the extension of the UNIFIL mandate by the Security Council in April 1985, the Secretary-General initiated a new effort to work out, in consultation with the Lebanese and Israeli authorities, arrangements which would lead to the full withdrawal of the Israeli forces, the deployment of UNIFIL to the international border and the establishment of international peace and security in the area. These efforts were not successful, and the Israeli forces proceeded with the third phase of the unilateral redeployment plan, without change, handing over their positions to SLA. On 10 June, the Israeli Government announced that the third phase had been completed. It indicated that, while all combat units had been withdrawn from Lebanese territory, some Israeli troops would continue to operate in the "security zone" for an unspecified period of time and act as advisers to SLA.

K.   Situation from 1985–1995

Israel maintains its occupation

Between 1985 and 1995, the situation in the UNIFIL area of operation remained essentially unchanged. The Israeli-controlled area (ICA), in which IDF/SLA had some 70 military positions, included territory adjacent to the armistice demarcation line, parts of the Fijian, Nepalese, Irish, and Finnish battalion sectors and the entire Norwegian battalion sector, as well as sizeable areas to the north of UNIFIL's area of operation. Israel continued its occupation on the grounds that this was necessary to ensure Israel's security so long as the Lebanese Government was not able to exercise effective authority and prevent its territory from being used to launch attacks against northern Israel.

The Government of Lebanon's position on the Israeli occupation of southern Lebanon was that there could be no possible justification for the continuation of Israel's occupation of Lebanese territory, which it viewed as the root cause of the continuing hostilities in the southern part of the country. The only solution to the conflict would be a withdrawal of Israeli forces from its territory, as required by Security Council resolution 425 (1978).

The Israeli authorities held that UNIFIL, as a peace-keeping force, was not capable of assuming this responsibility. Accordingly, IDF improved its fortifications along the border, many of them on Lebanese territory, and strengthened SLA. There was one notable exception: in October 1987, IDF/SLA withdrew from two positions near the village of Yatar which had come under frequent attack. As a result, quiet returned to that area and many people returned to their homes in the nearby villages. The Secretary-General continued his efforts to convince the Israeli authorities to complete the withdrawal of their forces from Lebanon.

IDF gradually established a civilian administration in the area it controlled. That administration assumed responsibility for police, intelligence, the collection of taxes and other levies and various other functions. It also issued permits required for residents of the ICA to travel to other parts of Lebanon. The establishment of the civilian administration was accompanied by threats against the civilian population, who often appealed to UNIFIL for support. Furthermore, IDF/SLA campaigned actively to recruit local men

[48]S/17557.

into SLA, employing coercion, arrests and threats. At times, villagers or their family members were expelled from their villages, sometimes for several months, for refusing to cooperate with that campaign. When possible, the United Nations intervened with the Israeli authorities on this matter. Movement between the ICA and the rest of Lebanon was strictly controlled; crossing points were closed frequently, and sometimes for long periods, causing difficulties for the inhabitants. The ICA remained economically dependent on Israel, and several thousand of its inhabitants held jobs in Israel; access to such jobs was controlled by SLA and the security services.

Israel also imposed restrictions on the movement of Lebanese fishermen in Lebanese territorial waters off the coast of southern Lebanon and enforced those restrictions by naval vessels. At times, this involved firing at or near fishing boats and temporary detention of Lebanese fishermen. UNIFIL intervened with the Israeli authorities repeatedly for the release of those detained.

UNIFIL also protested to the Israeli authorities over other actions by IDF/SLA, such as the demolition in November 1995 of civilian houses in Bayt Yahun village and, starting that same month, the forcing of families in Rshaf to spend nights in abandoned houses near an IDF/SLA position.

Tensions persist

As a consequence of the continued occupation, and indeed as forecast by the Secretary-General in his reports to the Security Council, the IDF/SLA positions in Lebanon remained targets for attacks by Lebanese groups opposed to the Israeli occupation. These groups included Amal, the Islamic Resistance (the military wing of the Shiite Muslim Hizbullah organization), and Palestinian groups. At first, Amal was most active in attacking IDF/SLA; later, the Islamic Resistance became responsible for the majority of attacks. Their attacks were generally on a small scale but occasionally involved sizeable and coordinated military operations leading sometimes to pitched battles. The main targets were the positions at the forward edge of the area occupied by Israeli forces, including those located inside UNIFIL battalion sectors. As a result, UNIFIL often found itself between two fires: on the one hand, the Lebanese groups attacking the Israeli forces and their Lebanese auxiliary, SLA; on the other hand, those very forces reacting, often with heavy weapons and with air support from Israel, to the attacks directed against them. The

situation in southern Lebanon remained tense and volatile, with occasional escalations to high levels of tension and hostilities, prompting third States to intensify their diplomatic efforts seeking to resolve such situations.

During the late 1980s, after the partial withdrawal of Israeli forces, the situation in the ICA remained tense with frequent attacks on IDF/SLA positions. About half of these attacks were directed against two positions near the village of Yatar, from which IDF/SLA withdrew in 1987. In response to attacks by armed elements, IDF/SLA carried out cordon-and-search operations against Shiite villages, including in the UNIFIL area, as well as long-range patrols. At a later stage, the emphasis of the IDF/SLA response shifted to artillery and aircraft. In the UNIFIL area, the situation was generally relatively calm and there was an increase in economic activity.

In the early 1990s, hostilities between Lebanese resistance groups and IDF/SLA in the UNIFIL area of operation intensified and the number of casualties rose. There was an increase both in attacks by armed elements against IDF/SLA and in retaliatory action by the latter. UNIFIL reported that clashes between the armed elements and IDF/SLA increased from an average of just over one per month during the first three months of 1991 to more than five per month during the subsequent seven months. There was a similar increase in resistance activities and IDF/SLA retaliation north of the UNIFIL area of operation.

IDF/SLA increasingly reacted to attacks by firing indiscriminately into nearby villages. They employed heavy artillery, tanks and sometimes helicopter gunships. UNIFIL, many of whose positions were located in or close to the population centres, was affected by these increased hostilities. IDF also staged air attacks over areas north of the Litani River.

A very tense situation developed in the wake of the killing on 16 February 1992 of Sheikh Abbas Musawi, the General Secretary of Hizbullah, together with his wife and young son, by Israeli forces who attacked his car with helicopters north of the Litani River. This was followed by heavy exchanges of artillery and rocket fire between Lebanese armed elements and IDF/SLA. The shelling affected towns in northern Israel and numerous villages in southern Lebanon. Within the UNIFIL area of operation, the Nepalese and Irish battalion sectors were mainly affected, and many of the inhabitants in these sectors fled their homes.

On 20 February 1992, an Israeli armoured force launched an incursion in the direction of

Kafra in the Nepalese battalion sector. UNIFIL took up blocking positions south of Kafra, which were manned by the Nepalese battalion, the Force Mobile Reserve and the Fijian Battalion Reserve and held up the Israeli force for two and one half hours. During this time many of the inhabitants fled the area. IDF bulldozers then pushed UNIFIL's obstacles aside, and the Israeli force was able to move forward towards Kafra. It was engaged by armed elements, who had come to stop the Israeli advance. During the incursion, the area was shelled by IDF/SLA artillery and mortars and strafed from Israeli helicopter gunships. The Israeli force withdrew the next morning after sustaining two fatalities. Five Fijian soldiers were wounded in an explosion caused by a missile fired from one of the helicopters; one of the five died from his wounds some weeks later.

The Secretary-General protested strongly to the Government of Israel about this incursion and instructed the Under- and Assistant Secretaries-General for Peace-keeping Operations to travel to the area to meet with high Lebanese and Israeli officials and hold discussions with the Force Commander of UNIFIL and his senior staff. Tension somewhat diminished towards the end of February.

Another dangerous situation developed after the killing, on 25 October 1992, of five Israeli soldiers by a roadside bomb in the Norwegian battalion sector. IDF/SLA responded with heavy shelling and air strikes against targets north of the UNIFIL area of operations. At least two persons died as a result of those attacks. Armed elements, for their part, fired rockets into Israel, killing one Israeli civilian and wounding five others. Following this, IDF brought up reinforcements to the border. A heightened state of tension persisted for several days.

Tensions rose even higher in a series of events which began with an Israeli air raid on 8 November 1992 in the southern Bekaa Valley, in which four persons were reportedly killed and four wounded. The next day, six persons were injured when a parachute flare dropped from an Israeli aircraft failed to ignite and fell down. This incident, initially reported as an Israeli air attack, was followed by retaliatory rocket fire into northern Israel and the ICA. IDF reinforced its artillery in southern Lebanon and subjected the area to heavy shelling. IDF also brought reinforcements up to the border. The firing in the area decreased gradually and tension subsided during the third week of November.

In early 1993, attacks by armed elements against Israeli and associated military targets on Lebanese territory were generally more effective than previous attacks, and the severity of Israeli retaliation rose concomitantly. A very serious escalation of hostilities took place in July 1993 involving the shelling of civilian targets in southern Lebanon and northern Israel. The incident culminated in an exceptionally intense week-long bombardment, from 25 to 31 July, by the Israeli air force and artillery of villages south and north of the Litani River. The effects of the bombardment were severe: according to Lebanese reports at the time, a total of 130 persons were killed and more than 500 injured. A large number of houses were destroyed or damaged, including schools and medical facilities; an estimated 200,000 inhabitants were temporarily displaced from UNIFIL's area. The heavy bombardment was followed by a lull, but in September hostilities returned to earlier levels.

Throughout 1994 and 1995, and particularly during the first half of both those years, there were again cases in which the parties fired at civilian targets, thereby raising tension in the area to sometimes high levels. These incidents were generally sparked by indiscriminate fire or the targeting of populated areas by IDF/SLA, followed by the firing of rockets into Israel, for which the Islamic Resistance claimed responsibility. In some instances, armed elements launched their attacks from the vicinity of villages in UNIFIL's area of deployment, drawing retaliatory fire.

The Secretary-General, conscious of the risk of escalation that is inherent in these exchanges, repeatedly expressed his concern at these actions and urged the parties to exercise restraint. In the field, UNIFIL maintained close contact with both sides, urging them to respect the non-combatant status of civilians.

UNIFIL's functions unchanged

UNIFIL continued to make every effort to limit the conflict and to protect the inhabitants from the hostilities. The Force maintained 45 checkpoints to control movement on the principal roads in UNIFIL's area; 95 observation posts to observe movement on and off the roads; and 29 checkpoints/observation posts which combined the functions of control and observation. Each was assigned responsibility for ensuring that hostile activities were not undertaken from the area surrounding it. This involved not only keeping watch from the position but also patrolling on foot or by vehicle in its vicinity. In addition, UNTSO military observers maintained five observation posts and operated five mobile teams in the area under Israeli control. The UNTSO observers served under the operational control of UNIFIL's Force Commander.

The Force continued to extend humanitarian assistance to the civilian population in the form of medical care, essential supplies and engineering work and repairs to buildings damaged as a result of hostilities. UNIFIL personnel also escorted farmers so that they could work their fields that were within range of IDF/SLA positions and assisted in putting out fires set off by firing by IDF/SLA. In addition, equipment or services for schools and social services were provided from resources made available by troop-contributing Governments. UNIFIL battalion medical centres and mobile teams continue to provide care to civilians at a rate of approximately 2,000–3,000 patients per month. The Force helped carry out a school project supported financially by UNICEF and the United Nations Educational, Scientific and Cultural Organization and assisted the United Nations Development Programme in its South Lebanon Emergency Rehabilitation Programme. The Force cooperated closely on these matters with the Lebanese authorities, United Nations agencies and programmes operating in Lebanon, ICRC and non-governmental organizations.

Lebanese Army deployment

On 22 October 1989, the Lebanese National Assembly, meeting in Taif, Saudi Arabia, adopted the Taif Agreement for national reconciliation. This Agreement made provision for the deployment of Lebanese government forces to restore central government authority over all Lebanese territory. In 1990, the Lebanese Army assumed control over the greater Beirut area. In 1991, the Government began to extend its authority beyond the greater Beirut area towards the north, east and south. Militias previously operating in those areas were disbanded and their weapons turned in to the Lebanese Army. In July 1991,

the Lebanese Army deployed in the Sidon and Tyre regions adjacent to the city of Jezzine and the UNIFIL area of operation. Subsequently, in accordance with its mandate of assisting the Government in ensuring the return of its effective authority in the UNIFIL area, UNIFIL and the Lebanese military authorities worked out arrangements for the transfer to the Lebanese Army of responsibility for the western part of the Force's Ghanaian battalion sector — an area of about 32 square kilometres with seven villages. The handover, which involved the vacating of eight UNIFIL positions, was completed in early April 1992. In a follow-up handover, additional area comprising the villages of Marakah, Jinnata and Yanuh, including the former Ghanaian battalion headquarters at Marakah, was handed over to the Lebanese Army on 16 February 1993. On 9 August 1993, after the serious escalation of hostilities in July and the establishment of a cease-fire, the Lebanese Government, after consultations with the United Nations, sent an army unit comprising some 300 all ranks to UNIFIL's area of operation for the purpose of maintaining law and order. In February 1994, the Lebanese Army established two permanent checkpoints inside the UNIFIL area for the purpose of controlling the influx of goods into the country. The Gendarmerie and custom authorities from time to time set up temporary checkpoints within UNIFIL's area for the same purpose. The presence of Lebanese Army personnel in the UNIFIL area proved especially helpful in defusing confrontations with armed elements.

The Lebanese authorities provided valuable assistance in connection with the rotation of UNIFIL troops and the increasing volume of logistic activities in Beirut. The Force continued to cooperate with the Lebanese internal security forces on matters pertaining to the maintenance of law and order. In December 1995, Lebanon and the United Nations concluded a status-of-the-Force agreement in respect to UNIFIL.

L. UNIFIL under fire

In carrying out its tasks, UNIFIL continued to be severely hampered by firing directed at its positions and personnel by both IDF/SLA and armed elements. The Secretary-General repeatedly

stressed the obligation of all concerned to respect UNIFIL's international and impartial status. All such incidents were protested to Israeli and Lebanese authorities respectively.

Clashes with armed elements

As part of its mandate, UNIFIL continued to oppose attempts by armed elements to use its area for hostile purposes. At times, this led to friction at UNIFIL's checkpoints and when UNIFIL foot patrols encountered armed elements, followed by harassment and threats directed at the members of the Force. Such cases were generally resolved through negotiations, and with the help of Lebanese Army personnel. In some cases, however, clashes with armed elements led to casualties among members of the Force. A serious crisis erupted following an incident late on 11 August 1986, during which two men, one of them a local leader of the Amal movement, were shot and killed by a French sentry in a confrontation at a checkpoint near the village of Abbasiyah. Shortly afterwards, members of Amal and other armed elements attacked 10 positions manned by French troops. This intense round of attacks ended in the early afternoon of the next day, but sporadic attacks by unidentified persons continued until 28 September 1986, resulting in 3 French soldiers being killed and 24 wounded.

In response to these and other events in which the Force had suffered casualties, UNIFIL took urgent measures to improve the security of its troops. A crash programme was launched to provide for additional shelters and to improve the physical defences at positions, certain vulnerable positions were closed, patrolling procedures were revised and additional security precautions were instituted. In December 1986–January 1987, a major redeployment took place following the withdrawal of the French infantry battalion. It resulted in a consolidation of the Force's deployment in fewer but more effective and better protected positions. In addition, the Force reserve, which had previously been drawn from the battalions as the need arose, was established as a permanent composite unit, the Force Mobile Reserve.

Nevertheless, clashes with armed elements continued. On 25 August 1987 a vehicle containing a company commander of the Nepalese battalion and four of his men were ambushed by armed elements, killing one soldier and wounding three others. UNIFIL established that the ambush was a deliberate attempt by armed elements to assassinate the company commander.

On 15 December 1988, four Lebanese civilians were abducted near the village of Tibnine and brought to the Khiam prison maintained by SLA. Apparently the vehicles used in this abduction had passed through a UNIFIL checkpoint without their purpose being detected. This incident led to an extremely tense situation in the Irish battalion sector. There were several threats to Irish positions and some of them came under fire by armed elements. The following day, a checkpoint was overrun and three Irish soldiers were kidnapped by armed elements. UNIFIL immediately mounted an intensive search operation, in which it received valuable assistance from the Lebanese Amal movement. On 17 December, Amal personnel intercepted the armed elements and secured the release of the Irish soldiers.

On 13 September 1991, six armed Palestinians landed in two rubber dinghies near UNIFIL headquarters in Naqoura. Three of the six were immediately apprehended by UNIFIL and subsequently handed over to the Lebanese authorities in Beirut. The other three landed south of Naqoura and detained 12 UNIFIL soldiers. UNIFIL representatives immediately began negotiations with the Palestinians. At the same time, SLA surrounded the building where the hostages were held. Israeli naval vessels came close inshore and Israeli helicopters hovered in the vicinity. While discussions were still under way, the building came under automatic weapons fire from all directions, killing a Swedish UNIFIL soldier and wounding three French and two Swedish UNIFIL soldiers. One of the Palestinians was killed and another seriously wounded. The United Nations protested to the PLO about the actions of its members in this incident. It similarly protested to the Government of Israel about the actions of IDF/SLA.

Another incident took place on 14 September 1991, when UNIFIL intercepted three armed men in the Nepalese battalion sector, who, in response fired a rocket-propelled grenade, killing a Nepalese UNIFIL soldier on the spot. The fire was returned and one of the three men was killed. The other two withdrew.

During the following years, dangerous confrontations between UNIFIL and the armed elements continued with casualties on both sides. One of the most serious incidents occurred on 3 June 1994, when a UNIFIL patrol encountered armed members of Hizbullah in the Fijian battalion sector. An exchange of fire ensued in which one Fijian soldier was seriously injured; he died two days later. One of the armed elements was killed in that incident. Following that clash, a number of Fijian positions and the camp of the Force Mobile Reserve came under intense fire from armed elements, resulting in injuries to two other Fijian soldiers. In the evening of the same day, two Fijian soldiers manning a checkpoint came under fire from a passing vehicle; one was killed and the other injured. The Lebanese authorities placed in custody one individual suspected of having been involved in that attack. The situation in the Fijian battalion sector was contained with the assistance of the Lebanese army, both locally and in Beirut.

Firing by IDF/SLA

IDF/SLA were responsible for most cases of firing close to or at UNIFIL positions. Sometimes this happened when IDF/SLA were responding to attacks by armed elements, but the firing was also frequently unprovoked and at times, apparently, deliberate. As a result of this firing UNIFIL suffered damage and casualties, including deaths. These firings were all strongly protested by the United Nations to Israeli authorities.

In January 1987, an Irish corporal at a clearly marked United Nations position in the village of Brashit was killed by a round fired from an Israeli tank during heavy bombardment of that village. According to an Israeli investigation, the position had been misidentified as an armed elements position. Later that year, on 4 October 1987, a tank and an armoured SLA personnel carrier were prevented from passing a checkpoint by troops from the Nepalese battalion who used an APC to block the road. Shortly thereafter, three rounds of light machine gun were fired by SLA at a Nepalese position nearby, wounding a sentry. As he was being evacuated in a fully marked United Nations ambulance, SLA fired three heavy machine gun rounds. One round hit the ambulance, killing the wounded sentry. On 19 February 1990, two Nepalese soldiers were killed and six were wounded when their position came under heavy mortar fire from an SLA position.

Another serious incident took place on 15 November 1991, when SLA shot and killed an Irish UNIFIL soldier at Tiri. In the same village, Irish UNIFIL soldiers narrowly escaped death and injury in the night of 22-23 December, when IDF/SLA fired two tank rounds, one of which hit a UNIFIL position.

During the bombardment of July 1993 [see above], there were 303 instances of firing by IDF/SLA at or close to UNIFIL positions and personnel, with the Finnish and Irish battalion sectors accounting for more than 70 per cent of the latter figure. The most serious incident occurred on 27 July, when Israeli aircraft bombed the Nepalese battalion headquarters, causing extensive damage.

The Norwegian battalion sector

The Norwegian battalion continued to be a special case. Its location was geographically separated from the rest of UNIFIL's area of deployment and, following the invasion of Lebanon in 1982, entirely within the ICA. UNIFIL nevertheless continued to do everything possible to ensure calm in this area, in accordance with its mandate. To accomplish that task, IDF/SLA cooperation was essential. It was pointed out to the Israeli authorities that IDF/SLA should not undertake any military operations in that sector. For a number of years UNIFIL's position in this regard was respected and the inhabitants of the area were able to lead comparatively peaceful lives. However, from 1988 onwards there was a growing tendency for IDF/SLA to undertake military operations in the sector. There were several cases of IDF/SLA forcing their way through Norwegian checkpoints in contravention of agreed informal procedures for the entry of non-UNIFIL personnel and vehicles. UNIFIL vigorously protested these violations of its area.

These incidents highlighted the anomaly of the situation in which the Force found itself in those parts of its area of deployment that were effectively under Israeli military occupation. After one particularly serious incident in July 1990, the Secretary-General again urged[49] the Government of Israel that its troops respect the Norwegian battalion's area of operation. He warned that if, however, Israeli forces insisted on operating in that area, it might become necessary for the Security Council to consider whether UNIFIL's role in that area should be changed.

There were also several cases of firing close to or at Norwegian battalion personnel. All serious cases, which were the subject of strong protests to IDF, took place at night and involved IDF tanks firing *fléchette* anti-personnel ammunition at UNIFIL foot patrols. The first of these incidents occurred on 18 February 1989; two soldiers were seriously injured. IDF investigated the incident and reported that it had been the result of a malfunction. Regretting the incident, IDF gave assurances that it had taken measures to prevent a recurrence. Nevertheless, in similar incidents, a Norwegian soldier was killed and another wounded on 27 December 1993 and, on 10 December 1995, three Norwegian soldiers were injured. As in the first incident, IDF investigated the matter and expressed its regrets. In the latter case, and recalling the previous instance, the United Nations asked

---

[49] S/21406/Add.1.

UNIFIL deployment as of July 1995

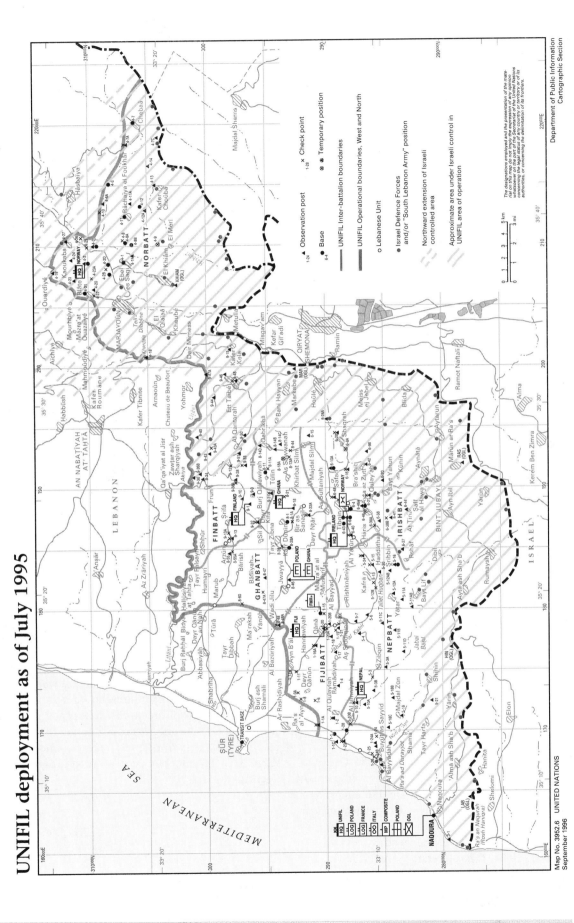

The designations employed and the presentation of the material on this map do not imply the expression of any opinion whatsoever on the part of the Secretariat of the United Nations concerning the legal status of any country or territory or of its authorities, or concerning the delimitation of its frontiers.

Legend:

- ▲ 1-24 Observation post
- × Check point
- ● 6-4 Base
- ⊗ 1-28 Temporary position
- —— UNIFIL Inter-battalion boundaries
- ▨ UNIFIL Operational boundaries, West and North
- ○ Lebanese Unit
- ● Israel Defence Forces and/or "South Lebanon Army" position
- Northward extension of Israeli controlled area
- ▨ Approximate area under Israeli control in UNIFIL area of operation

Scale: 0 1 2 3 4 5 km / 0 1 2 3 mi

Department of Public Information
Cartographic Section

Map No. 3952.6   UNITED NATIONS
September 1996

MEDITERRANEAN SEA

LEBANON

ISRAEL

the Israeli authorities to take effective measures, including disciplinary measures commensurate with the seriousness of the incident.

Casualties from mines

UNIFIL troops also undertook the exploding or dismantling of unexploded ordnance, mines, road-side bombs and other devices of war.

UNIFIL personnel as well as UNTSO military observers continued to suffer casualties by such devices. One tragic incident occurred on 21 March 1989, when three soldiers of the Irish battalion were killed in a mine explosion. A UNIFIL investigation concluded that the mines had been laid the previous night. No one claimed responsibility and the investigation was inconclusive as to the identity of those responsible.

M. Continuing importance of UNIFIL

As is clear from this chapter, UNIFIL continues to be prevented from implementing the mandate given to it by the Security Council. In these circumstances, the Force has used its best efforts to limit the conflict and to shield the inhabitants of the area from the worst effects of the violence. It has also provided humanitarian assistance to the population. Despite the continuing impasse, the Security Council has repeatedly extended the mandate of the Force at the request of the Government of Lebanon and on the recommendation of the Secretary-General.

Over the years, the Secretary-General has emphasized the role played by UNIFIL in controlling the level of violence in its area of operation and thus reducing the risk of a wider conflagration in the region; he has stressed its importance as a symbol of the international community's commitment to the sovereignty, independence and territorial integrity of Lebanon; and he has reiterated the conviction that the solution to the problems of southern Lebanon lies in the full implementation of Security Council resolution 425 (1978), which contains the original mandate of UNIFIL. The Secretary-General has also consistently pointed to the humanitarian assistance UNIFIL is able to provide from modest resources, which is especially important when hostile activities spread to populated areas.

The financial situation of the Organization has led the Secretary-General to implement two streamlining exercises in UNIFIL and to keep UNIFIL under close scrutiny with a view to making further savings.

Reporting[50] to the Security Council in January 1996, the Secretary-General stated that

although there had been no progress towards the implementation of UNIFIL's mandate, the Force's contribution to stability in the area and the protection it was able to afford the inhabitants remained important. He therefore recommended that the Security Council extend UNIFIL's mandate for another period of six months. The Council endorsed this recommendation by its resolution 1039 (1996) of 29 January 1996. In a presidential statement[51] adopted on the same day, the Council reaffirmed its commitment to the full sovereignty, independence, territorial integrity and national unity of Lebanon within its internationally recognized boundaries. In that context, the Council asserted that any State should "refrain from the threat or use of force against the territorial integrity or political independence of any State, or in any other manner inconsistent with the purposes of the United Nations".

When he recommended the extension of UNIFIL's mandate, the Secretary-General recalled that the Force, like other peace-keeping operations, was not an end to itself but should be viewed in the context of the broader objective of achieving a durable peace. In January 1996, renewed negotiations were under way between Israel and Syria in the framework of the Middle East peace process. It was hoped that progress could be made towards resolving the situation in the Israel-Lebanon theatre as well. To date, however, no such progress has been made.

[50]S/1996/45. [51]S/PRST/1996/5.

Chapter 7

Other operations in the Middle East: UNOGIL and UNYOM

Chapter 7

Other operations in the Middle East: UNOGIL and UNYOM

A. United Nations Observation Group in Lebanon (UNOGIL)

Background

In May 1958, armed rebellion broke out in Lebanon when President Camille Chamoun (a Maronite Christian) made known his intention to seek an amendment to the Constitution which would enable him to be re-elected for a second term. The disturbances, which started in the predominantly Moslem city of Tripoli, soon spread to Beirut and the northern and north-eastern areas near the Syrian border, and assumed the proportions of a civil war.

On 22 May, the Lebanese Government requested[1] a meeting of the Security Council to consider its complaint "in respect of a situation arising from the intervention of the United Arab Republic in the internal affairs of Lebanon, the continuance of which is likely to endanger the maintenance of international peace and security". It charged that the United Arab Republic[2] was encouraging and supporting the rebellion by the supply of large quantities of arms to subversive elements in Lebanon, by the infiltration of armed personnel from Syria into Lebanon, and by conducting a violent press and radio campaign against the Lebanese Government.

On 27 May, the Security Council decided to include the Lebanese complaint on its agenda but, at the request of Iraq, agreed to postpone the debate to permit the League of Arab States to try to find a settlement of the dispute. After the League had met for six days without reaching agreement, the Council took up the case and, on 11 June, adopted resolution 128 (1958), by which it decided to dispatch urgently to Lebanon an observation group "so as to ensure that there is no illegal infiltration of personnel or supply of arms or other *matériel* across the Lebanese borders". The Secretary-

General was authorized to take the necessary steps to dispatch the observation group, which was asked to keep the Council informed through him.

Resolution 128, supported by both Lebanon and the United Arab Republic, formed the basis for the establishment of the United Nations Observation Group in Lebanon (UNOGIL).

Creation of UNOGIL

Following adoption of the Security Council's 11 June resolution, Secretary-General Dag Hammarskjöld told the Council that the necessary preparatory steps had already been taken. The Observation Group proper would be made up of highly qualified and experienced men from various regions of the world. They would be assisted by military observers, some of whom would be drawn from UNTSO and could be in Beirut on the very next day. The Secretary-General stressed that the Group would not be a police force like the United Nations Emergency Force (UNEF) deployed in Sinai and the Gaza Strip.

Following the adoption of the resolution, the Secretary-General appointed Mr. Galo Plaza Lasso of Ecuador, Mr. Rajeshwar Dayal of India and Major-General Odd Bull of Norway as members of UNOGIL. Mr. Plaza acted as Chairman.

In order to start the operation without delay, 10 observers were immediately detached from UNTSO for assignment with UNOGIL. Five of them arrived in Beirut on 12 June and began active reconnaissance the following morning. The plan was to cover as many areas as possible and to probe further each day in the direction of the

[1]S/4007. [2]From February 1958 until October 1961, Egypt and Syria joined together to form the United Arab Republic.

Syrian border so as to observe any illegal infiltration of personnel and supply of arms across the border. The number of observers was rapidly increased with new arrivals and reached 100 by 16 June. They were drawn from 21 countries: Afghanistan, Argentina, Burma, Canada, Ceylon, Chile, Denmark, Ecuador, Finland, India, Indonesia, Ireland, Italy, Nepal, the Netherlands, New Zealand, Norway, Peru, Portugal, Sweden and Thailand.

The contributing countries were selected by the Secretary-General in accordance with the same criteria as those he had developed for UNEF in 1956, namely the agreement of the host Government and exclusion of nationals of the permanent members of the Security Council and of "special interest" countries. Two helicopters with Norwegian pilots were placed at the disposal of the Group on 23 June, and they were supplemented shortly thereafter by four light observation aircraft.

Method of operation

The three members of UNOGIL assembled in Beirut on 19 June under the personal chairmanship of Dag Hammarskjöld, who had arrived in the area the day before. As outlined by the Secretary-General, the role of UNOGIL was strictly limited to observation, to ascertain whether illegal infiltration of personnel or supply of arms or other *matériel* across the Lebanese borders was occurring. It was not UNOGIL's task to mediate, arbitrate or forcefully to prohibit illegal infiltration, although it was hoped that its very presence on the borders would deter any such traffic. The borders meant those between Lebanon and Syria, since the Armistice Demarcation Line between Israel and Lebanon was covered by UNTSO and not involved in the present case.

It was decided that the Group should discharge its duties by the following methods:[3]

(a) The UNOGIL military observers would conduct regular and frequent patrols of all accessible roads from dawn to dusk, primarily in border districts and the areas adjacent to the zones held by the opposition forces. Following the practice already established by UNTSO, the patrolling was to be carried out in white jeeps with United Nations markings, equipped with two-way radio sets.

(b) A system of permanent observation posts was to be established and manned by military observers. These posts were in continuous radio contact with UNOGIL headquarters in Beirut, with each other, and with the patrolling United

Nations jeeps. There were initially 10 such stations sited with a view to being as close as possible to the dividing-line between the opposing forces, as near to the frontier as possible or at points commanding supposed infiltration routes or distribution centres. The observers at these stations attempted to check all reported infiltration in their areas and to observe any suspicious development.

(c) An emergency reserve of military observers was to be stationed at headquarters and main observation posts for the purpose of making inquiries at short notice or investigating alleged instances of smuggling.

(d) An evaluation team was to be set up at headquarters to analyse, evaluate and coordinate all information received from observers and other sources.

(e) Aerial reconnaissance was to be conducted by light aeroplanes and helicopters, the former being equipped for aerial photography. The aircraft were in radio communication with headquarters and military observers in the field.

(f) The Lebanese Government would provide the Observation Group with all available information about suspected infiltration. Based on this information, instructions would be given to observers for maintenance of special vigilance within the areas in question. The Group would also request the military observers to make specific inquiries into alleged activities as occasion required.

First UNOGIL report to the Security Council

On 1 July 1958, UNOGIL submitted its first report[4] to the Security Council. The report, which dealt with the problems of observation arising from the political, military and geographical circumstances prevailing in Lebanon, indicated that the observers were facing difficulties in gaining access to much of the frontier area held by the opposition forces and could provide no substantiated or conclusive evidence of major infiltration.

The Lebanese Government criticized what it called the report's "inconclusive, misleading or unwarranted" conclusions.[5] It took strong exception to the report and insisted that the United Arab Republic was continuing "massive, illegal and unprovoked intervention in the affairs of Lebanon".

Initially, the military observers encountered serious difficulties in approaching the eastern and northern frontiers, where large areas were

[3]S/4040. [4]S/4040 and Add.1. [5]S/4043.

UNOGIL deployment as of July 1958

The boundaries and names shown and the designations used on this map do not imply official endorsement or acceptance by the United Nations.

MEDITERRANEAN SEA

LEBANON

UNOGIL HQ
BEIRUT

Arida
Aziziyé
Chadra
Notre-Dame du-Fort
Halba
Beino
Munié
Koussair
Tripoli
Sir Danié
Hermel
El Kah
Amioun
Ehden
Zabboud
Râs Baalbek
Hadeth Jobbé
El Laboué
Arsal
Aïnata
Yammouné
Btedaï
Baalbek
Dhour Choueir
A.U.E.F.
Rayak
Maarboûn
Chtaura
Jennta
Zahlé

BEKAA VALLEY

UNITED ARAB REPUBLIC (SYRIA)

Deïr el Kamar
Barouk
Masnaa
Aïta el Foukhar
Aïn Zebdé
Aïn Arab
Deïr el Aachayer
Awwali
Sidon
Kfar Mechki
Jezzine
Hasbani
El Haouch
Hasbaya
Marjayoûn
Chebaa
Deïr Mimass
Litani
Tyre
Kherouia

ISRAEL

Station
Sub-station
Observation post and Traffic check post
Station boundary
International boundary
Boundary of former Palestine Mandate

| 0 | 10 | 20 | 30 | 40 | 50 km |
| 0 | | 10 | | 20 | 30 mi |

35°30' 36° 36°30'
34°30'
34°
33°30'

Map No. 3952.7 UNITED NATIONS
September 1996

Department of Public Information
Cartographic Section

in opposition hands. In the early stage, these areas could only be patrolled by aircraft, including photographic and night reconnaissance. But the situation greatly improved by mid-July, when UNOGIL finally obtained full freedom of access to all sections of the Lebanese frontier and received assurances of complete freedom to conduct ground patrols throughout the area north of Tripoli and to establish permanent observation posts anywhere in that area. Arrangements were also made for inspection by military observers of all vehicles and cargoes entering Lebanon across the northern frontier.[6]

Dispatch of United States forces

In the meantime, however, new complications arose outside Lebanon's borders. On 14 July 1958, the Hashemite Kingdom of Iraq was overthrown in a *coup d'état* and replaced with a republican regime. This event had serious repercussions both on Lebanon and Jordan. On the same day, President Chamoun requested United States intervention to protect Lebanon's political independence and territorial integrity.

On 15 July, the Security Council was convened at the request of the representative of the United States, who informed it of his Government's decision to respond positively to the Lebanese request. He stated that United States forces were not in Lebanon to engage in hostilities of any kind but to help the Lebanese Government in its efforts to stabilize the situation, brought on by threats from outside, until such time as the United Nations could take the necessary steps to protect the integrity and independence of Lebanon. He added that his Government was the first to admit that the dispatch of United States forces to Lebanon was not an ideal way to solve the current problems and that these forces would be withdrawn as soon as the United Nations could take over.

Secretary-General's position

During the same meeting, the Secretary-General made a statement reviewing the actions he had taken under the mandate given to him in the Security Council's resolution of 11 June. He stated that he had acted solely with the purpose stated by the Council, "to ensure that there is no illegal infiltration of personnel or supply of arms or other *matériel* across the Lebanese borders". His actions had had no relation to developments that must be considered as the internal affairs of Leba-

non, nor had he concerned himself with the wider international aspects of the problem other than those referred to in the resolution. As a matter of course, he had striven to give the observation operation the highest possible efficiency. The Secretary-General also mentioned his own diplomatic efforts in support of the operation, which now had full freedom of movement in the northern area as well as in the rest of Lebanon.

On 16 July, UNOGIL submitted an interim report[7] stating that on the previous day it had completed the task of obtaining full freedom of access to all sections of the frontier of Lebanon. The next day, in a second interim report,[8] the Group expressed its intention to suggest to the Secretary-General that a force of unarmed non-commissioned personnel and other ranks should be assigned to it. It also indicated that the number of observers would have to be raised to 200, with additional aircraft and crews. With the envisaged increase in the observer force, and the addition of enlisted personnel and supporting equipment, it would be possible to undertake direct and constant patrolling of the actual frontier. In transmitting this report, the Secretary-General stated that he fully endorsed the plan contained in it.

Events in Jordan

On 17 July, the representative of Jordan requested[9] the Security Council to give urgent consideration to a complaint by his Government of interference in its domestic affairs by the United Arab Republic. The Council decided on the same day to consider this complaint concurrently with the Lebanese complaint.

During the ensuing discussions, the representative of the United Kingdom stated that his Government had no doubt that a fresh attempt was being prepared to overthrow the regime in Jordan. In response to an appeal by the Jordanian Government, British forces were being dispatched to Jordan to help its King and Government to preserve the country's political independence and territorial integrity. This action would be brought to an end if arrangements could be made by the Council to protect the lawful Government of Jordan from external threats and so maintain international peace and security.

At the beginning of the Council's debate, the Soviet Union submitted a draft resolution, later revised,[10] by which the Council would call upon the United Kingdom and the United States "to

---

[6]S/4051. [7]Ibid. [8]S/4052. [9]S/4053. [10]S/4047/Rev.1.

cease armed intervention in the domestic affairs of the Arab States and to remove their troops from the territories of Lebanon and Jordan immediately". The United States proposed a draft resolution[11] which would request the Secretary-General "immediately to consult the Government of Lebanon and other Member States as appropriate with a view to making arrangements for additional measures, including the contribution and use of contingents, as may be necessary to protect the territorial integrity and independence of Lebanon and to ensure that there is no illegal infiltration of personnel or supply of arms or other *matériel* across the Lebanese borders". A third draft resolution[12] was later submitted by Sweden to have the Council request the Secretary-General to suspend the activities of the observers in Lebanon until further notice.

The Soviet and Swedish draft resolutions were rejected by majorities, while the United States proposal was vetoed by the Soviet Union.

Following those votes, Japan proposed a draft resolution[13] under which the Secretary-General would be requested to make arrangements for such measures, in addition to those envisaged by the Council's resolution of 11 June 1958, as he might consider necessary in the light of the present circumstances, "with a view to enabling the United Nations to fulfil the general purposes established in that resolution, and which will, in accordance with the Charter, serve to ensure the territorial integrity and political independence of Lebanon, so as to make possible the withdrawal of the United States forces from Lebanon". This draft resolution was also rejected, owing to a Soviet negative vote.

Secretary-General's plan

Following the rejection of the Japanese proposal, the Secretary-General stated that, although the Security Council had failed to take additional action in the grave emergency facing it, the United Nations responsibility to make all efforts to live up to the purposes and principles of the Charter remained. He was sure that he would be acting in accordance with the Council's wishes if he used all opportunities offered to him, within the limits set by the Charter, towards developing those efforts, so as to help prevent a further deterioration of the situation in the Middle East and to assist in finding a road away from the dangerous point now reached. The continued operation of UNOGIL being acceptable to all Council members would imply concurrence in the further develop-

ment of the Group, so as to give it all the significance it could have, consistent with its basic character as determined by the Council in its resolution of 11 June 1958 and the purposes and principles of the Charter. He indicated that, should the members of the Council disapprove of the way these intentions were to be translated by him into practical steps, he would, of course, accept the consequences of its judgement.

The Secretary-General's plan was to increase the strength of UNOGIL as soon as possible to enable it to carry out fully its mission and thus expedite the withdrawal of the United States troops. The number of personnel, which stood at 200 on 17 July 1958, was increased to 287 by 20 September and to 591 in mid-November, including 32 non-commissioned officers in support of ground operations and 90 such officers in the air section. In November, UNOGIL had 18 aircraft, six helicopters and 290 vehicles, and 49 permanently manned posts of all types had been established.

Further UNOGIL report

On 30 July, UNOGIL submitted a periodic report[14] on its activities and observations. It stated that the military observers were operating with skill and devotion, often in conditions of considerable danger and difficulty. Intensive air patrolling had been carried out by day and by night, and air observations had been checked against the results of ground patrolling and observation. The Group reached the conclusion that the infiltration which might be taking place could not be anything more than of limited scale and was largely confined to small arms and ammunition.

With regard to illegal infiltration of personnel, UNOGIL stated that the nature of the frontier, the existence of traditional tribal and other bands on both sides of it and the free movement of produce in both directions were among the factors which must be taken into account in making an evaluation. In no case, however, had the observers, who had been vigilantly patrolling the opposition-held areas and had frequently observed armed bands there, been able to detect the presence of persons who had undoubtedly entered from across the border for the purpose of fighting. From the observations made of the arms and organization in the opposition-held areas, the fighting strength of opposition elements was not such as to be able successfully to cope with hostilities against a well-armed regular military force.

[11]S/4050/Rev.1.　[12]S/4054.　[13]S/4055/Rev.1.　[14]S/4069.

The United States troops, which had landed in Beirut on 15 July, were confined at all times to the beach area and there were no contacts between them and the United Nations military observers. However, UNOGIL indicated in its report that the impact of the landing of those forces in the Beirut area on the inhabitants of opposition-held areas had occasioned difficulties and caused setbacks in carrying out the tasks of the observers.

General Assembly emergency session

During the discussions in the Security Council in July, both the Soviet Union and the United States proposed the convening of an emergency special session of the General Assembly, but the matter was not taken up until 7 August. In the intervening period, the leaders of France, India, the Soviet Union, the United Kingdom and the United States held consultations through exchanges of letters in an effort to find a way out of the impasse. The idea of a "summit" meeting on the Middle East was advanced, but no agreement could be reached. On 7 August, the Security Council met again and decided to call an emergency special session of the Assembly.

That session took place from 8 to 21 August 1958. By the time the Assembly convened, two events which had an important bearing on the developments in the Middle East had occurred. First, General Fuad Chehab, who was acceptable to the Moslem leaders, had been elected President of Lebanon, and this effectively removed from the scene the controversial question of a second term for Mr. Chamoun. Second, the new Iraqi revolutionary Government had accepted the obligations of States under the United Nations Charter and had been recognized by the United Kingdom and the United States.

In a report[15] of 14 August, UNOGIL indicated that just before the election of President Chehab there had been a noticeable reduction of tension throughout the country and a comparable absence of armed clashes between Government and opposition forces. Since 31 July, there had been a virtual nationwide truce with only occasional reports of sporadic firing in some areas. The report also indicated that by dint of their perseverance and tact in dealing with difficult and often dangerous situations, the observers had won back the ground lost after 15 July. Most of the permanent stations in opposition-held areas envisaged by the Group had been established, and other stations were expected to be set up shortly.

At the end of the emergency special session, the General Assembly unanimously adopted, on 21 August, a proposal submitted by 10 Arab States. This became resolution 1237 (ES-III), by which the Assembly requested the Secretary-General to make forthwith, in consultation with the Governments concerned and in accordance with the Charter, such practical arrangements as would adequately help to uphold Charter purposes and principles in relation to Lebanon and Jordan in the present circumstances, and thereby facilitate the early withdrawal of the foreign troops from the two countries.

Secretary-General's Special Representative

In a report[16] dated 29 September to the General Assembly, the Secretary-General commented on the practical arrangements mentioned in the Assembly's August resolution. He noted that, in the case of Lebanon, the United Nations had already made extensive plans for observing the possible infiltration or smuggling of arms across the border. The work of the Observation Group had had to be re-evaluated within the new practical arrangements to be made. As to Jordan, its Government had indicated that it did not accept the stationing of a United Nations force in Jordan nor the organization of a broader observation group like UNOGIL. But it would accept a special representative of the Secretary-General to assist in the implementation of the resolution. Consequently, the Secretary-General asked Mr. Pier P. Spinelli, the Under-Secretary in charge of the United Nations Office at Geneva, to proceed to Amman and to serve as his Special Representative, on a preliminary basis.

With regard to the withdrawal issues, the Secretary-General had been informed that Lebanon and the United States were discussing a schedule for the completion of the withdrawal of the United States forces, and that they hoped this might take place by the end of October. Jordan and the United Kingdom were also discussing the fixing of dates for the withdrawal of the British troops from Jordan, which would begin during October.

In its fourth report[17] to the Security Council, which was circulated on 29 September 1958, UNOGIL stated that, during the period being reviewed, its military observers had not only been able to re-establish confidence in the independent nature of their activities, but had won for them-

[15]S/4085. [16]A/3934/Rev.1. [17]S/4100.

selves the trust and understanding of all sections of the population. Despite the presence of a considerable number of men under arms, there had been no significant clashes between the Lebanese army and organized opposition forces. No cases of infiltration had been detected and, if any infiltration was still taking place, its extent must be regarded as insignificant.

Withdrawal of United Kingdom and United States forces

In a letter[18] dated 1 October, the United Kingdom informed the Secretary-General that it had agreed with the Jordanian Government that the withdrawal of British troops should begin on 20 October. On 8 October, the United States announced[19] that, by agreement with the Lebanese Government, it had been decided to complete the withdrawal of United States forces by the end of October. The withdrawal of United States troops was completed by 25 October, and of the British troops by 2 November. Some of the UNOGIL observers played a role in assisting in the evacuation of the British forces from Jordan.

Termination of UNOGIL

In a letter dated[20] 16 November 1958, the Minister for Foreign Affairs of Lebanon stated that cordial and close relations between Lebanon and the United Arab Republic had resumed their normal course. In order to dispel any misunderstanding which might hamper such relations, the Lebanese Government requested the Security Council to delete the Lebanese complaint from its agenda.

In its final report, dated 17 November 1958,[21] UNOGIL recommended that the operation should be withdrawn since its task might be regarded as completed. On 21 November, the Secretary-General submitted[22] to the Security Council a plan for the withdrawal of the operation, formulated by the Observation Group, which was acceptable to Lebanon.

In accordance with that plan, the closing down of stations and substations preparatory to the withdrawal of UNOGIL began on 26 November and was completed by the end of the month. The observers were withdrawn in three phases, with the key staff, the personnel required for air service and the logistic components leaving last. The withdrawal was completed by 9 December.

B. United Nations Yemen Observation Mission (UNYOM)

Background

A civil war which broke out in Yemen in September 1962 contained the seeds of a wider conflict with international dimensions because of the involvement of Saudi Arabia and the United Arab Republic. Saudi Arabia shared an extended border with Yemen, much of it still undefined. The United Arab Republic (Egypt) had had a special relationship with Yemen in the past. In March 1958, Yemen joined it to form the United Arab States, but this association was dissolved in December 1961, shortly after Syria seceded from the United Arab Republic.

A further factor in the situation was that Yemen had long claimed that the Aden Protectorate was legally part of its territory. The British-controlled Government of the South Arabian Federation, which included the Aden Protectorate,

therefore also closely followed developments in Yemen.

On 19 September 1962, Imam Ahmed bin Yahya died and was succeeded by his son, Imam Mohammed Al-Badr. A week later, a rebellion led by the army overthrew the new Imam and proclaimed the Yemen Arab Republic. The new Government was recognized by the United Arab Republic on 29 September and by the Soviet Union the next day, but other major Powers with interests in the area, including the United Kingdom and the United States, withheld action on the question of recognition.

Following his overthrow, Imam Al-Badr managed to escape from San'a, the capital, and, with other members of the royal family, rallied the

[18]A/3937. [19] A/3942. [20]S/4113. [21]S/4114. [22]S/4116.

tribes in the northern part of the country. With financial and material support from external sources, the royalists fought a fierce guerrilla campaign against the republican forces. The revolutionary Government accused Saudi Arabia of harbouring and encouraging Yemeni royalists, and threatened to carry the war into Saudi Arabian territory. The Imam, on the other hand, claimed that the army rebellion was fostered and aided by Egypt, which denied the charge. At the beginning of October, large numbers of United Arab Republic forces were dispatched to Yemen at the request of the revolutionary Government to assist the republican forces in their fight against the royalists.

On 27 November, the Permanent Mission of Yemen to the United Nations, which was still staffed by the royalists, addressed a letter to the Secretary-General urging the United Nations to establish an inquiry to ascertain whether or not the rebellion was fostered from Cairo. This letter was informally circulated to the United Nations missions. A delegation of Yemeni republicans which had arrived in New York by that time let it be known that they would not object to a United Nations on-the-spot investigation.

The General Assembly, which began its seventeenth session in New York in September 1962, had before it credentials from both the royalist and republican regimes in Yemen. It took up the question of the representation of Yemen on 20 December, the very last day of its session. On that day, the Credentials Committee decided, by a vote of 6 to none, with 3 abstentions, to recommend that the Assembly accept the credentials submitted by the President of the Yemen Arab Republic. Later on the same day, the Assembly approved, by 73 votes to 4, with 23 abstentions, the Committee's report.

King Hussein of Jordan earlier that month had suggested that the presence of United Nations observers might be useful in finding a solution.

Secretary-General's initiative

Secretary-General U Thant undertook a peace initiative, which eventually led to the establishment of the United Nations Yemen Observation Mission (UNYOM).

In a report[23] dated 29 April 1963, the Secretary-General stated that, since the autumn of 1962, he had been consulting regularly with the representatives of the Governments of the Arab Republic of Yemen, Saudi Arabia and the United Arab Republic about "certain aspects of the situation in Yemen of external origin, with a view to making my office available to the parties for such assistance as might be desired towards ensuring against any developments in that situation which might threaten peace of the area". He had requested Mr. Ralph J. Bunche, Under-Secretary for Special Political Affairs, to undertake a fact-finding mission in the United Arab Republic and Yemen. As a result of the activities carried out by Mr. Bunche on his behalf, and by Mr. Ellsworth Bunker, who had been sent by the United States Government on a somewhat similar but unconnected mission, he had received from each of the three Governments concerned formal confirmation of their acceptance of identical terms of disengagement in Yemen.

Under those terms, Saudi Arabia would terminate all support and aid to the royalists of Yemen and would prohibit the use of Saudi Arabian territory by royalist leaders for carrying on the struggle in Yemen. Simultaneously with that suspension of aid, Egypt would undertake to begin withdrawal from Yemen of the troops that had been sent at the request of the new Government, the withdrawal to be phased and to take place as soon as possible. A demilitarized zone would be established to a distance of 20 kilometres on each side of the demarcated Saudi Arabia–Yemen border, and impartial observers would be stationed there to check on the observance of the terms of disengagement. They would also certify the suspension of activities in support of the royalists from Saudi Arabian territory and the outward movement of the Egyptian forces and equipment from the airports and seaports of Yemen.

The Secretary-General asked Lieutenant-General Carl C. von Horn (Sweden), Chief of Staff of UNTSO, to visit the three countries concerned to consult on the terms relating to the functioning of United Nations observers in implementation of the terms of disengagement.

In a second report,[24] dated 27 May, the Secretary-General told the Council that on the basis of information provided by General von Horn, he concluded that United Nations observers in the area were necessary and should be dispatched with the least possible delay. The personnel required would not exceed 200, and it was estimated that the observation function would not be required for more than four months. The military personnel in the Yemen operation would be employed under conditions similar to those applying to other United Nations operations of this nature. The total cost was estimated to be less than

[23]S/5298. [24]S/5321.

$1 million, and he hoped that the two parties principally involved, Saudi Arabia and Egypt, would undertake to bear this cost. He submitted more detailed estimates of the costs of the proposed Mission in a supplemental report[25] on 3 June.

In a further report,[26] submitted on 7 June, the Secretary-General informed the Security Council that Saudi Arabia had agreed to accept a "proportionate share" of the costs of the operation, while Egypt agreed in principle to provide $200,000 in assistance for a period of two months, which would be roughly half the costs of the operation for that period. Thus, there would be no financial implications for the United Nations in getting the Observation Mission established and for its maintenance for an initial two-month period. The Secretary-General announced his intention to proceed with the organization and dispatch of the Mission without delay.

Security Council action establishing UNYOM

The next day, the Soviet Union requested[27] the convening of the Council to consider the Secretary-General's reports on developments relating to Yemen, since the reports contained proposals concerning possible measures by the United Nations to maintain international peace and security, which, under the Charter, should be decided by the Council.

After considering the reports, the Council adopted, on 11 June 1963, resolution 179 (1963), requesting the Secretary-General to establish the observation operation as he had defined it, and urging the parties concerned to observe fully the terms of disengagement set out in his 29 April report and to refrain from any action that would increase tension in the area. The Council noted with satisfaction that Saudi Arabia and Egypt had agreed to defray, over a period of two months, the expenses of the observation function called for in the terms of disengagement.

This resolution constituted the basis for the establishment of UNYOM. It did not set a specific time-limit for the Mission, although two months was mentioned in the preamble in connection with its financing. The Secretary-General took the position that he could extend UNYOM without a decision of the Security Council if he considered that its task had not been completed, provided that he could obtain the necessary financial support.

Reports on UNYOM operations

In his first report[28] on the operation, which was submitted to the Security Council on 4 September 1963, the Secretary-General pointed out that the Mission's task would not be completed on the expiration of the two-month period, and for that reason he had sought and received assurances from both parties that they would defray the expenses of the operation for a further two months.

In his second report,[29] dated 28 October, the Secretary-General reported that there had been no decisive change in the situation in Yemen and, because of the limiting and restrictive character of the UNYOM mandate, the Mission would have to be withdrawn by 4 November 1963, since there would be no financial support for it after that date. However, three days later, he informed[30] the Council that Saudi Arabia and Egypt had agreed to participate in the financing of UNYOM for a further two-month period and, accordingly, preparations for the withdrawal of the Mission had been cancelled. He indicated that, although no Security Council meeting was required for the extension of UNYOM, he had consulted Council members to ascertain that there would be no objection to the proposed extension.

On 2 January 1964, before the expiration of the third two-month period, the Secretary-General reported[31] that he considered that the continuing functioning of UNYOM was highly desirable, that the two Governments concerned had agreed to continue their financial support for another two months, and that he had engaged in informal consultations with the members of the Council before announcing his intention to extend the Mission. This process was repeated at the beginning of March, May and July 1964, and UNYOM was extended for successive periods of two months until 4 September 1964.

In late August 1964, Saudi Arabia informed the Secretary-General that it found itself unable to continue the payment of expenses resulting from the disengagement agreement, and Egypt indicated that it had no objection to the termination of UNYOM on 4 September. The Secretary-General therefore advised[32] the Council of his intention to terminate the activities of the Mission on that date.

---

[25]S/5323. [26]S/5325. [27]S/5326. [28]S/5412. [29]S/5447. [30]S/5447/Add.1. [31]S/5501. [32]S/5927.

UNYOM deployment as of October 1963

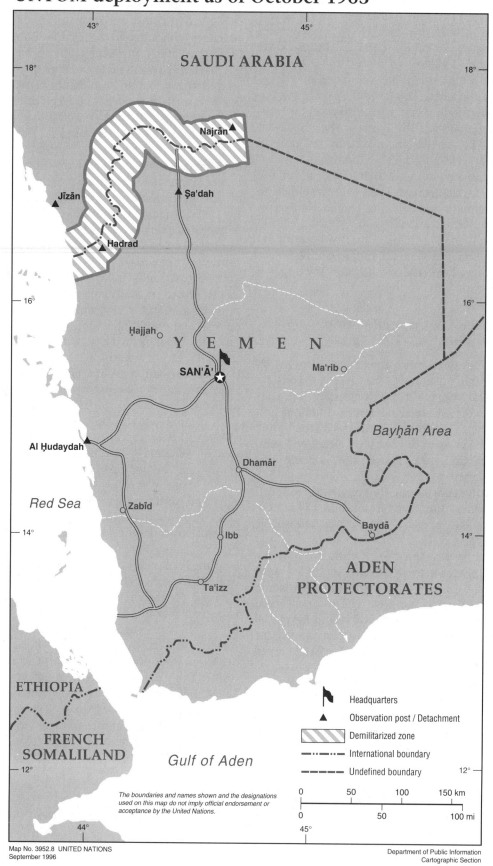

SAUDI ARABIA

Najrān ▲

Jīzān ▲

▲ Ṣa'dah

▲ Hadrad

Ḥajjah ○

Y E M E N

SAN'Ā' ☆

Ma'rib ○

Al Ḥudaydah ▲

Bayḥān Area

Dhamār ○

Red Sea

Zabīd ○

Ibb ○

Baydā ○

14°

Ta'izz ○

ADEN
PROTECTORATES

ETHIOPIA

FRENCH
SOMALILAND

Gulf of Aden

⚑ Headquarters

▲ Observation post / Detachment

▨ Demilitarized zone

International boundary

Undefined boundary

The boundaries and names shown and the designations
used on this map do not imply official endorsement or
acceptance by the United Nations.

0   50   100   150 km

0   50   100 mi

45°

Map No. 3952.8 UNITED NATIONS
September 1996

Department of Public Information
Cartographic Section

Organization of UNYOM

Following the adoption of resolution 179 (1963), the Secretary-General appointed General von Horn as Commander of UNYOM and took steps to provide the Mission with the required personnel and equipment. The resolution had requested the Secretary-General to establish UNYOM as he had defined it in his report of 29 April 1963, and he selected the various components of the Mission accordingly. In selecting those components and the contributing countries, he informally consulted the parties concerned. Practical considerations were also taken into account, including the proximity of the existing United Nations peace-keeping operations, namely UNTSO and UNEF.

In the initial stage, UNYOM was composed mainly of six military observers, a Yugoslav reconnaissance unit of 114 personnel and a Canadian air unit of 50 officers and men. In addition, 28 international staff members and a small military staff were assigned to UNYOM headquarters. The military observers were detailed from UNTSO and the reconnaissance unit personnel were drawn from the Yugoslav contingent of UNEF, which had experience in United Nations peace-keeping operations in similar terrain. The UNEF air base at El Arish provided support for the Canadian air unit, including six aircraft and a similar number of helicopters.

The strength and composition of UNYOM remained unchanged until November 1963, when a reappraisal of its requirements in terms of personnel and equipment was undertaken. It was felt that in view of the cooperation shown by the parties and the peaceful and friendly attitude of the people in the area covered by the Mission, it was no longer necessary to maintain a military unit in the demilitarized zone; therefore, it was decided to withdraw progressively the Yugoslav reconnaissance unit and to deploy instead up to 25 military observers, while the aircraft of the Mission were reduced to two. The new observers were provided by Denmark, Ghana, India, Italy, the Netherlands, Norway, Pakistan, Sweden and Yugoslavia.

With the arrival of General von Horn and the first group of military personnel, UNYOM began operations on 4 July 1963. In August, General von Horn resigned, and his deputy, Colonel Branko Pavlovic (Yugoslavia), took over as acting Commander until September 1963 when Lieutenant-General P. S. Gyani (India), then Commander of UNEF, was temporarily detailed from that Force and appointed Commander of UNYOM.

Secretary-General's Special Representative

At the end of October 1963, when the Secretary-General thought UNYOM had to be withdrawn for lack of financial support, he announced[33] his intention to maintain a civilian presence in Yemen after the withdrawal of the Observation Mission, and he had in mind the appointment of Mr. Pier P. Spinelli, head of the United Nations Office at Geneva, as his Special Representative for this purpose. After the withdrawal plan was cancelled, as mentioned earlier, the idea of appointing Mr. Spinelli was retained, particularly since General Gyani had to return to his command in UNEF.

In November 1963, upon the departure of General Gyani, Mr. Spinelli was appointed Special Representative of the Secretary-General, as well as head of UNYOM. He assumed this dual responsibility until the end of the Mission.

Functioning of UNYOM

The mandate of UNYOM stemmed from the disengagement agreement entered into by the three Governments concerned, namely, Saudi Arabia, the United Arab Republic and the Arab Republic of Yemen, set out in the report[34] of the Secretary-General of 29 April 1963. The function and authority of UNYOM as defined in the agreement were considerably more limited than in the case of other United Nations observation missions. For example, its establishment was not based on any cease-fire agreement and there was no cease-fire to supervise. The tasks of UNYOM were limited strictly to observing, certifying and reporting in connection with the intention of Saudi Arabia to end activities in support of the royalists in Yemen and the intention of Egypt to withdraw its troops from that country.

To carry out these tasks in the initial stage, detachments of the Yugoslav reconnaissance unit were stationed in Jizan, Najran and Sa'dah in the demilitarized zone and the surrounding areas. They manned check-posts and conducted ground patrolling. In addition, air patrolling was carried out by the Canadian air unit, which had bases at San'a as well as Jizan and Najran, particularly in the mountainous central part of the demilitarized zone where there were few passable roads. The six military observers detailed from UNTSO, who were stationed at San'a, and the two positions at Al

---

[33]S/5447. [34]S/5298.

Hudaydah were primarily responsible for observing and certifying the withdrawal of Egyptian troops.

In order to check on the reduction or cessation of assistance from Saudi Arabia to the royalists, a pattern of check-points and air/ground patrolling was established to cover all main roads and tracks leading into Yemen and the demilitarized zone. Air and ground patrols were carried out daily with varied timings and routes, the patrol plan being prepared and coordinated every evening.

Experience quickly showed that air and ground patrolling had two main limitations, namely, that traffic could be observed only by day while, for climatic reasons, travel during hours of darkness was customary in the area, and that cargoes could not be checked. These problems were met by periodically positioning United Nations military observers at various communication centres for 40 hours or more, so that traffic could be observed by day or night and cargoes checked as necessary. Arrangements were also made to have Saudi Arabian liaison officers assigned to United Nations check-points and check cargoes when requested by United Nations observers.

Various complaints were received by UNYOM from one or the other of the parties concerned. They fell mainly into two categories: on the one hand, allegations of offensive actions by Egyptian forces against the royalists in Yemen and in Saudi Arabian territory, and, on the other, alleged activities in support of the royalists emanating from Saudi Arabia. UNYOM authorities would transmit these complaints to the parties involved and, whenever possible and appropriate, investigate them.

In accordance with the disengagement agreement, the responsibilities of UNYOM concerned mainly, in addition to the cities of San'a and Al Hudaydah, the demilitarized zone on each side of the demarcated portion of the Saudi Arabia-Yemen border. It did not extend to the undefined portion of that border nor to the border between Yemen and the British-controlled South Arabian Federation.

From the very start, the Secretary-General pointed out that UNYOM, because of its limited size and function, could observe and report only certain indications of the implementation of the disengagement agreement. However, despite its shortcomings, the Mission did have a restraining influence on hostile activities in the area. The Secretary-General repeatedly expressed the view that the responsibility for implementing the agreement lay with Saudi Arabia and Egypt and progress

could be best achieved through negotiations between them.

With this in view, he informed the Security Council that UNYOM could, within limits, serve as an intermediary and as an endorser of good faith on behalf of the parties concerned, and that it was his intention to have the Mission perform these roles to the maximum of its capability. When Mr. Spinelli was appointed Special Representative of the Secretary-General and head of UNYOM in November 1963, he devoted a great deal of his time and attention to good-offices efforts and held extensive discussions with officials of the three Governments concerned. These discussions were of an exploratory character to try to ascertain whether there were areas of agreement between the parties which might, through bilateral discussions or otherwise, lead to further progress towards disengagement and the achievement of a peaceful situation in Yemen.

Secretary-General's assessment

The assessment of the Secretary-General on the functioning of UNYOM and the implementation of the disengagement agreement, as set out in his successive periodic reports to the Security Council, are outlined below.

In his first report[35] on this subject, which was dated 4 September 1963, the Secretary-General found no encouraging progress towards effective implementation of the agreement, although both parties had expressed a willingness to cooperate in good faith with UNYOM. He noted reluctance by each side to fulfil its undertakings regarding the agreement before the other side did so.

His second report,[36] which was submitted on 28 October 1963, indicated limited progress. He stated that although the developments observed by UNYOM were far short of the disengagement and regularization of the situation which had been hoped for, they were in a limited way encouraging in that the scale of fighting had been reduced and conditions of temporary truce applied in many areas.

On 2 January 1964, he reported[37] that UNYOM observations tended to confirm that, during the period under review, no military aid of significance had been provided to the royalists from Saudi Arabia, and that there had been a substantial net withdrawal of Egyptian troops from Yemen. Ground operations had further decreased in intensity. The Secretary-General reiterated his

[35]S/5412. [36]S/5447. [37]S/5501.

belief that the solution of the problem lay beyond the potential of UNYOM under its original mandate, and he referred to the extensive discussions his Special Representative had had with members of the three Governments concerned with a view to furthering progress towards disengagement and the achievement of a peaceful situation in Yemen.

A later report,[38] submitted on 3 March 1964, raised a new problem: Yemeni and Egyptian sources asserted that large quantities of supplies were being sent to the royalists from the Bayhan area across the frontier with the South Arabian Federation. The Secretary-General pointed out in this connection that since that frontier was not included in the disengagement agreement, United Nations observers did not operate in that area. However, he mentioned that the nature and extent of the military operations carried out by the royalists during January and February would seem to indicate that arms and ammunition in appreciable amounts had been reaching them from that source.

The Secretary-General also reported that the royalists appeared to be well provided with money and to have engaged foreign experts to train and direct their forces, and that they had recently launched attacks against Egyptian troops. From the developments observed by UNYOM, he felt that progress towards the implementation of the disengagement agreement had been very disappointing during the period under review; a state of political and military stalemate existed inside the country, which was unlikely to be changed as long as external intervention in various forms continued from either side. On the other hand, he noted certain encouraging factors, particularly the increasing unity of feeling and purpose within the Arab world arising from a Conference of Arab Heads of State held in Cairo in mid-January 1964 and the resulting improvement in relations between Saudi Arabia and Egypt. The Secretary-General expressed the hope that the meeting to be held between the two parties in Saudi Arabia would result in some progress towards the implementation of the agreement and towards an understanding between the two Governments to cooperate in promoting political progress and stability in Yemen.

In his report[39] dated 3 May 1964, the Secretary-General stated that there was no progress in troop reduction towards the implementation of the disengagement agreement and that no actual end of the fighting appeared to be in sight. He noted, however, that the two parties had reported noticeable progress in discussions of a number of problems at issue between them, and that a meeting between President Nasser of Egypt and Crown Prince Feisal of Saudi Arabia would be held in Cairo in the near future.

On 2 July, the Secretary-General reported[40] that the military situation in Yemen had remained fairly quiet over the past two months, that no military aid by Saudi Arabia to the Yemeni royalists had been observed and that some slight progress in Egyptian troop reduction appeared to have occurred. Once again he appealed to the parties concerned to meet at the highest level with a view to achieving full and rapid implementation of the disengagement agreement.

Termination of UNYOM

In his final report,[41] dated 2 September 1964, the Secretary-General again acknowledged the failure of the parties to implement the disengagement agreement and the difficulties UNYOM faced in observing and reporting on these matters. There had been a substantial reduction in the strength of the Egyptian forces in Yemen but it seemed that the withdrawal was a reflection of the improvement in the situation of the Yemeni republican forces rather than the beginning of a phased withdrawal in the sense of the agreement. There were also indications that the Yemeni royalists had continued to receive military supplies from external sources. Noting that UNYOM had been able to observe only limited progress towards the implementation of the agreement, he reiterated his view that UNYOM's terms of reference were restricted to observation and reporting only, and that the responsibility for implementation lay with the two parties to the agreement. He stated that UNYOM had actually accomplished much more than could have been expected of it in the circumstances, and that during the 14 months of its presence in Yemen, the Mission had exercised an important restraining influence on hostile activities in the area.

On 4 September 1964, the activities of UNYOM ended and its personnel and equipment were withdrawn.

Shortly after the withdrawal of UNYOM, relations between the parties steadily improved and issues were resolved between them. There has been no consideration of the matter in United Nations organs since the termination of that Mission.

[38]S/5572. [39]S/5681. [40]S/5794. [41]S/5927.

Part III
India and Pakistan

Chapter 8

United Nations Military Observer Group in India and Pakistan (UNMOGIP)

United Nations India-Pakistan Observation Mission (UNIPOM)

A. Background

B. United Nations Commission for India and Pakistan
Security Council action
Commission action
UNCIP mission

C. Supervision of the cease-fire, 1948–1965
Military adviser
Arrival of observers
Observers' tasks
Plebiscite Administrator
Supervision of the Karachi Agreement
Listing of cease-fire breaches
UNCIP report to the Security Council
Termination of UNCIP
Appointment of a United Nations representative
Continuance of UNMOGIP
Role and activities of UNMOGIP

D. The hostilities of 1965 and the establishment of UNIPOM
Background
Security Council action for a cease-fire
Establishment of UNIPOM
Further Security Council action
Tashkent agreement
Withdrawal plan
Termination of UNIPOM

E. Hostilities of 1971 and their aftermath

Chapter 8

United Nations Military Observer Group in India and Pakistan
(UNMOGIP)

United Nations India-Pakistan Observation Mission (UNIPOM)

A. Background

The United Nations Military Observer Group in India and Pakistan (UNMOGIP) had its origin in the conflict between India and Pakistan over the status of the State of Jammu and Kashmir (referred to here as Kashmir). The United Nations India-Pakistan Observation Mission (UNIPOM) was an administrative adjunct, created when conflict occurred in 1965 along the borders of the two countries outside the UNMOGIP area.

In August 1947, India and Pakistan became independent dominions, in accordance with a scheme of partition provided by the Indian Independence Act of 1947. Under that scheme, the State of Jammu and Kashmir was free to accede to India or Pakistan. The accession became a matter of dispute between the two countries and fighting broke out later that year.

The question first came before the Security Council in January 1948,[1] when India complained that tribesmen and others were invading Kashmir and that extensive fighting was taking place. India charged that Pakistan was assisting and participating in the invasion. Pakistan denied India's charges and declared that Kashmir's accession to India following India's independence in 1947 was illegal.

B. United Nations Commission for India and Pakistan

Security Council action

On 20 January, the Security Council adopted resolution 39 (1948) establishing a three-member United Nations Commission for India and Pakistan (UNCIP) "to investigate the facts pursuant to Article 34 of the Charter of the United Nations" and "to exercise . . . any mediatory influence likely to smooth away difficulties . . .".

Although India and Pakistan were consulted on the above resolution, serious disagreement arose between the two Governments regarding its implementation, and the proposed Commission could not be constituted.

On 21 April 1948, the Security Council met again and adopted resolution 47 (1948), by which it decided to enlarge the membership of the Commission from three to five (Argentina, Belgium, Colombia, Czechoslovakia and the United States), and instructed it to proceed at once to the

[1] S/628.

subcontinent. There it was to place its good offices at the disposal of the two Governments to facilitate the taking of the necessary measures with respect to both the restoration of peace and the holding of a plebiscite in the State of Jammu and Kashmir. The Commission was also to establish in Jammu and Kashmir such observers as it might require.

Commission action

The United Nations Commission for India and Pakistan arrived in the subcontinent on 7 July 1948 and immediately engaged in consultations with the Indian and Pakistan authorities. On 20 July, the Commission asked the Secretary-General to appoint and send, if possible at once, a high-ranking officer to act as military adviser to the Commission, and further to appoint officers and necessary personnel who would be ready to travel to the Indian subcontinent at a moment's notice

in order to supervise the cease-fire if and when it was reached.[2]

UNCIP mission

After undertaking a survey of the situation in the area, UNCIP unanimously adopted a resolution on 13 August,[3] proposing to India and Pakistan that their respective high commands order a cease-fire and refrain from reinforcing the troops under their control in Kashmir. The resolution provided for the appointment by the Commission of military observers who, under the Commission's authority and with the cooperation of both commands, would supervise the observance of the cease-fire order. It also proposed to the Governments that they accept certain principles as a basis for the formulation of a truce agreement, and stated that UNCIP would have observers stationed where it deemed necessary.

C. Supervision of the cease-fire, 1948–1965

Military adviser

On 19 November 1948, the Commission received an urgent communication[4] from the Minister for Foreign Affairs of Pakistan concerning alleged reinforcements of the Indian troops in Kashmir and attacks by those troops against positions held by forces of the Azad (Free) Kashmir movement. There was immediate need for an independent source of information on the military situation in the State, and UNCIP recommended urgently that a military adviser be appointed and proceed forthwith to the subcontinent. It further requested the Secretary-General to provide an adequate number of military observers to assist the adviser. On 11 December 1948, UNCIP submitted to India and Pakistan some new proposals[5] for the holding of a plebiscite in Kashmir upon the signing of a truce agreement, which were accepted by the two Governments.[6] On 1 January 1949, both Governments announced their agreement to order a cease-fire effective one minute before midnight, local time, on that day.[7]

Arrival of observers

The Secretary-General appointed Lieutenant-General Maurice Delvoie (Belgium) as Military Ad-

viser to the Commission. General Delvoie arrived in the mission area on 2 January 1949. On 15 January, the Indian and Pakistan high commands conferred in New Delhi and formalized the cease-fire in Kashmir. The UNCIP Military Adviser, who was invited to join the conference, presented to them a plan for the organization and deployment of the military observers in the area.[8] This plan was put into effect on the Pakistan side on 3 February, and on the Indian side on 10 February 1949. A first group of seven United Nations military observers had arrived on 24 January. Their number was increased to 20 in early February. These observers, under the command of the Military Adviser, formed the nucleus of UNMOGIP.

Observers' tasks

In accordance with the Military Adviser's plan, the observers were divided into two groups, one attached to each army. The senior officer of each group established a "control headquarters" under the direct command of the Military Adviser and in close liaison with the commander of the

[2]S/1100, annex 25. [3]S/995, section 1. [4]S/1196, annex 1. [5]S/1196, annex 3. [6]S/1196, annexes 4 and 5. [7]S/1196, annex 6. [8]S/1430, annex 47.

operations theatre on his side. Each group was divided into teams of two observers, attached to the tactical formations in the field and directly responsible to the control headquarters. The control headquarters on the Pakistan side was located at Rawalpindi. The one on the Indian side was first established at Jammu; later, at the end of March, it was transferred to Srinagar.

The tasks of the observers, as defined by the Military Adviser, were to accompany the local authorities in their investigations, gather as much information as possible, and report as completely, accurately and impartially as possible to the observer in charge of the group.

Any direct intervention by the observers between the opposing parties or any interference in the armies' orders were to be avoided. The local commanders might bring alleged violations of the cease-fire by the other side to the attention of the observers for their action. These arrangements remained in effect until the conclusion of the Karachi Agreement.

The administrative arrangements laid down for the UNMOGIP observers and the general principles under which they function are the same as those for the United Nations Truce Supervision Organization (UNTSO) [see chapter 2].

Plebiscite Administrator

With the entering into force of the cease-fire, the situation became quieter. After a brief visit to New York, UNCIP returned to the subcontinent on 4 February 1949 and resumed negotiations with the parties towards the full implementation of Security Council resolution 47 (1948). Earlier in the year, Fleet Admiral Chester W. Nimitz (United States) had been appointed by the Secretary-General, in consultation with the two parties and with UNCIP, as United Nations Plebiscite Administrator.

Supervision of the Karachi Agreement

On 18 July 1949, military representatives of the two Governments met at Karachi under the auspices of UNCIP, and on 27 July they signed an Agreement establishing a cease-fire line.[9] The Agreement specified that UNCIP would station observers where it deemed necessary, and that the cease-fire line would be verified mutually on the ground by local commanders on each side with the assistance of the United Nations military observers. Disagreements were to be referred to the Commission's Military Adviser, whose decision

would be final. After verification, the Adviser would issue to each high command a map on which would be marked the definitive cease-fire line. The Agreement further set forth certain activities which were prohibited on either side of the cease-fire line, such as the strengthening of defences or the increase of forces in certain areas, as well as the introduction of additional military potential into Kashmir.

Listing of cease-fire breaches

Interpretations of the Agreement were agreed upon during the demarcation of the cease-fire line on the ground and during the resulting adjustment of forward positions by both armies. An agreed list of acts to be considered as breaches of the cease-fire was established by the Military Adviser on 16 September 1949.

This list was later revised with the agreement of the parties and, in its final form,[10] encompassed six categories of activity, namely: (1) crossing of the cease-fire line, (2) firing and use of explosives within five miles of the line, (3) new wiring and mining of any positions, (4) reinforcing existing forward defended localities with men or warlike stores, (5) forward movement from outside Kashmir of any warlike stores, equipment and personnel, except for relief and maintenance, and (6) flying of aircraft over the other side's territory.

While the Karachi Agreement established a cease-fire line in Kashmir, it did not include the working boundary between Pakistan and that State, which runs in a general easterly direction from the southern extremity of the cease-fire line at Manawar. In this connection, the Chief Military Observer agreed on 11 February 1950, at the request of both parties, that the UNMOGIP observers would investigate all incidents on the boundary between Pakistan and Kashmir reported to them by both armies, solely for the purpose of determining whether or not military forces from either side were involved.

UNCIP report to the Security Council

In September 1949, UNCIP decided to return to New York to report to the Security Council. In a press statement[11] issued on 22 September on this subject, the Commission recalled that Security Council resolution 47 (1948) of 21 April 1948 envisaged three related but distinct steps: a cease-

[9]S/1430, annex 26. [10]S/6888. [11]S/1430, annex 41.

fire, a truce period during which the withdrawal of forces would take place and, finally, consultations to establish the conditions by means of which the free will of the people of Kashmir would be expressed. The first objective had been achieved but, despite the Commission's efforts, no agreement could be secured on the other two.

Concluding that the possibilities of its mediation had been exhausted, UNCIP decided to return to New York. However, it reaffirmed its belief that a peaceful solution of the problem of Kashmir could be reached, and expressed the hope that its report to the Council would further this purpose.

Termination of UNCIP

Before leaving the subcontinent, the Chairman of the Commission, on 19 September, addressed letters to the two Governments informing them of the above decision. In so doing, he stressed that the Military Adviser and the military observers would remain and pursue their normal activities.[12]

On 17 December 1949, following the Commission's return to New York, the Security Council decided to request the Council President, General A.G.L. McNaughton (Canada), to meet informally with the representatives of India and Pakistan and examine with them the possibility of finding a mutually satisfactory basis for dealing with the Kashmir problem. On 14 March 1950, after examining the reports of UNCIP and of General McNaughton, the Council adopted resolution 80 (1950), by which it decided to terminate the United Nations Commission for India and Pakistan.

Appointment of a United Nations representative

At the same time, the Security Council decided to appoint a United Nations representative who was to exercise all of the powers and responsibilities devolving upon UNCIP. Sir Owen Dixon (Australia) was appointed by the Council as United Nations Representative for India and Pakistan. A Chief Military Observer, Brigadier H.H. Angle (Canada), was appointed by the Secretary-General as head of UNMOGIP.

Continuance of UNMOGIP

By resolution 91 (1951) of 30 March 1951, the Security Council decided that UNMOGIP should continue to supervise the cease-fire in Kashmir, and requested the two Governments to ensure that their agreement regarding the cease-fire would continue to be faithfully observed. The United Nations Representative (at the time, Mr. Frank P. Graham (United States), who had succeeded Sir Owen Dixon) subsequently pointed out, in his report[13] of 15 October 1951, that the debate in the Security Council leading to the adoption of resolution 91 (1951) had indicated that it was the Council's intention that the Representative should deal only with the question of the demilitarization of Kashmir. The Representative was therefore not concerned with the existing arrangements for the supervision of the cease-fire, the responsibility for which the Council had placed with UNMOGIP.

Since that time, UNMOGIP has functioned as an autonomous operation, directed by the Chief Military Observer under the authority of the Secretary-General. Its headquarters alternates between Srinagar in summer (May to October) and Rawalpindi in winter. An operational staff office is maintained in one of those two cities when it is not hosting the headquarters. The supervision of the cease-fire in the field is carried out by a number of field observation teams stationed on both sides of the cease-fire line and also along the working boundary between Pakistan and Jammu.

Between 1949 and 1964, the number of military observers fluctuated between 35 and 67, according to need. Just before the outbreak of the hostilities of 1965, there were 45 observers, provided by 10 countries: Australia, Belgium, Canada, Chile, Denmark, Finland, Italy, New Zealand, Sweden and Uruguay.

Brigadier Angle served as Chief Military Observer until his death in an air crash in Kashmir in July 1950. Two other UNMOGIP military personnel and one civilian staff member were also among those killed in that crash. Brigadier Angle was later succeeded as Chief Military Observer by Lieutenant-General Robert H. Nimmo (Australia). Like the UNCIP Military Adviser, the Chief Military Observer of UNMOGIP, during the initial years, had the status of an observer, and continued to receive his military salary from his Government. In 1959, General Nimmo was given an appointment as an official of the United Nations Secretariat with the rank of Assistant Secretary-General. This administrative arrangement, which had also been applied to the Chief of Staff of UNTSO, was to become the general rule for all heads of United Nations peace-keeping operations.

[12] S/1430, annex 40. [13] S/2375.

Role and activities of UNMOGIP

With the conclusion of the Karachi Agreement in 1949, the situation along the cease-fire line became more stable. Incidents took place from time to time, but they were generally minor and were dealt with in accordance with the provisions of the Agreement. This situation continued until 1965.

The role and activities of UNMOGIP were described by the Secretary-General in a report[14] dated 3 September 1965 in this manner:

> The United Nations maintains UNMOGIP with its 45 observers along the CFL [cease-fire line] of almost 500 miles, about half of which is in high mountains and is very difficult of access. UNMOGIP exercises the quite limited function of observing and reporting, investigating complaints from either party of violations of the CFL and the cease-fire and submitting the resultant findings on those investigations to each party and to the Secretary-General, and keeping the Secretary-General informed in general on the way in which the cease-fire agreement is being kept. Because the role of UNMOGIP appears frequently to be misunderstood, it bears emphasis that the operation has no authority or function entitling it to enforce or prevent anything, or to try to ensure that the cease-fire is respected. Its very presence in the area, of course, has acted to some extent as a deterrent, but this is not the case at present. The Secretary-General exercises responsibility for the supervision and administrative control of the UNMOGIP operation.

D. The hostilities of 1965 and the establishment of UNIPOM

Background

In early 1965, relations between India and Pakistan were strained again because of their conflicting claims over the Rann of Kutch at the southern end of the international boundary.

The situation steadily deteriorated during the summer of 1965, and, in August, military hostilities between India and Pakistan erupted on a large scale along the cease-fire line in Kashmir. In his report[15] of 3 September 1965, the Secretary-General stressed that the cease-fire agreement of 27 July 1949 had collapsed and that a return to mutual observance of it by India and Pakistan would afford the most favourable climate in which to seek a resolution of political differences.

Security Council action for a cease-fire

On 4 September 1965, the Security Council, by resolution 209 (1965), called for a cease-fire and asked the two Governments to cooperate fully with UNMOGIP in its task of supervising the observance of the cease-fire. Two days later, the Council adopted resolution 210 (1965), by which it requested the Secretary-General "to exert every possible effort to give effect to the present resolution and to resolution 209 (1965), to take all measures possible to strengthen the United Nations Military Observer Group in India and Pakistan, and to keep the Council promptly and currently informed on the implementation of the resolutions and on the situation in the area".

From 7 to 16 September, the Secretary-General visited the subcontinent in pursuit of the mandate given to him by the Security Council. In his report[16] of 16 September to the Council, he noted that both sides had expressed their desire for a cessation of hostilities, but that each side had posed conditions which made the acceptance of a cease-fire very difficult for the other. In those circumstances, the Secretary-General suggested that the Security Council might take a number of steps: first, it might order the two Governments, pursuant to Article 40 of the United Nations Charter,[17] to desist from further military action; second, it

---

[14]S/6651. [15]Ibid. [16]S/6686. [17]In order to prevent an aggravation of a situation, the Security Council, under Article 40 of the Charter, before making recommendations or deciding on measures to be taken, may call upon the parties concerned to comply with provisional measures it deems necessary or desirable, without prejudice to the rights, claims or position of those parties.

might consider what assistance it could provide in ensuring the observance of the cease-fire and the withdrawal of all military personnel by both sides; and, third, it could request the two Heads of Government to meet in a country friendly to both in order to discuss the situation and the problems underlying it, as a first step in resolving the outstanding differences between their two countries.

On 20 September, after the hostilities had spread to the international border between India and West Pakistan, the Council adopted resolution 211 (1965), by which it demanded that a cease-fire take effect at 0700 hours GMT on 22 September 1965 and called for a subsequent withdrawal of all armed personnel to the positions held before 5 August. The Council also requested the Secretary-General to provide the necessary assistance to ensure supervision of the cease-fire and the withdrawal of all armed personnel.

Establishment of UNIPOM

In Kashmir, the supervision called for by the Security Council was exercised by the established machinery of UNMOGIP. For this purpose, its observer strength was increased to a total of 102 from the same contributing countries as before.

Since the hostilities extended beyond the Kashmir cease-fire line, the Secretary-General decided to set up an administrative adjunct of UNMOGIP, the United Nations India-Pakistan Observation Mission (UNIPOM), as a temporary measure for the sole purpose of supervising the cease-fire along the India-Pakistan border outside the State of Jammu and Kashmir.[18]

The function of UNIPOM was primarily to observe and report on breaches of the cease-fire as called for by the Security Council. In cases of breaches, the observers were to do all they could to persuade the local commanders to restore the cease-fire, but they had no authority or power to order a cessation of firing. Ninety observers from 10 countries — Brazil, Burma, Canada, Ceylon, Ethiopia, Ireland, Nepal, the Netherlands, Nigeria and Venezuela — were assigned to UNIPOM.

The Mission was closely coordinated both administratively and operationally with UNMOGIP. The Chief Military Observer of UNMOGIP, General Nimmo, was initially also placed in charge of UNIPOM. After the arrival of the newly appointed Chief Officer of UNIPOM, Major-General B.F. Macdonald (Canada) in October 1965, General Nimmo was asked by the Secretary-General to exercise oversight functions with regard to both operations.

Further Security Council action

On 27 September 1965, after learning that the cease-fire was not holding, the Security Council adopted resolution 214 (1965), by which it demanded that the parties urgently honour their commitments to the Council to observe the cease-fire, and called upon them to withdraw all armed personnel as necessary steps in the full implementation of resolution 211 (1965).

As cease-fire violations continued to occur and there were no prospects for the withdrawal of troops, the Security Council met again in November and adopted resolution 215 (1965) of 5 November. By this decision, the Council called upon the Governments of India and Pakistan to instruct their armed personnel to cooperate with the United Nations and cease all military activity.

The Security Council further demanded the prompt and unconditional execution of the proposal already agreed to in principle by India and Pakistan that their representatives meet with a representative of the Secretary-General to formulate an agreed plan and schedule of withdrawals. In this connection, the Secretary-General, after consultation with the parties, appointed Brigadier-General Tulio Marambio (Chile) as his representative on withdrawals.

On 15 December, the Secretary-General reported[19] that the two parties directly involved, India and Pakistan, had informed him of their desire that the United Nations should continue its observer function after 22 December 1965, which was the end of the first three months of the cease-fire demanded by the Security Council in its resolution 211 (1965) of 20 September 1965.

In the circumstances, the Secretary-General indicated his intention to continue the United Nations activities relating to the cease-fire and withdrawal provisions of the resolution by continuing UNIPOM for a second period of three months and maintaining the added strength of the Military Observer Group.

Tashkent agreement

On 10 January 1966, the Prime Minister of India and the President of Pakistan, who had met in Tashkent at the invitation of the Chairman of the Council of Ministers of the Soviet Union, announced their agreement that the withdrawal of all armed personnel of both sides to the positions they had held prior to 5 August 1965 should be

[18]S/6699/Add.3. [19]S/6699/Add.11.

completed by 25 February 1966 and that both sides should observe the terms of the cease-fire on the cease-fire line.[20]

Withdrawal plan

The principles of a plan and schedule of withdrawals were subsequently agreed upon by military representatives of India and Pakistan, who had held meetings for that purpose since 3 January 1966 at Lahore and Amritsar under the auspices of General Marambio, the Secretary-General's representative on withdrawals. The plan for disengagement and withdrawal was agreed upon by the military commanders of the Indian and Pakistan armies in New Delhi on 22 January.[21]

At a joint meeting on 25 January, under the auspices of the Secretary-General's representative, the parties agreed upon the ground rules for the implementation of the disengagement and withdrawal plan.[22] The plan was to be implemented in two stages and the good offices of UNMOGIP and UNIPOM were to be requested to ensure that the action agreed upon was fully implemented. In the event of disagreement between the parties, the decision of General Marambio would be final and binding on both sides. The good offices of UNMOGIP and UNIPOM were similarly requested for the implementation of the second stage of the agreement, as were the good offices of the Secretary-General's representative with regard to withdrawals of troops.

Termination of UNIPOM

On 26 February 1966, the Secretary-General reported[23] that the withdrawal of the troops by India and Pakistan had been completed on schedule on 25 February, and that the withdrawal provisions of the Security Council's resolutions had thus been fulfilled by the two parties. With regard to withdrawals, the responsibilities of the Secretary-General's representative came to an end on 28 February, and his mission ceased on that date. As planned, UNIPOM was terminated on 22 March 1966 and the 59 additional observers appointed in September 1965 to the Military Observer Group were gradually withdrawn. By the end of March 1966, the strength of UNMOGIP was reduced to 45 observers, drawn from the same 10 contributing countries. From that date until December 1971, UNMOGIP functioned on the basis of the Karachi Agreement in much the same way as it had before September 1965.

E. Hostilities of 1971 and their aftermath

At the end of 1971, hostilities broke out again between the forces of India and Pakistan. They started along the borders of East Pakistan and were related to the movement for independence which had developed in that region and which ultimately led to the creation of Bangladesh.

Secretary-General's actions

When tension was mounting in the summer of 1971, Secretary-General U Thant, invoking his responsibilities under the broad terms of Article 99[24] of the United Nations Charter, submitted a memorandum[25] to the Security Council on 20 July in which he drew attention to the deteriorating situation in the subcontinent and informed the Council of the action he had taken in the humanitarian field.

On 20 October, the Secretary-General sent identical messages[26] to the heads of the Governments of India and Pakistan expressing increasing anxiety over the situation and offering his good offices with a view to avoiding any development that might lead to disaster. In these messages, he recalled the efforts of the Chief Military Observer of UNMOGIP to ease tension and prevent military escalation along the cease-fire line in Kashmir.

In early December, after the outbreak of hostilities, the Secretary-General submitted a series of reports[27] to the Security Council on the situation along the cease-fire line in Kashmir, based on information received from the Chief Military Observer. The reports showed that from 20 October onwards both India and Pakistan had greatly reinforced their forces along the cease-fire line. Both sides admitted that violations of the Karachi Agreement were being committed by them, but

---

[20]S/7221. [21]S/6719/Add.5, annex. [22]Ibid. [23]S/6179/Add.6. [24]Article 99 of the Charter states: "The Secretary-General may bring to the attention of the Security Council any matter which in his opinion may threaten the maintenance of international peace and security." [25]S/10410. [26]Ibid. [27]S/10412 and Add.1,2.

they continued to use the machinery of UNMOGIP to prevent escalation. However, on 3 December, hostilities broke out along the cease-fire line, with exchanges of artillery and small-arms fire and air attacks by both sides. The Secretary-General pointed out that he could not report on military developments in other parts of the subcontinent since the United Nations had no observation machinery outside Kashmir.

General Assembly resolution

On 4 December, the Security Council met to consider the situation in the subcontinent, but it could not reach agreement and decided two days later to refer the matter to the General Assembly. On 7 December, the Assembly considered the question referred to it and adopted resolution 2793 (XXVI), calling upon India and Pakistan to take forthwith all measures for an immediate cease-fire and withdrawal of their armed forces to their respective territories.

Between 7 and 18 December, the Secretary-General submitted another series of reports[28] on the situation along the cease-fire line in Kashmir. Fighting continued, with varying intensity, until 17 December, 1930 hours local time, when a cease-fire announced by the two Governments went into effect. By that time, a number of positions on both sides of the 1949 cease-fire line had changed hands.

Security Council action

The Security Council met again on 12 December, and, on 21 December, adopted resolution 307 (1971), by which it demanded that a durable cease-fire in all areas of conflict remain in effect until all armed forces had withdrawn to their respective territories and to positions which fully respected the cease-fire line in Kashmir supervised by UNMOGIP.

Following the adoption of this resolution, the representative of India stated that Kashmir was an integral part of India. In order to avoid bloodshed, he added, his Government had respected the cease-fire line supervised by UNMOGIP, but there was a need to make some adjustments in that line and India intended to discuss and settle this matter directly with Pakistan. The representative of Pakistan insisted that Kashmir was disputed territory whose status should be settled by agreement under the aegis of the Security Council.

Reports on the cease-fire

Subsequent reports[29] of the Secretary-General indicated that following a period of relative quiet, complaints of violations of the cease-fire were received by the Chief Military Observer of UNMOGIP in late January from the military commands of both sides. The Secretary-General observed that, pending the withdrawals of the armed forces, the cease-fire under Security Council resolution 307 (1971) must be regarded, for the time being and for practical purposes, as a simple cease-fire requiring the parties to refrain from any firing or forward movement along the lines where the respective armies were in actual control at the time the cease-fire had come into effect on 17 December.

In order to report to the Secretary-General on the observance of the cease-fire, the observers needed the cooperation of the parties and freedom of movement and access along the lines of control, but these conditions were not met. In this connection, the Secretary-General remarked, discussions aimed at securing the cooperation of the parties had been satisfactorily completed with Pakistan but were still continuing with the Indian military authorities.

Functioning of UNMOGIP

On 12 May 1972, the Secretary-General reported[30] to the Security Council that, while the Pakistan military authorities continued to submit to UNMOGIP complaints of cease-fire violations by the other side, the Indian military authorities had stopped doing so. The situation concerning the functioning of UNMOGIP remained unchanged and, as a result, the Secretary-General could not keep the Council fully informed of developments relating to the observance of the cease-fire. The Secretary-General expressed the hope that, in keeping with the demand of the Security Council, the cease-fire would be strictly observed and that both sides would take effective measures to ensure that there was no recurrence of fighting. He noted in this connection that the UNMOGIP machinery continued to be available to the parties, if desired.

On the same day, India informed[31] the Secretary-General that its efforts to open direct negotiations with Pakistan had made some progress; it hoped the talks between the two countries would take place at the highest level as early as possible in a positive and constructive spirit, with

[28]S/10432 and Add.1-11. [29]S/10467 and Add.1-3. [30]S/10467/Add.4. [31]S/10648.

UNMOGIP deployment as of May 1996

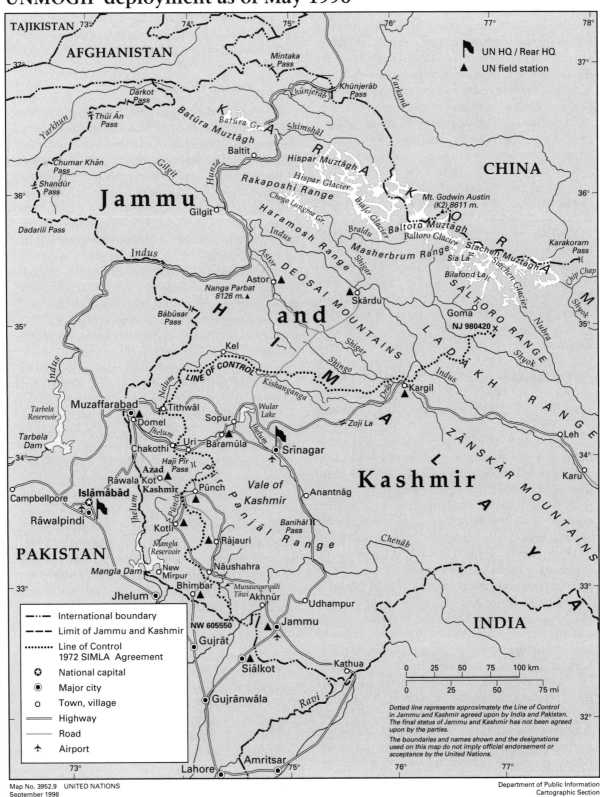

UN HQ / Rear HQ

▲ UN field station

International boundary

Limit of Jammu and Kashmir

Line of Control
1972 SIMLA Agreement

National capital

Major city

Town, village

Highway

Road

✈ Airport

Dotted line represents approximately the Line of Control
in Jammu and Kashmir agreed upon by India and Pakistan.
The final status of Jammu and Kashmir has not been agreed
upon by the parties.

The boundaries and names shown and the designations
used on this map do not imply official endorsement or
acceptance by the United Nations.

Map No. 3952.9   UNITED NATIONS
September 1996

Department of Public Information
Cartographic Section

a view to achieving durable peace in the subcontinent. India also indicated that many incidents had been satisfactorily settled at flag meetings between local commanders. India had refrained from sending to the Secretary-General lists of cease-fire violations by Pakistan in the firm belief that if Pakistan was indeed ready and willing to settle differences and disputes between the two countries in a truly friendly and cooperative spirit, direct negotiations provided the best means.

During May and June, Pakistan brought to the Secretary-General's attention long lists of alleged cease-fire violations by India in Kashmir and other sectors. In a letter[32] dated 5 June, Pakistan stated that there were no flag meetings between Pakistan and Indian military commanders with regard to incidents along the cease-fire line in Kashmir, although such meetings had been held for incidents along the working boundary between Jammu and Pakistan. It was clear that incidents along the cease-fire line should be investigated by UNMOGIP observers, and flag meetings held under the auspices of UNMOGIP, since both the 1949 Karachi Agreement and Security Council resolution 307 (1971) prescribed UNMOGIP's responsibilities in this regard. It was therefore the view of the Pakistan Government that the activation of the machinery of UNMOGIP on the Indian side of the cease-fire line in Kashmir would serve to prevent incidents.

India took a different position. As a result of the war, the Karachi Agreement of 1949 had, in India's view, ceased to be operative and the mandate of UNMOGIP had lapsed, since it had related specifically to the supervision of the cease-fire line under that Agreement and did not extend to the actual line of control that had come into existence in December 1971. India noted that there was no formal agreement on the location of that line or on the machinery for the maintenance of a durable cease-fire on all fronts.

In July 1972, the Prime Minister of India and the President of Pakistan agreed at Simla in India to define a Line of Control in Kashmir. The Line of Control was agreed by both parties in December 1972 and delineated on the ground by the representatives of the two armies. It followed, with minor deviations, the same course as the cease-fire line established in the Karachi Agreement of 1949. However, the positions of India and Pakistan on the functioning of UNMOGIP remained unchanged.

Financial aspects

Like UNTSO, UNMOGIP is financed from the regular budget of the United Nations. From the inception of its operation until December 1995, UNMOGIP's total expenditures were approximately $98,399,102.

Present situation

Given the disagreement between the two parties about UNMOGIP's mandate and functions, the Secretary-General's position has been that UNMOGIP can only be terminated by a decision of the Security Council. In the absence of such a decision, UNMOGIP has been maintained with the same administrative arrangements. Its task is to observe, to the extent possible, developments pertaining to the strict observance of the cease-fire of 17 December 1971 and to report thereon to the Secretary-General. The military authorities of Pakistan have continued to lodge with UNMOGIP complaints about cease-fire violations. UNMOGIP undertakes investigations of those complaints. The military authorities of India have lodged no complaints since January 1972 and have restricted the activities of the United Nations observers on the Indian side of the Line of Control. They have, however, continued to provide accommodation, transport and other facilities to UNMOGIP. The Observer Group's headquarters has continued to alternate between Rawalpindi and Srinagar.

As of 31 March 1996, UNMOGIP included 44 observers from eight contributing countries: Belgium, Chile, Denmark, Finland, Italy, Republic of Korea, Sweden and Uruguay. The Chief Military Observer was Major-General Alfonso Pessolano (Italy) who began his service in December 1994. He was preceded in that position by, from the inception of the Mission: Brigadier H.H. Angle (Canada) from November 1949 to July 1950; Colonel Siegfried Coblentz (United States) (Acting) from July to October 1950; Lieutenant-General R.H. Nimmo (Australia) from October 1950 to January 1966; Colonel J.H.J. Gauthier (Canada) (Acting) from January to July 1966; Lieutenant-General Luis Tassara-Gonzalez (Chile) from July 1966 to June 1977; Lieutenant-Colonel P. Bergevin (Canada) (Acting) from June 1977 to April 1978; Colonel P.P. Pospisil (Canada) (Acting) from April to June 1978; Brigadier-General Stig Waldenstrom (Swe-

[32]S/10681.

den) from June 1978 to June 1982; Brigadier-General Thor Johnsen (Norway) from June 1982 to May 1986; Lieutenant-Colonel G. Beltracchi (Italy) (Acting) from May to July 1986; Brigadier-General Alf Hammer (Norway) from August 1986 to August 1987; Lieutenant-Colonel G. Beltracchi (Italy) (Acting) from August to September 1987; Brigadier-General James Parker (Ireland) from September 1987 to May 1989; Lieutenant-Colonel Mario Fiorese (Italy) (Acting) from May to June 1989; Brigadier-General Jeremiah Enright (Ireland) from June 1989 to June 1992; and Major-General Ricardo Jorge Galarza-Chans (Uruguay) from June 1992 to December 1994.

Part IV
Cyprus

Chapter 9

United Nations Peace-keeping Force in Cyprus (UNFICYP)

Chapter 9

United Nations Peace-keeping Force in Cyprus (UNFICYP)

A. Background

The Constitution

The Republic of Cyprus became an independent State on 16 August 1960, and a Member of the United Nations one month later. The Constitution of the Republic, which came into effect on the day of independence, had its roots in agreements reached between the heads of Government of Greece and Turkey at Zurich on 11 February 1959. These were incorporated in agreements reached between those Governments and the United Kingdom in London on 19 February. On the same day, the representatives of the Greek Cypriot and Turkish Cypriot communities accepted the documents concerned, and accompanying declarations by the three Governments, as "the agreed foundation for the final settlement of the problem of Cyprus". The agreements were embodied in treaties — the Treaty of Establishment and the Treaty of Guarantee, signed by Cyprus, Greece, Turkey and the United Kingdom, and the Treaty of Alliance, signed by Cyprus, Greece and Turkey — and in the Constitution, signed in Nicosia on 16 August 1960.

The settlement of 1959 envisaged Cyprus becoming a republic with a regime specially adapted both to the ethnic composition of its population (approximately 80 per cent Greek Cypriot and 18 per cent Turkish Cypriot) and to what were recognized as special relationships between the Republic and the three other States concerned in the agreements. Thus, the agreements recognized a distinction between the two communities and sought to maintain a certain balance between their respective rights and interests. Greece, Turkey and the United Kingdom provided a multilateral guarantee of the basic articles of the Constitution. In the event of a breach of the Treaty of Guarantee, the three Powers undertook to consult on concerted action, and, if this proved impossible, each of them reserved the right to take action "with the sole aim of re-establishing the

state of affairs" set out in the Treaty. Both the union of Cyprus with any other State and the partitioning of the island were expressly forbidden. The settlement also permitted the United Kingdom to retain sovereignty over two areas to be maintained as military bases, these areas being in fact excluded from the territory of the Republic of Cyprus.

The Constitution assured the participation of each community in the exercise of the functions of the Government, while seeking in a number of matters to avoid supremacy on the part of the larger community and assuring also partial administrative autonomy to each community. Under the Constitution, the President, a Greek Cypriot, and the Vice-President, a Turkish Cypriot, were elected by their respective communities, and they designated separately the members of the Council of Ministers, comprising seven Greek Cypriots and three Turkish Cypriots. The agreement of the President and Vice-President was required for certain decisions and appointments, and they had veto rights, separately or jointly, in respect of certain types of legislation, including foreign affairs. Human rights and fundamental freedoms, as well as the supremacy of the Constitution, were guaranteed.

The application of the provisions of the Constitution encountered difficulties almost from the birth of the Republic and led to a succession of constitutional crises and to accumulating tension between the leaders of the two communities.

On 30 November 1963, the President of the Republic, Archbishop Makarios, publicly set forth 13 points on which he considered that the Constitution should be amended. He did so on the stated grounds that the existing Constitution created many difficulties in the smooth functioning of the State and the development and progress of the country, that its many *sui generis* provisions conflicted with internationally accepted democratic principles and created sources of friction between

Greek and Turkish Cypriots, and that its effects were causing the two communities to draw further apart rather than closer together.

The President's proposals would have, among other things, abolished the veto power of the President and the Vice-President, while having the latter deputize for the President in his absence. The Greek Cypriot President of the House of Representatives and the Turkish Cypriot Vice-President would have been elected by the House as a whole and not, as under the Constitution, separately by its Greek and Turkish members. The constitutional provisions regarding separate majorities for enactment of certain laws by the House of Representatives would have been abolished, unified municipalities established, and the administration of justice and the security forces unified. The proportion of Turkish Cypriots in the public service and the military forces would have been reduced, and the Greek Cypriot Communal Chamber abolished, though the Turkish community would have been able to retain its Chamber.

No immediate response was forthcoming from the Vice-President to this proposed programme, but the Turkish Government, to which the President's proposals had been communicated "for information purposes", rejected them promptly and categorically. Subsequently, the Turkish Cypriot Communal Chamber described the President's claim that the Constitution had proved an obstacle to the smooth functioning of the Republic as "false propaganda" and contended that the Greek Cypriots had never attempted to implement the Constitution in good faith. The Turkish Cypriots maintained that the structure of the Republic rested on the existence of two communities and not of a majority and a minority. They refused to consider the amendments proposed by the other side, which were in their opinion designed to weaken those parts which recognized the existence of the Turkish Cypriot community as such.

Whatever possibility might have existed at the time for calm and rational discussion of the President's proposals between the two communities disappeared indefinitely with the outbreak of violent disturbances between them a few days later, on 21 December 1963.

In the afternoon of 24 December 1963, the Turkish national contingent, stationed in Cyprus under the Treaty of Alliance and numbering 650 officers and other ranks, left its camp and took up positions at the northern outskirts of Nicosia in the area where disturbances were taking place. On 25 December, the Cyprus Government charged

that Turkish warplanes had flown at tree-level over Cyprus, and during the next several days there were persistent reports of military concentrations along the southern coast of Turkey and of Turkish naval movements off that coast.

Mission of the personal representative

In the face of the outbreak of intercommunal strife, the Governments of the United Kingdom, Greece and Turkey, on 24 December 1963, offered their joint good offices to the Government of Cyprus, and on 25 December they informed that Government, "including both the Greek and Turkish elements", of their readiness to assist, if invited to do so, in restoring peace and order by means of a joint peacemaking force under British command, composed of forces of the three Governments already stationed in Cyprus under the Treaties of Alliance and Establishment. This offer having been accepted by the Cyprus Government, the joint force was established on 26 December, a cease-fire was arranged on 29 December, and on 30 December it was agreed to create a neutral zone along the cease-fire line ("green line") between the areas occupied by the two communities in Nicosia. That zone was to be patrolled by the joint peacemaking force, but in practice the task was carried out almost exclusively by its British contingent. It was further agreed that a conference of representatives of the Governments of the United Kingdom, Greece and Turkey and of the two communities of Cyprus would be convened in London in January 1964. These arrangements were reported to the Security Council in a letter dated 8 January from the Permanent Representative of the United Kingdom to the United Nations.[1]

Meanwhile, on 26 December 1963, the Permanent Representative of Cyprus requested[2] an urgent meeting of the Security Council to consider his Government's complaint against Turkey. The meeting was held on 27 December. The Secretary-General met with the Permanent Representative of Cyprus to explore the best way in which the United Nations could assist in restoring quiet in the country. The representative of Cyprus, as well as the representatives of Greece, Turkey and the United Kingdom, requested the Secretary-General to appoint a personal representative to observe the peacemaking operation in Cyprus.

After consultations, during which agreement was reached with all concerned regarding the

[1] S/5508. [2] S/5488.

functions of the representative, the Secretary-General, on 17 January 1964, appointed Lieutenant-General P.S. Gyani (India) as his personal representative and observer, to go to Cyprus initially until the end of February. The Secretary-General stated that his function would be to observe the progress of the peacemaking operation. General Gyani was to report to the Secretary-General on how the United Nations observer could function and be most effective in fulfilling the task as outlined in the request made by the Government of Cyprus and agreed to by the Governments of Greece, Turkey and the United Kingdom. General Gyani's mandate was later extended until the end of March.

The London Conference, which met on 15 January 1964, failed to reach agreement, and proposals to strengthen the international peacemaking force were rejected by the Government of Cyprus, which insisted that any such force be placed under the control of the United Nations. From Nicosia, General Gyani reported a rapid and grave deterioration of the situation, involving scattered intercommunal fighting with heavy casualties, kidnappings and the taking of hostages (many of whom were killed), unbridled activities by irregular forces, separation of the members of the two communities, and disintegration of the machinery of government, as well as fears of military intervention by Turkey or Greece. The British peacemaking force was encountering increasing difficulties. While Gyani's presence had been helpful in a number of instances, attention was turning increasingly to the possibility of establishing a United Nations peace-keeping operation.

B. Establishment of the United Nations operation

Creation of the Force

On 15 February, the representatives of the United Kingdom and of Cyprus requested[3] urgent action by the Security Council. On the same day, the Secretary-General appealed[4] to all concerned for restraint. He was already engaged in intensive consultations with all the parties about the functions and organization of a United Nations force, and, on 4 March, the Security Council unanimously adopted resolution 186 (1964), by which it noted that the situation in Cyprus was likely to threaten international peace and security, and recommended the creation of a United Nations Peace-keeping Force in Cyprus (UNFICYP), with the consent of the Government of Cyprus.

The Council also called on all Member States to refrain from any action or threat of action likely to worsen the situation in the sovereign Republic of Cyprus or to endanger international peace, asked the Government of Cyprus, which had the responsibility for the maintenance and restoration of law and order, to take all additional measures necessary to stop violence and bloodshed in Cyprus, and called upon the communities in Cyprus and their leaders to act with the utmost restraint.

As for the Force, the Council said its composition and size were to be established by the Secretary-General, in consultation with the Governments of Cyprus, Greece, Turkey and the United Kingdom. The Commander of the Force was to be appointed by the Secretary-General and report to him. The Secretary-General, who was to keep the Governments providing the Force fully informed, was to report periodically to the Security Council on its operation. The Force's function should be, in the interest of preserving international peace and security, to use its best efforts to prevent a recurrence of fighting and, as necessary, to contribute to the maintenance and restoration of law and order and a return to normal conditions. The Council recommended that the stationing of the Force should be for a period of three months, all costs pertaining to it being met, in a manner to be agreed upon by them, by the Governments providing the contingents and by the Government of Cyprus. The Secretary-General was also authorized to accept voluntary contributions for that purpose. By the resolution, the Council also recommended the designation of a Mediator to promote a peaceful solution and an agreed settlement of the Cyprus problem.

[3]S/5543, S/5545. [4]S/5554.

The Minister for Foreign Affairs of Cyprus promptly informed[5] the Secretary-General that his Government consented to the establishment of the Force.

Operational establishment of UNFICYP

On 6 March, the Secretary-General reported[6] the appointment of General Gyani as Commander of UNFICYP, and referred to his approaches to several Governments about the provision of contingents. Negotiations with prospective troop-contributing Governments encountered certain delays, relating to political as well as financial aspects of the operation.

Meanwhile, as the situation in Cyprus deteriorated further, the Secretary-General on 9 March addressed messages to the President of Cyprus and to the Foreign Ministers of Greece and Turkey, appealing for restraint and a cessation of violence. The Government of Turkey sent messages to President Makarios on 12 March, and to the Secretary-General on 13 March, stating that unless assaults on the Turkish Cypriots ceased, Turkey would act unilaterally under the Treaty of Guarantee to send a Turkish force to Cyprus until the United Nations Force, which should include Turkish units, effectively performed its functions.[7] The Secretary-General replied immediately that measures to establish the United Nations Force were under way and making progress, and he appealed[8] to Turkey to refrain from action that would worsen the situation.

At the request[9] of the representative of Cyprus, the Security Council held an emergency meeting on 13 March and adopted resolution 187 (1964). The resolution noted the Secretary-General's assurances that the Force was about to be established, called on Member States to refrain from action or threats likely to worsen the situation in Cyprus or endanger international peace, and requested the Secretary-General to press on with his efforts to implement resolution 186 (1964).

Upon the arrival of troops of the Canadian contingent on 13 March, the Secretary-General reported[10] that the Force was in being. However, it did not become established operationally until 27 March, when sufficient troops were available to it in Cyprus to enable it to discharge its functions. The three-month duration of the mandate, as defined in resolution 186 (1964), began as of that date. This development marked a new phase in the Cyprus situation. The Secretary-General noted[11] that UNFICYP was a United Nations Force, operating exclusively under the mandate given to it by the Security Council and, within that mandate, under instructions given by the Secretary-General. It was an impartial, objective body which had no responsibility for political solutions and would not try to influence them one way or another.

The Force now consisted of the Canadian and British contingents (the latter's incorporation in UNFICYP having been negotiated with the British Government), and advance parties of Swedish, Irish and Finnish contingents. The main bodies of the last-mentioned three contingents arrived in April. A Danish contingent of approximately 1,000 as well as an Austrian field hospital arrived in May, along with additional Swedish troops transferred from the United Nations Operation in the Congo. By 8 June 1964, the Force had reached a strength of 6,411. As units of the new contingents arrived, certain units of the British contingent, which had formed part of the old peacemaking force and had been taken into UNFICYP, were repatriated. UNFICYP was thus established in 1964, with military contingents from Austria, Canada, Denmark, Finland, Ireland, Sweden and the United Kingdom, and civilian police units from Australia, Austria, Denmark, New Zealand and Sweden.

Under the terms of the 1960 Treaty of Alliance, Greece was given the right to maintain an army contingent of 950 officers and men on the island, and Turkey a contingent of 650. As already noted, the Turkish contingent left its camp when the intercommunal strife broke out and was deployed in tactical positions astride the Kyrenia road north of Nicosia, where it remained until 1974. The Government of Cyprus, contending that the Turkish move was a breach of the Treaty, unilaterally abrogated it on 4 April 1964. However, both contingents remained on the island.

During the early stages of the functioning of UNFICYP, the Secretary-General proposed that the Turkish Government should either order its contingent to retire to its barracks or accept his offer to put both the Greek and Turkish national contingents under United Nations command, though not as contingents of UNFICYP. Greece accepted the latter suggestion. Turkey put forward the condition that the Force Commander, before issuing orders to the Turkish contingent for any task or movement requiring a change in its present position, must have the prior consent of the Turkish Government. As the Secretary-General consid-

---

[5]S/5578. [6]S/5579. [7]S/5596. [8]S/5600. [9]S/5598. [10]S/5593/Add.2. [11]S/5593/Add.3.

ered this condition unacceptable, the two national contingents were not placed under United Nations command.

Force Commanders

Following the retirement of General Gyani in June 1964, General K.S. Thimayya (India) was appointed Force Commander and remained in that post until his death in December 1965. Brigadier A.J. Wilson (United Kingdom) served as Acting Commander until May 1966 when Lieutenant-General I.A.E. Martola (Finland) was appointed Commander. He was succeeded by Lieutenant-General Dewan Prem Chand (India) in December 1969, Major-General J.J. Quinn (Ireland) in December 1976, Major-General Günther G. Greindl (Austria) in March 1981, Major-General Clive Milner (Canada) in April 1988, Major-General Michael F. Minehane (Ireland) in April 1992, and Brigadier-General Ahti Toimi Paavali Vartiainen (Finland) in August 1994.

Special Representatives

In his report of 29 April 1964,[12] the Secretary-General referred to the necessity of appointing a high-level political officer, and on 11 May he announced the appointment of Mr. Galo Plaza Lasso as his Special Representative in Cyprus. Mr. Plaza served until his appointment as Mediator in September. The following have subsequently served as Special Representatives of the Secretary-General: Carlos A. Bernardes (1964-1967), P.P. Spinelli (Acting) (1967), Bibiano F. Osorio-Tafall (1967-1974), Luis Weckmann-Muñoz (1974-1975), Javier Pérez de Cuéllar (1975-1977), Rémy Gorgé (Acting) (1977-1978), Reynaldo Galindo-Pohl (1978-1980), Hugo J. Gobbi (1980-1984), James Holger (Acting) (1984-1988) and Oscar Camilión (1988-1993). Throughout all these years, Special Representatives or Acting Special Representatives were resident in Cyprus. In 1993, the Secretary-General decided to appoint a senior political figure to serve as his Special Representative for Cyprus, but on a non-resident basis. Accordingly, he appointed, in May 1993, Mr. Joe Clark, the former Prime Minister of Canada, as his Special Representative. In addition, he appointed Mr. Gustave Feissel (United States) as his Deputy Special Representative, resident in Cyprus.

In August 1994, in connection with the change of command from Major-General Minehane to Brigadier-General Vartiainen, Mr. Clark became Chief of Mission. The function of Chief of Mission reflects a unified arrangement for the United Nations operation in Cyprus and includes UNFICYP. In the absence of the Special Representative, the Deputy Special Representative assumed this function.

Mr. Clark served until April 1996, when he was succeeded by Mr. Han Sung-Joo, former Foreign Minister of the Republic of Korea. Mr. Feissel continued to serve as Deputy Special Representative, resident in Cyprus, and as Chief of Mission of the United Nations Operation in Cyprus.

Mediation

On 25 March 1964, in accordance with the Security Council's recommendation in resolution 186 (1964) that the Secretary-General designate a mediator for the purpose of promoting a peaceful solution and agreed settlement of the Cyprus problem, the Secretary-General appointed Mr. Sakari S. Tuomioja, a Finnish diplomat, as Mediator. Mr. Tuomioja died on 9 September. One week later, the Secretary-General appointed Galo Plaza Lasso (Ecuador) to succeed him. After several rounds of consultations with all concerned, the Mediator in March 1965 submitted a report[13] to the Secretary-General in which he analysed the situation on the island, the positions of the parties and the considerations that would have to be taken into account in devising a settlement. On that basis, the Mediator offered observations under three headings: independence, self-determination and international peace; the structure of the State; and the protection of individual and minority rights. The Mediator recommended that the parties concerned, and in the first instance the representatives of the two communities, should meet together for discussions on the basis of his observations.

The report was commented upon favourably by the Governments of Cyprus and Greece. Turkey, however, rejected the report in its entirety and considered that Mr. Plaza's functions as a Mediator had come to an end upon its publication. Mr. Plaza resigned in December 1965, and the Secretary-General's efforts to bring about a resumption of the mediation function did not meet with success.

In these circumstances, the Secretary-General, on 4 March 1966, instructed his Special Representative in Cyprus, Mr. Carlos A. Bernardes, to employ his good offices with the parties in and outside Cyprus with a view to discussions, at any

[12]S/5671. [13]S/6253.

level, of problems of a local or a broader nature. Thereafter, the Special Representatives of the Secretary-General were engaged in a mission of good offices on his behalf, with a view to promoting an agreed settlement. In 1975, the Security Council, by resolution 367 (1975), requested the Secretary-General to undertake a new mission of good offices, a mission the Council has reaffirmed periodically in connection with the extension of the mandate of UNFICYP.

C. UNFICYP operations until 1974

Deployment and organization

When UNFICYP was established in 1964, the contingents were deployed throughout the island and an effort was made as far as possible to match their areas of responsibility (zones or districts) with the island's administrative district boundaries. This was meant to facilitate a close working relationship with Cyprus Government District Officers, and with the local Turkish Cypriot leaders.

All districts were covered according to the intensity of the armed confrontation. The capital, Nicosia, initially was manned by two UNFICYP contingents (Canadian and Finnish), organized in a single Nicosia zone under Canadian command. The districts of Kyrenia and Lefka were manned by one contingent each. The remaining two contingents covered the districts of Larnaca, Limassol and Paphos.

Over the years, there have been numerous redeployments of UNFICYP contingents to secure better use of available troops in relation to the requirements of the mandate and to cover any new areas of tension.

In Nicosia, UNFICYP troops were positioned for an observation role along the length of the "green line". In two other districts, Kyrenia and Lefka, United Nations posts were deployed between the two defence lines; observation and patrolling took place from those posts. On the rest of the island, UNFICYP troops were generally deployed in areas where confrontation was likely to arise, and they were so positioned as to enable them to interpose themselves between the opposing sides in areas of tension and wherever incidents might cause a recurrence of fighting. Observation squads, backed by mobile patrols, were regularly deployed into areas that were likely to be potential areas of trouble.

Guiding principles for UNFICYP

On the basis of the experience gained during the first six months of operation of the Force, guiding principles, which remain in effect to this day, were summarized by the Secretary-General in his report[14] of 10 September 1964, as follows:

The Force is under the exclusive control and command of the United Nations at all times. The Commander of the Force is appointed by and responsible exclusively to the Secretary-General. The contingents comprising the Force are integral parts of it and take their orders exclusively from the Force Commander.

The Force undertakes no functions which are not consistent with the provisions of the Security Council's resolution of 4 March 1964. The troops of the Force carry arms which, however, are to be employed only for self-defence, should this become necessary in the discharge of its function, in the interest of preserving international peace and security, of seeking to prevent a recurrence of fighting, and contributing to the maintenance and restoration of law and order and a return to normal conditions. The personnel of the Force must act with restraint and with complete impartiality towards the members of the Greek and Turkish Cypriot communities.

As regards the principle of self-defence, it is explained that the expression "self-defence" includes the defence of United Nations posts, premises and vehicles under armed attack, as well as the support of other personnel of UNFICYP under

[14]S/5950.

UNFICYP deployment as of December 1965

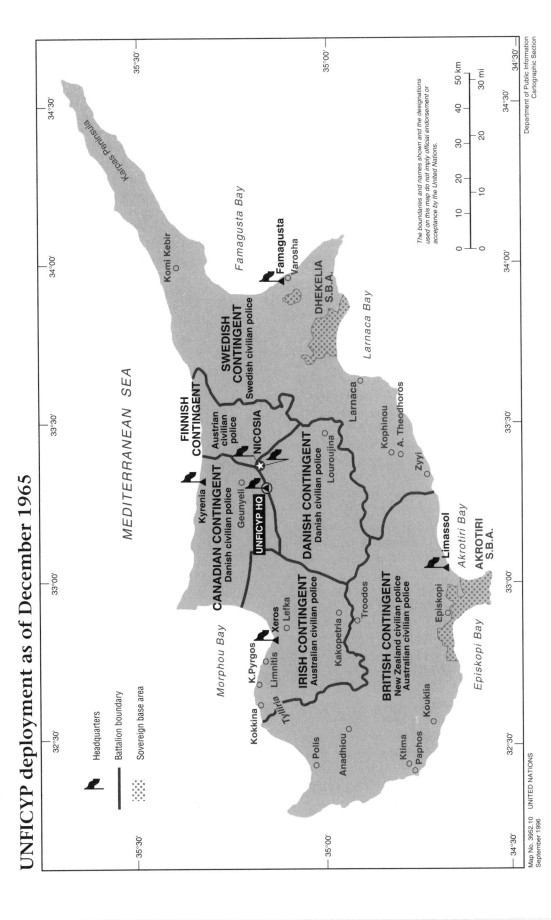

MEDITERRANEAN SEA

Karpas Peninsula

Komi Kebir

Famagusta Bay

Famagusta
Varosha

SWEDISH CONTINGENT
Swedish civilian police

DHEKELIA S.B.A.

Larnaca Bay

FINNISH CONTINGENT

Austrian civilian police

NICOSIA

Kyrenia

Geunyeli

CANADIAN CONTINGENT
Danish civilian police

UNFICYP HQ

DANISH CONTINGENT
Danish civilian police

Larnaca

Louroujina

Kophinou
A. Theodhoros

Zyyi

Akrotiri Bay

Limassol

AKROTIRI S.B.A.

Xeros

Lefka

Troodos

Kakopetria

Episkopi

BRITISH CONTINGENT
New Zealand civilian police
Australian civilian police

Episkopi Bay

K.Pyrgos

Limnitis

Tylliria

Kokkina

IRISH CONTINGENT
Australian civilian police

Kouklia

Ktima
Paphos

Anadhiou

Polis

Morphou Bay

Headquarters

Battalion boundary

Sovereign base area

35°30'   35°00'   34°30'   34°00'   33°30'   33°00'   32°30'

35°30'

35°00'

34°30'

The boundaries and names shown and the designations used on this map do not imply official endorsement or acceptance by the United Nations.

0   10   20   30   40   50 km
0   10   20   30 mi

Map No. 3952.10   UNITED NATIONS
September 1996

Department of Public Information
Cartographic Section

armed attack. When acting in self-defence, the principle of minimum force shall always be applied and armed force will be used only when all peaceful means of persuasion have failed. The decision as to when force may be used in these circumstances rests with the Commander on the spot. Examples in which troops may be authorized to use force include attempts by force to compel them to withdraw from a position which they occupy under orders from their commanders, attempts by force to disarm them, and attempts by force to prevent them from carrying out their responsibilities as ordered by their commanders.

With further reference to the question of the use of force, the Secretary-General had reported[15] to the Security Council on 29 April 1964 that the Force Commander was seeking to achieve the objectives of UNFICYP by peaceful means and without resorting to armed force, the arms of the Force being carried only for self-defence. Despite these efforts and the Secretary-General's appeals, fighting continued. The Secretary-General emphasized that "the United Nations Force was dispatched to Cyprus to try to save lives by preventing a recurrence of fighting. It would be incongruous, even a little insane, for that Force to set about killing Cypriots, whether Greek or Turkish, to prevent them from killing each other". Yet this was the dilemma facing UNFICYP, which could not stand idly by and see an undeclared war deliberately pursued or innocent civilians struck down.

When the UNFICYP Civilian Police (UNCIVPOL) became operational on 14 April 1964, the Secretary-General outlined[16] the following duties for it: establishing liaison with the Cypriot police; accompanying Cypriot police patrols which were to check vehicles on the roads for various traffic and other offences; manning United Nations police posts in certain sensitive areas, namely, areas where tension existed and might be alleviated by the presence of UNFICYP police elements; observing searches of vehicles by local police at road blocks; and investigating incidents where Greek or Turkish Cypriots were involved with the opposite community, including searches for persons reported as missing.

Liaison arrangements

In view of the comprehensive functions of UNFICYP as laid down by the Security Council in resolution 186 (1964), the United Nations operation in Cyprus became involved, from its inception, in carrying out a vast array of activities that affected almost every aspect of life in Cyprus, often in difficult conditions. All of UNFICYP's functions were of necessity carried out in contact and consultation with the Government of Cyprus and the Turkish Cypriot authorities, and also, on many occasions, with the Governments of Greece and Turkey, and depended for their success on the cooperation of all concerned.

The legal framework of relations with the host Government was provided on 31 March 1964, when the Secretary-General and the Foreign Minister of Cyprus concluded an exchange of letters constituting an agreement on the status of UNFICYP.[17]

From the outset, UNFICYP made arrangements for close and continuous liaison with the Government of Cyprus and with the Turkish Cypriot leadership. Liaison was likewise maintained at various levels of the administrative and military establishments of both sides, including field military units in the areas of confrontation.

In situations of military confrontation, UNFICYP, not being empowered to impose its views on either party, of necessity negotiated with both, since the consent of both was and is required if peaceful solutions are to be found and violence averted. Time and again, communications, messages and appeals were sent to civilian leaders and military commanders of both sides in Cyprus, calling upon them to exercise restraint, refrain from provocative actions, observe the cease-fire, cooperate with the Force and contribute to a return to normal conditions. This was done either with regard to specific problems or, as in October and November 1964, in an effort to generate an across-the-board programme of action in pursuance of the mandate.

At the same time, the efforts of UNFICYP to carry out its mandate were impeded by the parties' conflicting interpretations of the duties of the Force under that mandate. To the Cyprus Government, UNFICYP's task was to assist it in ending the rebellion of the Turkish Cypriots and extending its authority over the entire territory of the Republic. To the Turkish Cypriots, a "return to normal conditions" meant having UNFICYP restore, by force if necessary, the status of the Turkish Cypriot community under the 1960 Constitution, while the Cyprus Government and its acts should not be taken as legal. The Secretary-General in his reports rejected both these interpretations, which,

[15]S/5671. [16]S/5679. [17]S/5634, annexes I and II.

if followed, would have caused UNFICYP to affect basically the final settlement of the Cyprus problem. This he considered to be in the province of the Mediator, not of UNFICYP.

Freedom of movement of UNFICYP

The agreement on the status of UNFICYP mentioned above provides for the freedom of movement of the Force throughout Cyprus, subject to a minor qualification relating to large troop movements, and entitles UNFICYP to use roads, bridges, airfields, etc. Freedom of movement has been regarded from the outset as an essential condition for the proper functioning of the Force; indeed, the function of preventing a recurrence of fighting depends for its implementation entirely on the freedom of movement of the military and police elements of UNFICYP. The Force encountered many difficulties in this regard.

On 10 November 1964, the Force Commander reached an agreement with the Commander of the Cyprus National Guard, declaring the whole island open to UNFICYP except for certain stipulated areas (covering about 1.65 per cent of the country) that were accessible only to the Force Commander or to senior officers of UNFICYP. Arrangements were also negotiated for UNFICYP access to the Limassol docks, which were used by the Cyprus Government for the importation of military stores. Also in November 1964, it was agreed that the Cyprus security forces would henceforth refrain from searching UNFICYP personnel and vehicles.

During 1965, the Force Commander carried out a thorough review of UNFICYP's reconnaissance procedures, with a view to reducing friction to a minimum. Nevertheless, incidents of obstruction and harassment of UNFICYP continued. In certain cases, these even involved firing at UNFICYP soldiers, manhandling of UNFICYP officers and other unacceptable practices. Both the National Guard and Turkish Cypriot fighters were involved in incidents of this kind, especially during periods of tension.

Supervision of the cease-fire

UNFICYP's operating procedures to prevent a recurrence of fighting and to supervise the cease-fire were worked out pragmatically in the light of the impasse that persisted between the two sides. The Force instituted a system of fixed posts and frequent patrols, intervention on the spot and interposition to prevent incidents from escalating

into serious fighting, demarcation of cease-fire lines where appropriate, and the submission of proposals or plans for remedying situations of military tension or conflict. Thus, UNFICYP endeavoured to secure the withdrawal or elimination of fortifications erected by the two sides, and submitted numerous proposals to that end, designed to reduce the armed confrontation without prejudice to the security requirements of both sides. Wherever violent incidents broke out, UNFICYP made every effort, by persuasion, negotiation and interposition, to stop the fighting; it assisted civilians, evacuated the wounded and endeavoured to resolve the underlying security and other problems.

Despite the efforts of UNFICYP, sporadic violence continued on the island after the Force became operational, punctuated by outbreaks of severe fighting in which United Nations troops would find themselves at times fired upon by both sides, and forced to return the fire. Serious incidents occurred in the Tylliria area on 4 April 1964, at Ayios Theodhoros on 22 April, and in the area north of Nicosia from 25 to 29 April. A number of UNFICYP soldiers were killed as they sought to carry out their duties during continued scattered fighting in May. A major outbreak of fighting occurred from 5 to 8 August in the Tylliria area, reducing the Turkish Cypriot bridgehead there to the village of Kokkina. This was followed by aerial attacks on Government forces by Turkish fighter aircraft, and led on 8 and 9 August to meetings of the Security Council, which adopted resolution 193 (1964), which, *inter alia*, called for an immediate cease-fire. The Governments of Cyprus and Turkey accepted the cease-fire without conditions.[18]

In August and September 1964, the Secretary-General engaged in intensive negotiations with the parties on the explosive issue of the periodic partial rotation of the Turkish national contingent stationed in Cyprus under the Treaty of Alliance (which the Cyprus Government had abrogated, but which Turkey considered to remain valid). This was linked to the question of the reopening of the Nicosia-Kyrenia road, which the Turkish Cypriots had closed to Greek Cypriot traffic. On 25 September, U Thant announced in the Security Council that agreement had been reached for the reopening of the road under the exclusive control of UNFICYP, and for the unimpeded rotation of the Turkish national contingent.

The road was reopened on 26 October 1964, and UNFICYP continued until 1974 to supervise the movement of Greek Cypriot civilians on

[18]S/5879.

it and to ensure that no armed personnel except those of UNFICYP were allowed to use it. The first rotation of the Turkish national contingent under this agreement was carried out on the same day, with UNFICYP assistance and under UNFICYP observation. UNFICYP also performed observation functions in connection with checking the incoming Turkish troops and their stores by Cyprus Government officials at Famagusta harbour. These functions, too, continued to be carried out, twice a year, until 1974. It should be noted that the UNFICYP functions relating to the Turkish national contingent concerned relations between the Governments of Cyprus and Turkey and therefore did not fall strictly within the terms of UNFICYP's mandate; they were assumed at the request of all concerned, in the interest of maintaining the peace, reducing tension on the island, and creating favourable conditions for carrying out other aspects of UNFICYP's mandate.

As a result of this arrangement, the situation in Cyprus improved somewhat, and in his report[19] of December 1964, the Secretary-General reported that fighting had virtually ceased. However, the underlying tensions continued, and UNFICYP had little or no success in inducing the parties to scale down their military confrontation or dismantle their fortifications, which were the cause of recurrent incidents.

Return to normal conditions

UNFICYP normalization efforts evolved on an ad hoc basis and employed persuasion and negotiation exclusively. The principal objective was to restore conditions that would enable all the people of the island to go about their daily business without fear for their lives and without being victimized, and in this connection to restore governmental services and economic activities disrupted by the intercommunal strife. A significant aspect of UNFICYP's procedures under this heading concerned humanitarian and relief assistance. All of UNFICYP's efforts were so framed as to avoid prejudicing the positions and claims of the parties in respect of a final political settlement. However, its task was made difficult by the reluctance of the two communities to modify their positions in the absence of such a settlement.

From the beginning of the United Nations operation, UNFICYP undertook ad hoc measures designed to save lives, minimize suffering and, to the extent possible, restore essential civilian activities. These measures included:

(a) Escorts for essential civilian movements, including persons, food and essential merchandise, on the roads of Cyprus, especially for members of the Turkish Cypriot community who feared abduction.

(b) Harvest arrangements, including escorts and patrols, to enable farmers to till their lands in the vicinity of positions held by members of the other community; agricultural arrangements, including grain deliveries by the Turkish Cypriots to the Cyprus Grain Commission; maintenance of abandoned citrus orchards, etc.

(c) Arrangements for government property in Turkish Cypriot-controlled areas; water and electricity supplies to the Turkish Cypriot sectors; postal services; payment of social insurance benefits; efforts to normalize the public services, including arrangements to re-employ Turkish Cypriot civil servants, etc.

(d) Cooperation with the Red Cross and the Cyprus Joint Relief Commission in providing relief assistance for displaced persons (mainly Turkish Cypriots). UNFICYP also made intensive efforts to alleviate hardships resulting from the economic restrictions that had been imposed on the Turkish Cypriot community.

In October and November 1964, UNFICYP initiated a major effort to persuade the Government and the Turkish Cypriot leadership to drop most economic and security restrictions directed at members of the other community, to restore free movement and contacts for all, and to consider the return of displaced persons, with UNFICYP's assistance. This comprehensive approach resulted in some improvement of the situation, but the basic political problem continued to limit the effectiveness of UNFICYP's normalization efforts.

On 21 April 1965, President Makarios informed the Special Representative of the Secretary-General and the Force Commander that the Government planned a normalization programme in three districts — Larnaca, Limassol and Ktima. This move came in response to UNFICYP's suggestions for a withdrawal of troops from fortified posts, elimination of road-blocks and the lifting of economic restrictions. However, the Turkish Cypriots, noting the limited geographical scope of the programme and the continuation of economic restrictions, declined to remove their defences.

[19]S/6102.

The crisis of 1967

In January 1967, General George Grivas, the Greek Commander of the Cyprus National Guard, deployed a battalion of troops in the Kophinou area. These remained in place despite an understanding reached by UNFICYP with the local Turkish Cypriot commander to avoid incidents. As the National Guard unit was reinforced on 28 February, Turkish Cypriot fighters moved forward at nearby Ayios Theodhoros, where they also manhandled senior UNFICYP officers. There was severe friction between UNFICYP and Turkish Cypriot fighters in Kophinou, and the situation also deteriorated in the Paphos and Lefka districts.

In September 1967, the Government announced[20] a normalization programme that included the unmanning of armed posts and fortifications and complete freedom of movement, initially in the Paphos and Limassol districts. The Turkish Cypriot side assured UNFICYP that it would not seek to occupy the vacated positions.

In November 1967,[21] the Cyprus police sought to resume the practice of patrolling Ayios Theodhoros, passing through the Turkish Cypriot quarter, and informed UNFICYP that the National Guard would, if necessary, escort the policemen. On 15 November, heavy fighting broke out, and the National Guard overran most of Ayios Theodhoros and part of Kophinou. The Turkish Government protested to the Secretary-General, who requested the Cyprus and Greek Governments to bring about a withdrawal of the National Guard from the areas it had occupied. The withdrawal was carried out on 16 November. On 18 and 19 November, there were several Turkish overflights of Cyprus, and armed clashes spread to the Kokkina and Kyrenia areas.

These events set off a severe political crisis. The Secretary-General appealed[22] to the President of Cyprus and to the Prime Ministers of Greece and Turkey, on 22 and 24 November 1967, to avoid an outbreak of hostilities, and he sent a personal representative to the three capitals. In the second appeal, the Secretary-General urged the three parties to agree upon a staged reduction and ultimate withdrawal of non-Cypriot armed forces, other than those of the United Nations, and he offered the assistance of UNFICYP in working out a programme of phased withdrawals and helping to maintain calm.

The Security Council met on 24 November and, after consultations with the representatives of the parties, unanimously approved a consensus statement noting with satisfaction the efforts of the Secretary-General and calling upon all the parties to assist and cooperate in keeping the peace.

On 3 December 1967, the Secretary-General addressed a third appeal[23] to the President of Cyprus and to the Prime Ministers of Greece and Turkey, in which he called for Greece and Turkey to carry out an expeditious withdrawal of their forces in excess of their contingents in Cyprus. He added:

> With regard to any further role that it might be considered desirable for UNFICYP to undertake, I gather that this could involve, subject to the necessary action by the Security Council, enlarging the mandate of the Force so as to give it broader functions in regard to the realization of quiet and peace in Cyprus, including supervision of disarmament and the devising of practical arrangements to safeguard internal security, embracing the safety of all the people of Cyprus. My good offices in connection with such matters would, of course, be available to the parties on request.

All three Governments welcomed the Secretary-General's appeal,[24] and Turkey supported the enlargement of the UNFICYP mandate to include supervision of the disarmament in Cyprus of forces constituted after 1963. The Security Council, at a meeting on 22 December 1967, adopted resolution 244 (1967), by which, among other things, it noted the Secretary-General's three appeals and the replies of the three Governments.

In response to the Secretary-General's appeals, Greece and Turkey reached an agreement under which Greek national troops were withdrawn from Cyprus between 8 December 1967 and 16 January 1968. However, as no agreement was reached by Greece and Turkey on the issue of reciprocity, UNFICYP did not take on the task of checking that no Greek or Turkish forces in excess of their respective contingents remained in Cyprus.

At the same time, a formula was devised for informal meetings between Mr. Glafcos Clerides and Mr. Rauf R. Denktash, representing the Greek Cypriot and Turkish Cypriot communities, respectively. After an initial meeting in Beirut, Lebanon, on 2 June, they held meetings in Nicosia.

The intercommunal security situation in Cyprus improved during 1968, and in January 1969, President Makarios confirmed that he intended to extend normalization measures, includ-

---

[20]S/8141. [21]S/8248. [22]S/8248/Add.3,5. [23]S/8248, Add.6. [24]S/8248, Add.7,8.

ing freedom of movement for the Turkish Cypriots, throughout the island. The Secretary-General suggested that the Turkish Cypriot leadership should respond by allowing the free movement of Greek Cypriots through Turkish Cypriot areas, but this was not accepted.

Arms imports

From the beginning of the Cyprus operation, the Secretary-General reported that the influx of arms and military equipment was a cause of concern for UNFICYP with regard to the discharge of its mandate. UNFICYP kept a careful watch on all imports of such arms and equipment, but the question whether it could take any additional action in this regard under resolution 186 (1964) remained a controversial one. An agreement was concluded on 10 September 1964 to have UNFICYP present at the unloading of military equipment at Famagusta and Limassol, but additional material was being imported at Boghaz, unobserved by UNFICYP.

The issue came to a head when it became known in December 1966 that the Cyprus Government had imported a quantity of arms for distribution to the Cyprus police. On 12 January 1967, the Cyprus Government indicated to the Secretary-General that the imported arms would not be distributed for the time being, that the Secretary-General would be advised in due time if their distribution should become necessary, and that, in the meantime, the Force Commander could make periodic inspections.

In March 1970, increasing tension within the Greek Cypriot community culminated in an attempt on the life of President Makarios and the subsequent killing of a former Minister of the Interior, Mr. Polycarpos Georghadjis.

Clandestine activity by pro-*enosis* (union with Greece) elements continued in 1971, and in view of that, the Government of Cyprus in January 1972 imported a large quantity of arms and ammunition. To minimize the resultant increase in tension, UNFICYP negotiated a provisional agreement on 10 March, whereby the Cyprus Government undertook to keep the imported arms in safe-keeping and open to inspection by the Force Commander. On 21 April, the Secretary-General reported[25] that an improved arrangement had been agreed upon, under which the weapons and munitions, except for the high explosives, would be stored in a fenced area within the perimeter of an UNFICYP camp. The fenced area would be in the charge of unarmed Cyprus police personnel,

but control of the camp perimeter and access to it would be the responsibility of UNFICYP. The high-explosive munitions were stored at Cyprus police headquarters, but the fuses were removed and stored at the UNFICYP camp. A system of double locks and keys was devised for both storage areas.

UNFICYP continued to carry out its functions under both these agreements until 1974. Subsequently, the responsibility for their security rested with UNFICYP alone and the Cyprus police had no involvement with them other than periodic verification carried out jointly with UNFICYP.

UNFICYP reductions

The consolidation of the security situation that was achieved by the beginning of 1965, however limited and tenuous, made possible a gradual reduction of the strength of UNFICYP. From a total (military personnel and police) of 6,275 in December 1964, the Force was reduced one year later to 5,764, and to 4,610 by the end of 1966. The strength of the Force in December 1967 was 4,737.

The general lessening of tension throughout the island in 1968, in addition to creating a favourable atmosphere for the Clerides/Denktash intercommunal talks, also led to a further significant reduction in the strength of the Force. Steps were taken, in cooperation with the Government of Cyprus and the Turkish Cypriot leadership, to ensure that the effectiveness of the Force would not be adversely affected. Between April and December 1968, its strength was brought down to 3,708.

Further reductions took place gradually over the next two years; thereafter, the strength of UNFICYP from 1970 to 1972 remained stable at approximately 3,150. The strength of the Irish battalion was reduced from 420 to 150 during this period. In this connection, Austria, at the request of the Secretary-General, agreed in 1972 to augment its contingent, which had consisted of the UNFICYP field hospital and an UNCIVPOL unit, by providing also a battalion of 276 ground troops.

In October and November 1973, personnel of the Austrian, Finnish, Irish and Swedish contingents of UNFICYP were transferred to the Middle East to form the advance elements of the United Nations Emergency Force. Replacements for the Austrian, Finnish and Swedish personnel were promptly sent to Cyprus by the Governments concerned; however, at the request of the Secretary-

[25]S/10564/Add.1.

General, Ireland agreed to dispatch additional troops only to the Middle East, and the Irish contingent in Cyprus was reduced to a token detachment at UNFICYP headquarters.

A further reduction of 381 troops was made in the spring of 1974. However, this was soon overtaken by the events of July 1974, which made it necessary to increase the strength of the Force once again.

D. *Coup d'état* and Turkish intervention of 1974

Events from the *coup d'état* of 15 July to 30 July

On 15 July 1974, the National Guard, under the direction of Greek officers, staged a *coup d'état* against the Cyprus Government headed by President Makarios. In view of the seriousness of the matter in relation to international peace and security and in view of the United Nations involvement in Cyprus, the Secretary-General requested[26] the President of the Security Council on 16 July to convene a meeting of the Council. The Permanent Representative of Cyprus also requested[27] a meeting. The Council met on 16 and 19 July.

On 20 July, the Turkish Government, invoking the Treaty of Guarantee of 1960, launched an extensive military operation on the north coast of Cyprus which resulted eventually in the occupation of the main Turkish Cypriot enclave north of Nicosia and areas to the north, east and west of the enclave, including Kyrenia. The Council met on the same day and adopted resolution 353 (1974), by which it called upon all parties to cease firing and demanded an immediate end to foreign military intervention, requested the withdrawal of foreign military personnel present otherwise than under the authority of international agreements, and called on Greece, Turkey and the United Kingdom to enter into negotiations without delay for the restoration of peace in the area and constitutional government in Cyprus. The Council also called on all parties to cooperate fully with UNFICYP to enable it to carry out its mandate — thus indicating that UNFICYP was expected to continue to function despite the radically changed circumstances. The cease-fire called for by the Council was announced for 1600 hours, local time, on 22 July.

The fighting resumed on 23 July, especially in the vicinity of Nicosia International Airport, which, with the agreement of the local military commanders of both sides, was declared a United Nations–protected area and was occupied by UNFICYP troops. The Secretary-General re-

ported to the Council on the breakdown of the cease-fire, and sent messages[28] to the Prime Ministers of Greece and Turkey and to the Acting President of Cyprus, expressing his great anxiety and requesting measures to ensure observance of the cease-fire. The Council on 23 July adopted resolution 354 (1974), reaffirming the provisions of resolution 353 (1974) and demanding that the parties comply immediately with paragraph 2 of that resolution, which called on them to stop firing and refrain from action which might aggravate the situation.

UNFICYP activities

As a consequence of these events, UNFICYP was faced with a situation that had not been foreseen in its mandate. As laid down by the Security Council in resolution 186 (1964), the functions of UNFICYP were conceived in relation to the intercommunal conflict in Cyprus, not to large-scale hostilities arising from action by the armed forces of one of the guarantor Powers.

On 15 July, as soon as the *coup d'état* was reported, UNFICYP was brought to a high state of readiness. Additional liaison officers were deployed at all levels, and increased observation was maintained throughout the island in all areas of likely intercommunal confrontation. Special measures were taken to ensure the security of the Turkish Cypriot community. A few cases of firing into the Turkish enclave north of Nicosia were reported; the firing was stopped through liaison with the National Guard.

On 20 July, the day of the Turkish landings, UNFICYP was placed on full alert. An increased level of observation was maintained throughout the entire island and additional precautions were taken to safeguard isolated Turkish Cypriot villages. The National Guard reacted to the Turkish

---

[26]S/11334. [27]S/11335. [28]S/11368.

operations by strong simultaneous attacks in other parts of the island against most of the Turkish Cypriot quarters and villages. The best UNFICYP could achieve under the circumstances was to arrange local cease-fires to prevent further loss of life and damage to property, as the Turkish Cypriot fighters, who were mainly deployed to protect isolated villages and town sectors, were heavily outnumbered. When the war situation made it necessary on 21 July to evacuate foreign missions to the British Sovereign Base Area at Dhekelia, UNFICYP played a major part in the organization and execution of that humanitarian operation. In all areas, including the Kyrenia sector, intensified United Nations patrolling was carried out, a close watch was maintained over the battle zone and all possible efforts were made to promote the safety of civilians.

The Secretary-General reported to the Security Council his understanding that UNFICYP should, and indeed must, use its best efforts to ensure, as far as its capabilities permitted, that the cease-fire called for by the Council was maintained. Obviously, a United Nations peace-keeping force, in a deeply serious situation such as the one prevailing in Cyprus, could not be expected to stand by and not make the maximum effort to ensure that a resolution of the Security Council was put into effect. For this reason, the Special Representative, the Force Commander and all the personnel of UNFICYP made every effort to restore the cease-fire, to ensure that it was observed and to prevent any incidents from escalating into a full recurrence of fighting. In this connection, UNFICYP assisted in delineating the positions of the parties as at 1600 hours on 22 July. Additional United Nations observation posts were established in the confrontation areas, and extensive patrolling was carried out in order to maintain a United Nations presence throughout the island.

In addition, the Secretary-General requested reinforcements from the contributing countries; they arrived between 24 July and 14 August, increasing the total strength of the Force by 2,078 all ranks to a total of 4,444. UNFICYP was redeployed to meet the new situation, two new operational districts were established on both sides of the Turkish bridgehead, and the general level of surveillance throughout the island was increased accordingly. Because of the suffering caused by the hostilities, UNFICYP undertook an increasing number of humanitarian tasks to assist the afflicted population of both communities.

Tripartite Conference and the Geneva Declaration

As called for in Security Council resolution 353 (1974), the Foreign Ministers of Turkey, Greece and the United Kingdom began discussions in Geneva on 25 July, and on 30 July they agreed on the text of a declaration concerning the situation in Cyprus, which was immediately transmitted to the Secretary-General.[29] By the Geneva Declaration, the Foreign Ministers agreed on certain measures that involved action by UNFICYP. Thus:

(a) A security zone of a size to be determined by representatives of Greece, Turkey and the United Kingdom, in consultation with UNFICYP, was to be established at the limit of the areas occupied by the Turkish armed forces. This zone was to be entered by no forces other than those of UNFICYP, which was to supervise the prohibition of entry. Pending the determination of the size and character of the security zone, the existing area between the two forces was not to be entered by any forces.

(b) All the Turkish enclaves occupied by Greek or Greek Cypriot forces were to be immediately evacuated and would continue to be protected by UNFICYP. Other Turkish enclaves outside the area controlled by the Turkish armed forces would continue to be protected by an UNFICYP security zone and could, as before, maintain their own police and security forces.

(c) In mixed villages, the functions of security and police were to be carried out by UNFICYP.

(d) Military personnel and civilians detained as a result of the recent hostilities were to be either exchanged or released under the supervision of the International Committee of the Red Cross (ICRC) within the shortest time possible.

At the meeting of the Security Council held on 31 July, the Secretary-General made a statement referring to the above functions envisaged for UNFICYP. The Council, on 1 August, adopted resolution 355 (1974), taking note of the Secretary-General's statement and requesting him "to take appropriate action in the light of his statement and to present a full report to the Council, taking into account that the cease-fire will be the first step in the full implementation of Security Council resolution 353 (1974)".

Immediately after the adoption of resolution 355 (1974), the Secretary-General instructed

[29]S/11398.

his Special Representative in Cyprus and the Commander of UNFICYP to proceed, in cooperation with the parties, with the full implementation of the role of UNFICYP as provided for in that resolution. UNFICYP promptly informed the parties that it stood ready to carry out all the functions devolving upon it under the resolution and it repeatedly appealed for observance of the cease-fire.

The Secretary-General's interim report[30] of 10 August 1974 pursuant to resolution 355 (1974) gave an account of the action taken to carry out the various provisions of the Geneva Declaration. The military representatives of Greece, Turkey and the United Kingdom had been meeting since 2 August together with a representative of UNFICYP, but they had not as yet determined the size of the security zone. Accordingly, UNFICYP action regarding that zone had been limited to participation in the deliberations.

Concerning the Turkish enclaves occupied by Greek or Greek Cypriot forces, UNFICYP stood ready to assume its protective functions as soon as they had been evacuated by those forces. In the meantime, UNFICYP's protective functions in respect of Turkish enclaves had continued, including regular patrols, assistance to the population, escorts and convoys for relief supplies (food, medicaments, etc.), and visits to detainees, together with ICRC, to ensure that their treatment was satisfactory. These protective functions were also being carried out in the Turkish enclaves outside the area controlled by the Turkish forces mentioned in the Declaration, as well as in mixed villages.

On 12 August, the Secretary-General reported[31] that the National Guard had evacuated a number of Turkish Cypriot villages, and UNFICYP had assumed the responsibility for the protection of those areas.

The second round of fighting

Following the breakdown of the Geneva Conference on 14 August, fighting resumed in Cyprus. In the circumstances, UNFICYP resorted to ad hoc emergency operating procedures. Armoured reconnaissance units of UNFICYP maintained observation over the battle zone wherever possible. During the night of 14/15 August, and again on 15/16 August, UNFICYP achieved a partial cease-fire in Nicosia to allow all the non-combatants to be evacuated. It made major efforts throughout the country to put an end to the fighting, but was unable to do so in certain combat areas, where UNFICYP posts had to be withdrawn. In a few such areas, killing of civilians took place.

The resumption of heavy fighting on 14 August had placed UNFICYP units in an extremely difficult and dangerous position, resulting in severe casualties. The Security Council noted that development with concern in its resolution 359 (1974) of 15 August; it recalled that UNFICYP was stationed in Cyprus with the full consent of the Governments of Cyprus, Turkey and Greece; it demanded that all parties concerned fully respect the international status of the United Nations Force and refrain from any action which might endanger the lives and safety of its members; it further demanded that all parties cooperate with the Force in carrying out its tasks, including humanitarian functions, in all areas of Cyprus and in regard to all sections of the population. After negotiations, the Turkish forces declared a cease-fire at 1800 hours, local time, on 16 August.

On the same day, the Council adopted resolution 360 (1974), by which it recorded its "formal disapproval of the unilateral military actions undertaken against the Republic of Cyprus" and urged the parties to comply with its previous resolutions and to resume without delay the negotiations called for in resolution 353 (1974).

Humanitarian functions

During the events of July and August 1974, UNFICYP assumed important humanitarian functions, and the Security Council, in its resolution 359 (1974), took notice of these tasks. On 22 July, a special humanitarian and economics branch had been set up at UNFICYP headquarters. Every effort was made to protect the civilian population caught up in the hostilities — including both Cypriots and foreigners. In cooperation with ICRC, a wide range of relief assistance was organized for Greek and Turkish Cypriots. However, it soon became evident that a more systematic and larger scale of operation was needed, since approximately one third of the population of the island had become homeless or was otherwise in need. Accordingly, on 20 August, the Secretary-General designated the United Nations High Commissioner for Refugees as Coordinator of United Nations Humanitarian Assistance for Cyprus.[32] In resolution 361 (1974) of 30 August, the Security Council, noting that a large number of people in Cyprus were in dire need, and "mindful of the fact that it is one of the foremost purposes of the United Nations to lend humanitarian assistance in situations such as the one currently prevailing in

[30]S/11433. [31]S/11353/Add.20. [32]S/11488.

Cyprus", requested the Secretary-General to continue to provide emergency humanitarian assistance to all parts of the island's population in need of such assistance. UNFICYP assisted the Coordinator in carrying out his functions.

E.   UNFICYP since 1974

Since its establishment in 1964, the main objective of the United Nations operation in Cyprus, as of all other United Nations peace-keeping operations, has been to foster peaceful conditions in which the search for an agreed, just and lasting settlement of the problem could best be pursued. The main instrument for maintaining calm and preventing strife on the island has been and remains the United Nations Peace-keeping Force, which continues effectively to carry out its task of conflict control. Accordingly, the Secretary-General has reported to the Security Council, at the end of every six-month mandate period, that in the light of the situation on the ground and of political developments, the continued presence of UNFICYP remains indispensable, both in helping to maintain calm on the island and in creating the best conditions for his good offices efforts. For its part, the Security Council has regularly extended the mandate of the Force for six-month periods.

Until June 1983, the parties concerned consistently informed the Secretary-General of their concurrence in the proposed extension of the stationing of the Force on the island. Following the Turkish Cypriot proclamation on 15 November 1983 of the "Turkish Republic of Northern Cyprus", which was deplored and considered legally invalid by the Security Council, the Government of Cyprus as well as the Governments of Greece and the United Kingdom have continued to indicate their concurrence, but Turkey and the Turkish Cypriot community have indicated that the text of the resolution was unacceptable as a basis for extending the mandate. Nonetheless, all the parties have continued to cooperate with UNFICYP, both on the military and the civilian levels.

The function of the United Nations Peace-keeping Force in Cyprus was originally defined by the Security Council in its resolution 186 (1964) of 4 March 1964 in the following terms ". . . in the interest of preserving international peace and security, to use its best efforts to prevent a recurrence of fighting and, as necessary, to contribute to the maintenance and restoration of law and order and a return to normal conditions".

That mandate, which was conceived in the context of the confrontation between the Greek Cypriot and Turkish Cypriot communities in 1964, has been periodically extended by the Security Council. In connection with the hostilities in July and August 1974, the Security Council adopted a number of resolutions which have affected the functioning of UNFICYP and have required the Force to perform certain additional functions relating, in particular, to the maintenance of the cease-fire.

That cease-fire came into effect at 1800 hours on 16 August 1974. Immediately afterwards, UNFICYP inspected the areas of confrontation and recorded the deployment of the military forces on both sides. Lines drawn between the forward defended localities became respectively the National Guard and Turkish forces cease-fire lines. In the absence of a formal cease-fire agreement, the military status quo, as recorded by UNFICYP at the time, became the standard by which it was judged whether any changes constituted violations of the cease-fire. The military status quo was subsequently clarified further and adjusted in numerous local agreements between the units of UNFICYP and of the sides concerned. Most of those agreements were eventually consolidated in a simple set of rules, which UNFICYP communicated to the military forces on both sides in early 1989.

It is an essential feature of the cease-fire that neither side can exercise authority or jurisdiction or make any military moves beyond its own forward military lines. In the area between the lines, which is known as the United Nations buffer zone, UNFICYP maintains the status quo (including innocent civilian activity and the exercise of property rights) without prejudice to an eventual political settlement concerning the disposition of the area. UNFICYP discharges its responsibilities in

UNFICYP deployment as of June 1975

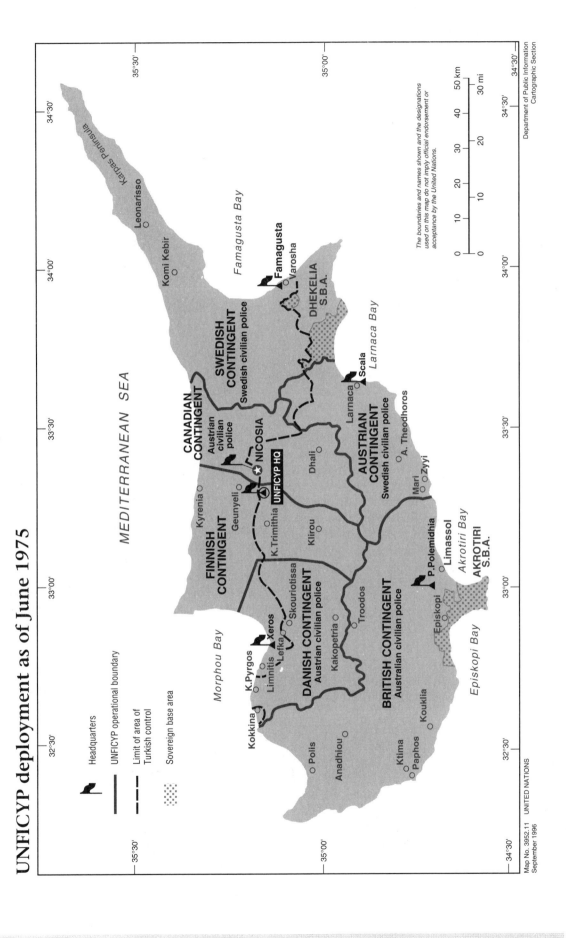

MEDITERRANEAN SEA

Karpas Peninsula

Leonarisso

Komi Kebir

Famagusta Bay

Famagusta
Varosha

DHEKELIA S.B.A.

Larnaca Bay

SWEDISH CONTINGENT
Swedish civilian police

Scala

Larnaca

AUSTRIAN CONTINGENT
Swedish civilian police

A. Theodhoros

CANADIAN CONTINGENT
Austrian civilian police

NICOSIA

UNFICYP HQ

Kyrenia

Geunyeli

K.Trimithia

Dhali

Klirou

Zyyi

Mari

FINNISH CONTINGENT

Skouriotissa

Troodos

Kakopetria

Limassol

Akrotiri Bay

P.Polemidhia

DANISH CONTINGENT
Austrian civilian police

Xeros

Lefka

Limnitis

K.Pyrgos

Kokkina

Polis

Anadhiou

Klima
Paphos

Kouklia

BRITISH CONTINGENT
Australian civilian police

Episkopi

AKROTIRI S.B.A.

Episkopi Bay

Morphou Bay

Headquarters

UNFICYP operational boundary

Limit of area of Turkish control

Sovereign base area

34°30'
34°00'
33°30'
33°00'
32°30'
35°30'
35°00'
34°30'

35°30'
35°00'

0   10   20   30   40   50 km
0   10   20   30 mi

The boundaries and names shown and the designations
used on this map do not imply official endorsement or
acceptance by the United Nations.

Map No. 3952.11   UNITED NATIONS
September 1996

Department of Public Information
Cartographic Section

165

that area, with a view to safeguarding the legitimate security requirements of both sides, while giving due regard to humanitarian considerations.[33]

The cease-fire lines extend approximately 180 kilometres from Kato Pyrgos on the north-west coast to the east coast at Dherinia. The United Nations buffer zone between the lines varies in width from less than 20 metres in Nicosia to some 7 kilometres near Athienou. It covers about 3 per cent of the island, including some of the most valuable agricultural land.

UNFICYP keeps the cease-fire lines and the buffer zone under constant surveillance through a system of observation posts and patrols. High-powered binoculars and night observation devices are used in this work. The Force maintains a patrol track, which runs the length of the buffer zone and is used for surveillance, monitoring of agricultural activities, the resupply of observation posts and rapid reaction to any incidents.

In Nicosia, the cease-fire lines of the two sides are in close proximity and, consequently, the most serious incidents have tended to occur there. In May 1989, UNFICYP reached an agreement with both sides whereby they unmanned their positions and ceased their patrols in certain sensitive locations. The opposing troops were thus moved further apart, although the cease-fire lines were left unchanged. As a result, the number of incidents in Nicosia has been reduced. UNFICYP has continued its efforts to extend the 1989 agreement to all areas of the buffer zone where the troops of both sides remain in close proximity to each other.

Both sides on the island have frequently expressed concern about the strength and development of the military forces of the other side. This subject is of concern to UNFICYP as well, and it has proposed to both sides that it conduct inspections to verify such developments. In the absence of any agreement on this proposal, UNFICYP monitors the opposing forces by overt means to the best of its ability.

In accordance with its mandate, UNFICYP encourages the fullest possible resumption of normal civilian activity in the buffer zone. To this end, four villages and certain other areas in the buffer zone have been designated as civilian use areas, which means that they are freely accessible and are policed by local civilian police. Elsewhere in the buffer zone, no civilian movement or activity is permitted unless specifically authorized by UNFICYP. In Nicosia, in view of the security implications, such authorization is given only with the concurrence of both sides. The main civilian activity in the buffer zone is farming.

UNFICYP provides its good offices, as necessary, in regard to the supply of electricity and water across the lines, facilitates normal contacts between Greek and Turkish Cypriots by making available meeting facilities, provides emergency medical services, including medical evacuations, and delivers mail and Red Cross messages across the lines.

UNFICYP discharges certain humanitarian functions for the Greek Cypriots living in the northern part of the island, mostly in the Karpas peninsula. The Force delivers to them supplies provided by the Cyprus Government and the Cyprus Red Cross Society as well as pension and welfare payments. Further, UNFICYP personnel verify that any permanent transfers to the southern part of the island are voluntary. UNFICYP also delivers supplies to the Maronites living in three villages in the northern part of the island and generally assists them in humanitarian matters.

UNFICYP periodically visits Turkish Cypriots living in the southern part of the island and helps them maintain contact with their relatives in the north.

United Nations civilian police maintain close cooperation and liaison with the Cyprus police and the Turkish Cypriot police on matters having intercommunal aspects. Together with the line units they contribute to law and order in the buffer zone and assist in investigations and in the Force's humanitarian activities.

UNFICYP cooperates with the United Nations High Commissioner for Refugees, as coordinator of United Nations humanitarian assistance to needy displaced persons in Cyprus, and with the United Nations Development Programme, in particular to facilitate projects involving both communities.

In the first part of 1995, UNFICYP conducted a humanitarian review with regard to the living conditions of Greek Cypriots and Maronites living in the northern part of the island and of Turkish Cypriots living in the southern part. In June 1995, UNFICYP shared with the Government of Cyprus and with the Turkish Cypriot authorities the outcome of its review and set out its concerns.

UNFICYP found that Turkish Cypriots living in the southern part of the island were not subject to a restrictive regime and under the law enjoyed the same rights as other citizens. At the same time, in several respects, it was found that

[33]S/12253.

Turkish Cypriots were often the victims of capricious discrimination or police harassment and thus did not enjoy a fully normal life. With regard to Greek Cypriots and Maronites living in the northern part of the island, the review confirmed that those communities were the objects of very severe restrictions imposed by the Turkish Cypriot authorities, "which curtailed the exercise of many basic freedoms and had the effect of ensuring that, inexorably with the passage of time, those communities would cease to exist in the northern part of the island".[34]

UNFICYP discussed extensively those issues with the authorities on both sides and made a number of recommendations for remedial action by the Government and by the Turkish Cypriot authorities respectively.

Secretary-General's good offices

Since the events of 1974, the situation in Cyprus has remained calm, although tension has arisen periodically. Both sides have generally respected the cease-fire and the military status quo. But, as the Secretary-General has repeatedly stated, the continuing quiet should not obscure the fact that there is only a cease-fire in Cyprus, not peace. The Security Council has declared on numerous occasions that the status quo is not an acceptable option. In the absence of progress towards a settlement between the two sides, the overall situation remains subject to sudden tensions, generated by events outside as well as within Cyprus.

It is now more than 30 years since the Secretary-General was first asked to use his good offices in Cyprus. After the events of 1974, the Security Council[35] requested the Secretary-General to undertake a new mission of good offices with the representatives of the two communities. Since then, the successive Secretaries-General and their Special Representatives have tried to find a formula acceptable to both the Greek Cypriots and the Turkish Cypriots. The Security Council has given detailed guidelines to the Secretary-General on the implementation of his mission of good offices.

In the 1990s, there has been an intensification of efforts which led to fleshing out the essential elements of an overall settlement. Most of the elements have been endorsed or set out in Security Council resolutions.[36] From 1990 through 1992, efforts focused on securing an agreement on a draft overall agreement, known as the "Set of Ideas", which included a map setting out a proposed territorial adjustment.[37] This document was endorsed by the Security Council in its resolution 774 (1992) as the basis for reaching an overall framework agreement. In November 1992, the Secretary-General informed the Security Council that it had not been possible to reach agreement on the Set of Ideas and suggested the adoption of confidence-building measures (CBMs) as a means of facilitating progress.

Extensive efforts were made during 1993 and the first half of 1994 to reach an agreement on CBMs. Main elements included the reopening of Nicosia International Airport for the equal benefit of both communities as well as the reopening of the fenced area of Varosha to its original inhabitants and as a centre of bicommunal contacts and trade. By mid-1994, the Secretary-General reported to the Security Council that agreement on the CBMs remained beyond reach.[38] In October 1994, at the suggestion of the Secretary-General, the leaders of the Greek Cypriot and Turkish Cypriot communities met together five times with the Deputy Special Representative to review the situation and to discuss a broad range of possible trade-offs for an overall settlement and for the implementation of the CBMs.

Since then, efforts continued to focus on achieving progress towards an overall settlement and on the implementation of confidence-building measures. As the Secretary-General has noted, all the elements for an overall settlement are on the table. If all concerned manifest the necessary political will, a just and lasting solution to the Cyprus problem is within reach.

Restructuring of UNFICYP

Until 1993, UNFICYP was the only United Nations peace-keeping operation not financed from assessed contributions by States Members of the Organization. In accordance with Security Council resolution 186 (1964), the costs of the Force were met by the Governments providing the military contingents and by voluntary contributions received for this purpose by the United Nations. In addition, the Government of Cyprus provided, at no cost, areas for the headquarters, camps and other premises of UNFICYP.

Under those arrangements, the troop-contributing Governments made available to the United Nations troops whose regular pay and

[34]S/1995/1020. [35]S/RES/367 (1975). [36]S/RES/649 (1990), S/RES/716 (1991), S/RES/750 (1992), S/RES/774 (1992), S/RES/789 (1992) and S/RES/939 (1994). [37]S/24472. [38]S/1994/629, S/1994/785.

UNFICYP deployment as of December 1995

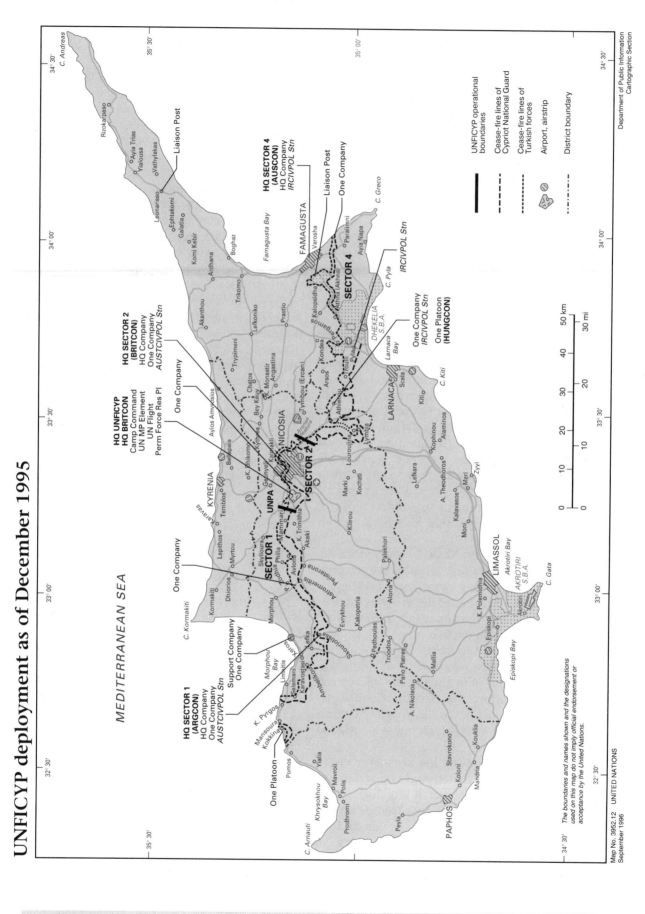

MEDITERRANEAN SEA

**HQ SECTOR 1
(ARGCON)**
HQ Company
One Company
AUSTCIVPOL Stn

Support Company
One Company

One Company

One Platoon

**HQ UNFICYP
HQ BRITCON**
Camp Command
UN MP Element
UN Flight
Perm Force Res Pl

**HQ SECTOR 2
(BRITCON)**
HQ Company
One Company
AUSTCIVPOL Stn

One Company

One Company

**HQ SECTOR 4
(AUSCON)**
HQ Company
IRCIVPOL Stn

Liaison Post

One Company

Liaison Post

IRCIVPOL Stn

One Company
IRCIVPOL Stn

One Platoon
(HUNGCON)

	UNFICYP operational boundaries
	Cease-fire lines of Cypriot National Guard
	Cease-fire lines of Turkish forces
	Airport, airstrip
	District boundary

The boundaries and names shown and the designations used on this map do not imply official endorsement or acceptance by the United Nations.

0   10   20   30   40   50 km
0   10   20   30 mi

SECTOR 1

SECTOR 2

UNPA

NICOSIA

KYRENIA

SECTOR 4

FAMAGUSTA

LARNACA

LIMASSOL

PAPHOS

DHEKELIA S.B.A.

AKROTIRI S.B.A.

Map No. 3952.12   UNITED NATIONS
September 1996

Department of Public Information
Cartographic Section

allowances and normal *matériel* expenses they had agreed to pay themselves. The United Nations was responsible for the operational costs for administrative and logistic support (e.g., rations, fuel, hire of vehicles, maintenance of premises, salaries and travel of non-military personnel) and for extra and extraordinary costs incurred by the troop-contributing Governments for which they sought reimbursement on the basis of separate agreements concluded by the United Nations with each of those Governments. These costs could be paid only from the voluntary contributions received for this purpose. Voluntary contributions, however, had consistently fallen short of the required funds, leaving the Special Account for UNFICYP with a total deficit of approximately $200 million for the period from the inception of the Force to June 1993. As a result, reimbursement claims from the troop-contributing countries were paid only up to December 1981.

The Secretary-General repeatedly voiced his profound concern about the worsening financial situation confronting UNFICYP. He suggested that the Force should be put on a sound and secure financial basis and that the best way to finance UNFICYP would be for its costs to be met from assessed contributions.

When, in October 1977 after more than 13 years of service, the Finnish battalion withdrew from UNFICYP, the Secretary-General, in consultation with the Government of Finland and with the parties concerned, decided not to replace the battalion. A compelling consideration in this regard was the critical financial condition of UNFICYP. In connection with the withdrawal of the battalion, a partial redeployment of the Force was carried out to fill the gap left in the area of the Nicosia International Airport.[39]

In February 1987, Sweden informed the Secretary-General that it had decided to withdraw its contingent by the end of the year, unless substantial improvements could be achieved both in the Force's financial situation, particularly through the introduction of financing by assessed contributions, and in the prospects for a political solution.[40] The subsequent withdrawal of the infantry battalion resulted in a major adjustment in the deployment of the Force. At the same time, Austria and Canada augmented their contingents, resulting in a net reduction of 206 in UNFICYP.[41]

In 1992, due to the deteriorating financial situation of the Force and frustration over the lack of progress towards a lasting political solution to the Cyprus problem, a number of troop-contributing Governments decided to reconsider their partici-

pation in UNFICYP. In his May 1992 report[42] on UNFICYP activities, the Secretary-General spoke of the need to consult with the troop-contributing countries on their intentions on participation in the Force, including the timing of any reductions or withdrawals of their contingents, and on the possible future options for UNFICYP. On 21 September, the Secretary-General informed[43] the Council that the troop-contributing Governments had given firm indications of their intention to reduce "the operational commitment" of their contingents, and he outlined a plan for a possible restructuring of UNFICYP.

In December 1992, the size of the Force was significantly reduced by the withdrawal of the Danish battalion (323 personnel) and reductions in the course of 1992 in the British, Austrian and Canadian contingents of 198, 63 and 61 personnel, respectively. This had reduced UNFICYP's strength by approximately 28 per cent.

In his 30 March 1993 report,[44] the Secretary-General stated that these reductions necessitated a major restructuring and reorganization of UNFICYP. The required operational and organizational adjustments had been put in place on 16 December 1992. He went on to say that further withdrawals announced by Canada and the United Kingdom would reduce the Force's strength from 1,513 to approximately 850 personnel and, unless the situation was redressed, UNFICYP would cease to be viable in June 1993. The Secretary-General presented his proposals for a further restructuring of the Force, stressing that they would be practical only if the Security Council changed the financing of UNFICYP from voluntary to assessed contributions.

In its resolution 831 (1993) of 27 May 1993, the Security Council decided that those costs of the Force that were not covered by voluntary contributions should be treated as expenses of the Organization, effective from the next extension of the Force's mandate on or before 15 June 1993. The Council also decided that UNFICYP should be restructured to a strength of three infantry battalions of approximately 350 personnel each, the minimum number required to maintain effective control of the buffer zone. A limited number of military observers were added to UNFICYP for reconnaissance, liaison and humanitarian tasks in 1993, but were discontinued in 1994.

As a result of reductions, the Force now covers the cease-fire lines more thinly than before.

---

[39] S/12463. [40] S/18880. [41] S/19304. [42] S/24050. [43] S/24581. [44] S/25492.

At the same time, the mandate of UNFICYP has remained unchanged, as essentially have the functions deriving from that mandate. The restructured UNFICYP continues to interpose itself between the Greek Cypriot and the Turkish Cypriot forces and to supervise the cease-fire lines that define the buffer zone, by observing and reporting any violations of the cease-fire and the military status quo.

For operational purposes, the Force is divided into three sectors and six line companies. In June 1993, the Canadian battalion was withdrawn, as scheduled. As a result, between June and September 1993, the Force's strength temporarily dipped below 1,000 and the Force Commander implemented an emergency contingency plan reorganizing UNFICYP in two sectors, covered by the Austrian and United Kingdom battalions. However, this did not last long; the decision of the Security Council to change the system of financing of the Force was followed by an offer by the Government of Argentina of a line battalion of some 350 personnel. The Force deployment was thus restored, as of 8 October 1993, to three line sectors/battalions as recommended by the Secretary-General and endorsed by Security Council resolution 831 (1993).

To offset the reductions in strength, the Force Commander adjusted the organization of UNFICYP by moving a greater portion of the battalions' strength into the buffer zone and reorganizing the system of observation posts, relying more heavily on mobile patrolling. He also handed over some humanitarian activities of the Force to the two sides.

In November 1993, the Secretary-General reported[45] to the Council in connection with its comprehensive reassessment of UNFICYP. The question of using large numbers of military observers in UNFICYP had been addressed in a review[46] of the Force carried out in 1990, and the matter was looked at again. The report concluded that a number of arguments continued to weigh heavily against the deployment of United Nations military observers.

As at 31 March 1996, the total strength (military personnel and civilian police) of UNFICYP was 1,200. The 1,165 military personnel were from Argentina (390), Austria (314), Canada (2), Finland (2), Hungary (39), Ireland (30) and the United Kingdom (388). There were 35 civilian police provided by Australia (20) and Ireland (15). In addition, UNFICYP had 360 civilian staff, 42 of whom were internationally recruited and 318 locally recruited.

F. Financial aspects

By its resolution 47/236 of 14 September 1993, the United Nations General Assembly decided that for the period beginning 16 June 1993 the costs of the Force not covered by voluntary contributions should be treated as expenses of the Organization to be borne by Member States in accordance with Article 17 of the United Nations Charter.

The rough cost of UNFICYP in 1996 is estimated at approximately $44 million. With effect from 16 June 1993, the financing of the Force consists of voluntary contributions of $6.5 million annually from the Government of Greece and one third of its cost from the Government of Cyprus. Thus, only some $22 million a year is financed from contributions assessed on the entire membership of the United Nations.

By resolution 48/244 of 10 May 1994, the General Assembly, among other things, requested the Secretary-General to continue his efforts in appealing for voluntary contributions to the account established for UNFICYP prior to 16 June 1993, when the Force was financed entirely by voluntary contributions. The accumulated shortfall of approximately $200 million remains unreimbursed to troop contributors for that period.

[45]S/26777. [46]S/21982.

Part V
Africa

Chapter 10

United Nations Operation in the Congo (ONUC)

Formation of the Adoula Government
Government ordinance on expulsions
Round-up of mercenaries
Attack on ONUC
Dag Hammarskjöld's death
Cease-fire, September 1961
Katangese violations of the cease-fire
ANC offensives
Security Council authorizes ONUC to remove mercenaries
Fighting of December 1961
Kitona Declaration
Secretary-General's Plan of National Reconciliation
End of the secession of Katanga

E. Consolidation of the Congolese Government (February 1963–June 1964)

Introduction
Civilian operations
Reorganization of the Congolese armed forces, 1960–1963

F. Winding up of ONUC

Situation in February 1963
General Assembly resolution of 18 October 1963
Secretary-General's report, 29 June 1964
Withdrawal of the Force

Chapter 10

United Nations Operation in the Congo (ONUC)

A. Introduction

Background

The United Nations Operation in the Congo (Opération des Nations Unies au Congo, or ONUC), which took place in the Republic of the Congo (now Zaire) from July 1960 until June 1964, marked a milestone in the history of United Nations peace-keeping in terms of the responsibilities it had to assume, the size of its area of operation and the manpower involved. It included, in addition to a peace-keeping force which comprised at its peak strength nearly 20,000 officers and men, an important Civilian Operations component. Originally mandated to provide the Congolese Government with the military and technical assistance it required following the collapse of many essential services and the military intervention by Belgian troops, ONUC became embroiled by the force of circumstances in a chaotic internal situation of extreme complexity and had to assume certain responsibilities which went beyond normal peace-keeping duties. The policy followed by Secretary-General Dag Hammarskjöld in the Congo brought him into direct conflict with the Soviet Union and serious disagreement with some other Powers. The Operation cost the Secretary-General his life and led to a grave political and financial crisis within the United Nations itself.

With an area of some 2,345,000 square kilometres (about 1 million square miles), approximately the size of Western Europe, the Congo/Zaire is the third largest country in Africa, after the Sudan and Algeria. Encompassing the greatest part of the Congo basin in the very heart of Africa, the country has an important strategic position. The Congo is also exceptionally rich in minerals, much of them in the province of Katanga.

At the time of independence, the Congo had a population of about 14 million. The wind of change that had swept across Africa after the Second World War left the Territory largely un-touched. The Belgian colonial administration practised a policy of paternalism which gave the indigenous population one of the highest living standards on the continent, but little political and educational advancement. Few Congolese studied beyond the secondary level and, at the time of independence, there were among them only 17 university graduates and no doctors, lawyers or engineers.

Little political activity was allowed the Congolese population until 1959. Early that year, the Belgian Government, confronted with increasing disturbances, announced its intention to prepare the Congo for independence, and soon embarked upon a radical decolonization plan. A charter granting freedom of speech, of the press and of association was put into effect in August 1959, and elections to municipal and territorial councils were held in December. In January 1960, at a round-table conference of Congolese leaders convened in Brussels, Belgium agreed to grant independence to the Congo as of 30 June that same year.

From then on it was a race against time to get the Congo ready for independence. Provisional executive councils with the participation of Congolese leaders were established at the central and provincial levels in March 1960. The "Loi fondamentale", which was to serve as the constitution for the Congo, was adopted by the Belgian Parliament and promulgated by King Baudouin of Belgium on 19 March. General and provincial elections leading to the establishment of the Congolese Parliament and the provincial assemblies were held during the same month.

The Parliament convened in the early part of June and, by 23 June, after lengthy debate, the newly elected representatives worked out a compromise whereby the two rival dominant Congolese leaders were elected to the two key positions in the new political structure: Mr. Joseph Kasa-Vubu as President of the Republic and Mr. Patrice

Lumumba as Prime Minister. Thus, the apparatus for the independent State was completed barely six days before independence.

On 29 June 1960, a treaty of friendship, assistance and cooperation between Belgium and the Congo was signed by the representatives of the two Governments (but never ratified). Under that treaty, most of the administrative and technical personnel of the colonial administration would remain in the Congo on secondment to the Congolese Government. The treaty also provided that the two military bases at Kamina and Kitona would be ceded to Belgium and that the Belgian Government could, at the request of the Congolese Government, call out the Belgian troops from the bases to assist the latter Government in maintaining law and order. Belgium hoped that with this massive assistance and the guarantees accompanying it, it would be possible to ensure a smooth transition from colonial status to independence. Its main hope lay in the Force publique, the 25,000-man security force which had maintained law and order in the country in a forceful and effective way during colonial times and which would continue to be commanded by Belgium's Lieutenant-General Emile Janssens, with an all-Belgian officer corps. It was what the Belgians called at the time the "*Pari congolais*", the Congolese gamble.

Secretary-General Dag Hammarskjöld, who had visited the Belgian Congo in January 1960, was keenly conscious of the serious problems that would confront the Congolese Government after independence. He felt that the Congo would need, in addition to massive assistance from Belgium, extensive United Nations technical aid that had no political strings attached. With this in mind, he asked his Under-Secretary for Special Political Affairs, Mr. Ralph J. Bunche, to attend the independence ceremony in Leopoldville (now Kinshasa) as his personal representative and to take the opportunity to discuss with the Congolese authorities the technical assistance which the United Nations could provide. Mr. Bunche arrived in Leopoldville on 26 June and stayed on after the independence ceremony to work out an extensive United Nations technical assistance programme for the country.

Shortly after independence, Congolese soldiers of the Force publique became restive and petitioned for more promotion opportunity. Their petition was dismissed by General Janssens. He made it clear that so far as the Force publique was

concerned, independence had changed nothing. On 5 July, a mutiny broke out in the Leopoldville garrison and spread to several other cities during the following days. As some mutineers attacked Belgians and other Europeans, and in some cases committed rape and other atrocities, most Belgian administrators and technicians fled the country, and this led to the collapse of a number of essential services throughout the country.

The Belgian Ambassador to the Congo repeatedly urged Prime Minister Lumumba to request the assistance of Belgian troops, under the friendship treaty, to maintain law and order, but Mr. Lumumba adamantly refused. Instead, he attempted to regain control of the Force publique by agreeing to the Congolese soldiers' demand for reform. He renamed the Force publique the Armée nationale congolaise (ANC), dismissed General Janssens and appointed Mr. Victor Lundula, a Congolese, as Commander of the Army with the rank of Major-General, and Mr. Joseph Mobutu, also a Congolese, as its Chief of Staff with the rank of Colonel. All Congolese soldiers and non-commissioned officers were promoted by one grade pending further measures to Africanize the entire officer corps.

As disorder spread and intensified, Ralph Bunche, who was in Leopoldville at the time, strongly advised the Belgian Ambassador not to call in Belgian troops without the prior agreement of the Congolese Government. At the same time, he was in close touch with the Congolese authorities and the Secretary-General in New York to work out a plan to help the Government control and strengthen the Congolese army through United Nations assistance. Secretary-General Hammarskjöld envisaged sending a large number of United Nations military advisers, experts and technicians for this purpose. He felt that if the Congolese Government were to request such military personnel as technical assistance of a military nature, rather than as military assistance, he could take immediate action on his own authority without referring the matter to the Security Council.

The Congolese Government agreed to this course of action and, on 10 July, submitted a formal request to the Secretary-General for technical assistance of a military nature, including military advisers, experts and technicians, to assist it in developing and strengthening the national army for the twin purposes of national defence and the maintenance of law and order.

Belgian intervention and Security Council action

However, a new situation developed on the next day when the Belgian Government ordered its troops into the Congo without the agreement of the Congolese Government, for the declared purpose of restoring law and order and protecting Belgian nationals. Belgian troops landed at Leopoldville, Matadi, Luluabourg (now Kananga) and Elisabethville (now Lubumbashi), in Katanga. Their intervention, which was followed in some cases by heavy fighting with Congolese soldiers, further increased tension and disorder throughout the country. On 11 July, shortly after the arrival of Belgian troops in Elisabethville, Mr. Moïse Tshombé, the provincial president, proclaimed the independence of Katanga, the richest province of the Congo, which provided the country with more than half of its revenues.

On 12 July, President Kasa-Vubu and Prime Minister Lumumba sent a joint telegram[1] to the Secretary-General requesting United Nations military assistance. They said that the essential purpose of the requested military aid was "to protect the national territory of the Congo against the present external aggression which is a threat to international peace". The next day, they cabled a further message[2] to the Secretary-General to make it clear that they were not asking for aid to restore the internal situation but to respond to Belgian aggression.

On 13 July, the Secretary-General, invoking Article 99 of the United Nations Charter — which empowers the Secretary-General to bring to the attention of the Security Council any matter which in his opinion may threaten international peace and security — requested an urgent meeting[3] of the Council to consider the situation in the Congo. The Council met on the same evening. In an opening statement, the Secretary-General outlined his ideas about the actions that the Council might take in response to the request of the Congolese Government. In essence, he recommended the establishment of a United Nations peace-keeping force to assist that Government in maintaining law and order until, with technical assistance from the United Nations, the Congolese national security forces were able fully to meet their tasks. He assumed that, were the United Nations to act as proposed, the Belgian Government would withdraw its forces from Congolese territory.

At the same meeting, during the night of 13/14 July, the Security Council adopted resolution 143 (1960), by which it called upon the Government of Belgium to withdraw its troops from the territory of the Congo and decided "to authorize the Secretary-General to take the necessary steps, in consultation with the Government of the Republic of the Congo, to provide the Government with such military assistance as might be necessary until, through that Government's efforts with United Nations technical assistance, the national security forces might be able, in the opinion of the Government, to meet fully their tasks". It requested the Secretary-General to report to the Security Council as appropriate.

The Council resolution was adopted by 8 votes in favour (including the Soviet Union and the United States) to none against, with 3 abstentions.

Secretary-General's principles governing the United Nations Force

In his first report[4] on the implementation of the resolution, the Secretary-General outlined the principles which would govern the organization and activities of the United Nations Force in the Congo, its composition and the action he had taken or envisaged taking to establish it.

The proposals the Secretary-General set out for the Force were as follows:

(a) The Force was to be regarded as a temporary security force to be deployed in the Congo with the consent of the Congolese Government until the national security forces were able, in the opinion of that Government, to meet fully their tasks.

(b) Although dispatched at the request of the Congolese Government and remaining there with its consent, and although it might be considered as serving as an arm of the Congolese Government for the maintenance of law and order and protection of life, the Force was necessarily under the exclusive command of the United Nations, vested in the Secretary-General under the control of the Security Council. The Force was thus not under the orders of the Congolese Government and could not be permitted to become a party to any internal conflict.

(c) The host Government, when exercising its sovereign rights with regard to the presence of the United Nations Force in its territory, should be guided by good faith in the interpretation of the Force's purpose. Similarly, the United Nations should be so guided when it considered the ques-

---

[1]S/4382. [2]Ibid. [3]S/4381. [4]S/4389.

tion of the maintenance of the Force in the host country.

(d) The United Nations should have free access to the area of operation and full freedom of movement within that area as well as all the communications and other facilities required to carry out its tasks. A further elaboration of this rule obviously required an agreement with the Government specifying what was to be considered the area of operation.

(e) The authority granted to the United Nations Force could not be exercised within the Congo either in competition with the representatives of its Government or in cooperation with them in any joint operation. This principle applied also *a fortiori* to representatives and military units of Governments other than the host Government. Thus, the United Nations Operation must be separate and distinct from activities by any national authorities.

(f) The units of the Force must not become parties to internal conflicts. They could not be used to enforce any specific political solution of pending problems or to influence the political balance decisive for such a solution.

(g) The basic rules of the United Nations for international service were applicable to all United Nations personnel employed in the Congo Operation, particularly as regards loyalty to the aims of the Organization.

(h) The United Nations military units were not authorized to use force except in self-defence. They were never to take the initiative in the use of force, but were entitled to respond with force to an attack with arms, including attacks intended to make them withdraw from positions they occupied under orders from the Commander, acting under the authority of the Security Council. The basic element of influence in this principle was clearly the prohibition of any initiative in the use of armed force.

With regard to the composition of the Force, the Secretary-General reiterated the principle that, while the United Nations must preserve its authority to decide on this matter, it should take full account of the views of the host Government. He recalled that in order to limit the scope of possible differences of opinion with host Governments, the United Nations had in recent operations followed two principles: not to include units from any of the permanent members of the Security Council or units from any country which, because of its geographical position or for other reasons, might be considered as having a special interest in the situation that had called for the

operation. He indicated his intention to seek, in the first place, the assistance of African States for the United Nations Force in the Congo. The Force would be built around a core of military units from African States and should also include suitable units from other regions to give it a truly international character. In selecting the contingents, the Secretary-General would necessarily be guided by considerations of availability of troops, language and geographical distribution within the region.

In order to set up the Force speedily, the Secretary-General said, he had accepted offers of troops by Ethiopia, Ghana, Guinea, Morocco and Tunisia. These five countries would provide seven battalions, with a total strength of 4,000 men. Arrangements were being made to airlift the battalions to the Congo as soon as possible. An offer of troops from Mali had also been received and would be activated at a later stage.

With the deployment of the seven battalions, the first phase of the build-up of the Force would be completed. For the second phase, the Secretary-General had requested troops from three European countries and one Asian and one Latin American country. In one of those cases — Sweden — he had asked and secured permission to transfer to the Congo on a temporary basis the Swedish battalion of the United Nations Emergency Force (UNEF) in Gaza, thus bringing the total strength of the Force to eight battalions.

Requests for aircraft, signal and other logistic support, as well as for air transport facilities, had been addressed to a number of non-African nations.

As soon as Security Council resolution 143 (1960) was adopted, the Secretary-General appointed Ralph Bunche as his Special Representative in the Congo to head the new Operation. He also appointed Lieutenant-General Carl C. von Horn (Sweden) as Supreme Commander of the United Nations Force in the Congo. General von Horn, who until then had occupied the post of Chief of Staff of the United Nations Truce Supervision Organization (UNTSO), would be assisted in the initial stage by a small personal staff of officers drawn from UNTSO.

On the evening of 15 July 1960, less than 48 hours after the adoption of the Council's resolution, an advance party of the Tunisian contingent, consisting of about 90 officers and men, landed at Leopoldville. They were followed on succeeding days by the remainder of the Tunisian battalion and personnel of the Ethiopian, Ghanaian, Guinean and Moroccan battalions. Mr. Bunche, who was appointed temporary Commander of the Force pending the arrival of General von Horn, immediately deployed these units in sensitive localities in Leopoldville, Stanleyville (now Kisangani), Matadi, Thysville and Coquilhatville (now Mbandaka). On 18 July, General von Horn and his staff officers arrived in Leopoldville and immediately set up Force headquarters at the airport.

As the responsibilities of the United Nations in the Congo expanded, the Secretary-General requested and obtained more battalions and support personnel. The Force reached a total of 19,828 at its peak strength by July 1961. From then on, as some of its responsibilities were fulfilled, the strength of the Force was progressively reduced. In addition to the military units, ONUC had a Civilian Operations component which employed some 2,000 experts and technicians to provide the Congolese Government with extensive assistance in the administrative, technical and humanitarian fields.

While its original mandate as outlined in Council resolution 143 (1960) remained valid, ONUC was given new responsibilities and new tasks during the four years of its operation. The history of ONUC may be divided into four periods, as follows: restoration of law and order and withdrawal of Belgian forces (July–August 1960); constitutional crisis (September 1960–September 1961); termination of the secession of Katanga (September 1961–February 1963); and consolidation of the Congolese Government (February 1963–June 1964). Each of these periods is dealt with separately below.

B. Restoration of law and order and withdrawal of Belgian forces (July–August 1960)

ONUC objectives

The two main objectives of ONUC during the initial phase were to help the Congolese Government restore law and order and to bring about the speedy withdrawal of the Belgian forces. These objectives were closely related.

In a statement made in the Security Council just before the adoption of resolution 143 (1960), the representative of Belgium stated that his Government had no political designs in the Congo and that when the United Nations Force had moved into position and was able to ensure the effective maintenance of order and the security of persons in the Congo, his Government would withdraw its forces.

Immediately after the adoption of the resolution, Mr. Bunche initiated negotiations with the Belgian Ambassador in Leopoldville in order to work out agreement for the speedy and orderly withdrawal of the Belgian forces in accordance with the resolution and in the light of the undertaking given by the Belgian Government. The United Nations plan was to bring its forces into the Congo as rapidly as possible and deploy them in various parts of the country, first of all in those positions occupied by Belgian troops. Once deployed, United Nations troops would restore law and order and ensure the protection of civilians in cooperation with the Congolese Government and speed up the withdrawal of the Belgian forces from the area.

Withdrawal of Belgian troops outside Katanga

The first troops of the United Nations Force arrived at Leopoldville on the evening of 15 July and were deployed the next morning at the radio station and the power station and along the main thoroughfare of the capital. Their presence had an immediate calming effect in an extremely tense situation. On 16 July, the Belgian Ambassador informed Mr. Bunche that, consequent upon the arrival of the United Nations troops, the first contingents of the Belgian armed forces had left Leopoldville and returned to their bases on that same day. On 19 July, Mr. Bunche reported to the Secretary-General that the United Nations was now in a position to guarantee that contingents of the United Nations Force drawn from both African and European countries would arrive during the week in sufficient numbers to ensure order and protect the entire population of Leopoldville, African and European. In the light of this assurance, it was decided that the Belgian forces would begin to withdraw completely from the Leopoldville area and return to their bases on 20 July. This withdrawal operation was to be completed by the afternoon of 23 July.

As more United Nations troops were flown into the Congo, they were deployed in other areas such as Thysville, Matadi, Luluabourg, Coquilhatville and Stanleyville. In each of these places, ONUC immediately began its task of maintaining law and order and protecting the local population, and initiated discussions with the Belgian representative to bring about the withdrawal of Belgian troops at an early date.

Although this speed could be achieved only through strenuous efforts, the Congolese Government did not consider it fast enough. On 17 July 1960, Mr. Lumumba and Mr. Kasa-Vubu addressed an ultimatum to the Secretary-General, warning that if the Belgian forces were not completely withdrawn within 48 hours, they would request troops from the Soviet Union. The Secretary-General brought the matter before the Security Council, which — by resolution 145 (1960) of 22 July 1960, adopted unanimously — commended the action taken by the Secretary-General and called upon Belgium to speed up the withdrawal of its troops.

The original plan was therefore continued without change. As soon as new United Nations contingents arrived, they were deployed in the positions occupied by Belgian troops. They brought about the complete withdrawal of the Belgian troops from Leopoldville and the surrounding area on 23 July 1960, and from the whole of the Congo, except Katanga and the two bases, by the beginning of August 1960.

Withdrawal from Katanga

The next step was the entry of United Nations troops into the province of Katanga. On this question, the Secretary-General ran into a grave conflict with Prime Minister Lumumba, who wanted ONUC to help his Government put down the secession of Katanga by force. The Secretary-General refused to do this, taking the position that under its mandate ONUC could not use force except in self-defence, and could not be a party to, or in any way intervene in or be used to influence the outcome of, any internal conflict in the Congo. He also encountered serious difficulties with the Katangese secessionist authorities and the Belgian Government. The Katangese authorities strongly opposed the entry of United Nations troops and, citing this opposition, the Belgian Government was reluctant to withdraw its forces from Katanga.

On 4 August 1960, the Secretary-General, who had arrived in Leopoldville a few days earlier, sent Mr. Bunche to Elisabethville to make arrangements with the Belgian representative there for the entry of United Nations troops into Katanga, which, if no difficulties arose, would take place on 6 August. But in the face of unqualified and unyielding opposition by the Katangese secessionist authorities, Mr. Bunche concluded that the entry of United Nations troops could not be achieved without bloodshed. The Secretary-General therefore decided to postpone the original plan and brought the matter before the Security Council.

By resolution 146 (1960) of 9 August 1960, the Security Council confirmed the authority conferred upon the Secretary-General by its previous resolutions and called upon Belgium immediately to withdraw its troops from Katanga, under speedy modalities determined by the Secretary-General. At the same time, while declaring that the entry of the United Nations Force into Katanga was necessary, the Council reaffirmed that the Force should not in any way intervene in any internal conflict in the Congo or be used to influence the outcome of any such conflict, constitutional or otherwise. The resolution was adopted by 9 votes to none, with 2 abstentions (France and Italy).

After the adoption of the resolution, the Secretary-General returned to the Congo and, on 12 August, personally led the first United Nations unit into Katanga. But Prime Minister Lumumba strongly criticized the manner in which the Secretary-General had implemented the Council's resolutions and refused thenceforth to cooperate with him. In view of the Prime Minister's reaction, the Secretary-General once again referred the matter to the Security Council.

The Council met on 21 August 1960, but did not vote on any resolution. During the discussion, the Secretary-General indicated that, in the absence of any new directive, he would consider his interpretation of the ONUC mandate as upheld. He also made known his intention to appoint an Advisory Committee, composed of Member States which had contributed troops to the United Nations Force, to advise him on future policy on the Congo.

The entry of United Nations troops into Katanga on 12 August 1960 set off a process of withdrawal of Belgian troops from the province, which was completed by the beginning of September. At that time, Belgian troops were also withdrawn from the military bases of Kamina and Kitona, which were taken over by ONUC.

Thus, despite difficult circumstances, ONUC brought about the withdrawal of Belgian troops from the whole of the Congo within six weeks. However, the secession of Katanga remained unresolved.

Maintenance of law and order

The maintenance of law and order was the heaviest of all the tasks falling upon ONUC. In order to carry out that task, the Secretary-General set up a United Nations Force which at its peak strength numbered nearly 20,000. But even at its peak strength, the Force was hardly sufficient and was severely strained, inasmuch as its responsibilities had to encompass such a vast land as the Congo.

On their arrival in the Congo, United Nations soldiers were officially instructed that they were members of a peace force, not a fighting force, that they had been asked to come in response to an appeal from the Congolese Government, that their task was to help in restoring order and calm in a troubled country and that they should give protection against acts of violence to all the people, Africans and Europeans alike. They were also told that although they carried arms, they were to use them only in self-defence; they were in the Congo to help everyone and to harm no one.

What ONUC sought to do was to assist the Congolese authorities to perform their normal duties, for instance by undertaking joint patrols with the local police for the maintenance of law and order in a given area. When, however, this was not possible on account of the breakdown of the security forces, the United Nations Force had to perform the normal security duties in the place of Congolese authorities. But in so doing it sought the consent and cooperation of the Congolese Government. Such was the case in Leopoldville during the Operation's first stage, when United Nations soldiers performed police duties along the city's main arteries to ensure the protection of its essential services.

Following these procedures, the Force restored law and order, protected life and property, and ensured the continued operation of essential services wherever it was deployed. In many areas it brought under control unruly ANC elements, many of whom laid down their arms voluntarily or at the request of their Government. Thus the Force carried out its task of maintaining law and order with success in the initial phase of the Operation.

However, the internal situation in August began to worsen rapidly. Tribal rivalries, which had plagued the country before independence, flared up that month with added intensity in Kasai between Baluba and Lulua tribesmen. The Baluba of the Luluabourg area fled en masse to their tribal lands in the Bakwanga region, where their leader, Mr. Albert Kalonji, proclaimed the secession of South Kasai.

In Equateur and Leopoldville provinces, there was increasing opposition to the Government. To put down opposition and secessionist movements, Prime Minister Lumumba arrested some opposition leaders, and anti-Government newspapers were suspended. At the end of August, ANC troops were sent to South Kasai, and many civilians were killed, including women and children. Other ANC troops were being massed near the northern border of Katanga in preparation for an invasion of the province. During those days, elements of the ANC, which the Government was using to achieve its political objectives but which it was not always able to control, were a constant danger to the civilian population.

Without the cooperation of the Congolese Government which it had come to assist, ONUC faced a frustrating situation. Its activities were further hampered when the Government itself resorted to actions which tended to endanger law and order, or restrict human rights. Whenever this happened, ONUC endeavoured to induce and persuade Congolese authorities to change their course of action, and, to the extent possible, took measures to ensure the protection of the threatened persons. But it refused to use force to subdue Congolese authorities, or the ANC under their orders. Even when its own personnel were attacked, ONUC intervened only to prevent further excesses and to urge the Congolese Government to take disciplinary action against the culprits.

C. Constitutional crisis (September 1960–September 1961)

Introduction

On 5 September 1960, a constitutional crisis developed, when President Kasa-Vubu, invoking the authority conferred upon him by the *Loi fondamentale*, decided[5] to dismiss Prime Minister Lumumba. The crisis lasted 11 months, during which time there was no legal government and the country was divided into four opposing camps, each with its own armed forces. ONUC therefore could only deal with de facto authority and do whatever it could to avert civil war and protect the civilian population. It attempted to prevent the leaders who wielded power from subduing opponents by force and at the same time encouraged those leaders to seek a solution through negotiation and conciliation.

Dismissal of Prime Minister

In the days following President Kasa-Vubu's dismissal of Prime Minister Lumumba, utter confusion prevailed in Leopoldville. The Prime Minister refused to recognize the President's decision and, in turn, dismissed President Kasa-Vubu as Chief of State. Parliament supported Mr. Lumumba, although it refused to endorse his decision to dismiss the Chief of State, but Parliament itself was soon suspended by President Kasa-Vubu. Each contending party sought the support of the army and, whenever it could, ordered the arrest of its opponents. On 14 September 1960, Colonel Joseph Mobutu imposed[6] by a coup an army-backed regime run by a Council of Commissioners (Collège des Commissaires) and supporting Mr. Kasa-Vubu. But the coup was not fully effective in that Mr. Lumumba and his supporters resisted the Commissioners' authority.

Emergency measures

At the outset of the crisis, ONUC took emergency measures[7] to avoid violence and bloodshed. It decided on the night of 5/6 September 1960 to close the Leopoldville airport to prevent the arrival of rival troops. The following day, in view of the likely dangerous effect of inflammatory speeches on an already disturbed populace and after a number of violent demonstrations had taken place in the city, it temporarily closed down the Leopoldville radio station. These measures were lifted by 13 September 1960, as soon as the tension had subsided to below the explosive level.

In response to appeals from political and other leaders of all sides in Leopoldville, ONUC agreed to protect the threatened leaders, and in so doing it endeavoured to show absolute impartiality. ONUC guards were stationed around the residences of both Mr. Kasa-Vubu and Mr. Lumumba. Protection was also given to the other leaders, though not to the same extent.

Containment of hostilities

In the following months, ONUC endeavoured to prevent or control hostilities between the various Congolese factions.

In South Kasai, ONUC helped in arranging a cease-fire between ANC troops and the Kalonji secessionist army and in establishing a neutral zone under ONUC control. It also persuaded the ANC command to withdraw its troops from the northern border of Katanga.

In northern Katanga, where violent fighting broke out between pro-Tshombé gendarmes and the anti-Tshombé Baluba population, ONUC put an end to the fighting by setting up, in agreement with both parties, neutral zones under its protection.

Protected areas were set up at various times and places, to which threatened persons, Africans and Europeans alike, could repair for safety. Neutral zones were established to stop tribal warfare. During this period of unrest, Europeans, many of whom were settlers in scattered, remote areas, were often threatened by hostile local authorities or populations. Whenever possible, ONUC took measures to rescue and protect them and, if they so desired, to evacuate them to safer areas.

The contending parties turned to ONUC for recognition and support. ONUC continued its policy of avoiding intervening or taking sides in the internal conflicts. While it recognized the unimpaired status of Mr. Kasa-Vubu as Chief of State, it refused to help him achieve political aims by

[5]S/4531. [6]S/4557. [7]S/4531.

force and, in particular, to recognize the Council of Commissioners supported by him.

Security Council and General Assembly consideration

The crisis was examined by the Security Council from 14 to 17 September 1960 and, when the Council failed to take a decision, by an emergency special session of the General Assembly from 17 to 20 September.

By resolution 1474 (ES-IV) of 20 September 1960, the Assembly requested the Secretary-General to continue to take vigorous action in line with the Security Council's resolutions. In an effort to resolve the constitutional crisis, it appealed to all Congolese to seek a speedy solution, by peaceful means, of all their internal conflicts, and requested the Advisory Committee on the Congo to appoint a conciliation commission to assist them in that endeavour.

The Conciliation Commission was composed of Ethiopia, the Federation of Malaya, Ghana, Guinea, India, Indonesia, Liberia, Mali, Morocco, Nigeria, Pakistan, Senegal, the Sudan, Tunisia and the United Arab Republic. Subsequently, Guinea, Indonesia, Mali and the United Arab Republic withdrew from the Commission.

During the meeting of the Security Council, two Congolese delegations, one appointed by Mr. Kasa-Vubu and the other by Mr. Lumumba, were sent to New York, but neither could win recognition. Two months later, during the fifteenth regular session of the General Assembly in December, Mr. Kasa-Vubu himself came to New York as the head of his delegation, which was seated by the Assembly after a long and heated debate. The Assembly's decision considerably enhanced Mr. Kasa-Vubu's personal prestige, but did not bring an immediate solution to the crisis.

Four rival groups

In the meantime, the internal situation rapidly worsened in the Congo. While the Council of Commissioners consolidated its position in Leopoldville, Mr. Antoine Gizenga, acting on behalf of Mr. Lumumba, succeeded in establishing a "government" in Stanleyville which was formally recognized as the legitimate government of the Republic by a number of Member States. With the support of the local ANC troops, led by General Victor Lundula, Mr. Gizenga extended his authority beyond Orientale province to Kivu and the northern part of Katanga.

At the same time, the secessionist authorities headed by Moïse Tshombé and Albert Kalonji consolidated their hold, respectively, over southern Katanga and South Kasai, with the active assistance of certain foreign Powers. Thus, the Congo came to be divided into four rival camps, each relying more on armed force than on popular support.

ONUC casualties

In carrying out its mission of peace, the United Nations Force suffered many casualties. On 8 November 1960, a patrol of 11 Irish soldiers was ambushed by tribesmen in northern Katanga and eight of them were killed. Another incident occurred on 24 November when ANC troops attacked the Ghanaian Embassy in Leopoldville. The Tunisian unit which guarded the Embassy incurred several casualties, including one fatality.

Here again, when the authorities in power indulged in actions which endangered peace and order, or violated human rights, ONUC could not always prevent those actions, but sought to redress the situation by the use of persuasion or good offices. Thus, ONUC could not prevent a number of political arrests made by the various local regimes. At the time, those regimes endeavoured to strengthen their armed forces by importing arms and military equipment from abroad. While ONUC did its best to stop such imports, its forces were insufficient to control all points of entry, and therefore it could not prevent quantities of arms and equipment from being smuggled into different parts of the country.

Patrice Lumumba's death

From the beginning of the constitutional crisis, ONUC troops vigilantly guarded Mr. Lumumba's residence and, so long as he remained there, he was safe. However, it was not possible to protect him when he voluntarily left his residence, as he did on the night of 27/28 November 1960, in an apparent attempt to get to Stanleyville, his political stronghold.[8] Before he could get there, he was arrested by ANC soldiers controlled by Colonel Mobutu near Port-Francqui (now Ilebo) and brought back to Leopoldville. Once he was arrested by the de facto authorities of Leopoldville, ONUC was not in a position to take forcible action to liberate him from his captors, but it exerted all possible pressure to secure lawful, humane treat-

[8]S/4571.

ment for him. Upon learning of the arrest, the Secretary-General sent a succession of messages[9] to President Kasa-Vubu, expressing his concern over the event and stressing the importance of giving the prisoner all the guarantees provided by law. Similarly repeated representations were later made to the President by Mr. Rajeshwar Dayal (India), at the time Special Representative of the Secretary-General in the Congo. ONUC could not do more without exceeding the mandate given it by the Security Council and without using force.

Mr. Lumumba remained detained in Thysville until 17 January, when he and two other political prisoners, Mr. Joseph Okito and Mr. Maurice Mpolo, were transferred to Elisabethville in Katanga. This move brought strong protests from both the Secretary-General and the United Nations Conciliation Commission for the Congo, which was then in the territory. In particular, the Secretary-General took immediate action to urge the authorities concerned to return Mr. Lumumba to Leopoldville province and to apply the normal legal rules. But no remedial action was taken, and, four weeks later, the news came from Katanga that the three prisoners had been murdered. The circumstances of their death were later investigated by a United Nations commission, which accepted as substantially true evidence indicating that the prisoners had been killed on 17 January 1961 and probably in the presence of high officials of the Katanga provincial government.

Following Mr. Lumumba's death, there was a series of reprisals and counter-reprisals by pro-Lumumba and anti-Lumumba factions, including summary executions of political leaders. The civil war, already under way in northern Katanga, threatened to spread to other regions.

Several troop-contributing countries withdrew their national contingents from ONUC, reducing its strength from 20,000 to less than 15,000. At United Nations Headquarters, the Soviet Union called for Secretary-General Hammarskjöld's dismissal and announced that it would not, henceforth, recognize him as Secretary-General.

Authorization to use force

The Security Council met again on 15 February 1961, and after long debate adopted, on 21 February, resolution 161 (1961), by which it authorized ONUC to use force, as a last resort, to prevent civil war in the Congo. It urged that the various Congolese armed units be reorganized and brought under discipline and control, and urged

the immediate evacuation of all Belgian and other foreign military and paramilitary personnel and political advisers not under United Nations command, as well as mercenaries. It also urged the convening of Parliament and the taking of the necessary protective measures in that connection.

Provisional government

After January 1961, a number of steps were taken by various Congolese leaders attempting to resolve the crisis. On 25 January, a preliminary round-table was sponsored by Mr. Kasa-Vubu in Leopoldville. It was boycotted by pro-Lumumba and pro-Tshombé leaders, which considerably limited its usefulness. However, at the end of the conference, Mr. Kasa-Vubu decided to replace the Council of Commissioners by a provisional government headed by Mr. Joseph Ileo, a decision which was considered by the United Nations Conciliation Commission as a step in the right direction.

Situation in the Congo: February–April 1961

The period immediately following the adoption of the Security Council's resolution of 21 February 1961 was a critical one for the United Nations Operation in the Congo. Thinly deployed throughout the country, the United Nations Force had great difficulty in coping with its overwhelming tasks, and this difficulty increased with its reduction in strength.

The difficulties were compounded by the hostile attitude of the de facto authorities of Leopoldville and Elisabethville. These authorities interpreted the Council's new resolution as an attempt to subdue them by force and, in retaliation, ordered a number of harassing measures against ONUC and its personnel. The most serious of these was an attack by ANC troops on the United Nations garrison in Matadi on 4 March 1961, which forced the garrison to withdraw from the port city.

In order to cope with these difficulties and to implement the resolution, the Secretary-General took urgent action to increase the strength of the United Nations Force. New contributions of personnel were obtained from several Governments, bringing the total of the United Nations troops to more than 18,000 in April 1961.

In April, the situation began to improve, first because of the increased strength of the Force,

[9]S/4571, annexes I and II.

ONUC deployment as of June 1961

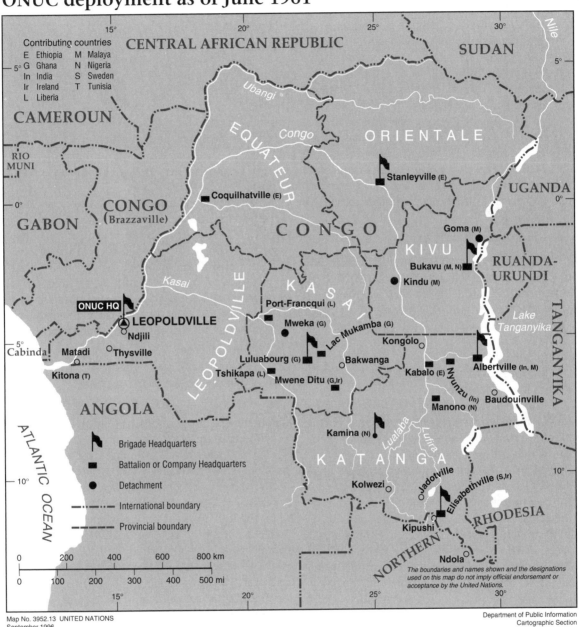

Contributing countries
E Ethiopia   M Malaya
G Ghana   N Nigeria
In India   S Sweden
Ir Ireland   T Tunisia
L Liberia

CENTRAL AFRICAN REPUBLIC

SUDAN

CAMEROUN

RIO MUNI

GABON

CONGO (Brazzaville)

Ubangi

Congo

EQUATEUR

ORIENTALE

Stanleyville (E)

UGANDA

Coquilhatville (E)

C O N G O

Goma (M)

KIVU

RUANDA-URUNDI

Bukavu (M, N)

Kindu (M)

Kasai

K A S A I

ONUC HQ

LEOPOLDVILLE

Ndjili

Matadi

Thysville

Cabinda

Kitona (T)

Port-Francqui (L)

Mweka (G)

Lac Mukamba (G)

Kongolo

Luluabourg (G)

Tshikapa (L)

Bakwanga

Albertville (In, M)

Mwene Ditu (G,Ir)

Kabalo (E)

Nyunzu (In)

Baudouinville

Manono (N)

Lake Tanganyika

TANGANYIKA

LEOPOLDVILLE

ANGOLA

ATLANTIC OCEAN

Brigade Headquarters

Battalion or Company Headquarters

Detachment

International boundary

Provincial boundary

Kamina (N)

K A T A N G A

Lualaba

Lufira

Kolwezi

Jadotville

Elisabethville (S,Ir)

Kipushi

RHODESIA

NORTHERN

Ndola

| 0 | 200 | 400 | 600 | 800 km |
| 0 | 100 | 200 | 300 | 400 | 500 mi |

The boundaries and names shown and the designations used on this map do not imply official endorsement or acceptance by the United Nations.

Map No. 3952.13 UNITED NATIONS
September 1996

Department of Public Information
Cartographic Section

185

and secondly because, after patient negotiations, ONUC reached an agreement with President Kasa-Vubu on 17 April 1961 for the implementation of the Security Council's February resolution.

The limited use of force, as authorized by the Council, was resorted to by ONUC at the beginning of April 1961 to stop the civil war, which was spreading dangerously in northern Katanga. Since mid-March 1961, Katangese gendarmerie led by foreign mercenaries had launched an offensive against the anti-Tshombé forces in northern Katanga in a determined effort to crush all opposition there. On 27 March, the United Nations Force Commander warned Mr. Tshombé to stop the offensive, but the warning was unheeded and his gendarmes entered Manono three days later and prepared to attack Kabalo. It was at this point that United Nations troops intervened, stopped the gendarmes and established control of the area between Kabalo and Albertville (now Kalemie).

Further casualties

At the end of April, a tragic incident occurred when a Ghanaian detachment of ONUC in Port-Francqui was suddenly attacked and overpowered by ANC troops, and 44 of its members ruthlessly massacred. It was generally agreed that this brutal assault was mainly an act by undisciplined and unpredictable armed troops. Thereafter, the ONUC command made it a rule not to station small units in isolated areas.

Another series of incidents was related to the ANC campaign, late in 1961, to occupy northern Katanga. In connection with this military campaign, which is described in the section below on the problem of Katanga, a number of grave incidents were caused by undisciplined ANC elements. At the beginning of November 1961, ANC soldiers of the Leopoldville group assaulted several Belgian women in Luluabourg. On 11 November, ANC soldiers of the Stanleyville group massacred 13 ONUC aircrew members of Italian nationality in Kindu. Two days later, ANC soldiers of the same group, who had just entered Albertville, began looting houses and threatening civilians there. On 1 January 1961, 22 European missionaries and an undetermined number of Africans were killed in Kongolo by ANC soldiers, also from Stanleyville, in an incident reminiscent of the Kindu massacre.

Conciliation efforts

During the first days of the constitutional crisis, ONUC endeavoured to prevent the leaders

holding the reins of power from using force to subdue their opponents within or outside the zones they controlled and, at the same time, it encouraged all leaders to seek a solution of their differences through negotiation and conciliation.

Conciliation efforts were also made by the United Nations Conciliation Commission, established under the Assembly's resolution of 20 September 1960. This Commission, which was composed of representatives of African and Asian countries which contributed troops to the United Nations Force, visited the Congo at the beginning of 1961. After spending seven weeks in that country, the Commission concluded that, while there was among most leaders a general feeling of weariness and a sincere desire to achieve a peaceful solution to the crisis, a small number of other leaders, among the very persons holding the reins of power, appeared to prefer a military rather than a political and constitutional solution. Because of those leaders' uncooperative and intransigent attitude, the Commission's attempts to reconcile the opposing groups had not led to positive results. The Commission also came to the conclusion that the crisis could be solved only if Parliament was reconvened and a national unity government was approved by it, and that one of the main obstacles to a speedy solution was foreign intervention in the internal affairs of the Congo.

Tananarive Conference

In the meantime, at the beginning of March 1961, a conference was held in Tananarive (now Antananarivo), Madagascar, on the proposal of Mr. Tshombé. It was attended by a number of top Congolese leaders, but Mr. Gizenga, who had at first agreed to come, did not show up. The Tananarive Conference proposed that the Congo be turned into a confederation of sovereign States. Under the proposed arrangement, the central Government would be abolished, and legislative and executive powers would be vested in the individual States. The Conference proposals also provided for the establishment of new States, but did not determine the criteria to be followed in that connection. This decision led some Congolese leaders, through personal ambition and tribal animosities, to lay claim for the creation of a score of new States. But the influence of the Tananarive Conference was short-lived. Soon afterwards, Mr. Kasa-Vubu and other leaders revised their positions and made it clear that the decisions of Tananarive were mere statements of intention and, unless approved by Parliament, had no force of law.

Coquilhatville meeting

The following month, on 24 April 1961, a more important conference was convened in Coquilhatville, on the proposal of President Kasa-Vubu. Mr. Gizenga again refused to attend. Mr. Tshombé came and sought to have the Conference endorse the Tananarive proposals. When his attempt was opposed by the overwhelming majority of the representatives, he decided to boycott the Conference. As he prepared to fly back to Elisabethville, he was arrested by the Leopoldville authorities, although he was released about a month later. The Conference continued nevertheless, and, at the conclusion of its work, it recommended a reorganization of the governmental structure of the Congo on a federal basis. From the outset, it had been made clear that Conference decisions would have to be endorsed by Parliament, and during the Conference, on 12 May, President Kasa-Vubu announced that Parliament would be reopened in the near future and requested United Nations assistance and protection for this purpose.

While carefully avoiding interference in the discussions between the Congolese leaders, ONUC assisted them whenever it was requested to do so. Thus it placed a guard at the site of the preliminary round-table conference in Leopoldville. It agreed to facilitate Mr. Gizenga's trip to Tananarive when he first accepted to go there. Before the Coquilhatville Conference, a Congolese leader, Mr. Cleophas Kamitatu, went to Stanleyville on an ONUC aeroplane in an effort to bring about a rapprochement between Mr. Gizenga and Mr. Kasa-Vubu. ONUC also made representations for Mr. Tshombé's release.

Reopening of Parliament

After President Kasa-Vubu announced his intention to reconvene Parliament, ONUC spared no effort to help achieve this purpose. An essential condition for reconvening Parliament was a rapprochement between leaders of the Leopoldville and Stanleyville groups. To these two groups belonged the great majority of parliamentarians, and if one of them refused to attend meetings of Parliament, there would be no quorum. But the memory of Patrice Lumumba's death and its aftermath was still vivid, and leaders of the two groups were divided by deep suspicion and distrust. Through good offices and persuasion, ONUC officials did everything possible to dissipate their mutual suspicion and lay the groundwork for negotiations between them.

After President Kasa-Vubu called the parliamentary session in Leopoldville, Mr. Gizenga condemned his action as illegal and ordered Parliament to meet in Kamina. Thanks to ONUC's good offices, Mr. Gizenga softened his stand and agreed not to insist on Kamina, provided that full protection was given to parliamentarians by ONUC. Later, a meeting[10] between Leopoldville and Stanleyville representatives was arranged at Leopoldville, under ONUC auspices, to consider the modalities of the reopening of Parliament. The Stanleyville representatives were brought to Leopoldville in an ONUC aircraft and the meeting took place at ONUC headquarters. After long discussions, an agreement was reached by the representatives of the two groups. At their joint request, ONUC accepted the responsibility for making arrangements for the session of Parliament and ensuring full protection to the parliamentarians.

In accordance with a request made by both delegations, ONUC also sought to persuade Congolese leaders of South Kasai and southern Katanga to subscribe to the agreement on the reconvening of Parliament. Both Mr. Kalonji and Mr. Tshombé, who was released from confinement by the Leopoldville authorities on 22 June 1961, promised to cooperate. Mr. Tshombé signed a protocol[11] calling for the reconvening of Parliament, but he changed his position after he returned to Elisabethville.

Parliament reopened on 22 July with more than 200 — out of a total of 221 — members attending. Most of them were brought to Leopoldville with the assistance of ONUC.

Government of national unity

On 2 August 1961, Prime Minister Cyrille Adoula, at the request of President Kasa-Vubu, constituted a Government of national unity, which was unanimously approved by both Chambers.[12]

With the act of approval of the national unity Government, the constitutional crisis was ended. In response to a letter from Prime Minister Adoula, the Secretary-General confirmed[13] that the United Nations would deal with his Government as the Central Government of the Republic and would render to it whatever aid and support the United Nations was in a position to give to the Congo.

[10]S/4841. [11]S/4841/Add.2. [12]S/4913. [13]S/4923.

Prime Minister Adoula endeavoured to secure Mr. Gizenga's cooperation, with the active assistance of other Stanleyville leaders and ONUC. His efforts seemed successful at first. On 7 August 1961, Mr. Gizenga recognized the Adoula Government as the sole legal Government of the Republic. Four weeks later, he came back to Leopoldville to assume the post of Deputy Prime Minister and accompanied Mr. Adoula in that capacity to a conference of non-aligned nations in Belgrade, Yugoslavia. However, Mr. Gizenga left again for Stanleyville at the beginning of October, ostensibly to collect some personal effects, and refused to return to Leopoldville despite the many appeals from Prime Minister Adoula. While he was in Stanleyville, he attempted to form a new party, the Parti national lumumbiste (PANALU), and made several statements strongly hostile to the Government.

On 8 January 1962, the Chamber of Representatives adopted a resolution[14] ordering Mr. Gizenga to return to Leopoldville without delay to answer charges of secessionism. Mr. Gizenga refused, and his defiant attitude led to fighting, on 13 January 1962, between gendarmes supporting him and ANC troops loyal to the Government, which was easily won by the latter. Thereafter, Mr. Gizenga was dismissed from the post of Deputy Prime Minister following a motion of censure[15] by the Chamber of Representatives.

D. Termination of the secession of Katanga (September 1961–February 1963)

United Nations resolutions

Along with the breakdown of law and order and foreign armed intervention, the secession of Katanga was one of the main problems which confronted the Congo when it appealed to the United Nations for help. However, the Security Council's resolution of 14 July 1960 contained no mention of this point. In a second resolution, of 22 July, the Council requested all States to refrain from any action which might undermine the territorial integrity and political independence of the Congo. In August, the Council called for the immediate withdrawal of Belgian troops from Katanga; however, it emphasized that the United Nations was not to take sides in Congolese internal conflicts, constitutional or otherwise, nor was the Organization to be used to influence the outcome of any such conflict.

Secretary-General's position

The Secretary-General's position was that, while ONUC originated from a request by the Congolese Government, the purpose of United Nations intervention as determined by the Security Council was not to achieve the domestic aims of the Government but to preserve international peace and security. The United Nations Force therefore could not, under the Council's decision, be used on behalf of the Central Government to subdue or to force the provincial government into a specific line of action in regard to an internal political controversy. At the same time, the problem of Katanga clearly had an international dimension.

What the United Nations sought to do was to encourage efforts at reconciliation and to eliminate foreign interference, which had been instrumental in bringing about the secession of Katanga and which had helped it to endure. The withdrawal of Belgian troops from Katanga, which occurred in August 1960, did not end the secession of the province, and the Tshombé secessionist regime was able to consolidate its hold over southern Katanga, with active foreign assistance. While Belgian officers, supplemented by an increasing number of foreign mercenaries, continued to strengthen the gendarmerie, Mr. Tshombé imported large quantities of arms and war *matériel*, including aircraft, from abroad. With his improved armed forces, he launched a merciless extermination campaign against the Baluba and other political and tribal enemies. Helping to maintain law and order in Katanga and protecting large parts of the Katangese population against the brutal lawlessness of the gendarmerie accordingly became one of the principal aspects of the ONUC effort, along with the removal of the foreign political

[14]S/5053/Add.1, annex I. [15]S/5053/Add.1, annex VI.

advisers, military and paramilitary personnel and mercenaries.

Union Minière du Haut-Katanga

In carrying out its functions in Katanga, ONUC continually found itself opposed by certain foreign financial interests which, in effect, controlled the economy of the province. These interests centred on the vast industrial and mining complex of the Union Minière du Haut-Katanga — with headquarters in Brussels, Belgium — which had apparently committed itself to Mr. Tshombé's secessionist policies.

The Union Minière supported Mr. Tshombé in four principal ways. Firstly, it paid nearly all of its taxes not to the Central Government, to which they were due, but to the Katangese provincial authorities. Secondly, it shipped its production not by way of the traditional "national" route, but by way of Portuguese Angola; this enabled it to credit hard-currency export duties to the account of the provincial government. Thirdly, the Congo's part of Union Minière stock was withheld from the Central Government and kept in Brussels. Fourthly, the firm allowed its industrial facilities at Elisabethville and other places to be used by the mercenary-led gendarmerie for military purposes, including the making of some implements of war.

Non-recognition of Katanga

Despite Mr. Tshombé's efforts and the powerful financial and political support he enjoyed, his separatist movement never gained official international recognition, either in Belgium or elsewhere. Moreover, neither Belgium nor any other Government publicly espoused the cause of Katangese secession. In fact, after the establishment of the coalition Government in Brussels in the spring of 1961, its Minister for Foreign Affairs, Mr. Paul-Henri Spaak, announced publicly his Government's opposition to the secession of Katanga.

Mercenaries

The problem of foreign elements who sought to influence the Congo's destiny in their own interests came to light soon after the country's accession to independence.

In the beginning, the bulk of these persons were Belgian professional military and civilian officials placed at the disposal of the Central Government of the Congo under the treaty of friendship with Belgium, which was signed in June 1960 but never ratified. After the severance of diplomatic relations between the Congo and Belgium, many of these men gathered in Katanga, where they gained prominent positions in the provincial administration and the gendarmerie. From these vantage points they vigorously promoted secession. In effect, they waged war on the Congolese Government at whose disposal they had been placed by their Government. Later, these Belgians were joined by other nationalities.

On 21 February 1961, the Security Council urged "the immediate withdrawal and evacuation from the Congo of all Belgian and other foreign military and paramilitary personnel and political advisers not under the United Nations Command, and mercenaries". Implicit in this language was the finding that while the Congo was admittedly and direly in need of assistance from outside, and especially of personnel to carry out technical and professional tasks which the Congolese had not hitherto been trained to perform, there were other types of foreign personnel whose actions were incompatible with genuine Congolese independence and unity. In certain parts of the Congo, and especially in Katanga, such personnel had come to play an increasingly questionable role, obstructing the application of United Nations resolutions and, in effect, working in their own interest and in the interest of certain financial concerns, to break up the country into a Balkanized congeries of politically and economically unviable states.

Secretary-General's efforts, 1961

Immediately after the adoption of the resolution of 21 February, the Secretary-General undertook intensive diplomatic efforts to bring about the withdrawal of the foreign military and political personnel.

The Belgian Government took the position that there must be no discrimination against Belgians in engaging non-Congolese technical personnel; as for military personnel and mercenaries, the Belgian Government divided them into several categories. Of these, it undertook to recall those whom it considered it had the legal right to request to return. But it would take no such action in respect of mercenaries or of Belgian personnel directly engaged by the Congolese Government, arguing that it was up to the Secretary-General to agree with the Congolese authorities on how to deal with them. The Secretary-General expressed the view that the measures indicated by the Belgian Government fell far short of full compliance with the Security Council's resolution.

The exchanges with Belgium continued, fairly inconclusively, until the change of government in the first half of 1961, when some progress was made. A new Belgian Government notified 23 of its nationals serving in Katanga as political advisers to return to Belgium. It also acted to prevent the recruitment of mercenaries proper. But the effectiveness of these efforts soon became open to doubt. On 30 October 1961, the Government at Brussels acknowledged that this was the case and took more vigorous steps — including the withdrawal of passports from recalcitrant Belgians.

Mr. Tshombé, however, would not cooperate with ONUC. He continued to recruit foreign personnel, whose influence in the councils of the provincial government in fact tended to rise sharply. The complexion of the group also changed noticeably as mercenaries replaced Belgian professional officials. Thus, the traditional colonial administrative and military elements were being supplemented through an influx of non-Belgian adventurers and soldiers of fortune, including outlawed elements previously involved in extremist, repressive and separatist policies. They drew political sustenance from the substantial non-Congolese community to which Katanga's extractive and processing industries had given rise.

Repatriation and expulsion of some foreign elements, 1961

Only after the United Nations had strengthened its position in April 1961 did the Katanga secessionist authorities, acting while Mr. Tshombé was under detention in the west, officially accept resolution 161 (1961) of 21 February.

Those authorities drew up lists of persons whom they considered as falling within the terms of the resolution. By the end of June 1961, 44 Belgian nationals were thus selected for repatriation and the cases of 22 others were under consideration. It was noted, however, that persons clearly not coming under the resolution had been included for political reasons, while others notorious for their activities had been omitted. ONUC representatives continued to press for revision of the lists, and brought home to the provincial authorities their determination to take drastic action, if need be, to comply with the United Nations mandate.

In April 1961, 30 members of a mercenary unit known as the "Compagnie internationale"

were apprehended[16] by ONUC personnel and evacuated from the Congo. By mid-June an estimated 60 more mercenaries had withdrawn from Katanga, and on 24 June the Compagnie was formally dissolved by the provincial government.

On 7 June 1961, following discussions with the Katangese authorities, the United Nations Force Commander dispatched a military mission to Katanga to help the authorities there to remove non-Congolese elements falling under the resolution. The mission reported that there were 510 foreign and non-commissioned officers active in the Katangese gendarmerie, as against 142 Congolese "cadres". Of the non-Congolese, 208 were the remaining Belgian professional military men; 302 were mercenaries.

But despite the unrelenting efforts of ONUC, the provincial authorities refused to take effective action to remove the foreign elements, without whom the secessionist movement might have collapsed. For its part, the Belgian Government said it was prepared to help in the removal of its professional and non-commissioned officers who had been serving the Congo and were currently in command of the gendarmerie, but it professed itself unable to do anything about "volunteers" and mercenaries. Persuasion by the Secretary-General, who discussed the matter with Foreign Minister Spaak at Geneva on 12 July 1961, was unavailing in this regard.

Gradually, the United Nations was compelled to shift to more vigorous and direct measures to achieve compliance with the Security Council's resolution. Mr. Tshombé's chief military adviser was compelled to leave in June 1961, and a prominent political adviser was apprehended, taken to Leopoldville, and evacuated in July. ONUC warned the Katangese authorities that it was prepared to compel the evacuation of other advisers and officers. Five French officers in politically sensitive gendarmerie posts were dismissed and repatriated, and a joint commission was established to list foreign political advisers, both those in official posts and others acting unofficially, who were to be repatriated.

Formation of the Adoula Government

The formation of the Adoula Government, enjoying unquestionable and internationally recognized authority, was of crucial importance in

[16]S/4790.

enabling the United Nations to proceed with the elimination of foreign elements.

Before the formation of a legal government, United Nations efforts had been restricted by the requirement of avoiding political interference or support of one Congolese faction against another. Now the United Nations was able to do more effectively what the 11-month constitutional crisis had impeded — that is, help the Government remove the foreign elements that had provided the teeth of the attempt to sever, in their own interests, the Congo's richest province from the rest of the country.

Government ordinance on expulsions

Soon after the reopening of Parliament, Mr. Tshombé somewhat softened his stand and allowed the parliamentarians of his party in Katanga to participate in the work of Parliament. However, he himself remained in Elisabethville and showed no intention of relinquishing the powers he held in Katanga. For weeks, ONUC representatives urged him to cooperate in removing the remaining foreign elements, but to little avail.

When all attempts at negotiations failed, in order to remove what it believed to be the main obstacle to a peaceful solution to the Katanga question, Prime Minister Adoula's Government formally requested the expulsion of the mercenaries serving in Katanga and requested ONUC to assist it in carrying out the decision. An ordinance[17] was issued on 24 August calling for expulsion of all foreign officers and mercenaries standing behind the secessionist policy.

Round-up of mercenaries

On 28 August 1961, ONUC proceeded to round up the mercenaries for deportation. In the face of inflammatory rumours about an invasion by the ANC which had been disseminated by Mr. Godefroid Munongo, the provincial Minister of the Interior, certain security precautions were taken by ONUC in Elisabethville, including surveillance over Radio Katanga, gendarmerie headquarters and some other key points. Inflammatory broadcasts were thus prevented, and appeals for calm were put on the air.

Mr. Tshombé, who had been fully informed of the objectives of ONUC's action, expressed his readiness to cooperate. He broadcast a statement[18] to the effect that the Katangese authorities accepted the decisions of the United Nations, and that the services of foreign military personnel were being terminated by his government.

At that point, ONUC representatives met with the Elisabethville consular corps, which offered to assume the responsibility, together with two senior Belgian officers formerly in the gendarmerie, for the orderly repatriation of the foreign personnel, most of whom were Belgians. In the interest of avoiding violence, ONUC accepted this arrangement, and suspended its own rounding-up operation.

However, the foreign military men being selected for repatriation were in the main personnel whose withdrawal had earlier been agreed to by the Belgian Government. By 9 September 1961, 273 had been evacuated and 65 were awaiting repatriation. But, while some of the volunteers and mercenaries had left, many others — about 104 of whom were known to be in Katanga — were "missing". They were reinfiltrating into the gendarmerie, distributing arms to groups of soldiers over whom they could assert control, and getting ready for violent resistance.

At the same time, the political police (Sûreté), under Mr. Munongo and largely directed by foreign officers, launched a campaign of assaults and persecution against anti-Tshombé Baluba tribesmen in Elisabethville. An effort was made to convince the world that ONUC's actions were causing disorder. The terrorized Baluba streamed out of the city and sought safety by camping in primitive conditions near ONUC troop quarters. ONUC arranged protection for the encampment, into which 35,000 Baluba had crowded by 9 September, creating a serious food and health problem, as well as a continuing danger of tribal violence.

Attack on ONUC

When ONUC realized that the Katangese authorities had no intention of fulfilling their promises, it pressed its demand for the evacuation of foreign personnel of the Katangese security police and of the remaining mercenaries. The Katangese, however, led by Mr. Tshombé, had manifestly fallen back under the domination of the foreign elements, and had let themselves be persuaded to launch violent action against ONUC. ONUC's plans for a solution of the difficulties in Elisabethville were rejected, and when, on 13 September 1961, it applied security precautions simi-

[17]S/4940, annex I. [18]S/4940.

lar to those of 28 August, the United Nations troops were violently attacked by gendarmes led by non-Congolese personnel.

In the morning of 13 September, Mr. Tshombé requested[19] a cease-fire, but the attacks on United Nations troops continued. From the building housing the Belgian Consulate in Elisabethville, where a number of Belgian officers were known to be staying, sustained firing was directed at United Nations troops. The United Nations base at Kamina was attacked, as were the United Nations garrison and installations at Albertville. Reluctantly, United Nations troops had to return the fire. All over Elisabethville, and elsewhere in Katanga, the foreign officers who had gone into hiding reappeared to lead operations against ONUC personnel.

Efforts to reinforce the troops were frustrated by the depredations of a Katangese jet fighter, piloted by a mercenary, which quickly managed to immobilize ONUC's unarmed air transport craft. The jet also played havoc with the ground movements of ONUC, which had deliberately refrained from securing offensive weapons such as fighter-planes or tanks as incompatible with its mission as a peace force.

Dag Hammarskjöld's death

In the meantime, the Secretary-General had arrived in Leopoldville at Prime Minister Adoula's invitation to discuss future prospects of the United Nations Operation in what was hoped would be a new setting created by the completion of the principal tasks assigned by the Security Council and the General Assembly. He intended also to bring about a reconciliation between Leopoldville and Elisabethville. Confronted instead with a situation of confused fighting in Elisabethville, the Secretary-General devoted himself to the task of securing a cessation of hostilities and achieving reconciliation among Congolese factions. In quest of a cease-fire, he flew to Ndola, in what was then Northern Rhodesia, to meet Mr. Tshombé. On this flight, on the night of 17 September 1961, his aeroplane crashed and he was killed, together with seven other United Nations staff members and the Swedish crew.[20]

Cease-fire, September 1961

The Secretary-General's mission was immediately taken up by the authorities of ONUC in Leopoldville. Mr. Mahmoud Khiari, the Chief of ONUC Civilian Operations, flew to Ndola and, on

behalf of the United Nations forces, signed a military cease-fire agreement[21] on 20 September. It was understood as an express condition that the agreement would not affect the application of the Security Council and General Assembly resolutions. A protocol[22] for carrying out the provisions of the cease-fire was signed on 13 October 1961 at Elisabethville. While the protocol allowed firing back in case of attack, it prohibited Katangese and ONUC troop movements. In approving this protocol, the United Nations stressed its military nature, re-emphasized its support of the unity, integrity and independence of the Congo, and insisted on continued enforcement of the Security Council resolution which called for the removal of mercenaries.

Katangese violations of the cease-fire

Although prisoners were exchanged and certain positions held by ONUC in Elisabethville during the fighting were duly released, in accordance with the protocol, the Tshombé regime was soon flouting the provisions of the cease-fire agreement. In Leopoldville, his emissaries made it clear that nothing less than independence along the lines of the Tananarive decisions would be acceptable to the Elisabethville authorities. Meanwhile, the remaining Katangese mercenaries were leading the gendarmerie in a long series of violations of the cease-fire agreement, going so far as to launch offensive air action along the Kasai-Katanga frontier. This was strongly protested by the United Nations. While strictly abiding by the cease-fire in Katanga, ONUC took steps to prevent the recurrence of the September situation when it had found itself powerless to stop the attacks of Katanga's jet fighters. Three Member States — Ethiopia, India and Sweden — provided jet fighter squadrons to the United Nations Force to strengthen its defensive capacity.

At the same time, however, the Force's ground strength was being whittled away. The Tunisian contingent had been withdrawn in August 1961 because of events in Tunisia; the Ghanaian contingent subsequently withdrew, and certain other ONUC units were reduced. Not unaware of these developments, Mr. Tshombé and the foreign elements supporting him were determined to turn secession into an accomplished fact. ONUC-sponsored talks between the Central Gov-

[19]S/4940/Add.2. [20]S/4940/Add.5,9. [21]S/4940/Add.7.
[22]S/4940/Add.11, annex I.

ernment and Katanga were subjected to stalling tactics. At least 237 persons, chiefly mercenaries falling under the provisions of the Security Council's resolution, remained in Katanga, many of whom donned civilian clothing.

ANC offensives

Despairing of a peaceful solution, the Central Government attempted to deal with Katanga's secession independently, by the use of force, in late October 1961. The strength of the national army was built up on the border of northern Katanga in preparation for entry into that region. At the beginning of November, a detachment of the ANC entered northern Katanga in the Kamina area, but was immediately repelled by Katangese gendarmes. Later, ANC units from Stanleyville succeeded in reaching Albertville, Nyunzu, Kongolo and other towns of northern Katanga. To facilitate this move, the Government had requested ONUC assistance for the transport of its troops. The request was turned down because, as had been the case from the outset, it remained against ONUC principles to become a party to an internal conflict.

Security Council authorizes ONUC to remove mercenaries

In the latter part of November 1961, the Security Council was convened once again to examine the situation in the Congo. By resolution 169 (1961) of 24 November 1961, the Council strongly deprecated the secessionist activities in Katanga and authorized the Secretary-General to use force to complete the removal of mercenaries.

After the adoption of the resolution, Mr. Tshombé launched an inflammatory propaganda campaign against ONUC which soon degenerated into incitement to violence. The results were not long in coming. On 28 November 1961, two senior United Nations officials in Elisabethville were abducted and badly beaten; later an Indian soldier was murdered and an Indian major abducted. Several members of the United Nations Force were detained, and others were killed or wounded. Roadblocks were established by the gendarmerie, impeding ONUC's freedom of movement and endangering its lifelines. It subsequently became known that this was part of a deliberate plan to cut off the United Nations troops in Elisabethville, and either force them to surrender or otherwise destroy them. For one week, United Nations officials sought to settle the crisis by peaceful nego-

tiations. But when it became evident that, in the face of the bad faith displayed by Katangese authorities, no commitments could be relied upon, and that, while pretending to negotiate, those authorities were preparing for more assaults, ONUC finally decided to take action to regain and assure its freedom of movement.

Fighting of December 1961

ONUC had few troops in Elisabethville when fighting broke out on 5 December 1961. Until 14 December, ONUC forces endeavoured to hold their positions and to maintain communications between units while reinforcements were hurriedly flown in from other parts of the Congo. On 15 December, having received enough reinforcements, ONUC troops moved to seize control of those positions in Elisabethville necessary to ensure their freedom of movement. In so doing, they worked their way around the perimeter of the city, in order to keep destruction and civilian casualties to the strict minimum. This objective was achieved within three days.[23]

From the outset of the hostilities, United Nations military and civilian officers did their best, in cooperation with the International Committee of the Red Cross, to relieve the distress caused to innocent civilians. Persons caught in areas where firing had been initiated by the gendarmerie were escorted to safety, at the risk of ONUC personnel's lives; food supplies were provided where needed; and special arrangements for the evacuation of women and children were made by ONUC. Notwithstanding the shortage of troops, ONUC employed a whole battalion to guard the Baluba refugee camp, where more than 40,000 anti-Tshombé Baluba lived under United Nations protection.[24] ONUC troops, on the one hand, prevented them from raiding Elisabethville and, on the other, protected them from the gendarmes who launched several attacks on the camp.

Kitona Declaration

On 19 December 1961, having ensured the positions necessary for its security, ONUC ordered its troops to hold fire unless fired upon.[25] The same day, Mr. Tshombé left Elisabethville to confer with Prime Minister Adoula at Kitona, the United Nations military base in Leopoldville province. After that, major fighting between ONUC and Katangese forces ceased. ONUC immediately

[23]S/4940/Add.18. [24]Ibid. [25]S/4940/Add.19.

turned its efforts to the re-establishment of normal conditions in Elisabethville. It cooperated closely with the local police to stop looting, to rid private houses of squatters and, in general, to restore and maintain law and order.

The Kitona meeting was arranged with the assistance of ONUC and the United States Ambassador in the Congo following a request by Mr. Tshombé on 14 December 1961, when the fighting in Elisabethville was in full swing. After meeting Prime Minister Adoula all day long on 20 December, Mr. Tshombé signed early in the morning of 21 December an eight-point Declaration.[26] In this Declaration, he accepted the application of the *Loi fondamentale*, recognized the authority of the Central Government in Leopoldville over all parts of the Congo and agreed to a number of steps aimed at ending the secession of Katanga. He also pledged himself to ensure respect for the resolutions of the Security Council and the General Assembly and to facilitate their implementation.

In accordance with the provisions of the Kitona Declaration, Mr. Tshombé sent 14 parliamentarians from Katanga to Leopoldville to participate in the session of Parliament. Three Katangese officials were also dispatched to the capital to participate in discussions for the modification of the constitutional structure of the Congo. In both cases, ONUC ensured the safety of the representatives during their journey to and from Leopoldville and their stay there.

While making the concessions contained in the Declaration, Mr. Tshombé stated that he had no authority to decide on the future of Katanga, and he summoned the provincial Assembly to meet in Elisabethville to discuss the Declaration. On 15 February, that Assembly decided to accept the "draft declaration" of Kitona only as a basis for discussions with the Central Government.

Following this action, Prime Minister Adoula invited Mr. Tshombé to meet with him in Leopoldville to discuss the procedure for carrying out the provisions of the Declaration,[27] but attempts at peaceful resolution through the talks failed; the agreement was not implemented owing to the procrastination and intransigence of the Katangese leader. The talks were suspended in June 1962 without agreement.[28]

Secretary-General's Plan of National Reconciliation

Given the failure of the negotiations, after consultation with various Member States, Secretary-General U Thant, in August 1962, proposed a "Plan of National Reconciliation",[29] which was ultimately accepted by both Prime Minister Adoula and Mr. Tshombé. It provided for: a federal system of government; division of revenues and foreign-exchange earnings between the Central and provincial governments; unification of currency; integration and unification of all military, para-military and gendarme units into the structure of a national army; general amnesty; reconstitution of the Central Government giving representation to all political and provincial groups; withdrawal of representatives abroad not serving the Central Government; and freedom of movement for United Nations personnel throughout the Congo.

End of the secession of Katanga

After acceptance of the Plan of National Reconciliation, a draft federal constitution[30] was prepared by United Nations experts, and amnesty was proclaimed by the Central Government in late November 1962. On the Katanga side, however, no substantial steps were taken to implement the Plan. In this situation, the Secretary-General requested[31] Member States, on 11 December, to bring economic pressure on the Katangese authorities, particularly by stopping Katanga's export of copper and cobalt. But before that action became effective, the Katangese fired, without provocation, on United Nations positions. Although the firing continued for six days, ONUC did not fire back but tried to resolve the situation by negotiation.

Immediately after the breakdown of the negotiations, ONUC began action to restore the security of its troops and their freedom of movement, the first phase being the clearing of the roadblocks from which Katangese troops had been directing fire at ONUC personnel. Ethiopian, Indian and Irish troops took part in the operations.

Wherever ONUC troops appeared, the gendarmerie offered little or no resistance. By 30 December 1962, all the Katangese roadblocks around Elisabethville had been cleared and ONUC forces were in effective control of an area extending approximately 20 kilometres around the city. Meanwhile, around Kamina, Ghanaian and Swedish troops, advancing in a two-pronged attack, had succeeded in occupying that town on the morning of 30 December. Thus, the first phase of the operations was completed.[32]

[26]S/5038. [27]S/5053/Add.8. [28]S/5053/Add.10, annex 46. [29]S/5053/ Add.13, annex I. [30]S/5053/Add.13, annex XI. [31]S/5053/Add.14, annexes XIII-XV. [32]S/5053/Add.14.

The second phase started on 31 December,[33] when Indian troops of the United Nations Force began to move towards Jadotville (now Likasi). The next day, ONUC advance elements reached the Lufira River, which they crossed by nightfall, although both bridges had been destroyed. On 2 January 1963, having met some gendarmerie resistance on the other side of that river, ONUC troops resumed their advance and reached Jadotville on 3 January, where they were greeted by the cheers of the population. At the same time, ONUC troops also reached the town of Kipushi, south of Elisabethville.

By 4 January, ONUC troops had secured themselves in the Elisabethville, Kipushi, Kamina and Jadotville areas. In all these areas, measures were taken to restore essential services and protect the local population.

In the meantime, Mr. Tshombé, who had left Elisabethville on 28 December 1962, had proceeded through Northern Rhodesia to Kolwezi, his last stronghold. To avoid useless bloodshed and destruction of industrial installations, the United Nations ordered its troops to slow their advance towards Kolwezi while the Secretary-General continued his efforts to persuade Mr. Tshombé to cease all resistance.

On 14 January 1963, the Secretary-General received, through Belgian Government channels, a message[34] from Mr. Tshombé and his ministers meeting at Kolwezi. They announced their readiness to end the secession of Katanga, to grant ONUC troops complete freedom of movement and to arrange for the implementation of the Plan of National Reconciliation. They asked that the Central Government immediately put into effect the amnesty called for in the Plan in order to guarantee the freedom and safety of the Katangese government and of all who worked under its authority.

The Secretary-General welcomed Mr. Tshombé's message and informed[35] him on 15 January that the United Nations would do its utmost to assist in the fulfilment of the promise implicit in his statement. On 15 January, President Kasa-Vubu and Prime Minister Adoula separately confirmed[36] that the amnesty proclamation of November 1962 remained valid. It was also announced, on 16 January, that Mr. Joseph Ileo had been appointed Minister of State Resident at Elisabethville, for the purpose of facilitating the process of reintegration.

On 16 January, Mr. Tshombé informed the Secretary-General that he was prepared to discuss at Elisabethville arrangements for ONUC's entry into Kolwezi. The next day, after four hours of discussions at ONUC headquarters, the Acting Representative of the United Nations at Elisabethville, the general officer commanding ONUC troops in the Katanga area and Mr. Tshombé signed a document[37] in which Mr. Tshombé undertook to facilitate the peaceful entry of ONUC into Kolwezi, to be completed by 21 January. It was understood that pending arrangements for the integration of the gendarmerie, the security of its members would be fully ensured by ONUC. They would not be treated as prisoners of war and would be able to continue to wear their uniforms in Kolwezi.

As agreed, Indian troops of ONUC entered Kolwezi in the afternoon of 21 January. Meanwhile, the situation became increasingly volatile in northern Katanga because of sizeable groups of disorganized but heavily armed gendarmes. Consequently, in the morning of 20 January, Indonesian troops disembarked at Baudouinville (now Moba) and shortly thereafter secured the town and its airport. On the same day, a Nigerian unit starting from Kongolo and a Malayan unit coming from Bukavu cleared the Kongolo pocket where there had remained a considerable gendarme force.

By 21 January, the United Nations Force had under its control all important centres hitherto held by the Katangese, and quickly restored law and order there. The Katangese gendarmerie ceased to exist as an organized fighting force. Thanks to the skill and restraint displayed by ONUC troops, the casualties incurred during the fighting were relatively light. In the 24 days of activity, ONUC casualties were 10 killed and 77 wounded. Katangese casualties also appeared to have been low.

At the beginning of January 1963, 22 officials and officers representing the Central Government arrived at Elisabethville to make up an administrative commission to prepare the way for the integration of the provincial administration into the Central Government. Mr. Ileo and his party arrived on 23 January to assume their duties. Shortly before that, Prime Minister Adoula had requested ONUC to give Mr. Ileo all the assistance and cooperation he might require. It had been agreed between the Central Government and ONUC that all the military forces in Katanga would be placed under the single command of ONUC. At ONUC's suggestion, Prime Minister Adoula declared that gendarmes who rejoined the Congolese

---

[33]Ibid. [34]S/5053/Add.15, annex V. [35]S/5053/ Add.15, annex VI. [36]S/5053/Add.15, annexes VII and VIII. [37]S/5053/ Add.15, annex IX.

National Army by a certain date would retain their ranks.

Progress was also achieved with regard to the economic reintegration of Katanga. On 15 January, an agreement on foreign exchange was signed at Leopoldville by the representatives of the Central Government and a representative of the Union Minière, who had come from Belgium, in the presence of the Director of the Bank of Katanga. In brief, that agreement provided that the Union Minière would remit all its export proceeds to the Congolese Monetary Council, which would in turn allocate to the Union Minière the foreign exchange it needed to carry out its operations. The allocation of foreign exchange by the Central Government to the provincial authorities was to be discussed separately by that Government and the provincial authorities of southern Katanga.

Under a decree of 9 January 1963, the Monetary Council assumed control of the "National Bank of Katanga" and ensured the resumption of the Bank's operations, with ONUC's assistance.

Thus, the secession of Katanga had been brought to an end, and with this an important phase of ONUC's operations had been completed.

E. Consolidation of the Congolese Government (February 1963–June 1964)

Introduction

While the period from the end of the Katangese secession until ONUC's withdrawal in June 1964 is the main subject of this section, with the Congolese Central Government authority now extended to the whole country, it is convenient first to consider ONUC's early efforts to assist that Government in regard to civilian operations and the retraining of the Congolese army and security forces.

Civilian operations

A main objective of ONUC was to provide the Congolese Government with technical assistance for the smooth operation of all essential services and the continued development of the national economy. The situation faced by ONUC at the beginning immediately assumed unprecedented proportions. In the absence of functioning governmental and economic machinery which could receive and use expert advice and training services, the Secretary-General at once mobilized the resources of the United Nations family of organizations under the authority of a Chief of Civilian Operations. A consultative group of experts was set up, consisting of senior officials of the United Nations and the specialized agencies concerned.

The first task was to restore or maintain minimum essential public services. Engineers, air traffic controllers, meteorologists, radio operators, postal experts, physicians, teachers and other specialists were rushed into the country. An emergency project was carried out to halt the silting of the port of Matadi and to restore navigation. In response to the Central Government's appeal, the United Nations agreed, in August 1960, to provide $5 million to finance essential governmental services as well as essential imports.

In the economic and financial fields, ONUC helped in setting up and managing monetary, foreign exchange and foreign trade controls, without which the country's slender resources might have been drained away and all semblance of a monetary system might have collapsed.

In all these fields, as well as in agriculture, labour and public administration, ONUC's efforts were designed chiefly to improve the ability of the Congolese authorities to discharge their responsibilities towards the population despite the precipitate departure of non-Congolese technicians and administrators. As it soon became obvious that the needs would continue for some time, the Secretary-General proposed and the General Assembly, by resolution 1474 (ES-IV) of 20 September 1960, approved the establishment of a United Nations Fund for the Congo, financed by voluntary contributions. Its purpose was to restore the economic life of the country and to carry on its public services as well as possible.

The Assembly's action coincided with the outbreak of the constitutional crisis of September 1960. As a result of that crisis, ONUC could not deal with any authorities, except for President

Joseph Kasa-Vubu, on the nationwide plane, and could not furnish advice at the ministerial level. As the emergency conditions continued, however, the ONUC effort did not flag, and was carried on in cooperation with those Congolese authorities exercising de facto control in the provinces or localities where United Nations Civilian Operations were being undertaken.

Famine conditions in some areas, and widespread unemployment, led the Secretary-General to institute refugee relief and relief-work programmes. The worst conditions developed in South Kasai in the second half of 1960, where it was reported that some 200 persons were dying daily from starvation as a result of disruptions caused by tribal warfare. For six months, the United Nations shipped and distributed food and medical supplies in the area. While several thousand persons died before the United Nations effort began, the number of lives saved approximated a quarter of a million.

In the meantime, foreign exchange reserves were running low, owing to the political and economic situation. Accordingly, in June 1961, an agreement was arrived at between President Kasa-Vubu and the Secretary-General, by which the United Nations put funds at the disposal of the Republic for financing a programme of essential imports. It was agreed that such assistance must benefit the population of the country as a whole.

Despite the constitutional crisis, United Nations training services continued as a long-range operation. They were regarded as an investment in the development of human resources so as to fill the huge void caused by the shortage of indigenous operational and executive personnel. Training courses were organized for air traffic controllers, agricultural assistants, farm mechanics, foresters, medical assistants, labour officials, police commissioners, etc. To train Congolese operators and instructors, a telecommunications training centre was set up; to train primary and secondary school teachers and inspectors, a national pedagogical institute was established. Undergraduate medical studies were fostered. A national school of law and administration was opened to produce competent civil servants; a technical college was set up to train junior engineers, public works foremen and the like. Fellowships for study abroad were awarded to school directors, medical students, police officers, social workers and others in need of training, for whom adequate facilities were not available in the Congo. Furthermore, a pro-gramme was prepared for the reorganization and retraining of the Congolese National Army.

In 1960 and 1961, ONUC Civilian Operations were able to provide about 600 experts and technicians to do the jobs of departing Belgian personnel. These experts and technicians, drawn from some 48 nationalities, were made available to the Congo by the United Nations and its specialized agencies for work in a variety of fields, such as finance and economics, health, transport, public administration, agriculture, civil aviation, public works, mining and natural resources, postal services, meteorology, telecommunications, judicature, labour, education, social welfare, youth training and community development. In addition, a large number of secondary school teachers were recruited with the assistance of the United Nations Educational, Scientific and Cultural Organization. These assistance programmes continued at about the same level until 1964, despite financial and other difficulties.

The end of the Katangese secession in January 1963 brought with it new responsibilities for the United Nations Civilian Operations programme, since experts became urgently needed to help the Central Government in the reintegration of services previously under Katangese rule, such as postal services, customs and excise, immigration, civil aviation, telecommunications and banking. An expert mission was required to survey the 40 rail and road bridges destroyed or damaged.

As a result of the various training programmes set up by ONUC, it became possible in 1963 to replace some international personnel by qualified Congolese, particularly in the postal, meteorological, telecommunications and civil aviation services. In 1963, 55 of the 130 medical assistants sent abroad for training in 1960–1961 under World Health Organization auspices returned to the Congo and were assigned to various parts of the country.

Reorganization of the Congolese armed forces, 1960–1963

Nearly all the grave incidents mentioned in earlier sections were caused by military elements of Congolese armed forces, whether they were part of the Congolese National Army, the Katangese gendarmerie or the Kalonji forces in South Kasai. From the outset, it was considered an essential task of ONUC to assist the Congolese Government in establishing discipline in the armed forces. These forces were to be brought under a unified command, the rebellious elements eliminated and the remaining ones reorganized and retrained. ONUC offered the Congolese Government full support and cooperation to achieve these objectives.

The United Nations Operation in the Congo took its first step towards the reorganization of the Congolese National Army when the Deputy Commander of the United Nations Force was appointed adviser to the ANC at the end of July 1960, at the request of Prime Minister Lumumba. Shortly thereafter, the ANC began to reform in new units and to engage in the training of its officers and men. This programme was interrupted at the end of August because of the Government's plan to invade Kasai and Katanga, and later ONUC was compelled to abandon it altogether because of the political struggle which began in September 1960.

After the Adoula Government was set up, in August 1961, ONUC's efforts were resumed and the new Deputy Force Commander prepared a reorganization programme to be carried out in full cooperation with the Government.

Nevertheless, difficulties were later encountered in regard to ONUC assistance in this area. After December 1962, it became clear that Prime Minister Adoula wanted the Secretary-General to request six countries — Belgium, Canada, Israel, Italy, Norway and the United States — to provide personnel and *matériel* for reorganizing and training the various armed services.[38]

The Secretary-General had doubts — which were shared by the Advisory Committee composed of ONUC troop-contributors — about the advisability of the United Nations assuming sponsorship of what was, essentially, bilateral military assistance by a particular group of States. He therefore concluded that it was not feasible to grant Prime Minister Adoula's specific request, although he continued to hope that a way would be found to make it possible for the ANC to receive the necessary training assistance through ONUC. That hope was not realized, however, and eventually the programme for the training of the ANC was carried out outside the United Nations.

F. Winding up of ONUC

Situation in February 1963

On 4 February 1963, the Secretary-General reported[39] to the Security Council on the extent to which the mandates given to ONUC by the Council's resolutions had been fulfilled and on the tasks still to be completed.

Regarding the maintenance of the territorial integrity and political independence of the Congo, the secession of Katanga was ended and there was no direct threat to Congo's independence from external sources. That part of the mandate was largely fulfilled.

The mandate to prevent civil war, given in February 1961, was also substantially fulfilled as was, for all practical purposes, the removal of foreign military and paramilitary personnel and mercenaries.

Assistance in maintaining law and order was continuing and, with the vast improvements in that regard, a substantial reduction of ONUC forces was being made.

In view of these accomplishments, the phase of active involvement of United Nations troops was concluded, and a new phase was begin-

ning, which would give greater emphasis to civilian operations and technical assistance.

General Assembly resolution of 18 October 1963

No specific termination date for the United Nations Force in the Congo had been set by any Security Council resolution. However, the General Assembly had, on 27 June 1963 at its fourth special session, adopted resolution 1876 (S-IV) appropriating funds for the Force, which, in the absence of any subsequent action, would in effect have established 31 December 1963 as the terminal date for ONUC's military phase.

In a report[40] to the Security Council dated 17 September 1963, the Secretary-General stated that, in the light of the Assembly's resolution, he was proceeding with a phasing-out schedule for the complete withdrawal of the Force by the end of 1963. He drew attention, however, to a letter dated 22 August 1963 from Prime Minister Adoula who, while agreeing with the substantial reduction

[38]S/5240/Add.2. [39]S/5240. [40]S/5428.

of the Force that had already been carried out, saw a need for the continued presence of a small United Nations force of about 3,000 officers and men through the first half of 1964.

In this connection, the Secretary-General expressed the opinion that cogent reasons existed in support of prolonging the stay of the Force. There could be no doubt that the presence of a United Nations Force in the Congo would continue to be helpful through the first half of 1964, or longer. But the time must come soon when the Government of the Congo would have to assume full responsibility for security and for law and order in the country.

Acting upon the Congolese Government's request for reduced military assistance up to 30 June 1964, the General Assembly decided, on 18 October 1963, by resolution 1885 (XVIII), to continue the ad hoc account for the United Nations Operation in the Congo until 30 June 1964, and authorized an expenditure of up to $18.2 million to that effect.

In accordance with the Assembly's resolution, the United Nations Force in the Congo was maintained beyond 1963, but its strength was gradually brought down from 6,535 in December 1963 to 3,297 in June 1964.

Secretary-General's report, 29 June 1964

The Secretary-General, in a report[41] of 29 June 1964, affirmed his earlier conclusions that most of ONUC's objectives had been fulfilled. He indicated his intention to continue technical assistance, within available financial resources, after ONUC's withdrawal.

As to maintenance of law and order, he noted considerable deterioration in a number of localities, especially in Kwilu, Kivu and northern Katanga. He observed, however, that maintenance of law and order, which was one of the main attributes of sovereignty, was principally the responsibility of the Congolese Government, and that ONUC's role had been limited to assisting the Government, to the extent of its means, when it was requested to do so.

The Secretary-General recalled the difficulties ONUC had encountered in attempting to assist the Government in training and reorganizing the Congolese security forces. He said the ANC was now an integrated body of 29,000 soldiers with a unified command, but was still insufficiently trained and officered to cope with a major crisis.

In view of the uncertainties affecting the Congo, the Secretary-General observed, the question was often asked why the stay of ONUC had not been extended beyond the end of June 1964. First, he said, the Congolese Government had not requested an extension. Secondly, a special session of the General Assembly would be required to extend any mandate.

In any case, the Secretary-General concluded, a further extension would provide no solution to the Congo's severe difficulties. The time had come when the Congolese Government would have to assume full responsibility for its own security, law and order, and territorial integrity. He believed this was the position of the Congolese Government, since it had not requested a further extension of ONUC.

Withdrawal of the Force

On 30 June 1964, the United Nations Force in the Congo withdrew from that country according to plan. With the completion of the military phase of ONUC, the Civilian Operations programme was formally discontinued. However, the overall programme of technical assistance which had been supplied by the United Nations family of organizations continued under the responsibility of the Office of the Resident Representative of the United Nations Development Programme.

[41]S/5784.

Chapter 11
United Nations Transition Assistance Group (UNTAG)

A. Introduction

B. Background

C. The structure and deployment of UNTAG

D. D-Day and its aftermath

E. The functions of UNTAG

F. Developments from the elections until the end of the mandate

G. Financial aspects

H. Conclusions

Chapter 11

United Nations Transition Assistance Group (UNTAG)

A. Introduction

The United Nations operation in Namibia marked the culmination of 70 years of pressure by the organized international community — through the League of Nations and then the United Nations — to enable the people of the Territory to live in peace, freedom and independence. Its climax came shortly after midnight on 21 March 1990, when the South African flag was lowered, the Namibian flag was raised, and the Secretary-General of the United Nations, Mr. Javier Pérez de Cuéllar, administered the oath of office to Mr. Sam Nujoma as President of the newly independent State.

Namibia had been the particular concern of the United Nations from its earliest days in 1946. In 1966, the General Assembly terminated the Mandate of South Africa to administer the Territory and placed it under the direct responsibility of the United Nations. From that time onwards, the pace of negotiation quickened, and led, though still at tortuous length and with great complexity, to the Security Council's decision on 16 February 1989 to implement a Settlement Proposal which had first been agreed in 1978.

The agreed settlement was a negotiated compromise and led to a most unusual, indeed *sui generis*, United Nations operation: the de facto but illegal occupying Power, South Africa, and the United Nations, in which *de jure* authority reposed but which had not previously been able to establish effective administration in Namibia, were to work together to enable the Namibian people to exercise their right of self-determination. The central objective of the United Nations operation was to create conditions for the holding of free and fair elections for a Constituent Assembly which would draw up a Constitution under which Namibia would proceed to independence as a free and sovereign State. The process, all of which was to take place under United Nations supervision and control, would move step by step from a cease-fire in a long and bitter war to the final moment

of transition, that of independence. Every step had to be completed, in a democratic manner, to the satisfaction of the Secretary-General's Special Representative.

At its height, nearly 8,000 men and women — civilians, police, military — from more than 120 countries were deployed in Namibia to assist this process. Every step was followed with the closest attention, not only by the people of Namibia themselves but by the members of the Security Council, who had set the process in motion, by the international community at large, by the media and by a multitude of non-governmental organizations.

The complexity of the operation and the intense interest it aroused led the Secretary-General to establish at Headquarters in New York a high-level Namibia Task Force, which met daily under his chairmanship, to coordinate the Secretariat's role and to provide policy guidance and maximum support to the Special Representative in the field. The Task Force comprised the Secretary-General's Chef de Cabinet, the Under-Secretary-General for Special Political Affairs, the Under-Secretary-General responsible for African questions, the Legal Counsel, the Military Adviser, the Secretary-General's Spokesman and supporting staff.

The United Nations Transition Assistance Group (UNTAG) was a political operation, in which the tasks of each element — civilian, police, military — were bonded together in the field under the Special Representative, with a view to achieving a structural change in society by means of a democratic process, in accordance with an agreed timetable. Though it had elements reminiscent of other United Nations field operations, which have monitored elections and law and order and patrolled borders with peace-keeping forces, it also had numerous novel aspects. It did not fit into the traditional mould of peace-keeping operations nor did it follow the pattern of the United Nations previous endeavours in the decolonization process. UNTAG was, in effect, in charge of the process, because each step had to be done to the satisfaction of the Secretary-General's Special Representative. The breadth and depth of the United Nations' political engagement with the process of change, and the integration of high-level Secretariat and UNTAG elements into this process, gave UNTAG its special character, with all tasks being conducted at a brisk pace, in conditions which posed daunting logistics and support problems.

B. Background

The context of the Settlement Proposal

Namibia, formerly South West Africa, with an area of 824,269 square kilometres, is a mainly arid country, with a sparse and widely dispersed population, estimated at 1.4 million, which is culturally and linguistically diverse. About half the inhabitants live in the relatively densely populated north-western border area adjacent to Angola.

In 1884, Germany annexed the Territory of South West Africa and retained control of it until the First World War, when an invasion by South Africa resulted in the defeat of German forces in July 1915.

In December 1920, the Permanent Mandates Commission of the League of Nations conferred upon the British Crown for and on behalf of the Government of South Africa (the Mandatory) a class C Mandate over South West Africa (i.e., the Territory could best be administered under the laws of the Mandatory "as an integral portion of the Union of South Africa"). Problems regarding South West Africa arose at almost every session of the Mandates Commission, and the people of the Territory often petitioned the League, complaining of South Africa's administration.

After the Second World War, however, when the Trusteeship Council of the United Nations assumed the responsibilities of the League's Permanent Mandates Commission, the validity of the mandate became a contentious issue. South Africa sought to incorporate South West Africa as a fifth province and, in 1948, ceased submitting annual reports to the United Nations. That same year, it granted whites living in the Territory direct representation in the South African parliament. In 1950, 1955 and 1956, the International Court of Justice (ICJ), at the request of the General Assembly, gave Advisory Opinions on the South West African question. In the 1950 Advisory Opinion, the Court concluded that South Africa had no legal obligation to conclude a trusteeship agreement with the United Nations, but also held that the Mandate was still in force, and that South Africa had no right to change the Territory's international status. The 1955 and 1956 Advisory Opinions dealt with the voting procedure of the General Assembly in considering reports and petitions on South West Africa and with its right to hear oral petitioners.

In 1962, Ethiopia and Liberia, the only African States which had been members of the League of Nations, brought action against South Africa at the ICJ, alleging failure on the part of South Africa to fulfil its international obligations in respect of South West Africa. While the case was in progress, a South African Government commission published and began to implement the Odendaal Report, a plan to divide the Territory into 12 regions or "homelands", with over 60 per cent of the land remaining under the control of whites. In 1966, a deeply divided ICJ ruled that Ethiopia and Liberia, even though they had been members of the League of Nations, did not have "any legal right or interest appertaining to them in the subject matter of the present claims, and that accordingly, the Court must decline to give effect to them".

In July 1966, the South West Africa People's Organization (SWAPO) —which, in 1976, was to be recognized by the United Nations General Assembly in resolution 31/146 as "the sole and authentic representative of the Namibian people" — resolved, if necessary, to employ all possible means to achieve national liberation, including armed struggle.

In October 1966, by resolution 2145 (XXI), the General Assembly revoked the Mandate and declared the Territory to be the direct responsibility of the United Nations. In May 1967, during its fifth special session, the Assembly, by resolution

2248 (S-V), established the United Nations Council for South West Africa, *inter alia*, "to administer South West Africa until independence, with the maximum possible participation of the people of the Territory". In 1968, it adopted the name "Namibia" for the Territory. By its resolutions 264 (1969) and 269 (1969), the Security Council endorsed the actions of the General Assembly.

In 1970, by resolution 276, the Security Council confirmed the illegality of South Africa's presence in the Territory. The same year, the Council decided to request an Advisory Opinion of the International Court of Justice as to the legal consequences for States of South Africa's continued presence in Namibia notwithstanding resolution 276 (1970). In 1971, in its Advisory Opinion, the Court confirmed the Assembly's revocation of the Mandate. It declared that South Africa must withdraw its administration and end its occupation and that Member States were under the obligation to refrain from any support or assistance to South Africa in Namibia.

In 1973, the General Assembly created the post of United Nations Commissioner for Namibia, to which Mr. Sean MacBride (Ireland) was appointed. He was succeeded by Mr. Martti Ahtisaari (Finland) (1977-1982), Mr. Brajesh Mishra (India) (1982-1987) and Mr. Bernt Carlsson (Sweden) (1987-1988).

South Africa, however, continued to pursue its own plans for the Territory. In 1975, it convened a constitutional conference in Windhoek of the leaders of the homelands set up under the Odendaal Plan. SWAPO was not invited. The Turnhalle group (named after the building where the conference took place) established an interim government and agreed to aim for independence at the end of 1976.

On 30 January of that year, the Security Council adopted resolution 385, in which it declared that it was imperative to hold free elections under United Nations supervision and control for the whole of Namibia as one political entity. South Africa did not initially accept this plan.

Five Western members of the Security Council — Canada, France, the Federal Republic of Germany, the United Kingdom and the United States — then began to seek a way of implementing resolution 385. This group, which became known as the "Contact Group", worked principally with South Africa, SWAPO and the front-line States (then comprising Angola, Botswana, Mozambique, the United Republic of Tanzania and Zambia) and maintained close contact with the Secretary-General and Mr. Ahtisaari, the United Nations Commissioner for Namibia at that time. A round of "proximity talks", held in New York in February 1978, produced the "Proposal for a settlement of the Namibian situation"[1] which, on 10 April 1978, was presented by the Contact Group to the President of the Security Council.

The Settlement Proposal and Security Council resolution 435 (1978)

The Settlement Proposal contained a negotiated compromise. Described as a "working arrangement" which would "in no way constitute recognition of the legality of the South African presence in and administration of Namibia", it allowed South Africa, through an Administrator-General designated by it, to administer elections, but under United Nations supervision and control exercised through a Special Representative of the Secretary-General, who would be assisted by a "United Nations Transition Assistance Group" (UNTAG). The Contact Group stated that the Proposal addressed all elements of resolution 385, but "the key to an internationally acceptable transition to independence is free elections for the whole of Namibia as one political entity with an appropriate United Nations role". All other elements of the Proposal were intended to facilitate this central objective of a democratic exercise in self-determination.

The Proposal's detailed provisions were accompanied by a timetable scheduling the actions required from the various parties. Approximately seven months were assigned for a complex series of steps culminating in the holding of elections. Implementation was to begin on "D-Day", as it was called, with a cease-fire in the war between South Africa and SWAPO, accompanied by the confinement to base of all combatants. Within six weeks of D-Day, the level of South Africa Defence Force (SADF) personnel was to be reduced to 12,000 and by 12 weeks after D-Day, to 1,500, confined to two bases in northern Namibia. As regards the local military and paramilitary forces established by South Africa, their command structures were to be dismantled and they were to be demobilized, their arms being placed under guarded supervision. By the beginning of the election campaign, due to start at the thirteenth week, all political prisoners and detainees, wherever they were held, were to be released and all discriminatory or restrictive laws which might abridge or

[1]S/12636.

inhibit the objective of free and fair elections were to be repealed. All Namibian refugees were to be allowed to return peacefully so that they could freely participate in the electoral process. Provision was to be made for the peaceful return of former SWAPO forces under United Nations supervision through designated entry points. While primary responsibility for maintaining law and order during the transition period was to remain with the existing police forces, the Administrator-General, to the satisfaction of the Special Representative, was to ensure their good conduct and to take the necessary action to ensure their suitability for continued employment during the transition period. The Special Representative was to make appropriate arrangements for United Nations personnel to accompany the police forces in the discharge of their duties.

As regards the political and electoral process, the Special Representative would have to satisfy himself at each stage as to the fairness and appropriateness of all measures affecting the political process at all levels of administration before such measures took effect. He himself would also be authorized to make proposals in regard to any aspect of the political process. Every adult Namibian was to be eligible, without discrimination or fear of intimidation from any source, to vote, campaign and stand for election to a Constituent Assembly which would draw up and adopt the Constitution for an independent and sovereign Namibia. Voting was to be by secret ballot, provision being made for those who could not read or write. There would be prompt decisions on the dates for the beginning of the electoral campaign and for the elections themselves, as well as on the electoral system, the preparation of voters' rolls and other aspects of electoral procedures. Full freedom of speech, assembly, movement and the press was to be guaranteed. Only when the Special Representative had satisfied himself as to the fairness and appropriateness of the electoral procedures was the official electoral campaign to commence. The implementation of the electoral process, including the proper registration of voters and the proper and timely tabulation and publication of voting results, was to be conducted to the satisfaction of the Special Representative. The Special Representative was also to take steps to guarantee against the possibility of intimidation or interference with the electoral process from any quarter.

One week after the date on which the Special Representative had certified the election, SADF was to withdraw its remaining personnel, SWAPO bases were to be closed, and the Constitu-

ent Assembly was to convene in order to draw up and adopt the Constitution. Whatever additional steps were necessary would be taken prior to the installation of the new Government, and independence. The Contact Group anticipated that this would occur, at the latest, by 31 December 1978.

Walvis Bay could not be included in the Settlement Plan. In 1977, after it had been administered for 55 years as if it were part of the territory of South West Africa, the South African President issued a proclamation by which it was provided that Walvis Bay would be administered as part of the South African Province of the Cape of Good Hope. In November 1977, the General Assembly declared Walvis Bay to be an integral part of Namibia. By resolution 432 (1978) the Security Council took a similar position: it "declared that the territorial integrity and unity of Namibia must be assured through the reintegration of Walvis Bay within its territory". In order not to further complicate the difficult negotiations on the conclusion of the Settlement Plan, it was decided to take up the issue of Walvis Bay as soon as the Settlement Plan was executed and Namibian independence achieved.

By Security Council resolution 431 (1978), the Secretary-General was requested to appoint a Special Representative for Namibia and to submit a report making recommendations concerning the implementation of the Settlement Proposal. The Secretary-General appointed Mr. Martti Ahtisaari as his Special Representative and dispatched a survey mission led by him to the Territory. Upon receiving the report[2] of the mission, the Secretary-General submitted to the Security Council on 29 August 1978 a plan to implement the Proposal and to provide the means that would be required to assist the Special Representative in doing so. He pointed out that it would obviously not be possible to complete the process by 31 December 1978 because the plan required approximately seven months for the completion of the stages prior to an election, and it would not be possible to abbreviate this consistently with the objective of holding free and fair elections. The Secretary-General's report stressed the resources that would be required to carry out the plan; with large civilian (including police) and military components and a substantial and complicated logistics structure.

On 29 September 1978, the Secretary-General made an explanatory statement[3] to the Security Council in reply to various questions which had been raised about his report. On the

[2]S/12827. [3]S/12869.

same day, the Security Council, by resolution 435, approved the Secretary-General's report and his explanatory statement.

From the adoption of resolution 435 to its implementation

Despite the protracted delay which occurred before implementation, and the extensive consultations which took place both within and outside the United Nations framework, resolution 435 established the definitive plan for Namibian independence.

Many rounds of further consultations on matters of detail led to what was planned as a "Pre-Implementation Meeting" of all parties concerned, at Geneva in January 1981. However, because of charges by the Turnhalle group of United Nations partiality in favour of SWAPO, the meeting failed to achieve its objective, namely, the setting of a date for a cease-fire and the start of implementation in the early part of 1981.[4] The Contact Group resumed its discussions later that year, as did the Secretary-General with all the parties. In July 1982, the Contact Group transmitted to the Secretary-General the text of "Principles concerning the Constituent Assembly and the Constitution for an independent Namibia".[5] These, they noted, had been put forward by their Governments, and all parties to the negotiations had accepted them. The Secretary-General stepped up his own consultations, and an updating of the Secretariat's implementation plans took place. However, other issues began to assume major importance, it being asserted that there could be no implementation of resolution 435 without parallel progress on the withdrawal of Cuban troops from Angola — the so-called "linkage" [see chapter 12].

In a report[6] to the Security Council on 19 May 1983, however, the Secretary-General emphasized the deteriorating situation in the region, and said that the delay in implementing resolution 435 was having widespread destructive consequences. So far as the United Nations was concerned, the sole outstanding questions related to the choice of an electoral system and the settlement of some final problems relating to UNTAG and its composition. He expressed deep concern "that factors which lie outside the scope of resolution 435" should hamper its implementation. The process of consultation continued thereafter, with the Secretary-General exploring every avenue with the parties to seek to bring about the agreed independence process in full accordance with resolution 435.

"Linkage" remained, however, an apparently insuperable obstacle until a series of meetings took place between Angola, Cuba and South Africa in London, Cairo, New York and Geneva, from May to August 1988, under the mediation of the United States and with the participation of the Soviet Union, with the aim of achieving a regional settlement to the conflict in south-western Africa. The three parties established "Principles for a peaceful settlement in south-western Africa",[7] and then a sequence of agreed steps necessary to prepare the way for the independence of Namibia in accordance with resolution 435, and to achieve peace in south-western Africa. The various elements of these agreements were embodied in the Geneva Protocol[8] of 8 August 1988, which provided, *inter alia*, for a cessation of hostile acts with effect from 10 August 1988. SWAPO, although not a party to the Protocol, informed[9] the Secretary-General that it had agreed to comply with the cessation of hostile acts embodied therein.

Immediately thereafter, the peace process began to move apace. The Secretary-General, who had remained actively involved in efforts to begin implementation of the resolution 435 process, was invited by the South African State President, Mr. P. W. Botha, to visit that country in September 1988 to discuss preparations for the implementation of resolution 435, and the general situation in the region. He told the State President, among other things, that the system of proportional representation had been agreed on for elections in Namibia. From South Africa, the Secretary-General proceeded to Luanda, where he met the President of Angola, Mr. José Eduardo dos Santos, to discuss with him progress in regard to the situation in south-western Africa.[10]

Further meetings between Angola, Cuba and South Africa took place in Brazzaville, Congo, under the continuing mediation of the United States, leading to the signature of the Brazzaville Protocol.[11] By this, the parties agreed to recommend that 1 April 1989 be established as the date for the beginning of implementation of resolution 435. They also agreed to establish a tripartite Joint Commission, which the Soviet Union and the United States would attend as observers. The three parties met on 22 December 1988 in New York, at United Nations Headquarters, for signature of a tripartite agreement between them, and for signature by Angola and Cuba of a bilateral agreement[12] relating to the phased withdrawal of Cuban

[4]S/14333. [5]S/15287. [6]S/15776. [7]S/20412, annex. [8]S/20109, annex. [9]S/20129. [10]S/20412. [11]S/20325. [12]S/20346, S/20345.

troops from Angola. In anticipation of the bilateral agreement, the Security Council had decided, in resolution 626 (1988) of 20 December 1988, to establish the United Nations Angola Verification Mission (UNAVEM), for a period of 31 months, to verify implementation of the Angolan-Cuban accord.

On 16 January 1989, the Security Council unanimously adopted resolution 629 (1989) in which it decided, *inter alia*, that 1 April 1989 would be the date on which implementation would begin. The Council called on South Africa to reduce the size of its police presence in Namibia, and requested the Secretary-General to prepare an updated report on the implementation of resolution 435, seeking cost-saving measures which would not prejudice the effectiveness of the operation. The Secretary-General's report[13] of 23 January 1989 responded to this request.

The Secretary-General referred to the serious concern which had been expressed to him, particularly by the permanent members of the Security Council, at the size and likely cost of the military component of UNTAG. Under the plan approved by the Council in 1978, this component would have accounted for more than 75 per cent of UNTAG's overall budgeted cost. However, the Movement of Non-Aligned Countries, the Organization of African Unity (OAU), front-line States and SWAPO had told him of their strong opposition to any reduction in its size. In these difficult circumstances, the Secretary-General proposed that the authorized upper limit for the military component of UNTAG should remain at 7,500 but that the Force should initially be deployed with a strength of only 4,650: three infantry battalions, each comprising five line companies, would be deployed, with four battalions in reserve in their home countries, instead of the previously planned deployment of six battalions of three line companies each, with one battalion in reserve. If the Special Representative reported a real need for additional military personnel, the Secretary-General would deploy as many of the reserve battalions as he judged to be necessary, subject to there being no objection from the Security Council.

Meanwhile, the Secretary-General proposed a concept of operations under which the military component would concentrate on certain specific tasks, namely: monitoring the disbandment of the citizen forces, commando units and ethnic forces, including the South West African Territorial Force (SWATF); monitoring SADF personnel in Namibia, as well as SWAPO forces in neighbouring countries; and securing installations in the northern border area. Other tasks approved under resolution 435, such as monitoring the cessation of hostile acts by all parties, keeping the borders under surveillance and preventing infiltration, would not, however, be eliminated. Some of them, which were previously to have been carried out by the battalions, would instead be done by military monitors or observers, whose numbers were to be increased from 200 to 300.

In view of the increase in the size of the existing police forces in the Territory, the Secretary-General also proposed an increase in the number of UNTAG police monitors from the 360 stipulated in 1978 to 500.

These changes in the plan resulted in a reduction in the overall budget from an estimated $700 million to $416 million, not including the cost of the repatriation and resettlement operation of the Office of the United Nations High Commissioner for Refugees (UNHCR), which would form the subject of a separate appeal for funding.

The Secretary-General's report also referred to agreements and understandings which had been reached by the parties since the adoption of resolution 435 (1978) and which formed part of the United Nations plan for Namibia. These included the 1982 agreement[14] that UNTAG would monitor SWAPO bases in Angola and Zambia; a number of informal understandings reached in 1982 on the question of impartiality (the "Impartiality Package"); the Constitutional Principles (also finalized in 1982);[15] and the 1985 agreement[16] on a system of proportional representation for the elections envisaged in resolution 435. The "Impartiality Package"[17] was published on 16 May 1989. It included undertakings by the Western Contact Group, the front-line States and Nigeria and SWAPO, with respect to activities within the United Nations system once the Security Council had met to authorize the implementation of resolution 435. It also included corresponding obligations on the part of South Africa in order to ensure free and fair elections in Namibia.

In an explanatory statement[18] on 9 February, the Secretary-General observed that the United Nations was now very close to the absolute minimum lead time required for the effective mobilization of UNTAG and its emplacement in Namibia; he emphasized the urgent need for the Council to adopt, without further delay, the necessary enabling resolution so that the date of 1 April 1989

---

[13]S/20412. [14]S/15776. [15]S/15287. [16]S/17658. [17]S/20635. [18]S/20457.

for the commencement of the implementation of the United Nations plan could be met.

If the operation began later than 1 April, it would not be possible to complete the electoral process before the onset of the rainy season in mid-November, which would make many tracks in northern Namibia impassable. In his contacts with all concerned, the Secretary-General also stressed that a minimum of six weeks would be needed for the deployment of UNTAG to the Territory. This could not begin until the General Assembly had approved the budget.

On 16 February, in resolution 632 (1989), the Council approved the Secretary-General's report and explanatory statement, and decided to implement resolution 435 "in its original and definitive form". Later that day, the Secretary-General presented the proposed UNTAG budget to the General Assembly, again stressing the extreme urgency if the 1 April date were to be maintained. He stated that the lead times for delivery of many essential items of equipment were already past. The Assembly, however, was especially concerned over certain aspects of the procurement of goods and services for UNTAG in southern Africa, and did not adopt the budget until 1 March. Until it had been adopted, the Secretary-General lacked the necessary authority to make official requests to Governments for the resources UNTAG required or to conclude commercial arrangements with other suppliers. Moreover, no reserves existed because of the severe financial crisis to which the Organization had been subjected for several years.

As regards the cease-fire envisaged in resolution 435, the Secretary-General had noted in his report of 23 January that South Africa and SWAPO had already agreed to a de facto cessation of hostilities with effect from 10 August 1988, as provided for in that month's Geneva Protocol. He would send identical letters to South Africa and SWAPO proposing a specific date and hour for the formal cease-fire. These letters were sent on 14 March, proposing that the cease-fire should begin at 0400 hours GMT on 1 April. The Secretary-General requested each of the parties to assure him in writing, no later than 22 March 1989, that it had accepted the terms of the cease-fire and had taken all necessary measures to cease all warlike acts and operations. These included tactical movements, cross-border movements and all acts of violence and intimidation in, or having effect in, Namibia. SWAPO and South Africa formally accepted the proposal on 18 and 21 March 1989 respectively. Each also recalled that it had previously informed the Secretary-General of its acceptance of the cessation of hostilities stipulated in the Geneva Protocol.

While it was inevitable that UNTAG's effective deployment would be retarded by several weeks, because of the delays in the Security Council and General Assembly over the size of the military component and aspects of the budget, resources were already pouring into Namibia and UNTAG's key personnel had begun to assemble there by the end of February. For 70 years, the Territory had been the subject of international debate and violent controversy, first in the League of Nations and then in the United Nations. On the eve of implementation of resolution 435, 31 March 1989, all at last seemed calm and auspicious. The Special Representative of the Secretary-General arrived at Windhoek airport on that day and was welcomed by his South African counterpart, the Administrator-General, Advocate Louis Pienaar.

C. The structure and deployment of UNTAG

UNTAG's mandate

UNTAG was essentially a political operation. Its basic mandate was to ensure that free and fair elections could be held in Namibia. Creating the conditions for such elections required UNTAG to carry out a wide variety of tasks, many of which went well beyond those previously undertaken by more traditional peace-keeping operations.

UNTAG had to monitor the cease-fire which was supposed to come formally into effect on the first day of the mandate (but which tragically did not do so, as is described in the next section of this chapter). It had to monitor the rapid reduction and eventual removal of the South African military presence in Namibia, which was an essential condition for free and fair elections and the subsequent transition to independence. It had the difficult task of ensuring that the remaining security forces, the South West Africa Police (SWAPOL), carried out their duties in a manner which was consistent with free and fair elections.

Above all, UNTAG had the political task of ensuring that a major change in political atmosphere took place so that there could be a free and fair campaign in a fully democratic climate. Numerous changes in law, attitude and society had to take place. But Namibia had had no tradition of political democracy and had been subjected to a harsh and discriminatory system of administration for a hundred years. UNTAG's task was to ensure that, despite this, the people of the country could feel sufficiently confident, free from intimidation from any quarter, and adequately informed, to exercise a free choice as regards their political future.

In carrying out these diverse tasks in the limited time available, the Special Representative of the Secretary-General had the assistance of UNTAG, an equally diverse group of international civilian and military personnel. Under the overall leadership of the Special Representative and his Deputy, Mr. Legwaila Joseph Legwaila (Botswana), UNTAG consisted of a civilian component, which included a large police element, and a military component, which was commanded by the Force Commander, Lieutenant-General Dewan Prem Chand (India). It was deployed at almost 200 locations throughout the Territory.

At maximum deployment, during the elections from 7 to 11 November 1989, UNTAG's overall strength was almost 8,000, consisting of just under 2,000 civilians (including local employees and more than 1,000 additional international personnel who came specifically for the elections), 1,500 police and approximately 4,500 military personnel.

The civilian component (excluding police)

The civilian component consisted of six elements, of which the largest, the police, is described in the next section. The other five were:

(a) the Special Representative's Office;

(b) the Independent Jurist;

(c) the Office of the United Nations High Commissioner for Refugees (UNHCR);

(d) the Electoral Division;

(e) the Division of Administration.

The Special Representative's Office had both coordinating and line functions. It was responsible for overall coordination and liaison with other UNTAG elements, with the Administrator-General's Office and his administration, with the political parties and local interest and community groups, and with the many governmental, and multitudinous non-governmental, observer missions that came to Namibia for the implementation process. Its line functions were mainly in the political and information areas. They involved responsibility for negotiations with the local administration on each of the political processes which had to unfold during implementation of the Settlement Plan and for an extensive information programme which was under the direct supervision of the Special Representative.

The Special Representative, his Deputy and his Office were located in Windhoek. Initially they operated from a series of makeshift offices, but a headquarters (the Troskie Building) became available at the end of April 1989 and its staffing, including liaison, legal and information personnel, was largely complete by early May 1989. In order to support the Special Representative's coordination, liaison, information and political activities and to provide him with a steady flow of information about developments throughout the Territory, 42 political offices were established throughout the length and breadth of Namibia. For this purpose, the Territory was divided into 10 regions: Oshakati, Rundu, Tsumeb, Otjiwarongo, Outjo, Swakopmund, Windhoek, Gobabis, Mariental and Keetmanshoop, with a regional director in charge of each one. Within the regions, 32 district centres were established, the largest number being in the relatively heavily populated Oshakati region.

Almost all these 42 offices were functioning by mid-May 1989, though one or two additional district centres were opened in the northern part of the Territory in early July 1989. A number of them closed immediately after the elections, but the basic structure of political offices remained, though at a somewhat reduced strength, until the mission closed in March 1990. One of their final tasks was to prepare for the United Nations Development Programme and for the other development agencies and programmes a comprehensive guide to the social, economic and political structures in their areas. This would ensure, during the next phase of international support for Namibia, that the extensive local knowledge acquired by UNTAG would not be lost.

The Settlement Proposal provided for the appointment of an Independent Jurist of international standing to advise on any disputes that might arise in connection with the release of political prisoners and detainees. Professor Carl Nörgaard (Denmark) was appointed to that position in 1978. His office was not subject to the direction of the Special Representative but had a quasi-autonomous status, despite being part of UNTAG and financed from its budget. It was located in central Windhoek, separately from the rest of UNTAG. Professor Nörgaard was himself present during the early months of the mission, when the majority of his work took place. His professional assistant remained in Windhoek until the close of the mission to deal with a residue of cases which continued to come forward until early 1990.

The Office of the UNHCR was responsible for the return of Namibian exiles, their reception and their resettlement. All were to be back in Namibia in time to vote, unless they indicated that they did not wish to return. The UNHCR operation was part of the Settlement Plan but was administered by UNHCR and was not financed from the UNTAG budget. However, it came under the overall political structure of UNTAG, and UNTAG facilitated its work. The operation was based at UNTAG headquarters in Windhoek, but UNHCR staff were deployed at many locations throughout Namibia, mostly in the northern half of the Territory. The designated entry points for the return of Namibian exiles were Windhoek, Grootfontein and Oshakati, where agreed formalities were completed before the returnees went to reception centres. In addition, a number of secondary reception centres were established for persons who had difficulty for one reason or another in quickly reintegrating into Namibian society.

UNHCR's key personnel arrived in Namibia on or about 1 April. The peak of their activity was during the repatriation operation, from June to September, but they maintained a presence in the Territory beyond independence in March 1990.

The Electoral Division was responsible for advising the Special Representative on all specialist and technical aspects of the election and for the supervision of the registration and electoral processes. It was also responsible for assisting the Special Representative in his and his deputy's negotiations with the South African Administrator-General concerning the electoral legislation and the manner in which the South African authorities would implement it. The Division was based at UNTAG headquarters in Windhoek. Its relatively small core staff was augmented by large numbers of additional staff, from the United Nations system and from Governments, during registration and the election itself.

For the purposes of registration and the elections, the Territory was divided into 23 electoral areas, in each of which an UNTAG official, usually from one of the regional or district political offices, was appointed district supervisor. All the 180 additional staff required for the registration of voters (3 July to 23 September) were provided from within the United Nations system. At the time of the elections themselves, from 7 to 11 November, the need for extra staff was so great that the Secretary-General sought the help of Member States. A total of 885 specialist personnel were made available by the Governments of the following 27 countries: Australia, Canada, China, Congo, Costa Rica, Denmark, Federal Republic of Germany, Finland, France, German Democratic Republic, Ghana, Greece, India, Japan, Kenya, Nigeria, Norway, Pakistan, Poland, Portugal, Singapore, Soviet Union, Sweden, Switzerland, Thailand, Trinidad and Tobago, United Kingdom.

The Division of Administration was responsible for all aspects of the administration of, and logistics support for, all elements of UNTAG, except for some of the military component, the police element and UNHCR, to the extent that they were self-administered or self-supported. UNTAG's policy was to fashion an integrated system of logistics support, with some items provided by the United Nations from its own resources, some by military logistics units and some by civilian contractors. This required the closest possible coordination and liaison between the Director of Administration and the Force Commander. Difficulties were encountered in the early weeks of the mission, both because of the pre-implementation delays already referred to and because of the tense situation which existed in the Territory following the events of early April. However, by the time of the elections in November, UNTAG's logistics were in key respects superior to those of the South African authorities, who found themselves having to rely on UNTAG's support during the elections, especially in the north.

The Division of Administration was located at UNTAG headquarters in Windhoek. The Director's deputy was based in Grootfontein, close to the concentration of civilian, police and military personnel in the northern part of the Territory. Many members of the Division of Administration were deployed for periods throughout the Territory from time to time. The Director of Administration arrived in Namibia in mid-February 1989, together with key personnel of his staff, and the Division built up rapidly thereafter. The majority departed at the conclusion of the mission after independence in March 1990 but a small "wind-up" team remained for several months thereafter.

UNTAG civilian deployment as of November 1989

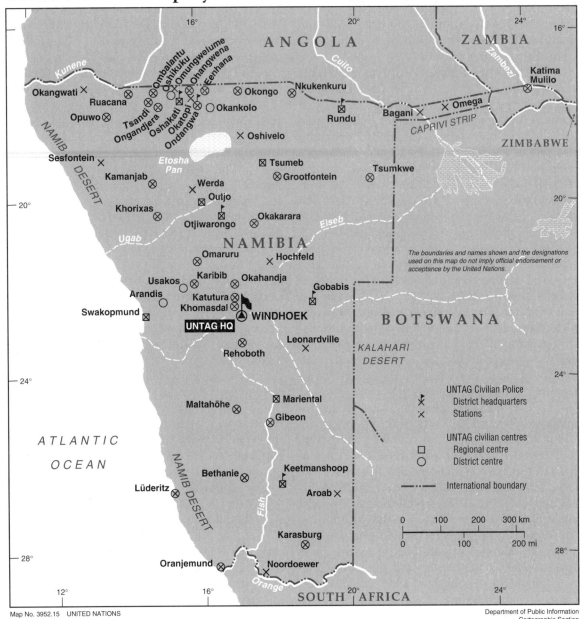

Map No. 3952.15   UNITED NATIONS
September 1996

Department of Public Information
Cartographic Section

Special efforts were devoted to the training of members of the United Nations Secretariat who were selected for political and electoral assignments with UNTAG. Training seminars took place in New York and Geneva in March 1989 for senior officials appointed to the Special Representative's Office and the 42 regional or district offices. These staff subsequently attended conferences in Windhoek at regular intervals during UNTAG's mandate period to discuss with the Special Representative the current situation, UNTAG's strategy and the carrying out of their responsibilities at each stage. As for electoral staff, they received training at special seminars in Windhoek and elsewhere in Namibia upon their arrival in the Territory.

The police element

The UNTAG civilian police (CIVPOL) were commanded by a Police Commissioner, who, as Police Adviser, also provided advice to the Special Representative and his Deputy on all police-related matters. Commissioner Steven Fanning (Ireland) was appointed to this post on 23 March 1989, having previously advised the Special Representative during the long preparations for the UNTAG mission. As Police Commissioner, he was responsible for the organization, deployment and operations of CIVPOL and shared responsibility with the Director of Administration for their administration and support. Their task was to ensure that the South West Africa Police fulfilled their duty of maintaining law and order in an efficient, professional and non-partisan way.

For police purposes, the Territory was divided in two, with a northern and a southern regional coordinator (later commander) providing coordination at the regional level. The country was further divided into six (later seven) UNTAG police districts. After the first group of 500 police officers had been deployed by May 1989, CIVPOL had 39 police stations; by September, the number had increased to 49.

The first tranche of 500 police monitors was largely deployed in the northern part of the Territory, because of the tense situation which persisted there after the events of early April. Continuing difficulties in the north caused the Special Representative to ask for a second tranche of 500 police monitors. After consulting the Security Council, the Secretary-General obtained the agreement of certain Member States to provide the additional officers, who arrived in the Territory between late June and late August. In the latter month, the Special Representative requested a third tranche of 500 in order to provide sufficient personnel during the election campaign and the elections themselves. After further consultations with the Security Council and contributing Governments, the Secretary-General began sending this group in mid-September and it was fully deployed by 31 October. The focus of CIVPOL's deployment continued to be in the north and on 1 December 1989, almost two thirds of its strength was in the northernmost quarter of the Territory.

The (finally) 1,500 police officers who served in CIVPOL were contributed, at the request of the Secretary-General, by the following Member States: Austria, Bangladesh, Barbados, Belgium, Canada, Egypt, Federal Republic of Germany, Fiji, German Democratic Republic, Ghana, Guyana, Hungary, India, Indonesia, Ireland, Jamaica, Kenya, Netherlands, New Zealand, Nigeria, Norway, Pakistan, Singapore, Sweden and Tunisia. Almost all CIVPOL personnel remained in Namibia until independence, after which they were rapidly repatriated, with the exception of officers from Ghana, India, Nigeria and Pakistan who, at the request of the incoming Government, remained for a time in Namibia under bilateral arrangements.

The military component

The military component was responsible for all military aspects of the Settlement Plan. The most important of these were monitoring the cease-fire and the confinement of the parties' armed forces to base; monitoring the dismantling of the South African military presence in Namibia; and maintaining some degree of surveillance over the Territory's borders. The military component was commanded by the Force Commander, who was appointed by the Secretary-General after consultation with the Security Council. The Force Commander also advised the Special Representative on military matters and reported through him to the Secretary-General. The Force Commander, and frequently also his deputy, participated in the Special Representative's daily morning meeting, as did the Deputy Special Representative, the Police Adviser and the Director of the Special Representative's Office, together with other senior officials as required.

Lieutenant-General Prem Chand had been appointed as Force Commander–designate in 1980 and had played an active part in the preparations for the UNTAG operation. He arrived in Namibia, with the advance party of the UNTAG military component, on 26 February 1989. The Deputy Force Commander was Brigadier-General Daniel Opande (Kenya). General Prem Chand established his headquarters at the Suiderhof base in Windhoek, on the other side of the city from the Troskie Building, where the Special Representative eventually established UNTAG's overall headquarters. Because of the limited accommodation available in Windhoek, it never proved possible to establish an integrated headquarters for both components of UNTAG. As a result, much travelling was required to ensure the close coordination necessitated by the complicated nature of the mission.

The military component, as deployed, consisted of three elements: 300 military monitors and observers; three infantry battalions; and a number of logistics units. The strength approved by the Security Council for initial deployment was 4,650, but the maximum number actually deployed was 4,493, this being due to a reduced requirement of personnel for air support.

The 300 military monitors and observers were contributed by the following Member States: Bangladesh, Czechoslovakia, Finland, India, Ireland, Kenya, Malaysia, Pakistan, Panama, Peru, Poland, Sudan, Togo and Yugoslavia. Of these, 291 had been deployed in Namibia before 1 April, though they were often without transport or communications because of the delays already referred to in the final decision-making for the establishment of UNTAG. The monitors, numbering about 200, were deployed at a variety of locations in Namibia and Angola to monitor the cease-fire, the confinement of the parties' forces to base and the dismantling of the South African military presence. In Namibia they were deployed at all the bases of SADF and SWATF units. In Angola, UNTAG (Angola) was based at Lubango, with outposts for several weeks at Chibemba, where SWAPO forces were concentrated after the events of early April, and with a liaison office in Luanda. They were withdrawn in early January 1990, following the return to Namibia of the great majority of the SWAPO forces, and the Luanda liaison office was closed a month later. UNTAG's military observers were deployed for border surveillance purposes in the Walvis Bay area and along Namibia's southern frontier with South Africa. The military monitors and observers left Namibia between January and April 1990.

The three enlarged infantry battalions approved for initial deployment were provided by Finland, Kenya and Malaysia. Four additional battalions were held in reserve, on seven days' notice to move to Namibia, by Bangladesh, Togo, Venezuela and Yugoslavia. In the event, the reserve battalions were not called to Namibia. The delays already referred to had made it clear that it was not going to be possible to deploy the infantry battalions to Namibia by D-Day, 1 April, as originally envisaged in the Settlement Plan. Under the revised plan, they were due to be deployed in late April/early May. The events of early April, however, led to an acceleration of this deployment by approximately two weeks. The Finnish battalion was deployed in the north-eastern part of the Territory by 17 April; the Malaysian battalion in the north-west by 1 May; and the Kenyan battalion in the centre and south, also by 1 May. All three battalions remained in Namibia until after independence, with the Finnish and Malaysian battalions leaving in early April 1990. The incoming Government asked Kenya to retain its battalion in Namibia after independence, under bilateral arrangements, for an initial period of three months, in order to fulfil various tasks, including helping with the training of a Namibian army.

As already noted, the logistics elements in UNTAG's military component worked closely with the civilian logistics elements to provide an integrated logistics support system for the whole operation. The military units consisted of: a signals unit (United Kingdom); an engineer squadron (Australia); an administrative company, including movement control and postal elements (Denmark); supply, transport and maintenance units (Canada and Poland, plus civilian personnel provided by the Federal Republic of Germany); a helicopter squadron (Italy); and a squadron of light transport aircraft (Spain). The military component also included a civilian medical unit contributed by Switzerland. In addition, the Soviet Union and the United States provided air transport for the initial deployment of UNTAG.

For the same reason that applied to the infantry battalions, the deployment of the logistics units was not completed before D-Day. Indeed most of them had little more than advance parties in Namibia at that time and most became fully operational only in late April or early May.

UNTAG military deployment as of November 1989

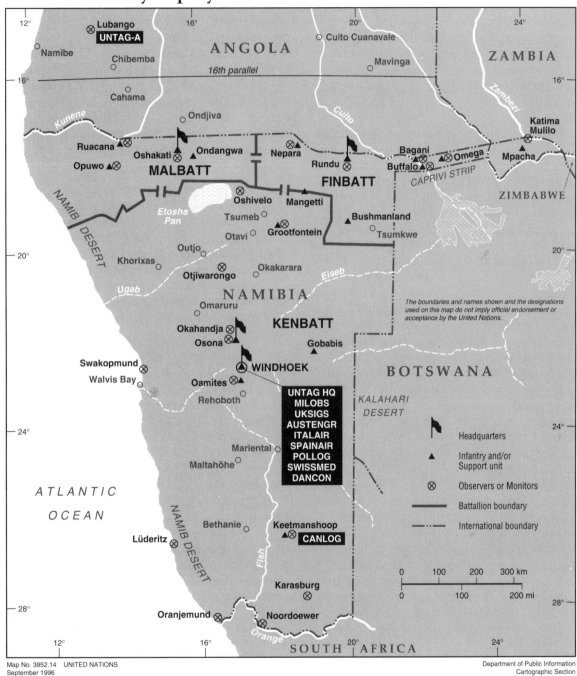

Map No. 3952.14   UNITED NATIONS
September 1996

Department of Public Information
Cartographic Section

D. D-Day and its aftermath

When the Special Representative arrived in Windhoek on 31 March 1989 to assume his duties in Namibia, hopes were high. What had seemed an interminable process of negotiation was at last to bear fruit and Namibia's independence seemed in sight. There was concern, of course, that — for the reasons already mentioned, which were beyond the Secretary-General's control — UNTAG would be far from fully deployed on D-Day and would become completely operational only a month or more later. It was recognized that this made it even more essential that all concerned should honour the commitments which they had entered into regarding all aspects of the Settlement Plan. But an informal cease-fire had been in effect, and largely respected, for over seven months and the parties had just reaffirmed in writing their acceptance of a formal cease-fire with effect from 0600 local time on the morning of 1 April.

The previous evening, however, the newly arrived Special Representative was told by the South African Administrator-General that heavily armed SWAPO forces, in combat uniform, had begun moving forward and crossing from Angola into Namibia, many others being poised to follow.

The following morning, while demonstrations and processions of welcome for UNTAG were occurring throughout the Territory, the Administrator-General told the Special Representative that further armed SWAPO personnel had crossed the border overnight and incidents were occurring on a broad front throughout the Ovambo area of northern Namibia. A series of similar reports came in during the day, indicating military action and casualties on a scale not seen for many years in the Namibian conflict. The Special Representative sent a team of senior UNTAG officials north to investigate. As already noted, UNTAG was not yet effectively deployed in the Territory. Apart from the military observers and monitors, few personnel, military or civilian, had arrived and their operational capability was severely hampered by the lack of vehicles and communications.

Later on 1 April, the South African Foreign Minister told the Secretary-General that if UNTAG was unable to contain the new situation, it would be necessary for his Government again to deploy its military forces which had, earlier that day, been confined to base under UNTAG monitoring in accordance with the Settlement Proposal; the South

West Africa Police were unable to deal with the incursion by heavily armed SWAPO groups. The Secretary-General immediately requested SWAPO representatives to do whatever they could to affect the situation positively.

Given all these circumstances, the Special Representative and the Force Commander sent to the Secretary-General an urgent joint recommendation that they be authorized to accept a strictly limited and temporary suspension of the SADF confinement to base. This recommendation was accepted. The arrangement under which this was to occur was in the following terms:

"Certain specified units, to be agreed, will be released from restriction to base to provide such support as may be needed by the existing police forces, in case they cannot handle the situation by themselves. The situation will be kept under constant review and the movement out of existing bases will throughout be monitored by UNTAG military observers."

The team of UNTAG officials sent to the north held discussions on 2 April with the South African security forces and interviewed two SWAPO prisoners captured the previous day. The latter said that they had been instructed by their commanders in Angola to enter Namibia, avoiding the South African security forces if possible, in order to establish bases in Namibia under United Nations supervision. Their units were to bring with them all their arms, including rockets and anti-aircraft devices.

In the light of the wide difference between the stated objectives of the captives, who had impressed the UNTAG team with their credibility, and those attributed to them by the South African security forces, who saw their intention as aggressive and hostile, the team immediately requested to see all the general staff of the South African security forces who were then present at Oshakati, together with a senior representative of the South African Foreign Ministry. The team emphasized the immense gravity of the situation and the serious disparity between the two versions of events. They stressed, in unambiguous language, the imperative need for maximum restraint by the security forces, while immediate efforts were made in all quarters to resolve the situation. In Windhoek, the Special Representative and Force Commander impressed the same message on the Administrator-General and his senior police and military personnel.

On 2 April, SWAPO emphatically denied that it had violated the cease-fire and stated that it was committed to honouring it in spirit and letter. On the contrary, SWAPO said, South African security forces had attacked its members who had been peacefully celebrating the beginning of the implementation of resolution 435 in northern Namibia and some of whom had been trying to come forward to hand over their weapons to UNTAG. South Africa, for its part, asserted that the incursion of heavily armed and uniformed SWAPO forces was continuing.

The Secretary-General reported on these grave developments to the Security Council in informal consultations on 3 April. He concluded his report as follows:

> "The mounting toll of Namibian and South African casualties, at the very moment when the long-delayed independence process has at last commenced, is especially tragic. On the basis of information so far available to it, UNTAG is of the view that SWAPO had infiltrated armed personnel and material into Namibia around the time of the cease-fire. UNTAG, however, feels that this infiltration may not have offensive intent, but instead may be aimed at the establishment of SWAPO camps inside the Territory, which SWAPO would then request UNTAG to monitor. SWAPO, for its part, has emphatically denied any infiltration and has stated that its supporters inside Namibia have been attacked. If the integrity of the Settlement Proposal, which took many years of difficult negotiation to conclude, is not respected by any party, then the people of Namibia will again be the principal sufferers. It is therefore most necessary for all concerned to exercise the maximum restraint at this time, and to advance and reinforce practical arrangements to implement each and every aspect of the Settlement Plan. This is a matter of the greatest political and humanitarian urgency, in view of the grave situation now existing along parts of the northern border of Namibia."

On 4 April, the South African Foreign Minister wrote[19] to the Secretary-General stating, *inter alia*, that more than 1,000 SWAPO armed forces had now infiltrated Namibia, and that major mechanized, tank and infantry elements of SWAPO had been deployed just north of the Namibian/Angolan border. Unless, he said, active and effective measures were taken to stem the rapid deterioration of the situation, the whole peace process in Namibia was in danger of collapse. On 5 April, he informed[20] the Secretary-General that the South African authorities were appealing by radio to SWAPO forces to return to Angola, and offering them safe conduct to locations north of the 16th parallel where, he said, it had been agreed, in the context of the Joint Commission agreements, that they would be confined.

On 5 April, the Secretary-General put proposals to South Africa and SWAPO for a cease-fire and the establishment of temporary assembly points under UNTAG supervision to which SWAPO armed personnel could report. They could then choose between being escorted across the border and to the north of the 16th parallel, with their arms, or handing over their weapons to UNTAG and returning as unarmed civilians to their homes in Namibia. If these proposals were accepted, South African security units would be required, 48 hours after the restoration of the cease-fire, to return to their bases under United Nations monitoring.

The Secretary-General communicated his proposals also to President Kenneth Kaunda of Zambia, Chairman of the front-line States. Following an emergency summit of the front-line States in Luanda on 6 April, President Kaunda informed the Secretary-General that the summit had accepted his proposals, but wished that the SWAPO forces, having handed over their arms to UNTAG, should remain at the assembly points until the SWAPO leadership returned to Namibia.

On 7 April, the Secretary-General again reported to the Security Council. Fighting was continuing, he said, and well over 200 persons had already been killed. Every effort was being made to expedite the arrival and deployment of UNTAG personnel throughout the Territory; members of the Council had offered fresh transport and logistics support to help to bring UNTAG rapidly up to operational strength. The Secretary-General went on to describe the cease-fire proposals which he had put forward.

[19] S/20565. [20] S/20567.

On 8 April, South Africa rejected the Secretary-General's proposals, which, it said, would be incompatible with the existing agreements. South Africa stated that it would respect all related agreements and that it would be impossible to complete the peace process unless all other parties did the same.

Also on 8 April, Mr. Sam Nujoma, the President of SWAPO, announced that the SWAPO leadership had decided to order its forces within Namibia to stop fighting, regroup and report to Angola within 72 hours under the escort of UNTAG.

Meanwhile, the Joint Commission established by the Brazzaville Protocol met in extraordinary session at Mount Etjo, in central Namibia, on 8 and 9 April. Angola, Cuba and South Africa attended, as did the United States and the Soviet Union, as observers. The Special Representative and the Administrator-General attended by invitation on 9 April. At the conclusion of the meeting, the parties adopted a Declaration of re-commitment to all aspects of the peace process, and urged the Secretary-General urgently to take all necessary measures for the most rapid and complete deployment of UNTAG so that it could fully and effectively carry out its mandate. In an annex to the Declaration, detailed agreement between the parties was recorded on Principles for a withdrawal procedure, and on a sequence of events for the implementation of the Declaration and Principles. These also were signed by the three Governments, having been agreed upon by all others in attendance at the meeting.

The withdrawal procedure was to be conducted under UNTAG supervision. SWAPO forces in Namibia were to present themselves at assembly points for safe passage to locations in Angola north of the 16th parallel. There they were to turn their arms over to UNTAG. They were to be informed of this process in local radio broadcasts in which a joint appeal by the Special Representative and the Administrator-General would be made. At the end of the process, and after information provided by SWAPO and joint verification by the Administrator-General and the Special Representative of the exit of all SWAPO forces from Namibian territory, the *status quo ante* 1 April would be deemed to have been reinstated. The parties, in agreeing to these provisions, further stated that they had taken note of the SWAPO announcement of 8 April.

On 9 April, the Secretary-General expressed his welcome for Mr. Nujoma's statement and the Mount Etjo Declaration; he believed that, in the light of these developments, the restoration of the cease-fire in Namibia would be facilitated, together with the process of implementing resolution 435. The next day, the Secretary-General again briefed the Security Council, expressing the hope that there would shortly be an end to the intense suffering and casualties that had scarred the start of UNTAG's work.

The Mount Etjo Declaration was an important step forward but it was not implemented in the manner envisaged. UNTAG found it impossible to persuade the South African security forces to keep their distance from the temporary assembly points. Perhaps as a result of this factor, among others, the SWAPO forces in Namibia chose to avoid them and only a handful, mostly sick or wounded, presented themselves for safe passage back to Angola. The vast majority preferred to make their own way across the border, without UNTAG protection. Unfortunately, a number of clashes occurred during this process. In a further meeting in northern Namibia on 20 April, the Joint Commission decided that in order to facilitate the return of SWAPO forces to Angola, all South African security forces would return to base for a period of 60 hours from 1800 hours local time on 26 April.

There was a further meeting of the Joint Commission in Cape Town, South Africa, from 27 to 29 April, about which the Secretary-General reported to the Security Council on 4 May. He said that he had asked the members of the Commission to ensure that the views of the United Nations were fully heard before the Commission adopted any decisions which would require action by UNTAG or otherwise affect the implementation of resolution 435. However, when the United Nations representatives were invited to join the Commission meetings, it was announced that certain agreements had already been arrived at, the main point being that for a two-week period, ending at 0600 hours local time on 13 May, the South African security forces would again be released from restriction in order to verify that SWAPO armed personnel had returned to Angola and to locate and lift arms caches. The Secretary-General told the Security Council that he would have preferred the outcome to have been a decision requiring that the restriction of South African security forces to their bases should continue without interruption. Regrettably, that had not been the case. He urged all parties to exercise maximum restraint, underlining the imperative need for SWAPO personnel to be given safe passage to the Angolan border.

In a further meeting of the Joint Commission at Cahama, Angola, on 19 May, the members noted the "positive steps" each had taken to fulfil its duties under the Mount Etjo agreement, as well as information provided by UNTAG that SWAPO forces were now confined to base under UNTAG monitoring north of the 16th parallel. The Special Representative and the Administrator-General confirmed that South African forces also had again been confined to base under UNTAG monitoring, with effect from 13 May, and that a de facto cessation of hostilities had been re-established in northern Namibia.

Meanwhile, the returning SWAPO forces and any others present on Angolan territory south of the 16th parallel had concentrated at Chibemba, south of Lubango, where their confinement to base by the Angolan armed forces was monitored by military officers of UNTAG (Angola). The SWAPO forces were later moved to bases closer to Lubango. These arrangements continued until the personnel concerned returned to Namibia as civilians under the repatriation programme described below.

Implementation of parts of the Settlement Proposal, which allowed a period of only seven months between D-Day and the elections, was now six weeks behind schedule. The intensity of the fighting revived the mistrust and division which had begun to be assuaged during the seven months of de facto cease-fire. UNTAG had been criticized in many quarters and its task of establishing its moral and political authority had been made more difficult. Between 300 and 400 combatants, mostly on the SWAPO side, had been killed. The counter-insurgency police, Koevoet, had been remobilized, and there would be much pain and tribulation before they were once again neutralized. It had been a nightmare beginning to an operation which had been launched with so much hope.

E. The functions of UNTAG

By mid-May the crisis created by the events of early April had been very largely resolved. UNTAG had also, by then, received most of its personnel, who had been deployed, or were in the process of being deployed, to their nearly 200 duty stations throughout the Territory. UNTAG had also received much, but still not all, of the equipment — vehicles, communications, accommodation — which it so sorely needed. It was thus able to get quickly into its stride in fulfilling the manifold functions assigned to it by the Security Council. These are described in this section.

Creating the political conditions for free and fair elections

As already noted, UNTAG was an essentially political operation whose central function was to create the conditions for free and fair elections to be held in Namibia, a Territory which had endured more than a hundred years of colonial rule and had had no previous experience of such elections. All UNTAG's activities were designed to serve this central function; all were subordinate to it. Implementation of the plan was supposed to begin on D-Day with the formal cease-fire and the confinement to base of South African and SWAPO forces. As described in the previous section, this situation was not, in the event, achieved until mid-May. Once it was achieved, the way was clear for UNTAG to start work on the practical measures which had to be taken, in less than six months, to create the political conditions for free and fair elections.

The South African military structure in Namibia had to be dismantled and the confinement of SWAPO forces to base in Angola monitored. The South West Africa Police had to be brought under effective monitoring. Discriminatory and restrictive legislation had to be repealed, political prisoners and detainees released, an amnesty for returnees proclaimed, and the many thousands of Namibian exiles, including political leaders, had to be enabled to return.

All these matters required negotiations with the South African Administrator-General and sometimes with the South African Government itself. The negotiations were conducted by the Special Representative and his various specialist teams, though on important occasions they had to be pursued in New York by the Secretary-General personally. Although satisfactory solutions were always found in the end, the Administrator-General's initial positions were rarely acceptable to the Secretary-General and his Special Representative, and in some cases negotiations were protracted and difficult.

It was recognized that if this painful process of negotiation was to be completed with the rapidity demanded by the timetable in the Settlement Plan, the necessary political momentum would have to be created. External interest and pressure had an important part to play but it was also necessary to take full advantage of the enthusiasm and support of the Namibian people for the independence process and for UNTAG's role.

As they completed their deployment throughout the Territory, UNTAG personnel found that the Namibian people were, in many cases, perplexed about what was happening and what UNTAG actually was. As a result of many years of colonialism and apartheid, Namibia had a public information system which was geared to maintain this situation, with deeply partisan newspapers and a public broadcasting system prone to disinformation. UNTAG had to neutralize these processes and to provide Namibians with relevant and objective information.

The effort was led by UNTAG's information service which used radio, television, all kinds of visual materials and print, as well as the traditional word-of-mouth. UNTAG's 42 political offices focused initially upon the need to reach out to all the people in their areas to tell them what was happening and what UNTAG was. They targeted local opinion-formers, often the churches, the farmers, the unions or political parties, or made direct contact with the people, often addressing gatherings under trees after church services. Information proved to be one of the key elements in UNTAG's operation; by the end, more than 200 radio broadcasts (usually translated into the country's many languages), 32 television programmes, and more than 590,000 separate information items had been produced.

The return of refugees, which began in mid-June 1989, gave a special boost to the process of informing the people about the independence process and about UNTAG's role. Quite suddenly, and shown in all the media, thousands of Namibians began to come home. By late June all but 1,500 of the South African troops had left Namibia and the local forces established by South Africa had been demobilized, all under the monitoring of UNTAG. Shortly after that, the law governing registration for the elections received the Special Representative's approval, and the process of registration began all over the country.

In late July, the political momentum accelerated further when the Secretary-General visited Namibia and travelled to many parts to see for himself how matters were proceeding. He convened at UNTAG headquarters a meeting of the leaders of all the parties which intended to contest the election. They had never met before in a single room. His message to them was that they should now unite, as Namibians, to build the new nation. He suggested they meet regularly, from then on, under his Special Representative's chairmanship, to iron out problems and begin a continuing and effective dialogue.

Thus was planted the seed of a political Code of Conduct which was then negotiated by the Special Representative with the party leaders and was followed by the parties during the pre-election campaigning, as well as during and after the elections. It laid down the ground rules for political conduct in a country which had never before enjoyed free and fair elections. It was essentially self-policing and self-enforcing and the parties undertook to publicize it by all available means, as did the Special Representative. In his report[21] to the Security Council of 6 October 1989, the Secretary-General described it as a document of "central importance. It gives reason to hope that the parties will conduct the election campaign in a truly democratic manner, that (despite some recent ugly incidents) they will ensure that their supporters do likewise and that they will all accept the outcome of the election. It is no exaggeration to say that Namibia's ability to make a peaceful and prosperous transition to independence will to a large extent depend upon the manner in which the political parties honour those pledges."

UNTAG made the fullest use of the Code, utilizing all its information techniques. Regular meetings were held with political leaders at all levels, and at each UNTAG regional and district centre, to deal with problems that had arisen and to pre-empt others before they could arise.

The Secretary-General's words became a reality, and the last month of the election campaign, which could have been marked by intimidation and disruption, instead saw an increasing tranquillity, with the elections themselves occurring in conditions of great serenity throughout the Territory.

The election legislation proposed by the Administrator-General again required arduous negotiations between teams led by the Special Representative and the Administrator-General, with

[21] S/20883.

frequent interventions from New York by the Secretary-General. Agreement on 6 October led to an intensive preparatory period in which election personnel were trained and a voter education campaign was conducted by UNTAG, by the Administrator-General, and by the political parties. Despite the much-criticized delays in the promulgation of the electoral legislation, the determination of the people of the country to decide their political destiny was made clear during the elections which took place from 7 to 11 November. More than 97 per cent of the registered electorate voted, with only a tiny percentage of spoilt ballots.

Throughout this political process, a helpful role was played by a Joint Working Group on All Aspects of Impartiality, which had been established in May 1989. Delegations from the Administrator-General's office and from that of the Special Representative dealt with the political problems arising from the day-to-day coexistence of the colonial Power and UNTAG. Allegations of minor misconduct by members of one or the other side, the bias of the broadcasting authorities, limitations on political activities by local public employees, allegations of prejudice in the control of public meetings, etc., were typical agenda items. Meeting weekly under alternating chairmanship, the Group successfully resolved many of the lesser problems that inevitably arose in, especially, the first months of the transition period, and usually managed to prevent them from becoming major bones of contention at the higher political levels.

Monitoring the dismantling of the South African military presence and the confinement of SWAPO forces to base

As already described, the cease-fire and confinement of forces to base which were supposed to come into effect on 1 April were not fully restored until 13 May.

The next step was the dismantling of the South African military presence in Namibia, through the withdrawal of almost all the SADF personnel and their equipment and the demobilization of the local military forces established by South Africa, namely the South West Africa Territorial Force (SWATF, otherwise known as the "ethnic forces"), the "citizen forces" and the "commandos".

Under the Plan, SADF strength was to be reduced to 1,500 all ranks, confined to base at Grootfontein and Oshivelo, by D-Day plus 12 weeks, i.e., 24 June. In spite of the hostilities of early April, which interrupted the planned SADF withdrawal, the reduction to 1,500 was achieved by 24 June, as required. Throughout the process, UNTAG officers monitored the bases and the withdrawal. The remaining 1,500, known as "the Merlyn Force", were withdrawn one week after the certification of the elections, on 21 November.

A number of other SADF personnel remained in Namibia fulfilling civilian functions. They too were monitored by UNTAG military officers. In early October, they totalled 796, of whom about two thirds were engaged in running airfields, with many of the remainder providing medical services to the population in the north. These arrangements, while in accordance with the Settlement Plan, caused some concern in the Security Council and other quarters because of the numbers of SADF personnel involved. Substantial and successful efforts were accordingly made by the Special Representative to find appropriate civilian replacements for these personnel inside Namibia and from other sources in the United Nations system, e.g., the International Civil Aviation Organization and the World Health Organization.

Of greater concern to the Security Council was the "civilianization" of other SADF personnel, some of them very senior, who were then assigned to the Administrator-General's office as a "Department of Defence Administration". Their functions included making bimonthly payments to former members of SWATF, who remained on the South African payroll until independence. Here, too, UNTAG pressed for, and gradually achieved, a substantial reduction in the numbers involved.

As regards the local forces established by South Africa, the "citizen forces" and "commandos", which were essentially part-time forces numbering 11,578 all ranks, had been demobilized before D-Day and their arms, military equipment and ammunition had been deposited in drill halls which were guarded by personnel from the UNTAG infantry battalions as soon as they arrived in the Territory. Some of the "citizen forces" and "commandos" were reactivated as a result of the events of early April, but by the end of May they had again been demobilized.

The most important element in the local forces, however, was SWATF, which numbered 21,661 all ranks on D-Day, most of the officers being on secondment from SADF. Their demobilization was completed by 1 June 1989, by which time all their arms, ammunition and military equipment had been deposited in drill halls where they were guarded by UNTAG infantry elements, the whole process having been closely monitored by UNTAG military monitors. However, the majority of the demobilized personnel retained their uniforms and, until after the elections, reported twice monthly to their erstwhile headquarters to receive their pay, in most cases from officers who had previously commanded them. This arrangement caused considerable concern to the Secretary-General and to the Security Council as being inconsistent with the requirement in the Settlement Plan that the command structures of SWATF should be dismantled. This remained a contentious issue between the Special Representative and the Administrator-General until after the elections.

Concerns were also expressed over the arrangements for the personnel of the two bushman battalions of SWATF. Unlike the other ex-members of SWATF, who could return to their places of origin after demobilization, the bushmen would have had no means of livelihood if sent away from their existing camps in the northern part of the Territory, where they had for many years lived with their families. All concerned sought a viable and humanitarian solution to this problem, but it was not possible to find a solution before UNTAG's mandate ended with the achievement of Namibia's independence.

Under the Settlement Plan, the military component of UNTAG was also required to monitor the cessation of hostile acts by all parties and to keep Namibia's borders under surveillance and prevent infiltration. As regards Namibia's border with South Africa, this task was entrusted to UNTAG's military observers, who established permanently manned checkpoints at all crossing-points from South Africa and patrolled regularly along the border. Similar arrangements were established around the enclave of Walvis Bay, where South Africa maintained an appreciable military presence after the reduction and eventual withdrawal of SADF from Namibia. The northern border presented a more difficult problem because of its extent, the presence of dense and closely related populations on both sides of the border and, as described below, repeated allegations of impending infiltration. The Finnish and Malaysian battalions accordingly mounted daily patrols along the border, a task in which they were assisted from time to time by the military monitors and by CIVPOL, who routinely accompanied SWAPOL on their own border patrols. The two infantry battalions, as well as the Kenyan battalion in the centre and the south, also undertook regular patrols in populated areas in order to advertise UNTAG's presence and give people the opportunity to raise with UNTAG their security concerns. This task also was, of course, shared with the military monitors and with CIVPOL who, as will be described, had the most important part to play in this context.

Throughout the period leading up to the elections, UNTAG had to address repeated allegations, mostly deriving from South African security sources, of imminent invasion of the north by SWAPO forces. It was asserted, on a number of occasions, that concentrations of armed SWAPO personnel were present in southern Angola, close to the Namibian border. These allegations were rejected by Angola and SWAPO. UNTAG's Angola-based monitors patrolled the areas and found no evidence to support them. The allegations nevertheless continued, even after almost all SWAPO forces had returned from Angola to Namibia as civilians to take part in the elections.

The persistence of these allegations caused the Joint Commission, which continued to meet throughout the transition period, to establish a Joint Intelligence Committee to look into all allegations of potential breaches of the basic agreements relating to the Angolan-Namibian border. This Committee, in turn, established a Verification Mechanism, which was empowered to investigate reports on the ground. UNTAG participated in these processes, its contribution being of particular importance because of its presence on the ground and the communications and other logistics support which it could provide.

The allegations nevertheless continued and culminated, a few days before the elections, in a claim by South Africa, on the basis of supposedly intercepted messages between UNTAG units, that an imminent incursion into Namibia by SWAPO forces had been verified by UNTAG military personnel. An investigation by the Special Representative of the transcripts of the alleged messages showed, rapidly and conclusively, that they were fraudulent and did not come from any UNTAG source. The South African Foreign Minister publicly withdrew the charges 48 hours later. This was the final episode in what had appeared to be a campaign by certain quarters to disrupt the independence process through disinformation and other, more direct, means, including an attack on UNTAG's regional office in Outjo, in which a local employee was killed, and a political assassination.

Monitoring the South West Africa Police

Following the confinement to base of the South African military forces and their subsequent return to South Africa or demobilization, the only

South African–controlled security forces remaining in the Territory were to be the South West Africa Police. The Settlement Plan had recognized that if conditions were to be created for the conduct of free and fair elections, without fear of intimidation from any quarter, it was essential that SWAPOL should fulfil its duty of maintaining law and order in an efficient, professional and non-partisan way. This in practice meant that SWAPOL had to change attitudes and practices which it had developed during the long years of war in the Territory. CIVPOL, as the police element of UNTAG was known, thus had a critical role to perform, a role which, as already indicated, required the Secretary-General, with the consent of the Security Council, to increase its strength from the originally envisaged 360 to a final total of 1,500.

CIVPOL could only carry out its monitoring function with the cooperation of SWAPOL itself. This was not readily provided, though the situation steadily improved during the transitional period. Cooperation was least effective in the north, the scene of former guerrilla warfare, especially in the early months of the mandate. CIVPOL also encountered major problems over the activities of the Koevoet counter-insurgency element in SWAPOL and the Security branch of SWAPOL. This problem of limited cooperation was the principal reason for the need to increase the strength of CIVPOL.

In fulfilment of its primary function of monitoring SWAPOL, CIVPOL accompanied SWAPOL on its patrols. Its ability to do so, however, depended on the necessary cooperation from SWAPOL, which was not always forthcoming, and, in the north, on the availability to UNTAG of mine-resistant vehicles, which was a problem at the beginning of the mission for both CIVPOL and the military component. CIVPOL also monitored SWAPOL's conduct of its investigations, its attendance at political rallies, and its presence during the registration and electoral processes. In principle, responsibility for the maintenance of law and order remained with the Administrator-General, and CIVPOL had no direct authority in this regard. It had no powers of arrest and could influence the standard of policing only indirectly. As the mission progressed, however, CIVPOL's role became more and more influential. CIVPOL was frequently present, and SWAPOL absent, from political gatherings, and CIVPOL often patrolled on its own, meeting the people and reassuring them by its presence.

The problem of monitoring the security police was never fully resolved. Nor was the Special Representative ever fully satisfied with CIVPOL's ability to investigate the many complaints made by the public about SWAPOL's activities, though this did greatly improve during the mission.

The Koevoet issue was one of the most difficult UNTAG had to face. This counter-insurgency unit, whose name means "crowbar" in Afrikaans, was formed by South Africa after the adoption of resolution 435, and was not, therefore, mentioned in the Settlement Proposal or related documents. Once Koevoet's role had become clear, the Secretary-General consistently took the position that it was a paramilitary unit and should therefore be disbanded, like other paramilitary units, upon implementation of the Settlement Proposal. About 2,000 of its members had been absorbed into SWAPOL before 1 April 1989, but they reverted to their former role against SWAPO in the events of early April, before once again being incorporated into SWAPOL in mid-May. The ex-Koevoet personnel, however, continued to operate as if they were a counter-insurgency unit, travelling around the north in armoured and heavily armed convoys, and habitually behaving in a violent, disruptive and intimidating manner. In June 1989, the Special Representative told the Administrator-General that this behaviour was totally inconsistent with the Settlement Proposal, which required the police to be lightly armed. Moreover, the vast majority of the ex-Koevoet personnel were quite unsuited for continued employment in the police forces, and this also was incompatible with the Settlement Plan. Unless the problem was dealt with, he would have no option but to halt the transition process.

There ensued a difficult process of negotiation with the South African Government, which continued for two months. The Secretary-General pressed for the removal of all ex-Koevoet elements from SWAPOL and the Special Representative brought to the Administrator-General's attention many complaints of misconduct by them. This was one of the main issues pursued by the Secretary-General during his visit to Namibia in July 1989. The Security Council, in its resolution 640 (1989) of 29 August, demanded the disbandment of Koevoet and the dismantling of its command structures. The Administrator-General, on the other hand, contended that there were repeated indications from his security personnel of imminent armed incursions by SWAPO and that it was necessary for him to maintain a counter-insurgency element in readiness. He also insisted that the Koevoet personnel were in fact trained policemen.

After continuing pressure by the United Nations on the South African authorities, the South African Foreign Minister announced on 28 September 1989 that some 1,200 ex-Koevoet members of SWAPOL would be demobilized with effect from the following day. A further 400 such personnel were demobilized on 30 October. These demobilizations were supervised by UNTAG military monitors.

This did not entirely eradicate the problem, as the demobilized personnel, fully paid until independence, were free to roam the sensitive and highly populated areas near the northern border. But CIVPOL was gradually able to contain the new situation, and, despite some ugly incidents, the political and electoral process in the northern areas continued with increasing tranquillity. As the United Nations had frequently emphasized, Koevoet personnel were a major part of the problem of law and order, rather than making, as was claimed, a contribution to its resolution.

Repeal of discriminatory laws, amnesty, release of prisoners and detainees

Preliminary discussions with South African officials about the repeal of discriminatory or restrictive laws which might abridge or inhibit the holding of free and fair elections in Namibia had begun, before implementation, in New York and Windhoek. Negotiations resumed in Windhoek, and in June 1989 a first tranche of legislation was repealed or substantially amended, followed by a second, more limited repeal. In all, 56 pieces of legislation were affected, among them some of the most conspicuous legal instruments of colonial repression and apartheid, though various "interim" governments in Namibia had already repealed much of the openly racist legislation that had accumulated there over the years. The first repeal proclamation also made provision for further repeals at the request of the public, although no member of the public in fact took advantage of this provision.

Particular controversy between the United Nations and the South African authorities arose over the law known as AG-8, which provided for a system of ethnic administration. This law was not repealed during the transition period, although its potentially disruptive effects were largely dissipated by other means. The Administrator-General took the position that the law fell outside the ambit of the Settlement Plan as it did not abridge or inhibit the holding of free and fair elections.

He asserted that its repeal during the transition period would entail a complete reconstruction of local administration, and that there were neither the resources nor the time to do this. In fact, few complaints were received by the Special Representative concerning discriminatory or restrictive laws after promulgation of the two repeal proclamations, although SWAPO and many foreign non-governmental organizations continued to emphasize the political unacceptability of AG-8, a position which was also consistently maintained by the Secretary-General and UNTAG.

The grant of a full and unqualified amnesty to all Namibian exiles was an essential prerequisite for their voluntary repatriation under the Settlement Plan. The scope of such an amnesty had been one of the most difficult areas of discussion between the United Nations and South Africa in the years following the adoption of resolution 435. South Africa sought to distinguish between Namibians accused or convicted of political crimes and those accused of common-law crimes. For reasons of principle and practicality, this could not be accepted by the United Nations, and, after implementation began, negotiations continued in Windhoek and New York on the subject. South Africa finally accepted the need for an unqualified amnesty, and the Amnesty Proclamation was promulgated on 6 June 1989, thus permitting implementation of the programme of repatriation, which had been delayed pending a satisfactory outcome. Each returnee received notice of amnesty as he or she re-entered Namibia.

The Settlement Plan required the release of all Namibian political prisoners and detainees. Immediately after implementation had begun, the Special Representative wrote to South Africa, SWAPO, Angola and Zambia, conveying lists of names of persons reported to have been detained or imprisoned. These had been forwarded to him by a number of non-governmental organizations which had been following the course of events in and relating to Namibia. The Special Representative inquired of the various parties whether they might have knowledge of such persons, who were alleged to have been, at one time or another, detained or imprisoned by their authorities or on their territory.

On 24 May 1989, UNTAG military monitors in Angola interviewed about 200 former detainees who had been released by SWAPO. These persons, and a number of others released by SWAPO, were duly repatriated. Meanwhile, discussions had taken place between the Special Representative and the Administrator-General regarding persons imprisoned or detained by the South African authorities. A number of disputed cases were referred to the Independent Jurist, Professor Nörgaard, and he advised upon them on 19 June 1989. Both the Special Representative and the Administrator-General accepted the Independent Jurist's advice, and 25 former political prisoners were consequently released on 20 July 1989. A number of other disputed cases were referred to the Independent Jurist during the remainder of the mission and, in each instance, his advice was followed and acted upon by UNTAG and South Africa.

However, it was persistently alleged, by both South Africa and SWAPO, that additional prisoners remained in detention and should have been released. In particular, allegations that prisoners remained in SWAPO hands became a major issue in the Namibian electoral campaign. For South Africa, the Administrator-General insisted that all persons on the lists submitted to him either had been released or were unknown to the South African authorities. As for SWAPO, it stated that it no longer held any detainees, and invited the international community to investigate allegations to the contrary.

For his part, the Special Representative sought to detach fact from allegation, and to produce, as accurately as possible, a verifiable list of Namibians who were missing or otherwise unaccounted for. He decided to send a mission to Angola and Zambia, with the cooperation of those Governments and of SWAPO, to look into the question. The mission spent several weeks during September 1989 visiting sites and seeking to check allegations. It found that no persons were detained at any of the reported locations. As a result of the information it obtained, and subsequently followed up, it was able to reduce an initial list of persons unaccounted for from 1,100 to 315. UNTAG continued to seek and obtain information on this question for the rest of its mandate. Many revisions of detail were made, and the data were subsequently refined, but the overall picture remained the same. The question of missing persons turned out to be one of the most divisive and emotionally charged issues that confronted UNTAG during its time in Namibia.

Return of refugees

The Settlement Plan required that all exiled Namibians be given the opportunity to return to their country in time to participate fully in the political and electoral process. Implementation was entrusted to UNHCR, although the operation formed part of the overall resolution 435 process of transition to independence. A number of other United Nations agencies and programmes contributed to the repatriation programme: the World Food Programme, the World Health Organization, the Food and Agriculture Organization of the United Nations, the United Nations Children's Fund and the United Nations Educational, Scientific and Cultural Organization. In Namibia, the Council of Churches in Namibia was UNHCR's implementing partner.

The great majority of returning Namibians came back from Angola, with smaller but significant numbers from Zambia. Altogether, returnees came from 46 countries, requiring a coordinated effort by UNHCR offices worldwide.

A massive airlift began in June, following proclamation of the general amnesty. Three air and three land entry points, as well as five reception centres, were established in northern and central Namibia to receive and register returnees and provide them with material assistance. Security at the reception centres was provided by the military component of UNTAG. A series of secondary reception centres was also established, but movement by returnees through the centres was, on the whole, brisk, due in large part to the assistance provided and to the resilient Namibian family structure which rapidly reabsorbed the exiles. The process of reintegration and rehabilitation was handled on an inter-agency basis, with special reference to questions of shelter, agriculture, water, health, education, income generation and family support.

The repatriation programme was conducted smoothly. The psychological impact of the return of so many exiles was perceptible throughout the country. Though various political issues were raised regarding one or another aspect of the repatriation process, its size, momentum and effectiveness helped to minimize political controversies. There were some problems in the north when ex-Koevoet elements searched villages for SWAPO returnees. This matter was kept under constant surveillance by UNTAG's police monitors, who in this area, as in others, played a valuable role in defusing local tensions and maintaining stability.

By the end of the process, 42,736 Namibians had been brought back from exile.

Registration and electoral supervision

All UNTAG's other functions were focused specifically upon the need to ensure that the whole electoral process, including registration, was transparently free and fair, so that Namibia could move to nationhood and independence through an impeccable act of self-determination. Though the electoral process was to be conducted by the South African Administrator-General, each and every element was to take place under the active supervision and control of the Special Representative and UNTAG. While the United Nations had previously participated as an observer in many final acts of decolonization, its role in Namibia was unique in terms of the degree of the Organization's involvement in the process of political change in the Territory and the central part played by UNTAG in that process.

Planning for the supervision and control of the electoral process had begun in the Special Representative's office immediately after the adoption of resolution 435 in 1978. As already mentioned, it had been decided well before implementation that a system of proportional representation would afford the most equitable and democratic means of ascertaining the popular will in the Namibian context.

As regards registration, a draft proclamation was published by the Administrator-General on 24 April 1989 for general information and comment. The Special Representative had desired that the fullest possible democratic consultation should take place prior to the finalization of the registration legislation. Many comments, often highly critical, were received on the draft and there ensued intensive negotiations between the Special Representative and the Administrator-General, which were closely directed by the Secretary-General from New York. On 26 June, the Special Representative indicated his consent to a much-amended Proclamation, which was duly issued.

The Special Representative's consent was conditional upon the Administrator-General's agreement to an exchange of letters which defined in detail UNTAG's role in the registration process. This contained, *inter alia*, the important provision that no application for registration could be rejected without the concurrence of an UNTAG official. Similar exchanges of letters were concluded between the Special Representative and the Administrator-General in connection with subsequent legislation concerning the other stages of the electoral process and the Constituent Assembly itself. They provided an important means of ensuring UNTAG's supervision and control of the election, in accordance with the Settlement Plan.

Registration began on 3 July and was originally scheduled to close on 15 September. However, the Special Representative requested that the period be extended to 23 September, so that all eligible voters would be given full opportunity to register, and this was done. The Proclamation identified the various categories of persons who would be qualified for registration. Anyone over the age of 18 could vote, if he or she was born in Namibia, or if they had been continuously resident there for four years, or if they were the child of a person born in Namibia. Provision was made for documentary or other proof of age and other qualifications. UNTAG's consent was required before a would-be registrant could be refused, and provision was made for appeals, and for the receipt of objections to registrations.

Seventy registration centres were established, together with 110 mobile registration teams which covered 2,200 points throughout the country. Each registration point was supervised by UNTAG officials, and CIVPOL was present at each location. The central register was also supervised by UNTAG computer experts, and a computerized list of registrants was made available on a weekly basis to all political parties. The number of registrants exceeded by 2.4 per cent the Administrator-General's projection of those likely to be qualified to register (701,483, as against 685,276). This confirmed UNTAG's assessment of the vast public enthusiasm for registration and the election generally.

As regards the election Proclamation, a draft was published by the Administrator-General on 21 July 1989, with a request for comments by the public within 21 days. The draft again evoked major criticisms from the public and from interested observers. The Secretary-General found it to be seriously deficient, and prolonged and difficult negotiations again ensued between the Special Representative and the Administrator-General. The Special Representative's legal staff was reinforced from New York, and the Secretary-General intervened personally at critical moments. The negotiations were not successfully concluded until 6 October. Prior to this, however, an agreed Proclamation was issued on the registration of political parties for the election. Ten parties registered. The electoral arrangements which were finally agreed and incorporated in the proclamation provided for elections on a nationwide basis (i.e., without constituencies) and for a dual system of ballots — ordinary and "tendered". Voters about whose registration or identity there was agreed to be some doubt would be required to use tendered ballots and to place them in a separate ballot box, such ballots being subject to a verification system. Voters would be expected to cast their ballots where they had registered; those who did not would be required to vote by tendered ballot.

Practical arrangements for the election were both complex and demanding, not only because of the terrain, but also because of language diversity, the unfamiliarity of many voters with the balloting procedure, the extensive measures taken to preclude fraudulent voting, and UNTAG's intensive supervision of each step. A total of 358 polling stations were established. The total number of United Nations personnel directly involved in the supervisory process was 1,758, including 885 specialist personnel made available by the Governments of 27 States. Three hundred and fifty-eight of the UNTAG personnel, acting as ballot-box supervisors, were drawn from the military component. The remaining electoral supervisors came from UNTAG's civilian component and the rest of the United Nations system. Additionally, 1,023 UNTAG police monitors were assigned to electoral duties.

All UNTAG election supervisory personnel were given specialist training. The process of voter education was inevitably delayed because of the difficult negotiations over the electoral law, which were not completed until one month before the elections. Once that had been agreed, however, a vigorous voter-education programme was carried out by UNTAG, by the Administrator-General and by the political parties. As the country moved towards elections, the atmosphere became increasingly peaceful, and the last weeks before the election saw a marked drop in allegations of intimidation.

While there had been many auspicious indications in the last weeks, and, indeed, UNTAG's whole strategy had aimed at this, few had anticipated the extraordinary response of the electorate. By the close of polling on 11 November, more than 97 per cent of the registered voters had voted in conditions of great tranquillity, and with memorable determination. In the first days, would-be voters

formed peaceful lines, often more than a kilometre in length, sometimes queuing up during the cold nights before the polling stations opened, or for hours in the sun during the day. Apart from logistical problems in the north, caused by an unexpected avalanche of voters in the first days, voting proceeded calmly, and the Special Representative had no hesitation in announcing, shortly after the polls had closed, that he was fully satisfied that the voting process had been free and fair.

Ballot-counting began on 13 November at the 23 election district centres and in Windhoek. Final results were declared on the evening of 14 November. They showed that no party had received a two-thirds majority, but that SWAPO had obtained 41 of the Assembly's 72 seats, that its main opponent, the Democratic Turnhalle Alliance (DTA), had 21 seats and that five of the remaining eight parties had also obtained representation. A very small percentage of ballots (1.4 per cent) had been rejected as invalid. A few minutes later, after informing the Secretary-General, the Special Representative, speaking to the press and public from the steps of UNTAG headquarters in Windhoek, certified, in fulfilment of his responsibility under the Settlement Proposal, that the electoral process in Namibia had, at every stage, been free and fair, and that it had been conducted to his satisfaction. In his statement, Mr. Ahtisaari said: "Its youngest democracy has given the whole world a shining lesson in democracy, exemplary as to commitment, restraint and tolerance." In his own statement, the Secretary-General, after paying tribute to the role played in the elections by the voters, the political parties, the South African authorities and UNTAG, said: "Namibia must become a united nation where the inhabitants of all political persuasions will be able to enjoy their inalienable rights without fear or favour. These were the aims and objectives of the United Nations when, 43 years ago, the issue of Namibia first came before the General Assembly."

F. Developments from the elections until the end of the mandate

On 21 November 1989, the newly elected Constituent Assembly convened, in accordance with the Settlement Plan and with a Constituent Assembly Proclamation. The latter had been promulgated after the usual difficult negotiations with the Special Representative on a draft which, in its first form, was largely unacceptable to the Secretary-General. The Constituent Assembly quickly elected officials and proceeded, initially in committees, to draw up a Constitution. The Constitution was adopted by consensus on 9 February 1990. It provided for independence six weeks later, on 21 March 1990. In his report[22] to the Security Council of 16 March 1990, the Secretary-General reported that the Constitution, which was annexed, was to enter into force on independence, and that it reflected the "Principles concerning the Constituent Assembly and the Constitution for an independent Namibia" adopted by all the parties concerned in 1982. The Special Representative had, as considered appropriate by the Assembly, made available his resources, when necessary, to assist in its deliberations and in the drafting of the Constitution.

In the period between the elections and independence, the Administrator-General remained responsible for the administration of the Territory, and his activities continued to be monitored by UNTAG and discussed as necessary with him by the Special Representative. After the elections, UNTAG closed some of its centres, and reduced staffing in others, and all were closed at independence. UNTAG's police monitors continued with their tasks until independence and there was no reduction in their strength until just before that time. Indeed, because of reductions in SWAPOL's manpower, after the elections, especially in the north, CIVPOL came to play an increasing role in maintaining calm and stability.

Numerous exercises in reconciliation between various elements were undertaken by UNTAG, particularly in the Kavango, Caprivi and Ovambo regions, with no small success.

The military component of UNTAG was gradually wound down in the early months of 1990, with certain logistics elements, and many monitors and observers, leaving during January and February. Meanwhile, however, a Tripartite Military Integration Committee was established, with UNTAG in the chair, to develop a concept for an integrated Namibian army. The Committee was to plan the integration of Namibian armed personnel who had fought on both sides of the war and develop a military structure for a future Namibian army. A team from the Kenyan battalion helped train the integrated nucleus of the new Namibian army, which participated in the independence ceremonies.

The independence ceremony, which took place just after midnight on 21 March, was attended by the Secretary-General, who administered the oath of office to President Sam Nujoma, in accordance with the terms of the Constitution, and by many leaders from around the world. In his final report[23] to the Security Council, on 28 March 1990, the Secretary-General reported: "Thus was achieved, in dignity and with great rejoicing, the goal of independence for Namibia for which the United Nations and its Member States have striven for so long."

G. Financial aspects

In his report[24] of 23 January 1989, the Secretary-General recommended to the Security Council that the costs of UNTAG should be considered as expenses of the Organization to be borne by Members in accordance with Article 17, paragraph 2, of the Charter. He also expressed his intention to recommend to the General Assembly that the assessments to be levied on Member States be credited to a special account which would be established for this purpose. This recommendation was duly accepted by the General Assembly in resolution 43/232 of 3 March 1989.

As discussed above, the Security Council's request to the Secretary-General in resolution 629 (1989) to "identify wherever possible tangible cost-saving measures without prejudice to his ability fully to carry out [UNTAG's] mandate" resulted in a reduction of the overall budget from approximately $700 million to $416 million. Considerable attention to economy during UNTAG's operation, together with voluntary contributions provided by Member States, meant that the total expenditures amounted to approximately $368,584,324.[25]

[22]S/20967/Add.2. [23]S/21215. [24]S/20412. [25]A/46/725.

H. Conclusions

The UNTAG operation had many novel features and constituted an evolutionary step beyond the United Nations traditional role of peace-keeping and the monitoring of self-determination processes. This was because of the far-reaching mandate given to the Secretary-General by the Security Council. UNTAG's principal function was to create the conditions for the holding of free and fair elections. This meant that it was required to be, and was, deeply involved in the whole political process of Namibia's transition from illegally occupied colony to sovereign and independent State. UNTAG thus had to play its part in monitoring and implementing a cease-fire, the withdrawal and demobilization of troops, monitoring a local police force, managing a political "normalization" process, supervising and controlling the resultant elections and assisting the transition to independence.

Because of the vast international interest in Namibia, a territory with a unique status under international law, each step was taken under a searchlight of public scrutiny and comment. The mandate made it one of the most political of United Nations operations, and the logistical dimensions, together with the strict timetable involved, caused it to be one of the most demanding, in practical terms, to be put in the field.

The foundation for the success of such operations remains, as ever, the full cooperation of the parties, the continuing support of the Security Council, and the timely provision of the necessary financial resources. If these are forthcoming, UNTAG showed how much the United Nations can achieve by making full use of all its resources, including the diverse skills, and the commitment, of its staff.

Chapter 12

United Nations Angola Verification Mission I, II and III
(UNAVEM I, II and III)

D. UNAVEM III

Chapter 12

United Nations Angola Verification Mission I, II and III

(UNAVEM I, II and III)

A. Background

At the time Angola emerged from its status as a Portuguese colony, the guerrilla war for independence had gone on for almost 15 years. In January 1975, the Portuguese Government sought to establish a programme for transition to independence in talks at Alvor, Portugal, with three separate Angolan liberation movements: the Movimento Popular de Libertação de Angola (MPLA), the Frente Nacional de Libertação de Angola (FNLA) and the União Nacional para a Independência Total de Angola (UNITA).

The agreement forged at Alvor soon fell apart, and the three groups fought one another with support from a variety of international sources, including Cuba, South Africa, the Soviet Union and the United States. South Africa sent troops to Angola opposing MPLA; MPLA, in turn, was backed by the Soviet Union and Cuba. MPLA emerged as the strongest of the three groups and, on 11 November 1975, established the People's Republic of Angola. FNLA's military importance subsequently dwindled, but UNITA continued to field troops, particularly in the countryside. The Soviet Union and Cuba maintained their support for MPLA, while UNITA received backing from South Africa and the United States.

The first United Nations Angola Verification Mission (UNAVEM), later known as UNAVEM I, was deployed at the beginning of 1989. It came about in a climate of declining cold-war rivalries as one aspect of intricate international negotiations on political arrangements throughout the region. While the negotiations were long and difficult and covered a range of issues, UNAVEM I accomplished its mandate in an atmosphere of cooperation. It was mandated by the Security Council to carry out a relatively straightforward assignment: monitoring the withdrawal of Cuban forces from Angola.

Once foreign troops were withdrawn from the country, the international community also saw a chance to end the long-standing conflict between the Angolan Government and UNITA. The second United Nations Angola Verification Mission (UNAVEM II) was launched in 1991. UNAVEM II took on the far more complex responsibilities characteristically faced by the new generation of peace-keeping operations in the post-cold-war era in monitoring the implementation of multi-component agreements. Those responsibilities included observing and verifying the first elections, efforts to demobilize troops and form a joint armed forces, monitoring the police and efforts to alleviate the suffering of the Angolan population.

The third United Nations Angola Verification Mission (UNAVEM III) was established in 1995. It represented an enlarged and reinforced role for the United Nations. UNAVEM III was to concentrate its efforts on helping the parties restore peace and achieve national reconciliation on the basis of the agreements they had reached in Lusaka, Zambia, in 1994. Its mandate would extend to five areas: political, military, police, humanitarian and electoral.

B. UNAVEM I

The deployment of UNAVEM I in January 1989 resulted from a complex diplomatic process which initiated both the implementation of Security Council resolution 435 (1978), leading to the independence of Namibia, and the withdrawal of Cuban troops from Angola [see chapter 11].

Intensive efforts to obtain the agreement of all concerned to the early implementation of Security Council resolution 435 (1978) on the independence of Namibia were halted by the failure in January 1981 of the "Pre-Implementation Meeting" in Geneva. Thereafter, the question of independence for Namibia became linked with that of the withdrawal of the Cuban troops which had been stationed in Angola since shortly before that country's independence in 1975. This "linkage" was opposed both by the General Assembly and by the Security Council which, in its resolution 566 (1985), rejected "South Africa's insistence on linking the independence of Namibia to irrelevant and extraneous issues as incompatible with resolution 435 (1978)". The United States Government nevertheless pursued its efforts, led by Mr. Chester Crocker, Assistant Secretary of State for African Affairs, to mediate between the countries primarily concerned in order to negotiate a complex of agreements relating both to Namibia's independence and to Cuban troop withdrawal from Angola.

Meanwhile, the military situation in southern Angola continued to deteriorate. The Namibian national liberation movement, the South West Africa People's Organization (SWAPO), carried out from bases there its armed struggle against the South African authorities in Namibia. The latter made frequent incursions into Angola, by land, sea and air, and at times occupied large tracts of that country's territory. The Security Council adopted a number of resolutions, including resolution 602 on 25 November 1987, in which it demanded unconditional withdrawal of South African forces from Angolan territory, to be monitored by the Secretary-General.

Technical mission

In response to this resolution, the Secretary-General dispatched a mission to Luanda to hold technical discussions with the Angolan Government. The mission, which spent one week in the region in early December 1987, was composed of United Nations civilian officials and three military officers seconded from the United Nations Truce Supervision Organization. It received detailed briefings on the continuing hostilities and travelled to Cunene province to investigate the situation on the ground. Upon its return to New York, it reported to the Secretary-General on South African troop concentrations and military activities in Angola.[1]

The 1988 agreements

During the course of 1988, considerable progress was made in the United States–mediated talks between Angola, Cuba and South Africa. In August of that year, the Governments concerned reached agreement on a series of practical steps that brought about a de facto cessation of hostilities in southern Angola and the withdrawal of South African forces from that country.

In November, provisional agreement was reached in Geneva on the redeployment and withdrawal of Cuban troops from Angola. On 13 December 1988, in Brazzaville, Congo, representatives of the three Governments signed a Protocol recommending to the Secretary-General that 1 April 1989 be established as the date for implementation of Security Council resolution 435.[2] They undertook to meet in New York the following week for the formal signature of two documents, a tripartite agreement between Angola, Cuba and South Africa, and a bilateral agreement between Angola and Cuba.

The two agreements were signed by the Foreign Ministers of the three countries at a ceremony at United Nations Headquarters on 22 December 1988 in the presence of the Secretary-General. In the tripartite agreement, Angola, Cuba and South Africa agreed to request the Secretary-General to seek authority from the Security Council to commence implementation of resolution 435 (1978) on Namibia's independence on 1 April 1989 and to cooperate fully with the Secretary-General in implementing the resolution. In addition, they undertook to ensure that their respective territories would not be used for acts of war, aggression or violence against the territorial integrity, inviolability of borders or the independence of any State of south-western Africa. In the bilateral

[1]S/19359. [2]S/20325, A/43/964.

agreement, Angola and Cuba agreed upon a timetable for the repatriation of the 50,000 Cuban troops which were then in Angola.[3]

Timetable of withdrawal

The timetable for withdrawal was set out in detail in an appendix to the bilateral agreement. By 1 April 1989, the first day of the implementation of resolution 435 (1978), 3,000 Cuban troops would have been withdrawn. In the ensuing 27 months, the remaining troops would redeploy northwards and would be repatriated in phases. By 1 August 1989, all Cuban soldiers would move to positions north of the "adjusted 15th parallel". By 31 October 1989, they would be redeployed to the north of the "adjusted 13th parallel".

Meanwhile, the original total of 50,000 Cuban troops would be steadily reduced. By 1 November 1989, 25,000 would be withdrawn (50 per cent); by 1 April 1990 this figure would rise to 33,000 (66 per cent), and by 1 October 1990 to 38,000 (76 per cent). The complete withdrawal of all Cuban troops would be achieved by 1 July 1991.

For the purposes of the operation, the "adjusted 15th parallel" was determined to be a direct line from a point on the coast 30 kilometres south of the Angolan provincial capital of Namibe to a point on the west bank of the Cunene River, 30 kilometres south of the 15th parallel; thence northwards up the west bank of the Cunene River to the 15th parallel; and thence eastwards along the 15th parallel to the Angolan-Zambian border. The "adjusted 13th parallel" is a line running 30 kilometres south of the 13th parallel from the coast to the 16th meridian; thence northwards up the 16th meridian to the 13th parallel; and thence eastwards to the Angolan-Zambian border.

United Nations involvement

It had for some years been envisaged that the United Nations could play a part in verification of any agreement that might be negotiated on the phased withdrawal of Cuban troops from Angola.

When it became clear that agreement was imminent on this matter, the Secretariat conducted consultations in New York with delegations from Angola and Cuba about the manner in which the United Nations would verify the withdrawal of Cuban troops, if so requested by the two parties and subject to the approval of the Security Council. Agreement was reached on a set of modalities which would enable United Nations military observers to keep an exact record of the movements of Cuban troops and military equipment through the ports and airport which the Angolan and Cuban authorities intended to use for the withdrawal. In the light of the continuing hostilities in Angola, these modalities also took account of the Cuban authorities' concerns that the military security of their troops should not be compromised.

Establishment of UNAVEM

On 17 December, prior to, but contingent upon, the signature of the two agreements described above, Cuba and Angola requested the Secretary-General to recommend to the Security Council the establishment of a United Nations military observer group.[4] Its task would be to verify compliance with the bilateral agreement, in accordance with the arrangements which had already been agreed between the two countries and the Secretariat.

On the same day, the Secretary-General issued a report containing his recommendations on how this task might be carried out. On 20 December, by resolution 626 (1988), the Security Council approved the Secretary-General's report and decided to establish UNAVEM for a period of 31 months, i.e., until one month after the planned completion of Cuban troop withdrawal on 1 July 1991. The necessary arrangements came into effect on 22 December when the tripartite and bilateral agreements between Angola, Cuba and South Africa were signed. Shortly thereafter, in a parallel move, the Security Council established the United Nations Transition Assistance Group in Namibia [see chapter 11].

Composition

UNAVEM consisted of a number of unarmed military observers, with command in the field being exercised by a Chief Military Observer (CMO). The observers were contributed by Algeria, Argentina, Brazil, Congo, Czechoslovakia, India, Jordan, Norway, Spain and Yugoslavia. On 23 December 1988, the Security Council accepted the Secretary-General's proposal that Brigadier-General Péricles Ferreira Gomes (Brazil) be appointed CMO.

---

[3]A/43/989, S/20346, S/20345. [4]S/20336, S/20337.

UNAVEM I deployment as of June 1990

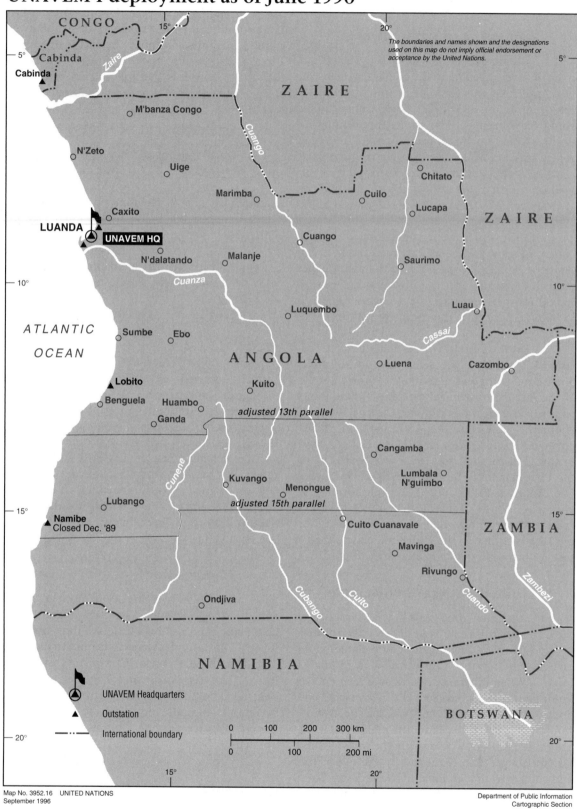

The boundaries and names shown and the designations used on this map do not imply official endorsement or acceptance by the United Nations.

CONGO

Cabinda
Cabinda ▲

ZAIRE

M'banza Congo

N'Zeto

Uige

Marimba

Caxito

LUANDA ⬛ **UNAVEM HQ**

N'dalatando

Malanje

Cuango

Chitato

Cuilo

Lucapa

Saurimo

ZAIRE

Cuanza

Luquembo

Luau

ATLANTIC

OCEAN

Sumbe   Ebo

ANGOLA

Cassai

Luena

Cazombo

Lobito ▲

Kuito

Benguela

Huambo

Ganda

adjusted 13th parallel

Cangamba

Lumbala
N'guimbo

Cunene

Kuvango

Menongue

adjusted 15th parallel

Lubango

Namibe ▲
Closed Dec. '89

Cuito Cuanavale

Mavinga

ZAMBIA

Rivungo

Zambezi

Cuando

Ondjiva

Cubango

Cuito

NAMIBIA

⬛ UNAVEM Headquarters

▲ Outstation

–··– International boundary

BOTSWANA

0   100   200   300 km

0   100   200 mi

Deployment

UNAVEM became operational on 3 January 1989 when an advance party of 18 military observers arrived in Luanda to verify the departure of the first 450 Cuban soldiers on 10 January. Thereafter, the strength rose to 70 military observers, assisted by international and local civilian staff.

The observer group's headquarters was located at Luanda, with small military teams deployed as needed at the ports (Cabinda, Lobito, Luanda and Namibe) and airport (Luanda) used for the arrival and departure of Cuban troops or military equipment. In addition, two mobile teams were established to confirm Cuban redeployment northwards in accordance with the agreed plan. The outstation at the provincial capital of Namibe was closed in December 1989, and the observer strength of the Mission was reduced to 60, after the completion of Cuban redeployment north of the "adjusted 13th parallel".

To permit effective verification, the Angolan and Cuban authorities were required to give the CMO at least seven days' notification of each departure or arrival of Cuban troops and/or equipment. As normal troop rotation continued during the withdrawal period, arrivals of troops and equipment were as carefully monitored and computed as departures. The net total of troops withdrawn could be simply calculated at any time by subtracting gross arrivals from gross departures. After each phase of the redeployment of Cuban troops northwards, the CMO dispatched one of the mobile teams to verify that no Cuban troops remained in the areas concerned. He was also authorized to conduct ad hoc inspections at any time, either on his own initiative or at the request of a member of the Security Council.

Joint Commission

To ensure liaison between the parties and the United Nations, a Joint Commission was established, consisting of the CMO as chairman and one senior officer appointed each by Angola and by Cuba. The Joint Commission's primary responsibilities were to coordinate United Nations verification of the bilateral agreement and to resolve any problems which arose. Angola and Cuba also assigned liaison officers to accompany the verification teams. In areas already vacated by the Cubans, the officers were Angolan.

Progress of withdrawal

In general, the provisions of the Angolan-Cuban agreement were scrupulously complied with and, on the whole, the withdrawal proceeded at a rate slightly ahead of the projected figures. However, the process was not immune to developments in the ongoing conflict in Angola. On 16 August 1989, President Fidel Castro of Cuba informed the Secretary-General by letter that UNITA forces had killed six Cuban soldiers in Benguela province and warned that any further incidents of this kind could have an adverse effect on compliance with the timetable for withdrawal of Cuban troops.[5] After a second attack by UNITA, this time on a Cuban water point near Lobito, in which four Cuban soldiers were killed, the withdrawal was suspended between 24 January and 25 February 1990. As a result, there was a shortfall of 619 in the 33,000 troops who were to have been withdrawn by 1 April 1990. By June 1990, however, the rhythm of the agreed withdrawal had been fully restored, and the entire process was completed by 25 May 1991, more than a month ahead of schedule.

Financial aspects

In resolution 626 (1988) of 20 December 1988, the Security Council accepted the Secretary-General's recommendation[6] that the cost of UNAVEM's operation should be considered as expenses of the Organization to be borne by Member States in accordance with Article 17, paragraph 2, of the United Nations Charter. On 16 February 1989, in resolution 43/231, the General Assembly requested the Secretary-General to establish a special account for this purpose, to which the assessments to be levied on Member States would be credited.

Expenditures for the operation of UNAVEM I during its mandate period amounted to $16,404,200 (net).

Conclusion

On 6 June 1991, the Secretary-General reported[7] to the Security Council that UNAVEM had carried out its mandate fully and effectively. He thanked the Governments of Angola and Cuba for their decision to complete the withdrawal ahead

[5] S/20799. [6] S/20338. [7] S/22678.

of schedule, thus allowing UNAVEM to concentrate its resources on the new tasks assigned by the Security Council in resolution 696 (1991) of 30 May 1991. The Secretary-General observed that the

"success of UNAVEM again demonstrates what can be achieved by a United Nations peace-keeping operation when it receives the full cooperation of the parties concerned."

C. UNAVEM II

In April 1990, the Government of Angola and UNITA began a series of talks with participation by Portugal as mediator and by the United States and the Soviet Union as observers. The negotiations eventually resulted in the Peace Accords for Angola (the Bicesse Accords or "Acordos de Paz para Angola"), which were initialled on 1 May 1991 at Estoril, Portugal, and signed by the President of Angola, Mr. José Eduardo dos Santos, and the President of UNITA, Mr. Jonas Savimbi, in Lisbon on 31 May 1991.

The Peace Accords for Angola

The Peace Accords for Angola included four documents: a cease-fire agreement, fundamental principles for the establishment of peace in Angola, concepts for resolving the issues still pending between the Government and UNITA, and the Protocol of Estoril. Overall political supervision of the cease-fire process would be the responsibility of the Angolan parties acting within the framework of a Joint Political-Military Commission (JPMC). Members of JPMC would comprise representatives of the Angolan Government and of UNITA, while representatives of Portugal, the Soviet Union and the United States would be observers. A representative of the United Nations could also be invited to participate in JPMC meetings.

The Cease-fire Agreement provided for a total and definitive cessation of hostilities throughout Angola. It would include the cessation of all hostile propaganda between the two parties and oblige both parties to refrain from acquiring lethal material. Both the United States and the Soviet Union undertook not to supply lethal aid to either party, and to encourage other countries not to do so. All civilian and military prisoners detained because of the conflict would be released. Observance of the cease-fire would be ensured by a Joint Verification and Monitoring Commission (JVMC) whose members would be representatives

of the Government and of UNITA, while representatives of Portugal, the Soviet Union and the United States would serve as observers. A representative of the United Nations would be invited to the meetings. Basically, the United Nations was asked to monitor the parties' verification activities. The Government and UNITA were to exchange information within the framework of JVMC on troops, organization of forces, equipment and armaments. JVMC would have the authority to create monitoring groups, comprising equal numbers of representatives from the Government and UNITA, which would travel unarmed and would be deployed full-time at assembly areas in which the troops of the two parties would canton, ports and airports and in general to monitor the cease-fire. Decisions of JVMC would be made by consensus between the Government and UNITA.

According to the agreed timetable for the cease-fire, a de facto suspension of hostilities was to take place at midnight on 15 May 1991, and JPMC and JVMC would take office by 31 May. Government and UNITA forces would begin to move to the areas of assembly by 1 July, and the process would be completed by 1 August 1991. It was later projected that 165,440 troops would be assembled, 115,640 for the Government's Forças Armadas Populares de Libertação de Angola (FAPLA) and 49,800 for UNITA's Forças Armadas de Libertação de Angola (FALA). By the date of the elections, the cease-fire process would be complete, and the verification and monitoring bodies would be abolished. Troops in the assembly areas would be demobilized or brought to training centres with a view to the formation of the new Angolan Armed Forces (FAA).

The "Fundamental principles for the establishment of peace in Angola" provided that UNITA would recognize the Angolan Government until the general elections were held and gave UNITA the right to participate in political activities when the cease-fire entered into force. They provided for free and fair elections for a new Government "under the supervision of international elections observers". They also noted that the new national army would be created by the date of elections. The "Concepts for resolving the issues still pending between the Government of the People's Republic of Angola and UNITA" stated that the two parties would determine the period within which elections would be held. The Government would discuss proposed changes in the Constitution with all political parties, and would work with them to draft electoral laws.

In the Protocol of Estoril, the parties noted their acceptance of a tripartite proposal by the mediator and the observers that national elections would take place between 1 September and 30 November 1992. The President would be elected by direct and secret suffrage through a majority system, "with recourse to a second round, if necessary", and a National Assembly would be elected through proportional representation at the national level. As for the length of an election campaign, a "technical opinion from a specialized international body such as the United Nations" would be obtained, but would not be binding.

The Protocol specified that the functions and activities of the police were the responsibility of the Government. To ensure neutrality of the police during the period between the beginning of the cease-fire and the elections, monitoring groups would be established. Each monitoring team would comprise two members designated by the Government, two by UNITA, and "one expert in police affairs to be designated by and subordinate to the United Nations command structure". UNITA would participate in the police force "consonant with the invitation from the Government".

In addition, the Protocol made detailed provisions relating to other questions, particularly the formation of FAA. By the date of the elections, the other armed forces would cease to exist. FAA would comprise an army with a strength of 40,000 to be drawn in equal numbers from Government and UNITA troops, an air force with a strength of 6,000 and a navy with a strength of 4,000. The Protocol noted that a Joint Commission for the Formation of the Armed Forces, subordinate to JPMC, would be created to direct this process.

The Peace Accords then provided for three possible roles for the United Nations, in addition to possible attendance at meetings of JPMC and attendance at meetings of JVMC. The cease-fire agreement specified that the United Nations would be invited to send monitors to support the Angolan parties and verify that they were assuming their responsibilities. This would include support in investigating and resolving alleged cease-fire violations. In addition, the United Nations would participate in monitoring the neutrality of the Angolan police during the cease-fire and might also be asked for advice on certain aspects of the elections.

Creation of UNAVEM II

A de facto suspension of hostilities came into effect on 15 May 1991. Two days later, the Secretary-General received a letter dated 8 May 1991 from the Minister for External Relations of Angola which included the texts of the Peace Accords.[8] The Minister asked the Secretary-General to take action in order to ensure participation by the United Nations in verifying the implementation of the Accords, and to inform the Security Council of the need to prolong UNAVEM's presence until general elections.

On 20 May 1991, Secretary-General Javier Pérez de Cuéllar recommended[9] that the Security Council entrust to UNAVEM the verification tasks attributed to the United Nations in the Peace Accords. This would entail the full-time deployment of unarmed United Nations military personnel at the 50 assembly areas (27 areas for Government troops and 23 for those of UNITA) and at 12 other "critical points" (at ports, airports and border posts) to verify the cease-fire arrangements throughout the country. United Nations observers would also make regular patrols and conduct investigations. Other tasks for the United Nations would include a role in monitoring neutrality of the police, and possible technical advice on electoral matters and supervision of the elections. The Secretary-General noted that he would inform the Council should the parties ask the United Nations to provide electoral advice and assistance. He also assured the Council that UNAVEM would continue to implement its mandate of verifying the total withdrawal of Cuban troops.

The new mandate would last from 31 May 1991, when the cease-fire entered into force, until the day following the completion of presidential and legislative elections. The Secretary-General also recommended that the rank of UNAVEM's CMO be raised to Major-General. UNAVEM would retain its headquarters at Luanda and include six regional headquarters collocated with JVMC regional headquarters. The new structure would comprise a group of up to 350 military observers

---

[8]S/22609. [9]S/22627.

who would work closely with the Angolan monitoring teams but would remain separate from them. The same procedure should apply in the case of up to 90 UNAVEM police observers.

On 30 May 1991, the Security Council established UNAVEM II for a period of 17 months.[10] The Secretary-General recommended[11] that an additional 14 countries should be added to the list of 10 countries already supplying troops to UNAVEM I. These additional countries would be Canada, Egypt, Guinea-Bissau, Hungary, Ireland, Malaysia, Morocco, the Netherlands, New Zealand, Nigeria, Senegal, Singapore, Sweden and Zimbabwe. On 1 October 1991, Major-General Edward Ushie Unimna (Nigeria) took over from Brigadier-General Ferreira Gomes as CMO of UNAVEM II.

Advance parties of military observers were deployed to five of UNAVEM II's six regional headquarters on 2 June 1991, three days after the Mission was established. Subsequent deployment occurred in stages — with minimum logistic support, partly because of a lengthy budget approval process — making it practically impossible to occupy all the assembly areas simultaneously. Furthermore, both Angolan parties were slow in establishing joint monitoring groups, in deploying their troops to assembly areas and in granting authorization to UNAVEM II to conduct reconnaissance there. Many of the planned assembly areas for Government and UNITA troops were subsequently changed to other locations. On 31 October, the Secretary-General reported[12] to the Security Council that deployment of observer teams to 46 assembly areas had been completed by 30 September 1991. Other areas were still under discussion or review or had not yet been established because of serious security problems. At this time, a UNAVEM II police presence had been established in all 18 provincial capitals.

As of 25 October, the Mission included 350 military observers, 14 military medical personnel, 89 police monitors, 54 international civilian staff and 41 local civilian staff. Police monitors came from nine Member States which also contributed military observers: Argentina, Brazil, Ireland, Malaysia, Morocco, Netherlands, Nigeria, Sweden and Zimbabwe. The Mission was organized with a command group chaired by the CMO, and also comprising the Deputy CMO, the Chief of Staff and Operations, the Senior Political Adviser and the Chief Administrative Officer. UNAVEM II was also equipped with a civilian air unit, made up of one fixed-wing cargo aircraft and 12 utility helicopters, supplemented when neces-

sary by hiring a heavy cargo aircraft and a small passenger aircraft.

As for the parties' compliance with the Peace Accords, there was considerable room for improvement. Furthermore, there were genuine logistical difficulties, especially in the provision of logistical support in troop assembly areas, which had to be established and maintained by the parties. By October 1991, troop assembly had fallen seriously behind schedule, and the two sides had failed to create joint police monitoring groups. The Secretary-General noted that these delays undermined confidence and trust between the parties.

With the agreement of the parties, UNAVEM II took the lead in monitoring some aspects of the Accords, including regular counting of troops and of weapons in all assembly areas and communicating relevant information to Luanda, and offered advice on ways to overcome practical difficulties in the assembly process. In addition, United Nations humanitarian agencies and programmes were heavily involved in the provision of food and other assistance to cantoned troops.

Hurdles on the road to elections

In the 15 months after the cease-fire fully took effect on 31 May 1991, there were no major violations of the cease-fire. Nevertheless, observance of the provisions of the cease-fire was affected by antagonisms and misunderstandings, placement of party interest before national interest, and lack of food and transport, as well as destroyed infrastructure and poor communications. While the parties chose to defuse many incidents through the joint monitoring and verification bodies established by the Peace Accords, the political and security atmosphere remained tense and fragile, with reports of violent incidents as well as of intimidation and provocation by both Government and UNITA supporters. In some cases, the heads of JPMC and observer delegations, as well as of UNAVEM II, travelled on an emergency basis to resolve the problems *in situ*.

Among the major deficiencies of this period was the failure of both sides to complete certain important tasks as provided in the Accords. The Secretary-General reported[13] to the Security Council in September 1992 that, more than one year after the deadline for confinement of Government and UNITA troops and weapons in 46 assembly areas, and despite massive international relief effort to such areas, the numbers of confined

[10]S/RES/696 (1991). [11]S/22716. [12]S/23191. [13]S/24145.

UNAVEM II deployment as of June 1992

Government troop (FAPLA) Assembly Area ▲
UNITA troop (FALA) Assembly Area ■
Government (FAPLA) "Critical Point" Ⓐ
UNITA (FALA) "Critical Point" ◉

Regional headquarters ⚑
Electoral Ⓔ

International boundary
UNAVEM II internal boundary

UNAVEM II Military Observers are located in the Assembly Areas and "Critical Points" shown on the map, except Assembly Areas of Dinge and Chimbuande.

CONGO

ZAIRE

Dinge ▲
Ⓔ ▲ Cabinda
■ Chimbuande
Soyo ▲
Ⓐ Noqui
Ⓔ ▲ M'banza Congo
■ Quimbele ◉
Nzeto Ⓐ
Kindege ■
Uige Ⓔ ■ Bungo
Quipedro ■ ▲ Negage
Dondo Ⓔ
Ⓔ Caxito
Marimba ◉
Cafunfo ▲
Xa-Cassau ■
Lucapa ▲
Luanda ⚑
UNAVEM HQ Ⓔ
N'dalatando Ⓔ
Quela ■
Malange ▲
Saurimo ▲ ⚑
Ⓔ
Cabo Ledo Ⓐ
Dondo ▲
Capanda ▲
Ⓔ
Muconda ■

ATLANTIC
OCEAN

Quibala ▲
Mussende ■
Quirima ■
Wako Kungo ■
Andulo ■ Nharea ■
Chicala ■ Luena ▲ ⚑
Cazombo ■
Sumbe Ⓔ
Bimbe ■
Kuemba ■
Ⓔ
Bailundo ▲
Bie/Cuito
Lobito ▲
Chingongo ■
Huambo ⚑
Ⓔ Cambandua
Benguela Ⓔ
Sambo ■
N'gove ▲
Chipindo ■
Lumbala-Nguimbo ◉
Quilengues ■
Menongue
Lubango ▲ ⚑
Matala ▲
Ⓔ
Namibe ▲
Mucuio ■
Cuito Cuanavale ▲
Mavinga ■ ⚑
Ⓔ
Cahama ▲
Licua ◉
Jamba ■
Xangongo Ⓐ
Ⓔ
Santa Clara Ⓐ
Mucusso ◉

ZAMBIA

NAMIBIA

BOTSWANA

0   100   200   300 km
0   100   200 mi

The boundaries and names shown and the designations used on this map do not imply official endorsement or acceptance by the United Nations.

Map No. 3952.17   UNITED NATIONS
September 1996

Department of Public Information
Cartographic Section

troops remained low, particularly in the case of FAPLA, and had even declined by comparison with the latter part of 1991. The length of stay in the assembly areas, poor living conditions and shortages of food and medicines had led to desertions and occasionally to riots, particularly in the Government assembly areas. UNAVEM, in cooperation with the World Food Programme (WFP), had to increase its assistance.

Beginning in March 1992, emphasis was placed on demobilization, the step which under the Peace Accords was to follow the assembly of troops (and which was to have been completed by the end of August 1992). This emphasis provided some incentive to the troops who had left their assembly areas without authorization to return to the areas to receive their demobilization papers, discharge allowance and clothes. New procedures introduced by JPMC and international assistance in transporting troops helped to accelerate the process somewhat. Beginning in July 1992, all troops, including those who had not been moved into the assembly areas, could be demobilized in their specific locations. This process involved the selection and transport of troops to the new FAA or to their home destinations; the transport of weapons and other military material to storage areas; a verification visit to the relevant assembly area by JVMC; followed by the formal closure of the assembly area by JPMC.

The new procedures notwithstanding, problems of organization, transport, logistics and resources continued to hamper the pace of demobilization. As of September 1992, a combined total of 61,994 (41 per cent) troops had been demobilized. The process had been faster on the Government's side (54,737, or 45 per cent) than on that of UNITA (7,257, or 24 per cent).

As for collection of weapons, most were stored either at the assembly areas or at other locations chosen by the Government and UNITA. Many were also in private hands and were to become a serious concern of the smaller political parties. Some progress was made through a directive designating locations where weapons belonging to FAPLA and FALA should be centralized and stored.

It was anticipated that UNAVEM military observers would remain in each assembly area until it was closed. As assembly areas closed, United Nations military observers would be required to verify the arms stored in the designated areas until such time as these weapons were either selected for FAA or destroyed. By September 1992, several assembly areas were near to closure but none had yet fulfilled all the conditions.

Formation of the 50,000-member FAA was also running behind schedule, although high-ranking officers from both sides were sworn in on 26 August 1992 to head the command structure. All troops not selected to form FAA were to be demobilized, and FAA was to come into existence before the elections. However, a solution was not found to the acute problem of obtaining tents to accommodate the troops selected for the new Armed Forces.

The two sides' joint police monitoring groups were established in all 18 provinces by June 1992. However, the activities of the monitoring mechanism remained weak because of mutual mistrust, political interference by the two parties and inadequate logistical support for the monitoring teams, which relied almost entirely on UNAVEM for their transport and communications.

Although the Peace Accords called for the Government to invite UNITA to participate in the national police, only 39 of the 183 UNITA personnel included in the first joint training course qualified for incorporation. The Government subsequently promised to accept an additional 1,011 UNITA members. Another major problem arose over UNITA's contention that the Government unilaterally and clandestinely transferred about 30,000 FAPLA troops into the "anti-riot", or emergency, police. The Government refuted those numbers, stating that the total strength of all its police, including the "anti-riot" police, was 39,830; that the total strength of the "anti-riot" police was only 1,030 and was planned to reach a strength of 1,516 by the end of December 1992; that Armed Forces personnel were incorporated into the police even before the Peace Accords took effect; and that the Government had until then recruited only 4,080 of its demobilized troops into the police. This question was a major concern of JPMC.

The extension of the Government's central administration throughout the whole country, as called for in the Peace Accords, was nearing completion by September 1992, but the process had not been accomplished with equal effectiveness in all areas. All 163 municipalities were covered, but 54 of the 542 communes remained without administration. In many cases, the delays in this process were caused as often as not by difficulties of logistics and infrastructure rather than by political factors.

As for the release of military and civilian prisoners, the International Committee of the Red Cross (ICRC) confirmed that the Government and UNITA completed the first phase in April 1992. While both sides subsequently stated that they held no more prisoners, each maintained outstanding claims against the other. In addition, ICRC had lists of missing persons presented to the Government and UNITA with a request for explanations.

Another difficult problem related to the province of Cabinda. Because of the activities of the Frente de Libertação do Enclave de Cabinda/ Forças Armadas de Cabinda (FLEC/FAC), led by Mr. N'zita Tiago, and the FLEC Renovada, led by Mr. José Tiburcio, the province was to a large extent left out of the peace process. The Government did not confine its troops to the two assembly areas in Cabinda because the troops, according to the Government, were in the province for combat duty against the armed FLEC factions. Meanwhile, UNITA kept only a small number of soldiers at its own assembly area in the province. The Government and UNITA agreed that negotiations could be held to address the issue of greater autonomy for the province and, in early July 1992, the Government arranged high-level talks with some FLEC leaders. The leaders of the FLEC/FAC armed factions did not, however, indicate their readiness to participate in negotiations.

Electoral process

The Peace Accords for Angola provided for "free and fair elections for a new Government" under "the supervision of international election observers". On 5 December 1991, the Secretary-General received two letters from the Minister for External Relations of Angola. One asked for United Nations technical assistance in preparing for and conducting the elections. The other requested that United Nations observers be sent to observe the Angolan electoral process until its completion. On 20 December 1991, the Secretary-General informed[14] the Security Council that he would recommend that it authorize an observation mission for the first-ever elections in Angola. In January 1992, the United Nations and the Angolan Government concluded an agreement on technical assistance.

On 6 February 1992, Secretary-General Boutros Boutros-Ghali informed[15] the Council of his decision to appoint Under-Secretary-General Margaret Joan Anstee as his Special Representative to coordinate the activities of the United Nations in connection with the Angola Peace Accords. She would also be Chief of Mission of UNAVEM II. On 3 March, after the Special Representative had visited Angola and met with the leaders of both sides, the Secretary-General submitted his recommendations[16] to the Council on the United Nations role in observing the elections. On 24 March, the Security Council, by resolution 747 (1992), decided to enlarge the mandate of UNAVEM II to include election observation in Angola.

In March 1992, the office of the Special Representative was established in Luanda to coordinate all United Nations activities related to the Angolan peace process. In addition to its deployed military and police observers and civilian staff, UNAVEM II was enlarged to include an Electoral Division, headed by a Chief Electoral Officer. Offices of the Electoral Division were established in Luanda, in the six Angolan regions and in the capitals of all 18 provinces to which approximately 100 international staff and the requisite number of local staff were deployed.

The United Nations role was to observe and verify the elections. The electoral process itself was organized and directed by the National Electoral Council (NEC), on which all legalized political parties in Angola were represented, and supported by technical assistance provided by experts and consultants from the United Nations Development Programme (UNDP). The electoral process comprised four phases: the registration of voters; the electoral campaign; the presidential and legislative elections; and the counting of the votes, investigation of complaints and announcement of the final results.

On 9 September 1992, the Secretary-General reported[17] to the Security Council that the results of the registration exercise, from 20 May to 10 August, had surpassed expectations, with NEC reporting the registration of 4.86 million eligible voters, representing some 92 per cent of an estimated voting population of 5.3 million.

The electoral campaign took place from 29 August to 28 September. It was conducted without major violence, although there were reports of intimidation by some political parties, notably UNITA and MPLA, as well as difficulties of access to certain areas, particularly those controlled by UNITA. The 18 political parties which had presented candidates campaigned actively. There were complaints, especially from the smaller parties, about the continued existence of the Government and UNITA armies, the slow progress in demobilization and in forming FAA, and lack of access to the Government-controlled radio and television, whose alleged partiality was criticized.

UNAVEM II electoral observers monitored the campaign, contributed to civic education pro-

[14]S/23556. [15]Ibid. [16]S/23671. [17]S/24556.

grammes and provided information on UNAVEM II's role. In addition, UNAVEM II and UNDP organized an air support operation, consisting of 45 helicopters and 15 fixed-wing aircraft, to overcome the logistical difficulties in reaching the more inaccessible polling stations. United Nations police observers also continued their work. Their role was particularly critical because the Angolan joint monitoring groups were almost entirely dependent on UNAVEM II for transport and communications.

On 27 September 1992, the Government and UNITA announced the disbandment of their armies. As the elections drew near, demobilization had formally accelerated. By 7 October, a total of 96,620 Government troops had been demobilized, representing 80 per cent of the projected figure. However, a much lower proportion of ex-FALA troops were demobilized. During this period, UNAVEM II continued to carry out its verification functions at the assembly areas.

Presidential and legislative elections were held on 29 and 30 September 1992. For the observation and verification of the voting, UNAVEM II deployed 400 electoral observers. Operating largely as two-person mobile teams, the observers covered all 18 provinces and most of the 164 municipalities, and visited about 4,000 of some 6,000 polling stations. On 1 October 1992, the Secretary-General's Special Representative issued a statement noting that the great majority of registered voters had cast their ballots in peaceful and orderly conditions, despite organizational and logistical difficulties. However, complaints were raised on 3 October and thereafter by UNITA and some other parties of widespread, massive and systematic irregularities and fraud during the elections. The Secretary-General urged the leader of UNITA, Mr. Savimbi, not to reject the results of the elections, pending investigation of UNITA's complaints, and emphasized the urgency of a meeting between him and President dos Santos. The complaints were investigated by NEC, with the active assistance of UNAVEM II. Investigative commissions were sent to all 18 provinces but found no conclusive evidence of systematic and massive fraud which would offset the overall results of the elections.

Meanwhile, a major violation of the Peace Accords occurred early in October when 11 former UNITA generals, including the commander of UNITA's army, withdrew from the new unified armed forces, in protest at what they called "fraud and cheating" in the elections.

In view of these developments, the Security Council sent to Angola, from 11 to 14 October, an ad hoc Commission, composed of the representatives of Cape Verde, Morocco, the Russian Federation and the United States, to support implementation of the Peace Accords. However, these diplomatic efforts proved incapable of preventing the continued deterioration of the political and military situation in the country.

On 17 October 1992, the President of NEC announced the official election results. More than 91 per cent of those registered had voted. MPLA had won the legislative elections, with 53.74 per cent, against UNITA's 34.1 per cent. In the presidential elections, President dos Santos had received 49.57 per cent, against Mr. Savimbi's 40.07 per cent. Since neither had achieved 50 per cent, the Electoral Law required a second round. The Special Representative issued a statement on 17 October saying there was no conclusive evidence of major systematic or widespread fraud. Irregularities had not been of a magnitude to have a significant effect on the official results announced on 17 October. She emphasized that, "with all deficiencies taken into account, the elections held on 29 and 30 September 1992 can be considered to have been generally free and fair". The statement was received in Angola with a campaign by UNITA-controlled mass media impugning the integrity and impartiality of the Special Representative and of UNAVEM II. Ms. Anstee received death threats and other UNAVEM II personnel were also threatened.

Aftermath of the elections

After the election results were announced, UNITA launched a nationwide operation to occupy municipalities by force and remove the Government's local administrative structures. The Secretary-General conveyed to the Security Council his serious concern at the rising tension. The Council once again[18] called upon both parties to abide by all their commitments under the Peace Accords, in particular the confinement of their troops and collection of weapons, demobilization and the formation of the unified armed forces. It requested UNITA to respect the results of the elections and urged the leaders of the two parties to engage in immediate dialogue to enable the second round of the presidential elections to be held.

[18] S/24720.

On 30 October, the Security Council, faced with further alarming reports of resumed hostilities in many parts of the country, adopted resolution 785 (1992), extending the existing mandate of UNAVEM II until 30 November 1992 and endorsing the statement by the Secretary-General's Special Representative that the elections had been generally free and fair.

Barely 23 hours later, on 31 October, heavy fighting broke out between the Government and UNITA forces, especially in Luanda and subsequently in several other cities. A large number of Angolans, in particular UNITA supporters, were killed. The Secretary-General's efforts, supported by a number of Member States, resulted in a cease-fire which came officially into effect on 2 November. UNAVEM II kept its military, police and civilian presence intact at 67 locations throughout the country and worked to maintain the cease-fire, patrolling trouble spots and using its good offices to foster dialogue between the parties.

Immediately after the cease-fire, the Government stipulated four conditions for resuming political dialogue with UNITA leader Jonas Savimbi: commitment by UNITA to uphold the cease-fire, pursue dialogue and renounce violence; commitment by UNITA to the principles of the Peace Accords; acceptance by UNITA of the results of the September 1992 legislative elections; and greater United Nations involvement in the peace process and the second round of the presidential elections.

To help the Special Representative put the peace process back on track, the Secretary-General sent Mr. Marrack Goulding, then Under-Secretary-General for Peace-keeping Operations, to Angola from 6 to 12 November. In discussions with President dos Santos and Mr. Savimbi, it became apparent that the main common ground between the two sides was their desire for an enlarged UNAVEM force to help with, among other things, mediation and good offices, troop reassembly and demobilization, formation of a joint police force, security for senior UNITA officials and a second round of elections. Following further negotiations, Mr. Savimbi confirmed in writing that UNITA had accepted on 16 November the results of the "recognizedly fraudulent and irregular" legislative elections in order to advance the peace process. At the same time, the Government proceeded with its plans to convene the newly elected Assembly and form what was called a government of national unity. While all the parties that had won seats were invited to participate, UNITA did not send a delegation, citing safety reasons, despite the

Special Representative's offers to provide transport and an escort of UNAVEM II military and police observers.

The Secretary-General reported[19] to the Security Council on 25 November 1992 that, although it was too soon to analyse the causes of the deteriorating situation in Angola, a "root cause" had been the incomplete fulfilment of key provisions in the Peace Accords. In particular, he pointed to the less than effective demobilization and storage of weapons; the delay in creating the unified armed forces, which only formally came into being two days before the elections; the failure to re-establish effective central administration in many parts of the country; and the delay in setting up a neutral police force. It had also been difficult to create in 16 months, after as many years of civil war, an atmosphere of mutual confidence, tolerance and respect.

At the same time, it was also too soon to despair of the Angolan peace process, for both parties had renewed their commitment to it. The Secretary-General recommended an extension of the mandate of UNAVEM II for a two-month period, until 31 January 1993. He made it clear that he could not recommend an enlargement of the mandate and strength of UNAVEM II unless both sides could convince him that they would genuinely adhere to and fulfil the Peace Accords, especially the key provisions relating to the dissolution of the existing armies and the creation of unified and non-partisan military and police forces.

On 30 November, the Security Council, by resolution 793 (1992), extended the mandate of UNAVEM II to 31 January 1993. The Council demanded that the Government and UNITA scrupulously observe the cease-fire, stop military confrontations and all offensive troop movements and create the conditions for completing the peace process in Angola. It appealed to the two parties to engage in a dialogue aimed at national reconciliation and at the participation of all parties in the democratic process, and to agree on a clear timetable for the fulfilment of their commitments under the Peace Accords.

Meanwhile, the efforts of the Secretary-General's Special Representative resulted in a meeting of high-level delegations from the Government and UNITA in the southern provincial capital of Namibe on 26 November 1992. Meeting under UNAVEM II auspices, the parties pledged themselves to full acceptance of the validity of the Peace Accords, to an effective cease-fire through-

[19]S/24858.

out the country and the immediate cessation of all offensive movements, and to the need for a larger United Nations involvement. However, almost immediately, this progress was followed by a setback when, on 29 November, UNITA forces took the northern provincial capital of Uíge and an important airbase nearby, Negage. Subsequent attempts to restore dialogue between the two sides failed, including a personal invitation from the Secretary-General to President dos Santos and Mr. Savimbi to meet with him.

Three options for UNAVEM II

The situation in Angola severely deteriorated in early 1993. There were outbreaks of heavy fighting in at least 10 provincial capitals and other population centres, with each side blaming the other for initiating those hostilities. The Secretary-General informed[20] the Security Council that, to all intents and purposes, Angola had returned to civil war and was probably in an even worse situation than before the Peace Accords were signed in May 1991. The conflict engulfed towns and population centres in a way unprecedented during the previous 16 years. There were disturbing but unconfirmed reports that new supplies of arms might be entering the country.

The widespread fighting and the absence of government administration in much of the countryside led to widespread hunger and the flight of large numbers of people from the towns involved in the conflict. An already serious humanitarian situation became catastrophic in many areas, and the capacity of international humanitarian agencies to provide assistance was severely disrupted.

The crisis thrust UNAVEM II into a central mediating role. At the same time, UNAVEM II teams in the field faced mounting dangers, which became so extensive that 45 of UNAVEM's 67 locations had to be evacuated. With the outbreak of violent and widespread hostilities, and the total collapse of the joint monitoring mechanisms, UNAVEM II's original mandate became less and less relevant. Even the mediating role was increasingly limited by the deteriorating security situation.

The Secretary-General outlined three options for the future of UNAVEM II. The first was to maintain the mission at its existing strength; the second was to reduce its provincial deployment to approximately six locations. The third option, which the Secretary-General preferred, was to confine UNAVEM II to the capital, Luanda, and

to one or two other locations but with the capability to deploy to six provincial sites if needed, to support his Special Representative's peacemaking efforts.

On 29 January 1993, the Security Council, by resolution 804 (1993), extended the mandate of UNAVEM II for a period of three months, until 30 April. As a provisional measure, for considerations of security, the Secretary-General was authorized to concentrate UNAVEM II's deployment in Luanda and, at his discretion, in other provincial locations, with the levels of personnel and equipment he deemed appropriate to allow for the subsequent expeditious redeployment of UNAVEM II as soon as that became feasible. The Council also demanded that the two parties establish a cease-fire immediately, restore continued and meaningful dialogue and agree on a clear timetable for the full implementation of the Peace Accords. When that did not happen, the Secretary-General decided to decrease temporarily the strength of the Mission.

Further efforts to restore peace

In the midst of the intensified fighting throughout Angola, particularly in the central provincial capital of Huambo, the Secretary-General's Special Representative continued efforts to arrange a dialogue between the Government and UNITA. The two sides agreed to hold talks in Addis Ababa, Ethiopia, focusing on the prerequisites for the effective relaunching of the peace process.

The first round was held from 27 to 30 January 1993 under United Nations auspices and the chairmanship of the Secretary-General's Special Representative. The Government and UNITA reached agreement on a number of questions, but some key issues remained to be resolved before a cease-fire could be arranged. The parties agreed to meet again in Addis Ababa on 10 February, but at the request of UNITA, the meeting was postponed to 26 February. It was then cancelled because the UNITA delegation failed to attend. In the light of the steadily worsening situation and the collapse of the Addis Ababa negotiations, the Secretary-General asked his Special Representative to come to New York from 9 to 12 March 1993 for consultations.

The Security Council, by resolution 811 (1993) of 12 March, demanded an immediate cease-fire throughout the country and called on the two parties, particularly UNITA, to produce

[20]S/25140.

early evidence that real progress had been made towards implementing the Peace Accords. The Council invited the Secretary-General to organize a meeting between the Government and UNITA at the highest possible level before 30 April 1993. The Secretary-General initiated consultations through his Special Representative, and agreement was reached on a meeting in Abidjan on 12 April 1993 at the invitation of the Government of Côte d'Ivoire. The Abidjan meeting, under the chairmanship of the Special Representative, lasted six weeks. It ended, on 21 May 1993, without full agreement on the text of what became known as the Protocol of Abidjan.

The Secretary-General described[21] the breakdown of the Abidjan talks as a major and tragic setback to the peace process. Having stated that it would be unthinkable for the United Nations to abandon Angola at such a critical juncture, he recommended a further interim extension of UNAVEM II, on a reduced basis, and in a manner which would respond to the evolution of the military and political situation. The Mission would consist of 40 international civilian staff, 50 military observers, 18 police observers and 11 medical and 75 local staff. It would provide good offices and mediation, with the goal of restoring a cease-fire and reinstating the peace process along the lines of the Peace Accords. At the same time, the Secretary-General stressed that with the humanitarian situation deteriorating daily, it would also be important during this interim period to devote increasing resources to coordination of humanitarian relief activities throughout Angola. To this end, a United Nations Humanitarian Assistance Coordination Unit (UCAH), headed by a senior official with extensive operational experience, was set up in Luanda in late April 1993, under the overall authority of the Special Representative of the Secretary-General.

On 27 May 1993, the Secretary-General announced[22] that he had agreed to accede to Ms. Anstee's wish to be released from her responsibilities. Subsequently, he appointed Mr. Alioune Blondin Beye, former Minister for Foreign Affairs of Mali, as his Special Representative for Angola, effective 28 June.

On 1 June 1993, the Security Council decided[23] to extend UNAVEM II's mandate for a period of forty-five days until 15 July and stressed the importance of the functions of good offices and mediation by UNAVEM II and the Special Representative. It also welcomed the steps taken by the Secretary-General to strengthen United Nations humanitarian activities in Angola. The Coun-cil extended[24] the mandate once again on 15 July for a period of two months until 15 September. It reiterated its demand that UNITA accept unreservedly the results of the elections and abide fully by the Peace Accords. In recommending the extension, the Secretary-General noted[25] that UNAVEM II was an essential factor in a continuous United Nations effort to facilitate the resumption of negotiations and to support humanitarian activities in the country, as well as an indispensable channel for communication between the parties. The Mission was deployed at five locations: Luanda, Lubango, Namibe, Benguela and Sumbe. UNAVEM II military and police observers patrolled the areas, maintained liaison with the respective local authorities, rendered support to humanitarian assistance operations, and conducted investigations and other activities.

Sanctions against UNITA

On 15 September 1993, the Security Council imposed[26] an embargo on the supply of arms and petroleum products to UNITA. The Council decided that all States should prevent the supply of weapons, ammunition and military equipment as well as petroleum products to Angola other than through points of entry named by the Government. The embargo was to enter into force in 10 days unless a cease-fire was established. The Council also expressed its readiness to consider the imposition of further measures, including trade measures against UNITA and restrictions on the travel of UNITA personnel, unless by 1 November 1993 the Secretary-General reported that an effective cease-fire had been established and that agreement had been reached on the full implementation of the Peace Accords and relevant resolutions of the Security Council. The Council established a committee to monitor the sanctions. The oil and arms embargo came into force at midnight on 25/26 September 1993. The Council also extended once again the existing mandate of UNAVEM II, this time for a period of three months. It reiterated its readiness to consider expanding substantially the United Nations presence in Angola in the event of significant progress in the peace process.

Meanwhile, the United Nations continued its efforts to facilitate the resumption of the peace process in consultation with the Angolan parties and interested countries, including, in particular,

---

[21]S/25840. [22]S/25882. [23]S/RES/834 (1993). [24]S/RES/851 (1993). [25]S/26060. [26]S/RES/864 (1993).

the observer States to the Peace Accords — Portugal, the Russian Federation and the United States. Following extensive consultations, the Government of Angola and UNITA began exploratory talks in Lusaka, Zambia, on 25 October 1993 under the auspices of the United Nations. These talks were made possible by positive steps taken by both sides, including UNITA's proclamation of a unilateral cease-fire, its acceptance of the general legal framework of the Peace Accords and its agreement to withdraw from the localities it had occupied following the resumption of the hostilities.

As requested by Security Council resolution 864 (1993), the Secretary-General reported[27] to the Council on 27 October. He stated that not enough progress had been made towards implementing the Peace Accords and relevant Council resolutions, and therefore recommended that the Council impose additional measures against UNITA. However, the Secretary-General said the Council should postpone such action until 1 December in view of the fact that the Angolan Government and UNITA were holding talks.

The Secretary-General also recommended that the authorized strength of UNAVEM II military and police observers be increased. These personnel would be deployed in the event of a breakthrough and would enhance the Mission's ability to verify major developments on the ground and to provide good offices. He appealed to the Government and UNITA to make full use of the opportunity and to consolidate the progress made up to that point in the search for a solution to the conflict in Angola. He also appealed to the international community for further generous support to meet the growing humanitarian needs, noting that stocks of relief supplies were inadequate.

The Security Council expressed[28] complete support for the Secretary-General and his Special Representative in their efforts to resolve the Angolan crisis. It also encouraged urgent contingency planning for the possible augmentation of the strength of the Mission. At the same time, it expressed its readiness to impose further sanctions against UNITA if it observed that UNITA was not cooperating in good faith to implement the cease-fire, the Peace Accords and relevant Council resolutions. It did not, however, take any action on the Secretary-General's recommendation to increase the strength of the Mission.

Peace talks begin

Exploratory talks were held from 25 to 31 October 1993 in Lusaka and in a short while resulted in the acceptance by UNITA of the validity of the 1991 Peace Accords and the validity of the results of the legislative and presidential elections of 29 and 30 September 1992. UNITA also agreed to withdraw its troops from the localities occupied since the resumption of the hostilities and to return its troops to United Nations–monitored areas as a transitional measure pending full implementation of the Peace Accords.

The Secretary-General's Special Representative, in consultation with the representatives of the three observer States, then set the date and venue for substantive talks which began at Lusaka on 15 November 1993. By 11 December 1993, there was agreement on the general and specific principles as well as on the modalities relating to all military issues on the agenda: the re-establishment of the cease-fire; the withdrawal, quartering and demilitarization of all UNITA military forces; the disarming of all civilians; and the completion of the formation of FAA.

In view of the encouraging progress being made at Lusaka, the Secretary-General recommended[29] that further sanctions on UNITA should be postponed. He also recommended that the mandate of UNAVEM II be extended for three months. The Security Council, by its resolution 890 (1993) of 15 December, accepted those recommendations and called on both parties to honour commitments already made at the talks in Lusaka, exercise maximum restraint and stop all military actions immediately. The Council urged agreement on the modalities for the establishment of an effective and sustainable cease-fire and the conclusion of a peaceful settlement as soon as possible.

Following the 11 December 1993 agreement on military issues, the discussions moved to political issues, including the questions related to the police and national reconciliation. On 31 January 1994, the parties agreed on the general and specific principles and on the modalities relating to the police. On 17 February 1994, following several rounds of proximity talks, an agreement was also reached on a revised text of the general principles concerning the question of national reconciliation.

[27]S/26644. [28]S/26677. [29]S/26872.

The Lusaka peace talks then focused on efforts to find ways to bridge the gap between the positions of the parties on the specific principles relating to the question of national reconciliation, which included the allocation of high-level government posts to UNITA. It was envisaged that once agreement was reached on that issue, the remaining items on the agenda would be resolved without much difficulty. Those included the future mandate of the United Nations and the role of the observer States, the conclusion of the electoral process and the re-establishment of a national administration throughout the country.

Meanwhile, fighting persisted in many parts of Angola. Several major cities remained under siege by one or the other side resulting in increased hardship for the civilian population and aggravating the already disastrous humanitarian situation. On 10 February 1994, the Security Council issued a statement[30] deploring the great loss of life and destruction of property caused by the fighting at several locations throughout Angola and stressed that the only way to achieve an effective, verifiable and sustainable cease-fire was for the Government and UNITA to conclude and sign a comprehensive peace agreement. The Council once again called upon the parties to honour their commitments, to exercise maximum restraint, to put an immediate halt to all offensive military actions and to commit themselves to the urgent conclusion of the Lusaka talks.

Expansion in principle of UNAVEM II

On 9 March 1994, the Secretary-General recommended[31] the extension of UNAVEM II for an additional three months and asked the Council to authorize in principle an increase in its existing strength. He stressed that swift deployment of the United Nations force would be important, especially in the most sensitive regions of the country, to avoid jeopardizing a settlement in its initial and most critical stages. The Secretary-General also recommended that the Council continue to take no action on the additional sanctions against UNITA.

On 16 March 1994, the Security Council adopted resolution 903 (1994), by which it decided to extend the mandate of UNAVEM II until 31 May 1994 and not to impose, at that time, additional measures against UNITA. The Council also declared its readiness, in principle, to consider promptly authorizing an increase in the strength of UNAVEM II to its previous level, following a report from the Secretary-General that the parties

had reached an agreement. Once again, it invited the Secretary-General to proceed with contingency planning in that regard. Demanding the end to all offensive military actions, the Council called upon both parties to honour commitments already made. It urged them to redouble their efforts to complete the remaining points on the agenda of the Lusaka talks, attain a sustainable cease-fire and conclude a peaceful settlement without "procrastination". In addition, it called for full cooperation of all the parties to guarantee the unimpeded delivery of humanitarian assistance.

Peace talks

Efforts continued at all levels to make further progress at the Lusaka peace talks. After February 1994, the talks focused on the specific principles and the modalities pertaining to the question of national reconciliation. Following consultations on proposals presented by the Special Representative, Mr. Beye, the Government and UNITA agreed on 12 of the 18 specific principles. However, one of the six remaining principles — the question of UNITA's participation in the management of State affairs, including the crucial issue of the allocation of senior government posts to UNITA — caused the talks to stall.

Despite the deadlock in negotiations, the Secretary-General remained convinced that the remaining issues relating to national reconciliation could be resolved if approached with realism and the necessary political will. On 31 March 1994, he reiterated[32] to the Security Council the need to strengthen UNAVEM II as soon as a comprehensive peace agreement had been reached and stressed the importance of adequate and timely financial resources in order to consolidate the agreement at its initial and most critical stage.

On 14 April 1994, the President of the Security Council, in a letter[33] to the Secretary-General, expressed concern at continuing outbreaks of hostilities in Angola and reaffirmed the importance its members attached to the "prompt and successful" conclusion of the Lusaka peace talks. The Council also reaffirmed its readiness, depending on the progress achieved towards the full implementation of the Peace Accords and relevant resolutions of the Security Council, to consider further action in accordance with its previous resolutions.

[30]S/PRST/1994/7. [31]S/1994/282. [32]S/1994/374. [33]S/1994/445.

Continued fighting

Agreement on the completion of the electoral process was reached between UNITA and the Government of Angola on 5 May 1994. Concerning the six remaining specific principles on the question of national reconciliation which had not yet been agreed, the Secretary-General's Special Representative and the three observer States submitted to both parties new proposals aimed at breaking the impasse.

While the intensity and scale of military activities decreased as of the second week of April 1994, small-scale operations, especially by UNITA, continued. On 19 April, Malange airport and the city itself were shelled while a World Food Programme (WFP) aircraft was unloading cargo, and humanitarian flights to the city were temporarily suspended. During May, the military situation remained tense throughout the country. As a result of the continuing hostilities, emergency relief flights to some locations were disrupted. UNAVEM II remained at its reduced strength, but while negotiations in Lusaka continued, the United Nations stepped up contingency planning in anticipation of a comprehensive settlement.

On 24 May 1994, the Secretary-General reported[34] to the Security Council that the Under-Secretary-General for Humanitarian Affairs had visited Angola from 15 to 18 April, reviewed the ongoing humanitarian operations there and discussed the expected increase in humanitarian needs in the event a peace agreement was concluded. United Nations organizations and non-governmental organizations (NGOs) continued to implement the emergency humanitarian assistance programme, which was aimed at providing relief to all accessible locations. However, the humanitarian needs of recently accessed areas had to be urgently met, as the populations in those locations were on the verge of starvation. It was very likely that similar conditions would be found in other inaccessible areas.

In its resolution 922 (1994) of 31 May 1994, the Security Council decided to extend the mandate of UNAVEM II until 30 June 1994. The Council stressed that its future decision concerning Angola would take into account the extent to which the parties demonstrated their political will to achieve a lasting peace. It encouraged both parties to finalize outstanding details in the peace process without further procrastination. The Security Council also decided not to impose additional measures against UNITA in view of the direct negotiations taking place, but reiterated its readiness

to consider further steps should the Secretary-General recommend additional measures or the review of those in effect.

Progress at Lusaka

The major problem at the Lusaka peace talks remained UNITA's insistence on the post of Governor of Huambo province. On 20 June 1994, the Secretary-General suggested[35] to the Security Council that it might wish not to impose further measures against UNITA if it gave an unequivocally positive response to the proposals put forward as a package by UNAVEM II and the observer States on UNITA's participation in the management of State affairs. If, however, UNITA persisted in its refusal to accept in their entirety the proposals which the Government of Angola had already accepted, the Council could consider their implementation.

On the military front, fighting escalated in late May and June, causing further loss of life and damage to infrastructures and hindering the delivery of humanitarian aid to many parts of the country. Both the Government and UNITA appeared to be determined to achieve their military objectives. The Council strongly deplored[36] the intensification of offensive military actions throughout Angola and condemned acts that imperilled humanitarian relief efforts. It urged both parties to grant immediate security clearances and guarantees for relief deliveries to all locations. The Council also declared its readiness to impose additional measures against UNITA if by 31 July 1994 UNITA had not formally accepted the complete set of proposals on national reconciliation put forward by the Special Representative and the three observer States. The mandate of UNAVEM II was extended until 30 September 1994.

Mr. Beye, representatives of the three observer States and a number of African leaders pushed the parties to conclude an agreement, but there was only limited progress at the peace talks in June and July 1994. Although agreements were reached on all the specific principles pertaining to national reconciliation, some aspects of the modalities for the implementation of those principles could not be agreed.

On 12 August 1994, the Security Council warned[37] that the peace process could not be delayed indefinitely and strongly urged UNITA to demonstrate its commitment to peace and to accept the complete set of proposals put forward by

[34]S/1994/611. [35]S/1994/740. [36]S/RES/932 (1994). [37]S/PRST/1994/45.

Mr. Beye and the representatives of the three observer States. On 5 September, the Special Representative obtained a letter from UNITA that conveyed its formal acceptance of the complete set of proposals on national reconciliation. Thus, the plan was accepted by both the Government and UNITA.

The Security Council acknowledged[38] the progress on 9 September 1994 and said that the way was clear for an early conclusion of the negotiations in Lusaka. However, the military situation in the country continued to be grim, with both parties fighting for last-minute advantage. There was heavy fighting in the oil-rich enclave of Cabinda, and in Lunda Norte and Kwanza Sul provinces. By the end of August, the military situation in the provinces of Bengo, Bié, Huambo and Kuando Kubango had also deteriorated. In other parts of the country, the situation remained tense.

In early September 1994, the Secretary-General sent a special mission to Angola, headed by former Under-Secretary-General James O. C. Jonah. The mission assessed United Nations efforts in peacemaking, peace-keeping and humanitarian relief at a time when the peace talks were in their final phase, with the parties negotiating the last item on their agenda, namely, the new mechanism for implementing the Peace Accords and the forthcoming Lusaka Protocol. The United Nations was to provide an important element of that mechanism.

The Secretary-General recommended[39] to the Security Council on 17 September that the mandate of UNAVEM II be extended for a further short period, until 30 November 1994, to allow time for the talks to conclude, for follow-up meetings between the military representatives of the Government and UNITA, for the signing of the Lusaka Protocol and for preparations for the expansion of UNAVEM II. The Council extended[40] the mandate until 31 October 1994 and urged the parties to make every effort to have the Lusaka Protocol formally signed before that date. The Council declared that any further "obstruction or procrastination" in the peace process would be unacceptable.

On 20 October 1994, in the expectation that an agreement would be concluded by 31 October, the Secretary-General recommended[41] that the existing mandate of UNAVEM II be extended until 31 November 1994. He also suggested that the Council might wish to consider authorizing the restoration of UNAVEM II to its previous strength so as to enable the Mission to consolidate implementation of the peace agreement in its in-

itial and most critical stage. The Secretary-General reiterated his appeal to both sides in Angola to exercise the utmost restraint and to desist from all military operations which could undermine the progress achieved in Lusaka.

On 27 October, the Security Council, by resolution 952 (1994), extended the mandate of UNAVEM II to 8 December 1994, and authorized the restoration of the Mission's strength to its previous level of 350 military and 126 police observers, once the Secretary-General reported that a peace agreement had been initialled and an effective cease-fire was in place. The Council also reaffirmed its readiness to consider promptly, once the Lusaka Protocol had been formally signed, any recommendation from the Secretary-General for an expanded United Nations presence in Angola.

Lusaka Protocol

A comprehensive peace agreement, the Lusaka Protocol, was initialled on 31 October 1994. In commending both sides for the achievement, the Secretary-General noted[42] that talks between high-ranking military representatives set to begin shortly should be brought quickly to a successful conclusion so that there was no delay in the formal signing of the Protocol by mid-November. He expressed hope that the necessary momentum had been created for the immediate establishment of an effective cease-fire and appealed to the Government and UNITA to declare one without delay.

Nevertheless, heavy fighting continued throughout Angola. As a result of major offensives, Government forces were able to retake many strategically important areas of the country, including all provincial capitals, some of which had been occupied by UNITA for many months. While the Security Council welcomed[43] the initialling of the Protocol, it expressed grave concern over the intensification of military operations, in particular those towards Huambo, which put the lives of Angolan citizens at risk and jeopardized the successful completion of the peace process. The Council stressed once again that any obstruction to the peace process would be unacceptable, and urged the Government of Angola to exercise its authority to bring an immediate end to the military activities. It called upon the parties to honour their commitments, to exercise maximum restraint and responsibility, and to refrain from any action that

---

[38]S/PRST/1994/52. [39]S/1994/1069. [40]S/RES/945 (1994). [41]S/1994/1197. [42]SG/SM/5463. [43]S/PRST/1994/63.

could jeopardize the signing of the Protocol on 15 November 1994.

The continued fighting, in which the city of Huambo fell to Government forces, delayed the talks between high-ranking military representatives. On 16 November, after a meeting with the Special Representative and the three observer States in Lusaka, the Government and UNITA stated that they would sign the peace agreement on 20 November 1994. They also agreed to establish a truce as of 16 November, until the formal cease-fire provided for in the Protocol came into effect. On 18 November, the Security Council expressed concern[44] at allegations that the truce was not being respected. The President of the Council sent identical messages[45] to Angolan President dos Santos and UNITA President Savimbi, calling on them to ensure that their forces adhered strictly to the terms of the truce, and urging them to sign the Protocol as agreed.

The Protocol was signed on 20 November in Lusaka by the Minister for External Relations of Angola, Mr. Venâncio de Moura, and by the Secretary-General of UNITA and its chief negotiator at Lusaka, Mr. Eugénio Manuvakola, in the presence of President dos Santos. The ceremony was witnessed by several heads of State, a number of foreign ministers and other dignitaries. Citing security concerns, Mr. Savimbi did not travel to the Zambian capital.

The Lusaka Protocol consisted of 10 annexes, each relating to a particular issue on the agenda of the peace talks, covering legal, military and political issues. The main military issues centred on the re-establishment of the cease-fire; the withdrawal, quartering and demilitarization of all UNITA military forces; the disarming of civilians; and the completion of the formation of FAA. The major political issues included the neutrality of the national police and the integration of UNITA elements into its ranks; the mandate of the United Nations and the role of the observers of the Peace Accords; the completion of the electoral process; and the question of national reconciliation.

On 21 November, the Security Council welcomed[46] the signing of the Lusaka Protocol. In the Council's view, the Protocol, along with the 1991 Peace Accords, should lay the foundation for lasting peace in Angola. The parties should continue to demonstrate their commitment to peace through the full and timely implementation of its provisions. At the same time, the Council noted with concern reports that the fighting in Angola was continuing. It called for full respect for the cease-fire which was to go into effect on 22 No-

vember. The Secretary-General also issued a statement[47] saying that the United Nations would be ready to start deploying UNAVEM II observers to former combat zones as soon as the cease-fire was effective and to begin implementation of provisions of resolution 952 (1994) concerning enlargement of the Mission.

The high-level military talks and the negotiations regarding the security arrangements for Mr. Savimbi and other senior UNITA leaders concluded at Lusaka on 23 November. It was agreed that further talks would be held at Luanda on 29 November. However, the talks did not resume as scheduled since the UNITA delegation, citing logistical and transport problems, delayed its arrival at Luanda.

A shaky cease-fire

Even after the cease-fire formally went into effect on 22 November, the military situation in many parts of Angola remained tense, with some fighting reported between Government forces and UNITA. In order to enhance the verification capabilities of UNAVEM II and as an additional confidence-building measure, the Special Representative decided to deploy to the countryside small teams of military and police personnel already serving with the Mission. Accordingly, on 27–29 November, UNAVEM II regional headquarters were established in the cities of Huambo, Luena, Menongue, Saurimo and Uíge, in addition to one already existing in Lubango. The Secretary-General also dispatched a small group of specialists from the United Nations Secretariat to Angola to conduct a technical survey. On the basis of the team's proposals, he intended subsequently to present to the Security Council comprehensive recommendations for the overall role of the United Nations in the implementation of the Lusaka Protocol.

The Secretary-General reiterated[48] to the Security Council on 4 December 1994 that once his Special Representative reported that the cease-fire was effective, he would proceed with the expansion of UNAVEM II to its previous level. Pending that, the Secretary-General recommended that the mandate of UNAVEM II be extended for a further period, until 31 January 1995. It was his expectation that the cease-fire would solidify during this period and that the international community would be reassured of the commitment of the

---

[44]S/PRST/1994/63. [45]SC/5940, SC/5941. [46]S/PRST/1994/70.
[47]SG/SM/ 5492. [48]S/1994/1376.

Angolan parties to national reconciliation and the implementation of other key provisions of the Lusaka Protocol.

Reports from the Special Representative indicated that the cease-fire was generally holding, despite some initial difficulties. Moreover, the Government and UNITA were reasonably satisfied with the status of the cease-fire and wanted the planned enlargement of UNAVEM II to take place as soon as possible. The Secretary-General informed[49] the Security Council that he therefore intended to proceed with the restoration of the strength of UNAVEM II to its previous level and the deployment of the Mission throughout the country. In addition to existing tasks, the Mission would monitor and verify all major elements of the Lusaka Protocol and provide good offices to the parties, including at the local level. Also in early December, the Secretary-General's Special Representative came to New York and briefed the Security Council on the situation in Angola.

On 8 December 1994, the Security Council extended[50] the mandate of UNAVEM II to 8 February 1995 to enable it to monitor the cease-fire established by the Protocol. It welcomed the Secretary-General's intention to restore UNAVEM II to its previous level, contingent on strict observance of an effective cease-fire and on guarantees of security for United Nations personnel. The Council welcomed the Secretary-General's continued planning regarding a possible mandate for a new United Nations operation in Angola.

Humanitarian situation

A particularly harsh element of the situation in Angola was the severe toll of the conflict on the civilian population. It was estimated that during 1993 close to 1,000 persons died every day from the direct or indirect effects of the war. Children, women and the elderly were among the worst hit. United Nations agencies and programmes made intensive efforts to provide humanitarian assistance to those in need, but it was often impossible to reach those in the interior of the country. Only in October 1993, following intensive negotiations with the two parties on humanitarian access and a general decrease in the level of fighting country-wide, were relief flights able to reach besieged cities such as Kuito and Huambo, whose populations had been cut off from international assistance for many months. In many of these previously inaccessible communities, people were found to be starving to death, and the malnutrition rates in many cases were higher than 35 per cent. The United Nations started a massive programme of humanitarian assistance. WFP spearheaded the effort by providing air transport of relief supplies for other United Nations agencies, such as the United Nations Children's Fund and the Office of the United Nations High Commissioner for Refugees (UNHCR).

Six months of relative stability and steady progress in relief efforts between November 1993 and April 1994 were followed by intensified conflict and a near standstill in humanitarian assistance to critical areas of the country. United Nations officials negotiated with both sides in the conflict in order to secure access to people in need. But between mid-May and mid-August 1994, the delivery of humanitarian relief dropped sharply, due to increased security risks and curtailment or suspension of relief flights.

In June 1994, the Secretary-General drew[51] the Security Council's attention to the dramatic escalation in the number of serious violations of humanitarian law in Angola, the rapid deterioration in the humanitarian situation in places where access was being denied, and threats to the safety of relief workers. The Security Council deplored[52] the worsening of the humanitarian situation and urged the parties to grant all necessary security guarantees and to refrain from actions endangering relief personnel or disrupting humanitarian assistance.

Despite major logistical difficulties, United Nations relief programmes did manage to provide relief to accessible populations in need. In the coastal provinces and other areas considered secure, national and international NGOs worked with the United Nations to provide food and other emergency assistance to large numbers of Angolans displaced by the war or affected by the country-wide economic decline. UCAH played a major role in that process. On 21 May 1993, the United Nations Department of Humanitarian Affairs launched an inter-agency appeal for Angola, seeking some $226 million in emergency humanitarian assistance for 2 million Angolans in need. Donors provided nearly 50 per cent of that figure by the end of January 1994.

Between February and September 1994, the Department of Humanitarian Affairs twice revised and updated the consolidated inter-agency appeals to support humanitarian action in Angola. An appeal for the period February to June initially sought $179 million. By mid-August, donors had

---

[49]S/1994/1395. [50]S/RES/966 (1994). [51]S/1994/740/Add.1. [52]S/RES/ 932 (1994).

pledged nearly 70 per cent of that amount and had responded particularly well with commitments in the agricultural sector. Funds for basic non-food relief and survival items were not forthcoming, however, and the affected population receiving assistance was 10 per cent larger than the figure anticipated in February. In September, the Department of Humanitarian Affairs further updated the appeal, seeking $61 million to cover the estimated shortfall in funding for relief activities until the end of the year and estimated at $188 million the total requirements for humanitarian assistance in Angola for the period February to December 1994. Most of that sum was for food aid, followed by assistance particularly targeted at children and mothers. Pledges towards this overall total remained at roughly 70 per cent of requirements at the end of 1994.

In early 1995, some 3.5 million Angolans living in accessible areas were receiving humanitarian aid. Supplies went by air and road to an average of 15 cities every week. Approximately 112,000 returnees and other vulnerable groups living near resettlement areas were receiving aid from UNHCR. Some 280,000 Angolan refugees in the Congo, Namibia, Zaire and Zambia were expected to begin returning as conditions improved in Angola. A particular problem was posed by landmines. Angola, a country with an estimated population of 11 million, was reported to be the "most mine-polluted country in the world", with an estimated 10 million unexploded pieces of ordnance distributed throughout the territory. On 1 February 1995, the Department of Humanitarian Affairs issued a consolidated inter-agency appeal for Angola in the amount of $213 million. Of that, $55.8 million was for demobilization and reintegration and $12.4 million for mine action.

Final period

On 1 February 1995, the Secretary-General presented[53] to the Security Council the possible mandate for a new United Nations operation in the country, UNAVEM III. At the same time, he reported that UNAVEM II had been steadily increased in strength. As of 27 January, the number of military observers had increased from 50 to 171, and civilian police observers had increased from 18 to 122. With the easing of initial logistical difficulties and the improved security conditions on the ground, it became possible to establish 22 team sites throughout the country. By the beginning of February, over 30 outstations were established in the most critical areas.

Composition of UNAVEM II

UNAVEM II was headed by a Chief Military Observer until the appointment on 6 February 1993 of Under-Secretary-General Margaret Anstee (United Kingdom) as the Special Representative of the Secretary-General and Chief of Mission. Ms. Anstee was succeeded by Mr. Alioune Blondin Beye (Mali) on 28 June 1993. The CMO at the inception of UNAVEM II was Brigadier-General Péricles Ferreira Gomes (Brazil). His successor, Major-General Edward Ushie Unimna (Nigeria), took over on 1 October 1991 and served until 14 December 1992. After a period when Brigadier-General Michael Nyambuya (Zimbabwe) served as Acting CMO, Major-General Chris Abutu Garuba (Nigeria) assumed command on 9 July 1993.

The original authorized strength of UNAVEM II was 350 military observers and 90 police observers. There were also a civilian air unit and a medical unit, as well as some 87 international and 155 local civilian staff. In May 1992, the Security Council acted on the recommendation of the Secretary-General to increase the police strength of the Mission to 126 officers. Military and police observers were provided by Algeria, Argentina, Brazil, Canada, Colombia, Congo, Czechoslovakia (later Slovakia), Egypt, Guinea-Bissau, Hungary, India, Ireland, Jordan, Malaysia, Morocco, Netherlands, New Zealand, Nigeria, Norway, Senegal, Singapore, Spain, Sweden, Yugoslavia and Zimbabwe. In addition, during the polling, the Electoral Division fielded a total of 400 electoral observers. They were of some 90 nationalities and included staff members from the United Nations system and observers contributed by Member States. UNAVEM II military and police observers also participated in the observation of the electoral process.

Following the outbreak of the post-election fighting, the strength of UNAVEM II was reduced to 50 military observers, 18 police observers and 11 military paramedics. The Mission also included some 50 international civilian staff and approximately 70 local staff. In October 1994, in anticipation of a new peace agreement in Angola, the Security Council authorized the restoration of UNAVEM II's strength to its previous level.

[53] S/1995/97.

Financial aspects

The costs of UNAVEM II were met by assessed contributions from United Nations Member States. Expenditures for the operation of the Mission amounted to $175,802,600 net.[54]

Conclusion

UNAVEM II operated in a dangerous and complex conflict situation requiring flexibility and innovation. While the scope of its mandate was limited by the Bicesse Accords, UNAVEM II, from its very inception, had to take the lead in actively assisting the parties in overcoming obstacles to the implementation of the Peace Accords. Its political role, however, remained restricted. UNAVEM II also made a major contribution to the impressive achievement represented by the successful, internationally monitored conduct of elections in a war-torn country. In the period after the renewal of hostilities, UNAVEM II maintained its political and military presence and became an essential factor in a continuous United Nations effort to facilitate the resumption of negotiations to advance the peace process as well as in monitoring the dramatically evolving situation in the country. As a neutral body, UNAVEM II was an indispensable channel for communications and repeatedly drew the warring parties back to the negotiating process while fulfilling other vital functions, such as its support for humanitarian activities. To some extent, the Mission became important as a preventive measure to check further escalation.

At the same time, the setbacks experienced by UNAVEM II show the risks faced by the United Nations when its mandate and resources are inadequate in relation to the complexities of the task, especially in circumstances where the parties do not demonstrate the necessary political will for peace. The short time-frame allotted for the cantonment and the demobilization of troops and for national reconciliation, and the narrow scope of United Nations activities in assuring compliance with major provisions of the Peace Accords, had a negative impact on the overall situation. Following the aftermath of the elections, the Secretary-General observed[55] that "the deliberately limited role assigned by the two parties and the observers in the Peace Accords to UNAVEM II in military matters, which was only to verify the efficient working of joint monitoring mechanisms to be established and chaired by the parties themselves, hampered its ability to correct the drift towards non-compliance".

D. UNAVEM III

The signing of the Lusaka Protocol[56] on 20 November 1994 marked a new stage in the Angolan peace process. The signing was followed by a cease-fire on 22 November 1994 and a gradual improvement in conditions for the delivery of humanitarian aid. Contributing to the improvement of the situation were a meeting on 10 January 1995 of Chiefs of Staff of the armed forces of both sides and the work of the Joint Commission, established under the Lusaka Protocol to watch over the implementation of the Peace Accords and the Lusaka Protocol. The Commission consisted of the Government and UNITA as members, the Special Representative as Chairman, and Portugal, the Russian Federation and the United States as observers.

On 24 January, the President of Angola wrote[57] to the Secretary-General reiterating his Government's commitment to the full implementation of the Lusaka Protocol and noting a number of initiatives that had contributed to the growing mutual trust between former enemies. He expressed the hope that the Security Council would soon establish UNAVEM III to assist in the implementation of the Lusaka Protocol.

On 1 February 1995, the Secretary-General recommended[58] to the Security Council that "a new United Nations operation in Angola, UNAVEM III, immediately take over from UNAVEM II". In doing so, he stressed the reaffirmation by both the Government and UNITA of their commitment to respect and implement the Peace Accords, the relevant resolutions of the Security Council and the Lusaka Protocol, and their agreement, with the full participation of the three observer States, on an enlarged and reinforced role for the United Nations. The breadth of that role would require a sizeable presence in the country.

[54]A/50/651/Add.3. [55]S/25140. [56]S/PRST/1994/70. [57]S/1995/94. [58]S/1995/97.

For the international community there were obvious risks involved in investing in a new peace-keeping operation in Angola. If the Government and UNITA were found to be lacking the political will to abide by their commitments, the Secretary-General would not hesitate to "invite the Security Council to reconsider its commitments".

Main objectives and mandate

In setting out the concept of operations, special consideration was given to the geography of Angola and the prevailing conditions. The country had a total area of 1,246,700 square kilometres with a varied and difficult terrain. Its basic infrastructure had been devastated, in some areas almost totally, by 34 years of struggle for independence and civil war. The humanitarian situation was extremely grave, with approximately 30 per cent of the estimated population — some 3.5 million people — refugees, displaced and/or in need of relief assistance. The very large number of mines laid throughout the country posed a serious hazard for the population and for United Nations activities.

The Secretary-General recommended a new mandate for the United Nations in Angola with five main features:

(1) Political. UNAVEM III would assist in the implementation of the Lusaka Protocol by providing good offices and mediation to the parties and taking appropriate initiatives, as necessary, to give impetus to the peace process. The Special Representative would chair meetings of the Joint Commission. UNAVEM III would monitor and verify the extension of State administration throughout the country and the process of national reconciliation.

(2) Military. The military component of UNAVEM III would supervise, control and verify the disengagement of forces and monitor the cease-fire. It would verify information received from the Government and UNITA regarding their forces, and monitor all troop movements. It would help to establish quartering areas, verify and monitor the withdrawal, quartering and demobilization of UNITA forces, and supervise the collection and storage of UNITA armaments. It would verify the movement of the Government army to barracks, and verify and monitor the completion of the formation of FAA, the joint national army. Finally, it would verify the free circulation of persons and goods.

(3) Police. UNAVEM III observers would verify and monitor the neutrality of the Angolan National Police, the disarming of civilians, the quartering of the Government rapid reaction police, and the security arrangements for UNITA leaders.

(4) Humanitarian. UNAVEM III would coordinate, facilitate and support humanitarian activities directly linked to the peace process, in particular those relating to the quartering and demobilization of troops and their reintegration in civilian life, as well as participate in mine-clearing activities.

(5) Electoral. UNAVEM III would declare formally that all essential requirements for the holding of the second round of presidential elections had been fulfilled, and it would support, verify and monitor the entire electoral process.

The activities of the components would be coordinated and integrated as necessary. The Secretary-General's Special Representative would exercise executive authority over all aspects of the operation, which would be completed in the time-frame envisaged in the Lusaka Protocol. The Angolan parties would be expected to keep in mind that the international community would not entertain delays in the fulfilment of their obligations under the Protocol or extensions of the mandate of the Mission. The Secretary-General recommended that the rules of engagement allow, in accordance with normal practice, the use of force in self-defence. That would include the use of force against forcible attempts to impede the discharge of the operation's mandate.

Concept of operations

To accomplish the mandated political tasks of good offices and mediation, the Special Representative would require substantive and support staff able to certify that requisite conditions had been fulfilled for the normalization of the State administration throughout the country. To do that, and in order for the Special Representative to be able to determine whether all conditions for the holding of the second round of presidential elections had been fulfilled, a minimum political presence would be maintained in each of the Mission's six regional bases. Staff outposted to these centres would determine that the necessary security guarantees had been extended to UNITA leaders and that they participated in the management of State affairs. Mission staff would also determine if there was free circulation of people and goods, and if an atmosphere of tolerance had been established. To promote a climate of confidence through the mass media, the Mission would create a section to monitor and verify compliance with the cessation of all hostile propaganda. That section would also disseminate public information about the goals of the peace process and the mandate of UNAVEM III. The Secretary-General noted that a United Nations radio station, "appropriately staffed and equipped, would play a very useful role".

The military monitoring and verification responsibilities of UNAVEM III would be carried out by observers stationed at 59 sites throughout the country. The Secretary-General envisaged the need for military observers and 22 to 24 self-sustained infantry companies to be deployed in 14 quartering areas and 8 main weapons storage locations throughout the country. The UNAVEM III Force Commander would supervise the establishment and management of quartering areas and the registration and subsequent demobilization of UNITA personnel. Three independent engineer squadrons/companies would be deployed along with the infantry to help establish quartering areas, clear mines, set up water supply points and help repair main access routes and perform other specialized tasks.

The formed infantry units would be supported by a signals company. There would be a small field hospital in Luanda, with two advance dressing stations. Other support elements would include eight helicopters and a naval unit of three patrol boats (the latter was not actually deployed). In view of the ravaged infrastructure of the country, a logistic unit or three independent logistic companies would be needed. The United Nations would provide military de-mining specialists and help establish a de-mining school. The infantry and support units would comprise 7,000 all ranks, in addition to 265 military staff personnel, 350 military observers and 56 de-mining experts. The formed units would stay in Angola for up to 12 months after deployment.

The civilian police component of UNAVEM III would consist of 260 observers, stationed in all 18 provinces of Angola, and headed by a Chief Superintendent of Police. The component would monitor the activities of the Angolan National Police in order to guarantee its neutrality and verify the quartering of the rapid reaction police in eight locations. UNAVEM III would thoroughly verify the whole process of integration of 5,500 UNITA personnel into the National Police. Among other duties, United Nations police teams would regularly visit local police facilities and conduct independent investigations on reported violations. The component would freely receive complaints and relevant information.

UCAH would continue to serve as the coordinating body for all humanitarian operations, supporting and coordinating the efforts of the operational agencies of the United Nations while mobilizing increased participation by other agencies and NGOs. UCAH would extend its presence throughout the country through regional field advisers. The new Demobilization and Reintegration Office would coordinate the supply of food, clothing, health services and agricultural construction and domestic kits to soldiers in quartering areas. The Unit would consist of 38 international staff, 50 United Nations Volunteers (UNVs) and 45 local staff. A social reintegration programme would be carried out in each quartering area. UCAH's Central Mine Action Office would coordinate all activities relating to mines and other explosive devices, and develop a comprehensive mine action plan in cooperation with the Mission, United Nations agencies and NGOs.

UNAVEM III deployment

By its resolution 976 (1995) of 8 February 1995, the Security Council authorized the establishment of UNAVEM III as recommended by the Secretary-General. According to the timetable, deployment of infantry units would begin on 9 May 1995. The Council decided that this deployment would be contingent on an effective cessation of hostilities, the provision of all relevant military data, the designation of all quartering areas and other vital tasks. The Council also encouraged the Secretary-General to pursue urgently the Government's offer of direct assistance, and to explore with the Government and UNITA substantial additional assistance related to peace-keeping. On 5 March 1995, the Secretary-General told[59] the Council that, given logistical constraints, deployment of the infantry units by 9 May would be feasible only if he could notify the Council by 25 March that the parties had substantially met the Council's conditions. He urged the Government and UNITA to take the necessary concrete action.

Meanwhile, the expansion of UNAVEM III continued in accordance with earlier Security Council resolutions. As of 1 March, there were 418 military observers and police observers, deployed to 38 sites outside Luanda. Deployment to the countryside was slowed by incidents of shooting at UNAVEM III aircraft by UNITA, in particular in

[59]S/1995/177.

Quibaxe on 13 February and Licua on 18 February, and restrictions by both parties on freedom of movement. The Secretary-General described the situation in Angola as tense but hopeful. Complaints of cease-fire violations, difficulties related to implementation of troop disengagement and other matters were being addressed through the Joint Commission, chaired by the Special Representative.

Concerned at the slow pace of implementation of the Lusaka Protocol, the Secretary-General sent Under-Secretary-General Ismat Kittani to Angola from 17 to 22 March 1995 to deliver letters from him to President dos Santos and to Mr. Savimbi and to discuss with them the measures they should urgently take. In the light of Mr. Kittani's assessment and the increasing need to assist the parties to overcome their mutual mistrust, the Secretary-General recommended[60] to the Security Council that he proceed with preparations for the deployment of infantry units to Angola. The Council welcomed[61] that course of action.

Humanitarian aspects

By mid-1995, the improving situation in Angola had had two diametrically opposite results. On the one hand, the opening of overland routes and de-mining activities had made it easier to provide relief to people in need throughout the country. In some areas, the need for relief itself had decreased, allowing aid agencies to suspend general food distribution there. On the other hand, donor response to appeals for assistance had fallen sharply. In June 1995, the Secretary-General reported[62] that the pattern of food pledges and deliveries to WFP could result in a "major disruption in supply as early as July" and could in turn jeopardize delivery to the troop quartering areas, where the provision of food was a key element. In the non-food sectors, the response to the 1995 appeal for humanitarian aid had yielded only 3 per cent of what was needed. This threatened to put all relief programmes in Angola at risk with potentially "dramatic consequences for the civilian population".

Encouraging developments

As of 31 March 1995, UNAVEM III military and civilian police personnel stood at 527. Although progress had been made in the consolidation of the cease-fire, in the disengagement of forces and in other critical areas, the Secretary-General reported[63] to the Council on 7 April that further resolute steps were needed to ensure that the peace process could be pursued with confidence. There were still many causes for serious concern, namely the fragility of the cease-fire, reports of military preparations and major troop movements and indications of the continued acquisition of weapons from abroad. In addition, the attacks on unarmed United Nations military and police observers and on NGO personnel raised doubts about the willingness of the parties to cooperate in good faith in implementation of the provisions of the Lusaka Protocol.

The Secretary-General reminded the parties that, unless they complied without delay with the immediate requirements of the Lusaka Protocol and provided UNAVEM III with indispensable logistic support, it would not be possible to initiate the deployment of United Nations infantry units to Angola in May. In this connection, he also warned against undue expectations that the arrival of United Nations troops would in itself solve the pressing problems that the Angolans should resolve themselves: disengagement of their troops country-wide, establishment of reliable verification mechanisms and communication links, provision to the United Nations of all necessary military data, initiation of the quartering process, release of prisoners, and so on. The Secretary-General appealed once again to President dos Santos and Mr. Savimbi to proceed with the necessary preparations for a meeting between them at the earliest possible opportunity. Such a meeting could provide a strong impetus to the process of national reconciliation.

The Security Council welcomed[64] the progress that had been made and commended the parties for their efforts in that regard. At the same time, the Council reminded the Angolan parties that they must implement without delay the requirements of the Lusaka Protocol and provide UNAVEM III with logistical support.

During the month of April 1995, there was a further reduction in the number of cease-fire violations, but the situation in several areas remained tense. Both sides continued to occupy forward positions, sporadically attacking the local population and conducting movements of their troops. Nevertheless, the second phase of disengagement was almost completed. On 20 April 1995, the parties agreed on the principle of "global incorporation" of UNITA soldiers into the national army, to be followed by gradual demobilization,

---

[60]S/1995/230. [61]S/PRST/1995/18. [62]S/1995/458. [63]S/1995/274. [64]S/PRST/1995/18.

until FAA reached the level of 90,000 troops, a figure that both parties had accepted. As for the establishment of communications links among the parties and UNAVEM III, contacts with Government troops were successfully established in all regions, but effective communication with UNITA existed only in the regions of Huambo and Uíge. UNAVEM III also continued efforts to accelerate the start of country-wide de-mining.

The advance party of the logistics battalion provided by the United Kingdom arrived in Lobito/Catumbela to make the necessary preparations for the deployment in May of UNAVEM III infantry units. In the meantime, the deployment of military observers to all 53 team sites was completed. With the arrival of the Police Commissioner, the civilian police component of UNAVEM III had become fully operational. As of 26 April, UNAVEM III had a strength of 875, including 690 military and support personnel and 185 civilian police observers.

On 3 May 1995, the Secretary-General reported[65] to the Council that there had been a marked improvement in the overall political climate in the country and in the attitude of the parties. With the active support of the representatives of the three observer States and regional leaders, the Special Representative maintained frequent contacts with President dos Santos and with Mr. Savimbi, with a view to convening a long-awaited meeting between them. Preparations for such a meeting were reported to be at an advanced stage. Agreement had been reached on the agenda for the meeting, as well as on a number of other practical details.

Important breakthrough

President dos Santos and Mr. Savimbi met in Lusaka on 6 May 1995. In their discussions, they covered all aspects of the peace process and pledged their cooperation to consolidate peace in Angola and to implement the provisions of the Lusaka Protocol. They also agreed that their next meeting would take place in Luanda, at an unspecified date. The Secretary-General strongly encouraged President dos Santos and Mr. Savimbi "to pursue actively the issues discussed at their last meeting and, as agreed, to convene a second meeting in Luanda as soon as possible".[66]

By June 1995, the United Nations logistic battalion deployed in Lobito/Catumbela and Luanda had become fully operational. An engineer squadron, a signals unit, a field hospital and advance parties of several other units had also been deployed. According to the revised timetable, the first infantry battalion was arriving in Angola during the first week of June, deployment of the second was planned for the first half of July, and the third for the second half of July. The further dispatch of United Nations infantry would depend on the progress made by the parties in opening up major access roads and in mine clearance. As of 30 May, UNAVEM III strength stood at 1,813, including 1,603 military and support personnel and 210 civilian police observers.

On 15 June, the Security Council welcomed[67] the positive developments in Angola and, strongly supporting the ongoing dialogue between the two Angolan parties, encouraged a further meeting between President dos Santos and Mr. Savimbi. At the same time, it noted with concern that implementation of the provisions of the Lusaka Protocol continued behind schedule.

Intensified activity

Following the meeting between President dos Santos and Mr. Savimbi in Lusaka, high-level contacts between members of the Government and UNITA intensified. On 25 May, the Government delegation to the Joint Commission travelled to Bailundo — the headquarters of UNITA — to deliver a message to Mr. Savimbi from President dos Santos. In addition, President dos Santos and Mr. Savimbi were in regular contact by telephone. In late June, a high-level UNITA delegation visited Luanda to review with the Government the practical modalities for accelerating the implementation of the Lusaka Protocol. The review culminated in a comprehensive working document signed by the two parties and submitted to the Joint Commission. From 19 June to 1 July, high-level Government and UNITA delegations reached agreement on a timetable to make up for the delays. They concurred on the location of almost all quartering areas and the sequence of the quartering process, on basic conditions for assembly areas, on the modalities of FAA withdrawal to barracks and on the need to eliminate checkpoints and organize additional humanitarian road convoys to formerly inaccessible areas. However, on certain aspects, such as the incorporation of UNITA troops into FAA, agreement was not reached.

Despite formidable difficulties, the overall humanitarian situation in Angola continued to improve, as a direct result of the peace process and the expanded presence of UNAVEM III in the coun-

[65]S/1995/350. [66]S/1995/458. [67]S/1995/487.

try. United Nations road convoys from Luanda to Lobito and from Uíge to Negage facilitated humanitarian activities by making new areas accessible by road and reducing the need for costly deliveries by air. In June 1995, for the first time since 1992, WFP was able to dispatch road convoys from Lobito to Sumbe and from Lobito to Huambo and Kuito. Varying degrees of progress were also achieved in opening the Kuito-Menongue, Luanda-Malange and Lobito-Lubango routes.

The Secretary-General emphasized[68] to the Security Council on 17 July 1995 the importance of humanitarian assistance in consolidating the Angolan peace process, especially in the demobilization and reintegration exercise. This activity would rely largely on external resources to support demobilized UNITA troops and their dependants. Although many donors had expressed interest, less than 1 per cent of the voluntary funds sought for this purpose under the 1995 humanitarian appeal had been contributed. He appealed to Member States to respond with generous and timely financial contributions to the humanitarian effort.

In order to review the progress made and to assess the situation on the ground, Secretary-General Boutros-Ghali visited Angola from 14 to 16 July. During the visit, he discussed with the Government and UNITA ways and means of expediting the implementation of the provisions of the Lusaka Protocol and consolidating the efforts to bring about lasting peace and reconciliation in Angola. He also reviewed with the parties the reconstruction needs of the country. The Secretary-General met with President dos Santos and Mr. Savimbi, both of whom committed themselves to support the peace process in order to make it irreversible.

UNAVEM III mandate extended

As of 4 July 1995, in addition to the 6 regional headquarters, 337 military observers of UNAVEM III had been deployed to 55 sites throughout Angola. Deployment of the formed units, whose total strength had reached 1,970 personnel, was generally proceeding in accordance with the adjusted time-frame. There were 208 staff officers and military support personnel. In addition, 209 United Nations civilian police observers from 19 countries had been deployed to 29 team sites throughout Angola, including most provincial capitals. In response to complaints about human rights violations and in accordance with the provisions of the Lusaka Protocol, UNAVEM III established a small unit to deal with relevant issues and to contribute to civil education in the country.

On 7 August, the Security Council extended[69] the mandate of UNAVEM III for a further six months, until 8 February 1996. At the same time, the Council urged the Government and UNITA to adhere strictly to the revised timetable on the implementation of the Lusaka Protocol and make concerted efforts to accelerate that process.

Consolidating the peace process

President dos Santos and Mr. Savimbi met again in Franceville (Gabon) on 10 August and in Brussels on 25 September. The two leaders agreed on modalities for continuation of their discussions on the completion of the formation of FAA, including the global incorporation of UNITA troops. General understandings were also reached on ways to define the powers and responsibilities of the two Vice-Presidents and on various aspects of holding legislative and presidential elections. Meeting in October in Brussels, they consulted further on those issues and reached agreement on consolidating the peace process. The Secretary-General viewed[70] these meetings, as well as the continuing dialogue between the Government and UNITA in the framework of the Joint Commission, as "gradually generating greater mutual trust and confidence, although there is still some tension at lower levels in certain regions". It was important that the parties continue to demonstrate their political will by backing up their declarations with concrete actions on the ground. The Security Council was encouraged by the meetings[71] but expressed concern at delays in the implementation of the provisions of the Lusaka Protocol.

While preparations for the quartering process in particular were slow, overall progress was nevertheless significant. During August and September 1995, UNAVEM III reconnoitred all 15 proposed quartering areas. Of these, 11 were accepted by the parties, and work began on establishing a number of them; the confirmation of the four others was delayed because of the absence of either FAA or UNITA personnel on the joint reconnaissance missions arranged by UNAVEM III. The Mission also set up a coordination group chaired by the deputy to the Special Representative to enhance internal coordination and decision-making. UNVs, who would carry out the registration in the areas, started to arrive in Angola.

[68]S/1995/588. [69]S/RES/1008 (1995). [70]S/1995/842. [71]S/PRST/1995/51.

In September 1995, cease-fire violations were at their lowest level recorded. The situation in most regions was relatively calm, except for some clashes and numerous acts of banditry. However, tensions persisted, particularly in the diamond-rich area of Lucapa in the north-east, where both sides were seeking to consolidate and enlarge their areas of control. Reinforcements and sporadic shelling by the two sides were also reported in the northern region. UNAVEM III investigated all cease-fire violations and troop movements, and mediated between the parties to defuse tension and avert a resumption of hostilities. Limited de-mining activities by FAA and UNITA continued, in a few cases jointly. Disturbing reports about renewed laying of mines were investigated by UNAVEM III. With the exception of the infantry units assigned to the eastern and south-eastern regions, the deployment of United Nations troops proceeded satisfactorily.

Frequent violations of human rights continued, in particular by elements of the armed forces and police of both sides. The decision of the Joint Commission to inscribe human rights on the agenda of all its regular sessions and to request UNAVEM III to report periodically on the general human rights situation in Angola was viewed as a positive development. United Nations police observers assisted in the investigation of complaints about human rights violations.

Progress is slow

It was expected that the meetings between President dos Santos and Mr. Savimbi, together with the resumption of military talks between the two parties and the commencement of the quartering of UNITA troops on 20 November 1995, would foster a climate of mutual trust and confidence between the Government and UNITA. However, a serious setback occurred towards the end of 1995, when FAA took control of several locations in the oil-producing region of Soyo. In response, UNITA suspended the quartering of its troops, withdrew its assistance to UNAVEM III in the construction of quartering areas and, in some areas under its control, imposed restrictions on the movement of UNAVEM III and other international personnel, including NGOs.

Following persistent efforts by the Secretary-General's Special Representative, and subsequent to President dos Santos's visit to Washington, a government delegation met with UNITA leaders on 21 December 1995 to review the implementation of the Lusaka Protocol. The two parties undertook to start fulfilling their respective obligations as soon as possible. These included the definitive cessation of all military activities, the conclusion of military talks, the release of prisoners, an end to hostile propaganda, the resumption of the quartering of UNITA troops, the quartering of the government rapid reaction police and the withdrawal of FAA to the nearest barracks.

Further diplomatic efforts resulted, on 12 January 1996, in the acceptance by the two parties of a new timetable for the implementation of the understandings of 21 December. Also, by mid-January, military delegations of the two parties reached a framework understanding with regard to the formation of the Angolan Armed Forces.

Following the recommendation[72] of the Secretary-General, the Security Council extended[73] the mandate of UNAVEM III until 8 May 1996. At the same time, the Council expressed deep concern at the continuing delays in the implementation of the Lusaka Protocol and urged the Government of Angola and UNITA to maintain an effective cease-fire, conclude their military talks on integration of the armed forces, undertake active engagement in the de-mining process, and commence the integration of UNITA personnel into administrative and governmental institutions. By extending the mandate of UNAVEM III for only three months, the Council clearly signalled that, while it was prepared to continue to support the peace process, the parties should demonstrate their commitment to implement the Lusaka Protocol without further delay.

In the following weeks, there was some movement towards meeting the goals established in the timetable, including a decrease in the number of cease-fire violations; a further reduction in hostile propaganda; the release of additional prisoners registered with ICRC; the disengagement of government forces from some forward positions; and continued quartering of the rapid reaction police in 3 out of the 10 planned quartering areas.

However, the implementation of many other elements was still behind schedule, particularly the crucial quartering of UNITA troops. Delays in this process affected the implementation of other key provisions of the Lusaka Protocol, including the extension of State administration throughout the country. The Secretary-General's Special Representative and the three observer States then presented to the Government and UNITA a revised timetable which envisaged sub-

[72]S/1996/75. [73]S/RES/1045 (1996).

UNAVEM III deployment as of March 1996

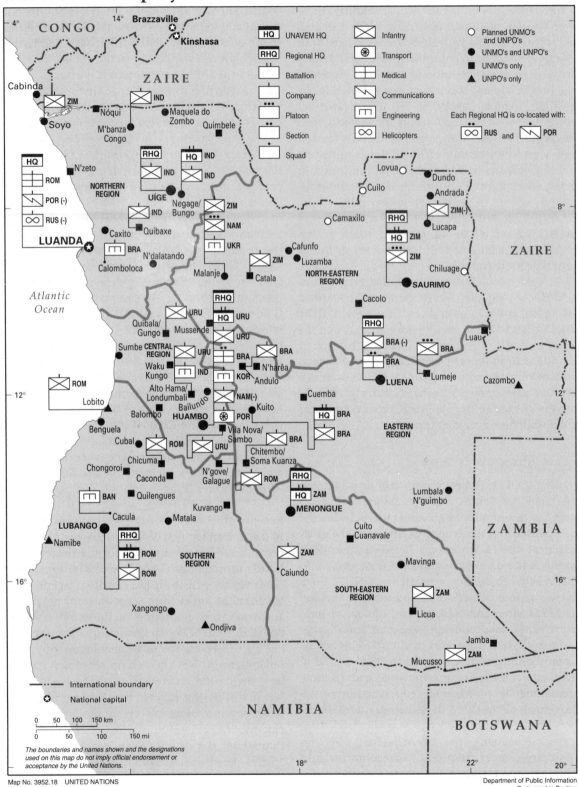

Map No. 3952.18   UNITED NATIONS
September 1996

Department of Public Information
Cartographic Section

stantial acceleration of the entire peace process. Following a meeting at Bailundo on 19 February between Mr. Savimbi and a high-level government delegation, the Joint Commission approved this timetable on 28 February.

The fourth meeting between President dos Santos and Mr. Savimbi took place on 1 March 1996 at Libreville, Gabon. Mr. Savimbi promised to complete the quartering of UNITA troops by June 1996, and both sides agreed to start the process of selection of UNITA troops for incorporation into FAA and to complete by June the formation of the unified armed forces. They also agreed to form by June or July the Government of Unity and National Reconciliation. Mr. Savimbi promised to respond to an official offer to assume the post of a Vice-President and submitted to President dos Santos a list of officials proposed for the various posts reserved for UNITA in the Government and the administration. It was agreed that the mandate of the National Assembly would be extended following adequate consultations, and that President dos Santos would declare an amnesty for offences resulting from the Angolan conflict.

Situation improves

Following that meeting, the political atmosphere in the country improved. Although implementation of the adjusted timetable fell behind schedule, progress was achieved particularly with respect to military aspects. The dialogue between the Government and UNITA continued within and outside the framework of the Joint Commission. High-level government delegations travelled to Bailundo and other UNITA-controlled areas for talks with Mr. Savimbi and his senior aides. Meetings took place at Luanda on an almost daily basis between government and UNITA delegations to the Joint Commission.

The military situation remained stable, with only occasional incidents in diamond-producing and cattle-raising areas, and in Malange province. The Government/UNITA conflict-prevention mechanism operating under United Nations auspices was instrumental in preventing serious cease-fire violations. FAA agreed to withdraw from the areas around Andrada, Lucapa and Cafunfo which had been taken over in December 1995 and February 1996. This made it possible for both parties to disengage their troops and to begin clearing the Malange-Saurimo road of mines. On 21 March, the Government handed over to UNAVEM III a plan for the first phase of the withdrawal of FAA, including its heavy weapons, to the nearest barracks in Bengo, Huambo, Kuando Kubango and Uíge provinces. This process began on 25 March and was closely monitored by UNAVEM III.

As of 29 March 1996, out of the declared 62,500 UNITA military personnel, 18,595 UNITA soldiers had registered in the first five quartering areas and had handed over a total of 15,169 weapons. Some 10,000 family members of UNITA troops were also encamped in the vicinity of the quartering areas. The Secretary-General's Special Representative and the members of the Joint Commission visited both the operational quartering areas and those under preparation to assess living conditions. Overall discipline in the camps remained good and, despite complaints, the Joint Commission found conditions there to be generally acceptable. The United Nations, its agencies and NGOs operating in Angola were doing everything possible to provide quartering areas with adequate supplies and services, including food, health facilities and civic education for the demobilized soldiers.

The civilian police component of UNAVEM III focused on monitoring the neutrality of the Angolan National Police, the general law and order situation, the free circulation of people and the provision of assistance to the Mission's Human Rights Unit. In addition, the component verified and monitored the quartering of the rapid reaction police and provided the quartered police with training. UNAVEM III police observers also closely monitored the activities of the Angolan National Police in providing security to UNITA leaders residing in Luanda.

UNAVEM III team sites reported numerous violations of basic human rights in various parts of Angola. United Nations human rights personnel and police observers monitored the situation and investigated complaints presented by the Government and UNITA, as well as by private individuals. At the same time, UNAVEM III finalized a plan of action, for which a special voluntary trust fund would be established, aimed at promoting human rights education. On 27 February, in implementation of this plan, UNAVEM III organized a seminar for law enforcement officers in Benguela province. In the meantime, the European Union agreed to provide support to a UNAVEM III project to train Angolan nationals involved in human rights education. The programme was to be prepared in cooperation with the Centre for Human Rights of the United Nations Secretariat. The Union also provided funds for several additional human rights monitors.

UNAVEM III, United Nations agencies and specialized international NGOs continued de-mining operations in eight provinces of Angola. Mine survey and clearance was expected to accelerate along the main access road from Malange to the eastern border of the country; UNITA had finally lifted its objections to the opening of this vital route. Demining courses for former FAA and UNITA soldiers conducted at the Central Mine Action Training School also continued. It was planned that the school would train up to 500 Angolan deminers by the end of 1996.

Humanitarian activities

As the peace process gradually consolidated in September and October 1995, humanitarian activities continued to expand, with priority given to internally displaced persons returning to their home areas. Preparations were also under way for the repatriation of Angolan refugees from neighbouring countries. Despite the reopening of some new roads, however, road access remained an obstacle to humanitarian assistance and to food security, particularly in the eastern half of the country. The Government and UNITA issued a joint statement on 25 August reinforcing their commitment to the principle of free circulation of people and goods all over Angola.

The focus of assistance then began to shift to economic and social concerns, and United Nations programmes and agencies elaborated plans for increased participation in development activities and for better coordination of their efforts. In that context, a programme of community rehabilitation and national reconciliation was presented to the first Round-Table Conference of donors held in Brussels on 25 and 26 September 1995 in which both President dos Santos and Mr. Savimbi participated. The donor community responded at the Round-Table Conference with pledges of over $993 million for small-scale community rehabilitation activities aimed at restoring rural production and mobilizing civil society for the massive reconstruction task as well as for humanitarian assistance. At the meeting, donors were also requested to give priority to complete funding of the programmes outlined in the United Nations 1995 inter-agency humanitarian appeal for Angola. Those programmes were complementary to the Government's plan for community rehabilitation and national reconciliation.

Following the renewed hostilities in December 1995, security for humanitarian assistance activities deteriorated in many parts of the country, especially in those controlled by UNITA. In some areas, UNITA imposed restrictions on relief flights, and road convoys had to be cancelled when UNAVEM III could not obtain security guarantees. There were also incidents of confiscation of relief goods, vehicles and radios, as well as harassment of humanitarian personnel and, in a few cases, their temporary detention. Humanitarian assistance activities were none the less carried out wherever possible.

Joint missions by representatives of UNAVEM III, UCAH, UNITA and the International Organization for Migration visited centres for disabled UNITA soldiers in order to prepare for their future demobilization. UCAH also prepared the final draft of the 1996 updated appeal for Angola, in close collaboration with United Nations agencies and NGOs. The appeal reflected resources needed in 1996 for emergency assistance, de-mining and quartering, demobilization and reintegration of former combatants.

As tensions eased, humanitarian assistance activities, including road convoys and relief flights, returned to normal in January and February 1996. WFP was able to transport over 80 per cent of relief items overland. For the first time, a humanitarian convoy travelled from Huambo to Andulo via Mungo in Bié province. The opening of this route facilitated access to the nearby quartering area and to needy populations in the neighbourhood. In response to reports of food shortages in northern Angola, various relief agencies started humanitarian operations in that region. However, access to many municipalities was still restricted as a result of bad road conditions, mines and lack of adequate security. In eastern and central Angola, isolated security incidents led to the temporary suspension of relief activities.

The spontaneous return of internally displaced persons continued on a limited scale, particularly in the provinces of Benguela and Kwanza Sul. Some displaced families were also departing from villages near Jamba and efforts were under way to help them resettle in the central highlands. In areas bordering Zaire and Zambia, UNHCR, in cooperation with partner NGOs, was preparing conditions for the reception of returning refugees. On 22 March, UNHCR issued an appeal for $30.8 million for its 1996 repatriation programme for some 300,000 Angolans.

Composition

The Chief of Mission of UNAVEM III is the Secretary-General's Special Representative for

Angola, Mr. Alioune Blondin Beye. Major-General Chris Abutu Garuba, who served as Chief Military Observer of UNAVEM II beginning in July 1993, also served as Force Commander of UNAVEM III until he completed his tour of duty on 30 September 1995. He was succeeded by Major-General Phillip Valerio Sibanda (Zimbabwe).

As of 31 March 1996, 336 military observers, 6,576 troops and support personnel and 226 civilian police officers were deployed in Angola. The following countries were contributing military and civilian police personnel to UNAVEM III as of that date: Algeria, Bangladesh, Brazil, Bulgaria, Congo, Egypt, Fiji, France, Guinea-Bissau, Hungary, India, Italy, Jordan, Kenya, Malaysia, Mali, Namibia, Netherlands, New Zealand, Nigeria, Norway, Pakistan, Poland, Portugal, Republic of Korea, Romania, Russian Federation, Senegal, Slovak Republic, Sweden, Tanzania, Ukraine, United Kingdom, Uruguay, Zambia and Zimbabwe.

Financial aspects

Expenditures for operating UNAVEM III from inception through 8 May 1996 were estimated at $366,523,900.[74] This cost is an expense of the Organization, shared by Member States. Requirements through voluntary contributions for humanitarian assistance for demobilization and re-integration were $104.5 million, of which $54.4 million was for assistance to the quartering areas.[75]

The Angolan Government expressed[76] its willingness to contribute significantly to various programmes associated with the peace process. Specifically, it would provide UNAVEM III with a residential compound, aircraft and vehicle parking facilities, harbour space, warehouses and office space in ports and airports and fuel at rates below the international price. Exemption from customs formalities and availability of land for the Mission were also pledged.

[74]A/50/651/Add.3. [75]S/1995/842. [76]S/1994/1451.

Chapter 13

United Nations Mission for the Referendum in Western Sahara (MINURSO)

A. Background

Implementation plan of the settlement proposals

B. MINURSO: 1991–1995

Establishment of MINURSO

Cease-fire

Differences remain

Compromise proposal

Secretary-General remains hopeful

Referendum rescheduled

Voter registration

Options before the Security Council

Identification and registration

Timetable revised

Major difficulties remain

Security Council mission

Further delays

Other aspects

MINURSO mandate further extended

Modified procedure proposed

C. Suspension of the identification process

D. Composition of MINURSO

E. Financial aspects

Chapter 13

United Nations Mission for the Referendum in Western Sahara (MINURSO)

A. Background

Western Sahara, a Territory on the northwest coast of Africa bordered by Morocco, Mauritania and Algeria, was administered by Spain until 1976. Both Morocco and Mauritania affirmed their claim to the Territory, a claim opposed by the Popular Front for the Liberation of Saguia el-Hamra and Rio de Oro (Frente POLISARIO).

The United Nations has considered the situation in the Territory since 1963. Over the years, the General Assembly reaffirmed the right of the people of Western Sahara to self-determination, and called on the administering Power to take steps to ensure the realization of that right. In response to a request by the General Assembly for an advisory opinion, the International Court of Justice concluded in 1975 that the materials and information presented to it showed the existence, at the time of Spanish colonization, of legal ties of allegiance between the Sultan of Morocco and some of the tribes living in the Territory. They equally showed the existence of rights, including some rights relating to the land, which constituted legal ties between Mauritania and the Territory. Nevertheless, they did not establish any tie of territorial sovereignty between Western Sahara and Morocco or Mauritania. Thus, the Court did not find legal ties of such a nature as to affect the application of the 1960 General Assembly resolution 1514 (XV) in the decolonization of Western Sahara and, in particular, of the principle of self-determination. Also in 1975, Spain, Morocco and Mauritania agreed upon a Declaration of Principles by which Spain confirmed its resolve to decolonize the Territory by 28 February 1976. Under that agreement, Spain would institute a temporary administration in which Morocco and Mauritania would participate, in collaboration with the Jema'a (a local assembly set up by Spain in 1967) expressing the views of the Saharan population.

Spain completed its withdrawal on 26 February 1976, stating that, although it did not consider that the people of Western Sahara had exercised their right to self-determination, it considered itself released from international responsibility towards the Territory. On 27 February, the Secretary-General received a message, through Morocco, from the President of the Jema'a informing him that the Jema'a had approved the "reintegration" of the Territory with Morocco and Mauritania. On the same day, another body, the pro-POLISARIO Provisional Sahrawi National Council, proclaimed the founding of an independent state, the "Saharan Arab Democratic Republic" (SADR), and stated that it would engage in an armed struggle to achieve the right of self-determination for the people of the Territory. By then, serious fighting had broken out between the Frente POLISARIO forces and the Moroccan and Mauritanian armed forces. Part of the Saharan population left the Territory to follow the Frente POLISARIO and settle in camps in the Tindouf area of south-western Algeria. In April, Mauritania and Morocco announced an agreement whereby the northern two thirds of the Territory would be integrated with Morocco and the southern part with Mauritania. The Frente POLISARIO and Algeria opposed the arrangement, maintaining that the Jema'a had not been democratically elected.

Following a change of Government, Mauritania in 1979 signed a peace agreement in Algiers with the Frente POLISARIO by which it renounced all claims to Western Sahara. Morocco declared the accord null and void, and Moroccan troops took over the Mauritanian sector of Western Sahara. The Frente POLISARIO stepped up its attacks on Moroccan forces, and fighting in the Territory continued in the following years.

Besides the United Nations, the Organization of African Unity (OAU) became involved in seeking a peaceful settlement. In 1979, OAU called for a referendum so that the people of the Territory might exercise their right to self-determination. It established a committee to work out the modalities in cooperation with the United Nations. At the 1981 summit of OAU, the King of Morocco announced that he was prepared to agree to a cease-fire and to a referendum under international supervision. Welcoming the announcement, the summit called for a cease-fire and a referendum to be held in cooperation with the United Nations. Also in 1981, the General Assembly appealed to Morocco and the Frente POLISARIO to begin negotiation on a cease-fire. However, Morocco made it clear that it was not prepared to negotiate directly with the Frente POLISARIO. In 1982, after 26 OAU member States had recognized SADR, it was admitted to the OAU Council of Ministers. Morocco withdrew from OAU when the Frente POLISARIO was seated at the 1984 OAU summit.

In 1985, Secretary-General Javier Pérez de Cuéllar, in cooperation with the Chairman of the OAU Assembly of Heads of State and Government, initiated a joint mission of good offices. Some three years later, on 11 August 1988, the Secretary-General and the Special Envoy of the Chairman presented, in separate meetings, to Morocco and the Frente POLISARIO a document referred to as "the settlement proposals". The document, to which the two parties agreed in principle on 30 August 1988, contained proposals for a just and definitive solution of the question of Western Sahara in conformity with General Assembly resolution 1514 (XV). This would be accomplished by means of a cease-fire and the holding of a referendum without military or administrative constraints, to enable the people of Western Sahara, in the exercise of their right to self-determination, to choose between independence and integration with Morocco.

The Security Council then adopted resolution 621 (1988) of 20 September 1988 authorizing the appointment of a special representative. The Secretary-General accordingly appointed Mr. Hector Gros Espiell (Uruguay) as Special Representative with effect from 19 October 1988. Mr. Gros Espiell was succeeded, with effect from 19 January 1990, by Mr. Johannes Manz (Switzerland).

On 27 June 1990, the Security Council, in its resolution 658 (1990), approved a report[1] of the Secretary-General containing the full text of the settlement proposals and an outline of the

Secretary-General's plan for implementing those proposals.

Implementation plan of the settlement proposals

The implementation plan (also referred to as the "settlement plan" or the "peace plan") provided for a transitional period during which the Special Representative of the Secretary-General, acting under the authority of the Secretary-General, would have sole and exclusive responsibility over all matters relating to the referendum, including its organization and conduct. The Special Representative would be assisted in his tasks by a deputy special representative and by an integrated group of United Nations civilian, military and civilian police personnel. This group would be known as the United Nations Mission for the Referendum in Western Sahara (MINURSO). The civilian component would range in size from about 800 to 1,000 personnel, depending on the requirements of the various phases of the transitional period. At full strength, the military component would consist of approximately 1,700 personnel, and the security unit of about 300 police officers.

The transitional period would begin with the coming into effect of a cease-fire and end with the proclamation of the results of the referendum. Following the announcement of a cease-fire, MINURSO would verify the reduction of Moroccan troops in the Territory; monitor the confinement of Moroccan and Frente POLISARIO troops to designated locations; take steps with the parties to ensure the release of all Western Saharan political prisoners or detainees; oversee the exchange of prisoners of war (International Committee of the Red Cross); implement the repatriation programme; identify and register qualified voters; organize and ensure a free referendum; and proclaim the results.

Morocco was prepared to reduce its troops in the Territory to a level not exceeding 65,000 all ranks, within a period of 11 weeks from the beginning of the transitional period. This was accepted by the United Nations as an appropriate, substantial and phased reduction in accordance with the settlement proposals. All remaining Moroccan troops would be located in static or defensive positions along the sandwall, known as the berm, with limited exceptions. MINURSO military observers would monitor these troops and, towards this end, would be co-located with Moroc-

[1]S/21360.

can subsector headquarters and with the Moroccan support and logistics units remaining elsewhere in the Territory. MINURSO military observers would conduct extensive patrols by land and air to ensure observance of the cease-fire and the confinement of the Moroccan troops to the designated locations. In addition, they would monitor the custody of certain arms and ammunition.

The Special Representative was to designate the locations to which Frente POLISARIO troops would be confined, with their arms, ammunition and military equipment. MINURSO military observers would be deployed at each of the designated locations in order to monitor the Frente POLISARIO troops. The plan specified that an independent jurist, appointed by the Secretary-General, would take steps in cooperation with the parties to ensure the release of all Saharan political prisoners and detainees before the beginning of the referendum campaign, so that they could participate freely and without restriction in the referendum.

All Saharans counted in a 1974 census taken by the Spanish authorities and aged 18 years or over would have the right to vote in the referendum. The plan provided for an Identification Commission, set up by the Secretary-General in consultation with OAU, to be responsible for reviewing the 1974 census and updating it. It also provided for the establishment of a Referendum Commission to assist the Special Representative in the organization and conduct of the referendum. The Referendum Commission would absorb appropriately qualified staff of the Identification Commission, upon completion of the latter's tasks of identification and registration.

As an integral part of the MINURSO operation, the repatriation programme for those Western Saharans who were identified as eligible to vote in the referendum and who wished to return to the Territory was to be carried out by the United Nations High Commissioner for Refugees (UNHCR). UNHCR's task would be threefold: to ascertain and record the repatriation wishes of each Western Saharan as he or she was registered as a voter by the Identification Commission; to issue the necessary documentation to the members of his or her immediate family; and to establish and manage, in cooperation with MINURSO, which would provide security, the reception centres that would be established in the Territory for the returnees.

B. MINURSO: 1991–1995

Establishment of MINURSO

On 29 April 1991, the Security Council, in its resolution 690 (1991), decided to establish MINURSO, in accordance with a report[2] of the Secretary-General which further detailed the implementation plan. In approving the plan, the Security Council also accepted the timetable proposed in the Secretary-General's report. It was envisaged that the transitional period would begin no later than 16 weeks after the General Assembly approved the MINURSO budget and would last for 20 weeks. MINURSO would remain in the Territory for up to 26 weeks from the coming into effect of the cease-fire. The Secretary-General indicated, however, that the periods of time allowed for the various processes were estimates that could require adjustment.

The budget for MINURSO was approved by the General Assembly on 17 May 1991.

Cease-fire

On 24 May 1991, in accordance with the plan, the Secretary-General proposed that the cease-fire should enter into effect on 6 September. Both parties accepted that date.[3] During the following three months, however, it became clear that it would not be possible to complete before 6 September a number of tasks that were to be completed before the cease-fire. It also became clear that, notwithstanding the parties' earlier acceptance of the settlement plan, substantial areas of difference between them remained. One party, therefore, was not able to agree that the transition period should begin on 6 September 1991.

Meanwhile, hostilities had broken out in the Territory, interrupting an informal cease-fire that had been in effect for over two years. In these circumstances, the Secretary-General decided that

[2]S/22464. [3]S/22779.

the formal cease-fire should come into effect on 6 September as initially agreed, on the understanding that the transition period would begin as soon as the outstanding tasks had been completed. The Security Council supported his proposal that, during this delay, 100 military observers should be deployed in the Territory to verify the cease-fire and the cessation of hostilities in certain areas.[4] The number of military observers was subsequently increased to 228, and certain logistics and administrative support staff were also sent to the field.

The primary function of MINURSO was restricted to verifying the cease-fire and cessation of hostilities. This was done by direct observation of military forces and activities carried out by either party and verifying complaints of alleged cease-fire violations. United Nations military observers were deployed to 10 team sites/observation posts in the northern and southern sectors of the Territory to monitor the cease-fire in mobile patrols. Helicopter-borne patrols were also conducted to enhance MINURSO monitoring capability and react at short notice to complaints and violations.

The headquarters of the Mission was established in the capital, Laayoune, with two regional headquarters in the northern and southern sectors of the Territory. A liaison office was also established in Tindouf to maintain contact with the Algerian authorities and the Frente POLISARIO.

Differences remain

According to the settlement plan, the referendum in Western Sahara should have taken place in January 1992. However, it was not possible to proceed in conformity with the original timetable. While both Morocco and the Frente POLISARIO reiterated their confidence in the United Nations, their commitment to the settlement plan and their willingness to restore the momentum of the peace process, they continued to have divergent views and different interpretations of some of the key elements contained in the plan, including those with regard to the question of criteria for eligibility to vote in the referendum.

Criteria for voter eligibility were enunciated by the Secretary-General on 19 December 1991.[5] While considering them to be unduly restrictive, Morocco nevertheless accepted them. For its part, the Frente POLISARIO maintained that, in the initial agreement, the two parties had agreed that the list of Saharans counted in the census conducted by the Spanish administration in the Territory in 1974 would be the exclusive basis of the electorate. In its view, the criteria of 19 December 1991 would unduly expand the electorate beyond the 1974 census list and were incompatible therefore with the relevant provisions of the settlement plan.

In the meantime, Mr. Manz resigned as Special Representative to assume functions in the service of his country. On 25 March 1992, Secretary-General Boutros Boutros-Ghali informed[6] the Security Council of the appointment of Sahabzada Yaqub-Khan as the new Special Representative. In the hope of breaking the deadlock, the Special Representative held, in August and September 1992, a series of separate talks with the two parties on the interpretation and application of the criteria. The purpose of such talks was to find ways of ensuring that both parties arrived at the same interpretation of the criteria.

In spite of intensive efforts by Secretary-General Boutros-Ghali and his Special Representative to find mutually acceptable solutions, the implementation plan could not be put back on track. Moreover, an attempt to organize a meeting of 38 Western Saharan tribal chiefs in Geneva, at the end of November 1992, had to be cancelled because of the differences relating to the powers of some participants designated by the Moroccan party.

On 26 January 1993, the Secretary-General told[7] the Security Council that the cancellation of the meeting in Geneva demonstrated the futility of the efforts undertaken "with vigour and resource" by his Special Representative over the preceding eight months to seek a way out of the existing deadlock. He suggested three possible options available under the circumstances.

A first option suggested the continuation and, if possible, the intensification of talks. The Secretary-General believed, however, that the chances for success under this option were very slim. A second option required the immediate implementation of the settlement plan on the basis of the instructions for the review of applications for participation in the referendum, appearing in the annex to the 19 December 1991 report of the Secretary-General to the Security Council. This could mean, the Secretary-General pointed out, that the implementation would have to proceed without the cooperation of one of the parties. A third option was to adopt an alternative approach not based on the settlement plan.

---

[4]S/23008, S/23009. [5]S/23299, annex. [6]S/23754. [7]S/25170.

On 2 March 1993, the Security Council, by its resolution 809 (1993), invited the Secretary-General to intensify efforts to resolve outstanding issues, and to make the necessary preparations for the referendum and to consult accordingly with the parties for the purpose of commencing voter registration starting with the updated lists of the 1974 census. The Council urged the two parties to cooperate fully with the Secretary-General in implementing the settlement plan and to resolve their differences regarding the criteria for voter eligibility.

The Special Representative then initiated consultations with the parties on a possible compromise regarding the interpretation and application of the criteria. Discussions were also held with the parties on a number of issues relating to an early registration of voters. After both sides confirmed their desire to proceed promptly with the registration of voters and to cooperate with MINURSO in this regard, it was decided to establish an Identification Commission for the Referendum in Western Sahara.[8] On 23 April 1993, the Secretary-General appointed Mr. Erik Jensen (Malaysia) as Chairman of the Commission.

Compromise proposal

The parties continued to have fundamentally divergent positions on the establishment of the electorate. One party, Morocco, wanted to make all Saharans eligible to participate in the referendum, while the other, the Frente POLISARIO, wanted to limit participation, so far as possible, to those counted in the Territory in the 1974 census, in order to avoid including those it regarded as foreign to the Territory.

During a visit to the area from 31 May to 4 June 1993, the Secretary-General presented to the parties a comprehensive proposal regarding the interpretation and application of the criteria for voter eligibility. He believed that it represented a practical and valid, although imperfect, basis for a preliminary selection of potential voters and a compromise between conflicting positions that was even-handed and fair.

Another round of meetings was held by the Special Representative from 5 to 20 June 1993. During these and subsequent consultations, both parties reaffirmed their commitment to the implementation of the peace plan in its entirety and their determination to move towards an early referendum. Both sides stressed that they did not reject the proposed compromise but expressed reservations on certain provisions of the text. In spite of its reservations, Morocco subsequently acquiesced in the compromise. For its part, the Frente POLISARIO, while finally conveying its acceptance of all the eligibility criteria of 19 December 1991, maintained substantial reservations on, and requested several amendments to, the compromise text.

On 28 July 1993, the Secretary-General reported[9] to the Security Council that shortly after his visit to the area, the two parties agreed to initiate direct talks and to ask for the assistance of the United Nations in holding this meeting. The delegations of Morocco and the Frente POLISARIO met from 17 to 19 July 1993 at Laayoune, in the presence of the Special Representative as United Nations observer. The Secretary-General described this event as an encouraging sign and expressed his hope that such talks would be resumed soon. In the meantime, the Chairman of the Identification Commission travelled to the region in order to prepare for the initiation of the process of identification and registration of voters.

Secretary-General remains hopeful

The direct talks between the Government of Morocco and the Frente POLISARIO were scheduled to resume on 25 October 1993 in New York. While ground rules laid down for the resumption of talks gave to each party the right to choose the composition of its delegation, the POLISARIO delegation "found it impossible" to meet with the other party because of the presence of former POLISARIO officials in the Moroccan delegation. Despite efforts by the Secretary-General's Special Representative to find ways of overcoming the procedural difficulties, the talks did not take place.

On 27 October, the Secretary-General issued a statement[10] in which he deeply regretted the failure of the parties to meet. At the same time, he remained hopeful that a dialogue between the two parties might be resumed in due course. In the meantime, he was determined to continue efforts for the implementation of the settlement plan and to proceed with the identification and registration of potential voters in the referendum.

Referendum rescheduled

The Secretary-General informed[11] the Security Council on 24 November 1993 that, in view of the remaining difficulties in the implementa-

---

[8]S/25818. [9]S/26185. [10]SG/SM/5142. [11]S/26797.

tion of the settlement plan, it would not be possible to fulfil the goal of holding a free and fair referendum by the end of 1993. However, on the assumption that those difficulties were settled and progress made in the initial stages of the voter registration process, he hoped to be able to propose to the Council early in 1994 a detailed timetable for holding the referendum in mid-1994. He further proposed to maintain the existing military and civilian strength of MINURSO until his next report to the Council. The Council agreed[12] that the Secretary-General's compromise proposal was a sound framework for determining potential participation in the referendum in Western Sahara as foreseen in the settlement plan, and expected that any difficulties with the compromise would be resolved by early 1994. The Council also welcomed the Secretary-General's determination to move ahead and proceed with voter registration and identification.

Voter registration

After the Chairman of the Identification Commission arrived in the mission area towards the end of May 1993, he assembled the members of the Commission and a team of registration officers. The former group arrived in Laayoune in June. The Chairman and his team held intensive discussions with the authorities of both parties on modalities which would enable identification and registration to proceed in a thorough and judicious manner. They also made essential arrangements for voter registration both in Western Sahara and in the Tindouf (Algeria) area.

On 3 November 1993, after several rounds of discussions with both parties, the Chairman of the Commission officially announced the launching of the process leading to identification and registration. He then held a further series of discussions with both the Government of Morocco and the Frente POLISARIO urging them to adhere as far as possible to a timetable agreed upon by the parties in October 1993. During these consultations, both sides confirmed their intention to proceed expeditiously with the initial stage of the registration process in cooperation with MINURSO.

In late November 1993, the revised lists of the 1974 census, together with the supplement listing the names of additional persons expected to reach 18 years of age by 31 December 1993, were made accessible in Laayoune and in the El-Aiun refugee camp in the Tindouf area. Beginning in December 1993, application forms were sup-

plied and distributed, initially through centres in Laayoune and in the Tindouf area. Additional registration offices were opened in the other population centres in the Territory as well as in a few locations outside the Territory where numbers of Western Saharans were known to be living.

The Special Representative visited the mission area from 2 to 13 January 1994 for consultations with the parties and the neighbouring countries on the situation and ways of resolving the remaining difficulties. He provided assurances to allay the concerns of the Frente POLISARIO that, on the basis of the compromise, thousands of individuals foreign to the Territory might be included in the electorate. These assurances were confirmed and further elaborated in a letter[13] dated 4 February 1994 from the Special Representative to the representative of the Frente POLISARIO in New York.

Options before the Security Council

Although the preliminary registration of applicants for participation in the referendum proceeded in Laayoune and the Tindouf area, the completion of the identification and final registration of all eligible voters remained uncertain in the absence of agreement by the Frente POLISARIO to the compromise as a whole. On 10 March 1994, the Secretary-General told[14] the Security Council that, following protracted delays since the inception of MINURSO, every possible avenue had been explored by himself and his Special Representative to break the deadlock over the criteria and their interpretation so that the plan could be implemented. The fact that these efforts had not succeeded confronted the Security Council with a difficult choice. The Secretary-General presented three options.

Under option A, the Council would decide that the United Nations should proceed to hold the referendum regardless of the cooperation of either party. Registration and identification of eligible voters would proceed based on the compromise, the terms of reference of the Identification Commission and the relevant provisions of the settlement plan. The transitional period would commence on 1 August 1994. The Identification Commission would analyse voter applications from March to May 1994 and would begin registration in June, at which time it would also announce the arrangements for the appeals process.

---

[12]S/26848. [13]S/1994/283, annex. [14]S/1994/283.

By September, voter registration would be completed and the final list of voters would be published. The United Nations would also undertake other activities called for in the original settlement plan. From 7 to 15 December 1994, the referendum would be held, the results would be proclaimed, and the withdrawal of MINURSO personnel would commence. MINURSO's monitoring responsibilities would end by 31 December 1994.

Option B would have the Council decide that the Identification Commission should continue its work while the United Nations continued its efforts to obtain the cooperation of both parties based on the compromise proposal put forward by the Secretary-General. At the end of a prescribed period, the Council would review progress achieved and would decide on its next course of action. Until that time, the Identification Commission would be expected to complete its analysis of voter applications and begin registration of potential voters. Under option C, the Council would conclude that the cooperation of the parties in completing the registration process could not be obtained at that time and would decide either that the whole MINURSO operation should be phased out within a given time-frame or that the registration and identification process should be suspended, but that a reduced United Nations military presence should be retained in order to encourage respect for the cease-fire.

The Secretary-General noted that either option A or option B would require Member States to be willing to provide military personnel. Even maintenance of MINURSO at its existing strength would require urgent action to obtain replacements for the contingents whose withdrawal had already been announced by their Governments.

In the meantime, on 15 March 1994, the Secretary-General appointed the Chairman of the Identification Commission, Mr. Erik Jensen, as his Deputy Special Representative for Western Sahara, in addition to his responsibility as Chairman.

On 29 March 1994, the Security Council, by its resolution 907 (1994), agreed to the course of action as outlined in option B of the Secretary-General's report and requested him to report no later than 15 July 1994 on progress achieved in the Identification Commission's work as well as on other aspects of the settlement plan. It also decided that, in the event the Secretary-General reported that the referendum could not be held by the end of 1994, it would consider MINURSO's future, including an examination of options regarding its mandate and continued operations.

Identification and registration

Following the adoption of resolution 907 (1994), the Identification Commission focused its efforts on achieving the agreement and cooperation of both parties in order to proceed with the identification of potential voters. As a result, the Commission succeeded in completing all the necessary groundwork for launching the process. That event was to have taken place on 8 June 1994 with the assistance of the tribal chiefs and in the presence of observers of both parties and OAU. However, it could not start as scheduled because of Morocco's reservations over the designation of OAU observers.

As requested, the Secretary-General reported[15] to the Security Council on 12 July 1994. He noted the progress made towards the implementation of the settlement plan for Western Sahara and pointed to the remaining difficulties. In light of delays in the identification and registration process, the Secretary-General intended to propose that the transitional period in Western Sahara should start on 1 October 1994 and that the referendum should take place on 14 February 1995.

The Security Council welcomed[16] the progress made, took note of the proposed revised timetable and urged the parties to continue to cooperate with the Secretary-General and MINURSO to ensure the earliest possible implementation of the settlement plan.

As a result of the Secretary-General's extensive discussions with the leaders of OAU and other interested parties, the question of OAU observers was resolved. The identification and registration operation was finally launched on 28 August 1994, with opening ceremonies held simultaneously at Laayoune in Western Sahara and at the El-Aiun camp in the Tindouf area. At the same time, the United Nations intensified work on other political and military aspects relevant to the fulfilment of the settlement plan.

Timetable revised

The identification and registration operation proved to be far more complex than expected, as members of the same tribal subgroups, who had to be identified individually with the assistance of their respective sheikhs, were dispersed in different locations, and means of communication were limited. By the end of October, only some 4,000 potential voters from five Saharan tribal subfrac-

[15]S/1994/819. [16]S/PRST/1994/39.

tions had been interviewed, equivalent to less than 2 per cent of the total number of application forms. The situation became even more complex when, on 25 October — the deadline set for the submission of applications — MINURSO received a flood of completed forms, which exceeded the number previously submitted. By then, only about 50,000 (about 21 per cent of the total) had been computerized and analysed. This meant further lengthy delays in the identification process.

On 4 November 1994, the Secretary-General told[17] the Security Council that it had become clear that many months would be required to make sufficient progress in the identification process to be close to determining a date for the referendum and a revised timetable for the steps still to be taken to implement the settlement plan. He stated that he would report further to the Council on the organization and timing of the referendum after the consultations he intended to hold during a visit to the area in November 1994. In the meantime, the Secretary-General dispatched a technical team to MINURSO to review the requirements with regard to the logistic, personnel and other resources for the deployment of the Mission at full strength.

The Security Council expressed[18] concern over the slow speed of the identification process and urged the two parties to exert all possible efforts to facilitate MINURSO's work. It welcomed the Secretary-General's decision to visit the region, and looked forward to receiving his report and the report of the technical team charged with reassessing requirements for the deployment of MINURSO at full strength. The Council strongly believed that there should be no further delay in the holding of a free, fair and impartial referendum.

The Secretary-General travelled to the region from 25 to 29 November 1994. During the visit, he held discussions on the question of Western Sahara with Algerian authorities in Algiers, the representatives of the Frente POLISARIO in the Tindouf area, and Moroccan authorities in Laayoune and Rabat. He reported[19] to the Council that his consultations with the parties indicated that, despite the difficulties encountered and the delays experienced, the political will existed to move the process forward. Furthermore, the four identification teams working at Laayoune and Tindouf (two at each centre) had achieved a weekly output of 1,000 potential voters interviewed and identified. Given the large number of applications received, the only way to complete identification and registration in a reasonable time would be through a major reinforcement of personnel and other resources.

It had been estimated that 25 teams working simultaneously at an increased number of identification and registration centres would be required. Consultations had started with the parties regarding the location, equipping and opening of additional centres. Under the proposal, the Identification Commission would be expanded by 51 additional staff. Approximately 13 civilian police would also be required to provide security and assist with the identification activities at each centre, and 4 civilian police were required for each mobile team. Thus, an additional 105 civilian police were required, including 10 officers at the civilian police headquarters.

The Secretary-General hoped that by 31 March 1995 progress achieved in the identification and registration process would reach a level that would enable him to recommend 1 June 1995 as the date (D-Day) for the start of the transitional period. In mid-August, the identification and registration of voters would be completed and the final list of voters published. The repatriation programme would be completed by the end of September. That date would coincide with the start of the referendum campaign in time to permit the referendum to take place in October 1995.

On 13 January 1995, the Security Council adopted resolution 973 (1995), in which it approved the expansion of MINURSO and extended its mandate until 31 May 1995, with the possibility of a further extension.

Major difficulties remain

In the following months, the identification of applicants for participation in the referendum progressed slowly but incrementally. In February and March 1995, the number of identification centres was increased from four to seven, and MINURSO achieved its goal of processing at least 150 persons a day at each centre. On 3 April, the eighth centre became operational, at the Dakhla camp 180 kilometres south of Tindouf.

Despite increased operational capabilities, however, the rate of identification was uneven, and major difficulties remained. It had been agreed that identification could take place only when two sheikhs, one from each side, were present to testify. The representatives of the two parties and an OAU observer were also expected to attend. The

[17]S/1994/1257. [18]S/1994/PRST/67. [19]S/1994/1420.

operation was interrupted periodically by difficulties relating to the timely availability of sheikhs and party representatives and to weather conditions and logistics. Work had to be suspended when one side or the other experienced difficulties in making its sheikh available or, preferring a delay, had its sheikh fail to arrive, arrive late or leave the centre. Moreover, both sides' insistence on strict reciprocity meant that whenever, for whatever reason, identification could not take place at a centre on one side, work was automatically suspended at a centre on the other.

In addition, the process of identifying each potential voter was very time-consuming. This work required meticulous examination of material evidence and detailed interviews with applicants. The difficulties were complicated by the vast distances, in a territory of 266,000 square kilometres, and the dispersal of the members of each tribal subgroup throughout the towns of Western Sahara and the camps near Tindouf. As of 15 May 1995, 35,851 persons had been identified. This was far below the figure that MINURSO would be technically capable of achieving if the full cooperation of the parties was invariably forthcoming.

If MINURSO was permitted to proceed rapidly with identification, the referendum could take place in early 1996. Meanwhile, and before confirming the date for the start of the transitional period, progress must be achieved on other important aspects of the settlement plan. In this regard, the Secretary-General intended, in early July 1995, to forward to the parties the final text of the code of conduct during the referendum campaign. In August, he would inform the Council of the progress made by the independent jurist on the release of political prisoners and in September he would make a ruling on the confinement of the Frente POLISARIO troops. By that time, the Secretary-General hoped to receive confirmation from the Government of Morocco on the arrangements for the reduction of its troops in the Territory.

The Secretary-General believed that monitoring these benchmarks would enable the Security Council to assess the parties' willingness to press ahead with the implementation of the settlement plan. He recommended[20] that the Council extend the mandate of MINURSO for a period of four months. With a view to accelerating the implementation of the plan, the Council decided[21] to send a mission of the Council to the region, and to extend the mandate of MINURSO until 30 June 1995, pending the findings and recommendations of its mission.

Security Council mission

The six-member Council delegation visited Morocco, Algeria, Mauritania, Tindouf and Laayoune from 3 to 9 June 1995. Its objective was to impress upon the parties the necessity of fully cooperating with MINURSO in the implementation of all aspects of the settlement plan, to assess progress and identify problems in the identification process, and to identify problems in other areas relevant to the fulfilment of the plan. The mission observed,[22] among other things, that there was continuing suspicion and lack of trust between the parties. As a result, in the course of identification, technical problems that could have been resolved easily had there been goodwill had become politicized and blown out of proportion, with each party blaming the other for the lack of progress. This could make it nearly impossible for MINURSO to meet its objectives unless both parties improved their performance. The mission felt that there was a real risk that the identification process might be extended beyond the time previously envisaged and the referendum might not be held in January 1996.

Among many recommendations made, the mission called upon the Government of Morocco to conduct preliminary vetting of the 100,000 applicants not residing in the Territory at that time prior to examination by the Identification Commission, in order to enable MINURSO to maintain its timetable for completing the identification process. MINURSO should without delay commence the identification operation for applicants living in Mauritania with a view to completing that operation as soon as possible. The Deputy Special Representative of the Secretary-General should seek ways to secure a date in the near future for the reduction and confinement of troops in order to allow the Secretary-General to make his ruling in the matter in early September. The mission also recommended that the Deputy Special Representative should consult with the two parties on the exchange of prisoners of war and the release of political detainees, so that those issues could be removed from the timetable and linked closely to the commencement of the transitional period.

The Security Council endorsed[23] the recommendations of the mission concerning the identification process and other aspects of the settlement plan. It decided to extend the mandate of MINURSO until 30 September 1995, as recom-

---

[20]S/1995/404. [21]S/RES/995 (1995). [22]S/1995/498.
[23]S/RES/1002 (1995)

mended by the Secretary-General, and to consider the possible extension of the mandate of MINURSO after that date on the basis of the Secretary-General's report and in the light of progress achieved towards the holding of the referendum and the implementation of the settlement plan.

Further delays

On 23 June 1995, the Frente POLISARIO announced[24] that it was suspending its participation in the identification process and was withdrawing its observers. This was in protest against the sentencing by Morocco of eight Saharans to prison terms of 15 to 20 years for having participated in a demonstration in Laayoune, and the announcement by Morocco to the Council mission of its intention to present for identification 100,000 applicants residing outside the Territory. In response, the Moroccan Prime Minister, Mr. Abdellatif Filali, stated[25] that Morocco could not accept an indefinite postponement of the referendum and called upon the Security Council to take all necessary steps to ensure the resumption of the process with a view to holding the referendum on schedule.

The identification operation resumed in late July, after the details concerning its resumption had been clarified and practical measures taken to reopen the centres. As of early September 1995, a total of over 53,000 persons in the Territory and in the refugee camps near Tindouf had been identified since the process began. However, the Frente POLISARIO continued to dismiss categorically the 100,000 applications from persons living outside the Territory in southern Morocco and had major reservations about members of certain tribal groupings also in the Territory, namely the "Tribus del Norte", "Tribus Costeras y del Sur" and "Chorfa". From among these, they rejected three groups as in no sense "belonging to the Territory". With respect to other groups, while not contesting the right of their members who were included in the 1974 census to be identified, the Frente POLISARIO agreed to participate in identification on the assumption that the number would be modest and the individuals would be identified by one sheikh from each side. The Government of Morocco, on the other hand, was insistent that there should be no discrimination between applicants, irrespective of whether they were currently residing in or outside the Territory and irrespective of the criterion under which they applied to be included in the electoral roll.

Other aspects

As to other aspects relevant to the fulfilment of the settlement plan, Morocco reiterated its commitment to reduce its troops in the Territory to the agreed level at the appropriate time in accordance with the plan. The Secretary-General intended to request the Government of Morocco to provide information on the strength and location of its military forces in the Territory, with a plan and timetable for their reduction to the agreed level of 65,000 all ranks.

Major differences remained with regard to the confinement of troops in designated locations. The Frente POLISARIO objected to the suggestion that its troops be confined outside the Territory, while Morocco refused to agree that the Frente POLISARIO troops be confined in the area between the sandwall (berm) and the international border of Western Sahara.

The code of conduct for the period of the referendum campaign was finalized and sent to the two parties on 17 August 1995. Both sides, however, indicated their inability to accept the document as submitted to them. Therefore, a further revision of the code was required.

UNHCR continued preparations for the repatriation of refugees after the start of the transitional period. UNHCR officers were deployed in Laayoune and Tindouf to determine the logistic requirements for repatriation and to coordinate UNHCR activities in the region. For planning purposes, UNHCR was proceeding with a pre-registration of refugees before completing its preparatory work. Both sides cooperated with the efforts of UNHCR and pledged their support to the smooth repatriation of refugees after the start of the transitional period.

In the meantime, pending the fulfilment of the conditions necessary for the commencement of the transitional period, MINURSO's military mandate remained restricted to monitoring and verifying the 6 September 1991 cease-fire. The activities of the civilian police component continued to be linked to those of the Identification Commission. In this connection, MINURSO civilian police maintained a 24-hour security presence at the identification centres and provided technical assistance to the Commission.

In anticipation of Security Council authorization of the transitional period, plans for the full deployment of MINURSO underwent an in-depth review. As a result, it was estimated that

---

[24]S/1995/524, annex. [25]S/1995/514, annex.

a force of about 1,780 (all ranks) would be required in order for MINURSO to implement effectively its military mandate. The concept of operations for the full deployment of the civilian police component was also reviewed.

MINURSO mandate further extended

Reviewing the situation in Western Sahara in September 1995, the Secretary-General observed[26] that progress in the implementation of the settlement plan in the preceding three months had been "disappointing". The benchmarks he had proposed had not been achieved for the most part. Both parties maintained their respective positions concerning the confinement of the Frente POLISARIO troops. In addition, they objected to the terms of the proposed code of conduct, despite the efforts made by the Secretariat to reconcile their differences.

On the other hand, there were some positive results achieved. In circumstances largely without precedent and under particularly adverse conditions, over 40 per cent of the applicants in the Territory and more than 51 per cent of those in the refugee camps had been identified. In addition, many more had already been convoked, sometimes repeatedly. A detailed programme for the identification of most of the remaining applicants had been prepared. Were both parties to cooperate fully, the process of identification in all four refugee camps and three of the four centres in the Territory (with the exception of Laayoune) could be completed in approximately five weeks. There would then remain those individuals who belonged to an assortment of tribal groups widely dispersed and thinly represented in any one place in the Territory or in the camps. Special arrangements would have to be made in cooperation with the parties to group those people for identification.

The Secretary-General appealed to the parties to make every effort to permit the expeditious implementation of the settlement plan. He believed that although the process could not continue indefinitely, premature withdrawal of MINURSO would undoubtedly have very grave and far-reaching implications for the parties and for the whole subregion. The Secretary-General proposed, therefore, the extension of MINURSO's mandate until 31 January 1996. If, before then, however, the conditions necessary for the start of the transitional period were not in place, he would present the Security Council with alternative options for consideration, including the possibility of MINURSO's withdrawal. The Security Council extended[27] MINURSO's mandate as recommended by the Secretary-General. It requested him, in close consultation with the parties, to produce specific and detailed proposals to resolve the problems hindering the completion of the identification process.

Modified procedure proposed

The basic obstacle to completing the identification process continued to be the refusal of the Frente POLISARIO to participate in the identification of three tribal subfractions (out of 88 subfractions and equivalent groups included in the 1974 census) and persons not resident in the Territory. Since MINURSO had an obligation to consider all applications which had been correctly submitted, a compromise solution had to be found to enable the Mission to meet its obligation in circumstances where the Frente POLISARIO was unwilling or unable to make a sheikh available. As a way forward, the Secretary-General suggested that in such circumstances identification should be based on documentary evidence. In a letter[28] to the President of the Security Council dated 27 October 1995, he elaborated his proposal, which had already been explained to both parties.

In a letter dated 26 October 1995, the Frente POLISARIO assured the Acting Special Representative of its willingness to cooperate in the identification of all persons whose applications had been received in the Territory and outside, in the camps and the Tindouf region and in Mauritania, in conformity with the settlement plan. The Moroccan Government, in communications dated 25 and 29 October, rejected any change in the procedure and considered the suggested simplification of the procedure as a radical departure from the settlement plan.

In November 1995, in an effort to break the deadlock, the Secretary-General proposed[29] a modified procedure for the identification of those persons. In accordance with established practice, both parties would be invited to present a sheikh, or alternate, of the subfraction concerned and to be represented during the identification process. An OAU observer was also expected to attend. When two sheikhs, or alternates, were present — one from each side — identification would take place according to the normal proceeding. When one party did not provide a sheikh or alternate, identification would take place on the basis of

[26]S/1995/779. [27]S/RES/1017 (1995). [28]S/1995/924. [29]S/1995/986.

MINURSO deployment as of November 1995

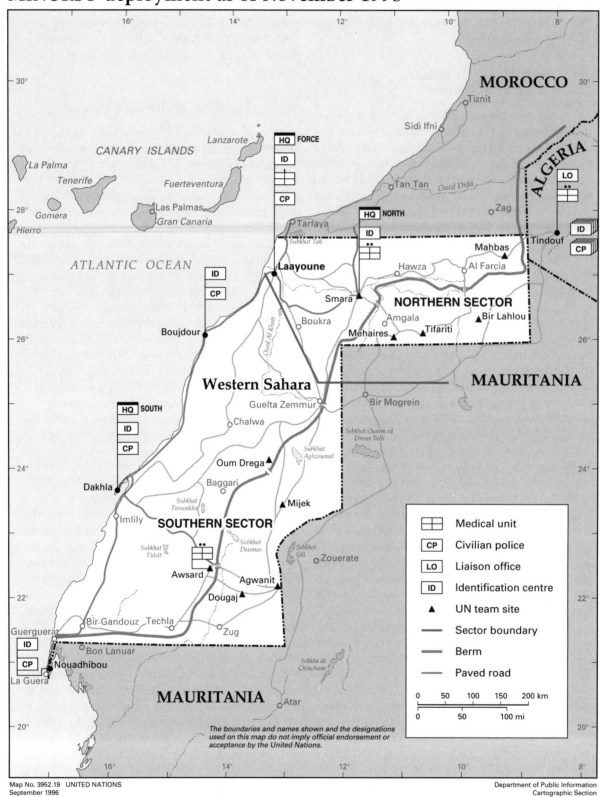

MOROCCO

Tiznit

Sidi Ifni

Tan Tan Oued Drâa

ALGERIA

CANARY ISLANDS

Lanzarote

La Palma

Tenerife

Fuerteventura

Gomera

Las Palmas

Gran Canaria

Hierro

ATLANTIC OCEAN

HQ FORCE

ID

CP

Tarfaya

Subkhat Tah

HQ NORTH

ID

Laayoune

ID

CP

Zag

Mahbas

Tindouf

LO

ID

CP

Hawza Al Farcia

Smara

Boukra

NORTHERN SECTOR

Amgala

Bir Lahlou

Mehaires Tifariti

Boujdour

Western Sahara

Oued Al Khatt

MAURITANIA

Guelta Zemmur

Bir Mogrein

HQ SOUTH

ID

CP

Chalwa

Sebkhet Oumm ed
Drous Telli

Subkhat
Aghzoumal

Oum Drega

Baggari

Subkhat
Tamwakka

Subkhat
Tidsit

Mijek

SOUTHERN SECTOR

Imlily

Dakhla

Subkhat
Doumas

Awsard

Agwanit

Sebkhet
Ijill

Zouerate

Dougaj

Guerguerat

Bir-Gandouz Techla

Zug

ID

CP

Bon Lanuar

Nouadhibou

La Guera

MAURITANIA

Atar

Sebkha de
Chinchane

	Medical unit
CP	Civilian police
LO	Liaison office
ID	Identification centre
▲	UN team site
——	Sector boundary
——	Berm
——	Paved road

0 50 100 150 200 km

0 50 100 mi

The boundaries and names shown and the designations
used on this map do not imply official endorsement or
acceptance by the United Nations.

Map No. 3952.19 UNITED NATIONS
September 1996

Department of Public Information
Cartographic Section

appropriate documentation, with the assistance of only one sheikh present. In the case that neither party was willing or able to make available a sheikh or alternate, identification would be based on documentary evidence only.

Neither party was satisfied with the Secretary-General's proposal. Morocco wanted to limit, to the extent possible, the role of documentary evidence and give privilege to that of oral testimony. The Frente POLISARIO considered that the implementation of the new approach would allow for the introduction of applicants who had no ties with Western Sahara. Despite objections, however, the Secretary-General concluded that the new approach was the only way the process could be carried forward. He hoped that both parties would be persuaded to cooperate and give the identification operation a chance.

As of 18 November 1995, 233,487 applications had been processed (176,533 in the Territory and on the Moroccan side, 42,468 in the camps and Tindouf area, and 14,486 in Mauritania). Of those, 75,794 persons had been convoked (46,701 in the Territory and 29,093 in the camps),

of whom 58,947 had been identified (37,708 in the Territory and 21,239 in the camps).

A total of 157,693 applicants remained. The Secretary-General envisaged[30] that if identification was allowed to proceed in accordance with the new procedures and without interruption, a total of 12 centres should be able to complete identification within about four months, at a rate of 36,000 applicants per month. Should it fail to proceed with the necessary speed, it would be the Secretary-General's intention to "present for the consideration of the Council alternative options, including the possibility of MINURSO's withdrawal".

On 19 December 1995, the Security Council welcomed[31] the Secretary-General's decision to intensify consultations with the Government of Morocco and the Frente POLISARIO. In the event that the consultations failed to produce agreement, the Secretary-General was requested to provide the Council with options for its consideration, including a programme for the orderly withdrawal of MINURSO.

C. Suspension of the identification process

All further United Nations efforts to obtain the parties' agreement to a plan to resolve their differences hindering the timely completion of the identification process proved unsuccessful. Although both the Government of Morocco and the Frente POLISARIO continued to confirm their commitment and desire to hold a free and fair referendum on the future status of Western Sahara, each of them insisted that there was no room left for additional concessions on its part. Thus, the impasse reached at the end of 1995 persisted.

In the absence of any meaningful progress towards completion of the settlement plan, the Secretary-General, in May 1996, recommended[32] that the identification process be suspended "until such time as both parties provide convincing evidence that they are committed to resuming and completing it without further obstacles, in accordance with the settlement plan, as mandated by the Security Council". The members of the Identification Commission would leave the mission area and the records of the Commission would be transferred to the United Nations Office at Geneva for

safe keeping. Suspension of identification would also entail the withdrawal of the civilian police component, except for a small number of officers to maintain contacts with the authorities on both sides and to plan for eventual resumption of the identification process. On the military side, the Secretary-General proposed a reduction in the strength of the military component of MINURSO by 20 per cent.

At the same time, the Secretary-General stressed that his proposals did not imply lessening of resolve to discharge the mandate entrusted to him by the Security Council and that the United Nations could not abandon its responsibility. He recommended the extension of MINURSO's mandate for a period of six months at the reduced strength. In a continuing effort to overcome existing obstacles, he also proposed to maintain a political office, headed by his Acting Special Representative, in Laayoune, with a liaison office in Tindouf. That office would maintain a dialogue

[30]S/1995/986. [31]S/RES/1033 (1995). [32]S/1996/343.

with the parties and the two neighbouring countries (Algeria and Mauritania) and would facilitate any other effort that could help set the parties on a course towards an agreed formula for the resolution of their differences.

The Security Council agreed[33] with the Secretary-General's recommendations and decided to extend the mandate of MINURSO until 30 November 1996. The Council reiterated its commitment to the holding, as soon as possible, of a free, fair and impartial referendum for the self-determination of the people of Western Sahara and urged the two parties to demonstrate without further delay the political will, cooperation and flexibility necessary to permit the resumption and early completion of the identification process and the implementation of the settlement plan.

D. Composition of MINURSO

The Security Council authorized the appointment of a special representative in its resolution 621 (1988) of 20 September 1988. Mr. Hector Gros Espiell (Uruguay) served as Special Representative with effect from 19 October 1988. Upon his resignation, Mr. Gros Espiell was succeeded by Mr. Johannes Manz (Switzerland) with effect from 19 January 1990. When Mr. Manz resigned to assume other functions in the service of his country, the Secretary-General informed the Security Council on 25 March 1992 of the appointment of Sahabzada Yaqub-Khan (Pakistan) as the new Special Representative. On 15 March 1994, the Secretary-General appointed Mr. Erik Jensen (Malaysia) to serve as Deputy Special Representative for Western Sahara, in addition to his responsibility as Chairman of the Identification Commission. In conformity with the settlement plan, the Deputy Special Representative was in charge of the Mission during any absence of the Special Representative from the Mission area. In August 1995, Mr. Jensen was designated Acting Special Representative.

From its inception to 24 April 1992, Major-General Armand Roy (Canada) served as Force Commander of MINURSO. From that date to 30 September 1992, the Deputy Force Commander, Brigadier-General Luis Block Urban (Peru) served as Acting Force Commander. With effect from 1 October 1992, the Secretary-General appointed Brigadier-General André Van Baelen (Belgium) to the post of Acting Force Commander. Subsequently, General Van Baelen was designated as Force Commander of MINURSO. With effect from 1 April 1996, Brigadier-General Van Baelen was succeeded by Major-General José Leandro (Portugal).

The civilian police component of MINURSO was deployed in June 1993. The Police Commissioner, Colonel Jürgen Friedrich Reimann (Germany) served as Civilian Police Commissioner until March 1995, when he was succeeded by Colonel Wolf-Dieter Krampe (Germany). Colonel Krampe served until 20 August 1995 and, pending the designation of his replacement, Lieutenant-Colonel Jan Walmann (Norway) was designated Acting Civilian Police Commissioner. On 4 January 1996, Brigadier-General Walter Fallmann (Austria) assumed his duties as Civilian Police Commissioner.

The foreseen full strength of MINURSO was approximately 1,700 military observers and troops, 300 police officers and 800 to 1,000 civilian personnel. The strength of the Mission in early May 1996, in its limited deployment, included 228 military observers, 48 military support personnel and 44 civilian police. Originally, the military personnel were provided by Argentina, Australia, Austria, Bangladesh, Belgium, Canada, China, Egypt, France, Ghana, Greece, Guinea, Honduras, Ireland, Italy, Kenya, Malaysia, Nigeria, Pakistan, Poland, Russian Federation, Switzerland, Tunisia, United Kingdom, United States and Venezuela. In October 1993, the Government of the United Kingdom withdrew its military observers. Australia withdrew its signals contingent in May 1994. Its communications duties have been taken over by military observers. The Canadian movement control was withdrawn in June 1994 and replaced by civilian staff. In August 1994, a medical unit from the Republic of South Korea replaced the Swiss medical contingent. Civilian police personnel were provided by Austria, Egypt, Germany, Ghana, Hungary, Ireland, Nigeria, Norway, Togo and Uruguay.

[33]S/RES/1056 (1996).

In early May 1996, military personnel were provided by the following countries: Argentina, Austria, Bangladesh, China, Egypt, El Salvador, France, Ghana, Greece, Guinea, Honduras, Ireland, Italy, Kenya, Malaysia, Nigeria, Pakistan, Poland, Portugal (Force Commander), Republic of Korea, Russian Federation, Tunisia, United States, Uruguay and Venezuela. Civilian police personnel were provided by Austria, Germany, Hungary, Norway, Togo and Uruguay.

MINURSO's authorized civilian staff level was 251, including Professional staff (81), General Service staff (78), Field Service staff (37) and local staff (55).

In May 1996, with the suspension of the identification process, the Security Council authorized withdrawal of the civilian police component, except for a small number of officers to maintain contacts with the authorities on both sides. It further decided to reduce the strength of the military component of MINURSO by 20 per cent. The civilian staff was also reduced.

MINURSO has suffered a number of casualties, including from landmines, and a number of fatalities. In one incident, in June 1993, an aircraft belonging to the Swiss Medical Unit crashed while taking off from team site Awsard in the southern sector. The Swiss pilot, an Australian doctor and a Norwegian technician died in the crash; the third passenger, a Swiss nurse, was seriously injured.

E. Financial aspects

MINURSO is funded by assessed contributions of United Nations Member States. Estimated expenditures from the inception of MINURSO to 31 May 1996 amounted to $224,813,800 net.

Chapter 14

United Nations Operation in Somalia I and II (UNOSOM I and II)

A. Background

B. UNOSOM I

C. UNITAF

D. UNOSOM II: March 1993–July 1994

E. UNOSOM II: August 1994–March 1995
UNOSOM II downsized
Grave concern
Secretary-General takes stock
Security Council mission
Final extension of mandate
Inter-agency statement
SNA/SSA agreements
Withdrawal

F. Conclusion

G. Composition of UNOSOM

H. Financial aspects

Chapter 14

United Nations Operation in Somalia I and II (UNOSOM I and II)

A. Background

The story of the United Nations Operations in Somalia began with the Organization's efforts to facilitate humanitarian aid to people trapped by civil war and famine and developed into a broad attempt to help stop the conflict and reconstitute the basic institutions of a viable State. Somalia occupies a strategically important geopolitical position, stretching from the Equator to the Gulf of Aden over most of the Horn of Africa. It is about 2 per cent arable and given to periodic droughts. The political culture is influenced by competition among a number of clans and clan-based factions.

In 1960, Italian and British colonial territories united to become independent Somalia. From its inception, the country had a dispute with Ethiopia over the arid stretches of the Ogaden, where a nomadic population kept to no firm boundaries. As the parties tried to resolve the matter militarily, they sought military aid from the United States and the Soviet Union. In October 1969, the Soviet-trained army, led by General Mohamed Siad Barre, seized power in Somalia. In pro-Western Ethiopia, Emperor Haille Selassie was deposed in a 1975 *coup*. The Soviet Union provided the new Ethiopian Government with military aid, and Cuban troops arrived for service in the Ogaden. Somalia switched sides in the cold war. The United States, which had lost its base in Ethiopia, provided Somalia with military aid and helped develop the port of Berbera.

The Army Chief of Staff when General Siad Barre took power was General Mohamed Farah Aidid. General Aidid soon found himself out of favour and in prison. He was released six years later to fight in the 1977–1978 war with Ethiopia. In 1989, after serving as Somalia's ambassador to India, Mr. Aidid returned to join the forces in armed opposition to President Siad Barre and was credited for driving him from power in early 1991. However, in late January 1992, the United Somali

Congress (USC), to which General Aidid belonged, appointed as president, in a temporary capacity, Mr. Ali Mahdi Mohamed, also of the Hawiye clan, a businessman. Mr. Ali Mahdi was confirmed to remain as "interim President" of Somalia for two years at a conference on reconciliation convened by the President of Djibouti in July 1991. However, this was not accepted by General Aidid and his followers, presaging the later contest for power between General Aidid and Mr. Ali Mahdi. Further complicating the political competition between the two was the competition between the Hawiye clan and the Darod clan to which ex-President Siad Barre belonged.

From November 1991, there was heavy fighting in Mogadishu. Heavily armed elements controlled parts of the city, including the seaport and the airport, some allied to General Aidid, others allied to Mr. Ali Mahdi, and yet others that were controlled by neither. In addition to Mogadishu, there was conflict in Kismayo, the main port in the southern part of the country. In the south-west, the ousted President of the country was marshalling his forces, and in the north-west, local leaders were pushing to create an independent "Somaliland". The country as a whole was without any form of central government. Banditry was rife.

The fighting that followed, with clans and sub-clans constituted in loose alliances without central control, took place at a time of serious drought. That combination proved disastrous for the population at large. By 1992, almost 4.5 million people, more than half the total number in the country, were threatened with starvation, severe malnutrition and related diseases. The magnitude of suffering was immense. During the worst period it was estimated that in the famine zones approximately one third of all Somali children under the age of five died from starvation and diseases related to malnutrition. Overall, some

300,000 people were estimated to have died. In the fighting, farms were destroyed, livestock killed, food harvests burned and homes razed to the ground. Some 2 million people violently displaced from their home areas fled either to neighbouring countries or elsewhere within Somalia. All institutions of governance and at least 60 per cent of the country's basic infrastructure disintegrated. The only security available was provided by armed groups, sometimes outside any command structure and subject to no political control.

Under such conditions, international efforts to help the people of Somalia were hampered by the rampant lawlessness. In some areas, it became virtually impossible to deliver humanitarian aid because supplies were looted by combatants for their own use. Despite the turmoil, the humanitarian agencies of the United Nations, in particular the United Nations Children's Fund (UNICEF) and the World Food Programme (WFP), continued their efforts. By March 1991, they were fully engaged in the country, but over the following months the volatile security situation forced them on several occasions to temporarily withdraw their personnel. Humanitarian activities continued to the extent possible in cooperation with the International Committee of the Red Cross (ICRC) and other non-governmental organizations (NGOs).

How United Nations involvement began

The conflict within the country threatened the fragile stability of the region as a whole. On 27 December 1991, just days before the end of his term in office, Secretary-General Javier Pérez de Cuéllar informed the President of the Security Council of his intention to take an initiative to restore peace in Somalia. After consulting incoming Secretary-General Boutros Boutros-Ghali, he asked Mr. James Jonah, then Under-Secretary-General for Special Political Affairs, to visit the area. In early January 1992, Mr. Jonah led a team of senior United Nations officials to Somalia for talks that sought to further political reconciliation and to secure access by international aid agencies to civilians in areas of need. During that visit, support for a cease-fire in Mogadishu was expressed by all faction leaders, except General Aidid. There was unanimous support, however, for a United Nations role in bringing about national reconciliation. Against that background, the Security Council placed Somalia on its agenda on 23 January 1992.

The Council received from Somalia's United Nations mission in New York a letter[1] trans-mitting two communications from the country's "interim Prime Minister". One asked that the topic of "the unsettled situation in Somalia" be included in the agenda of the Council; the other, addressed to the Somali mission, authorized it to present to the Council "the deteriorating situation in Somalia, particularly the fighting in Mogadishu".

Arms embargo

At its meeting on 23 January, the Security Council unanimously adopted resolution 733 (1992), saying it was gravely alarmed at the rapid deterioration of the situation in Somalia and the heavy loss of human life and widespread material damage. Aware of its consequences for regional stability and concerned that the situation constituted a threat to international peace and security, the Council decided under Chapter VII of the United Nations Charter to impose a general and complete embargo on all deliveries of weapons and military equipment to Somalia.

The Council asked the Secretary-General, in cooperation with the heads of the Organization of African Unity (OAU) and the League of Arab States (LAS) "immediately to contact all parties in the conflict, to seek their commitment to the cessation of hostilities to permit the humanitarian assistance to be distributed, to promote a cease-fire and compliance therewith, and to assist in the process of a political settlement of the conflict in Somalia". It also asked the Secretary-General "immediately to undertake the necessary actions to increase humanitarian assistance of the United Nations and its specialized agencies to the affected population in all parts of Somalia in liaison with the other international humanitarian organizations, and to this end, appoint a coordinator to oversee the effective delivery of this assistance".

On 11 March 1992, the Secretary-General reported[2] to the Security Council that while Mr. Ali Mahdi had confirmed his acceptance of resolution 733 (1992), General Aidid had raised some questions and called for reconsideration by the Council. General Aidid did not "indicate specifically whether or not he accepted the resolution". Both sides did, however, send delegations to New York for consultations on a cease-fire and on the framework for a sustained peacemaking effort. The Secretary-General also reported that although 68 States had informed him of their strict implementation of the arms embargo, "both Somali factions have claimed that the other side was receiving

[1]S/23445. [2]S/23693.

arms from some of the countries in the region". This observation continued to be made in successive reports the Secretary-General submitted to the Security Council. Although the Security Council set up a committee of the whole to monitor the implementation of the arms embargo, the flow of weapons into Somalia did not stop.

New York talks

The Secretary-General invited both factions of Mogadishu led by Mr. Ali Mahdi and General Aidid respectively to New York for consultations. The talks that began on 12 February 1992 had two main objectives. One was to get the commitment of the belligerent parties in Mogadishu to a cessation of hostilities and cease-fire that would permit the distribution of humanitarian aid. The second was to help the process of a political settlement by convening a conference on national reconciliation and unity. At a meeting on 12 February with the representatives of OAU, LAS, and the Organization of the Islamic Conference (OIC), who were also invited for consultations, the Secretary-General stressed the need for a common and cooperative approach and underlined the importance of the involvement of the regional and intergovernmental organizations. He also said that the consultations involving the belligerent factions in Mogadishu constituted an essential first step towards achieving durable peace. "They did not in any way imply recognition of any Somali faction".

On 13 February, the Secretary-General met separately with representatives of the two factions. On the same day and the next, Under-Secretary-General James Jonah headed a joint delegation of the United Nations, OAU, LAS and OIC in separate meetings with the representatives. Both sides committed themselves to an immediate cessation of hostilities and to a visit to Mogadishu by a delegation comprised of representatives of the United Nations and OAU, LAS and OIC, with the aim of working out an agreement to maintain the cease-fire. The representative of Mr. Ali Mahdi asserted in this connection that a cease-fire agreement without international monitoring and supervision would not hold.

Joint delegation

A joint delegation of the United Nations, OAU, LAS and OIC arrived in Mogadishu on 29 February. Over the next four days, the delegation met separately with Mr. Ali Mahdi and General Aidid, and on 3 March the two signed an "Agreement on the Implementation of a Cease-fire." Mr. Ali Mahdi had pressed unsuccessfully for a United Nations peace-keeping force to implement the cease-fire agreement, disarm civilians and protect the stockpiling and distribution of humanitarian aid. General Aidid only agreed to a United Nations security component for humanitarian aid convoys and military monitors — in civilian clothes, with blue berets and arm bands — for the cease-fire.

The implementation of the cease-fire involved the following arrangements: (1) The parties would order their forces to disengage and refrain from all hostilities and further deployment or action to extend territory under their control. (2) Commanders on both sides would ensure that their troops remained at their respective positions. (3) Both parties would facilitate the unimpeded flow and delivery of humanitarian aid to all in need. (4) Both parties would encourage and support the withdrawal of forces from airports and seaports to agreed locations, and turn over monitoring and security arrangements at the ports to the United Nations.

The two sides also agreed that a United Nations technical team would visit Mogadishu to work out a possible United Nations monitoring mechanism to stabilize the cease-fire. In principle, the mechanism would have as its civilian head a Special Representative of the Secretary-General, assisted by senior officials from the three regional organizations. Together, they would constitute a Joint Monitoring Commission (JMC) which would have under it United Nations military observers. In addition, a contingent of United Nations civilian police would be made available to JMC to facilitate the delivery of humanitarian aid in and around Mogadishu. As for the convening of a conference on national reconciliation, differences persisted on a variety of matters.

The Security Council on 17 March unanimously adopted resolution 746 (1992), urging the continuation of the United Nations humanitarian work in Somalia and strongly supporting the Secretary-General's decision to dispatch a technical team. It asked that the technical team develop a "high priority plan to establish mechanisms to ensure the unimpeded delivery of humanitarian assistance". Three days later, the Secretary-General appointed Mr. David Bassiouni as Coordinator to oversee the effective delivery of humanitarian aid to Somalia. Also on 20 March, the Secretary-General appointed a 15-member Technical Team for Somalia. Led by Mr. Robert Gallagher, the team included representatives of LAS, OAU, and OIC.

First technical team

The Technical Team found that General Aidid and Mr. Ali Mahdi continued to differ on United Nations involvement in dealing with the crisis. General Aidid reiterated his opposition to a United Nations peace-keeping force in Mogadishu and to any identifiable United Nations military presence. He called instead for international aid to be distributed by the United Somáli Congress/ Somali National Alliance (USC/SNA), of which he was chairman. Mr. Ali Mahdi, in contrast, said that without such a force, it would be impossible to maintain security and stability in Mogadishu or distribute humanitarian aid. On 27 and 28 March, agreements were, however, signed with the rival parties in Mogadishu to (a) deploy United Nations observers to monitor the cease-fire and (b) deploy United Nations security personnel to protect its personnel and safeguard its activities in continuing to provide humanitarian and other relief assistance in and around Mogadishu.

The Secretary-General then recommended[3] the establishment of the United Nations Operation in Somalia (UNOSOM), comprising 50 military observers to monitor the cease-fire, and a 500-strong infantry unit to "provide the United Nations convoys of relief supplies with a sufficiently strong military escort to deter attack and to fire effectively in self-defence if deterrence should not prove effective". Given the lack of suitable accommodation in Mogadishu, as well as security considerations, the Secretary-General recommended that the security personnel "as far as possible be accommodated on a ship which would perform the functions of a base camp, including the provision of logistic support to the mission". He also urged that UNOSOM be given the "usual civilian administrative support services" and that its vehicles "have distinctive United Nations colours and markings".

The Secretary-General submitted a 90-Day Plan of Action[4] to provide food and non-food supplies to some 1.5 million people immediately at risk and to help an additional 3.5 million people with food, seeds and basic health and water supply.

The latter group included many thousands of soldiers and other armed groups in programmes of disarmament and demobilization. The Plan called for increased United Nations humanitarian presence, with substantial expansion in the activities of UNICEF, the Office of the United Nations High Commissioner for Refugees (UNHCR) and WFP, backstopped by the United Nations Development Programme (UNDP), including the United Nations Volunteers (UNVs). They would all work closely with ICRC and other non-governmental aid agencies.

The effectiveness of the 90-day Plan of Action and subsequent programmes would be determined by all parties' observance of the basic principles of international humanitarian assistance. Distribution of relief assistance would be based upon equity and need, not political or geographical considerations. Designated corridors as well as zones of peace should be maintained to ensure the passage and distribution of assistance. These zones included seaports, airports and areas in which United Nations and non-governmental organization activities were under way. The inviolability of United Nations–flagged ships, aircraft and relief convoys and protection of relief workers were fundamental requisites. The principles incorporated the activities and security of all NGOs providing humanitarian assistance.

On 28 April 1992, the Secretary-General appointed Mr. Mohamed Sahnoun (Algeria) as Special Representative. Mr. Sahnoun took up residence in Mogadishu on 4 May and began a round of consultations with Somali leaders, including the traditional repositories of authority, the Elders of the clans. Accompanied by the representatives of OAU, LAS and OIC, he solicited the views of personalities throughout the country on the three major elements of his mandate. These were the monitoring of the cease-fire in Mogadishu and the cessation of hostilities throughout the country, the effective delivery of humanitarian assistance, and support for the process of national reconciliation.

[3]S/23829. [4]S/23829 Add.1.

B. UNOSOM I

UNOSOM established

On 24 April 1992, the Security Council, by resolution 751 (1992), decided to establish UNOSOM. The Council asked the Secretary-General to deploy immediately 50 unarmed but uniformed United Nations military observers and to continue consultations with the parties in Mogadishu in that regard. It took nearly two months for those consultations. On 23 June, the Secretary-General informed the Security Council that both principal factions in Mogadishu had agreed to the deployment of the unarmed observers. The observers, from Austria, Bangladesh, Czechoslovakia, Egypt, Fiji, Finland, Indonesia, Jordan, Morocco and Zimbabwe, were under a Chief Military Observer (CMO), Brigadier-General Imtiaz Shaheen of Pakistan.

The CMO and 3 observers arrived in Mogadishu on 5 July, only to be met with an immediate crisis. On 25 June, an Antonov aircraft with United Nations markings, which had been under charter by WFP, was alleged to have illegally carried Somali currency and military equipment from Nairobi for delivery to the Ali Mahdi faction in Mogadishu. Accusing United Nations personnel of bias, General Aidid then ordered the suspension of the deployment of United Nations observers. United Nations Headquarters, however, instructed CMO Shaheen to remain at his post, whereupon USC/SNA (headed by General Aidid) served him and his party with an expulsion notice. Deployment resumed after Mr. Sahnoun secured Mr. Ali Mahdi's agreement that the currency obtained from Nairobi would not be put into circulation.

Meanwhile, conditions within Somalia continued to deteriorate for the great majority of its people. To deal with this situation, the Secretary-General proposed[5] that the United Nations should enlarge its efforts to help bring about an effective cease-fire throughout the country, while at the same time pressing forward with parallel efforts to promote national reconciliation. It should establish a presence in all regions and adopt a comprehensive approach dealing with all aspects of the Somalia situation, namely humanitarian relief and recovery, the cessation of hostilities and security, the peace process and national reconciliation in a consolidated framework.

Operations should be structured in four zones: the north-west (Berbera), the north-east (Bossasso), the central rangelands and Mogadishu (Mogadishu), and the south (Kismayo). In each zone, a consolidated United Nations operation would carry out humanitarian activities, monitor the cease-fire and maintain security while helping combatants demobilize and disarm. The whole would be in the framework of national reconciliation efforts. A technical team would examine how the cease-fire could be monitored outside Mogadishu, the possible deployment of observers on the border with Kenya in the south-west, the feasibility of an "arms for food exchange programme, bearing in mind that this would require military personnel adequately armed and equipped", the military needs for the escort and protection of humanitarian aid convoys and a possible role for the United Nations in re-establishing local police forces.

The Secretary-General reported that all political leaders and Elders in Somalia had requested United Nations assistance in disarming the population and demobilizing the irregular forces. Such a programme had begun in some areas, such as north Mogadishu and parts of the north-west and the north-east, on the initiative of the local leaders themselves. Some leaders preferred the arms to be destroyed while others suggested that they should be retained for the new regular forces which would be created. The Secretary-General's Special Representative, working with the technical team, was to develop a plan for all areas of the country. There was similar wide support for rebuilding police forces.

"The desperate and complex situation in Somalia will require energetic and sustained efforts on the part of the international community to break the circle of violence and hunger" the Secretary-General said. The United Nations could support the process, but the conflict could only be resolved by the people of Somalia themselves. The Special Representative had already shown that he could help defuse potential local crises and facilitate the delivery of aid. The "new, comprehensive approach" was "intended to be a catalyst for achieving the vital objective of national reconciliation and the construction of peaceful, stable and democratic Somalia".

---

[5] S/24343.

Second technical team

In resolution 767 (1992) of 27 July, the Security Council approved the proposal to establish the four operational zones and strongly endorsed the sending of a technical team. The Secretary-General then asked former Assistant Secretary-General Peter Hansen (then with the Commission on Global Governance in Geneva, and later Under-Secretary-General for Humanitarian Affairs) to head the team, which visited Somalia from 6 to 15 August. It obtained the agreement of those concerned for the deployment of United Nations security units in two parts of the country. The first was for Bossasso in the north-east, to help provide security at the port, escort convoys of relief supplies to distribution centres and protect them during distribution. The second was to escort relief convoys overland to a new "preventive zone" in the Gedo region of Somalia along the border with Kenya. UNHCR would take the lead in establishing the zone, in order to reduce the swelling cross-border flow of refugees from Somalia.

UNOSOM grows

On 12 August, the Secretary-General reported to the Council that agreement had been reached on the deployment in Mogadishu of the 500-strong unit authorized under resolution 751 and that Pakistan had agreed to provide it. On 24 August 1992, he requested[6] an increase in the authorized strength of UNOSOM to create the four security zones. For each zone, he proposed that UNOSOM be provided with a unit of 750, all ranks. In addition to the two agreed areas, he proposed that units be posted to Berbera and Kismayo as soon as consultations with leaders there made it possible. The total strength of United Nations security personnel envisaged for Somalia thus rose to 3,500. On 28 August, the Security Council, by resolution 775 (1992), authorized the increase of UNOSOM as recommended. On 8 September, it agreed to a further addition of three logistical units with a total of 719 personnel, raising the total authorized strength of UNOSOM to 4,219 troops and 50 military observers. The first group of security personnel arrived in Mogadishu on 14 September 1992.

100-day plan

In tandem with these preparations, the Secretary-General took the initiative to improve planning and coordination of humanitarian ac-

tion. In the second week of September, Mr. Jan Eliasson, then Under-Secretary-General in the newly created Department of Humanitarian Affairs, led a high-level inter-agency mission to Somalia. After looking at the work being done by the six main United Nations organizations at work in Somalia (UNICEF, WFP, UNHCR, the Food and Agriculture Organization of the United Nations, the World Health Organization, and UNDP) and their 30 or so non-governmental partners in the field, the mission recommended that a 100-Day Action Programme for Accelerated Humanitarian Assistance be developed.

This plan was reviewed at a Coordination Meeting on Humanitarian Assistance to Somalia, chaired by the Special Representative, Mr. Sahnoun, in Geneva on 12–13 October 1992. The 100-Day plan had eight main objectives: (1) massive infusion of food aid; (2) aggressive expansion of supplementary feeding; (3) provision of basic health services and mass measles immunization; (4) urgent provision of clean water, sanitation and hygiene; (5) provision of shelter materials, including blankets and clothes; (6) simultaneous delivery of seeds, tools and animal vaccines with food rations; (7) prevention of further refugee outflows and the promotion of returnee programmes; (8) institution-building and rehabilitation of civil society. Of the $82.7 million requested for its implementation, $67.3 million was received.

Growing difficulties

The actual implementation of the programme proved difficult. The country-wide and more effective deployment of UNOSOM was impossible in the face of continuing disagreements among Somali factions on the role of the United Nations. Mr. Sahnoun resigned, and on 3 November it was announced that he would be replaced by Mr. Ismat Kittani, an Iraqi diplomat with long-standing connections to the United Nations.

The Secretary-General informed[7] the Security Council on 24 November of a number of disturbing developments immediately preceding the 8 November arrival of Mr. Kittani in Mogadishu. On 28 October, General Aidid declared that the Pakistani battalion would no longer be tolerated in the streets of Mogadishu. He also ordered the expulsion within 48 hours of the UNOSOM Coordinator for Humanitarian Assistance, Mr. Bassiouni, on the grounds that his activities went counter to the interests of the Somali

[6]S/24480. [7]S/24859.

people. He warned that any forcible UNOSOM deployment would be met by violence and that the deployment of United Nations troops in Kismayo and Berbera was no longer acceptable.

At the request of General Shaheen, who was by then UNOSOM Force Commander, the expulsion order on Mr. Bassiouni was extended by seven days, but General Aidid would not rescind it. Another disturbing trend was that "apparently at the instigation of local faction leaders" there was a widespread perception among Somalis that the United Nations had "decided to abandon its policy of cooperation" and was planning to "invade" the country. Despite a statement[8] to reassure Somalis issued by a spokesman for the Secretary-General on 2 November, "apprehensions over the alleged intention of the United Nations to resort to forcible action in Somalia" persisted.

General Aidid's forces shelled and shot at UNOSOM forces controlling the airport, and Mr. Ali Mahdi's forces shelled ships carrying food as they attempted to enter Mogadishu port. General Aidid objected to United Nations control of the airport; Mr. Ali Mahdi wanted UNOSOM to take full control of the port. On 13 November, after being shot at with machine-guns, rifles and mortars, the Pakistani troops in control of the airport returned fire. Although they remained in control of their position, the overall situation was bad.

In the absence of a government or governing authority capable of maintaining law and order, Somali authorities at all levels were competing for anything of value. International aid had become a major (and in some areas the only) source of income and was the target of all the authorities, sometimes no more than two or three bandits with guns. In essence, humanitarian supplies became the basis of an otherwise non-existent Somali economy.

Relief organizations experienced increased hijacking of vehicles, looting of convoys and warehouses and detention of expatriate staff. In the south-west, the confrontation between the supporters of General Aidid and those of former President Siad Barre made delivery of humanitarian aid extremely difficult. Massive amounts of relief supplies sat in storage, but the aid that reached hungry people was "often barely more than a trickle". The Secretary-General did not exclude the possibility that it might become necessary to review the basic premises and principles of the United Nations effort in Somalia.

The Security Council concluded that the situation was intolerable. On 25 November, it expressed strong support for the Secretary-General's view that it was time to move into Chapter VII of the Charter and asked him for specific recommendations on what the United Nations could do. The same afternoon, the Secretary-General received a visit from Mr. Lawrence Eagleburger, then Acting Secretary of State of the United States, who indicated that should the Security Council decide to authorize use of force by Member States to ensure the delivery of humanitarian aid in Somalia, his country would be ready to take the lead in organizing and commanding the operation.

Options for United Nations action

On 30 November 1992, the Secretary-General set out[9] five options for action. Two options did not involve the possible use of force: the withdrawal of military protection for the humanitarian effort and the continuation of existing operations without change. However, the Secretary-General dismissed these options as inadequate, noting that the Security Council had "no alternative but to decide to adopt more forceful measures to secure the humanitarian operations in Somalia".

As no government existed in Somalia that could request and allow the use of force, it would "be necessary for the Security Council to make a determination under Article 39 of the Charter that a threat to the peace exists, as a result of the repercussions of the Somali conflict on the entire region, and to decide what measures should be taken to maintain international peace and security. The Council would also have to determine that non-military measures as referred to in Chapter VII were not capable of giving effect to the Council's decisions".

Another factor was the military capability of the parties against which force was to be used. The troops in Mogadishu numbered several thousand when counting all the clans, sub-clans and free-roaming bandits. In south Mogadishu alone, there were approximately 150 "technical" vehicles, each of which carried a heavy machine-gun or 106 mm RR anti-tank gun and 8 to 12 soldiers armed mainly with AK 47s, G3 rifles and anti-armour RPG-7. The local forces had no uniforms and no communication. Vehicles were of different types, colours, patterns and shapes. The state of training was unknown but almost all would have had some kind of combat and weapons experience. The condition of their weapons was surprisingly good; ammunition was old but plentiful. In addi-

[8]SG/SM/4848. [9]S/24868.

tion, they had several operational armoured wheeled vehicles with cannons of 20 mm and dump trucks with twin 30mm AA guns. It was assumed that the equivalent military force existed in north Mogadishu. Both sides had indirect fire capabilities (mortars, field guns and free flight rockets).

Force would be used to ensure, on a lasting basis, that the violence against the international relief effort was brought to an end. To achieve that, it would be necessary for at least the heavy weapons of the organized factions to be neutralized and brought under international control and for the irregular forces and gangs to be disarmed. That action would help de facto to bring about a cease-fire.

The Secretary-General offered three options for consideration by the Council: (1) A show of force in Mogadishu by UNOSOM troops "to deter factions and other armed groups there and elsewhere in Somalia from withholding cooperation from UNOSOM". (2) A country-wide enforcement operation undertaken by a group of Member States authorized to do so by the Security Council. (3) A countrywide enforcement action undertaken under United Nations command and control.

In explaining the second option, the Secretary-General informed the Council of the offer by the United States to take the lead in such an operation. In the event the Security Council

chose that option, the enabling resolution could underline that the military operation was being authorized in support of the wider mandate entrusted to the Secretary-General to provide humanitarian relief and promote national reconciliation and reconstruction. The initial authorization could be for a specific period of time, followed by Security Council review at regular intervals. The enabling resolution might state the purpose of the operation was to resolve the immediate security problem and that it would be replaced with a United Nations peace-keeping operation as soon as the irregular groups had been disarmed and the heavy weapons of the organized factions brought under international control. The resolution could further stipulate that the operation would be conducted with full respect for international humanitarian law.

With regard to the final option — command and control of an enforcement action by the United Nations itself — the Secretary-General pointed out that while that would be consistent with the recent expansion of the Organization's role in the maintenance of international peace and security, the Secretariat was already overstretched in managing greatly enlarged peace-keeping commitments and did not have the capability to undertake an operation of the size and urgency required in Somalia.

C. UNITAF

Use of force

On 3 December 1992, the Security Council unanimously adopted resolution 794 (1992) welcoming the offer by a Member State to help create a secure environment for the delivery of humanitarian aid in Somalia and authorizing, under Chapter VII of the Charter, the use of "all necessary means" to do so. Statements in the Council before and after the adoption of the resolution included several by developing country members stressing that the uniqueness of the situation had necessitated resort to the enforcement provisions of the Charter.

Resolution 794 asked States to provide military forces and to make contributions in cash or kind. Appropriate mechanisms for coordination between the United Nations and those military

forces should be established by the Secretary-General and States participating in the operation, including attachment by the Secretary-General of a small UNOSOM liaison staff to the field headquarters of the unified command. Regular reports on progress in establishing a secure environment in Somalia should be provided by the Secretary-General and the participating States. The Council also asked the Secretary-General to provide a plan to ensure that UNOSOM would be able to fulfil its mandate upon the withdrawal of the unified command.

As for UNOSOM itself, the Security Council left it to the Secretary-General to decide when to further deploy the 3,500 personnel authorized by resolution 775 of 28 August. The Council did not, as the Secretary-General had suggested, set a time limit on its delegation of authority. Nor did it mention disarmament of the irregulars and controlling the heavy weaponry of the factions.

Operation Restore Hope

United States President George Bush responded to Security Council resolution 794 (1992) with a decision on 4 December to initiate "Operation Restore Hope". The Secretary-General wrote to President Bush on 8 December. Among other things, he described his concept of a division of labour between the United Nations and the United States in the following terms: "The United States has undertaken to take the lead in creating the secure environment which is an inescapable condition for the United Nations to provide humanitarian relief and promote national reconciliation and economic reconstruction, objectives which have from the outset been included in the various Security Council resolutions on Somalia".[10]

The first elements of the Unified Task Force (UNITAF) came ashore on the beaches of Mogadishu without opposition on 9 December 1992. On 13 December, the United States forces had secured the airfield at Baledogle, and by 16 December they had seized Baidoa. The first report of UNITAF was submitted to the Security Council on 17 December.[11] According to the report, the operation was proceeding generally as planned and was primarily driven by the ability of the Somalia port and airfield infrastructure to support the deployment of UNITAF forces. The United States Central Command, which was in charge of the combined operation, was following a four-phase programme to realize the objectives of securing major airports and seaports, key installations and food distribution points, and providing open and free passage of relief supplies, with security for convoys and relief organizations and those supplying humanitarian relief.

The first phase involved securing the airfield and seaport at Mogadishu with United States marine amphibious forces and elements of UNITAF and then expanding the operation to Baledogle and Baidoa with follow-on United States marine elements. In the second phase, a brigade of the United States army and UNITAF forces was to secure Baidoa and expand the lodgement area to secure the relief centres of Oddur, Belet Weyne and Gialassi. In the third phase, the operation would be extended to the south to secure the port and airfield at Kismayo, Bardera and the land route from Bardera to Baidoa. The final phase would be the transfer of responsibility to UNOSOM. As a

measure of the success of the operation, the report noted that the seaport in Mogadishu was open to traffic and relief supplies were said to be moving throughout the city.

The number of United States forces was expected to build to approximately 28,000 personnel, to be augmented by 17,000 UNITAF troops from over 20 countries, the report said. In addition to the United States forces, UNITAF included military units from Australia, Belgium, Botswana, Canada, Egypt, France, Germany, Greece, India, Italy, Kuwait, Morocco, New Zealand, Nigeria, Norway, Pakistan, Saudi Arabia, Sweden, Tunisia, Turkey, United Arab Emirates, United Kingdom and Zimbabwe.

In his letter to President Bush, the Secretary-General also stressed the importance of two conditions in relation to how and when the transition to continued peace-keeping operations could be made. Those two conditions were: (1) that UNITAF should take effective action to ensure that the heavy weapons of the organized factions were neutralized and brought under international control and that the irregular forces and gangs were disarmed before UNITAF withdrew; and (2) that UNITAF's authority be exercised throughout Somalia.

The Secretary-General established a policy group on Somalia at Headquarters in New York to meet with senior representatives of the United States Government to review the progress of the operation, composition of the Force, funding and planning for the future role of UNOSOM. Other coordinating mechanisms included an operational task force, and, in Somalia, close contacts between Special Representative Kittani and Force Commander Shaheen and UNITAF Commander Lieutenant-General Robert Johnson and the United States Special Envoy, Ambassador Robert Oakley. A small UNOSOM liaison staff was attached to UNITAF headquarters. The Secretary-General also initiated regular meetings to which all States participating in the Force were invited.

The fund requested by the Security Council in paragraph 11 of resolution 794 (1992) was established by the Secretariat. Known as the Trust Fund for Somalia—Unified Command, its initial target figure was set at $400 million.

National reconciliation

In the light of his Special Representative's continuing contacts with Somali parties and the results of a technical meeting between the United

[10]S/24992. [11]S/24976.

Nations and various Somali groups at Addis Ababa from 3 to 5 December, the Secretary-General decided to initiate the process of national reconciliation during the first phase of action by UNITAF. To that end, he convened an informal preparatory meeting for a conference of national reconciliation and unity to prepare a framework to enable the Somali people themselves to develop ideas and suggest arrangements for the formation of a government in accordance with their own traditions and values. The meeting was to seek consensus on the date, venue and list of participants of the formal conference and, if possible, a draft agenda.

The meeting lasted from 4 to 15 January 1993. Fourteen Somali political movements attended: Somali Africans Muki Organization (SAMO), Somali Democratic Alliance (SDA), Somali Democratic Movement (SDM), Somali National Democratic Union (SNDU), Somali National Front (SNF), Somali National Union (SNU), Somali Patriotic Movement (SPM), Somali Patriotic Movement (SPM)/(sna), Somali Salvation Democratic Front (SSDF), Southern Somali National Movement (SSNM)/(sna), United Somali Congress (USC)/(sna), United Somali Congress (USC), United Somali Front (USF) and United Somali Party (USP). Participants also included the Secretaries-General of LAS, OAU and OIC and the Chairman of the Standing Committee of the Countries of the Horn, as well as representatives of the Chairman of the Movement of Non-Aligned Countries.

The following three agreements were concluded and signed at the meeting: (1) General Agreement of 8 January 1993; (2) Agreement on implementing the cease-fire and on modalities of disarmament; (3) Agreement on the establishment of an ad hoc committee to help resolve the criteria for participation at, and the agenda for, the conference on national reconciliation, as well as any other issues pending from the informal meeting. Among other things, the informal meeting also agreed on the convening of a conference on national reconciliation in Addis Ababa on 15 March 1993. The Somali parties requested the United Nations, in consultation with the relevant regional and subregional organizations, to provide logistic support both prior to and during the conference.[12]

Transition from UNITAF to UNOSOM II

On 3 March 1993, the Secretary-General submitted to the Security Council his recommendations[13] for effecting the transition from UNITAF to UNOSOM II. He indicated that since the adoption of Council resolution 794 (1992) in December 1992, UNITAF had deployed approximately 37,000 troops in southern and central Somalia, covering approximately 40 per cent of the country's territory. The presence and operations of UNITAF had a positive impact on the security situation in Somalia and on the effective delivery of humanitarian assistance. He pointed out, however, that despite the improvement, a secure environment had not yet been established, and incidents of violence continued. There was still no effective functioning government in the country, no organized civilian police force and no disciplined national armed force. The security threat to personnel of the United Nations and its agencies, UNITAF, ICRC and NGOs was still high in some areas of Mogadishu and other places in Somalia. Moreover, there was no deployment of UNITAF or UNOSOM troops to the north-east and north-west, or along the Kenyan-Somali border, where security continued to be a matter of grave concern.

The Secretary-General concluded, therefore, that, should the Security Council determine that the time had come for the transition from UNITAF to UNOSOM II, the latter should be endowed with enforcement powers under Chapter VII of the United Nations Charter so as to be able to establish a secure environment throughout Somalia. To that end, UNOSOM II, under the mandate recommended by the Secretary-General, would seek to complete, through disarmament and reconciliation, the task begun by UNITAF for the restoration of peace, stability, law and order. The mandate would also empower UNOSOM II to provide assistance to the Somali people in rebuilding their economy and social and political life, re-establishing the country's institutional structure, achieving national political reconciliation, recreating a Somali State based on democratic governance and rehabilitating the country's economy and infrastructure.

The mandate of UNOSOM II, covering the whole territory of Somalia, would include the following military tasks: (a) monitoring that all factions continued to respect the cessation of hostilities and other agreements to which they had consented; (b) preventing any resumption of violence and, if necessary, taking appropriate action against any faction that violated or threatened to violate the cessation of hostilities; (c) maintaining control of the heavy weapons of the organized factions which would have been brought under international control pending their eventual de-

---

[12]S/25168 and annexes. [13]S/25354.

struction or transfer to a newly constituted national army; (d) seizing the small arms of all unauthorized armed elements and assisting in the registration and security of such arms; (e) securing or maintaining security at all ports, airports and lines of communications required for the delivery of humanitarian assistance; (f) protecting the personnel, installations and equipment of the United Nations and its agencies, ICRC as well as NGOs, and taking such forceful action as might be required to neutralize armed elements that attacked, or threatened to attack, such facilities and personnel, pending the establishment of a new Somali police force which could assume this responsibility; (g) continuing the programme for mineclearing in the most afflicted areas; (h) assisting in the repatriation of refugees and displaced persons within Somalia; (i) carrying out such other functions as might be authorized by the Security Council.

On the basis of the Addis Ababa agreements, a planning committee composed of senior officers from both UNITAF and UNOSOM had developed a "Somalia cease-fire disarmament concept". It would require the establishment of cantonments, the storage of heavy weapons, and sites for the temporary accommodation of factional forces. At those sites, they would turn in their small arms, register for future support from the government or non-governmental organizations and receive training for eventual reintegration into civilian life. Cantonment and transition sites would be separated from each other to prevent any possibility of factions or groups seizing the heavy weapons. Those failing to comply with timetables or other modalities of the disarmament process would have their weapons and equipment confiscated and/or destroyed.

According to the Secretary-General, UNOSOM II military operations would be conducted in four phases: (1) the transition of operational control from UNITAF, with continuing military support to relief activities and the disarming of factions; (2) the effective deployment and consolidation of United Nations operational con-

trol throughout Somalia and the border regions; (3) the reduction of UNOSOM II military activity, and assistance to civil authorities in exercising greater responsibility (phase three would end when a Somali national police force became operational and major United Nations military operations were no longer required); (4) the redeployment or reduction of UNOSOM II forces. The exact timing of transition from phase to phase would be determined to a large extent by political reconciliation efforts and rehabilitation programmes.

The deployment of UNOSOM II would be at the discretion of the Secretary-General, his Special Representative and the Force Commander acting under the authority of the Security Council. It would not be subject to the agreement of any local faction leaders. The Secretary-General estimated that it would be necessary to deploy a military component of 20,000 all ranks to carry out the assigned tasks and an additional 8,000 personnel to provide the logistic support. The United States Government agreed in principle to provide a tactical quick reaction force in support of the Force Commander of UNOSOM II. The United Nations force would also include civilian staff of approximately 2,800 individuals.

The Secretary-General suggested 1 May 1993 as the date of transfer of budgetary and administrative control from UNITAF to UNOSOM II. It was subsequently decided that the transfer of the military command would take place on 4 May. To head the new phase of operations, the Secretary-General appointed Admiral Jonathan Howe (Ret.) (United States) as his new Special Representative for Somalia for an initial period of three months, effective 9 March 1993. Admiral Howe was asked to oversee the transition from UNITAF to UNOSOM II and continue the tasks of promoting political reconciliation, coordinating humanitarian assistance and paving the way for rehabilitation and reconstruction of the country. Earlier, the Secretary-General had appointed Lieutenant-General Çevik Bir of Turkey as Force Commander of UNOSOM II.

D. UNOSOM II: March 1993–July 1994

Security Council acts

The Security Council acted unanimously on these recommendations in resolution 814 (1993) of 26 March 1993. The Council invoked Chapter VII of the Charter to expand the size and mandate of UNOSOM, authorizing it initially through 31 October 1993. It demanded that all Somali parties comply fully with the commitments they had undertaken, and in particular with the Agreement on Implementing the Cease-fire and on Modalities of Disarmament, and that they ensure the safety of the personnel of all organizations engaged in humanitarian and other assistance to Somalia. All States, in particular neighbouring ones, were called upon to cooperate in the implementation of the arms embargo established under resolution 733 (1992).

The Council also requested the Secretary-General, with assistance from all relevant United Nations entities, offices and specialized agencies, to provide humanitarian and other assistance to the people of Somalia in rehabilitating their political institutions and economy and promoting political settlement and national reconciliation. In addition to economic relief and rehabilitation of Somalia, the assistance was to include the repatriation of refugees and displaced persons within Somalia, the re-establishment of national and regional institutions and civil administration in the entire country, the re-establishment of Somali police, mine-clearance and public information activities in support of the United Nations activities in Somalia.

Humanitarian aid conference

The deployment of UNITAF forces improved the security situation and facilitated the flow of food and other emergency relief supplies into the neediest areas of Somalia. The level of malnutrition and death from starvation fell dramatically in many areas. In spite of the improvements, however, the humanitarian and political situation in many parts of the country remained difficult and tense. In the southern and central parts of Somalia, large numbers of people remained destitute and totally dependent on emergency aid. Measles, diarrhoea and other infections continued to take a heavy toll, particularly on small children. Lack of access to clean water sources and poor sanitation continued to present major health threats.

The Secretary-General viewed a secure environment as essential for the effective delivery of humanitarian assistance and for the reconstruction of Somalia. He identified three major challenges facing the United Nations in 1993: (1) facilitate the voluntary return of approximately 300,000 refugees and internally displaced persons; (2) help provide jobs and work for the many millions of unemployed Somalis, including members of armed gangs, militias and various private armies; (3) help the Somalis rebuild their society and rehabilitate its decayed infrastructure.

To achieve these aims, the United Nations, with the active participation of the Somalis, United Nations agencies, ICRC and NGOs, put together a new Relief and Rehabilitation Programme and convened a United Nations Conference on Humanitarian Assistance to Somalia, from 11 to 13 March 1993 in Addis Ababa under the chairmanship of the United Nations Under-Secretary-General for Humanitarian Affairs. The Conference was attended by some 190 Somali representatives, as well as senior representatives of donor Governments, international agencies, regional organizations and NGOs. The programme they adopted covered the period until December 1993, and included action in 10 priority areas: (1) re-establish local administrative capacity; (2) re-establish national and local police forces; (3) provide support services for women, particularly victims of violence and trauma; (4) repatriate some 300,000 refugees and over 1 million displaced persons within Somalia; (5) develop a food security system; (6) establish a basic health-care system; (7) increase the availability of potable water and of sanitation; (8) expand agriculture and enhance holdings of livestock; (9) create employment; and (10) re-establish primary education and vocational training.

Donors attending the conference pledged over $130 million of the estimated cost of $166.5 million to implement the Programme. It was anticipated that more funding would become available as the implementation of the various projects gained momentum.

National reconciliation conference

As agreed at the January 1993 informal meeting and following considerable preparatory work, the Conference on National Reconciliation in Somalia met on 15 March 1993 in Addis Ababa. It was chaired by the Secretary-General's Deputy Special Representative for Somalia, Mr. Lansana Kouyaté (Guinea), and attended by the leaders of 15 Somali political movements, as well as the representatives of LAS, OAU, OIC, the Standing Committee of the Countries of the Horn and the Non-Aligned Movement. After almost two weeks of intensive negotiations, the leaders of all 15 Somali political movements signed, on 27 March 1993, an Agreement of the First Session of the Conference of National Reconciliation in Somalia. At the closing session of the Conference on 28 March, the Agreement was unanimously endorsed, including by representatives of women's and community organizations, as well as elders and scholars.

The Agreement had four parts: disarmament and security, rehabilitation and reconstruction, restoration of property and settlement of disputes, and transitional mechanisms. The Somali parties resolved to put an end to armed conflict and to reconcile their differences through peaceful means. They agreed to consolidate and carry forward advances in peace, security and dialogue made since the beginning of 1993 and reaffirmed commitment to comply fully with the January 1993 Addis Ababa cease-fire agreement, which provided for the handing over of weapons and ammunition to UNITAF and UNOSOM II.

Over a two-year transitional period from 27 March 1993 the agreement provided for the following four basic organs of authority:

- Transitional National Council (TNC): The repository of Somali sovereignty and the prime political authority, with legislative powers. To consist of 74 members, with three representatives (two men and one woman) from each of the 18 regions of the country, one from each of the 15 political movements, and five from Mogadishu. It would appoint a committee to draft a transitional Charter, guided by the basic principles of the Universal Declaration of Human Rights and Somalia's traditional ethics.

- Central Administrative Departments: Responsible for the re-establishment and operation of departments of civil administration and social, economic and humanitarian affairs, thus preparing for the restoration of a formal Government.

- Regional Councils: One in each of the 18 regions of the country, with 3 representatives from each district council.

- District councils: One in each of the 92 districts in the country. Members to be appointed through election or through consensus-based selection in accordance with Somali traditions.

The Somali parties invited the Secretary-General and his Special Representative to extend all necessary assistance to the people of Somalia to implement the agreement.

Incidents on 5 June

Following the transition from UNITAF to UNOSOM II in May 1993, it became clear that, although signatory to the March Agreement, General Aidid's faction would not cooperate in the Agreement's implementation. Attempts by UNOSOM II to implement disarmament led to increasing tensions and, on 5 June, to violence. In a series of armed attacks against UNOSOM II troops throughout south Mogadishu by Somali militia apparently belonging to General Aidid's faction, 25 Pakistani soldiers were killed, 10 were reported missing and 54 wounded. The bodies of the victims were mutilated and subjected to other forms of degrading treatment. The Secretary-General, on 6 June,[14] strongly condemned this "treacherous act" against peace-keepers "who were on a mission of peace, reconciliation and reconstruction" and urged prompt and firm action against the perpetrators. Special Representative Howe stated that the soldiers were "murdered as they sought to serve the neediest people in the city". He said that 12 of the soldiers were helping unload food at a feeding station "when they were foully attacked by cowards who placed women and children in front of armed men".

The Security Council reacted to these developments in resolution 837 (1993) on 6 June. It strongly condemned the unprovoked armed attacks against UNOSOM II which "appear to have been part of a calculated and premeditated series of cease-fire violations to prevent by intimidation

[14]SG/SM/5005.

UNOSOM II from carrying out its mandate". It reaffirmed that the Secretary-General was authorized under resolution 814 (1993) to take all necessary measures against those responsible for the armed attacks and for publicly inciting them, including their arrest and detention for prosecution, trial and punishment. The Council requested him to investigate the incident, particularly on the role of the factional leaders involved.

The Council demanded that all Somali parties comply fully with their commitments regarding political reconciliation, cease-fire and disarmament. It reaffirmed the crucial importance of the early implementation of the disarmament of all Somali parties and of neutralizing radio broadcasting systems that contributed to the violence and attacks against UNOSOM II. On 8 June, 11 Somali parties condemned the attacks and expressed support for Security Council resolution 837 (1993).

UNOSOM II responds militarily

To implement resolution 837 (1993), UNOSOM II initiated military action on 12 June 1993, conducting a series of air and ground military actions in south Mogadishu. UNOSOM II removed Radio Mogadishu from the control of USC/SNA (General Aidid's faction), and disabled or destroyed militia weapons and equipment in a number of storage sites and clandestine military facilities. The Secretary-General, in a statement[15] released on the same day, said that the objective of the action was to restore peace to Mogadishu "so that the political reconciliation, rehabilitation and disarmament process can continue to move forward throughout Somalia". He stated that this should be seen in the context of the international community's commitment to the national disarmament programme endorsed by all Somali parties at Addis Ababa on 27 March 1993.

The action by UNOSOM II was strongly supported by the Security Council.[16] At the same time, the Council expressed deep regret at any civilian casualties caused, adding that an investigation was under way into an incident on 13 June which had involved such casualties among the Somalis. Preliminary reports indicated that General Aidid and his supporters had used civilians, including women and children, as human shields for attacks on UNOSOM II.

On 18 June, the Security Council condemned[17] the practice of "some Somali factions and movements in using women and children as human shields to perpetrate their attacks against UNOSOM", and deplored the civilian deaths that

had resulted "despite the timely measures adopted to prevent this from happening".

Aidid asked to surrender

In parallel with its disarmament operations, UNOSOM II instituted an investigation of the 5 June incident. On 17 June, citing mounting evidence implicating SNA militia in the attack, the Special Representative called on General Aidid to surrender peacefully to UNOSOM II and to urge his followers to surrender their arms. He directed the UNOSOM Force Commander to detain General Aidid for investigation of the 5 June attack and of the public incitement of such attacks. General Aidid would be treated "decently, fairly and with justice", the Special Representative said. However, efforts to capture General Aidid proved unsuccessful, and attacks on UNOSOM II by his militia continued.

The Secretary-General reported[18] to the Security Council that the short-sighted attitude of leaders of a few factions aggravated the already difficult situation. The ambushing of UNOSOM II personnel on 5 June and on subsequent occasions left UNOSOM II with no choice but to take forceful action to effect the disarming required by all Somali factions under the Addis Ababa agreement. The Secretary-General again asserted that effective disarmament of all the factions and warlords was a precondition for implementing other aspects of UNOSOM's mandate, be they political, civil, humanitarian, rehabilitation or reconstruction. He said that Somalia would not enjoy stability until criminal elements were apprehended and brought to justice as demanded by Security Council resolution 837 (1993).

On 22 September 1993, the Security Council, in resolution 865 (1993), reaffirmed the importance it attached to the successful fulfillment, on an urgent and accelerated basis, of UNOSOM II's objectives—facilitation of humanitarian assistance and the restoration of law and order and of national reconciliation in a free, democratic and sovereign Somalia—so that the mission could be completed by March 1995. In that context, the Council requested the Secretary-General to direct urgent preparation of a detailed concerted strategy with regard to UNOSOM II's humanitarian, political and security activities. The Security Council also approved the Secretary-General's recommendations relating to the re-establishment of the Somali police, judicial and penal systems.

[15]SG/SM/5009. [16]SC/5647. [17]SC/5650. [18]S/26317.

3 October incidents

After the June 1993 events, UNOSOM II pursued a coercive disarmament programme in south Mogadishu. Active patrolling, weapons confiscations and operations were directed at the militia and depots of General Aidid's faction (USC/SNA). A public information campaign was instituted to explain these activities to the population. Concurrently, UNOSOM II encouraged "cooperative" or voluntary disarmament by the Somali factions. UNOSOM II also continued its efforts to apprehend those responsible for instigating and committing armed attacks against United Nations personnel.

In support of the UNOSOM II mandate, United States forces—the United States Rangers and the Quick Reaction Force—were deployed in Mogadishu. These forces were not under United Nations command and control. As part of the coercive programme, the Rangers launched an operation in south Mogadishu on 3 October 1993, aimed at capturing a number of key aides of General Aidid who were suspected of complicity in the 5 June attack, as well as subsequent attacks on United Nations personnel and facilities. The operation succeeded in apprehending 24 suspects, including two key aides to General Aidid. During the course of the operation, two United States helicopters were shot down by Somali militiamen using automatic weapons and rocket-propelled grenades. While evacuating the 24 USC/SNA detainees, the Rangers came under concentrated fire. Eighteen United States soldiers lost their lives and 75 were wounded. One United States helicopter pilot was captured and subsequently released on 14 October 1993. The bodies of the United States soldiers were subjected to public acts of outrage, and the scenes were broadcast by television stations around the world.

Following these events, the United States reinforced its Quick Reaction Force with a joint task force consisting of air, naval and ground forces equipped with M1A1 tanks and Bradley fighting vehicles. At the same time, United States President William Clinton announced the intention of his country to withdraw its forces from Somalia by 31 March 1994.

On 9 October 1993, USC/SNA declared a unilateral cessation of hostilities against UNOSOM II forces. After this declaration the situation was generally quiet, but Mogadishu remained tense and, in the capital and elsewhere, major factions were reportedly rearming, in apparent anticipation of renewed fighting.

Secretary-General reviews situation

The Secretary-General travelled to the Horn of Africa in October 1993 to consult with the leaders of the region on the future of UNOSOM II and on a concerted strategy for humanitarian, political and security activities. He met with President Hosni Mubarak of Egypt, President Hassan Gouled of Djibouti, President Daniel Arap Moi of Kenya and President Meles Zenawi of Ethiopia. He also visited Baidoa and Mogadishu, where he met with military and civilian officials of UNOSOM II as well as with Somali elders, and attended a meeting convened in Cairo by President Mubarak, then OAU Chairman, attended by the Secretaries-General of OAU, LAS and OIC.

After his return to New York, the Secretary-General addressed a letter[19] to the Security Council on 28 October 1993, asking for an interim extension of the UNOSOM II mandate, which was to expire on 31 October. This was to allow time for further consultations aimed at preparing a detailed report. The Security Council, by its resolution 878 (1993) of 29 October, extended the UNOSOM II mandate until 18 November 1993.

On 12 November 1993, the Secretary-General reviewed[20] for the Security Council the priorities of the United Nations role in Somalia—the highest of which was humanitarian relief. He pointed to the dramatic and visible success that had been achieved in reducing starvation deaths and conditions of famine in the country. Significant improvements had also been made in the fields of public health, education, agriculture and other areas. Some 32 hospitals were operating throughout the country by November 1993, as well as 81 maternal and child health centres. One hundred and three mobile vaccination teams were covering the country, working towards sustainable immunization coverage. It was estimated that about 75 per cent of children under 5 years of age had received vaccination against measles. Medicines, supplies, and other equipment were being made available to hospitals, health centres and pharmacies through United Nations agencies and NGOs.

City water-supply systems in a number of cities, including Mogadishu, were rehabilitated. United Nations agencies and NGOs were continuing to pursue sanitation and employment projects with food-for-work programmes. In Mogadishu alone, there were 120 such projects that provided food for teachers and hospitals. Similar projects

[19]S/26663. [20]S/26738.

were supported throughout Somalia. United Nations agencies and NGOs were also assisting in re-opening schools, supplying school lunches, providing education kits, textbooks and incentives to teachers.

In the agricultural sector, which had provided two thirds of Somalia's pre-war employment and nearly three quarters of the country's foreign exchange earnings, the food production and livestock sectors had been revived. The United Nations system had provided seeds and agricultural tools, and with the end of the drought, it had been possible to raise food production significantly. In the livestock sector, the supply of veterinary drugs and the vaccination of animals facilitated the resuscitation of exports.

Commercial and trading activities were also showing encouraging signs of recovery. Commercial traffic at Somalia's ports had increased dramatically since December 1992. Civilian ship movements at Mogadishu port increased tenfold in the first half of 1993. Joint ventures between Somali and foreign investors were on the rise. Telecommunication services became available in parts of Mogadishu. Local companies were also providing fuel throughout the country.

At the request of UNOSOM II, a draft framework for planning of long-term reconstruction and recovery had been prepared by a task force comprising donors, United Nations agencies and NGOs, under the coordination of the World Bank. The objectives of the framework were to: (a) establish a common vision of the economic and social reconstruction, rehabilitation and development of Somalia; (b) identify criteria and establish priorities for reconstruction and rehabilitation; (c) construct a mechanism for coordinated action in an environment of constrained human and capital resources. An informal meeting of donors, United Nations agencies and NGOs in Paris, the third in a series organized by the World Bank, reviewed the draft framework and discussed the implementation of the programme on 22 October 1993.

By November 1993, of some 1.7 million people displaced as a result of the turmoil and the famine in Somalia, more than 1 million had crossed into Kenya and Ethiopia. Over 250,000 persons moved to Mogadishu, and about 60,000 persons to Kismayo and Baidoa. The northern regions were supporting at least 250,000 refugees and internally displaced persons. The number of refugees returning from camps in Kenya was increasing. It was estimated that about 70,000 refugees in the Mombasa area had returned by boat to Kismayo, Mogadishu and Bossasso. Assistance was being provided to approximately 800 refugees a week returning to the Gedo region and to those spontaneously moving into the Lower and Middle Juba areas.

The Secretary-General told the Council that his Special Representative and staff were continuing efforts to rebuild political institutions in Somalia. Thirty-nine district councils, considered to be a foundation for civil government, had been established. In Mogadishu, consultations had begun on the establishment of district councils. Efforts were continuing to expedite the formation of regional councils, the next layer of political reconstruction. By November 1993, regional councils had been established in six areas.

UNOSOM II continued to attach high priority to the national reconciliation process in Somalia. In this regard, it undertook to resolve conflicts at the regional level and to assist in reconciliation among the Somali people. A regional peace conference convened in Kismayo, one of the most conflict-ridden areas of the country, brought together 152 elders from throughout the Juba region; on 6 August 1993, they signed the Jubaland peace agreement, committing the more than 20 clans in the region. A series of similar reconciliation meetings were held in other regions of Somalia.

In the north-east and central regions, from Bossasso to Galkayo, the Deputy Special Representative and UNOSOM II political affairs officers facilitated the reconciliation of the leadership of two competing wings of the Somali Salvation Democratic Front (SSDF). There was also a reconciliation of clans in the north-west, in Erigavo, and in the Gedo region. In Mogadishu, several meetings were held between UNOSOM II officials and a 47-member supreme committee of the Hawiye sub-clan. From 30 September to 1 October 1993, an all-Somali conference attended by 600 delegates was supported by UNOSOM II. Another pan-Hawiye conference took place in Mogadishu from 14 to 16 October 1993 with the participation of Habr Gedir sub-clan (to which General Aidid belonged).

The Secretary-General also told the Council that UNOSOM II was continuing to support small locally based police forces in its areas of operations as a step towards establishing a neutral and professional Somali police force. Since May 1993, 5,000 former Somali policemen had been hired to assist in the performance of police functions. UNOSOM II was finalizing a basic police training programme for Somali policemen. Meanwhile, a number of States pledged contributions for various programmes to re-establish the Somali judicial and penal systems. Some countries provided police advisers or trainers.

In order to investigate violations of international humanitarian law, UNOSOM II was planning to establish an Office of Human Rights. A team of international specialists, in cooperation with Somali police, were to investigate violations such as mass murder of Somali citizens and attacks and threats made against international assistance workers and UNOSOM II personnel.

Critical juncture

Despite the progress achieved in many areas, however, the Secretary-General stressed that UNOSOM II was at a critical juncture, as the situation in Somalia was continuously evolving. There was still no effectively functioning government, no disciplined national armed force, and no organized civilian police force or judiciary, although impressive progress had been achieved in initiating the recreation of the police and judiciary.

UNOSOM II's record of general progress throughout most of Somalia was seriously marred by the incidents that had taken place between 5 June and 3 October 1993. Those incidents challenged the cause of disarmament and reconciliation in Somalia, created a situation of instability in south Mogadishu, and stimulated factional elements elsewhere to prepare for a future of renewed fighting. The Secretary-General reiterated his firm belief that without effective disarmament of all the factions and warlords in Somalia it would not be possible for the country to enjoy lasting peace and stability.

Voluntary disarmament had nevertheless succeeded to some extent both during UNITAF and in the early weeks of UNOSOM II. It was only after 5 June 1993 that it became necessary for UNOSOM II to resort to coercive methods. The situation in Somalia, he observed, would continue to remain complex and complicated for the foreseeable future, and the Security Council would have to display flexibility as well as firmness in any decision that it would take while renewing the mandate of UNOSOM II.

In presenting his recommendations on a renewed mandate for UNOSOM II, the Secretary-General pointed out that, following the events of 3 October 1993, the United States had announced its intention to withdraw all its combat troops and the bulk of its logistics support troops by 31 March 1994. He stressed that the troop-contributing countries could not be expected to maintain their generosity forever, nor could Member States be expected to maintain funding on the present scale. The Governments of Belgium, France and Sweden had earlier announced their decisions to withdraw their contingents from UNOSOM II. The Secretary-General wrote to 42 Member States inviting them to contribute, or to increase their contribution, in terms of troops and logistics support.

Three options

In light of the changing circumstances, the Secretary-General went on to present three options for the Security Council to consider in re-examining the mandate of UNOSOM II. In the first option, the mandate of UNOSOM II, as laid down by the Security Council in its resolutions 814 (1993), 837 (1993), 865 (1993) and 878 (1993), would remain essentially unchanged. UNOSOM II would not take the initiative to resort systematically to coercive methods to enforce disarmament. It was hoped that all factions, including USC/SNA, would cooperate to ensure peaceful conditions. In Mogadishu, USC/SNA would have to remove its roadblocks and strong points so that UNOSOM II could escort humanitarian convoys. Should these expectations not be met, UNOSOM II should retain the capability for coercive disarmament and retaliation against attacks on its personnel. UNOSOM II would also pursue its plans to re-establish an impartial and professional Somali police force and judicial system. The objective would be to create and maintain secure conditions for humanitarian assistance, foster national reconciliation and implement other parts of the existing mandate.

Under this option, UNOSOM II would need the reauthorization of its troop strength, as well as the deployment of an additional brigade. In addition, the Member States should fulfil their financial obligations, promptly and in full, of approximately $1 billion annually.

In the second option, the Security Council would decide that UNOSOM II would not use coercive methods anywhere in the country, rely on the cooperation of the Somali parties in discharging its mandate and use force only in self-defence. Disarmament would be entirely voluntary. Under this option, UNOSOM II would have to retain some capability to defend its personnel should inter-clan fighting resume. The emphasis would be on ensuring the unimpeded flow of humanitarian assistance, the rehabilitation of the Somali infrastructure, the repatriation of refugees, political reconciliation, the reorganization of the Somali

UNOSOM II deployment as of November 1993

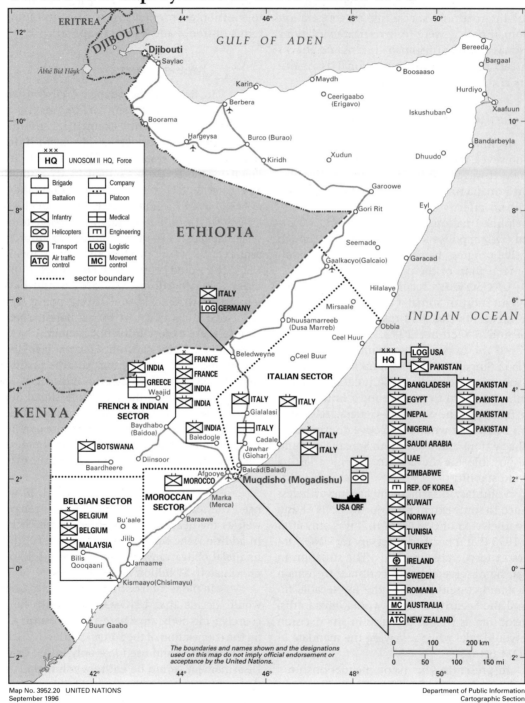

Map No. 3952.20 UNITED NATIONS
September 1996

Department of Public Information
Cartographic Section

police and judicial system and keeping secure the main supply routes between Mogadishu and outside areas.

The troop requirement under this option would be approximately 16,000 all ranks, with one brigade deployed in Mogadishu, one assigned to convoy duty and one for the security of refugees and of critical areas in need of assistance. A Force Logistics Supply Command of about 2,500 all ranks would also be needed. The financial requirements for this option would be considerably less than the first option.

Under the third option, UNOSOM II would be limited to keeping secure the airport and port in Mogadishu, as well as important ports and airports in other parts of the country, to maintain open supply routes for humanitarian purposes. It would assist in the delivery of humanitarian aid, help development agencies and programmes, and continue training a Somali police force. That option would presuppose cooperation of local authorities and would focus on the regions, rather than on Mogadishu. It would call for the deployment of about 5,000 all ranks and a financial requirement substantially less than the other two options.

The Secretary-General further noted that, in the mean time, UNOSOM II troop strength was adequate for the present purpose. UNOSOM II would not use coercive methods to ensure a secure environment which, by and large, was lacking mainly in south Mogadishu. UNOSOM II would continue its efforts to initiate a political dialogue with all the factions, including USC/SNA. In this, UNOSOM II would seek and welcome support from Somalia's neighbours, Djibouti, Ethiopia and Kenya, and from OAU, LAS and OIC. At the same time, UNOSOM II would stand ready to protect its own personnel as well as the personnel of other intergovernmental and non-governmental organizations. UNOSOM II might also have to be prepared to use force to keep open the lines of communication and supply routes in Mogadishu and elsewhere.

Commission of inquiry

On 16 November 1993, the Security Council adopted resolution 885 (1993) authorizing a Commission of Inquiry, in further implementation of its resolutions 814 (1993) and 837 (1993), to investigate armed attacks on UNOSOM II personnel which led to casualties among them. The Secretary-General recommended[21] a three-member Commission of Inquiry comprised of the Honour-

able Matthew S.W. Ngulube, the Chief Justice of Zambia (Chairman), General Emmanuel Erskine (Ret.) of Ghana and General Gustav Hagglund of Finland. Mr. Winston Tubman of the United Nations Office of Legal Affairs and former Minister of Justice of Liberia was designated as Executive Secretary of the Commission.

In accordance with the decision of the Council, pending the completion of the report of the Commission, UNOSOM II suspended arrest actions against those suspected, and, by the end of November 1993, all but eight of those arrested and detained following the June 1993 incidents were released. Like most of the others, these were officials of General Aidid's faction. On 17 January 1994, the last eight detainees were released. The Secretary-General ordered their release after receiving a report from Mr. Enoch Dumbutshena, the independent jurist and former Chief Justice of Zimbabwe, who had been asked to review the cases of the detainees. Also, from 13 to 16 January, a Hirab Peace Conference was held. The Habr Gedir and Abgal sub-clans concluded a peace agreement at the Conference. Although neither Mr. Ali Mahdi nor General Aidid attended that meeting, it was considered to be a development conducive to reconciliation between the two sub-clans to which they belonged.

Review of mandate set

In renewing the mandate of UNOSOM II for a period of six months to 31 May 1994, the Security Council, on 18 November 1993, decided in resolution 886 (1993) that it would fundamentally review that mandate by 1 February 1994. It asked for a report from the Secretary-General on or before 15 January on the progress made by the Somali people towards national reconciliation. The Council further requested the Secretary-General to supply, as part of his report, an updated plan for UNOSOM II's future humanitarian, political and security strategies.

Affirming that the Addis Ababa agreements of 8 January and 27 March 1993 had established a sound basis for resolving the problems in Somalia, the Council reminded all the parties that continued United Nations involvement in Somalia depended on their active cooperation and tangible progress towards a political settlement. The Council expressed concern at the destabilizing effects of cross-border arms flows in the region and called for the cessation of such flows and reaffirmed the

[21]S/26823.

obligation of all States to fully implement the embargo on weapons and military equipment to Somalia. In addition, the Council condemned the continued armed attacks against persons engaged in humanitarian and peace-keeping efforts and paid tribute to those troops and humanitarian personnel who had been killed or injured while serving in Somalia.

Comprehensive review

To facilitate the Council's fundamental review of the UNOSOM II mandate, the Secretary-General submitted a comprehensive report[22] on 6 January 1994. He pointed to two primary obstacles on the political level: (1) deep divisions between the two main factional alliances, the Group of 12 supporting Mr. Ali Mahdi and SNA led by General Aidid; (2) the continued rejection by USC/SNA of all political initiatives undertaken by UNOSOM II.

From 2 to 11 December 1993, at the invitation of the Ethiopian Government and with the support of UNOSOM II, representatives of the two main alliances, the Group of 12 and SNA, met to discuss outstanding matters and disputes between them. Despite warnings from the international community that failure to achieve progress on the political front could drive away the needed international assistance, the factional representatives failed to agree on a structure for face-to-face talks between their leaders.

There were also sharp differences of opinion between the Group of 12 and SNA on a number of other key issues, including the status of the district and regional councils, and SNA's suggestion that the Addis Ababa agreement be revised. Moreover, SNA continued to insist that the United Nations had no role to play in political reconciliation in Somalia, preferring this to be done by regional Powers, while the Group of 12 held the view that UNOSOM II should remain in Somalia and that the United Nations must play a key role in the Somali political process.

The Secretary-General saw support of national reconciliation as a key task of UNOSOM II. Simultaneously, it would continue to convey the message to Somali factional leaders that the international community was not prepared to wait indefinitely for an improved security environment in which to work on behalf of the Somali people.

Fourteen additional district councils had been certified during November and December 1993, bringing the total to 52 out of 81 districts (excluding the north-west). A primary obstacle to the effective establishment of district councils in

Somalia had been the opposition of SNA, which had refused to participate in the process and had in some instances attempted to block their formation through intimidation or the creation of shadow SNA district councils. Eight regional councils had been formed. In all 13 were needed, excluding the north-west. With the exception of the SNA factions, participants in the Addis Ababa political meetings had expressed a strong intention to work towards the rapid establishment of TNC. At that time, UNOSOM II had received nine nominations for representatives from the 15 political factions, each of which might nominate one representative to TNC. In addition, regional councils, to nominate three representatives each, began deliberations for the selection of their representatives to TNC.

UNITAF/UNOSOM II had re-established 107 police stations in Somalia's districts. Nationally, there were 6,737 policemen at the regional and district levels, 311 judicial personnel in 8 regions and 26 districts, and over 700 prison officers in two regions. It was also planned to put in place a Somali police rapid deployment force, known as Darawishta, by March 1994. The re-establishment of police forces and justice systems was particularly important in the north-east, where no United Nations military forces had been deployed.

UNOSOM II had renewed its effort to place humanitarian programmes at the forefront of its work in Somalia. However, despite successful efforts to end famine in the country, there were indications that malnutrition levels were on the rise again in parts of Somalia, including Mogadishu and the Juba valley, two areas of ongoing conflict and insecurity. Consequently, the Division for the Coordination of Humanitarian Affairs of UNOSOM II, United Nations agencies and NGOs had stepped up efforts to provide emergency food relief and medical treatment to the affected population.

Although resettlement programmes were slowed by insecurity in parts of Somalia, UNOSOM II continued to cooperate with UNHCR and other agencies to facilitate the safe and orderly return of Somali refugees and internally displaced persons. Particularly successful resettlement projects were undertaken in the Juba valley, where, since October 1993, over 3,000 persons had returned from camps in Kenya, and from those in Kismayo and Mogadishu.

The Fourth Coordination Meeting on Humanitarian Assistance for Somalia was held at Ad-

[22]S/1994/12.

dis Ababa from 29 November to 1 December 1993. Representatives from Somali regions, political movements and the international donor community reaffirmed their commitment to accelerate Somali control of the rehabilitation and development process. In the Declaration of the meeting, the participants reaffirmed the commitment of the international community to provide unconditionally essential emergency assistance to vulnerable groups. Assistance would be provided in those areas where stability and security had been attained. The Declaration called for Somali initiatives in establishing viable civil institutions and appropriate mechanisms to facilitate the reconstruction and recovery of Somalia. The Somali representatives committed themselves to establish preconditions to end insecurity, and the donor community agreed to support fully mechanisms established to determine rehabilitation priorities, funding modalities and implementation and to develop a common approach among themselves for the allocation of resources. For its part, UNOSOM committed itself to work with all concerned agencies and organizations to strengthen coordination of all aspects of the United Nations efforts throughout Somalia — humanitarian, political and peace-keeping.

The Declaration called for an aid coordination body composed of representatives of donors, United Nations agencies and programmes, NGOs and other multilateral and regional institutions and organizations. Technical support for the regional committees would be provided by the United Nations Office of Development, under the umbrella of the Humanitarian Division of UNOSOM II. The Office would also serve as secretariat for the development council and for the aid coordinating body. The participants agreed that the Declaration should be translated into a plan of action.

As for the security situation, banditry continued to plague parts of the countryside, and there were outbreaks of localized inter-clan fighting. A number of incidents involving threats and actual attacks against international agencies in outlying regions forced several NGOs to temporarily suspend their operations. In Mogadishu itself, while direct armed confrontation between USC/SNA and UNOSOM II forces had been avoided, armed banditry grew considerably, making movement for Somali commercial traffic, UNOSOM personnel and international humanitarian relief supplies increasingly dangerous. Security for international staff remained a troublesome issue. In a number of separate incidents, casualties were suffered by UNOSOM civilian and NGO staff, both international and local, on the streets of Mogadishu. As a result, there was a significant reduction in the presence of international NGOs willing to work in such an environment.

The Secretary-General reaffirmed that general disarmament was a prerequisite for the establishment of the peaceful and secure environment. However, despite UNOSOM II efforts to promote voluntary disarmament by the Somali parties, there were growing indications that the major factions were actively rearming in anticipation of renewed hostilities in the coming months. The Secretary-General appealed to the parties to commit themselves once again to the disarmament process agreed upon at Addis Ababa and to work constructively with UNOSOM II in order to determine how to implement these commitments.

Progress notwithstanding, the Secretary-General concluded that the mandate of UNOSOM II was far from being achieved. Only when the Addis Ababa agreement of March 1993 was fully implemented, culminating in the holding of general elections and the installation of a popularly elected Government could that mandate be considered fully implemented. A spirit of cooperation, compromise and commitment on the part of the Somali people and the continued involvement of the international community were needed to reach that goal.

Without the continued stabilizing presence of an adequate United Nations force, there would be an early resumption of civil strife and an unravelling of all that had been achieved, the Secretary-General said. The peace-building process, therefore, would depend on the willingness of United Nations Member States to see the Somalia operation to its successful conclusion. He was doubtful that UNOSOM II would have the required level of resources after 31 March 1994, when the military strength would be reduced to 19,700. Although the Secretary-General had approached a large number of United Nations Member States for contributions to UNOSOM II's military component, not a single positive response had been received. Another important question was the availability of timely and adequate financing for UNOSOM II operations.

The Secretary-General recalled that, in his 12 November 1993 report, he had outlined three options relating to the mandate and functioning of UNOSOM II. The first option, which he preferred, had to be excluded because of the inadequacy of human, material and financial resources. He therefore recommended the second option for consideration by the Security Council. Under it, UNOSOM II would not use coercive methods but would rely on the cooperation of the Somali parties. In the event that inter-clan fighting resumed in different parts of the country, UNOSOM II, while not becoming involved in the fighting, would retain some capability to defend its personnel. UNOSOM II would protect the important ports and airports in the country as well as the essential infrastructure of Somalia; keep open the main supply routes between Mogadishu and outlying areas; pursue as a matter of utmost priority the reorganization of the Somali police and judicial systems; and help with the repatriation of refugees. UNOSOM II would also continue its efforts to provide emergency humanitarian relief supplies to all in need throughout the country.

UNOSOM II would continue to coordinate rehabilitation and development activities so as to assist international programmes of assistance in areas of their choice. The Secretary-General recalled that the donor community had made it clear at the Fourth Humanitarian Conference in Addis Ababa that aid would go only to those regions where security prevailed and where counterpart Somali institutions were available. As for the political processes in Somalia, UNOSOM II would continue to play a role as desired by the Somali people.

Mandate revised

By its resolution 897 (1994) of 4 February 1994, the Security Council approved the Secretary-General's recommendation for the continuation of UNOSOM II, with a mandate to: assist the Somali parties in implementing the Addis Ababa Agreements, particularly in their cooperative disarmament and cease-fire efforts; protect major ports, airports and essential infrastructure; provide humanitarian relief to all in need throughout the country; assist the reorganization of the Somali police and judicial system; help repatriate and resettle refugees and displaced people; assist the political process in Somalia; and protect the personnel, installations and equipment of the United Nations and its agencies as well as of NGOs providing humanitarian and reconstruction assistance. The Council authorized a gradual reduction of UNOSOM II to a force level of 22,000. It underlined the vital importance of providing UNOSOM II with the material means and military assets needed for discharging its responsibilities and defending its personnel. It encouraged Member States to contribute urgently troops, civilian personnel, equipment, financial and logistical support to the Operation.

Expressing serious concern at reports of a rearming and troop build-up by Somali factions, the Council called upon all parties to cooperate fully with UNOSOM II and respect all cease-fire arrangements and other commitments. It demanded that the parties refrain from acts of intimidation or violence against humanitarian or peace-keeping personnel. The Council approved the direction of international reconstruction resources first to those regions of the country where security was being re-established. Resources would also be directed to local Somali institutions ready to cooperate with the international community in setting development priorities as contained in the Declaration of the Fourth Humanitarian Conference in Addis Ababa.

The Council requested the Secretary-General, in consultation with OAU and LAS, to consider establishing contacts with Somali parties to agree on a timetable for implementing the Addis Ababa Agreements. The objective would be to complete the process by March 1995. The Secretary-General was also asked to report back as soon as the situation warranted, and in any case before 31 May 1994.

Coordinating aid

The inaugural meeting of the Somali Aid Coordination Body (SACB), whose membership included major bilateral and multilateral donors, United Nations agencies and non-governmental groups, was held in Nairobi on 1 and 2 February 1994. Formed in response to the call by the Fourth Humanitarian Conference on Somalia, SACB was mandated to identify means of involving Somalis and their organizations in its efforts. At the meeting, SACB endorsed the Plan of Action, prepared as a follow-up to the Conference, which reconfirmed that international rehabilitation and reconstruction assistance would be provided to areas of Somalia able to achieve sufficient levels of peace and security to allow long-term donor involvement.

In view of the long-term nature of reconstruction and development programmes, the Secretary-General approved the transfer of the Development Office from UNOSOM II to a UNDP project on 15 March 1994. The Development Office would function as an integral component of United Nations activities in Somalia and in that context would cooperate closely with UNOSOM II.

Nairobi declaration

Upon completion by Admiral Howe of his year-long assignment as Special Representative, the Secretary-General appointed Deputy Special Representative Kouyaté as Acting Special Representative in February 1994. Mr. Kouyaté then began efforts to ease the relationship between UNOSOM II and SNA, and to help the Somali faction leaders in restoring dialogue and personal relationships among themselves. To those ends, he held a series of informal consultations on the overall political and security situation in Somalia with leaders of Somali political factions. In March, he convened a meeting in Nairobi to deal with the situation in Kismayo, where inter-clan fighting had continued since early February 1994. The occasion also provided an opportunity to reactivate the political process in Somalia. On 17 March 1994, Mr. Ali Mahdi of the Somali Salvation Alliance (SSA) and General Aidid, leader of SNA, met in Nairobi, under the auspices of the Acting Special Representative. It was the first meeting of the two political leaders since December 1992.

On 24 March, after a series of intensive consultations in Nairobi, Mr. Ali Mahdi and General Aidid signed, respectively for the Group of 12 and SNA, a declaration on national reconciliation.[23] The Somali faction leaders repudiated any form of violence as a means of resolving conflicts and committed themselves to implement a cease-fire and voluntary disarmament. They also agreed to restore peace throughout Somalia, giving priority wherever conflicts existed. It was agreed that in order to restore the sovereignty of the Somali State, a National Reconciliation Conference would be convened on 15 May 1994 to elect a President and Vice-Presidents, and to appoint a Prime Minister. The Somali factions which had signed the March 1993 Addis Ababa Peace Agreement and the Somali National Movement (SNM) would meet on 15 April 1994 in Mogadishu to prepare for the Conference. They would also discuss the establishment of a Legislative Assembly after the formation of a national Government. The Secretary-General welcomed the signing of the Nairobi Declaration and congratulated Somali political leaders for showing wisdom and political maturity during the negotiations. However, the ongoing factional disputes and conflicts and disagreements concerning modalities led to repeated postponements of the preparatory meeting for the National Reconciliation Conference.

On 27 March, the parties directly involved in the conflict in Kismayo — the Somali Patriotic Movement (SPM) and SNA — signed an agreement calling for a cease-fire as of 27 March and a Lower Juba Reconciliation Conference to be convened on 8 April 1994 in Kismayo. The parties also agreed to appoint a committee to work out the details of its agenda. The Lower Juba Reconciliation Conference, after considerable delays, was held from 24 May to 19 June 1994 at Kismayo. It resulted in the signing of a nine-point agreement including a general cease-fire to take effect in the region on 24 June 1994. On 19 June, General Mohamed Said Hersi "Morgan" (SPM) and Mr. Osman Atto (SNA) — the leaders of the two dominant factions in the area — signed a statement pledging the support of their factions for implementation of the Agreement.

Extension of mandate

Reporting[24] to the Security Council on 24 May 1994, the Secretary-General provided a negative assessment of the political and security situations. He nevertheless believed that "the Somali people deserve a last chance". But that must be firmly tied to evidence of serious and productive pursuit of the reconciliation process, strict observance of the cease-fire and cooperation with UNOSOM II in preventing the recurrence of clashes and resolving local clan and factional conflicts. He based his recommendation that the Security Council extend UNOSOM II's mandate for a six-month period on the assumption that the Somali leaders would prove able and willing to pursue the path to political reconciliation. Should that not be the case, he stated that he would not rule out recommending that the Council consider the withdrawal of UNOSOM II in part or in full.

The Security Council, by resolution 923 (1994) of 31 May 1994, renewed the mandate of UNOSOM II until 30 September 1994, subject to a review no later than 29 July, after which the Council might request the Secretary-General to prepare options regarding UNOSOM's mandate and future operations. The Council demanded that all parties in Somalia refrain from any acts of intimidation or violence against personnel engaged in humanitarian or peace-keeping work in the country.

Little progress

In June and July, the security situation was marred by clashes among clans and sub-clans, es-

23S/1994/614, annex I. 24S/1994/614.

pecially in Mogadishu, and by a further increase in banditry. The recurring outbreaks of inter-clan fighting brought all humanitarian activities in Mogadishu and its immediate vicinity to a near-standstill for several weeks. There were further attacks against UNOSOM II personnel resulting in a number of fatal casualties.

UNOSOM II focused on consolidating activities both inside Mogadishu and in outlying areas by securing key installations and facilities, maintaining its presence along key routes and within areas of responsibility through patrolling, and providing security for humanitarian aid convoys. In addition, it intensified its work related to the training of local police personnel. As of 8 July 1994, police recruits totalled 7,869, and 96 of the 125 police stations had become operational. The mission also continued its work in the judicial, correctional, juvenile justice, crime prevention and human rights fields. As at 10 July, the force strength of UNOSOM II was 18,790.

There was some progress in overcoming the emergency humanitarian situation and moving into the recovery phase because the situation of the most vulnerable improved, particularly of women and children. The outbreak of a cholera epidemic in February 1994 created an unexpected health emergency. Under the auspices of UNOSOM II, a Cholera Task Force was quickly established to coordinate the efforts to contain the epidemic. Responses to new outbreaks were prompt, resulting in a low fatality rate. There were, at the same time, several important setbacks, which included the interruption, for security reasons, of WFP activities in Kismayo, as well as those of UNHCR in Afmadu and Buale and of the non-governmental Save the Children Fund in Mogadishu.

There was no progress on national reconciliation. The National Reconciliation Conference and its preparatory meeting were repeatedly postponed, new subgroups of factions emerged and there was no clear reconciliation process. The Secretary-General expressed[25] the view to the Security Council that some leaders did not yet seem ready to subordinate their personal ambitions for power to the cause of peace and stability in Somalia. There was, in fact, little or no reason to believe that the target of completing the national reconciliation process by March 1995 could be achieved.

From 1 July 1994, the Secretary-General appointed Mr. James Victor Gbeho (Ghana) as Special Representative. He then asked the Special Representative to prepare an in-depth assessment of the prospects for national reconciliation in So-

malia. He informed the Security Council that he had decided to undertake a comprehensive review of the current troop strength of UNOSOM II. He also told the Council that he intended to dispatch a special mission to discuss with the Special Representative and the Force Commander the feasibility of a reduction in the troop level currently deployed. The views of the humanitarian agencies and the non-governmental organizations would also be taken into account.

National reconciliation prospects

On 17 August, the Secretary-General[26] reported to the Security Council that conflicts within the dominant Hawiye clan, to which both Mr. Ali Mahdi and General Aidid belonged, constituted the major obstacle to national reconciliation. No meaningful progress could be made in the political process without first finding a solution to the conflict among the Hawiye sub-clans (Habr Gedir, Abgal, Hawadle and Murosade). The root causes of dissension and tension among the 15 factions were also by and large attributable to rivalries within the Hawiye clan. Those rivalries had precipitated the crisis in Mogadishu and its environs in 1991 and were the main cause of the resumption of fighting since June 1994.

The Special Representative believed that if Hawiye reconciliation could be attained and the differences between Mr. Ali Mahdi and General Aidid resolved, the prospects for national reconciliation and the establishment of a national government would be significantly improved. Both General Aidid and Mr. Ali Mahdi had expressed their willingness to participate in a Hawiye reconciliation conference with the cooperation of other concerned factions and political leaders. The Special Representative believed that with the cooperation of the parties concerned and the support of the international community, the reconciliation of the Hawiye should be achieved in good time to create a favourable climate for the convening of a conference on national reconciliation and the establishment of an interim government in the last quarter of 1994. That would leave three months for consolidating agreed transitional arrangements for the interim government before the scheduled completion of the mission of UNOSOM II at the end of March 1995.

The Secretary-General said that he was inclined to agree with the Special Representative's

[25]S/1994/839. [26]S/1994/977.

assessment. Although there were no clear signs that the parties were preparing for a Hawiye conference, he nevertheless instructed the Special Representative to provide all possible support to the efforts deployed by the parties concerned to convene such a conference.

E. UNOSOM II: August 1994–March 1995

UNOSOM II downsized

The special mission sent by the Secretary-General visited Somalia from 28 July to 4 August 1994. It found that the Special Representative and the Force Commander were in consensus on reducing the number of troops to about 17,200 all ranks by the end of September 1994. The authorized strength of UNOSOM II was then 22,000 all ranks and the actual strength on 2 August was 18,761. The special mission recommended that any further reductions should be carefully decided and take into account evolving circumstances. A troop level of approximately 15,000 represented the critical minimum below which the mandated tasks could not be implemented. The gradual reduction to the level of 15,000 could be achieved by the end of October or during November 1994.

Grave concern

On 25 August, the Security Council expressed[27] grave concern at the deteriorating security situation in Somalia and deplored attacks and harassment directed against UNOSOM II and other international personnel. The Council was also concerned by the lack of progress towards reconciliation among Somali factions. It attached great importance to accelerated inter-clan reconciliation, in particular among the Hawiye sub-clans, with the involvement of all concerned.

The Council agreed with the Secretary-General's proposed initial reduction, and stressed that priority attention should be given to ensuring the security of UNOSOM II and other international personnel, including the staff of NGOs. It invited the Secretary-General to submit, well before 30 September 1994, a report on prospects for national reconciliation in Somalia and on the possible options for the future of UNOSOM II.

In the following weeks, Special Representative Gbeho conducted intensive consultations with Mr. Ali Mahdi, General Aidid and the Imam of Hirab (who had also been attempting to mediate between the two). The Imam of Hirab advised the Special Representative that it would be necessary to arrange separate meetings between the Habr Gedir and the other sub-clans before proceeding to a plenary session of the Hawiye peace conference. Several such meetings were convened with some positive results.

The Secretary-General informed[28] the Security Council on 17 September that because of the deteriorating security situation, the UNOSOM Force Commander had been forced to begin concentrating troops in four key areas. By doing that, he hoped to prevent a repetition of the kind of incident that occurred in Belet Weyne on 29 July 1994 when a small UNOSOM contingent was overrun by a strong militia force. As a result of the concentration of forces and the reduction process, troops had been withdrawn from Bardera, Hoddur, Wajid and Balad. It was expected that by the end of October, UNOSOM II would be concentrated mainly in three locations: the Mogadishu area, Baidoa and Kismayo.

In the Secretary-General's view, the end of September would be a crucial period for both the national reconciliation process and the continued involvement of the United Nations in Somalia. He expected to be in a position by mid-October to submit to the Council his assessment of the prospects for national reconciliation and recommendations for the future of the United Nations operation in Somalia. In the mean time, he recommended that the Council consider extending the mandate of UNOSOM II for a period of one month.

On 30 September, the Security Council, by resolution 946 (1994), extended the mandate of UNOSOM II until 31 October 1994. It also encouraged the Secretary-General to continue with and intensify preparations for possible contingency arrangements, including the withdrawal of UNOSOM II within a specified time-frame.

[27]S/PRST/1994/46. [28]S/1994/1068.

Secretary-General takes stock

The Under-Secretary-General for Peace-keeping Operations, Mr. Kofi Annan, visited Mogadishu in preparation for the report[29] the Secretary-General submitted to the Security Council on 14 October. In that report, the Secretary-General said that the process of national reconciliation had not kept pace with achievements in the humanitarian area. Security had been progressively deteriorating, especially in Mogadishu, and the Somali leaders had not carried out commitments entered into under the Addis Ababa Agreement and the Nairobi Declaration. UNOSOM's goal of assisting the process of political reconciliation was becoming ever more elusive, while the burden and cost of maintaining a high troop level was proving increasingly difficult for Member States to justify.

The protracted political impasse, the Secretary-General continued, had created a vacuum of civil authority and of governmental structure in Somalia, leaving the United Nations with no function to build on. The presence of UNOSOM II troops had limited impact on the peace process and on security in the face of continuing inter-clan fighting and banditry. If the Council maintained its previous decision to end the Mission in March 1995 and to withdraw all UNOSOM II forces and assets, time would be required to ensure that the withdrawal took place in a secure, orderly and expeditious manner. This might take as long as 120 days. Extensive air and sea support from Member States might also be required.

In the light of those considerations, the Secretary-General recommended that the Security Council extend the Mission's mandate until 31 March 1995. He believed that the five-month extension would give the Somali leaders time to begin consolidating any positive achievements which might arise from the ongoing process of political reconciliation. Accordingly, the Secretary-General instructed his Special Representative to maintain his efforts to help the Somali leaders achieve national reconciliation.

The Secretary-General noted that the humanitarian organizations were committed to continuing their work in Somalia, but they could only go on doing so in a secure environment. Somali leaders would bear the ultimate responsibility for the safety of international and national relief personnel and their assets.

In the Secretary-General's view, only the Somalis themselves could establish a viable and acceptable peace. The international community could only help in that process. Such assistance, however, could not be sustained indefinitely. The withdrawal of UNOSOM II would not mean United Nations abandonment of Somalia. Should the Somali leaders succeed in creating and maintaining favourable security conditions, the United Nations and the international community could continue to play a role in the country's rehabilitation and reconstruction. The United Nations could also retain a certain presence after the withdrawal of UNOSOM II to continue assisting the Somali political organizations and factions in the process of national reconciliation. However, the Secretary-General warned that the feasibility of international assistance of this kind would be very much dependent on the degree of security prevailing in the country.

Security Council mission

In resolution 946 (1994) of 30 September 1994, the Security Council had declared its readiness to consider sending a mission to Somalia to convey directly to the Somali political parties the Council's views on the situation, and on the future of the United Nations involvement. On 20 October, during informal consultations, the Council decided to send such a mission to Somalia. The seven-member mission, headed by Ambassador Colin Keating, Permanent Representative of New Zealand, visited Somalia from 26 to 27 October. In addition to United Nations officials there, it met with Somali faction leaders, representatives of United Nations agencies and NGOs operating in Somalia.

The mission concluded[30] that 31 March 1995 was the appropriate date for the end of the mandate of UNOSOM II. None of the Somali factions had requested a longer extension; nor did the humanitarian agencies or NGOs. On 31 October, the Security Council extended the mandate of UNOSOM II, which was expiring on that day, for an interim period until 4 November 1994, to allow time to complete the review of the mandate of UNOSOM II and decide on its future.[31]

Final extension of mandate

On 4 November 1994, the Security Council, by resolution 954 (1994), decided to extend the mandate of UNOSOM II for a final period until 31 March 1995. It affirmed that the primary purpose of UNOSOM II until its termination was to facilitate political reconciliation in Somalia. The

[29]S/1994/1166. [30]S/1994/1245. [31]S/RES/953 (1994).

Council decided that every effort should be made to withdraw the UNOSOM II military force and assets from Somalia in a secure and orderly manner. To that end it authorized UNOSOM II to take the actions necessary to protect the withdrawal. It also requested Member States to assist with the withdrawal of the Operation. The Council demanded that the Somali parties refrain from any acts of intimidation or violence against UNOSOM II and other personnel engaged in humanitarian activities. It also urged them to negotiate an effective cease-fire and the formation of a transitional government of national unity.

Inter-agency statement

On 10 November 1994, the Secretary-General drew attention[32] to a statement issued by the Inter-Agency Standing Committee (IASC), a body established by the General Assembly in 1991[33] and comprised of the heads of United Nations operational agencies, ICRC, the International Organization of Migration, the International Federation of the Red Cross, and the representatives of three international non-governmental organizations. IASC reaffirmed the commitment of the humanitarian agencies of the United Nations to continue emergency and rehabilitation activities in Somalia to the maximum extent possible after the withdrawal of UNOSOM II. To that end, IASC decided to adopt a common and coordinated approach to retain or replace the essential programme support and operational services formerly provided by UNOSOM II and to develop a common framework of action with the full support of all operational partners.

IASC proposed the creation of a United Nations Coordination Team of senior representatives of organizations active in Somalia, to be chaired by the Resident Coordinator of UNDP (who served also as the Humanitarian Coordinator). IASC urged the Security Council to support the process of transition from UNOSOM-protected humanitarian activities to those following UNOSOM II's withdrawal. Specifically, IASC asked that the Security Council consider: (1) establishing protected humanitarian operational bases at essential ports and airports; (2) authorizing the transfer of UNOSOM II equipment and assets to operational United Nations organizations and international NGOs; and (3) making UNOSOM II humanitarian and security staff available to the new coordination arrangement. The United Nations organizations also urged that security arrangements in the post–UNOSOM period be funded

from a special allocation so as to prevent the diversion of voluntary funds for humanitarian activities.

The Council took note[34] of the IASC statement on 7 December 1994 and welcomed the commitment of the agencies to continue emergency and rehabilitation activities in post-UNOSOM Somalia. The Council encouraged the Secretary-General to play a facilitating or mediating political role in Somalia after March 1995 if the parties to the conflict in Somalia were willing to cooperate with the United Nations and if this was the wish of the Somali people.

SNA/SSA agreements

Following the Security Council's decision to end UNOSOM's mandate on 31 March 1995, the rival factions in Mogadishu began to work together. On 19 February 1995, Mr. Ali Mahdi and Mr. Osman Ali Atto, a high-ranking official of SNA, had a meeting that led to significant political developments during the last two weeks of UNOSOM II's withdrawal. On 21 February 1995, a peace agreement was signed by General Aidid and Mr. Ali Mahdi on behalf of SNA and SSA respectively to promote national reconciliation and a peaceful settlement. In that agreement, the two sides accepted the principle of power-sharing. They pledged not to seek the presidency through military means but through democratic elections, agreed to the resolution of disputes through dialogue and peaceful means and agreed on a common platform for tackling problems. The Agreement also included provisions for the confinement of "technicals" to designated areas and discouraged the open carrying of arms in the streets of Mogadishu. In addition, it called for the removal of roadblocks and the reopening of the main markets.

On 23 February, the two sides reached agreement on the establishment of two joint committees to manage the operations of the airport and seaport. Endorsed by Mr. Ali Mahdi and General Aidid, the agreement provided for cooperation of the rival factions with the United Nations system. On 8 March, the two leaders initialled yet another agreement, this one on security arrangements. A security committee was set up to ensure the exclusion of unauthorized "technicals" from the airport and seaport and ensure security within those facilities. Joint militias with specially marked "technicals" were set up to secure the outer per-

[32]S/1994/1392. [33]A/RES/46/182. [34]S/1994/1393.

imeters as well as the delivery routes in use from and to the ports. The seaport was opened for commercial traffic under the administration of the joint committee on 9 March.

Withdrawal

The initial phase of withdrawal of UNOSOM II forces entailed redeploying troops to Mogadishu from Baidoa, Baledogle, Afgoye and Kismayo. The pull-back from Kismayo was supported by an Indian naval task force, comprising two frigates, one logistic ship and six helicopters. Between 28 December 1994 and 5 January 1995, the Zimbabwean and Malaysian contingents were repatriated. The personnel of the Pakistani hospital were repatriated on 11 January 1995. Headquarters staff were reduced by 50 per cent by 15 January 1995 and relocated from the Embassy compound to the Mogadishu airport.

By 2 February 1995, with the repatriation of the Indian, Zimbabwean and Malaysian contingents, some headquarters personnel and those of the Pakistani hospital, UNOSOM II troop strength was reduced to 7,956, comprising Pakistani, Egyptian and Bangladeshi contingents and the remaining headquarters personnel. As the withdrawal accelerated, military support provided by UNOSOM troops to United Nations agencies, human rights organizations and NGOs still engaged in humanitarian activities was greatly reduced. With the major reductions starting in mid-February, it was no longer possible for UNOSOM II troops to extend the necessary protection even within Mogadishu. Agencies were then advised to evacuate their international staff to Nairobi by 14 February 1995.

During the first two months of 1995, the various compounds occupied by different functional units of UNOSOM II were vacated. The humanitarian and southern compounds were vacated on 30 January, leaving one platoon of the Pakistani brigade to secure buildings in the southern compound necessary for the tactical defence of the airport. The administration of UNOSOM II moved ahead of schedule, vacating the university and embassy compounds by 31 January. That allowed the relocation of the Pakistani brigade to the airport on 2 February, and the concentration of all troops in the airport, new seaport complex and the old seaport area.

After a final review of preparations by Under-Secretary-General Kofi Annan, who visited Somalia from 8 to 10 February, the final phase of withdrawal got under way. Support was provided

by a combined task force, known as "United Shield", composed of forces from France, India, Italy, Malaysia, Pakistan, the United Kingdom and the United States, under Lieutenant-General Anthony Zinni of the United States. From 12 to 15 February approximately 1,750 Pakistani personnel left Mogadishu, followed by 1,160 members of the Egyptian brigade who were repatriated from 17 to 20 February. An additional 2,600 men from the Pakistani contingent were taken out between 23 and 27 February, leaving a rearguard of 2,500 Pakistani and Bangladeshi military personnel and UNOSOM headquarters staff.

Mogadishu seaport was handed over to the combined task force and closed to commercial traffic on 28 February. The Secretary-General's Special Representative, his staff and the UNOSOM Force Commander left Mogadishu by air on 28 February. The withdrawal of the UNOSOM II rearguard was completed on 2 March, with the combined task force providing cover. Among the last to leave were 25 United Nations civilian personnel and 11 contractual logistic staff, accompanied by one representative of a shipping company, who had stayed after the withdrawal of all other international staff on 28 February in order to supervise the shipment of the last consignment of UNOSOM II material. The personnel of the combined task force, who had come ashore on 28 February, also withdrew on 3 March, concluding the operation without casualties.

In addition to contingent-owned equipment, over 156,000 cubic metres of United Nations–owned and –leased assets, valued at some $120 million, were shipped out of Somalia during the last two months. Equipment worth $235,761, considered vital for the support of local communities, was donated to Somali district councils. Some material was transferred to United Nations agencies which continued humanitarian activities in the country, and some was sold at depreciated cost. Communications equipment worth half a million dollars went with the Secretary-General's Special Representative to Nairobi. Plans called for its return as soon as conditions allowed the resumption of United Nations political and agency offices in Mogadishu. Mr. Gbeho invited the chairmen of the two committees to visit Nairobi for consultations aimed at reactivating civilian operations at the airport and seaport. Among the subjects to be discussed was the return to Mogadishu of the equipment for operating the seaport and airport facilities, without which only small ships could be serviced. This equipment was stored in the United Nations logistics base in Brindisi, Italy.

F. Conclusion

The withdrawal of UNOSOM II marked "a point of transition in the efforts of the United Nations to succour a people and a country caught in the throes of famine, civil war and the collapse of all institutions of government".[35] The major political achievement of the United Nations in Somalia was to help bring about a cease-fire, first in Mogadishu and then nationally. Although its ambitious plan to rebuild the internal structures of a functioning State did not prove possible in the face of the inability of the Somali factions to come to terms with each other, the United Nations did help to put in place 52 (of a possible 92) district councils, and 8 regional councils (of a possible 18). Opposition to the formation of these councils from SNA prevented the creation of the Transitional National Council envisaged in the Addis Ababa agreement of March 1993.

Another element of the United Nations achievement in Somalia was the long-term effect of two major conferences. The first was the National Reconciliation Conference in March 1993, which produced the Addis Ababa Agreement. The second was the "consultation" of all the factions in Nairobi in March 1994. The significant representation of the civil society of Somalia at the Addis Ababa conference (where more than 250 representatives of community organizations, elders, scholars, as well as women's groups, were present), and the substantial number of elders at the Nairobi meetings, signalled an unprecedented broadening of political participation. Although the implementation of agreements reached at those meetings was forestalled by subsequent developments, the agreements continued to serve as the major frame of reference in the political life of Somalia.

Success was greatest in the humanitarian field. The operational arms of the United Nations system, in particular UNICEF, WFP, UNDP and UNESCO, worked with a host of governmental and non-governmental agencies to meet the vast humanitarian challenge. Millions of Somalis benefited from these activities and, at a minimum, an estimated quarter of a million lives were saved. Despite the withdrawal of the United Nations peace-keeping force, the agencies and programmes of the United Nations system continued to be involved in humanitarian and development-related work in Somalia. The expectation was that this work would take place for the foreseeable future in a context of political unrest and against a background of uncertainty. Furthermore, in the absence of national institutions capable of coping even with minor emergencies, Somalia would remain vulnerable to future disasters.

There were also achievements in terms of reviving the Somali police: some 8,000 were deployed in 82 district stations. By March 1995, there were 46 district courts, 11 regional courts and 11 appeals courts, all functioning because the United Nations had helped with funds, training and rebuilding of infrastructure.

Reporting[36] to the Security Council on 28 March 1995, the Secretary-General emphasized that the Council had been prepared to pursue its peace-keeping efforts as long as it felt that the United Nations presence was receiving the cooperation of the Somali factions. However, over the preceding few months, it had been concluded that the United Nations presence in Somalia was no longer promoting national reconciliation. Agreements reached under United Nations auspices unravelled and security continued to deteriorate, especially in Mogadishu. United Nations peace-keepers and humanitarian convoys were threatened and, in a number of instances, viciously attacked. The Somali leaders did not heed repeated warnings that if they did not show a minimum of political will the United Nations presence would have to be reconsidered. In these circumstances, continuation of UNOSOM II could no longer be justified.

In the Secretary-General's view, the experience of UNOSOM II had confirmed the validity of the point that the Security Council had consistently stressed in its resolutions on Somalia, namely that the responsibility for political compromise and national reconciliation must be borne by the leaders and people concerned. It was they who bore the main responsibility for creating the political and security conditions in which peace-making and peace-keeping could be effective. The international community could only facilitate, prod, encourage and assist. It could neither impose peace nor coerce unwilling parties into accepting it.

The Secretary-General observed that there were important lessons to be learned about the "theory and practice of multifunctional peace-keeping operations in conditions of civil war and

35S/1995/231. 36Ibid.

chaos and especially about the clear line that needs to be drawn between peace-keeping and enforcement action". The world had changed and so had the nature of the conflict situations which the United Nations was asked to deal with. There was a need for careful and creative rethinking about peacemaking, peace-keeping and peace-building in the context of the Somali operation.

The withdrawal of UNOSOM II did not mean that the United Nations was abandoning Somalia. The United Nations agencies and organizations, as well as NGOs, were determined to continue humanitarian operations in Somalia. In the post-UNOSOM II era, they would focus on rehabilitation, recovery and reconstruction, without prejudice to emergency relief where that was necessary.

The experience of UNOSOM II, the Secretary-General continued, had demonstrated the vital link between humanitarian assistance and assistance in achieving national reconciliation. The former was geared towards the immediate amelioration of emergency situations, while the latter was necessary to ensure stability in the long term so that the positive results of humanitarian assistance could be preserved and a recurrence of the tragedy avoided. He stressed that he would continue to make available his good offices to assist the Somali factions to arrive at a political settlement and would maintain a political presence in the area for that purpose. Its location should be in Mogadishu but this would depend on security considerations. In the mean time, the Secretary-General's Special Representative would remain in Nairobi in order to monitor the situation in Somalia and coordinate United Nations humanitarian activities there.

For its part, the Security Council underlined[37] that the timely intervention of UNOSOM II and the humanitarian assistance given to Somalia had helped to save many lives and much property, mitigate general suffering and contributed to the search for peace in Somalia. However, "the continuing lack of progress in the peace process and in national reconciliation, in particular the lack of sufficient cooperation from the Somali parties over security issues, undermined the United Nations objectives in Somalia and prevented the continuation of UNOSOM II mandate beyond 31 March 1995". The Council reaffirmed that the people of Somalia bore the ultimate responsibility for achieving national reconciliation and restoring peace to Somalia. The international community could only facilitate, encourage and assist the process, but not try to impose any particular solution on it. The Council, therefore, called upon the Somali parties to pursue national reconciliation, rehabilitation and reconstruction in the interest of peace, security and development.

The Security Council supported the view of the Secretary-General that Somalia should not be abandoned by the United Nations and stated that the Organization would continue to assist the Somali people to achieve a political settlement and to provide humanitarian and other support services, "provided that the Somalis themselves demonstrate a disposition to peaceful resolution of the conflict and to cooperation with the international community". It welcomed the Secretary-General's intention to continue a small political mission, should the Somali parties so wish, to assist them in national reconciliation. The Security Council expressed its appreciation to those Governments and agencies that had provided the personnel, humanitarian assistance and other support to the peace-keeping operation in Somalia, including those Governments which had participated in the multinational operation for UNOSOM's withdrawal.

The Council reaffirmed the obligations of States to implement fully the embargo on all deliveries of weapons and military equipment to Somalia imposed by its resolution 733 (1992), and called on States, especially neighbouring States, to refrain from actions capable of exacerbating the conflict in Somalia.

[37]S/PRST/1995/15.

G. Composition of UNOSOM

The command structure for UNOSOM included a Special Representative of the Secretary-General as political head. The first Special Representative was Mr. Mohamed Sahnoun (Algeria). Upon his resignation, Mr. Ismat Kittani (Iraq) was appointed on 3 November 1992. He was in turn succeeded in March 1993 by Admiral Jonathan Howe (Ret.) (United States). In February 1994, upon Admiral Howe's completion of his year-long assignment, his Deputy, Mr. Lansana Kouyaté (Guinea), was appointed as Acting Special Representative. The Secretary-General appointed Mr. James Victor Gbeho (Ghana) as his Special Representative from 1 July 1994, and Mr. Kouyaté then took up a new assignment at United Nations Headquarters. Mr. Gbeho served as Special Representative until April 1995.

The Chief Military Observer of UNOSOM I was Brigadier-General Imtiaz Shaheen of Pakistan, appointed on 23 June 1992. The authorized strength of UNOSOM I according to resolution 751 (1992) was 50 military observers. They were provided to UNOSOM I by Austria, Bangladesh, Czechoslovakia, Egypt, Fiji, Finland, Indonesia, Jordan, Morocco, Pakistan and Zimbabwe. Resolution 751 also authorized a 500-strong security unit, which Pakistan later agreed to provide. The first group of security personnel arrived in Mogadishu on 14 September 1992. General Shaheen then served as Force Commander.

On 28 August 1992, the Security Council, by resolution 775 (1992), authorized the increase of the total strength of United Nations security personnel to 3,500, and on 8 September, it agreed to a further addition of three logistical units, raising the total authorized strength of UNOSOM to 4,219 troops and 50 military observers. Only a few of this authorized number of troops—some 900—were deployed during the UNOSOM I period. In addition to the 500 troops contributed by Pakistan, troops were also contributed by Australia, Belgium, Canada, New Zealand and Norway. These forces remained in Mogadishu under UNOSOM I command following the deployment of UNITAF in December 1992.

The first Force Commander of UNOSOM II was Lieutenant-General Çevik Bir (Turkey), appointed in April 1993. On 18 January 1994, he was succeeded by Lieutenant-General Aboo Samah Bin Aboo Bakar (Malaysia).

The original authorized strength of UNOSOM II under resolution 814 (1993) was approximately 28,000 military personnel and some 2,800 civilian staff. Military personnel were provided by the following countries: Australia, Bangladesh, Belgium, Botswana, Canada, Egypt, France, Germany, Greece, India, Indonesia, Ireland, Italy, Kuwait, Malaysia, Morocco, Nepal, New Zealand, Nigeria, Norway, Pakistan, Republic of Korea, Romania, Saudi Arabia, Sweden, Tunisia, Turkey, United Arab Emirates, United States and Zimbabwe.

Supporting UNOSOM II in the field, but not part of it, were as many as 17,700 troops of the United States Joint Task Force in Somalia. A Quick Reaction Force was part of the United States presence. These troops remained under United States command.

In the course of 1993, a number of Member States informed the Secretary-General of their intention to withdraw their troops from UNOSOM II. Accordingly, at the end of 1993, Belgium (950), France (1,100) and Sweden (150 field hospital staff) withdrew from UNOSOM II. The United States withdrew 1,400 military logistics personnel at the end of 1993 and all of its troops and the rest of its logistics personnel (1,400) by the end of March 1994.

On 1 January 1994, UNOSOM II strength was 25,945. Italy (2,300), Germany (1,350), Turkey (320) and Norway (140) pulled out their troops at the end of March 1994. Greece, Kuwait, Morocco, the Republic of Korea, Saudi Arabia, Tunisia, Turkey and the United Arab Emirates also withdrew their contingents. At the same time, a number of other contributing countries increased their contingent strength. The troop strength available to UNOSOM II at the end of July 1994 was 18,775. Before the final withdrawal began, the troop level of UNOSOM II had been brought down to 15,000 all ranks.

The Office of the Special Representative was composed of civilian international and local staff and included specialized staff seconded from Governments. During the period of UNOSOM I, the Office comprised units dealing with humanitarian, political and public information aspects, including a spokesman. During the period of UNOSOM II, additional offices were added to deal with matters relating to justice; police; and disarmament, demobilization and de-mining.

Under the UNOSOM II civilian police programme started by UNITAF, police advisers and personnel were contributed by a number of countries. After May 1994, these included Australia, Bangladesh, Egypt, Ghana, Ireland, Italy, Malaysia, Netherlands, Nigeria, Philippines, Republic of Korea, Sweden, Zambia and Zimbabwe. Maximum strength of 54 was reached in July 1994, reduced to about 30 by October and thereafter. From April to June 1994, the Police Commissioner was Chief Superintendent Mike Murphy (Ireland), and from June 1994 to February 1995, Chief Superintendent Selwyn Mettle (Ghana).

H. Financial aspects

For the operation of UNOSOM I, expenditures amounted to $42,931,700 net. For the operation of UNOSOM II, expenditures amounted to $1,643,485,500 net. These costs were met by assessed contributions from United Nations Member States.

The Security Council, by resolution 794 (1992) of 3 December 1992, requested the Secretary-General to establish a fund through which contributions could be channelled to States or operations involved in establishing a secure environment for humanitarian relief operations in Somalia. In its resolution 814 (1993), the Security Council requested the Secretary-General to maintain the Fund for the additional purpose of receiving contributions for the maintenance of UNOSOM II forces following the departure of UNITAF forces in early May 1993 and for the establishment of a Somali police force. It was the intention of the Secretary-General to continue the police and justice programmes once the situation in Somalia improved.[38]

[38]A/50/741.

Chapter 15

United Nations Operation in Mozambique (ONUMOZ)

Chapter 15
United Nations Operation in Mozambique (ONUMOZ)

A. Background

Mozambique obtained its independence from Portugal in June 1975 after a protracted liberation war led by the Frente da Libertação de Moçambique (FRELIMO). Under an agreement signed on 7 September 1974, the Government of Portugal handed the administration of Mozambique to a transitional Government headed by Mr. Joaquim Chissano.

In 1977, FRELIMO declared itself to be a Marxist-Leninist party and the Government signed aid agreements with the Union of Soviet Socialist Republics and Cuba. Covert assistance from the minority regime in Southern Rhodesia was then stepped up and directly channelled to the Resistência Nacional Moçambicana (RENAMO). In October 1979, following the death in combat of Mr. André Matsangaiza, RENAMO's first leader, Mr. Afonso Dhlakama became president of RENAMO. Following the independence of Zimbabwe, aid from South Africa and some groups in Western countries increased substantially.

RENAMO tactics included disruption and destruction of Mozambique's transport and supply facilities, in particular the Beira and Limpopo corridors. This aroused the concern of Zimbabwe and Malawi, which depended on these routes for much of their foreign trade. In November 1982, with the consent of the Government of Mozambique, Zimbabwe sent more than 10,000 troops to protect the Beira transport corridor. A smaller contingent of troops from the United Republic of Tanzania was sent to patrol the Nacala transport route in the north.

The conflict in Mozambique reached its widest extent during the second half of the 1980s. As a result of the war between the Government and RENAMO, close to one million Mozambicans died, either directly through fighting or due to widespread hunger and disease. In addition, by the late 1980s, at least 3.2 million people had been displaced from the countryside; by 1989, as many as 4.6 million had been severely affected. Approximately one and a half million Mozambicans fled the fighting into neighbouring countries.

By 1990, the Government had undertaken far-reaching economic reforms, instituting a new system favouring political liberalization and promulgating a new Constitution guaranteeing individual rights and a multi-party system of government. However, in the conflict between the Government and RENAMO, neither party was capable of imposing a military solution, and the stalemate continued. Tentative negotiations through Catholic Church intermediaries began in 1988 and subsequently involved a number of African Governments, among them Kenya and Zimbabwe, followed by Botswana, Malawi and others, including South Africa. In late 1989, the process gained momentum and came to be supported by the efforts of Italy, Portugal, the United Kingdom and the United States, as well as by the United Nations.

General Peace Agreement

On 4 October 1992, Mr. Chissano, who had become President of the Republic of Mozambique in 1986, and Mr. Dhlakama signed in Rome a General Peace Agreement[1] establishing the principles and modalities for the achievement of peace in Mozambique. The Agreement called for United Nations participation in monitoring its implementation, in providing technical assistance for the general elections and in monitoring those elections.

Under the Agreement, negotiated with the help of a number of mediators and observers including at the final stages of talks United Nations experts, a cease-fire was to come into effect not later than 15 October 1992 (which was designated as E-Day). The Agreement itself and its seven pro-

---

[1]S/24635, annex.

tocols called for the cease-fire to be followed rapidly by the separation of the two sides' forces and their concentration in certain assembly areas. Demobilization was to begin immediately thereafter of those troops who would not serve in the new Mozambican Defence Force (FADM). Demobilization would have to be completed six months after E-Day. Meanwhile, preparations would be made for elections, scheduled to take place not later than 15 October 1993. A 16 July 1992 Declaration by the Government of Mozambique and RENAMO on guiding principles for humanitarian assistance, a Joint Declaration signed in Rome on 7 August 1992, as well as a Joint Communiqué of 10 July 1990 and an earlier accord on a partial cease-fire dated 1 December 1990, all formed integral parts of the General Peace Agreement.

The United Nations was requested to undertake a major role in monitoring the implementation of the Agreement and was asked to perform specific functions in relation to the cease-fire, the elections and humanitarian assistance. The implementation of the Agreement was to be supervised by a Supervisory and Monitoring Commission chaired by the United Nations. On 9 October 1992, Secretary-General Boutros Boutros-Ghali submitted to the Security Council a report[2] on the proposed United Nations role in Mozambique, in which he recommended an immediate plan of action and stated his intention, subject to the Council's approval, to appoint an interim Special Representative. On 13 October, the Security Council adopted resolution 782 (1992), by which it welcomed the signature of the General Peace Agreement and approved the appointment by the Secretary-General of an interim Special Representative and the dispatch to Mozambique of a team of up to 25 military observers.

Agreement enters into force

The Secretary-General then appointed Mr. Aldo Ajello (Italy) as his interim Special Representative for Mozambique, and later — in March 1993 — appointed him Special Representative. The Secretary-General asked the Special Representative to proceed to Mozambique to assist the parties in setting up the joint monitoring machinery, in finalizing the modalities and conditions for the military arrangements and in carrying out the various other actions that were required of them at the very beginning of the peace process. The interim Special Representative and a team of 21 military observers, drawn from existing United Nations peace-keeping missions, arrived in Mozambique on 15 October 1992, the day the Agreement entered into force. On 20 October, two teams of military observers were also deployed to the provincial capitals of Beira and Nampula. Later, two additional outposts were established to verify the withdrawal of foreign troops from Mozambique, an important element of the Agreement.

Both the Government and RENAMO committed themselves to undertake, immediately after, and in some instances before, the entry into effect of the Agreement, specific actions to set in motion the joint mechanisms to monitor and verify its implementation. However, no such actions had been initiated at the time the interim Special Representative arrived in Mozambique, and he immediately started extensive discussions with the two parties.

Meanwhile, violations of the cease-fire were reported in various areas of the country, and the parties presented official complaints to the interim Special Representative about military attacks and movement of troops. He urged them to refrain from any type of military operation and to discuss and settle all disputes through negotiations. On 27 October 1992, the Security Council expressed[3] its deep concern over the reports of major violations of the cease-fire, called upon the parties to halt such violations immediately and urged them to cooperate fully with the interim Special Representative.

Monitoring mechanism

In an attempt to avoid a deterioration of the situation, the interim Special Representative called for an early informal meeting of the Government and RENAMO. Both parties sent high-level delegations to their first meeting in Maputo; thereafter, the two delegations met on numerous occasions, both bilaterally and together with the Special Representative. On 4 November 1992, the Supervisory and Monitoring Commission (CSC) was established to guarantee the implementation of the Agreement, assume responsibility for authentic interpretation of it, settle any disputes that might arise between the parties and guide and coordinate the activities of the subsidiary Commissions. CSC was chaired by the United Nations and initially composed of government and RENAMO delegations, with representatives of Italy (the mediator party at the Rome talks), France, Portugal, the United Kingdom, the United States (which acted as observers in Rome) and the Organization

[2]S/24642. [3]S/24719.

of African Unity (OAU). In December 1992, Germany also became a member of CSC. At its first meeting on 4 November 1992, CSC appointed the main subsidiary commissions: the Cease-fire Commission (CCF), composed of government and RENAMO delegations, with representatives of Botswana, Egypt, France, Italy, Nigeria, Portugal, the United Kingdom and the United States and chaired by the United Nations; the Reintegration Commission (CORE), composed of government and RENAMO delegations, with representatives of Denmark, France, Germany, Italy, the Netherlands, Norway, Portugal, South Africa, Spain, Sweden, Switzerland, the United Kingdom, the United States and the European Community and chaired by the United Nations; and the Joint Commission for the Formation of the Mozambican Defence Force (CCFADM), composed of government and RENAMO delegations, with representatives of France, Portugal and the United Kingdom.

B. Establishment of ONUMOZ

On 3 December 1992, the Secretary-General submitted to the Security Council a report[4] presenting a detailed operational plan for the United Nations Operation in Mozambique (ONUMOZ). Describing the difficulties of the operation, he referred to the size of the country, the devastated state of its infrastructure, the disruption of its economy by war and drought, the limited capacity of the Government to cope with the new tasks arising from the Agreement and the complexity of the processes envisaged in the Agreement. He also referred to the breadth of responsibilities entrusted to the United Nations under the Agreement.

The Secretary-General expressed his conviction that it would not be possible to create the conditions for successful elections in Mozambique unless the military situation had been brought fully under control, and that the Agreement would not be implemented unless the Mozambican parties made a determined effort in good faith to honour their commitments. In recommending to the Security Council the establishment and deployment of ONUMOZ, the Secretary-General stated that "in the light of recent experiences elsewhere, the recommendations in the present report may be thought to invite the international community to take a risk. I believe that the risk is worth taking; but I cannot disguise that it exists."

On 16 December 1992, the Security Council, by its resolution 797 (1992), approved the Secretary-General's report and decided to establish ONUMOZ until 31 October 1993. The Council endorsed the Secretary-General's recommendation that the elections not take place until the military aspects of the Agreement had been fully implemented. It called upon the Government and RENAMO to cooperate fully with the United Nations and to respect scrupulously the cease-fire and their obligations under the Agreement.

ONUMOZ mandate

In accordance with the General Peace Agreement, the mandate of ONUMOZ included four important elements: political, military, electoral and humanitarian. The operational concept of ONUMOZ was based on the strong interrelationship between those four components, requiring a fully integrated approach and coordination by the interim Special Representative. Without sufficient humanitarian aid, and especially food supplies, the security situation in the country might deteriorate and the demobilization process might stall. Without adequate military protection, the humanitarian aid would not reach its destination. Without sufficient progress in the political area, the confidence required for the disarmament and rehabilitation process would not exist. The electoral process, in turn, required prompt demobilization and formation of the new armed forces, without which the conditions would not exist for successful elections.

The Office of the Special Representative was to provide overall direction of United Nations activities in Mozambique and would be responsible for political guidance of the peace process, including facilitating the implementation of the Agreement, in particular by chairing the Supervisory and Monitoring Commission and its subsidiary commissions. This office would require up to 20 international staff and an adequate number of locally recruited staff.

[4] S/24892.

ONUMOZ's verification of the arrangements for the cease-fire and other military aspects of the peace process in Mozambique was to be carried out mainly by teams of United Nations military observers at 49 assembly areas in three military regions and elsewhere in the field. Teams were also to be deployed at airports, ports and other critical areas, including RENAMO headquarters.

ONUMOZ was to monitor and verify the cease-fire, the separation and concentration of forces of the two parties, their demobilization and the collection, storage and destruction of weapons; monitor and verify the complete withdrawal of foreign forces, and provide security in the four transport corridors; monitor and verify the disbanding of private and irregular armed groups; authorize security arrangements for vital infrastructures; and provide security for United Nations and other international activities in support of the peace process.

The military aspects of the United Nations operation in Mozambique were to be closely linked with the humanitarian effort. The approximately 100,000 soldiers who were to come to the assembly areas were to be disarmed, demobilized and reintegrated into civil society. They would need food and other support as soon as the assembly areas were established. An ONUMOZ technical unit, staffed by civilian personnel, was to assist in implementing the demobilization programme and to collaborate closely with the United Nations Office for Humanitarian Assistance Coordination (UNOHAC) on the programme's humanitarian aspects.

The Agreement provided for the withdrawal of foreign troops to be initiated following the entry into force of the cease-fire. Simultaneously, the Supervisory and Monitoring Commission, through the Cease-fire Commission, was to assume immediate responsibility "for verifying and ensuring security of strategic and trading routes", of which the most important were the four transport corridors (Beira, Limpopo, Nampula and National Highway No. 1). ONUMOZ was to assume transitional responsibility for the security of the corridors in order to protect humanitarian convoys using them, pending the formation of the new unified armed forces. Bearing this in mind, ONUMOZ infantry battalions were to be deployed in the corridors.

The military component would require the deployment of a Headquarters company and military police platoon; 354 military observers; 5 logistically self-sufficient infantry battalions, each composed of up to 850 personnel; 1 engineer battalion, with contracted assistance as needed; 3 logistics companies; and air, communications, medical and movement control support units. The Secretary-General also suggested the deployment of a civilian technical unit to support the logistic tasks relating to the demobilization programme in the assembly areas, with adequate resources.

While the Agreement did not provide a specific role for United Nations civilian police in monitoring the neutrality of the Mozambican police, the Secretary-General proposed to leave open the possibility of incorporating a police component into ONUMOZ, if both Mozambican parties requested it. His initial recommendation in this regard (which at that stage was not supported by the Government) was to deploy, should the parties concur, 128 police officers to monitor civil liberties and to provide technical advice.

Under the terms of the Agreement, legislative and presidential elections were to be held simultaneously one year after the date of signature of the Agreement. This period might be extended if warranted by the prevailing circumstances. The ONUMOZ Electoral Division was to monitor and verify all aspects and stages of the electoral process which would be organized by the National Elections Commission. The Division was to provide overall direction and maintain contacts with the Government, RENAMO, the National Elections Commission and the main political parties. In addition, the Secretary-General's Special Representative was to coordinate technical assistance to the whole electoral process in Mozambique, which was to be provided through the United Nations Development Programme (UNDP), other existing mechanisms of the United Nations system and bilateral channels.

The Secretary-General recommended that the Electoral Division consist of up to 148 international electoral officers and support staff, from the start of the electoral component of the peace process, followed by the deployment of some 1,200 international observers for the elections themselves and the periods immediately preceding and following them.

As for humanitarian aspects, the 1992 Agreement set out two objectives for international humanitarian assistance to Mozambique: to serve as an instrument of reconciliation, and to assist the return of people displaced by war and hunger, whether they had taken refuge in neighbouring countries or in provincial and district centres within Mozambique. ONUMOZ's integral component for humanitarian operations, UNOHAC, was to be established in Maputo, with suboffices at the regional and provincial levels. It was to replace the office of the United Nations Special Coordinator for Emergency Relief Operations which had been responsible for humanitarian assistance programmes in Mozambique. Headed by the Humanitarian Affairs Coordinator, and under the overall authority of the Special Representative, it was to function as an integrated component of ONUMOZ. Operational agencies and the non-governmental aid community were asked to provide representatives to work within UNOHAC.

UNOHAC was also to make available food and other relief for distribution by a technical unit of ONUMOZ to the soldiers in the assembly areas. In order to achieve the successful reintegration of demobilized soldiers, UNOHAC proposed a three-pronged strategy centred on identification of training and employment opportunities, a vocational kits and credit scheme, and a counselling and referral service.

Early difficulties

On 14 February 1993, Major-General Lélio Gonçalves Rodrigues da Silva (Brazil), appointed with the concurrence of the Security Council, assumed his duties as Force Commander of ONUMOZ. Meanwhile, from the outset of ONUMOZ operations, various delays and difficulties of a political, administrative, as well as of a logistical nature seriously impeded the implementation of the Agreement. On 2 April 1993, the Secretary-General informed[5] the Security Council that although the cease-fire had largely held, many of the timetables established in the Agreement had proved to be unrealistic. Continuing deep mistrust had resulted in reluctance to begin assembly and demobilization of troops and contributed to the delay in the deployment of United Nations military observers. Another complication was RENAMO's insistence that 65 per cent of ONUMOZ troops be deployed in Mozambique before the assembly process began. There were administrative delays in the deployment of ONUMOZ-formed military units. A number of logistical and legal problems also arose from the initial absence of a status-of-forces agreement with the Mozambican Government.

As to the elections, the Secretary-General stressed that the military situation in Mozambique should be fully under control for conditions to be created in which a successful election could take place. Having found it evident that the elections could not be held in October 1993 as originally scheduled, he indicated that he would continue discussions with the parties on new dates.

On 14 April 1993, the Security Council, in resolution 818 (1993), stressed its concern about delays and difficulties impeding the peace process in Mozambique, and strongly urged the Government and RENAMO to finalize the precise timetable for the full implementation of the provisions of the Agreement, including the separation, concentration and demobilization of forces, as well as for the elections. The Council also urged both sides urgently to comply with their commitments under the Agreement and to cooperate with the Secretary-General and his Special Representative in the full and timely implementation of the mandate of ONUMOZ.

New timetable

In the following weeks, due to determined efforts undertaken by the United Nations, many of the difficulties were overcome and, by the beginning of May 1993, ONUMOZ was fully deployed and its military infrastructure established in all three operational regions. Other positive developments included the establishment on 10 May of the voluntary trust fund to assist RENAMO to establish itself as a political entity, i.e., obtain office space, accommodation and equipment. The work of the Joint Commissions also resumed, and there was a massive international effort in the humanitarian field, with a sharp increase in the return of refugees and displaced persons. The withdrawal of foreign troops, from Malawi and Zimbabwe, as provided for in the Agreement, was successfully completed. After intensive negotiations, a status-of-forces agreement was signed between the Government and the United Nations on 14 May, facilitating the entire range of work of ONUMOZ.

However, the establishment of the National Elections Commission and the Commission of State Administration was still pending, and cantonment and demobilization of troops as well as the formation of the new army had not commenced. The Secretary-General told[6] the Security Council on 30 June 1993 that, unless the major provisions of the Agreement were implemented, the future stability of the country would remain uncertain. There should be no further delay in finalizing a new and realistic timetable for the implementation of the Agreement. He insisted that the cantonment and demobilization of troops

[5]S/25518. [6]S/26034.

should start soon and be completed early in 1994, and the training of a new Mozambican army should be initiated as soon as possible. To assist in that process, the Secretary-General was willing to accede to the request that ONUMOZ, with the consent of the Security Council, assume chairmanship of the Joint Commission for the Formation of the Mozambican Defence Force on the understanding that it would not entail any obligation on the part of the United Nations for training or establishing the new armed forces.

The revised timetable, as presented by the Secretary-General at that time, took as its point of departure the resumption of the work of the Joint Commissions beginning on 3 June 1993 and concluded 16 months later with the holding of elections in October 1994. The concentration and demobilization of Government and RENAMO troops, to be carried out in stages, was expected to take eight or nine months. The concentration of troops was scheduled to begin in September 1993 and would be followed a month later by the beginning of demobilization. It was expected that 50 per cent of the soldiers should have been demobilized by January 1994, and the demobilization of troops should be completed by May 1994.

It was expected that approximately 30,000 soldiers would be absorbed into the new army and that the remainder were to return to civilian life. Half the new army was to be operational by May 1994 and its formation was to be completed by September 1994. Home transportation of soldiers who would not be part of the new army was to start in October 1993, after demobilization began, and was to be concluded by April 1994 in order to enable the demobilized soldiers to register for the elections. Voter registration was expected to take three months and was scheduled to be carried out from April to June 1994. The repatriation of refugees and displaced persons was expected to be largely completed by April 1994 so that the resettled population might register in time for the elections.

The Secretary-General told the Council that, although the general parameters of the new timetable had been thoroughly discussed, he was still awaiting final agreement from both parties.

In resolution 850 (1993) of 9 July, the Security Council welcomed the progress made in the implementation of the Agreement but expressed concern over continuing delays, particularly in the assembly and demobilization of forces, the formation of the new unified armed forces, and the finalizing of election arrangements. It approved the Secretary-General's recommendation that ONUMOZ should chair the Joint Commission for the Formation of the Mozambican Defence Force. Further, the Council invited the Government and RENAMO to agree without delay to the revised timetable to implement the provisions of the Agreement based on the general parameters described by the Secretary-General.

Two major agreements

Direct talks between President Chissano and Mr. Dhlakama began on 23 August 1993 in Maputo. Although the revised timetable had not yet been formally approved by the Supervisory and Monitoring Commission, important progress was made in key areas. The Government explicitly agreed to the October 1994 deadline for the holding of the elections, while RENAMO also expressed its implicit agreement. The Secretary-General instructed his Special Representative to follow as closely as possible the revised timetable for assembly and demobilization of forces and the formation of the unified armed forces. He also strongly urged the parties to turn their dialogue into an ongoing and action-oriented process aimed at bringing the peace process to a successful conclusion.[7]

Two major agreements[8] were signed between the Government and RENAMO on 3 September 1993 as the outcome of the first meetings between the President of Mozambique and the President of RENAMO since the signing of the Agreement in October 1992. By the first agreement, the Government and RENAMO would integrate into the State administration the areas that had been under RENAMO control. By the second agreement, concerning the impartiality of the national police, the parties concurred to request the United Nations to monitor all police activities in the country, to monitor the rights and liberties of citizens and to provide technical support to the Police Commission (COMPOL) established under the Agreement. In particular, the proposed United Nations police contingent would be responsible for verifying that all police activities in the country were consistent with the Agreement.

The Secretary-General informed[9] the Council on 10 September that he planned to send to Mozambique a small survey team of experts and, based on their findings, make recommendations concerning the size of the police component. While awaiting those recommendations, preparations would commence to deploy the 128 ONUMOZ

---

[7]S/26385. [8]S/26432, annex. [9]S/26385/Add.1.

police observers already authorized by resolution 797 (1992) of 16 December 1992.

On 13 September 1993, the Security Council, by resolution 863 (1993), strongly urged the Government and RENAMO "to apply, without further postponement" the revised timetable for implementing the Agreement, and encouraged the President of Mozambique and the President of RENAMO to continue their direct talks. Further, it urged RENAMO to join the Government in authorizing immediate assembly of forces, and urged both parties to begin demobilizing troops, in accordance with the revised timetable and without preconditions.

Deploring the lack of progress in the multi-party consultative conference, the Security Council urged RENAMO and other political parties to join with the Government in quickly agreeing on an electoral law, which should include provision for an effective National Elections Commission. The Council called on the Government and RENAMO to make operational, without further delay, the National Commission for Administration, the National Information Commission and the Police Commission. The Council requested the Secretary-General to examine expeditiously the proposal of the Government and RENAMO for United Nations monitoring of police activities in the country, and welcomed his intention to send a survey team.

Secretary-General visits Mozambique

In an attempt to break the stalemate in the peace process, the Secretary-General visited Mozambique from 17 to 20 October 1993. He met with President Chissano and Mr. Dhlakama as well as with leaders of other political parties and representatives of the international community. On 20 October, the Secretary-General announced a breakthrough in the peace process. Major agreements had been reached between the Government and RENAMO on, among other things, the assembly and demobilization of RENAMO and Government troops as well as the simultaneous disarmament of paramilitary forces, militia and irregular troops; the composition of the National Elections Commission and the system and timetable for finalizing the Electoral Law; and the establishment of local Police Commission subcommittees to monitor the activities of the Mozambican police. Following those and other agreements, the revised timetable for the implementation of the Agreement was approved by the Supervisory and Monitoring Commission on 22 October 1993.

On 29 October 1993, the Security Council, by its resolution 879 (1993), decided to extend ONUMOZ's mandate for a short interim period. The Secretary-General submitted his further report[10] on 1 November 1993, and, on 5 November, the Security Council by resolution 882 (1993) renewed the mandate of ONUMOZ for six months, subject to a review within 90 days. The Council requested the Secretary-General to report by 31 January 1994 and every three months thereafter on whether the parties had made "sufficient and tangible progress" towards implementing the Agreement and meeting the revised timetable.

C. Operational activities

In fulfilling its mandate, ONUMOZ carried out extensive operational activities throughout Mozambique. The security of the four corridors and main roads was ensured by regular road and aerial patrol as well as by vehicle and train escorts provided by United Nations forces. They also provided security to oil-pumping stations, airports, United Nations warehouses, ONUMOZ headquarters and to temporary and permanent arms depots collected from Government and RENAMO troops. ONUMOZ's military component also contributed to humanitarian activities in the country by providing engineering and medical assistance. ONUMOZ military observers conducted inspections into allegations of cease-fire violations and assisted in the establishment and preparation of assembly areas. The observers supervised the process of cantonment of troops since its inception.

Security Council resolution 882 (1993) urged the parties to commence assembly of troops in November 1993 and to initiate demobilization

[10]S/26666.

by January 1994 with a view to ensuring the completion of the demobilization process by May 1994, in accordance with the timetable signed by the two parties in October 1993. On 30 November 1993, following a series of lengthy negotiations, troop cantonment formally commenced. An initial 20 of the total 49 assembly areas were opened (12 for the Government and 8 for RENAMO), and the assembly of troops began. Fifteen additional assembly areas were opened on 20 December. During the initial stages of cantonment, Government troops assembled in much larger numbers than RENAMO forces. This trend, however, was reversed by mid-December 1993. After delays in the dismantling of Government paramilitary forces and militia, scheduled to begin simultaneously with the assembly and demobilization of regular troops, the process was eventually initiated on 12 January 1994.

Notifications of alleged cease-fire violations were dealt with by the Cease-fire Commission with the active participation of ONUMOZ. On the whole, formally confirmed cease-fire violations were relatively few and presented no serious threat to the peace process. Basically, they fell into three categories: illegal detention of individuals, alleged movement of troops and occupation of new positions.

Formation of Mozambican Defence Force

On 22 July 1993, the Joint Commission for the Formation of the Mozambican Defence Force, under United Nations chairmanship, approved the Lisbon Declaration by which France, Portugal and the United Kingdom set out a programme aimed at assisting in the formation of the new unified army. The Commission decided to initiate the training of instructors for the new Mozambican army by sending 540 officers from the Government and RENAMO to a training facility at Nyanga, Zimbabwe. This training, conducted by the United Kingdom, was completed by 20 December 1993, and these officers were then transported by ONUMOZ to Mozambique on 12 January 1994 to help in training infantry soldiers at the three Mozambican Defence Force training centres. France and Portugal also conducted training programmes for different branches of the national armed forces.

Meanwhile, the Joint Commission approved a total of 19 documents relating to a number of matters including the organization, operating procedures, uniforms, ranking symbols and training of the unified armed forces.

Electoral process

On 26 March 1993, the Government prepared and distributed a draft electoral law to RENAMO and the other political parties. A multi-party consultative conference to discuss this document was convened on 27 April 1993. However, RENAMO initially refused to attend the meeting on the grounds that it had not had sufficient time to study the text. Smaller parties did attend, but walked out after having presented a declaration demanding material and financial support and alleging that there had been insufficient time for them to analyse the draft.

Although the conference resumed its work on 2 August 1993, with the presence of all political parties, including RENAMO, it reached a deadlock over an article on the composition of the National Elections Commission, meant to be the representative and impartial body responsible for organizing the parliamentary and presidential elections. This led to a breakdown of discussions. The deadlock was broken during the Secretary-General's visit to Mozambique from 17 to 20 October 1993 when agreements were reached between the Government and RENAMO on the issues of composition and chairmanship of the National Elections Commission. Subsequent discussions, however, reached an impasse over four other questions: (a) voting rights for expatriate Mozambicans; (b) composition of the provincial and district elections commissions; (c) composition of the Technical Secretariat for Electoral Administration; and (d) establishment and composition of an electoral tribunal. On 26 November 1993, a consensus on those questions was finally reached after a number of meetings were held between President Chissano and Mr. Dhlakama in consultation with the Special Representative.

Following these agreements, the Electoral Law was approved by the Mozambican National Assembly on 9 December 1993, nine days later than envisaged in the agreed timetable. It was promulgated by President Chissano shortly thereafter and entered into force on 12 January 1994. The members of the National Elections Commission were appointed on 21 January 1994.

Police component authorized

Despite significant progress, the Secretary-General told the Security Council at the end of January 1994, that several serious problems were unresolved. These included the opening of the remaining assembly sites, initiation and subsequent completion of the actual demobilization, transfer of weapons from assembly areas to regional warehouses, dismantling of the paramilitary forces, provision of financial support for the transformation of RENAMO from a military movement into a political party, and formation of a well-functioning national defence force.

The Secretary-General stated that it was the Mozambicans themselves who bore the main responsibility for success in the implementation of the Agreement. It was imperative that the two parties honour their commitments and cooperate closely with the United Nations in overcoming existing obstacles.

He also told the Council that recent political developments in Mozambique had evolved in such a way as to allow an increasing shift of focus from monitoring cease-fire arrangements to general verification of police activities in the country and the respect of civil rights. Therefore, he recommended[11] the establishment of a 1,144-strong ONUMOZ civilian police component inclusive of the 128 police officers already authorized by the Council. Being aware of the additional costs associated with the establishment of a sizeable United Nations police presence in the country, he proposed, following the expected completion of the demobilization of troops in May 1994, to begin a gradual decrease of ONUMOZ military elements.

On 23 February 1994, the Security Council, by resolution 898 (1994), authorized the establishment of the police component, as recommended by the Secretary-General. At the same time, concerned with cost implications, it requested him to prepare immediately specific proposals for the drawdown of military personnel so as to ensure that there be no increase in the Mission's costs. He was also requested to prepare a timetable for the completion of the ONUMOZ mandate, including withdrawal of its personnel by the end of November 1994 when the elected Government should assume office.

The ONUMOZ civilian police component (CIVPOL) was mandated to monitor all police activities in the country and verify that their actions were consistent with the Agreement. It was to monitor respect of citizens' rights and civil liberties, provide technical support to the National Police Commission and verify that the activities of private protection and security agencies did not violate the Agreement. In addition, CIVPOL would verify the strength and location of the Government police forces and their *matériel* and monitor and verify the process of reorganization and retraining of the rapid reaction police, including its activities, weapons and equipment. CIVPOL, together with other ONUMOZ components, monitored the proper conduct of the electoral campaign and verified that political rights of individuals, groups and political organizations were respected.

CIVPOL became a separate component of ONUMOZ under the command of a Chief Police Observer reporting directly to the Special Representative of the Secretary-General. It worked closely with the existing electoral, military, humanitarian and administrative components of ONUMOZ. After a period of difficulties, appropriate liaison arrangements were established with the national police at all levels, and CIVPOL itself had a presence at all strategic locations throughout the country. Despite some resistance, especially at the initial stages of the operation, it sought unrestricted access to the general public. It conducted all its own investigations and, when necessary, recommended corrective action.

As the Secretary-General recommended, CIVPOL was deployed progressively. The initial phase, during which the central headquarters and regional and provincial capitals teams were fully established, was completed in March 1994. The second phase coincided with the voter registration process, starting in April, during which some 60 to 70 per cent of CIVPOL posts and stations throughout the countryside became operational. The remainder of the component was deployed approximately one month before the beginning of the electoral campaign, originally scheduled for 1 September but in fact delayed till 22 September.

Progress on several fronts

In the course of March and April 1994, a number of important developments took place in Mozambique. During that period, there were no military activities in the country that posed a serious threat to the cease-fire or to the peace process as a whole. When demobilization began on 10 March 1994, the implementation of the Agreement entered into another critical phase. All 49 planned assembly areas were open and operational by 21 February. By mid-April, 55 per cent of Government

[11]S/1994/89/Add.1.

and 81 per cent of RENAMO soldiers were cantoned. As of 18 April, a total of 12,756 troops (12,195 Government and 561 RENAMO) were demobilized and transported to the districts of their choice. This corresponded to 20 per cent of Government and 3 per cent of RENAMO soldiers. The training programme for FADM, the new Mozambican armed forces, inaugurated in March, provided training for some 2,000 soldiers. The leaders of FADM, Generals Lagos Lidimo of the Government and Mateus Ngonhamo of RENAMO, took office on 6 April as joint commanders of the new army.

On 11 April, the President of Mozambique announced that the general elections would take place on 27 and 28 October 1994. The National Elections Commission had been inaugurated in February 1994, and its 10 provincial offices established by the end of March. The Technical Secretariat for Elections Administration had initiated its activities on 11 February. The Government decree that officially established the Secretariat was promulgated on 13 April.

By early 1994, considerable progress had also been made in resettling internally displaced persons and Mozambican refugees returning from neighbouring countries. The United Nations, in collaboration with other organizations concerned and bilateral donors, was pursuing programmes to assist the remaining 1 million internally displaced persons and 800,000 refugees to be resettled.

In the mean time, on 1 March 1994, the Secretary-General informed the Security Council of his decision to appoint Major-General Mohammad Abdus Salam (Bangladesh) to succeed Major-General Rodrigues da Silva as Force Commander. The appointment became effective on 23 March 1994.

In spite of the positive developments, some serious difficulties continued to hinder the timely completion of the peace process. Especially worrying were the delays in the assembly of Government troops, the demobilization of RENAMO troops and the training of FADM. In addition, the National Elections Commission might face potential practical difficulties in the complex process of voter registration. A number of problems also persisted in the areas of logistics, finance, the identification of party representatives and free access by the political parties to all districts of Mozambique.

By the end of April 1994, the Secretary-General was able to report[12] to the Security Council that the major political conditions for the timely completion of the Mission were in place. As ONUMOZ continued to play a vital role in the peace process, he recommended that the Council extend its mandate to 31 October 1994. He expected that liquidation of the Mission would be completed by 31 January 1995 and was making every effort to ensure that the deployment of the civilian police component would not entail an overall increase in the costs of the Mission. As requested by Security Council resolution 898 (1994) of 23 February, he outlined his plans for the reduction of the military elements of ONUMOZ. As of 18 April 1994, the military component totalled 5,914 all ranks, inclusive of 375 military observers. The Secretary-General foresaw a drawdown of some 2,000 ONUMOZ troops by the end of May. He did not recommend, however, any further reductions before the elections. Some redeployment of the military units was also recommended.

On 5 May 1994, the Security Council, by resolution 916 (1994), renewed the mandate of ONUMOZ at a reduced strength for a final period until 15 November 1994, subject to review. The Council also urged the two parties to meet the target dates of 1 June 1994 for the completion of the assembly of forces and 15 July 1994 for the completion of demobilization. While RENAMO accepted the deadlines, the Government declared that it would not be able to meet the target dates, but would conclude troop assembly by 1 July and demobilization by 15 August.

Security Council mission

The Government had declared in November 1992 that it would send 61,638 troops to its 29 assembly areas, with an additional 14,767 registered outside the assembly areas, for a total of 76,405. In April 1994, however, it presented substantially lower figures, saying that it had not deducted some 13,776 soldiers demobilized before the Agreement had been signed. RENAMO did not accept these figures. On 17 June 1994, following protracted investigations and negotiations, the two parties signed a joint declaration. Based on revised estimates, the new overall strength of the Government troops was established at 64,466, of which 49,638 would be registered in assembly areas. RENAMO agreed to use the revised Government figure as a working estimate and as a point of reference, on the condition that it would be verified by the Cease-fire Commission after the assembly of Government troops was completed.

The self-imposed 1 July deadline was not met. As of 4 July 1994, the Government had de-

[12]S/1994/511.

ONUMOZ military deployment as of October 1994

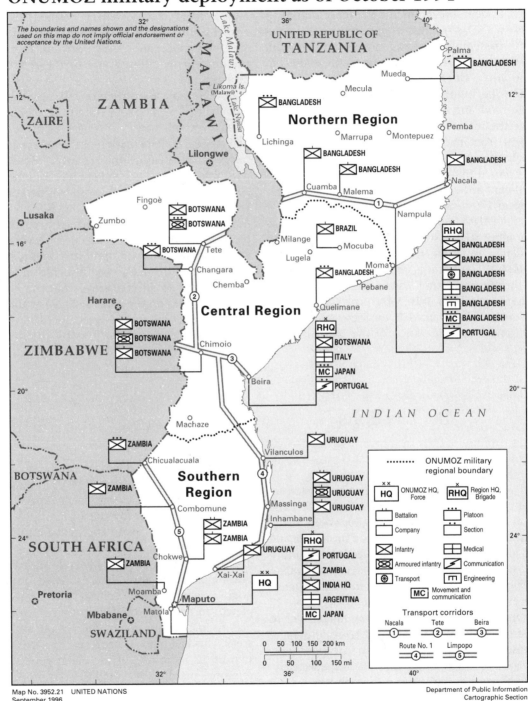

The boundaries and names shown and the designations used on this map do not imply official endorsement or acceptance by the United Nations.

Map No. 3952.21   UNITED NATIONS
September 1996

Department of Public Information
Cartographic Section

mobilized 22,832 soldiers, or 46 per cent of the expected total, while RENAMO had demobilized 5,138 soldiers, or 54 per cent of the expected total. The Secretary-General told[13] the Council on 7 July that a dramatic effort was required to complete the demobilization process by 15 August. In addition, delays in demobilization and the selection of soldiers for FADM resulted in prolonged waiting periods in assembly areas and mounting frustration, demonstrations and even rioting by the soldiers in some areas. On a number of occasions, United Nations personnel were attacked and threatened, while food and other supplied were looted. Because the main body of the Italian infantry contingent from the central region of Mozambique had been repatriated, the Secretary-General told the Council that he had decided to deploy in July a self-contained infantry company with a strength of up to 170 personnel provided by Brazil.

FADM, according to the Agreement, was to number 30,000 soldiers, half of this number to be drawn from the Government and half from RENAMO. The training programme sponsored by the three participating States covered only 15,000 soldiers, and by 4 July 1994 only 3,000 FADM soldiers had been trained. In the Secretary-General's view, and in consideration of the difficulties in-volved, it would be preferable for the soldiers covered by the training programmes to be formed prior to the elections, and the second group after the elections. However, with the approach of the elections and the delays experienced in troop assembly and demobilization and the formation of FADM, the Secretary-General warned that three armies could potentially be in existence during the election period, thus posing a serious threat to the stability of the country and of the entire peace process.

In these circumstances, the Security Council decided[14] to send a mission to Mozambique to discuss with the parties how best to ensure the full and timely implementation of the Agreement. The mission consisted of nine Security Council members: Brazil, China, Czech Republic, Djibouti, New Zealand, Nigeria, Oman, Russian Federation and United States. Visiting Mozambique from 7 to 12 August 1994, the mission formed a positive impression of the pace of the peace process and maintained a cautious optimism about its prospects, despite the delays and difficulties. The mission stressed to all concerned that the elections should be held on the dates agreed and under the conditions set out in the Agreement.[15]

D. Elections

Run-up period

Voter registration for elections began on 1 June and was extended until 2 September. The initial estimate of 8.5 million eligible voters, based on the 1980 census, was considered inaccurate and was lowered by the National Elections Commission. Of the new estimate — 7,894,850 — more than three-quarters had been registered by 22 August. The electoral campaign was set to begin on 22 September, and a trust fund was established to assist the political parties to organize and prepare themselves for active participation in the elections.

Reporting[16] on 26 August 1994, the Secretary-General advised the Security Council that several of the difficulties he had previously cited had been overcome. He also pointed to the considerable progress in implementing humanitarian programmes, contributing to the overall efforts to achieve national reconciliation. About 75 per cent of those who were internally displaced at the time of signature of the Agreement had been resettled. There were still an estimated 342,000 refugees in neighbouring countries who were expected to return to Mozambique by the end of 1994. Some progress was also made in the de-mining programme. Security, however, remained a serious concern. Rioting among soldiers, both inside and outside assembly areas, had escalated until early August, when demobilization was nearly completed. In addition, the level of criminal activity had risen dramatically in both rural and urban areas. This had made it necessary for ONUMOZ to step up its patrolling of the major routes and to reinforce guarding of United Nations property and key locations. The most significant role for the United Nations during September and October would involve technical preparations for the conduct of the poll and assistance in bringing about

[13]S/1994/803. [14]S/1994/931. [15]S/1994/1009. [16]S/1994/1002.

the conditions necessary for the holding of free and fair elections, as well as in the creation of an environment conducive to a stable and peaceful transition to a democratically elected Government.

By 21 October, the Secretary-General was able to report[17] to the Security Council that Mozambique was ready to hold free and fair elections as scheduled. There had been no violation of the cease-fire for many months; voter registration had concluded in an orderly manner; and the electoral campaign was in its active phase. More than 75,000 soldiers had been demobilized and approximately 10,000 soldiers had been incorporated into the unified army. The number of incidents of violent rioting in the country had fallen, and the political situation was relatively calm.

On the negative side, the Secretary-General noted that the atmosphere during the electoral campaign was tense and that armed banditry had become widespread. This situation was exacerbated by the continuing proliferation of weapons despite the fact that 111,539 weapons had been collected from troops of the two parties and 43,491 from the paramilitary forces. There had also been a number of public pronouncements by certain candidates which could cast doubt on their commitment to accept the results of the elections.

The Secretary-General further stated that there was an obvious risk that the political temperature would rise before and immediately after the poll and that particular caution and statesmanship would be required at that time by all concerned. The future of Mozambique, he concluded, lay in the hands of its people and their leaders.

The Security Council, in a statement by its President, also expressed[18] its belief that the necessary conditions had been established for holding free and fair elections on 27 and 28 October under effective national and international monitoring. The Council appealed to all concerned to ensure that the election campaign and subsequent voting be calmly and responsibly conducted and that the elections be held freely and fairly. It also appealed that those in authority act with complete impartiality and that there be no violence or threat of violence during the election days and their aftermath. The Council reminded the parties of their obligation, under the Agreement, fully to abide by the results of the elections.

The vote

On the eve of the elections, the international community deployed approximately 2,300 electoral observers, including some 900 from the United Nations, to observe and verify the polling and the counting of votes in all provinces of the country. Several organizations, including OAU, the European Union and the Association of European Parliamentarians for Southern Africa, sent teams of their own electoral observers. As scheduled, polling stations opened on 27 October 1994.

The peace process had been threatened, however, when, on 26 October, the President of RENAMO alleged irregularities in the election process and announced his decision to withdraw. The Security Council immediately appealed[19] to Mr. Dhlakama to reconsider his decision, saying that appropriate procedures were in place through the National Elections Commission whereby any concern RENAMO might have could be addressed. The Secretary-General also emphasized[20] that the parties should fully honour their commitments and the elections should go ahead as planned and agreed by the parties.

The Special Representative engaged in an intensive effort to resolve the situation and established contact with Mr. Dhlakama. His efforts were fully supported by the ambassadors of the States members of the Supervision and Control Commission and by other ambassadors in Maputo. The Presidents of South Africa, Zimbabwe and several other countries of the region urged Mr. Dhlakama to reconsider his decision.

Despite Mr. Dhlakama's call to boycott the elections, United Nations monitors reported large turnouts and no major irregularities at polling stations; more than half of the registered voters cast their ballots on the first day. RENAMO monitors were present at most polling stations. On 28 October, Mr. Dhlakama reversed his position and decided to vote. The voting period was extended by one day to 29 October to allow all registered voters to exercise their rights. Meanwhile, the National Elections Commission in close cooperation with ONUMOZ undertook to make every effort to ensure that the complaints about irregularities submitted by RENAMO and some other parties were fully investigated.

According to a preliminary statement[21] by the Special Representative of the Secretary-General, the elections had been conducted peacefully, in a well-organized manner, and without any

[17]S/1994/1196. [18]S/PRST/1994/61. [19]SC/5922. [20]SG/SM/5456. [21]S/1994/1282, annex

major irregularities or incidents. In some provinces, more than 90 per cent of the registered electorate had voted. The Special Representative stressed that United Nations observation could not support any claim of fraud or intimidation, or any other pattern of incidents that could affect the credibility of the elections. He said that the counting of ballots was under way, and that ONUMOZ would maintain its vigilance. Once the count was completed, he would be in a position to make an official pronouncement on the freedom and fairness of the entire electoral process.

ONUMOZ mandate extended

The installation of the new Government was expected to take place by 15 December 1994, following the publication of the final electoral results. On 15 November, however, the mandate of ONUMOZ was scheduled to expire. The Secretary-General therefore recommended[22] to the Security Council that the mandate be extended accordingly until the Government was installed. During that period, ONUMOZ would continue its functions of good offices, as well as its verification and monitoring activities, as mandated by the relevant Security Council resolutions.

On 15 November, the Security Council, by its resolution 957 (1994), extended the mandate of ONUMOZ until the new Government took office, but no later than 15 December, and authorized it to complete residual operations prior to its withdrawal on or before 31 January 1995. The Council welcomed the peaceful manner under which the elections had been conducted and reiterated its intention to endorse the results, should the United Nations declare the elections free and fair. It called on the parties to accept and fully abide by them.

Elections declared free and fair

Announcement of the results was to take place 15 days after the close of the polls. However, the announcement by the National Elections Commission came on 19 November 1994. This delay was mainly due to the need to ensure absolute accuracy and transparency under the scrutiny of political party monitors and United Nations observers. In addition, computer program errors complicated the computerization of the data at the provincial level.

The incumbent President, Mr. Chissano, won the presidential election with 2,633,740 votes, amounting to 53.3 per cent. The leader of RENAMO, Mr. Dhlakama, received 1,666,965 votes, or 33.7 per cent. The candidate receiving the third largest number of votes (2.9 per cent) was Mr. Wehia Ripua of the Partido Democrático de Mozambique. A total of 5,402,940 persons, representing 87.9 per cent of all registered voters, participated in the presidential election. Blank votes amounted to 5.8 per cent, while 2.8 per cent were considered invalid by the National Elections Commission.

In the legislative election, FRELIMO received the largest share of the votes with 2,115,793 (44.3 per cent), followed by RENAMO with 1,803,506 votes (37.8 per cent) and the União Democrática (UD) with 245,793 votes (5.2 per cent). The 250 seats in the new parliament were apportioned as follows: FRELIMO, 129; RENAMO, 109; and UD, 12.

The Secretary-General's Special Representative issued a statement[23] on 19 November saying that the electoral process had been characterized by the impartiality, dedication and high professionalism of the electoral authorities. It had been distinguished by the strong commitment of the political players to let the principles of democracy prevail and had confirmed the will of the Mozambican people to live in peace and harmony. The Special Representative noted that, although there had been problems, minor irregularities and disruption, there was no event or series of events, throughout the entire process, which could affect the overall credibility of the elections. On behalf of the United Nations, he therefore declared that the elections held in Mozambique from 27 to 29 October 1994 had been free and fair. The Secretary-General also issued a statement[24] in which he congratulated the people and the leaders of Mozambique on the successful outcome of the elections. He called on all Mozambicans to pursue the task of national reconciliation and to ensure that peace and stability prevailed in their country and region. The Security Council endorsed the results of the elections by its resolution 960 (1994) of 21 November 1994.

After the new Parliament was installed in Maputo on 8 December, and Mr. Chissano was inaugurated as President the following day, the mandate of ONUMOZ formally came to an end at midnight on 9 December. The Special Representative of the Secretary-General left Mozambique on 13 December 1994. The final liquidation of ONUMOZ assets in Mozambique was accomplished by the end of January 1995. When the last

[22]S/1994/1282. [23]SG/SM/5488. [24]SG/SM/5489.

members of the Mission left the country, other United Nations personnel remained, working in a variety of economic and social assistance programmes aimed at helping Mozambique recover from the long period of war.

E. Humanitarian programme

The Agreement placed humanitarian assistance firmly within the context of peacemaking and peace-keeping. The declaration on guiding principles for humanitarian assistance, signed in July 1992, specifically called on the United Nations to coordinate the provision of humanitarian assistance to Mozambique. UNOHAC, as the practical expression of the coordination role of the United Nations Department of Humanitarian Affairs, was transformed by the Security Council in its resolution 797 (1992) into the humanitarian component of ONUMOZ.

The international community contributed directly more than 78 per cent of the approximately $650 million required to meet Mozambique's needs for humanitarian assistance during the period of the ONUMOZ mandate. The United Nations system of organizations and agencies, international public and non-governmental organizations, as well as a number of Mozambican entities, played an essential role in the design and implementation of both the individual and the overall humanitarian programmes. The Coordinated Programme of Assistance, which was developed in cooperation with the donor community and the two major parties, placed emphasis on the restoration of essential services in rural areas, particularly for the returning refugees and displaced persons.

At the end of the ONUMOZ mandate, UNOHAC transferred its coordination responsibilities to the United Nations Resident Coordinator in Maputo. The ongoing mine-clearance programme became a joint responsibility of UNDP and the Department of Humanitarian Affairs.

Reintegration

A major goal of the ONUMOZ humanitarian assistance programme was to respond effectively to the reintegration needs of all Mozambicans, particularly those returning to resettle in their original communities. It had been projected that approximately 6 million Mozambicans would resettle during a period of two years, including about 4.0 to 4.5 million internally displaced persons, 1.5 million refugees and 370,000 demobilized soldiers and their dependants. This situation necessitated a shift in emphasis from emergency humanitarian relief towards reintegration and rehabilitation. Humanitarian assistance committees convened by UNOHAC's field officers in the provinces expanded contacts among all concerned parties.

By the end of 1993, the Office of the United Nations High Commissioner for Refugees (UNHCR) estimated that more than half of Mozambique's 1.5 million refugees had returned to the country. A further 350,000 were expected to return by the end of 1994, with the remaining 375,000 expected to repatriate during 1995. By October 1994, the international humanitarian assistance programme had also aided the resettlement and reintegration of some 3 million internally displaced persons and 200,000 former combatants and their dependants. During the demobilization process, UNOHAC focused particular attention on its programme for the reintegration of former combatants into civilian life and worked through informal tripartite discussions within the Reintegration Commission to secure agreement on a strategy to address the needs of ex-soldiers.

Since some 20,000 more Government and RENAMO soldiers than the originally envisaged 57,103 were demobilized, the budget for the Reintegration Support Scheme increased to $31.9 million, of which $27.6 million was pledged and only $8.9 million received. The scheme, which was implemented by UNDP, included cash payments, vocational training, promotion of small-scale economic activities and credit facilities for the demobilized soldiers, and was essential for the successful reintegration of the ex-combatants into civilian life.

By the time ONUMOZ drew to a close in December 1994, approximately 4.3 million people had returned to their original areas of residence. In addition, emergency assistance was being distributed by over 40 organizations to beneficiaries at more than 300 delivery points within previously inaccessible areas.

Landmines

It was estimated that more than two million uncleared landmines were scattered throughout Mozambique. Following the signing of the Agreement, the United Nations was asked to provide assistance for mine-clearance activities. Accordingly, the Security Council approved mine clearance as part of the ONUMOZ mandate. A total of $11 million was set aside in the ONUMOZ budget for this purpose, and a further $7.5 million was contributed to a trust fund of the Department of Humanitarian Affairs. In addition, Mozambique benefited from some bilateral assistance. Overall management of the mine-clearance programme was assigned to UNDP in October 1993.

Although mine-clearance programmes were slow to reach the implementation stage, major hurdles were overcome and a National Mine-Clearance Plan began coordinating efforts to clear 4,000 km of roads in the initial phase, to develop mine awareness programmes and train Mozambican nationals in mine clearance and related technologies. In May 1994, UNOHAC assumed responsibility for assuring that the objectives of the ONUMOZ mandate for mine clearance were achieved expeditiously. The accelerated programme was aimed at creating and fostering a national capacity for mine clearance.

By the end of the mandate of ONUMOZ, the programme had been able to train 450 Mozambicans to man 10 de-mining teams operating in the southern areas of Maputo province. They cleared some 40,000 square metres and disabled over 555 mines. The programme also achieved a significant number of other goals, including the training of de-mining team supervisors, minefield surveyors, paramedics, explosive ordnance disposal specialists and logisticians, and for general administrative and other functions.

The accelerated de-mining programme relied on funds from the ONUMOZ budget and a contribution by the Government of Italy, and on personnel provided for the most part by the Governments of Australia, Bangladesh, Germany, the Netherlands and New Zealand. In July 1994, UNDP and the Office for Project Services contracted a commercial firm to clear mines from certain priority roads. International non-governmental organizations and a number of commercial firms were also clearing mines. Parties concerned with de-mining in Mozambique shared the view that there was a need for the establishment of an entity at the national level to provide the various de-mining organizations and companies with policy orientation, operational standards and coherence.

Other programmes

At the time of the establishment of ONUMOZ, 80 per cent of the primary schools in Mozambique had either been closed or destroyed and the availability of other social services was minimal. With the help of UNHCR and a number of non-governmental organizations, more than 700 primary schools and 250 health facilities were built in rural areas. Among other programmes, reconstruction of another 310 health posts was planned through a joint project of the World Bank and the World Food Programme (WFP). Approximately 2,000 wells were opened or rehabilitated, and the national Programme for Rural Water Supply was working in concert with the United Nations Children's Fund (UNICEF) to provide one water source per 500 people. In addition, WFP and local authorities worked together to distribute increasing amounts of seed.

F. ONUMOZ in review

The original authorized strength estimates of ONUMOZ included a military contingent of 6,625 personnel, a military observer group of 354 officers, some 355 international staff and 506 local staff. On 23 February 1994, the Security Council, by its resolution 898 (1994), authorized the establishment of a 1,144-strong civilian police component inclusive of the 128 civilian police authorized earlier.

During the course of the mission the following States provided military and civilian police personnel: Argentina, Australia, Austria, Bangladesh, Bolivia, Botswana, Brazil, Canada, Cape Verde, China, Czech Republic, Egypt, Finland, Ghana, Guinea Bissau, Guyana, Hungary, India, Indonesia, Ireland, Italy, Japan, Jordan, Malaysia, Nepal, Netherlands, New Zealand, Nigeria, Norway, Pakistan, Portugal, Russian Federation, Spain, Sri Lanka, Sweden, Switzerland, Togo, United States, Uruguay, Zambia.

Mr. Aldo Ajello (Italy) served as Special Representative of the Secretary-General for Mozambique from 13 October 1992. The Office of the Special Representative was comprised of a small number of international professional and support staff as well as an adequate number of locally recruited personnel. On 12 February 1993, Major-General Lélio Gonçalves Rodrigues da Silva (Brazil) assumed his duties as Force Commander of ONUMOZ. He was succeeded as Force Commander on 23 March 1994 by Major-General Mohammad Abdus Salam (Bangladesh).

The ONUMOZ Electoral Division included some 148 international electoral officers. During the polling itself, ONUMOZ deployed approximately 900 United Nations electoral observers throughout the country. They were supported by some 1,400 various international observers assisting in the verification.

Some 250 international professional and support staff and about 500 local staff provided secretariat functions and administrative support to the military, electoral and humanitarian components of ONUMOZ, as well as to the Commissions chaired by the United Nations. UNOHAC had a small number of international professional staff to coordinate and monitor all humanitarian assistance in Mozambique; it was assisted by an ONUMOZ technical unit in the humanitarian aspects of the demobilization process.

Costs of ONUMOZ were considered an expense of the Organization to be borne by Member States in accordance with Article 17, paragraph 2, of the United Nations Charter. Expenditures for the period 15 October 1992 to 15 November 1994 amounted to $471,199,200. For the liquidation period from 16 November 1994 to 31 March 1995, the General Assembly decided, by its resolution 49/235 of 10 March 1995, to appropriate to the ONUMOZ Special Account the amount of $39,053,300 net.

ONUMOZ carried out its mandate over a two-year period, twelve months longer than initially planned. It verified and monitored the implementation of the General Peace Agreement signed on 4 October 1992 in Rome, from the verification of the cease-fire arrangements and establishment of the implementation structures to the assembly of approximately 92,000 troops and demobilization of 80,000 of them. Within its limited mandate, it assisted in the formation of a new army constituted of soldiers who had fought on opposite sides in a bitter civil war. One of the largest police components in the history of United Nations peace-keeping operations verified all the activities of the national police, enhancing confidence among the population. ONUMOZ coordinated and monitored humanitarian assistance operations that benefited millions of people, initiated a reintegration programme for demobilized soldiers and began training Mozambicans to undertake long-term programmes to remove landmines. With the assistance of the United Nations and its agencies, more than four million people voluntarily returned to their place of origin, including one and a half million who had been refugees in neighbouring countries. With technical assistance and diplomatic skill, ONUMOZ steered a war-torn society through the entire electoral process, culminating in free and fair elections in October 1994.

The Secretary-General described the accomplishment of the mandate as a remarkable achievement.[25] A number of factors had been involved in this success. Among them were the strong commitment to peace and reconciliation demonstrated by the Mozambican people and their leaders and the political pragmatism shown by the parties to the General Peace Agreement. Other factors were the clarity of the ONUMOZ mandate, the consistent support provided by the Security Council and the international community's significant political, financial and technical support of the peace process. ONUMOZ represented an example of what could be achieved through the United Nations when all forces joined together in one common endeavour towards a common goal.

Although all major aspects of the General Peace Agreement and the ONUMOZ mandate were implemented, many issues remained. These included the existence of arms caches in the country and the safe keeping of weapons collected by ONUMOZ; the incomplete integration of the territorial administration; and the continued presence of mines throughout the country. It would also be essential to continue to train and equip the new armed forces and to upgrade the national police. Mozambique's democratic institutions would also need to be strengthened and economic and social reconstruction promoted in order to

[25]S/1994/1449.

ensure that peace, democracy and development could be sustained.

For its part, the Security Council welcomed[26] the installation of the President and the inauguration of the new Assembly of the Republic. In congratulating the people and the parties of Mozambique for the fulfillment of the General Peace Agreement, the Council emphasized the continuing need in the post-election period for the assistance of the international community in the reconstruction and redevelopment of the country. The Council urged all States and relevant international organizations to contribute actively to those efforts.

[26]S/PRST/1994/80.

Chapter 16

United Nations Observer Mission Uganda-Rwanda (UNOMUR)

United Nations Assistance Mission for Rwanda (UNAMIR)

F. October 1994–May 1995
UNAMIR fully deployed
Security in the camps
Challenges remain
Displaced persons camps
Commission of Experts
International Tribunal
Security Council mission to Rwanda
The Kibeho tragedy
Humanitarian aspects
Security measures in the refugee camps
HRFOR
UNAMIR activities

G. June–December 1995
A new situation
Arms embargo lifted
August 1995 refugee crisis
Political situation in Rwanda
UNAMIR downsized
Other developments
Security Council welcomes progress
Regional conference

H. Final period
Commission of inquiry
UNAMIR's mandate ends

I. Composition of UNOMUR and UNAMIR

J. Financial aspects

Chapter 16

United Nations Observer Mission Uganda-Rwanda (UNOMUR)

United Nations Assistance Mission for Rwanda (UNAMIR)

A. Background

Rwanda is one of the most densely populated countries in the world. It is located in central Africa, bordered on the north by Uganda, to the northwest and west by Zaire, to the south by Burundi and to the east by Tanzania. The country was a German colony from 1884 to 1916 and was then placed by the League of Nations, and subsequently by the United Nations, under Belgian trusteeship from 1918 to 1962. Rwanda became independent in 1962.

Its population of over 7 million is divided into three ethnic groups, the Hutu (about 85 per cent), the Tutsi (about 14 per cent) and the Twa (about 1 per cent). The three groups speak the same language and share the same culture. Transition from the Hutu group to the Tutsi group, and vice versa, was possible. The Belgian colonial authorities, however, required that identity cards specify ethnic group. From then on, membership of an ethnic group was strictly defined for administrative purposes, and social categories became increasingly rigid. The Tutsi dominated the country's political and economic life until 1959, when the Hutu "social revolution" put an end to the monarchy. With the ensuing ethnic violence, a large number of Tutsi left Rwanda and sought refuge in neighbouring countries, especially in Uganda, although they repeatedly attempted to stage an armed comeback. There were about 10 such attempts until 1967, each giving rise to renewed ethnic violence and retaliation.

In 1973, when ethnic unrest and violence were at their height, Major-General Juvénal Habyarimana took power in a military *coup d'état*. He founded the second Republic, dominated by a single party, the National Revolutionary Movement for Democracy and Development. Previous practices of ethnic discrimination were institutionalized during this period through a policy known as "establishing ethnic and regional balance". Most of the country's political and social life became subject to quotas established according to "ethnic proportions", which determined the posts and resources allocated to the various ethnic groups (10 per cent for the Tutsi). As from 1973, regional rivalries were added to this ethnic antagonism (President Habyarimana was from the north).

A few months after the announcement by the President that the country would be opened to multi-party rule and democratization, an attack was launched across the Rwanda-Uganda border in October 1990 by the Rwandese Patriotic Front (RPF), an armed force consisting mainly of Tutsi refugees living in Uganda. The result of this attack, and of a policy of deliberately targeted government propaganda, was that all Tutsi inside the country were collectively labelled as accomplices of RPF. In addition, some members of the opposition parties, though Hutu themselves, were also accused of betraying their country because of their opposition to the Government in power and their attempts to enter into a dialogue with RPF.[1]

---

[1] E/CN.4/1994/7/Add.1.

B. United Nations involvement

A number of cease-fire agreements followed the outbreak of fighting in 1990, including one negotiated at Arusha, United Republic of Tanzania, on 22 July 1992, which arranged for the presence in Rwanda of a 50-member Neutral Military Observer Group (NMOG I) furnished by the Organization of African Unity (OAU). Hostilities resumed in the northern part of the country in early February 1993, interrupting comprehensive negotiations, supported by OAU and facilitated by Tanzania, between the Government of Rwanda and RPF.

Meanwhile, Rwanda continued to accuse Uganda of supporting RPF; Uganda denied the allegations. On 22 February 1993, both countries asked the United Nations to help establish the facts. In separate letters[2] to the President of the United Nations Security Council, the two countries called for the deployment of United Nations military observers along their 150-kilometre common border in order to prevent the military use of the area, especially the transportation of military supplies.

Secretary-General Boutros Boutros-Ghali decided to send a goodwill mission to Rwanda and Uganda from 4 to 18 March 1993. Meanwhile, efforts by OAU and Tanzania led to a meeting between the Government of Rwanda and RPF from 5 to 7 March in Dar es Salaam, the capital of Tanzania. In a joint communiqué, the Government of Rwanda and RPF agreed to reinstate the cease-fire on 9 March and to resume peace talks in Arusha. On 12 March 1993, the Security Council, by its resolution 812 (1993), called on the Government of Rwanda and RPF to respect the renewed cease-fire and requested the Secretary-General to examine the requests of Rwanda and Uganda for the deployment of observers.

A technical mission dispatched by the Secretary-General to the border area visited Uganda from 2 to 5 April and Rwanda on 6 April. The mission reported that it would be possible to deploy United Nations military observers to monitor the border between Uganda and Rwanda and verify that no military assistance was being provided across it. Because RPF control of the border area was extensive, the military observers had to be deployed on the Ugandan side of the border.[3]

Security Council authorizes UNOMUR

On 22 June 1993, the Security Council, by its resolution 846 (1993), authorized the establishment of the United Nations Observer Mission Uganda-Rwanda (UNOMUR) on the Uganda side of the common border, for an initial period of six months, subject to review every six months. The Council decided that the verification would focus primarily on transit or transport, by roads or tracks which could accommodate vehicles, of lethal weapons and ammunition across the border, as well as any other material which could be of military use.

The Council welcomed the Secretary-General's decision to support the peace-keeping efforts of OAU by putting two military experts at its disposal to help expedite the deployment of OAU's expanded NMOG to Rwanda. It also urged the Government of Rwanda and RPF to conclude quickly a comprehensive peace agreement, and requested the Secretary-General to report on the contribution the United Nations could make to assist OAU in implementing this agreement and to begin contingency planning in the event that the Council decided that such a contribution was needed. On 29 June 1993, the Secretary-General informed[4] the Council of his intention to appoint Brigadier-General Romeo A. Dallaire (Canada) as Chief Military Observer (CMO) of UNOMUR.

As requested by resolution 846 (1993), the United Nations undertook consultations with the Government of Uganda with a view to concluding a status of mission agreement for UNOMUR. The agreement was finalized and entered into force on 16 August 1993. This opened the way to deployment of an advance party which arrived in the mission area on 18 August. UNOMUR established its headquarters in Kabale, Uganda, about 20 kilometres north of the border with Rwanda. By the end of September, the Mission had reached its authorized strength of 81 military observers and was fully operational. Observers were provided by the following countries: Bangladesh, Botswana, Brazil, Hungary, Netherlands, Senegal, Slovak Republic and Zimbabwe.

[2]S/25355, S/25356. [3]S/25810. [4]S/26019.

Arusha peace talks

Meanwhile, the Arusha talks reconvened on 16 March 1993. The United Nations Secretary-General was represented by Mr. Macaire Pédanou, head of the United Nations goodwill mission that visited Rwanda earlier that month. On 11 June, the two parties called[5] on the United Nations to send a reconnaissance mission to Rwanda to prepare for the quick deployment of a neutral international force as soon as the peace agreement was signed, and welcomed the OAU suggestion that the United Nations assume responsibility for the force. The force would assist in the maintenance of public security and in the delivery of humanitarian aid and in searches for weapons caches, neutralization of armed bands, de-mining, disarmament of civilians and the cessation of hostilities. The parties also requested that the international force oversee the demobilization of existing armed forces and of all aspects of the formation of the new National Army and National Gendarmerie.

The talks in Arusha were finally concluded on 4 August 1993. The comprehensive peace agreement called for a democratically elected government and provided for the establishment of a broad-based transitional Government until the elections, in addition to repatriation of refugees and integration of the armed forces of the two sides. Both sides asked the United Nations to assist in the implementation of the agreement. In early August 1993, NMOG I was replaced by an expanded NMOG II force, composed of some 130 personnel to operate as an interim measure pending the deployment of the neutral international force.

UNAMIR recommended

A United Nations reconnaissance mission visited Rwanda from 19 to 31 August 1993. Its senior officials also consulted with the Government of Tanzania and the Secretary-General of OAU.[6] On the basis of the mission's findings, the Secretary-General recommended[7] to the Security Council the establishment of a United Nations Assistance Mission for Rwanda (UNAMIR), with the mandate of "contributing to the establishment and maintenance of a climate conducive to the secure installation and subsequent operation of the transitional Government".

The principal functions of UNAMIR would be to assist in ensuring the security of the capital city of Kigali; monitor the cease-fire agreement, including establishment of an expanded demilitarized zone (DMZ) and demobilization procedures; monitor the security situation during the final period of the transitional Government's mandate leading up to elections; and assist with mine-clearance. The Mission would also investigate alleged non-compliance with any provisions of the peace agreement and provide security for the repatriation of Rwandese refugees and displaced persons. In addition, it would assist in the coordination of humanitarian assistance activities in conjunction with relief operations.

The Secretary-General proposed that the military observers of UNOMUR come under the command of the new Mission, while maintaining their separate monitoring tasks on the Uganda-Rwanda border. UNAMIR would also incorporate elements of NMOG II which was mandated by OAU to supervise the cease-fire until 31 October 1993.

The operation would be conducted in four phases. The first phase would begin on the day the Security Council established UNAMIR and would end on the day the transitional Government was installed, estimated in late 1993. UNAMIR's objective would be to establish conditions for the secure installation of such a Government, and its strength, by the end of phase one, would total 1,428 military personnel. During phase two, expected to last 90 days or until the process of disengagement, demobilization and integration of the Armed Forces and Gendarmerie began, the build-up of the Mission would continue to a total of 2,548 military personnel. UNAMIR would continue to monitor the DMZ, to assist in providing security in Kigali and in the demarcation of the assembly zones, and to ensure that all preparations for disengagement, demobilization and integration were in place.

During phase three, which would last about 9 months, the Mission would establish, supervise and monitor a new DMZ and continue to provide security in Kigali. The disengagement, demobilization and integration of the Forces and the Gendarmerie would be completed in this stage, and the Mission would reduce its staff to approximately 1,240 personnel. Phase four, which would last about four months, would see a further reduction of the Mission's strength to the minimum level of approximately 930 military personnel. UNAMIR would assist in ensuring the secure atmosphere required in the final stages of the transitional period leading up to the elections.

[5]S/25951. [6]S/26350. [7]S/26488.

In order to verify that law and order were maintained effectively and impartially, the Secretary-General proposed to deploy a small United Nations civilian police unit in Kigali and the nine prefecture capitals of Rwanda and in specific police installations.

Humanitarian assistance

In early 1993, there had been a threefold increase in the number of displaced persons. Local capacity was overwhelmed. As the result of a request by the President of Rwanda to the Secretary-General, the United Nations launched an inter-agency appeal on 15 April 1993 for international assistance to Rwanda to cover the period from April to December 1993, amounting to $78 million to meet the needs of over 900,000 war-displaced people, or approximately 13 per cent of the nation's population.

Most of the displaced people were living in and around 30 camps, where serious malnutri-tion and disease were prevalent. The situation was exacerbated by Rwanda's already precarious economic condition, overpopulation and rapidly declining agricultural production. An inter-agency mission was fielded between 18 and 25 March 1993 to prepare a consolidated appeal focusing on food, nutrition, health, water and sanitation, shelter and household items and education. By late 1993, contributions in cash and in kind amounting to some $33 million had been made available to the United Nations agencies carrying out humanitarian activities in Rwanda. With the signing of the Arusha Peace Agreement, it was estimated that some 600,000 individuals returned home, thus easing the emergency situation. The emphasis of the humanitarian assistance efforts then shifted to meeting the needs of the displaced returning home. At the same time, some 300,000 people who remained displaced continued to rely on emergency assistance in the camps.

C. October 1993–March 1994

UNAMIR established

UNAMIR was established on 5 October by Security Council resolution 872 (1993) for an initial period of six months with the proviso that it would be extended beyond the initial 90 days only upon a review by the Council. UNAMIR's mandate was to end following national elections and the installation of a new government in Rwanda, events scheduled to occur by October 1995, but no later than December 1995. The Council then authorized the Secretary-General to deploy a first contingent to Kigali, which would permit the establishment of the transitional institutions and implementation of the other relevant provisions of the Peace Agreement.

The Council also urged the parties to implement the Arusha Agreement in good faith and called upon Member States, United Nations specialized agencies and non-governmental organizations to provide and intensify their economic, financial and humanitarian assistance. It welcomed the intention of the Secretary-General to appoint a Special Representative who would lead UNAMIR in the field and exercise authority over all its elements.

On 18 October 1993, the Secretary-General informed[8] the Council that he would appoint Brigadier-General Dallaire, then CMO of UNOMUR, as UNAMIR Force Commander. General Dallaire arrived in Kigali on 22 October 1993, followed by an advance party of 21 military personnel on 27 October. A status of forces agreement was signed by the Government on 5 November 1993, and a copy was forwarded to RPF, which confirmed its readiness to cooperate in its implementation. On 12 November, the Secretary-General informed[9] the Council that he had decided to appoint as his Special Representative for Rwanda Mr. Jacques-Roger Booh-Booh, former Minister for External Relations of Cameroon. Mr. Booh-Booh arrived in Kigali on 23 November 1993.

UNOMUR activities in the border area

Meanwhile, UNOMUR established observation posts at two major crossing sites and three secondary sites on the Ugandan side of the border. The mission monitored the border area through

[8]S/26593. [9]S/26730.

mobile patrols enhanced by airborne coverage. It also facilitated the transit of vehicles transporting food and medical supplies to Rwanda. The Secretary-General noted[10] on 15 December 1993 that UNOMUR was "a factor of stability in the area and that it was playing a useful role as a confidence-building mechanism". Upon his recommendation, the Security Council, by its resolution 891 (1993) of 20 December 1993, extended UNOMUR's mandate by six months. The Council expressed its appreciation to the Government of Uganda for its cooperation and support for UNOMUR and also underlined the importance of a cooperative attitude on the part of the civilian and military authorities in the mission area.

Deployment and delay

UNAMIR's demilitarized zone sector headquarters was established upon the arrival of the advance party and became operational on 1 November 1993, when the NMOG II elements were absorbed into UNAMIR. Deployment of the UNAMIR battalion in Kigali, composed of contingents from Belgium and Bangladesh, was completed in the first part of December 1993, and the Kigali weapons-secure area was established on 24 December.

At a meeting initiated by the Special Representative, the Government and RPF issued a joint declaration on 10 December 1993 reaffirming their commitment to the provisions of the Arusha Peace Agreement. They agreed to set up a broad-based transitional Government and the Transitional National Assembly before 31 December 1993. Most of the projected tasks of phase one of the implementation plan were accomplished by 30 December 1993. Despite signs of intransigence, the parties showed good will and cooperation with each other and with the United Nations. The Secretary-General therefore recommended to the Council that UNAMIR continue to implement its mandate. In this regard, he intended to proceed with the implementation plan, including the early deployment of the second battalion in the DMZ.[11] The Security Council endorsed these proposals by its resolution 893 (1994) of 6 January 1994.

With the arrival of the UNAMIR Police Commissioner, Colonel Manfred Bliem (Austria), on 26 December 1993 and of the police units in January and February 1994, the UNAMIR civilian police contingent (CIVPOL) set up its headquarters in Kigali and reached its authorized strength of 60 civilian police monitors. In carrying out its mandate, which was to assist in maintaining public security through the monitoring and verification of the activities of the Gendarmerie and the Communal Police, CIVPOL worked closely with both bodies in Kigali.

The Arusha Peace Agreement provided that the incumbent head of State would remain in office until the elections. Accordingly, Major-General Juvénal Habyarimana was sworn in as President of Rwanda on 5 January 1994. However, the transitional Government and the Transitional National Assembly were not installed because the parties could not agree on several issues, including the lists of members of those bodies. This failure delayed the completion of phase one and contributed to a deterioration of the security situation. January and February 1994 saw increasingly violent demonstrations, roadblocks, assassination of political leaders and assaults on and murders of civilians. In late February, two prominent political leaders were assassinated and a UNAMIR-escorted RPF convoy was ambushed. The Government then imposed a curfew in Kigali and in a number of other cities. UNAMIR provided increased support to the National Gendarmerie, and the security situation began to stabilize.

Notwithstanding the increased tensions and insecurity, the cease-fire generally held. UNAMIR forces, whose operational capacity was enhanced with the deployment of additional personnel and equipment, continued to play a stabilizing role. UNAMIR forces earmarked for phase two were in place and ready to begin operations on short notice. Preparations for phase three were also under way.

Extension of UNAMIR mandate

The Secretary-General told[12] the Security Council on 30 March 1994 that, in spite of increasing tensions, he was encouraged that the parties had maintained the process of dialogue. He believed that UNAMIR should continue to support that dialogue. Therefore, he recommended that the Council extend the mandate of UNAMIR for a period of six months, during which time he would keep the Council informed of the pace of progress. However, if the transitional institutions were not installed within two months and sufficient progress had not been achieved, the Council should then review the situation, including the role of the United Nations.

On April 5, 1994, the Security Council, by its resolution 909 (1994), decided to extend the

[10]S/26878. [11]S/26927. [12]S/1994/360.

mandate of UNAMIR until 29 July 1994. At the same time, it expressed its deep concern at the delay in the establishment of the transitional institutions and at the deterioration in security. It noted that, lacking progress, it would review the situation within six weeks.

D. April 1994–June 1994

Mass murder and civil war

On 6 April 1994, an aircraft carrying President Juvénal Habyarimana of Rwanda and President Cyprien Ntaryamira of Burundi crashed at Kigali airport, killing all those on board. The two Presidents had been attending a regional meeting at Dar es Salaam. It was not possible to carry out a full investigation of the causes of the crash, which remain unknown.

The crash was followed over the next three months by a series of events whose speed and ferocity taxed to the utmost the attempts of the international community to respond. The horror that engulfed Rwanda during this period was threefold: mass murders throughout the country amounting to genocide; a brief but violent civil war that swept government forces out of the country; and refugee flows that created a humanitarian and ecological crisis of unprecedented dimensions.

The genocide in Rwanda claimed between 500,000 and one million victims, primarily members of the Tutsi minority and "moderate" Hutus, including the intelligentsia, suspected of sympathizing with the Tutsi. The killers included members of the Rwandese government forces, but in the main were drawn from the Presidential Guard and the youth militias, primarily the *interahamwe*, recruited and formed by the late President's party.

Beginning in Kigali and then throughout the country, civilian men, women and children were shot, blown up by rockets or grenades, hacked to death by machete or buried or burned alive. Many were attacked in the churches in which they had sought refuge. Tens of thousands of bodies were hurled into the rivers and carried downstream. These facts were independently and overwhelmingly attested to by eyewitnesses belonging to governmental, intergovernmental and non-governmental sources, as well as the international media, and were fully reported by an impartial Commission of Experts established by the Security Council [see below].

Victims included Prime Minister Agathe Uwilingiyimana and 10 Belgian United Nations peace-keepers assigned to protect her.

The Secretary-General condemned the acts of violence in the strongest terms.

The crash of the Presidents' aircraft and the massacres which followed also spurred the civil war into a new, more violent and decisive phase. On the second day after the crash, RPF launched an offensive from the positions they occupied in Rwanda and attacked the "interim government" which had been set up on 8 April 1994 in the wake of President Habyarimana's death. The "interim government" left Kigali on 12 April 1994 as fighting between the armed forces and RPF intensified, establishing itself in Gitarama, 40 kilometres to the south-west. By the end of May 1994, RPF had occupied about half of the territory of Rwanda, including strong positions in and around Kigali.

Effect on UNAMIR

The Government of Belgium then decided to withdraw its battalion from UNAMIR. Finding it impossible to carry on with its original mandate, UNAMIR concentrated on securing a cease-fire to be followed by political negotiations; protecting civilians; negotiating a truce to permit the evacuation of expatriates; assisting in evacuations; rescuing those trapped in the fighting; and providing humanitarian assistance to large groups of displaced persons under UNAMIR protection.

Despite direct contacts under the auspices of UNAMIR, both sides adopted rigid positions, undermining negotiations for a cease-fire. Violence continued in the streets, as did fighting between Rwandese Government Forces (RGF) and RPF forces. UNAMIR headquarters was hit on 19 April, although there were no casualties. On 20 April, the Secretary-General informed[13] the Council that UNAMIR personnel could not be left at risk indefinitely with no possibility of performing the

[13]S/1994/470.

tasks for which they were dispatched. With the departure of the Belgian contingent and non-essential personnel, UNAMIR strength stood at 1,515 military personnel, down from 2,165, and 190 military observers, down from 321.

Three alternatives were put forward. Assuming no realistic prospect for an effective cease-fire agreement, combat and massacres could only be averted by an immediate and massive reinforcement of UNAMIR. This would require several thousand additional troops and could require that UNAMIR be given enforcement powers under Chapter VII of the United Nations Charter. Alternatively, a small group, headed by the Force Commander, would remain in Kigali to act as an intermediary between the two parties. This effort would require 270 military personnel. Finally, the Secretary-General noted that UNAMIR could be completely withdrawn. He did not favour this alternative since the cost in human lives could be very severe.

On 21 April 1994, the Security Council decided in its resolution 912 (1994) to reduce UNAMIR to the numbers recommended by the Secretary-General in his second alternative. According to its adjusted mandate, UNAMIR would act as an intermediary between the parties in an attempt to secure their agreement to a cease-fire; assist in the resumption of humanitarian relief operations to the extent feasible; and monitor developments in Rwanda, including the safety and security of civilians who sought refuge with UNAMIR.

On 22 and 23 April, the Secretary-General's Special Representative participated in the Arusha talks at which a cease-fire statement was presented. Although cease-fire negotiations could not take place, the meeting contributed to a unilateral declaration of a cease-fire by RPF.

The humanitarian response

Although the evacuation of humanitarian personnel was recommended on 9 April 1994, and humanitarian activities were temporarily suspended, the United Nations agencies participating in the United Nations Disaster Management Team in Rwanda recommenced their coordination efforts in Nairobi within days of the evacuation, under the aegis of the newly created United Nations Rwanda Emergency Office (UNREO). There was limited cross-border humanitarian assistance, primarily from Uganda but also from Burundi. The World Food Programme (WFP) was able to carry out lim-

ited food distribution from existing WFP stocks in southern Rwanda.

As the massacres continued, Under-Secretary-General for Humanitarian Affairs Peter Hansen led an inter-agency Advance Humanitarian Team (AHT) into Kigali on 23 April 1994. Composed of members of the United Nations Department of Humanitarian Affairs, the United Nations Development Programme (UNDP), the Office of the United Nations High Commissioner for Refugees (UNHCR), the United Nations Children's Fund (UNICEF) and the World Health Organization (WHO), the team assessed needs in the Kigali area and in most RPF-controlled areas as well. AHT immediately initiated aid efforts in Kigali, in close collaboration with UNAMIR, but efforts to obtain access to WFP food stocks held in warehouses were repeatedly blocked by hostile fire.

A suboffice of UNREO was then set up in Kabale, Uganda. Staffed with personnel seconded by UNHCR and non-governmental organizations (NGOs), the Kabale office helped coordinate cross-border relief efforts. Uganda-based efforts to provide humanitarian aid in RPF-controlled areas expanded rapidly as security conditions allowed. These efforts included a number of international NGOs and were coordinated closely with the work of the International Committee of the Red Cross (ICRC). Access to most of the needy population in RGF-controlled areas, where the number of internally displaced people was estimated to be as many as a million, continued to prove virtually impossible. United Nations agencies based in Burundi, especially UNHCR, UNICEF and WFP, continued efforts to obtain first-hand information on needs in these areas, and to provide aid whenever the security situation allowed. On 25 April, the Department of Humanitarian Affairs launched a "flash appeal" for $8 million. This appeal received a mixed response from donors.

The humanitarian situation subsequently changed dramatically. In the most rapid exodus of this scale UNHCR had ever recorded, more than 250,000 Rwandese refugees entered Tanzania over the Rusumo Falls border-crossing point within 24 hours. Although UNHCR had pre-positioned food, blankets, and other relief supplies for 50,000 persons, the continued exodus along this border forced the creation of a massive relief operation. The international relief community, with overall coordination by UNHCR, rushed to help the Tanzanian Government and local residents cope with the massive influx of refugees. UNHCR made an urgent appeal to donors for an additional $56 million to meet the needs of refugees in the region, and particularly those crossing into Tanzania.

Secretary-General seeks further action

By the end of April 1994, Kigali was effectively divided into sectors controlled by RGF and RPF, with frequent exchanges of artillery and mortar fire. UNAMIR reported strong evidence of preparations for further massacres of civilians in the city, while massacres continued on a large scale in the countryside, especially in the south. The developments raised serious questions about the viability of UNAMIR's revised mandate. In the Secretary-General's view,[14] it had become clear that UNAMIR did not have the power to take effective action to halt the continuing massacres and would be unable to protect threatened people in Kigali if a new wave of massacres were to start. According to some estimates, as many as 200,000 people had died over the previous three weeks.

While some of the massacres were the work of uncontrolled military personnel, most were perpetrated by armed groups of civilians taking advantage of the complete breakdown of law and order in Kigali and many other parts of Rwanda. Convinced that massacres could be prevented only if law and order were restored, the Secretary-General urged the Security Council to consider again what action, including forceful action, it could take or could authorize Member States to take. Such action, however, would require a commitment of human and material resources on a scale which Member States had so far proved reluctant to contemplate. The Secretary-General nevertheless felt that the degree of human suffering and its implications for regional stability left the Security Council with no alternative but to examine this possibility.

On 30 April 1994, the Security Council demanded[15] that the interim Government of Rwanda and RPF take effective measures to prevent any attacks on civilians in areas under their control and recalled that persons who instigate or participate in such acts are individually responsible. The Council noted that the killing of members of an ethnic group with the intention of destroying such a group in whole or in part constitutes a crime punishable under international law. The Council also asked the Secretary-General, in consultation with the Secretary-General of OAU, to report further on how to help restore law and order in Rwanda and provide security for displaced persons and to explore urgently ways of extending hu-

manitarian relief assistance to refugees and displaced persons.

On 4 May, the Secretary-General publicly called the situation genocide and warned that the United Nations, if it did not act quickly, might later be accused of passivity. On 6 May, the Security Council asked[16] the Secretary-General to prepare contingency plans to deliver humanitarian assistance and support of displaced persons, and indicated that the Council might later seek indications on logistics and financial implications of an expanded United Nations or international presence in Rwanda.

Adjustment of tasks

When it was initially deployed, UNOMUR restricted its monitoring activities in Uganda along the area of the border with Rwanda controlled by RPF. After RPF gained control of the entire Uganda-Rwanda border, the Mission extended its observation and monitoring activities to that area. This necessitated the readjustment of tasks and the reassignment of military observers. UNOMUR carried out its tasks essentially through patrolling, monitoring and surveillance of the whole stretch of the operational area, involving both mobile and fixed observations as well as on-site investigations of suspected cross-border traffic. The arrival in the mission area of three helicopters in early April 1993 strengthened UNOMUR's overall operational capacity.

As for UNAMIR, its strength stood at 444 all ranks in Rwanda by early May 1994, with 179 military observers at Nairobi pending repatriation or redeployment to the Mission.

UNAMIR, UNREO, the operational United Nations agencies and NGOs working in Rwanda agreed on a division of labour for humanitarian assistance and on a set of principles to serve as the basis for operations. These included ensuring the security of relief efforts; joint identification of distribution sites by responsible authorities and United Nations humanitarian organizations; clear identification of interlocutors to represent the authorities for discussion of humanitarian operations; acceptance by authorities of the monitoring and reporting responsibilities of the United Nations organizations regarding the distribution and use of relief materials; and an understanding that aid should be provided based on need, regardless of race, ethnic group, religion or political affili-

[14]S/1994/518. [15]S/PRST/1994/21. [16]S/1994/546.

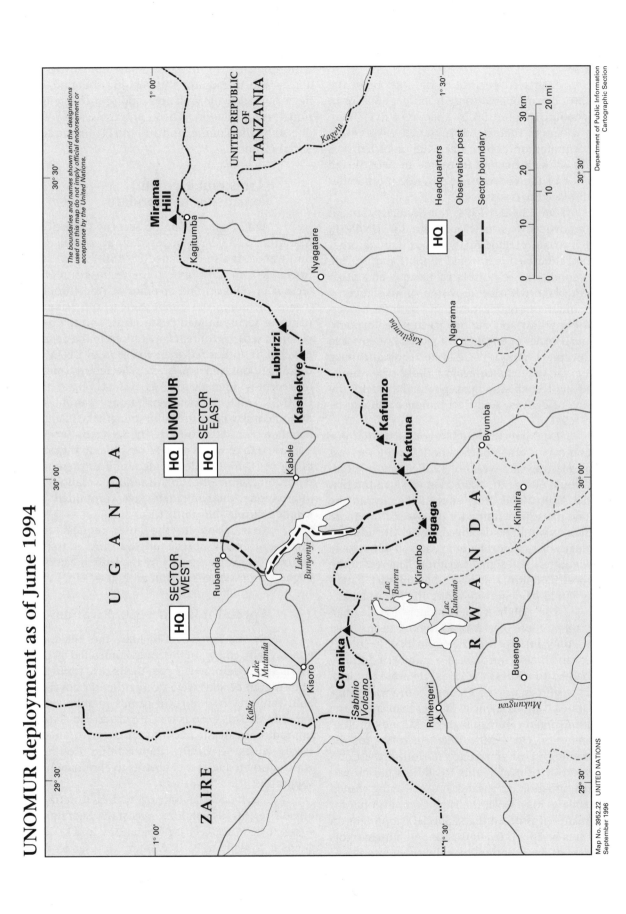

UNOMUR deployment as of June 1994

UNITED REPUBLIC
OF
TANZANIA

Mirama
Hill

Kagitumba

Nyagatare

Ngarama

Kagera

Kagitumba

Lubirizi

Kashekye

Kafunzo

Katuna

Byumba

Kabale

UGANDA

UNOMUR

SECTOR
EAST

SECTOR
WEST

Rubanda

*Lake
Bunyonyi*

Bigaga

Kirambo

Kinihira

*Lac
Burera*

RWANDA

Kisoro

*Lake
Mutanda*

Kaku

Cyanika

*Sabinio
Volcano*

*Lac
Ruhondo*

Busengo

Ruhengeri

Mukungwa

ZAIRE

HQ UNOMUR
HQ
HQ

Headquarters
Observation post
Sector boundary

HQ

0   10   20   30 km
0   10   20 mi

29° 30'
30° 00'
30° 30'

1° 00'
1° 30'

Map No. 3952.22   UNITED NATIONS
September 1996

Department of Public Information
Cartographic Section

ation. Both sides subsequently agreed on the principles.

Displaced persons in the interior of the country outnumbered those in border areas or in neighbouring countries by a factor of five. There was a danger that, if humanitarian efforts were concentrated on border areas, the protected sites could act as a magnet to people in need in the interior of the country and increase the number of displaced persons.

On 13 May 1994, the Secretary-General recommended[17] a new mandate for UNAMIR, which would include 5,500 troops. Among other things, the new force would support and provide safe conditions for displaced persons and other groups, help with the provision of assistance by humanitarian organizations, and monitor border-crossing points and the two parties' deployment. While its rules of engagement would not envisage enforcement action, it could be required to take action in self-defence against those who threatened protected sites and populations and the means of delivery and distribution of humanitarian relief.

Deployment would be conducted in three phases over a one-month period. During the first phase, lasting one week, one full-strength battalion would ensure the protection of Kigali International Airport and other sites in the city. In the second phase, extending for two weeks, two more battalions would be deployed, along with advance elements of a support battalion and all of the force headquarters and signal squadron. The rest of the support battalion and two other infantry battalions would be deployed during the third phase.

The High Commissioner for Human Rights, Mr. José Ayala Lasso, who had assumed office only a day before the outbreak of hostilities in Rwanda, also introduced a number of timely initiatives to address the crisis. He acted immediately to spur an urgent response from a wide range of United Nations agencies and mechanisms of the Commission on Human Rights, OAU and the NGO community. On 4 May 1994, he called for the convening of an emergency session of the Commission of Human Rights to address the human rights situation in Rwanda. After having visited Rwanda in May 1994, the High Commissioner for Human Rights urged that a Special Rapporteur on Rwanda be appointed to examine all human rights aspects of the situation, including root causes and responsibilities for the atrocities. The Commission subsequently designated Mr. René Dégni-Ségui as Special Rapporteur for Rwanda. The High Commissioner also proposed that the Special Rapporteur should be supported by a field operation, staffed with specialists to investigate past human rights abuses and to monitor the ongoing situation, to deter human rights violations and to promote national reconciliation. These proposals were endorsed by the Commission and the Economic and Social Council.

Arms embargo and expansion of mandate

On 17 May 1994, the Security Council in resolution 918 (1994) imposed an arms embargo on Rwanda. It also expanded UNAMIR's mandate to enable it to contribute to the security and protection of refugees and civilians at risk, through means including the establishment and maintenance of secure humanitarian areas, and the provision of security for relief operations to the degree possible. It authorized the expansion of UNAMIR to 5,500 troops, and requested the Secretary-General to redeploy immediately, as a first phase, the UNAMIR military observers from Nairobi to Rwanda, and to bring up to full strength the infantry battalion then in the country. The Secretary-General was asked to report as soon as possible on the next phase of UNAMIR's deployment and to present a report on the investigation of serious violations of international humanitarian law committed in Rwanda during the conflict.

In response to the latter request, the Secretary-General subsequently transmitted to the Security Council a report[18] by the United Nations High Commissioner for Human Rights.

Special mission visits Rwanda

By the latter part of May, the RPF zone was virtually empty. In the zones controlled by the Rwandese government force, increasing numbers of displaced persons were fleeing the RPF advance and were seeking refuge in camps in subhuman conditions. This exodus was in part due to alarming radio broadcasts from Rwandese government forces zones, especially Radio Mille Collines, which also broadcast incitements to eliminate RPF supporters.

To move the warring parties towards a cease-fire, Mr. Iqbal Riza, Assistant Secretary-General for Peace-keeping Operations, and Major-General J. Maurice Baril, Military Adviser to the Secretary-General, visited the area from 22 to 27 May 1994. Despite assurances of an informal

[17]S/1994/565. [18]S/1994/867.

truce during the visit, firing and shelling continued. During discussions with the mission, both sides recognized that only a political settlement could bring stability to Rwanda. However, while both sides declared that the principles of the Arusha Peace Agreement remained valid as a framework, each stated that the new circumstances would necessitate renegotiation of certain parts of the agreement.

The special mission was informed that those responsible for the genocide included members of the Rwandese government forces, but in the main were drawn from the Presidential Guard and the *interahamwe*. Allegations by representatives of the interim Government and the Rwandese Armed Forces and the Gendarmerie that the RPF bore equal culpability for the killings were not corroborated by other sources.

The special mission obtained the agreement of the two sides to initiate talks for the establishment of a cease-fire as called for by Security Council resolution 918 (1994). RPF's insistence that it would not deal, directly or indirectly, with the de facto authorities in Gitarama was accepted by the other side. A working paper, to serve as a basis for the talks, was prepared by the special mission and the Force Commander, and the first meeting was held between military staff officers on 30 May at UNAMIR headquarters. The Deputy Force Commander acted as intermediary.

UNAMIR's mandate extended

On 31 May 1994, the Secretary-General informed the Security Council that the repercussions of the massacres in Rwanda were enormous, with displaced persons in the range of 1.5 million and an additional 400,000 refugees in bordering countries. These figures would mean that over a quarter of Rwanda's population had been afflicted. There was no effective humanitarian assistance programme, beyond sporadic deliveries, in zones controlled by Rwandese government forces. More systematic humanitarian assistance programmes had begun in the RPF zone, but worked under strict RPF controls.

In the Secretary-General's view, the international community's delayed reaction to the genocide in Rwanda "demonstrated graphically its extreme inadequacy to respond with prompt and decisive action to humanitarian crises entwined with armed conflict". He added that while attempting to redeem the failings in the Rwandese crisis, the entire system required review to strengthen its reactive capacity. There was little doubt that the killing in Rwanda constituted genocide, but the continuing hostilities impeded a full investigation.

Since national reconciliation was unlikely to be swift, the Secretary-General recommended[19] to the Security Council on 31 May 1994 that UNAMIR's expanded mandate be authorized by the Council for at least six months, with the anticipation that at least another six-month renewal would be required. The special mission had secured assurances from both parties of cooperation with the mandate established by resolution 918 (1994). In the Secretary-General's view, the implementation of phase one remained urgent and had to be commenced even before a cease-fire was effected. He informed the Council that the Government of Ghana was prepared to dispatch troops immediately, but these were waiting for necessary equipment, especially armoured personnel carriers, to be made available by other Member States. It was estimated that phase one would not be operational for another four to six weeks. Considering the projected delays, the Secretary-General recommended that phase two should be initiated immediately, in close synchronization with phase one, while urgent preparations for phase three should continue.

The Secretary-General also declared his intention to establish a special trust fund to support effective rehabilitation programmes in Rwanda.

In its resolution 925 on 8 June 1994, the Security Council endorsed the Secretary-General's recommendations for the deployment of an expanded UNAMIR, invited the international community to contribute generously to the trust fund for Rwanda and demanded that all parties to the conflict cease hostilities. By its resolution 935 of 1 July 1994, the Security Council expressed its grave concern at reports of violations of international law, including genocide. It requested the Secretary-General to establish as a matter of urgency an impartial Commission of Experts that would provide him with its conclusions about the evidence of these violations. The Council also called on States, relevant United Nations bodies and organizations to inform the commission within 30 days of substantiated grave violations. The Secretary-General notified the Council on 26 July that he had established the Commission of Experts.[20] The Commission was to be based in Geneva and would benefit from the resources of the High Commissioner for Human Rights and, in particular, those already made available to the Spe-

[19]S/1994/640. [20]S/1994/879.

cial Rapporteur of the Commission on Human Rights in Geneva and in the field.

Decision to close UNOMUR

On 16 June 1994, the Secretary-General reported[21] to the Security Council that UNOMUR had been particularly critical as UNAMIR sought to defuse tensions resulting from the resumption of hostilities. The Mission's activities allowed UNAMIR to address, at least to some degree, the issue of outside interference in the Rwandese civil war. Its presence was a factor of stability in the area. Nevertheless, there appeared to be little rationale for monitoring one of Rwanda's borders and not the others. He believed that UNOMUR should continue its monitoring activities until an effective cease-fire was established. He therefore recommended that UNOMUR's mandate be renewed for a period of three months. During that period, the number of military observers would be reduced by phases, adjusting to operational requirements. UNOMUR would be closed down by 21 September 1994. The Security Council endorsed the Secretary-General's recommendations on 20 June 1994 by its resolution 928 (1994).

E. June–September 1994

Operation Turquoise

The Secretary-General informed[22] the Security Council on 19 June 1994 that the United Nations expected, in the best of circumstances, to complete the deployment of the first phase of UNAMIR in the first week of July 1994; deployment of the second phase could not be determined lacking final confirmations of required resources. The Security Council might therefore wish to consider the offer of the Government of France to undertake a French-commanded multinational operation, subject to Security Council authorization, under Chapter VII of the Charter, to assure the security and protection of displaced persons and civilians at risk. Such an operation would last about three months, until UNAMIR was brought up to the necessary strength to take over from the multinational force. The activities of the multinational force and those of UNAMIR would be closely coordinated by the respective force commanders.

On 22 June 1994, acting under Chapter VII of the Charter, the Council, by its resolution 929 (1994), authorized Member States to conduct the operation using all necessary means to achieve their humanitarian objectives. The operation would be limited to two months, unless UNAMIR was able to carry out its mandate before then. Costs of implementing the operation would be borne by the Member States concerned. The French initiative, named Operation Turquoise, was launched on 23 June 1994. On 2 July, France announced that Operation Turquoise would establish a "humanitarian protected zone" in the Cyangugu-Kibuye-Gikongoro triangle in southwestern Rwanda, covering about one fifth of Rwandese territory. While expressing its strong opposition to the French move, RPF did not seek confrontation with French forces which, on their side, avoided provocation.

From the start, close cooperation at all levels was established between UNAMIR and Operation Turquoise. In the first week of July an UNREO/Department of Humanitarian Affairs officer was dispatched to the French military base of operations at Goma in order to establish communications and ensure liaison between the command of Operation Turquoise, United Nations agencies and some 30 NGOs engaged in humanitarian assistance in the region. On 11 July, the Prime Minister of France informed the Security Council and the Secretary-General of the French Government's decision to commence its withdrawal by 31 July.

RPF establishes control

On 1 July 1994, the Secretary-General called for a halt to military operations in Rwanda. His new Special Representative, Mr. Shaharyar M. Khan (Pakistan), arrived in Kigali on 4 July and immediately established direct contact with the parties, emphasizing the importance of achieving a cease-fire. This was followed on 14 July by a demand[23] by the Security Council for an immediate and unconditional cease-fire.

[21] S/1994/715. [22] S/1994/728. [23] S/PRST/1994/34.

RPF established military control over most of the country in July 1994, taking Kigali on 4 July, Butare (the second largest city) on 5 July and Ruhengeri (the former Government's stronghold) on 14 July. Retreating RGF forces concentrated in and around Gisenyi in the north-west and thereafter withdrew into Zaire. On 17 July, RPF took Gisenyi and on 18 July unilaterally declared a cease-fire, effectively ending the civil war. On 19 July, a Broad-Based Government of National Unity was formed and subsequently extended its control over the whole national territory.

At the same time, the flight of civilians continued, spurred on by inflammatory broadcasts from radio stations controlled by the "interim government". Over a two-week period in July, some 1.5 million Rwandese sought refuge in Zaire. Retreating soldiers urged and forced whole populations to leave their homes and follow them into exile. In some cases, massacres were even perpetrated deliberately in order to create situations of panic, chaos and fear.

The protracted violence in Rwanda created an almost unprecedented humanitarian crisis. Of a total population of approximately 7 million, 3 million persons were displaced internally and more than 2 million Hutus had fled to neighbouring countries. Among those who had fled Rwanda, an outbreak of cholera had already claimed as many as 20,000 lives — and would eventually claim some 50,000. The logistics of arranging the daily supply and distribution of 30 million litres of drinking water and 1,000 tons of food were daunting. As many as 2 million internally displaced Hutus were estimated to be in the humanitarian protected zone in south-west Rwanda. To prevent an outflow of this group into Zaire, it was necessary to ensure the capacity of UNAMIR to take over responsibility in the area and to increase the humanitarian presence and activities there.

A $434.8 million consolidated interagency appeal for the Rwandese crisis was launched by the Secretary-General on 22 July 1994.[24] In the Secretary-General's view, the deterioration of the situation was beyond the resources and capacity of the United Nations humanitarian agencies and non-governmental organizations. The international community was confronted with four basic humanitarian challenges: to respond to the immediate life-saving needs of refugees; to facilitate the early return of those who had fled their homes; to restore basic infrastructure in Rwanda; and to ensure a smooth transition in the humanitarian protected zone established by French forces. The Secretary-General also an-

nounced that he was immediately sending the Under-Secretary-General for Humanitarian Affairs to the region.

During his visit to Rwanda from 24 to 28 July, the Under-Secretary-General met with senior officials of the new Government to discuss how humanitarian aid could be delivered to all parts of the country and the urgent steps required to re-establish a climate conducive to the return of refugees and displaced persons. The Government indicated its commitment to encourage people to return to Rwanda, to ensure their protection and to permit full access to all those in need throughout the country. UNREO, headquartered in Kigali and with offices in Goma (Zaire), Kabale (Uganda) and Bujumbura (Burundi), continued to work with the United Nations agencies and the growing number of humanitarian NGOs to identify needs in Rwanda by sector and region.

UNAMIR's main tasks in the changed situation were to ensure stability and security in the north-western and south-western regions of Rwanda; to stabilize and monitor the situation in all regions of Rwanda to encourage the return of the displaced population; to provide security and support for humanitarian assistance operations inside Rwanda; and to promote, through mediation and good offices, national reconciliation in Rwanda. UNAMIR had already deployed a company along the border near Goma, as well as a number of observers in that region and in the zone controlled by Operation Turquoise. In the expectation that UNAMIR would eventually receive the 5,500 troops authorized by the Security Council, the Force Commander had planned deployment in five sectors. The Force headquarters would remain at Kigali, with the minimum units required for protection, along with specialized units for communications and logistics, as well as the field hospital. United Nations military observers and United Nations civilian police monitors would be deployed in all sectors according to operations requirements.

The principal areas of concern were in the north-west to resettle returning refugees, and in the south-west to avert possible outbreaks of violence. In the north-west, substantial numbers of the former Rwandese government forces and militia, as well as extremist elements suspected of involvement in the massacres of the Hutu opposition and RPF supporters, were mingled with the refugees in Zaire, and were reportedly trying to prevent their return. In the south-west, a more

[24]S/1994/924.

volatile situation prevailed where armed elements of the Rwandese government forces had sought refuge in the French-protected zone; this situation was particularly pressing in view of the anxiety of the French Government to complete its withdrawal by 21 August. In discussions with UNAMIR, the new Rwandese Government had indicated that it would not insist on taking control of this area immediately, provided that UNAMIR would ensure its stability.

On 3 August 1994, the Secretary-General told[25] the Council that the international community, by failing to intervene sooner in Rwanda, had in fact acquiesced in the horrifying loss of human life and suffering of an entire people. At the very least, the international community should ensure that those individuals responsible in their personal and official capacities for unleashing and instigating the genocide were brought to justice. To avoid problems of coordination, all foreign forces engaged in support of humanitarian efforts in the area should ideally be part of UNAMIR. If this was not possible, deployment of foreign forces should be authorized by the Security Council even if their mandate was purely humanitarian, and formal liaison arrangements should be established between them and UNAMIR, as had been the case with Operation Turquoise.

The need for reinforcements for UNAMIR remained urgent. Two and a half months after the Security Council expanded UNAMIR's mandate, fewer than 500 troops were on the ground apart from a number of military observers.[26]

The Security Council urged the country's former leadership and those who had assumed political responsibility in refugee camps to cooperate with the new Rwandese Government in reconciliation and repatriation efforts and to cease propaganda campaigns inducing refugees to stay in exile. The Council called upon the new Government to ensure that there were no reprisals against returnees and to cooperate with the United Nations in ensuring that those guilty of atrocities were brought to justice. In this connection, it welcomed the Government's statement supporting the establishment of an international tribunal.[27]

Signs of stabilization

The Broad-based Government of National Unity, while suffering from a severe lack of basic resources, undertook efforts to normalize the situation and to put in place civilian structures. It encouraged members of the former Rwandese government forces to join the Rwandese Patriotic Army (RPA). Land tenure and rival claims to property rights presented a particular problem. Long-standing Tutsi refugees had returned from Burundi and Uganda to reclaim property, and Hutu refugees who had fled more recently were returning home to find their property held by others. Although the Government emphasized that the wrongful occupation of another person's home or property was unlawful, it was encountering difficulty in implementing that policy.

The main objective of UNAMIR deployment during this time was to promote security in all sectors of Rwanda and to create a climate conducive to the safe return of refugees and displaced persons, as well as to support humanitarian operations. Relations between UNAMIR and RPA were cordial and cooperative, although movement restrictions were sometimes imposed on UNAMIR troops. UNAMIR began deploying troops in the humanitarian protection zone on 10 August 1994, and on 21 August it assumed responsibility from Operation Turquoise. As the Government undertook the restoration of civil administration and the gradual deployment of its troops in the zone, it made a concerted effort to reassure the population, averting a renewed major exodus of civilians to Zaire. Members of the Government also made several visits to the refugee camps in Zaire to encourage voluntary return of the refugees.

The Government also urged the Commission of Experts to conclude its work expeditiously and gave assurances that it would make every effort to prevent summary trials, revenge executions and other acts of violence and would arrest those accused of such crimes. In August, during the second visit to Rwanda by the United Nations High Commissioner for Human Rights, the Government concluded an agreement to increase the number of human rights officers deployed to Rwanda to 147. By 30 September, their number stood at 17. In the agreement, the objectives and functions of the operation were defined as follows: (a) carrying out investigations into violations of human rights and humanitarian law, including possible acts of genocide; (b) monitoring the ongoing human rights situation, and helping to prevent such violations through the presence of human rights field officers; (c) cooperating with other international agencies to re-establish confidence and facilitate the return of refugees and displaced persons and the rebuilding of civil society; and (d) implementing programmes of technical cooperation in the field of human rights, particularly in the area of

[25]Ibid. [26]S/1994/923. [27]S/PRST/1994/42.

the administration of justice, to help Rwanda re-build its shattered judiciary and to provide human rights education to all levels of Rwandese society.

The Government sought the urgent assistance of UNAMIR in establishing a new, integrated, national police force. On 16 August, UNAMIR initiated a training programme with students selected by the Government as volunteers from different social and ethnic groups. CIVPOL was also charged with monitoring the activities of local police and gendarmerie and those of the civil authorities with regard to human rights violations.

Conclusion of UNOMUR

Reduction of UNOMUR was carried out in four phases with a gradual scaling down of monitoring activities. Phase one took effect on 15 August, and the Mission's total strength of 80 military observers was reduced by 25. In phase two, effective from 30 August, the Mission was further reduced by nine military observers. In phase three, effective from 6 September, an additional 12 military observers left, leaving a total strength of 34. In the final phase, all remaining military and civilian personnel were to leave the area by 21 September. The formal closing ceremony was presided by the Under-Secretary-General for Peace-keeping Operations, Mr. Kofi Annan.

The Secretary-General informed[28] the Security Council that, while the tragic turn of events in Rwanda had prevented UNOMUR from fully implementing its mandate, the Mission had played a useful role in efforts to build confidence, defuse tensions and facilitate the implementation of the Arusha Agreement. Following the Security Council's authorization on 17 May to expand UNAMIR, UNOMUR became a forward base to back up the movement of UNAMIR personnel, equipment and supplies into Rwanda. During the closure of Kigali airport, Entebbe airport in Uganda functioned as the only air base from which those personnel and supplies were routed by land to Rwanda. A team of UNOMUR military observers was stationed at Entebbe to coordinate logistic activities, and UNOMUR observers escorted convoys of logistic material and foodstuffs to the Uganda-Rwanda border for use by UNAMIR. UNOMUR also facilitated the transport of UNAMIR and other United Nations personnel between Kabale and Entebbe and between Kabale and Goma and Bukavu in Zaire. The evacuation of UNAMIR casualties was carried out with UNOMUR assistance.

The Secretary-General expressed his appreciation to the Government of Uganda for the cooperation and assistance it had extended to the Mission. He commended both the military and the civilian personnel of UNOMUR for the dedication and professionalism with which they had carried out their tasks.

F.   October 1994–May 1995

UNAMIR fully deployed

UNAMIR reached its full authorized strength of 5,500 all ranks in October 1994. By 15 November, 80 of the 90 police observers authorized for UNAMIR were also deployed. The troops and military observers were deployed in six sectors: north-east, south-east, south, south-west, north-west and Kigali City. UNAMIR assisted with the transport of refugees and internally displaced persons, maintained protection for populations at risk, and worked with the humanitarian agencies and the Government to develop and implement a strategy to close the displaced persons camps in Rwanda gradually by ensuring voluntary return. UNAMIR troops and observers also intensified their monitoring, observation and patrol duties.

The human rights field operation had about 60 human rights officers and special investigators at seven regional offices. Another 40 human rights observers and teams of forensic experts were expected by the end of December 1994. The Special Rapporteur, Mr. René Dégni-Ségui, visited Rwanda from 15 to 22 October, and the Commission of Experts visited Rwanda from 29 October to 10 November.

[28]S/1994/1073.

Security in the camps

The Secretary-General reported[29] to the Security Council in early October that the first priority in Rwanda remained the resolution of the humanitarian crisis. According to the estimates, Rwanda's pre-war population of 7.9 million had fallen to 5 million and the number of internally displaced persons ranged from 800,000 to 2 million. There were more than 2 million refugees in Zaire, Tanzania, Burundi and Uganda. At the same time, it was estimated that some 360,000 refugees had returned to Rwanda spontaneously since the cease-fire on 18 July. The victims of the genocidal slaughter could number as many as 1 million. In the refugee camps, the Government was concerned about elements who continued to incite people to flee from Rwanda, and to threaten those who might return home. In addition, reports and preliminary investigations suggested that returning refugees might have been subjected to reprisals by Government troops.

UNHCR estimated that the camps in Zaire held approximately 1.2 million Rwandese refugees in overcrowded, chaotic and increasingly insecure conditions. The refugees were completely dependent on United Nations and relief agencies for basic needs assistance.

The former Rwandese political leaders, government forces and militia who controlled the camps were determined to ensure by force, if necessary, that the refugees did not repatriate to Rwanda. They were believed to be preparing for an armed invasion of Rwanda and might be stockpiling and selling food distributed by relief agencies in preparation for such an invasion. Security was further undermined by general lawlessness, extortion, banditry and gang warfare between groups fighting for control. The lives of relief workers were repeatedly threatened. The law and order enforcement agents in the countries of asylum were not adequately equipped to cope with the situation. As a result, NGOs responsible for the distribution of relief supplies had begun to withdraw.

It was estimated that there were approximately 230 Rwandese political leaders in Zaire, including former ministers, senior civilian and military officials, members of parliament and other political personalities, many of whom were living in good conditions outside the refugee camps. The number of former Rwandese government forces personnel in Zaire was estimated at about 50,000 persons, including dependants, and some estimates indicated that the armed militia could amount to some 10,000 or more.

The Secretary-General identified[30] for the Security Council three major military options for addressing the worsening security situation in the refugee camps, namely: (a) a United Nations peace-keeping operation to establish security progressively in the camps; (b) a United Nations force, set up under Chapter VII of the Charter, to separate the former political leaders, military personnel and militia from the ordinary refugee population of the camps; (c) a multinational force, authorized by the Security Council under Chapter VII of the Charter but not under United Nations command. Associated with any of the options, foreign security experts could train and monitor the local security forces. A peace-keeping force of 3,000 all ranks would take 24 to 30 months to complete the operation, while a force of 5,000 would require 14 to 20 months. The mandate would be separate from that of UNAMIR but would be under the operational control of, and supported logistically by, UNAMIR. Such an operation, although the most realistic way of progressively improving security in the camps, would be difficult, complex and, to some extent, unprecedented.

The Security Council responded[31] that the options raised complex issues which required further elucidation. It requested the Secretary-General to consult potential troop contributors. Further, the Council encouraged him to assess initial measures for immediate assistance to the Zairian security forces in the camps, including deploying security experts to train and monitor the local security forces.

Challenges remain

On 30 November 1994 in its resolution 965, the Security Council extended[32] the mandate of UNAMIR to 9 June 1995, as recommended by the Secretary-General.[33] It also expanded the mandate to enable the Mission to contribute to the security in Rwanda of personnel of the International Tribunal for Rwanda [see below] and of human rights officers, including full time protection of the Prosecutor's office. UNAMIR would also assist in the establishment and training of a new, integrated, national police force.

On 20 December 1994, the Government of Rwanda was formally renamed the "Government of National Unity", a modification which

[29] S/1994/1133. [30] S/1994/1308. [31] S/PRST/1994/75. [32] S/RES/965 (1994). [33] S/1994/1344.

placed primary emphasis on national reconciliation. The National Assembly, officially installed in Kigali on 25 November 1994, opened its first working session on 12 December. On that occasion, the Prime Minister presented an eight-point programme reiterating the goals of rehabilitation and reconstruction that the Government first set out when it was installed on 19 July 1994. To help reunify the army, some 2,242 members of the former RGF were retrained and RGF officers were given new appointments, including that of Deputy Chief of Staff and Chief of the Gendarmerie.

The Government also established a commission to finalize and implement a programme for the repatriation and reintegration of refugees, as provided for in the Arusha Peace Agreement, composed of two representatives each of the Government, UNHCR and the refugee community, as well as a representative of OAU. On 14 January 1995, the Government and UNAMIR signed an agreement on the establishment of United Nations radio in Kigali, followed by discussions regarding the necessary technical details. Radio UNAMIR began operations on 16 February, with broadcasts seven days a week in three languages.

Rwanda's court system was not yet functioning, its prisons were overcrowded and thousands of suspects were awaiting trial. The United Nations Human Rights Field Operation in Rwanda was active in helping the Government to rehabilitate the justice system, but substantially more technical and financial assistance was required. As a result of a needs assessment mission undertaken in December 1994, the High Commissioner for Human Rights developed a programme of technical assistance in the administration of justice, which included review of criminal cases of detainees, improvement in prison administration, establishment of civil dispute resolution mechanisms and recruitment and training of civilian police.

Furthermore, reports persisted of summary executions, secret detention and torture, as well as reports of banditry and other violent acts against civilians, both in Kigali and in the countryside. In an incident on 7 January, elements of RPA attacked a displaced persons camp at Busanze, killing 18 people, including women and children, and wounding 36 others. The Government condemned the attack and detained some of the soldiers reportedly involved, assuring the United Nations that the isolated act of misconduct did not represent official policy.

In the eight camps in Tanzania, with 600,000 Hutu refugees, a security force created by the refugee population was cooperating with some 310 Tanzanian police to provide security. In the camps in Zaire, with 1.4 million refugees, the Government of Zaire took steps to enhance security, but the situation remained potentially explosive, with the most acute security situation in the camps north of Lake Kivu, in the Goma region, where approximately 850,000 refugees were located. The threat to the safety of international relief workers was also significant.

A joint technical team from the Department of Peace-keeping Operations and UNHCR was dispatched from 11 to 19 December 1994 to review the situation. The team explored the possibility of deployment in the camps of Zairian security forces, with approximately 150 to 200 United Nations civilian police officers to train and monitor them and about 30 to 50 military observers to liaise with them at the command level. The Government of Zaire indicated that it would be prepared to deploy a national security force of about 1,500 to 2,500 troops to the camps.

Following the team's visit, the Secretary-General reported[34] that nearly 50 Member States had been contacted to ascertain their willingness to provide police personnel. As of 23 January, only four countries had expressed an interest and only one was French-speaking. Furthermore, only one of the countries contributing military observers to UNAMIR would be prepared to allow them to operate in Zaire. As to the camps in Tanzania, the Government indicated that it could increase its force to 500 but required logistic and operational support. Some support in that regard was being provided by the Government of the Netherlands through UNHCR.

The Secretary-General also reported that only one of 60 potential troop-contributing countries had formally offered a unit for a possible peace-keeping operation to ensure security in the camps. That option was thus not feasible. Another proposal, the provision of training and monitoring support to the local security forces through contractual arrangements, would be too costly. UNHCR would therefore conclude appropriate arrangements with the Government of Zaire, and continue to explore means of augmenting support to the Tanzanian Government. In Burundi, UNHCR indicated that the security situation in those camps was being adequately addressed at that time. The close relationship between improving both security in the refugee camps and conditions inside Rwanda to encourage voluntary return was emphasized by the Presidents of Burundi,

---

[34] S/1995/65.

Kenya, Rwanda, Tanzania, Uganda and Zambia and the Prime Minister of Zaire at their summit meeting in Nairobi on 7 January 1995.

On 27 January 1995, the Zairian Ministers of Defence and Justice and the UNHCR Special Envoy to Countries of the Great Lakes Region signed an aide-mémoire outlining specific measures aimed at improving the security situation. Under that agreement, the Government of Zaire was to deploy 1,500 experienced military and police security personnel to the camps in the Goma region, north of Lake Kivu, and in the Bukavu and Uvira regions, south of Lake Kivu. Those personnel would assist in the maintenance of law and order in the camps; take measures to prevent violence against and intimidation of refugees; provide protection for relief workers and for the storage and delivery of humanitarian assistance; and escort to the border of Rwanda those refugees who voluntarily chose to return to their homes. In accordance with its mandate, UNAMIR would provide assistance in escorting the repatriated refugees to their home communities.

UNHCR, for its part, would ensure liaison between UNHCR and the commanders of the Zairian security units, provide technical advice and, to the extent possible, provide to the local security units some financial and logistic support. The first phase would last from February to June 1995. UNHCR would seek contributions from Member States to defray costs. The Security Council welcomed[35] the agreement and encouraged the Government of Rwanda to continue to provide a framework for the action to be taken to repatriate the refugees, to promote national reconciliation and to reinvigorate the political process.

Displaced persons camps

The violent harassment and misinformation in the refugee camps on the borders, especially in Zaire, paralleled the situation of internally displaced persons in Rwanda. The urgent need to bring these persons back to their home communities was thwarted by intimidation within the camps and fear of reprisals. In addition, a perception that the camp population had a better life than those outside generated tension between local and camp populations. At the same time, the camp sites occupied much-needed farmland and were increasingly an ecological hazard. The Special Representative, in close collaboration with the Government, and through the United Nations Emergency Relief Coordinator, formulated an integrated humanitarian response to address the issue of the internally displaced persons.

UNAMIR undertook an operation in the Kibeho and Ndago displaced persons camps from 13 to 15 December to help create conditions for voluntary return. After screening disruptive elements, a total of 44 people were detained and handed over to the Rwandese authorities. UNAMIR discovered and confiscated caches of grenades, machetes and spears. The operation was undertaken in the presence of human rights monitors and representatives of ICRC. RPA provided liaison officers and established a security perimeter a few kilometres from the camps but did not participate in the actual operation. The success of the operation helped to establish suitable conditions for the launching, on 29 December 1994, of Opération Retour, an integrated inter-agency initiative using the combined assets of the United Nations system aimed at facilitating the safe resettlement of internally displaced persons. Activities included the provision of security to ensure that displaced persons could travel safely to their homes and were protected once they reached them, as well as the provision of medical, food, water, sanitation and other basic assistance in the home communes.

Commission of Experts

On 9 December 1994, the Secretary-General transmitted to the Security Council the final report of the Commission of Experts.[36] Located at the United Nations office in Geneva, the Commission had begun its work on 15 August 1994. The Chairman was Mr. Atsu-Koffi Amega, a former President of the Supreme Court and former Foreign Minister of Togo. Other members were Mrs. Habi Dieng, Attorney-General of Guinea, and Mr. Salifou Fomba, Professor of International Law from Mali and a Member of the United Nations International Law Commission.[37]

During the first stage of its work, the Commission reviewed available information and carried out its own investigations in Rwanda. In its second stage, it drew up its conclusions on the evidence of specific violations of international humanitarian law, and, in particular, of acts of genocide, on the basis of which identification of persons responsible for those violations could be made. In the light of those conclusions, the Commission examined the question of the jurisdiction, international or national, before which such persons should be brought to trial.

[35]S/PRST/1995/7. [36]S/1994/879. [37]S/1994/906.

On 1 October, the Secretary-General transmitted to the Security Council the Commission's interim report.[38] The Commission recommended that the Security Council take action to ensure that the individuals responsible for crimes under international law were brought to justice before an independent and impartial international criminal tribunal. The Commission further recommended that the Council amend the Statute of the International Criminal Tribunal for the former Yugoslavia so that it could consider such crimes committed during the armed conflict in Rwanda.

In its 9 December report,[39] the Commission concluded as follows: (a) There existed overwhelming evidence to prove that acts of genocide against the Tutsi ethnic group were committed by Hutu elements in a concerted, planned, systematic and methodical way, in violation of article II of the Convention on the Prevention and Punishment of the Crime of Genocide, 1948; (b) Crimes against humanity and serious violations of international humanitarian law were committed by individuals of both sides, but there was no evidence to suggest that acts committed by Tutsi elements were perpetrated with an intent to destroy the Hutu ethnic group as such, within the meaning of the Genocide Convention; the Commission recommended, however, that investigation of violations of international humanitarian law and of human rights law attributed to the Rwandese Patriotic Front be continued by the Prosecutor of the International Tribunal for Rwanda.

International Tribunal

By its resolution 955 (1994) of 8 November 1994, the Security Council had decided to establish an international tribunal to prosecute persons responsible for genocide and other violations of international humanitarian law committed in Rwanda and Rwandese citizens responsible for such acts in neighbouring States between 1 January and 31 December 1994, and to this end to adopt the Statute of the International Criminal Tribunal for Rwanda. It decided that the Tribunal would consist of the Chambers, the Prosecutor and the Registry. The Prosecutor of the International Tribunal for the Former Yugoslavia would also serve as the Prosecutor for the International Tribunal for Rwanda. The Council requested the Secretary-General to make practical arrangements for the effective functioning of the International Tribunal, including recommendations to the Council as to possible locations for the seat of the Tribunal.

The Prosecutor of the International Tribunal for Rwanda, Judge Richard Goldstone, paid his first visit to the country on 19 and 20 December. He held detailed discussions with senior government officials as well as with the Secretary-General's Special Representative, and also met with representatives of United Nations agencies and NGOs operating in Rwanda.

The first stage of the operation of the Tribunal began with the establishment of an investigative/prosecutorial unit in Kigali. The unit's main functions were to establish the Prosecutor's Office, gather documents and information, initiate the process of recruitment, and develop the investigative strategy and field operating procedures. Initially, the Office of the Prosecutor in Kigali was almost entirely staffed by personnel contributed by Member States under agreements concluded between the United Nations and respective Governments.

Mr. Honoré Rakotomanana (Madagascar) was appointed as Deputy Prosecutor to assist with prosecutions before the International Tribunal. In January 1995, he initiated the process of investigations and officially took office on 20 March 1995. Investigations were to be carried out inside and outside Rwanda, notably in other African countries, Europe and North America, covering 400 identified suspects, most of whom had sought refuge abroad. Under article 28 of the statute of the Rwanda Tribunal,[40] States were under an obligation to cooperate with the International Tribunal and to comply with any of its requests, including the arrest or detention of persons and the surrender or transfer of suspects.

The Secretary-General's search for the seat of the International Tribunal was guided by the Security Council's indication of a preference for an "African seat". Among the criteria for choosing the site were justice and fairness, which would require that trial proceedings be held in neutral territory, security and economy. A technical mission to identify suitable premises visited Rwanda and two of its neighbouring countries, Kenya and Tanzania, in the second half of December 1994. In view of the severe shortage of premises in Kigali and the decision by the Kenyan Government that it was unable to provide a seat for the Tribunal, the team concluded that the Arusha International Conference Centre could constitute suitable premises. The Secretary-General therefore recommended[41] to the Security Council that, subject to appropriate arrangements acceptable to the Coun-

[38]S/1994/1125. [39]S/1994/1405, annex. [40]See resolution 955 (1994), annex. [41]S/1995/134.

cil, Arusha be determined as the seat of the International Tribunal for Rwanda. He drew the attention of the Council to the position of the Government of Rwanda that the seat of the Tribunal should be located in Kigali for the moral and educational value that its presence there would have for the local population. In a spirit of compromise and cooperation, however, the Rwandese Government had indicated that it would raise no objection to locating the seat of the Tribunal in a neighbouring State.

On 22 February, the Security Council, by its resolution 977 (1995), decided that, subject to the conclusion of appropriate arrangements between the United Nations and the Government of Tanzania, the International Tribunal for Rwanda should have its seat at Arusha. By resolution 978 (1995), adopted on 27 February, the Council urged States to arrest and detain, in accordance with their national law and relevant standards of international law, pending prosecution by the International Tribunal for Rwanda or by the appropriate national authorities, persons found within their territory against whom there was sufficient evidence that they were responsible for acts within the jurisdiction of the International Tribunal for Rwanda. It urged States to cooperate with representatives of ICRC and investigators for the International Tribunal, in order to secure unimpeded access to those persons. It also urged States, on whose territory serious acts of violence in the refugee camps had taken place, to arrest and submit to the appropriate authorities for prosecution persons against whom there was sufficient evidence that they had incited or participated in such acts.

On 7 March 1995, the Secretary-General addressed a letter to all States Members of the United Nations, as well as to non-member States maintaining permanent observer missions at United Nations Headquarters, inviting them to nominate judges for the Tribunal by 7 April 1995. Subsequently, the Security Council, by its resolution 989 (1995) of 24 April 1995, established a list of 12 candidates. On 25 May, six judges for the Trial Chambers were elected by the General Assembly. They were sworn in and their first plenary session was held from 26 to 30 June at The Hague. During that session, the judges elected Judge Laïty Kama (Senegal) President and Judge Yakov A. Ostrovsky (Russian Federation) Vice-President and adopted the rules of procedure and evidence of the Tribunal.

Security Council mission to Rwanda

The Security Council took advantage of its second fact-finding mission to Burundi to visit Rwanda on 12 and 13 February 1995. The mission was composed of China, the Czech Republic, Germany, Honduras, Indonesia, Nigeria and the United States. In its report[42] to the Security Council on 28 February, the mission put forward a number of recommendations, including Government action in regard to (a) reinvigorating the political process; (b) a civic education programme; (c) an effective mechanism to protect property rights; (d) a transparent and effective judiciary; (e) a trained police force; (f) effective civil administration throughout the country; and (g) unimpeded access throughout the country for UNAMIR, humanitarian personnel and human rights monitors. The mission considered that, while national reconciliation was principally a task for the Rwandese themselves, the process could be facilitated by promoting repatriation and rehabilitation and by concrete movement in the area of justice.

The Kibeho tragedy

From February through May 1995, the security situation deteriorated, with reports that the armed forces of the former Rwandese Government were training and rearming. A number of those forces were apprehended in Rwanda, carrying arms, grenades and anti-personnel mines, with the result that RPA tightened security. These measures led to incidents involving United Nations and international staff. RPA denied UNAMIR access to parts of the country, searched and seized UNAMIR vehicles and other equipment and participated in anti-UNAMIR demonstrations. UNAMIR personnel were delayed or denied entry at Kigali airport. In addition, the fortnightly meetings between UNAMIR and RPA were suspended. Government authorities at the middle and lower levels were often uncooperative. In March, Radio Rwanda initiated a virulent propaganda campaign against UNAMIR. There were also cases of deliberate and unprovoked attacks on UNAMIR military personnel. Members of the Government expressed regret for the attacks, indicating that they were isolated acts.

[42]S/1995/164.

Several factors contributed to the climate of tensions and frustrations. The military activities and reports of arms deliveries to elements of the former Rwandese government forces in neighbouring countries were sources of serious concern for the Government. The Government was also concerned that no effective limitations were seen to be placed on military training of those elements or on the delivery to them of arms supplies, while the arms embargo continued to apply to Rwanda. Another factor was the delay in bringing those responsible for the genocide to justice. In the Government's view, many of those responsible for the genocide continued to operate openly from abroad, the Tribunal had not yet begun its work, and the national judicial system, severely short of personnel and resources, was dependent on international support. Delivery of needed economic assistance was slow.

The Kibeho tragedy underscored the tensions and fears. On 18 April, the Rwandese Government took action to cordon off and close the eight remaining camps for internally displaced persons in the Gikongoro region, of which Kibeho was by far the largest. The Government considered the camps to be sanctuaries of elements of the former Rwandese government forces and militia; they were a destabilizing factor and represented a security threat. Negotiations were taking place between the Government and the United Nations for the voluntary closure of the camps when the decision to act was taken without notice or consultation. Seven of the camps were closed without serious incident. However, at Kibeho an estimated 80,000 internally displaced persons attempted to break out on 22 April, after spending 5 days on a single hill without adequate space, shelter, food or sanitation. A large number of deaths occurred from firing by government forces, trampling and crushing during the stampede and machete attacks by hardliners in the camp, who assaulted and intimidated those who wished to leave.

UNAMIR reacted immediately to provide transportation to displaced persons, casualty collection posts and emergency medical assistance and road repairs to facilitate movement of humanitarian convoys. Sick and injured internally displaced persons were evacuated by UNAMIR troops to medical facilities operated by NGOs in Butare. This evacuation procedure was at times hindered by restrictions on movement and denial of passage. The presence of UNAMIR troops at open relief centres, way stations and transit centres was increased, and patrols and monitoring were intensified. Senior UNAMIR officials, including the Spe-cial Representative and the Force Commander, visited Kibeho and the surrounding areas on several occasions to assess the situation on the ground, urge restraint and help to coordinate the activities of UNAMIR personnel and relief agencies.

The Secretary-General dispatched Mr. Aldo Ajello to Kigali as Special Envoy to convey his concern to the Rwandese leaders and urge the Government to undertake an impartial investigation. On 27 April, the Government announced that an independent International Commission of Inquiry would be set up consisting of representatives of Belgium, Canada, France, Germany, the Netherlands, the United Kingdom, the United States, OAU, the United Nations and the Government of Rwanda. After 3 weeks of persuasion through the combined efforts of UNAMIR and the Government of Rwanda, the approximately 2,500 internally displaced persons who had remained in Kibeho returned to their communes.

The report[43] of the Independent Commission of Inquiry concluded that the tragedy of Kibeho was neither premeditated nor an accident that could not have been prevented. It recognized the efforts made by the Special Representative, UNAMIR, the Government of Rwanda and other organizations to keep the situation under control. It concluded that there was sufficient reliable evidence that unarmed internally displaced persons were subjected to serious human rights abuses committed by both RPA and armed elements in the camp. The Commission welcomed the initiative taken by the Rwandese Government to carry out an investigation at the national level. It also recommended that the international community continue encouraging and assisting Rwanda in its efforts to achieve justice, national reconciliation and reconstruction.

Humanitarian aspects

The consequences of the forced closure of internally displaced persons camps required a rapid and coordinated response of UNAMIR, UNREO, United Nations agencies, intergovernmental organizations, in particular the International Organization for Migration (IOM), and NGOs. The efforts were undertaken in cooperation with national and local authorities. Transportation assistance was provided by UNHCR, IOM, UNAMIR and NGOs to over 70,000 people; emergency medical facilities were set up to tend to the sick and wounded, mainly in Butare; way stations and open relief

[43] S/1995/411.

centres, managed and supported by NGOs, served as first-aid points and provided food, water and other emergency items to the former occupants of internally displaced persons camps.

During the month of May, WFP undertook the distribution of food items to a total of 420,000 beneficiaries from vulnerable groups. Emergency non-food assistance was continued to former camp populations. Other programmes of assistance included rehabilitation of hospitals and health centres by UNHCR, health training programmes undertaken by WHO and the United Nations Population Fund, water supply projects undertaken by UNICEF, and assistance by UNICEF to some 2,000 unaccompanied minors, of whom approximately 70 per cent were under the age of 5.

The relief effort was hampered by inadequate funding. As of 15 May, only $80 million was pledged against a total requirement of $219 million. The total contributions actually received amounted to $6.3 million only.

Security measures in the refugee camps

Deployment of the Zairian Camp Security Contingent got under way in early February. It reached 913 troops by 11 April and was operating in Kibumba, Katale/Kahindo and Mugunga/Lac Vert. Experts from the Netherlands and Switzerland arrived in Goma to serve in the Civilian Security Liaison Group, and the Governments of Benin, Burkina Faso and Cameroon each offered to provide between 10 and 20 experts to serve in the Group. UNHCR appointed Brigadier-General (retired) Ian Douglas of Canada as Commander of the Group. General Douglas took up his duties in Goma on 27 March 1995. The total cost of the security operation in Zaire, through the end of June, was estimated at $9.7 million.

A matter of concern was the persistent report of arms shipments into Goma airport, allegedly to arm the former Rwandese government forces, and of the training of these forces on Zairian territory. The allegations were rejected by the Chargé d'affaires of the Permanent Mission of Zaire to the United Nations. Furthermore, on the occasion of the OAU/UNHCR Regional Conference on Assistance to Refugees, Returnees and Displaced Persons in the Great Lakes Region, which took place from 15 to 17 February 1995 in Bujumbura, the Minister for Foreign Affairs of Zaire requested that an independent commission of inquiry be established to investigate and report on the matter.

HRFOR

During the first few months of 1995, the Human Rights Field Operation in Rwanda (HRFOR) became fully operational. As of 1 April 1995, HRFOR was composed of 113 staff in 11 field offices, including 67 fixed-term staff, 34 United Nations Volunteers, and 12 human rights officers contributed by the Commission of the European Communities. In addition, there were 6 experts in investigations provided by the Governments of the Netherlands and Switzerland. The above number grew to 125 by the end of May.

The mandate of HRFOR was designed according to a three-pronged approach to confidence-building with a view towards eventual national reconciliation. First, HRFOR carried out extensive investigations of genocide and other serious violations of human rights and humanitarian law that took place during the April to July 1994 armed conflict. Second, it established a comprehensive presence of human rights field officers throughout the country to monitor the ongoing human rights situation. Third, it initiated a broad-based programme of promotional activities in the field of human rights, ranging from projects for the rebuilding of the Rwandese administration of justice to human rights education.

With regard to the investigation of the genocide, a special investigations unit was established to gather evidence which might otherwise have been lost or destroyed. All collected information was regularly forwarded to the High Commissioner for Human Rights, the Special Rapporteur and the International Tribunal. The information placed before the Special Rapporteur and the Commission of Experts during 1994 was forwarded to the International Tribunal in January 1995. HRFOR continued its genocide-related investigations until the Deputy Prosecutor's Office, with its own investigations unit, was established in Kigali. Thereafter, the emphasis of HRFOR's investigative work shifted to coordinating activities of the field teams with the work of the International Tribunal. Information and evidentiary materials that were collected subsequently were again made available to the Special Rapporteur and personally handed over by the High Commissioner to the Deputy Prosecutor of the International Tribunal on 2 April 1995 in Kigali.

In addition, monitoring and reporting on the prevailing human rights situation constituted essential elements of HRFOR's mandate. It had been considered important for the post-genocide rehabilitation of Rwanda that the ongoing human rights situation be closely observed, that patterns of violations be identified and immediate action taken. During his third visit to Rwanda from 1 to 3 April 1995, the High Commissioner for Human Rights had the opportunity to discuss the most pressing problems confronting Rwanda with Government officials, particularly the establishment of an effective justice system. The Government fully recognized respect for human rights as a prerequisite for genuine confidence-building and national reconciliation and supported HRFOR's efforts in this regard. The Foreign Minister again conveyed the Government's wish that the number of Human Rights Officers be increased to 300.

Moreover, HRFOR played an important role in the process of repatriation and resettlement of refugees and internally displaced persons. In this context, HRFOR closely coordinated its activities with UNHCR. HRFOR's aim was to ensure that basic human rights were not violated at any stage of return, resettlement and reintegration, including the evaluation of the state of readiness of home communes as regards reception of returnees, as well as assisting these communes in the resettlement process and monitoring the subsequent treatment and security of resettled returnees.

Another priority for HRFOR was the serious situation in prisons and local detention centres. By the end of May 1995, there were approximately 42,000 detainees throughout the country, many of them held in inhumane conditions. Most of those detained were arrested outside the procedures laid down in Rwandese law, on accusations of involvement in the genocide, and there were initially no case files recording the allegations against them. HRFOR actively promoted respect for legal procedures governing arrest and detention, and, as an increasing number of Rwandese judicial officials were trained and deployed, there was gradual progress in this respect.

To cope with the tragedy of genocide and its aftermath and to make possible steps towards national reconciliation and rebuilding the principal organs of State administration, the re-establishment of the administration of justice was seen as a priority. HRFOR worked to assist in the rehabilitation of the justice system at national and local levels. The close contacts developed by HRFOR's field teams with local judicial officials enabled HRFOR to enhance judicial functions despite limitations of the system. HRFOR was thus able to assist in channelling material assistance made available by UNDP and donor countries to meet local needs, and to promote the gradual re-

sumption of judicial functions. Three legal experts worked with the Ministry of Justice, and HRFOR developed, in cooperation with the Ministry of Justice and UNDP, a plan to deploy 50 foreign legal experts to assist the Government in restarting the judiciary. In September 1995, the Government asked to suspend this project for reexamination.

HRFOR actively supported respect for Rwandese law and human rights standards through efforts focused on establishing or re-establishing the governmental and non-governmental institutions necessary for the protection of human rights. It also provided training in international human rights standards to government officials, the Gendarmerie or RPA.

UNAMIR activities

During the first half of 1995, the UNAMIR military component maintained its authorized strength of 5,500 troops and 320 military observers. By February, UNAMIR's force structure and deployment had been adjusted as a result of security developments in the displaced persons camps and an increase in armed attacks by groups infiltrating across the border with Zaire as well as the additional security tasks under resolution 965. UNAMIR logistic resources were made available throughout the country, particularly to transport internally displaced persons and returning refugees and to help in the restoration of essential services and facilities, including the reconstruction of bridges, the repair of roads and water supply schemes. UNAMIR military observers maintained constant contact and coordination with the Government, human rights observers and United Nations agencies for the purpose of smooth and efficient movement and follow-up monitoring of resettled refugees and internally displaced persons.

CIVPOL had 89 observers on the ground by February. However, only 25 were French-speaking, putting a considerable strain on UNAMIR's ability to carry out its civilian police functions effectively. Additional personnel were also required to meet CIVPOL's expanded functions under resolution 965 (1994). The Secretary-General therefore proposed[44] on 6 February that the component's authorized strength be raised from 90 to 120 police observers. The Security Council subsequently agreed.[45] Notwithstanding this authorization and despite repeated requests to Member States, CIVPOL faced an acute shortage of personnel. By April 1995,

[44] S/1995/107. [45] S/1995/130.

UNAMIR deployment as of May 1995

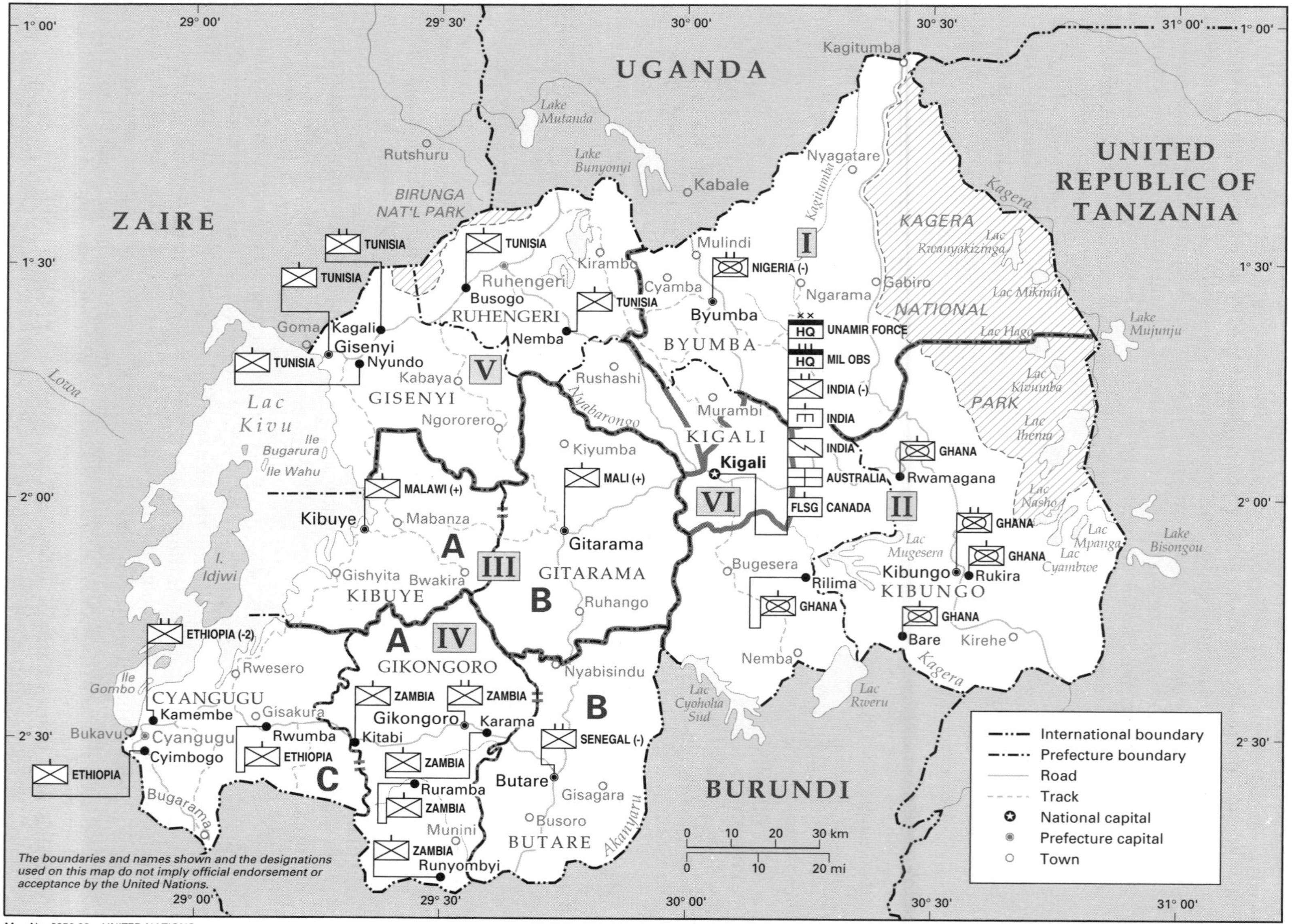

Map No. 3952.23   UNITED NATIONS
September 1996

Department of Public Information
Cartographic Section

The boundaries and names shown and the designations
used on this map do not imply official endorsement or
acceptance by the United Nations.

CIVPOL strength had fallen to 58 police observers; by May the number had only risen to 64.

A major CIVPOL activity was the training of a new integrated national police force. A group of 300 gendarmes and 20 instructors completed an intensive 16-week training programme on 29 April and arrangements were made to start training 400 additional candidates in June over a period of four months. This was to be followed by the training of 100 instructors selected from the already-trained gendarmes. Other CIVPOL activities included monitoring the increasingly difficult situation in Rwanda's overcrowded prisons and provided monitoring and investigatory assistance to the human rights officers and the military and civilian components of UNAMIR. CIVPOL had teams of 3 to 4 observers in each of the 11 prefectures in the country working in close cooperation with local authorities, United Nations agencies and non-governmental organizations.

G. June–December 1995

A new situation

On 4 June 1995, the Secretary-General informed[46] the Council that the Government of Rwanda had raised questions about the future role of UNAMIR, whose mandate would expire on 9 June. Designed at a time when Rwanda was in the midst of a devastating genocide and civil war, UNAMIR's mandate included the responsibility of contributing to the security and protection of displaced persons, refugees and civilians at risk. The war and the genocide had come to an end with the establishment of the new Government on 19 July 1994. The Government made it clear that it would insist on a sharp reduction both in the scope of UNAMIR's tasks and in troop levels.

The Secretary-General suggested shifting the focus of the mandate from peace-keeping to confidence-building. This role would entail: (a) tasks specifically required to sustain a United Nations peace-keeping presence, including the protection of United Nations premises, protection of International Tribunal personnel and, as required, of United Nations agencies and NGOs; (b) tasks aimed at assisting the Government of Rwanda in confidence-building and in the promotion of a climate conducive to stability and to the return of refugees and displaced persons. These tasks would entail monitoring throughout the country with military/police observers, as a complement to human rights monitors; helping in the distribution of humanitarian assistance; facilitating the return and reintegration of refugees; providing assistance and expertise in engineering, logistics, medical care and de-mining; and stationing a limited reserve of formed troops in certain provinces to assist in the performance of the above tasks, as required.

The Secretary-General estimated that UNAMIR would require approximately 2,330 formed troops, 320 military observers and 65 civilian police. The proposed force would be structured along the following lines: an infantry battalion of 800 all ranks, based in Kigali and reinforced by essential support units; in addition, one independent infantry company would be deployed in each of the UNAMIR sectors of operation and would include elements from the support units or specialists, as required for specific humanitarian tasks. The reduction in UNAMIR's strength would begin as soon as possible and be implemented gradually, on the understanding that, after 9 June 1995, the infantry battalions currently deployed in the provinces would change over from their present tasks to those outlined above.

In consultations with the Special Representative, the Rwandese Government proposed a more limited role for UNAMIR. In the Government's view, national security and the protection of humanitarian convoys were its responsibility, as was border monitoring. The training programme carried out by CIVPOL should be replaced by bilateral arrangements. The Government proposed that UNAMIR be reduced to a maximum of 1,800 formed troops, deployed in Kigali and in the provinces. UNAMIR's mandate would be extended for six months with no further extensions.

In the Secretary-General's view, UNAMIR would not have the strength under the Government's proposal to perform adequately the tasks he had outlined. Because UNAMIR's continued presence in Rwanda depended on the consent and

[46]S/1995/457.

active cooperation of the Government, he intended to continue consultations with the Government. In the mean time, he recommended that the Security Council renew the mandate of UNAMIR, adjusted to accommodate the tasks he had outlined, for a period of six months ending on 9 December 1995. UNAMIR, in cooperation with UNDP, United Nations agencies and NGOs, would also assist in the implementation of an integrated multifunctional plan of action in the field of rehabilitation, resettlement, repair of infrastructure and the revival of justice. The funds committed to such projects could be channelled by donor countries through the Rwanda Trust Fund.

By its resolution 997 of 9 June 1995, the Security Council extended UNAMIR's mandate until 8 December 1995. It authorized a reduction of the force level to 2,330 troops within three months and to 1,800 troops within four months. It maintained the existing level of observers and police monitors. According to its adjusted mandate, UNAMIR would exercise its good offices, assist the Government in facilitating the voluntary and safe return of refugees, support the provision of humanitarian aid, assist in the training of a national police force, and contribute to the security of United Nations personnel and premises and, in case of need, to the security of humanitarian agencies. The Council also called upon States neighbouring Rwanda to ensure that arms and *matériel*, as specified in resolution 918, were not transferred to Rwandese camps within their territories. It requested the Secretary-General to consult with the Governments of those States on the possible deployment of United Nations military observers to monitor the sale or supply of arms and *matériel* as specified in resolution 918 (1994).

In the following weeks, the Government of Rwanda continued its efforts to enhance the administration of justice, establish law and order, promote national reconciliation and encourage the voluntary return of refugees. Steps were taken to improve relations with neighbouring countries, and Burundi, Rwanda and Zaire agreed to organize joint border patrols. Nevertheless, reports of infiltration and sabotage by armed elements, as well as allegations that members of the former government forces and militias were conducting military training and receiving deliveries of arms, had heightened tensions in the border areas and led the Government of Rwanda to enhance security measures. The Governments of Zaire and Rwanda accused each other of involvement. Rwanda re-

quested that restrictions on its acquisition of arms be lifted.

To carry out consultations regarding deployment of United Nations military observers in countries neighbouring Rwanda, the Secretary-General appointed Mr. Aldo Ajello as his Special Envoy. Mr. Ajello visited the region from 20 to 28 June 1995. The countries concerned saw the uncontrolled circulation of arms, including to civilians and refugees in the subregion, as a major cause of destabilization, especially in Rwanda and Burundi. There were mixed reactions, however, to the idea of deploying military observers in neighbouring countries. While Rwanda supported the idea, some countries were reluctant to have such military observers stationed in their territory.[47]

Secretary-General Boutros-Ghali visited Rwanda on 13 and 14 July 1995. During the visit, he held detailed discussions with senior government officials, including President Pasteur Bizimungu, Vice-President Paul Kagame and Prime Minister Faustin Twagiramungu. National reconciliation, the maintenance of security within the country and along its borders, reconstruction and reports of the growing threat of destabilization beyond Rwanda's borders were high on the agenda in his discussions. The Secretary-General also had discussions in Uganda and Burundi. He reported a clear consensus that instability in any State in the area could have a dramatic effect on all its neighbours; destabilizing influences should be prevented through cooperative efforts. Strong interest was expressed by some countries in the establishment of an international commission, under the auspices of the United Nations, to address allegations of arms flows to former government forces.

The Secretary-General also discussed the idea of convening a regional conference that would consider the interrelated problems of peace, security and development, having in mind the adoption of a specific programme of action. In order to address the more urgent problems facing the repatriation of refugees, he suggested to convene a regional meeting aimed at developing concrete measures to fulfil commitments already entered into by Rwanda, neighbouring countries hosting Rwandese refugees and humanitarian agencies.[48]

---

[47]S/1995/552. [48]S/1995/678.

Arms embargo lifted

By its resolution 1011 (1995) of 16 August, the Security Council unanimously decided to lift its embargo on the sale of arms and related *matériel* to Rwanda until 1 September 1996, effective immediately. The flow of arms and *matériel* would be allowed through certain points of entry to be designated by the Rwandese Government. On 1 September 1996, the embargo would be terminated, unless otherwise decided by the Council. The Council continued its prohibition on the sale and supply of arms and related *matériel* to non-governmental forces in Rwanda and in neighbouring countries if they were for use in Rwanda.

The Government of Zaire expressed strong opposition to the lifting of the arms embargo on Rwanda, fearing an increase in tension and in the flow of refugees. It would be forced to derogate from the principle of non-refoulement of refugees for reasons of national security and in order to protect its own population. In a letter[49] to the Secretary-General, the Prime Minister of Zaire stated that the adoption of resolution 1011 (1995) left him no choice but to request the Secretary-General to indicate "the arrangements made at the United Nations level in relation to the new country or countries of asylum to which the Rwandese and Burundi refugees should be evacuated". In the absence of any clear indication, the Government would "evacuate them to their country of origin at the expense of the United Nations Assistance Mission for Rwanda, the United Nations and the Governments of their respective countries".

August 1995 refugee crisis

Despite the Secretary-General's urgent appeal, Zaire began forced repatriation of refugees on 19 August. To calm the crisis, the Secretary-General asked United Nations High Commissioner for Refugees Sadako Ogata to travel to Zaire. On 23 August, the Security Council called[50] on the Government of Zaire to stand by its humanitarian obligations regarding refugees and to reconsider and halt its declared policy of forcible repatriation. It encouraged all Governments in the region to cooperate with UNHCR to achieve the voluntary and orderly repatriation of refugees.

Strong international pressure helped to avert a new tragedy. On 24 August, the Government of Zaire suspended its expulsion policy. Its announcement followed the forcible expulsion of approximately 13,000 people to Rwanda and the outflow of some 170,000 refugees, many from Burundi, out of the refugee camps into the hills of Zaire to avoid forced repatriation. The Government also welcomed a visit by the High Commissioner.

Mrs. Ogata met with the Prime Minister of Zaire in Geneva on 29 August. The Prime Minister wished the repatriation to be completed by 31 December 1995. The High Commissioner made it clear that a policy of forcible repatriation would not solve the problem. From 31 August to 7 September, the High Commissioner visited Burundi, Rwanda, Tanzania and Zaire. Mrs. Ogata found a strong convergence of interest on the importance of a safe, accelerated, organized and voluntary return of refugees. UNHCR would be able to set in motion such a repatriation if all commitments made during the High Commissioner's mission were respected. At the same time, there was need for immediate support from the international community for the efforts of UNHCR.

A meeting of the Tripartite Commission involving Rwanda, Tanzania and UNHCR met from 18 to 21 September at Arusha, at which practical measures were agreed for starting large-scale repatriation of the more than 600,000 Rwandese refugees in Tanzania. A meeting of the Tripartite Commission involving Zaire, Rwanda and UNHCR was held at Geneva on 25 September. In a joint communiqué, the parties reaffirmed commitments to create conditions for repatriation to Rwanda in a safe and organized manner. In anticipation of an increased rate of return, UNHCR augmented its facilities at official border entry points and, in cooperation with UNDP, expanded activities in the communes of origin.

Meanwhile, repatriation of Rwandese refugees from Burundi gained momentum. Between 5 and 25 September 1995, more than 4,000 refugees were repatriated under UNHCR auspices, bringing to a total of some 18,000 the refugees assisted by UNHCR since June 1995. UNHCR further estimated that an equal number had repatriated spontaneously. The number of Rwandese refugees remaining in Burundi was 155,000. From Zaire, which as of September 1995 hosted 1 million Rwandese refugees, UNHCR believed that a realistic target for voluntary repatriation was between 500,000 and 600,000 persons by the end of 1995.

[49]S/1995/722. [50]S/PRST/1995/41.

Political situation in Rwanda

In August and September 1995, the political situation and the process of national reconciliation in Rwanda were influenced by two additional major events. The first was the departure of Prime Minister Faustin Twagiramungu, who left office on 28 August together with four other Cabinet Ministers. The second event was the killing of 110 villagers at Kanama, in northwestern Rwanda, on 11 and 12 September, another in a spate of killings which had taken the lives of local and provincial government officials, clergymen and judges. The Government reacted quickly and managed to contain and counteract those events: first, it appointed a new Prime Minister, Mr. Pierre Celestin Rwigema, and replaced the departing Cabinet Ministers; secondly, the Vice-President and Defence Minister, Major-General Paul Kagame, visited Kanama the day after the killings, acknowledged RPA excesses and promised punishment of the guilty.

In the second part of October and November, a climate of relative security and stability continued to prevail within Rwanda. Some improvement in the socio-economic sectors also occurred, and the first effective steps towards the revival of the national judicial system were taken by the Government, with the appointment of the Supreme Court on 17 October.

At the same time, the former Rwandese Government Forces and armed militia continued their infiltration and sabotage campaigns along the Zaire-Rwanda border. These attacks, which usually triggered counter-measures and retaliation by Rwandese security forces, remained the most disturbing security problem facing Rwanda.

UNAMIR downsized

In accordance with the adjusted mandate, the activities of UNAMIR's military component shifted from providing security to assisting in the normalization of the country. The component also assisted in the delivery of humanitarian aid and the provision of engineering and logistical support. Furthermore, its strength was drawn down. As at 3 August 1995, there were 3,571 UNAMIR troops, all ranks; by 31 October, the force stood at 1,821 troops and 286 military observers.

During this period, UNAMIR helped construct and renovate detention centres to relieve the overcrowding in jails and assisted in the construction or repair of bridges, roads and schools and in the transport of humanitarian assistance, including food and medicines. Between 19 and 24 August, when Rwandese refugees were forced across the border from Zaire, UNAMIR troops and military observers, in coordination with UNHCR and other United Nations agencies, supported the Government's resettlement efforts by helping to construct transit camps. UNAMIR provided vehicles to help transport the returnees and contributed to a sense of confidence by its presence at the border checkpoints, in transit camps and in communes of destination.

As for CIVPOL activities, some 900 of the estimated 6,000 gendarmes needed had been trained. However, the training of the communal police was delayed because of the ongoing rehabilitation of the Communal Police Training Centre. CIVPOL also continued to carry out monitoring duties, together with the military observers, in areas including the prisons and other places of detention. As at 31 October 1995, a total of 85 police observers from 12 countries were deployed.

Other developments

A Headquarters Agreement relating to the seat of the Tribunal was signed on 31 August between the United Nations and Tanzania and a Memorandum of Understanding with the Government of Rwanda covering the Prosecutor's office at Kigali was under negotiation. The President of the International Tribunal, the Prosecutor and the Registrar travelled to Rwanda for a three-day visit to discuss the Tribunal's operations, including the functioning of the Prosecutor's office in Rwanda. They also visited the seat of the Tribunal at Arusha, to inspect the premises designated for it, as well as a proposed prison site and accommodation arrangements for the Tribunal's staff.

By August, over 50,000 people were incarcerated in 12 prisons and various places of detention, although the prison capacity was only 12,250. At the beginning of October 1995, more than 52,000 people were incarcerated. As part of the working group established by the Special Representative, Mr. Khan, the Human Rights Field Operation worked to facilitate the processing of detainees' cases and to coordinate short- and medium-term initiatives for rehabilitating the judicial system. A Plan of Action, drafted by representatives of the Government of Rwanda and UNDP, for urgent action on prisons and in the justice sector was circulated to the international community. It was estimated that more than $43 million would be required for these purposes.

In September, the Nsinda detention centre, built with the assistance of UNAMIR, UNDP and ICRC, was completed. Two of seven temporary sites were near completion, and, in view of the gravity of the situation, WFP made five warehouses available as temporary detention sites.

As at 12 July 1995, the United Nations Trust Fund for Rwanda had received contributions amounting to $6.54 million. The Fund financed projects aimed at meeting emergency and rehabilitation needs, as well as the urgent requirements of essential government ministries. As at 1 August, a total of $116 million had been pledged against the sum of $219 million outlined in the 1995 Consolidated Inter-Agency Emergency Appeal for Rwanda.

In the field of economic and social assistance, donor countries and United Nations agencies met at Kigali on 6 and 7 July for a mid-term review of the Round-Table Conference held at Geneva in January 1995. Progress in rebuilding the country's infrastructure was reported, as was an increase in agricultural production. Formidable challenges remained, however, in the areas of resettlement, budgetary support, national capacity-building and industrial production. Following the mid-term review, there was a sizeable increase in the commitment and disbursement of funds pledged for the Government's Programme of National Reconciliation and Socio-Economic Rehabilitation and Recovery. As at 14 September, $523 million had been committed (up from $345 million in July) and $252 million disbursed (up from $86 million in July) against total pledges of $587 million made at Geneva in January 1995. In fact, since the Geneva Conference, total pledges had risen to $1,089 million. Some of these additional funds were to be disbursed over the period 1996-1997.

A joint programme of the World Bank, the International Monetary Fund and UNDP was developed to strengthen the Government's capacity to manage its economic, financial and human resources. By October 1995, through several food-for-work and income-generating activities, WFP was providing food for some 100,000 persons and assisting Rwanda's agricultural recovery, rehabilitation of destroyed infrastructure and construction of new houses, schools and water facilities. UNICEF, ICRC and several NGOs were also training local communities to manage their own water points. In addition, the international community continued to pursue a series of initiatives designed to help reinvigorate the Rwandese judicial system.

The United Nations Rwanda Emergency Office structure was officially closed at the end of October 1995. The United Nations Resident Coordinator subsequently assumed the responsibilities of United Nations Humanitarian Coordinator and a support office was established to facilitate operations. It was foreseen that one of the principal activities of the Humanitarian Coordinator would be to ensure the continuity of humanitarian assistance to Rwanda following the departure of UNAMIR.[51]

During September and October 1995, a total of 32,190 refugees returned to Rwanda, mainly in UNHCR-organized convoys. The rate of return from Tanzania increased from 1,000 returnees in September to 2,000 in October, of whom 1,144 were new caseload refugees. Approximately 19,000 refugees returned from Zaire, 94 per cent of whom came under UNHCR auspices. Voluntary repatriation from Burundi, however, fell from 7,773 in September to 1,012 in October. According to most observers, the low number of returnees was to be attributed to the continuing campaign of intimidation and misinformation in the refugee camps.

Security Council welcomes progress

On 17 October, the Security Council welcomed[52] progress made by the Government of Rwanda in the reconciliation process. To foster that process, an effective and credible national judiciary had to be established. At the same time, the Council reaffirmed its view that genuine reconciliation and long-lasting stability in the region as a whole could not be attained without the safe, voluntary and organized return to their country of all Rwandese refugees. The Council also called on Member States to comply with their obligations regarding cooperation with the International Tribunal for Rwanda, which should begin its proceedings as soon as possible.

The Council underlined that sound economic foundations were vital for achieving lasting stability in Rwanda. At the same time, it reiterated its concern at reports about continuing cross-border infiltrations from neighbouring countries, and at the danger for peace and stability in the Great Lakes Region which would be caused by uncontrolled arms flows. As for UNAMIR, the Council reaffirmed the Mission's important role in Rwanda and the subregion and was ready to study any further recommendations on the issue of force reductions in relation to the fulfilment of the mandate of UNAMIR.

[51]S/1996/61. [52]S/PRST/1995/53.

Regional conference

The Secretary-General, convinced that stability in Rwanda went beyond its borders, continued his efforts to prepare the Regional Conference on Security, Stability and Development in the Great Lakes Region of Central Africa. His Special Envoy on the matter, Mr. José Luis Jésus (Cape Verde), held high-level consultations with OAU and the Governments of Burundi, Ethiopia, Kenya, Rwanda, Uganda and Tanzania.

OAU and most of those Governments supported the idea. The Government of Rwanda, on the other hand, expressed strong opposition, and the Government of Uganda indicated that it was not keen to have the United Nations actively involved in this process. In the mean time, the Secretary-General welcomed a regional conference with similar objectives organized by former United States President Jimmy Carter in Cairo, Egypt.[53] The conference was attended by the heads of State of Burundi, Rwanda, Uganda and Zaire and a representative of Tanzania. In a final declaration[54] on 29 November 1995, the parties pledged to take concrete actions to advance peace, justice, reconciliation, stability and development in the region. Zaire and the United Republic of Tanzania pledged to isolate those elements in the camps who were intimidating refugees, and Rwanda guaranteed the safety of the returning refugees. The parties believed that the number of returning refugees should rise to 10,000 a day within a short time.

H. Final period

The Secretary-General advised[55] the Security Council on 1 December 1995 that national reconciliation in Rwanda required the rapid creation of conditions to facilitate the safe return of refugees. Forced repatriation could well result in another humanitarian disaster. Efforts to induce a large-scale return would need a time-frame extending over three to six months. A large part of the international community therefore believed that a further six-month extension of UNAMIR's mandate was desirable. This view was shared among donor countries, most UNAMIR troop contributors, UNHCR, the International Tribunal, the High Commissioner for Human Rights, United Nations agencies, the Secretary-General of OAU, NGOs and Rwanda's neighbours. They felt that if UNAMIR was to be perceived as abandoning Rwanda at a critical time, it would send a discouraging message to the refugees, to the region and to the international community at large.

The Government of Rwanda, however, officially informed[56] the Secretary-General that it did not agree to an extension of UNAMIR's mandate beyond its expiration on 8 December on the basis that, as a peace-keeping mission, UNAMIR did not respond to Rwanda's priority needs. However, the Government indicated that it would be receptive to a continued United Nations presence, provided its purpose was to assist Rwanda in its pressing tasks of rehabilitation and reconstruction, including the provision of technical expertise, financial assistance and equipment.

Since UNAMIR could not remain in Rwanda without the consent of the Government, the Secretary-General stated his intention to initiate the drawdown of the operation as of 8 December. He estimated that the withdrawal process would take two to three months to complete. During this period, UNAMIR would no longer be able to fulfil its mandate but would concentrate on ensuring its smooth and peaceful departure.

In the Secretary-General's view, the overarching objective of the United Nations was the restoration of peace and stability not only in Rwanda but in the region as a whole. The United Nations still had a useful role to play in political efforts to this end. He recommended, therefore, that the United Nations should maintain a political presence in Rwanda after the withdrawal of UNAMIR. A United Nations office, headed by the Special Representative, could be established with a view to furthering, in consultation with the Government of Rwanda, the search for peace and stability through justice and reconciliation. The Special Representative would continue to have overall authority for the coordination of international assistance for rehabilitation and reconstruction.

[53]SG/T/1996. [54]S/1995/1001, annex. [55]S/1995/1002. [56]S/1995/1018, annex.

Following an extension[57] of UNAMIR's mandate from 8 to 12 December 1995, the Security Council, by its resolution 1029 (1995) of 12 December, extended the mandate for a final period until 8 March 1996. During that time, UNAMIR would exercise its good offices, assist in voluntary and safe repatriation of refugees, support the Government's efforts to promote a climate of confidence and trust, and assist UNHCR and the agencies in the provision of logistical support for repatriation. It would also contribute to the protection of the International Tribunal as an interim measure until alternative arrangements agreed with the Government could be put in place. The Council requested the Secretary-General to withdraw CIVPOL and to reduce the force level to 1,200 troops and 200 military observers and military support staff. Final withdrawal of all UNAMIR elements was to take place six weeks after the end of the mandate.

The UNAMIR Force Commander, General Tousignant, left the mission area on 15 December 1995 upon completion of his tour of duty, and Brigadier-General Siva Kumar (India) was designated as Acting Force Commander. By January 1996, the civilian police component of UNAMIR ceased its activities and all remaining CIVPOL personnel were repatriated.

On 16 January 1996, the Permanent Representative of Canada formally notified[58] the Secretary-General that his Government had decided to withdraw its participation in UNAMIR. The Government considered that the UNAMIR mandate, as adjusted in December 1995, was not viable in the light of the reduction of the force level. With the departure of this key logistic support unit, and unable to make alternative arrangements in the time remaining, the Acting Force Commander took steps to restrict the remaining UNAMIR strength to a garrison mode in Kigali.

The reduction of the UNAMIR force level to 1,200 formed troops and 200 military observers and headquarters staff was achieved by early February. In addition to the formed troops in Kigali, UNAMIR logistic bases, consisting of about 40 personnel each, were deployed at Nyundo, near Gisenyi, and Shagasha, near Cyangugu, to assist in the return of refugees. The troops stationed in Kigali were tasked, among other things, to contribute to the security of the Tribunal, the provision of humanitarian assistance and the protection of United Nations property and assets. A small contingent was also deployed at Kibuye for the protection of members of the Tribunal working in that town.

When the Burundi authorities closed the camp of Ntamba in the first week of February, UNAMIR troops and military observers, working in support of UNHCR and other agencies, provided assistance to resettle the returnees. Tasks performed by UNAMIR also included the construction and improvement of transit camps, transportation on behalf of United Nations agencies and other partners, and engineering work, including road and bridge repair. UNAMIR assisted RPA in transporting a number of weapons systems and major pieces of equipment belonging to Rwanda, which were returned by Zaire on 13 February. Military observers continued to patrol and monitor the situation. However, the reduction in the number of military observers curtailed the Mission's reporting and investigation capabilities.

UNHCR, Rwanda and the countries hosting some 1.7 million Rwandese refugees, namely, Zaire, Burundi and Tanzania, made a concerted effort to accelerate the voluntary return of refugees. From an average of around 5,000 a month through much of 1995, January 1996 saw the number of returnees increase to more than 14,000. In the first three weeks of February alone, refugee returns topped 20,000.

The pace of return, however, was not uniform. Following intensive discussions among Zaire, Rwanda and UNHCR to implement decisions taken by the Tripartite Commission at its meeting in December 1995, which included a proposal for targeted voluntary repatriation leading to the closure of camps, an operation launched by Zaire began on 13 February. However, the number of refugees returning from Zaire remained very low.

Refugee returns from Burundi increased dramatically in February in the wake of fighting in the northern part of the country, which emptied two Rwandese refugee camps. Following the abandonment of the Ntamba camp in Burundi by some 14,000 refugees fearing the spread of ethnic fighting, on 27 January a delegation led by Rwanda's Minister for Rehabilitation and Social Integration visited Ntamba to urge refugees who had returned to the camp to go back to Rwanda. Members of the Burundi/Rwanda/UNHCR Tripartite Commission and a second delegation from Rwanda also made efforts to persuade those remaining to repatriate rather than follow the bulk of the camp's residents into the United Republic of Tanzania. As a result, more than 4,400 Rwandese decided to repatriate during the first two days of February and the camp was subsequently closed.[59]

[57]S/RES/1028 (1995). [58]S/1996/35. [59]S/1996/149.

Commission of inquiry

On 13 March 1996, the Secretary-General transmitted to the Security Council the final report of the International Commission of Inquiry. Under the terms of its resolution 1011 (1995) of 16 August 1995, the Security Council had requested the Secretary-General to make recommendations on the establishment of a commission mandated to conduct a full investigation of alleged arms flows to former Rwandese government forces in the Great Lakes region of Central Africa. The Secretary-General did so on 25 August.

According to the recommendations,[60] the proposed commission would collect information and investigate reports relating to the sale or supply of arms and related *matériel* to former Rwandese government forces and attempt to identify parties aiding or abetting the illegal acquisition of arms and recommend measures to curb their illegal flow. It would also investigate allegations that such forces were receiving military training. The Secretary-General noted that the proposal to establish such a commission had initially been made by the Government of Zaire. He therefore recommended that the commission commence its work in Zaire. In the mean time, he would pursue consultations with the other concerned countries in the region, so that the commission could extend its work to those countries.

The Security Council, by its resolution 1013 (1995) of 7 September, requested the Secretary-General to establish the commission, as a matter of urgency. On 16 October 1995, the Secretary-General informed[61] the Council that arrangements had been completed. The Commission consisted of six members, as follows: Ambassador Mahmoud Kassem, Egypt (Chairman); Inspector Jean-Michel Hanssens, Canada; Colonel Jürgen G. H. Almeling, Germany; Lt. Colonel Jan Meijvogel, Netherlands; Brigadier Mujahid Alam, Pakistan; Colonel Lamek Mutanda, Zimbabwe. The International Commission of Inquiry began its work in the Great Lakes region on 3 November and submitted an interim report[62] to the Council on 26 January 1996.

In its final report,[63] the Commission found that a "highly probable" violation of the arms embargo had taken place in June 1994 involving more than 80 tons of weapons purchased in Seychelles by Colonel Théoneste Bagosora, a high-ranking officer of the former Rwandese government forces. Since Colonel Bagosora had bought the weapons on the authority of an end-user certificate apparently signed by the Zairian Vice-Minister of Defence, had signed for the weapons on behalf of the Forces Armées Zaïroises and had chartered an Air Zaire DC-8 aircraft to transport them to Goma airport in Zaire before delivering them to the Rwandese army in Gisenyi, the Commission also concluded that the Government of Zaire, or elements within it, had aided and abetted in this violation of the embargo.

The Commission's recommendations concerned mechanisms to monitor, implement and enforce Security Council resolutions, to gather information and preserve evidence; measures designed to foster stability in the subregion; confidence-building measures designed to reduce the flow of arms in the subregion; the further investigation of violations which had or might have taken place; and measures to deter further violations of the embargo.

On 23 April 1996, the Security Council adopted resolution 1053 (1996), requesting the Secretary-General to retain the Commission to maintain contacts with the Governments of the Great Lakes region, to follow up its earlier investigations, to respond to any further allegations of violations and to make periodic reports to the Council on the evolution of the situation with regard to compliance with relevant Council resolutions. The Commission was expected to return to the Great Lakes region for these purposes and to report in September 1996.

UNAMIR's mandate ends

On 8 March 1996, as UNAMIR's mandate was ending, the Security Council, in its resolution 1050 (1996), paid tribute to the work of UNAMIR and to the personnel who served in it. It also took note of arrangements for the withdrawal of UNAMIR starting on 9 March. The Council authorized those elements of UNAMIR remaining in Rwanda prior to their final withdrawal to contribute, with the agreement of the Government, to the protection of the personnel and premises of the International Tribunal. At the same time, the Council encouraged the Secretary-General to maintain a United Nations office in Rwanda for the purpose of supporting the efforts of the Government to promote national reconciliation, strengthen the judicial system, facilitate the return of refugees and rehabilitate the country's infrastructure, and of coordinating United Nations efforts to that end.

[60]S/1995/761. [61]S/1995/879. [62]S/1996/67. [63]S/1996/195.

Throughout March and April 1996, discussions continued between the United Nations and the Government on modalities of the United Nations presence in Rwanda following the withdrawal of UNAMIR. That withdrawal was completed on 19 April. On 24 April, following a visit by the Under-Secretary-General for Political Affairs, Mr. Marrack Goulding, the Government announced that it had agreed to the establishment of the United Nations Office in Rwanda.

Although the Government consistently supported the presence of the Human Rights Field Operation in Rwanda and expressed the wish that it be maintained after the departure of UNAMIR, by mid-March 1996 the number of human rights monitors had decreased to 78 of a total staff on the ground of 95. The United Nations High Commissioner for Human Rights considered that 120 human rights field officers constituted the minimum presence necessary. However the absence of sufficient financial resources made it impossible to maintain that number.

I. Composition of UNOMUR and UNAMIR

When UNOMUR was set up on 22 June 1993, it was put under the command in the field of the Chief Military Observer, Major-General Romeo A. Dallaire (Canada). From October 1993, when UNAMIR was established, UNOMUR came under the command of the new Mission, while maintaining its separate monitoring tasks. Observers were provided by the following countries: Bangladesh, Botswana, Brazil, Hungary, Netherlands, Senegal, Slovak Republic and Zimbabwe.

In November 1993, the Secretary-General announced his intention to appoint Mr. Jacques-Roger Booh-Booh (Cameroon) as Special Representative and Head of Mission. Mr. Booh-Booh served as Special Representative until June 1994 when he was succeeded by Mr. Shaharyar M. Khan (Pakistan). Two military officers have served as UNAMIR Force Commander: Major-General Romeo A. Dallaire (Canada), from October 1993 to August 1994; and Major-General Guy Tousignant (Canada) who took up his duties on 19 August 1994. Upon General Tousignant's departure on 15 December 1995, Brigadier-General Siva Kumar (India) was designated Acting Force Commander.

At UNAMIR's inception, its authorized peak military strength was 2,548 military personnel, including 2,217 formed troops and 331 military observers. As of 31 March 1994, UNAMIR had a strength of 2,539 military personnel. At that time, the Mission also comprised 60 civilian police monitors. Following the outbreak of violence in April 1994, the Security Council adjusted UNAMIR's mandate and decided to reduce the Mission to 270 military personnel. After the situation in Rwanda further deteriorated, the Council authorized an expansion of UNAMIR's mandate and authorized an increase of the UNAMIR force level up to 5,500 troops.

The larger mission was to include five infantry battalions numbering some 4,000 all ranks, a force support battalion of approximately 721 personnel, a military observer group of 320 officers, 219 headquarters personnel, a helicopter squadron of some 110 all ranks and 16 helicopters, 50 military police personnel and a force of 90 civilian police. UNAMIR reached its full authorized strength of 5,500 all ranks in October 1994. In February 1995, the Security Council decided to increase the strength of UNAMIR's civilian police component from 90 to 120 police observers.

By its resolution 997 of 9 June 1995, the Security Council authorized a reduction of the force level to 2,330 troops within three months and to 1,800 troops within four months. It maintained the existing level of observers and police monitors. By its resolution 1029 (1995) of 12 December, the Council requested the Secretary-General to withdraw CIVPOL and to reduce the force level to 1,200 troops and 200 military observers and military support staff. It extended UNAMIR's mandate for a final period until 8 March 1996. On 19 April 1996, UNAMIR completed its withdrawal when the last UNAMIR troops left the country.

During the course of the Mission and for various periods, the following countries contributed troops and/or observers to UNAMIR: Argentina, Australia, Austria, Bangladesh, Belgium, Brazil, Canada, Chad, Congo, Djibouti, Egypt, Ethiopia, Fiji, Ghana, Guinea, Guinea Bissau, India, Jordan, Kenya, Malawi, Mali, Netherlands, Niger,

Nigeria, Pakistan, Poland, Romania, Russian Federation, Senegal, Slovak Republic, Spain, Togo, Tunisia, United Kingdom, Uruguay, Zambia and Zimbabwe. Police monitors were contributed by: Austria, Bangladesh, Belgium, Chad, Djibouti, Germany, Ghana, Guinea, Guinea Bissau, Guyana, Jordan, Mali, Niger, Nigeria, Switzerland, Togo, Tunisia and Zambia.

For the period beginning on 22 June 1993, UNOMUR was authorized to have 17 international civilian personnel and 7 local staff. UNAMIR's authorized staffing from 5 October until 4 April included 126 international staff and 68 local staff. For the period April to December 1994, UNAMIR was authorized to have 225 international staff and 173 local staff.

J. Financial aspects

The Secretary-General recommended that the costs of UNOMUR should be considered as an expense of the Organization to be borne by Member States in accordance with Article 17, paragraph 2, of the Charter and that the assessment be credited to a special account for that purpose. He made a similar recommendation regarding the costs of UNAMIR.

Net operating costs for UNOMUR for the period from its inception until 21 December 1993 amounted to $2,298,500 net. By 22 December 1993, UNOMUR had been integrated administratively within UNAMIR. After that date, costs related to UNOMUR were reflected in cost estimates for UNAMIR.

Estimated expenses for UNAMIR and, after 22 December 1993, UNOMUR amounted to $437,430,100 net. Costs for the administrative close-down of UNAMIR were estimated at $4,102,000 net.[64]

[64]A/50/712/Add.1.

Chapter 17

United Nations Observer Mission in Liberia (UNOMIL)

F. July–November 1995
Abuja Agreement
Implementation of the Agreement
New mandate and concept of operations
Humanitarian aspects

G. A turn for the worse

H. Composition of UNOMIL

I. Financial aspects

Chapter 17
United Nations Observer Mission in Liberia (UNOMIL)

A. Background

Civil war in Liberia claimed the lives of between 100,000 and 150,000 civilians and led to a complete breakdown of law and order. It displaced scores of people, both internally and beyond the borders, resulting in some 700,000 refugees in the neighbouring countries. Fighting began in late 1989, and, by early 1990, several hundred deaths had already occurred in confrontations between government forces and fighters who claimed membership in an oppostion group, the National Patriotic Front of Liberia (NPFL), led by a former government official, Mr. Charles Taylor.

From the outset of the conflict, a subregional organization, the Economic Community of West African States (ECOWAS),[1] undertook various initiatives aimed at a peaceful settlement. These included creating the ECOWAS Monitoring Group (ECOMOG) in August 1990. The Group initially comprised about 4,000 troops from the Gambia, Ghana, Guinea, Nigeria and Sierra Leone. Although the President of Liberia, Mr. Samuel Doe, had agreed to accept ECOMOG, as did Mr. Prince Johnson, leader of an NPFL faction challenging the leadership of Charles Taylor, Mr. Taylor opposed the ECOMOG intervention. On 10 September 1990, President Doe was killed after having been taken prisoner by Johnson forces. The following year, in June 1991, former supporters of the late President were to create another group, the United Liberation Movement of Liberia for Democracy (ULIMO).

Other ECOWAS efforts to achieve a peaceful settlement in Liberia included the mediation of a series of agreements which became the basis for the peace plan of November 1990, including the establishment of an Interim Government of National Unity (IGNU). Dr. Amos Sawyer was inducted into office as the President of the interim government. On 30 October 1991, ECOWAS brokered the Yamoussoukro IV Accord[2] which outlined steps to implement the peace plan, including the encampment and disarmament of warring factions under the supervision of an expanded ECOMOG, as well as the establishment of transitional institutions to carry out free and fair elections.

The United Nations supported the efforts of the ECOWAS member States. In addition, it provided humanitarian assistance to the affected areas in Liberia through coordinated activities of the United Nations Development Programme (UNDP), the Food and Agriculture Organization (FAO), the United Nations Population Fund, the United Nations Children's Fund (UNICEF), the World Food Programme (WFP) and the World Health Organization (WHO). The United Nations Special Coordinator's Office (UNSCOL) opened in December 1990; its operation, initially focusing on the desperate situation in the Monrovia area, was expanded in 1991 to respond to the needs of Liberians throughout the country. Regional arrangements were also made to assist those who fled to the neighbouring countries, mainly Guinea, Côte d'Ivoire and Sierra Leone.

United Nations actions on Liberia

The Security Council first took up the question of Liberia on 22 January 1991. The Council commended[3] the efforts of the ECOWAS heads of State and called upon the parties to the conflict to respect the cease-fire agreement. On 7 May 1992, the Council again commended[4] ECOWAS and indicated that the Yamoussoukro IV Accord offered the best possible framework for a peaceful resolution of the conflict in Liberia.

On 19 November 1992, the Security Council, by adopting resolution 788 (1992), imposed a

---

[1]ECOWAS membership comprises Benin, Burkina Faso, Cape Verde, Côte d'Ivoire, Gambia, Ghana, Guinea, Guinea-Bissau, Liberia, Mali, Mauritania, Niger, Nigeria, Senegal, Sierra Leone and Togo. [2]S/24815, annex. [3]S/22133. [4]S/23886.

general and complete embargo on all deliveries of weapons and military equipment to Liberia—except for those destined for the sole use of the peace-keeping forces of ECOWAS. The Council also called on the Member States of the United Nations to exert self-restraint in their relations with all parties to the conflict in Liberia, and to refrain from taking any action that would be inimical to the peace process. Further, it requested the Secretary-General to dispatch urgently a special representative to Liberia who would evaluate the situation and make recommendations as soon as possible.

On 20 November 1992, Secretary-General Boutros Boutros-Ghali appointed[5] Mr. Trevor Livingston Gordon-Somers (Jamaica) as his Special Representative for Liberia. Following his appointment, the Special Representative visited Liberia as well as Benin, Burkina Faso, Côte d'Ivoire, the Gambia, Guinea, Nigeria, Senegal and Sierra Leone.

The Secretary-General reported[6] to the Security Council on 12 March 1993 that the discussions his Special Representative had held with the parties concerned, including the Executive Secretary and member States of ECOWAS, indicated the existence of general consensus that the United Nations should assume a larger role in the search for peace in Liberia. Reaffirming his commitment to a "systematic cooperation between the United Nations and a regional organization, as envisaged in Chapter VIII of the Charter" and stating his intention to continue working with ECOWAS in the peace process, the Secretary-General outlined three areas in which the United Nations could play a role in Liberia: political reconciliation, humanitarian assistance and electoral assistance.

Further, the Secretary-General proposed that ECOWAS convene a meeting at the summit level where the President of the Interim Government and the warring factions in Liberia would conclude and sign an agreement, reaffirming their commitment to implementing promptly the peace process as envisaged in the Yamoussoukro IV Accord.

On 26 March, the Security Council, by resolution 813 (1993), requested the Secretary-General to consider the possibility of convening a meeting of the Liberian parties to reaffirm their commitment to the implementation of the Yamoussoukro IV Accord, and also to discuss with ECOWAS and the parties concerned the contribution which the United Nations could make in support of the Yamoussoukro IV Accord, including the deployment of United Nations observers.

Massacre of civilians

On the morning of 6 June 1993, nearly 600 Liberians, mainly displaced people, including children and the elderly, were killed in an armed attack near Harbel, Liberia. The Security Council strongly condemned[7] the killings and warned that those responsible would be held accountable for the serious violations of international humanitarian law. It requested the Secretary-General to commence immediately an investigation into the massacre.

After a preliminary investigation by his Special Representative, the Secretary-General, on 7 August, appointed a Panel of Inquiry composed of Mr. Amos Wako of Kenya as Chairman, and Mr. Robert Gersony of the United States and Mr. Mahmoud Kassem of Egypt as members, to undertake a more comprehensive investigation.[8] In a report dated 10 September 1993, the Panel concluded that the killings were planned and executed by units of the military arm of IGNU — the Armed Forces of Liberia (AFL) — and that NPFL, to which the act of violence had initially been attributed, had no role in it. The Panel named three AFL soldiers who had participated in the massacre and recommended that criminal investigations be undertaken with a view to prosecuting them. The Panel added, however, that this finding did not mitigate or diminish the responsibility of NPFL, ULIMO and others alleged to have engaged in similar atrocities against unarmed, innocent civilians throughout the conflict. It further recommended investigations into a number of major atrocities attributed to all parties to the Liberian conflict.

Cotonou Peace Agreement

In July 1993, a three-day meeting was held in Cotonou, Benin, under the co-chairmanship of the Secretary-General's Special Representative, President Canaan Banana of the Organization of African Unity (OAU) and Mr. Abass Bundu, Executive Secretary of ECOWAS. At the conclusion of the meeting on 25 July, IGNU, NPFL and ULIMO signed the Cotonou Peace Agreement.[9] The Agreement laid out a continuum of action, from the cease-fire through disarmament and demobilization to the holding of national elections.

On military aspects, the Agreement provided for a cease-fire to take effect on 1 August

[5]S/24834. [6]S/25402. [7]S/25918. [8]S/26265. [9]S/26272, annex.

1993 and outlined steps for the encampment, disarmament and demobilization of military units. To ensure against any violation of the cease-fire between 1 August and the arrival of some 4,000 additional ECOMOG troops, including from OAU countries outside the West African subregion, as well as the main body of a United Nations observer contingent, the parties agreed to establish a Joint Cease-fire Monitoring Committee, comprising representatives of the three Liberian sides, ECOMOG and the United Nations. For that period, the United Nations was asked to consider dispatching 30 advance military observers to participate in the work of the Committee.

On the political side, the parties reaffirmed the Yamoussoukro IV Accord. They agreed that there should be a single Liberian National Transitional Government which would have three branches: legislative, executive and judicial. The Agreement also provided for general and presidential elections to take place within seven months from the signing of the Agreement and set out the modalities for the elections to be supervised by a reconstituted Electoral Commission.

On humanitarian issues, the parties agreed that every effort should be made to deliver humanitarian assistance throughout Liberia using the most direct routes and under inspection, to ensure compliance with the embargo provisions of the Agreement. The United Nations, in particular the United Nations High Commissioner for Refugees (UNHCR), was requested to facilitate the speedy return of refugees and their reintegration into their communities.

On 4 August 1993, the Secretary-General told[10] the Security Council that, while he recognized the difficulties ahead, he welcomed the Agreement as offering the "hope that the violent and destructive civil war which has afflicted Liberia may at long last be brought to an end." On 10 August, the Security Council, by resolution 856 (1993), authorized the Secretary-General to dispatch an advance team of 30 United Nations military observers to Liberia.

B. September–December 1993

UNOMIL is established

The Security Council established UNOMIL on 22 September 1993 by resolution 866 (1993), for an initial period of seven months, to work with ECOMOG in the implementation of the Cotonou Peace Agreement. UNOMIL was the first United Nations peace-keeping mission undertaken in cooperation with a peace-keeping operation already set up by another organization. The Mission was set up under the command of the United Nations, vested in the Secretary-General under the authority of the Security Council and led in the field by the Special Representative of the Secretary-General. It was to be composed of military and civilian components. Command of the military component was entrusted to the Chief Military Observer (CMO) reporting to the Secretary-General through the Special Representative. The civilian component would include humanitarian assistance and electoral assistance, as well as the necessary political and administrative staff. The deployment plan called for the Mission to operate out of its headquarters in Monrovia, as well as four regional headquarters, co-located with ECOMOG's four sector headquarters, in the eastern, northern and western regions and Greater Monrovia.

Relationship with ECOMOG

It was envisaged that UNOMIL and ECOMOG would work closely together in facilitating the implementation of the military aspects of the Cotonou Peace Agreement. In accordance with the Agreement, ECOMOG had primary responsibility for ensuring implementation. UNOMIL's role was to monitor the implementation procedures in order to verify their impartial application. UNOMIL's concept of operations and deployment would therefore be parallel to those of ECOMOG. UNOMIL and ECOMOG were to have separate chains of command, but the missions were to consult formally, through established committees, as well as informally, on matters affecting them both. UNOMIL would also keep ECOMOG informed, as necessary, of its activities in pursuance of other aspects of its mandate.

On 9 September 1993, the Secretary-General had reported[11] to the Security Council

---

[10]S/26200. [11]S/26422.

that the cooperation of ECOMOG would be critical to UNOMIL's success. He warned that failure by ECOMOG to deploy additional troops or their premature withdrawal would gravely jeopardize the peace process. "In such an event," he declared, "I shall immediately bring the situation to the attention of the Security Council; depending on the prevalent circumstances, I might be obliged to recommend the withdrawal of UNOMIL." He announced his intention to conclude with ECOWAS a formal agreement defining the relationship between UNOMIL and ECOMOG. The agreement, concluded in November 1993, set in place a formal consultative process and mechanisms for coordination.

Although financing ECOMOG troops was not the responsibility of the United Nations, it was proposed to establish a trust fund, under the auspices of the United Nations, to enable African countries to send reinforcements to ECOMOG, to provide necessary assistance to countries already participating in ECOMOG, and for humanitarian assistance, elections and demobilization. With the endorsement of the Security Council,[12] the Secretary-General took steps to set up the fund.

UNOMIL components

The military component of UNOMIL was to monitor and verify compliance with the cease-fire, the embargo on delivery of arms and military equipment, as well as the cantonment, disarmament and demobilization of combatants. The Secretary-General estimated that 303 military observers would be required, including 41 teams composed of 6 observers per team for investigation, airports, seaports, border crossings and cantonment sites, 25 observers stationed at UNOMIL headquarters and 8 observers at each of four regional headquarters. In addition, a military medical unit of some 20 staff and a communications unit of about 25 civilian staff would be required.

The civilian component was to include political, humanitarian, and electoral personnel. The humanitarian assistance element would work closely with UNDP, the United Nations specialized agencies and non-governmental organizations (NGOs) in assisting in the coordination of relief activities and facilitating the return of refugees, the resettlement of displaced persons and the reintegration of ex-combatants.

The electoral assistance element would observe and verify the entire election process, from the registration of voters until the voting itself. The work would be carried out by 13 international staff, 40 United Nations Volunteers and necessary support staff. Organizing and holding elections would be the responsibility of the transitional government, through the Liberian Elections Commission consisting of representatives of the three Liberian parties. The elections were originally scheduled for February/March 1994. Several potential bottlenecks to the holding of elections on that date were foreseen, including operationalizing the Electoral Commission, repatriating refugees, settling internally displaced population and completing demobilization.

Developments during the first months

Following the adoption of Security Council resolution 856 (1993) on 10 August 1993, the advance party of military observers began arriving in Liberia. The Chief Military Observer arrived in the country on 10 October 1993 and by mid-December there were 166 UNOMIL military observers.

The first meeting of the Joint Cease-fire Monitoring Committee was chaired by the United Nations on 13 August. The Committee was to monitor, investigate and report all cease-fire violations between the period when the cease-fire came into force on 1 August 1993 and the arrival of the additional ECOMOG troops and the full contingent of UNOMIL. In addition to regular patrolling and cease-fire monitoring through the Joint Committee, UNOMIL military observers conducted reconnaissance missions in cooperation with ECOMOG in many areas of the country in preparation for their deployment to these areas and in preparation for disarmament and demobilization.

The five members of the Council of State were selected on 17 August 1993, following consultations among the Liberian parties. The swearing in of the Council, however, did not take place as it was awaiting the beginning of disarmament, the start of which, in accordance with the Cotonou Agreement, was dependent on the expansion of ECOMOG and the provision by the parties of necessary information on the number and location of their combatants, weapons and mines.

Throughout the negotiations leading to the Cotonou Agreement in July 1993, the expansion of ECOMOG had been viewed as a crucial prerequisite for progress towards a lasting peace in Liberia. On 30 September 1993, the United

[12]S/26376.

States pledged $19.83 million to the Trust Fund, exclusively to meet the cost of deployment, equipment and maintenance needs of the expanded ECOMOG troops. On the basis of consultations with potential troop contributing countries and discussions with ECOMOG, and in accordance with the terms of reference of the Trust Fund, a budget estimate covering the requirements of the expanded ECOMOG battalions was developed.

The International Foundation for Election Systems undertook a joint mission to Liberia in October 1993 to assess the requirements for holding elections and to evaluate the probability of maintaining the timetable set out in the Peace Agreement. The mission concluded that the timetable, which provided for holding elections in February/March 1994, was optimistic but that elections could possibly be held in May 1994, on the assumption that disarmament and demobilization, installation of the transitional government and unification of the country were achieved expeditiously.

The Chairman of ECOWAS, President Nicéphore Dieudonné Soglo of Benin, arranged for consultations among the parties at a meeting in Cotonou from 3 to 5 November 1993. At that meeting, the parties agreed on the distribution of 13 of a total of 17 cabinet posts. The distribution of the remaining 4 ministerial portfolios, as well as other issues related to the installation of the transitional government, would await further talks. The parties also reached agreement on the composition of the Elections Commission, on the Speaker of the Legislature and the members of the Supreme Court.

In establishing UNOMIL, the Security Council had stipulated that the Mission would continue beyond 16 December 1993 only upon a review by the Council based on a report from the Secretary-General on whether or not substantive progress had been made towards the implementation of the Peace Agreement and other measures aimed at establishing a lasting peace. The Secretary-General submitted the report[13] on 13 December.

He informed the Council that planning and preparation for disarmament and demobilization, undertaken by UNOMIL in consultation with the Liberian parties, ECOMOG, United Nations specialized agencies and NGOs, were well under way. The commencement of actual disarmament, linked to the expansion of ECOMOG, was delayed.

The Secretary-General hoped that the additional ECOMOG troops would soon be deployed to Liberia, thus enabling the disarmament and demobilization to start immediately.

The Secretary-General noted that the timetable called for disarmament to begin within 30 days of signature of the Agreement, concomitant with the establishment of the transitional government. From the beginning of the peace process, all parties had been aware that the timetable was "highly ambitious, especially given the complexities in establishing the joint UNOMIL/ECOMOG peace-keeping mission, including the deployment of additional ECOMOG troops". In spite of delays in the implementation of the Agreement, there were no major violations of the cease-fire, and the Liberian parties displayed a willingness to move the peace process forward. The Secretary-General recommended that UNOMIL continue to implement the mandate entrusted to it under resolution 866 (1993), although it was unlikely that the original timetable for elections would be met.

In a letter dated 16 December 1993 from the President of the Security Council, the members of the Council informed the Secretary-General that they shared his expectation that, despite the unavoidable delays, disarmament would begin presently, the transitional government would soon be installed and the elections would be held in the first half of 1994.

Inter-agency appeal

On 16 December 1993, the United Nations launched a Consolidated Inter-Agency Appeal for $284 million for emergency humanitarian assistance to Liberia covering a broad spectrum of activities to facilitate Liberia's transition from a war-torn nation to a peaceful and democratic State. United Nations agencies had identified priority needs, amounting to $96.41 million through the first quarter of 1994. The total appeal for $284 million was for 13 months, through December 1994. Later, following renewed hostilities, this figure was revised down to $168.4 million, to reflect limits on implementation of rehabilitation activities.

[13] S/26868.

C.   December 1993–August 1994

Difficulties remain

In December 1993, the Liberian parties resumed their talks on the composition of the transitional government. After two weeks of intense negotiations, however, they failed to reach agreement on the disposition of the four remaining ministerial portfolios of defence, foreign affairs, justice and finance. They were also unable to agree on the date for the seating of the transitional government and for the beginning of encampment, disarmament and demobilization of combatants.

UNOMIL attained its total authorized strength in early January 1994 and began deployment of its military observers throughout Liberia. As to the expansion of ECOMOG, battalions from the United Republic of Tanzania and Uganda arrived in Monrovia on 8 January and 28 January 1994 respectively and started preparations for deployment to the northern and eastern regions of the country.

On 18 January 1994, the Security Council expressed[14] its concern over delays in the implementation of the Cotonou Agreement and over difficulties in delivering humanitarian assistance to all parts of the country. The continued support of the international community for the efforts of UNOMIL would depend on the full and prompt implementation of the Agreement. The Secretary-General's Special Representative subsequently held bilateral consultations with each of the three Liberian parties and relayed to them the Security Council's message, namely that the Council expected to see tangible progress in the peace process. The parties reiterated their willingness to cooperate in the effective implementation of the Peace Agreement.

Following arrival of the additional battalions, consultations with ECOMOG and the parties on the date for disarmament intensified. Ten encampment sites were identified, two for AFL, four for NPFL and four for ULIMO. The parties agreed that the disarmament of their forces would commence simultaneously and was likely to continue over a two–to–three–month period. At the same time, UNOMIL developed a plan for the demobilization and reintegration of ex-combatants into civilian society, covering the continuum from military disarmament to reintegration into civilian society and involving the coordination of activities to be implemented by United Nations agencies and NGOs.

The Secretary-General urged the Liberian parties to make a renewed and determined effort to reach consensus and cooperate in good faith with UNOMIL and ECOMOG. The impasse in the implementation of the Cotonou Agreement resulted, in his view,[15] from differences among the parties on the date for the installation of the transitional government and the commencement of disarmament. He believed that the remaining outstanding issues were not insurmountable. He also called upon the parties to create the necessary conditions to ensure the unimpeded delivery of humanitarian assistance to all parts of Liberia. He urged the international community to contribute the necessary logistical and financial resources to both the existing and expanded ECOMOG troops.

Transitional government installed

Meeting in Monrovia on 15 February 1994, the Liberian parties reached agreement on most of the outstanding issues impeding the commencement of disarmament and the installation of the transitional government. They then set 7 March 1994 as the date for commencement of disarmament and the installation of the transitional government. Free and fair elections would be held on 7 September 1994. The question of the disposition of the four remaining cabinet posts was not resolved.[16]   The Security Council welcomed the agreement but warned that the support of the international community would not continue in the absence of tangible progress towards full and prompt implementation of the Agreement, in particular, the revised timetable.[17]

On 7 March 1994, the Council of State of the Transitional Government was installed in Monrovia. Three demobilization centres, one for each of the warring parties, were opened on the same day. On 11 March, the Transitional Legislative Assembly was inducted into office, with ULIMO being given the responsibility for naming the Speaker of the Assembly. The Supreme Court of Liberia opened for the 1994 term on 14 March.

In his 7 March acceptance speech, the Chairman of the Council of State confirmed that

---

[14]S/1994/51. [15]S/1994/168. [16]S/1994/168/Add.1. [17]S/PRST/1994/9.

the holding of elections on 7 September 1994 was a foremost concern of the transitional government. The Elections Commission had intensified its organizational work in order to finalize a calendar of activities leading up to the elections and submitted a draft electoral budget to the Council of State for its consideration. It estimated that $13.7 million would be required for the electoral process, of which the transitional government would attempt to provide some $8.5 million and would seek international support for the remaining $5.2 million.

Deployment continues

Meanwhile, UNOMIL proceeded with deployment throughout the country. By April 1994, the Mission had deployed its military observers in 27 team sites out of a total of 39 projected sites. Four regional headquarters were established at Monrovia (central region), Tubmanburg (western region), Gbarnga (northern region) and Tapeta (eastern region). The military observers were engaged in the patrolling of border crossings and other entry points, observation and verification of disarmament and demobilization and the investigation of cease-fire violations.

ECOMOG deployed into the western (Tubmanburg) and northern (Gbarnga) regions. Deployment of both UNOMIL and ECOMOG in Upper Lofa was impeded by insecurity in the area. Likewise, deployment in the south-east was curtailed by the activities of the Liberian Peace Council (LPC), which emerged in the south-eastern part of Liberia after the Cotonou Agreement was signed in July 1993. UNOMIL and ECOMOG were engaged in consultations with ULIMO and with NPFL and LPC in order to reach agreement on further deployment in the western and south-eastern regions. It was reported that the total number of combatants of all factions was approximately 60,000 soldiers. In the first month of disarmament, more than 2,000 combatants, from all parties, were disarmed and demobilized. Owing to political difficulties, however, disarmament was slower than anticipated. Assuming the full cooperation of the parties, it was estimated that disarmament could be completed in two months.

Following the deployment of UNOMIL and ECOMOG, the Joint Cease-fire Monitoring Committee was replaced by a Violations Committee, as foreseen in the Cotonou Agreement. The Violations Committee was chaired by the UNOMIL CMO.

Some progress achieved

On 18 April 1994, the Secretary-General informed[18] the Security Council that the Liberian parties had achieved progress in their search for peace, but a number of obstacles still existed, including the disposition of the four remaining cabinet posts, the question of allocation of posts to head the public corporations and autonomous agencies, continued military conflict involving various parties, and the slow pace of the disarmament and demobilization process. A number of issues in the electoral process were also left to be addressed, including voter education, the repatriation of refugees and displaced persons and the mobilization of resources required for the elections. Taking into account progress achieved, he recommended that the Security Council extend the mandate of UNOMIL for a further period of six months, which would include the elections scheduled for September 1994. Provision would also be made for the liquidation phase of the Mission, which would end by 31 December 1994. The Secretary-General stated, however, that if the disposition of the four remaining ministries was not resolved within two weeks, and if there was no further progress in the peace process within this period, he would request the Council to review the mandate of UNOMIL.

Meeting on 21 April 1994, the Security Council was informed[19] by the representative of Liberia that the Ministers of Defence, Finance and Justice had been designated on 19 April 1994 and that the appointment of the Minister for Foreign Affairs would follow. The Council extended[20] the mandate of UNOMIL until 22 October 1994, on the understanding that it would review by 18 May 1994 the situation in Liberia and UNOMIL's role there. That review would be based on whether the transitional government had been fully installed, and whether there had been substantial progress in implementing the peace process. The Council decided to conduct by 30 June 1994 a further review focusing on the effective operation of the transitional government, progress in disarmament and demobilization, and preparations for the holding of elections.

The Security Council called on the Liberian parties to give urgent priority to the complete installation, by 18 May 1994, of the transitional government, especially the seating of the full Cabinet and the Transitional National Assembly, so that a unified civil administration of the country could

[18]S/1994/463. [19]S/PV.3366. [20]S/RES/911 (1994).

be established and appropriate arrangements completed for national elections to be held on 7 September. It also urged the parties to cease hostilities immediately and cooperate with ECOMOG to complete the disarmament process. It encouraged Member States to contribute to the Trust Fund for the Implementation of the Cotonou Agreement or to provide other assistance to facilitate the work of ECOMOG, and to assist in humanitarian, development and electoral assistance.

Continued fighting

On 20 April 1994, the Council of State of the Liberian Transitional Government was fully installed, and the Ministers for Justice, Defence and Finance were confirmed by the Transitional Legislative Assembly, with the newly appointed Minister for Foreign Affairs scheduled to be formally inducted on 19 May.

At the same time, a dispute arose within the leadership of ULIMO, along ethnic lines, between Chairman Alhaji Kromah (Mandingo) and General Roosevelt Johnson (Krahn) over ULIMO nominees to the Council of State. The dispute resulted in an outbreak of fighting in the western region among the ULIMO forces. Fighting also erupted in the eastern part of Liberia between NPFL and LPC. The transitional government, UNOMIL and ECOMOG undertook efforts to bring about a cease-fire between the two groups and to bring LPC into the disarmament and demobilization process.[21]

The continuing fighting within and between the parties constituted one of the most serious obstacles in the way of the peace process. Mediation efforts to resolve the dispute within ULIMO resulted on 6 May in a cease-fire and an agreement for further negotiations. However, the negotiations collapsed and serious fighting resumed on 26 May. In the eastern part of Liberia, attacks by LPC against NPFL also continued. All attempts to negotiate the end of hostilities were unsuccessful.

Moreover, the parties' mistrust for one another extended, in the case of some of them, to ECOMOG. Soldiers of the Nigerian and Ugandan contingents were abducted and held for varying lengths of time by elements of ULIMO and LPC, both of which claimed that ECOMOG had lost its impartiality and was involved in the conflict. NPFL also asserted complicity between some elements of ECOMOG and AFL in supplying material and logistical support to LPC. All these assertions added difficulties to ECOMOG's ability to carry out its peace-keeping responsibilities.

As a result of mistrust and hostilities between and within some factions, and despite the efforts of ECOMOG and UNOMIL, the parties refused to engage actively in the disarmament of their combatants or to give up control of territory. Three months after the start of demobilization, a total of only 3,192 combatants had been demobilized. Insecurity in some areas of the country also impeded full deployment of ECOMOG and UNOMIL.

The Secretary-General reiterated[22] to the Security Council on 24 June his belief that UNOMIL's efforts were critical to the implementation of the Cotonou Agreement and to assisting the transitional government and the Liberian people to achieve national reconciliation. It was imperative that all the Liberian parties extend greater cooperation to ECOMOG and UNOMIL and that the transitional government bring all the parties together to agree on specific steps to ensure that the elections were held on schedule. Should the parties fail to maintain their commitment to the peace process, the Secretary-General warned, he would have no alternative but to recommend to the Security Council that the involvement of the United Nations in Liberia be reconsidered. On 13 July, the Council called[23] on the transitional government, in cooperation with ECOWAS and OAU with the support of UNOMIL, to convene a meeting of the Liberian factions not later than 31 July in order to agree on a realistic plan for resumption of disarmament and to set a target date for its completion.

Fact-finding mission dispatched

The transitional government did not meet the deadline. During July and August 1994, the situation in Liberia seriously deteriorated, and the Council of State remained ineffective. Fighting continued between the Krahn and Mandingo elements of ULIMO in the west of the country, and between LPC and NPFL in the south-east. There were also signs of a split within the NPFL hierarchy. All factions were experiencing command and control problems, resulting in an increase in banditry and harassment of civilians, including NGOs and unarmed United Nations military observers. Disarmament virtually ceased, and there was no clear prospect as to when elections would or could be held. Population displacement from the coun-

---

[21]S/1994/588.　[22]S/1994/760.　[23]S/PRST/1994/33.

ties in the south-east and west continued to grow with every new wave of fighting and with each report of atrocities against civilians. ECOMOG was still not fully deployed and UNOMIL withdrew from the western region due to lack of security. On 26 August, the Secretary-General informed[24] the Security Council that he had decided to dispatch to Liberia a fact-finding mission to review the situation in the country and advise him on the most appropriate course of action. On the basis of the mission's report, the Secretary-General would submit to the Council his recommendations with regard to the future United Nations role in Liberia. The mission was headed by the Secretary-General's Special Envoy, Mr. Lakhdar Brahimi, and visited the area from 16 to 26 August.

D. September–December 1994

Akosombo Agreement

On 7 September 1994, the Chairman of ECOWAS, President Jerry Rawlings of Ghana, convened a meeting of the leaders of the warring factions at Akosombo, Ghana. The meeting was attended by NPFL, both wings of ULIMO and AFL. LPC and the Lofa Defence Force (LDF) — the second faction which emerged in Liberia after the signing of the Cotonou Agreement — declined to attend the meeting. Representatives of the United Nations and OAU were present as facilitators. The meeting culminated in the signing, on 12 September, of a supplementary agreement[25] to the Cotonou Agreement, which reaffirmed the Cotonou Agreement as the only framework for peace in Liberia. It also sought to give the transitional government a more central role in the supervision and monitoring of the implementation of that Agreement. The factions would be permitted to review the status of their appointees to the Council of State, and participation in the Transitional Legislative Assembly would be broadened by adding 13 representatives from the various counties.

The Akosombo Agreement called for an immediate cease-fire and provided more details concerning its implementation, the disengagement of forces and the responsibilities of the factions with regard to assembly and disarmament of combatants. It foresaw elections by October 1995 and specified that, if any faction or group refused to desist from acts in violation of the Agreement, the transitional government, in collaboration with ECOMOG, would have the power to use the necessary force to assure compliance. The transitional government would also conclude a status-of-forces agreement with ECOWAS. Soon after its signing, however, the Akosombo Agreement became engulfed in controversy, and there was no movement towards its implementation.

Liberian National Conference

At the initiative of private citizens, a Liberian National Conference convened on 24 August 1994 to deliberate on the many aspects of the peace process. After extended sessions, lasting until 3 October, the Conference adopted a set of resolutions concerning the peace process. It then suspended further consultations for a period of two months, after which it planned to reconvene to assess progress made in disarmament and demobilization. The Conference reaffirmed the Cotonou Agreement as the only framework for restoring peace in Liberia and sought to enable the transitional government to play a more central role in its implementation.

Liberia in a "desperate state"

Overall, the military situation during September and October remained confused, with alignment and realignment of groups depending on their short-term interests, and the breakdown of command and control within factions. Warlords, without any particular political agenda but with control of a certain number of soldiers, were seeking territory for the sake of adding to their own claim to power. The results were not large military victories, but deaths mostly of civilians, the decimation of entire villages and the breakdown of any semblance of law and order.

On 8 September, the Alhaji Kromah wing of ULIMO attacked Gbarnga and took control of NPFL headquarters. Forces of a coalition formed by AFL, LPC and ULIMO-Johnson then launched attacks against NPFL forces in northern and eastern regions. Troops of the coalition had already begun to gather in mid-August, reportedly to defeat NPFL

---

[24]S/1994/1006. [25]S/1994/1174.

and capture Gbarnga, an objective said to be supported by breakaway NPFL ministers in the transitional government. On 15 September, a dissident group within AFL attempted to stage a *coup* against the transitional government. The attempted *coup* was successfully foiled by ECOMOG's decisive action.

The factional fighting resulted in some 200,000 persons being uprooted from their places of temporary or permanent residence. Because of insecurity, international and local relief organizations located in Liberia were unable to deal with the growing tragedy inside the country. Movement of relief supplies became impossible, including across the border from Côte d'Ivoire, leaving thousands without access to assistance. As a result, almost all international humanitarian assistance operations ceased, except at Buchanan and Monrovia.

The continued fighting significantly limited the ability of UNOMIL to perform its functions. Moreover, on a number of occasions, unarmed United Nations military observers were themselves the target of harassment and violence. On 9 September, in what might have been a premeditated action to use the observers as a shield and to secure reliable communications and transportation facilities, NPFL elements detained 43 UNOMIL observers and 6 NGO personnel at nine sites in the northern and eastern regions and confiscated their transport, communications and most other equipment. UNOMIL immediately undertook round-the-clock contacts with faction representatives, NPFL interlocutors, neighbouring countries and ECOMOG in order to secure the release of those detained. On 14 September, 33 observers were released and found their way to relative safety. However, an attempted helicopter rescue of observers at Harper was aborted when the helicopter was shot at by NPFL elements. On the same day an ECOMOG contingent with six observers and six NGO personnel moving from Gbarnga to Monrovia was attacked by elements of ULIMO-Johnson, suffering casualties. The troops eventually reached Kakata, but were looted of their arms and equipment by NPFL. Although all military observers and NGO personnel had been released by 18 September, some of them had been mistreated and beaten.

Given the breakdown in the cease-fire and the inability of ECOMOG to provide security for UNOMIL observers, UNOMIL was unable to carry out many of its mandated activities. All UNOMIL team sites were evacuated except for those in the Monrovia area. As of 12 October, the strength of

UNOMIL military personnel was reduced to approximately 90 observers from the authorized strength of 368. This temporary reduction was matched by a commensurate reduction in the civilian staff of UNOMIL. The lack of progress in the peace process, as well as the lack of financial resources, also led ECOWAS to consider withdrawing from Liberia. ECOWAS Chairman Jerry Rawlings, President of Ghana, said that he would consider withdrawing his Government's contingent of ECOMOG if there was no progress by the end of 1994. Nigeria had reportedly reduced its presence, and Uganda and the United Republic of Tanzania indicated they might withdraw their contingents.

The Secretary-General told[26] the Security Council on 14 October 1994 that the political, military and humanitarian developments of the preceding month had left Liberia in a desperate state. The transitional government, the factions and the people of Liberia needed to focus on political accommodation to stop the country from sliding deeper into chaos. The Secretary-General decided to dispatch a high-level mission to consult the ECOWAS countries on how best the international community could continue to assist Liberia in bringing about a cessation of hostilities. In order to allow the high-level mission time to conduct its work and present its conclusions, he recommended that the Council extend the mandate of UNOMIL for a period of two months.

On 21 October, the Security Council, by its resolution 950 (1994), extended the mandate of UNOMIL until 13 January 1995. It recognized that circumstances in Liberia had warranted the Secretary-General's decision to reduce UNOMIL's strength, and stated that any decision to return it to the authorized level should depend on a real improvement in the situation on the ground, particularly the security situation. The Council condemned the widespread killings of civilians and other violations of international humanitarian law and demanded that the factions strictly respect the status of ECOMOG and UNOMIL.

Humanitarian crisis

By June 1994, approximately 1.1 million people were receiving humanitarian assistance, of an estimated 1.5 million in need. Approximately 400,000 people were inaccessible because of factional fighting. Of the total number of beneficiaries, 800,000 were registered as displaced, of whom

[26] S/1994/1167.

150,000 had been displaced within the preceding six months. Since the beginning of 1994, 70 per cent of the estimated food needs had been mobilized by the international relief community. Organized voluntary repatriation of the 700,000 Liberian refugees had been adversely affected by the slow pace in the peace process. However, UNHCR continued to facilitate spontaneous repatriation, with an average of 1,000 persons returning every month from Guinea, Côte d'Ivoire and Sierra Leone.

The number of people in need of humanitarian assistance grew to an estimated 1.8 million by August, with assistance and rehabilitation activities limited to the areas immediately in and around Monrovia and Buchanan. By 12 November 1994, the United Nations Resident Coordinator in Liberia was reporting that the crisis had affected more than 700,000 innocent civilians in rural Liberia and 1.2 million residents and displaced persons in Monrovia, its environs and the rest of Montserrado country. He noted that continued fighting severely restricted most relief activities, and that the plight of those suffering in rural Liberia could not be significantly eased until minimum conditions of security existed that would permit an orderly resumption of emergency food deliveries.

At the end of November 1994, donors had provided approximately 49 per cent of the $168.4 million in prioritized needs requested in the Consolidated Inter-Agency Appeal, covering the period from November 1993 to December 1994.

Mission to ECOWAS member States

In its resolution 950 (1994), the Security Council welcomed the Secretary-General's proposal to send a high-level mission to discuss the deteriorating situation in Liberia with ECOWAS member States. The mission was led by Mr. Lansana Kouyaté, Assistant Secretary-General for Political Affairs, and visited Ghana, Côte d'Ivoire, Nigeria, Liberia, Guinea and Sierra Leone. Consultations were held with the Chairman of ECOWAS, President Rawlings of Ghana, President Lansana Conté of Guinea, Chairman Valentine Strasser of Sierra Leone, President Konan Bédié of Côte d'Ivoire, and the ECOWAS Committee of Nine, which coordinates ECOWAS activities on Liberia and is composed of the foreign ministers of Burkina Faso, Côte d'Ivoire, the Gambia, Ghana, Guinea, Mali, Nigeria, Senegal and Sierra Leone. Discussions were also held with Liberia's Council of State, including its Chairman, Mr. David Kpomakpor,

diplomatic missions, United Nations organizations and NGOs, as well as with the Liberian faction leaders, who were meeting in Accra at the invitation of President Rawlings.

In all its consultations with ECOWAS member States, the mission emphasized that an enduring political accommodation among the factions in Liberia would be possible only if it was underpinned by a common policy on the part of the six ECOWAS countries most directly involved with Liberia, namely, Burkina Faso, Côte d'Ivoire, Ghana, Guinea, Nigeria and Sierra Leone. The mission concluded that, notwithstanding the tireless efforts of the Chairman of ECOWAS, the Liberian political and factional leaders were not yet committed to a sustainable peace in their country. Accordingly, the mission submitted the following recommendations for ending the conflict in Liberia: (a) the Liberian political and factions leaders must be brought to understand that, in the absence of political accommodation and reconciliation, continued support from the international community would not be forthcoming; (b) ECOWAS member States, particularly the six directly involved with Liberia, should urgently organize an extraordinary meeting of Heads of State to resolve their differences and harmonize their policies on Liberia; (c) if the above could be accomplished, ECOWAS should be encouraged to consider strengthening ECOMOG and restructuring it in order to achieve a better balance of troops, including contributions from other African countries; (d) international support, including financial support, logistics and equipment, should be sought to enable ECOMOG to carry out its mandate, particularly with respect to deployment, encampment and disarmament; (e) the future of UNOMIL should depend on the successful implementation of the above steps. Meanwhile, UNOMIL's mandate should be extended for a limited period of three months from 13 January 1995.

Accra Agreement

The Akosombo Agreement continued to be a source of significant controversy among those Liberian parties and interest groups which had not taken part in the negotiations. Faced with opposition to the Agreement, the Chairman of ECOWAS dispatched delegations to Liberia and to several ECOWAS member States to seek a compromise. In November 1994, the Liberian parties carried out negotiations in Accra for about three weeks. These led to the presentation by Ghana of a compromise proposal, which sought to address the key issues of an agreement: representation and timing of the seating of a new Council of State; selection and status of its Chairman; decision-making by the Council; appointment of ministers; establishment of safe havens; cease-fire; and encampment and disarmament. Although agreement was reached in several areas, the parties failed to reconcile their differences over the composition of the Council of State and the process of selecting its members.

After further discussions, the parties returned to Accra on 18 December 1994. On 21 December, having resolved their key differences, they were able to sign two agreements, known collectively as the Accra Agreement. One clarified the Akosombo Agreement, which had been signed by NPFL, Alhaji Kromah's wing of ULIMO and AFL. The other enabled the non-signatories to the Akosombo Agreement — ULIMO-Johnson, LPC, LDF, the Central Revolutionary Council (CRC-NPFL) and the Liberian National Conference (LNC) — to accept that Agreement. CRC-NPFL was a breakaway faction of NPFL.

The Accra Agreement stipulated that a cease-fire would come into effect by midnight on 28 December 1994. A new, five-member Council of State would be installed within 14 days thereafter, composed of one member chosen by each of NPFL, ULIMO, AFL/Coalition and LNC and Mr. Tamba Taylor, a traditional chief chosen by NPFL and ULIMO. Elections would be held on 14 November 1995 and a new Government installed on 1 January 1996.

In the mean time, the Secretary-General informed[27] the Security Council that Mr. Trevor Gordon-Somers would shortly be completing his assignment as Special Representative for Liberia. It was the Secretary-General's intention to appoint Mr. Anthony B. Nyakyi, former Permanent Representative of the United Republic of Tanzania to the United Nations, to succeed Mr. Gordon-Somers. Mr. Nyakyi took up his duties in Monrovia on 28 December 1994.

The cease-fire came into effect as stipulated in the Accra Agreement. However, the military situation remained highly charged and unstable. Hostilities had spread to over 80 per cent of the country and the fighting had caused massive population displacement. Because of insecurity and serious logistical difficulties, ECOMOG had been deployed in less than 15 per cent of the country. Its absence from major points along the borders was a factor in the continuous breach of the arms embargo.

E. January–June 1995

Political stalemate continues

On 6 January 1995, the Secretary-General recommended[28] that the Security Council extend UNOMIL's mandate for a further period of three months. During that period, the Liberian parties would be expected to respect the cease-fire and implement the other relevant aspects of the Accra Agreement, including the installation of the new Council of State. During that period also, his Special Representative would conduct an in-depth assessment of the role the United Nations could play in support of the peace process. Without the full commitment of the Liberian factions to the peace process, ECOWAS and the international community would not be in a position to continue to assist them in the search for peace in their country. The Security Council extended the mandate of UNOMIL until 13 April by its resolution 972 (1995) of 13 January.

In accordance with the timetable set out in the Accra agreement, the Liberian parties were to have nominated a new five-member Council of State by 11 January 1995. However, when they met in Accra under the auspices of ECOWAS on 9 January, they were unable to reach agreement on the composition and chairmanship of the Council. The main bottleneck was the inability of AFL and Coalition forces (ULIMO-J, LDF, LPC and CRC-NPFL) to reach agreement on their joint nominee. Nominees from the other parties included Mr. Charles Taylor, President of NPFL; Mr. Alhaji Kromah, Chairman of ULIMO-K; and Mr. Oscar Quiah, representative of LNC.

The Security Council expressed deep concern[29] at the failure of the Liberian parties to reach agreement on the composition of the Council of State and called upon them to work together to

[27]S/1994/1340. [28]S/1995/9. [29]S/RES/972 (1995).

implement the Accra Agreement by upholding the cease-fire, resuming disarmament and demobilization of combatants and implementing the other relevant aspects of the agreement in accordance with the timetable, including the prompt installation of the New Council of State. With regard to returning UNOMIL and its civilian staff to the level authorized under resolution 866 (1993), the Council requested that the Secretary-General base any decision to do so on the existence of an effective cease-fire and on UNOMIL's ability to carry out its mandate. The Council urged Member States to provide support for the peace process in Liberia by contributing to the United Nations Trust Fund for Liberia, and by providing financial, logistical and other assistance in support of the troops participating in ECOMOG.

During the following two weeks, the Chairman of ECOWAS, supported by the Secretary-General's Special Representative, continued discussions in Accra in an attempt to bring the parties to agreement. On 30 January, however, after almost one month of intensive but unsuccessful efforts, the Chairman of ECOWAS informed the parties that they should return to Liberia to continue their deliberations.

Technical team

By resolution 972 (1995), the Security Council requested the Secretary-General to report on the role of UNOMIL and of ECOMOG in Liberia and the resource requirements of ECOWAS States to maintain their troops in ECOMOG. The Secretary-General dispatched a small technical team to Monrovia, which held detailed consultations from 6 to 10 February 1995.

ECOMOG informed the technical team that its strength was about 8,430 troops, organized in 10 self-contained infantry battalions. The Government of Nigeria contributed the bulk of the force (4,908), while troops were also provided by the Governments of Ghana (1,028), Guinea (609), the United Republic of Tanzania (747), Uganda (760) and Sierra Leone (359). Smaller contingents were also provided by the Gambia (10) and Mali (10).

The main military functions of ECOMOG, in accordance with the Cotonou and Accra agreements, were the protection of civilians in safe havens; establishment and provision of security for assembly sites, where the combatants would initially congregate pending disarmament; establishment and provision of security for encampment sites where ECOMOG would disarm combatants

and carry out other activities related to demobilization; assistance in the enforcement of the arms embargo through the establishment of border-crossing points and patrols; and maintenance of general security throughout the country.

In order to carry out its responsibilities under the Accra agreement, ECOMOG indicated that it would require a force of some 12,000 all ranks. That would require seven additional self-contained battalions (about 4,250 troops), taking into account the proposed withdrawal of the Tanzanian contingent. The technical team found that the resources and logistical assets available to ECOMOG were clearly insufficient for it to carry out its tasks effectively. Accordingly, the team concluded that estimates of ECOMOG's logistical support requirements, provided by its Force Commander, were justified. The team was not convinced, however, that seven additional battalions would be required for the implementation of ECOMOG's concept of operations.

Humanitarian situation

In the absence of credible security guarantees, relief activities continued to be limited to greater Monrovia and Buchanan town, and to those areas of Grand Bassa, Margibi and Montserrado counties that were controlled by ECOMOG. The humanitarian crisis in Monrovia itself was of particular concern and continued to be aggravated by a steady flow of internally displaced persons seeking refuge, and a small number of combatants wishing to demobilize.

On 3 February, the Secretary-General launched an inter-agency consolidated appeal for Liberia, for the six-month period January to June 1995, seeking the $65 million in extrabudgetary resources required by United Nations agencies to continue to carry out life-saving interventions in a number of key emergency sectors. While the appeal sought funds for activities to be undertaken in those areas of Liberia secured by ECOMOG, it also made allowance for the possibility of expanding humanitarian assistance programmes to other areas, should security conditions allow. In accordance with this strategy, a number of United Nations agencies and NGOs undertook exploratory initiatives in January 1995 to expand the scope of their operations. Several international NGOs also made preliminary overtures to the factions concerning the possibility of commencing activities on a larger scale.

The February appeal covered a wide range of humanitarian programmes in the following sectors: food and nutrition, agriculture and food, health and medical relief, water and sanitation, emergency shelter, education and training. Special projects for children and women were also prepared. Agencies taking part in the appeal included FAO, the United Nations Centre for Human Settlements (Habitat) in conjunction with the United Nations Development Programme (UNDP), UNICEF, WFP, WHO and the United Nations Department of Humanitarian Affairs.

Options before the Security Council

On 24 February 1995, the Secretary-General advised[30] the Security Council that, because of the security situation, the 78 military observers and seven paramedical staff serving with UNOMIL were deployed only in the greater Monrovia area, including Buchanan and Kakata. Two months after the signing of the Accra Agreement, the Liberian factions and political leaders were still haggling over the composition and chairmanship of the Council of State and had yet to show that they were genuinely committed to the fulfilment of their obligations under the Agreement. Moreover, their inability to re-establish a cease-fire verification committee threatened the already fragile cease-fire. Under the circumstances, the Secretary-General felt that the time had come to consider carefully how the international community could continue to assist in the search for peace and stability in Liberia and what form this assistance should take. In this regard, the Secretary-General presented a number of options which the Council would have to consider when the mandate of UNOMIL expired on 13 April.

If the Liberian parties demonstrated a clear willingness to implement the Accra agreement, the Council's options would be: (a) to maintain UNOMIL as currently mandated under resolution 866 (1993). It was imperative that ECOMOG be provided with the resources required to carry out its responsibilities. The viability of this option would also depend on a restructuring of ECOMOG, effective enforcement of the arms embargo and more effective harmonization of the policies of the ECOWAS member States towards Liberia; or (b) to consider an enhanced role of the United Nations in Liberia through the establishment of a United Nations peace-keeping force to help the parties implement all aspects of the Accra Agreement.

However, if the current political stalemate continued, the Secretary-General said, the Coun-

cil's options would be: (a) to reduce further UNOMIL's military component and limit the Mission's mandate to the provision of good offices, until the parties clearly demonstrated the political will necessary to reactivate the peace process; or (b) to withdraw UNOMIL, a decision that would send a signal to ECOWAS and the Liberian people that the international community had given up its effort to help to find a peaceful solution to the conflict in Liberia.

During the following weeks, the peace process in Liberia remained at an impasse. All further efforts to reach agreement on the new Council of State proved unsuccessful. Moreover, military activities intensified throughout the country. The civilian population continued to suffer and the factions' military activities impeded the delivery of essential relief items to most areas of the country other than Buchanan, Kakata and Monrovia. In the mean time, in addition to the Government of the United Republic of Tanzania, the Government of Uganda had indicated its intention to withdraw from ECOMOG. The withdrawal of both contingents would bring the strength of ECOMOG down from 8,430 to approximately 6,843 all ranks.

In its resolution 972 (1995), the Security Council had expressed the hope that the member States of ECOWAS would convene a summit with a view to harmonizing their policies on Liberia, including tightening the application of the arms embargo. Meeting in Copenhagen on 11 March 1995, the Secretary-General and President Rawlings agreed that the summit should take place as soon as possible and should bring together the heads of State of the ECOWAS Committee of Nine and also involve the leaders of the Liberian parties.

On 10 April 1995, the Secretary-General told[31] the Security Council that the proposed ECOWAS summit offered a possibility that the peace process might shortly be relaunched. In those circumstances, it would be premature to withdraw UNOMIL. Accordingly, he recommended that the Security Council extend the mandate of UNOMIL until 30 June 1995. However, given the fact that the security situation prevented UNOMIL from carrying out many aspects of its mandate, it was his intention to reduce its military strength by a further 20 observers. He hoped that, during that period, ECOWAS would have sufficient time to prepare for and convene its summit and that the parties would finally cooperate fully with the ongoing efforts of ECOWAS and the international community to restore peace in Liberia.

[30]S/1995/158. [31]S/1995/279.

On 13 April, the Security Council, by its resolution 985 (1995) decided to extend the mandate of UNOMIL until 30 June 1995 and urged all Liberian parties to implement the Akosombo and Accra Agreements. The Council urged all States, and in particular all neighbouring States, to comply fully with the embargo on all deliveries of weapons and military equipment to Liberia imposed by resolution 788 (1992), and to that end decided to establish a Committee of the Security Council, consisting of all the members of the Council, to monitor and help improve the embargo's effectiveness, and to recommend measures in response to violations. The Council expressed its appreciation to the Chairman of ECOWAS for his initiative in organizing a regional summit on Liberia and to the Government of Nigeria for agreeing to host it.

ECOWAS summit

The Third Meeting of Heads of State and Government of the ECOWAS Committee of Nine on Liberia was held at Abuja from 17 to 20 May 1995. The meeting was also attended by representatives of the United Nations, OAU and the United States. The following Liberian parties sent their delegations: AFL, LNC, LPC, NPFL, CRC-NPFL, ULIMO-K, and ULIMO-J. Mr. David Kpomakpor, the Chairman of the Council of State, also participated in the meeting. Delegations of all the Liberian factions except NPFL were headed by their respective leaders.

Despite four days of discussions and the emergence of a substantial measure of agreement on nearly all the outstanding issues, the Liberian parties were unable to reach a final agreement on the composition of the Council of State. In a final communiqué[32] dated 20 May 1995, the heads of State and Government requested the leaders of the Liberian parties to conduct the necessary consultations towards a definitive solution, and entrusted the Ministers of the Committee of Nine with responsibility for reconvening a meeting of the Liberian parties within a short period in order finally to resolve the outstanding issues.

The ECOWAS leaders expressed their concern over the continued flow of arms into Liberia, in violation of the arms embargo. They requested ECOMOG and UNOMIL to improve the existing monitoring mechanisms and appealed to the international community to provide logistical support to ECOWAS in order to facilitate the effective patrolling of Liberia's borders and stem the flow of arms into the country.

In the mean time, fighting in Liberia continued between ULIMO-K and ULIMO-J in Grand Cape Mount and Bomi counties; between NPFL and ULIMO-K in Lofa county; between NPFL and ULIMO-J in Bong and Margibi counties; and between NPFL and LPC in Grand Bassa and Maryland counties. Several towns changed hands, and there were reports of human rights abuses as combatants moved into or out of a particular area. All this resulted in a continued influx of displaced persons into the ECOMOG-controlled areas of Buchanan and Kakata. Contending factions continued to block access routes into inhabited areas, resulting in the disruption of the delivery of relief supplies and unnecessary suffering of civilians. Because of the unstable security situation, ECOMOG's deployment remained restricted to the central region and to some areas of the western region. United Nations military observers were co-deployed with ECOMOG in Buchanan, Kakata and Monrovia.

Although the humanitarian situation continued to remain critical, there was some expansion of humanitarian assistance activities in Bomi and Cape Mount counties. The declaration in mid-April by ECOMOG that the areas around Bo Waterside, Tiene, Kle and Tubmanburg were "safe havens" resulted in the increased delivery of assistance to those regions. At the same time, in the areas around Gbarnga, Kakata and Bong Mines, the factions continued to prevent the delivery of relief supplies. To formulate a comprehensive programme of disarmament, demobilization and reintegration of ex-combatants, the Secretary-General's Special Representative convened a task force consisting of representatives of UNOMIL, ECOMOG, the UNDP Resident Coordinator, the transitional government, donor Governments and NGOs.

In collaboration with United Nations agencies in Liberia, national and international NGOs and local counterparts, the office of the Coordinator continued to develop a strategy for the delivery of humanitarian assistance. By June 1995, the United Nations consolidated interagency appeal for Liberia had received $49 million of the total $65 million requested, most of it in support of food aid needs.

UNOMIL's mandate extended

On 10 June 1995, the Secretary-General recommended[33] to the Security Council the extension of UNOMIL's mandate for a period of three

---

[32]S/1995/473, annex I. [33]S/1995/473.

months. He expressed hope that during that period the Liberian parties would reach agreement on the outstanding issues and demonstrate, through concrete steps, the political will necessary to bring the long-standing crisis to an end. These steps would include the installation and functioning of the Council of State; a comprehensive cease-fire; the disengagement of forces; and an agreed timetable and schedule for the implementation of other aspects of their agreements, in particular the disarmament process. In the event that the political stalemate continued, UNOMIL would, subject to the consent of the Security Council, be terminated and converted into a good offices mission, including a small military cell, which would maintain liaison with ECOMOG. If, on the other hand, significant progress was made, the Secretary-General would recommend that the Council consider restoring UNOMIL to its full strength. The Mission's role, however, and its relationship with ECOMOG would have to be adjusted to enable both operations to carry out their respective functions more effectively.

The Secretary-General called on the Liberian faction leaders to do all they could to "give peace a chance, to save innocent civilians from death and suffering, and to avoid the continuing destruction of Liberia as a result of their inability to settle their differences". By its resolution 1001 (1995) of 30 June, the Security Council extended UNOMIL's mandate until 15 September 1995 and declared that unless serious and substantial progress was made towards a peaceful settlement, the Mission's mandate would not be renewed.

F. July–November 1995

Abuja Agreement

Following the adoption of resolution 1001 (1995), diplomatic efforts aimed at moving the peace process forward intensified. In July, the Liberian parties held a series of meetings in Monrovia. Liberian faction leaders also consulted extensively with the Chairman of ECOWAS, President Jerry Rawlings of Ghana, and other leaders of the subregion. In addition, the Secretary-General's Special Representative and the representatives of ECOWAS and OAU continued their efforts to facilitate the peace process.

Meeting on 28 and 29 July at Accra, the ECOWAS Heads of State adopted a resolution[34] stating that the withdrawal of UNOMIL would compromise the efforts made by ECOMOG and affect the situation in the subregion. They called on the Security Council to review its decision to withdraw UNOMIL from Liberia if the peace process had not progressed significantly. The Chairman of ECOWAS then convened a meeting of the Liberian factions at Abuja from 16 to 19 August. The leaders of all the parties, as well as Chief Tamba Taylor, representing the traditional chiefs, attended the meeting. Representatives of the Nigerian Government, the Eminent Person of OAU for Liberia and the Secretary-General's Special Representative were also present as facilitators.

After four days of intensive discussions, the Abuja talks culminated on 19 August 1995 in the signing by the Liberian parties of an agreement,[35] amending and supplementing the Cotonou and Akosombo accords, as subsequently clarified by the Accra agreements. In accordance with provisions of the Abuja Agreement, a comprehensive cease-fire was established on 26 August at midnight and a new six-member Council was installed on 1 September, one day ahead of schedule. The Council comprised Mr. Wilton Sankawolo as its Chairman; Dr. George Boley, representing the coalition of LPC, CRC-NPFL and LDF; Mr. Alhaji Kromah of ULIMO; Mr. Oscar Quiah of LNC; Chief Tamba Taylor; and Mr. Charles Taylor of NPFL. AFL was given the defence portfolio, while General Roosevelt Johnson's wing of ULIMO (ULIMO-J) was given a number of ministerial posts. The new Council of State would remain in power for one year, until the holding of elections on 20 August 1996. The Agreement also included a schedule of implementation and a formula for the distribution of government posts.

Implementation of the Agreement

An ECOWAS delegation visited Liberia from 25 to 27 August to assess the situation on the ground and confirmed that the factions had sent instructions to their forces to lay down arms and

[34] S/1995/701, annex. [35] S/1995/742, annex.

observe the cease-fire. In the mean time, UNOMIL and ECOMOG began active preparations for the implementation of the Agreement. The Cease-fire Violations Committee, chaired by UNOMIL and consisting of ECOMOG and representatives of the transitional government and the factions, met in the beginning of September to review with the factions plans for monitoring the cease-fire and the implementation of the other provisions of the Agreement, including disarmament and demobilization. A Disarmament Committee, chaired by ECOMOG and comprising UNOMIL, the transitional government and representatives of the armed factions, with the participation of the International Committee of the Red Cross, was established to draw up plans for the disengagement of forces, disarmament and the exchange of prisoners of war. The international community was urgently requested to provide support for ECOMOG as well as for the disarmament, demobilization and reintegration of combatants.

The humanitarian situation in several parts of Liberia also improved. Negotiations between UNOMIL, ECOMOG and a number of factions resulted in the opening of critical roads from Kakata to Gbarnga and from Kakata to Bong Mines. This allowed United Nations agencies and NGOs to begin delivering aid to previously cut-off locations in central and northern Liberia. In addition to increasing their activities in new areas, relief agencies continued to provide relatively unimpeded assistance to needy populations in ECOMOG-controlled areas. However, logistical constraints and the absence of credible security guarantees for other parts of Liberia continued to prevent sustained humanitarian activity in much of the country, including Lofa county and southwest Liberia.

The Secretary-General observed[36] to the Security Council on 13 September 1995 that "... the prospects for peace in Liberia are perhaps better now than they have been at any time since the outbreak of the civil war". He emphasized, however, that ultimately it was the Liberian leaders who were primarily responsible for the restoration of peace in their country. He recommended that the Council consider extending the mandate of UNOMIL until 31 January 1996 and identified several elements which, in his view, were crucial for the success of the peace process in Liberia. Among them, he pointed to the need for international assistance in rebuilding the country's economy and infrastructure and strengthening governmental institutions. Another important factor was the disarmament and demobilization of Liberia's esti-

mated 50,000 to 60,000 combatants, of whom as many as 25 per cent were children, and their effective reintegration into civilian life. The country's national police force did not have the capacity to maintain law and order and, therefore, technical and logistic assistance should be provided in that area.

There was also an urgent need to provide ECOMOG with adequate financial and logistic resources to enable it to carry out its responsibilities in Liberia effectively. The Secretary-General intended to dispatch a mission to Liberia in order to assess the requirements involved in the implementation of the Abuja Agreement. He also informed the Council of his intention to deploy 42 additional military observers to UNOMIL, in order for the Mission to carry out its responsibilities in monitoring the cease-fire and the disengagement of forces. At the same time, UNOMIL would continue to work with ECOMOG on the adoption of a new joint concept of operations. The Security Council welcomed[37] the steps to resolve the conflict in Liberia peacefully and extended the mandate of UNOMIL as recommended by the Secretary-General.

New mandate and concept of operations

A United Nations technical team visited Liberia from 19 to 30 September to consult with the Liberian leaders and other interested parties on the requirements for the implementation of the Abuja Agreement. The team subsequently travelled to Accra for consultations with ECOWAS on 2 October. On 23 October, the Secretary-General submitted[38] his recommendations to the Security Council on a new mandate and concept of operations for UNOMIL, based on the findings of the mission and the lessons learned since the Mission had been established in September 1993.

In accordance with the peace agreements, ECOWAS would continue to play the lead role in the peace process in Liberia, while ECOMOG would retain the primary responsibility for assisting the transitional government in the implementation of the military provisions of the agreements. Under the proposed adjustment of UNOMIL's mandate, the Mission' main functions would be to exercise its good offices to support the efforts of ECOWAS and the transitional government; investigate allegations of reported cease-fire violations; recommend measures, in cooperation with

---

[36]S/1995/781. [37]S/RES/1014 (1995). [38]S/1995/881 and Add.1.

ECOMOG and the transitional government, to prevent their recurrence and report to the Secretary-General accordingly; monitor compliance with the other military provisions of the peace agreements and verify their impartial application, especially disarming and demobilization of combatants; and assist in the maintenance of assembly sites agreed upon by ECOMOG, the transitional government and the factions, and in the implementation of a programme for demobilization of combatants, in cooperation with the transitional government, donor agencies and NGOs. UNOMIL would require 160 military observers to carry out these tasks. They would be co-located with ECOMOG.

UNOMIL would also support humanitarian assistance activities as appropriate; investigate and report to the Secretary-General on violations of human rights; assist local human rights groups in raising voluntary assistance for training and logistic support; observe and verify the election process, in consultation with OAU and ECOWAS, including the legislative and presidential elections, scheduled to take place on 20 August 1996.

The functions of ECOMOG had been defined to include the following tasks: to monitor the borders of Liberia and man the main entry points by land, sea or air in order to ensure that no arms or ammunition were brought into the country; to assemble and disarm combatants of all factions; to establish checkpoints to verify the movement of arms and assist in the return of refugees and internally displaced persons; and to carry out intensive patrols throughout the country to build confidence and create an atmosphere conducive to the holding of free and fair elections. For operational purposes, ECOMOG divided the country into three sectors, each under the control of a brigade. Accordingly, ECOMOG brigade headquarters would be established at Gbarnga, Greenville and Tubmanburg. ECOMOG force headquarters would remain in Monrovia.

ECOMOG strength in October 1995 was 7,269 all ranks. In order to fulfil its new tasks, ECOMOG planned to increase its strength to some 12,000 all ranks and to deploy its forces to nine safe havens (6,600 all ranks), 10 to 13 assembly sites (3,400 all ranks) and at 14 border-crossing points (2,000 all ranks). Nigeria had indicated its readiness to provide two additional battalions, and Ghana and Guinea had also indicated their readiness to provide one each. Other ECOWAS countries were in principle prepared to contribute troops, subject to the availability of the required financial and logistical support.

By its resolution 1020 (1995) of 10 November, the Security Council decided to adjust UNOMIL's mandate and concept of operations, as recommended by the Secretary-General. The Council urged the transitional government to act to avoid cease-fire violations and to maintain the momentum of the peace process. The Council also urged all Member States to contribute to the United Nations Trust Fund for Liberia, and to provide logistical and other assistance to ECOMOG.

Humanitarian aspects

As of October 1995, some 1.5 million people, out of a total population of approximately 2.3 million, continued to require humanitarian assistance, including some 700,000 displaced persons. In addition, UNHCR estimated that 727,000 Liberian refugees had sought asylum in neighbouring countries: 367,300 in Côte d'Ivoire, 395,000 in Guinea, 14,000 in Ghana, 4,600 in Sierra Leone and 4,000 in Nigeria. Following improvement in the political and security situation, new requirements for humanitarian assistance included extending relief aid to civilians in previously inaccessible areas, providing for the repatriation of refugees and resettlement of internally displaced persons, and addressing the humanitarian aspects of the demobilization of former combatants and their integration into civilian life.

To expand and strengthen the coordination mechanisms, the Secretary-General appointed, in November 1995, a United Nations Humanitarian Coordinator. Serving under the overall authority of the Special Representative, the Humanitarian Coordinator would support and coordinate the efforts of the operational agencies of the United Nations such as UNICEF, UNHCR and WFP, while mobilizing increased participation by FAO, UNDP and WHO in relief and resettlement activities and in the provision of assistance to demobilizing soldiers. Other United Nations agencies, such as the International Labour Organisation, the United Nations Educational, Scientific and Cultural Organization and the United Nations Volunteers, would contribute in areas related to their mandates. The Humanitarian Coordinator would also support the efforts of the wider humanitarian community, including non-governmental, international and multilateral organizations. In order to support the Humanitarian Coordinator in carrying out these functions, a Humanitarian Assistance Coordination Unit was established. The Unit consisted of two offices: a Humanitarian Assistance Coordination Office and a Demobilization and Reintegration Office.

G.   A turn for the worse

By the end of 1995, following some initial progress in the implementation of the peace agreements and improvement in the security and humanitarian conditions in the country, the situation in Liberia began to take another turn for the worse. The implementation of the Abuja Agreement was behind schedule. The critical aspects of the Agreement, disarmament and demobilization, did not begin at the time foreseen. There were serious violations of the cease-fire. These violations included intermittent fighting between Alhaji Kromah's forces (ULIMO-K) and Roosevelt Johnson's forces (ULIMO-J). Fighting also occurred between LPC and NPFL and between NPFL and ULIMO-K. There were also delays in deploying ECOMOG personnel and equipment throughout the country. At the end of December 1995, heavy fighting broke out at Tubmanburg as a result of attacks on ECOMOG by ULIMO-J troops. Casualties were suffered by the combatants and by the civilian population.

Despite intensive efforts by ECOWAS and the United Nations to put the peace process back on track, the first months of 1996 saw further deterioration of the situation. Intensified skirmishes between different factions created discord among members of the Council of State. As large numbers of fighters came into Monrovia, purportedly to protect their leaders, security in the city deteriorated. On 6 April, the attempted arrest of General Roosevelt Johnson of ULIMO-J sparked fierce fighting in Monrovia between combined NPFL/ULIMO-K forces and ULIMO-J/LPC/AFL fighters. This was accompanied by the complete breakdown of law and order in the city. Fighters from all factions systematically looted the commercial district of the city as well as United Nations offices and warehouses. Houses were broken into, buildings were set on fire and vehicles were commandeered.

Civilians were caught in the crossfire. More than half of Monrovia's 1.3 million citizens were displaced, with many thousands concentrated in several locations in an attempt to escape the fighting. Thousands of others sought refuge in neighbouring countries.

During the first days of the crisis, United Nations staff members were forced from their homes and offices; they were robbed and harassed while seeking safety and when the vehicles they were driving were hijacked. On a number of occasions, local United Nations staff displayed particular bravery in assisting United Nations international personnel to safety.

UNOMIL and the United Nations agencies were forced to relocate all non-essential personnel to neighbouring countries or to repatriate them. Eighty-eight of UNOMIL's 93 military observers were relocated to Freetown and Dakar, with the assistance of the United States Government. Subsequently, most of these observers were repatriated. However, five military observers, including the Chief Military Observer, remained in Monrovia to support the political efforts aimed at peacefully resolving the crisis. Their tasks included monitoring military developments, patrolling the city, convening meetings of the Cease-fire Violations Committee and organizing security escorts for faction representatives participating in consultations to resolve the crisis. Ten additional observers remained on standby in Freetown to return to Monrovia as conditions permitted.

ECOMOG was unable to halt the hostilities. It maintained that the fighting was a matter between the factions and that it could not intervene in view of its limited manpower and resources, as well as the nature of its mandate as a peacekeeping force. Given these constraints, ECOMOG was also unable to provide protection for United Nations personnel and property. However, once ECOMOG received reinforcements from outlying areas, it assigned a security detail to the United Nations residential compound at Riverview and for the Secretary-General's Special Representative, as well as for the mediation team and some faction representatives involved in consultations to end the crisis.

In accordance with the cease-fire arrangements that went into effect on 19 April, ECOMOG deployed in central Monrovia establishing checkpoints and undertaking patrols, as fighters started to withdraw from the city. UNOMIL also patrolled the city. Fighters continued to move freely, however, and when the cease-fire broke down on 29 April, ECOMOG withdrew to specific locations in sufficient numbers to deter attack from the factions. As of mid-May 1996, ECOMOG was deployed on Bushrod Island and maintained a presence at the telecommunications headquarters, the two bridges leading to the north and the airport. ECOMOG also maintained a presence at the seaport and around the Riverview compound. Outside Monrovia, ECOMOG continued to maintain its presence in Buchanan and Kakata. However, ECOMOG completely withdrew from Gbarnga, Bo, Tiene and Sinjie and reduced its strength in Buchanan and Kakata, to provide reinforcements for Monrovia. ECOMOG suffered a number of casualties following the resumption of fighting.

In the mean time, diplomatic efforts aimed at resuming the peace process in Liberia continued. At their meeting held on 7 and 8 May in Accra, the ECOWAS Foreign Ministers reaffirmed the Abuja Agreement as the only basis for peace in Liberia and agreed upon a number of steps necessary to resume its implementation. ECOWAS warned the faction leaders that if they did not implement those steps, it would have to reconsider its involvement in Liberia at its next summit meeting scheduled for August 1996.

Reporting[39] to the Security Council on 21 May, the Secretary-General observed that in the existing insecure and unstable conditions that prevailed in Monrovia and throughout Liberia, there was little that UNOMIL could accomplish with respect to implementing its original mandate. At the same time, through the use of its good offices, UNOMIL continued to play an important role in supporting the efforts of ECOWAS to facilitate the resumption of the peace process. The Secretary-General, therefore, recommended that the Council extend the mandate of UNOMIL for three months, until 31 August. During that period, UNOMIL's strength would remain at the level of approximately 25 civilian and military personnel. At the same time, the Secretary-General indicated that, following the ECOWAS Summit, he would submit to the Council recommendations on the role, if any, that UNOMIL could play after 31 August. These recommendations would depend on the ECOWAS decisions regarding its own role in Liberia.

The Security Council agreed[40] with the Secretary-General's recommendation and called upon the Liberian parties to implement fully and expeditiously all the agreements and commitments they had already entered into, in particular the Abuja Agreement. The Council demanded that the parties restore an effective and comprehensive cease-fire, withdraw all fighters and arms from Monrovia, allow the deployment of ECOMOG and restore Monrovia as a safe haven.

H. Composition of UNOMIL

On 20 November 1992, the Secretary-General appointed Mr. Trevor Livingston Gordon-Somers (Jamaica) as his Special Representative for Liberia. When UNOMIL was established on 22 September 1993, Mr. Gordon-Somers, as Special Representative, also served as head of mission. He was succeeded as Special Representative and head of mission by Mr. Anthony B. Nyakyi (United Republic of Tanzania) on 28 December 1994. Major-General Daniel Ishmael Opande (Kenya) served as Chief Military Observer of UNOMIL from October 1993 until 30 May 1995, when he completed his tour of duty. On 16 November 1995, the Secretary-General informed the Security Council of his intention to appoint Major-General Mahmoud Talha (Egypt) as the new Chief Military Observer of UNOMIL.

When it was established, the authorized strength of the Mission was 303 military observers, 20 military medical personnel and 45 military engineers. UNOMIL reached full strength in January 1994. In October 1994, given the deteriorating circumstances in Liberia, the Secretary-General decided to reduce UNOMIL's strength to some 90 military personnel. He further reduced the strength by 20 in May 1995 and again in July 1995,

[39]S/1996/362. [40]S/RES/1059 (1996).

UNOMIL deployment as of December 1995

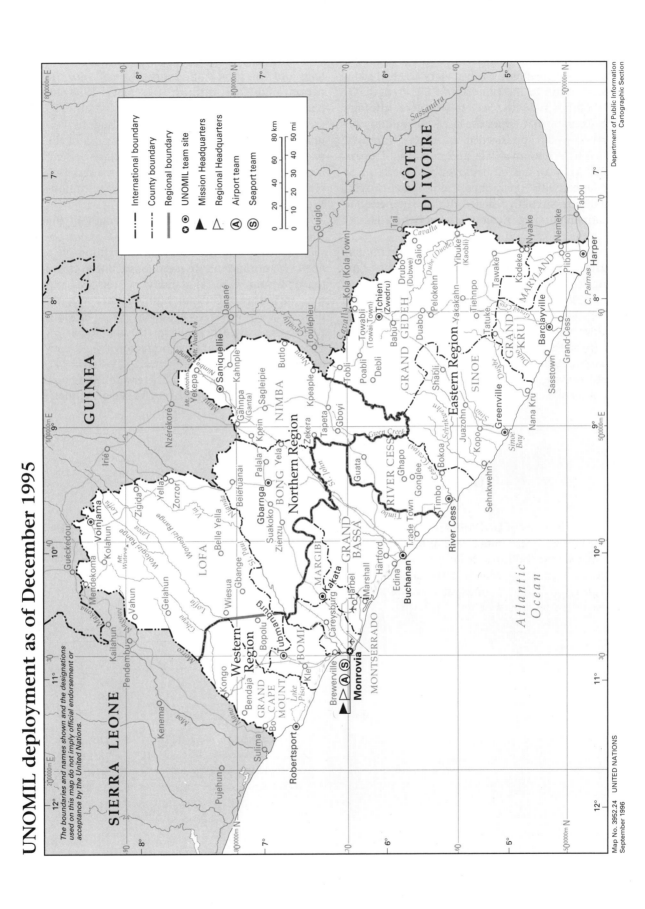

The boundaries and names shown and the designations used on this map do not imply official endorsement or acceptance by the United Nations.

Department of Public Information
Cartographic Section

Map No. 3952.24   UNITED NATIONS
September 1996

when 17 observers were redeployed to the United Nations operation in Rwanda. After the signing of the Abuja Agreement, the Secretary-General stated his intention to increase UNOMIL's strength. On 23 October 1995, the Secretary-General informed the Council that approximately 160 military observers would be needed in connection with UNOMIL's new mandate and concept of operations. They would be deployed to Liberia in accordance with operational requirements, with maximum strength reached during the period of disarmament and demobilization scheduled for December 1995 and January 1996.

The following countries provided military personnel throughout the mandate period beginning from late 1993, except as otherwise noted, as of 31 December 1995: Austria (until October 1994), Bangladesh, China, Czech Republic, Egypt, Guinea-Bissau, Hungary (until January 1994), India (from February 1994), Jordan, Kenya, Malaysia, Pakistan, Slovak Republic (until October 1994) and Uruguay. Strength at 31 December 1995 was 68 observers and 8 medical staff.

There was also a provision for 89 civilian international personnel, 58 United Nations Volunteers and 136 local staff. Budget estimates for the period mid-1995 through December 1995 included provision for 54 international staff, 110 locally recruited staff, and 7 United Nations Volunteers. In connection with the expansion of the mandate in October 1995, the Secretary-General increased those estimates by 51 international civilian staff, 442 local staff and 103 United Nations Volunteers.

As of 5 April 1996, the strength of the UNOMIL's military component stood at 93 observers. Following the outbreak of fighting on 6 April, the number of observers was reduced to 15, ten of whom were on standby in Freetown and five, including the Chief Military Observer, remained in Monrovia. As at 15 May, those in Monrovia were provided by Egypt (2) and India (3). The observers on standby in Freetown were contributed by Bangladesh (3), India (2), Kenya (1), Malaysia (2) and Pakistan (2). There were also a number of international and local civilian personnel.

I. Financial aspects

The costs of UNOMIL are met by assessed contributions from United Nations Member States. Estimated expenditures from the inception of UNOMIL until 31 March 1996 amounted to $77,981,100.[41] It was anticipated, however, that these estimates would be revised down.

Contributions to the Trust Fund for the Implementation of the Cotonou Agreement in Liberia amounted to $24 million as of 31 March 1996.

[41]A/50/650/Add.3.

Chapter 18

United Nations Aouzou Strip Observer Group (UNASOG)

Background
United Nations reconnaissance mission
Establishment of UNASOG
Operations

Chapter 18

United Nations Aouzou Strip Observer Group (UNASOG)

Background

Ownership of the Aouzou Strip — an area between the Republic of Chad and the Socialist People's Libyan Arab Jamahiriya — was contested by the two countries beginning in 1973. Following the resumption of diplomatic relations between them on 3 October 1988, both States proclaimed their willingness to resolve the dispute over the Strip by peaceful means. On 31 August 1989, the two Governments signed, in Algiers, a Framework Agreement on the Peaceful Settlement of the Territorial Dispute.[1] In September 1990, after several rounds of inconclusive talks, Chad and the Libyan Arab Jamahiriya referred the dispute to the International Court of Justice (ICJ).

The Libyan Arab Jamahiriya based its claims to the area on rights and titles including those of the indigenous inhabitants, of the Senoussi Order (a religious grouping founded during the early part of the nineteenth century) and of a succession of sovereign States — the Ottoman Empire, Italy, and Libya itself. Meanwhile, the Republic of Chad claimed the boundary was established by a Treaty of Friendship and Good Neighbourliness[2] concluded by the French Republic and the United Kingdom of Libya on 10 August 1955, among other arguments.

In its Judgment, delivered on 3 February 1994, the ICJ found that the boundary between Chad and the Libyan Arab Jamahiriya had been defined by the Treaty of Friendship and Good-Neighbourliness. According to the 16-1 decision, the boundary ran "From the point of intersection of the 24th meridian east with the parallel 19°30' of latitude north, a straight line to the point of intersection of the Tropic of Cancer with the 16th meridian east; and from that point a straight line to the point of intersection of the 15th meridian east and the parallel 23° of latitude north."

In March 1994, both Governments pledged[3] to abide by the ICJ Judgment and noted that it had brought a definite solution to the territorial dispute. After further talks, an agreement[4] was signed on 4 April 1994 establishing the prac-tical modalities for the implementation of the Judgment. Among other things, the agreement provided for the withdrawal of the Libyan administration and forces from the Aouzou Strip, removal of mines, crossing points for persons and property, study of the question of monitoring the frontier, maintenance of good-neighbourliness, demarcation of the boundary, further cooperation and notification of the agreement to the United Nations.

United Nations reconnaissance mission

According to the agreement, the withdrawal operation of the Libyan administration and forces was to commence on 15 April 1994, under the supervision of a mixed team composed of 25 Libyan and 25 Chadian military officers, and to end on 30 May 1994. United Nations observers would be present during the withdrawal operations and would establish that the withdrawal was actually effected.

Following consultations in New York between United Nations Secretariat and Chadian and Libyan officials, both Governments agreed that a United Nations reconnaissance team composed of civilian and military personnel would visit the area to conduct a brief survey of conditions on the ground.

The reconnaissance mission was endorsed by the Security Council in its resolution 910 (1994) of 14 April 1994. The team arrived in Tripoli on 15 April and proceeded to the Aouzou Strip on 17 April. On the basis of the discussions with the Chadian and Libyan authorities and of the preliminary assessment of conditions on the ground, the team reported that it would be possible to deploy United Nations observers to perform the functions envisaged in the 4 April 1994 agreement.

[1]United Nations, *Treaty Series*, No. 26801. [2]Ibid, No. 27943. [3]S/1994/296, S/1994/332. [4]S/1994/402, annex; S/1994/424, annex.

UNASOG deployment

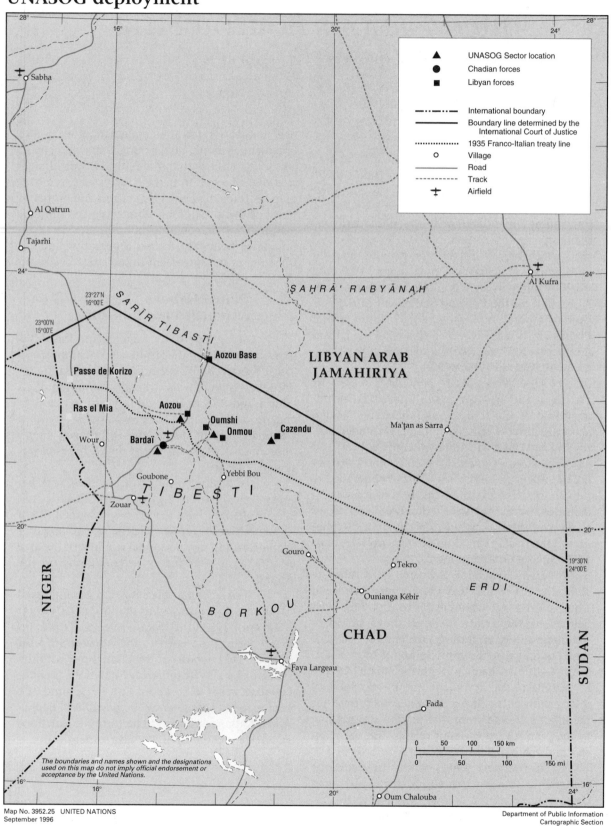

Establishment of UNASOG

On 27 April 1994, the Secretary-General recommended[5] to the Security Council the deployment of the United Nations Aouzou Strip Observer Group (UNASOG) for a period of approximately 40 days from the date of adoption of the relevant decision of the Council. The Secretary-General envisaged that, subject to the approval of the Council, UNASOG would be deployed immediately. The reconnaissance team, with five military observers already in the area, would become the advance party of the operation. Because the withdrawal of the Libyan administration and forces was to begin on 15 April 1994, the team would continue to monitor the withdrawal until the establishment of UNASOG.

On 4 May 1994, the Security Council, by its resolution 915 (1994), established UNASOG in accordance with the recommendations of the Secretary-General, and authorized its deployment for a single period of up to 40 days from the date of the resolution. It called upon the parties to cooperate fully with the Secretary-General in verifying implementation of the 4 April agreement and, in particular, to grant UNASOG freedom of movement and all the services it required in order to fulfil its functions.

With the adoption of resolution 915, the reconnaissance team became the advance party of UNASOG. Four other observers joined the mission on 12 May 1994.

The authorized strength of UNASOG was 9 military observers and 6 international civilian staff. The military observers as well as most of the civilian staff were drawn from the United Nations Mission for the Referendum in Western Sahara. The observers came from Bangladesh, Ghana, Honduras, Kenya, Malaysia and Nigeria. The Chief Military Observer was Colonel Mazlan Bahamuddin (Malaysia).

Net expenditures amounted to $67,471, appropriated through the United Nations regular budget.

Operations

The Libyan Arab Jamahiriya/Chad mixed team, after consultations with the reconnaissance team, established a list of locations from which the withdrawals of the Libyan forces were to be effected. The mixed team also agreed on a schedule for withdrawal and evacuation of the Libyan forces. These operations were carried out according to the established schedule. Each time a withdrawal was effected, it was certified by a member of the Libyan team and of the Chadian team. UNASOG was present for each withdrawal and witnessed the certification by the teams. The parties agreed that all outstanding issues would be settled within the framework of the 4 April agreement.

On 30 May 1994, Mr. Abderrahman Izzo Miskine, Minister of Interior and Security of Chad, and Mr. Mohamed Mahmud Al Hijazi, Secretary of the General People's Committee for Justice and Public Security of the Libyan Arab Jamahiriya, signed a Joint Declaration[6] on behalf of their Governments. According to the Declaration, the withdrawal of the Libyan administration and forces from the Aouzou Strip had been effected to the satisfaction of both parties and monitored by UNASOG. The Chief Military Observer of UNASOG signed the Declaration as a witness.

The Secretary-General reported[7] to the Security Council on 6 June 1994 that UNASOG had successfully completed its task and that the mission could therefore be considered as terminated. In his view, the accomplishment of UNASOG's mandate demonstrated the useful role which the United Nations could play in the peaceful settlement of disputes. He thanked the two Governments for the cooperation they had extended to UNASOG and for the spirit of friendship they had exhibited towards each other during the operation.

By its resolution 926 (1994) of 13 June 1994, the Security Council commended the work of the members of UNASOG and noted with appreciation the cooperation extended by the two Governments.

[5]S/1994/512. [6]S/1994/672, annex. [7]S/1994/672.

Part VI
Central America

Chapter 19
General review

Chapter 19
General review

A complex and difficult process of negotiations, beginning in 1983, has reversed the cycle of turmoil which engulfed Central America for many years. At its various stages, the process has involved countries from inside and outside the region, as well as the opposing parties within several of the Central American countries. These initiatives have been actively supported and facilitated by the United Nations. As a result of the negotiations and the agreements reached, the United Nations has been called on to establish a number of mechanisms for observing and verifying commitments. These include the United Nations Observer Group in Central America (ONUCA), the United Nations Observer Mission to verify the electoral process in Nicaragua (ONUVEN), the International Support and Verification Commission (CIAV), the United Nations Observer Mission in El Salvador (ONUSAL), the United Nations Mission in El Salvador (MINUSAL) and the United Nations Mission for the Verification of Human Rights in Guatemala (MINUGUA). Two of these, ONUCA and ONUSAL, were peace-keeping operations.

A negotiated settlement

The desire to find a negotiated settlement inspired peace initiatives by the Governments of Colombia, Mexico, Panama and Venezuela — known as the Contadora Group — in 1983, and then by the Presidents of Costa Rica, El Salvador, Guatemala, Honduras and Nicaragua. After preliminary consultations in Esquipulas, Guatemala, in 1986, Costa Rican President Oscar Arias Sánchez drafted a comprehensive regional peace plan, based on the principle of solving several interrelated problems simultaneously. The plan, for which President Arias was awarded the 1987 Nobel Peace Prize, was embodied in the final declaration of a summit of the five Central American Presidents held in Guatemala in August 1987.

Esquipulas II Agreement

The "Procedure for the Establishment of a Firm and Lasting Peace in Central America", known both as the Esquipulas II Agreement and the Guatemala Procedure, dealt with issues of national reconciliation; an end to hostilities; democratization; free elections; termination of aid to irregular forces and insurrectionist movements; non-use of the territory of one State to attack other States; negotiations on security, verification and the control and limitation of weapons; refugees and displaced persons; cooperation, democracy and freedom for peace and development; international verification and follow-up; and a timetable for the fulfilment of commitments.

In conjunction with the Organization of American States (OAS), the United Nations was requested to verify free elections and to participate in an International Verification and Follow-up Commission (CIVS). The Commission would comprise the Secretary-General of the United Nations, the Secretary-General of OAS, or their representatives, and the Ministers for Foreign Affairs of the Central American countries, the Contadora Group and the Support Group (the Support Group consisting of Argentina, Brazil, Peru and Uruguay). It was to be responsible for verifying and monitoring fulfilment of the commitments contained in the Agreement.[1]

United Nations endorsement

The subject of peace in Central America had been on the agenda of the General Assembly since 1983 and had been addressed in Security Council resolutions 530 (1983) of 19 May 1983 and 562 (1985) of 10 May 1985. In the latter, the Council had called upon all States "to refrain from carrying out, supporting or promoting political, economic or military actions of any kind against any State in the region".

On 7 October 1987, in resolution 42/1, the General Assembly expressed its "firmest support" of the Esquipulas II Agreement. It requested the Secretary-General to afford the fullest assistance to the Central American Governments in their effort to achieve peace, especially by responding to the specific requests made of him in the Agreement. Meanwhile, the Secretaries-General of both

[1]S/19085.

the United Nations and OAS had agreed to participate in CIVS, which held its inaugural session in Caracas, Venezuela, on 22 August 1987.

In October 1987, a joint United Nations/OAS mission visited the five Central American countries to evaluate the need for on-site verification of the security commitments in the Esquipulas II Agreement, and in November it undertook a second round of consultations with representatives of the Central American Governments. However, because of lack of agreement among the five Central American Governments, the mission concluded that the conditions did not exist at that time for on-site verification.

Costa del Sol Declaration

On 8 February 1989, the Ministers for Foreign Affairs of the five Central American countries met the United Nations Secretary-General in New York to prepare for a presidential summit in El Salvador the following week. The Ministers requested the Secretary-General to appoint a technical group of the Secretariat to elaborate, with representatives of their countries, terms of reference for a mechanism to verify the security aspects of Esquipulas II and to draft a proposal for its establishment. Six days later, the presidential summit issued a Joint Declaration, known as the Costa del Sol Declaration or Tesoro Beach Agreement, which, *inter alia*, announced the decision by the President of Nicaragua to hold elections no later than 25 February 1990. In addition, the Presidents undertook to draw up within 90 days a joint plan for the voluntary demobilization, repatriation or relocation in Nicaragua or third countries of members of the Nicaraguan Resistance and their families. The Executive Commission (which consisted of the Ministers for Foreign Affairs of the five Central American countries) was entrusted with the task of immediately organizing technical meetings to establish, in accordance with the talks held with the Secretary-General of the United Nations, the most appropriate and efficient mechanism for verifying security commitments.[2]

Technical discussions

Representatives of the Central American Governments held detailed discussions in mid-March with the United Nations Secretariat on the creation of the United Nations verification mechanism. On 31 March 1989, the five Ministers for Foreign Affairs officially requested the Secretary-General to take the necessary steps to set it in motion.[3] However, it became clear that progress could be made on this aspect of the Central American peace process only when Nicaragua had agreed to postpone a pending legal action against Honduras at the International Court of Justice.

ONUVEN

Meanwhile, however, progress was achieved in another area. The Secretary-General of the United Nations responded positively to a request by the Government of Nicaragua for the United Nations to monitor the elections to be held there.[4] Several missions were accordingly sent to Nicaragua to observe the revision of electoral laws and the laws regulating the mass media, as well as to carry out a study of the new legislation. The foundations were thus laid for the establishment of ONUVEN, which became operational on 25 August 1989. As ONUVEN did not involve the use of military personnel, it is not considered to be a peace-keeping operation and is not further discussed in the present work. It should, however, be recorded that its very successful fulfilment of its mandate enhanced the role of the United Nations in the Central American peace process and thus facilitated the work of ONUCA, especially in Nicaragua.

Tela Accord

On 27 July 1989, in an effort to revive the momentum of the peace process, the Security Council unanimously adopted resolution 637 (1989). In it the Council, *inter alia*, expressed its firmest support for the Esquipulas II Agreement and subsequent joint declarations by the Presidents and called upon them "to continue their efforts to achieve a firm and lasting peace in Central America". It also lent the Security Council's full support to the Secretary-General to continue his mission of good offices.

Considerable progress was made at the summit held at Tela, Honduras, between 5 and 7 August 1989, when the Presidents issued a Declaration and a "Joint Plan for the voluntary demobilization, repatriation or relocation of the members of the Nicaraguan Resistance and their families, as well as assistance in the demobilization of all those involved in armed actions in the countries of the region when they voluntarily seek it".[5] The support for this process would be provided by an International Support and Verification Com-

[2]S/20491. [3]S/20642. [4]A/44/210, A/44/375. [5]S/20778, annex.

mission (CIAV), which the Secretaries-General of the United Nations and OAS were requested to establish.

Among the functions assigned to CIAV, both those of a humanitarian nature and those relating to development would be entrusted to the United Nations High Commissioner for Refugees and the United Nations Development Programme. CIAV was also to be entrusted with receiving arms, equipment and military supplies from the members of the Nicaraguan Resistance and storing them until the five Presidents decided how they should be disposed of.

The Joint Plan also addressed the necessity of an immediate and effective end to the hostilities in El Salvador and the issue of the voluntary demobilization of the members of the Salvadorian resistance front, the Frente Farabundo Martí para la Liberación Nacional (FMLN).

On 25 August, the Secretaries-General of the United Nations and OAS, meeting at United Nations Headquarters, decided to establish CIAV with effect from 6 September 1989. On 1 September 1989, Secretary-General Pérez de Cuéllar appointed Assistant Secretary-General Alvaro de Soto as his Personal Representative for the peace process in Central America. On 21 September, he informed[6] the President of the Security Council of the establishment of CIAV and expressed the view that the demobilization of the members of the Nicaraguan Resistance was an operation of a clearly military nature, which would have to be launched by the Security Council.

At the Tela Summit an agreement was also reached between Honduras and Nicaragua regarding the pending litigation between the two countries at the International Court of Justice. With this obstacle out of the way, the Secretary-General was able to send a reconnaissance mission to the region from 3 to 23 September 1989. Brigadier-General Péricles Ferreira Gomes (Brazil), Chief Military Observer of the United Nations Angola Verification Mission, led the mission, which comprised senior United Nations officials and military personnel provided by Member States. On the basis of the information furnished by the mission, the Secretary-General duly recommended[7] to the Security Council the deployment of ONUCA.

The Secretary-General also reported[8] to the Security Council and the General Assembly that the Government of El Salvador and FMLN had reached an agreement in Mexico City on 15 September "to initiate a dialogue aimed at ending the armed conflict in El Salvador by political means". Both parties had invited the Secretary-General to send a representative, as a witness, to the subsequent talks in San José, Costa Rica.

[6]S/20856. [7]S/20895. [8]S/20699/Add.1-A/44/344/Add.1.

Chapter 20

United Nations Observer Group in Central America (ONUCA)

Chapter 20

United Nations Observer Group in Central America (ONUCA)

ONUCA was established by the Security Council on 7 November 1989. The Group's mandate was set out by the Secretary-General in his report[1] to the Council of 11 October 1989. ONUCA would conduct on-site verification of the security undertakings contained in the Esquipulas II Agreement, namely (a) the cessation of aid to irregular forces and insurrectionist movements, and (b) the non-use of the territory of one State for attacks on other States. The latter undertaking was to include preventing the establishment or use of facilities for radio or television transmissions for the specific purpose of directing or assisting the military operations of irregular forces or insurrectionist movements in any of the five countries.

Because the nature of the terrain in the region would have limited the efficacy of static observation posts, it was judged that the best results would be achieved by establishing mobile teams of at least seven military observers, who would carry out regular patrols by road vehicles with cross-country capability, by helicopter and, in the Gulf of Fonseca and certain other coastal areas and rivers, by patrol boats and light speedboats. A small fixed-wing aircraft would be required to transport the Chief Military Observer (CMO) and his senior staff between the capitals of the five countries and to rotate military observers from one duty station to another.

The mobile teams would also make spot checks on their own initiative and would be instructed to undertake immediate ad hoc inspections to investigate allegations of violations of the undertakings. The observers would be grouped in verification centres located as close as possible to sensitive areas where violations of the undertakings on cessation of assistance and non-use of territory would be most likely to occur.

Command of ONUCA in the field would be exercised by the CMO, who would be under the command of the United Nations, vested in the Secretary-General, under the authority of the Security Council. The 260 military observers, who would be unarmed, would be provided by Member States, at the request of the Secretary-General.

In resolution 644 (1989) of 7 November 1989, the Security Council approved the Secretary-General's report and decided to set up ONUCA immediately for a period of six months. On 21 November 1989 the Security Council approved[2] the appointment of Major-General Agustín Quesada Gómez (Spain) as CMO.

Deployment

It was envisaged that ONUCA would be deployed in four phases. In phase one, an advance party would proceed to the region following the adoption of the enabling resolution by the Security Council. During phase two, ONUCA would establish a capacity to investigate complaints and a limited capability to carry out patrolling and spot inspections. Ninety-nine observers would be required, along with a number of helicopters and naval vessels. During phase three, some three months after the adoption of the necessary resolution, a further 63 observers would be deployed, with additional helicopters. Deployment during phase four would be determined in light of the progress and results achieved during the first three phases and other relevant factors. During this phase, a further 98 military observers would be required, for a total strength of 260 military observers.

On 3 December 1989, an advance party led by the CMO and consisting of approximately 30 military officers and United Nations civilian officials established the Group's headquarters in Tegucigalpa, Honduras. The team made visits to the five countries of the region to set up liaison offices in each capital and make the necessary preparations for the subsequent establishment of verification centres there and elsewhere. In the light of the prevailing security conditions, the El Salvador liaison office could not be established

[1]S/20895. [2]S/20982.

in San Salvador until 17 January 1990. ONUCA reached its full strength on 5 June 1990, at which time, in addition to the liaison offices in the five capitals, it was manning 14 verification centres, five of them in the capitals, and 3 operational posts. In June 1990, four fast patrol boats joined the mission and began operating from a naval verification centre at San Lorenzo, Honduras.

Operations

ONUCA operations involved mobile teams of military observers patrolling from verification centres, each manned by up to 10 observers, and smaller operational posts in forward areas. Patrols were carried out daily by land, by air and occasionally by river, covering terrain that was mostly rugged and densely forested, with limited access by road. Under such conditions, helicopters proved indispensable for observation purposes and for transporting observers and supplies. ONUCA monitoring concentrated in those areas where activities contrary to the security undertakings in the Esquipulas II Agreement were alleged to occur, mostly in the areas adjacent to the borders between Costa Rica and Nicaragua, between Honduras and Nicaragua, between Honduras and El Salvador and between Guatemala and El Salvador, together with the north-eastern part of Nicaragua and the south-western part of Honduras. When a complaint was registered with ONUCA, the practice was to communicate it to the Government complained against, which was asked to extend to ONUCA full cooperation in an investigation. The results of the investigation were then transmitted to both Governments concerned. ONUCA received relatively few complaints in that process.

First expansion of the mandate

On 12 December 1989, the five Central American Presidents issued the "Declaration of San Isidro de Coronado"[3] in which, *inter alia*, they requested that ONUCA's mandate be expanded to include verification of any cessation of hostilities and demobilization of irregular forces that might be agreed upon in the region.

On 15 March, soon after the elections in Nicaragua, the Secretary-General reported to the Security Council that, in consultations between the Nicaraguan Government, the Government-elect and the United Nations, agreement had been reached in principle on modalities for the demobilization of the members of the Nicaraguan Re-

sistance. Those in Honduras would be demobilized at their existing camps and then repatriated without delay. For those in Nicaragua at the time of demobilization, ONUCA would establish temporary assembly points where they would be demobilized and where ONUCA would ensure their security pending their resettlement, which was to be arranged by the International Support and Verification Commission without delay. ONUCA would be responsible for taking delivery of their weapons, *matériel* and military equipment, including military uniforms. Armed personnel would be required for these tasks. The Secretary-General accordingly asked[4] the Security Council, on a contingency basis, to enlarge ONUCA's mandate for this purpose and to authorize the addition of armed personnel to its strength. No additional troops would be deployed until agreement existed among all concerned on the voluntary demobilization of the Nicaraguan Resistance.

In resolution 650 (1990) of 27 March 1990, the Security Council unanimously approved the Secretary-General's report and decided to authorize, on a contingency basis in accordance with the report, an enlargement of the mandate of ONUCA and the addition of armed personnel to its strength in order to enable it to play a part in the voluntary demobilization of the Nicaraguan Resistance. The Council requested the Secretary-General to keep it fully informed of further developments regarding the implementation of the resolution.

On 2–3 April 1990, the five Central American Presidents agreed[5] to the Secretary-General's proposal that the weapons and other equipment received from the members of the Nicaraguan Resistance should be destroyed *in situ* by ONUCA.

Demobilization in Honduras

The first company of an armed infantry battalion, contributed by Venezuela, was accordingly deployed to Honduras on 10 April 1990, after agreement had been reached on the demobilization of the two principal groups of the Nicaraguan Resistance remaining in that country. On 16 April 1990, it demobilized 260 members of the Atlantic Front (Yatama) of the Nicaraguan Resistance at La Kiatara in eastern Honduras and destroyed their weapons and military equipment. On 18 April, at the main Nicaraguan Resistance camp at Yamales in Honduras, large quantities of weapons, most of them obsolete and unserviceable, were

[3]S/21019, annex. [4]S/21194. [5]S/21235, annex.

handed over to ONUCA for destruction. But no personnel were demobilized on this occasion as all active combatants previously located at Yamales had apparently returned to Nicaragua.

Second expansion of the mandate

Before the transfer of political power in Nicaragua on 25 April 1990, intensive negotiations took place between the Nicaraguan Government, representatives of the President-elect and representatives of the Northern, Central and Atlantic Fronts of the Nicaraguan Resistance, with the participation of the Archbishop of Managua, Cardinal Obando y Bravo. The CMO of ONUCA and Mr. Iqbal Riza, the Secretary-General's Alternate Personal Representative for the Central American peace process, also took part.

On the night of 18–19 April, the Nicaraguan parties signed a complex of agreements relating to the voluntary demobilization of the members of the Nicaraguan Resistance in Nicaragua during the period from 25 April to 10 June 1990. A cease-fire would come into effect at 12 noon local time on 19 April and a separation of forces would take place as a result of the withdrawal of the Nicaraguan Government's forces from certain "security zones" which were to be established in Nicaragua and in which the members of the Nicaraguan Resistance would concentrate for the purposes of demobilization. ONUCA was asked to monitor both the cease-fire and the separation of forces.

On the basis of these agreements, the Secretary-General sought[6] the Security Council's approval of a further expansion of ONUCA's mandate to cover these functions. That approval was granted by resolution 653 (1990) of 20 April 1990.

By resolution 654 (1990) of 4 May 1990 the Security Council decided to extend the mandate of ONUCA, as defined in resolutions 644 (1989), 650 (1990) and 653 (1990), for a further period of six months, on the understanding that the additional tasks of monitoring the cease-fire and separation of forces and demobilizing the members of the Nicaraguan Resistance would lapse not later than 10 June 1990.

"Security zones"

Five "security zones" were established on 22 April following the withdrawal of the Nicaraguan Government's forces from the areas in question during the preceding three days. Within each

zone, ONUCA personnel — both unarmed observers and armed members of the Venezuelan battalion — were deployed in a "demobilization and logistics support area" where the hand-over of weapons and other activities connected with the demobilization of the members of the Nicaraguan Resistance took place. Each zone was 500–600 square kilometres in area and was surrounded by a demilitarized zone of some 20 kilometres in width. Two additional zones were subsequently established on the Atlantic Coast for the demobilization of the members of the "Yatama" front. These zones covered a total of 2,550 square kilometres.

Progress of demobilization

Although all the necessary arrangements had been made by ONUCA, in coordination with leaders of the Nicaraguan Resistance, for demobilization to begin on 25 April at El Amparo in Zone 1, the members of the Resistance who had assembled there declined to lay down their weapons after their commander told them that the minimum conditions for demobilization had not been met. In the ensuing days, only a few members of the Resistance demobilized.

On 4 May 1990, after further consultations, the Nicaraguan Government and the leadership of the Nicaraguan Resistance issued the "Managua Declaration", in which, *inter alia*, the Nicaraguan Resistance declared that it would continue its voluntary demobilization and that the process would be completed in all the "security zones" by 10 June at the latest. Demobilization began on 8 May. But during the next two weeks only small numbers came forward for demobilization, and it soon became clear that the pace was insufficient to ensure completion by 10 June. The leaders of the Nicaraguan Resistance complained of breaches by the Nicaraguan Army of the agreements relating to the cease-fire and separation of forces.

On 22 and 23 May 1990, the Security Council met to discuss this grave situation, and on 23 May the President of the Security Council made a statement[7] expressing the Council's concern at the slow pace of demobilization.

ONUCA, meanwhile, investigated complaints from both sides relating, on the one hand, to the presence of armed civilians and militia personnel in the "security zones" and demilitarized zones, and, on the other, to the presence outside

6 S/21259. 7 S/21331.

the "security zones" of armed members of the Nicaraguan Resistance, some of whom had allegedly committed various criminal acts. However, it remained the Secretary-General's assessment that there had been no serious violations of the cease-fire.

This serious situation was resolved on 30 May when a meeting between President Violeta Chamorro of Nicaragua, the leaders of the Nicaraguan Resistance and the Archbishop of Managua resulted in an agreement entitled the "Managua Protocol".[8] Under its terms, the Nicaraguan Government responded to a number of the Resistance's publicly stated concerns, notably through the establishment of "development areas" in which demobilized members of the Resistance would be resettled. The Resistance reaffirmed its commitment to demobilize by 10 June 1990 at the latest and, to this end, undertook that at least 100 combatants would be demobilized each day in each of the "security zones".

Completion of demobilization

After 30 May, demobilization generally proceeded rapidly. On 8 June the Secretary-General reported[9] to the Security Council that there had been a marked increase in the rate at which the members of the "Northern Front" and "Central Front" were being demobilized. However, demobilization of the "Atlantic Front", which had begun on 21 May, was proceeding at a less satisfactory pace than that of the main group, largely because of logistic difficulties in concentrating the members at demobilization areas in the large security zones concerned.

In light of the progress of the demobilization, the Secretary-General recommended that the Security Council extend the relevant part of ONUCA's mandate for a brief and clearly defined period. By resolution 656 (1990) of 8 June 1990, the Council accordingly decided that ONUCA's tasks of monitoring the cease-fire and separation of forces in Nicaragua and demobilizing the Resistance should be extended, on the understanding, as recommended by the Secretary-General, that these tasks would lapse with the completion of the demobilization process not later than 29 June 1990.

During the following three weeks, demobilization proceeded in all zones. The process reached a peak on 10 June, when 1,886 members of the Nicaraguan Resistance were demobilized. On 18 June, an eighth "security zone" became

operational to facilitate the demobilization of members of the "Southern Front".

On 29 June 1990, the Secretary-General informed[10] the Security Council that at 1900 hours local time on 28 June 1990, demobilization of all armed and unarmed members of the Nicaraguan Resistance had been completed at all locations, except for one in Nicaragua where a handful of members remained to be demobilized. This was soon accomplished, and the final zone was closed on 5 July 1990.

By the time the process was completed, a total of 19,614 armed and unarmed members of the Nicaraguan Resistance had been demobilized in Nicaragua and 2,759 in Honduras. Weapons handed over to ONUCA by members of the Nicaraguan Resistance included 15,144 small arms (including AK 47s, other assault rifles, rifles and light machine-guns), as well as heavy machine-guns, mortars, grenade launchers, grenades, mines and missiles.

Completing the original mandate

The early part of the mandate period, dominated by ONUCA's role in the demoblization of the members of the Nicaraguan Resistance, was thus ending. The Secretary-General reported[11] that ONUCA observers in the five countries had then reverted to their original mandate, which required patrolling of areas where violations of the Esquipulas II security undertakings seemed most likely to occur. ONUCA maintained a regular and visible presence in those areas. ONUCA's role was thus one of verification; it did not have the authority or the capacity to prevent by physical means either the movement of armed persons or warlike material across borders or other violations of the undertakings. Nor was it staffed or equipped for the detection of clandestine activities.

Responding to a request from the five Central American Governments, the Secretary-General recommended to the Security Council on 26 October 1990 that ONUCA should continue its operations for a further period of six months, until 7 May 1991. He also recommended a reduction of ONUCA's strength, which as of October was 254 military observers. Liaison offices and verification centres in each of the five capitals would be merged to form in each case an Observer Group headquarters, and the number of verification centres would also be reduced. Given ONUCA's

[8]S/21341, annex. [9]S/21349. [10]S/21379. [11]S/21909.

ONUCA deployment as of June 1990

ONUCA Headquarters

Liaison office

Verification centre

Operational post

Security zone

International boundary

0   100   200   300 km

0   100   200 mi

The boundaries and names shown and the designations used on this map
do not imply official endorsement or acceptance by the United Nations.

Map No. 3952.26   UNITED NATIONS
September 1996

Department of Public Information
Cartographic Section

smaller size, the rank of the CMO would be reduced from Major-General to Brigadier-General. The Security Council approved the Secretary-General's report in its resolution 675 (1990) of 5 November 1990.

The necessary retrenchment was completed by the middle of December 1990, and Major-General Quesada Gómez relinquished his command on 20 December. Pending the appointment of a successor, the Deputy Chief Military Observer, Brigadier-General Lewis MacKenzie (Canada), exercised the command of ONUCA as Chief Military Observer a.i.

A further extension of ONUCA's mandate, until 7 November 1991, was approved by the Council in its resolution 691 (1991) of 6 May 1991. In recommending[12] that extension to the Council, the Secretary-General had also recommended a further reduction in ONUCA's strength, which in April 1991 stood at 158 military observers. Based on a study into the cost-effectiveness of the Group's methods of operations, it had been determined that, while ONUCA should continue to maintain its regular and visible presence, emphasis of that presence in the border areas should be more directly focused on liaison and the exchange of information with the security authorities of the States concerned. In the ensuing months, ONUCA intensified those activities. The Secretary-General also informed the Council that he had taken steps to appoint Brigadier-General Víctor Suanzes Pardo (Spain) as CMO. General Suanzes Pardo assumed his command with effect from 13 May 1991. Among his other activities, the CMO attended meetings of the Central American Security Commission, at the Commission's invitation.

On 28 October 1991, the Secretary-General informed[13] the Security Council that the situation in the region had continued to improve. The five Governments were making efforts to arrive at new collective security arrangements for the region. Furthermore, "[t]hose Powers that were earlier actively supporting opposing sides in Central America appear to be disengaging themselves and have publicly announced their intention to revise their policies vis-à-vis Central America, emphasizing their support for negotiated political solutions to conflicts and assistance for economic and social development rather than military purposes". The five countries also continued their efforts to honour their commitments under the Esquipulas II Agreement. Although violations continued to occur, they were increasingly linked to criminal activity for pecuniary rather than political motives. At the same time, there was

no evidence to indicate that the irregular armed groups that had re-emerged in Nicaragua were being helped from abroad. In relation to the conflict in El Salvador, ONUCA had confirmed that neighbouring countries had adopted measures, with varying degrees of vigour, to prevent activities from their territories that would violate the Agreement. However, considering the large quantities of weapons in private hands or hidden away, considerable potential for breaches of the Agreement continued in relation to the conflict in El Salvador.

In the prevailing "fluid and dynamic situation", the Secretary-General did not think "it would be right to withdraw ONUCA or further reduce the scope of its operations". At that time, the number of military observers stood at 132. He therefore suggested an extension of the mandate until 30 April 1992, during which time the Security Council might reconsider ONUCA's future if developments warranted. The Security Council extended the mandate in resolution 719 (1991) of 6 November 1991, bearing in mind the Secretary-General's report and the need to monitor expenditures carefully during a period of increasing demands on peace-keeping resources.

In the meantime, there were major developments relating to settlement of the armed conflict in El Salvador, including additional verification tasks assigned to the United Nations Observer Mission in El Salvador (ONUSAL). The new Secretary-General, Mr. Boutros Boutros-Ghali, informed[14] the Council of these tasks on 10 January 1992. He then stated his intention to meet as much as possible of the personnel requirements of ONUSAL's Military Division by transferring to it officers then serving with ONUCA. Aircraft, vehicles and other equipment would be similarly transferred. He had informed the Governments of the five countries where ONUCA was deployed of his intention to recommend the termination of ONUCA. Reporting[15] on 14 January, he recalled that, in a previous report to the Council, his predecessor, Mr. Javier Pérez de Cuéllar, had referred to the cost of meeting the ever-growing demand for peacemaking and peace-keeping activities by the United Nations and to the widely held view that peace-keeping operations should be set up to do a specific task for a specific period and then be disbanded. With this in mind, the Secretary-General proposed that the Security Council decide to terminate ONUCA's operational mandate with effect from 17 January 1992. The Security Council, by its resolution 730 (1992) of 16 January, ap-

[12]S/22543. [13]S/23171. [14]S/23402. [15]S/23421.

proved the Secretary-General's report and decided to terminate ONUCA's mandate.

On 24 January 1992, 131 military observers serving with ONUCA were transferred to ONUSAL. To supervise the closing of the Mission, a number of international and local staff serving with ONUCA were retained and subsequently phased out over a period of three and a half months.[16]

Composition

Major-General Agustín Quesada Gómez (Spain) served as Chief Military Observer of ONUCA from 21 November 1989 to 20 December 1990. Following ONUCA's reduction in size, Brigadier-General Lewis MacKenzie (Canada) served as acting CMO from 18 December 1990 to the end of his tour of duty on 13 May 1991. Brigadier-General Victor Suanzes Pardo (Spain) took up his command as CMO on 17 May 1991.

ONUCA's authorized military strength included 260 military observers, as well as crews and support personnel for an air wing and a naval unit. Initially, military observers were contributed by Canada, Colombia, Ireland, Spain and Venezuela. Subsequently, they were joined by military observers from Brazil, Ecuador, India and Sweden. A helicopter unit was contributed by Canada. Argentina provided four fast patrol boats, with crews, for maritime patrolling duties in the Gulf of Fonseca. The Federal Republic of Germany provided a civilian medical unit and a fixed-wing aircraft with civilian crew. After the enlargement of ONUCA's mandate, Venezuela contributed an infantry battalion to undertake the demobilization of the members of the Nicaraguan Resistance from April to June 1990. The mission also included international and locally recruited civilian staff and a number of civilian aircrew and maintenance personnel for commercially chartered helicopters.

From November 1990 until January 1991, 16 military observers were temporarily detached from ONUCA to serve as security observers in the United Nations Observer Group for the Verification of the Elections in Haiti (ONUVEH).

Financial aspects

Reporting to the Security Council on 11 October 1989, the Secretary-General recommended that the costs of ONUCA should be considered as expenses of the Organization to be borne by the Members in accordance with Article 17, paragraph 2, of the United Nations Charter. Subsequently, by resolution 44/44 of 7 December 1989, the General Assembly accepted his recommendation that the assessments to be levied on Member States should be credited to a special account which would be established for this purpose. By its resolution 46/240 of 22 May 1992, the General Assembly decided that the special accounts for ONUCA and ONUSAL should be merged. Expenditures related to the operation of ONUCA amounted to $88,573,157.

Conclusion

ONUCA vividly illustrated the complex demands made of the Organization's peacemaking and peace-keeping skills and the varied role it played in advancing the peace process in Central America. Although initially established with the limited mandate of verifying only one aspect of that process, the tasks entrusted to it evolved, and it was able to assist the parties concerned to control and resolve the conflicts in the region. Its role in the demoblization of the members of the Nicaraguan Resistance marked an important step forward in the process of national reconciliation in Nicaragua. In his report recommending the termination of the Mission, the Secretary-General paid tribute to the military and civilian personnel who served in ONUCA for their great success in establishing the first large-scale peace-keeping operation of the United Nations in the Americas and for the contribution which they made to the restoration of peace and stability in Central America.

[16]A/47/556.

Chapter 21

United Nations Observer Mission in El Salvador (ONUSAL)

Chapter 21

United Nations Observer Mission in El Salvador (ONUSAL)

A. Background

Negotiating process

The establishment in 1991 of the United Nations Observer Mission in El Salvador (ONUSAL) resulted from a complex negotiating process initiated by the Government of El Salvador and the Frente Farabundo Martí para la Liberación Nacional (FMLN) in September 1989 and conducted by the parties under the auspices of the United Nations Secretary-General. The objective of the negotiations was to achieve a series of political agreements aimed at resolving the prolonged armed conflict in El Salvador by political means as speedily as possible, promoting democratization in the country, guaranteeing unrestricted respect for human rights and reunifying Salvadorian society. It was envisaged that implementation of all agreements that might be signed between the two parties would be subject to verification by the United Nations.

The first substantive agreement was achieved on 26 July 1990, when the two sides signed, at San José, Costa Rica, the Agreement on Human Rights.[1] That Agreement pledged both sides to unrestricted respect for international human rights laws and standards. It called for a United Nations verification mission that would: (1) receive communications on human rights violations from any individual, group or organization in El Salvador; (2) interview anyone freely and privately; (3) visit any place or establishment freely and without prior notice; (4) carry out an educational and informational campaign on human rights and on the functions of the mission; and (5) take whatever legal action it deemed appropriate to promote and defend human rights and fundamental freedoms.

At an informal meeting of the Security Council on 3 August 1990, Secretary-General Javier Pérez de Cuéllar reviewed[2] the sequence of agreements that had led to the San José Agreement. He recalled that the initial objective of the peace process was "to achieve political agreements for a halt to the armed confrontation and any acts that infringe the rights of the civilian population, which will have to be verified by the United Nations, subject to the approval of the Security Council". The issues on which agreements were needed related to: (1) armed forces; (2) human rights; (3) judicial system; (4) electoral system; (5) constitutional reform; (6) economic and social issues; (7) verification by the United Nations.

At their May 1990 round of talks in Caracas, Venezuela, the parties had set a target of mid-September 1990 for the achievement of synchronized political agreements in these areas, with implementation schedules that would allow for coordinated action. It had been envisaged that this would allow the March 1991 elections in El Salvador to be conducted in a tranquil atmosphere free from intimidation. Although it was not clear whether the target would be met or, given the complexity of the issues, whether the process would be successful at all, the Secretary-General set out for the Council the broad concept of the operational plan the United Nations would follow. Core activities would include the verification of a cease-fire, the monitoring of the electoral process and the verification of respect for human rights. The Secretary-General recommended that these operations be carried out as parts of an integrated operation rather than separately. On 29 August 1990, he sought[3] and subsequently received[4] the concurrence of the Council for making the necessary arrangements, including the possible establishment of a small preparatory office in El Salvador, to be set up at the appropriate time. Verification itself would await further consultations with the Council.

But such action did not follow immediately. Reporting[5] to the Security Council on 21 De-

---

[1]A/44/971-S/21541. [2]S/22031, annex. [3]S/21717. [4]S/21718. [5]S/22031.

cember 1990, the Secretary-General noted that, while the San José Agreement marked significant progress in the peace talks, problems had been encountered on the issue of armed forces, "the most sensitive and complex issue on the agenda". Given the pervasive character of that question, it had not been possible to make progress on other items. "Conscious of the need to reinvigorate the negotiating process," the Secretary-General informed the Council, "the two parties, with the participation of my Representative [Assistant Secretary-General Alvaro de Soto], agreed on 31 October 1990 at a direct meeting held at Mexico City to make adjustments in the mechanics of the negotiations, laying greater emphasis on the active role of my Representative and on the confidential nature of the process." Referring to his statement to the informal meeting of the Council on 3 August 1990, the Secretary-General repeated his recommendation for an integrated and coordinated United Nations verification operation.

The San José Agreement had envisaged that the verification operation would begin after the cessation of armed conflict in the country, but both parties had since asked to have the human rights mechanism in place as soon as possible, without waiting for other agreements. In view of the fact that such action would be in keeping with the Esquipulas II Agreement, the Secretary-General said that he would soon request authorization for ONUSAL. Pending the conclusion of other agreements, he would recommend that, as a first step towards establishing an integrated operation, the human rights verification component be put in place as soon as preparations had been made on the ground, in particular, a determination of the extent to which it could perform its functions in the absence of a cease-fire. A preliminary mission was sent in March 1991 to help the Secretary-General determine the feasibility of acceding to the request. The mission was supported by a small preparatory office which had been established in San Salvador in January 1991.

On 16 April 1991, the Secretary-General reported[6] to the Council that the preliminary mission had found "a strong and widespread desire in all sectors of opinion in El Salvador that the United Nations commence, as soon as possible, the verification of the Agreement without awaiting a cease-fire". Explicit assurances of support from the military, security and judicial authorities and FMLN made such action feasible. While the lack of a cease-fire could pose risks to the security of personnel not usually encountered in United Nations verification missions, these were not to a degree that should prevent action. Personnel might also be subjected to intimidation by certain extremist groups, and the Secretary-General would advise caution in this regard. He then informed the Council that he had decided to accept the recommendation of the preliminary mission that the "human rights component of ONUSAL be established at the earliest feasible moment in advance of an agreement on a cease-fire".

Mexico City Agreement

Meanwhile, negotiations between the parties continued to make progress, and on 27 April 1991 an Agreement[7] was signed in Mexico City on a number of constitutional reforms that could be presented to the Legislative Assembly of El Salvador before its term expired at the end of the month. Reform of the Constitution required action by two successive Legislative Assemblies, with a two-thirds majority in the second. The agreements on constitutional reforms focused on the armed forces, the judicial system and human rights, and the electoral system. In addition, there was agreement on the creation of a three-member Commission on the Truth which would contribute to the reconciliation of El Salvador society by investigating serious acts of violence since 1980. The Commission was to transmit a final report with its conclusions and recommendations to the parties and to the United Nations Secretary-General, who would make it public and would take the decisions and initiatives that he deemed appropriate. The parties undertook to carry out the Commission's recommendations. On 10 December 1991, after extensive consultation with the parties, the Secretary-General appointed Mr. Belisario Betancur, former President of Colombia, Mr. Reinaldo Figueredo Planchart, former Foreign Minister of Venezuela, and Mr. Thomas Buergenthal, former President of the Inter-American Court of Human Rights, as members of the Commission on the Truth.

[6]S/22494. [7]A/46/553-S/23130, annex.

B. Establishment of ONUSAL

Security Council action

On 20 May 1991, the Security Council, by resolution 693 (1991), decided to establish ONUSAL, as an integrated peace-keeping operation, to monitor all agreements concluded between the Government of El Salvador and FMLN. As recommended by the Secretary-General, the Mission's initial mandate was to verify the compliance by the parties with the San José Agreement on Human Rights. At that stage, the tasks of the Mission included actively monitoring the human rights situation in El Salvador; investigating specific cases of alleged human rights violations; promoting human rights in the country; making recommendations for the elimination of violations; and reporting on these matters to the Secretary-General and, through him, to the United Nations General Assembly and Security Council.

ONUSAL begins work

ONUSAL was launched on 26 July 1991, at which time it absorbed the small preparatory office. The Secretary-General appointed Mr. Iqbal Riza, a member of the United Nations Secretariat, as Chief of Mission with the rank of Assistant Secretary-General. In assuming its initial tasks, ONUSAL adopted a two-phase approach. During the preparatory phase, from July through September, ONUSAL set up its regional offices and laid the operational and conceptual bases for its future work. On 1 October 1991, the Mission entered its second phase of operations, in which it began to investigate cases and situations involving allegations of human rights violations and to follow them up systematically with the competent State organs and with FMLN. The purpose of these activities was to establish the veracity of such allegations and, where required, to follow the actions taken to identify and punish those responsible and to deter such violations in future. During this phase, ONUSAL significantly expanded its contacts with the parties, establishing flexible, stable coordination mechanisms with them. In addition, the Mission initiated both a human rights education programme and an information campaign on human rights.

First enlargement of mandate

Meanwhile, steady progress was made in the negotiations on other political agreements aimed at ending the armed conflict in El Salvador. Following meetings in New York which lasted from 16 to 25 September 1991, the parties agreed on a compressed agenda for negotiations covering all outstanding matters.[8] In addition, they signed the New York Agreement,[9] in which they decided, among other things: (1) to create a National Commission for the Consolidation of Peace (COPAZ), mandated to oversee the implementation of all political agreements reached by the parties; (2) to "purify" the armed forces and to reduce their size; (3) to redefine the doctrine of the armed forces with regard to their function; (4) to begin immediately to organize the new National Civil Police (PNC).

Then, on 31 December 1991, following more than two weeks of intensive negotiations at United Nations Headquarters in New York, the parties signed the Act of New York[10] which, combined with the previously signed Agreements of San José (26 July 1990), Mexico City (27 April 1991) and New York (25 September 1991), completed the negotiations on all substantive issues of the peace process.

Before the agreements reached in New York were formalized in a Peace Agreement, the newly-elected Secretary-General, Mr. Boutros Boutros-Ghali, reported[11] to the Security Council on the need for an immediate and substantial increase in ONUSAL's strength. The agreement on the cessation of the armed conflict would require ONUSAL to verify all aspects of the cease-fire and the separation of forces. The agreement on PNC would involve ONUSAL in monitoring the maintenance of public order during the transition period while the new PNC was being set up. The Secretary-General recommended the creation of two new ONUSAL divisions to deal with military and with police affairs. The military division would be commanded by an officer in the rank of Brigadier-General appointed by the Secretary-

---

[8]A/46/502/Add.1-S/23082/Add.1, annex. [9]A/46/502-S/23082, annex. [10]S/23402, annex. [11]S/23402 and Add.1.

General with the consent of the Security Council and reporting to the Chief of Mission.

On 14 January 1992, the Security Council, by resolution 729 (1992), unanimously decided to enlarge both the mandate and strength of ONUSAL. After signature of the Peace Agreement[12] at Chapultepec Castle in Mexico City on 16 January 1992, the Secretary-General took immediate steps to enable the Mission to implement its expanded mandate. In addition to the existing Human Rights Division, two new Divisions — Military and Police — were established. All three were under the overall direction of the Chief of Mission, whose office was responsible for monitoring and promoting the implementation of all the political aspects of the Peace Agreement.

Peace Agreement

The text signed at Chapultepec, with its nine chapters and several annexes, was the result of a complex negotiating process which succeeded in achieving agreement on the reform of some of the key institutions of Salvadorian society. The principles on which the "doctrine of the armed forces" were to be based were set out in the first chapter of the Agreement. The mission of the armed forces in national defence was differentiated from national security; the "obedient, professional, apolitical and non-deliberative" character of the armed forces was emphasized. Respect for the political order determined by the sovereign will of the people was enjoined. "As a State institution, the armed forces play an instrumental, non-decision-making role in the political field", the text said. "Consequently, only the President of the Republic and the basic organs of government may use the armed forces to implement the provisions they have adopted, within their respective constitutional areas of competence, to enforce the Constitution."

Other sections of the text dealt with the educational system of the armed forces, the "purification" of the force of those guilty of human rights violations or other unprofessional conduct, and the reduction of the forces to "a size appropriate to their doctrine". The parties recognized the need to "clarify and put an end to any indication of impunity on the part of officers of the armed forces, particularly in cases where respect for human rights is jeopardized". To that end, they referred the issue to the Commission on the Truth. The National Intelligence Department was to be abolished under the Agreement and provision made for the creation of a new State Intelligence Agency, with a rigorous check on the transfer of personnel from the former to the latter. The Agreement acknowledged the need to proscribe paramilitary forces or groups except those duly constituted under law for civil defence and as reserves for the armed forces. Forcible recruitment was to be suspended, pending passage of laws under which military service would become universal, non-discriminatory and compulsory.

The Agreement also set out in equal detail the parameters for the reform of the police, the judiciary and the electoral system. In a section on economic and social questions, the parties agreed that one of the "prerequisites for the democratic reunification of Salvadorian society" was sustained development. To that end, the parties agreed on certain actions and guidelines to address the question of land reform, agricultural credit, technical assistance, consumer protection, privatization and procedures for direct external cooperation for community development and assistance projects. It was agreed to establish a forum for consultations on economic and social issues, open to representatives of the Government, labour and business, and re-integration programmes for ex-combatants and war-disabled.

A timetable was set under the Peace Agreement for political participation by FMLN. It included the passage of legislation ensuring full civil and political rights to former FMLN combatants, the freeing of all political prisoners, the return of exiles, and licences for FMLN mass media.

The Agreement conceived of the cessation of the armed conflict as a "brief, dynamic and irreversible process of predetermined duration which must be implemented throughout the national territory of El Salvador". There were four elements to ending the conflict: (1) the cease-fire; (2) the separation of forces; (3) the end of the military structure of FMLN and the reintegration of its members into society; and (4) United Nations verification of all those activities. Specifically, ONUSAL was to verify the cease-fire and the subsequent separation and consolidation of forces and equipment of both sides in pre-determined locations. It was to prevent movements of forces except for strictly limited purposes (supply, de-mining operations, sick or medical leave), and only if the movements did not jeopardize the cease-fire. FMLN was to destroy all arms and equipment deposited in designated locations under ONUSAL supervision and verification.

---

[12]A/46/864-S/23501, annex.

ONUSAL structure

To undertake the enormously wide range of its responsibilities, ONUSAL was constituted into three separate divisions.

(1) Human Rights Division. The Human Rights Division consisted of approximately 30 human rights observers and legal advisers. In addition, the Mission's Regional Coordinators also dealt with all the human rights aspects of the Mission's mandate and reported directly to the Director of the Division. During the course of the Mission, the Director of the Human Rights Division prepared 13 periodic reports reflecting the situation of human rights in the country. These reports were submitted by the Secretary-General to the General Assembly and the Security Council. They traced a slow improvement that, by the time ONUSAL's mission ended, led to an overall transformation of the situation of human rights. The process was, however, ongoing. As the reports consistently pointed out, the effective enjoyment of human rights depended primarily on strengthening the national institutions that were responsible, directly or indirectly, for protecting and defending those rights. In particular, it depended on the proper functioning of the institutional framework provided for in the peace agreements to ensure that the State's activities in respect of human rights were in keeping with the law.

The active verification carried out by the Division was directed not only at an objective recording of facts, but also at the exercise of good offices aimed at assisting efforts by Salvadorians to find a remedy to violations. The Division also cooperated with Salvadorian institutions to strengthen their ability to work in promoting human rights. Of particular importance in this regard was the Division's cooperation with the National Counsel for the Defence of Human Rights and the Division's activities with human rights non-governmental organizations, with a view to contributing to the training of their personnel and enhancing their leadership capacity. In sum, this was, as the Director of the Human Rights Division said in his final submission[13] to the Secretary-General in April 1995, "the most extensive human rights verification operation ever undertaken in any country with the support of the international community, and a process unprecedented in the history of United Nations peace-keeping operations".

(2) Military Division. When ONUSAL was established in July 1991, 15 military officers from Canada, Brazil, Ecuador, Spain and Venezuela maintained liaison with the military chiefs of the two parties to the conflict. They also carried out, jointly with the United Nations Observer Mission in Central America, operations through which FMLN commanders in the field were escorted from their respective conflict zones to and from the negotiations in Mexico and New York.

ONUSAL's Military Division was established on 20 January 1992, once the Peace Agreement was signed, with an authorized strength of 380 military observers. The Division verified the cessation of the armed conflict, the redeployment of the Armed Forces of El Salvador to the positions they would maintain in normal peace time, and the concentration of FMLN forces in agreed designated locations in the areas of conflict. It monitored the troops of both parties in those locations, verified the inventories of weapons and personnel, authorized and accompanied the movements of both forces, and received and investigated complaints of violations. The Division coordinated the Plan for the Prevention of Accidents from Mines, and helped control and coordinate the clearing of 425 mine-fields. The Division was reduced in number following the culmination, on 15 December 1992, of the cease-fire process. It was further reduced after 31 May 1993 and again in December 1994, given the advances in the peace process. In the final phase of ONUSAL, the number of military observers dropped to 3.

(3) Police Division. From ONUSAL's inception, 16 police officials from Spain, France and Italy participated in the Mission's work. Following signature of the Peace Agreement, ONUSAL was expanded to include a Police Division. One of the Agreement's fundamental components was the creation of a new Salvadorian police force, PNC, to replace the old public security structures. The Police Division of ONUSAL, composed mostly of specialists in the organization and operation of civilian police forces, monitored National Police activities during the transition from armed conflict to national reconciliation. In a country where the police had been one of the primary factors in human rights abuses, this provided the Salvadorian people with a sense of security. The authorized strength of the Police Division was 631, although this number was never reached. The deployment of police observers throughout the territory of El Salvador began on 7 February 1992.

ONUSAL police observers also supervised and provided instruction to the Auxiliary Transitory Police (PAT), which operated between

[13] A/49/888-S/1995/281.

ONUSAL deployment as of April 1992

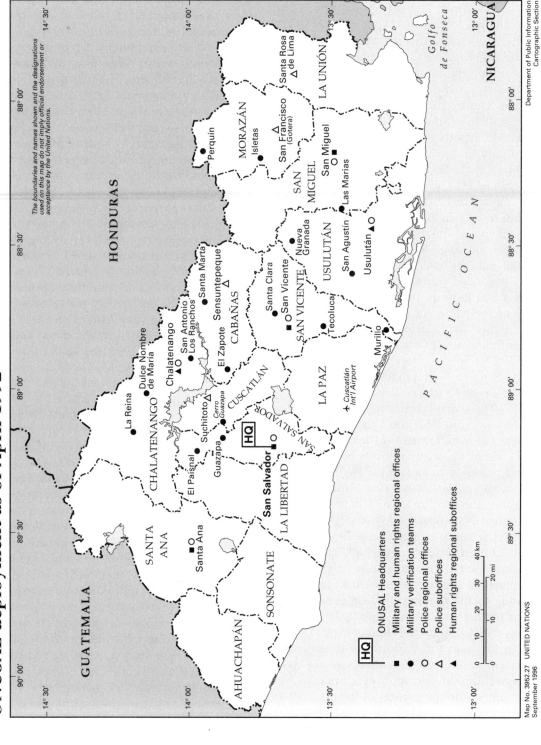

The boundaries and names shown and the designations used on this map do not imply official endorsement or acceptance by the United Nations.

GUATEMALA

HONDURAS

NICARAGUA

PACIFIC OCEAN

Golfo de Fonseca

SANTA ANA
Santa Ana

SONSONATE

AHUACHAPÁN

CHALATENANGO
La Reina
Dulce Nombre de Maria
Chalatenango
San Antonio Los Ranchos
El Paisnal
Guazapa
Cerro Guazapa
Suchitoto

Santa Marta
Sensuntepeque
CABAÑAS
El Zapote

MORAZÁN
Perquin
Isletas
San Francisco (Gotera)

Santa Rosa de Lima
LA UNIÓN

SAN MIGUEL
San Miguel
Las Marias
Nueva Granada
San Agustin
Usulután

USULUTÁN

CUSCATLÁN

SAN SALVADOR
HQ
San Salvador
LA LIBERTAD

Cuscatlán Int'l Airport

LA PAZ
Tecoluca
Murillo

Santa Clara
San Vicente
SAN VICENTE

Legend

HQ ONUSAL Headquarters
■ Military and human rights regional offices
● Military verification teams
○ Police regional offices
△ Police suboffices
▲ Human rights regional suboffices

40 km
20 mi

Map No. 3952.27   UNITED NATIONS
September 1996

Department of Public Information
Cartographic Section

October 1992 and July 1993. PAT was responsible for maintaining public order and security in the former zones of conflict until their substitution by the new PNC. PAT was made up of recruits from the National Public Security Academy, which began its activities on 1 September 1992. ONUSAL monitored the admission examinations to the Academy and recommended improvements where necessary. The presence of an ONUSAL observer in the Academic Council greatly strengthened its capacity for effective monitoring. ONUSAL also provided support to the Academy to strengthen its training courses on human rights.

The Police Division assumed additional functions as territorial deployment of PNC began in March 1993. In response to a request from the Government and in close coordination with the international technical team that provided advice to the Director-General of PNC, the Division carried out, between 1 April and 30 September 1993, an evaluation of the performance of the new police force in the field and provided it with technical advice and logistical support. On 27 July 1994, PNC and ONUSAL signed a framework agreement. PNC also had memorandums of understanding on technical cooperation with the Police Division and Human Rights Division of ONUSAL, respectively. The Division assisted in efforts to locate illegal arms caches and supported the Human Rights Division. Police observers conducted special inquiries when required and ensured that appropriate security measures were provided for FMLN leaders, as established by the Peace Accords. Support was also provided to the Electoral Division when it was established in September 1993 [see below].

Adjustments to the timetable

The cease-fire in El Salvador was informally observed from 16 to 31 January 1992. It officially took hold on 1 February. On the same day, ONUSAL's Military Division began its verification activities. The Secretary-General reported[14] to the Security Council on 25 February that, under ONUSAL's supervision, the first stage of the separation of forces had been completed without any major incident. Under the original plan, ONUSAL's Military Division was to be reduced after June 1. On 20 May 1992, however, the Secretary-General informed[15] the Council of the need to maintain the Division's strength beyond that date. He explained in his report[16] of 26 May that the process of ending a 12-year old civil war, consolidating peace and returning El Salvador politics to normalcy was not an easy one. While both the Gov-

ernment and FMLN were to be commended for not breaking the cease-fire and threatening the fragile first phase of national reconciliation, there were serious delays in implementing the various provisions of the agreements. That had "undermined each side's confidence in the other's good faith". Both sides had failed to concentrate all their forces in designated locations. There were doubts about whether the inventories of arms presented by FMLN were accurate, and suspicion persisted that FMLN was retaining clandestine arms caches. The Government had failed to establish the National Public Security Academy and begin recruitment for PNC by 1 May 1992. It had also not begun promoting the legislation to legalize FMLN as a political party. While the breach of one part of the agreement could not be used as an excuse to break another part of it, the Secretary-General noted that the timetable for implementing the Peace Agreement was not a "haphazard sequence of actions that can easily be altered. It is, on the contrary, an intricately designed and carefully negotiated mechanism whose purpose is to synchronize (a) the reintegration of FMLN's ex-combatants into civilian life and (b) the measures that the Government has committed itself to undertake in order to facilitate that process, especially as regards agriculture, political activity and recruitment into the National Civil Police".

"ONUSAL is operating in an atmosphere of deep distrust", the Secretary-General said. "Its insistence on maintaining its impartiality is sometimes misperceived by each side as being partiality towards the other. In this context, I regret to have to report to the Security Council that there has recently been a recurrence of threats against the security of the Mission and its personnel". The Secretary-General informed the Council of his contacts with both sides on the issue of delays in implementing the peace agreement, adding that each side had assured him that they were making efforts to bring the process back on course.

On 19 June, the Secretary-General reported[17] to the Security Council on agreements to resolve the issues that had delayed the implementation of the peace process. Under the revised timetable, the forces of both sides would be fully concentrated at designated locations by 25 June 1992. By 30 June, the first contingent of former FMLN combatants would commence their reintegration into civilian life, and the process for all those in that category would be completed (as in the original timetable) by 31 October 1992. By

[14]S/23642. [15]S/23987. [16]S/23999. [17]S/23999/Add.1.

15 July, the National Academy for Public Security would begin its first course for training recruits for the new PNC, including personnel from the existing National Police and former FMLN combatants in agreed proportions. By 30 June, the Government would present in the legislature a bill for the definitive abolition of the National Guard and the Treasury Police, and establish a "Special Brigade for Military Security" with no civilian security responsibilities. Also by that date, the Government would propose reforms to the Electoral Code to facilitate the legalization of FMLN and take steps related to land reform.

Despite this agreed timetable, difficulties continued in ensuring that political agreements were implemented together with agreements related to the demobilization of FMLN forces. On 30 September 1992, FMLN informed the United Nations that, in order to maintain the link in the original timetable between the key undertakings of the two parties, it would suspend demobilization until new dates had been set for the start of the transfer of land and other aspects of the Agreements that had fallen behind schedule. On 13 October, the Secretary-General presented a proposal to the two parties regarding the solution of the land issue. He later informed[18] the Council that his proposal had been accepted.

While an agreement on the land issue was reached, it became evident that the complete dismantling of the FMLN military structure by 31 October 1992 would be difficult to achieve. On 23 October, the Secretary-General proposed to the parties a set of adjustments to the timetable according to which the phase of the cessation of the armed conflict would be completed on 15 December 1992. FMLN accepted the proposal contingent upon its acceptance by the Government. The Government, however, reserved its position on some aspects of the proposal and suspended the restructuring, reduction and demobilization of its Armed Forces.

To help resolve the situation, Mr. Marrack Goulding, who was Under-Secretary-General for Peace-keeping Operations, and Assistant Secretary-General Alvaro de Soto were sent to San Salvador. The consultations that followed led to arrangements for the formal ending of the armed conflict on 15 December. The arrangements also included agreement by the President of El Salvador, Mr. Alfredo Cristiani, to complete implementation of the recommendations of the Ad Hoc Commission on Purification of the Armed Forces. The Commission, which was provided for under the Peace Agreements, was set up on 19 May 1992, and had submitted its confidential report to President Cristiani and to the Secretary-General on 22 September. Its recommendations were for the dismissal or transfer of 103 officers, including several very senior officers.

ONUSAL closely followed all issues related to the creation of the new PNC, the political participation of FMLN, the restoration of public administration in former zones of conflict, and reforms of the judicial and electoral systems. In addition, the Mission participated as an observer in COPAZ.

C. December 1992–September 1993

End of the armed conflict

On 23 December 1992, the Secretary-General reported[19] to the Security Council that the armed conflict between the Government of El Salvador and FMLN had been brought formally to an end on 15 December. This event, which had been preceded the previous evening by the legalization of FMLN as a political party, was marked by a ceremony presided over by President Cristiani and attended by the Secretary-General and a number of international statesmen. The Secretary-General described the event as "a defining moment in the history of El Salvador, whose long-suffering people can now look forward to a future in which political, economic and social arguments will be settled through the processes of democracy and not by war". At the same time, he stressed that it did not mark the end of the peace process in El Salvador. It was important that both parties, and the international community, should persevere in their efforts to ensure implementation of the remaining provisions of the Peace Agreements.

[18]S/24688, S/24833. [19]S/25006.

Second enlargement of mandate

The mandate of ONUSAL was enlarged a second time after the Government of El Salvador, on 8 January 1993, formally requested United Nations observation of the elections for the presidency, the Legislative Assembly, mayors and municipal councils, all set for March 1994. The Secretary-General informed[20] the Security Council of the request and indicated his intention to recommend that the Council accept it. A technical mission visited El Salvador from 18 to 28 April 1993 to define the terms of reference, concept of operations and financial implications of expanding the ONUSAL mandate. The Secretary-General summarized the main findings of the mission in his 21 May 1993 report[21] to the Security Council and stated that the elections were likely to be the culminating point of the entire peace process. The Salvadorian Supreme Electoral Tribunal would receive full cooperation from ONUSAL should the Security Council approve his recommendation that the Mission be authorized to observe the electoral process.

The Electoral Division was to be established in five stages. The preparatory stage, from 1 to 30 June 1993, was devoted to organization at the central and regional levels; during the period July to December, the main tasks would be to verify citizens' registration and to follow political activities; from December 1993 to March 1994, efforts were to be concentrated on observation of the electoral campaign; the Division would then observe the elections, set for 20 March 1994, the counting of votes and the announcements of results. Should the first round yield a definitive result, the activities of the Division would conclude on 31 March 1994. Should a second round of elections for the presidency be necessary, observation would continue from 1 to 30 April 1994.

The Security Council approved the Secretary-General's report by its resolution 832 (1993) of 27 May 1993 and decided to enlarge ONUSAL's mandate to include observation of the electoral process. The Council welcomed the continuing adaptation by the Secretary-General of the activities and strength of ONUSAL, taking into account progress made in implementing the peace process.

Shift in focus

The Secretary-General also reported that the peace process in El Salvador had been successfully advanced to a stage where the priority assigned to military aspects could be shifted to other provisions of the agreements. Implementation of several key commitments had continued to progress. However, the deployment of PNC was behind schedule and difficulties continued to plague the transfer of land and other programmes essential to the reintegration of former combatants on both sides. The Military Division continued its verification of the destruction of FMLN weapons and the reduction of the Armed Forces of El Salvador. In the area of human rights, the National Counsel for the Defence of Human Rights had opened regional offices. In addition, the Commission on the Truth had submitted its report.

Commission on the Truth

The Commission on the Truth had been formally installed in the presence of the Secretary-General at United Nations Headquarters in New York on 13 July 1992. The members then travelled to El Salvador to commence the activities of the Commission. During the next few months, it received over 22,000 complaints of "serious acts of violence" that had occurred between January 1980 and July 1991. These were classified as violence by agents of the State; massacres of peasants by the Armed Forces; assassinations by death squads; violence by FMLN; and assassinations of judges. The report of the Commission, entitled "From Madness to Hope: The 12-year war in El Salvador",[22] was presented to the Secretary-General on 15 March 1993. Its recommendations were in four categories: (1) those arising from the results of its own investigations; (2) eradication of structural causes directly connected with the incidents investigated; (3) institutional reforms to prevent the repetition of such events; and (4) measures for national reconciliation. The Security Council welcomed[23] the report and called on the parties to comply with its recommendations.

The Secretary-General reported,[24] however, that the question of implementing those recommendations had given rise to controversy and remained outstanding. He instructed that a detailed analysis be made of the Commission's recommendations, examining whether any of them were outside the Commission's mandate or incompatible with the Constitution. The analysis should also identify what action was required by whom and in what time-frame. The Secretary-General conveyed the analysis[25] to the Government, FMLN and COPAZ on 20 May 1993. He requested each

---

[20]S/25241. [21]S/25812. [22]S/25500, annex. [23]S/25427. [24]S/25812. [25]S/25812/Add.3.

to inform him by 20 June 1993 of the action it had taken or planned to take to implement the recommendations for which it was designated as an addressee and to promote the implementation of the other recommendations. The Secretary-General later reported[26] that the Commission's recommendations had been the subject of active exchanges of views and communications between the United Nations Secretariat and the Government, FMLN and COPAZ. Although some action had been taken on a large number of the recommendations, no implementation had been reported with regard to others. At a high-level meeting on 8 September 1993, in which ONUSAL participated, the Government and FMLN agreed on the need to step up the implementation process with a view to "sweeping the table clear" before the electoral campaign began.

Discovery of FMLN arms caches

The discovery in Nicaragua on 23 May 1993 of an illegal arms cache belonging to FMLN and the latter's subsequent admission that it had maintained large quantities of weapons both within and outside El Salvador marked a serious violation of the Peace Accords. The Secretary-General reported to the Council[27] that he had made continuous efforts directly and through ONUSAL to establish the facts, to ensure that all remaining clandestine caches were declared to it and their contents destroyed and to limit the repercussions on the peace process. He also reported that the right of FMLN to maintain its status as a political party in these circumstances had been questioned in some quarters. It was his view that the cancellation or suspension of FMLN's status as a political party could deal a severe blow to the peace process.

On 12 July, the Security Council took note[28] of the Secretary-General's report and noted FMLN's promise to disclose all its holdings of arms and munitions and subsequently to destroy them by 4 August 1993. The members of the Council stressed that the complete disarmament of FMLN, and the reintegration of its members into the civil, political and institutional life of the country, formed an essential part of the peace process. They shared the Secretary-General's assessment that it was an indication of the strength and irreversibility of the peace process that a serious incident of this nature had not been allowed to derail the implementation of the Peace Agreements.

Purification of the Armed Forces

On 7 July 1993, the Secretary-General was also able to confirm[29] that the Government had taken the steps it had promised to bring it into broad compliance with the recommendations of the Ad Hoc Commission on the Purification of the Armed Forces. Following the President's agreement in November 1992 to complete implementation of the Commission's recommendations, the Secretary-General had raised the matter with President Cristiani on a number of occasions. In January 1993, he wrote[30] to the Security Council, stressing that he had "from the outset been conscious of the particular difficulty and sensitivity of this aspect of the Peace Accords". While he had been at that time ready to accept as satisfactory the measures adopted and implemented by the Government with respect to 87 of 102 officers, and another officer was no longer serving, the measures adopted in respect of the 15 others were not in conformity with the Peace Accords. He had therefore asked President Cristiani to take early action in this regard. By 2 April, the Secretary-General was able to write[31] to the Council that the President's plan would, when implemented, bring the Government into broad compliance with the Ad Hoc Commission's recommendations. The Security Council welcomed[32] the Secretary-General's confirmation and said that the actions taken by the Government represented a significant achievement in the consolidation of the peace process.

Completion of a process

The Secretary-General reported[33] to the Security Council on 30 August 1993 that the overall process of verification and destruction of FMLN weapons and equipment mandated by the Peace Agreements had been completed on 18 August. The process had included two distinct phases. The first covered the period until the accidental discovery of the illegal arms cache in Managua, Nicaragua, on 23 May 1993. The second phase covered ONUSAL's operations with respect to arms discovered in the immediate aftermath of the Managua incident and those declared by FMLN in compliance with its renewed commitment to disclose all its remaining weapons. The Secretary-General also confirmed to the Council that the military structure of FMLN had been effectively dismantled and

---

[26]S/26581. [27]S/26005. [28]S/26071. [29]S/26052. [30]S/25078. [31]S/25516. [32]S/26077. [33]S/26371.

that its former combatants had been demobilized and reintegrated into the civil, institutional and political life of the country.

The Supreme Electoral Tribunal of El Salvador was also informed by the Secretary-General, in accordance with its request, that the residual arms deposits declared by FMLN had been verified and destroyed by ONUSAL. This enabled FMLN to continue as a legally recognized political party. On 5 September 1993, FMLN held its national convention at which it decided to participate in the elections and chose its candidates.

D. Electoral period

ONUSAL Electoral Division

The Electoral Division of ONUSAL was established in September 1993 with a mandate to observe the electoral process before, during and after the elections under the following terms of reference: (a) to observe that measures and decisions made by all electoral authorities were impartial and consistent with the holding of free and fair elections; (b) to observe that appropriate steps were taken to ensure that eligible voters were included in the electoral rolls, thus enabling them to exercise their right to vote; (c) to observe that mechanisms were in place effectively to prevent multiple voting, given that a complete screening of the electoral rolls prior to the elections was not feasible; (d) to observe that freedom of expression, organization, movement and assembly were respected without restrictions; (e) to observe that potential voters had sufficient knowledge of the mechanisms for participating in the election; (f) to examine, analyse and assess criticisms made, objections raised and attempts undertaken to delegitimize the electoral process and, if required, to convey such information to the Supreme Electoral Tribunal; (g) to inform the Supreme Electoral Tribunal of complaints received regarding irregularities in electoral advertising or possible interference with the electoral process; when appropriate, to request information on corrective measures taken by the Tribunal; (h) to place observers at all polling sites on election day to verify that the right to vote was fully respected.

The Division functioned with 36 Professional staff deployed throughout the Mission's 6 regional offices. Despite the rather small number of staff, the Division performed its observation duties on the basis of coordination with and close collaboration of the other components of ONUSAL.

Beginning in October 1993, the Secretary-General submitted regular reports to the Council on the activities of the ONUSAL Electoral Division and the unfolding of the electoral process. In his first report,[34] the Secretary-General stated that the Division's chief task in its initial phase had been to verify the registration of citizens on the electoral rolls and to observe the political activities of the period preceding the electoral campaign. He then explained that the institutional framework of the electoral process had been established. On 20 March 1994, four elections would be held simultaneously, namely, elections for the President, with a second round within the ensuing 30 days if no candidate had obtained an absolute majority; parliamentary elections for the 84 seats in the National Assembly on the basis of proportional representation; municipal elections in 262 mayoral districts on the basis of a simple majority; and for the Central American Parliament, treated as a single national district, for which 20 deputies would be elected on the basis of proportional representation. The Supreme Electoral Tribunal had already set up offices in all departments and municipalities of the country. The electoral law called for a Board of Vigilance consisting of representatives of all the political parties with authority to supervise the work of all Supreme Electoral Tribunal offices. Twelve political parties would take part in the elections.

Secretary-General's concerns

On 23 November 1993, the Secretary-General reported[35] to the Council that on the whole the implementation of the Peace Accords had progressed well, but it was a matter of serious concern that the electoral campaign should have begun when important elements in the Accords remained only partially implemented and when there were signs of the reappearance of some disturbing features of El Salvador's past.

[34]S/26606. [35]S/26790.

Several key aspects of the Peace Accords continued to suffer serious delays, including the programme for the transfer of lands and the reintegration programmes for ex-combatants and war disabled. One year after the agreement on the land programme, and in spite of commitments by the two parties to accelerate the process, land titles had been issued to fewer than 10 per cent of the potential beneficiaries. The main problem still related to determining who should be entitled to land. The difficulties encountered and the slow rate of progress were also discouraging potential donors from making new commitments to the programme. The Secretary-General appealed to the two parties to exercise flexibility in the belief that the remaining technical, financial and legal difficulties could be solved if the political will to do so existed.

Serious difficulties affected the operation of the National Public Security Academy and the deployment of PNC. There were also problems over the lack of a plan for phasing out the National Police and the establishment of functional divisions of PNC. While the Secretary-General acknowledged the complexity of establishing a completely new police force and transferring responsibility for public order to it in the aftermath of a long civil war, the impression had been created of a lack of commitment at some levels in the Government to the objectives of the Peace Accords. This was reflected in the denial to PNC of the necessary logistical and technical resources, the introduction into PNC of military personnel, the prolongation of the existence of the National Police and the denial to ONUSAL of the information it required for verification purposes. Concerns also persisted that the military intelligence establishment might still be involving itself with internal security matters.

As for the collection of weapons issued for the exclusive use of the personnel of the Armed Forces of El Salvador, implementation of that provision of the Peace Agreement was incomplete.

Human rights

With regard to human rights, the Secretary-General reported that important legal reforms were in progress, although many of them were only in the proposal stage. Deficiencies in judicial practice persisted. The ONUSAL Human Rights Division had continued its active verification and its programmes in support of the institutions responsible for the administration of justice and protection of human rights. Of special relevance were activities being carried out with the Supreme Court of Justice for the training of judges and magistrates and support to the Armed Forces of El Salvador in the development of a new democratic doctrine and the revision of curricula in the military academy relating to human rights and constitutional law. The Division was cooperating with the Office of the National Counsel for the Defence of Human Rights, with which it had signed an agreement aimed at the transfer to the Council's Office of experience and investigative technology upon ONUSAL's withdrawal from El Salvador. A permanent consultative mechanism existed at the highest level between the Division and the Counsel's office with a view to conducting joint verification activities in the near future.

The human rights situation had shown in some areas signs of improvement and in others an increase in serious violations. Problems relating to the right to life, individual liberty, personal integrity and due process had intensified. A number of murders and assaults in preceding weeks had raised fears about the possible resurgence of illegal armed groups with political objectives, including the "death squads". The emergence of criminal organizations of this type seriously affected the stability of the peace process by eroding confidence and security. The Human Rights Division of ONUSAL had alerted the Government to this danger and stressed the usefulness of establishing an autonomous mechanism for the investigation of these incidents. The subsequent killings of two senior FMLN leaders, a member of the governing party — the Alianza Republicana Nacionalista (ARENA) — and two former municipal officers belonging to that party brought this issue into sharper focus.

In view of these killings and the ONUSAL position, the Government created an Inter-institutional Commission to investigate this type of crime. With the agreement of FMLN, foreign experts were invited to participate in the work of a subgroup of the Commission to investigate the cases of the two senior FMLN leaders. Although this subgroup did not meet United Nations criteria for the investigation of summary executions, ONUSAL closely followed its work.

The Secretary-General conveyed[36] his concerns to the President of the Security Council on 3 November. In reply, the Council endorsed[37] the Secretary-General's decision that the Human Rights Division should work with the National Counsel for the Defence of Human Rights. It

[36]S/26689. [37]S/26695.

would do so in order to help the Government carry out the recommendation of the Commission on the Truth that a thorough investigation of illegal armed groups be undertaken immediately.

With regard to the implementation of other recommendations of the Commission on the Truth and, at the same time, of those of the ONUSAL Human Rights Division, which had been fully endorsed by the Commission, a positive step was taken when the Ministry of Justice submitted to the Legislative Assembly a number of draft laws aimed at perfecting the guarantees for due process. Also included was the proposed repeal of a law which violated some of the fundamental rights enshrined in international instruments.

Other matters

The Secretary-General reported[38] to the Council that he had asked his Special Representative to obtain the agreement of the Government and FMLN to a new timetable that would set the firmest possible dates for completing the implementation of the most important outstanding points. It was also important that, following the elections, the new Government should maintain its predecessor's commitment to implement the Accords in their entirety. In this regard, responding to an initiative by the Special Representative, six of the seven presidential candidates signed a statement in which they solemnly committed themselves to maintain the constructive evolution of the peace process and to implement all the commitments contained in the Peace Accords. The seventh candidate later explained that, although he agreed with its objectives, he had not signed the statement because he believed that it should contain more detailed commitments to specific measures.

The Secretary-General also recommended that ONUSAL continue its activities for a further mandate period through 31 May 1994. After that time, it would probably be necessary to keep the Mission in existence at a reduced strength for a few months to verify the implementation of major points in the Peace Accords.

On 30 November, the Council, by resolution 888 (1993), extended the mandate of ONUSAL through 31 May 1994. It condemned acts of violence and urged the Government and FMLN to make determined efforts to prevent political violence and accelerate compliance with their commitments under the Peace Accords. It also requested the Secretary-General to report by 1 May so that it might review ONUSAL's size and scope for the period after 31 May.

Investigation of illegal groups

In a letter[39] to the President of the Council on 7 December 1993, the Secretary-General recalled the Council's approval[40] on 5 November of his ideas on how the United Nations should help in an investigation of illegal groups. From 8 to 15 November, the Secretary-General had dispatched a mission to El Salvador, led by Under-Secretary-General for Political Affairs Marrack Goulding, which resulted in progress towards principles for the establishment of a joint group for the investigation of politically-motivated illegal armed groups. Following further consultations, the Joint Group was established on 8 December. Its membership consisted of the National Counsel for the Defence of Human Rights, the Director of the ONUSAL Human Rights Division and two representatives of the Government of El Salvador nominated by the President. The Security Council informed[41] the Secretary-General that it supported the principles for the establishment of the group as well as the Secretary-General's role in ensuring the effectiveness and credibility of investigations. The Joint Group presented its report[42] on 28 July 1994. The report contained the Group's findings regarding politically-motivated violence in El Salvador and its recommendations for the strengthening of the investigative structure of PNC and for appropriate reforms within the judicial system.

Run-up to elections

The electoral campaign opened officially on 20 November 1993 for the election of the President and on 20 January 1994 for the election of the Legislative Assembly. The campaign for the municipal elections would begin officially on 20 February 1994. During the period from November 1993 to January 1994, ONUSAL's Electoral Division focused on observing voter registration, monitoring the election campaign and providing assistance in the drawing up of an electoral roll.

The Division held joint meetings on a regular basis with the Supreme Electoral Tribunal, the Board of Vigilance, made up of representatives of all political parties, and the party campaign managers with a view to solving any possible problem arising during the electoral process. In addition, a system had been set up to receive and process allegations of violations of the Electoral Code. These allegations were then transmitted in writing to the Supreme Electoral Tribunal, which

[38]S/26790. [39]S/26865. [40]S/26695. [41]S/26866. [42]S/1994/989.

was asked to report on the follow-up action taken.[43]

During the campaign period, ONUSAL teams made an average of 9 observation visits to each of the country's 262 towns, or more than 2,350 visits, and dispatched a total of 3,700 patrols. ONUSAL promoted discussions with a view to obtaining the signing of codes of conduct by political parties. Pacts of this kind were signed by all contending parties in each of the 14 departments of El Salvador as well as in a number of municipalities. On 10 March, at ONUSAL headquarters, all presidential candidates signed a declaration in which they declared their rejection of violence and their commitment to respect the results of the elections and to comply with the Peace Accords. The Electoral Division held periodic meetings with political parties at the central and local levels in order to discuss ongoing problems and viable solutions. At these meetings, technical proposals to improve the registration process were discussed and evaluated.[44]

ONUSAL teams attended more than 800 events, mainly political meetings and demonstrations, and monitored political advertising through the mass media. Complaints of irregularities in electoral publicity and other aspects of the electoral process were transmitted in a timely manner by ONUSAL to the Supreme Electoral Tribunal in accordance with the terms of reference of the Electoral Division.

Communication with the Tribunal included not only complaints presented to ONUSAL by claimants from different sources, mostly political parties, but also reports on problems identified in the field by ONUSAL observers. In some cases, problems were solved through action by the Tribunal. In this connection, ONUSAL made recommendations to the Tribunal as appropriate. Some 300 complaints were presented to ONUSAL during the campaign period dealing with arbitrary or illegitimate action by public authorities (23 per cent), acts of intimidation (21 per cent), destruction of propaganda materials (18 per cent), aggression (9 per cent), murder (7 per cent) and miscellaneous complaints (22 per cent).

Election day

Election day was 20 March 1994, with the participation of an estimated 1.5 million voters, or 55 per cent of persons on the electoral rolls. ONUSAL monitored proceedings from the time the polling stations were set up until the completion of the count by deploying nearly 900 observers of 56 nationalities who covered all polling centres with teams of between 2 and 30 observers. This massive presence of ONUSAL made it possible throughout election day to resolve countless practical problems of organization of the voting. The observers collected information on the events of election day on more than 7,000 forms (one for each of the 6,984 polling stations and the 355 polling centres) which were subsequently compiled by the Electoral Division and which constituted the basic documentary source for evaluating the conduct of the elections.

ONUSAL made a quick count based on a random sample of 291 polling stations, making it possible to have a reliable projection of the outcome of the presidential election two hours after the polls closed. The information was transmitted by the ONUSAL Chief of Mission to the Supreme Electoral Tribunal. The difference between the quick count and the provisional results provided by the Tribunal was 0.5 per cent.

On 21 March, the Special Representative of the Secretary-General stated[45] that, in the light of the information gathered by the observers on election day, and in view of the systematic observation of the electoral process over the preceding six months, ONUSAL believed that in general the elections had taken place under appropriate conditions in terms of freedom, competitiveness and security. Despite serious flaws regarding organization and transparency, the elections could be considered acceptable.

In his general assessment[46] of election day, the Secretary-General noted that participation, while substantially higher than in earlier elections, had been lower than many had hoped. He attributed this, at least in part, to some structural problems of the system, including the complexities of Salvadorian registration and the limited number of polling centres. Pending announcement of the official results, the provisional count indicated that no candidate had obtained the required absolute majority in the presidential race. A second round would therefore be necessary, probably on 24 April. It would be some time before the results of the elections for the Legislative Assembly and the municipalities were known, although available data seemed to indicate that one political party, ARENA, would have a relative majority in the Assembly and that it had won most of the mayoral districts.

The Secretary-General stated that the general conduct of the electoral process and the

[43]S/1994/179. [44]S/1994/304. [45]S/1994/375. [46]S/1994/375.

campaign had many positive aspects: massive expansion of the electoral rolls; participation by the political parties throughout the process and at all levels of the electoral authorities; peaceful exercise of the right to organize, of the right to freedom of expression and of the right of assembly; publicity by the parties in all the media; conduct of campaign activities without violent incidents; and proper functioning on the part of the security forces and armed forces.

He also pointed out that no party had rejected the results of the presidential election, and ONUSAL observers had not recorded any fraudulent acts that could have had a significant impact on the outcome. In general, the Assembly and municipal elections had been conducted under the same conditions as the presidential election. However, the smaller size of constituencies at this electoral level, which meant that problems affecting a small number of votes could have a significant impact on the outcome, had given rise to a number of challenges. Such challenges were being dealt with in the manner laid down by the legislation, and ONUSAL would continue to observe how cases evolved until definitive solutions were found.

First round results

The official results[47] of the first round of the presidential election, based on a count by the Supreme Electoral Tribunal, were as follows: ARENA: 49.03 per cent; Coalition Convergencia Demócratica (CD)-FMLN-Movimiento Nacional Revolucionaria (MNR): 24.9 per cent; Partido Demócrata Cristiano (PDC): 17.87 per cent; Partido Conciliación Nacional (PCN): 5.39 per cent; Partido Movimiento de Unidad (PMU): 2.41 per cent; Movimiento de Solidaridad Nacional (MSN): 1.06 per cent; and Movimiento Auténtico Cristiano (MAC): 0.83 per cent. The 84 seats of the Legislative Assembly went to: ARENA: 39; FMLN: 21; PDC: 18; PCN: 4; CD: 1; PMU: 1. The 262 mayoralties went to: ARENA: 206; PDC: 29; FMLN: 16; PCN: 10; MAC: 1. ONUSAL had assigned a team of 40 specialized observers to monitor the official count of the votes in the Supreme Electoral Tribunal.

Continuing concerns

Meanwhile, on 28 March 1994, the Secretary-General addressed a letter[48] to the President of the Security Council in which he raised continuing concerns regarding the implementation of certain aspects of the original Peace Accords. It was essential to have an updated agreement between the parties on a timetable for the implementation of pending matters so that the process should suffer no further delays during the transition to the new Government.

According to the Secretary-General, little progress had been achieved in certain aspects related to public security. PNC was still being denied resources, there was no clear accounting of the transfer to PNC of military personnel, and there seemed to be a desire to de-link the deployment of PNC from the phasing out of the National Police. ONUSAL was being hindered from properly carrying out its verification responsibilities in this regard.

Notwithstanding progress in the reintegration of FMLN into the political life of El Salvador, much remained to be done in other critical areas. The transfer of land, through which most former combatants and supporters of FMLN were to be reintegrated was the most important of these; the process was well short of the agreed goal. Also delayed was the implementation of the recommendations of the Commission on the Truth that required constitutional amendments, particularly with regard to the decentralization of the powers and competence of the Supreme Court. The Secretary-General stated that urgent action to implement those amendments was needed.

On 7 April, responding to the Secretary-General's report of 31 March and his letter of 28 March in a presidential statement,[49] the Council congratulated the people of El Salvador on the historic elections and called for the correction of shortcomings reported in the first round of voting. It also called for the full implementation of the Peace Accords and shared the concerns expressed by the Secretary-General in his letter.

Second round of voting

Since no candidate in the presidential election obtained the required absolute majority, a second round of voting was scheduled for 24 April 1994 between the two candidates with the highest number of votes, namely, Mr. Armando Calderón Sol of ARENA and Mr. Rubén Zamora of the CD-FMLN-MNR coalition. Stating that the anomalies recorded in the first round should be eliminated in the second, the Secretary-General reported[50] that ONUSAL had expressed its views to the Tribunal regarding measures to deal with the shortcomings. Recommendations related to

---

[47]S/1994/486. [48]S/1994/361. [49]S/PRST/1994/15. [50]S/1994/375.

discrepancies in the electoral rolls; reform of the Electoral Code; the number of polling centres; the training of electoral personnel; sufficient public transport; illegal electoral publicity; and a public information campaign. In monitoring the implementation of these measures, the Electoral Division posted observers in five areas of work: registration, computation, printing, electoral project unit and training. In addition, ONUSAL observers were present at campaign activities during the two-week campaign preceding the election. Up to 18 April, the campaign was conducted in a tense atmosphere. After that date, however, the tone of the campaign improved, following signature by the two presidential candidates of a joint statement expressing their commitment to the future governance of El Salvador, their determination to conduct a decent campaign and their pledge to make every effort during the following two years to overhaul the electoral system.

On voting day, 24 April, ONUSAL deployed 900 observers in all the voting centres in the country, from the opening of the polling stations until completion of the first count of the votes from the ballot boxes. On 25 April, ONUSAL issued a statement[51] in which it reported that in general, the election had proceeded without serious incidents affecting public order or ballot-tampering. There were also signs of a clear improvement in the conditions in which the election was held, such as the management of the voting centres, the deployment of guides to direct voters to their voting places, identification on the electoral register, free public transport and early information on the night of 24 April concerning the election results. All those factors, the statement

went on, made it possible to have a better-organized election day thanks to the joint efforts of the two presidential candidates, the political institutions which nominated them, the Supreme Electoral Tribunal and the donor countries.

At the same time, ONUSAL registered a number of irregularities. Some polling stations were not opened or closed on time and both parties complained of illegal campaigning inside the voting centres. It was also reported that a considerable number of citizens had been unable to cast their ballots despite having voting cards.

The preliminary vote count on 24 April showed Mr. Calderón Sol as apparent President-elect. His opponent, Mr. Rubén Zamora, acknowledged the victory of his adversary. In his public statement on the night of 24 April, the President-elect reaffirmed his commitment to the process of peace and reconciliation in El Salvador.

Final results

The results[52] of the second round of the presidential elections, according to the final count by the Supreme Electoral Tribunal, were announced on 27 April 1994. They were as follows: ARENA — 818,264 votes (68.35 per cent); Coalition — 378,980 votes (31.65 per cent); making a total of 1,197,244 valid votes. The total number of votes cast was 1,246,220, of which 3,467 were challenged, 40,048 were invalid and 5,461 were abstentions. ONUSAL's quick count, available two hours after the polls had closed on 24 April, was based on a sample of 294 polling stations. It had indicated 67.88 per cent for ARENA and 32.12 per cent for the Coalition.

E. Completion of the mandate

New timetable for unresolved issues

According to the agreed timetable, almost all aspects of the Peace Accords were to have been implemented before the new Government assumed office on 1 June 1994. The main exceptions were the deployment of PNC and the demobilization of the National Police, which were to be completed on 28 July and 31 October 1994 respectively. As for the land transfer programme, the Secretary-General reported[53] to the Security

Council on 11 May 1994 that it would have to be extended into 1995.

While a vestigial presence of ONUSAL had been expected for the period after 1 June 1994, serious shortcomings in the implementation of the Accords meant that on 1 June 1994 much would remain to be done, in spite of all the efforts to make up for lost time. The Secretary-General, believing that the United Nations had a continuing

[51]CA/89. [52]S/1994/536. [53]S/1994/561.

responsibility to honour its undertaking to verify compliance with the Peace Accords, held the view that the mandate of ONUSAL should be extended for a further six months, that is, until 30 November 1994. During this time, the Secretary-General would continue to reduce the size of ONUSAL as rapidly as implementation of the outstanding agreements permitted. He appealed to the Government of El Salvador, both the outgoing and incoming administrations, and to all others concerned, to make the effort necessary to ensure that their remaining commitments were implemented with the least possible delay.

On 24 May, the Secretary-General informed[54] the Security Council that on 19 May the two Salvadorian parties had reached agreement on a new "Timetable for the implementation of the most important outstanding agreements". He also informed the Council that the President-elect of El Salvador, Mr. Calderón Sol, had reiterated to the Secretary-General his personal commitment to the terms of the Peace Accords and his desire to see those Accords implemented without delay.

ONUSAL's final months

The Security Council extended the mandate of ONUSAL on two further occasions. Under the terms recommended by the Secretary-General in his report of 11 May 1994,[55] the Council, by its resolution 920 (1994) of 26 May, extended the mandate until 30 November. Then, under the terms of the Secretary-General's report[56] of 31 October 1994, the Council extended the mandate for one final period until 30 April 1995 by its resolution 961 (1994) of 23 November 1994.

During the last phases of its activity, ONUSAL emphasized institution-building and strengthening, and the Secretary-General used maximum suasion, both directly and through his Special Representative, to remind the parties of the international community's expectation that each would honour its commitments in full and promptly. In the period following the inauguration of President Calderón Sol on 1 June 1994, progress achieved in implementing the 19 May timetable, in particular those areas most relevant to the strengthening and modernization of democratic institutions, reflected the new Government's decision to establish firmly the rule of law in El Salvador, the Secretary-General reported[57] on 26 August. The high-level governmental team responsible for follow-up activities at the political level had been maintained, the fortnightly tripartite meetings envisaged by the 19 May 1994 agree-

ment were held regularly, and joint working groups on various outstanding issues continued to function. The Government had expressed its determination to take decisive action against all those involved in criminal activities within the public security apparatus. COPAZ and several of its subcommissions continued to function, and the election by consensus of the new Supreme Court of Justice was a laudable decision. The new Vice-Minister for Public Security and the new Director-General of PNC were appointed.

The Secretary-General also reported that, beginning on 1 May 1994, the Salvadorian Legislative Assembly had functioned with the participation of FMLN as the country's second political force, as well as with that of other political parties. In addition, the Government and FMLN signed a joint declaration[58] on 4 October 1994 reconfirming their commitment to complete implementation of the Peace Accords.

By the time of his report[59] of 24 March 1995, the Secretary-General was able to inform the Security Council that, following the demobilization of the National Police in December 1994, PNC had taken over practically all security functions from the former security forces. PNC then had a strength of slightly more than 7,000 agents and approximately 220 middle- and high-level officers, all of whom were graduates of the National Public Security Academy. Although a new Supreme Court made up of eminent professionals had been set up in 1994, reforms to ensure that its decisions were effectively implemented remained pending, included the adoption of a new criminal code and criminal procedures code, the decentralization of functions then carried out by the Supreme Court, the elimination of extrajudicial confessions, and the facilitation of *habeas corpus* proceedings. The National Counsel for the Defence of Human Rights had established offices in all departments but required further strengthening. Helped by political stability, the Salvadorian economy also continued to recover.

Although the conditions necessary to ensure the full and final implementation of the Peace Accords seemed to be in place, there continued to be a number of outstanding problems. There were indications of intelligence activity carried out by certain members of the armed forces contrary to their Constitutional mandate, and there were delays in the programme to transfer land to former combatants of the Armed Forces and of FMLN and

[54]S/1994/612.　[55]S/1994/561 and Add.1.　[56]S/1994/1212 and Add.1.
[57]S/1994/1000.　[58]S/1994/1144.　[59]S/1995/220.

to landholders. By the end of August 1994, the total number of beneficiaries had not yet been determined, and the number of persons who had received title to the land was still below the target for the end of 1993 which both parties had accepted as feasible. The virtual paralysis of the programme had given rise to tension. Although there was marked progress at the end of 1994, the programme again came to a halt in January 1995 only to be followed by a slow improvement. By March 1995, only 45 per cent of the potential beneficiaries had received title.

With regard to the transition to PNC, the process had taken longer and been more difficult that originally conceived. Resistance and lack of cooperation from certain sectors had been evident, and there had been reluctance to dismantle the old military command structure and the National Police. The decision in March 1994 to use military patrols to deter crime in rural areas was not in compliance with the constitutional procedures. A law was necessary to specify the exceptional circumstances under which the Armed Forces could be used for public security. Furthermore, legal voids still affected the functioning of PNC, and the machinery to regulate it required strengthening.

Most officials still felt free to ignore the non-binding recommendations of the National Counsel for the Defence of Human Rights, which had not yet taken real advantage of its power to seek judicial remedies. In regard to military weapons in the hands of civilians or State institutions, ONUSAL closely monitored the adoption and implementation of legislative and administrative measures taken to collect those weapons. Nevertheless, while a limited number of registered arms still needed to be collected, the major problem lay with the unknown but large number of weapons of which there was no record. Voluntary surrender had been negligible.

Thus, at the close of the Mission, various important obligations were pending. The strengthening of PNC, and particularly of its investigative capacity and internal disciplinary mechanisms, was essential to provide protection from crime and to punish it in an effective manner, while at the same time ensuring that public security fell within civilian competence, as provided in the agreements. The continued purification and modernization of the judiciary was crucial to the protection of the rule of law and the eradication of impunity. The still pending adoption and ratification of international human rights instruments, as recommended by the Commission on the Truth, would extend the benefits of protection mechanisms in

the event of possible future abuses. Efforts to ensure that the pending reforms of electoral legislation were approved would be needed if they were to be in place before new elections. The land programme continued to be a source of serious concern, as well as agreement on modalities for the transfer of human settlements. In light of those aspects of the Peace Agreements still pending, the Secretary-General recommended that COPAZ, as the national institution for verifying implementation of the Accords, should remain in existence.

Drawing down of ONUSAL

In his report[60] of 26 August 1994, the Secretary-General stated that he had already reduced the military component of the Mission to 12 military observers and 7 medical personnel from a total of 30 on 1 May 1994. By 1 October, he expected further reductions. The Secretary-General intended to reduce the size of the Police Division to 145 by 1 October, excluding 15 police instructors posted to the National Police Academy. He also intended to begin the progressive phasing out of the substantive civilian staff of ONUSAL. By 30 November 1994, ONUSAL had a strength of 3 military observers and 31 police observers.

Reporting to the Security Council on 24 March 1995, the Secretary-General said that preparations to dismantle ONUSAL were well under way. The transfer of vehicles, equipment, furniture and supplies to other Missions and United Nations organizations had commenced in June 1994. By February 1995, nearly all assets not directly required at that time had been disposed of by transfer or commercial sale. After the official closure of ONUSAL at the end of April 1995, a small team of civilian personnel would remain to deal with outstanding claims and to handle the final disposal of property and equipment.

MINUSAL

In his report to the Security Council of 31 October 1994, the Secretary-General had noted the widely held view that the termination of ONUSAL in April 1995 should not mark the end of United Nations efforts to consolidate peace in El Salvador. He was then invited[61] by the Council to prepare, in consultation with competent specialized agencies, regional organizations and Members States, modalities for further assistance to El Salvador for the period after 30 April 1995.

[60]S/1994/1000. [61]S/RES/961 (1994).

When he reported on 24 March 1995, the Secretary-General recalled that a number of commitments under the Peace Accords remained unfulfilled. Those commitments pertained to aspects of such importance that they "will call into question the irreversibility of the peace process as a whole as long as they are unfulfilled". Some of the issues were "potentially explosive and need to be defused urgently".

On the basis of these problems, he said, "a strong case could have been made for maintaining ONUSAL after 30 April 1995" and the Secretary-General had given serious consideration to that possibility. He had refrained from recommending it "in the light of clear indications from members of the Council that the time had come to bring ONUSAL to a close". It was against that background that he had informed[62] the Security Council on 6 February 1995 that "following the withdrawal of ONUSAL he proposed to leave behind a small team that would conduct the remaining verification and good offices responsibilities of the United Nations". The Council welcomed[63] the Secretary-General's proposal.

The United Nations Mission in El Salvador (MINUSAL) began its work on 1 May 1995, led by the Secretary-General's Special Representative, Mr. Enrique ter Horst. In order to support the Mission's activities, the Secretary-General established the Trust Fund for MINUSAL.

F. Composition of ONUSAL

From the establishment of ONUSAL on 20 May 1991 until it completed its mandate on 30 April 1995, there were three successive Special Representatives of the Secretary-General, who also served as Chief of Mission of ONUSAL. The first was Mr. Iqbal Riza (Pakistan) who served from the inception of ONUSAL until March 1993. Mr. Augusto Ramirez-Ocampo (Colombia) then served in the post until March 1994, when he was succeeded by Mr. Enrique ter Horst (Venezuela). At its peak strength in February 1992, ONUSAL's Military Division, headed by Brigadier-General Victor Suanzes Pardo (Spain), comprised 368 military observers. The authorized strength of the Police Division, headed by General Homero Vaz Bresque (Uruguay), was 631, although this figure was never realized. As the peace process progressed, the strength of both Divisions was gradually reduced. By 30 November 1994, the military component, then headed by Colonel Luis Alejandre Sintes (Spain) was down to 3 military observers, and the Police Division, by then headed by Comisario Principal Alfredo Carballo (Spain), had a strength of 31.

ONUSAL military observers were provided by Brazil, Canada, Colombia, Ecuador, India, Ireland, Spain, Sweden and Venezuela. In addition, medical officers came from Argentina and Spain. Police observers from Austria, Brazil, Chile, Colombia, France, Guyana, Italy, Mexico, Spain and Sweden served with ONUSAL.

The Electoral Division, under the direction of Mr. Rafael Lopez Pintor, consisted of 36 core observers. During the elections of 20 March and 24 April 1994, the number of observers increased to 900.

The Human Rights Division was staffed by some 30 international civil servants. It was initially headed by Mr. Philippe Texier, who was succeeded in late 1992 by Mr. Diego Garcia-Sayan and by Mr. Reed Broody in 1994. Many of the Division's personnel were recruited from human rights organizations for the ONUSAL mission.

[62] S/1995/143. [63] S/1995/144.

G. Financial aspects

Costs for the operation of ONUSAL were apportioned among the Member States of the United Nations as expenses of the Organization. Expenditures amounted to $107,003,650.

H. Conclusions

The Secretary-General appraised[64] the United Nations undertaking in El Salvador as innovative in a variety of ways. The Organization had played a central role in the negotiation of the Peace Accords from start to finish and had overseen a multidimensional peace-keeping and peace-building operation in whose design it had played a key part. Although he reported[65] that a number of commitments remained unfulfilled before the Salvadorian peace process could be pronounced a success, there was, nevertheless, "much reason for satisfaction at what has been accomplished by the Salvadorians during this time. ONUSAL can take credit for having helped the Salvadorians to take giant strides away from a violent and closed society towards a democratic order where institutions for the protection of human rights and free discourse are being consolidated". At the end of its mandate, the United Nations would be closing down "a paradigmatic, multifunctional peace-keeping operation 45 months after the opening of the pioneering human rights-monitoring mission that was its initial stage and 39 months after the formal cease-fire that accompanied full deployment".

In its resolution 991 (1995) of 28 April 1995, the Security Council paid tribute to the accomplishments of ONUSAL, under the authority of the Secretary-General and his Special Representatives, and recognized with satisfaction that El Salvador had evolved from a country riven by conflict into a democratic and peaceful nation.

[64]S/1994/1212. [65]S/1995/220.

Part VII
Cambodia

Chapter 22

United Nations Advance Mission in Cambodia (UNAMIC)

United Nations Transitional Authority in Cambodia (UNTAC)

G. Electoral period (April–May 1993)
Campaigning begins
The elections

H. Post-electoral period (June–September 1993)
Withdrawal plans
Mandate ends
United Nations liaison team in Cambodia

I. A brief review of UNTAC
Electoral component
UNTAC human rights role
Military component
Mine clearance
Civil administration
Civilian police
Repatriation
Information/education activities
Rehabilitation
UNTAC Composition
Financial Aspects
Conclusion

Chapter 22

United Nations Advance Mission in Cambodia (UNAMIC)

United Nations Transitional Authority in Cambodia (UNTAC)

A. Background

The Agreements on a Comprehensive Political Settlement of the Cambodia Conflict were signed in Paris on 23 October 1991 at the final meeting of the Paris Conference on Cambodia. They were the culmination of more than a decade of negotiations in which the United Nations had been closely involved from the outset. The Agreements, also known as the Paris Agreements, invited the Security Council to establish the United Nations Transitional Authority in Cambodia (UNTAC) and to provide it with the mandate set out in the Agreements. The Council fully supported the Paris Agreements in its resolution 718 (1991) of 31 October 1991 and requested the Secretary-General to prepare a detailed plan of implementation.

In signing the Agreements along with 18 other States, Cambodia took a vital step in its emergence from years of internal conflict and relative isolation. In the 1950s, French colonialism had given way to a period of political instability and civil conflict, exacerbated in the 1960s and 1970s by the spillover of the war in Viet Nam, including bombardment by United States forces. From 1975 to 1979, the country suffered a vastly destructive regime under Pol Pot. The cities were emptied of their populations and the general mass of people were subjected to harsh labour and political re-education. It is estimated that more than 1 million people died in a brutal process of "social reconstruction". Pol Pot's regime — the "Khmer Rouge" — was ended by the intervention of Vietnamese troops in late 1978 and the installation of a new government in Phnom Penh.

But the battle for control of the country continued. Three factions opposed the Phnom Penh government: the United National Front for an Independent, Neutral, Peaceful and Cooperative Cambodia (FUNCINPEC), led by Prince Norodom Sihanouk; the Khmer People's Liberation Front (KPNLF); and the Party of Democratic Kampuchea (PDK), also known as the Khmer Rouge. In 1982, the three factions formed a coalition party under the name Coalition Government of Democratic Kampuchea, later called the National Government of Cambodia, and led by Prince Sihanouk. The coalition occupied the seat reserved for Cambodia at the United Nations from 1982 until the signing of the Paris Agreements.

The Phnom Penh government — the People's Republic of Kampuchea — was backed by Viet Nam and the Soviet Union, and fielded an army thought to total approximately 50,000. It controlled some 80 to 90 per cent of the country. The coalition was backed by China, the United States and the Association of South East Asian Nations (ASEAN) (Brunei Darussalam, Indonesia, Malaysia, Philippines, Singapore and Thailand). It had combined forces of between 50,000 and 60,000 and operated from areas along the border with Thailand and in north-western Cambodia.

International Conference on Kampuchea

The Security Council first considered the question of Cambodia[1] in early 1979, following

[1] S/PV.2108.

the intervention by Viet Nam, but could take no action for lack of agreement among its permanent members (China, France, Soviet Union, United Kingdom, United States). The General Assembly then took up the matter, and in November 1979, as it did annually for most of the decade that followed, called[2] for the withdrawal of foreign forces from Cambodia and self-determination for its people. The Assembly also welcomed efforts begun by the Secretary-General to coordinate relief assistance to the Cambodian people, who in this turbulent period, fled their country in large numbers. Over three hundred thousand found refuge in Thailand.

In July 1981, an International Conference on Kampuchea was convened by the General Assembly.[3] Although Viet Nam did not attend, it did accept the offer of good offices by the Secretary-General. Mr. Rafeeuddin Ahmed, the Secretary-General's Special Representative for Humanitarian Affairs in South-East Asia, visited the area many times during this period.

By 1985, the Secretary-General had identified, through quiet diplomacy, a set of objectives[4] to be achieved by negotiation. These were elaborated into proposals for action following a December 1987 meeting between Prince Sihanouk and the Prime Minister of the Phnom Penh government, Mr. Hun Sen. That meeting took place at the invitation of the Government of France which, with Indonesia, assumed a lead role in the ongoing effort to end the war in Cambodia.

Paris Conference

In July 1988, the representatives of the Phnom Penh government and the three Cambodian opposition parties met informally in Indonesia. That first direct contact, followed by another in February 1989, set the scene for the Paris Conference on Cambodia. The Conference was held from 30 July to 30 August 1989 and was attended by the representatives of all four Cambodian parties and of 18 other States: Australia, Brunei Darussalam, Canada, China, France, India, Indonesia, Japan, Laos, Malaysia, Philippines, Singapore, Soviet Union, Thailand, United Kingdom, United States, Viet Nam and Zimbabwe. Zimbabwe was then chairman of the Non-Aligned Movement. Secretary-General Javier Pérez de Cuéllar was present, as was his Special Representative for Humanitarian Affairs. France and Indonesia co-chaired the Conference which, although mapping out a broad strategy to move towards peace, was unable to agree on a comprehensive settlement. The major

unresolved issues were the power-sharing formula during a transitional period before elections and the drafting of a new constitution, and the role of PDK. The conference was suspended without being able to agree on an international mechanism to verify the withdrawal of Vietnamese troops from Cambodia. That withdrawal, as announced[5] by Viet Nam, was undertaken without international verification in September 1989. In Phnom Penh, the government of Mr. Hun Sen continued in power. Since May 1989, that government had been known as the Government of the State of Cambodia (SOC).

Intense diplomatic activity

There was intense diplomatic activity in the first half of 1990. The Cambodian parties met in Indonesia in February 1990 and in Tokyo in June 1990. In addition, a series of consultations was undertaken by the five permanent members of the Security Council beginning in January 1990. The basis for their discussions was a proposal put forward by Australia the previous October. After the first meeting on 15 and 16 January 1990, the Five issued a summary of conclusions[6] in which they agreed to be guided by the following principles in working for a resolution of the Cambodia problem:

(1) No acceptable solution could be achieved by force of arms. (2) An enduring peace could only be achieved through a comprehensive political settlement, including the verified withdrawal of foreign forces, a cease-fire and cessation of outside military assistance. (3) The goal should be self-determination for the Cambodian people through free, fair and democratic elections. (4) All accepted an enhanced United Nations role in the resolution of the Cambodian problem. (5) There was an urgent need to speed up diplomatic efforts to achieve a settlement. (6) The complete withdrawal of foreign forces must be verified by the United Nations. (7) The five would welcome an early resumption of a constructive dialogue among the Cambodian factions which was essential to facilitating the transition process, which should not be dominated by any one of them. (8) An effective United Nations presence would be required during the transition period in order to assure internal security. (9) A Special Representative of the United Nations Secretary-General was needed in Cambodia to supervise United

[2]A/RES/34/22. [3]A/RES/35/6. [4]A/40/759. [5]A/44/214-S/20572, annex. [6]S/21087.

Nations activities during a transition period culminating in the inauguration of a democratically elected government. (10) The scale of the United Nations operation should be consistent with the successful implementation of a Cambodian settlement, and its planning and execution should take account of the heavy financial burden that might be placed on Member States. (11) Free and fair elections must be conducted under direct United Nations administration. (12) The elections must be conducted in a neutral political environment in which no party would gain advantage. (13) The five permanent members committed themselves to honouring the results of free and fair elections. (14) All Cambodians should enjoy the same rights, freedoms and opportunities to participate in the election process. (15) A Supreme National Council might be the repository of Cambodian sovereignty during the transition process. (16) Questions involving Cambodian sovereignty should be resolved with the agreement of the Cambodian parties. (17) The Five supported all responsible efforts by regional parties to achieve a comprehensive political settlement, and would remain in close touch with them with a view to reconvening the Paris Conference at an appropriate time.

P-5 proposal

The United Nations, in preparation for a peace-keeping operation in Cambodia, sent several fact-finding missions to the country to study its devastated administrative, economic and social infrastructure and the requirements for the repatriation of refugees. The findings helped shape an August 1990 proposal[7] from the five permanent members of the Security Council for a comprehensive settlement in Cambodia. The proposal was accepted by the four Cambodian parties at an "Informal Meeting on Cambodia" in Jakarta on 10 September. They agreed to constitute a Supreme National Council (SNC) of 12 members and to accept Prince Sihanouk's proposal that the 12 members might elect a chairman. The Security Council in resolution 668 (1990) of 20 September endorsed the proposal. Indonesia and France then took charge of the negotiations to fill out the framework proposal into a peace agreement. At a meeting in Paris from 21 to 23 December 1990, they presented the draft agreements[8] on a comprehensive political settlement to the 12 members of SNC. After some discussion, and the submission of an explanatory note[9] by the five permanent members, SNC accepted the draft. It was then presented to Thailand and Viet Nam in February 1991.

Cease-fire

On 22 April 1991, the Secretary-General appealed[10] jointly with France and Indonesia for a temporary cessation of hostilities in Cambodia as a gesture of good faith. As a result, a cease-fire went into effect on a voluntary basis and was generally observed over the next several months as negotiations continued. Meeting in July, SNC decided to elect Prince Sihanouk as its chairman. It also decided to send a letter signed by Prince Sihanouk asking the United Nations to dispatch a survey mission to Cambodia. In response, on 8 August, the Secretary-General informed[11] the Security Council of his intention to proceed with the necessary arrangements. On 26 August, Prince Sihanouk wrote[12] to the Secretary-General asking "to have at least 200 United Nations personnel sent to Cambodia as 'observers' in September 1991 in order to assist SNC in controlling the cease-fire and the cessation of foreign military assistance, as a first step within the framework of a comprehensive political settlement."

B. UNAMIC

The Secretary-General reiterated[13] to the Security Council on 30 September 1991 that the United Nations could help in maintaining the cease-fire by deploying in Cambodia a small advance mission consisting mainly of military liaison officers in order to help the parties to address and resolve any violations or alleged violations of the cease-fire. Such an advance mission could be envisaged as the first stage of the good offices mission foreseen in the draft peace agreements. On that basis, the Secretary-General recommended that the

[7]A/45/472-S/21689. [8]A/46/61-S/22059, annex II. [9]A/46/61-S/22059, annex III. [10]A/46/161-S/22552. [11]S/22945. [12]A/46/494-S/23066. [13]S/23097.

Security Council authorize the United Nations Advance Mission in Cambodia (UNAMIC), to become operational as soon as the Paris Agreements were signed. UNAMIC would be absorbed into UNTAC once UNTAC was established by the Security Council and its budget adopted by the General Assembly.

The Secretary-General recommended that UNAMIC operate under the authority of the Security Council and United Nations command. The mission would be led in the field by a civilian Chief Liaison Officer, who, in addition to duties in relation to UNAMIC, would have responsibility for maintaining contact with SNC on preparations for the deployment of UNTAC and on other matters related to the role of the United Nations. A Senior Military Liaison Officer, appointed with the consent of the Security Council, would report to the Secretary-General through the Chief Liaison Officer. The Secretary-General would, in turn, "report regularly to the Security Council on the operations of UNAMIC. All matters that might affect the nature or the continued effective functioning of the Mission would be referred to the Security Council for its decision".

UNAMIC would deploy small teams of military personnel with experience in training civilian populations on how to avoid injury from mines or booby traps. Initially, the teams would give priority to populations living in or close to areas of recent military confrontation. The Secretary-General envisaged the eventual expansion of the programme, in close consultation with the United Nations High Commissioner for Refugees (UNHCR), to repatriation routes, reception centres and resettlement areas for refugees. These activities would need to be carefully coordinated with the mine-awareness programme begun earlier in 1991 for Cambodian refugees and displaced persons in the camps along the Cambodia-Thailand border.

UNAMIC was estimated to require 8 civilian liaison staff, 50 military liaison officers, 20 other military personnel to form the mine awareness unit, and approximately 75 international and 75 local civilian support staff. In addition, there would be a military communications unit of some 40 persons, provided by Australia as a voluntary contribution. An air unit of four utility helicopters and one fixed-wing aircraft would also be needed. The deployment was planned in two stages. In the first, the head of mission, accompanied by his chief aides, would arrive in Phnom Penh within ten days of the signature of the agreements on a comprehensive political settlement. The second

phase would begin as soon as the necessary vehicles, generators, accommodation, and other items had been procured and delivered to the general military headquarters of each of the Cambodian parties, whereupon the military liaison teams would be deployed. The mine-awareness unit would be deployed as soon as possible after that.

The Secretary-General also informed[14] the Security Council that, operationally, UNAMIC would be headquartered in Phnom Penh, deploying military liaison units to the general military headquarters of each of the Cambodian parties. In addition, teams would be deployed to two forward positions, Battambang and Siem Reap, which were also to be main bases for the mine-awareness programme. UNAMIC would require an effective and independent round-the-clock communications system, open to the Cambodian parties so as to facilitate communications between them and help resolve problems with the maintenance of the cease-fire. The Secretary-General expected full deployment between mid-November and mid-December 1991. He estimated the first six-months of operations, including start-up and capital equipment costs, would run to $19.9 million.

UNAMIC becomes operational

The Security Council, in its resolution 717 (1991) of 16 October 1991, authorized UNAMIC as recommended by the Secretary-General. UNAMIC became operational on 9 November 1991 when Mr. A.H.S. Ataul Karim (Bangladesh) assumed his functions as Chief Liaison Officer of UNAMIC in Phnom Penh. Brigadier-General Michel Loridon (France), Senior Military Liaison Officer, assumed command of the military elements of UNAMIC on 12 November and, on the same day, an air operations unit contributed by France arrived in Phnom Penh. Officers and other military personnel were contributed by Algeria, Argentina, Australia, Austria, Belgium, Canada, China, France, Germany, Ghana, India, Indonesia, Ireland, Malaysia, New Zealand, Pakistan, Poland, Senegal, Tunisia, Soviet Union, United Kingdom, United States and Uruguay.

On 27 November 1991, the PDK delegation arrived in Phnom Penh. It was forced to flee, however, after demonstrations against the delegation became violent, and its members were attacked. On 3 December, SNC held an emergency meeting in Pataya, Thailand to discuss, among

[14]S/23097/Add.1.

other things, the security measures for SNC members.

Demonstrations against corruption in the Phnom Penh administration, which started around 17 December, also became violent, and the security situation in the city deteriorated during the next few days. Although the SNC meeting scheduled for 21 December did not materialize, Prince Sihanouk chaired a special meeting of the SNC Secretariat to assess the situation. Also discussed was the deployment of UNAMIC liaison teams to the parties' headquarters and the activation of the mixed military working group (MMWG) stipulated in the Paris Agreements. The deployment of the liaison teams was completed on 22 December, and the first meeting of MMWG was held with the participation of all four parties on 28 December. The meeting appealed to the Secretary-General for the early deployment of UNTAC and the appointment of the Special Representative of the Secretary-General.

Expansion of mandate

At the end of December 1991, the Secretary-General reported[15] to the Security Council on the need to expand the mandate of UNAMIC to undertake on an urgent basis a major de-mining effort in Cambodia. This effort should begin even before the establishment of UNTAC to prepare the ground for the safe and orderly repatriation of Cambodian refugees and displaced persons.

The Secretary-General recommended the addition of 1,090 military personnel. Forty of these would be assigned to a planning and liaison unit to liaise with the National Mine Clearance Commission established by SNC, as well as with UNHCR and other international agencies. The unit would gather information on all known mine fields in the country and would develop a training programme for Cambodians in mine-detection and clearance, establish priorities for action and allocate work among different units.

The Secretary-General also recommended the addition of a field engineer battalion of 700 personnel to begin clearing repatriation routes, reception centres and resettlement areas and to carry out emergency repair and rehabilitation work on roads and bridges already cleared. Other requirements included 200 personnel to comprise expert teams to train local military personnel made available by the four Cambodian parties, and 150 logistic support personnel. The Secretary-General estimated[16] the cost of this expansion at $24.7 million through the end of the mandate on 30 April. On 8 January 1992, by its resolution 728 (1992), the Council expanded the mandate of UNAMIC as recommended by the Secretary-General. In this connection, an engineering battalion from Thailand was deployed in the Sisophon/Battambang area on 21-22 February.

Cease-fire violations

Until January 1992, the cease-fire was generally maintained. However, in Kompong Thom, where forces of all four Cambodian parties were present, there were armed clashes in January between forces of SOC and forces of PDK. UNAMIC deployed a military liaison team to the area on 29 January. Although UNAMIC's presence contributed to calming the situation, the atmosphere remained tense.

On 26 February, a United Nations helicopter on a reconnaissance mission in the Kompong Thom area came under fire, and a member of the Australian contingent was wounded. This was the first attack against United Nations peace-keepers in Cambodia. UNAMIC immediately undertook an investigation.

C. Second session of the Paris Conference

The second session of the Paris Conference on Cambodia met from 1 to 23 October 1991. Cambodia was represented by SNC, with Prince Sihanouk as its Chairman. Also present were the five permanent members of the Security Council, the six members of ASEAN, Australia, Canada, India, Japan, Laos and Viet Nam. Yugoslavia attended in its capacity as Chairman of the Non-Aligned Movement, replacing Zimbabwe in that capacity. The peace plan that emerged from the Paris Conference was known as the Agreements on a Comprehensive Political Settlement of the Cambodia Conflict. The Agreements consisted of a Final Act

[15]S/23331. [16]S/23331/Add.1.

and three instruments: the Agreement on a Comprehensive Political Settlement of the Cambodia Conflict; the Agreement concerning the Sovereignty, Independence, Territorial Integrity and Inviolability, Neutrality and National Unity of Cambodia; and the Declaration on the Rehabilitation and Reconstruction of Cambodia.

Political agreement

The first instrument consisted of 9 parts, with 32 articles and 5 detailed annexes, including one which set out the mandate of UNTAC. It also defined a transitional period beginning with the entry into force of the Paris Agreements, i.e. 23 October 1991, and ending when a Constituent Assembly, elected in conformity with the Agreements, approved the new Cambodian Constitution and transformed itself into a legislative assembly, creating a new Cambodian Government. SNC was declared the "unique legitimate body and source of authority in which, throughout the transitional period, the sovereignty, independence and unity of Cambodia are enshrined". SNC would represent Cambodia externally and would occupy the seat of Cambodia at the United Nations. The members of SNC were "committed to the holding of free and fair elections organized and conducted by the United Nations as the basis for forming a new and legitimate government".

The United Nations Security Council was to establish a transitional authority, UNTAC, and the Secretary-General would designate a Special Representative to act on his behalf. SNC would delegate to the United Nations "all powers necessary to ensure the implementation" of the Agreement. SNC would offer advice to UNTAC, which would comply provided there was consensus among the members of SNC and provided the advice was consistent with the objectives of the Agreement. In the absence of consensus, the Chairman of SNC would be entitled to make the decision on what advice to offer to UNTAC, taking fully into account the views expressed in SNC. Should the Chairman be unable to make such a decision, his power of decision would transfer to the Secretary-General's Special Representative, who would make the final decision, taking fully into account the views expressed in SNC. Similar provisions applied to any power to act regarding the implementation of the Agreement. In all cases, the Secretary-General's Special Representative or his delegate would determine whether the advice or action of SNC was consistent with the Agreement. The Special Representative would attend the meetings of SNC and of any subsidiary body which might be established by it and give its members "all necessary information on the decisions taken by UNTAC".

Administrative agencies, bodies and offices which could directly influence the outcome of elections would be placed under direct United Nations supervision or control. In that context, special attention would be given to foreign affairs, national defence, finance, public security and information. The Special Representative of the Secretary-General was given power to issue directives to those agencies, bodies and offices, with binding effect and to install United Nations personnel with unrestricted access to information and administrative operations, and to remove existing officers or reassign them. The civil police was to operate under UNTAC supervision and control. In consultation with SNC, UNTAC was also to supervise other law enforcement and judicial processes throughout Cambodia. Further, UNTAC was empowered to investigate and take remedial action on complaints and allegations against existing administrative structures regarding actions that were inconsistent with a comprehensive political settlement or worked against it.

A cease-fire and disengagement of forces, to be effected immediately after the signature of the Agreements, would be followed by the provision of information to UNTAC about the total strength of forces, their deployment, armaments, and locations, including the detailed record of mine fields and booby-traps. All forces were committed to refrain from all hostilities and from any deployment, movement or action which would extend the territory they controlled or which might lead to renewed fighting. Any foreign forces, advisers, and military personnel remaining in Cambodia, together with their weapons, ammunition, and equipment would be withdrawn from the country with verification by UNTAC. The forces of the Cambodian parties would be regrouped and restricted to cantonment areas, their weapons and ammunition stored, under arrangements verified by UNTAC, which was also charged with the investigation of violations. Prisoners of war and political prisoners would be released, and displaced Cambodians resettled. To ensure the smooth performance of all these functions, the Agreement called for the establishment of a mixed military working group with representatives of all Cambodian parties.

In consultation with SNC, UNTAC was to establish a system of laws, procedures and administrative measures necessary for the holding of a free and fair election in Cambodia. Included were an electoral law and a code of conduct regulating participation in the election in a manner consistent with respect for human rights and prohibiting coercion or financial inducement in order to influence voter preference. Existing laws which could defeat the objectives and purposes of the Agreement would be nullified. UNTAC was to design and implement a system of registering individual voters and parties, a system of balloting to ensure a free and fair vote, and arrangements to facilitate the presence of foreign observers of the campaign and voting. UNTAC would investigate complaints of electoral irregularities, take appropriate corrective action and determine whether the voting was free and fair. It would then certify the list of people duly elected. The duration of the whole process was not to exceed nine months from the commencement of voter registration.

In other provisions of the Agreement, Cambodia undertook to ensure respect for human rights and fundamental freedoms and their observance in Cambodia. UNTAC was to develop and implement a programme of education to promote understanding of human rights and to provide for general human rights oversight during the transitional period. It would investigate complaints of abuse, taking corrective action when appropriate. The Agreement also set out the right of Cambodian refugees and displaced persons to return to their homes, as well as commitments by all signatories and acceding States to implement the Agreement. In the event of a violation or threat of violation, the two Co-Chairmen of the Paris Conference were committed, upon the request of the Secretary-General and without prejudice to the prerogatives of the Security Council, to "immediately undertake appropriate consultations with a view to taking appropriate steps" to remedy the situation.

Sovereignty and rehabilitation

In the second of the three instruments, Cambodia undertook to "maintain, preserve and defend its sovereignty, independence, territorial integrity and inviolability, neutrality and national unity" and to refrain from action that might affect the sovereignty, independence, territorial integrity and inviolability of other States, and to refrain from entering into any military alliances or other military agreements with other States that could be inconsistent with its neutrality. It also committed itself to refrain from permitting the introduction or stationing of foreign forces, including military personnel, in Cambodia unless it was done

so pursuant to United Nations authorization for the implementation of the political settlement.

In the declaration on the rehabilitation and reconstruction of Cambodia, it was agreed that implementation of an international aid effort would have to be phased in over a period that acknowledged realistically the political and technical imperatives. The United Nations Secretary-General could help in the first phase by appointing a coordinator to meet immediate needs and lay the groundwork for future action. Longer term priorities for reconstruction were left to the government of Cambodia after the elections. Nevertheless, seeing the need to harmonize and monitor contributions, the Paris Conference suggested the formation of an International Committee on the Reconstruction of Cambodia (ICORC) and asked the Secretary-General to make special arrangements to support ICORC.

UNTAC implementation plan

The Secretary-General informed[17] the Security Council of the adoption of the Paris Agreements on 30 October 1991. The Council welcomed[18] the Agreements and noted the intention of the Secretary-General to send a survey mission to Cambodia to prepare a plan for the Council's approval. The Council also asked for a detailed estimate of the cost of UNTAC, "on the understanding that this report would be the basis on which the Council would authorize the establishment of the Authority, the budget of which is to be subsequently considered and approved in accordance with the provisions of Article 17 of the Charter of the United Nations".

On 9 January 1992, Mr. Boutros Boutros-Ghali, having succeeded Mr. Pérez de Cuéllar as Secretary-General, appointed Under-Secretary-General Yasushi Akashi (Japan) as his Special Representative for Cambodia. On 18 January 1992, in a letter[19] to the President of the Security Council, the Secretary-General noted the widely recognized need for the urgent deployment of UNTAC and recalled the considerable lead time required to launch an operation. He had therefore decided to submit to the General Assembly a proposal for an initial appropriation of $200 million, which, upon approval of the implementation plan by the Security Council, should be made immediately available to pay for accommodation, transportation, communication and other support equipment and

<hr>

[17]S/23179. [18]S/RES/718 (1991). [19]S/23458.

services. The General Assembly acceded[20] to this request on 14 February 1992.

Action plan

On 19 February 1992, the Secretary-General submitted to the Security Council the implementation plan for UNTAC and subsequently submitted an indication of administrative and financial aspects.[21] UNTAC would consist of seven distinct components: human rights, electoral, military, civil administration, civilian police, repatriation and rehabilitation.

Human rights component. The human rights component would concentrate its efforts in encouraging SNC to ratify relevant international human rights instruments, conduct an extensive campaign of human rights education, investigate allegations of human rights abuses and exercise general oversight of human rights aspects of every component of UNTAC. A human rights office would be established to be the central policy-making and coordinating body. Staff would include specialists in human rights advocacy, civil education and investigation.

Electoral component. The Paris Agreements entrusted UNTAC with organizing and carrying out free and fair elections in Cambodia. The Special Representative would be assisted in these responsibilities by a Chief Electoral Officer. Other personnel needs included 198 international staff operating from headquarters and from 21 provincial and municipal centres, and some 400 United Nations Volunteers operating from each of 200 districts. These personnel would undertake duties related to electoral operations, information, training, communications, compliance and complaints, and coordination. They would be supplemented by some 4,000 Cambodian personnel during the registration process, and, during the polling process, by 1,000 international supervisors and 56,000 Cambodian personnel organized into 8,000 polling teams. To maximize efficiency and minimize costs, the electoral process would be computerized.

The Secretary-General recommended that registration of voters begin in October 1992 and proceed for three months, discretion being allowed to the Special Representative to extend that period if necessary. Elections would be scheduled for the period extending from the end of April to the beginning of May 1993.

Military component. Information provided by the Cambodian parties to the military survey mission sent by the Secretary-General in November–December 1991 indicated total forces of over 200,000 deployed in some 650 separate locations. In addition, militias totalling some 250,000 operated in almost all villages. These forces were armed with over 350,000 weapons and some 80 million rounds of ammunition.

Based on this and other information, the Secretary-General recommended that UNTAC have a military component of 15,900 all ranks to be headed by a Force Commander. Personnel would include headquarters staff (204), a military observer group (485), an infantry element (10,200), an engineer element (2,230), an air support group (326) to operate and maintain 10 fixed-wing aircraft and 26 helicopters, a signals unit (582), a medical unit (541), a composite military police company (160), a logistics battalion (872), and a naval element (376) to operate 6 sea patrol boats, 9 river patrol boats, 3 landing craft and 12 other boats. Force headquarters would be in Phnom Penh. For operational reasons, Cambodia would be divided into nine sectors, two of them with separate sector headquarters.

The military component would have four main functions: (1) to verify the withdrawal and non-return of all categories of foreign forces and their arms and equipment; (2) to supervise the cease-fire and related measures including regroupment, cantonment, disarming and demobilization; (3) to control weapons, including monitoring the cessation of outside military assistance; and (4) to assist in mine-clearing, including training and mine awareness programmes. The Secretary-General recommended that the military component be fully deployed by the end of May 1992 and that the regrouping and cantonment process, as well as demobilization of at least 70 per cent of the cantoned forces, be achieved by the end of September 1992. At that time, the strength of the military component could be reduced, followed by a further gradual reduction after the election.

The Agreements provided that all forces of the parties, with their weapons, should be regrouped and cantoned. This activity, however, would require massive deployment of UNTAC military personnel for an extended period and entail a serious disruption of the social and economic life of Cambodia, since most militia members were also engaged in farming and other civilian activities. In order to achieve economy of operation of UNTAC and avoid crippling the economy of Cambodia, the Secretary-General reported that practical arrangements had been worked out

[20]A/RES/46/222. [21]S/23613 and Add.1.

and agreed by the parties whereby the militia forces would not be physically cantoned but would report to locations designated by UNTAC to hand over their weapons. UNTAC would transfer the weapons to more secure centralized storage areas.

In consultation with the parties, the number of regrouping areas for regular forces was set at 95, reduced from 325 as originally proposed. The number of cantonment areas was set at 52, down from 317. Of these, 48 of the regrouping areas and 33 cantonment sites were designated for the forces of SOC, the Cambodian People's Armed Forces (CPAF). The forces of PDK, the National Army of Democratic Kampuchea (NADK), would regroup in 30 centres and canton in 10 others. Eight regroupment centres and 6 cantonment sites were designated for the forces of KPNLF, the Khmer People's National Liberation Armed Forces (KPNLAF). FUNCINPEC forces, the National Army of Independent Kampuchea (ANKI), would regroup in 9 areas and be cantoned at 3 locations. The number of cantonment centres was later revised upward to 55 (33 for CPAF, 14 for NADK, 5 for KPNLAF, and 3 for ANKI);[22] CPAF naval forces, totalling some 4,000 and equipped with 18 naval and 38 river vessels were to be dealt with in the same manner as the land forces, except that a few would be retained to patrol coastal and river areas under the close supervision and control of UNTAC. Engineer and logistic units of the regular forces would also be subject to special arrangements in view of their role in the de-mining programme, as well as in supplying and supporting the cantoned forces.

The Secretary-General informed the Security Council that all the Cambodian parties would need scrupulously to fulfil their commitments and extend full cooperation to the UNTAC military component, which would require freedom of movement and communication. The successful accomplishment of the component's tasks would depend on the timely availability of resources and the capacity of the infrastructure, including roads, airfields, ports, fuel supply, power supply, communications, warehousing space and personnel accommodation. Considering the state of the country's infrastructure, the Secretary-General saw the need for a "sizeable and concerted engineering effort to be deployed urgently" for basic repair before the onset of the rainy season in May.

Civil administration component. The civil administration functions envisioned in the Paris Agreements provided for UNTAC to exercise control over existing administrative structures having impact on the outcome of the elections. The Secretary-General proposed establishing offices to deal with those areas under direct UNTAC control, that is foreign affairs, national defence, finance, public security and information. An office would also be established to deal with areas under less direct control, and other offices would deal with training and complaints and investigation. Twenty-one provincial offices would parallel the existing administrative structure in the country. At each centre, international staff would be assigned duties under the civil administration mandate, in addition to other related duties, such as dissemination of UNTAC information and human rights. The civil administration component and the human rights component would together consist of some 224 specialists assisted by 84 international support staff. In terms of implementation, UNTAC would rely upon codes of conduct and guidelines and would maintain liaison officers in the various areas. Furthermore, UNTAC had been accorded the right to issue binding directives as necessary.

Civilian police component. The Paris Agreements stipulated that the Special Representative, in consultation with the parties, would determine those civil police required to perform law enforcement in the country. While the management of the civil police would remain the responsibility of the Cambodian parties, their operation would come under UNTAC supervision and control. The Secretary-General recommended a total of some 3,600 UNTAC civilian police monitors. At that number, and based on UNTAC's preliminary estimate of 50,000 Cambodian civil police, there would be one UNTAC monitor for every 15 local civil police. The structure of the component would include a policy and management unit at headquarters, 21 units at the provincial level and 200 district-level units. The main function of the UNTAC police monitors would be to supervise or control the local civil police in order to ensure that law and order were maintained effectively and impartially, and that human rights and fundamental freedoms were fully protected. To assist the monitors, use would be made as appropriate of codes of conduct and other operational guidelines developed by the United Nations. Monitors would also assume other responsibilities relating to the elections and to security requirements within UNTAC itself.

Repatriation component. According to the Paris Agreements, all Cambodian refugees and displaced persons had the right of voluntary return to Cambodia, to the place of their choice, in full

---

[22]S/23870.

respect for their human rights and fundamental freedoms. The Agreements also reaffirmed the Secretary-General's designation of UNHCR as lead agency in this respect. UNHCR had determined that there were more than 360,000 potential returnees, of whom over 90 per cent were under the age of 45 and almost half under the age of 15. Some 60 per cent of them originated from the provinces along the Thai-Cambodian border, and over two thirds of them had lived in the refugee camps along the border for over a decade.

An objective had been set for returning the refugees and displaced persons from the camps within a period of nine months. It would be necessary to identify and provide agricultural and settlement land for 360,000 returnees and to provide them with installment assistance as well as reintegration assistance and food supplies for an average of one year. Provision would also have to be made for food and installation assistance for up to 30,000 spontaneous returnees. The Secretary-General, on the recommendation of UNHCR, would appoint a director to head the repatriation and resettlement, which would be funded from voluntary contributions.

Rehabilitation component. Urgent needs to be met during the rehabilitation phase included humanitarian needs, such as food, health, housing and other essential needs, particularly of the disadvantaged, the handicapped, women and children; resettlement and reintegration needs, including those of the returnees, some 170,000 displaced persons and the estimated 150,000 or more Cambodian military forces to be demobilized; and essential restoration, maintenance and support of basic infrastructure. The Secretary-General would appoint a coordinator who would make ongoing assessments to ensure that requirements were being met without duplication or overlap. From $9 million to $14 million would be required for reintegration assistance in respect of demobilized military forces, to be funded as part of UNTAC's regular budget. With regard to other activities undertaken in the rehabilitation phase, the Secretary-General estimated that resource needs would amount to about $800 million, to be funded from voluntary donor contributions.

Other aspects. Given the magnitude of UNTAC's mandate, all UNTAC components would need to be computerized. The Secretary-General suggested that elements be integrated to enhance efficiency and control. At the same time, components would have specific information needs that could not be met under existing conditions in Cambodia. Furthermore, information would have to be provided to Cambodians to acquaint them with the Paris Agreements, with UNTAC, its purposes, activities and goals. The Secretary-General therefore suggested the establishment of an information office at UNTAC headquarters to act as the sole production point and conduit for information to be disseminated to the Cambodian people by UNTAC.

UNTAC components would be assisted by an estimated 7,000 locally recruited support personnel, including some 2,500 interpreters and by additional temporary staff as might be required.

D. UNTAC's initial period (March–April 1992)

By resolution 745 (1992) of 28 February, the Security Council established UNTAC for a period not to exceed 18 months. Meanwhile, UNAMIC continued to function until UNTAC became operational, at which time the Mission and its functions were subsumed by UNTAC. The initial phase of UNTAC's deployment began on 15 March 1992 with the arrival in Phnom Penh of the Secretary-General's Special Representative accompanied by his senior aides, including the Force Commander, Lieutenant-General John Sanderson (Australia).

UNTAC established a constructive working relationship with SNC and its President, Prince Sihanouk. For this purpose, UNTAC used the Secretariat of SNC, which SNC had created to deal with administrative and procedural matters. In addition, a "hot line" service linked the Special Representative and the Force Commander with a representative of each of the four Cambodian parties beginning on 1 April.

The Special Representative, in close consultation with Prince Sihanouk, took the initiative in drawing up agendas for SNC meetings and in

making proposals for consideration. Of the 21 ordinary meetings of SNC held during the UNTAC
period, five were held between the beginning of
UNTAC's deployment and the end of April 1992.
On the advice of the Special Representative, it
established a number of technical advisory committees to be chaired by an UNTAC official to deal
with a major area of UNTAC responsibility. A draft
electoral law drawn up by UNTAC was presented
to SNC on 1 April, followed by a series of consultations.

Following reports of violent incidents involving political figures, the Special Representative
issued a statement on 19 March 1992 stressing
UNTAC's determination to foster an environment
in which human rights would be assured so as to
permit the exercise of fundamental freedoms.
Members of the human rights, civil administration
and police components established a quick response
mechanism for investigating alleged human rights
violations. The first training programme in human
rights also got under way, initially provided to
UNTAC police monitors.

By the end of the first six weeks, that is
at the end of April 1992, the number of UNTAC
troops deployed to Cambodia rose to 3,694. In
Kompong Thom, where the situation had remained highly volatile, UNTAC deployed 200
troops, which effectuated a cease-fire. By the end
of April, the United Nations presence there expanded to 244 troops, and the situation remained
generally calm. With regard to the incident of
26 February involving the United Nations helicopter, UNTAC's investigation implicated members of
NADK, although NADK denied responsibility.

Progress was also made in the establishment of regroupment and cantonment areas.
Although a total of 52 cantonment areas had been
foreseen, it was agreed, following discussions
with the Cambodian parties, to establish a total
of 55 sites: 33 for CPAF, 14 for NADK, 5 for
KPNLAF and 3 ANKI.

In accordance with the mandate, UNTAC
military observers were to verify the withdrawal
and non-return of foreign forces. It had been envisaged to undertake this task by establishing a
total of 24 check-points. Of these, 18 would be
along the country's borders: 9 on the border with
Viet Nam, 7 on the border with Thailand, and
2 on the border with Laos. There would be one
each at the ports of Kompong Som and Phnom
Penh and the airports at Phnom Penh, Battambang, Siem Reap and Strung Treng. There would
also be a number of mobile monitoring teams.
During UNTAC's initial period of deployment, three

check-points were set up along the border with
Viet Nam.

UNTAC deployed six mine-clearing training teams in north-western Cambodia by the end
of April and another four teams were about to
begin work. It was planned that some 5,000 Cambodians would be trained in mine detection and
clearance by the end of the year, many of them
demobilized soldiers of the four Cambodian parties. Their new skills would aid in efforts at rehabilitation and creation of employment.

Repatriation of refugees began on 30
March 1992 with the return to Cambodia of 526
men, women and children. They were welcomed
at the reception centre at Sisophon in north-west
Cambodia by Prince Sihanouk and the Special Representative. By the end of April, 5,763 people had
returned. Concerns were being raised, however,
that because of the difficulty of finding suitable
mine-free land for the returnees, the congestion of
urban areas, the unsatisfactory health situation
within the country and the delays expected during
the rainy season, a number of the returnees would
be unable to take part in the electoral process. The
Secretary-General saw the need for "maximum
flexibility" in the search for viable options for
reintegration if the returnees were to register in
time for the elections.[23] A geographical widening
of land settlement options and diversification of
non-agricultural solutions offered to returnees
were being actively pursued.

By the end of April 1992, a total of 193
civilian police monitors had arrived in Cambodia.
Priority in their deployment was given to Sisophon
and Battambang where refugees and displaced persons were being resettled. Further deployments
were to be made in consultation with UNHCR as
the repatriation proceeded. Police monitors were
also deployed during this time to the three border
check-points established by UNTAC's military
component and to the Phnom Penh area. In all,
plans called for 3,600 UNTAC police monitors.
Their role was foreseen to be crucial in creating an
environment conducive to the holding of free and
fair elections. However, as of the end of April, there
was a substantial shortfall in commitments from
Member States to provide the monitors.

The civil administration component drew
up operating procedures for the exercise of the
right of assembly and freedom of association
which were presented to SNC by the Special Representative on 6 April. Recruitment to the component was slow in the first weeks, however, owing

[23]S/23870.

in particular to the high degree of specialization of its functions. Control of the agencies, bodies and offices dealing with Cambodian information media began in late April 1992, once the technical means for monitoring Cambodian broadcast news media were in place.

To provide information to the Cambodian people, UNTAC arranged access to existing radio transmission facilities in South-east Asia for the broadcast of UNTAC information and educational programmes. An UNTAC information bulletin was also initiated.

The Secretary-General visited Cambodia from 18 to 20 April 1992, attending a meeting of SNC on 20 April at which the members signed the International Covenant on Civil and Political Rights and the International Covenant on Eco-nomic, Social and Cultural Rights. During his visit, the Secretary-General formally launched an appeal for $593 million in international aid for Cambodia to fund the broad-based rehabilitation effort. The funds were to be used for food, health services, shelter, education, training and the restoration of the country's basic infrastructure, public utilities and support institutions to initiate the process of rehabilitation during the transition period. In-cluded in the aid figure was $116 million, esti-mated to be the cost of repatriating refugees from Thailand, which had been the subject of an earlier appeal.

On 1 May 1992, in his report[24] to the Security Council, the Secretary-General told the Security Council that UNTAC had made a "gener-ally good start".

E. Second phase of cease-fire (May–November 1992)

Announcement of phase II

On 9 May 1992, UNTAC announced that phase I of the cease-fire, in effect since the signing of the Paris Agreements, would be followed on 13 June by phase II, the cantonment, disarming and demobilization phase. The Force Commander took this step in consultation with the four Cam-bodian parties and after having obtained from each of them assurances that it would grant free-dom of movement to UNTAC personnel, vehicles and aircraft; mark minefields in the areas under its control; provide to UNTAC by 20 May information on troops, arms, ammunition and equipment; and adhere to the Paris Agreements, in particular not interfere with troops moving to regroupment and cantonment areas, and inform its troops of the plan for regroupment and cantonment.

However, following this announcement, it became clear that of the four signatory parties PDK was not cooperating. In particular, there was interference with UNTAC's freedom of movement. At a meeting of SNC on 26 May, the Special Rep-resentative called on the parties to show their readiness to comply with phase II by taking twelve steps, including, among others, permitting full and unrestricted freedom of movement to UNTAC, marking minefields, providing detailed informa-tion on troops to be cantoned, and undertaking a phased and balanced demobilization of at least 70 per cent of their forces. Three of the parties responded positively, but PDK did not provide the information requested. On 30 May, senior UNTAC officials, including the Special Representative and the Force Commander, were prevented by PDK from proceeding through PDK areas.

The Secretary-General then addressed a personal appeal to Mr. Khieu Samphan, President of PDK, urging that PDK take the necessary steps to enable UNTAC to begin implementation of phase II on 13 June. The reply did not contain the requested assurances. A further appeal for full com-pliance with the provisions of the Paris Agreements was made by the Special Representative at the SNC meeting on 5 June. On 9 June, PDK informed the Special Representative by letter that it was not in a position to allow UNTAC to proceed with deploy-ment in areas under its control. PDK again failed to respond positively when, at the SNC meeting on 10 June, the Special Representative called on PDK to meet in full its obligations under the Paris Agreements, to comply with the 12 points and to enter phase II of the cease-fire on 13 June.

In explanation of its position, PDK as-serted that foreign military personnel remained present in Cambodia. Its own security required deferring compliance with phase II until the with-drawal and non-return of foreign forces had been verified by UNTAC. PDK also raised concerns re-

[24]Ibid.

garding the effective control of existing administrative structures.

UNTAC rejected this view but took a number of steps designed to meet the concerns of PDK. It established a total of ten check-points — one more than foreseen — on the Cambodian border with Viet Nam at an earlier date than planned. It also invited the four parties to participate in manning those checkpoints. Mobile teams were launched empowered to carry out investigations, including allegations of the presence of foreign forces. Although PDK presented UNTAC with a list in writing of allegations regarding the presence of foreign forces, it did not provide personnel to accompany UNTAC's investigations.

On 30 May 1992, Viet Nam confirmed[25] in writing to UNTAC that its forces, volunteers and all equipment had been completely withdrawn from Cambodia by 26 September 1989 and that they had not been reintroduced. Viet Nam also stated that military assistance to Cambodia had ended in September 1989 and no country had been allowed to use Vietnamese territory to provide such aid to the Cambodian parties.

Phase II of the cease-fire depended critically on the cooperation of all parties. However, despite the lack of cooperation from PDK, the Secretary-General concluded that phase II should commence on 13 June as scheduled. In his view, as related[26] to the Security Council on 12 June 1992, any delay would result in a loss of momentum and would jeopardize UNTAC's ability to organize and conduct elections by April or May 1993. The Special Representative was consulting with the other three parties to ensure that the process of regrouping and cantonment of forces would minimize any military disadvantage they would suffer *vis-à-vis* PDK. This could, however, be only a short-term solution; it was imperative that all efforts be made to persuade PDK to join the other parties in good faith in implementing the comprehensive political settlement. The Secretary-General concluded that the Security Council itself might wish to consider what action it could take to achieve this objective. For its part, the Council, in a Presidential statement,[27] reaffirmed the importance of the full and timely implementation of the Paris Agreements and stressed the need that the second phase of the military arrangements should begin on 13 June 1992.

Tokyo Conference

A Ministerial Conference on the Rehabilitation and Reconstruction of Cambodia met in Tokyo on 20 and 22 June 1992. Participating were Australia, Austria, Belgium, Brunei Darussalam, Cambodia, Canada, China, Denmark, Finland, France, Germany, India, Indonesia, Ireland, Italy, Japan, Laos, Malaysia, Netherlands, New Zealand, Norway, Philippines, Portugal, Republic of Korea, Russian Federation, Singapore, Spain, Sweden, Switzerland, Thailand, United Kingdom, United States and Viet Nam. A number of inter-governmental organizations were also represented, including the European Community and the programmes of the United Nations system.

The Conference issued two declarations which were adopted by consensus. One focused on the peace process,[28] the other on rehabilitation and reconstruction of Cambodia.[29] In the latter, the participants agreed to establish a consultative body to be called the International Committee on the Reconstruction of Cambodia. Under the chairmanship of Japan, it was to be the coordinating mechanism of the international community with the democratically elected government of Cambodia on matters of medium- and longer-term reconstruction of the country. Pledges of aid to Cambodia amounted to $880 million, surpassing the $593 million appeal.

The Conference also drew up an informal proposal[30] for discussion, setting out a number of measures designed to meet some of the concerns expressed by PDK. On the same day, 22 June, at an extraordinary meeting of SNC convened in Tokyo, the four Cambodian parties were asked to respond to the proposal. Three of them accepted it; PDK promised to consider the proposal and make known its views at a later time.

UNTAC's negotiation with PDK

On 2 July, at a working session of SNC, PDK introduced its own proposals regarding the role and powers of SNC and the administrative structures in the zone under the control of SOC. On 7 July, the Secretary-General addressed a letter to Mr. Khieu Samphan, assuring him that the Special Representative would pursue his efforts to take into account, on the basis of the Tokyo proposal, the legitimate concern expressed by PDK as well as those of the other three parties. At the SNC meeting on 8 July, Mr. Khieu Samphan repeated the PDK proposals and took the same position in a letter dated 9 July addressed to the Secretary-General.

[25] S/24082. [26] S/24090. [27] S/24091. [28] A/47/285-S/24183, annex I. [29] A/47/285-S/24183, annex II. [30] S/24286, annex.

In addition to meetings of SNC, the Special Representative met three times with Mr. Khieu Samphan to secure PDK's agreement to the Tokyo proposal and to persuade it to take the necessary steps to comply with the Paris Agreements. At the meetings, PDK elaborated its positions and, in particular, called for the dissolution of the main institutions and structures established in the zones under SOC control. In response, the Special Representative explained that, according to the Paris Agreements, UNTAC's control should be exercised through the existing administrative structures of each of the four Cambodian parties, of which the Phnom Penh authorities formed part.

Situation by the end of July 1992

During this time, UNTAC accelerated its efforts to recruit and deploy its civil administration staff, in order to exercise its mandate under the Agreements of direct control over the five areas of foreign affairs, national defence, finance, public security and information, and supervision of other areas, of the existing administrative structures. UNTAC also sought agreement with PDK on the establishment of a mechanism for keeping the four Cambodian parties informed and involved with regard to UNTAC's exercise of direct control over the five areas. Comprehensive plans to introduce this control throughout the territory of Cambodia were announced by the Special Representative on 26 June. Control over SOC administrative structures dealing with foreign affairs and national defence was established on 1 July. Plans called for the progressive introduction of control in finance between 1 July and 1 September, and in public security the staff concerned was to be fully deployed by 15 July. A Media Working Group composed of representatives of the four parties was established on 10 June 1992.

UNTAC's military component was almost fully deployed by July, with some 14,300 troops in the country and the remainder en route. There were 1,780 UNTAC civilian police monitors deployed throughout the country to supervise the fair and impartial enforcement of law and order. Some 100 cases of human rights violations had been investigated in SOC zones, and investigations would soon begin in the zones of the other two parties.

Following the beginning of phase II on 13 June, UNTAC was to have completed the regroupment and cantonment process within four weeks, i.e. by 11 July. As of 10 July, of the esti-mated 200,000 troops, the numbers of cantoned troops were as follows: CPAF, 9,003; ANKI, 3,187; KPNLAF, 1,322. However, reflecting PDK's position of non-cooperation, no NADK troops were cantoned.

In light of the situation, the Secretary-General, in a report[31] to the Security Council on 14 July, pointed to two possible courses of action: to suspend the operation until all parties complied with the Paris Agreements, or to pursue the process, thus demonstrating the international community's determination to assist the Cambodian people despite the lack of cooperation from PDK. Considering the latter approach to be appropriate, he had requested his Special Representative to press forward with the regrouping and cantonment process, albeit cautiously and selectively, taking great care to maintain security in the countryside and concentrating on areas where there was no military confrontation. The main questions were how to persuade PDK to comply with its obligations, how to underscore the determination of the international community to implement the Agreements and how to obtain the full and active support of the signatories for UNTAC efforts to carry out its mandate.

By resolution 766 (1992) of 21 July, the Security Council approved the efforts of the Secretary-General to continue implementing the Paris Agreements despite the difficulties. It demanded that PDK permit the deployment of UNTAC in the areas under its control and implement phase II of the cease-fire as well as other aspects of the Agreements. It also requested the Secretary-General to ensure that international assistance to the rehabilitation and reconstruction of Cambodia from then on benefit only the parties fulfilling their obligations under the Agreements and cooperating fully with UNTAC.

At the end of July 1992, the Special Representative wrote[32] to the Secretary-General that the military situation had somewhat worsened, with aggressive action by NADK in the north and parts of the centre and south, while the acceptance of cantonment by the three parties had created a vacuum. At the same time, some NADK soldiers had shown interest in being cantoned and joining their families, but their leaders had managed to keep tight control. Although UNTAC had addressed issues of genuine concern to PDK, no cooperation had been forthcoming. PDK would be satisfied with no less than a radical "depolitiza-

---

[31]S/24286. [32]See *The United Nations and Cambodia*, United Nations Blue Book Series, Volume II, p. 206.

tion" dealing a crippling blow to the Phnom Penh regime, thus gaining what it had been unable to obtain either on the battlefield or in the Paris negotiations. In the meantime, PDK radio was broadcasting allegations linking UNTAC with SOC and Viet Nam.

There were other problems as well. In the countryside, the security situation had worsened. The economic situation was precarious, and hyperinflation was imminent. UNTAC was grappling with the task of keeping the country afloat and having Cambodians focus on their common national priorities. The prospects were daunting, but the Special Representative remained basically optimistic. There was a substantial reservoir of resources and goodwill, as well as the unanimous support of the entire international community. Furthermore, the great majority of Cambodians wanted to build a new, peaceful country.

Adoption of the electoral law

The electoral law, which had been submitted to SNC by UNTAC on 1 April 1992, was adopted by SNC on August 5 and promulgated on 12 August. The law differed from the 1 April draft in two respects. In order to meet the concern expressed by the Cambodian parties that the franchise be restricted to "Cambodian persons", the text of the Paris Agreements would be interpreted as giving the right to register to "every Cambodian person", defined as follows: (a) a person born in Cambodia, at least one of whose parents was born in Cambodia; or (b) a person, wherever born, at least one of whose parents was a Cambodian person within the meaning of paragraph (a). Secondly, the draft law was amended to permit overseas Cambodians to vote at one polling station in Europe, one in North America and one in Australia. However, registration of voters was still to take place exclusively in Cambodia.

PDK, however, did not withdraw its objection. The Special Representative decided to exercise his power under the Paris Agreements, and the draft law was adopted at the SNC meeting despite the objection of PDK.

The adoption of the electoral law was followed on 15 August by the beginning of the provisional registration of parties. The Secretary-General remained convinced that the electoral process should be carried out in accordance with the implementation timetable. UNTAC was also studying a proposal to hold a presidential election. While much support for the election had been voiced by the Cambodian parties and by Prince

Sihanouk himself, such an election was not provided for in the Paris Agreements.

Failure of international efforts to persuade PDK

Notwithstanding the continuing refusal of PDK to grant UNTAC access to its zones of control or to commit its forces to cantonment, the Secretary-General reported[33] to the Security Council on 21 September 1992 that UNTAC had acquired a powerful momentum. Its presence had already achieved a "profound and probably lasting impact" on Cambodia. UNTAC was close to full deployment over most of the territory of Cambodia, including a strong police presence extending down to village level. Supervision and control over the administrative structures of the country had been established and progressively strengthened, and Cambodians continued to be informed and educated on human rights issues. More than 115,000 refugees and displaced persons had been repatriated.

UNTAC consistently stressed that the door remained open for full and constructive participation by PDK in the peace process. However, the persistent failure of PDK to meet its obligations under the Paris Agreements continued to obstruct their full implementation. In his 21 September report, the Secretary-General suggested that the Security Council consider further action to impress upon the parties the international community's firm determination to press ahead with the implementation of the Paris Agreements. He also indicated his intention, subject to Security Council approval, to request the co-Chairmen of the Paris Conference — the Foreign Ministers of France and Indonesia — to undertake, within a definite timeframe, consultations with the aim of finding a way out of the impasse or, if that should prove impossible, exploring appropriate steps to ensure the realization of the fundamental objectives of the Agreements.

On 13 October, the Security Council, by its resolution 783 (1992), confirmed that the electoral process should proceed according to the implementation timetable. The Council, among other things, demanded that PDK fulfil immediately its obligations under the Paris Agreements, and invited the Governments of Japan and Thailand, which had been actively involved in finding solutions to the current problems, to continue their efforts and to report the results to the Secretary-

[33] S/24578.

General and to the co-Chairmen of the Paris Conference. The Council also invited the Secretary-General to ask the co-Chairmen immediately on receipt of that report to undertake appropriate consultations with a view to implementing fully the peace process. It requested the Secretary-General to report to the Council no later than 15 November 1992 on the implementation of resolution 783 (1992).

The Governments of Japan and Thailand undertook consultations with PDK on 22 and 29 October 1992, but concluded that tripartite consultation was no longer the appropriate means to address the impasse.[34] On 7 and 8 November, the Co-Chairmen of the Paris Conference met in Beijing with Prince Sihanouk, members of SNC representing the four Cambodian parties and representatives of the five permanent members of the Security Council, as well as Australia, Germany, Japan and Thailand. The Special Representative also participated. The Co-Chairmen subsequently informed[35] the Secretary-General that it had become clear that PDK was still not prepared to cooperate in the further implementation of the Paris Agreements. Furthermore, PDK had indicated its intention not to take part in the electoral process so long as, in its view, a neutral political condition was not ensured.

Suspension of phase II process

Voter registration opened in Phnom Penh on 5 October 1992, in four other provinces on 19 October, and progressively in the other provinces. In the first weeks, about a million Cambodians registered to vote. When Radio UNTAC began broadcasts on 9 November 1992, the programmes concentrated on information regarding voter registration and the electoral process.

As for the cantonment process, which had begun in June with the declaration of phase II, some 55,000 troops of the three participating factions, or approximately a quarter of the estimated total number of troops, entered the cantonment sites and handed over their weapons. This process, however, had to be suspended, due to the noncompliance by PDK and the deterioration of the military situation. Some 40,000 cantoned troops were subsequently released on agricultural leave, subject to recall by UNTAC.

Reporting[36] to the Security Council on 15 November 1992, the Secretary-General said that the difficulties encountered in implementing phase II of the cease-fire had led to the effective suspension of the cantonment, disarmament and demobilization process. Although he concurred with the Co-Chairmen that the implementation of the peace process should continue and the timetable be maintained, he expressed his concern that the elections would take place with the two largest armed forces mostly intact, and with some of the forces of the other two parties still in the field.

The Secretary-General nevertheless continued to believe that patient diplomacy remained the best means of getting the peace process back on track. He stated that UNTAC would continue its dialogue with PDK in an effort to meet that party's concerns and persuade it to comply with its obligations under the Paris Agreements. In the circumstances, however, the projected reduction of the strength of the military component was no longer feasible until after the elections. It would also be necessary to adjust deployment in order to foster a general sense of security among the Cambodian people and enhance the component's ability to protect the voter registration and polling processes, particularly in remote or insecure areas.

The issue of foreign residents and immigrants was another matter that deeply disturbed many Cambodians. Killings of Vietnamese-speaking villagers had aroused serious concerns about public security and had implications for the creation of a neutral political environment. UNTAC investigations indicated that units of NADK had been responsible for two such incidents.

On 30 November, the Security Council in resolution 792 (1992) confirmed that the elections for a constituent assembly in Cambodia would be held no later than May 1993, and noted the Secretary-General's instruction for contingency planning for a presidential election. It condemned PDK for failing to comply with its obligations under the Paris Agreements and demanded, among other things, that it immediately fulfil those obligations, facilitate full deployment of UNTAC in the areas under its control, and not impede voter registration or the activities of other political parties in those areas. The Council determined that UNTAC should proceed with preparations for the holding of elections in all areas of Cambodia to which UNTAC had full access as at 31 January 1993. It requested the Secretary-General to consider the implications which the failure by PDK to canton and demobilize its forces would have for the electoral process and, accordingly, to take all appropriate steps to ensure the successful implementation of the process.

---

[34]S/24800, annex I. [35]S/24800, annexes II and III. [36]S/24800.

UNTAC military deployment for electoral support

The boundaries and names shown and the designations used on this map do not imply official endorsement or acceptance by the United Nations.

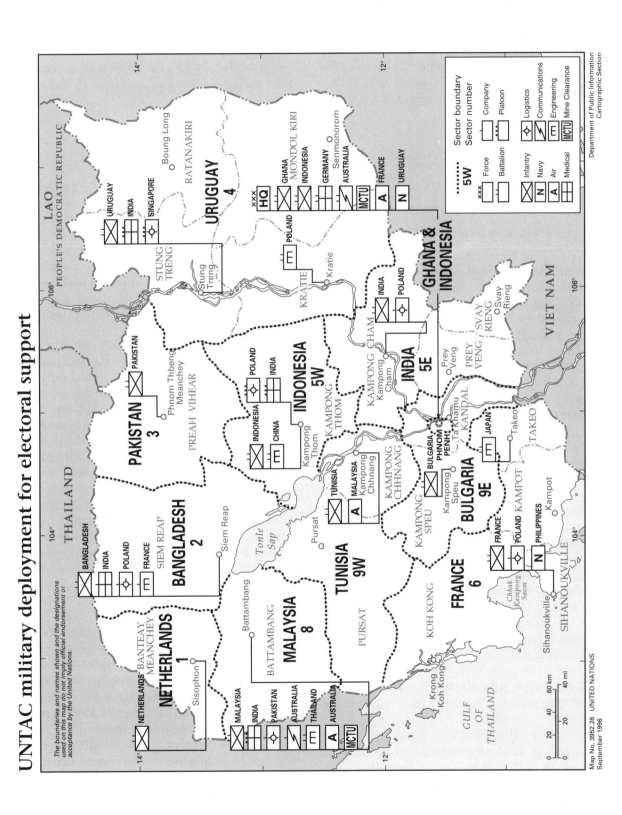

Map No. 3952.28 UNITED NATIONS
September 1996

Department of Public Information
Cartographic Section

The Security Council also supported the 22 September decision of SNC to set a country-wide moratorium on the export of logs from Cambodia in order to protect the country's natural resources, and requested UNTAC to take appropriate measures to secure the implementation of this moratorium. The Council requested SNC to consider adopting a similar moratorium on the export of minerals and gems. In addition, it called for measures to prevent the supply of petroleum products from reaching areas occupied by any Cambodian signatory party not complying with the military provisions of the Paris Agreements. The Council invited UNTAC to establish all necessary border checkpoints, as recommended by the Secretary-General.

F. Before the elections (December 1992–March 1993)

Deteriorating security situation

With the onset of the dry season, cease-fire violations increased, mostly in Kompong Thom, Siem Reap and Battambang provinces in central and north-west Cambodia. The violations typically took the form of artillery duels, which drove villagers from their homes without causing extensive casualties on either side. SOC, claiming that NADK had made territorial gains, called on the Special Representative to restore the military balance. Reports from UNTAC military observers indicated that CPAF was attempting to recover territory over which NADK had extended its influence during the rainy season, while NADK was attempting to consolidate its gains and interrupt CPAF's communications.

The Special Representative had issued a call for military restraint on 4 November, and the Secretary-General had appealed to all parties to respect the cease-fire in his 15 November report to the Security Council. Cease-fire violations continued, however, and in December, two serious violations occurred. Frequent exchanges of shelling took place between NADK and CPAF throughout the month in the Bavel area of Battambang province, causing about 15,000 local residents to flee their homes. On 24 and 25 December, NADK artillery shells landed near a location occupied by UNTAC troops from the Bangladesh battalion in Siem Reap province. The area came under shelling again on 31 December.

Since December 1992, there were several incidents of temporary detention of UNTAC personnel by NADK units. On 20 December, PDK informed the Special Representative by letter that UNTAC should not enter PDK-controlled zones without prior authorization and that UNTAC must assume full responsibility for incidents that occurred as a result of its failure to obtain such authorization. The Special Representative and the Force Commander replied on 22 December, pointing out the distortion contained in the declaration. The President of the Security Council also issued a statement[37] in which the Council strongly condemned the illegal detention of UNTAC personnel by elements of NADK.

Other problems surfaced as well. The inability of UNTAC to gain access to the administrative structure of PDK gave rise to a hardening of SOC's position regarding supervision and control by UNTAC of SOC administrative structures. This growing reluctance, while having emerged as early as October 1992, became particularly evident as the military situation deteriorated and applied to nearly all fields of control and supervision entrusted to UNTAC.

Furthermore, a spate of violent incidents — "politically-motivated attacks on political party offices and staff, attacks on Vietnamese-speaking persons, and killings having no particular political motivation" — heightened a sense of insecurity among Cambodians. The Secretary-General's Special Representative had stated publicly in November that free and fair elections could not be held in circumstances where people faced threats to their lives, property and personal security for attempting to exercise their political rights. However, political parties, and in particular FUNCINPEC and the Buddhist Liberal Democratic Party (BLDP), the political wing of KPNLF, subjected to attacks on their offices and workers, complained that they were not provided with effective protection by local administrative structures.

In addition to investigating these incidents, UNTAC's civilian police, military, and civil administration components, together with the

[37]S/25003.

human rights component, developed measures to prevent and deal with threats to public order. UNTAC announced that it would give priority to ensuring freedom from intimidation, freedom of party affiliation and freedom of action for political parties. On 6 January 1993, the Special Representative issued a directive establishing procedures for the prosecution of persons responsible for human rights violations; as a result, UNTAC assumed powers to arrest, detain and prosecute suspects in cases of serious violations. For this purpose, the Special Representative established the office of the Special Prosecutor.[38]

Relations with SNC

Since September 1992, Prince Sihanouk had intermittently stayed in Beijing for medical treatment. The Special Representative, in order to keep close relations with SNC, organized working sessions of SNC in Phnom Penh, with the approval of the Prince. Through the working sessions, UNTAC continued to consult with SNC members on subjects related to the implementation of the Paris Agreements.

On 20 December, Prince Sihanouk announced that SNC membership would be increased by one, to 13, to allow for a second FUNCINPEC representative.

On 4 January 1993, citing persistent violent attacks on FUNCINPEC staff, Prince Sihanouk informed the Special Representative that he could no longer cooperate with UNTAC or SOC. Prince Norodom Ranariddh, the leader of FUNCINPEC, also said he would suspend working relations with UNTAC until effective measures were taken to put an end to the climate of violence. The Special Representative met with both leaders to inform them of measures taken by UNTAC to promote a neutral political environment. Both leaders showed their understanding. Prince Ranariddh subsequently expressed gratitude for UNTAC's efforts to address this problem and stressed that FUNCINPEC had always cooperated with UNTAC and would continue to do so. Prince Sihanouk used the occasion of a special SNC meeting on 28 January in Beijing to express publicly his renewed support for UNTAC. He assured the meeting of his continuing cooperation with the United Nations in the implementation of the Paris Agreements.

Prince Sihanouk had also confirmed to the Special Representative on 4 January that he would be a candidate in presidential elections. However, at the meeting of SNC on 28 January the Prince announced his decision not to advance his candi-dacy. Instead, he wished to wait until the new Constitution had been adopted before holding the elections, so that the President could be elected in accordance with the modalities, the term of office and powers laid down in the Constitution.

At the 28 January meeting, SNC set the dates of the constituent assembly elections for 23 to 25 May 1993. These dates were later expanded to allow for polling at mobile stations on 27 and 28 May. Prince Sihanouk also issued, in his own name and in the name of SNC members belonging to FUNCINPEC, KPNLF and SOC, a statement[39] condemning violence against Cambodians or foreign persons in Cambodia and any act which threatened the dignity, fundamental freedoms, rights, security and personal safety of any member of UNTAC.

Continuing difficulties

In January and February 1993, cease-fire violations continued, including exchanges of artillery and mortar fire between CPAF and NADK and movement of troops. CPAF forces launched attacks on NADK forces in a number of districts and moved closer to the PDK-held district town of Pailin in the province of Battambang. UNTAC protested the moves as exceeding the bounds of self-defence.[40] The Special Representative called on SOC to desist from violating the cease-fire and to exercise self-restraint. In the meantime, PDK tightened restrictions on the UNTAC team deployed in Pailin, subjecting them at one point to virtual house arrest.

An attack by NADK on a village in Siem Reap province in January resulted in eight casualties, four of them UNTAC personnel. Two Cambodian women, members of an UNTAC voter registration team, died from their wounds. In January, February and March, six UNTAC military and civilian personnel were injured and two were killed by hostile action against UNTAC, including a Bangladeshi soldier killed by a mortar believed to be fired by NADK.

Incidence of violence and intimidation, which had peaked in December 1992, fell significantly in January 1993. However, political violence increased somewhat in early February. Many of the incidents were concentrated in the provinces of Battambang and Kompong Cham, and the victims in the vast majority of cases were members of FUNCINPEC.

While PDK radio had commonly attacked UNTAC, and its broadcasts had become increasingly

[38]S/25124. [39]S/25289, annex. [40]S/25289.

hostile, the Phnom Penh authorities also undertook a media campaign against UNTAC, asserting
that only SOC could defend the country against
PDK and so deserved electoral support, while UN-
TAC could not be trusted to protect Cambodians.

Attacks against Vietnamese-speaking
Cambodians also continued. On 10 March, members of an NADK unit attacked a floating village
in Siem Reap province, killing 33 people, including 12 children, and injuring 24. The village was
inhabited primarily by Cambodian-born persons
of Vietnamese descent. On 24 March, a group of
assailants attacked fishing boats in Kompong
Chhnang Province resulting in 8 deaths, including
three children. And on 29 March in Phnom Penh,
a coordinated attack with hand-grenades on four
premises frequented or owned by Vietnamese-
speaking persons resulted in 2 deaths and at least
20 injuries.

Registration of voters and political parties

On 21 December, the Special Representative announced that the voter registration
period would be extended to 31 January 1993. At
its completion, over 4.6 million people, or some
96 per cent of the estimated eligible population,
had been registered. Returnees were given the opportunity to be registered on their return to Cambodia, either in their final destination or in six
reception centres. As the end of the registration
period approached, a special arrangement was
made between UNTAC's repatriation and electoral
components to enable registration of the remaining eligible population in the border camps. They
were temporarily listed in Thailand during the
month of January and received their registration
cards upon return to Cambodia.

As for the political parties, on 27 January
1993, 20 out of the 22 provisionally-registered
political parties had applied for official registration, in accordance with the Electoral Law, by
submitting a list of at least 5,000 registered voters
who were members of the party. Neither PDK nor

its political party, the National Unity of Cambodia
Party formed in November 1992, filed official registration to take part in the elections.

At a meeting of SNC on 10 February,
UNTAC announced its decision that the electoral
campaign would begin on 7 April 1993 and end
on 19 May, followed by a four-day cooling-off period before polling. During the campaign, UNTAC
would make its information and broadcasting facilities available to all political parties in order to
ensure fair access to the media. On 11 March, the
Special Representative met with the leaders of the
20 political parties to inform them of their rights
and responsibilities as party leaders under the Electoral Law.

Protection of natural resources

In its resolution 792 (1992), the Security
Council had adopted a number of measures aimed
at protecting Cambodia's natural resources, particularly timber, minerals and gems. An appeal by
UNTAC to Cambodia's neighbouring countries resulted in announcements by Laos, Thailand and
Viet Nam that they would impose a complete ban
on the import of logs from Cambodia beginning
1 January 1993. UNTAC deployed border guards
to monitor the situation on land and sea. However,
numerous and large-scale violations by both routes
continued. Personnel of all the Cambodian parties
were involved in the export of logs, but because
PDK refused to allow UNTAC monitors in the zone
it controlled, it had not been possible to obtain
figures for the bulk of log exports from there.

At the SNC meeting on 28 January 1993,
UNTAC proposed that the moratorium on log
exports be extended to minerals and gems. At the
initiative of FUNCINPEC, the moratorium was
widened to include the commercial extraction of
mineral resources onshore and offshore. This proposal was supported by three of the Cambodian
parties. The matter was raised again at the SNC
meeting of 10 February, when the moratorium
was adopted despite the continued objections of
PDK.

G. Electoral period (April–May 1993)

Campaigning begins

On 4 April 1993, PDK formally announced to SNC its decision not to participate in the elections, asserting that "Vietnamese forces of aggression" continued to occupy Cambodia and that a neutral political environment did not exist. On 13 April, the President of PDK wrote to Prince Sihanouk that his party could no longer attend SNC meetings in Phnom Penh because there was insufficient security. PDK would therefore withdraw temporarily from the city.

The electoral campaign officially began on 7 April, and the 20 political parties participated actively. During his second visit to Cambodia on 7 and 8 April, the Secretary-General told SNC that, in his judgement and in all due caution, the basic acceptable conditions for the conduct of an electoral campaign did exist. He was encouraged that electoral campaigning was being conducted peacefully with the participation of tens of thousands of Cambodians.[41]

Despite these encouraging signs, violence and intimidation remained a major challenge to the creation and maintenance of a neutral political environment. Victims included members of all four Cambodian parties. Many acts of violence had apparent political or ethnic overtones, but some killings had no identifiable motivation and took place in an environment where, after years of war, there was an oversupply of weapons.

As a result of the series of attacks on Vietnamese-speaking persons, several thousand members of the Vietnamese community in Cambodia began to migrate from their homes towards the Vietnamese border, many by boat. Between 21 March and 28 April, 21,659 people were recorded crossing the border into Viet Nam at border checkpoints manned by UNTAC personnel. UNTAC naval units and civilian police closely monitored these movements to ensure that the local authorities assumed their responsibility to protect the migrants.

During his visit to Cambodia, the Secretary-General issued an urgent appeal for an end to violence. Prince Sihanouk issued a strong declaration demanding that his "armed compatriots" refrain from acts of violence against UNTAC. His declaration was endorsed by SOC, KPNLF and FUNCINPEC.[42]

All units of UNTAC's military component in all locations had been directed to increase vigilance and enhance security measures and procedures. UNTAC further refined and strengthened measures to help ensure the security of the electoral process and the safety of the Cambodian political parties and of UNTAC staff under conditions of instability. Teams of military observers worked with UNTAC civilian police in monitoring political rallies and gatherings throughout the country. Personnel from both components assisted electoral staff with the civil education campaign. The military component's defensive positions, particularly in Siem Reap and Kompong Thom provinces, were reinforced and expanded to allow the construction of bunkers and overhead protection as well as firing bays, defensive pits from which soldiers could return fire.

It was also decided that, during the election itself, no polling would be conducted in areas controlled by PDK, to which UNTAC had not been permitted access, nor in some remote areas in which NADK had been operating. Other parts of the country were designated as high-, medium-, and low-risk areas. Different levels of security measures were established for each level of risk. In high-risk zones, it was decided to station armed UNTAC military personnel at and around polling stations and to issue protective gear to UNTAC staff. Quick reaction forces and medical support units were identified for the high-risk sites. In response to the heightened threat in one province, UNTAC civilian personnel were withdrawn from some locations and the number of polling sites was reduced. Security at UNTAC headquarters was also strengthened.

Despite initial indications of a relative decline in violence during April, deaths and injuries from violence continued. Many of the casualties resulted from attacks on civilians and on SOC by NADK, and by unidentified groups, and attacks on other political parties by SOC and unidentified groups.

Further attacks also took place against UNTAC personnel. In April, seven UNTAC personnel were killed and fifteen injured by hostile action against UNTAC. The killing of a Japanese United Nations Volunteer and his Cambodian interpreter was a shocking incident. In Kompong Speu, in three separate incidents, four Bulgarian military personnel were killed and nine wounded. In two

---

[41]S/25719. [42]S/25784.

incidents in early May, UNTAC vehicles were attacked in Kompong Cham and Banteay Meanchey, resulting in thirteen military and civilian police personnel wounded and one civilian police monitor (a Japanese) killed. On 21 May in Kompong Cham province, an attack by NADK on an SOC police station resulted in the death of two UNTAC military observers when a rocket overshot its target and hit the Chinese Engineer Company compound nearby.

The Security Council, by its resolution 826 (1993) of 20 May 1993, condemned all acts of violence committed on political and ethnic grounds, intimidation and attacks on UNTAC. At the same time, the Council commended those participating in the election campaign in accordance with the Paris Agreements despite the violence and intimidation. It expressed its satisfaction with the arrangements made by the United Nations for the elections and fully supported the decision of the Secretary-General that the elections be held as scheduled. At the same time, the Council demanded that all parties abide by the Paris Agreements and give UNTAC the full cooperation required under it.

The elections

The elections were the focal point of the comprehensive settlement. As stipulated in the Agreements, the election of 120 members to the constituent assembly was held throughout Cambodia on a provincial basis in accordance with a system of proportional representation. Every Cambodian person 18 years of age or older was eligible to vote. The Agreements provided for a multi-party electoral system. Voting was for political parties, and all political parties were registered by UNTAC in order to participate in the elections. The list of party candidates for each province was published before the elections.

The Special Representative promulgated a number of minor revisions to the Electoral Law in order to respond to security or other considerations as they arose or were anticipated. The process to register over 4.7 million Cambodian voters, beginning on 5 October 1992 for a three-month period and subsequently extended until 31 January 1993, was scrutinized by representatives of the political parties with the right to challenge registrants whom they deemed to be unqualified. Voters' lists were complied by UNTAC's computer support system, designed to store up to 5.2 million voter registration records. UNTAC was not given access to PDK-controlled areas, which were considered to

be populated by about 5 per cent of the total population of Cambodia.

During the electoral campaign, from 7 April to 19 May 1993, scores of political meetings and rallies were held daily and peacefully with the participation of tens of thousands of people in virtually all parts of Cambodia. UNTAC itself organized multi-party meetings.

On 21 April at a meeting of SNC, the Special Representative expressed the view that the freeness and fairness of the elections would be judged in accordance with three main criteria: the extent to which the campaign and voting were marred by violence, intimidation and harassment; the extent to which SOC, which controlled the largest zones and had the most extensive administrative structure, enjoyed unfair advantages; and the technical conduct of the poll. UNTAC raised the issue of the separation of party and State several times both in public and in private meetings with the Phnom Penh authorities, particularly regarding access of other political parties to the media and their right to freedom of movement. All political parties had access to Radio UNTAC and to UNTAC video productions. Three political parties requested and received assistance from UNTAC with air transport facilities for campaign purposes.

The election took place from 23 to 28 May 1993. During the first three days of the elections, some 1,400 large, medium and small fixed polling stations operated throughout the country, as well as 200 mobile teams in remote or difficult areas. A Cambodian presiding officer was in charge of each station, with support and assistance from an international polling station officer. Some fixed stations were converted to mobile operations on 26 May and worked as mobile teams on 27 and 28 May. Mobile teams operated for the entire six-day period. Counting of the ballots by UNTAC began on the morning of 29 May. The Special Representative declared the conduct of the poll free and fair in a statement[43] made on behalf of the Secretary-General and the United Nations at a meeting of SNC on 29 May.

The Security Council endorsed this declaration in resolution 835 (1993) of 2 June and called upon all parties to stand by their obligations to respect fully the results. Reporting[44] on 10 June 1993 on the holding and the results of the elections, the Secretary-General informed the Council that three of the four Cambodian parties signatory to the Paris Agreements had taken part in the electoral process — SOC, through the Cambodian

[43]S/25879. [44]S/25913.

People's Party (CPP); FUNCINPEC; and KPNLF/BLDP. PDK, the fourth Cambodian signatory party, had failed to register as a political party, had taken no part in the election and had threatened to disrupt it with violence. Aside from a few incidents, however, polling was conducted in a peaceful and often festive atmosphere, with voters sometimes walking several miles to cast their ballots, apparently undaunted by threats of violence or banditry, by rough terrain or the heavy rain that swept much of the country.

A total of 4,267,192 voters, representing 89.56 per cent of the registered voters, had turned out to vote. The count of the 4,011,631 valid ballots indicated that, nationwide, FUNCINPEC had won 1,824,188 votes, or 45.47 per cent, to CPP's 1,533,471 votes, or 38.23 per cent. BLDP won 152,764 votes, or 3.81 per cent, and the other 17 political parties won the remainder. The number of seats won in the constituent assembly was 58 for FUNCINPEC, 51 for CPP, 10 for BLDP and 1 for a fourth political party, MOLINAKA. At a meeting of SNC, held on 10 June and presided by Prince Norodom Sihanouk, the Special Representative of the Secretary-General issued a statement[45] declaring, on behalf of the Secretary-General and the United Nations, that the elections as a whole had been free and fair.

The Security Council endorsed the results of the elections by resolution 840 (1993) of 15 June. It also expressed full support for the newly elected, 120-member Constituent Assembly, which was to draw up a constitution and then transform itself into a legislative assembly to establish a new government for all Cambodians. The Council emphasized the necessity for the assembly to complete its work as soon as possible and within the three-month time-frame stipulated in the Agreements. It requested UNTAC to continue to play its role in conjunction with SNC during the transitional period.

H.   Post-electoral period (June–September 1993)

Notwithstanding the successful holding of the elections and the creation of a Constituent Assembly, the post-election period was not without difficulties. Despite the fact that CPP, at the 29 May meeting of SNC, issued a statement of its satisfaction at the excellent result of the electoral process, CPP began to make numerous allegations of electoral irregularities as the counting proceeded. It also requested UNTAC to hold new elections in seven provinces. At the 10 June meeting of SNC, CPP announced that it could not recognize the result of the elections and demanded an investigation of the irregularities.

UNTAC conducted intensive discussions with CPP in this regard, asking it to provide details to support the allegations. Every concrete allegation was promptly investigated by UNTAC. The Special Representative and his associates also corresponded with the President of CPP, Mr. Chea Sim, listing all the measures UNTAC had taken to rectify anomalies of which it was aware. UNTAC also made it clear that the alleged irregularities did not amount to fraud and that none of CPP's allegations, even if true, would affect the outcome of the elections. UNTAC firmly maintained that its own actions were impartial and that the elections were free and fair.

In early June, some elements of SOC declared a "secession" in three eastern provinces: Kompong Cham, Prey Veng and Svay Rieng. As tension increased in those provinces, there were anti-UNTAC demonstrations and a number of attacks against UNTAC personnel and property. This led UNTAC to withdraw its non-essential civilian personnel on 12 and 13 June. The Special Representative requested Prince Sihanouk to cooperate with UNTAC in calming the situation, and also contacted the leaders of CPP and FUNCINPEC. On 12 June, the Prince made an appeal for the peaceful settlement and normalization of the situation. The Special Representative also encouraged a dialogue between SOC and FUNCINPEC.

The duly elected Constituent Assembly began work on 14 June 1993. At the inaugural session, it adopted a resolution to make Prince Sihanouk Head of State retroactive to 1970, thus making the *coup d'état* of 18 March 1970 null and void. The Assembly gave the Prince full powers as head of State. The following day, Prince Sihanouk

_____
[45]S/25913, annex.

proposed the formation of an Interim Joint Administration (GNPC) with Prince Ranariddh and Mr. Hun Sen as Co-chairmen.

During the course of these developments, CPP gradually softened its position. With support for the secession dissipating, the secession collapsed. On 21 June, CPP issued a statement recognizing the result of the elections, while suspending judgement regarding the alleged electoral irregularities. UNTAC agreed to form a committee of inquiry (the Electoral Advisory Committee) in order to deal with this issue. PDK also declared that it would accept the outcome of the elections. By 24 June, CPP, FUNCINPEC and BLDP had agreed to the proposal to form GNPC and the list of the cabinet was submitted to the Constituent Assembly.

On 30 June, the Constituent Assembly elected its President and two Vice-Presidents and adopted its Rules of Procedure. It also established two permanent committees: the Committee for Drafting the Constitution and the Committee on Rules of Procedure. At the request of the Cambodian parties, UNTAC provided logistical and operational assistance, as well as technical advice, to the Assembly. The Assembly held a vote of confidence on 1 July 1993.

The Secretary-General informed[46] the Security Council that the establishment of GNPC, although not foreseen under the Paris Agreements, provided for a cooperative framework between all parties which held seats in the Constituent Assembly. The Administration, which would operate during the transitional period, should be viewed as an attempt to fuse three of the existing administrative structures, with Prince Sihanouk as head of State. Furthermore, tentative discussions took place between the parties participating in the Administration and PDK aimed at achieving national reconciliation.

Withdrawal plans

Although the main body of troops and civilian staff remained in Cambodia after the elections, a substantial number had already been withdrawn as their functions came to an end. The whole of the repatriation component and the great majority of the staff of the electoral component had already been withdrawn by June 1993. Due to security considerations, the timing of the withdrawal of the civilian staff from the district and provincial levels was closely coordinated with the military withdrawal plan. The latter was difficult to implement because it involved moving thousands of troops at the height of the rainy season over severely degraded infrastructure. Furthermore, the security situation was anything but settled, for banditry was rife. According to the Secretary-General's withdrawal plan,[47] physical preparations for withdrawal were to end by 31 July, and the phased movement of troops out of the country to be completed by 15 November 1993.

In putting forward his proposal for the final withdrawal of UNTAC, the Secretary-General noted that Cambodia clearly required continued international assistance and support. The country still faced enormous problems of security, stability, mine-clearance, infrastructure improvement and general economic and social development. Future assistance, however, should be clearly separate from the UNTAC presence. UNTAC was an operation with a clearly defined mandate and duration and specific resources. In order to coordinate the full range of civilian activities that would be undertaken by various agencies of the United Nations system, in accordance with their existing mandates, to promote development, provide humanitarian assistance and foster respect for human rights in Cambodia, the Secretary-General reiterated his intention to establish in Phnom Penh an integrated office headed by a United Nations representative. The office would also deal with a number of residual issues arising from the Paris Agreements and UNTAC's presence in the country. The Secretary-General would not recommend at that stage the retention of United Nations military personnel in Cambodia after the departure of UNTAC, but would give careful consideration to such a request if the new Government were to make one.

On 27 August 1993, the Security Council in its resolution 860 (1993) approved the UNTAC withdrawal plan and set 15 November 1993 as the deadline for the completion of the process. However, acting on the recommendation[48] of the Secretary-General, the Security Council, in its resolution 880 of 4 November, extended the period of withdrawal of the Mine Clearance and Training Unit until 30 November 1993. It also extended until 31 December at the latest the withdrawal period for elements of the military police and medical components. The Secretary-General had noted that, in view of the deterioration of security conditions in Cambodia, a number of military police officers and members of a medical unit were needed in order to ensure the safety and security of UNTAC personnel and equipment as the withdrawal was being completed. Between 16

[46]S/26090. [47]S/26090, S/26360. [48]S/26675.

and 30 November, 71 military police officers were required, along with 10 members of a medical unit. In December, the number was reduced to 30 and 8 respectively.

Mandate ends

On 21 September 1993, the Constituent Assembly adopted the new Constitution. The vote was 113 in favour and 5 against, with two abstentions.

The mandate entrusted to UNTAC was concluded on 24 September 1993 when Prince Norodom Sihanouk formally promulgated the new Constitution of the Kingdom of Cambodia, making the country a constitutional monarchy, independent, sovereign, peaceful, neutral and non-aligned. The same day, Prince Sihanouk was elected King of Cambodia by the Royal Council of the Throne. In accordance with the Constitution and the Paris Agreements, the Constituent Assembly was transformed into a legislative assembly. The King appointed Prince Norodom Ranariddh, leader of FUNCINPEC, first Prime Minister in the new Government and Mr. Hun Sen, leader of CPP, second Prime Minister. The Special Representative left Cambodia on 26 September 1993.

The Council expressed[49] its satisfaction at the auspicious developments that had taken place in Cambodia since the holding of the elections and stressed the importance of the continued support of the international community to the consolidation of peace and democracy and the promotion of development in Cambodia.

United Nations liaison team in Cambodia

On 26 September 1993, the First and Second Prime Ministers of Cambodia jointly requested the Secretary-General to consider the possibility of dispatching some 20 or 30 unarmed United Nations military observers to Cambodia for a period of six months following the end of UNTAC's mandate. The two Prime Ministers subsequently reiterated to the Secretary-General their conviction that such a presence would strengthen confidence among the people and thus enhance the stability of Cambodia and its new Government at a critical time.[50] The Security Council indicated[51] its agreement in principle and asked the Secretary-General to submit a detailed proposal on the matter.

The task of a military liaison team, as recommended[52] by the Secretary-General, would be to maintain close liaison with the Government and report to the Secretary-General on matters affecting security. The team would also help the Government in dealing with residual military matters related to the Paris Agreements. It would consist of 20 unarmed military officers and be headed by a Chief Military Liaison Officer (CMLO) designated by the Secretary-General with the consent of the Security Council. The team, based in Phnom Penh, would be distinct from the integrated United Nations office the Secretary-General intended to establish, although in practice, the CMLO would maintain regular contact with the United Nations representative. The Secretary-General estimated the cost at $1.06 million for six-months. By its resolution 880 (1993) of 4 November, the Security Council decided to establish a military liaison team for a single period of six months.

The United Nations Military Liaison Team was set up in Phnom Penh on 15 November 1993, with Colonel Muniruz Zaman (Bangladesh) as CMLO. Other countries contributing officers were Austria, Belgium, China, France, India, Indonesia, Malaysia, New Zealand, Pakistan, Poland, Russian Federation, Thailand and Uruguay. Liaison was conducted at the ministerial, executive and ambassadorial levels by the CMLO, and at the functional level by other officers, who reported daily to United Nations Headquarters on security conditions and developments. Officers were also dispatched in mobile teams to observe areas outside Phnom Penh when requested by the Government and when the CMLO deemed that the issue related to the mandate.[53]

In the meantime, on 29 March 1994, the Secretary-General appointed Mr. Benny Widyono as his representative in Cambodia.[54] On 2 May, the Government requested an extension of the Team's mandate for a further period. However, as an alternative, the Council decided to endorse the Secretary-General's proposal to attach three military advisers to the office of the representative to assist him in fulfilling his mandate. Three military advisers, from Belgium, France and Malaysia, were retained in Cambodia for this purpose following the Team's departure when it ceased operations on 15 May 1994.[55] After April 1995, one military adviser was attached to the representative's office whose mandate was subsequently extended through March 1996.[56]

---

[49]S/26531. [50]S/26546. [51]S/26570. [52]S/26649. [53]S/1994/169. [54]S/1994/389. [55]S/1994/645. [56]S/1995/870.

I. A brief review of UNTAC

Each UNTAC component had a distinctive role, including, as discussed above, that of the Special Representative and his Office in maintaining relations with SNC and the Cambodian parties. The activities of the components were coordinated as necessary to allow for the most efficient and cost-effective use of resources. The level of activity in each case varied during the course of the transitional period.

Electoral component

The activities of the electoral component and the central importance of the electoral process have already been related in detail. Special mention, however, should be made of the 465 United Nations Volunteers (UNVs) serving as district electoral supervisors, many of them in remote, and sometimes contested, areas. They played a vital role in the programme of civic education about the election as well as in convincing the electorate that their vote was secret. Among their other duties was the training of Cambodian electoral staff. Following an incident on 8 April 1993 in which a district electoral supervisor was killed, UNTAC instituted emergency provisional arrangements to improve security. UNVs in areas considered to present security risks were instructed to withdraw from the countryside and not to travel without an armed escort until further notice.

Prior to UNTAC's establishment, compilation of socio-demographic and cartographic data was initially undertaken by the Advance Election Planning Unit, set up in late 1991. That unit was subsequently integrated into the electoral component. Other electoral staff were progressively deployed throughout the country. Staff at headquarters during the registration period included about 280 Cambodian data entry clerks, working in three 8-hour shifts.

Following the elections, a skeleton staff remained in Phnom Penh to advise the Special Representative's Electoral Advisory Committee on CPP complaints and, subsequently, to assist with the establishment of the Constituent Assembly and with its work on the constitution, as requested.

UNTAC human rights role

The Paris Agreements gave UNTAC the responsibility during the transitional period for fostering an environment in which respect for human rights and fundamental freedoms were ensured and where free and fair elections might take place. UNTAC activities in this regard comprised three aspects: a human rights education programme; general human rights oversight of all existing administrative structures in Cambodia; and the investigation of allegations of human rights abuses occurring during the transitional period.

The UNTAC human rights component was active in three broad areas. First, it encouraged SNC to adhere to relevant international human rights instruments and undertook a review of the existing judicial and penal systems in the light of international provisions. Secondly, it conducted an extensive human rights information and education campaign in close cooperation with the Information/Education Division of UNTAC. Thirdly, it investigated human rights-related complaints and took corrective measures where necessary. Human rights officers were progressively deployed in all 21 provinces in Cambodia, including in the zones controlled by FUNCINPEC and KPNLF. However, the component had no access to the zones controlled by PDK.

On 20 April 1992, SNC ratified the International Covenants on Civil and Political Rights and on Economic, Social and Cultural Rights. On 10 September, it agreed to accede to the Convention against Torture and Other Cruel, Inhuman or Degrading Treatment or Punishment; the International Convention on the Elimination of All Forms of Discrimination against Women; the Convention on the Rights of the Child; and the Convention and Protocol relating to the Status of Refugees.

UNTAC developed a human rights education programme with particular reference to teacher training, dissemination of relevant international instruments, education of health professionals, training of public and political officials and support for local human rights organizations. Educational materials, posters, leaflets, stickers and other printed materials were disseminated throughout the country. Human rights training was introduced into the Cambodian education system, and human rights studies were incorporated in the curriculum of Phnom Penh University's Law School and Medical Faculty. Collaboration with local human rights organizations was an important aspect of UNTAC's work. UNTAC provided them with materials, training and expertise as well as

STRUCTURE OF UNTAC

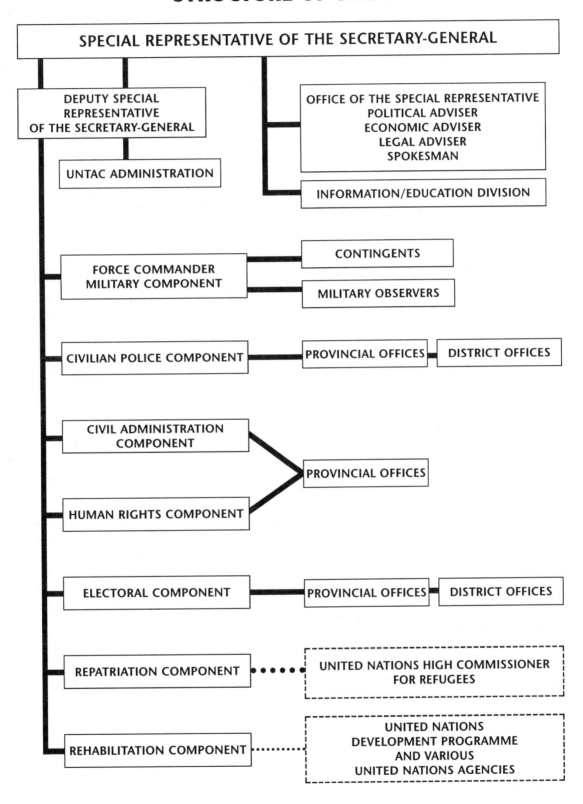

small grants for basic office expenses. It organized an International Symposium on Human Rights in Cambodia from 30 November to 2 December 1992, and conducted a special course for human rights advocates, including a training programme on United Nations human rights procedures and a special training programme dealing with human rights issues in the electoral process.

As part of the effort to promote the development of an independent judiciary, a major programme of training for judges, defence lawyers and public defenders was initiated. Training sessions for officials of the existing administrative structures and professional or activist groups were undertaken in almost every province. Participants included representatives of political parties, members of human rights associations, teacher trainees, justice officials and police. UNTAC closely monitored conditions of detention in civil prisons throughout Cambodia and pressed local authorities to improve the situation to the extent possible within the means available to the prison administration. It investigated all cases of prisoners whose detention might be politically motivated.

On 19 February 1993, the United Nations Commission on Human Rights adopted a resolution providing for the first time for the operational involvement of the United Nations Centre for Human Rights in Cambodia in the post-UNTAC period. One of the major tasks of UNTAC's human rights component was to prepare for this operational presence. In 1996, this presence continued to be a factor in Cambodia's political life.

Military component

The objectives of the military arrangements during the transitional period were to stabilize the security situation and build confidence among the parties to the conflict. Achieving those objectives was a necessary precursor to the successful conduct of the functions of the other components. In addition to its tasks related to the cease-fire and the cantonment process, the military component also carried out other tasks, including weapons control and assistance to other components such as the repatriation component. It carried out activities related to essential engineering, de-mining, logistics and communications, and patrolling and observation, and participated in a border control mechanism established by UNTAC. The military component also undertook civil action programmes.

Between the beginning of the phase II cantonment process in June 1992 and mid-November 1992, UNTAC cantoned some 55,000 troops of the three cooperating parties. However, the refusal of PDK to enter phase II of the cease-fire resulted in the suspension of the cantonment, disarming and demobilization process.

Under these circumstances, the Secretary-General proposed that the level of deployment of the military component be maintained until the elections. The deployment pattern, which was originally based on the requirements of regrouping and cantonment, was realigned to correspond with the borders of the Cambodian provinces. This deployment, which also conformed to the deployment of the electoral teams, reflected the component's new priority task of enhancing UNTAC's ability to protect voter registration and the electoral and polling processes, particularly in areas with a higher potential for conflict.

During the registration period, military observers accompanied electoral teams in order to negotiate, where necessary, with local authorities or forces that tried to hinder registration. Security of the polling stations and their vicinity was provided by UNTAC alone. However the military component concluded agreements with the armed forces of SOC, FUNCINPEC and KPNLF. The armed forces of the factions assisted UNTAC, conveyed information on possible or actual threats to the elections and ensured security in the zones under their control.

UNTAC devoted serious attention to the question of the possible presence of foreign forces in Cambodia. It repeatedly requested the Cambodian parties to provide it with verifiable information relating to foreign forces, but none did so. It also established Strategic Investigation Teams to follow up on allegations. UNTAC found no evidence of the presence of any formed units of such forces in areas to which it had access, although some seven men were identified as "foreign forces" within the meaning of the definition approved by SNC.

Mine clearance

UNTAC took over the landmine programmes begun by UNAMIC and expanded them. For its part, SNC on 20 April 1992 decided to establish the Cambodian Mine Action Centre (CMAC) under the Presidency of Prince Norodom Sihanouk and the Vice Presidency of the Special Representative. Each were to appoint five members to a ten-member Governing Council. CMAC would then undertake long-term programmes in mine-awareness, marking and clearance. The Governing

Council held its first meeting on 4 November 1992.

UNTAC's Mine Clearance Training Unit (MCTU), comprising some 183 officers and men, taught Cambodians to identify, locate and destroy land mines and to mark minefields, and promoted mine awareness among the general public. The Unit was organized into mine clearance training teams and mine clearance supervisory teams. Towards the end of its mandate, MCTU worked to equip CMAC to function after UNTAC's withdrawal.

By August 1993, as a result of the work done by UNTAC, in collaboration with the Cambodian parties and with non-governmental organizations, more than 4 million square metres of Cambodian territory had been cleared of mines. About 37,000 mines and other unexploded ordnance had been destroyed, and some 2,300 Cambodians trained in mine-clearance techniques. CMAC continued this work in the post-UNTAC period. In this regard, the Secretary-General appealed to the international donor community to render assistance. Pending alternate funding arrangements acceptable to donors and in consultation with the new Cambodian Government, he intended to maintain the United Nations Trust Fund for Demining Programmes in Cambodia.

Civil administration

UNTAC's civil administration component used three complementary means of control. One was control and appraisal, achieved through the receipt of all documentation dealing with the operation of the existing administrative structures, including the lines of decision-making, personnel policies and questions. A second form of control was achieved through the authority to obtain prior knowledge of decisions reached by the administrative structures, as well as the authority to change decisions dealing, for instance, with personnel, finance and the sale of assets. A third form of control involved the proposal of improvements in the operations of the existing administrative structures. On a day-to-day basis, these three means of direct control were exercised in various ways, including the physical presence of civil administration personnel alongside their highest-ranking counterparts in the existing administrative structures, regular meetings between UNTAC staff and these officials and the establishment of clear lines of decision-making.

On 1 July 1992, the civil administration component began to exercise full control over the five key areas in the Phnom Penh administration, as specified in the Paris Agreements: foreign affairs, national defence, public security, finance and information. By 15 July, UNTAC civil administration offices had been established in all 21 provinces, although, like the other components of UNTAC, civil administration personnel were denied access to PDK-controlled areas. In addition, UNTAC established optional control over other administrative structures identified as having direct influence over the outcome of elections. In accordance with the implementation plan, the civil administration component requested the four Cambodian parties to submit a list of their current laws for review by UNTAC. With the exception of PDK, all parties complied. At the initiative of UNTAC, SNC adopted laws enshrining the rights of freedom of association and of assembly, and approved a set of principles relating to the legal system, penal law and penal procedure with a view to establishing uniform standards for the judiciary and for substantive law that would be applicable throughout Cambodia.

In the area of foreign affairs, UNTAC had control over the receipt and distribution of foreign aid and the issuance of passports and visas. It also exercised control over the various border functions, such as immigration, customs and the implementation of SNC moratoriums on timber, gems and minerals. A border control unit was established with responsibility for liaison between UNTAC components and the existing administrative structures.

In the area of defence, UNTAC inspected the defence structures of the three parties and established other modalities, including the monitoring of incoming and outgoing correspondence, in order to control any actions that might impair the neutrality of the political environment. The leaders of the armed forces of the three factions complying with the Paris Agreements signed the directive prepared by UNTAC regulating the political activity of military personnel. At the request of UNTAC, the SOC ministry of defence established a committee to investigate allegations of illegal activity on the part of CPAF armed forces.

UNTAC's activities with regard to public security included the training of judges, prosecutors and police officers of the existing administrative structures in the implementation of the Penal Code adopted by SNC on UNTAC's initiative, and a programme of regular prison visits. Working groups on road safety and banditry were established. The Special Representative issued a directive prohibiting the illegal possession and carrying of weapons and explosives.

In the area of finance, UNTAC worked with the administrative structures to put in place controls over expenditure, sources of revenue, central bank functions and the sale of public assets. SNC adopted a financial control directive prepared by the Special Representative on the transfer of public assets in order to introduce orderly and transparent procedures into the process of privatization of property owned by the existing administrative structures.

Another dimension of UNTAC's work was the effort to stabilize the country's economy in order to reduce possible causes of unrest that might have an adverse effect on the electoral environment. Control teams were set up to supplement the regular supervision that UNTAC exercised over the existing administrative structures, particularly outside Phnom Penh. Each team was headed by an inspector assisted by Finance and Public Security Services staff, representatives of the military and civilian police components, and analysts and interpreters from the Information/Education Division.

Following the elections, the component streamlined its activities to help ensure a smooth transition from the existing administrative structures to the new Government. At the provincial level, civil administration staff maintained their contacts with the personnel of the existing administrative structures, promoted dialogue and national reconciliation, monitored any sale, transfer or disposal of public assets, followed up on allegations of human rights violations or political intimidation, and facilitated the work of United Nations agencies. On the national level, civil administration staff focused their efforts on the judiciary and the administration of justice, on monitoring the implementation of SNC moratoria on timber, gems and minerals, on border and customs control, and on the control and safeguarding of public funds and State assets. Financial control activities continued through the transitional period at both the national and provincial levels.

Civilian police

UNTAC's civilian police component worked in close cooperation with the human rights, electoral, military, civil administration and repatriation components. The police presence, like that of the military, helped assure Cambodians of UNTAC's commitment to the peace process. It also promoted the creation of a neutral political envi-

ronment by making Cambodians aware that the arbitrary abuse of power would not be tolerated.

Much of the daily work of the 3,600 UNTAC civilian police focused on its main function, the supervision or control of local police activities. In carrying out this function, the component provided local police with training in basic police methods, including operations, traffic control, human rights observance, criminal law, criminal investigation, crime prevention, and demonstration and riot control. It also provided local police with basic information on the roles of UNTAC and the civilian police component. Special instruction was provided to police officers and judges in the implementation of the new penal code adopted by SNC.

Priority in initial deployment was given to areas were Cambodian refugees and displaced persons were being resettled. The component eventually extended its activities to all provinces. Police monitors were posted at border checkpoints and cooperated with the military component in arrangements concerning supervision of checkpoints and patrols operated by local police forces in sensitive areas. Joint checkpoints manned by UNTAC and local police resulted in the confiscation of a large number of unauthorized firearms. The component also directed the efforts of local police against the growing problem of banditry in the interior.

Some 60 per cent of UNTAC civilian police were directly involved in assisting the voter registration process. During the electoral campaign, following the steep rise in attacks against the offices of political parties, UNTAC civilian police, in collaboration with other components, launched a special operation which included intensive patrols and static guard duty to curb the attacks. UNTAC civilian police also monitored political rallies and meetings. During the voting, they were present at all polling stations.

The police component undertook independently hundreds of investigations into serious crimes, particularly those considered to be politically or ethnically motivated. In a number of those cases, the Special Prosecutor had enough evidence to issue a warrant. Where cases involved political or ethnic considerations, the Special Representative also raised the matter with SNC or in private meetings with party leaders.

Repatriation

Some 365,000 Cambodian refugees and displaced persons from camps on the Thai border and elsewhere were repatriated under United Nations auspices in an inter-agency effort under the overall authority of UNTAC. UNHCR acted as lead agency and oversaw the movement of returnees, the provision of immediate assistance and food, and a reintegration programme. The repatriation component of UNTAC was headed by a director, appointed by the Secretary-General and reporting to the Special Representative as well as to the High Commissioner for Refugees.

The repatriation exercise began on 30 March 1992. On 30 March 1993, the largest and last of the refugee camps, Site 2, was closed at an official ceremony presided by the United Nations High Commissioner for Refugees. Some 365,000 refugees and displaced persons had returned to Cambodia under United Nations auspices. The monthly rate of return rose from 4,000 in April to 20,000 in June. By July, some 30,000 Cambodians were returning home each month. Difficult travelling conditions during the rainy season were largely overcome by the use of rail and, in some cases, waterways. By November, the rate of return rose to 35,000 a month and reached a peak of 40,000 in the months of January and February 1993. Though the great bulk of the returnees came from Thailand, some 2,000 were also repatriated from Indonesia, Viet Nam and Malaysia. Most refugees chose to settle in areas controlled by the Phnom Penh authorities. Of the rest, about 33,000 chose to settle in the KPNLF zone, while several thousand settled in the PDK and FUNCINPEC zones.

In addition to rations for 400 days and a domestic kit, returnees had the choice of several forms of assistance, including agricultural land, a housing plot and a cash grant in lieu of building materials. Most returnees, some 88 percent, chose the cash grant. UNHCR advised returnees on the situation prevailing in their communes of final destination, particularly when they were unsafe or inaccessible. In cooperation with other UNTAC components, United Nations agencies and non-governmental organizations, UNHCR established a country-wide mechanism for monitoring the condition of returnees. Quick-impact projects were also implemented to help communities absorb the returnees. These included road and bridge repair, mine-clearance, agricultural development, digging of wells and water ponds and improvement and construction of sanitation, health and education facilities. All eligible returnees were given the opportunity to register to vote, either in their final destination along with the local population or in the six reception centres. In January 1993, as the deadline for the end of the electoral registration period was approaching, a special arrangement was made between UNTAC's repatriation and electoral components to enable registration of the remaining eligible population in the border camps whereby they were temporarily "listed" in Thailand and received their registration cards upon return to Cambodia.

Information/education activities

After two decades of fighting and isolation, many Cambodians were little aware of the international community's efforts to assist their country. Many were skeptical about the applicability in Cambodia of basic concepts of human rights, including free and fair elections and multi-party political campaigning. The flow of information between UNTAC and the people of Cambodia was thus considered essential to UNTAC's operation. The arrangements in this regard was another unprecedented aspect of UNTAC.

The Information/Education Division of UNTAC was responsible for producing information material in the Khmer language and disseminating it to the Cambodian people. It published media guidelines aimed at lifting legal restrictions and encouraging the operation of a free and responsible press, and launched a Cambodian Media Association of all Cambodian journalists. It pursued efforts to exercise control over the administrative structures dealing with information. The Special Representative issued a directive on fair access to the media during the electoral campaign, and UNTAC made its own television/video, radio and other information facilities available to the 20 political parties participating in the elections.

UNTAC had its own radio station. On 9 November 1992, the station began broadcasting from a Phnom Penh-based transmitter loaned by SOC for UNTAC's exclusive use. By April 1993, relay stations brought the UNTAC message to all parts of the country and, by early May, programming had expanded to 15 hours per day. In addition, under arrangements made with the Thai Foreign Ministry and Voice of America (VOA), UNTAC materials were broadcast via a VOA transmitter in Thailand at prime time twice daily. The broadcasts concentrated on information regarding the electoral process, human rights and other aspects of the UNTAC mandate. During the electoral campaign particular emphasis was given to the secrecy of the ballot. In accordance with the directive of the Special Representative on fair access to the media during the electoral campaign, Radio UNTAC offered weekly segments to each political party for the broadcast of political material and allowed a "right of response" to a political party, candidate or official in cases of unfair attack or misrepresentation of public statements.

UNTAC also produced a variety of videos, posters, information leaflets, flyers, banners, billboards and advertisements for public display to illustrate the work of UNTAC and to inform Cambodians of the events of the electoral process and encourage their full participation in it. Activity during the campaign included disseminating information on various political party platforms, building confidence in the secrecy of the ballot and instructing voters in voting procedures. Information videos, including round-table discussions involving representatives of the 20 political parties contesting the elections, were shown in Phnom Penh and distributed throughout the country. Translations and analyses of the Khmer-language radio and print output of all four Cambodian parties signatory to the Paris Agreements were provided to the Special Representative and all UNTAC components. Information officers conducted regular opinion surveys among Cambodians to assess the impact of UNTAC's information programme and to monitor the attitude of the people towards UNTAC and its implementation of the peace process.

Rehabilitation

The rehabilitation phase ran from the signing of the Paris Agreements and the establishment of UNTAC until the formation of a new Cambodian Government following free and fair elections. UNTAC's rehabilitation component focused on food security, health, housing, training, education, the transport network and the restoration of Cambodia's basic infrastructure, including public utilities. The component's director, appointed by the Secretary-General and reporting to the Special Representative, ensured effective coordination of rehabilitation activities, and made ongoing assessments of needs. Shortly after the establishment of UNTAC in Cambodia, a technical advisory committee of SNC was set up under the chairmanship of the UNTAC Director of Rehabilitation in order to facilitate the approval of projects by the Cambodian parties. In addition, the director had responsibilities related to raising resources through donor contributions.

On 23 July 1992, SNC established a technical advisory committee to review and assess existing contractual arrangements relating to the exploitation of natural resources such as timber stock and gem mines. On the committee's recommendation, SNC, on 22 September, instituted a country-wide moratorium on the export of logs — a decision supported by the Security Council in its resolution 792 (1992). Compliance with the moratorium was monitored by the rehabilitation component, in close coordination with UNTAC military observers, civil administration and civilian police personnel deployed at border checkpoints. On 10 February 1993, SNC adopted supplementary measures aimed at discouraging further tree felling by reducing the volume of sawn timber allowed to be exported from Cambodia. In March 1993, SNC approved the UNTAC draft action plan on the implementation of the Declaration on Mining and Export of Minerals and Gems from Cambodia. The Declaration placed a moratorium on the commercial extraction of mineral resources on land and offshore and on the export of minerals and gems from Cambodia, effective 28 February 1993. Also in 1993, SNC approved the proposal made by UNTAC in collaboration with the United Nations Educational, Scientific and Cultural Organization for the establishment of a National Heritage Protection Authority of Cambodia to coordinate efforts aimed at protecting and administering the physical cultural heritage of Cambodia.

Of the nearly $880 million pledged at the Ministerial Conference on the Rehabilitation and Reconstruction of Cambodia in Tokyo, the Secretary-General reported that the actual level of disbursements by early 1993 stood at no more than $95 million. Further, the lack of funding for certain specific sectors, including training and maintenance of essential social services, also gave rise to concern that these deficiencies might compromise the overall rehabilitation effort. These issues of concern were discussed at a meeting of donors in Phnom Penh on 25 February 1993. The participants recognized the need for speedy disbursement of the commitments made in Tokyo. They reviewed the emerging priority needs and agreed that arrangements be made for meetings, following the elections, of the International Committee on the Reconstruction of Cambodia. As of mid-August 1993, approximately $200 million had been disbursed. A meeting of the Committee was held in Paris on 8 and 9 September 1993 at which new pledges amounting to $120 million were made.

Towards the end of the transition period, the rehabilitation component concentrated on the implementation of small-scale rehabilitation projects yielding quick results. These projects involved the repair and maintenance of public utilities and education and health facilities. Most projects were highly labour-intensive, thus creating jobs. Donor response to the component's initiative to implement these projects was relatively positive after the elections had taken place.

UNTAC Composition

UNTAC was headed by the Special Representative of the Secretary-General, Mr. Yasushi Akashi (Japan). Lieutenant-General John Sanderson (Australia) served as Force Commander. Budget provision[57] made for UNTAC personnel included up to 15,547 troops, 893 military observers, and 3,500 civilian police. Other components of UNTAC consisted of staff members of the United Nations and its specialized agencies, United Nations Volunteers, staff seconded from Member States, and local staff. Provision included up to 1,149 international civilian staff, 465 United Nations Volunteers and 4,830 local staff, supplemented by international contractual staff. During the electoral period, more than 50,000 Cambodians served as electoral staff and some 900 international polling station officers were seconded from 44 countries and the Interparliamentary Union.

Military personnel were provided by Algeria, Argentina, Australia, Austria, Bangladesh, Belgium, Brunei Darussalam, Bulgaria, Cameroon, Canada, Chile, China, France, Germany, Ghana, India, Indonesia, Ireland, Japan, Malaysia, Namibia, Netherlands, New Zealand, Pakistan, Philippines, Poland, Russian Federation, Senegal, Singapore, Thailand, Tunisia, United Kingdom, United States and Uruguay.

Civilian police personnel were provided by Algeria, Australia, Austria, Bangladesh, Brunei Darussalam, Bulgaria, Cameroon, Colombia, Egypt, Fiji, France, Germany, Ghana, Hungary, India, Indonesia, Ireland, Italy, Japan, Jordan, Kenya, Malaysia, Morocco, Nepal, Netherlands, Nigeria, Norway, Pakistan, Philippines, Singapore, Sweden, and Tunisia.

Financial Aspects

Expenditures for UNAMIC and UNTAC amounted to $1,620,963,300. Repatriation and resettlement of refugees and displaced persons, as well as rehabilitation assistance, were funded from voluntary contributions.

Conclusion

In its resolution 880 (1993) of 4 November 1993, the Security Council noted with great satisfaction that, with the conclusion of UNTAC's mission, the goal of the Paris Agreements — restoring to the Cambodian people and their democratically elected leaders their primary responsibility for peace, stability, national reconciliation and reconstruction — had been fulfilled. The Council paid tribute to the work of UNTAC, whose success constituted a major achievement for the United Nations. The Secretary-General believed the international community could take satisfaction in the fact that, despite serious difficulties, UNTAC was able to accomplish its central task of holding a free and fair election in Cambodia and laying a sound foundation for the people of Cambodia to build a stable and peaceful future.[58]

[57] A/48/701. [58] S/26360.

Part VIII

The former Yugoslavia

Chapter 23

United Nations efforts in the former Yugoslavia: Overview

Chapter 23

United Nations efforts in the former Yugoslavia: Overview

A. Background

Fighting begins

The Socialist Federal Republic of Yugoslavia consisted of six republics: Bosnia and Herzegovina, Croatia, Macedonia, Montenegro, Serbia and Slovenia. Within the republic of Serbia, there were two autonomous regions: Vojvodina and Kosovo. For the sake of convenience, the country is referred to here as Yugoslavia.

Yugoslavia's internal boundaries rarely coincided with demographic distribution. Among the major communities, all of them Slavic, were Croats, Muslims and Serbs; in addition, there were numbers of Macedonians, Montenegrins and Slovenes, as well as those who referred to themselves as Yugoslavs. The population also included a number of ethnic Albanians, Hungarians and others. According to the 1991 census, Serbs comprised about 36 per cent of a total population of some 23.5 million people, Croats about 20 per cent and Muslims about 10 per cent. In Serbia, Serbs comprised some 66 per cent of the population, Muslims 2.5 per cent and Croats 1.1 per cent; more than 81 per cent of the population in Kosovo was ethnic Albanian, and in Vojvodina there was a large minority of ethnic Hungarians. In Bosnia and Herzegovina, 44 per cent of the population were Muslims, 31 per cent were Serbs and 17 per cent Croats. In Croatia, 78 per cent were Croats, 12 per cent Serbs and fewer than 1 per cent Muslims. During the administration headed by President Josip Broz Tito, the political life of the country and of the republics was structured to balance the diversity of the population and knit it together.

In July 1971, President Tito introduced a system of collective leadership and regular rotation of personnel among posts. He established and himself led the collective State presidency until his death in May 1980. The 1974 Constitution gave the different republics much autonomous power, the federal government remaining responsible only for national defence, foreign policy and the single national market. In 1979, the principle of rotating leadership was also extended to the secretaryship of the League of Communists of Yugoslavia (LCY). Following the death of President Tito, his responsibilities passed smoothly to the collective presidency and the LCY presidium.

The 1980s were marked by economic and political crises in the country, social and nationalist unrest and increasing evidence of inter-ethnic tensions. The collective federal presidency and its six rotating Presidents were unable to negotiate a revised national structure or to devise effective means to deal with the changing circumstances. By June 1991, following popular referendums in Croatia and Slovenia, those two republics declared themselves independent. A referendum in the republic of Macedonia on 8 September also supported independence as did a vote in the assembly of the republic of Bosnia and Herzegovina in October. The vote in the assembly was supported by Bosnian Muslims and Bosnian Croats, but it caused the Bosnian Serb members to walk out and the Bosnian Serb community to affirm separateness. The republic of Serbia strongly disapproved the declarations of independence and expressed grave concern over the fate of Serbs resident in Croatia and of Serbs resident in Bosnia and Herzegovina.

Fighting in Croatia began in June 1991 when Serbs living in Croatia, with the support of the Yugoslav People's Army (JNA), opposed the declaration of independence. In Slovenia, where there was not any significant Serb minority, fighting was brief and JNA withdrew after an agreement brokered by the European Community [now the European Union] entered into force at the beginning of July 1991. However, efforts by the European Community to stop hostilities in Croatia and to resolve the crisis in the framework of the Conference on Yugoslavia proved unsuccessful.

United Nations involvement

The United Nations involvement in the former Yugoslavia began on 25 September 1991 when the Security Council, meeting at the ministerial level, unanimously adopted its resolution 713 (1991) calling on all States to implement immediately a "general and complete embargo on all deliveries of weapons and military equipment to Yugoslavia". The Council commended the efforts of the European Community, with the support of the States participating in the Conference on Security and Cooperation in Europe (CSCE) [now the Organization for Security and Cooperation in Europe (OSCE)], to restore peace and dialogue in Yugoslavia and invited the Secretary-General to offer his assistance.

Secretary-General Javier Pérez de Cuéllar appointed Mr. Cyrus Vance, former United States Secretary of State, as his Personal Envoy for Yugoslavia on 8 October 1991. On 23 November 1991, Mr. Vance convened in Geneva a meeting which was attended by the President of Serbia, the President of Croatia, the Secretary of State for National Defence of Yugoslavia and Lord Carrington, Chairman of the European Community's Conference on Yugoslavia. The parties reached agreement on an immediate cease-fire and expressed the wish to see the speedy establishment of a United Nations peace-keeping operation. However, while progress was made on other issues, the cease-fire broke down almost immediately. By its resolution 721 (1991) of 27 November 1991, the Security Council endorsed the Personal Envoy's statement to the parties that the deployment of a United Nations peace-keeping operation could not be envisaged without full compliance by all parties with the Geneva agreement.

By its resolution 724 (1991) of 15 December, the Security Council approved a report by the Secretary-General which contained a plan for a possible peace-keeping operation. A small group of military officers, civilian police and United Nations Secretariat staff travelled to the area to prepare for the implementation of this plan. On 2 January 1992, the Personal Envoy convened in Sarajevo a meeting between military representatives of the Republic of Croatia and representatives of JNA, at which the Implementing Accord on the unconditional cease-fire was signed. With the Security Council's concurrence, Secretary-General Boutros Boutros-Ghali then sent to the area a group of 50 military liaison officers, with the task of using their good offices to promote maintenance of the cease-fire by facilitating communication between the opposing parties and by helping them to resolve difficulties that might arise.

UNPROFOR established

On 15 February 1992, notwithstanding differences voiced by some of those concerned regarding the United Nations plan, the Secretary-General recommended to the Security Council the establishment of the United Nations Protection Force (UNPROFOR). In his view, the danger that a United Nations peace-keeping operation would fail for lack of cooperation from the parties was less grievous than the danger that delay in its dispatch would lead to a breakdown of the cease-fire and to a new conflagration.

On 21 February, the Security Council, by its resolution 743 (1992), established UNPROFOR for an initial period of 12 months as an interim arrangement to create the conditions of peace and security required for the negotiation of an overall settlement of the crisis within the framework of the European Community's Conference on Yugoslavia. The Council requested the Secretary-General to deploy immediately those elements of UNPROFOR which could assist in developing an implementation plan. The Security Council authorized the full deployment of the Force by its resolution 749 (1992) of 7 April 1992.

B. General review of peace-keeping in the former Yugoslavia, 1992–1995

UNPROFOR was first deployed in Croatia. Subsequently, its mandate was extended to Bosnia and Herzegovina and to the former Yugoslav Republic of Macedonia. It also had an operational mandate in the Federal Republic of Yugoslavia (Serbia and Montenegro) and a liaison presence in

Slovenia. UNPROFOR established its headquarters in Sarajevo, in Bosnia and Herzegovina. The headquarters was later moved to Zagreb, in Croatia.

From March 1992 to April 1993, UNPROFOR was headed by its Force Commander. In May 1993, the Secretary-General appointed Mr. Thorvald Stoltenberg (Norway) as his Special Representative for the former Yugoslavia and first civilian head of UNPROFOR. In January 1994, he was succeeded by Mr. Yasushi Akashi (Japan) as Special Representative and Head of UNPROFOR.

From March 1992 to March 1995, five military officers served as UNPROFOR Force Commander: Lieutenant-General Satish Nambiar (India), from March 1992 to March 1993; Lieutenant-General Lars-Eric Wahlgren (Sweden), from March 1993 to June 1993; Lieutenant-General Jean Cot (France), from June 1993 to March 1994; General Bertrand de Lapresle (France), from March 1994 to March 1995; and General Bernard Janvier (France) who took up his duties on 1 March 1995.

In March 1995, UNPROFOR's three operational commands were headed as follows: UNPROFOR (Croatia) led by Major-General Eid Kamel Al-Rodan of Jordan, UNPROFOR (Bosnia and Herzegovina) led by Lieutenant-General Rupert Smith of the United Kingdom of Great Britain and Northern Ireland, and UNPROFOR (the former Yugoslav Republic of Macedonia) led by Brigadier-General Juha Engström of Finland.

UNPROFOR included military, civil affairs (including civilian police), public information and administrative components. As of 20 March 1995, the strength of the military component, commanded by the Force Commander, Lieutenant-General Janvier, amounted to 38,599, including 684 United Nations military observers, from 39 countries. The Head of Civil Affairs reported to the Special Representative and was responsible for the civil affairs component which also included 803 civilian police. There were 2,017 other international civilian staff (including 1,526 contractual personnel who were not members of the international civil service) and 2,615 local staff. During its three years of existence, UNPROFOR suffered 156 fatalities as of 20 March 1995.

On 31 March 1995, the Security Council decided to replace UNPROFOR by three separate but interlinked peace-keeping operations. In Bosnia and Herzegovina, the Council retained the mandate and name of UNPROFOR. In Croatia, it established the United Nations Confidence Restoration Operation in Croatia, to be known as UNCRO. Within the former Yugoslav Republic of Mace-donia, the Council decided that UNPROFOR would become the United Nations Preventive Deployment Force (UNPREDEP). Their joint theatre headquarters, known as United Nations Peace Forces headquarters (UNPF-HQ), was established in Zagreb, the capital of Croatia. UNPF-HQ was also responsible for liaison with the Government of the Federal Republic of Yugoslavia (Serbia and Montenegro), other concerned Governments and the North Atlantic Treaty Organization (NATO).

Following the restructuring of UNPROFOR in March 1995, Mr. Akashi continued to serve as the Secretary-General's Special Representative and Chief of all United Nations peace-keeping forces in the former Yugoslavia. General Bernard Janvier was appointed Theatre Force Commander responsible for all three operations. Effective 1 November 1995, Mr. Kofi Annan (Ghana) succeeded Mr. Akashi as the Secretary-General's Special Envoy to the Former Yugoslavia and in this context to NATO.

The authorized strength of the military component of UNPF (UNPROFOR, UNCRO, UNPREDEP and UNPF-HQ) was 57,370 all ranks. In addition, there was a provision for 940 civilian police monitors, 822 international civilian staff, 3,214 local staff, 149 United Nations Volunteers and 1,500 international contractual personnel. Each separate component of UNPF was headed by a civilian chief of mission and had its own military commander.

UNCRO was headed by Mr. Byung Suk Min (Republic of Korea), and its military commander was Major-General Eid Kamal Al-Rodan (Jordan). Its strength, as of November 1995, was 6,581 troops, 164 military observers and 296 civilian police. There were also 30 military observers in the Prevlaka peninsula.

UNPROFOR was headed by Mr. Antonio Pedauye (Spain), and its military commander was Lieutenant-General Rupert Smith (United Kingdom). As of November 1995, its troop strength, including the Rapid Reaction Force, was 24,178 troops. In addition, there were 311 military observers and 45 civilian police.

UNPREDEP was headed by Mr. Henryk Sokalski (Poland) and its military commander was Brigadier-General Juha Engström (Finland). Its strength as of November 1995 was 1,050 troops, 24 military observers and 25 civilian police.

In addition, in other locations in the former Yugoslavia, there were 47 airfield monitors, whose task was to monitor the no-fly-zone.

UNPROFOR ceased to exist on 20 December 1995 when authority was transferred from UNPROFOR to the International Implementation

UNPROFOR deployment as of March 1995

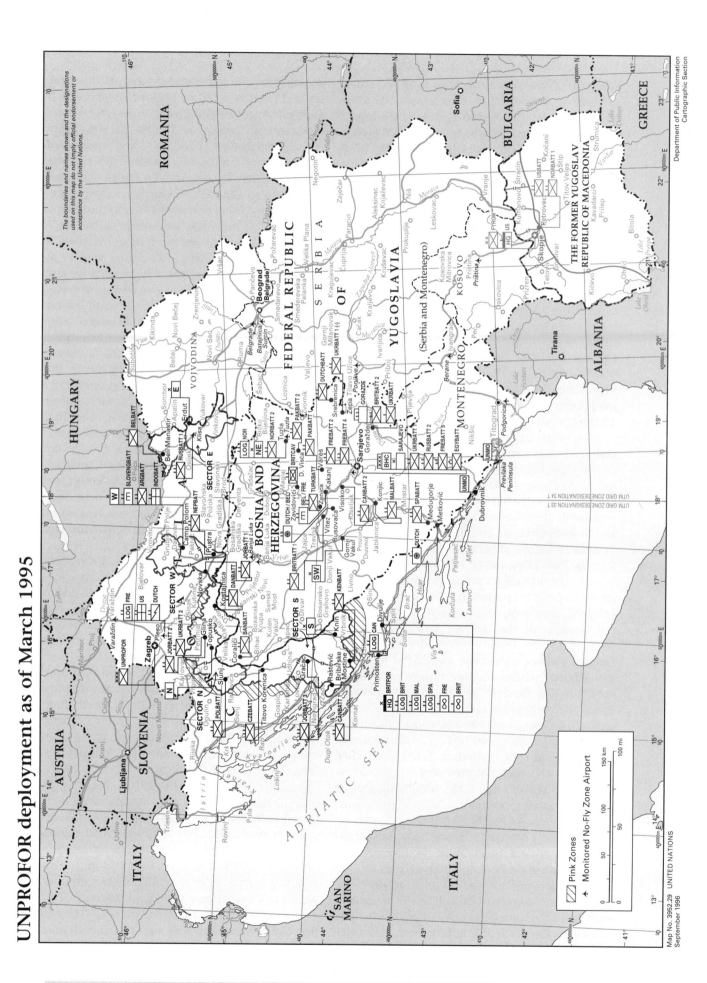

Department of Public Information
Cartographic Section

Map No. 3952.29 UNITED NATIONS
September 1996

Force, as provided for in the Peace Agreement [see below].

By other provisions of the Agreement, the United Nations was requested to set up a United Nations International Police Task Force (IPTF) in Bosnia and Herzegovina. IPTF was established by the Security Council on 21 December 1995 by its resolution 1035 (1995). It required a total of 1,721 police monitors, 254 international staff and 811 locally recruited staff. To coordinate United Nations activities, the Secretary-General appointed Mr. Iqbal Riza (Pakistan) as his Special Representative and Coordinator of United Nations Operations in Bosnia and Herzegovina. Mr. Peter FitzGerald (Ireland) was appointed IPTF Commissioner, reporting to the Coordinator. IPTF and the civilian office subsequently became known as the United Nations Mission in Bosnia and Herzegovina (UNMIBH).

The mandate of UNCRO terminated on 15 January 1996. On the same date, the Security Council decided by its resolution 1037 (1996) to establish for an initial period of 12 months a United Nations peace-keeping operation, with both military and civilian components, under the name United Nations Transitional Administration for Eastern Slavonia, Baranja and Western Sirmium (UNTAES). This was in accordance with the Basic Agreement [see below] which requested the United Nations to set up a transitional administration in Eastern Slavonia, Baranja and Western Sirmium and an international force to assist in the implementation of the agreement. UNTAES would have

an initial deployment of 5,000 troops. Mr. Jacques Klein (United States) was appointed Transitional Administrator and Major-General Jozef Schoups (Belgium) was appointed Force Commander.

The Security Council also authorized United Nations military observers to continue monitoring the demilitarization of the Prevlaka peninsula. Twenty-eight United Nations military observers in the Prevlaka area would be under the command and direction of a Chief Military Observer, who would report directly to United Nations Headquarters in New York. By provisions of resolution 1038 (1996), the mission was authorized for a period of three months, with the possibility of an extension. The mission would be known as the United Nations Mission of Observers in Prevlaka (UNMOP). Colonel Göran Gunnarsson (Sweden) was appointed Chief Military Observer.

On 30 November 1995, the Security Council extended UNPREDEP's mandate for a period terminating on 30 May 1996. Subsequently, on 1 February 1996, the Security Council concurred[1] in principle with the Secretary-General's recommendation that UNPREDEP become an independent mission. By its resolution 1046 (1996) of 13 February, the Council authorized an increase in the Force's strength by 50 military personnel for the duration of its existing mandate and approved the establishment of the position of Force Commander of UNPREDEP. As of 1 March 1996, Brigadier-General Bo Lennart Wranker (Sweden) was to take up those functions.[2]

C. Membership in the United Nations

On 22 May 1992, on the Security Council's recommendations, the General Assembly, by its resolutions 46/236, 46/237 and 46/238, decided to admit the Republic of Slovenia, the Republic of Bosnia and Herzegovina, and the Republic of Croatia to membership in the United Nations.

The former Socialist Federal Republic of Yugoslavia was a founding Member of the United Nations. On 19 September 1992, however, the Security Council, by its resolution 777 (1992), considered that this membership could not be continued automatically by the Federal Republic of Yugoslavia (Serbia and Montenegro). The General Assembly, by its resolution 47/1, agreed with

the Council that the Federal Republic of Yugoslavia (Serbia and Montenegro) should apply for membership in the United Nations and that it should not participate in the Assembly's work. On 29 April 1993, by its resolution 47/229, the Assembly further decided that the Federal Republic of Yugoslavia (Serbia and Montenegro) should not participate in the work of the Economic and Social Council.

On 7 April 1993, the Security Council recommended that the General Assembly admit the former Yugoslav Republic of Macedonia to United Nations membership. In its resolution 817 (1993),

[1]S/1996/76. [2]S/1996/118, S/1996/119.

the Council noted the difference which had arisen over the name of the State and welcomed the readiness of the Co-Chairmen of the Steering Committee of the International Conference on the Former Yugoslavia to use their good offices to settle the matter. On 8 April, the General Assembly admitted to membership in the United Nations the State being provisionally referred to for all purposes within the United Nations as the former Yugoslav Republic of Macedonia pending settlement of the difference that had arisen over the name of the State.

On 8 July 1993, the Secretary-General appointed Mr. Cyrus Vance to carry out his good offices in the difference between the former Yugoslav Republic of Macedonia and Greece. The appointment was made in accordance with Security Council resolution 845 (1993), which called on the Secretary-General to continue his efforts for a speedy settlement of the remaining issues between the two parties. An interim accord between Greece and the former Yugoslav Republic of Macedonia was signed in September 1995 [see below].

D. Peacemaking in the former Yugoslavia

International Conference on the Former Yugoslavia

On 24 July 1992, the Security Council invited the European Community in cooperation with the Secretary-General to examine the possibility of broadening the European Community's Conference on Yugoslavia. The European Community then invited the Secretary-General to co-chair with the President of the Council of Ministers of the European Community the International Conference on the Former Yugoslavia (ICFY), which was convened in London on 26–28 August 1992.

The Conference adopted a Statement of Principles for a negotiated settlement and established, under the overall direction of the Permanent Co-Chairmen of the Conference, a Steering Committee co-chaired by the Secretary-General's Personal Envoy, Mr. Cyrus Vance, and Lord David Owen, who succeeded Lord Carrington as European Community mediator. Mr. Vance was succeeded in May 1993 by Mr. Thorvald Stoltenberg, and Lord Owen by Mr. Carl Bildt in June 1995.

The Co-Chairmen were to direct six Working Groups and prepare the basis for a general settlement and associated measures. They commenced work in continuous sessions at the United Nations Office at Geneva, beginning in September 1992.

ICFY provided a forum for discussion and negotiation, often directly between the parties in conflict, throughout the former Yugoslavia. ICFY helped to negotiate a new cease-fire agreement on 29 March 1994 in Croatia; prepared successive blueprints for peace in Bosnia and Herzegovina; recommended the preventive deployment of UNPROFOR in the former Yugoslav Republic of Macedonia; negotiated joint understandings between the Governments of the Republic of Croatia and the Federal Republic of Yugoslavia (Serbia and Montenegro); provided a framework for addressing humanitarian issues; negotiated confidence-building measures; defused tensions involving ethnic and national communities and minorities; and sponsored efforts looking towards reconstruction and economic development in the area.

In early August 1994, the Federal Republic of Yugoslavia (Serbia and Montenegro) severed economic and political relations with the Bosnian Serb leaders and closed its 300-mile border with areas of Bosnia and Herzegovina under the control of Bosnian Serb forces to all traffic except for food, clothing and medical assistance. In September, authorities of the Federal Republic agreed to the presence of a civilian ICFY mission which would control the effective delivery of humanitarian assistance at designated crossing-points and would have freedom of access elsewhere in the country. The Mission would report to the Co-Chairmen of the Steering Committee and, through them, to the Secretary-General of the United Nations and the Presidency of the European Union. The ICFY Mission eventually included 152 international personnel from Belgium, Canada, Czech Republic, Denmark, Finland, France, Germany, Greece, Ireland, Italy, Netherlands, Norway, Portugal, Russian Federation, Spain, Sweden, United Kingdom of Great Britain and Northern Ireland and United States of America. It was headed by the Mission Coordinator, Mr. Bo Pellnäs (Sweden), and subsequently by Mr. Tauno Nieminen (Finland).

ICFY also negotiated the economic agreement of 2 December 1994 between the Government of the Republic of Croatia and the local Serb authorities; worked, with representatives of the Russian Federation and the United States of America, on a draft agreement relating to a political solution of the conflict in Croatia; collaborated closely with the Contact Group for Bosnia and Herzegovina and helped to develop a territorial proposal and constitutional arrangements; and initiated and worked on the implementation of a population census in the former Yugoslav Republic of Macedonia, needed as a basis for discussions among the various population groups. ICFY also contributed to defusing tensions in that country in the run-up to and during the elections held in October 1994; negotiated a draft treaty on succession issues; exercised its good offices to promote mutual recognition among successor States in the former Yugoslavia; and brought together the Foreign Ministers of the Republic of Croatia and the Federal Republic of Yugoslavia (Serbia and Montenegro) for what was hoped would be regular meetings in their respective capitals.

In accordance with the decisions adopted at the Peace Implementation Conference on 8 and 9 December 1995 [see below] and the Secretary-General's report of 13 December 1995 [see chapter 25], ICFY ceased to exist on 31 January 1996.

Vance-Owen Peace Plan

On 4 January 1993, the Co-Chairmen put to the Bosnian Government, the Bosnian Croats and the Bosnian Serbs a comprehensive package as the basis for a fair, just and lasting peace in Bosnia and Herzegovina. The package, which became known as the Vance-Owen peace plan, included a set of constitutional principles along with a map setting out the organization of the country into 10 provinces, and an agreement for peace. The Co-Chairmen explained that all three elements of the package were inextricably linked and could not be implemented separately. The Co-Chairman also introduced an additional component — an agreement on arrangements for the governance of the country in the interim period between the signing of a peace settlement and the holding of elections under a new constitution.

In the course of intense negotiations in Geneva and in New York, the following elements were signed: on 30 January 1993, the constitutional principles element was signed by President Alija Izetbegovic of Bosnia and Herzegovina, Mr. Mate Boban, the leader of the Bosnian

Croats, and Dr. Radovan Karadzic, the leader of the Bosnian Serbs; the agreement for peace was signed by the Bosnian Croats and the Bosnian Serbs on 30 January and by the Bosnian Government on 3 March; the interim arrangements agreement by the Bosnian Croats and the Bosnian Government on 25 March; and a revised map on provincial boundaries by the Bosnian Croats and the Bosnian Government on 25 March.

On 25 March, the Security Council, in a statement by its President, welcomed the signing by President Izetbegovic and Mr. Boban of all four documents of the peace plan. It called on the remaining party to sign without delay the two documents it had not yet endorsed, and to cease its violence, offensive military actions, "ethnic cleansing" and obstruction of humanitarian assistance. The Council stated its readiness to take the steps required to bring about the peace settlement.

The Vance-Owen peace plan provided for a wide range of measures requiring the deployment of additional peace-keeping troops in Bosnia and Herzegovina. These measures included the cessation of hostilities throughout Bosnia and Herzegovina, the restoration of infrastructure, the opening of routes, the separation of forces, the demilitarization of Sarajevo, the monitoring of the borders of Bosnia and Herzegovina, and the return of forces to designated provinces.

The Secretary-General pointed out[3] that the multitude of tasks envisaged in the peace plan would exceed the planning capability of the United Nations Secretariat and that of UNPROFOR. Therefore, consultations were initiated with NATO which indicated that it would consider a formal request to undertake detailed planning for the implementation of the plan and making available a core headquarters structure into which other potential troop contributors could be incorporated. NATO experts estimated that some 60,000 to 75,000 troops would be required for the implementation of the various military tasks envisaged in the peace plan.

The Secretary-General indicated that the implementation of the plan would involve a United Nations operation conducted under the authority of the Security Council and financed collectively by United Nations Member States under the peace-keeping scale of assessments. As to the principal civilian tasks of the peace plan, they included the restoration of law, order and civil authority throughout Bosnia and Herzegovina in conformity with the nine constitutional principles;

[3] S/25668.

the preparation of a constitution in accordance with the nine principles; the resolution of problems concerning provincial borders, and related political issues; the preparation of internationally supervised, free and fair elections to be held for the central government as well as the provincial governments; the provision of arrangements for the highest level of internationally recognized human rights through domestic and international mechanisms; the reversal of "ethnic cleansing" and the establishment of conditions in which those refugees and displaced persons who wished to return to their homes might do so; and the provision of humanitarian aid and appropriate levels of relief and rehabilitation assistance.

On 29 April 1993, the Co-Chairmen of the ICFY Steering Committee, Mr. Vance and Lord Owen, together with Co-Chairman-designate Mr. Thorvald Stoltenberg, convened a further meeting of the three parties to the conflict in Bosnia and Herzegovina. In addition to President Izetbegovic, Mr. Boban and Dr. Karadzic, the meeting was attended by President Franjo Tudjman of Croatia, President Dobrica Cosic of the Federal Republic of Yugoslavia (Serbia and Montenegro), President Slobodan Milosevic of Serbia and President Momir Bulatovic of Montenegro. The two-day meeting resulted in Dr. Karadzic's signing, on 2 May, the remaining two documents of the Vance-Owen peace plan. Dr. Karadzic indicated, however, that the documents would have to be approved by the Bosnian Serb "Assembly".

On 5 May, notwithstanding Dr. Karadzic's signature and the strong pressure from the international community and the Federal Republic of Yugoslavia (Serbia and Montenegro), the Bosnian Serb "Assembly" again rejected the peace plan and instead voted to hold a referendum on the subject.

By the end of May 1993, it had become clear that the international will was lacking to continue pushing for the 10-province solution proposed under the Vance-Owen peace plan and the substantial Bosnian-Serb military roll-back that was implied. In addition, the Bosnian Croats, whose relations with the Bosnian Muslims were already under strain, had started to consolidate their own republic — "Herzeg-Bosna". As a result, fighting increased between Muslim-led Bosnian Government forces and the forces of the Bosnian Croats.

Despite the set-backs, the Co-Chairmen continued throughout the summer their search for a negotiated settlement to the conflict in Bosnia and Herzegovina. In their contacts in June 1993,

the concept of a confederation for Bosnia and Herzegovina was revived. According to this concept, first proposed in March 1992 but rejected at that time by the Bosnian Government, the Bosnian Croats, the Bosnian Muslims and the Bosnian Serbs would each have a republic within the state of Bosnia and Herzegovina.

Following discussions held at Geneva and Brussels in December, there was agreement among all three sides that Bosnia and Herzegovina should be organized as a Union of three republics; the Muslim-majority republic should have a minimum 33.3 per cent of territory and the Croat-majority republic should have 17.5 per cent, leaving the Bosnian Serbs with 49.2 per cent; a holiday truce would cover the period 23 December 1993 to 15 January 1994; the three sides would return to Geneva on 15 January 1994, to continue the search for peace. In addition, working groups were established to look into the following issues and to help reach agreement on them by 15 January: the definition of the Mostar city area that would be placed under the temporary administration of the European Union, technical arrangements for providing the Muslim-majority republic with road and rail access to Brcko and the Sava river, access of the Muslim-majority republic to the Adriatic Sea, continued discussions on territorial delimitation. All three sides were asked to consult their respective Assemblies beforehand so that any agreement concluded at Geneva would come into force immediately upon signature.

Bosniac-Croat federation agreement

In efforts to establish a Bosniac–Croat federation and a confederation between Croatia and the federation, the Government of the United States took the lead. In late February 1994, talks were held in Washington D.C. between the leaders of the Bosnian Muslims and of the Bosnian Croats, as well as the Foreign Minister of Croatia. On 1 March, two documents were signed: the Framework Agreement establishing a Federation in the Areas of the Republic of Bosnia and Herzegovina with a Majority Bosniac and Croat Population, and the Outline of a Preliminary Agreement for a Confederation between the Republic of Croatia and the Federation. After further talks, the Government of Bosnia and Herzegovina, the Government of Croatia and the Bosnian Croat side signed, on 10 May, the Washington accords for the creation of the Bosniac–Croat Federation.

Contact group

Meanwhile on 25 April 1994, a Contact Group was established involving, at ministerial level, the Foreign Ministers of France, Germany, the Russian Federation, the United Kingdom, the United States, the European Union Commissioner for Foreign Affairs and the two Co-Chairmen of the ICFY Steering Committee.

The Contact Group drew up a map for the allocation of territory between the Bosniac-Croat Federation and the Bosnian Serb entity (the so-called "Republika Srpska"). The map allocated 51 per cent to the Bosniac-Croat Federation and 49 per cent to the Bosnian Serbs. The Contact Group, supported by the Security Council and the Council of Ministers of the European Union, as well as by Governments and organizations worldwide, informed the parties that the proposed map would have to be accepted as presented, unless the parties could agree between themselves on changes. At the end of July 1994, the Bosniac-Croat Federation, the Republic of Croatia and the Federal Republic of Yugoslavia (Serbia and Montenegro) accepted the map. Leaders of the Federal Republic of Yugoslavia (Serbia and Montenegro) urged the Bosnian Serb leadership to accept the map. The Bosnian Serb side, however, rejected it.

Peace Agreement

In 1995, at the same time as fighting was raging in Bosnia and Herzegovina, the United States, with the support of the Security Council, the Contact Group and the Co-Chairmen of the ICFY Steering Committee, continued actively to pursue the peace initiative it had begun during the summer. On 5 October 1995, the United States delegation secured a country-wide cease-fire agreement that included non-military elements such as humane treatment for detained persons, freedom of movement and the right of displaced persons to return to their original homes.

The Security Council welcomed[4] the agreement as well as the decision of the Governments of Bosnia and Herzegovina, Croatia and the Federal Republic of Yugoslavia (Serbia and Montenegro) to attend peace talks at the end of October to be followed by a peace conference.

On 1 November 1995, at the invitation of the United States Government, President Alija Izetbegovic of Bosnia and Herzegovina, President Slobodan Milosevic of Serbia [President Milosevic assumed the authority to conduct negotiations on behalf of the Bosnian Serbs], and President Franjo Tudjman of Croatia began talks to end the Bosnian conflict in Dayton, Ohio (United States). The question of Eastern Slavonia, the last Serb-held area of Croatia, was also to be addressed.

After three weeks of intensive negotiations in Dayton, the parties initialled, on 21 November, the General Framework Agreement for Peace in Bosnia and Herzegovina and the Annexes thereto (collectively the Peace Agreement)[5] by the Republic of Bosnia and Herzegovina, the Republic of Croatia and the Federal Republic of Yugoslavia. The Peace Agreement was formally signed by the parties at a ceremony in Paris on 14 December 1995. The signing was preceded by a Peace Implementation Conference convened in London on 8 and 9 December, which had adopted a document known as "the London conclusions."[6]

The parties to the Peace Agreement undertook to respect each other's sovereign equality, to settle disputes by peaceful means and to refrain from any action against the territorial integrity and independence of Bosnia and Herzegovina or any other State. They affirmed their commitment to the agreed basic principles,[7] which included the continued existence of Bosnia and Herzegovina within its existing international borders, but consisting of two democratic entities — the Bosniac-Croat Federation and a Serb Republic called Republika Srpska — with a 51 per cent to 49 per cent territorial division between them. Both entities would have the right to establish parallel special relationships with neighbouring countries.

Military aspects of the settlement included the cessation of hostilities agreement, the withdrawal of forces "not of local origin" from Bosnia and Herzegovina and the phased redeployment of forces around Sarajevo, Gorazde and other locations. The parties — the Republic of Bosnia and Herzegovina, the Republic of Croatia, the Federal Republic of Yugoslavia, the Federation of Bosnia and Herzegovina and the Republika Srpska — invited the Security Council to adopt a resolution authorizing Member States or regional organizations and arrangements to establish a multinational military Implementation Force (IFOR) to help ensure compliance with the provisions of the Peace Agreement. IFOR would be composed of ground, air and maritime units from the members of NATO and from non-NATO States. The Agreement also covered UNPROFOR's withdrawal, establishment of a Joint Military Commission to be chaired by the IFOR Commander, and prisoner

---

[4]S/PRST/1995/50. [5]A/50/790, S/1995/999, annex. [6]S/1995/1029, annex. [7]S/1995/780.

exchanges. It stipulated full cooperation by the parties with all entities involved in the implementation of the Agreement, including the International Criminal Tribunal for the Former Yugoslavia [see below].

The Agreement outlined regional stabilization measures, including confidence- and security-building measures and measures for regional and subregional arms control. It detailed the agreement between the Republic of Bosnia and Herzegovina, the Federation of Bosnia and Herzegovina and the Republika Srpska on the "Inter-Entity Boundary Line" and related issues concerning their respective territories, stipulating that a transitional period be designated in areas transferring from one entity to another.

Also covered in the document are the parties' agreement on the holding of democratic elections, including the role of OSCE and the Provisional Election Commission; the Constitution of Bosnia and Herzegovina; arrangements for observation of human rights; return and repatriation of refugees and displaced persons; amnesty for such returnees (except in cases of serious violations of international law as defined in the statute of the International Tribunal).

On the civilian implementation of the peace settlement, the parties broadly agreed that a wide range of activities would be involved, including: continuation of the humanitarian aid effort for as long as necessary; rehabilitation of infrastructure and economic reconstruction; the establishment of political and constitutional institutions in Bosnia and Herzegovina; promotion of respect for human rights and the return of displaced persons and refugees; and the holding of free and fair elections. The parties' efforts towards those ends would be facilitated by the High Representative, who would mobilize and coordinate the activities of organizations and agencies involved in civilian aspects of the peace settlement, and monitor the implementation of that settlement. The High Representative's mandate would include coordination and liaison and staffing. He was designated as the final authority in theatre on interpretation of the agreement on civilian implementation of the Peace Agreement. The London Peace Implementation Conference designated Mr. Carl Bildt to the post of the High Representative and the Security Council approved[8] the appointment.

Also detailed in the agreement were arrangements for civilian law enforcement, which included a request by the parties to the Council for establishment of a United Nations International Police Task Force (IPTF) to carry out a mandated programme of assistance in Bosnia and Herzegovina. That programme would include monitoring of law enforcement activities and facilities, advice and training, and response to requests for assistance. The agreement stipulated that any obstruction of IPTF activities would constitute a failure to cooperate with the IPTF, with such failure communicated by the IPTF Commissioner to the High Representative.

Basic Agreement

Throughout September and October 1995, the Secretary-General's Special Envoy, Mr. Stoltenberg, and the United States Ambassador to Croatia, Mr. Peter Galbraith, undertook intensive local negotiations in Croatia. Further negotiations were undertaken in November at the peace talks in Dayton, Ohio. On 3 November, a commitment was reached between President Milosevic and President Tudjman to reinvigorate local negotiations. These concluded with the signing of the Basic Agreement on the Region of Eastern Slavonia, Baranja and Western Sirmium[9] on 12 November 1995.

The Basic Agreement, which the Secretary-General described as "a landmark accomplishment",[10] provided for the peaceful integration into Croatia of the region known as Sector East. It also opened the way for the return to their homes of all Croatian displaced persons who so wished. The Agreement requested the Security Council to establish a transitional administration to govern the region during the transitional period of 12 months, which might be extended by up to a further 12 months, and to authorize an international force to maintain peace and security during the transitional period and to otherwise assist in the implementation of the agreement.

Interim Accord

On 13 September 1995, Greece and the former Yugoslav Republic of Macedonia signed a wide-ranging Interim Accord,[11] which opened a way for the establishment of a new relationship between them based on international law and peaceful, friendly relations. This was a result of difficult and lengthy negotiations facilitated since July 1993 by the Secretary-General's Special Envoy, Mr. Vance. The Security Council welcomed[12] the Interim Accord and encouraged the parties to

[8]S/RES/1031 (1995). [9]S/1995/951. [10]S/1995/987. [11]S/1995/794, annex I. [12]S/PRST/1995/46.

continue their efforts to resolve the remaining differences between them.

The Accord provided that each party would respect the sovereignty, territorial integrity and political independence of the other and confirmed their common existing frontier as an enduring and inviolable international border. The two countries would establish liaison offices in each other's capitals.

The Accord also provided that the former Yugoslav Republic of Macedonia would cease to use in any manner the symbol that was at that time on its national flag and that its Constitution would be consistent with the principles of international law and good-neighbourly relations. The Accord provided for unimpeded movement of people and goods between the two countries, and, by its terms, for terminating the economic blockade imposed by Greece in February 1994 and for replacing it by an open and cooperative economic relationship. The parties agreed to continue negotiations with respect to the outstanding difference between them.

The Interim Accord also paved the way for the former Yugoslav Republic of Macedonia's admission to a number of European organizations, but did not lead to recognition by the Federal Republic of Yugoslavia, the only neighbouring country not to recognize it.

Arms embargo

On 25 September 1991, the Security Council, by its resolution 713 (1991), unanimously called on all States to implement a general and complete embargo on the delivery of weapons and military equipment to Yugoslavia. It subsequently established a Committee to undertake a number of tasks relative to the embargo.

On 18 December 1992, the General Assembly adopted resolution 47/121 which urged the Security Council to exempt the Republic of Bosnia and Herzegovina from the arms embargo in order to exercise its inherent right of self-defence. On 29 June 1993, the Security Council failed to adopt an exemption by a vote of 6 in favour, 0 against and 9 abstentions. At its 48th session, the General Assembly, in its resolution 48/88 adopted on 20 December 1993, reaffirmed that, as the Republic of Bosnia and Herzegovina was a sovereign, independent State and a Member of the United Nations, it was entitled to all rights provided for in the Charter of the United Nations, including the right to self-defence, and again urged the Council to consider exempting Bosnia and Herzegovina

from the arms embargo. By its resolution 49/10 of 3 November 1994, the General Assembly again encouraged the Security Council to exempt the Republic and the Federation of Bosnia and Herzegovina from the embargo and urged members of the international community to extend their cooperation to Bosnia and Herzegovina in exercise of its inherent right of individual and collective self-defence in accordance with Article 51 of the Charter. The Security Council discussed the issue on 8 and 9 November 1994, but took no decision.

In November 1995, the Security Council welcomed[13] the initialling of the Peace Agreement by Bosnia and Herzegovina, Croatia and the Federal Republic of Yugoslavia and decided to terminate the arms embargo imposed by resolution 713 (1991) as soon as the Secretary-General reported that the parties had formally signed the Agreement. It also decided that the provisions of the embargo should remain in place during the first 90 days following the submission of the Secretary-General's report. During the second 90 days, all provisions should be terminated, except that the delivery of heavy weapons and ammunition for them, mines, military aircraft and helicopters should continue to be prohibited until an arms control agreement took effect. After 180 days, and after a report from the Secretary-General on the implementation of Annex 1B of the Peace Agreement (Agreement on Regional Stabilization), all provisions would terminate unless the Council decided otherwise. On 18 June 1996, the Chairman of the Committee established by the Council issued a statement[14] on behalf of the members to the effect that all provisions of the embargo on deliveries of weapons and military equipment imposed by resolution 713 (1991) were terminated.

Sanctions

On 30 May 1992, acting under Chapter VII of the United Nations Charter, the Security Council, in its resolution 757 (1992), imposed wide-ranging sanctions on the Federal Republic of Yugoslavia (which by then consisted of Serbia and Montenegro), in order to help achieve a peaceful solution to the conflict. The sanctions were to apply until the Security Council decided that the authorities in the Federal Republic had taken effective measures to fulfil the requirements of resolution 752 (1992). They included, among other things, provisions banning trade with the Federal Republic, air service, sporting exchanges and sci-

[13]S/RES/1021 (1995). [14]SC/6235.

entific and technical cooperation and cultural exchanges, and reducing the level of diplomatic staff.

On 17 April 1993, the Security Council adopted its resolution 820 (1993), by which it commended the Vance-Owen peace plan for Bosnia and Herzegovina and welcomed the fact that the plan had been accepted in full by two of the Bosnian parties. The Council expressed grave concern at the refusal of the Bosnian Serb party to accept the Agreement on Interim Arrangements and the provisional provincial map, and called on that party to accept the peace plan in full. The Council decided to strengthen the sanctions regime imposed against the Federal Republic of Yugoslavia (Serbia and Montenegro), effective nine days after the date of adoption of the resolution, unless the Bosnian Serb party signed the peace plan and ceased its military attacks in Bosnia and Herzegovina. Among other provisions, the Council adopted certain measures affecting the territory in Bosnia and Herzegovina under the control of Bosnian Serb forces.

The Security Council expressed its readiness to review all such measures pending acceptance by all three Bosnian parties of the peace plan and evidence that the Bosnian Serb party was cooperating in good faith. Despite the efforts of the Co-Chairmen of the ICFY Steering Committee, the deadline established by Security Council resolution 820 (1993) passed, and the new sanctions regime against the Federal Republic of Yugoslavia (Serbia and Montenegro) came into force at midnight on 26 April 1993.

The further sanctions against the Federal Republic of Yugoslavia (Serbia and Montenegro) included: preventing the diversion to it of commodities and products said to be destined for other places; authorization by the Sanctions Committee for the transshipment of commodities and products through that country on the Danube; forbidding any vessels registered in that country, owned by it, operated by it or suspected of violating Council resolutions, to pass through installations within the territory of Member States; authorizing Member States to freeze any funds in their territory belonging to that country, to ensure that they were not made available for the benefit of the Yugoslav authorities.

On 23 September 1994, the Security Council, by its resolution 942 (1994), welcomed the territorial settlement for Bosnia and Herze-

govina proposed by the Contact Group, strongly condemned the Bosnian Serb party for their refusal to accept it and decided to strengthen the sanctions against the Bosnian Serbs. The sanctions, applied to "all activities of an economic nature, including commercial, financial and industrial activities and transactions". The resolution referred in particular to all economic activities involving property — funds, financial, tangible and intangible assets, property rights, and publicly and privately traded securities and debt instruments and any other financial and economic resources. Excepted from the sanctions were medical supplies, foodstuffs and goods for essential humanitarian needs.

The Council then decided, by its resolution 943 (1994) of 23 September, to suspend several economic sanctions against the Federal Republic of Yugoslavia (Serbia and Montenegro) for an initial period of 100 days following the receipt by the Secretary-General of a certification that the authorities of the republic were effectively implementing their decision to close the border with Bosnia and Herzegovina. The Council also requested that every 30 days the Secretary-General report on the republic's implementation of the decision. The Council extended the suspension of the sanctions for another 100 days by its resolution 970 (1995) of 12 January 1995; until 15 July by its resolution 988 (1995) of 21 April 1995; until 18 September by its resolution 1003 (1995) of 15 July 1995; and until 18 March 1996 by its resolution 1015 (1995) of 15 September 1995.

On 22 November 1995, the Security Council decided[15] to suspend indefinitely its sanctions against the Federal Republic of Yugoslavia, with the proviso that they would be automatically reimposed if the Federal Republic did not sign the Peace Agreement reached in Dayton. The Council specified that the suspension of sanctions would not apply to the Bosnian Serb party until the day after all Bosnian Serb forces had withdrawn behind the zones of separation established in the Peace Agreement. The withdrawal took place and the sanctions were lifted on 27 February 1996. The Council decided that the sanctions would be terminated on the tenth day following the holding of free and fair elections provided for in the Peace Agreement, provided the Bosnian Serbs had withdrawn from and respected the zones of separation.

[15] S/RES/1022 (1995).

E. Humanitarian relief

By December 1991, it was estimated that there were approximately 500,000 refugees, displaced persons and other victims of the conflict in the former Yugoslavia requiring assistance and protection. As the conflict intensified and extended to Bosnia and Herzegovina, the humanitarian problems increased dramatically with the growing number of refugees and displaced persons, widespread violations of basic human rights and international humanitarian law. Under such difficult circumstances, the Office of the United Nations High Commissioner for Refugees (UNHCR) and other United Nations agencies concerned, the International Committee of the Red Cross (ICRC) and many other non-governmental organizations (NGOs) did their utmost to address the humanitarian needs of the conflict-affected population.

In November 1991, the Secretary-General named UNHCR as lead United Nations agency coordinating the provision of humanitarian assistance in the former Yugoslavia. As lead agency, UNHCR undertook and maintained intensive contacts with all relevant counterparts in the region. The High Commissioner also chaired the ICFY Working Group on Humanitarian Issues. The purpose of the group was to promote humanitarian relief in all its aspects, including refugees.

On 29 July 1992 in Geneva, the International Meeting on Humanitarian Aid to the Victims of Conflict in the Former Yugoslavia endorsed a seven-point Comprehensive Humanitarian Response proposed by the High Commissioner. The elements of the plan were: respect for human rights and humanitarian law, preventive protection, humanitarian access to those in need, measures to meet special humanitarian needs, temporary protection measures, material assistance, and return and rehabilitation. Participants at the Meeting also agreed on the need for concerted humanitarian action and a greatly enhanced level of international and inter-agency cooperation.

To fund the effort to provide humanitarian assistance, 12 appeals were launched for the years 1991 through 1995. The first appeal, on 3 December 1991, was launched by UNHCR jointly with the United Nations Children's Fund (UNICEF) and the World Health Organization (WHO). The appeal of 20 November 1995 was launched on behalf of nine United Nations bodies — UNHCR, World Food Programme, UNICEF, WHO, Food and Agriculture Organization, United Nations Development Programme, United Nations Educational, Scientific and Cultural Organization, United Nations Volunteers and the Department of Humanitarian Affairs — as well as the International Organization for Migration.

The magnitude and complexity of the humanitarian operation was reflected in the numerous appeals. The 3 December 1991 appeal targeted 500,000 planned beneficiaries. By December 1992, a revised appeal was issued to benefit 3.8 million beneficiaries. In October 1993, there were some 4.3 million planned beneficiaries, including some 2.74 million people in Bosnia and Herzegovina, 800,000 in Croatia, 647,000 in the Federal Republic of Yugoslavia (Serbia and Montenegro), 27,000 in the former Yugoslav Republic of Macedonia and 45,000 in Slovenia. In September 1995, assistance was targeted to 3.5 million beneficiaries.

In the 1991 appeal, total estimated requirements amounted to $24.3 million. In 1992, there were three appeals with total estimated requirements for 1992 amounting to $467.6 million. In 1993, two appeals were launched with total estimated requirements for 1993 amounting to $990 million. Three appeals were launched in both 1994 and 1995. Total revised requirements for 1994 were $721.2 million, and for 1995 $514.8 million. For 1996, revised requirements amounted to $823.2 million.

The international community's efforts to provide humanitarian assistance were greatly obstructed by the warring parties as they tried to achieve political or military objectives. Security conditions throughout the entire period were fragile. Humanitarian aid convoys were subject to harassment and delays at checkpoints, and indiscriminate fighting was a major obstacle. Humanitarian personnel were deliberately targeted, resulting in fatalities among them. Relief supplies were stolen and vehicles were hijacked. As the conflict continued, the prohibition of humanitarian relief was increasingly used as a weapon of war. Humanitarian access was also hampered on occasion by the arbitrary, hostile behaviour of the population, as well as by political considerations, such as the republic of departure of the aid and the route chosen. In spite of these difficulties, during the four-year period from December 1991 to December 1995, UNHCR provided humanitarian aid totalling more than 1 million tons.

Beginning with its resolution 724 (1991) of 15 December 1991, the Security Council encouraged the Secretary-General to pursue humanitarian relief efforts in the former Yugoslavia. By its resolution 752 (1992) of 15 May, the Council called on all parties concerned to ensure that conditions were established for the effective and unhindered delivery of humanitarian assistance. By its resolution 757 (1992) of 30 May, the Council included in this demand the establishment of a security zone encompassing Sarajevo and its airport. Among other measures relating to humanitarian aid, the Security Council, in its resolution 787 (1992) of 16 November 1992, condemned "all violations of international humanitarian law, including in particular the practice of 'ethnic cleansing' and the deliberate impeding of the delivery of food and medical supplies to the civilian population of the Republic of Bosnia and Herzegovina, and reaffirms that those that commit or order the commission of such acts will be held individually responsible in respect of such acts".

In response to the deteriorating humanitarian situation in Bosnia and Herzegovina, UNPROFOR's mandate and strength were expanded several times. Sarajevo airport was reopened in July 1992 under the exclusive authority of the United Nations for the delivery of humanitarian supplies and related purposes. In September 1992, the Security Council authorized the enlargement of the mandate of UNPROFOR to provide protection, when necessary, for UNHCR convoys delivering humanitarian relief throughout Bosnia and Herzegovina. UNPROFOR also provided engineering support for road repair works, air and ground transport for medical evacuation operations, assessment of infrastructure needs and capabilities, loading and unloading aircraft, and support and coordination of airlift and airdrop operations.

As for displaced persons, United Nations policy was that such individuals had the right to return voluntarily to their homes of origin in safety and dignity with the assistance of the international community. The lead in that matter was to be taken by the humanitarian agencies with UNPROFOR providing all appropriate support.

Within the framework of the humanitarian assistance programme, UNHCR began the longest running airlift operation in history as the conflict escalated into a siege of Sarajevo. The Sarajevo airlift was begun on 3 July 1992 and ended on 9 January 1996. It was suspended for brief periods for security reasons, for example following the incident on 3 September 1992 in which

an Italian Air Force G-222 cargo plane was downed and all four crewmen aboard were killed. On 8 April 1995, after a series of serious shooting incidents, the airlift was suspended until mid-September. In all, there were more than 270 security incidents involving the airlift.

Over a period of three and one half years, some 20 nations and at least five organizations would participate; among other things, UNPROFOR provided security at the airport. The operation averaged 15 to 17 flights per day and transported more than 144,827 metric tons of food and 15,850 metric tons of medicine, equipment and other supplies. During many months, the airlift provided more than 85 per cent of all aid reaching Sarajevo. It also helped with the medical evacuations of more than 1,100 patients.

Five nations flew regularly: Canada flew 1,806 flights; France, 2,133; Germany 1,279; the United Kingdom, 1,902; and the United States, 4,597. Italy provided planes and facilities at Ancona. Other participating States included Algeria, Belgium, Denmark, Germany, Greece, Jordan, Kuwait, Netherlands, Norway, Poland, Portugal, Saudi Arabia, Spain, Sweden, Tunisia and Turkey.[16]

Humanitarian relief was also provided to certain inaccessible areas in Bosnia and Herzegovina by means of airdrops. That operation, initiated by the United States in collaboration with Germany and France, distributed some 20,500 tons of assistance between March 1993 and August 1994.

With the signing on 14 December 1995 of the Peace Agreement for Bosnia and Herzegovina, the overall situation there significantly improved. The Agreement entrusted UNHCR with continuing as lead agency in coordinating humanitarian relief assistance, and with implementing a plan for the return of refugees and displaced persons. UNHCR's operations were therefore slated to undergo a transition from relief and assistance to the return and reintegration of refugees and internally displaced persons. For a phased and orderly voluntary return programme, UNHCR planned to concentrate on three broad categories of returnees: an estimated 1 million internally displaced persons inside Bosnia and Herzegovina; more than half a million refugees from Bosnia and Herzegovina living in Croatia, the Federal Republic of Yugoslavia, Slovenia, and the former Yugoslav Republic of Macedonia; and some of the estimated 700,000 people from the former Yugoslavia under temporary protection in other countries.[17]

[16]REF/1130. [17]REF/1131.

F. Human rights

"Ethnic cleansing" and other violations

Throughout the conflict, massive and systematic violations of human rights, as well as grave violations of humanitarian law, occurred in most of the territory of the former Yugoslavia, in particular in Bosnia and Herzegovina and in Croatia. "Ethnic cleansing" — the elimination, by the ethnic group exercising control over a given territory, of members of other ethnic groups — was the cause of the vast majority of human rights violations. The practice of "ethnic cleansing", involving a variety of methods aimed at expelling the unwanted group, included harassment, discrimination, beatings, torture, rape, summary executions, forced relocation and displacement of populations, confiscation of property and destruction of homes, places of worship and cultural institutions.

In a series of resolutions and presidential statements, the Security Council condemned the practice of "ethnic cleansing" and other violations of human rights and international humanitarian law. On 13 July 1992, for example, in its resolution 764 (1992), the Council reaffirmed that all parties were bound to comply with the obligations under international humanitarian law and in particular the Geneva Conventions of 12 August 1949 for the protection of war victims, and that persons who committed or ordered the commission of grave breaches of the Conventions were individually responsible in respect of such breaches. On another occasion, concerned about the continuing reports of widespread violations of international humanitarian law and, in particular, reports of the imprisonment and abuse of civilians in camps, prisons and detention centres within the territory of the former Yugoslavia and especially in Bosnia and Herzegovina, the Council, in a presidential statement,[18] condemned any such violations and abuses. It also demanded that relevant international organizations, and in particular ICRC, be granted immediate, unimpeded and continued access to all such places.

On 13 August, by its resolution 771 (1992), the Security Council reaffirmed that all parties to the conflict were bound to comply with their obligations under international humanitarian law, and strongly condemned violations, including "ethnic cleansing". It further called on States and international humanitarian organiza-

tions to collate substantiated information relating to violations of international humanitarian law, and requested the Secretary-General to submit such information to the Council with recommendations on an appropriate follow-up response.

The General Assembly, too, condemned on a number of occasions the massive violations of human rights and international humanitarian law. On one such occasion, for example, the Assembly[19] condemned in particular the practice of "ethnic cleansing", and demanded that that practice be brought to an end immediately. It called for further steps to stop the massive and forcible displacement of population from and within Bosnia and Herzegovina, as well as all other forms of violation of human rights in the former Yugoslavia. On another occasion, the Assembly strongly condemned[20] the "abhorrent practice" of rape and abuse of women and children in the areas of armed conflict in the former Yugoslavia and demanded that those involved immediately cease those acts. It subsequently expressed[21] its outrage at the systematic use of rape as a weapon of war and an instrument of "ethnic cleansing" against women and children in Bosnia and Herzegovina.

The United Nations Commission on Human Rights also repeatedly condemned violations of human rights and expressed its concern for raped and abused women. In its resolution 1992/S-2/1 of 30 November 1992, for example, the Commission condemned again all human rights violations and "ethnic cleansing" in the territory of the former Yugoslavia and called upon all States to consider whether the acts committed in Bosnia and Herzegovina and in Croatia constituted genocide. In its resolution 1995/89, adopted on 8 March 1995, the Commission renewed its expression of outrage at the systematic practice of rape as a weapon of war against women and children and as an instrument of "ethnic cleansing", and recognized that rape in these circumstances constituted a war crime.

Special rapporteur

On 13-14 August 1992, the Commission on Human Rights convened a special session — the first ever in its history — on the human rights situation in the former Yugoslavia. The Commis-

[18]S/24378. [19]A/RES/46/242. [20]A/RES/48/143. [21]A/RES/49/205.

sion, in its resolution 1992/S-1/1, asked that its Chairman appoint a Special Rapporteur to investigate firsthand the human rights situation in the former Yugoslavia, in particular within Bosnia and Herzegovina, to make recommendations for ending human rights violations as well as for preventing future occurrences, and to gather systematically information on possible human rights violations which might constitute war crimes. Mr. Tadeusz Mazowiecki, former Prime Minister of Poland, was appointed as Special Rapporteur. He served until 27 July 1995 when he resigned. He was succeeded by Mrs. Elisabeth Rehn, former Defence Minister of Finland.

Mr. Mazowiecki submitted 18 periodic or special reports[22] based on information gathered through various sources, including a number of field trips undertaken by the Special Rapporteur's staff and his own visits to the territory of the former Yugoslavia. In the first report of 28 August 1992, and reconfirmed in his second report of 27 October 1992, the Special Rapporteur concluded that human rights violations were being perpetrated by all parties to the conflicts, with victims on all sides; however, the situation of the Muslim population was particularly tragic.

In the third report, considered at the second special session of the Commission on Human Rights on 30 November–1 December 1992, the Special Rapporteur indicated that "ethnic cleansing" not only continued, but in some regions had intensified, with the primary responsibility falling on the Serb authorities in de facto control of certain territories in Bosnia and Herzegovina and in the United Nations Protected Areas in Croatia. The command of JNA and the political leadership of the Republic of Serbia were also identified as sharing responsibility. According to this report, Albanians, Croats, Hungarians, Muslims and other minority groups were discriminated against in Kosovo, Vojvodina and Sandzak (Muslim denomination of a region located partly in Serbia and partly in Montenegro). At the same time, discrimination and serious violations of the human rights of Serbs also occurred in territories controlled by the Government of Bosnia and Herzegovina, and to a somewhat greater extent in territory under the control of Bosnian Croats. Discrimination and other human rights abuses also occurred in Croatia, in particular against Serbs.

In his report to the 49th session of the Commission on Human Rights in February 1993, the Special Rapporteur stated that evidence was mounting of war crimes during the conflicts in both Croatia and in Bosnia and Herzegovina. Numerous cases had been documented of summary executions and death threats, disappearances, torture and ill-treatment of detainees and destruction of property including religious sites. Rape of women was widespread. There were victims among all ethnic groups and there were rapists among the armed forces of all parties. In addition, the Special Rapporteur sent a team of medical experts to the area to investigate reports of widespread occurrence of rape. According to the experts' report, the majority of the rapes they documented had been committed by ethnic Serb forces against Muslim women from Bosnia and Herzegovina.

With the consent of the Governments concerned, the Centre for Human Rights set up in March 1993 human rights field offices in Zagreb and in Skopje, and later in Sarajevo and Mostar. The Federal Republic of Yugoslavia and the de facto authorities in Bosnian Serb-controlled areas of Bosnia and Herzegovina did not allow field office operations in territories under their control until early 1996. On a number of occasions, following investigation by the field staff, the Special Rapporteur intervened with the authorities to draw their attention to particular instances or allegations of human rights abuses, urging them to investigate and, where necessary, to remedy the situation without delay.

The reports dated 5 May 1993 and 19 May 1993 drew attention to specific situations of "ethnic cleansing" and other violations of fundamental human rights in eastern and central Bosnia. The reports dated 26 August 1993 and 6 September 1993 conveyed the Special Rapporteur's grave concern regarding the human rights situation in the towns of Sarajevo and Mostar. In the report of 17 November 1993, the Special Rapporteur drew attention to the widespread abuse of the fundamental rights of residents in Croatia, Bosnia and Herzegovina and the Federal Republic of Yugoslavia (Serbia and Montenegro).

The report issued on 21 February 1994 dealt with the human rights situation in all countries covered by the Special Rapporteur's mandate, i.e. Bosnia and Herzegovina, Croatia, the Federal Republic of Yugoslavia (Serbia and Montenegro), the former Yugoslav Republic of Macedonia and Slovenia. The report also brought a comprehensive analysis of the situation of children. In describing the situation in Bosnia and Herzegovina, the Spe-

---

[22]S/24516; S/24766; S/24809; S/25341; S/25792; S/26469; S/26383; S/26415; S/26765; S/1994/265; S/1994/743; S/1994/967; S/1994/1252; S/1995/80; S/1995/79; S/1995/597; S/1995/575; S/1995/801.

cial Rapporteur was concerned by such issues as "ethnic cleansing", rape, summary executions, arbitrary arrests and military attacks on civilians and aid workers. He drew particular attention to the attacks by all sides on aid convoys. The Special Rapporteur pointed out that prolongation of the conflict in Bosnia and Herzegovina would lead to atrocities by all sides and the persecution of peoples of every ethnic origin.

Concerning Croatia, the Special Rapporteur pointed to arbitrary executions and "ethnic cleansing" committed by Croatian forces in the predominantly Serb Medak "pocket" on 9 September 1993. He also noted other human rights concerns, such as arbitrary detention, illegal and enforced evictions, the problematic effects of citizenship laws, the destruction of property, the situation of the media and treatment of Muslim minorities and refugees.

With regard to the Federal Republic of Yugoslavia (Serbia and Montenegro), the Special Rapporteur described the discrimination against ethnic Albanians in Kosovo, including their treatment by the police and in the courts, and linguistic and educational discrimination. Other key areas of concern were security of the person, freedom of assembly and association, freedom of expression and the media and discriminatory treatment against minorities in the Sandzak and Vojvodina areas.

The Special Rapporteur pointed out that, in the former Yugoslav Republic of Macedonia, the legal structure had not yet been completed and the administration of justice had not been fully operational. He pointed out that despite certain irregularities concerning the right of national minorities, these problems were being approached within the framework of the Constitution. He also noted that the situation of the mass media gave reason for concern.

With regard to Slovenia, the Special Rapporteur pointed out that certain human rights problems still existed in connection with citizenship law and freedom of the media. Nevertheless, he reiterated his opinion that the human rights situation was by and large satisfactory and recommended that Slovenia should be excluded from his mandate.

The Special Rapporteur placed very strong emphasis on the situation of children. He described the tragic fate of children in war and pointed out that many children had been placed in detention centres and several of them had been tortured there. Children had been deprived of adequate food and medicines. He pointed out the far-reaching consequences arising from disruption of education. He also described the situation of refugee and displaced children, many of whom had been abandoned or were unaccompanied.

The report issued on 10 June 1994 dealt with the deteriorating human rights situation in the eastern Bosnian "safe area" of Gorazde. According to the report, Bosnian Serb forces had committed massive violations of human rights during their March/April 1994 offensive. At the same time, the Special Rapporteur noted that government forces had also been responsible for violations of human rights, though not on a scale comparable to that of the Bosnian Serb forces. In his report of 4 August 1994, the Special Rapporteur expressed, among other things, his grave concern about the significant internal conflict in Mostar and Bihac. Of special concern was the plight of detainees in Bihac.

In his report of 4 November 1994, the Special Rapporteur concluded that, in Bosnia and Herzegovina, Bosnian Serb de facto authorities continued to be responsible for large-scale violations of human rights and, both directly and indirectly, for displacement of people from areas under their control, for systematic military attacks on civilians in the "safe areas" and elsewhere, and for disruption of humanitarian aid and medical evacuation programmes. He also concluded that certain violations of human rights had been perpetrated by governmental authorities and Bosnian Croat local authorities. In Croatia, he reported that while violations of international humanitarian law had decreased, serious human rights violations and discriminatory treatment against minority groups continued, along with arbitrary practices on the part of the Croatian authorities. The Special Rapporteur recommended that all necessary measures be taken to strengthen the independence of the judiciary, that all evictions be suspended and that Croatia grant access to all bona fide refugees from Bosnia and Herzegovina. In the United Nations Protected Areas, a cause for particular concern was the ongoing violence, harassment and intimidation directed against minorities.

Regarding the human rights situation in the Federal Republic of Yugoslavia (Serbia and Montenegro), the Special Rapporteur pointed to the following problems: decline of the rule of law and continuing violence, cases of discrimination on ethnic and political grounds, cases of discriminatory treatment of members of independent trade unions and lack of clear regulations governing citizenship. He was also concerned with the human rights situation in Kosovo, Vojvodina and

Sandzak. In addition, there were reports that police had used unjustifiable force and that other human rights violations had been committed by law enforcement institutions.

Concerning the former Yugoslav Republic of Macedonia, the Special Rapporteur drew attention to the negative impact on the human rights situation of the delay in the implementation of the basic laws related to the juridical structure of the State, the reported limited enjoyment of the right to a fair trial, the excessive use of force by the police and the negative influence of the economic situation on the social stability of the country.

On 10 December 1994, the Special Rapporteur issued a special report on the media and their role in the former Yugoslavia. He concluded that most of the media were controlled, directly or indirectly, by Governments and the ruling parties, and thus were closely bound up with the formulation and defence of their nationalist policies. False information, nationalistic rhetoric and sweeping attacks and slurs against other peoples had been the dominant feature of news propagated in the former Yugoslavia's media since the start of the conflicts.

The report submitted on April 1995 concerned the practice of "ethnic cleansing" in the Banja Luka region of Bosnia and Herzegovina. The Special Rapporteur stated that the de facto Bosnian Serb authorities were very close to attaining their apparent aim of achieving "ethnic purity" in territory under their control. Non-Serbs had been subjected to unrelenting terrorization and discrimination, and a large amount of evidence suggested that the de facto authorities were personally and directly responsible for the massive human rights abuses. Such evidence included the authorities' failure to take even minimal steps for the protection of victimized populations. In addition, the de facto authorities continued to compel non-Serbs to serve in forced-labour brigades and refused to allow access of human rights monitors into territories under their control.

The July 1995 report covered the situation in Western Slavonia following the 1 May 1995 Croatian offensive there [see chapter 25], and the situation in Bosnia and Herzegovina. According to the Special Rapporteur, the Croatian authorities were responsible for violations of human rights and humanitarian law during and after the operation, many of which were of a serious character but did not appear to occur on a massive scale. The Croatian Government's denial to international observers of access to affected areas during the first week of the offensive created serious obstacles to verifying pertinent facts. The Special Rapporteur stated that the vast majority of the Serb population had either already left or was determined to leave Western Slavonia, the main reason for the exodus apparently being fear of possible repercussions. For their part, the authorities of the so-called Republic of Serb Krajina were responsible for shelling a number of civilian areas, a serious violation of humanitarian law.

In the United Nations-designated "safe areas" in Bosnia and Herzegovina, the Special Rapporteur reported a violent escalation of military attacks on civilians by Bosnian Serb forces, resulting in the large-scale loss of life and injury. The humanitarian situation was grave in the areas owing to constant interference by the Bosnian Serb de facto authorities with the transport of humanitarian supplies. In addition, the intimidation and harassment of United Nations personnel had reached an unprecedented scale. Both the Government and the Bosnian Serb de facto authorities were responsible but the latter bore a far greater degree of responsibility in terms of the severity of acts.

On 27 July 1995, Mr. Mazowiecki informed[23] the Chairman of the Commission on Human Rights, as well as the Secretary-General, of his decision to resign his mandate. In his final periodic report, he gave his findings on events which had taken place up to the date of his resignation, including violations of human rights and humanitarian law following the fall of Srebrenica [see chapter 25]. The report noted significant direct and circumstantial evidence indicating that summary executions had occurred and that mass executions of large numbers of people at one time may have occurred. Thousands of people were still missing, and it had not been possible to verify reports that they were being held in detention. There were many instances of inhuman and degrading treatment of the population, credible accounts of rape, although probably not on a mass scale, and disregard for the mental suffering caused by the expulsion of the population from Srebrenica, particularly with reference to the destruction of ties of family, friendship and community.

The report also presented the Special Rapporteur's analysis of the development and implementation of the concept of "safe areas", a concept that could not substitute for a permanent peace agreement but should be considered as a tempo-

[23]A/50/441-S/1995/801, annex.

rary solution aimed at solving humanitarian and not political problems. The "safe areas" established in Bosnia and Herzegovina had offered at least partial protection to a number of local inhabitants and displaced persons. Nevertheless, in the Special Rapporteur's view, lack of determination on the part of the international community and prolongation of the war resulted in the collapse of that concept. The fall of Srebrenica and Zepa had brought tragedy, loss of life and serious human rights violations to the inhabitants of those areas. At the same time, it had seriously undermined the credibility of the United Nations.

Following her appointment on 27 September 1995, the new Special Rapporteur, Mrs. Rehn, conducted her first mission to the region, visiting Bosnia and Herzegovina, Croatia and the Federal Republic of Yugoslavia. In her report[24] on the mission, she stated that the human rights situation in various regions gave reason for serious concern. Cases of mass killings of civilians, torture, other forms of harassment, looting of property, and the burning of houses were still being reported. A large number of people were unaccounted for and new cases of missing persons had been reported.

According to the report, children had been one of the most vulnerable groups affected by the conflict. Their development was significantly obstructed by suffering from war-related trauma and the instability of their lives.

In Bosnia and Herzegovina, of particular and immediate concern was the fate of the approximately 8,000 Bosnian Muslims, mainly males, from Srebrenica who were still unaccounted for. There was ongoing persecution and harassment of the remaining Bosnian Muslim and Bosnian Croat minorities in Banja Luka and other areas controlled by the Bosnian Serb forces. And many Bosnian males were unaccounted for following the expulsions from north-western Bosnia and Herzegovina.

Following the August offensive by the Croatian Army in the former sectors North and South, the fate of the remaining Croatian Serb population, composed mainly of disabled and elderly people, was of particular concern. In addition, the report said, the Government had not provided for adequate living conditions for approximately 25,000 Bosnian Muslim refugees from the Velika Kladusa region while they were stranded as refugees on Croatian territory. Nor had the responsible authorities of Bosnia and Herzegovina created conditions for their return. For its part, the Federal Republic of Yugoslavia was facing serious humanitarian problems, owing to the influx of over 100,000 refugees from Croatia.

G. Commission of Experts

By its resolution 780 (1992) of 6 October 1992, the Security Council requested the Secretary-General to establish an impartial Commission of Experts to provide its conclusions on the evidence of grave breaches of the 1949 Geneva Conventions and other violations of international humanitarian law committed in the territory of the former Yugoslavia. On 23 October, the Secretary-General informed the Council that he had appointed the following five persons as the members of the Commission: Professor Fritz Kalshoven (Netherlands), Chairman; Professor Cherif Bassiouni (Egypt); Mr. William Fenrick (Canada); Judge Keba Mbaye (Senegal); and Professor Torkel Opsahl (Norway). Following the resignation for health reasons of Professor Kalshoven and the untimely death of Professor Opsahl in September 1993, the Secretary-General appointed Professor Christine Cleiren (Netherlands) and Judge Hanne Sophie Greve (Norway) as members of the Commission. Professor Bassiouni was appointed as the new Chairman of the Commission.

To support the activities of the Commission, the Secretary-General established a Trust Fund open to voluntary financial contributions from States, intergovernmental organizations, national institutions and non-governmental organizations as well as natural and juridical persons.

The Commission commenced its work early in November 1992 and carried out four main tasks: the examination and analysis of information obtained from various sources, identification of cases warranting in-depth investigation, verification of facts and consideration of issues of law. In its first interim report, the Commission informed the Secretary-General that it had received

[24]S/1995/933.

several thousand pages of documentation as well as video information on allegations of grave breaches of the Geneva Conventions and international humanitarian law, and that a database was being designed to provide a comprehensive, consistent and manageable record of all reported crimes.

Subsequent Commission activities were of two basic types: (a) collecting, evaluating and analysing information with the help of the database and (b) sending investigative missions to the former Yugoslavia to collect and verify the information, to investigate specific incidents as well as to obtain testimonies, to interview victims and witnesses and to hear alleged perpetrators. On 6 September 1993, the Commission submitted its second interim report.

Following the appointment of an Acting Deputy-Prosecutor for the International Tribunal, the Secretary-General, in consultation with the Se-curity Council, decided that the Commission should conclude its work on 30 April 1994.

The Commission's final report included its views on selected legal issues, a general study on the military structure of the "warring factions" and the strategies and tactics employed by them, and substantive findings on alleged crimes of "ethnic cleansing", genocide and other massive violations of elementary dictates of humanity, systematic rape and sexual assault and destruction of cultural property committed in various parts of the former Yugoslavia.

The database and all of the information gathered by the Commission were forwarded to the Office of the Prosecutor of the International Tribunal. The Secretary-General informed[25] the Council on 24 May 1994 that he was confident that the material collected and analysed by the Commission would greatly facilitate the task of the Tribunal in carrying out its mandate.

H. International Tribunal

The decision that an international tribunal should be established was taken by the Security Council on 22 February 1993 in its resolution 808 (1993). In so deciding, the Council took into account the interim report of the Commission of Experts and noted the recommendation by the Co-Chairmen of the ICFY Steering Committee for the establishment of such a tribunal. At the request of the Council, the Secretary-General submitted on 3 May 1993 a detailed report[26] on all aspects of the decision. A Statute of the Tribunal, covering such issues as jurisdiction, organization, investigations, pre-trial, trial and post-trial proceedings and cooperation and judicial assistance, was annexed to the report.

In the report, the Secretary-General stated that such a Tribunal should be established under Chapter VII of the United Nations Charter as a subsidiary organ of the Security Council. It should perform its functions independently of political considerations and not be subject to the authority or control of the Council with regard to the performance of its judicial functions. Its life span should be linked to the restoration and maintenance of international peace and security in the territory of the former Yugoslavia. The seat of the Tribunal should be at The Hague, Netherlands.

The Secretary-General proposed that the Tribunal should consist of three organs: two Trial Chambers and an Appeals Chamber; the Prosecutor; and a Registry, servicing both the Chambers and the Prosecutor. The Chambers would be composed of a total of 11 judges — three in each Trial Chamber and five in the Appeals Chamber. Judges should be elected for a four-year term by the United Nations General Assembly from a list of nominees put forward by Member States and short-listed by the Security Council to a number no less than 22 and no more than 33.

On 25 May, the Security Council, by its resolution 827 (1993), approved the Secretary-General's report and decided to establish an International Tribunal "for the sole purpose of prosecuting persons responsible for serious violations of international humanitarian law committed in the territory of the former Yugoslavia between 1 January 1991 and a date to be determined by the Security Council upon the restoration of peace ...". The Council also adopted the Statute of the Tribunal and decided that all States must cooperate fully with the Tribunal and take any measures necessary under their domestic law

[25] S/1994/674. [26] S/25704.

to implement its Statute. The Secretary-General was requested to make urgently practical arrangements for the effective functioning of the Tribunal.

On 20 August, the Council adopted its resolution 857 (1993), by which it established a list of 23 candidates, each from a different country and representing all major legal systems, to be presented to the General Assembly. In accordance with the Statute of the Tribunal, 11 judges were elected by the General Assembly on 17 September 1993 for a four-year term. They would be eligible for re-election. Their terms and conditions of service would correspond to those of the judges of the International Court of Justice. The elected judges were: Mr. Georges Abi-Saab (Egypt), Mr. Antonio Cassese (Italy), Mr. Jules Deschenes (Canada), Mr. Adolphus Karibi-Whyte (Nigeria), Mr. Germain Le Foyer de Costil (France), Mr. Haopei Li (China), Ms. Gabrielle Kirk McDonald (United States), Ms. Elizabeth Odio Benito (Costa Rica), Mr. Rustam Sidhwa (Pakistan), Sir Ninian Stephen (Australia), Mr. Datuk Wira Lal Vohrah (Malaysia). After the resignation of Mr. Germain Le Foyer de Costil on 1 January 1994, the Secretary-General, following consultations with the Presidents of the Security Council and the General Assembly, appointed Mr. Claude Jorda (France) as Judge of the International Tribunal. Following the resignation of Judge Abi-Saab, he was succeeded in the same manner by Mr. Fouad Abdel-Moneim Riad (Egypt).

The International Tribunal was inaugurated on 17 November 1993 at the Peace Palace in The Hague. The Security Council, by its resolution 877 (1993) of 21 October 1993, appointed Mr. Ramón Escovar-Salom, Attorney General of Venezuela, as Prosecutor. During the Tribunal's second session, however, the Prosecutor-designate announced his intention not to take up office in order to assume a high governmental position in his own country. On 8 February 1994, the Secretary-General appointed Mr. Graham Blewitt (Australia) as the Acting Deputy Prosecutor.

Mr. Theodoor C. van Boven (Netherlands) was appointed by the Secretary-General as Acting Registrar of the Tribunal on 21 January 1994. Upon Mr. van Boven's resignation, Ms. Dorothee Margarete Elizabeth de Sampayo Garrido-Nijgh (Netherlands) was appointed Registrar on 29 December 1994.

The first annual report[27] of the Tribunal, submitted in August 1994, noted that the Office of the Prosecutor, responsible for the initiation and conduct of investigations and prosecutions, had been handicapped by the delay in the appointment of a Prosecutor. Even so, the Acting Deputy Prosecutor had managed to make substantial progress in establishing the necessary infrastructure. It was not until 8 July 1994 that the Security Council, by its resolution 936 (1994), appointed Mr. Richard J. Goldstone, Judge of the Appellate Division of the Supreme Court of South Africa, as Prosecutor of the International Tribunal. Judge Goldstone took office on 15 August 1994.

With the appointment of the Prosecutor, the Office of the Prosecutor was able to complete some of the major investigations. On 18 October 1994, the Tribunal held its first public hearing in The Hague. In early November, the Prosecutor issued a first indictment. On 24 April 1995, the Prosecutor announced that he was investigating the responsibility of the Bosnian Serb leadership for a wide range of war crimes. Subsequent indictments were confirmed against the Bosnian Serb leaders Dr. Radovan Karadzic and General Ratko Mladic. An indictment was also confirmed against the leader of the Krajina Serbs, Mr. Milan Martic. In each case where an indictment was confirmed, arrest warrants for the accused were issued and transmitted to the appropriate authorities.

Given that most warrants of arrest issued by the Tribunal have not yet been served on the accused, the Tribunal has commenced proceedings under Rule 61 of the Rules of Procedure and Evidence. Under this Rule, if within a reasonable time a warrant of arrest has not be executed, a Judge who confirmed the indictment shall order a review of the indictment. The Prosecutor will resubmit the indictment in open court together with all relevant evidence, and if the Trial Chamber is satisfied that there are reasonable grounds for believing that the accused has committed the crimes charged in the indictment, it shall have the relevant parts of the indictment read out by the Prosecutor. Proceedings under Rule 61 do not provide for a finding of guilt. If, however, the Trial Chamber is satisfied that the failure to effect personal service was due to the refusal of a State to cooperate with the Tribunal, the President of the Tribunal shall notify the Security Council accordingly. The President of the Tribunal availed himself of this procedure in the *Nikolic* case when, following Rule 61 proceedings, he informed the Council of the refusal of the Bosnian-Serb Administration in Pale to comply with the orders of the Tribunal.[28]

The Prosecutor also submitted three Applications for deferral of investigations and criminal proceedings to the competence of the

---

[27]A/49/342; S/1994/1007. [28]S/1995/910.

International Tribunal. According to Rule 9 (iii) of the Rules of Procedure and Evidence, an Application for deferral may be requested when what is in issue is related to, or otherwise involves, significant factual and legal questions which may have implications for investigations or prosecutions before the Tribunal.

The work of the International Tribunal is financed by assessed contributions separately from the regular budget of the United Nations. In addition, the General Assembly invited Member States and other interested parties to make voluntary contributions to the International Tribunal both in cash and in the form of services and supplies acceptable to the Secretary-General. The appropriation for the period 1994–1995 amounted to $38.8 million. Requirements for 1996 were estimated at $40.8 million. Voluntary contributions totalling $8.9 million had been received or pledged as of mid-1995, excluding the cost of staff and experts on loan from Governments and international organizations and institutions. A number of Member States and institutions also made contributions of equipment.[29]

I. Decisions by the International Court of Justice

On 8 April 1993, the International Court of Justice issued an Order of provisional measures, in which it stated that the Government of the Federal Republic of Yugoslavia (Serbia and Montenegro) "should in particular ensure that any military, paramilitary or irregular armed units which may be directed or supported by it, as well as any organizations and persons which may be subject to its control, direction or influence, do not commit any acts of genocide, of conspiracy to commit genocide, of direct and public incitement to commit genocide, or of complicity in genocide, whether directed against the Muslim population of Bosnia and Herzegovina or against any other national, ethnical, racial or religious group". The Court also held that neither party should aggravate or extend the existing dispute over the prevention or punishment of the crime of genocide.

The Court issued these provisional measures in response to a suit initiated by the Government of Bosnia and Herzegovina on 20 March 1993. The Court found that it had *prima facie* jurisdiction to issue its Order under the Convention on the Prevention and Punishment of the Crime of Genocide concluded by the United Nations in 1948. The Convention describes as genocide acts "committed with the intent to destroy, in whole or in part, a national, ethnical, racial or religious group".

A judgment on the merits of the case would be handed down only after the parties fully briefed and argued it. The Court's Order emphasized that the facts and law of the dispute meanwhile remained unsettled. Under its Statute, the Court has the power to indicate provisional measures for preserving the rights of either party, pending judgment on the merits of the case. The Court noted that it was not able to indicate measures for the protection of any disputed rights which fell outside the scope of the Genocide Convention.

On 29 July 1993, Bosnia and Herzegovina filed a second request with the International Court of Justice calling for provisional measures against the Federal Republic of Yugoslavia (Serbia and Montenegro) to prevent commission of the crime of genocide. The request stated that additional measures were necessary because the Federal Republic of Yugoslavia (Serbia and Montenegro) had violated all of the protective measures indicated by the Court in its Order of 8 April.

On 10 August 1993, the Federal Republic of Yugoslavia (Serbia and Montenegro), alleging genocide against the Serb people in Bosnia and Herzegovina by the authorities of that country, requested the International Court of Justice to indicate, as a provisional measure, that the Government of the "so-called Republic of Bosnia and Herzegovina" immediately take all measures within its power to prevent the commission of the crime of genocide against the Serb ethnic group.

On 13 September 1993, the Court issued an interim Order of provisional measures which, in effect, reaffirmed its earlier Order. It stated that "the present perilous situation demands not an indication of provisional measures additional to those indicated by the Court's Order of 8 April 1993, but immediate and effective implementation of those measures".

[29]A/C.5/50/41.

The Court declined to adopt the more far-reaching injunctions requested by Bosnia and Herzegovina because it could order interim measures only within the scope of the jurisdiction conferred on it by the anti-Genocide Convention and was not entitled to deal with broader claims. It also declined to order an injunction sought by the Federal Republic of Yugoslavia (Serbia and Montenegro) requiring Bosnia and Herzegovina to take all measures within its power to prevent commission of the crime of genocide against the Serbs in Bosnia and Herzegovina. The Court declared that it was "not satisfied that all that might have been done has been done" to prevent genocide in Bosnia and Herzegovina, and reminded the parties to the case that they were obliged to take the Court's provisional measure "seriously into account".

Chapter 24

United Nations Protection Force
(UNPROFOR), February 1992–March 1995

Chapter 24

United Nations Protection Force (UNPROFOR), February 1992–March 1995

A. Introduction

The United Nations Protection Force (UNPROFOR) was established by Security Council resolution 743 (1992) of 21 February 1992 for an initial period of 12 months. In that resolution, the Council recalled that, in accordance with the United Nations peace-keeping plan, UNPROFOR should be an interim arrangement to create conditions of peace and security required for the negotiation of an overall settlement of the Yugoslav crisis. UNPROFOR's first mandate related to Croatia. In June 1992, the mandate was expanded to include Bosnia and Herzegovina and later that year the former Yugoslav Republic of Macedonia.

Between the end of the first mandate period in February 1993 and UNPROFOR's restructuring in March 1995, the Security Council decided to extend UNPROFOR's mandate on eight occasions: on 19 February 1993 (S/RES/807 (1993)) until 31 March 1993; on 30 March 1993 (S/RES/815 (1993)) until 30 June 1993; on 30 June 1993 (S/RES/847 (1993)) until 30 September 1993; on 30 September 1993 (S/RES/869 (1993)) for 24 hours; on 1 October 1993 (S/RES/870 (1993)) until 5 October 1993; on 4 October 1993 (S/RES/871 (1993)) until 31 March 1994; on 31 March 1994 (S/RES/908 (1994)) until 30 September 1994; and on 30 September 1994 (S/RES/947 (1994)) until 31 March 1995.

B. Croatia

UNPAs

Following its establishment in February 1992, UNPROFOR was deployed in certain areas in Croatia designated as United Nations Protected Areas (UNPAs). The UNPAs were areas in which Serbs constituted the majority or a substantial minority of the population and where inter-ethnic tensions had led to armed conflict. The Security Council judged that special interim arrangements were required in the UNPAs to ensure that a lasting cease-fire was maintained. For United Nations purposes, the UNPAS were divided into four sectors — East, North, South and West — in the areas of Eastern Slavonia, Western Slavonia and Krajina.

The original United Nations plan in Croatia[1] rested on two central elements: (a) the withdrawal of the Yugoslav People's Army (JNA) from all of Croatia and the demilitarization of the UNPAs; and (b) the continuing functioning, on an interim

basis, of the existing local authorities and police, under United Nations supervision, pending the achievement of an overall political solution to the crisis.

UNPROFOR's mandate was to ensure that the UNPAs were demilitarized, through the withdrawal or disbandment of all armed forces in them, and that UNPA residents were protected from fear of armed attack. To this end, UNPROFOR was authorized to control access to the UNPAs, to ensure that the UNPAs remained demilitarized, and to monitor the functioning of the local police to help ensure non-discrimination and the protection of human rights. Outside the UNPAs, UNPROFOR military observers were to verify the withdrawal of all JNA and irregular forces from Croatia, other than those disbanded and demobilized there. In

[1] S/23280.

support of the work of United Nations humanitarian agencies, UNPROFOR was also to facilitate the return, in conditions of safety and security, of civilian displaced persons to their homes in the UNPAs.

UNPROFOR included military, police and civilian components. The original authorized strength of the military component was 12 enlarged infantry battalions (10,400 all ranks); headquarters, logistics and other support elements totalling about 2,480 all ranks; and 100 military observers. The police component was to consist of approximately 530 police personnel.

The Force Commander, Lieutenant-General Satish Nambiar, and his principal staff members arrived in Belgrade on 8 March 1992. After initial consultations there and in Zagreb, they proceeded to Sarajevo where they established UNPROFOR's headquarters on 13 March 1992. Following the arrival of advance teams of military elements in mid-March, active preparations for the full deployment of the Force began. By the end of April 1992, UNPROFOR had a strength of 8,332, including 7,975 military personnel. Its headquarters was fully operational, with the majority of the headquarters military personnel already there. Logistic bases were established in Belgrade and Zagreb.

Enlargements of mandate in 1992

The original mandate of UNPROFOR in Croatia underwent several enlargements. On 30 June 1992, the Security Council, by its resolution 762 (1992), authorized UNPROFOR to undertake monitoring functions in the "pink zones" — certain areas of Croatia which had earlier been controlled by JNA and populated largely by Serbs, but which were outside the agreed UNPA boundaries. It also recommended the establishment of a Joint Commission chaired by UNPROFOR and consisting of representatives of the Government of Croatia and of the local authorities in the region, with the participation of the European Community Monitoring Mission, to oversee and monitor the restoration of authority by the Croatian Government in the "pink zones".

On 7 August 1992, the Security Council, by its resolution 769 (1992), authorized the enlargement of UNPROFOR's strength and mandate to enable it to control the entry of civilians into the UNPAs and to perform immigration and customs functions at the UNPA borders at international frontiers.

The third enlargement of UNPROFOR's mandate in Croatia came about on 6 October 1992, when the Security Council adopted its resolution 779 (1992), authorizing UNPROFOR to assume responsibility for monitoring the demilitarization of the Prevlaka Peninsula near Dubrovnik. By the same resolution, the Council approved the Secretary-General's action to ensure the control by UNPROFOR of the vitally important Peruca dam, situated in one of the "pink zones".

Renewed hostilities

On 22 January 1993, the Croatian Army launched an offensive in a number of locations in the southern part of UNPROFOR's Sector South and the adjacent "pink zones", citing as a reason its impatience with the slow progress of negotiations in respect of various economic facilities in and adjacent to the UNPAs and "pink zones". On 27 January, the Croatian Army attacked and captured the Peruca dam. The local Serbs responded to the Croatian offensive by breaking into a number of United Nations weapons storage areas, which were under joint control under a double-lock system in the UNPAs, and by removing their arms, including heavy weapons.

UNPROFOR warned both the Croatian Government and the local Serb authorities against further violations. The Force also sought to limit the damage caused by the fighting, to prevent escalation and to bring about a cease-fire.

On 25 January, the Security Council adopted its resolution 802 (1993), by which it demanded an immediate cessation of hostile activities by the Croatian armed forces within or adjacent to the UNPAs and their withdrawal from those areas, and strongly condemned the attacks by those forces against UNPROFOR personnel. The Council demanded also the return of all heavy weapons seized from UNPROFOR-controlled storage areas, and strict compliance by all parties and others concerned with the terms of cease-fire arrangements, including the disbanding and demobilization of Serb Territorial Defence units or other units of similar functions. It called upon them to cooperate fully with the International Conference on the Former Yugoslavia (ICFY) and to refrain from any actions which might undermine efforts aimed at reaching a political settlement.

On 26 January, the Croatian Government informed the Force Commander of UNPROFOR that, upon compliance by the Serb side with the various provisions of the resolution, they would remove their military personnel, but not their police, from the areas they had taken. For its part, the Serb side stated that Croatia must return to its pre-22 January positions before the implementation of the remainder of resolution 802 (1993) could be considered.

UNPROFOR's first year in Croatia

During UNPROFOR's first year, the experience in Croatia was a mixed one. Its principal success was in ensuring the complete withdrawal of JNA from the territory of Croatia, including the Prevlaka Peninsula. Until the fourth week of January 1993, UNPROFOR's presence also helped to prevent a recurrence of hostilities in the UNPAs and the "pink zones". However, the uncooperative attitude of the local Serb authorities prevented UNPROFOR from achieving the demilitarization of the UNPAs and the disarming of the Serb Territorial Defence and irregular forces. As a result, UNPROFOR was not able to establish the conditions of peace and security that would have permitted the voluntary return of refugees and displaced persons to their homes in these areas. Nor was it able to establish border controls.

An atmosphere of terror and intimidation in many parts of the four sectors characterized much of the first ten months of the mandate period. Efforts of United Nations civilian police to prevent discrimination and human rights abuses in the UNPAs did not prove fully successful. Beginning in November 1992, however, the situation did show improvement in all but a few areas, and the maintenance of law and order was gradually enhanced through the reorganization and redeployment of the local police.

While the non-cooperation of the local Serb authorities seriously impeded implementation of the United Nations peace-keeping plan, the Croatian offensive of January 1993 significantly altered the situation on the ground. The President of Croatia, Mr. Franjo Tudjman, declared that the willingness of his Government to agree to an extension of UNPROFOR's mandate after its initial 12 months was dependent on progress in a number of areas, including the complete disarmament of all paramilitary forces and militia in the UNPAs and the "pink zones" with a destruction of their heavy weapons, voluntary and unconditional return of all refugees and displaced persons to their homes in the UNPAs, maintenance of tight controls by UNPROFOR in those border areas where the boundaries of the UNPAs coincided with internationally recognized frontiers of Croatia; and restoration of Croatian authority in the "pink zones". He also urged the Council to grant UNPROFOR an enforcement mandate.

For its part, the Serb leadership in the UNPAs felt "betrayed" by what it saw as UNPROFOR's failure to protect them. It therefore rearmed and remobilized its forces in response to the Croatian offensive and received substantial reinforcements of Serb fighters from elsewhere in the former Yugoslavia. Serb militias broke into storage depots holding heavy weapons placed there under the peace-keeping plan. The Serb side also refused to enter into negotiations with the Croat side, or to return the heavy weapons taken from storage, unless the Croatian armed forces withdrew to the positions they occupied before the offensive. Such a withdrawal was categorically rejected by the Croatian authorities.

The peace-keeping plan had been envisaged as an interim arrangement pending an overall political solution to the Yugoslav crisis. The Government of Croatia claimed there was no longer any "overall political solution" to negotiate. The only issue was the return of the UNPAs and the "pink zones" to Croatian control. The Krajina Serb leadership in the UNPAs, however, refused to consider those territories to be a part of Croatia and rejected talks on that basis, recalling that the plan was explicitly not intended to prejudge a political solution to the Yugoslav crisis. Further, the Krajina Serbs argued that two parties to the original plan, the President of Serbia and the Federal Yugoslav military authorities in Belgrade, no longer had recognized legal status in the areas where UNPROFOR was deployed. Therefore, the mandate and deployment of UNPROFOR needed to be discussed anew with the authorities representing the so-called "Republic of Serb Krajina".

In these circumstances, the Secretary-General saw three options with regard to UNPROFOR's mandate in Croatia as the initial period of 12 months drew to a close. UNPROFOR could withdraw, but withdrawal from the UNPAs would almost certainly result in the resumption of large-scale hostilities, nullifying the political effort and the material resources already invested. The mandate could be modified, but any enforcement capability "would be a fundamental contradiction of the nature and purpose of UNPROFOR's deployment in Croatia, as a peace-keeping force entrusted with the implementation of a plan agreed by all parties." Or the mandate could be renewed with no change.

In the Secretary-General's judgement, the difficulties which UNPROFOR and the Security

Council faced in Croatia could be attributed to two principal factors: the inability to implement the peace-keeping plan; and the lack of an agreed settlement to the conflict between the Republic of Croatia and the Serb populations living in the UNPAs and the "pink zones". Unless those two factors were addressed, a sound basis would not exist for renewing UNPROFOR's mandate in Croatia. Urgent efforts needed to be made to resolve the problems arising from the Croatian offensive, to establish a basis for completing the implementation of the peace-keeping plan and to agree on a framework for negotiating, within the principles of the International Conference on the Former Yugoslavia, a settlement of the underlying dispute. The Secretary-General told the Security Council that he had asked the Co-Chairmen of the ICFY Steering Committee to address these questions urgently with a view to establishing a basis on which to recommend an extension of UNPROFOR's mandate. On 10 February 1993, he recommended that the Security Council extend UNPROFOR's existing mandate for an interim period up to 31 March 1993, in order to give the Co-Chairmen the necessary time.[2]

Extensions of the mandate

On 19 February 1993, the Security Council adopted resolution 807 (1993), by which it extended UNPROFOR's mandate for an interim period until 31 March 1993. The Council demanded that the parties and others concerned comply fully with the United Nations peace-keeping plan in Croatia and their other commitments, and refrain from positioning their forces near the UNPAs and in the "pink zones". It invited the Secretary-General to take all appropriate measures to strengthen the security of UNPROFOR, in particular by providing it with the necessary defensive means.

The Council urged the parties and others concerned to cooperate fully with the Co-Chairmen of the ICFY Steering Committee in the discussions under their auspices. The Co-Chairmen held several rounds of talks in New York and Geneva with representatives of the Government of Croatia and the Serb populations living in the UNPAs and the "pink zones". While some progress was made in these talks, fundamental differences remained between the two sides. The Secretary-General told the Security Council that more time would be needed to bring the negotiations to a meaningful conclusion. He therefore recom-

mended the extension of UNPROFOR's mandate for a further interim period of three months.[3]

On 30 March, the Security Council, by resolution 815 (1993), extended the mandate of UNPROFOR for an additional interim period until 30 June 1993. It also reaffirmed its commitment to ensure respect for the sovereignty and territorial integrity of Croatia (as well as of the other Republics where UNPROFOR was deployed). The Council thus made it clear formally that the international community would not entertain the claim of the local Serb authorities to recognition as a sovereign entity.[4] The Secretary-General later reported[5] to the Council that the local Serb authorities viewed the resolution as prejudging the outcome of the political negotiations, and that, following its adoption, their resistance to any dialogue had intensified.

The Council also decided to reconsider within one month, or at any time at the request of the Secretary-General, UNPROFOR's mandate in light of developments of ICFY and the situation on the ground. It requested the Secretary-General to report to it on how the peace plan for Croatia could be effectively implemented.

On 24 June, the Secretary-General drew the attention of the Security Council to the failure of the parties to permit implementation of the United Nations plan and to cooperate in establishing a political process leading to an early settlement. He noted, nevertheless, that the presence of UNPROFOR was indispensable for controlling the conflict, fostering a climate in which negotiations between the parties could be promoted, preventing the resumption or escalation of conflict, providing a breathing-space for the continued efforts of the peacemakers and for supporting the provision of essential humanitarian assistance. He also informed the Council that the termination of UNPROFOR's mandate at that point would risk the resumption of a major conflict in the region and cause severe adverse consequences for humanitarian relief operations in Bosnia and Herzegovina. The Secretary-General recommended that the Security Council extend the mandate of UNPROFOR by a further three months, to 30 September 1993.[6]

In doing so, by its resolution 847 (1993) of 30 June 1993, the Security Council also requested the Secretary-General to report within one month on progress towards implementation of the peace-keeping plan and all relevant Security Council resolutions. On 16 August, the Secretary-

[2]S/25264 and Corr.1. [3]S/25470 and Add.1. [4]S/25777. [5]S/1994/300. [6]S/25993.

General recommended[7] to the Council that no further action should be taken at that stage.

Implementation of resolution 802

Following the renewed outbreak of hostilities in Croatia, precipitated by the Croatian incursion into the UNPAs and "pink zones" on 22 January 1993, intensive efforts were made within the framework of the International Conference and by UNPROFOR to bring about a cease-fire and a restoration of the prior status in accordance with Security Council resolution 802 (1993) of 25 January 1993.

On 6 April 1993, the representatives of the Government of Croatia and the local Serb authorities signed an agreement[8] regarding the implementation of resolution 802. The agreement was to enter into force when the Co-Chairmen of the ICFY Steering Committee received from both parties assurances regarding the stationing of police in the areas from which the Croatian Government's armed forces were withdrawn, and their agreement that UNPROFOR should exclusively fulfil all police functions in those areas during an interim period. Croatian authorities orally gave that assurance at the time of signature; the Serb assurance required the approval of their "Assembly". That approval was not forthcoming and the agreement therefore did not enter into force.

The parties also agreed to begin talks, under the auspices of the Co-Chairmen of the Steering Committee, within 15 days of implementation of the agreement in order to resolve outstanding obstacles to the full implementation of the United Nations plan for Croatia.

The UNPROFOR Force Commander assessed the additional resources required to implement the agreement and recommended that UNPROFOR be augmented by two mechanized infantry battalions of some 900 all ranks each, one engineer company of up to 150 troops all ranks, and 50 additional military observers. The Secretary-General recommended that, once the agreement entered into force, the Security Council approve the recommended changes to UNPROFOR's strength and mandate.

However, on 6 July 1993, new tensions arose following the decision of the Croatian Government to take unilateral actions aimed at rebuilding and reopening the Maslenica bridge on 18 July. On 15-16 July 1993, the Erdut/Zagreb agreement was concluded, which required the withdrawal of Croatian armed forces and police from the area of the Maslenica bridge by 31 July 1993, and the placing of the bridge under the exclusive control of UNPROFOR. UNPROFOR moved 2,000 troops into the areas adjacent to those from which the Croatian forces were to withdraw. The UNPROFOR troops could not be deployed, however, because the Croatian military authorities would not allow UNPROFOR full access to the areas concerned.

Despite Croatia's failure to withdraw and the Serb shelling and the sinking of one of the pontoons of the Maslenica bridge on 2 August 1993, the Co-Chairmen nevertheless concluded that there was still enough common ground to continue negotiations. The parties accepted the invitation of the Co-Chairmen, and negotiations began in Geneva on 12 August 1993 on a cease-fire which would include the elements of the original Erdut/Zagreb agreement. Despite intensive discussions in Geneva, Zagreb and Knin, an overall cease-fire agreement could not be achieved.

On 9 September, after several days of grave incidents in the UNPAs and the "pink zones", and rising tensions, shelling intensified on both sides of the confrontation line. The Croatian Army once again carried out a military incursion in the area of Medak, where three Serb villages were seized. Hostilities worsened on 10 and 11 September. Following the intervention of the Secretary-General's Special Representative and the UNPROFOR Force Commander, and a call[9] from the Security Council, the parties finally agreed to a cease-fire on 15 September. UNPROFOR moved some 500 to 600 troops into the area to replace the Croatian armed forces which eventually withdrew to positions occupied before the incursion began.

Mandate renewed

On 20 September 1993, the Secretary-General recommended[10] that the Security Council renew the mandate of UNPROFOR for a period of six months. Referring to Croatia, the Secretary-General said that he had been "sorely tempted" to recommend the withdrawal of UNPROFOR altogether. Key parts of the original United Nations peace-keeping plan had been difficult, if not impossible, to implement, and had become more so since the resumption of hostilities following the Croatian incursion of 22 January 1993. The fundamental solution to the problem had to be sought through political dialogue. In this process, the

[7]S/26310. [8]S/25555, annex. [9]S/26436. [10]S/26470.

principal objective of UNPROFOR could only be to keep the peace, thereby permitting negotiations to take place. To enhance the security of UNPROFOR, he requested the extension of close air support to the territory of Croatia. The Security Council had already authorized Member States to take all necessary measures, through the use of air power, in support of UNPROFOR in and around the "safe areas" in Bosnia and Herzegovina.

Should the Council decide to extend UNPROFOR's mandate, the Secretary-General stated that he would give "favourable consideration" to a suggestion by the President of Croatia that UNPROFOR be divided into three parts — UNPROFOR (Croatia), UNPROFOR (Bosnia and Herzegovina) and UNPROFOR (the former Yugoslav Republic of Macedonia) — while retaining its integrated military, logistical and administrative structure under the command of one Special Representative of the Secretary-General and one theatre Force Commander.

In the meantime, on 24 September, the Security Council was informed[11] by the Croatian Government that if the mandate of UNPROFOR was not amended to promote energetic implementation of the relevant resolutions of the Security Council, Croatia would be forced to request UNPROFOR to leave the country not later than 30 November 1993.

UNPROFOR's mandate was set to expire on 30 September 1993. In the midst of intensive consultations, the Security Council extended the mandate for 24 hours on 30 September and for four days on 1 October.[12] On 4 October, the Council, by its resolution 871 (1993), extended the mandate for a period of six months, through 31 March 1994. It took this action under Chapter VII of the Charter, reiterating its determination to ensure the security of UNPROFOR and its freedom of movement.

The Council reaffirmed the crucial importance of the full and prompt implementation of the United Nations peace-keeping plan for Croatia and called upon the signatories of the plan and all others concerned, in particular the Federal Republic of Yugoslavia (Serbia and Montenegro), to cooperate in its full implementation. Declaring that continued non-cooperation in the implementation of relevant resolutions would have serious consequences, the Council affirmed that full normalization of the international community's position towards those concerned would take into account their actions in implementing those resolutions, including those relating to the United Nations peace-keeping plan for Croatia.

The Council called for an immediate cease-fire agreement between the Croatian Government and the local Serb authorities in the UNPAs, mediated under the auspices of ICFY. It urged all parties to cooperate with UNPROFOR in reaching and implementing an agreement on confidence-building measures, including the restoration of electricity, water and communications in all regions of Croatia. Stressing the importance of restoring Croatian authority in the "pink zones", the Council called for the revival of the Joint Commission established under the chairmanship of UNPROFOR.

The Council decided to continue to review urgently the extension of close air support to UNPROFOR in the territory of Croatia as recommended by the Secretary-General. It authorized UNPROFOR, in carrying out its mandate in Croatia, acting in self-defence, to take the necessary measures, including the use of force, to ensure its security and its freedom of movement.

Christmas truce in Croatia

As requested by Security Council resolution 871 (1993), the Secretary-General reported[13] to the Council on 1 December 1993. In view of various initiatives under way, he would not recommend that the Council reconsider the mandate of UNPROFOR in Croatia at that stage. Talks aimed at achieving a comprehensive cease-fire in and around the UNPAs in Croatia and initiating discussions on economic confidence-building steps were continuing within the framework of ICFY.

On 17 December 1993, Croat representatives and local Serb authorities in Croatia signed a Christmas Truce Agreement, mediated by UNPROFOR. The two parties undertook to cease all armed hostilities along all existing confrontation lines from midnight on 23 December 1993 until midnight on 15 January 1994. They also agreed to implement certain confidence-building measures, and to open negotiations as soon as the truce took effect on a "general and lasting" cease-fire, with the separation of forces on both sides. Subsequently, the truce was extended beyond 15 January.

Cease-fire agreement in Croatia

On 29 March 1994, in Zagreb, representatives of the Government of Croatia and the

---

[11]S/26491, annex. [12]S/RES/869 (1993) and S/RES/870 (1993). [13]S/26828.

local Serb authorities in UNPAs concluded a cease-fire agreement[14] aiming to achieve a lasting cessation of hostilities. The agreement was concluded in the presence of the representatives of the Russian Federation and of the United States, and witnessed by the ICFY representatives and the Force Commander of UNPROFOR.

In a 30 March 1994 letter[15] to the President of the Security Council, the Secretary-General reported that the implementation of this cease-fire agreement would involve, *inter alia*, the interpositioning of UNPROFOR forces in a zone of separation of varying width, the establishment of additional control points, observation posts and patrols, as well as the monitoring of the withdrawal of heavy weapons out of range of the contact line. In order to enable UNPROFOR to perform the functions called for in the agreement, the Secretary-General recommended that the Council increase the authorized strength of the Force by four mechanized infantry companies (one mechanized infantry battalion of 1,000 all ranks) and four engineer companies (600 all ranks). In addition, a helicopter squadron of at least six helicopters with 200 all ranks would be needed for effective monitoring of the cease-fire agreement.

Recommendation to the Council

As the mandate period approached its expiration at the end of March 1994, criticism of the effectiveness of UNPROFOR, mounting threats to the safety and security of United Nations personnel, and the continuing failure of Member States to honour their financial obligations had led the Secretary-General to consider seriously whether the continuation of UNPROFOR constituted a worthwhile use of the limited peace-keeping resources of the United Nations. He told[16] the Security Council on 16 March 1994 that the diversity and scope of the problems in the former Yugoslavia required the deployment of more military forces than troop-contributing nations appeared to be prepared, at that time, to make available. Nevertheless, UNPROFOR's deployment embodied the will of the international community to help the parties to arrive at an overall political settlement. The Secretary-General therefore recommended its prolongation, adding that it was the responsibility of the parties to seize the opportunity to demonstrate that they were seriously committed to pursuing the path of peace.

Monitoring the cease-fire

On 31 March 1994, the Security Council, by its resolution 908 (1994), extended the mandate of UNPROFOR for an additional six-month period terminating on 30 September 1994. In relation to Croatia, the Council also decided that Member States might take all necessary measures to extend close air support to the territory of Croatia in defence of UNPROFOR personnel in the performance of its mandate, under the authority of the Council and subject to close coordination with the Secretary-General and UNPROFOR.

UNPROFOR activities in Croatia focused on the monitoring of the general cease-fire agreement of 29 March 1994. By the end of May 1994, UNPROFOR reported almost total compliance, characterized by a general cessation of hostilities, withdrawal of forces beyond fixed lines of separation and the placement of heavy weapons in agreed storage sites. UNPROFOR assumed exclusive control over the zone of separation, covering an area of over 1,300 square kilometres.

It was hoped that the parties would then begin comprehensive discussions on issues of mutual economic benefit. However, during the months of April and May, local Serb authorities issued from their headquarters in Knin a number of statements that appeared to close the door on political reconciliation. They announced their intention to pursue full integration with other Serb areas in the former Yugoslavia and stipulated unrealistic preconditions for talks. It proved impossible to open negotiations at that stage.

In August, following renewed mediation efforts by ICFY, senior officials from the Croatian Government and local Serb authorities were brought together for discussions in Knin. Committing themselves to continuing the negotiating process, they agreed to establish eight expert groups to prepare for future negotiation on specific economic issues.

In another development, in early July, the Association of Displaced Persons of Croatia, with the support of the Croatian authorities, imposed a blockade on all the crossing-points into or within the UNPAs, in order to draw attention to their plight and apply pressure on UNPROFOR to expedite their return to their homes in the Protected Areas. After a series of high-level discussions between UNPROFOR and Croatian authorities, the blockade was eventually lifted on 19 August. Although by September 1994,

[14]S/1994/367, annex. [15]S/1994/367. [16]S/1994/300.

17 of the 19 crossing-points were reopened, tensions persisted on this issue.

UNPROFOR mandate further extended

In reviewing the mandate period, the Secretary-General reported[17] to the Security Council that the conflicts in the former Yugoslavia were closely interrelated. In that context, the work of the Contact Group, which had emerged in April 1994 and involved five major Powers working with the Co-Chairmen of the ICFY Steering Committee, could be of great significance for UNPROFOR's future.

With regard to UNPROFOR's mandate in Croatia, the Secretary-General outlined four problem areas: the demilitarization of the UNPAs; the restoration of Croatian authority in the "pink zones"; the establishment of border controls; and assistance for the return of refugees and displaced persons to their homes. All four required either enforcement or the consent of both parties for their implementation. UNPROFOR had neither the means nor the mandate for enforcement action of this nature, and the cooperation of the parties was elusive.

The successful implementation of the cease-fire agreement had nevertheless opened the possibility for progress, reduced dramatically the number of war casualties and allowed for increasing normalization of life. UNPROFOR, however, continued to be criticized by the Croatian Government and media for its inability to fulfil its entire mandate, and to be threatened with unrealistic deadlines. While recriminations were related to the Croatian domestic political process, they also reflected certain incompatibilities in UNPROFOR's mandate. The resultant gap between Croatian expectations and what UNPROFOR was actually mandated to do and capable of achieving became increasingly difficult to bridge.

The Secretary-General stated that he remained alert to the possibility that the situation on the ground could be frozen in a stalemate in which UNPROFOR's continued presence contributed only to the maintenance of an unsatisfactory status quo. It was of the greatest importance, however, to secure continued respect for the cease-fire agreement and, at the same time, further efforts would have to be made in order to create a basis for the reopening of negotiations. These tasks required the continued presence of UNPROFOR. On 30 September 1994, the Security Council, by resolution 947 (1994), extended UNPROFOR's mandate until 31 March 1995.

Seeking a new mandate in Croatia

The March 1994 cease-fire agreement helped to create a climate conducive for negotiations pursued under ICFY auspices as well as for follow-up measures undertaken by UNPROFOR. Another step towards confidence-building and an eventual resolution of the conflict in Croatia was made on 2 December 1994, when the Croatian sides concluded an agreement on economic issues.[18] The agreement provided for the re-establishment of water and electricity services, the reopening in Croatia of the Zagreb-Belgrade highway and the re-opening of the oil pipeline through the Krajina. In parallel with the economic negotiations, two ICFY negotiators together with the Ambassadors to Croatia of the Russian Federation and the United States — the "Zagreb-Four" — worked on a plan for a political settlement of the conflict between the Croatian Government and the local Serb authorities in the UNPAs.

No progress was made on the deployment of international monitors on Croatia's international borders with Bosnia and Herzegovina and the Federal Republic of Yugoslavia (Serbia and Montenegro). There was a continuing increase in the restrictions on UNPROFOR's freedom of movement imposed by both sides, coupled with a significant decrease in their willingness to cooperate. The number of violations of the cease-fire agreement also increased.

On 12 January 1995, the President of Croatia informed[19] the Secretary-General of his Government's decision not to agree to a further extension of UNPROFOR's mandate beyond 31 March 1995. President Tudjman stated that "Croatia's overall experience during the past two years" had brought him to the conclusion "that, although UNPROFOR has played an important role in stopping violence and major conflicts in Croatia, it is an indisputable fact that the present character of the UNPROFOR mission does not provide conditions necessary for establishing lasting peace and order ...."

The Secretary-General expressed[20] to the Security Council his hope that the Croatian Government would reconsider its position. He would, however, undertake a detailed study of the practi-

[17]S/1994/1067. [18]S/1994/1375, annex. [19]S/1995/28, annex. [20]S/1995/38.

cal consequences and financial implications of a withdrawal of UNPROFOR from Croatia. His principal concern was that the withdrawal would considerably increase the likelihood of a resumption of hostilities. He reiterated his conviction that the fundamental solution to the problem in Croatia could be sought only through political dialogue.

On 17 January, by a presidential statement,[21] the Security Council reiterated its commitment to the sovereignty and territorial integrity of Croatia within its internationally recognized borders. The Council understood the concerns of the Croatian Government about the lack of implementation of major provisions of the United Nations peace-keeping plan for Croatia, and would not accept the status quo becoming an indefinite situation. It believed, however, that UNPROFOR's continued presence in Croatia was of vital importance for regional peace and security, and that the United Nations in general and UNPROFOR in particular had a positive role to play in achieving the further implementation of the peace-keeping plan and bringing about a political settlement. The Council hoped that discussions would lead Croatia to a re-examination of its position.

The following months witnessed a significant escalation in military activity and tension. Violations of the cease-fire agreement increased from 133 on 12 January 1995 to 218 on 7 March 1995. The climate of uncertainty was compounded by the decision of the self-proclaimed Serb Assembly in Knin on 8 March 1995 to declare a state of "immediate war alert". Military preparations intensified on both sides.

Nevertheless, they both continued publicly to maintain their commitment to a peaceful resolution and to cooperate fully in implementing the economic agreement. On 8 February, however, the Serb Assembly decided to postpone further negotiations and implementation — except for continued cooperation regarding the Zagreb-Lipovac highway and the oil pipeline through UNPA Sector North — until UNPROFOR's future presence in the protected areas was assured.

In the meantime, the "Zagreb-Four" ambassadors, comprising the United States and Russian ambassadors to Croatia and Ambassadors Ahrens and Eide from ICFY, presented a "Draft agreement on the Krajina, Slavonia, Southern Baranja and Western Sirmium" to both sides on 30 January 1995. While the Croatian Government accepted the plan as a basis for negotiation, the Serbs in Knin refused to receive it until the future presence of UNPROFOR was assured.

Other international efforts intensified to find a compromise solution which would allow the continuing United Nations peace-keeping presence in Croatia. Those efforts, led by the United States, resulted in a joint announcement[22] on 12 March 1995 by the President of Croatia and the Vice-President of the United States, which opened the way to a solution. The Government of Croatia agreed, working with the United Nations Security Council and its partners in the international community, to negotiate a new mandate for an international presence in Croatia. Pending the successful negotiation of such a mandate, the Government of Croatia agreed that the existing international presence might continue to perform functions related to its mission in Bosnia and Herzegovina. It might also continue to perform functions essential to the continued implementation of the cease-fire agreement of 29 March 1994 and the economic agreement of 2 December 1994.

The Secretary-General instructed Mr. Thorvald Stoltenberg, acting as his Special Envoy, to conduct negotiations with the parties to define the mandate of a future United Nations peace-keeping force, with which both sides would commit themselves to cooperate.

As of mid-March 1995, UNPROFOR in Croatia included 14,825 troops and military support personnel, 256 military observers and 731 civilian police.

C. Bosnia and Herzegovina

Although the mandate of UNPROFOR originally related only to Croatia, it was envisaged that following the demilitarization of the UNPAs, 100 UNPROFOR military observers would be redeployed from Croatia to certain parts of Bosnia and Herzegovina. However, in light of the deteriorating situation in Bosnia and Herzegovina, the Secretary-General decided[23] to accelerate this de-

[21]S/PRST/1995/2. [22]A/50/111, S/1995/206, annex. [23]S/23836.

ployment by sending 40 military observers to the Mostar region on 30 April 1992. In May, despite all diplomatic efforts by the European Community, the Secretary-General's representatives and UNPROFOR to negotiate a lasting cease-fire, the conflict between the Bosnian Muslims and the Bosnian Croats on the one side and the Bosnian Serbs on the other intensified. On 14 May, when risks to their lives reached an unacceptable level, the UNPROFOR observers were withdrawn from the area and redeployed in the UNPAs in Croatia. About two thirds of UNPROFOR headquarters personnel also withdrew from Sarajevo on 16 and 17 May, leaving behind some 100 military personnel and civilian staff who lent their good offices to promote local cease-fires and humanitarian activities.

In a series of resolutions and statements, the Security Council appealed to all parties to bring about a cease-fire and a negotiated political solution, and demanded that all forms of interference from outside Bosnia and Herzegovina, including by JNA, as well as by the Croatian Army, cease immediately and that all local irregular forces be disbanded and disarmed. On 30 May 1992, acting under Chapter VII of the United Nations Charter, the Security Council, in its resolution 757 (1992), imposed wide-ranging sanctions on the Federal Republic of Yugoslavia (Serbia and Montenegro).

Security at Sarajevo airport

In keeping with the Council's request, UNPROFOR pursued negotiations with the parties to the conflict aimed at stopping the fighting around the airport and reopening it for humanitarian purposes. On 5 June 1992, UNPROFOR negotiated an agreement[24] for the handing over to UNPROFOR of the Sarajevo airport. On 8 June, the Security Council, by its resolution 758 (1992), approved the enlargement of UNPROFOR's mandate and strength and authorized the Secretary-General to deploy military observers and related personnel and equipment to Sarajevo to supervise the withdrawal of anti-aircraft weapons and the concentration of heavy weapons at agreed locations in the city.

Following intensive work by UNPROFOR to establish modalities of implementation of the 5 June agreement, and a visit to Sarajevo by President François Mitterrand of France on 28 June, the Secretary-General reported[25] to the Security Council that Bosnian Serb forces had been withdrawing from the Sarajevo airport, and that both sides — the Bosnian Serb and the Bosnian government forces

— had begun to concentrate their heavy weapons in locations to be supervised by UNPROFOR. On the same day, the Council, by resolution 761 (1992), authorized deployment of additional elements of UNPROFOR to ensure the security and functioning of the airport. By 3 July, despite continued fighting in the area, United Nations observers and troops were deployed at the airport and at other locations in Sarajevo, and the airport was reopened for the humanitarian airlift.

UNPROFOR's authorized strength in Bosnia and Herzegovina at this time was a reinforced infantry battalion of some 1,000 personnel, 60 military observers, additional military and civilian staff for the Sarajevo sector headquarters, 40 civilian police to supervise the peaceful functioning of the airport, and a number of technical personnel, engineers and airport staff.

Protection of humanitarian convoys

The situation prevailing in Sarajevo severely complicated UNPROFOR's efforts to ensure the security and functioning of Sarajevo airport and the delivery of humanitarian assistance. On 13 August 1992, the Security Council adopted resolution 770 (1992). Acting under Chapter VII of the United Nations Charter, the Council called on States to "take nationally or through regional agencies or arrangements all measures necessary" to facilitate, in coordination with the United Nations, the delivery of humanitarian assistance to Sarajevo and wherever needed in other parts of Bosnia and Herzegovina.

In further discussions, however, it was decided that that task should be entrusted to UNPROFOR. On 10 September, following consultations with a number of Governments, the Secretary-General recommended[26] to the Security Council the expansion of UNPROFOR's mandate and strength in Bosnia and Herzegovina. He proposed that UNPROFOR's task, under its enlarged mandate, would be to support efforts by the United Nations High Commissioner for Refugees (UNHCR) to deliver humanitarian relief throughout Bosnia and Herzegovina, and in particular to provide protection, at UNHCR's request, where and when UNHCR considered such protection necessary. In addition, UNPROFOR could be used to protect convoys of released civilian detainees if the International Committee of the Red Cross (ICRC) so requested and if the Force Commander agreed

[24]S/24075. [25]S/24201. [26]S/24540.

that the request was practicable. UNPROFOR would be deployed in four or five new zones. In each zone, there would be an infantry battalion group, whose headquarters would also include civilian staff to undertake political and information functions and liaison with UNHCR. UNPROFOR troops would follow normal peace-keeping rules of engagement, which authorized them to use force in self-defence, including situations in which armed persons attempted by force to prevent them from carrying out their mandate.

In resolution 776 (1992), which was adopted on 14 September 1992 and which made no reference to Chapter VII of the Charter, the Security Council approved the Secretary-General's report and authorized the enlargement of UNPROFOR's mandate and strength in Bosnia and Herzegovina for these purposes. A separate Bosnia and Herzegovina Command was established within UNPROFOR to implement resolution 776 (1992), in addition to Sector Sarajevo.

"No-fly zone"

The Security Council, on 9 October 1992, banned[27] all military flights in the airspace of Bosnia and Herzegovina, except for those of UNPROFOR and other flights in support of United Nations operations, including humanitarian assistance. The Council requested UNPROFOR to monitor compliance with the ban and to place observers, where necessary, at airfields in the former Yugoslavia. The Council also requested that UNPROFOR employ "an appropriate mechanism for approval and inspection" to ensure that the purpose of other flights to and from Bosnia and Herzegovina was consistent with its resolutions. It also called on States to provide technical assistance to UNPROFOR in its monitoring efforts. On 10 November, the Security Council adopted its resolution 786 (1992) authorizing the expansion of UNPROFOR's strength by 75 military observers to enable it to monitor airfields in Bosnia and Herzegovina, Croatia and the Federal Republic of Yugoslavia (Serbia and Montenegro).

Border observers

On 16 November 1992, the Security Council decided[28] that observers should be deployed on the borders of Bosnia and Herzegovina. This was done to facilitate the implementation of Council resolution 713 (1991), which established a general and complete embargo on all deliveries of weapons and military equipment to Yugoslavia; resolu-

tion 752 (1992), which demanded that all forms of interference from outside Bosnia and Herzegovina, including by units of JNA as well as elements of the Croatian Army, cease immediately; resolution 757 (1992), which imposed comprehensive mandatory economic sanctions against the Federal Republic of Yugoslavia (Serbia and Montenegro); and resolution 787 (1992), which demanded that all forms of interference from outside Bosnia and Herzegovina, including infiltration into the country of irregular units and personnel, cease immediately.

On 21 December, the Secretary-General recommended[29] to the Council to give UNPROFOR a mandate which would include the right not only to search but also to turn back or confiscate military personnel, weapons, or sanctioned goods whose passage into or out of Bosnia and Herzegovina would be contrary to the decisions of the Council. He pointed out that a symbolic presence at selected crossing points would "not only fail to fulfil the Council's requirements, but would also undermine the already strained credibility of UNPROFOR". He proposed, therefore, an enlargement of UNPROFOR with some 10,000 additional troops to provide for a 24-hour observation and search operation at 123 crossing points on Bosnia and Herzegovina's border with neighbouring countries.

UNPROFOR's first year in Bosnia and Herzegovina

The Secretary-General reported[30] to the Security Council in February 1993 that UNPROFOR's efforts in Bosnia and Herzegovina had been characterized by a regrettable tendency on the part of the host Government to blame UNPROFOR for a variety of shortcomings, whether real or imagined. The criticism had largely been directed at UNPROFOR's failure to fulfil tasks that it had not been mandated, authorized, equipped, staffed or financed to fulfil. There had been a number of attacks on UNPROFOR by the Government and by elements answerable to it, both in public statements and declarations and, more seriously, through violence, resulting in several UNPROFOR fatalities.

The operation to protect humanitarian convoys throughout the Republic was persistently thwarted by obstruction, mines, hostile fire and the refusal of the parties on the ground, particu-

---

[27]S/RES/781 (1992). [28]S/RES/787 (1992). [29]S/25000 and Add.1. [30]S/25264 and Corr.1.

larly, but not exclusively, the Bosnian Serb party, to cooperate with UNPROFOR. None the less, from the deployment of additional UNPROFOR battalions for this purpose in November 1992 until January 1993, a total of some 34,600 tons of relief supplies had been delivered to an estimated 800,000 beneficiaries in 110 locations throughout Bosnia and Herzegovina.

UNPROFOR also succeeded in keeping Sarajevo airport open, despite interruptions as a result of hostile military action against humanitarian aircraft. From 3 July 1992 to 31 January 1993, the humanitarian airlift organized by UNHCR under UNPROFOR protection brought in 2,476 aircraft carrying 27,460 tons of food, medicines and other relief goods.

Although the ban on military flights in the airspace of Bosnia and Herzegovina was violated by all three parties on nearly 400 occasions in its first four months, it achieved its principal purpose of preventing the use of air power in military combat in the Republic. UNPROFOR observers, using AWACS information made available by the North Atlantic Treaty Organization (NATO), found no evidence to suggest that any party had flown combat air missions, or conducted hostilities from the air, since the interdiction regime was established by the Council.

"No-fly zone" enforcement

On 13 March 1993, however, three aircraft dropped bombs on two villages east of Srebrenica before leaving in the direction of the Federal Republic of Yugoslavia (Serbia and Montenegro). UNPROFOR was not able to determine to whom the aircraft belonged. The Security Council, in a statement[31] by its President, strongly condemned all violations of its relevant resolutions and underlined the fact that since the beginning of the monitoring operations in early November 1992, the United Nations had reported 465 violations of the "no-fly zone". The Council demanded from the Bosnian Serbs an immediate explanation of the violations and particularly of the aerial bombardment of the two villages, and requested the Secretary-General to ensure that an investigation was made of the reported possible use of the territory of the Federal Republic of Yugoslavia (Serbia and Montenegro) to launch air strikes against Bosnia and Herzegovina.

The Federal Republic of Yugoslavia (Serbia and Montenegro) responded to a request for information with a note verbale.[32] The note conveyed a statement by the Government affirming that "airplanes and helicopters of the Air Forces of the Army of Yugoslavia have not violated the airspace of Bosnia and Herzegovina since the no-fly zone came into effect".

On 31 March, the Security Council adopted its resolution 816 (1993), by which it extended the ban on military flights to cover flights by all fixed-wing and rotary-wing aircraft in the airspace of Bosnia and Herzegovina. Acting under Chapter VII of the Charter, the Council authorized Member States, seven days after the adoption of the resolution, acting nationally or through regional arrangements, to take, under the authority of the Security Council and subject to close coordination with the Secretary-General and UNPROFOR, "all necessary measures" in the airspace of Bosnia and Herzegovina to ensure compliance with the ban on flights, and proportionate to the specific circumstances and the nature of flights. It also requested the Member States concerned, the Secretary-General and UNPROFOR to coordinate closely on those measures and on the starting date of the implementation, which was to be no later than 14 days from the date of the resolution, and to report on the starting date to the Council.

On 9 April, the Secretary-General transmitted[33] to the Security Council a letter from the Secretary General of NATO, Dr. Manfred Wörner, informing him that the North Atlantic Council had adopted the "necessary arrangements" to ensure compliance with the ban on military flights and that it was prepared to begin the operation at noon GMT on 12 April 1993. Dr. Wörner also reported that France, the Netherlands, Turkey, the United Kingdom and the United States had offered to make aircraft available for the operation. In order to commence the enforcement operation on time, aircraft from France, the Netherlands and the United States were initially deployed in the region and liaison cells were established at UNPROFOR's headquarters in Zagreb and in Bosnia and Herzegovina (Kiseljak). In addition, UNPROFOR would send a liaison team to the command headquarters of the NATO countries concerned.

The operations authorized by resolution 816 (1993) started, as scheduled, on 12 April at 1200 GMT. Subsequently, the Secretary-General was informed by NATO that all the countries offering to make aircraft available for the operation would participate fully in it.

Since the establishment of the "no-fly zone" on 9 October 1992 through 19 December

---

[31]S/25426. [32]S/25450. [33]S/25567.

1995, the total number of flights assessed as apparent violations of the ban was 7,552.[34] The most serious incident took place on 28 February 1994. After UNPROFOR personnel observed four Galeb aircraft taking off from Udbina airstrip in UNPA Sector South in Croatia, AWACS made radar contact southwest of Banja Luka, in Bosnia and Herzegovina. NATO fighter aircraft investigated and issued warnings to which there was no reaction. UNPROFOR personnel then observed two Galebs dropping bombs on an ammunition factory in Novi Travnik; at the same time, UNPROFOR personnel in Bugojno observed four Galebs dropping bombs, hitting an ammunition dump and a hospital. The NATO fighters then shot down four of the six jets.[35] On 21 November 1994, after aircraft of the Krajina Serbs had crossed the border with Bosnia and Herzegovina and attacked targets in the Bihac enclave on 18 and 19 November, NATO fighters launched an air strike on the Udbina airstrip [see below].

"Safe areas"

In March 1993, fighting intensified in eastern Bosnia and Herzegovina, with Bosnian Serb paramilitary units attacking several cities in the area, including Srebrenica. The military attacks resulted in a heavy loss of life among the civilian population and severely impeded United Nations humanitarian relief efforts in the area. In mid-March, UNHCR reported that thousands of Muslims were seeking refuge in Srebrenica from surrounding areas which were being attacked and occupied by Bosnian Serb forces, and that 30 or 40 persons were dying daily from military action, starvation, exposure to cold or lack of medical treatment. In April, despite strong political pressure from the international community and the Security Council, and the efforts by UNPROFOR and UNHCR in the field, the fighting persisted and the humanitarian situation in the area continued to deteriorate.

On 16 April, the Security Council, acting under Chapter VII of the Charter, adopted resolution 819 (1993), in which it demanded that all parties treat Srebrenica and its surroundings as a "safe area" which should be free from any armed attack or any other hostile act. It demanded the immediate withdrawal of Bosnian Serb paramilitary units from areas surrounding Srebrenica and the cessation of armed attacks against that town. The Council requested the Secretary-General to take steps to increase the presence of UNPROFOR in Srebrenica and to arrange for the safe transfer of the ill and wounded, and demanded the unimpeded delivery of humanitarian assistance to all parts of Bosnia and Herzegovina, in particular to the civilian population of Srebrenica.

By other provisions of the resolution, the Council condemned and rejected the deliberate actions of the Bosnian Serb party to force the evacuation of civilians from Srebrenica and other parts of Bosnia and Herzegovina in its campaign of "ethnic cleansing". It also decided to send a mission of Council members to ascertain, first-hand, the situation in Bosnia and Herzegovina.

Following the adoption of the resolution, UNPROFOR's Force Commander, the Commander of the Serb forces and the Commander of the Bosnian Muslim forces signed, on 17 April, an agreement for the demilitarization of Srebrenica.[36] On 21 April, UNPROFOR's Force Commander reported that 170 UNPROFOR troops, civilian police and military observers had been deployed in Srebrenica to collect weapons, ammunition, mines, explosives and combat supplies and that by noon on 21 April they had successfully demilitarized the town.

The Security Council's fact-finding mission, composed of representatives of France, Hungary, New Zealand, Pakistan, the Russian Federation and Venezuela, visited the region from 22 to 27 April. Having considered the mission's report and recommendations,[37] the Security Council adopted resolution 824 (1993) of 6 May, in which it declared that, in addition to Srebrenica, Sarajevo and other such threatened areas, in particular the towns of Tuzla, Zepa, Gorazde, Bihac and their surroundings, should be treated as safe areas by all the parties concerned. The Council further declared that in those areas armed attacks must cease, all Bosnian Serb military or paramilitary units must withdraw and all parties must allow UNPROFOR and the international humanitarian agencies free and unimpeded access to all safe areas. It authorized the strengthening of UNPROFOR's mandate by an additional 50 military observers to monitor the humanitarian situation in those areas.

On 4 June, the Security Council, by its resolution 836 (1993), acting under Chapter VII of the United Nations Charter, further expanded the mandate of UNPROFOR to enable it to deter attacks against the safe areas, to monitor the cease-fire, to promote the withdrawal of military or paramilitary units other than those of the Bosnian Government and to occupy some key points on

[34] S/1995/5/Add.67.   [35] S/1994/5/Add.13.   [36] S/25700, annex II.
[37] S/25700.

the ground. The Council authorized UNPROFOR, acting in self-defence, to take necessary measures, including the use of force, in reply to bombardments against the safe areas or to armed incursion into them or in the event of any deliberate obstruction to the freedom of movement of UNPROFOR or of protected humanitarian convoys. The Council also decided that Member States, acting nationally or through regional arrangements, might take, under its authority, all necessary measures, through the use of air power, in and around the safe areas, to support UNPROFOR.

In response to the Council's invitation to report to it on the requirements for implementing the resolution, the Secretary-General, in his report dated 14 June 1993,[38] indicated that it would be necessary to deploy additional troops on the ground and to provide air support. While the UNPROFOR Force Commander had estimated an additional troop requirement of approximately 34,000 to obtain deterrence through strength, the Secretary-General noted that it was possible to start implementing the resolution under a "light option", with a minimal troop reinforcement of around 7,600. That option represented an initial approach and had limited objectives. It assumed the consent and cooperation of the parties and provided a basic level of deterrence.

As to the air support, the Secretary-General reported that he had initiated contacts with Member States and had invited NATO to coordinate with him the use of air power in support of UNPROFOR. The Secretary-General pointed out that the first decision to initiate the use of air resources in this context would be taken by him in consultation with the members of the Security Council.

In adopting resolution 844 (1993) of 18 June, the Security Council authorized an additional reinforcement of UNPROFOR initially by 7,600 troops and reaffirmed the use of air power, in and around the declared safe areas in Bosnia and Herzegovina, in support of UNPROFOR.

On 18 August, the Secretary-General informed[39] the Security Council that following the necessary training exercises in coordination with NATO, the United Nations had the operational capability for the use of air power in support of UNPROFOR.

Hostilities in central Bosnia

The situation was further aggravated when, in May 1993, intense fighting between the forces of the Bosnian Croats — the Croat Defence Council (HVO) — and the Government of Bosnia

and Herzegovina erupted in southern and central Bosnia and Herzegovina. In the city of Mostar, Muslims were forced across the Neretva river by HVO to the eastern part of the city, which was under Government control, dividing the population along ethnic lines. There were reports of shelling from HVO positions on the west bank, and sniper fire originated from both sides, preventing repair to the water pumping stations. On the east bank, food and medical supplies were at a critical level.[40] Despite numerous efforts, UNHCR was able to bring in relief supplies only at the end of August, the first delivery since 15 June. The forced evictions were accompanied by mass arrests, mostly of draft-age Muslim men in Mostar and the Bosnian Croat areas around Mostar. Detainees were held in extremely harsh conditions.[41]

Despite the calls by the Security Council, efforts of the Co-Chairmen of the Steering Committee and UNPROFOR, hostilities between the two former allies continued. The fighting intermittently blocked the main supply routes for humanitarian assistance into northern Bosnia, and severely restricted the freedom of movement of UNPROFOR and UNHCR in the area. In this connection, UNPROFOR and UNHCR initiated a humanitarian "Operation Lifeline" to keep the main routes open to help ensure the survival of up to 2.7 million people in Bosnia and Herzegovina during the winter.

Options for border control

On 10 June 1993, the Security Council, by its resolution 838 (1993), requested the Secretary-General to submit a further report on options for the deployment of international observers on the borders of Bosnia and Herzegovina, with priority being given to its borders with the Federal Republic of Yugoslavia (Serbia and Montenegro), to monitor the implementation of the relevant Security Council resolutions. The observers would be drawn from the United Nations and, if appropriate, from Member States.

In his report,[42] the Secretary-General said that full border control would require a capability to deny passage and to act where borders had already been crossed. It would also mean that UNPROFOR would supersede the national authorities in respect of certain border-control functions. Border monitoring, another option, would involve observation and reporting by ob-

---

[38]S/25939 and Add.1. [39]S/26335. [40]S/26415. [41]REF/1034.
[42]S/26018 and Add.1 and Corr.1.

servers, who would not be in a position to check the nature of goods coming into and out of the republic. Both options would require substantial additional resources, and the necessary personnel and financing might not be available.

The Security Council, however, continued to believe that international observers should be deployed. They invited the Secretary-General, bearing in mind his observations, to contact Member States to establish whether they were ready, individually or through regional organizations or arrangements, to make qualified personnel available; and to continue to explore all possibilities for implementation of the border monitors concept.[43]

Deteriorating conditions

Although numerous cease-fire agreements were signed by the warring parties in Bosnia and Herzegovina, practically none of them were respected and the military situation remained grave. Notwithstanding the Joint Declarations on the delivery of humanitarian assistance, signed by the three sides at Geneva on 18 and 29 November 1993, the level of violence, the imposition of bureaucratic procedures hindering the transport of relief goods or the denial of clearance for the passage of UNHCR convoys reduced deliveries of humanitarian assistance to half the amount required. Furthermore, elements of all three sides deliberately fired upon relief convoys and United Nations personnel.

On 9 November 1993, the Security Council expressed[44] deep concern at the deterioration of the situation in central Bosnia and Herzegovina where increased military activities posed a serious threat to the security of the civilian population. The Council also condemned[45] all attacks and hostile acts against UNPROFOR by all parties in Bosnia and Herzegovina, as well as in Croatia, "which have become more frequent over the last weeks", and demanded that "they cease forthwith". On 7 January 1994, a Security Council statement[46] condemned any hostilities in United Nations-designated "safe areas", particularly the relentless bombardment of Sarajevo by Bosnian Serb forces, and demanded an immediate end to attacks against Sarajevo, which had resulted in a large number of civilian casualties, disrupted essential services, and aggravated an already severe humanitarian situation.

On 28 January 1994, in a letter[47] to the President of the Security Council, the Prime Minister of Bosnia and Herzegovina reported that military formations of the regular armed forces of Croatia, supplemented by heavy artillery, armoured vehicles and other war materials, were involved in military actions on his country's territory. The Secretary-General subsequently reported[48] that the Croatian Army (HV) had been directly supporting HVO — the Croat Defence Council — with manpower, equipment and weapons for some time. The number of Croatian soldiers had apparently increased following successful offensives of Bosnian Government forces against HVO. It was assessed that in total there were approximately 3,000 to 5,000 Croatian regular army personnel in Bosnia and Herzegovina. This was, however, an estimate, as it was impossible with UNPROFOR's assets to obtain required information for a more accurate account.

The Council issued a Presidential statement[49] on 3 February strongly condemning Croatia for deploying elements of its army and heavy military equipment in the central and southern parts of Bosnia and Herzegovina, and demanded that they be withdrawn. The Council stated that it would consider "other serious measures", if Croatia failed to put an immediate end to "all forms of interference".

The Secretary-General informed[50] the Council on 17 February 1994 that despite its demand for non-interference in Bosnia and Herzegovina, some 5,000 Croatian Army troops were still believed to remain in that country. Also, no action had been taken regarding the proposed establishment of a monitoring mechanism to verify troop withdrawals. The Secretary-General also stated that, while no HV command posts nor any full HV brigades operating as formed units had been identified, it appeared that HV troops might be removing their insignia while in Bosnia and Herzegovina. UNPROFOR believed that HV insignia on a number of vehicles had also been erased or repainted.

Question of air strikes

The Heads of State and Government participating in the NATO summit meeting on 10 and 11 January 1994 issued a Declaration[51] expressing their continued belief that the conflict in Bosnia and Herzegovina must be settled at the negotiating table. They were determined to "eliminate obstacles to the accomplishment of the UNPROFOR mandate" and reaffirmed their readiness under the

---

[43]S/26049. [44]S/26716. [45]S/26717. [46]S/PRST/1994/1. [47]S/1994/95, annex. [48]S/1994/109. [49]S/PRST/1994/6. [50]S/1994/190. [51]S/1994/50.

authority of the Security Council "to carry out air strikes in order to prevent the strangulation of Sarajevo, the safe areas and other threatened areas in Bosnia and Herzegovina".

Since early December 1993, UNPROFOR had faced Bosnian Serb opposition to the replacement of Canadian troops in Srebrenica and of Ukrainian troops in Zepa by elements of the incoming Netherlands battalion. In Tuzla, as a result of the HVO blockades in southern and central Bosnia and Herzegovina, UNPROFOR had been engaged in efforts to open the airport for the delivery of humanitarian assistance to the Tuzla safe area. The NATO Declaration urged UNPROFOR to draw up urgently plans to ensure that the blocked rotation could take place and to examine how the Tuzla airport could be opened.

On 12 January, the Secretary-General instructed his Special Representative to undertake an urgent preparatory study of the proposal. He subsequently indicated to the Security Council that in both cases the use of air power to attain proposed objectives would require military assets in excess of what was available to UNPROFOR in Bosnia and Herzegovina. Furthermore, UNPROFOR had previously been allowed to use air support only in defence of United Nations personnel. The new proposal implied that UNPROFOR could launch offensive action against Bosnian Serb elements which obstructed or threatened to obstruct its operations.

The Secretary-General stated that he would not hesitate to initiate the use of close air support if UNPROFOR were attacked while implementing plans to rotate peace-keepers in Srebrenica and Zepa and to open Tuzla airport. He hoped that the troops could be rotated and the airport opened by mutual agreement. However, he noted that UNPROFOR's mandate regarding safe areas in Bosnia and Herzegovina had been adopted under Chapter VII of the United Nations Charter, and UNPROFOR did not have to seek the consent of the parties for operations falling within its mandate.

At the same time, he distinguished between close air support involving the use of air power for self-defence, which had already been authorized by NATO, and air strikes for pre-emptive or punitive purposes. NATO forces were not authorized to launch the latter types of air strikes without a decision of the North Atlantic Council (NAC). Nevertheless, the Secretary-General instructed his Special Representative to "pursue actively", in direct contact with the Government of Bosnia and Herzegovina and the leadership of the Bosnian Serbs, the implementation of the two plans. In the specific circumstances of UNPROFOR operations in Srebrenica and Tuzla, the Secretary-General delegated to his Special Representative the authority to approve a request for close air support from the Force Commander.

On 1 March 1994, the Bosnian Serbs, following talks with high-ranking officials of the Russian Federation in Moscow, agreed in principle to open the Tuzla airport for humanitarian purposes. Deployment of UNPROFOR troops around the airport began in early March in preparation for an airlift that was expected to bring relief supplies to hundreds of thousands of people in the area. Although some UNPROFOR flights subsequently landed in Tuzla, no agreement could be reached with the parties ensuring security for humanitarian flights and thus enabling the operation of the airport on a permanent basis.

The rotation of troops in Srebrenica, after protracted negotiations with the Bosnian Serb side, was completed on 10 March 1994, with the Dutch troops replacing the Canadian contingent.

Meanwhile, fighting in and around Sarajevo continued unabated, including lethal mortar attacks against civilian targets. On 5 February 1994, a 120-mm mortar round fired at the central market killed at least 58 civilians and wounded 142 others in the worst single incident of 22 months of war. This followed a similar attack on one of the suburbs of Sarajevo on 4 February 1994 in which 10 civilians were killed and 18 injured. These acts were strongly condemned by the international community. The Secretary-General immediately instructed his Special Representative and the Force Commander of UNPROFOR to proceed to Sarajevo in order to supervise the investigation of the incidents and to prevent further atrocities.

After an initial investigation, UNPROFOR established that the round fired on 4 February had come from a Bosnian Serb position, but it had not been possible to locate the source of the attack against the central market on 5 February. A team was then established by UNPROFOR to conduct a comprehensive follow-up investigation. That team also reported[52] the lack of physical evidence to determine which side — the forces of the Bosnian Government or the Bosnian Serbs — had fired the mortar bomb on 5 February 1993.

In a letter[53] dated 6 February to the President of the Security Council, the Secretary-General stated that those two incidents made it necessary,

[52]S/1994/182. [53]S/1994/131.

in accordance with resolution 836 (1993),[54] to prepare urgently for the use of air strikes to deter further such attacks. The Secretary-General also informed the Council that he had requested the Secretary General of NATO to obtain "a decision by the North Atlantic Council to authorize the Commander-in-Chief of NATO's Southern Command to launch air strikes, at the request of the United Nations, against artillery or mortar positions in and around Sarajevo which are determined by UNPROFOR to be responsible for attacks against civilian targets in that city".

On 9 February, moving to end the strangulation of Sarajevo, NAC issued a statement calling "for the withdrawal, or regrouping and placing under UNPROFOR control, within ten days, of heavy weapons (including tanks, artillery pieces, mortars, multiple rocket launchers, missiles and anti-aircraft weapons) of the Bosnian Serb forces located in the area within 20 kilometres (about 12.4 miles) of the centre of Sarajevo, and excluding the area within 2 kilometres (about 1.2 miles) of the centre of Pale", a city located east of Sarajevo which served as headquarters of the Bosnian Serbs. NAC also called upon the Muslim-led Government of Bosnia and Herzegovina, within the same period, "to place the heavy weapons in its possession within the Sarajevo exclusion zone described above under UNPROFOR control, and to refrain from attacks launched from within the current confrontation lines in the city".

NAC decided that, ten days from 2400 GMT 10 February 1994, heavy weapons of any of the parties found within the Sarajevo exclusion zone, unless controlled by UNPROFOR, would, along with their direct and essential military support facilities, be subject to NATO air strikes. The strikes would be conducted in close coordination with the United Nations Secretary-General. NAC accepted the 6 February 1994 request of the United Nations Secretary-General and authorized the Commander-in-Chief, Allied Forces Southern Europe, to launch air strikes, at the request of the United Nations, against artillery or mortar positions in or around Sarajevo, including any outside the exclusion zone, which were determined by UNPROFOR to be responsible for attacks against civilian targets in that city.

In a parallel development, a few hours prior to the announcement of the NATO decision of 9 February, a cease-fire agreement was reached between the warring parties in Bosnia and Herzegovina regarding the area in and around Sarajevo. The agreement followed intensive discussions at the political and military levels brokered by UNPROFOR. The agreement involved the positioning of UNPROFOR troops in sensitive areas, monitoring, and the placing of all heavy weapons under UNPROFOR's control.

Immediately following the decision by NATO, the United Nations Secretary-General instructed his Special Representative for the former Yugoslavia to finalize, with the Commander-in-Chief, Allied Forces Southern Europe, detailed procedures for the initiation and conduct of air strikes. He delegated to the Special Representative the authority to approve a request from the UNPROFOR Force Commander for close air support for the defence of United Nations personnel anywhere in Bosnia and Herzegovina.

The Secretary-General also instructed him and UNPROFOR military authorities to negotiate arrangements under which: (a) there would be an effective cease-fire in and around Sarajevo; (b) the heavy weapons of the Bosnian Serb forces would be withdrawn or regrouped and placed under UNPROFOR control; and (c) the heavy weapons of the Government of Bosnia and Herzegovina would be placed under UNPROFOR control.

On 10 February 1994, the Ministry of Foreign Affairs of the Russian Federation stated[55] that NATO's call for the parties — both the Bosnian Serbs and the Bosnian Government — to place the heavy weapons deployed in the Sarajevo area under United Nations control or to withdraw them from the area was close to the Russian position. At the same time, however, the Russian Federation could not agree with the position of a number of NATO members which interpreted the NATO decision as "a one-sided ultimatum to the Bosnian Serbs, who are being threatened by air strikes". It requested an urgent meeting of the United Nations Security Council, open to all countries concerned, to consider practical ways to demilitarize Sarajevo and to introduce a United Nations administration there.

Over the course of four meetings on 14 and 15 February 1994, the Council heard 58 speakers. Many Member States welcomed the decision by NATO and the steps taken by the Secretary-General to prepare for the use of force, adding that

[54]In paragraph 9 of resolution 836 (1993), the Security Council authorized UNPROFOR, "... acting in self-defence, to take the necessary measures, including the use of force, in reply to bombardments against the safe areas by any of the parties ...". In paragraph 10 of the same resolution, the Council decided that "... Member States, acting nationally or through regional organizations or arrangements, may take, under the authority of the Security Council and subject to close coordination with the Secretary-General and UNPROFOR, all necessary measures, through the use of air power, in and around the safe areas in the Republic of Bosnia and Herzegovina, to support UNPROFOR in the performance of its mandate ...". [55]S/1994/152, annex.

those actions had been fully authorized by existing Council resolutions. They emphasized that force was designed to underpin efforts by the United Nations and the European Union to achieve a negotiated settlement, and that air strikes had to be carried out with caution and precision. Although the NATO ultimatum received wide support, a number of Member States opposed it or expressed concern that, as a result of air strikes, UNPROFOR might become a target for retaliatory measures. No Security Council resolution or statement was put forward during the meetings.

On 17 February 1994, following a meeting with Russian officials in Bosnia and Herzegovina, the Bosnian Serbs agreed to withdraw within two days all their heavy weapons from the exclusion zone set by NATO. On 18 February, after discussions in Sarajevo with Bosnian Serb leader Dr. Radovan Karadzic and Bosnian President Alija Izetbegovic, and later in Zagreb with the Commander-in-Chief of NATO Southern Command, the Secretary-General's Special Representative reported that progress was being made towards achieving a durable cease-fire, disarmament and disengagement, with a clear-cut role for UNPROFOR.

It was agreed that UNPROFOR should patrol unhindered within the weapons exclusion zone covering the 20-kilometre radius from the centre of Sarajevo. Heavy weapons not withdrawn from the exclusion zone would be grouped and placed in seven different sites, under the control of armed UNPROFOR elements. An agreement was also reached with regard to communications, with the full assurance that hot-lines would be established between UNPROFOR and the Bosnian Serb and Bosnian government sides.

On 20 February 1994, the Security Council met in informal consultations at the request of the Russian Federation, with the NATO deadline scheduled for midnight that night. The Council was briefed by the Under-Secretary-General for Peace-keeping Operations, Mr. Kofi Annan, who reported that, according to the Secretary-General's Special Representative for the former Yugoslavia, the UNPROFOR Force Commander and NATO, Bosnian Serb compliance with the ultimatum had been effective. Certain weapons on both the Bosnian Serb and Bosnian government sides, which had not been removed from the exclusion zone, would be monitored in place by UNPROFOR. As a result, the Council decided, in coordination with NATO, not to recommend that air strikes be carried out at that time.

The Under-Secretary-General also urged Member States to contribute additional troops

with equipment to facilitate the monitoring of the weapons withdrawal and the cease-fire in and around Sarajevo. United Nations troops had been temporarily redeployed for that purpose from other parts of Bosnia and Herzegovina and from Croatia, but they were still needed in those areas.

Agreement on cease-fire

In another positive development, military representatives of the Bosnian Government and the Bosnian Croat sides signed, on 23 February 1994, a cease-fire agreement.[56] Under this agreement, reached at a meeting hosted by the Force Commander of UNPROFOR at Camp Pleso in Zagreb, Croatia, the two parties agreed to the immediate and total cessation of hostilities with effect from noon on Friday, 25 February 1994, a halt to all forms of propaganda against one another, and a fixing of lines of contact and positions as of the time of the cease-fire. UNPROFOR forces were to be positioned at key points; heavy weapons were to be withdrawn or put under UNPROFOR control; and a Joint Commission was to be established, with representatives of both sides and chaired by UNPROFOR.

Also in late February 1994, talks began in Washington D.C. between the Bosnian Government and the leaders of the Bosnian Croats, as well as the Foreign Minister of Croatia, culminating on 1 March in a framework federation agreement for areas within Bosnia and Herzegovina and the outline of an confederation agreement. After further talks, the Government of Bosnia and Herzegovina, the Government of Croatia and the Bosnian Croat side signed, on 10 May, the Washington accords for the creation of the Bosniac–Croat Federation [see chapter 23].

These measures brought a large degree of stability to central Bosnia and western Herzegovina.

Increased strength is authorized

On 4 March 1994, the Security Council adopted resolution 900 (1994) by which it called on all parties in Bosnia and Herzegovina to cooperate with UNPROFOR in the consolidation of the cease-fire in and around Sarajevo; to achieve complete freedom of movement for the civilian population and humanitarian goods to, from and within Sarajevo; and to help restore normal life to the city. It requested the Secretary-General to ap-

---

[56] S/1994/291, annex.

point a senior civilian official to draw up an overall assessment and plan of action for the restoration of essential public services in the various *opstinas* of Sarajevo, other than the city of Pale; and invited him to establish a voluntary trust fund for that purpose. It also requested him to present a report on the feasibility and modalities for the application of protection, defined in resolutions 824 (1993) and 836 (1993), to Maglaj, Mostar and Vitez.

The Secretary-General informed the Council on 11 March that the implementation of resolution 900 (1994) would require an increase of the authorized strength of UNPROFOR by a total of 8,250 additional troops, 150 military observers and 275 civilian police monitors. Of these additional troops, 2,200 would be required for the operation in and around Sarajevo and 6,050 for operations in central Bosnia, including Mostar and Vitez. A further 1,500 troops would be needed if the Council were to extend the safe area concept to Maglaj.[57]

A voluntary trust fund for the restoration of essential public services in and around Sarajevo was established on 21 March 1994. On 30 March, the Secretary-General appointed Mr. William L. Eagleton (United States) as the Special Coordinator for Sarajevo.

On 31 March 1994, the Security Council, by its resolution 908 (1994), extended the mandate of UNPROFOR for an additional six-month period terminating on 30 September 1994 and decided, as an initial step, to increase UNPROFOR's strength by an additional 3,500 troops. It decided to take action by 30 April 1994 at the latest on further troop requirements recommended by the Secretary-General in his reports of 11 March and of 16 March 1994 and his letter of 30 March 1994.

By the same resolution, the Council demanded that the Bosnian Serb party cease all military operations against the town of Maglaj and requested the Secretary-General to keep the situation there under review. It also authorized UNPROFOR to carry out tasks relating to the cease-fire entered into by the Government of Bosnia and Herzegovina and the Bosnian Croat party.

On 27 April 1994, the Security Council, by its resolution 914 (1994), authorized, as recommended by the Secretary-General, an increase in the strength of UNPROFOR of up to 6,550 additional troops, 150 military observers and 275 civilian police monitors, in addition to the reinforcement already approved in resolution 908 (1994).

Situation in Gorazde

At the end of March 1994, the Bosnian Serb forces launched an infantry and artillery offensive against the safe area of Gorazde. The indiscriminate shelling of the city and of the outlying villages led to considerable casualties among the civilian population.

Despite the Council's demand[58] that attacks cease, and UNPROFOR's efforts to arrange for a cease-fire, attacks against Gorazde continued unabated. After United Nations military observers in the city were endangered by Bosnian Serb shelling, UNPROFOR Command requested NATO to use close air support for self-defence of United Nations personnel. Consequently, on 10 and 11 April 1994, aircraft belonging to NATO bombed Bosnian Serb positions. The Bosnian Serbs then imposed major obstructions to the freedom of movement of UNPROFOR personnel stationed in territory under their control. On 14 April, 15 Canadian UNPROFOR troops were detained for several days at an observation post in Ilijas, and by 19 April some 130 United Nations personnel — 50 military observers and 80 other UNPROFOR personnel — were being detained.

On 18 April, the situation had become extremely dire. The Secretary-General asked NATO to authorize the use of air strikes against artillery, mortar positions or tanks attacking civilians in Gorazde, as well as in four other safe areas, namely the towns of Tuzla, Zepa, Bihac and Srebrenica. In a letter[59] to the NATO Secretary General, he noted that permission for such air strikes had already been given regarding Sarajevo. The tragic events in Gorazde demonstrated the need for NAC to take similar decisions on the other safe areas in Bosnia and Herzegovina.

On 22 April 1994, NAC authorized[60] the use of air strikes against Bosnian Serb military targets around Gorazde if the Bosnian Serbs did not end their attacks immediately, pull their forces back three kilometres from the city centre by 0001 GMT on 24 April 1994, and allow United Nations forces and humanitarian relief convoys freedom of movement there. NAC agreed that a "military exclusion zone" (within the territory of Bosnia and Herzegovina) be established for 20 kilometres around Gorazde, which called for all Bosnian Serb heavy weapons (including tanks, artillery pieces, mortars, multiple rocket launchers, missiles and anti-aircraft weapons) to be withdrawn by 0001

---

[57]S/1994/291 and Add.1. [58]S/PRST/1994/14. [59]S/1994/466, annex. [60]S/1994/495, annex.

GMT on 27 April 1994. NAC also agreed[61] on similar arrangements for four other safe areas if they were attacked by heavy weapons from any range or if there was a concentration or movement of heavy weapons within a radius of 20 kilometres of these areas.

On the same day, the Security Council, by its resolution 913 (1994), condemned the shelling and attacks by Bosnian Serb forces against the safe area of Gorazde and demanded the withdrawal of those forces and their weapons to a distance from which they would cease to threaten the safe area. The Council also demanded an end to any provocative action, the immediate release of all United Nations personnel held by Bosnian Serb forces and unimpeded freedom of movement for UNPROFOR. Underlying the urgent need to intensify efforts towards an overall political settlement, the Council called for the intensification of close consultation between the United States and the Russian Federation and the United Nations and the European Union with the aim of bringing together diplomatic initiatives.

By other terms of the resolution, the Council invited the Secretary-General to take necessary steps to ensure that UNPROFOR was able to monitor the situation in Gorazde and to ensure respect for any cease-fire and disengagement of military forces, including measures to put heavy weapons under United Nations control.

On 23 April, an agreement was reached between UNPROFOR and the Bosnian Serb civilian and military authorities. It called for an immediate and total cease-fire in and around Gorazde from 1000 hours GMT on 23 April and the urgent deployment of an UNPROFOR battalion in an area within a three-kilometre radius from the centre of the city. It was also agreed that heavy weapons would be withdrawn, not later than 2200 hours GMT on 26 April, out of an area within a 20-kilometre radius from the centre of Gorazde.

Although the Bosnian Serbs had not yet fully complied when the 24 April deadline expired, the Force Commander of UNPROFOR decided against the immediate use of air strikes. UNPROFOR felt that significant progress was being made and that the Serbs would soon comply with the ultimatum. It addition, it was important to get United Nations troops and medical units into Gorazde as quickly as possible, and the air strikes might have jeopardized that operation.

The first UNPROFOR convoy arrived in Gorazde during the night of 23-24 April, including some 100 infantry, 40 medical and about 26 civil affairs and civilian police personnel. These person-nel were subsequently reinforced to bring their number to some 432. UNPROFOR interpositioned itself between the opposing forces and deployed its soldiers, civilian and police staff within the urban area on both banks of the Drina river. The situation was further eased by the evacuation of urgent medical cases, the arrival of UNHCR humanitarian assistance convoys and by other measures aimed at restoring security and confidence among the civilian population, including the Serb minority.

On 26 April 1994, the United Nations Secretary-General announced that Bosnian Serb forces had complied with the demand that they cease their attacks on Gorazde and pulled their forces and heavy weapons out of the 20-kilometre exclusion zone around the city. He subsequently reported[62] to the Security Council that the cease-fire within the 3-km total exclusion zone, as well as the 20-km heavy weapon exclusion zone, had been largely respected. An anti-sniping agreement was concluded in Gorazde on 28 August 1994.

Refining safe-area concept

Pursuant to Security Council resolutions 836 (1993) and 844 (1993) and further to his previous reports[63] dealing with the safe areas, the Secretary-General, on 9 May 1994, informed[64] the Council of results achieved and lessons learned, and proposed some improvements with a view to ensuring more effective implementation of the concept of safe areas.

The safe areas were a temporary mechanism by which some vulnerable populations could have been protected pending a comprehensive negotiated political settlement. A particularly serious problem in that regard was the failure of the warring parties to understand or fully respect the safe-area concept. This was starkly evident in Gorazde. The Bosnian Government expected UNPROFOR to intervene to protect as much of the territory under its control as possible, and called for the early employment of large-scale air strikes in order to break the offensive capability of Serb forces. Government forces armed themselves and conducted military activities from within the safe area. The Bosnian Serbs, on the other hand, regarded UNPROFOR's very limited use of close air support as an intervention on behalf of their opponents, and did not hesitate to attack a populated area. UNPROFOR's neutrality and credibility were

[61]S/1994/498, annex. [62]S/1994/600. [63]S/1994/291, S/1994/300.
[64]S/1994/555.

strongly challenged by the different attitudes and expectations of each party, and their respective demands and complaints heightened tension with the United Nations and for a time seriously impaired working relationships.

The Secretary-General identified three overriding principles for the successful implementation of the safe area concept. First, the intention of safe areas was primarily to enhance the security of the population and not to defend territory. UNPROFOR's protection of these areas was not intended to make it a party to the conflict. Second, methods of carrying out the safe-area task should enhance UNPROFOR's original mandates in Bosnia and Herzegovina, namely the support of humanitarian assistance operations and contribution to the overall peace process through the implementation of cease-fires and local disengagements. Third, any mandate had to take into account UNPROFOR's resource limitations and the conflicting priorities that inevitably arose from unfolding events.

In the Secretary-General's view, as related to the Security Council on 9 May 1994, UNPROFOR's safe area mission should be clearly defined and the safe areas should be delineated, as proposed by UNPROFOR, and respected. Complete freedom of movement, on a "notification" (as opposed to "clearance") basis, should be ensured for the provision of humanitarian aid to the safe areas, as a prelude to further normalization, including the resumption of commercial traffic.

Other developments

In a further attempt to stabilize the situation in Bosnia and Herzegovina, a meeting was held with the delegations of the Government and of the Bosnian Serb side in Geneva from 6 to 8 June. On 8 June, after three rounds of discussions held with both sides, the parties signed an agreement according to which they would not engage in any offensive military operations or provocative actions for one month. The agreement came into effect from 1200 hours GMT on 10 June 1994. The agreement also provided for the immediate release, under the auspices of ICRC, of prisoners-of-war and detainees and the exchange of information on persons whose whereabouts were unknown.

While that agreement was still in effect, Bosnian government forces attempted to capture dominating terrain or to secure routes in the areas of Ozren and Travnik. At the same time, Bosnian Serb elements continued to expel Muslim civilians

from the Banja Luka and Bijeljina areas and imposed new restrictions on the movement of UNHCR convoys. The agreement, which was renewed for an additional month in July, lapsed on 8 August 1994.

Elsewhere in Bosnia and Herzegovina, UNPROFOR was instrumental in achieving a breakthrough in an agreement on freedom of movement in the Mostar area, which was implemented on 23 May, and resulted in a rapid improvement in the quality of life for the Muslim residents on the eastern bank of the Neretva River. UNPROFOR also played an important role in monitoring the demilitarization of Mostar, a precondition for the establishment of the European Union administration in that city on 23 July 1994. In central Bosnia, UNPROFOR undertook negotiations on freedom of movement both for the population and for commercial traffic, resulting in the movement of some commercial convoys from the coast to southern, central and northern Bosnia, under the security provided by UNPROFOR's presence.

UNPROFOR also mediated between the parties when tensions mounted in and around the strategically important Posavina corridor in late April, with frequent artillery, mortar and rocket exchanges affecting the Brcko, Tuzla and Orasje areas. UNPROFOR eventually deployed United Nations military observers in the Brcko area in an attempt to reduce tension and decrease the likelihood of an offensive by either side.

In western Bosnia, Government forces launched an offensive and defeated the forces of the self-proclaimed "Autonomous Province of Western Bosnia" in the Bihac area, resulting in an exodus of an estimated 35,000 mostly Muslim refugees to the UNPA Sector North in Croatia. The "Autonomous Province" had its stronghold at Velika Kladusa and was headed by the breakaway Muslim leader Mr. Fikret Abdic. Meanwhile Government forces resumed operations in the Ozren and Travnik areas and advanced south from the areas of Breza and Dastansko. These activities were met by heavy Bosnian Serb shelling and local counter-attacks at many points along the confrontation line. UNPROFOR made several unavailing attempts to persuade both sides to seek a negotiated rather than a military solution.

To assist the Security Council in its deliberations as the March–September 1994 mandate period drew to a close, the Secretary-General provided the Council on 17 September with an account[65] of developments affecting UNPROFOR's

[65]S/1994/1067.

operations. He did not recommend a withdrawal. Nevertheless, the significant constraints on UNPROFOR's ability to perform its responsibilities in the safe areas remained largely unchanged. Furthermore, the exclusion zones around Sarajevo and Gorazde, although highly successful in protecting the civilian population from mortar, artillery and tank fire, were expensive in manpower and difficult to enforce and could not be maintained indefinitely. UNPROFOR personnel, widely dispersed at weapons collection points, were vulnerable to any determined effort to remove weapons or take hostages. In addition, the supervision and enforcement of weapons exclusion zones placed additional strains on UNPROFOR as an impartial force.

The Secretary-General noted that UNPROFOR continued to experience serious restrictions on its freedom of movement imposed by all sides, and especially by the Bosnian Serbs. Particularly serious were actions by the Bosnian Government and the Bosnian Serb sides that had led to the repeated closure of the Sarajevo airport. In the absence of improved relations between the Government and the Bosnian Serb party, these difficulties would continue and might intensify.

While he was aware that some Member States might have come to view as inadequate the strategy of deploying a peace-keeping force dependent upon the active cooperation of the parties, the Secretary-General noted that the use of "disincentives", such as the general imposition and stricter enforcement of exclusion zones, or, as called for by some Member States, the lifting of the arms embargo in favour of the Government of Bosnia and Herzegovina, would change the nature of the United Nations presence in the area and imply unacceptable risks to UNPROFOR. The former action would place UNPROFOR unambiguously on one side of an ongoing conflict, and the latter step would be tantamount to fanning the flames. In both cases the result would be a fundamental shift from the logic of peace-keeping to the logic of war and would require the withdrawal of UNPROFOR from Bosnia and Herzegovina.

The Secretary-General instructed UNPROFOR to finalize plans for a withdrawal at short notice. Should this withdrawal become necessary, it would have to take place under extremely difficult conditions and require at minimum a 60-day period of preparation. In a number of foreseeable circumstances, protecting the withdrawing troops could be achieved only by the temporary introduction of a significant number of highly combat-capable ground forces provided by Member States outside the United Nations framework. Any decision that would necessitate the withdrawal of UNPROFOR would also have immediate implications for its ability to implement its existing mandates.

On the other hand, in the absence of an overall political settlement, UNPROFOR's presence and activities in Bosnia and Herzegovina remained invaluable and represented, in a society faced with the challenges of reconciliation and restoration, the principles and objectives of the Charter of the United Nations. Its usefulness in supporting humanitarian activities, facilitating local cease-fires and disengagements and fostering reconciliation and cooperation between communities argued in favour of a further renewal of its mandate.

Speaking of humanitarian activities, the Secretary-General noted that although increasingly secure movement of humanitarian relief convoys was possible throughout the contiguous territory controlled by the Bosniac-Croat Federation, security problems remained in relation to land access to Sarajevo and other safe areas. UNPROFOR's assistance was essential. If land access to the safe areas was denied by the Bosnian and Krajina Serbs, some aid could continue to be delivered by air drops. However, this would not be adequate for Sarajevo, where the airlift could effectively be halted by a single shell or even a single armed individual.

As for human rights, the Secretary-General stated that the continued harassment of minorities, particularly by the Bosnian Serbs, had underlined the need for a more comprehensive mandate for the United Nations civilian police (UNCIVPOL). At that time, civilian police had a limited mandate to operate in Srebrenica, Tuzla and Mostar, an unofficial agreement to operate in Sarajevo and Gorazde, and no formal mandate to operate in other areas, including Velika Kladusa. The Secretary-General recommended that the Security Council consider providing UNPROFOR with a uniform UNCIVPOL mandate for the whole mission area, similar to that already mandated for Croatia in resolution 743 (1992) of 21 February 1992.

On 30 September 1994, the Security Council, by its resolution 947 (1994), extended UNPROFOR's mandate for an additional period terminating on 31 March 1995, and approved proposals made by the Secretary-General relating to civilian police, mine-clearance and public information.

Security situation deteriorates

In August and September 1994, the security situation in Bosnia and Herzegovina deteriorated. Despite the August anti-sniping agreement in Sarajevo, attacks by snipers escalated in frequency and deadly effect. The extent of heavy weapons attacks also increased. Attacks on many occasions were directed at residences, pedestrians and moving vehicles, such as trams packed with people. United Nations personnel were also targeted and suffered fatalities. Twice, in August and September, UNPROFOR called in NATO warplanes to hit Bosnian Serb heavy weapons violating the exclusion zone around Sarajevo.

A key humanitarian route in Sarajevo was closed by Bosnian Serb forces, thus greatly impeding the delivery of aid not only to the city, but also to many points in northern and eastern Bosnia. Attacks both by Bosnian Serbs and by Government forces on Sarajevo airport resulted in its frequent closure. Attacks and interference with humanitarian aid were reported in Gorazde, Maglaj, Travnik, Bugojno, Srebrenica and Tuzla. In a number of other locations, the situation also remained tense.

In resolution 941 (1994) adopted on 23 September, the Security Council demanded that Bosnian Serb authorities immediately cease their campaign of "ethnic cleansing" in the Republic of Bosnia and Herzegovina and authorize immediate and unimpeded access for representatives of the United Nations and of ICRC to Banja Luka, Bijeljina and other areas of concern. The Council also requested the Secretary-General to arrange the deployment of UNPROFOR troops and United Nations monitors to those areas. It strongly condemned violations of international humanitarian law, particularly "ethnic cleansing", and reaffirmed that those committing or ordering such acts would be held individually responsible; and that parties to the conflict were bound to comply with international humanitarian law, in particular the Geneva Conventions of 12 August 1949.

Fighting in Bihac pocket

In October 1994, after defeating the Abdic forces in western Bosnia during the summer, the Bosnian Government army, acting in cooperation with Bosnian Croat units, mounted a large and, initially, successful offensive operation against Bosnian Serb forces in and around the Bihac pocket.

In early November, however, after regrouping, Bosnian Serb forces launched a major counteroffensive. They were supported by the Krajina Serb forces acting from across the border with Croatia and forces loyal to Mr. Abdic. By mid-November, the Bosnian Serbs regained most of the territory lost during the earlier Bosnian Government offensive and advanced on the United Nations-designated safe area of Bihac. Both the offensive by the Bosnian Government army and the Bosnian Serb counteroffensive resulted in civilian casualties and a new flow of refugees and displaced persons in the region.

UNHCR reported that since May 1994, only 12 aid convoys carrying less than 2,000 metric tons of food had reached the 400,000 people besieged in the Bihac enclave. Another 131 UNHCR convoys loaded with humanitarian aid had been denied access, despite repeated promises from the Krajina Serb authorities to allow them to pass. Re-supply convoys for UNPROFOR's Bangladeshi battalion stationed in Bihac had also not been allowed.

All diplomatic efforts and the activities of UNPROFOR on the ground failed to stop the attack on Bihac, Velika Kladusa and other areas in the pocket. Moreover, on 18 November, in a clear violation of Bihac's status as a safe area, aircraft belonging to the Krajina Serb forces flying from Udbina airstrip in the UNPA Sector South in Croatia crossed the border with Bosnia and Herzegovina and dropped napalm and cluster bombs in southwest Bihac. On 19 November, aircraft belonging to the Krajina Serb forces bombed the town of Cazin, about 10 miles north of Bihac. One of the aircraft crashed into an apartment block housing displaced persons who had fled the war in other parts of Bosnia and Herzegovina. Several people were killed or wounded in the incident.

On 18 November, the Security Council, in a Presidential statement,[66] strongly condemned the attack. By its resolution 958 (1994) of 19 November, the Council decided that the authorization given to Member States under resolution 836 (1993) — to take, under its authority and subject to close coordination with the Secretary-General and UNPROFOR, all necessary measures, through the use of air power, in and around the safe areas of Bosnia and Herzegovina to support UNPROFOR in the performance of its mandate — also applied to such measures taken in the Republic of Croatia. On the same day, the Council adopted resolution 959 (1994), in which it condemned violations of the international border between Croatia and Bosnia and Herzegovina. By the same resolution, the

---

[66]S/PRST/1994/69.

Secretary-General was requested to update his recommendations on the modalities of the implementation of the concept of safe areas and to encourage UNPROFOR to achieve agreements on the strengthening of the safe areas regimes.

On 21 November, in accordance with resolution 958 (1994), NATO launched an air strike on the Udbina airstrip located in the UNPA Sector South in Croatia. The raid came after the aircraft of the Krajina Serbs attacked targets in the Bihac enclave on 18 and 19 November. A total of 39 warplanes from France, the Netherlands, the United Kingdom and the United States took part in the attack on the Udbina airfield in close cooperation with UNPROFOR. The Secretary-General's Special Representative described that action as a necessary and proportionate response. He noted that NATO had targeted the airstrip at Udbina, and not the aircraft operating from it, in order to limit collateral damage and casualties.

On 23 November, after Bosnian Serb forces fired missiles at two British Harrier jets patrolling the Bihac area and locked their radar on NATO reconnaissance aircraft, NATO conducted air strikes against surface-to-air missile sites in the area. On 25 November, after Bosnian Serb forces began shelling the town of Bihac, NATO planes were again called in by UNPROFOR to protect United Nations troops. The planes flew for 60 minutes but could not initiate any attack without endangering both UNPROFOR troops and civilians.

Despite all efforts and warnings, the Bosnian Serbs continued their attack and eventually captured some high ground within the Bihac safe area but did not move into the town of Bihac itself. Also, in apparent retaliation for NATO air strikes, the Bosnian Serbs detained a number of United Nations personnel throughout Bosnia and Herzegovina, restricted UNPROFOR movement and stopped most humanitarian and supply convoys in territories under Bosnian Serb control.

On 26 November, the Security Council issued a statement[67] demanding the withdrawal of all Bosnian Serb forces from the Bihac safe area and condemned in the strongest possible terms all violations, in particular, the "flagrant and blatant" entry of Bosnian Serb forces into the safe area. It demanded that all parties agree to an immediate and unconditional cease-fire in the Bihac region, particularly in and around the safe area.

The Council also demanded that all hostile acts across the border between Croatia and Bosnia and Herzegovina cease immediately and that the Krajina Serb forces withdraw immediately from the territory of Bosnia and Herzegovina. It called for an end to hostilities throughout Bosnia and Herzegovina in pursuit of the territorial settlement proposed by the Contact Group [see chapter 23], reiterated its full support for the settlement, and demanded that the Bosnian Serb party accept it unconditionally and in full.

Plan for safe areas

In order to achieve the overriding objective of the safe areas, i.e. protection of the civilian population and delivery of humanitarian assistance, the Secretary-General proposed[68] to the Council that the safe areas should be clearly delineated and completely demilitarized. Demilitarization should be accompanied by the cessation of hostilities and of provocative actions in and around the safe areas.

The ability of one party to retain troops, weapons and military installations within a safe area, the Secretary-General continued, created an unstable situation and drew attacks from the opposing party. The use of force by UNPROFOR to repel such attacks in defence of the safe area was inevitably construed as "taking sides" and could have a destabilizing effect throughout Bosnia and Herzegovina. Moreover, UNPROFOR was not equipped to repel such attacks, and air power was frequently an inappropriate means of doing so.

The Secretary-General observed that until complete demilitarization of safe areas could be achieved, the party controlling a safe area should be obliged to refrain from attacks and hostile or provocative actions from within the safe area directed against opposing forces or targets outside the safe area. No weapons or weapon systems larger than 81 mm in diameter, or military headquarters or similar installations or factories producing *matériel* for military use should be located within the safe areas. The safe areas should not be used by a party to the conflict as a haven for its troops or for training or equipping troops. Meanwhile, complete freedom of movement for the local population, as well as for UNPROFOR and humanitarian relief agencies, should be guaranteed to, from and within the safe areas.

The Secretary-General did not believe that UNPROFOR should be given the mandate to enforce compliance with the safe-area regime. The use of force would prevent UNPROFOR from carrying out its overall mandate in the former Yugoslavia, turn it into a combatant and further destabilize the situation in Bosnia and Herzegovina. Such a mandate would

[67]S/PRST/1994/71. [68]S/1994/1389.

be incompatible with the role of UNPROFOR as a peace-keeping force.

The Secretary-General recommended that the Security Council redefine the regime of safe areas in accordance with his proposals, and demand that all the parties and others concerned agree on the concrete steps to be taken to ensure compliance with the modified safe-area regime. The Council should also demand that all the parties and others concerned comply with the interim measures pending complete demilitarization of the safe areas, and mandate UNPROFOR to define the operational boundaries of the safe areas with or without the agreement of the parties.

In the meantime, UNPROFOR proposed a three-point plan for an immediate and unconditional cease-fire for the Bihac safe area, involving the demilitarization of the safe area, turning it over to UNPROFOR, and interposition of peace-keepers in the sensitive areas. The proposal, which was delivered to both parties on 27 November, was accepted in principle by the Bosnian Government. The Bosnian Serb side indicated that it needed more time to review the proposal. The efforts of UNPROFOR were actively supported by the Contact Group and the Secretary-General.

The Secretary-General visited Sarajevo on 30 November. He met with President Izetbegovic to discuss the effectiveness of United Nations operations and specific action to reach agreement on immediate measures to bring the military situation under control and create conditions in which negotiations for a political settlement could reach a successful conclusion. Dr. Karadzic had declined an invitation to meet with the Secretary-General.

Cease-fire agreement signed

Immediately after the Secretary-General's visit, his Special Representative initiated intense negotiations for a cease-fire and a cessation of hostilities. The visit of former United States President Jimmy Carter to Sarajevo and Pale in mid-December greatly facilitated that process and led to the Bosnian Serbs announcing their willingness to agree to a cease-fire. Following President Carter's visit, the Special Representative succeeded in securing a cease-fire agreement between the sides on 23 December 1994 and a cessation-of-hostilities agreement on 31 December 1994.[69] The latter agreement, which came into effect on 1 January 1995, included nine basic elements: a four-month cessation of hostilities; the establishment of a joint commission to oversee implementation of the agreement; an exchange of liaison officers; the

separation of forces, withdrawal of heavy weapons and interpositioning of UNPROFOR troops along the line of confrontation; freedom of movement for UNPROFOR and UNHCR, particularly for the purpose of delivering aid and monitoring human rights; compliance with earlier agreements concerning Sarajevo and certain areas in eastern Bosnia; restoration of utilities and joint economic activities; release of prisoners and provision of information on missing persons; and cooperation with UNPROFOR in the monitoring and withdrawal of foreign troops. On 2 January 1995, Bosnian Croat leaders joined those agreements.

In the first month following the cease-fire and cessation-of-hostilities agreements, military activities of all the parties declined substantially throughout Bosnia and Herzegovina, except in the area of Bihac. There was a marked improvement in the quality of life for the citizens of Sarajevo and significant gains in freedom of movement and in the humanitarian situation throughout the country.

However, despite the general success of the cease-fire agreement and some success on the provisions of the cessation-of-hostilities agreement, little progress was achieved in January on the provisions relating to the separation of forces, interpositioning of UNPROFOR troops and the withdrawal of heavy weapons. Moreover, a continued lack of cooperation on those issues in February 1995, military preparations by the Bosnian parties, persistent attacks and counter-attacks in the Bihac area gave grounds for fearing renewed hostilities at or before the expiration of the four-month cessation-of-hostilities agreement.

In addition, the Bosnian Government made it clear that it would not extend the agreement if the Bosnian Serbs were still unwilling to accept the Contact Group's peace plan, at least as a starting point for negotiations. Government forces began to apply restrictions on UNPROFOR's freedom of movement in government-controlled territory. In addition, in violation of the cease-fire, they initiated offensives around Travnik and Tuzla. The Bosnian Serbs, for their part, also began restricting UNPROFOR's freedom of movement in the areas controlled by them and increased obstruction of humanitarian assistance. The security situation in Sarajevo began to deteriorate, with increasing sniping at civilians and targeting of UNPROFOR and UNHCR aircraft. Despite UNPROFOR's repeated efforts to achieve a cease-fire, fighting and blockage of delivery of supplies continued in the Bihac pocket in north-western Bosnia.

[69]S/1995/8.

As of mid-March 1995, UNPROFOR in Bosnia included 21,994 troops and military support personnel, 305 military observers and 45 civilian police.

D. The former Yugoslav Republic of Macedonia

First United Nations preventive operation authorized

On 11 November 1992, the President of the former Yugoslav Republic of Macedonia requested the deployment of United Nations observers in view of his concern about the possible impact of fighting elsewhere in the former Yugoslavia. Such deployment was also recommended by the Co-Chairmen of the ICFY Steering Committee. With the Security Council's approval,[70] the Secretary-General sent a group of military, police and civilian personnel to assess the situation.[71]

On 9 December 1992, the Secretary-General recommended[72] to the Council an expansion of UNPROFOR's mandate and strength to establish a United Nations presence on the republic's borders with Albania and the Federal Republic of Yugoslavia (Serbia and Montenegro). The mandate would be essentially preventive, to monitor and report any developments in the border areas which could undermine confidence and stability in the republic and threaten its territory. The enlargement would comprise a battalion of up to 700 all ranks, 35 military observers, 26 civilian police monitors, 10 civil affairs staff, 45 administrative staff and local interpreters. The headquarters would be in the capital, Skopje.

The Security Council authorized the establishment of UNPROFOR's presence in the former Yugoslav Republic of Macedonia by its resolution 795 (1992) of 11 December. Subsequently, on 18 June 1993, the Council welcomed the offer by the United States to provide about 300 troops to reinforce UNPROFOR's presence in the republic and, in its resolution 842 (1993), authorized the deployment of the additional personnel.

The first civilian police monitors arrived in Skopje on 27 December 1992. They were subsequently deployed along the northern and western borders of the republic. As at mid-May 1993, there were 24 monitors. A joint Nordic battalion, consisting of contingents from Finland, Norway and Sweden, became operational on 18 February 1993. It took over from the Canadian company which had been deployed on an interim basis on 7 January, pending the arrival of the joint battalion. The battalion, a 434-man force composed of three rifle companies, was deployed on the western border from Debar northward and on the northern border up to the border with Bulgaria. The western border area south of Debar was covered by United Nations military observers, who constituted the main United Nations presence there. As at mid-May 1993, there were 19 military observers in the area of operations. The United States contingent of some 300 soldiers arrived in the Skopje area in the first two weeks of July 1993, deploying to the republic's side of the border with the Federal Republic of Yugoslavia (Serbia and Montenegro) on 20 August.

Military situation

Beginning in early January 1993, the northern border and the western border north of Debar were constantly monitored by UNPROFOR from observation posts and by regular patrols. One of the difficulties encountered by the peace-keepers from the very beginning of the mission was the fact that the republic's border with the Federal Republic of Yugoslavia (Serbia and Montenegro) had not been definitively delineated and the two Governments had yet to establish a joint border commission to resolve this matter conclusively. This resulted in border crossings and encounters between the military patrols from the two sides. Most of those incidents, however, were non-confrontational, indicating that neither party seemed to wish to provoke conflict.

Beginning in April 1994, there was a rise in the frequency of encounters. UNPROFOR successfully mediated several tense situations, achieving the withdrawal of soldiers on both sides. In those activities, UNPROFOR maintained close coordination with other international bodies, including ICFY and CSCE. Following further border incidents in the summer of 1994, UNPROFOR negotiated a military administrative boundary between the two parties that determined the northern

[70] S/24852.   [71] S/24851.   [72] S/24923.

limit of the area of operation of UNPROFOR troops. Although neither Government acknowledged that boundary as the legitimate international border, both sides used it for the reporting and management of border-crossing incidents.

Apart from the border incidents, the overall military situation in the republic remained relatively calm and stable. The Secretary-General repeatedly reported to the Security Council that UNPROFOR was successful in its preventive mandate and that there was no military threat to the former Yugoslav Republic of Macedonia. It was believed that the more likely sources of instability were internal rather than external.

As of mid-March 1995, UNPROFOR in the former Yugoslav Republic of Macedonia included 1,096 troops and military support personnel, 24 military observers and 24 civilian police.

Situation in the country

The internal political situation in the republic remained very complex. Tensions persisted between the Government and elements among the ethnic Albanian population, who were demanding improvements in their political, economic, social, cultural and educational status. There were also tensions between the Government and nationalist elements among the ethnic Macedonian majority. In order to establish accurate estimates of the ethnic composition of the population, the Government conducted a nationwide population census from 25 June to 11 July 1994. The census was monitored, financed and partly organized by the Council of Europe and the European Union. The results showed that 67 per cent of the resident population in the Republic were ethnic Macedonians, 23 per cent were ethnic Albanians, and the remaining 10 per cent consisted of Turks, Serbs, Vlachs, Gypsies and people of non-identified ethnicity. Despite verification by international observers of the veracity of the results and the proper conduct of the census, ethnic Albanian leaders disputed the results.

Internal political and social stability were also endangered by rising unemployment and a declining economy resulting, among other things, from the effects of the economic blockade imposed by Greece on 17 February 1994 and of the United Nations sanctions against the Federal Republic of Yugoslavia (Serbia and Montenegro), formerly the country's primary trading partners. In addition, international investors showed reluctance to invest in the country.

Given the complex interrelation of external and internal factors contributing to economic and political uncertainty, and rising social tensions, the Security Council, by its resolution 908 (1994) of 31 March 1994, encouraged the Secretary-General's Special Representative, in cooperation with the authorities of the republic, to use his good offices as appropriate to contribute to the maintenance of peace and stability. Accordingly, UNPROFOR began effectively monitoring developments in the country, including possible areas of conflict, with a view to promoting reconciliation among various political and ethnic groups. The mission maintained close cooperation with the CSCE monitoring mission and enjoyed an excellent cooperative relationship with the host Government.

Within the good offices function of the Special Representative, his delegate, upon the invitation of the President of the Parliament, joined CSCE, the Council of Europe and other international organizations in monitoring the parliamentary and presidential elections held in October 1994. While certain irregularities were noted in the elections, the overall opinion of the observers was that the elections had been conducted in a generally orderly, regular and peaceful manner. However, the two major opposition parties within the country, VRMO-DPMNE and the Democratic Party, considered the first round of the elections to have been fraudulent and boycotted the second round. As a result, the parties already in power secured an overwhelming majority of 95 of the 120 seats in Parliament [see chapter 25].

E. Restructuring UNPROFOR

The mandate of UNPROFOR had been authorized until 31 March 1995. On 22 March 1995, the Secretary-General informed[73] the Security Council that, in Croatia, the retention of UNPROFOR in its existing form and with its existing mandate would not enjoy the consent of the Government of Croatia. It was equally clear that the Chapter VII option was not feasible either politically or in resource terms. At the same time, the total withdrawal of all United Nations peace-keeping forces from Croatia would result immediately in a grave threat to peace and security extending beyond the borders of Croatia. Nor was it clear whether the peace-keeping operation in Bosnia and Herzegovina could be continued without a substantial United Nations presence and support facilities in Croatia. The maintenance of a reduced force in Croatia under a new mandate seemed the only way to reduce the risks of a renewed major war, while permitting continued progress in implementing the economic agreement and beginning political negotiations.

The Secretary-General also noted, in reference to Mr. Stoltenberg's negotiations with the parties, that an agreement on the details of the new mandate and the modalities of the United Nations peace-keeping operation in Croatia required further work. The gulf between the positions of the Government of Croatia and the Krajina Serb authorities on the role and functions of the new force remained wide, particularly with regard to the nature, size and functions of the force in the zone of separation and in the protected areas. Deployment patterns (e.g., fixed posts or mobile patrols or a combination of the two) and mode of functioning (e.g., monitor and report, as opposed to stop and search) of the United Nations force in the zone of separation and on the international borders also required further discussion.

The Secretary-General believed that the mandate of the force should include support for implementation of the cease-fire agreement of 29 March 1994 and the economic agreement of 2 December 1994, as well as implementation of those elements of the existing United Nations peace-keeping plan for Croatia that had been accepted by both parties as having continuing relevance. These would include, but not be limited to, maintenance of a United Nations presence on the international borders of the Republic of Croatia and confidence-building and humanitarian tasks, such as assistance to refugees and displaced persons, protection of ethnic minorities, mine-clearance and convoy assistance.

In addition, the new force would continue to perform functions arising from the accord on the Prevlaka peninsula and from relevant resolutions of the Security Council, such as those dealing with the monitoring of the "no-fly zone" and the extension of close air support in Croatia.

With regard to Bosnia and Herzegovina, the Secretary-General viewed UNPROFOR's performance as a mixture of achievements and setbacks. More than ever before, the country faced the probability of renewed hostilities. UNPROFOR's stabilization of the situation on the ground had not been matched by political progress on a negotiated settlement. The impasse on the Contact Group's proposal had created a vacuum in which UNPROFOR had little or no political context for the pursuit of local initiatives. While UNPROFOR continued to perform humanitarian and confidence-building tasks, the lack of progress on the fundamental political questions had created a situation in which it could do little but to delay rather than prevent a renewed outbreak of hostilities. That could also have negative consequences for the future of the Federation, which could not remain immune from the processes in other parts of Bosnia and Herzegovina or the mission area as a whole.

Speaking of relations between UNPROFOR and NATO, the Secretary-General said that they had continued to be excellent, despite the delicate balance required as a result of the different mandates and objectives of the two organizations. The joint NATO/Western European Union operation "Sharp Guard" enforced the Adriatic embargo in accordance with Council resolution 820 (1993). NATO operation "Deny Flight" continued to provide aerial monitoring and enforcement of the "no-fly-zone", as well as protective close air support, air strikes and the enhancement of the security of the United Nations-designated safe areas within Bosnia and Herzegovina when requested by UNPROFOR. In the event that United Nations personnel had to be withdrawn from any part of the theatre, it would be of great value to the United Nations to be able to call on NATO to protect or conduct a withdrawal operation.

[73]S/1995/222.

In the former Yugoslav Republic of Macedonia, UNPROFOR, acting in full cooperation with the authorities of the republic as well as with other external organizations such as OSCE and ICFY, had made a modest but important contribution to helping the authorities and various ethnic groups to maintain peace and stability and build a workable future. If external or internal threats to the Republic's peace and stability were to significantly increase and warrant a new mandate, the Secretary-General would submit the appropriate recommendations to the Security Council.

Throughout the mission, the Secretary-General continued, UNPROFOR had maintained a presence in the Federal Republic of Yugoslavia (Serbia and Montenegro) to discharge political liaison and public information functions and monitor the Prevlaka peninsula and airfields. The presence of UNPROFOR in the Federal Republic of Yugoslavia (Serbia and Montenegro) and the cooperation it had received from the federal authorities in Belgrade had proved vital to the effective functioning of all three of the operation's commands. The United Nations peace-keeping presence should be maintained there with unaltered functions.

The Secretary-General informed the Security Council that the Governments of Croatia and of the former Yugoslav Republic of Macedonia had expressed the wish that the United Nations forces in their countries should be separate from UNPROFOR. The Government of Bosnia and Herzegovina had also expressed a wish for possible changes in the existing arrangements. In order to respond to those wishes, the Secretary-General proposed that UNPROFOR be replaced by three separate but interlinked peace-keeping operations. Each of the three operations would be headed by a civilian Chief of Mission and would have its own military commander. In view of the interlinked nature of the problems in the area and in order to avoid the expense of duplicating existing structures, overall command and control of the three operations would be exercised by the Special Representative of the Secretary-General and a Theatre Force Commander commanding the military elements of the Force under his authority. Their theatre headquarters would be in Zagreb, Croatia.

Chapter 25
United Nations operations in the former Yugoslavia after March 1995

Chapter 25

United Nations operations in the former Yugoslavia after March 1995

A. United Nations Peace Forces (UNPF)

On 31 March 1995, the Security Council, by adopting three resolutions, decided to restructure UNPROFOR replacing it with three separate but interlinked operations in Croatia, Bosnia and Herzegovina and the former Yugoslav Republic of Macedonia, with mandates extending until 30 November 1995. Known collectively as the United Nations Peace Forces (UNPF), with headquarters in Zagreb, Croatia, the three operations were under the overall command and control of the Special Representative of the Secretary-General. Under his authority, the Theatre Force Commander exercised overall command of military elements of the three operations. Each operation also had its own civilian chief of mission and military commander.

By resolution 981 (1995), the Council established the United Nations Confidence Restoration Operation in Croatia, to be known as UNCRO, and requested the Secretary-General to take the measures necessary to ensure its earliest possible deployment. The mandate of the Force should include: (a) performing fully the functions envisaged in the cease-fire agreement of 29 March 1994; (b) facilitating implementation of the Economic Agreement of 2 December 1994; (c) facilitating implementation of all relevant Security Council resolutions; (d) assisting in controlling, by monitoring and reporting, the crossing of military personnel, equipment, supplies and weapons, over the international borders between the Republic of Croatia and the Republic of Bosnia and Herzegovina, and the Republic of Croatia and the Federal Republic of Yugoslavia (Serbia and Montenegro) at the border crossings for which UNCRO was responsible; (e) facilitating the delivery of international humanitarian assistance to the Republic of Bosnia and Herzegovina through the territory of the Republic of Croatia; (f) monitoring the demilitarization of the Prevlaka peninsula.

The Council decided that UNCRO would be an interim arrangement to create the conditions that would facilitate a negotiated settlement consistent with the territorial integrity of the Republic of Croatia and which would guarantee the security and rights of all communities. The Council requested the Secretary-General to continue his consultations with all concerned on the implementation of the new mandate and to report to it not later than 21 April 1995 for its approval.

The Council also decided that Member States, acting nationally or through regional organizations or arrangements, might take, under the authority of the Security Council and subject to close coordination with the Secretary-General and the United Nations Theatre Force Commander, all necessary measures to extend close air support to the territory of the Republic of Croatia in defence of UNCRO personnel in the performance of UNCRO's mandate.

By resolution 982 (1995), the Security Council extended UNPROFOR's mandate in the Republic of Bosnia and Herzegovina for an additional period terminating on 30 November 1995 and further decided that all previous relevant resolutions relating to UNPROFOR should continue to apply. It authorized the Secretary-General to redeploy before 30 June 1995 all UNPROFOR personnel and assets from Croatia, with the exception of those whose continued presence there was required for UNCRO operations.

The Council also decided that UNPROFOR should continue to perform fully the functions envisaged in the implementation of the cease-fire agreement of 29 March 1994 and the economic agreement of 2 December 1994 between the Republic of Croatia and the local Serb authorities and

UNPF deployment as of November 1995

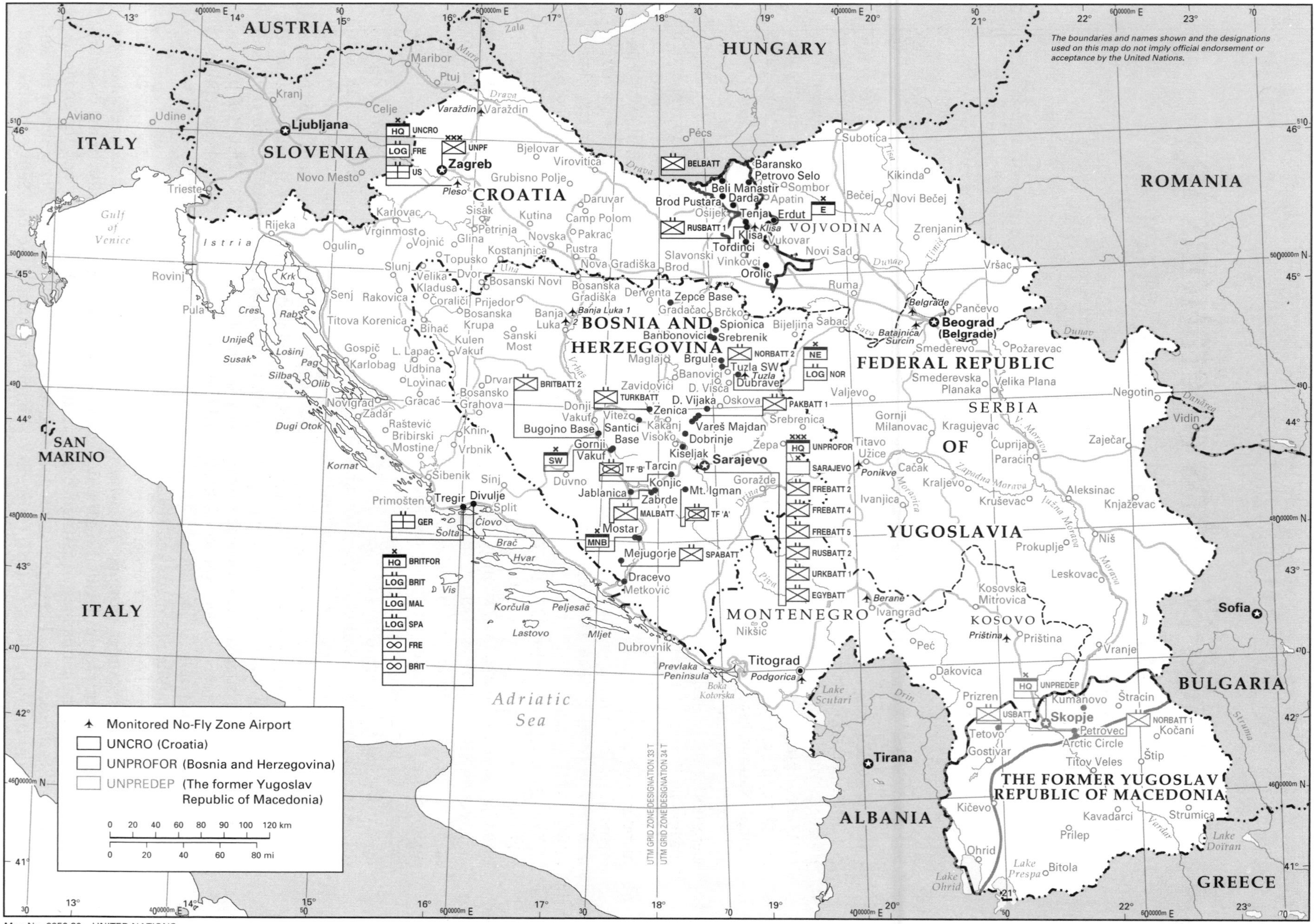

The boundaries and names shown and the designations used on this map do not imply official endorsement or acceptance by the United Nations.

AUSTRIA

HUNGARY

ROMANIA

ITALY

SLOVENIA

CROATIA

BOSNIA AND HERZEGOVINA

FEDERAL REPUBLIC OF YUGOSLAVIA

SERBIA

KOSOVO

MONTENEGRO

BULGARIA

THE FORMER YUGOSLAV REPUBLIC OF MACEDONIA

GREECE

ALBANIA

SAN MARINO

Adriatic Sea

Gulf of Venice

Ljubljana

Zagreb

Beograd (Belgrade)

Sarajevo

Skopje

Sofia

Tirana

Titograd (Podgorica)

Legend

Monitored No-Fly Zone Airport

UNCRO (Croatia)

UNPROFOR (Bosnia and Herzegovina)

UNPREDEP (The former Yugoslav Republic of Macedonia)

0 20 40 60 80 100 120 km
0 20 40 60 80 mi

UTM GRID ZONE DESIGNATION 34 T
UTM GRID ZONE DESIGNATION 33 T

Map No. 3952.30 UNITED NATIONS
September 1996

Department of Public Information
Cartographic Section

STRUCTURE OF UNPF

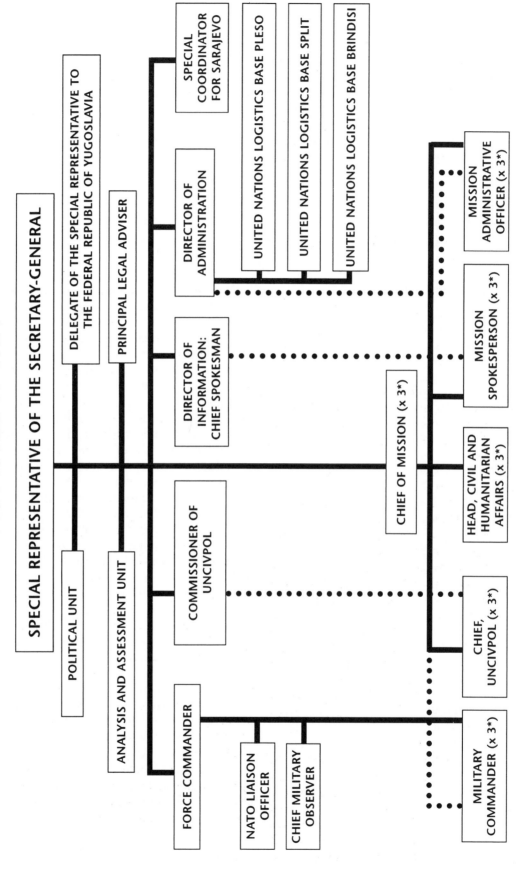

SPECIAL REPRESENTATIVE OF THE SECRETARY-GENERAL

POLITICAL UNIT

ANALYSIS AND ASSESSMENT UNIT

DELEGATE OF THE SPECIAL REPRESENTATIVE TO THE FEDERAL REPUBLIC OF YUGOSLAVIA

PRINCIPAL LEGAL ADVISER

FORCE COMMANDER

NATO LIAISON OFFICER

CHIEF MILITARY OBSERVER

COMMISSIONER OF UNCIVPOL

DIRECTOR OF INFORMATION: CHIEF SPOKESMAN

DIRECTOR OF ADMINISTRATION

SPECIAL COORDINATOR FOR SARAJEVO

UNITED NATIONS LOGISTICS BASE PLESO

UNITED NATIONS LOGISTICS BASE SPLIT

UNITED NATIONS LOGISTICS BASE BRINDISI

CHIEF OF MISSION (x 3*)

HEAD, CIVIL AND HUMANITARIAN AFFAIRS (x 3*)

CHIEF, UNCIVPOL (x 3*)

MILITARY COMMANDER (x 3*)

MISSION SPOKESPERSON (x 3*)

MISSION ADMINISTRATIVE OFFICER (x 3*)

*UNPROFOR, UNCRO, UNPREDEP

547

all relevant Security Council resolutions, and to facilitate the delivery of international humanitarian assistance to the Republic of Bosnia and Herzegovina through the territory of the Republic of Croatia until the effective deployment of UNCRO or 30 June 1995, whichever was sooner.

The Council reiterated the importance of full compliance with the agreements between the Bosnian parties on a cease-fire and on a complete cessation of hostilities in Bosnia and Herzegovina, and called upon them to agree to a further extension and implementation of those agreements beyond 30 April 1995 and to use that period to negotiate an overall peaceful settlement on the basis of the acceptance of the Contact Group peace plan as a starting point.

By resolution 983 (1995), the Security Council decided that UNPROFOR within the former Yugoslav Republic of Macedonia should be known as the United Nations Preventive Deployment Force (UNPREDEP) with mandate, responsibilities and composition identical to those in place.

B. UNCRO

Implementation plan

As requested by resolution 981 (1995) of 31 March 1995, the Secretary-General's Special Envoy, Mr. Stoltenberg, continued his consultations regarding the implementation of UNCRO's mandate and met with all concerned, including military authorities on both sides. The consultations were carried out in close contact with the Special Representative for the former Yugoslavia and the Force Commander of the United Nations Peace Forces in Zagreb.

On the basis of those consultations, the Secretary-General reported[1] to the Security Council on 18 April 1995 on the detailed implementation of the new United Nations mandate in Croatia. In accordance with the functions envisaged in the cease-fire agreement of 29 March 1994, UNCRO would: (a) monitor the area between the forward troop deployment lines; (b) verify that all weapons systems were deployed in accordance with the provisions of the agreement; (c) occupy checkpoints at all crossing-points specified in the agreement; (d) chair the Joint Commissions at all levels; (e) conduct the liaison activities required to ensure the implementation of the agreement.

To perform those functions fully, UNCRO would have exclusive control of the area between the forward troop deployment lines. It would establish static posts as well as carry out patrols on foot, by vehicle and by helicopter. UNCRO would also have full freedom of movement to monitor the deployment of troops and weapons systems. In addition, CIVPOL would supervise the local police which, under the cease-fire agreement, were obliged to assist UNCRO in the prevention of crime and maintenance of law and order in the area between the forward troop deployment lines. CIVPOL would also patrol the area between the forward troop deployment lines in order to enhance confidence and identify policing requirements.

In order to advance the process of reconciliation and the restoration of normal life, UNCRO would: (a) facilitate and support the opening of transportation networks, as well as of water and energy facilities, within the limits of its resources; (b) support the negotiation and implementation of further economic and humanitarian measures included in the economic agreement or which may be agreed in subsequent negotiations.

In order to maintain conditions of peace and security and to restore confidence, thereby also facilitating the negotiation of a political solution, UNCRO would: (a) provide assistance to needy individuals and communities (Croat, Serb and others), in cooperation with international agencies; (b) monitor the human rights situation of individuals and communities (Croat, Serb and others) to ensure that there was no discrimination and that human rights were protected; (c) facilitate the voluntary return of refugees and displaced persons (Croat, Serb and others) in accordance with established international principles and in coordination with UNHCR; (d) support local confidence-building measures, including socio-economic and reconstruction activities, people-to-people contacts and information exchanges of mutual benefit.

UNCRO would also assist in controlling, by monitoring and reporting, the crossing of military personnel, equipment, supplies and weapons, over the international borders between Croatia

[1]S/1995/320.

and Bosnia and Herzegovina, and Croatia and the Federal Republic of Yugoslavia (Serbia and Montenegro). UNCRO would carry out those monitoring and reporting functions at designated border crossing-points. Traffic crossing over the international borders would be monitored for military personnel, equipment, supplies and weapons. All information concerning the movement of military personnel, equipment, supplies and weapons would be reported to the Security Council through the Secretary-General.

UNCRO would carry out its tasks at designated border crossing-points by deploying with a strength sufficient to perform these tasks and maintain troop safety and security. All vehicles and personnel would stop at the border crossing-points and would be visually checked. In cases where military personnel, equipment, supplies and weapons were detected, UNCRO would give notice that the crossing of such personnel and items would be in violation of Security Council resolutions and would be reported to the Security Council. UNCRO would also compile any information on the crossing of such personnel and items and report that information to the Security Council through the Secretary-General.

To facilitate the delivery of international humanitarian assistance to Bosnia and Herzegovina through the territory of Croatia, UNCRO would concentrate on providing advice and assistance to agencies involved in international humanitarian deliveries to Bosnia and Herzegovina through the territory of Croatia. UNCRO would facilitate convoy and route clearances from the Government of Croatia and from the local Serb authorities; escort humanitarian convoys as required for their security and protection; and maintain routes when required and within the limits of its resources.

In order to monitor the demilitarization of the Prevlaka peninsula, United Nations military observers would patrol and maintain a permanent presence on the most southerly portion of the peninsula. They would also monitor the area 5 kilometres on either side of the border and report on the presence of any military forces. This task would continue to be performed by unarmed military observers only and would require the cooperation of both sides and their commitment to demilitarization.

The Secretary-General's Special Representative and the Theatre Force Commander assessed that an overall total of some 8,750 troops would be required for the implementation of UNCRO's mandate, on the assumption that the operation would enjoy the necessary cooperation of all concerned. The necessary civilian staff, United Nations military observers and CIVPOL, as well as administrative and logistical support elements would also be required. It was expected that the strength of the United Nations forces in Croatia could be reduced to the proposed level of 8,750 and their deployment completed by 30 June 1995.

While there appeared to be enough common ground between the Government of Croatia and the local Serb authorities to make it possible to implement resolution 981 (1995), the Secretary-General emphasized that the implementation plan did not have the formal acceptance and full support of either the Government of Croatia or the local Serb authorities. The risk therefore remained that either or both sides would fail to cooperate. On the other hand, the proposed plan provided for a pragmatic implementation of Security Council resolution 981 (1995). The alternative to its adoption would be the withdrawal of United Nations forces and the resumption of war. The Secretary-General therefore recommended that the Security Council approve the proposed arrangements and authorize the deployment of UNCRO to implement them.

On 28 April 1995, the Security Council, by its resolution 990 (1995), approved the arrangements proposed by the Secretary-General for the implementation of UNCRO's mandate and decided to authorize the deployment of the force as set out in his 18 April report. The Council called upon the Government of Croatia and the local Serb authorities to cooperate fully with UNCRO in the implementation of its mandate.

May 1995 offensive

In the meantime, the peace efforts in Croatia suffered a major setback. On 24 April 1995, the Croatian Serb leadership closed the Zagreb-Belgrade highway in Sector West — Western Slavonia — for 24 hours because of claims that the highway was not of equal benefit to the Croatian Serbs. Shortly following its reopening, a series of incidents took place on the highway, after which the situation around the highway deteriorated rapidly. On the morning of 1 May 1995, the Croatian Army, in violation of the cease-fire agreement of 29 March 1994, launched a military offensive in the areas of Sector West under Croatian Serb control. Despite an immediate call[2] by the Security Council to stop the offensive, hostilities continued. In the afternoon of 1 May, the Secretary-General's Special Representative brought the

---

[2] S/PRST/1995/23.

parties together in Zagreb and presented a proposal for a cease-fire which was accepted by the Croatian Serbs, but not by Croatia. By 2 May, the Croatian Army had essentially secured all militarily important positions in Sector West. The Krajina Serbs responded by firing missiles on both 2 and 3 May into urban areas of Zagreb and the Pleso airfield and shelling the towns of Karlovac and Sisak.

The offensive was initially described by the Croatian Government as a police action intended only to restore security on the highway. However, further Croatian military movements in the central part of Sector West and against the mainly Serb-inhabited town of Okucani, indicated that the intention was to establish complete control over the Sector. Following intensive negotiations in Knin and Zagreb, an agreement was reached on 3 May on a cessation of hostilities in all areas, including Sector West, and on arrangements to ensure safe passage from Sector West into Bosnian Serb-controlled parts of Bosnia and Herzegovina for those remaining Croatian Serb civilians and soldiers (with sidearms only) who wished to leave under UNCRO and UNHCR surveillance.

Hostilities resumed on 4 May, when the Croatian Army shelled the Croatian Serb-inhabited part of Pakrac and captured a large group of Croatian Serb soldiers and the remaining residents. In Sectors South, North and East, tensions between Croatian and Krajina Serb forces also rose to an extremely high level. The Croatian Army advanced and took up improved tactical positions in the zone of separation near Osijek in Sector East, Petrinja in Sector North and Gospic and Medak in Sector South. The most significant Croatian Serb advance into the zone of separation in response to the Croatian Army attack was in Sector East. Elsewhere, Croatian Serbs removed heavy weapons from storage sites and impeded United Nations freedom of movement. The Security Council's demand[3] to withdraw all forces from the zone of separation and to re-establish the authority of UNCRO in Sector West and other affected areas was not met.

The Croatian offensive had a major impact on the Croatian Serb population in Sector West. During the first days, more than 10,000 Croatian Serbs living in areas immediately affected by the fighting crossed the Sava bridge into Bosnia and Herzegovina. Human rights violations against local Serb residents were reported, including looting of household items, livestock and vehicles by Croatian army personnel; forced eviction of families from their dwellings; burning or blowing up of scores of abandoned houses; harassment and intimidation; and confiscation of personal documents, such as driving licences and car registration papers. Most of the Croatian Serbs remaining in the Sector expressed their determination to leave.

The Croatian Army imposed total restriction of movement on UNCRO in Sector West for the first seven days of May. This precluded normal patrolling and hindered access to places that might have needed prompt humanitarian assistance and human rights monitoring. Subsequently, restrictions on movement were lifted. Following the Croatian offensive, reduction of UNPROFOR troop levels required by Security Council resolution 990 (1995) could not be implemented.

The international response to events in Sector West included assistance from United Nations and European agencies, including UNHCR, the United Nations Office at Vienna, the European Community Monitoring Mission, the European Community Task Force and ICRC. Human rights monitoring was undertaken by UNCRO, the Centre for Human Rights and other organizations.

On 17 May, the Security Council, in its resolution 994 (1995) made three principal demands: (a) that the warring parties complete without further delay the withdrawal of all their troops from the zone of separation and that they refrain from taking any further military measures or actions that could lead to the escalation of the situation; (b) that the Government of Croatia respect fully the rights of the Serb population, including their freedom of movement, and access to them by international humanitarian organizations; and (c) that the authority of UNCRO be re-established, that its status and mandate, as well as the safety and security of its personnel, be respected and that necessary arrangements be made in order to ensure its full deployment.

UNCRO remains in place

Despite repeated demands by the Security Council, hostilities continued. On 4 June, the Croatian Army and Bosnian Croat forces launched a combined small-scale infantry and artillery attack in the area of Mount Dinara, 20 kilometres south-east of Knin, shelling several villages in the environs. On 6 June, a similar attack was again carried out from the direction of Mount Dinara, resulting in several bouts of shelling, with three rounds impacting inside the camp of UNCRO's Kenyan battalion at Civiljane in Sector South.

Reporting[4] to the Council on 9 June, the Secretary-General observed that although some

[3]S/PRST/1995/26. [4]S/1995/467.

progress had been achieved, resolution 994 (1995) had yet to be implemented. The Croatian offensive in Sector West had taken place despite the presence of United Nations peace-keepers; this underlined the reality that, without the cooperation of the parties, peace-keeping forces could not keep the peace. In the Secretary-General's view, the presence of United Nations forces and negotiators had been critical for achieving the cessation-of-hostilities agreement of 3 May 1995, for preventing escalation and for subsequently monitoring the human rights situation of Croatian Serbs in the Sector. However, such presence had not been sufficient to prevent the sequence of events leading to the Croatian offensive nor to forestall the offensive itself.

Furthermore, on the Croatian Serb side, there was anger and hostility at UNCRO's inability to prevent the Croatian offensive or to fulfil its role under the cessation-of-hostilities agreement of 3 May 1995. Krajina Serb leaders expressed their mistrust of the Security Council but affirmed their agreement to the continuation of the United Nations operation on the basis of its original mandate in the United Nations peace-keeping plan for Croatia[5] and the functions under the cease-fire agreement of 29 March 1994. The Government of Croatia also agreed to a continued UNCRO presence in Sector West for the purposes of implementing its mandate, in particular with reference to the monitoring of the human rights situation.

Arrangements were made with the Croatian Government for the comprehensive deployment throughout Sector West of UNCIVPOL and civil affairs personnel. Their functions included the provision of assistance to needy individuals and communities in cooperation with international agencies; monitoring the human rights of individuals and communities to ensure that there was no discrimination and that human rights were protected; facilitating the voluntary return of refugees and displaced persons in accordance with international principles and in coordination with UNHCR; and supporting local confidence-building measures between communities.

August 1995 offensive

Following the Croatian Army's takeover of Sector West, tensions remained high in the other Sectors. Croatian Army mobilization, continuous skirmishes, exchanges of fire, incidents and troop deployments within the zone of separation and violations of the heavy weapons withdrawal zones increased throughout June and July.

On 19 July, the Krajina Serb army ("ARSK") and the forces loyal to Mr. Fikret Abdic launched offensives against the Bosnian Army forces in the Bihac pocket. The attacks were supported by Bosnian Serb shell fire along the southern confrontation line. The following day, the Minister for Foreign Affairs of Croatia warned[6] the Security Council that "the displacement of the population of Bihac ... would be considered a serious threat to the security and stability of Croatia ... [and] Croatia may be compelled to undertake necessary measures to secure its status and territory".

On 22 July, the Presidents of Croatia and Bosnia and Herzegovina signed the Split Declaration, which committed the Croatian Government to assist militarily Bosnian forces in the Bihac pocket. On 28 July, the combined forces of the Croatian Army and the Bosnian Croat Defence Council captured Bosansko Grahovo and Glamoc in western Bosnia and Herzegovina, severing the Krajina Serbs' main supply route from Banja Luka to Knin. In response, the Krajina Serbs and the Bosnian Serbs declared a state of war and mobilized their respective armies.

Within Croatia, the Croatian Army continued a major build-up of troops around Sectors North and South. The leadership of the Croatian and Bosnian Serbs, meanwhile, convened a session of their joint Supreme Defence Council on 1 August at Drvar in Bosnia and Herzegovina. The meeting resulted in an appeal to "all Serbs", including the Government of the Federal Republic of Yugoslavia (Serbia and Montenegro), to assist in the defence of "Serb territory".

All efforts by the United Nations and by various Member States to prevent the conflicts in July and early August through negotiations were met with delays and intransigence. Over the period from 29 July to 3 August 1995, the Secretary-General's Special Representative and the Co-Chairman of the ICFY Steering Committee, with the support of the Security Council,[7] made a series of attempts to avert the war. Their efforts, however, did not succeed, as both sides adopted irreconcilable positions. The UNPF Theatre Force Commander attempted to arrange a meeting between the military commanders of the Croatian Army and the Krajina Serb forces on 31 July, but the Croatian Army Commander did not attend.

On 4 August 1995, the Croatian Army launched an attack in Sectors North and South (the Krajina region). Despite an immediate demand[8] by

[5]S/23280, annex III.   [6]S/1995/601, annex.   [7]S/PRST/1995/37.
[8]S/PRST/1995/38.

the Security Council to cease all military activity, the offensive continued and Knin fell on 5 August, following concentrated shelling. The majority of the civilian population fled from Sector South to Bosnian Serb-held territory. Resistance was stronger in Sector North. Meanwhile, the Bosnian Army launched a cross-border offensive against the Krajina Serbs, linking up with the Croatian Army. The situation in Sector East became tense and some civilians departed the area, fearing that a Croatian offensive was imminent.

In Sector North, 7 August attempts to conclude an agreement on the surrender of Krajina Serb elements collapsed when they tried to take heavy weapons systems with them as they withdrew. This led to continued fighting. A cease-fire was, however, successfully concluded for the Topusko and Glina areas on 8 August, to come into effect the following day. It provided for the surrender of Croatian Serb heavy weapons, the withdrawal of Krajina Serb forces with side arms only, and the safe passage of civilians from the area.

A total of 98 United Nations observation posts were overrun and destroyed by the Croatian Army during its offensive in Sectors North and South. Reports indicated that Croatian soldiers directly and indirectly fired upon observation posts, used peace-keepers as human shields, arrested and temporarily disarmed United Nations soldiers and took United Nations equipment. In all, three United Nations peace-keepers died as a result of actions by Croatian troops during the offensive and one died as a result of action by Krajina Serbs. In addition, 16 peace-keepers were injured. These incidents were vigorously protested by UNPF.

In response to the deteriorating military situation that was threatening the security of United Nations troops in Sector South, a request was made on 4 August 1995 for NATO air presence over the sector. This was granted by the Theatre Force Commander in order to deter hostile action against United Nations personnel. For its part, the Security Council demanded[9] that the Government of Croatia fully respect the status of United Nations personnel, refrain from any attacks against them, bring to justice those responsible for any such attacks, and ensure the safety and freedom of movement of United Nations personnel at all times.

Following the launching of the Croatian offensive, the situation in Sector East — Eastern Slavonia, Baranja and Western Sirmium — deteriorated rapidly. Local Serb forces and the Croatian Army exchanged artillery, mortar and small arms fire, and units from both sides deployed into the zone of separation. The situation became increasingly tense as events in Sectors North and South unfolded. The level of uncertainty was reflected in a breakdown of law and order which saw the hijacking of United Nations vehicles, harassment of United Nations personnel and the temporary detention of five Sector headquarters staff.

Both the Croatian Army and local Serb forces adopted an aggressive stance towards UNCRO personnel stationed in Sector East. Sixteen United Nations observation posts were taken over; 14 by the Croatian Army and 2 by the Serb forces. In addition, both sides fired on UNCRO positions, with one peace-keeper being wounded by direct fire from local Serb forces. Severe restrictions on all United Nations movements were imposed by both sides. This, as well as local lawlessness, severely hampered the ability of UNCRO to implement its mandate.

The mass exodus of the Krajina Serb population created a humanitarian crisis of significant proportions. As many as 200,000 people, more than 90 per cent of the Serb population of the area, fled former Sectors North and South following the Croatian offensive. Most of the refugees (approximately 150,000) fled to the Federal Republic of Yugoslavia (Serbia and Montenegro). A group of up to 15,000 moved to the area of Banja Luka in Bosnia and Herzegovina. Simultaneously, another group of refugees, numbering approximately 21,000 and consisting largely of Bosnian Muslims from the former "Autonomous Province of Western Bosnia", led by Mr. Abdic, made its way north from Velika Kladusa into Croatia. As a result of the massive influx of Krajina Serb refugees in the Banja Luka area in Bosnia and Herzegovina, harassment of members of the minority Croat and Muslim communities there intensified and they began to leave the area in large numbers. Reports of expulsions of Bosnian Croats and Muslims from their homes in the area continued.

On 6 August, the Secretary-General's Special Representative concluded a nine-point agreement[10] with the head of the Croatian Commission for Relations with UNCRO to allow the United Nations, together with other international organizations, to cope with the humanitarian difficulties, to monitor the human rights situation and to permit the safe return of displaced persons in the Krajina and Western Slavonia.

The Special Representative established a humanitarian crisis cell to collate information and coordinate responses. The cell, composed of UNPF

[9]S/RES/1009 (1995). [10]S/1995/666, annex III.

staff, communicated with all international agencies involved in humanitarian affairs and coordinated the work of four human rights action teams in the field led by officers of the Centre for Human Rights. In accordance with the 6 August agreement, the role of these teams was to report on the observance of human rights. Following the Croatian offensive in the Krajina, numerous violations of human rights of the Serb population were reported, including killing of civilians during and after the military operation, massive burning and looting of property belonging to Croatian Serbs, harassment and ill-treatment of civilians, and inadequate care and protection of the remaining Serb population, composed mainly of vulnerable persons. Alarmed by this situation, the Security Council demanded[11] that the Government of Croatia immediately investigate all such reports and take appropriate measures to put an end to such acts.

Implications for UNCRO

Croatia's reintegration by force of the former Sectors West, South and North effectively eliminated the need for United Nations infantry battalions in these areas. The Theatre Force Commander therefore initiated the immediate reduction of UNCRO's troop strength to within the authorized ceiling of 8,750 troops. In addition, the Secretary-General recommended[12] that the Security Council approve the further repatriation, during the remainder of the existing mandate, of all remaining battalions, except the two in Sector East.

The mandate of UNCRO in Sector East remained essentially unchanged. Its implementation had, however, been seriously affected by high levels of tension, lack of cooperation by both sides, and a volatile military situation that had persisted since the Croatian offensive into Sector West in May 1995. The Secretary-General reported[13] to the Security Council that neither of the parties had objected in principle to the continued application in Sector East of the cease-fire agreement of 29 March 1994. But he warned that if UNCRO's presence in Sector East was to be made effective, it was essential that both sides reaffirm their commitment to existing agreements and cooperate with UNCRO in stabilizing the military situation and reducing tension. Unless there was a significant change in the attitude of the parties, and much improved cooperation with UNCRO in enabling it to fulfil its existing mandate, including border monitoring and patrolling on both sides of

the confrontation line, the continuation of UNCRO's deployment in Sector East would be difficult to justify.

In the course of September, further discussions on UNCRO's tasks were held with the Croatian Government, with Serb leaders in Belgrade and local Serb authorities in Sector East. On the basis of these consultations, the Secretary-General reported[14] to the Security Council on 29 September.

The plan proposed for Sector East envisaged that UNCRO would perform fully the functions under the Cease-fire Agreement of 29 March 1994; facilitate the implementation of the sections of the Economic Agreement of 2 December 1994 which were relevant to Sector East and arranging local economic initiatives as appropriate; facilitate the implementation of all relevant Security Council resolutions, in particular the continuation of confidence-building and humanitarian tasks, such as assistance to refugees and displaced persons and the monitoring of the treatment of ethnic minorities; and assist in controlling, by monitoring and reporting, the crossing of military personnel, equipment, supplies and weapons, over the international borders between the Republic of Croatia and the Federal Republic of Yugoslavia (Serbia and Montenegro) at the border crossings in Sector East where UNCRO was deployed.

Elsewhere in Croatia, UNCRO would monitor the demilitarization of the Prevlaka peninsula in accordance with Security Council resolution 779 (1992); and observe and report on military incidents in the vicinity of the international border between the Republic of Croatia and the Republic of Bosnia and Herzegovina.

The Security Council agreed[15] with the proposed arrangements for UNCRO for the remainder of its mandate, which was due to expire on 30 November 1995, pending, in the case of Eastern Slavonia, Baranja and Western Sirmium (Sector East), the outcome of negotiations on the subject.

In the meantime, after intensive consultations with both sides, the Special Representative was assured by the parties that they were willing to resolve the issue of Sector East through negotiation. In addition, both sides undertook to improve their level of compliance with existing agreements, and with specific regard to cooperation with UNCRO. The Croatian Government stated that Croatian Serbs were welcome to live in

[11]S/PRST/1995/44. [12]S/1995/730. [13]S/1995/730. [14]S/1995/835. [15]S/1995/859.

Croatia and that those Serbs who had fled following the recapture of Sectors West, North and South were welcome to return.

Termination of UNCRO's mandate

In the following weeks, against a background of rising military tension in Sector East and repeated statements by Croatian authorities of their intention to recapture the area if negotiations for a peaceful reintegration were unsuccessful, UNCRO sought to uphold the integrity of the zone of separation between the two sides and to monitor the conditions of minorities in the former United Nations protected areas of Sectors South, North and West. At the same time, it was withdrawing and repatriating all United Nations military personnel from the former sectors and closing the Sector headquarters and UNCRO military headquarters. United Nations military observers in the Prevlaka and Dubrovnik areas helped to control tensions in these potentially explosive regions.

As of mid-November 1995, UNCRO's overall strength was 6,581 troops and military support personnel, 164 military observers and 296 civilian police. Deployment was as follows: Sector East — 1,605 troops, 48 military observers and 16 civilian police; former Sector North — 591 troops, 31 military observers and 61 civilian police; former Sector South — 540 troops, 34 military observers and 71 civilian police; former Sector West — 165 troops, 12 military observers and 99 civilian police. There were also 3,386 military support personnel. In addition, UNCRO's headquarters in Zagreb, Split and Ploce included 294 troops, 39 military observers and 49 civilian police.

Following the signing of the Basic Agreement on the Region of Eastern Slavonia, Baranja and Western Sirmium [see chapter 23] on 12 November 1995, the Security Council expressed[16] its readiness to consider expeditiously the request to establish a transitional administration and authorize an appropriate international force. The Council requested[17] the Secretary-General to submit a report on all aspects of an operation consisting of a transitional administration and a transitional peace-keeping force to implement the Basic Agreement. It also decided that, in order to allow for the orderly establishment of such an operation, the mandate of UNCRO would terminate after an interim period ending on 15 January 1996 or when the Council had decided on the deployment of the transitional peace-keeping force, whichever was sooner.

UNTAES and UNMOP established

In his report[18] on the aspects of establishing a transitional administration and transitional peace-keeping force in Eastern Slavonia, Baranja and Western Sirmium, submitted to the Security Council on 13 December, the Secretary-General stated that the operation as envisaged in the Basic Agreement would be a complex and difficult one. He recalled that the past record of the parties to the Agreement in honouring their commitments was not encouraging. Also, with the Agreement's imprecise nature and risk of differing interpretations, ready compliance could not be assumed. The force deployed must therefore have a mandate under Chapter VII of the Charter, must have the capacity to take the necessary action to maintain peace and security, must be sufficiently credible to deter attack from any side and must be capable of defending itself. In the Secretary-General's view, the minimum strength needed to implement the Basic Agreement and deter attacks from other forces in the region would require a mechanized division of two brigades, with combat capability, air support and a strong armoured reserve, comprising 9,300 combat and 2,000 logistics troops.

"Anything less than a well-armed division-sized force would only risk repeating the failures of the recent past", the Secretary-General stated. "The concept of deterrence by mere presence, as attempted in the 'safe areas' in Bosnia and Herzegovina, would be no likelier to succeed on this occasion. Should there be a mismatch between the international force's mandate and its resources, there would be a risk of failure, of international casualties, and of undermined credibility for those who had put the force in the field." The Secretary-General expressed the view that the deployment and command of the force would best be entrusted to a coalition of Member States rather than to the United Nations. The Council could authorize Member States to establish such a force.

However, if the Council instead accepted some Member States' preference for the Agreement to be implemented by the United Nations, its force should have a Chapter VII mandate, a combat capability and air support. Arguing that the United Nations would find it hard to assemble and deploy such a force in the time-frame envisaged by the parties, he expressed reservations about the Organization's ability to undertake such an enforce-

[16]S/RES/1023 (1995). [17]S/RES/1025 (1995). [18]S/1995/1028.

ment operation. Still, the Council had the option of entrusting the operation to a United Nations force. He cautioned that the mission would not succeed without active and sustained political support from the Council, as well as the immediate provision by Members States of troops and guarantees of adequate funding.

The Basic Agreement, the Secretary-General noted, also requested the Security Council to set up a transitional administration to govern the region for an initial period of 12 months, which could be extended to two years at the request of one of the parties. The transitional administration was to help reintegrate the region peacefully into Croatia's legal and constitutional system. The Secretary-General proposed that the administration be led by the "transitional administrator", a United Nations official working under and reporting to him. If the international force was a United Nations force, it would be under the authority of the transitional administrator.

Regarding the administration's structure, the Secretary-General proposed that it should have a transitional council, chaired by the administrator. The council would include a representative each of Croatia's Government, local Serbs, local Croats and other local minorities. It would be solely advisory, with executive power in the hands of the administrator who would set up implementation committees on the police, civil administration, restoration of public services, education and culture, the return of displaced persons, human rights, elections and records.

Recalling resolution 1025 (1995), the Secretary-General said that the mandate of UNCRO would lapse on 15 January 1996, and the United Nations military observers and civilian police monitors performing these functions would be withdrawn. However, and on the basis of consultations with the parties in the area, he recommended that the monitoring of the demilitarization of the Prevlaka peninsula in accordance with Council resolution 779 (1992) continue. He also proposed that the authorized strength of this United Nations military observer operation be increased from 14 to 28. That would permit it to be self-sufficient, to more reliably patrol the areas concerned and to maintain liaison teams in Dubrovnik and Herzeg Novi.

After having considered the Secretary-General's report, the Security Council decided, by adopting its resolution 1037 (1996) of 15 January, to establish for an initial period of 12 months a United Nations peace-keeping operation, with both military and civilian components, under the name "United Nations Transitional Administration for Eastern Slavonia, Baranja and Western Sirmium" (UNTAES). The Council also decided that the military component of UNTAES would have an initial deployment of 5,000 troops; that Member States, acting nationally or through regional organizations, might take all necessary measures, including close air support to defend or help withdraw UNTAES, and that such actions would be based on UNTAES' request and procedures communicated to the United Nations. UNTAES and the multinational implementation force (IFOR) in Bosnia and Herzegovina were requested to cooperate with each other and with the High Representative [see below].

The Council decided that the demilitarization of the region, as provided in the Basic Agreement, should be completed within 30 days from the date the Secretary-General informed the Council that the military component of UNTAES had been deployed and was ready to undertake its mission. The component would then supervise and facilitate the demilitarization of the region, according to the schedule and procedures to be established by UNTAES; monitor the voluntary and safe return of refugees and displaced persons to their home of origin in cooperation with UNHCR; contribute, by its presence, to the maintenance of peace and security in the region; and otherwise assist in implementation of the Basic Agreement.

The civilian component of UNTAES would establish a temporary police force, define its structure and size, develop a training programme and oversee its implementation, and monitor treatment of offenders and the prison system; undertake tasks relating to civil administration; undertake tasks relating to the functioning of public services; facilitate the return of refugees; organize elections, assist in their conduct, and certify the results. The component would also undertake other activities relevant to the basic Agreement, including assistance in the coordination of plans for the development and economic reconstruction of the Region; and monitoring of the parties' compliance with their commitments to respect the highest standards of human rights and fundamental freedoms, promote an atmosphere of confidence among all local residents irrespective of their ethnic origin, monitor and facilitate the demining of territory within the Region, and maintain an active public affairs element.

The Council further stressed that UNTAES would cooperate with the International Criminal Tribunal for the Former Yugoslavia in performing its mandate, and reaffirmed that all States must cooperate with the Tribunal and its organs and comply with requests for help or order issued by a Trial Chamber of the Tribunal.

The Secretary-General estimated[19] that the costs associated with the emplacement and maintenance of the United Nations transitional administration and transitional peace-keeping force in Eastern Slavonia, Baranja and Western Sirmium for an initial period of six months would be approximately $128.5 million. This estimate provided for 5,000 contingent personnel, 600 civilian police, 469 international civilian staff and 681 locally recruited staff.

By another resolution,[20] the Council authorized United Nations military observers to continue monitoring the demilitarization of the Prevlaka peninsula for a period of three months, to be extended for an additional three months upon a report by the Secretary-General that an extension would continue to help decrease tension there. In that context, the Council requested the Secretary-General to submit to it by 15 March 1996 a report on the situation in the Prevlaka peninsula as well as on the progress made by Croatia and the Federal Republic of Yugoslavia towards a peaceful settlement of their differences. The report should also examine the possibility that the existing mandate be extended or that another international organization might assume the task of monitoring the demilitarization of the peninsula.

Twenty-eight United Nations military observers in the Prevlaka area would be under the command and direction of a Chief Military Observer, who would report directly to United Nations Headquarters in New York. The mission would be known as United Nations Mission of Observers in Prevlaka (UNMOP).

C. UNPROFOR

Cease-fire collapses

From March to November 1995, the situation in Bosnia and Herzegovina was dominated by three main developments. First, there was an unprecedented level of military activity, including offensives by all sides, accompanied by major movements of refugees and displaced persons and violations of international humanitarian law, particularly by Bosnian Serb forces. Secondly, both UNPROFOR and NATO used force against the Bosnian Serbs. Thirdly, the United States-led peace initiative, together with a country-wide decrease in fighting in October and November, provided a solid opportunity for a political solution to the conflict.

The continued lack of diplomatic progress and the breakdown in March 1995 of the 31 December 1994 cessation-of-hostilities agreement caused fighting to spread from the Bihac area to central Bosnia and Tuzla and then to Sarajevo. Bosnian Serb forces increased pressure on the city, by harassing convoys, hijacking United Nations vehicles, closing the airport to humanitarian and civilian traffic, sniping and firing heavy weapons at the Mount Igman road. Government forces were also responsible for a number of incidents. Fighting around Sarajevo further intensified after the cessation-of-hostilities agreement had expired on 1 May 1995, despite the persistent efforts of the Special Representative to obtain its renewal. The use of heavy weapons by the two sides and sustained shelling of Sarajevo resulted in numerous civilian and UNPROFOR casualties and mounting calls for stricter enforcement of the exclusion zone. Although by mid-May, UNPROFOR had managed to restore some stability, tension persisted.

On 24 May 1995, after Bosnian Serb forces had removed several heavy weapons from a weapons collection point, fighting erupted again, with Bosnian Serb forces firing heavy weapons from within a number of weapons collection points and the government forces firing from various positions within Sarajevo. A statement by the Secretary-General's Special Representative emphasizing the seriousness of the situation was followed by a warning by the Commander of UNPROFOR to the Bosnian Government and the Bosnian Serb party that their forces would be attacked from the air if, by 1200 hours the next day, all heavy weapons did not cease firing and the Bosnian Serbs did not return them to collection points. A second deadline, 24 hours later, was established for the removal out of range, or the placement in weapons

---

[19]S/1995/1028/Add.1. [20]S/RES/1038 (1996).

collection points, of all heavy weapons that had been introduced into the area by the two sides.

After the failure of the Bosnian Serbs to respect the deadline for the return of heavy weapons, two NATO air strikes, on 25 and 26 May, were conducted against an ammunition dump near Pale. Bosnian Serb forces reacted by surrounding additional weapons collection points. They also took over 300 UNPROFOR personnel as hostages, using some of them as human shields to deter further air attacks on potential targets. They also cut electricity to the city. Fighting between UNPROFOR troops and the Bosnian Serbs erupted on 27 May, when Bosnian Serb elements seized an observation post at the Vrbanja bridge in Sarajevo and detained some United Nations soldiers. The position was recaptured by UNPROFOR at the cost of 2 dead and 14 wounded; on the Bosnian Serb side there were also casualties.

As to the second deadline, constraints on observation from both the ground and the air made it difficult to verify compliance by both sides. While relative calm returned to Sarajevo, the situation with respect to UNPROFOR detainees remained uncertain and dangerous. For these reasons, it was decided to review the situation before considering further military action. The hostage crisis was subsequently resolved through negotiations.

Options for UNPROFOR

At the end of May 1995, United Nations forces in the Sarajevo area found themselves in complete isolation and targeted by both sides. UNPROFOR had also lost control over heavy weapons in collection points from which its personnel had been removed and was subjected to further restrictions on its freedom of movement. There was a complete breakdown in negotiations to re-open Sarajevo airport and utilities were again being cut. The problem of resupply in Sarajevo and the eastern enclaves was further aggravated. Moreover, the ability of United Nations forces to operate effectively, efficiently and safely throughout much of Bosnia and Herzegovina, on the basis of impartiality and the consent of all parties, was seriously compromised.

Reporting[21] to the Security Council on 30 May, the Secretary-General stated that UNPROFOR's role was untenable and had to be changed. The United Nations faced a truly defining moment in its reaction to events in Bosnia and Herzegovina. Three interconnected objectives represented the Organization's very essence: the quest for peace, the protection of human life and the rejection of a culture of death.

The Secretary-General put forward a number of options for consideration by the Council, including a revision of the mandate so that it included only those tasks that a peace-keeping operation could realistically be expected to perform in the prevailing circumstances. Those would include good offices, liaison and negotiation; monitoring cease-fires, etc. as long as the parties remained willing to implement them; maintaining a presence in the safe areas, after negotiating appropriate regimes for them but without any actual or implied commitment to use force to deter attacks against them; operation of Sarajevo airport with the consent of the parties; facilitating the normalization of life in Sarajevo; escorting humanitarian convoys and supporting other humanitarian activities; border monitoring, if accepted by the parties; and the use of force, including air power, only in self-defence. This revision would probably require some redeployment and could eventually lead to a reduction in UNPROFOR's strength. It would also reduce the risks to which UNPROFOR personnel were exposed in the safe areas, at weapons collection points and elsewhere when air power was used at the Force's request. It would give UNPROFOR a realistic mandate that would enable it to help to contain the situation in Bosnia and Herzegovina without creating expectations that it could either enforce an end to the war or join it to fight on the side of one of the parties.

The option of withdrawal would be tantamount to abandonment of the people of Bosnia and Herzegovina and an admission of the United Nations inability to help to resolve the war. As for maintaining the status quo, UNPROFOR's effectiveness would be further reduced and would bring more United Nations casualties and more damage to the Organization's credibility. UNPROFOR's use of force would not be appropriate for a peace-keeping operation. It would be necessary to replace UNPROFOR with a multinational force authorized by the Council but under the command of one or more of the countries contributing troops to it, as had been the case in Somalia and Haiti.

The Secretary-General warned, however, that any option which would involve the continuing presence of UNPROFOR in Bosnia and Herzegovina would need to be accompanied by measures, including the possible deployment of additional forces, to provide better security both for UNPROFOR personnel and for the personnel

[21]S/1995/444.

of UNHCR and other civilian agencies. He added that decisions by the Council on the future of UNPROFOR should be accompanied by a significant new political initiative, possibly in a new format.

Rapid Reaction Force

A group of countries (France, the Netherlands and the United Kingdom) expressed[22] their readiness to provide military reinforcements for UNPROFOR in order to reduce the vulnerability of its personnel and to enhance its capacity to carry out its existing mandate.

Under the proposal, the tasks of the rapid reaction force (RRF) could include: emergency actions and responses to assist isolated or threatened United Nations units; helping redeployment of elements of UNPROFOR; and facilitating freedom of movement where necessary. RRF would be an integral part of UNPF/UNPROFOR, would be financed through normal peace-keeping assessments, and would be under the existing United Nations chain of command. RRF would operate under existing United Nations rules of engagement. The proposal stated that while the rapid reaction force gave the commander a capacity between "strong protest and air strikes", it would not change the United Nations role from peace-keeping to peace enforcement. The status of UNPROFOR and its impartiality would not be affected.

The Secretary-General recommended that the Security Council accept the proposal. In his view, the proposed reinforcement would enhance UNPROFOR's ability to continue its humanitarian efforts, with less danger to its personnel.[23] The troops proposed for RRF amounted to about 15,000, of whom 2,500 were already in the theatre, necessitating an increase in the ceiling for UNPROFOR's strength by 12,500. The total authorized strength of United Nations Peace Forces in the former Yugoslavia would then rise from 44,870 all ranks to 57,370 all ranks, including a stand-by force in France of 4,000 troops. The cost of the increase was estimated at $414.3 million for a 6-month period.[24]

The Security Council, by its resolution 998 (1995) of 16 June, welcomed the establishment of a rapid reaction force and decided accordingly to authorize an increase in UNPF/UNPROFOR personnel by up to 12,500 additional troops.

RRF was expected to become operational by 15 July. However, the Governments of Croatia and of Bosnia and Herzegovina took the position that RRF troops were not covered by the Status of Forces Agreement (SOFA) covering other UNPF/UNPROFOR troop deployments, significantly delaying deployment of major RRF elements. Moreover, those RRF elements already inside Bosnia and Herzegovina encountered restrictions on their movements. The Secretary-General warned[25] that those delays and restrictions could have serious consequences for the effectiveness of the United Nations mission in Bosnia and Herzegovina. On 19 August, the Security Council called[26] on the two Governments immediately to remove all impediments to give clear undertakings concerning the freedom of movement and provision of facilities for the force. It further called upon them to resolve forthwith within the framework of the existing SOFAs any outstanding difficulties with the relevant United Nations authorities.

Srebrenica and Zepa fall

After the adoption of resolution 998 (1995), the situation further deteriorated. Intense fighting in and around Sarajevo resumed, involving the use of mortars and heavy machine-guns. There were also reports regarding the Bosnian Government build-up north of the city. Freedom of movement of UNPROFOR continued to be severely restricted by both sides. On several occasions, UNPROFOR and relief personnel came under direct attack in various parts of the Republic.

The humanitarian situation remained a major concern. The escalation of the conflict deeply affected UNHCR's ability to continue to provide assistance in Bosnia and Herzegovina, to the point that operations became almost completely blocked in Bosnian Serb-held territories as well as in the eastern enclaves. UNPROFOR and UNHCR warned of developing humanitarian disasters in Sarajevo, Bihac, Gorazde, Srebrenica and Zepa. Due to obstructive actions by Bosnian Serb forces, humanitarian supplies and relief personnel had difficulty in reaching those areas. In June, UNHCR was able to deliver only 20 per cent of targeted supplies to the six safe areas and only 8 per cent to Sarajevo.

On 6 July, the Bosnian Serbs launched a full-scale assault against the safe area of Srebrenica. UNPROFOR positions were overrun. During and after the offensive a large number of human rights abuses were inflicted on the population, including mass arbitrary detention of civilian men and boys, and summary executions. An estimated 25,000

---

[22]S/1995/470, annex. [23]S/1995/470. [24]S/1995/470/Add.1. [25]S/1995/707. [26]S/PRST/1995/40.

people were forcibly evacuated on a convoy of buses and trucks organized by the Bosnian Serb authorities. Thousands of people were unaccounted for. Despite a call by the Security Council[27] and all efforts at the field level, adequate access to affected areas or to the detained was denied by Bosnian Serb authorities. The Council's demand[28] that the Bosnian Serb forces cease their offensive and withdraw from the safe area of Srebrenica was also ignored.

After the fall of Srebrenica on 11 July, the Serbs began an attack on the nearby safe area of Zepa, which fell to their forces on 25 July. Deeply concerned at the plight of the civilian population in Srebrenica and Zepa, the Security Council demanded[29] that the Bosnian Serb party give immediate access for UNHCR, ICRC and other international agencies to persons displaced from those areas, and that the Bosnian Serb party permit representatives of ICRC to visit and register any persons detained against their will. The Council reiterated that all those who committed violations of international humanitarian law would be held individually responsible in respect of such acts.

On 21 July, as the Serbs were attacking Zepa, the foreign ministers of the Contact Group, NATO and UNPROFOR troop-contributing nations met in London to discuss future action in the light of the inability of UNPROFOR to deter attacks on the safe areas. Following this, the parties to the conflict, in particular the Bosnian Serbs, were warned that further violations of the safe areas would be met with decisive force, including the use of NATO air strikes.

Despite this warning, on 28 August 1995, 5 mortar rounds landed in the vicinity of Sarajevo's Markale market place, 1 of which killed 37 people and wounded more than 80 others. In order to restore the heavy weapons exclusion zone around Sarajevo and to deter any further attacks on safe areas, multiple NATO air strikes were conducted with the approval of the UNPF Force Commander against Bosnian Serb anti-aircraft systems and heavy weapons in the vicinity of Sarajevo, as well as against ammunition supply depots and other military facilities throughout eastern Bosnia. During this operation, RRF mortars and artillery engaged Bosnian Serb targets in the area of Sarajevo.

The air strikes were suspended on 14 September for three days, following an agreement signed in Belgrade by Bosnian Serb military and political leaders, in which they committed themselves to withdraw their heavy weapons from the 20-kilometre "exclusion zone" around Sarajevo. After the Bosnian Serbs fulfilled those commit-

ments and allowed the re-opening of Sarajevo airport, NATO and UNPROFOR agreed not to resume the air strikes.

In the meantime, the military situation in north-western and western Bosnia and Herzegovina had changed dramatically in August and September. In early August, Bosnian government and Bosnian Croat forces, supported by the Croatian Army, launched an offensive in north-western Bosnia and defeated the forces of the "Autonomous Republic of Western Bosnia" of rebel Muslim leader Fikret Abdic. This resulted in the exodus of some 25,000 Abdic followers to Croatia. Allegations of human rights abuses committed against Abdic followers during and after the offensive were subsequently confirmed by the Commission on Human Rights Special Rapporteur.[30]

Soon after NATO began air operations in eastern Bosnia, Bosnian government and Bosnian Croat forces began to advance in the western part of the country. In the week of 10 September 1995, Bosnian government forces took much of the Ozren salient, while, simultaneously, Bosnian Croat forces made sweeping advances in the southwest of the country, including the capture of areas traditionally populated by Bosnian Serbs. As a result of that offensive, an estimated 50,000 Bosnian Serbs were displaced to Banja Luka — a city which had already received a large number of refugees from the Krajina region in August. At the same time, the eviction of Muslim and Croat minorities from the Banja Luka area continued. The influx of thousands of displaced Bosnian Serbs further exacerbated the situation.

On 27 November 1995, at the request of the Security Council,[31] the Secretary-General submitted a report[32] according to which there was undeniable evidence that summary executions, rape, mass expulsions and large-scale disappearances had occurred around Srebrenica, Zepa, Banja Luka and Sanski Most. The full horror of atrocities had yet to be revealed, the Secretary-General said, adding that the international community should insist that the Bosnian Serb leadership cooperate fully with all relevant international mechanisms so that the events might be thoroughly investigated and the truth established. The International Tribunal for the Former Yugoslavia must have the ability to perform the task for which it had been created.

"The moral responsibility of the international community is heavy indeed," the Secretary-General concluded. "The world surely must not

[27]S/PRST/1995/32.   [28]S/RES/1004 (1995).   [29]S/RES/1010 (1995).   [30]A/50/727, S/1995/933. [31]S/RES/1019 (1995). [32]S/1995/988.

allow such acts to go unpunished, wherever and by whomever they are committed. If it does, these and similar crimes will happen again."

Country-wide cease-fire agreement

The peace initiative undertaken by the United States with the support of the Security Council, the Contact Group and the Co-Chairmen of the ICFY Steering Committee, resulted on 5 October 1995 in a country-wide cease-fire agreement. UNPROFOR military and civilian personnel immediately undertook various measures to ensure the successful implementation of the agreement, including de-mining activities that were necessary for the repair and reopening of utilities for Sarajevo. The Chief of Mission of UNPROFOR, Mr. Antonio Pedauye, conducted the negotiations that led to the entry into force of the cease-fire on 12 October 1995.

After 12 October, neither side engaged in offensive activity, and all parties participated constructively in joint military commissions. United Nations military observers were allowed to operate in Bosnian Serb-held areas, and UNPROFOR and humanitarian convoys, as well as escorted civilian vehicles, moved freely in and out of Sarajevo and Gorazde. Sarajevo airport resumed its operations and operated safely and without hindrance. Releases of prisoners of war and detainees took place. However, restrictions were still being imposed by Bosnian Croat military units on UNPROFOR patrols in north-western Bosnia. Some restrictions on UNPROFOR movement were also imposed by Bosnian Government forces and Bosnian Serb forces.

Peace agreement

The diplomatic initiative to end the Bosnian conflict culminated in talks held in Dayton, Ohio in November 1995 [see chapter 23]. On 21 November, the Peace Agreement was initialled and, on 14 December, formally signed at a ceremony in Paris.[33]

Along with plans for the withdrawal of UNPROFOR, the agreement included a request by the parties — the Republic of Bosnia and Herzegovina, the Republic of Croatia, the Federal Republic of Yugoslavia, the Federation of Bosnia and Herzegovina and the Republika Srpska — to the Security Council to adopt a resolution authorizing Member States or regional organizations and arrangements to establish a multinational military Implementation Force (IFOR) to help ensure compliance with the provisions of the Peace Agreement. IFOR would be composed of ground, air and maritime units from the members of NATO and from non-NATO States. The parties also requested the Security Council to establish a United Nations International Police Task Force (IPTF).

The Secretary-General subsequently recommended[34] that IPTF central and regional headquarters should, where possible, be co-located with IFOR headquarters. On the basis of a ratio of 1 monitor to 30 local police officers and taking into account the need to monitor parts of the judicial and prison systems, the recommended civilian police structure, including supervisory personnel at all locations, would require a total of 1,721 police monitors. It was estimated[35] that the cost associated with the emplacement and maintenance of IPTF, which would also include 254 international staff and 811 locally recruited staff, for an initial period of six months would be approximately $90 million.

IPTF tasks would include: (a) monitoring, observing and inspecting law enforcement activities and facilities, including associated judicial organizations, structures and proceedings; (b) advising law enforcement personnel and forces; (c) training law enforcement personnel; (d) facilitating, within the IPTF mission of assistance, the parties' law enforcement activities; (e) assessing threats to public order and advising on the capability of law enforcement agencies to deal with such threats; (f) advising government authorities in Bosnia and Herzegovina on the organization of effective civilian law enforcement agencies; and (g) assisting by accompanying the parties' law enforcement personnel as they carry out their responsibilities, as the Task Force deems appropriate. In addition, the Task Force would consider requests from the parties or law enforcement agencies in Bosnia and Herzegovina for assistance, with priority being given to assisting the parties in carrying out their responsibility to ensure the existence of conditions for free and fair elections, including the protection of international personnel in Bosnia and Herzegovina in connection with the elections provided for in the Peace Agreement.

Final extension of UNPROFOR's mandate

Reporting[36] to the Security Council on 23 November, the Secretary-General pointed to UNPROFOR's improved ability to carry out its

[33]S/1995/999. [34]A/1995/987. [35]S/1995/1031/Add.1. [36]S/1995/987.

mandate, due primarily to the revitalization of the peace process and enhanced compliance by the parties with the cease-fire of 12 October. The assumption by President Milosevic of the authority to conduct negotiations on behalf of the Republika Srpska was also an important factor. Another critical element was the increased deterrence achieved as a result of the manner in which NATO air power and the rapid reaction force were employed in August and September, following redeployments that greatly reduced UNPROFOR's vulnerability throughout Bosnia and Herzegovina.

During the transition to IFOR, a primary task for UNPROFOR would be to arrange for the transfer of responsibility. The Secretary-General accepted the recommendations of his Special Representative and the Force Commander that only essential UNPROFOR forces should be retained. He recommended that UNPROFOR's existing mandate be extended for two months, or until an appropriate transfer of authority. By its resolution 1026 (1995) of 30 November, the Council extended the mandate of UNPROFOR until 31 January 1996.

IFOR and UNMIBH

The Secretary-General then informed[37] the Council of his intention to appoint a United Nations official to serve in Sarajevo under the Secretary-General's authority as the United Nations Coordinator. The Coordinator would exercise authority over the IPTF Commissioner and coordinate other United Nations activities in Bosnia and Herzegovina, maintaining close liaison with the High Representative.

In the Secretary-General's view, it would be appropriate to dissolve the International Conference on the Former Yugoslavia as well as its Steering Committee not later than 31 January 1996. However, the ICFY Mission on the border between the Federal Republic of Yugoslavia and Bosnia and Herzegovina, and such of the ICFY working groups as were still required, would continue their work, with their existing terms of reference, reporting to the High Representative. The office of the Special Coordinator for Sarajevo should be subsumed, with effect from 30 April 1996, in arrangements for rehabilitation to be established by the World Bank, the European Commission and others. The Secretary-General further recommended that UNPROFOR's responsibilities concerning monitoring of the ban on military flights in the airspace of Bosnia and Herzegovina be discontinued and that responsibility for operating Sarajevo airport, Tuzla airport and other airfields be transferred to IFOR.

As regards UNPF, the Secretary-General believed that the time had come to wind down its headquarters in Zagreb and to make the three United Nations operations in the former Yugoslavia fully independent of one another. At the same time, it was clear that the complex and time-consuming process of dismantling elements of UNPROFOR and UNCRO, handing over to IFOR and mounting new civilian operations in Bosnia and Herzegovina and in Croatia would necessitate the retention of a coordinated civilian and military capacity at UNPF headquarters in Zagreb for at least six months beyond the expiry of the mandates of UNPROFOR and UNCRO. He intended to restructure and drastically reduce the civilian and military personnel of the headquarters, including the Office of the Special Representative, which could be phased out by the end of February 1996. In view of the complex interrelationships between the three missions and all the parties in the mission area, it was considered essential that there continue to be small but adequately staffed United Nations liaison offices in Zagreb and Belgrade.

The Secretary-General stressed the need for continuity of the mines information networks and databases established by the Mine Action Centre at UNPF headquarters in Zagreb. He therefore proposed that four military mines information officers remain for the time being in Bosnia and Herzegovina to maintain accurate and up-to-date records under the direction of the United Nations coordinator.

The Secretary-General welcomed the agreement of the London Peace Implementation Conference that the High Representative or his representative should chair a human rights task force in Sarajevo. He noted that the United Nations High Commissioner for Human Rights had identified three areas in which experience gained from existing efforts in Bosnia and Herzegovina could contribute to the process: training of personnel charged with human rights monitoring; making available to the High Representative a limited number of experienced and trained human rights officers; and continuing to support the work of the Special Rapporteur and the Expert on the special process dealing with missing persons in the former Yugoslavia, both of them appointed by the Commission on Human Rights.

OSCE was entrusted by the Peace Agreement with responsibility for electoral aspects; the

[37]S/1995/1031.

United Nations would be ready to make available to OSCE technical advice based on its extensive experience in providing such assistance. The Secretary-General went on to say that while the World Bank and the European Commission would take the lead in international efforts for rehabilitation and reconstruction in Bosnia and Herzegovina, he had no doubt that the specialized agencies and other programmes, funds and offices of the United Nations would be ready to play their usual part in such endeavours.

By its resolution 1031 (1995) of 15 December, the Security Council, acting under Chapter VII of the Charter, authorized Member States to establish IFOR, under unified control and command and composed of ground, air and maritime units from NATO and non-NATO nations. The Council also authorized Member States concerned to take all necessary measures to effect implementation of the Peace Agreement and ensure compliance with its provisions. It stressed that the parties to the Agreement would be held equally responsible for such compliance, and equally subject to such enforcement action by IFOR as might be necessary to ensure implementation of the Peace Agreement and the protection of IFOR. Demanding that the parties respect the security and freedom of movement of IFOR and other international personnel, the Council recognized IFOR's right to take all necessary measures to defend itself from attack or threat of attack.

The Security Council decided to review the situation one year after the transfer of authority from UNPROFOR to IFOR, in order to determine whether to end the authorizations granted by the resolution. It further decided to terminate UNPROFOR's mandate with effect from the day the Secretary-General reported to it that the transfer of authority from UNPROFOR to IFOR had taken place. It approved the arrangements set out by the Secretary-General on the withdrawal of UNPROFOR and headquarters elements from UNPF headquarters. At the same time, it stipulated that civilian, police, de-mining and other personnel required to carry out the tasks outlined by the Secretary-General should remain in theatre. It also decided to act swiftly on the Secretary-General's recommendation on the establishment of a United Nations civilian police force in Bosnia and Herzegovina.

In a separate resolution[38] adopted on 21 December, the Security Council decided to establish IPTF and a United Nations civilian office for a period of one year from the transfer of authority from UNPROFOR to IFOR. Subsequently, this operation became known as the United Nations Mission in Bosnia and Herzegovina (UNMIBH).

IFOR takes over from UNPROFOR

In keeping with the Peace Agreement and Security Council resolution 1031 (1995), UNPROFOR began withdrawing from Bosnia and Herzegovina those parts of the Force which were not to be incorporated into IFOR. UNPROFOR also facilitated preparations for the arrival of IFOR. On 20 December 1995,[39] the transfer of authority from UNPROFOR to IFOR took place, with the IFOR commander, Admiral Leighton Smith (United States), assuming command. At that date a number of UNPROFOR troops had already left the theatre as part of a restructuring exercise and, of the approximately 21,000 UNPROFOR and rapid reaction force troops that remained, about 18,500 were designated to stay on as part of IFOR. The repatriation of the remaining 2,500 troops began in late December 1995.

As of mid-January 1996, over 50 per cent of the ground component of IFOR, numbering more than 35,000 troops, were deployed. Fifteen of the 16 NATO countries contributed forces to IFOR; Iceland contributed medical personnel. In addition, the NATO Secretary General issued written invitations to 16 non-NATO countries to contribute forces to IFOR. These were Austria, the Czech Republic, Egypt, Estonia, Finland, Hungary, Latvia, Lithuania, Malaysia, Pakistan, Poland, Romania, the Russian Federation, Slovakia, Sweden and Ukraine. Discussions were also under way concerning possible force contributions from Bulgaria, Bangladesh, Morocco and Jordan.

As to the new United Nations mission in Bosnia and Herzegovina, a number of steps were taken to establish it as quickly as possible. Mr. Antonio Pedauye was appointed Interim United Nations Coordinator for UNMIBH from 5 to 31 January and was succeeded by Mr. Iqbal Riza who was appointed Special Representative of the Secretary-General and Coordinator of United Nations Operations in Bosnia and Herzegovina on 1 February 1996. In conjunction with the end of the UNCRO mandate, most of the remaining United Nations civilian police monitors in Croatia were redeployed. At the end of January 1996, there were about 230 monitors in Bosnia and Herzegovina, deployed under the supervision of Commissioner Peter FitzGerald, who arrived in theatre on 29 January.

[38]S/RES/1035 (1995). [39]S/1995/1050.

As at 22 January, 43 of the 51 Member States approached by the Secretariat had responded, offering a total of 1,970 monitors for employment with IPTF.

Conclusion

Since the start of its deployment in Bosnia and Herzegovina, UNPROFOR's mandate was plagued by ambiguities that affected the Force's performance as well as its credibility with the parties, with the members of the Security Council and with the public at large. UNPROFOR was not a peace-enforcement operation in spite of references to Chapter VII of the Charter of the United Nations in some Security Council resolutions relating to its mandate. In May 1995, the Secretary-General told[40] the Security Council that many of the concerns raised by members of the Council and the Government of the Republic of Bosnia and Herzegovina on the implementation of the mandate reflected this confusion.

UNPROFOR was not deployed to end the war in Bosnia and Herzegovina. In the Secretary-General's view, that was a task for the peacemakers. Nor was it an army sent out to fight on one side in the war, though it was often criticized as if it had failed to prosecute a war effectively. It was, instead, a mission deployed by the Security Council to fulfil three purposes: to alleviate the consequences of the war, notably through helping in the provision of humanitarian aid; to contain the conflict, and mitigate its consequences, by imposing constraints on the belligerents, through the establishment of such arrangements as a "no-fly zone", safe areas and exclusion zones; and to promote the prospects for peace by negotiating local cease-fires and other arrangements, maintaining these where possible and providing support for measures aimed at an overall political settlement. UNPROFOR had considerable success in fulfilling these purposes. They were not, however, an end in themselves but attempted to produce conditions that would enable the peacemakers to negotiate an overall solution.

UNPROFOR's original peace-keeping mandate, which could not be implemented without the cooperation of the parties, was gradually enlarged to include elements of enforcement. This caused it to be seen as a party to the conflict. The safe-areas mandate, for instance, required it to cooperate and negotiate daily with a party upon whom it was also expected to call air strikes in certain circumstances. Similarly, the United Nations imposed sanctions on one party but at the same time set up a Force that was obliged to work with the consent and cooperation of that party. The result was that Bosnian Serb leaders largely withdrew their consent and cooperation from UNPROFOR, declaring that they were applying their own "sanctions" to the United Nations in response to United Nations sanctions on them. UNPROFOR thus found itself obstructed, targeted by all sides, denied resupply, restricted in its movements and subjected to constant criticism.

The Secretary-General strongly disputed the allegation that the United Nations involvement in the former Yugoslavia was not a success.[41] The original and primary purpose in deploying United Nations peace-keepers in Bosnia and Herzegovina was to protect humanitarian activities. That mission was successfully carried out, thanks to the courage and dedication of the civilian workers concerned but also thanks to the protection, logistics support and other services afforded to them by UNPROFOR. In the Secretary-General's view, UNPROFOR also deserved credit for its successes in negotiating and helping to implement cease-fires and other military arrangements, without which many more people would have died and material destruction would have been even greater. The lessons learned would benefit future peacemaking and peace-keeping endeavours.

The price, however, was high, the Secretary-General continued. United Nations personnel were killed or suffered crippling injuries. The conflicts in the former Yugoslavia dominated the Organization's agenda in the peace and security field and distorted its peacemaking and peace-keeping efforts at the expense of other parts of the world. At the time of peak deployment, in August 1995, the former Yugoslavia accounted for nearly 70 per cent of peace-keepers worldwide and over two thirds of peace-keeping costs. The Secretary-General welcomed the fact that the vast task of helping to implement the Peace Agreement in Bosnia and Herzegovina would not be entrusted to the United Nations alone. Only a cooperative effort between many international organizations and Member States could generate the skills and resources and, above all, the political will required to end the fighting and start building the peace in Bosnia and Herzegovina.

[40]S/1995/444. [41]S/1995/1031.

D. UNPREDEP

Activities of UNPREDEP

Pursuant to Security Council resolution 983 (1995) of 31 March, UNPREDEP was established as a distinct operating entity in the former Yugoslav Republic of Macedonia. The resolution, however, did not change the nature of the United Nations presence in the republic nor its basic mandate, strength and troop composition.

In conjunction with its major tasks of monitoring and reporting on the situation along the borders with the Federal Republic of Yugoslavia and Albania, the military component of UNPREDEP continued to cooperate with a number of civilian agencies and offered ad hoc community services, as well as humanitarian assistance, to the local population. At the end of 1995, UNPREDEP operated 24 permanent observation posts along a 420-kilometre stretch on the Macedonian side of the border with the Federal Republic of Yugoslavia and Albania. It also operated 33 temporary observation posts. Close to 40 border and community patrols were conducted daily. The United Nations military observers complemented the work of the battalions.

In accordance with Security Council resolution 908 (1994), UNPREDEP continued to monitor developments in the country with a view to promoting reconciliation among various political and ethnic groups. The presence of civilian police monitors considerably strengthened the mission's outreach to local civil authorities and institutions, in particular the police. Civilian police also played an indispensable role in regular monitoring of areas populated by ethnic minorities. The mission's press and information unit were active in raising public awareness on the unique role of UNPREDEP as the first United Nations preventive deployment operation of its kind.

To enhance its effectiveness and fulfil its mandate, UNPREDEP cooperated with various regional organizations, including the OSCE mission established in 1992. Also, since its establishment, UNPREDEP worked closely with ICFY. This cooperation mainly involved two areas: humanitarian issues and the promotion of dialogue on human rights issues involving ethnic communities and national minorities. UNPREDEP and the Humanitarian Issues Working Group of ICFY provided a valuable framework for peacemaking, peace-building and humanitarian activities. Another area of coop-

eration related to ethnic and minority rights. In this connection, UNPREDEP and the ICFY Working Group on Ethnic and National Communities and Minorities cooperated in promoting legislative and practical improvements in favour of Albanian and other nationalities.

Mutually beneficial contacts were initiated by the UNPREDEP Commander with the military authorities of Albania and the Federal Republic of Yugoslavia. There was consent on both sides that more tolerance should be displayed during border encounters and that potentially explosive but minor border crossings would be considered as "honest mistakes". Consequently, the number of border incidents between patrols of the two sides significantly decreased.

At the end of 1995, the UNPREDEP military troop component consisted of two mechanized infantry battalions: a Nordic composite battalion and a United States Army task force, supported by a heavy engineering platoon from Indonesia. The total strength of the military component was 1,000. In addition, there were 35 United Nations military observers and 26 United Nations civilian police monitors. The authorized strength of the civilian component was 168. Civilian and military personnel were drawn from 42 nations.

Reporting[42] to the Security Council on 23 November, the Secretary-General observed that UNPREDEP's preventive deployment role had contributed greatly to the peace and stability on the former Yugoslav Republic of Macedonia and in the southern Balkans. He recommended that the mandate of UNPREDEP should be renewed for a further 12-month period irrespective of developments elsewhere in the theatre. At the same time, the Secretary-General pointed to the need to revert to the Council, as soon as practicable, on the establishment of UNPREDEP on a fully independent footing, reporting directly to United Nations Headquarters. This would require adjustments to the administrative, logistic and military support structures of the mission and thus minor adjustments to its authorized strength.

The Council extended[43] UNPREDEP's mandate for a period terminating on 30 May 1996. It also requested the Secretary-General to keep the Council regularly informed of any developments

[42]S/1995/987. [43]S/RES/1027 (1995).

on the ground and other circumstances affecting the mandate of UNPREDEP and, in the light of developments in the region, to submit a report on all aspects of UNPREDEP by 31 January 1996 for review by the Council.

Situation on the ground

In the course of 1995, the Government of the former Yugoslav Republic of Macedonia continued its internal reforms and foreign policy initiatives. Although opposition parties continued to challenge the outcome of the 1994 parliamentary elections, the ruling coalition's majority in the legislature made it possible to pass several important laws in the areas of democratization, privatization, formation of political parties, local self-government and education. The most significant single political event in the country in 1995 was the attempt, in October, on the life of President Kiro Gligorov. This terrorist act, which was unanimously condemned by all major political forces in the country, fortunately neither destabilized national life nor slowed down the process of reforms. President Gligorov resumed his official duties in January 1996.

Notwithstanding considerable progress in many areas, the political scene remained divided across ideological and ethnic lines. Political partisanship was fierce and ran particularly deep between the non-parliamentary opposition parties and the ruling coalition, on the one hand, and between the ethnic Albanian community, the government coalition and the ethnic Macedonian parties, on the other. The absence of an effective parliamentary opposition added to the political controversy, as did the lack of a viable dialogue on the country's future among the various political forces.

A complex network of ethnic problems, in particular between ethnic Macedonians and ethnic Albanians, contributed considerably to political uncertainty and social tensions. Claims and aspirations of other ethnic groups, including Rhomas, Serbs, Turks and Vlachs, also constituted a source of concern. In taking gradual steps towards reconciliation, the Government took a position that the main demands of the ethnic Albanian community (i.e. status as a constituent nation; university-level education to be conducted in Albanian, including the establishment of a special university at Tetovo; proportional representation in all institutions of public life; and recognition of Albanian as a second official language) could not be met immediately on constitutional grounds or for reasons of time

to rectify the situation. The state of the country's economy remained precarious, in part due to the cost of sanctions against the Federal Republic of Yugoslavia and that of the economic blockade from the south.

Change in UNPREDEP's status

The positive developments elsewhere in the former Yugoslavia, the termination of the mandates of UNCRO, UNPROFOR and UNPF-HQ and the establishment of two new United Nations missions in Bosnia and Herzegovina and Croatia[44] had significant practical ramifications for the functioning of UNPREDEP.

The Secretary-General reviewed the status of UNPREDEP in his 30 January 1996 report[45] and informed the Council of the Republic's strong preference for a longer extension of the mandate, since the reasons which had led to its establishment continued to exist. The Government had expressed the wish that the mission should continue until three conditions were met, namely, mutual recognition and normalization of relations with the Federal Republic of Yugoslavia and the commencement of negotiations on the demarcation of the border between the two States; the full implementation of the peace agreement in the Republic of Bosnia and Herzegovina, including its arms control and confidence-building measures; and the attainment of sufficient national indigenous defensive capability.

The Secretary-General shared the view that the continuation of the UNPREDEP mission was an important contribution to the maintenance of peace and stability in the region. Therefore he recommended to the Council that the mandate of UNPREDEP should not only be continued but that effective on 1 February 1996, it should become an independent mission, reporting directly to United Nations Headquarters in New York, while maintaining its basic mandate, strength and composition. The Security Council concurred[46] in principle with these recommendations. On 13 February 1996, by its resolution 1046 (1996), the Council authorized an increase of 50 in UNPREDEP's military strength in order to provide a continuing engineering capability in support of its operations. It also approved the establishment of the position of Force Commander of UNPREDEP.

The Secretary-General estimated[47] that the cost associated with the change in UNPREDEP's

---

[44]S/RES/1035 (1995) and S/RES/1037 (1996). [45]S/1996/65. [46]S/1996/76. [47]S/1996/94.

status for a six-month period would be $29 million. The estimate provided for 1,050 contingent personnel, 35 military observers, 26 civilian police, 73 international civilian staff and 127 locally recruited staff.

Conclusion

The United Nations operation in the former Yugoslav Republic of Macedonia has demonstrated that preventive deployment is an effective form of peace-keeping and that results can be achieved even with a small, almost symbolic deployment of United Nations peace-keepers, if it is done at the right time and with a clear mandate. In November 1995, the Secretary-General reported[48] to the Security Council that the fundamental objective of the operation, that the conflict in the former Yugoslavia be prevented from spreading, had been achieved. However, the causes that led to the establishment of the United Nations preventive deployment operation had not ceased to exist and the continued presence of UNPREDEP remained vital to the maintenance of peace and stability in the country.

[48]S/1995/987.

Part IX

Republics of the former Soviet Union

Chapter 26

United Nations Observer Mission in Georgia (UNOMIG)

Chapter 26

United Nations Observer Mission in Georgia (UNOMIG)

A. Background

The conflict in Abkhazia, strategically located on the Black Sea in the northwestern region of the Republic of Georgia, began with social unrest and the attempts by the local authorities to separate from the Republic. It escalated into a series of armed confrontations in the summer of 1992 when the Government of Georgia, concluding that the railway and certain communication links had to be protected, deployed 2,000 Georgian troops in Abkhazia. Fierce fighting broke out on 14 August 1992 when the Georgian troops entered Abkhazia, resulting in some 200 dead and hundreds wounded. The Abkhaz leadership abandoned the Abkhaz capital of Sukhumi and retreated to the town of Gudauta.

The relations between the Abkhaz and the Georgians have been tense for many decades. Historically, the Abkhaz attempted several times to separate from Georgia. Most recently, in August 1990, the Abkhaz Supreme Soviet declared Abkhazia a sovereign republic of the Soviet Union independent of Georgia. This was immediately annulled by the Georgian Supreme Soviet.

As a compromise for remaining in Georgia, the Abkhaz were given disproportionate representation in the Supreme Council of Abkhazia. At that time, of the total population in Abkhazia of 540,000, only about 18 per cent were Abkhaz. The majority were Georgian (about 47 per cent), and others included Armenians (about 18 per cent) and Russians (about 13 per cent). In December 1991, a new Supreme Council was elected, which allocated 28 seats to the Abkhaz, 26 seats to the Georgians and 11 seats to the remaining 35 per cent of the population. This did not ease the tension between the Abkhaz and Georgians. The Supreme Council split into two opposing factions, and for all intents and purposes, it ceased to function.

The 1992 cease-fire agreement

A cease-fire agreement[1] was reached on 3 September 1992 in Moscow by the Republic of Georgia, the leadership of Abkhazia and the Russian Federation. The agreement stipulated that "the territorial integrity of the Republic of Georgia shall be ensured". It also set out, as the basis of the peace settlement, a cease-fire to take effect as of 5 September 1992; the establishment of a Monitoring and Inspection Commission composed of representatives of Georgia, Abkhazia and the Russian Federation to ensure compliance with the agreement; the disarming and withdrawal of all illegal armed formations that had come from outside Georgia; the reduction of the armed forces of Georgia in Abkhazia to an agreed number required to protect railway and certain other installations; the exchange of detainees, prisoners and hostages by 10 September 1992; the removal of all impediments to the free movement of goods and persons; the return of refugees to their homes; the search for missing persons; and the resumption of the normal functions by the legitimate authorities of Abkhazia by 15 September 1992.

The agreement also included an appeal to the United Nations and the Conference on Security and Cooperation in Europe (CSCE) [now redesignated the Organization for Security and Cooperation in Europe (OSCE)] to assist in the implementation of the peace settlement. The Security Council then requested the Secretary-General to keep it informed periodically of developments in Abkhazia and took note of his intention to send a goodwill mission.

Situation deteriorates

The agreement was never fully implemented. Both sides accused one another of cease-

---

[1] S/24523, annex.

fire violations. The situation remained very tense, as confirmed by the United Nations mission to the region from 12 to 20 September 1992. On 1 October 1992, the cease-fire collapsed, and the fighting resumed in all areas. The Abkhaz forces, supported by fighters from the North Caucasus region, quickly captured the major towns, and threatened to bring nearly 80 per cent of Abkhazia, including the capital city of Sukhumi, under their control. The raging fighting forced some 30,000 civilians to flee across the border to the Russian Federation. The parties to the conflict accused one another of human rights violations committed against the civilian population.

By November 1992, the outbreak of inter-ethnic fighting in the North Caucasus region of the Russian Federation added another dimension to the already tense situation in the area.

United Nations efforts

The United Nations sought to revive the peace process by diplomatic means, consulting with CSCE so as to ensure effective coordination of activities. Secretary-General Boutros Boutros-Ghali sent a second mission in mid-October 1992 to explore specific ways in which the United Nations could support the implementation of the 3 September agreement, including the possible deployment of civilian and/or military observers. Two United Nations civilian personnel remained on the spot to provide an initial United Nations presence. In November 1992, a United Nations office opened in the Georgian capital of Tbilisi to provide an integrated United Nations approach in the region and to assist in the peace-making efforts of the Secretary-General.

It was the Secretary-General's view that more active support by the international community was required to restore the viability of the peace process. He felt, however, that dispatching another United Nations mission at that time "would not be an adequate approach in attempting to revive the peace process", and that a more concentrated effort was needed.[2]

After the necessary consultations, the Secretary-General, on 11 May 1993, appointed Mr. Edouard Brunner (Switzerland) as his Special Envoy for Georgia for an initial period of three months. Mr. Brunner's tasks, based on the 1992 agreement, were to obtain agreement on a cease-fire; to assist the parties in reviving the process of negotiations to find a political solution to the conflict; and to enlist the support of neighbouring countries and others concerned in achieving the above objectives. The Special Envoy was to consult closely with the Chairman-in-Office of CSCE.[3]

The first mission undertaken by the Special Envoy, from 20 to 31 May 1993, reaffirmed that all parties supported an active role by the United Nations in reaching a peaceful resolution to the conflict. The Secretary-General held the view, endorsed by the Security Council, that an integrated peace package should be implemented, which pursued a solution on three tracks: consolidation of the cease-fire; the launching of a political negotiating process; and support for these two processes by the neighbouring countries, particularly the Russian Federation, which had been active in mediating the conflict.

To this end, the Secretary-General proposed the deployment of United Nations military observers, as well as the holding of a peace conference under the auspices of the United Nations. The Secretary-General acknowledged the risks in deploying United Nations personnel to an area where an agreed cease-fire was not being respected. He asserted, however, that such a move was justified given the urgent need to get the conflict in Abkhazia under control.

When the Special Envoy presented the Secretary-General's approach during his mission, it was determined that the Republic of Georgia fully supported all aspects of the approach; the Abkhaz side favoured the conference but not, at the time, the deployment of military observers; and the Russian Federation favoured the deployment of United Nations military observers, but had reservations about the conference. Meanwhile, the situation on the ground deteriorated again. A cease-fire, agreed on 14 May 1993, came into effect on 20 May but held for only two weeks. Between 2 and 7 July, hospitals in the area of fighting reported that 77 Georgian soldiers were killed and 481 wounded; during the same period, 6 civilians were killed and 43 wounded. Two hundred fifty wounded Abkhaz were reportedly counted in one hospital in Gudauta by an independent observer.

Given the military situation, the Secretary-General believed it would not be wise to proceed with the actual deployment of 50 military observers, as proposed in his report of 1 July, until the cease-fire had been re-established and was being respected.[4] On 9 July 1993, the Security Council adopted resolution 849 (1993), by which it approved the deployment of military observers as soon as the cease-fire was implemented. The Secretary-General, who was asked to make necessary prepa-

[2]S/25198. [3]S/25756. [4]S/26023 and Add.1.

rations and to notify the Council when conditions permitted the deployment of the observers, announced, on 19 July, that he was sending a technical planning mission to the area.

Cease-fire is reached

On 27 July 1993, a new agreement[5] was concluded, through the mediation efforts of the Russian Federation, between the Government of Georgia and the Abkhaz authorities in Gudauta, which re-established a cease-fire as of 28 July. The agreement provided for the immediate commencement of a phased demilitarization of the conflict zone. To monitor this process, international observers were to be deployed within 10 to 15 days of the date of the cease-fire. On 4 August, the Secretary-General proposed[6] the deployment of an advance team of up to 10 observers to help verify compliance with the cease-fire, and the Security Council agreed.[7] The advance team would then become part of the observer group if the Council decided to establish one.

At the same time, the Secretary-General expressed to the Council his view that conditions permitted the deployment of the proposed military observer mission. Based on the report of the technical planning team which had been in Georgia from 19 to 26 July, the Secretary-General concluded[8] that an expanded mandate and additional military observers than had been previously envisaged would strengthen the effectiveness of the United Nations observation mission considerably. He recommended the deployment of 88 military observers and support staff without delay.

Advance team is deployed

The advance team of 9 military observers and 8 civilian support staff arrived in Abkhazia on 8 August 1993 and established its headquarters in the city of Sukhumi. The team then initiated regular road patrols to monitor compliance with the 27 July cease-fire. As envisaged, the observers established liaison with the tripartite Georgian-Abkhaz-Russian interim monitoring groups responsible for the supervision of the cease-fire on the ground. The leader of the team participated as an observer in the work of the tripartite "Joint Commission" following its establishment on 5 August. Initial reports received from the team confirmed that the cease-fire was holding.

B. August 1993–June 1994

UNOMIG is deployed

On 24 August 1993, the Security Council, by its resolution 858 (1993), decided to establish the United Nations Observer Mission in Georgia (UNOMIG), comprising up to 88 military observers, plus minimal civilian support staff. UNOMIG was given the following mandate: to verify compliance with the cease-fire agreement of 27 July with special attention to the situation in the city of Sukhumi; to investigate reports of cease-fire violations and to attempt to resolve such incidents with the parties involved; and to report to the Secretary-General on the implementation of its mandate, including, in particular, violations of the cease-fire agreement.

The Council established UNOMIG for a period of six months subject to the proviso that it would be extended beyond the initial 90 days "only upon a review by the Council based on a report from the Secretary-General whether or not substantive progress had been made towards implementing measures aimed at establishing a lasting peace". It requested the Secretary-General, through his Special Envoy, to pursue efforts to facilitate the peace process and negotiations towards the achievement of a comprehensive political settlement of the conflict. On 27 August, the Secretary-General informed[9] the Council of his intention to appoint Brigadier-General John Hvidegaard (Denmark) as Chief Military Observer (CMO). General Hvidegaard took up his command in Sukhumi on 10 September 1993.

On 16 September, the cease-fire broke down. Abkhaz forces, with armed support from outside Abkhazia, launched attacks on Sukhumi and Ochamchira. Notwithstanding the Security Council's call[10] for the immediate cessation of hostilities and its condemnation of the violation of the cease-fire by the Abkhaz side, fighting continued. As a result of the intensity of the shelling

---

[5]S/26250, annex. [6]S/26254. [7]S/RES/854 (1993). [8]S/26250. [9]S/26391. [10]S/26463.

and other hostilities, the UNOMIG observers were obliged to suspend all patrols as of 17 September. In the next few days, the military situation developed rapidly, with loss of life among the local civilian population. The Georgian authorities made appeals for assistance to the Russian Federation, to CSCE and to the United Nations Secretary-General. The Abkhaz side occupied the city of Sukhumi on 27 September and a few days later all of Abkhazia. As a result of the fighting, hundreds of thousands of civilians, mostly Georgians, were displaced.

Following the breakdown of the cease-fire, further deployment of UNOMIG was suspended. The strength of UNOMIG in Sukhumi was limited to four military observers, including the CMO, and four civilians. Seven observers remained in Sochi, a city on the territory of the Russian Federation, where they were when the hostilities resumed. One observer remained in Tbilisi.

The general breakdown of the cease-fire and the collapse of the tripartite machinery responsible for its implementation led the Secretary-General to inform[11] the Security Council that UNOMIG's mandate had been invalidated. He was exploring with the parties and with the Russian Federation the possible need for and usefulness of the continuing presence of UNOMIG with a revised mandate adapted to the radically changed circumstances. In the meantime, he proposed maintaining the existing strength of UNOMIG in Sukhumi. The CMO had already established contact with Abkhaz military and civilian officials and was assured of their cooperation and of UNOMIG's freedom of movement in monitoring the situation there.

By its resolution 876 (1993) adopted on 19 October, the Security Council reaffirmed its condemnation of the violation by Abkhaz forces of the cease-fire agreement and their subsequent violations of international humanitarian law. It also condemned the killing of the Chairman of the Defence Council and Council of Ministers of the Autonomous Republic of Abkhazia, and demanded that all parties to the conflict refrain from the use of force and from any violations of international humanitarian law. The Council welcomed the Secretary-General's decision to send a fact-finding mission to Georgia, in particular to investigate reports of "ethnic cleansing". The Council reiterated its support for the efforts of the Secretary-General and his Special Envoy. While welcoming the humanitarian assistance already provided to victims of the conflict, the Council urged Member States to contribute to relief efforts being carried out by international aid agencies.

The Secretary-General dispatched a fact-finding mission from 22 to 30 October 1993 to investigate the situation of human rights in Abkhazia. The mission noted numerous and serious human rights violations committed in Abkhazia since the outbreak of the armed conflict in August 1992. Civilians, including women, children and elderly persons, as well as combatants who were no longer actively participating in armed confrontations, were victims of violations of the right to life and physical integrity and of the rights to personal security and property. The victims included members of all ethnic groups inhabiting Abkhazia.

The mission reported that both Georgian government forces and Abkhazian forces, as well as irregulars and civilians cooperating with them, were responsible for such human rights violations. In addition to the loss of numerous lives, the conflict had led to the almost complete devastation of vast areas and the massive displacement of population.[12]

On 4 November 1993, the Security Council, by its resolution 881 (1993), approved the continued presence of UNOMIG in Georgia until 31 January 1994. As recommended[13] by the Secretary-General, it would have the following interim mandate: to maintain contacts with both sides to the conflict and with Russian military contingents, and to monitor and report on the situation, with particular reference to developments relevant to United Nations efforts to promote a comprehensive political settlement. UNOMIG would not be extended beyond 31 January unless the Secretary-General reported that there had been substantive progress towards a lasting peace or that the peace process would be served by a prolongation.

At that time, there were four military observers with minimal support staff in Sukhumi; a fifth military observer provided liaison services in Tbilisi.

Discussions and negotiations

On 6 and 7 October 1993, the Special Envoy for Georgia had discussions in Geneva with Abkhaz representatives, and on 17 and 18 October with Georgian representatives. He was also invited for discussions in early November with the Russian Deputy Foreign Minister. In view of those developments, the Special Envoy held a first round of

[11]S/26551. [12]S/26795. [13]S/26646.

discussions with both parties. The round took place in late November in Geneva, under the auspices of the United Nations and with the Russian Federation present as facilitator. CSCE was invited to attend as a participant. The discussions focused on the question of a political settlement of the conflict.

A Memorandum of Understanding[14] was signed by the parties to the conflict on 1 December 1993 in the presence of representatives of the United Nations, the Russian Federation and CSCE. The Memorandum covered three vital areas — political, humanitarian and war damage issues — and included major commitments towards the peaceful resolution of the conflict: not to use force or threat of force against each other for the period of continuing negotiations; to exchange prisoners of war and assist in finding those missing before 20 December 1993; and to return hundreds of thousands of refugees, as well as occupied homes and properties.

The Secretary-General believed that the signing of the Memorandum manifested encouraging progress towards lasting peace in the area. He therefore recommended[15] that the Council authorize the deployment of up to 50 additional military observers, together with a minimal number of civilian support staff. In his view, a reinforced UNOMIG would be better placed to ascertain the actual conditions on the ground, and to plan and prepare for a further expansion beyond the 50, should the next round of negotiations scheduled in January 1994 warrant it. By its resolution 892 (1993) of 22 December 1993, the Security Council welcomed the signature of the Memorandum of Understanding and authorized the phased deployment of additional military observers.

A second round of negotiations, chaired by the Secretary-General's Special Envoy, took place in Geneva from 11 to 13 January 1994. On the last day of the talks, the representatives of the Abkhaz and Georgian sides signed a communiqué[16] noting that the provisions of the Memorandum of Understanding were, for the most part, being implemented. An exchange of prisoners had taken place on the principle of "all for all"; representatives of the United Nations High Commissioner for Refugees (UNHCR) had carried out a first preparatory visit; and on 15 and 16 December 1993 a group of experts had met in Moscow to prepare recommendations on the political status of Abkhazia. The two sides reaffirmed their commitment not to use force and agreed that the deployment of a full-scale peace-keeping operation

in Abkhazia would contribute to the establishment of favourable conditions for further progress. It was agreed that the third round of negotiations would be held on 22 February 1994.

Options before the Security Council

To permit time for the parties to demonstrate their willingness to make substantive progress, the Secretary-General recommended[17] to the Security Council on 25 January that UNOMIG be maintained to 15 March 1994. He postponed making a substantive recommendation on an expanded international military presence in Abkhazia. However, that presence could take a number of possible forms. Two options, in particular, were discussed with the Secretary-General's Special Envoy and with the group of Member States that had constituted themselves as the "Friends of Georgia" (France, Germany, Russian Federation, United Kingdom and United States).

Under the first option, the Council could establish a traditional United Nations peace-keeping force of some 2,500 troops, under United Nations command and control, to operate initially in the areas of the Gali region and the Inguri and Psou rivers. It would aim to carry out an effective separation of forces, monitor the disarmament and withdrawal of armed units, and help create conditions conducive to the return of refugees and displaced persons. Under the second option, the Council could authorize a multinational force, not under United Nations command, consisting of contingents made available by interested Member States, including the Russian Federation, to carry out the same functions. UNOMIG would be entrusted with the tasks of monitoring the operations of the force, liaising with the local authorities in Abkhazia and observing developments on the ground. This option would require up to 200 military observers, with the necessary civilian support.

On 31 January 1994, the Security Council, by its resolution 896 (1994), extended the mandate of UNOMIG until 7 March 1994 at its authorized strength of up to 55 observers and urged the parties to demonstrate stronger willingness to achieve progress towards a comprehensive political settlement. Declaring its readiness to act before 7 March to increase the strength of UNOMIG, the Council requested the Secretary-General to report on any progress at the third round of negotiations and on the situation on the ground, with special attention

[14]S/26875, appendix. [15]S/26901. [16]S/1994/32. [17]S/1994/80.

to circumstances which might warrant a peace-keeping force and on the modalities for such a force.

Further political efforts

The third round of negotiations, chaired by the Secretary-General's Special Envoy, took place in Geneva from 22 to 25 February 1994. By the final day of the negotiations, the Chairman put forward a draft political declaration, most of which was acceptable to both parties. There remained, however, a significant difference over the issue of the territorial integrity of Georgia and the relationship of Abkhazia to Georgia. The Abkhaz side declined to sign any document that included recognition of Georgia's territorial integrity. In a separate working group, chaired by UNHCR, agreement was reached on a draft quadripartite agreement on the voluntary return of refugees and displaced persons, except for one phrase referring to whether immunity should apply to persons who had taken part in hostilities and who continued to pose a real threat to security.

Despite every effort to find a compromise, neither of the two documents was signed, and the Chairman suspended the third round of negotiations in order to give the parties time for reflection. It was decided that the session should be resumed at United Nations Headquarters in New York on 7 March 1994.

The Secretary-General informed[18] the Security Council on 3 March 1994 that its requirement for substantive progress in the political negotiations had not yet been met. Furthermore, he reported a new outbreak of hostilities in early February 1994 in the Gali district of Abkhazia. While the deployment of an international military presence could contribute to stability, the conditions for making it possible did not exist at that time. The Secretary-General strongly urged the parties to make necessary compromises at the resumed negotiations on 7 March. In the meantime, he recommended a short extension of UNOMIG under the existing mandate. By its resolution 901 (1994) of 4 March, the Security Council extended UNOMIG's mandate until 31 March 1994.

Negotiations resumed in New York from 7 to 9 March with representatives of CSCE and of UNHCR in attendance. The Russian Federation again participated as facilitator. Despite three days of intensive discussions, the parties to the conflict remained far apart on three major issues: recognition of the territorial integrity of Georgia, the repatriation of refugees and displaced persons, and

the role and area of deployment of a possible peace-keeping force.

On 18 March 1994, the Secretary-General reported[19] that developments in the latest round of negotiations gave no reason to alter his earlier judgement. Furthermore, the negotiation process was greatly complicated by the absence of any spirit of reconciliation. It had not been possible to identify measures that might create a more propitious climate to resolve seemingly intractable issues. The level of tension in the area remained high, and there was an increasing risk of return to war. Stressing that the international community should not abandon its efforts to assist the parties to find the road to peace, the Secretary-General stated his intention to ask the Special Envoy to resume contacts with the parties, as well as with the Russian Federation. The Secretary-General recommended that UNOMIG's mandate be extended for a further three months and that its strength — 22 military observers at that time — be maintained.

On 25 March 1994, the Security Council, by its resolution 906 (1994), urged the parties to resume the negotiations and to achieve substantive progress towards a political settlement, including the political status of Abkhazia, respecting fully the sovereignty and territorial integrity of the Republic of Georgia. The Council extended the mandate of UNOMIG for an additional interim period terminating on 30 June 1994.

Two documents signed

On 4 April 1994, at resumed negotiations held in Moscow, the representatives of the Georgian and Abkhaz sides signed two documents: the "Declaration on measures for a political settlement of the Georgian-Abkhaz conflict" and the "Quadripartite agreement on voluntary return of refugees and displaced persons".[20]

By signing the Declaration, the parties committed themselves to a formal cease-fire and reaffirmed their commitment to the non-use of force or threat of the use of force against each other. By other provisions, the parties reaffirmed their request for the early deployment of a peace-keeping operation and for the participation of a Russian military contingent in the United Nations peace-keeping force. They also appealed to the Security Council to expand the mandate of UNOMIG.

In the Quadripartite Agreement, signed by the parties and by the Russian Federation and

---

[18]S/1994/253. [19]S/1994/312 and Add.1. [20]S/1994/397, annex.

UNHCR, the parties agreed to "cooperate and interact in planning and conducting the activities aimed to safeguard and guarantee the safe, secure and dignified return of people who had fled from areas of the conflict zone to the areas of their previous permanent residence".

The Security Council considered[21] the signing of the two documents as an encouraging event which laid the basis for further progress. The Council supported a further increase in the deployed strength of UNOMIG up to the limit specified in resolution 892 (1993), if the Secretary-General considered the conditions on the ground appropriate. The Council stressed the need for progress in the next round of talks so that it might consider establishing a peace-keeping force in Abkhazia, Georgia.

Cease-fire and separation of forces agreement

Following the signature of the two documents, further negotiations were held in three areas: repatriation of refugees and displaced persons; the possible establishment of a peace-keeping force; and the achievement of a comprehensive political settlement of the conflict.

At a meeting on 15 April 1994, the Council of Heads of State of the Commonwealth of Independent States (CIS) expressed readiness to send a peace-keeping force to the region should the Security Council decide not to send a comparable United Nations force. Since the necessary preconditions for the establishment of a United Nations presence had not been achieved, the Secretary-General proposed[22] three broad options for the Council's consideration, one of which included the acceptance of the CIS offer. If the Council accepted that offer, UNOMIG should monitor the operation of the CIS force, and United Nations efforts towards a comprehensive political settlement should continue.

Following further talks, the Georgian and Abkhaz sides signed in Moscow on 14 May the Agreement on a Cease-fire and Separation of Forces.[23] The parties agreed that a CIS peace-keeping force should be deployed to monitor compliance with the Agreement. They also appealed to the Security Council to "expand the mandate of the United Nations military observers in order to provide for their participation in the operations" envisaged under the Agreement. From 23 to 26 May 1994, the United Nations Secretariat held technical discussions with representatives of the Russian Federation regarding the possible role of the United Nations observers and their relationship with the CIS peace-keeping force. The Secretary-General sought an early indication of the views of the members of the Council. Subject to those views, he intended, as a first step, to increase the number of military observers of UNOMIG to 55, as authorized by resolution 892 (1994).[24]

The Council informed the Secretary-General that it stood ready to consider detailed recommendations on the expansion of UNOMIG, following his further consultations with the parties concerned.[25] On 16 June 1994, the Secretary-General reported[26] to the Security Council that he was continuing his urgent consultations and recommended that the existing mandate of UNOMIG be extended for a period of one month. He also informed the Council on the preparations for the voluntary return of refugees and displaced persons and on the further efforts to achieve a political settlement in Abkhazia. UNOMIG's mandate was extended until 21 July by Council resolution 934 (1994) of 30 June 1994.

C. The situation after July 1994

UNOMIG's mandate expanded

The United Nations continued consultations with the Government of Georgia, the Abkhaz authorities and representatives of the Russian Federation and of CIS to reach a clear understanding on the Security Council's decision to amend UNOMIG's mandate and to increase its strength. In his 12 July report, the Secretary-General informed the Security Council of the results of his consultations. On the basis of those consultations, he recommended that the Council extend UNOMIG for a period of six months and expand its mandate to include a number of tasks.

The expanded UNOMIG would maintain its headquarters in Sukhumi and would establish three sector headquarters — in Sukhumi, Gali and

---

[21]S/PRST/1994/17. [22]S/1994/529. [23]S/1994/583, annex. [24]S/1994/529/Add.1. [25]S/1994/714. [26]S/1994/725.

Zugdidi — and a liaison office in Tbilisi. To perform its monitoring functions effectively, UNOMIG would need a combination of static teams and mobile patrols. Helicopter patrols would be conducted of mountainous and less accessible areas. The Secretary-General envisaged that UNOMIG would require a total strength of 136 military personnel, including the necessary medical personnel, supported by international and local civilian staff. UNOMIG would operate independently of the CIS peace-keeping force but in close cooperation and coordination with it. The Mission also would maintain close contacts with both parties and with military contingents of the Russian Federation in the zone of conflict.

On 21 July, the Security Council, by its resolution 937 (1994), decided to increase the strength of UNOMIG to up to 136 military observers, and extended the period of the mandate until 13 January 1995. In addition, it expanded the Mission's mandate to include the following tasks: (a) to monitor and verify the implementation by the parties of the Agreement on a Cease-fire and Separation of Forces signed in Moscow on 14 May 1994; (b) to observe the operation of the CIS peace-keeping force within the framework of the implementation of the Agreement; (c) to verify through observation and patrolling that troops of the parties did not remain in or re-enter the security zone and heavy military equipment did not remain or was not reintroduced in the security zone or the restricted weapons zone; (d) to monitor the storage areas for heavy military equipment withdrawn from the security zone and the restricted weapons zone in cooperation with the CIS peace-keeping force as appropriate; (e) to monitor the withdrawal of troops of the Republic of Georgia from the Kodori valley to places beyond the boundaries of Abkhazia, Republic of Georgia; (f) to patrol regularly the Kodori valley; (g) to investigate, at the request of either party or the CIS peace-keeping force or on its own initiative, reported or alleged violations of the Agreement and to attempt to resolve or contribute to the resolution of such incidents; (h) to report regularly to the Secretary-General within its mandate, in particular on the implementation of the Agreement, any violations and their investigation by UNOMIG, as well as other relevant developments; and (i) to maintain close contacts with both parties to the conflict and to cooperate with the CIS peace-keeping force and, by its presence in the area, to contribute to conditions conducive to the safe and orderly return of refugees and displaced persons. The Council also welcomed the contribution made by the Russian Federation, and indications of further contributions from other members of the CIS, of a peace-keeping force, and requested the Secretary-General to establish an appropriate arrangement for delineating the respective roles and responsibilities of UNOMIG and the CIS peace-keeping force.

Differences remain

In the meantime, the Special Envoy, Mr. Brunner, visited the area for discussions with both sides, followed by political negotiations held in Sochi on 7 and 8 July 1994. A further round of political negotiations, convened by the Special Envoy, took place at Geneva from 31 August to 2 September 1994. The discussions focused on refugee issues, military aspects concerning the Kodori valley and political matters. Regarding refugee matters, a statement was signed recognizing that returnees would be informed through UNHCR about the Abkhaz requirement to comply with the laws in force in Abkhazia. With regard to political questions, both sides were given a non-paper outlining political and legal elements for a comprehensive settlement of the conflict, which had been drafted by the Special Envoy in collaboration with CSCE and the Russian Federation.

The negotiations in the Quadripartite Commission, established on 1 June 1994 and including both parties to the conflict, the Russian Federation and UNHCR, were difficult, and progress was slow. Differences remained, particularly regarding conditions and the rhythm of repatriation and the delay in the organized return of refugees and displaced persons to Abkhazia. During the eighth meeting of the Commission, held at Sochi on 28 September, the parties reached a consensus on the need to restore the necessary security conditions in the area where refugees were to return and on the choice of adequate measures to do so. Following that meeting, the Abkhaz authorities accepted the first group of 100 repatriation applications concerning 460 persons, out of a total of approximately 7,000 applications concerning 26,000 persons.

In view of the large number of mines remaining in the area, UNHCR, after an assessment mission undertaken in August, began preparation of a mine awareness education programme aimed at improving security conditions.

Compliance with 14 May Agreement

The Secretary-General informed[27] the Council on 14 October that the Government of Georgia and the Abkhaz authorities had largely complied with the 14 May Agreement. All armed forces and heavy military equipment were withdrawn from the security zone, and no heavy military equipment remained in the restricted weapons zone. All volunteer formations from outside the boundaries of Abkhazia were disbanded. In the Kodori valley, in accordance with the Agreement, troops of the Republic of Georgia were withdrawn to their places of deployment beyond the boundaries of Abkhazia as confirmed by UNOMIG.

By 12 October, UNOMIG strength stood at 90 military observers. The Mission was operating in the security and restricted weapons zones and in the Kodori valley, and was monitoring the weapons storage sites. Patrols were being conducted either by UNOMIG observers or jointly with personnel from the CIS peace-keeping force. The Government of Georgia and the Abkhaz authorities were cooperating with the Mission, and cooperation with the CIS peace-keeping force was proceeding in a satisfactory manner.

Abkhazia adopts a constitution

A further round of talks between the Georgian and Abkhaz parties was held on 15–18 November 1994 in Geneva under the chairmanship of Special Envoy Brunner, but ended without any agreement on the voluntary return of refugees and displaced persons as well as little substantive progress on political matters. While the parties agreed to consider a draft paper outlining possible political and legal components of the future status of Abkhazia within a union State as a basis for further discussion, the Georgian side withdrew its acceptance on 12 December 1994.

There were also plans to convene a larger meeting, under the chairmanship of the Secretary-General, involving the Chairman of Parliament and the Head of State of Georgia, Mr. Eduard Shevardnadze; the Abkhaz leader, Mr. Vladislav Ardzinba; the Foreign Minister of the Russian Federation, Mr. Andrei Kozyrev; and the Chairman of CSCE, Foreign Minister of Italy, Mr. Antonio Martino.

The political process, however, suffered a setback when on 26 November the Supreme Soviet of Abkhazia adopted a constitution declaring Abkhazia a "sovereign democratic State". The Supreme Soviet, in a statement issued the same day, declared that "Abkhazia ... is not breaking off the process of negotiations with Georgia, but is prepared to pursue it with a view to the establishment of a union State of two equal subjects, and it proposes that the process should be invigorated".

The Head of State of Georgia requested[28] the President of the Security Council to convene urgently a meeting of the Council "since recent events in the Abkhaz Autonomous Republic" might have "unforeseeable consequences and lead to further escalation of the conflict". He stated that he expected that "swift and dramatic measures" would be taken by the Council "to curb the aggressive separatism".

After a meeting convened on 2 December 1994, the Security Council, in a statement by its President, said that any unilateral act purporting to establish "a sovereign Abkhaz entity" would violate the commitments assumed by the Abkhaz side in the search for a comprehensive political settlement of the Georgian-Abkhaz conflict. The Council reaffirmed its commitment to the sovereignty and territorial integrity of the Republic of Georgia, and called upon all parties, in particular the Abkhaz side, to reach substantive progress in the negotiations, including on the political status of Abkhazia, respecting fully the sovereignty and territorial integrity of the Republic of Georgia.

The Abkhaz leader, Mr. Ardzinba, was "inaugurated" "President of the Republic" on 6 December 1994.

In early January 1995, the Secretary-General summarized[29] the political process as being at a standstill. The core question of the Georgian/Abkhaz conflict — the identification of a political status for Abkhazia acceptable to both sides — remained far from being resolved. The security situation had continued to prevent a successful resolution of the humanitarian problems of the refugees and displaced persons. Also missing were the basic elements of stability and security that were essential for the eventual return of normalcy to the peoples of the region.

Mandate extended

As to UNOMIG, the Secretary-General reported on 6 January 1995 that the Mission had reached its full authorized strength of 136 military observers and had continued to fulfil its tasks as mandated by the Security Council in resolution 937 (1994). He recommended that its mandate, set

[27]S/1994/1160. [28]S/1994/1357, annex. [29]S/1995/10.

to expire on 13 January, should be extended to 15 May, the date on which the mandate of the CIS peace-keeping force would end. The Security Council did so on 12 January 1995 by its resolution 971 (1995). It also requested the Secretary-General to report within two months on all aspects of the situation in Abkhazia, Republic of Georgia.

Negotiations resume

In an effort to make progress towards a comprehensive settlement, the Secretary-General's Special Envoy convened a further round of negotiations in Geneva from 7 to 9 February 1995. The negotiations were also attended by representatives of the Russian Federation as facilitator, OSCE and UNHCR. Despite all efforts, the Abkhaz authorities continued to oppose a timetable for the speedier return of refugees and displaced persons. They maintained their position that progress on the question of refugees must be linked to progress on political issues.

Negotiations on the question of the political status of Abkhazia were conducted on the basis of the political paper circulated to both sides at the previous round of negotiations. In the course of talks, both sides reached, for the first time, an understanding on certain provisions of a future agreement concerning a State within the boundaries of the former Georgian Soviet Socialist Republic as at 21 December 1991, including the establishment of a "federal legislative organ" and a "supreme organ of executive power", acting within the bounds of agreed competences.

During follow-up expert group meetings, convened by the Special Envoy in February and March in Moscow, some further progress was achieved on formulations for basic provisions of an agreement on a political settlement. However, core areas of disagreement remained, including recognition of the territorial integrity of Georgia, characterization of the union State as federal in nature, the issue of a joint army and popular legitimization of an agreement.

Some movement reported

Reporting to the Council on all aspects of the situation, as requested, the Secretary-General stated, on 6 March 1995, that there had been "some movement, albeit not extensive". For the first time, there was a productive dialogue between the two sides; negotiations and expert discussions were constructive and businesslike, and a certain substantive momentum was tentatively estab-

lished. On the other hand, the continued stalemate on the question of the orderly return of refugees and displaced persons to Abkhazia was creating pressures which could result in explosive developments leading to the resumption of war. Every effort should therefore be made to obtain Abkhaz agreement to a timetable ensuring the early return of a substantial number of persons to their homes by mid-1995, in particular in the Gali region.

With regard to the situation on the ground, the Secretary-General described it as tense, except in the Kodori valley, where it had been calm. In spite of the positive effect of the CIS peace-keeping force's presence and UNOMIG's extensive patrolling of certain areas, the crime rate throughout the Mission's area of operation, especially in Abkhazia, remained high. Incidents of violations of human rights, largely against the Georgian population, had been reported. UNOMIG believed that armed elements, beyond the control of either the Government of Georgia or the Abkhaz authorities, had been responsible for those acts. Further, attempts to reintroduce heavy military equipment and armament into the security and restricted weapons zones had been made by both sides. UNOMIG and the CIS peace-keeping force had protested all such attempts.

The Secretary-General believed that the presence of UNOMIG and the CIS peace-keeping force in the region had contributed greatly to preventing a resumption of hostilities and paved the way for continued political negotiations.

On 17 March 1995, the Security Council reaffirmed its commitment to the sovereignty and territorial integrity of the Republic of Georgia but was deeply concerned about the lack of progress regarding the return of refugees and displaced persons.[30]

Violence and negotiations

A further round of negotiations for a comprehensive settlement was planned for early April in Moscow. However, an upsurge in violence in the Gali region in mid-March and early April precluded any face-to-face meetings by the two sides. Despite this setback, diplomatic efforts continued. On 19 and 20 April, the Special Envoy held in Moscow separate consultations with Russian representatives, the Georgian side and the Abkhaz side. The discussions focused on the latest draft of the political paper prepared by the Russian Federation, which had developed the elements consid-

[30]S/PRST/1995/12.

ered on earlier occasions, providing for a solution on the basis of a federal State within the borders of Georgia as of 21 December 1991, with certain competences for Abkhazia. During the April discussions, the Georgian side said that, in recognizing a federal solution to the conflict, the draft text went as far as Georgia was prepared to go. The Abkhaz side rejected the draft on the basis that, in their view, all it offered to Abkhazia was autonomy, not a union State in which relations would be determined by horizontal ties between two equal States.

In March and April 1995, the situation in the security and restricted weapons zones, especially in the Gali region, where most of the refugees were expected to return, was extremely unstable. Criminal activities, incidents of looting and burning of houses and tea plantations were reported. The most pressing problem in the security zone on both banks of the Inguri was the level of armaments. UNOMIG reported the existence of a large number of unauthorized weapons among the population on both sides. In addition, the Abkhaz authorities carried out two militia operations, reportedly to "clamp down on subversive elements" and to "check the identification cards" of the residents. On the positive side, it was reported that the situation in the Kodori valley had remained calm.

Political stalemate

The Secretary-General indicated[31] to the Security Council on 1 May 1995 that "the constructive dialogue that seemed to be leading towards progress has once again encountered difficulties". He noted that experience had shown that tense political stalemates in which neither peace nor war prevailed did not allow the creation of the stability and public confidence essential for economic assistance, reconstruction and a return to normalcy.

Although UNOMIG had been able to implement the tasks assigned, its presence had not had the intended effect of contributing substantially to the creation of conditions conducive to the safe and orderly return of refugees and internally displaced persons. The principal reason for that situation was that neither the Government of Georgia nor the Abkhaz authorities had been able to guarantee the safety of the displaced persons and the protection of the repatriants. The Secretary-General pointed out that unless the parties demonstrated the necessary will, it would be

impossible to improve security conditions in the security and restricted weapons zones.

Notwithstanding these difficulties, the Secretary-General believed that the untimely withdrawal of the CIS peace-keeping force and UNOMIG would lead to open confrontation and the resumption of conflict. He therefore recommended to the Security Council that it extend the mandate of UNOMIG for a six-month period. That extension would be subject to revision in the light of the decision to be taken by the CIS Council of Heads of State regarding the mandate of the CIS peace-keeping force.

The Security Council, by its resolution 993 (1995) of 12 May, extended the mandate of UNOMIG for an additional period terminating on 12 January 1996, subject to review by the Council in the event of any changes in the mandate of the CIS peace-keeping force. The Council called upon the parties to reach substantive progress in the negotiations under the auspices of the United Nations and with the assistance of the Russian Federation as facilitator and with participation of OSCE representatives. On 26 May 1995, the CIS Council of Heads of State decided to extend the length of stay of the CIS peace-keeping force in Abkhazia until 31 December 1995.

UNOMIG criticized

During the months of May, June and July 1995, UNOMIG maintained its full strength of 136 military observers. It also had 55 international and 69 local civilian staff. It maintained six team sites. Operations were based on mobile patrols operating from sector headquarters and the teamsites. Although cooperation with the parties remained at an acceptable level, both sides criticized UNOMIG: the Georgians over the lack of progress in the repatriation of the refugees, and the Abkhaz over the Mission's alleged failure to prevent the infiltration of armed elements into the security zone on the west bank of the Inguri river.

The situation in the security zone remained unstable, although the number of spontaneous returns to the Gali region increased during the period. Returnees were still fearful that the Abkhaz militia would take action against them, concerns which were not unjustified in view of the militia's violent behaviour towards the local population. Looting and destruction of property also continued. Furthermore, despite claims to the contrary by the local Georgian authorities, not all

[31]S/1995/342.

elements of the forces of the Ministry of the Interior, in UNOMIG's view, were fully under their control.

The presence of the CIS peace-keeping force and that of UNOMIG contributed significantly to the decrease in the number of serious incidents in the Gali region. However, defensive preparations by the Abkhaz side continued in the restricted weapons zone, in particular along the Gali canal. The Abkhaz were particularly sensitive over access to the canal and to the area immediately south of Ochamchira. In addition, UNOMIG experienced increasing difficulties with respect to its inspection of the heavy weapons storage sites maintained by the Government of Georgia and the Abkhaz authorities.

Appointment of Deputy

On 7 August 1995, the Secretary-General told the Security Council that much remained to be done if a political settlement was to be found.[32] While efforts continued to draft the text of a protocol that might provide the basis for a settlement, and the Special Envoy maintained his regular discussions with the authorities involved, those efforts did not bring any progress. Stalemate also persisted with respect to the return of refugees and displaced persons. Both sides continued to take positions "that cannot, as yet, be bridged". The Georgian side believed that it had made as many concessions of principle as it could, whereas the Abkhaz side believed its position had been consistent from the beginning and was unwilling to change it. Both sides, however, agreed that the negotiation process should continue.

The Secretary-General stated further that even if it proved possible to find agreement on the draft protocol under discussion, there would then have to be a prolonged period of detailed negotiations on specific ways to implement the constitutional, economic, human rights and other practical aspects of the settlement. Such negotiations would require continuous attention *in situ*. He had therefore decided to appoint a deputy to his Special Envoy, who would be resident in the area and thus able to provide a continuous presence at a senior political level. The Deputy would also be the Head of Mission of UNOMIG. With effect from 1 October 1995, the Secretary-General appointed Mr. Liviu Bota resident Deputy to his Special Envoy and Head of Mission of UNOMIG.[33]

Stalemate continues

In the view of the Secretary-General, a comprehensive settlement of the Georgian/Abkhaz conflict should be based on three essential elements: the safe and early return of the refugees and internally displaced persons; maintenance of the territorial integrity of the Republic of Georgia; and a special status for Abkhazia. Without all three being met, the risk would remain that instability would continue and conflict would eventually break out again.

Furthermore, the economy of Abkhazia was at a virtual standstill and would continue to be so until the displaced population were permitted to return to their homes and normal social, economic, communication, legal, energy, transport and other links with the rest of Georgia were restored. The economy of Georgia continued to be extremely weak and could not be properly rebuilt when political and other energies and resources had to be diverted to the troubles in Abkhazia and South Ossetia.

On 24 August, the Georgian parliament adopted the text of a new constitution, which was signed by the Head of State on 17 October. The Constitution declared the Republic of Georgia to be an independent, single and indivisible State. Internal territorial state arrangements would be defined when Georgia's jurisdiction over its whole territory had been restored.

In mid-September, a governmental delegation of the Russian Federation headed by Prime Minister Viktor Chernomyrdin paid an official visit to Georgia. The two sides reaffirmed their adherence to the principles of respect of sovereignty, territorial integrity of States and inviolability of existing borders, and condemned aggressive separatism and terrorism in any form. The Abkhaz authorities were critical of the agreements, arguing that they seriously affected their interests and complicated the situation both inside and around Abkhazia. On 24 October, the Georgian and Abkhaz sides had a further round of negotiations with senior officials of the Russian Federation. No progress was achieved and the peace process remained deadlocked. It appeared that the continuing standstill in the search for a political solution was due primarily to the Abkhaz side's unwillingness to offer concessions on its future political status.

In the following months, the Russian Federation undertook further efforts aimed at bring-

[32]S/1995/675. [33]S/1995/839.

ing the two sides closer to compromise solutions. In addition, several direct contacts between representatives of the two sides took place in Moscow. Those efforts were actively supported by the Secretary-General's Special Envoy and his resident Deputy, who continued to maintain close contact with the Georgian and Abkhaz leadership, and held regular consultations with senior government officials of the Russian Federation and senior representatives of OSCE. In mid-February 1996, the Secretary-General discussed the Georgian-Abkhaz problem with the Secretary-General of OSCE, Mr. Wilhelm Höynck. In addition, when his Special Envoy was indisposed, the Secretary-General asked his Special Adviser, Mr. Ismat Kittani, to travel to the region. Mr. Kittani held consultations from 14 to 18 March 1996 with Mr. Shevardnadze at Tbilisi, with Mr. Ardzinba at Sukhumi and with the Russian First Deputy Foreign Minister, Mr. Pastukhov, in Moscow.

Despite all these diplomatic efforts, however, little progress was achieved and the Georgian-Abkhaz peace process remained stalled. The sides continued to hold divergent views on the core issue of the conflict — the future political status of Abkhazia. In early 1996, the Abkhaz leadership accepted that Abkhazia would be part of a single Georgian State within the boundaries of the former Georgian Soviet Socialist Republic as at 21 December 1991. It also agreed that the State should be "federative" in nature. But pronounced differences remained over the constitutional definition of the Georgian State. While the Georgian side insisted that Georgia was one single federal State within which Abkhazia enjoyed certain State powers and rights, the Abkhaz side described the State as a union which came about as the result of a treaty between two subjects of equal status under international law.

Further political developments

Presidential and parliamentary elections were held in Georgia in November 1995. According to international monitors, the elections were conducted without major infringements of the election law. Mr. Shevardnadze was elected President of Georgia by an overwhelming majority, and a new Parliament was formed. Elections were not held in the districts of Abkhazia where the central Government of Georgia did not exercise de facto jurisdiction. In accordance with the election law, parliamentarians from Abkhazia in the Georgian

Parliament had their mandates extended until such time as elections could be held in Abkhazia.

President Shevardnadze then proposed an enlargement of the mandate of the CIS peace-keeping force, which should also be deployed throughout the whole territory of Abkhazia and not only in the Gali district.[34] The Council of Heads of State of CIS met in Moscow on 19 January 1996 and adopted, among other things, two decisions regarding the conflict. One of them extended the mandate of the CIS peace-keeping force for three months, to 19 April 1996, and requested the Council of Ministers of Foreign Affairs and the Council of Ministers of Defence of CIS to prepare by 19 February an agreed draft of a new mandate for the CIS peace-keeping force on the basis of the Georgian proposals, with a possible extension up to 19 July 1996.[35] By the end of March 1996, no agreement on a new mandate had been reached nor was there any decision on the continuation of the mandate of the CIS force. The CIS Foreign Ministers' Council asked the Executive Secretary of CIS to continue to examine the issue. In the meantime, the CIS troops would remain.

Another document adopted at the January meeting was the "Decision on measures to settle the conflict in Abkhazia, Georgia".[36] It condemned "the destructive position of the Abkhaz side, which is preventing the achievement of mutually acceptable agreements on a political settlement of the conflict and the safe and dignified return of the refugees and displaced persons to their places of permanent residence" and included a series of measures aimed at influencing the Abkhaz side.

The Abkhaz authorities took exception to these decisions. They stated that they would not recognize a new mandate of the CIS peace-keeping force based on the Georgian proposals and that the existing mandate could be changed only with the consent of the two parties. They also reacted negatively to subsequent enforcement measures taken by the Russian authorities to implement the January decisions.[37]

At the end of 1995, the Governments of Georgia and the Russian Federation had reached a number of agreements and measures of relevance to the conflict. These concerned such matters as consular affairs, trade facilities, restoration of the railway line from Sochi to Tbilisi, Yerevan and Baku, as well as other matters. The Georgian Parliament also ratified the Treaty on Friendship,

[34]S/1996/5. [35]A/51/62-S/1996/74, annex III. [36]A/51/62-S/1996/74, annex IV. [37]S/1996/284.

Cooperation and Good-Neighbourliness, signed between the two countries on 3 February 1994.

In mid-March 1996, President Shevardnadze paid an official visit to the Russian Federation and met President Boris Yeltsin. Both Presidents reaffirmed their commitment to the principles of the territorial integrity of States and the inviolability of existing borders and strongly condemned separatism and terrorism in all their aspects. Regarding the conflict in Abkhazia, they expressed their conviction that all the possibilities for settling the conflict through peaceful political means had not yet been exhausted and that there was no reasonable alternative to settling the conflict in this manner. The Presidents called upon the member States of CIS strictly to observe its decisions of 19 January 1996 regarding Abkhazia.

UNOMIG continues

While the impasse in the peace process persisted, the situation on the ground remained unsettled, especially in the Gali sector. UNOMIG continued to fulfil its tasks, operating in parts of the security and restricted weapons zones and the Kodori valley. The Head of Mission and Deputy Special Envoy continued to operate from both Tbilisi and Sukhumi, and the Chief Military Observer was based at Sukhumi. In November 1995, there was a change in the disposition of UNOMIG on the ground to allow more military observers to be positioned permanently in the security zone and to enable those elements of the military operations who were previously located in Pitsunda to be redeployed to Sukhumi. The concept of operations, however, remained unchanged. The main headquarters of UNOMIG was at Sukhumi, the administrative headquarters was at Pitsunda, and there were two sector headquarters at Gali and Zugdidi, which had 54 and 39 military observers respectively. There were four military observers at Tbilisi, three of whom were attached to the liaison office and one to the air operations office. In March 1996, the Mission had seven team bases (four in the Gali sector, at Inguri Ges, Otobaya, Zemo-Bargevi and Gali; and three in the Zugdidi sector, at Dzvari, Darcheli and Zugdidi). These bases were designed to provide a constant presence in sensitive areas and enable UNOMIG to cooperate closely with the CIS peace-keeping force.

However, because of the threat posed by mines in the security and restricted weapons zones in the Gali sector — a mine had already cost the life of one military observer — UNOMIG suspended temporarily its patrolling in the area. These temporary restrictions on movement kept the observers out of harm's way but, in effect, prevented them from implementing their mandate fully. UNOMIG then began exploring with the Government of Georgia, the Abkhaz authorities and the CIS peace-keeping force measures they could take to improve the safety of UNOMIG personnel in the area where the force was deployed. In the meantime, a team of de-mining experts was sent to the area to train the observers in mine awareness and the use of mine-detection equipment.

On 12 January 1996, acting on the recommendation of the Secretary-General,[38] the Security Council extended[39] the mandate of UNOMIG for an additional period terminating on 12 July 1996. At the same time, the Council stood ready to review UNOMIG's mandate in the event of any changes that might be made in the mandate of the CIS peace-keeping force.

D. Composition of UNOMIG

Secretary-General Boutros-Ghali appointed Mr. Edouard Brunner (Switzerland) as his Special Envoy for Georgia on 11 May 1993. With effect from 1 October 1995, the Secretary-General appointed Mr. Liviu Bota (Romania) as resident Deputy to the Special Envoy to provide continuous attention *in situ* to negotiations. Mr. Bota also serves as Head of Mission. UNOMIG's first CMO was Brigadier-General John Hvidegaard (Denmark), who took up his command on 10 September 1993. After completing two years of duty, General Hvidegaard relinquished command on 7 August 1995. On 28 October 1995, Major-General Per Källström (Sweden) assumed duties as CMO of UNOMIG.

The current authorized strength of UNOMIG is 136 military observers under the command of the CMO. The mission is supported by 55 interna-

[38] S/1996/5. [39] S/RES/1036 (1996).

UNOMIG deployment as of December 1995

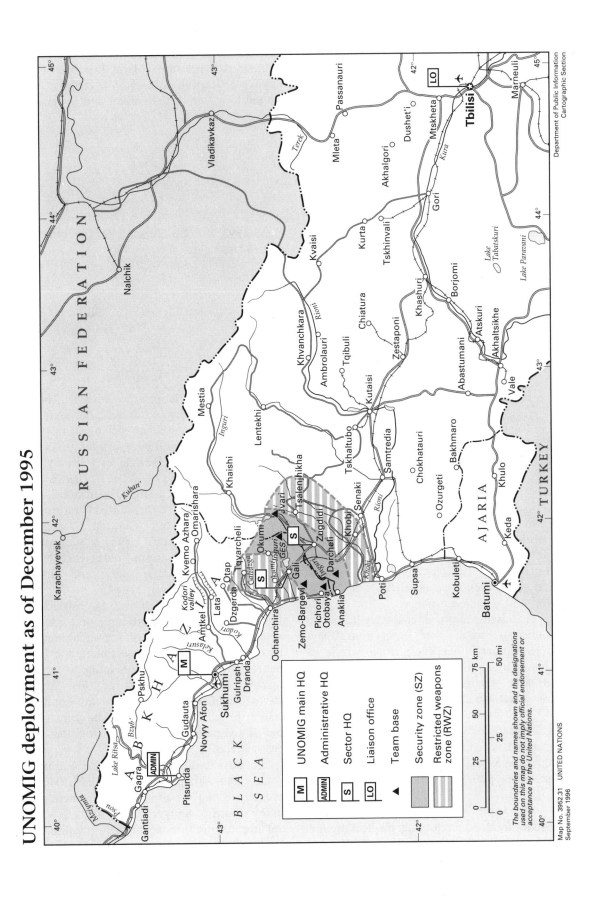

Department of Public Information
Cartographic Section

Map No. 3952.31   UNITED NATIONS
September 1996

Legend

M	UNOMIG main HQ
ADMIN	Administrative HQ
S	Sector HQ
LO	Liaison office
▲	Team base
	Security zone (SZ)
	Restricted weapons zone (RWZ)

The boundaries and names shown and the designations
used on this map do not imply official endorsement or
acceptance by the United Nations.

RUSSIAN FEDERATION

TURKEY

AJARIA

ABKHAZIA

BLACK SEA

Tbilisi

tional and 75 local civilian staff. A civilian-pattern aircraft is being made available to UNOMIG by the Government of Switzerland at no cost to the United Nations. Military observers have been provided by the following countries: Albania, Austria, Bangladesh, Cuba, Czech Republic, Denmark, Egypt, France, Germany, Greece, Hungary, Indonesia, Jordan, Pakistan, Poland, Republic of Korea, Russian Federation, Sweden, Switzerland, Turkey, United Kingdom, United States and Uruguay.

E. Financial aspects

The costs of UNOMIG are met by assessed contributions from United Nations Member States. Estimated expenditures for the period from 7 August 1993 to 30 June 1996 amounted to $30,742,460 net.[40]

F. Other aspects

Humanitarian situation

The fighting in Abkhazia resulted in a massive displacement of civilians. According to inter-agency estimates, close to 250,000 persons fled from Abkhazia and either became displaced persons in other regions of Georgia or sought refuge in other countries. The Georgian authorities issued an urgent appeal to Governments for humanitarian assistance. The United Nations Representative in Tbilisi convened a meeting of representatives of the United Nations system, diplomatic community and non-governmental organizations to review the situation and arrange assistance.

A United Nations inter-agency humanitarian assessment mission visited Georgia from 30 January to 16 February 1993. The mission, which was coordinated by the United Nations Department of Humanitarian Affairs, included representatives of the United Nations Children's Fund (UNICEF), the World Food Programme (WFP) and UNHCR. Based on its findings, the Department of Humanitarian Affairs issued a consolidated appeal for emergency humanitarian assistance for Georgia with total requirements of $20.9 million through December 1993.

The appeal called particular attention to the need for food, warm clothing, medical supplies and logistic support for the transport of relief supplies. A United Nations relief flight was then organized. The head of the United Nations interim office and a second United Nations official maintained a United Nations presence in Tbilisi to monitor the delivery of humanitarian relief.

A full scale inter-agency needs assessment mission organized by the Department of Humanitarian Affairs visited Georgia in February–March 1994. Representatives of UNHCR, UNICEF, WFP, the Food and Agriculture Organization of the United Nations (FAO), the United Nations Educational, Scientific and Cultural Organization (UNESCO), the World Health Organization (WHO), the United Nations Volunteers (UNV) and the International Organization for Migration (IOM) participated.

In Abkhazia there was extensive destruction of homes and infrastructure, and it was estimated that 75 per cent of the inhabitants had departed. Following the assessment, the Department of Humanitarian Affairs launched an Inter-Agency Consolidated Appeal for Armenia, Azerbaijan and Georgia in a total amount of $100 million for all three countries. The principal sectors of assistance were food aid, logistics, health and shelter.

As a result of the signing on 4 April 1994 by Georgian, Abkhazian, Russian and UNHCR representatives of a "Quadripartite agreement on voluntary return of refugees and displaced persons", and after further inter-agency consultation, an addendum to the appeal for Armenia, Azerbaijan and Georgia was issued. In the addendum, $31 million

---

[40]A/50/731/Add.1.

was requested for food, logistics, shelter and domestic needs in order to promote voluntary return of refugees and displaced persons to Abkhazia/Georgia.

The voluntary repatriation to Abkhazia of refugees and internally displaced persons started in mid-October 1994. Out of an estimated total of 250,000 refugees and displaced persons, however, only some 300 persons had returned under the procedures established by the Quadripartite Commission. UNHCR proposed that a timetable be set for the repatriation. Meanwhile, reports by both UNHCR and UNOMIG indicated that a significant number of persons, estimated at several thousands, had repatriated spontaneously.

During the Geneva talks held in November 1994, a statement on the question of refugees and displaced persons was issued jointly by the United Nations, CSCE and the Russian Federation, requesting the parties to take a number of specific steps to speed up the pace of repatriation.

Since the end of November 1994, however, formal repatriation has virtually halted. The issue of the timetable was again addressed at the meeting of the Quadripartite Commission in February 1995, but no progress was achieved. The security situation in the Gali region remained extremely precarious and several serious security threats were reported. Those were attributed to actions carried out by uncontrolled groups and formations. Inevitably, humanitarian programmes were affected by the unstable security situation. In addition, there continued to be a danger of mines.

The stalemate in repatriation also represented a major constraint in addressing the needs of spontaneous returnees and other affected members of the population, and imposed a heavy additional burden on the rest of Georgia. In addition, in the absence of a clear commitment by the parties to the quadripartite process, the financing of humanitarian programmes had become difficult.

The Secretary-General has repeatedly drawn the attention of Member States to the critical humanitarian situation in Georgia. In his report to the Security Council of 6 March 1995, he cited UNHCR reports that, despite the presence of the CIS peace-keeping force and UNOMIG, conditions in the security zone had deteriorated to the point where it had become increasingly difficult to deliver relief supplies to target groups without their being looted and without placing the intended beneficiaries at risk. Furthermore, UNHCR's implementing partners were reluctant to operate in those areas.

The insufficient funding for UNHCR's programmes in Georgia continued to be critical and even compelled UNHCR to reduce its presence in the country. The inter-agency consolidated appeal aimed at bringing emergency relief to people displaced by the fighting in Abkhazia, covering the period through March 1995, had a 52 per cent shortfall in contributions.

Despite all constraints and adverse conditions, UNHCR remained committed to the quadripartite process of voluntary return of refugees and displaced persons. UNHCR continued to maintain a presence in Georgia, including Abkhazia, where it monitored the security situation in the Gali region so as to determine when conditions conducive to the safe and orderly return of refugees were present and to monitor the situation of the 311 returnees. UNHCR also monitored the security situation of the refugees and internally displaced persons in the Zugdidi region.

From 29 January to 4 February 1995, an inter-agency assessment mission to the Caucasus visited the region and evaluated the needs of Georgia and the other countries in the region for 1995, for the purposes of preparing the next inter-agency consolidated appeal for the Caucasus (April 1995–March 1996). The mission included representatives of WFP, UNICEF, UNHCR, FAO, WHO, ILO, UNV and IOM, and was accompanied by a representative of the United States Agency for International Development. The mission took note of the fact that there was a severe energy situation that had consequences for industrial and agricultural production and also affected the most vulnerable population groups. The food supply situation was also a cause for concern.

The appeal to fund humanitarian programmes in Armenia, Azerbaijan and Georgia was launched on 23 March, covering the most urgent needs of refugees, internally displaced persons and other vulnerable segments of the population in the three countries. The appeal for Georgia aimed at securing $36,473,385 in financial assistance for United Nations–system agency projects. As of 31 December 1995, approximately $20.6 million, or 56.1 per cent of the total requested, had been received. The Appeal Supplement, covering the period January–May 1996, showed a total amount received (as of 29 March 1996) of $2.7 million against a revised requirement of $16.9 million.

Social and economic aspects

Emergency relief and humanitarian aid continued to be the predominant modes of United

Nations assistance and other donors' support to Georgia. At the same time, there was increasing awareness of the need to support transitional activities as Georgia moves into a post-emergency phase. This was reconfirmed at the appeal meeting, organized by the Department of Humanitarian Affairs in March 1996, where donors, United Nations agencies, international organizations, non-governmental organizations and government officials from Azerbaijan, Armenia and Georgia met to discuss humanitarian needs in the region.

However, there was a wide range of other development initiatives. The Bretton Woods institutions, the European Union, the United Nations Development Programme (UNDP) and bilateral donors were assisting Georgia to evolve from a mere recipient of humanitarian and development aid into a self-reliant and genuine United Nations partner in development cooperation. The International Monetary Fund (IMF) provided stand-by arrangements and enhanced its structural adjustment facility for Georgia, and provided senior monetary advisers. IMF technical assistance also covered the fields of banking, taxation and support for the introduction of the new national currency, the lari.

As for other United Nations specialized agencies and programmes, UNICEF, WHO and the United Nations Population Fund (UNFPA) were operationally supporting basic social services that should normally be provided by government. This support also involved capacity-building in the sectors of education, health and family planning. UNDP, the Economic Commission for Europe (ECE), UNESCO, FAO and the United Nations Conference on Trade and Development (UNCTAD) were providing the Government of Georgia with policy advice for capacity-building in the economic and public administration sectors. The United Nations Industrial Development Organization (UNIDO) assisted the Government in developing a plan for the restructuring of Georgia's industry.

Human rights

The Security Council, by its resolution 993 (1995), requested the Secretary-General to consider ways of improving observance of human rights in the region. At the request of the Secretary-General,

the High Commissioner for Human Rights dispatched, from 24 June to 2 July 1995, a senior human rights officer to Georgia to discuss the possible establishment of a human rights monitoring mission there. The Secretary-General's Special Envoy also discussed this question with both sides during his visit to the region from 15 to 18 July.

The Government of Georgia strongly supported the establishment of a human rights monitoring mission in the Gali region operating from Georgian-controlled territory. The Abkhaz authorities also offered full cooperation with a possible human rights mission. However, they expressed the view that, for the time being, periodic visits by human rights monitors would be more acceptable than a permanent monitoring presence.

In his reports to the Security Council of 8 November 1995[41] and 2 January 1996,[42] the Secretary-General noted the initiative of the Special Envoy and his Deputy to hold consultations on a programme for human rights. This initiative was welcomed by the High Commissioner for Human Rights, Mr. Ayala Lasso, and, on 12 January 1996, the Security Council, in its resolution 1036 (1996), expressed its full support for the elaboration of a programme for the protection and promotion of human rights in Abkhazia, Georgia.

A United Nations mission, with OSCE participation, was dispatched to the region from 21 to 24 February 1996 to discuss potential concrete actions. An outline for a Programme for the Protection and Promotion of Human Rights was elaborated and, after lengthy negotiations, agreed with Abkhaz authorities. The Programme was to be carried out in cooperation with OSCE, with the participation of interested United Nations agencies and organizations, including UNHCR.

The draft Programme foresaw the establishment of a human rights office in Sukhumi with a limited number of experienced United Nations and OSCE international staff. Its objectives were to be the promotion and protection of human rights in Abkhazia, contribution to the safe return of refugees and internally displaced persons and reporting on human rights developments. The Programme would include monitoring, advisory services, seminars and other educational activities.

41 S/1995/937. 42 S/1996/5.

Chapter 27

United Nations Mission of Observers in Tajikistan (UNMOT)

A. Background

B. UNMOT established

C. Composition

D. Financial aspects

E. Economic and social activities

Chapter 27

United Nations Mission of Observers in Tajikistan (UNMOT)

A. Background

The conflict in Tajikistan has resulted in thousands of deaths and an estimated 700,000–900,000 refugees and displaced persons. It is a struggle influenced by economic, social, demographic, religious and ideological factors. These factors were further aggravated by the rapid pace of change associated with the disintegration of the Soviet Union, which disrupted existing political and economic structures. Regions and groups that had traditionally been excluded from power began to expect fuller participation in the country's affairs. As a result, a struggle arose between different clans for a redistribution of power.

The inhabitants of Tajikistan form a traditional society, characterized by clan and ethnic divisions. Before the civil conflict, twenty-five per cent of the 5.5 million population of Tajikistan were Uzbeks. Uzbeks ethnically belong to the Turkic group of peoples, while Tajik culture and language are closely linked to those of the Persian-speaking peoples. Many Uzbeks remain in Tajikistan, though the numbers are uncertain. The population of Uzbekistan itself includes more than 1 million Tajiks. Before the war, 10 per cent or more of Tajikistan's population consisted of minorities, particularly Russians, Ukrainians and Germans, and smaller groups of Koreans, Tatars, Georgians, Armenians, Bashkirs and others; most of these minority populations have left. Clans in Tajikistan are generally divided by region, except in the Kurgan-Tyube area, where the population is mixed and which has been the scene of the worst fighting.

Independence also made possible a revival of Islam and its politization in the country. Some members of the Tajik Islamic clergy, which is based in northern Afghanistan, Iran and Pakistan, are leading the armed opposition to the current Government. Some 70,000 Tajik refugees fled to those areas, and approximately 20,000 remain there.

The Republic of Tajikistan (formerly the Tajik Soviet Socialist Republic) is situated in south-east Central Asia. To the north and west it borders Uzbekistan (formerly the Uzbek Soviet Socialist Republic), to the north-east Kyrgyzstan (formerly the Kyrgyz Soviet Socialist Republic), to the east the People's Republic of China and to the south Afghanistan.

Coup d'état and civil war

The Tajik Supreme Soviet voted to proclaim Tajikistan an independent State on 9 September 1991. This vote followed the failed conservative *coup d'état* in Moscow in August of that year which marked the beginning of the disintegration of the Soviet Union. The Republic of Tajikistan became a Member of the United Nations on 2 March 1992.

In May 1992, the Tajik opposition — an informal coalition of Islamic and other groups — seized power de facto after two months of non-stop demonstrations. Further tensions and frequent incidents of violence dragged Tajikistan into civil war. After suffering defeat from the government forces in December 1992, most of those opposition forces crossed over into the territory of Afghanistan. Although the civil war as such ended at the start of 1993, the Government remained concerned with regard to armed insurgency of the opposition forces, in particular from across the Tajik-Afghan border. To protect the border, the Governments of Tajikistan and the Russian Federation agreed that Russian border forces would continue to be deployed along the Pyanj river, which forms the Tajik-Afghan border.

Early United Nations involvement

There have been a number of international and regional diplomatic efforts to find a lasting peaceful solution to the conflict in Tajikistan, including those by the Russian Federation, by neighbouring and a number of other countries, and by the Conference on Security and Cooperation in Europe (CSCE) [now the Organization for Security and Cooperation in Europe (OSCE)].

The United Nations became actively involved in the situation in Tajikistan in September 1992, when Secretary-General Boutros Boutros-Ghali, in response to a letter from the President of Uzbekistan, dispatched a fact-finding mission to Uzbekistan and Tajikistan from 13 to 23 September to make a first-hand assessment of the situation on the ground. He then sent a United Nations good-offices mission to the region on the basis of two communications from the Acting President of the Republic of Tajikistan, on 29 September and 15 October.[1] The mission visited Tajikistan, Kazakhstan, Kyrgyzstan, the Russian Federation and Uzbekistan in November 1992 and held a series of discussions with Government officials in those countries.

The Security Council welcomed this mission, including a humanitarian assistance mission, led by the Department of Humanitarian Affairs, as a contribution by the United Nations to resolving the conflict. At the same time, it called on all parties to the conflict to end the fighting and to enter into political dialogue. The Council welcomed the efforts made by the member countries of the Commonwealth of Independent States (CIS) and those undertaken by other States to help Tajikistan to resolve the crisis.[2]

The Secretary-General informed the Security Council of his intention to send to Tajikistan a small United Nations unit of political, military and humanitarian officers. The unit would monitor the situation on the ground, provide liaison services and constitute a core for any future United Nations role there. The mission became operational on 21 January 1993. It provided the Secretary-General with up-to-date information and was instrumental in coordinating the international community's response to the humanitarian situation.

Special Envoy appointed

In April 1993, reports from the United Nations mission led the Secretary-General to conclude that there could be an escalation of the conflict. This was especially true in the border areas between Tajikistan and Afghanistan. Urgent action was required to establish a cease-fire and start a political dialogue among all concerned for the earliest possible solution of the problem.

In this context, the Secretary-General decided[3] to appoint Mr. Ismat Kittani as his Special Envoy for Tajikistan for an initial period of three months. His mandate would be: to obtain agreement on a cease-fire and make recommendations on appropriate international monitoring mechanisms; to ascertain the positions of all the concerned parties and make good offices available to assist in the establishment of a process of negotiations for a political solution; and to enlist the help of neighbouring countries and others concerned in achieving those objectives. The Secretary-General also recommended extending the mandate of the United Nations mission in Tajikistan for an additional three months to continue its monitoring and humanitarian efforts as well as to provide support to the Special Envoy. The Security Council welcomed the decision to appoint the Special Envoy and the proposal to extend the mandate of mission.[4]

In the following months, the Special Envoy visited Tajikistan and held discussions with the President and other Government officials. He also travelled to Uzbekistan, the Russian Federation, Kyrgyzstan, Kazakhstan, the Islamic Republic of Iran, Pakistan and Saudi Arabia, for talks with their leaders. In Tajikistan and Iran, he met with leaders of various groups opposing the Tajik Government and other prominent opposition personalities.

Regional efforts

In the meantime, the regional search for a peaceful solution of the Tajik conflict continued. In July 1993, on the initiative of President Rabbani of Afghanistan, agreement was reached at a summit meeting of the countries members of the Economic Cooperation Organization (ECO) in Istanbul, Turkey, to establish a commission, composed of representatives of Afghanistan, Tajikistan, Uzbekistan and the Russian Federation, to find a peaceful solution to the problem on the border between Tajikistan and Afghanistan.

President Boris Yeltsin of the Russian Federation approved a decree on 28 July 1993 on the settlement of the situation at the Tajik-Afghan border, appointing the Foreign Minister of the Federation as his Special Representative for Tajikistan. The Foreign Minister was authorized to implement measures to promote talks between the Government of Tajikistan and the Tajik opposition and to facilitate the dialogue between Kazakhstan, Kyrgyzstan, Turkmenistan and Uzbekistan on the set-

[1]S/24739. [2]S/24742. [3]S/25697. [4]S/25698.

tlement of the conflict. President Yeltsin also took the initiative of hosting on 7 August 1993 a summit meeting of heads of State and Government from Kazakhstan, Kyrgyzstan, the Russian Federation, Tajikistan and Uzbekistan on the situation in Tajikistan. A representative of the President of Turkmenistan also attended. The leaders emphasized that a political settlement in Tajikistan remained the main priority and called on the international community to support efforts in this regard. At the same time, the Tajik Government expressed its intention to develop a dialogue with opposition forces. Efforts to find a peaceful solution were also actively supported by CSCE.

Special Envoy's mandate extended

In August 1993, the mandates of the Special Envoy and the mission were extended for a further three months until 31 October.[5] This action was taken in a concerted effort to persuade the Government and all major tendencies in the opposition to accept the need of a political solution and to participate in a negotiating process. In view of the escalating hostilities along the Tajik-Afghan border, the Secretary-General's Special Envoy visited Afghanistan to ascertain the views of the Tajik opposition leaders residing in the country[6] and to have discussions with the Afghan authorities and other authorities in the region.

Following consultations in Afghanistan, Tajikistan, the Islamic Republic of Iran and Pakistan from 17 to 26 August 1993, the Secretary-General informed the Security Council that his Special Envoy had found an emerging consensus on the need for a political settlement of the conflict in Tajikistan.[7] The Secretary-General himself discussed the problem of Tajikistan with many heads of State and Foreign Ministers, including President Rakhmonov of Tajikistan and President Karimov of Uzbekistan in particular, who were attending the regular session of the United Nations General Assembly.

Situation remains tense

These diplomatic efforts notwithstanding, the situation in Tajikistan, and especially on the Tajik-Afghan border, remained tense. Cross-border infiltration from Afghanistan by armed opposition groups occurred on a daily basis, provoking fighting between those groups and the Russian border forces. In addition, armed confrontation was intensifying inside the country, particularly in the Khatlon and Gorno-Badakhshan regions. Instabil-

ity and fighting in neighbouring Afghanistan continued to have a negative effect on the situation in Tajikistan.

The humanitarian situation in the country also continued to deteriorate. Instability and fighting had brought economic life to a halt in many districts of the Khatlon, Gorno-Badakhshan and Garm regions. The population was suffering from shortages of food, medical attention and shelter. Refugees and internally displaced persons returning to their places of origin were among the most vulnerable.

As part of the efforts to stabilize the situation in Tajikistan, the Governments of Kazakhstan, Kyrgyzstan, the Russian Federation, Tajikistan and Uzbekistan decided, at a meeting held in Moscow on 24 September 1993, to establish the CIS Collective Peace-keeping Forces in Tajikistan. These forces, comprised of Kazakh, Kyrgyz, Russian and Uzbek contingents, have the following mandate: (a) to assist in the normalization of the situation on the Tajik-Afghan border with a view to stabilizing the overall situation in Tajikistan and creating conditions conducive to progress in the dialogue between all interested parties on ways of achieving a political settlement of the conflict; and (b) to assist in the delivery, protection and distribution of emergency and other humanitarian aid, create conditions for the safe return of refugees to their places of permanent residence and guard the infrastructure and other vitally important facilities required for the foregoing purpose.

New Special Envoy

On 14 November, the Secretary-General informed[8] the Security Council that he would be ready to respond positively to any reasonable request by the parties and to recommend to the Council an appropriate international monitoring mechanism to help to implement possible future agreements concluded by them. He told the Council that he had decided to extend the mandate of his Special Envoy for Tajikistan for a further five months, until 31 March 1994 and proposed that the small team of United Nations officials in Tajikistan should continue to perform their functions until a United Nations integrated office was established in Dushanbe. The establishment of such an office was requested by the Government of Tajikistan to provide advice and assistance in developing the economic and social infrastructure and to coordinate the humanitarian efforts of the inter-

[5]S/26341. [6]S/26311. [7]S/26744. [8]S/26743.

national community. The Government also sought United Nations advisory services in the field of human rights and democratic institutions.

In December 1993, having appointed Mr. Kittani as his Senior Adviser in the United Nations Secretariat, the Secretary-General appointed Mr. Ramiro Píriz-Ballón, Permanent Representative of Uruguay to the United Nations, as his Special Envoy for Tajikistan.

Agreement on peace talks

In January and February 1994, the new Special Envoy undertook two trips to the region for discussions with the Government of Tajikistan and the leaders of the opposition. He also had talks in the Islamic Republic of Iran, Pakistan, the Russian Federation and Uzbekistan. The establishment of a serious negotiation process between the Tajik parties, its venue, participants and format were discussed extensively with all parties concerned.

The efforts of the Special Envoy were actively supported by countries in the region, including the Russian Federation, which agreed with the opposition's request to have unofficial consultations with them before the start of the political dialogue between the Tajik parties. In March 1994, the Tajik opposition agreed to have Moscow as the venue for the talks. The venue would then rotate to Tehran and then to Islamabad. It was also agreed that Afghanistan, the Islamic Republic of Iran, Kazakhstan, Kyrgyzstan, Pakistan, the Russian Federation and Uzbekistan would be observers at the talks.

The President of Tajikistan accepted the format of negotiations in a letter of 23 March 1994 to the Special Envoy. He also stated that his Government was prepared to start negotiations with the opposition in Moscow as soon as possible.

The Secretary-General then instructed the Special Envoy to invite the Tajik parties to a first round of talks to be held in Moscow and to inform the observers. On the Secretary-General's recommendation,[9] the Security Council expanded[10] the mandate of the Special Envoy to enable him to provide good offices during the political negotiations. It also extended his mandate for another three months until the end of June 1994 and decided to continue the presence of the United Nations mission in Tajikistan for the same period.

Moscow round of talks

The first round of inter-Tajik talks on national reconciliation, under United Nations auspices, took place in Moscow from 5 to 19 April

1994 with the participation of observers from Afghanistan, the Islamic Republic of Iran, Kazakhstan, Kyrgyzstan, Pakistan, the Russian Federation and Uzbekistan. At the request of the parties concerned, the talks were chaired by the Secretary-General's Special Envoy.

During these talks, the two parties were able to work out a comprehensive agenda for the duration of inter-Tajik negotiations. The agenda included three clusters of issues: (a) measures aimed at a political settlement in Tajikistan; (b) solution of the problem of refugees and internally displaced persons; and (c) fundamental institutional issues and consolidation of the statehood of Tajikistan.

The parties agreed that in the future they would consider all three clusters of issues as a single package and would negotiate compromise solutions based on that approach. Both parties reaffirmed their commitment to political dialogue as the only means of achieving national reconciliation and included this principle in their joint communiqué. They also signed a number of other documents, including a joint statement which contained an appeal "to refrain from any act that could complicate the process of . . . negotiations", and a protocol on the establishment of a joint commission on problems relating to refugees and displaced persons from Tajikistan.[11]

Tehran round of talks

The second round of inter-Tajik talks took place in Tehran from 18 to 28 June 1994 with the participation of observers from Afghanistan, the Islamic Republic of Iran, Kazakhstan, Kyrgyzstan, Pakistan, the Russian Federation and CSCE. During 10 days of intensive discussions, the Tajik parties focused on one main objective: agreement on a cease-fire and the cessation of other hostile acts. Despite the fact that the talks were inconclusive, the parties agreed on a comprehensive definition of "the cease-fire and the cessation of other hostile acts" and on a joint communiqué[12] in which they again reaffirmed their commitment to political dialogue as the only means to achieve national reconciliation.

The concept of the cessation of hostilities included:[13]

"(a) The cessation by the Parties of all military actions, including all violations of the Tajik-Afghan border, offensive operations within the country, the

[9]S/1994/379. [10]S/1994/494. [11]S/1994/542. [12]S/1994/893.
[13]S/1994/1102, annex I.

shelling of adjacent territory, the conduct of all forms of military training, the redeployment of regular or irregular military formations in Tajikistan, which might result in the breakdown of the agreement;

"*Note*: The Collective Peace-keeping Forces of the Commonwealth of Independent States and the Russian troops in Tajikistan shall carry out their duties in keeping with the principle of neutrality, which is part of their mandate, and shall cooperate with United Nations military observers.

"(b) The cessation by the Parties of acts of terrorism and sabotage on the Tajik-Afghan border, within the Republic and in other countries;

"(c) The prevention by the Parties of murders, the taking of hostages, unlawful arrest and detention, and acts of pillage against the civilian population and servicemen in the Republic and other countries;

"(d) The prevention of the blockades of populated areas, national economic and military installations and of all means of communication;

"(e) The cessation of the use of all forms of communication and mass media to undermine the process of national reconciliation;

"(f) The Parties shall refrain from using religion and the religious feelings of believers, as well as any ideology, for hostile purposes."

Third round preparations suspended

In July, however, the peace process suffered a serious setback when the Supreme Soviet of Tajikistan endorsed a political plan providing for a referendum on a new constitution, to be held in September 1994, and simultaneous elections for the post of President. The implementation of the plan, which did not provide for the participation of the opposition and ignored the agreed agenda of the inter-Tajik talks, threatened to jeopardize the negotiations. The issue of the inter-Tajik talks was not even raised.

For its part, the opposition intensified its armed struggle through border infiltrations and acts of terrorism and sabotage inside the country. It cited the continuing lack of "seriousness and sincerity" on the Government side in the negotiations.

In those circumstances, the Secretary-General decided to suspend preparations for the third round of talks in Islamabad until the Tajik parties took new and substantive steps that would give unequivocal proof of their sincerity and their commitment to pursue the negotiations. In the meantime, he requested his Special Envoy to maintain the necessary contacts with the Tajik parties and the Governments in the region.[14]

In the following weeks, the Tajik Government adopted an amnesty decree, released some opposition members, upgraded the level of its delegation at the negotiations and postponed the presidential election and referendum. Taking into account these positive developments, the Secretary-General instructed his Special Envoy to undertake consultations with the Tajik parties and certain Governments in the region with a view to arranging the next round of inter-Tajik talks. As a result, the two sides agreed to high-level consultations to discuss the prospects for a third round in Islamabad.

The consultations were held in Tehran from 9 to 18 September 1994. The delegation of the Tajik Government was led by Mr. A. Dostiev, First Deputy Chairman of the Supreme Soviet of the Republic of Tajikistan; the delegation of the Tajik opposition was led by Mr. Akbar Turajonzodah, First Deputy Chairman of the Islamic Revival Movement of Tajikistan. Talks were also held with Mr. Abdullo Nuri, leader of the Islamic Revival Movement of Tajikistan. The Special Envoy served as mediator. High-ranking representatives of the Islamic Republic of Iran, Pakistan and the Russian Federation facilitated the consultations.

Tehran Agreement

On 17 September, the Government and the opposition signed the Agreement on a Temporary Cease-fire and the Cessation of Other Hostile Acts on the Tajik-Afghan Border and within the Country for the Duration of the Talks[15] (also known as the Tehran Agreement). The two sides agreed to halt, on a temporary basis, hostile acts on the Tajik-Afghan border and within the country. The concept of "cessation of hostilities", which was worked out during the second round of talks

[14]S/1994/893. [15]S/1994/1080, annex I.

in June 1994, was incorporated into the signed agreement. They also agreed that within one month the Tajik Government would release those opposition members who had been arrested and sentenced, in conformity with the list provided by the opposition, and the opposition would release their prisoners of war in conformity with the list annexed to the Agreement.

In order to ensure effective implementation of the Agreement, the parties agreed to establish a Joint Commission consisting of representatives of the Government and of the opposition, as the principal monitoring mechanism. They requested the Security Council to assist the work of the Commission by providing political good offices and dispatching United Nations military observers to the conflict areas. It was agreed that the Tehran Agreement would enter into force as soon as United Nations observers were deployed.

The parties also reaffirmed their commitment to resolve the conflict through political dialogue and agreed in a joint communiqué[16] to hold the next round of inter-Tajik talks in Islamabad in October 1994.

On 22 September, the Security Council welcomed the Tehran Agreement and invited the Secretary-General to present urgently his recommendations regarding the request of the Tajik parties for United Nations support.[17] Those recommendations,[18] presented to the Council on 27 September, included extending the mandates of the Special Envoy and the small group of United Nations officials for a further period of four months. As a provisional measure, the group was to be strengthened with up to 15 military observers drawn from existing peace-keeping operations, pending a decision by the Security Council to establish a new United Nations observer mission in Tajikistan. A technical survey mission would travel to Tajikistan to assess the modalities for establishing an observer mission.

The technical survey team visited Tajikistan from 4 to 12 October 1994. Also during October, 15 military observers, under the command of Brigadier-General Hasan Abaza (Jordan), arrived in Tajikistan and were deployed in Dushanbe, Garm, Kurgan-Tyube and Pyanj. The cease-fire came into effect as from 0800 hours local time on 20 October 1994, following a public announcement by the head of the United Nations office in Dushanbe, Mr. Liviu Bota.

Islamabad round of talks

The third round of inter-Tajik talks on national reconciliation took place in Islamabad from 20 October to 1 November 1994 with the participation of observers from Afghanistan, the Islamic Republic of Iran, Kazakhstan, Pakistan, the Russian Federation, Uzbekistan, CSCE and the Organization of the Islamic Conference (OIC). The talks were chaired by the Special Envoy of the Secretary-General, Mr. Píriz-Ballón.

Although fundamental institutional issues and consolidation of the statehood of Tajikistan had previously been identified as the main themes on the agenda of the third round, the extension of the Tehran Agreement de facto became the main issue negotiated in Islamabad. After 10 days of difficult discussions, the parties succeeded in extending the Agreement for another three months until 6 February 1995. That decision was reflected in the joint communiqué signed by the parties on 1 November 1994.[19] The two sides also signed the Protocol on the Joint Commission to monitor the implementation of the Tehran Agreement.[20] The Protocol defined the role the parties wished the United Nations to assume in assisting the work of the Joint Commission.[21]

Both Tajik parties reaffirmed their commitment to political dialogue as the only means of achieving national reconciliation and included this principle in the joint communiqué. They agreed to hold the next round of talks in early December 1994 in Moscow. To be discussed, on a priority basis, were such issues as arrangements for free and democratic elections to the Tajik parliament and provincial and district legislative bodies, scheduled for late February 1995; confidence-building measures, including lifting the ban on political parties and movements in the context of national reconciliation, as well as the constructive engagement of the mass media in Tajikistan and beyond, with the aim of facilitating the restoration of peace and normalcy in the country.

In the meantime, the Joint Commission, established under the Tehran Agreement as the formal machinery for its implementation, held its first meeting on 14 November 1994 at Dushanbe and began to perform its functions assisted by the United Nations military observers already in the country.

[16]S/1994/1102, annex II. [17]S/PRST/1994/56. [18]S/1994/1102.
[19]S/1994/1253, annex. [20]S/1994/1253, annex. [21]S/1994/1253, annex.

B. UNMOT established

On 30 November, the Secretary-General outlined[22] to the Security Council the composition and functions of a possible United Nations peace-keeping operation. According to the proposed concept of operations, the United Nations mission in Tajikistan would act on its own initiative or at the request of the Joint Commission. In case of a complaint about a cease-fire violation, the mission would investigate, establish the facts and report its findings to the Joint Commission and to United Nations Headquarters. It would also provide good offices as stipulated in the Tehran Agreement. The Mission would be an integrated civilian-military operation, headed by a person with political experience and supported by a small civil affairs staff as well as military observers. The personnel would be deployed in teams at a number of offices in the country. Each office would serve as a base from which the teams would cover a geographic area of responsibility.

The mission would be under the exclusive direction of the United Nations Secretary-General. The parties would be required to respect the international status of the mission and its personnel and to cooperate fully with it in the implementation of its mandate.

The concept of operations did not require a large mission. A military complement of 40 officers would suffice to strengthen the headquarters in Dushanbe and the offices in Kurgan-Tyube, Pyanj and Garm, and to open additional offices, for example in Tavildara and Khorog. The Chief of Mission would need to be supported in his headquarters by a small civilian staff; it would also be desirable to have some additional civil affairs officers for work away from headquarters. Depending on the level of activities, they could be permanently stationed in some of the field offices. The international support staff would need to be strengthened to deal with the increased requirements. Similarly, a number of staff, including interpreters, would need to be recruited locally.

The United Nations mission would be quite distinct from the Russian border forces and the CIS Collective Peace-keeping Forces in Tajikistan. It would, however, maintain close liaison with them and rely on their cooperation as appropriate.

On 16 December 1994, the Security Council, by its resolution 968 (1994), welcomed the agreement on the extension of the Tehran Agreement. It decided to set up the United Nations Mission of Observers in Tajikistan (UNMOT) in accordance with the plan outlined by the Secretary-General. UNMOT was established for a period of up to six months subject to the proviso that it would continue beyond 6 February 1995 only if the Secretary-General reported to the Council that the Tajik parties had agreed to extend the Tehran Agreement, and that they remained committed to an effective cease-fire, national reconciliation and the promotion of democracy.

UNMOT deployed

By the end of January 1995, UNMOT's total personnel numbered 55, of which 22 were military observers, 11 were international civilian staff and 22 were local staff. The military observers had been provided by Austria, Bangladesh, Denmark, Hungary, Jordan and Uruguay. In addition to its headquarters at Dushanbe, UNMOT established field stations at Garm, Kurgan-Tube and Pyanj. Additional field stations were to be opened as soon as the necessary personnel and equipment had arrived.

UNMOT maintained close liaison with the parties to the conflict as well as with the CIS Collective Peace-keeping Forces and the Russian border forces on matters relating to the maintenance of the cease-fire. It was also in close touch with the representatives of the States and international organizations that were observers at the inter-Tajik talks. However, maintaining regular contact with the opposition in Afghanistan proved difficult, with most liaison being maintained through its members in the Joint Commission. The United Nations Secretariat maintained telephone contacts with political leaders of the Tajik opposition based in the Islamic Republic of Iran. UNMOT also continued to provide political liaison and coordination for humanitarian assistance to Tajikistan.

From late December 1994, there were a number of reports by the Russian border forces about attempts by armed members of the opposition to infiltrate Tajikistan from Afghanistan across the Pyanj River. For their part, the opposition reported shelling of Afghan villages by the Russian border forces and, on several occasions in January 1995, UNMOT's team at Pyanj reported shelling by the Russian border forces towards Afghanistan.

[22]S/1994/1363.

The Joint Commission carried out an investigation at the end of January in northern Afghanistan in response to a complaint by the opposition.

UNMOT was closely involved in the work of the Joint Commission. UNMOT chaired its meetings, and UNMOT military observers participated in the Commission's field investigations. Cooperation between the Commission's members was smooth and its findings were adopted by consensus. There were, however, financial and logistic difficulties in the work of the Commission. The Secretary-General made arrangements for a trust fund to support the Joint Commission in accordance with resolution 968 (1994) and sent an appeal to Member States to contribute to it.

Further consultations

Although the two sides had agreed to hold the next round of inter-Tajik talks in Moscow in early December 1994, delays occurred. The Secretary-General instructed his Special Envoy to undertake consultations with the Tajik Government, leaders of the opposition and certain Governments in the region. From 12 to 21 December 1994, the Special Envoy visited Dushanbe, Moscow and Tashkent.

During those consultations, President Rakhmonov of Tajikistan supported the idea of an early fourth round of inter-Tajik negotiations in Moscow, with the aim of extending the Tehran Agreement and achieving further progress in mutual confidence-building measures with the opposition. He also indicated his willingness to postpone the elections scheduled for 26 February 1995, provided the leaders of the opposition would state that they were willing to participate in the elections and to recognize their results. It was believed that such a postponement would provide an opportunity to introduce necessary reforms in Tajikistan, creating the requisite environment for free and fair elections under international monitoring.

From 12 to 15 January 1995, a team dispatched from United Nations Headquarters held consultations with the Tajik opposition leaders in Tehran and with high-ranking officials of the Islamic Republic of Iran. The Tajik opposition leaders showed no interest in participating at that stage in parliamentary elections, even if they were to be postponed for a few months and appropriate conditions were created for them. In addition, they stated that Moscow was not acceptable as the venue for the next round of talks, regardless of the previous agreement, unless the Russian Federation would officially recognize the Tehran Agreement, return to the opposition the weapons and ammunition seized since the Agreement had come into force, remove the new checkpoints established on the road connecting the towns of Khorog and Kalaikhumb in Gorno-Badakhshan, and delegate a representative of the border forces to the Russian observer team during the negotiations.

The election to the Parliament (Majlis-i Oli) took place as originally scheduled, on 26 February 1995. Following the election, the Government of Tajikistan announced[23] that a total of 2,650,267 people had been included in the electoral rolls for the election of people's deputies, and 2,413,722 voters, or 91.07 per cent, had participated in the voting. The deputies elected included representatives of four political parties registered with the Ministry of Justice: the People's Party, the Communist Party, the Economic Recovery Party and the Unity and Concord Party. There was also a large bloc of non-party deputies.

Extension of the Tehran Agreement

The Tehran Agreement was scheduled to expire on 6 February 1995. On 25 January, in a letter[24] addressed to the Secretary-General, President Rakhmonov stated that the Government of Tajikistan was prepared to extend the Tehran Agreement "for any length of time and without any additional conditions". The President also reconfirmed the commitment of his Government to ensure the continuation of the talks.

The head of the Tajik opposition delegation, Mr. Turajonzodah, also emphasized in a letter[25] to the Secretary-General dated 27 January 1995 the need to resolve the conflict through political means at the negotiating table. He declared a one-month extension — until 6 March 1995 — of the Tehran Agreement, in connection with the holy month of Ramadan. He had expressed the hope that this would give an opportunity to continue the inter-Tajik political talks and lead to significant progress in resolving the fundamental issues on the agenda of the talks. Mr. Turajonzodah had also stated that, in view of the constructive and stabilizing role of UNMOT, the Tajik opposition hoped that the Secretary-General would recommend to the Security Council the extension of the Mission's mandate.

On 3 February 1995, a delegation of the Tajik opposition headed by Mr. Turajonzodah visited United Nations Headquarters in New York. Senior Secretariat officials urged the delegation to

[23] S/1995/237, annex. [24] S/1995/105, annex I. [25] S/1995/105, annex II.

accept that the fourth round of talks should take place at an early date in Moscow, as had been agreed at the third round in Islamabad. Mr. Turajonzodah stated that the opposition was ready to participate in the fourth round of talks at any time but that it could not agree that it should be held in Moscow. This was because of actions by the Russian border forces which the opposition considered to be violations of the Tehran Agreement. The opposition was, however, ready to meet in any other capital of a member of CIS.

UNMOT to continue

Mindful of the Security Council's proviso that UNMOT would continue only if certain conditions were met, the Secretary-General reported[26] to the Council on 4 February that the Tajik parties had complied only partially with the requirements of resolution 968 (1994). Both had agreed to an extension of the cease-fire beyond 6 February 1995, though the opposition's agreement was to an extension of only one month. Both had also stated their commitment to a continuing political process. But the opposition's unwillingness to accept Moscow as a venue for the next round of inter-Tajik talks made it impossible for the Secretary-General to report to the Council that negotiations were being actively pursued. The importance of UNMOT as a stabilizing factor was recognized by both Tajik parties. The Secretary-General recommended that UNMOT's presence in Tajikistan be continued for another month, until 6 March 1995, on the understanding that every effort would be made during that period to obtain agreement on the holding of the next round of talks as soon as possible.

On 6 February 1995, the Security Council endorsed[27] the Secretary-General's recommendation. It also urged the Tajik parties to reconfirm through concrete steps their commitment to resolve the conflict only through political means, and their commitment to national reconciliation and to the promotion of democracy.

Search for peace continues

In an effort to revitalize the negotiating process, during the temporary absence of his Special Envoy, Mr. Píriz-Ballón, the Secretary-General asked Under-Secretary-General Aldo Ajello to undertake consultations with senior government officials of the Russian Federation and Tajikistan, and leaders of the Tajik opposition. Mr. Ajello was to discuss the venue, date and agenda for the fourth round and to obtain agreement on the extension of the cease-fire. He had consultations in Moscow from 24 to 27 February, in Dushanbe from 28 February to 1 March, in Islamabad from 2 to 4 March, and once again in Moscow from 5 to 9 March. As a result of the negotiations, the parties agreed to extend the cease-fire agreement until 26 April 1995. On that basis, the Security Council agreed[28] to the Secretary-General's recommendation[29] that UNMOT's presence in Tajikistan be continued until 26 April 1995.

The Secretary-General asked Mr. Ajello to continue his mission in an effort to resolve the remaining difficulties. Progress was made in addressing some of the problems that the opposition presented as preconditions for holding the next round of inter-Tajik talks in Moscow. One of the issues was the existence of discrepancies between the mandate of the Russian border forces, which had broad powers of search and arrest in the border areas, and the provisions of the cease-fire. This had been the subject of a continuing dialogue with the Russian authorities and, in particular, with the Russian border forces in Tajikistan in order to find a way for those forces to carry out their mandate within the spirit and provisions of the Tehran Agreement. Finally, the Russian Foreign Ministry agreed to issue a statement recognizing the validity of the Tehran Agreement for the Russian border guards and servicemen of the CIS Collective Peacekeeping Forces in Tajikistan. However, other issues remained unresolved, and the opposition continued to insist on various conditions, particularly the withdrawal of 350 Tajik government soldiers deployed in Gorno-Badakhshan in violation of the Tehran Agreement.

New consultations were undertaken by the Secretary-General's Special Envoy, Mr. Píriz-Ballón, in early April 1995 in Moscow and Dushanbe, and an understanding was reached on the removal of the 350 soldiers. However, the Tajik Government withdrew the understanding after an attack by the opposition on a convoy of the Russian border forces on 7 April 1995.

During the first three months of 1995, the situation in Tajikistan was relatively quiet, although the period was marked by increasing tension arising from attempts at infiltration by opposition fighters from Afghanistan and the continued presence of 350 Tajik government troops in Gorno-Badakhshan. Beginning on 7 April 1995, the situation deteriorated and the cease-fire was repeatedly broken in a series of violent incidents,

[26]S/1995/105. [27]S/1995/109. [28]S/1995/189. [29]S/1995/179.

involving attacks by Tajik opposition fighters against the Russian border forces and retaliation by those forces against targets on Afghan territory. Those hostilities caused numerous casualties on both sides.

The Security Council expressed[30] its deep concern at the escalation of military activities on the Tajik-Afghan border. It called on the Tajik opposition and the Government of Tajikistan to comply strictly with their obligations under the Tehran Agreement and called on the Tajik opposition in particular to extend it for a substantial period beyond 26 April 1995.

In an effort to stop the ensuing escalation of hostilities, the Special Envoy arranged high-level consultations in Moscow from 19 to 26 April. In a joint statement[31] at the end of the consultations, the two sides reconfirmed their commitment to settling the conflict and achieving national reconciliation through exclusively peaceful political means on the basis of mutual concessions and compromise. They also enhanced the effectiveness of the Tehran Agreement by including a number of additions to its text,[32] the most significant of which stipulated that all the provisions of the Tehran Agreement would be binding for the opposition groups in the territory of Afghanistan. The Joint Commission and United Nations military observers would carry out monitoring functions in the territory of Afghanistan when they received the official agreement of the Afghan authorities. The Special Envoy pressed for an extension of the Tehran Agreement by six months, but the parties agreed to a one month extension to 26 May 1995. The opposition did not accept the longer extension so long as the Government refused to withdraw its 350 soldiers from Gorno-Badakhshan.

Agreement was also reached on measures to strengthen the role of the Joint Commission. The two parties decided to expand the Commission's membership from 10 to 14, with 7 from each side. Furthermore, the fourth round of inter-Tajik talks would be held in Almaty beginning on 22 May 1995 and include on the agenda the fundamental institutional issues and consolidation of the statehood of Tajikistan, as set forth during the first round in April 1994.

On 26 April 1995, while awaiting further developments in the peace process, the Security Council, on the recommendation[33] of the Secretary-General, decided[34] that UNMOT should continue its presence in Tajikistan.

Secretary-General sums up

Reporting on the situation in Tajikistan and the activities of UNMOT, the Secretary-General told[35] the Security Council on 12 May that the Mission, which numbered at that time 69 over all including 36 military observers and 33 civilian staff, continued to maintain close liaison with the parties as well as with the CIS forces and the Russian border troops on matters relating to the maintenance of the cease-fire. In late March, UNMOT established a radio link with the opposition's headquarters in Taloqan in northern Afghanistan. UNMOT also provided political liaison and coordination for humanitarian assistance to Tajikistan. The economic situation remained very difficult, especially in the areas of Pyanj, Garm and Gorno-Badakhshan.

The Secretary-General observed that a number of factors had created serious difficulties for the political process. Those factors included the Government's position regarding the deployment of its troops to Gorno-Badakhshan and the manner in which it carried through the elections on 26 February; the refusal of the opposition to participate in elections, its attempt to introduce preconditions to the holding of the fourth round of negotiations and its de facto withdrawal from the Joint Commission; and the escalation of hostilities in April.

Some problems had been resolved, including agreement on the fourth round of negotiations, which provided grounds for continuing United Nations efforts and maintaining UNMOT. He appealed to the Tajik parties to comply strictly with their obligations under the Tehran Agreement and to refrain from any steps that could aggravate the situation or complicate the peace process at this critical juncture. He underlined the need to strengthen the Joint Commission and to enable it to assume the central role envisaged for it.

Fourth round of talks

A meeting between President Rakhmonov and the Chairman of the Islamic Revival Movement of Tajikistan, Mr. Nuri, took place at the President's initiative in Kabul from 17 to 19 May 1995. In their joint statement,[36] both sides confirmed their readiness to solve the inter-Tajik conflict, to repatriate all the refugees to their places of origin and to stabilize fully the political situation in Tajikistan. They also agreed to extend the Tehran Agreement until 26 August 1995 and

---

[30]S/PRST/1995/16. [31]S/1995/337, annex. [32]S/1995/390, annex.
[33]S/1995/331. [34]S/1995/332. [35]S/1995/390. [36]S/1995/429.

to define further the results of their summit at the fourth round of inter-Tajik talks.

The fourth round was held under United Nations auspices at Almaty from 22 May to 1 June 1995, with the participation of observers from Afghanistan, the Islamic Republic of Iran, Kazakhstan, Kyrgyzstan, Pakistan, the Russian Federation, Uzbekistan, OSCE and OIC. The delegation of the Government of Tajikistan was led by Mr. Makhmadsaid Ubaidulloev, First Deputy Prime Minister, and the delegation of the Tajik opposition by Mr. Turajonzodah.

For the first time, the parties had an in-depth discussion of fundamental institutional issues and the consolidation of the statehood of Tajikistan, although they were unable to reach mutually acceptable decisions on those issues. As a result of the fourth round, the two sides adopted a joint statement.[37] They agreed to exchange an equal number of detainees and prisoners of war by 20 July 1995 and to ensure unobstructed access of representatives of the International Committee of the Red Cross and members of the Joint Commission to places where detainees and prisoners of war were being held. The parties were to step up their efforts to ensure the voluntary, safe and dignified return of all refugees and internally displaced persons to their places of permanent residence and adopted concrete measures to that end. The delegation of the Government of Tajikistan agreed to take the necessary measures to suspend, for the duration of the inter-Tajik talks, the death sentences of opposition members and subsequently to review those sentences.

UNMOT mandate extended

On 16 June, after having considered the report[38] of the Secretary-General on the results of the fourth round, the Security Council by its resolution 999 (1995) decided to extend UNMOT's mandate until 15 December 1995 subject to the proviso that the Tehran Agreement remained in force and the parties continued to be committed to an effective cease-fire, to national reconciliation and to the promotion of democracy.

Protocol on fundamental principles

Following the fourth round of talks, the Secretary-General instructed his Special Envoy to explore with the two Tajik sides and the observer countries ways to achieve better progress on the fundamental political and institutional issues.

In that connection, he appealed to President Rakhmonov and Mr. Nuri to continue their direct dialogue.

President Rakhmonov and Mr. Nuri met again in Tehran on 19 July. In a joint statement, both sides agreed to establish a consultative forum of Tajik peoples, the modalities of which would be worked out during the fifth round of inter-Tajik talks. From 2 to 17 August, the Secretary-General's Special Envoy, by shuttling between Dushanbe and Kabul, facilitated indirect talks between President Rakhmonov and Mr. Nuri. The negotiations resulted in the signing, on 17 August, of a protocol on the fundamental principles for establishing peace and national accord in Tajikistan.[39]

In the Protocol, the two sides agreed on the fundamental principles for a comprehensive political solution of the conflict and concluded that further negotiations should result in the signing of a general agreement on the establishment of peace and national accord. The general agreement would consist of seven separate protocols on the following groups of problems: (a) fundamental principles for establishing peace and national accord; (b) political problems; (c) military problems; (d) repatriation and reintegration of refugees; (e) a commission on monitoring and control; (f) guarantees; and (g) a donor conference. By signing the first of these protocols, the President of Tajikistan and the leader of the opposition agreed on the main parameters of other clusters of problems that would be negotiated in the future. During the negotiations, the two sides also agreed to extend the Tehran Agreement for another six months, until 26 February 1996.

Agreement was also reached to modify the format of inter-Tajik negotiations and to hold them in a continuous round, beginning on 18 September 1995. However, the issue of the venue for these negotiations remained undetermined, and it was agreed that this should be resolved by the sides through the good offices of the Special Envoy. The Government insisted that the talks be held at Ashkhabad, the capital of Turkmenistan, while the opposition wanted Tehran, Vienna or Almaty, but not Ashkhabad.

In the following weeks, efforts to break the stalemate continued. The possibility of holding the talks in more than one venue was accordingly explored. In this double-venue scenario, the talks were either to begin at Ashkhabad and continue at Vienna, Tehran or elsewhere, or vice versa. Even-

[37]S/1995/460, annex. [38]S/1995/472 and Corr.1 and Add.1.
[39]S/1995/720, annex.

tually, the Tajik opposition agreed to Ashkhabad as the venue of the continuous round of inter-Tajik dialogue.

Situation on the ground

Delays in the negotiating process were accompanied by an increase in hostilities in several regions and serious violations of the Tehran Agreement. In Gorno-Badakhshan, where the authorities and the opposition forces coexist side by side, the situation continued to be tense and there was increased friction between the Russian border forces and the so-called Self-Defence Forces (SDF), which also oppose the Government. The field commanders of SDF and another opposition group, the Islamic Revival Movement, threatened reprisals against the Russian border forces for alleged harassment of civilians at checkpoints. (The opposition makes no secret of the fact that their fighters routinely cross the border between Afghanistan and Gorno-Badakhshan.) On a number of occasions, the Russian border forces fired across the border into Afghanistan for the stated purpose of preventing illegal border crossings by persons believed to be either opposition fighters or drug smugglers. In other sectors of the border (Pyanj and Moskovskiy), however, the situation improved and the number of firing incidents decreased.

A tense situation developed at the end of June 1995 in the Garm area, involving a series of killings and clashes between local armed groups and government security forces. During the ensuing period of instability, there were numerous attacks against State police and internal security personnel. The Government blamed the opposition for those attacks, while the opposition leadership denied any responsibility for them. UNMOT was not able to confirm the identity of the attackers.

In Kurgan-Tyube, a conflict developed in June following the assassination of a commander of the Eleventh Brigade of the Tajik National Army, allegedly perpetrated by the members of the First Brigade also deployed in the region, and the subsequent arrest by the government security forces of a delegate to the regional parliament. After intense negotiations, assisted by UNMOT, the situation was brought under control. However, tensions persisted between the First and Eleventh brigades of the Tajik Army. The conflict culminated in mid-September in a serious military confrontation, in the course of which a United Nations military observer was shot and killed. In view of the situation prevailing in the area, UNMOT tem-

porarily withdrew its team from Kurgan-Tyube. Following intervention by high-ranking Government officials and the withdrawal of elements of the two brigades to the places of their permanent location, the situation normalized. The UNMOT team was re-established on 22 November, after assurances by the Tajik authorities of its security and that the trial of those responsible for the death of the military observer would take place in the near future.

After elements of the Eleventh Tajik Army Brigade were redeployed to the areas of Garm and Tavildara, hostilities broke out, in mid-October, in the Tavildara area between Tajik government forces and local opposition groups, who had been reinforced by fighters redeployed from Gorno-Badakhshan. The situation in the area remained very tense.

UNMOT and the Joint Commission received numerous complaints of alleged violations of the Tehran Agreement. The complaints submitted by the Government dealt mainly with the deployment of opposition fighters to the Garm, Tavildara and Gorno-Badakhshan regions and attacks directed against government installations and personnel. The complaints submitted by the opposition were mainly about the deployment of the government troops to the Garm and Tavildara regions and about the detention of persons without charge and their treatment while in detention. Most of those complaints were investigated either by the Joint Commission with the support of UNMOT or by UNMOT alone.

On 6 November 1995, the Security Council agreed[40] with the Secretary-General's proposal[41] to establish a liaison post of UNMOT in Taloqan (northern Afghanistan), and supported his recommendation to increase the staff of UNMOT by five military observers and three civil affairs officers.

Continuous talks begin

The continuous round of inter-Tajik negotiations began in Ashkhabad on 30 November 1995. However, the resumed fighting north-east of Tavildara between government and opposition forces and increased attacks by opposition fighters against border posts in the Moskovskiy district overshadowed the beginning of the talks; the first working plenary session was held only on 7 December.

---

[40]S/PRST/1995/54. [41]S/1995/799.

UNMOT deployment as of December 1995

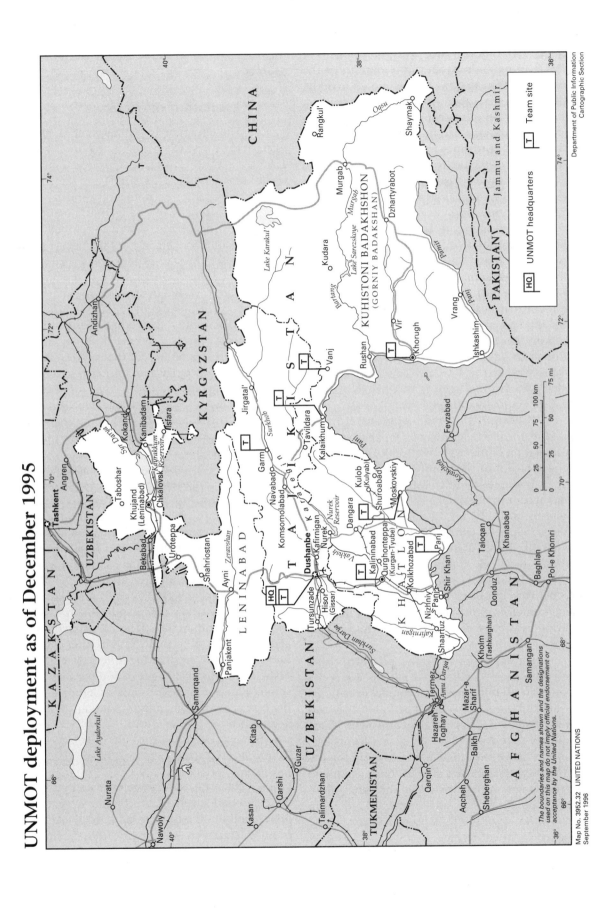

603

Reporting[42] to the Security Council on 8 December, the Secretary-General expressed his concern that, one year after the establishment of UNMOT, progress towards the resolution of the conflict had been so slow. The deterioration of the situation on the ground was equally worrying. Nevertheless, he was encouraged by the resumption of negotiations. He therefore proposed that UNMOT be extended for another six months. On 14 December 1995, by its resolution 1030 (1995), the Security Council extended the mandate of UNMOT until 15 June 1996 with the same proviso as in earlier resolutions.

In the meantime, on 13 December 1995, the two delegations to the Ashkhabad talks adopted a joint declaration,[43] in which they deplored the violations of the Tehran agreement and pledged to respect it in the future. The fighting nevertheless continued. On 14 and 15 December, the Secretary-General's Special Envoy visited Moscow for consultations. On 17 December, an UNMOT team was stationed in Tavildara. After joint efforts by the Government of the Russian Federation and the United Nations, the fighting was halted and the situation gradually calmed down.

Following this restoration of a fragile cease-fire, the two delegations in Ashkhabad began consideration of the main political issues included in the protocol of 17 August 1995 on the fundamental principles for establishing peace and national accord in Tajikistan. The delegation of the Government, led by Mr. Ubaidulloev, presented a position paper in which the establishment of a consultative forum of the peoples of Tajikistan was the main proposal. The delegation of the United Tajik Opposition (UTU), led by Mr. Turajonzodah, rejected that proposal, alleging that the Government wanted to avoid the consideration of other political issues by concentrating exclusively on this issue.

The opposition delegation presented elaborate proposals on political and military issues, including the establishment of a council of national reconciliation for a transitional period of up to two years, which would replace the Parliament. These proposals were rejected by the government delegation as unconstitutional and as having the potential to destabilize the country once again and provoke a new cycle of civil war. The opposition's own proposals on the establishment of the consultative forum of the Tajik peoples were also not accepted by the other side.

This phase of the talks, which ended on 22 December 1995, marked the first time that the two sides discussed the central political issues, including possible ways of power-sharing. However, they were not able to reach agreements on them because of the wide gap between their approaches.

Escalation of violence

The situation in Tajikistan took another turn for the worse when, beginning on 27 January 1996, armed anti-Government insurrections flared up in Kurgan-Tyube, Tursunzade and Khojand. Although the situation in Khojand normalized soon afterwards, a potentially dangerous situation developed in Tursunzade, where the armed group involved took members of the Tajik border guards hostage, and in Kurgan-Tyube, where the First Brigade of the Tajik National Army took control of the city and subsequently deployed towards Dushanbe. The insurgents made a number of demands, including the replacement of senior government officials, the partition of Khatlon province and an amnesty for themselves. The situation was defused without bloodshed after the Government complied with some of these demands, including the replacement of some officials and the amnesty. The insurgents in Tursunzade laid down their arms and the First Brigade returned to its barracks.

While the country was preoccupied with this crisis, fighting resumed between government and opposition forces in the Tavildara area on 29 January. In the following two weeks, the opposition forces advanced approximately 30 kilometres towards Tavildara, coming within 18 kilometres of the city. In the Garm area, the situation was also very tense, despite a meeting arranged by UNMOT on 12 February between the Joint Commission and the chief opposition commander in the area. At Vanj, the opposition seized the government offices and forced the officials to resign. After intervention by UNMOT, most of the offices were vacated. There were also exchanges of fire between opposition fighters and the Russian border forces along the border with Afghanistan, between Pyanj and Shuroabad.

Second phase of continued talks

The escalation of violence and instability on the ground adversely affected the second phase of the continuous talks in Ashkhabad, which lasted from 26 January to 18 February 1996. During that

[42]S/1995/1024. [43]S/1996/212, annex I.

phase, the delegation of the Government, led by Mr. Talbak Nazarov, Minister for Foreign Affairs, presented a position paper which included proposals to hold a special session of the Parliament to consider the inter-Tajik negotiations; to discuss the modalities of the integration of opposition representatives into the Government and local executive committees; and to consider ways for integration of opposition military units into the government forces. The opposition delegation agreed to participate in the special session. The agreement on holding the special session was included in the Ashkhabad Declaration.[44]

The government delegation accepted the opposition's proposals, made during the first phase of the talks, on the establishment of the consultative forum of the Tajik peoples. However, the two sides disagreed on the timing of its convening. Nevertheless, the two sides agreed that the draft agreement would remain open for signature after the problem of timing was resolved.

The opposition delegation, headed by Mr. Turajonzodah, did not present new proposals, but reiterated its positions on political issues as formulated during the first phase of the talks. In view of the continued differences between the positions of the two Tajik sides, the Secretary-General's Special Envoy presented compromise proposals[45] on the political and military clusters of issues contained in the 17 August protocol. The government delegation accepted the proposals as the basis for further negotiations. The opposition delegation accepted some proposals but disagreed with others.

The question of the extension of the cease-fire agreement was also discussed. The government delegation agreed to a further six-month extension, while the opposition delegation agreed only to a three-month extension, provided the Government accepted three conditions: an exchange of prisoners of war and detainees (150 on each side) in one month; respect for the frontline in the Tavildara sector as it was on 17 February; and respect for the status quo established in the Vanj district as of 17 February. The government delegation was prepared to discuss the exchange of prisoners of war and detainees but rejected the other two conditions. The talks ended on 18 February without agreement on an extension of the cease-fire.

Cease-fire agreement extended

Further efforts by the United Nations and others, notably the Islamic Republic of Iran and the Russian Federation, to establish agreement on extension of the cease-fire were negatively affected when in Dushanbe, on 24 February, Mr. Zafar Rakhmonov, the opposition co-chairman of the Joint Commission, was reported to have been kidnapped by unknown individuals. At the time, he was unprotected, as the security detail provided by the Government for the opposition members of the Joint Commission had been withdrawn and, despite repeated *démarches* by UNMOT, had not been replaced. The other four opposition members of the Joint Commission in Dushanbe have since left Tajikistan on security grounds.

The seriousness of the problems related to the extension of the cease-fire agreement and the participation of the opposition delegation in the special session of the Parliament required an urgent diplomatic initiative. Since, by that time, Mr. Píriz-Ballón had returned to his country's service, the Secretary-General asked Mr. Ismat Kittani, his Special Adviser and, formerly, his Special Envoy for Tajikistan, to visit Tehran and Dushanbe in an effort to resolve these two issues.

On 9 and 10 March 1996, Mr. Kittani had intensive talks in Tehran with Mr. Nuri, leader of UTU, as well as consulted with Mr. Vaezi, Deputy Foreign Minister of the Islamic Republic of Iran. As a result, the Tajik opposition agreed to extend the cease-fire agreement for another three months until 26 May 1996. On the negative side, however, the Tajik opposition leaders decided not to participate in the special session of the Parliament. Security concerns were given as the main reason for their decision. But Mr. Nuri unequivocally indicated the intention of the opposition to continue the inter-Tajik political dialogue and expressed the will to resume negotiations as soon as possible.

The special session was held on 11 March 1996. The Parliament considered the issue of the inter-Tajik negotiations and problems related to national reconciliation. An absolute majority of the speakers, including President Rakhmonov, strongly supported the continuation of the inter-Tajik negotiations as the only way out of the current crisis. They expressed regret over the absence of the opposition leaders.

[44]S/1996/129, annex. [45]S/1996/212, annex II.

C. Composition

On 26 April 1993, the Secretary-General informed the Security Council of his decision to appoint Mr. Ismat Kittani (Iraq) as his Special Envoy for Tajikistan. Mr. Kittani was succeeded by Mr. Ramiro Píriz-Ballón, Permanent Representative of Uruguay to the United Nations, who served until February 1996. The Secretary-General subsequently informed the Security Council of his decision to appoint Mr. Gerd Merrem (Germany) as his Special Representative for Tajikistan and Head of Mission of UNMOT. The Council welcomed this decision on 2 May 1996.

Mr. Liviu Bota (Romania) served as Head of Mission of UNMOT from its inception until March 1995. At that time, he was succeeded by Mr. Darko Silovic (Croatia). Subsequently, Mr. Silovic was also given the title of Deputy Special Envoy of the Secretary-General for Tajikistan, to reflect the mandate to assist the Special Envoy in his functions. He performed these duties until May 1996. Brigadier-General Hasan Abaza (Jordan) has been the Chief Military Observer from the inception of the Mission to date.

At its inception, the authorized strength of UNMOT was 40 military observers. On 6 November 1995, the Security Council authorized 5 additional observers. There was also provision for a number of international civilian staff and locally recruited staff. Over the course of the Mission, the following countries have provided military observers: Austria, Bangladesh, Bulgaria, Denmark, Hungary, Jordan, Poland, Switzerland, Ukraine and Uruguay.

As at March 1996, UNMOT had an overall strength of 89, including 45 military observers from Austria, Bangladesh, Bulgaria, Denmark, Jordan, Poland, Switzerland, Ukraine and Uruguay and 44 civilian staff, of whom 18 were recruited internationally and 26 locally. In addition to its headquarters at Dushanbe, UNMOT maintained teams at Garm, Kalaikhumb, Khorog, Kurgan Tyube/Moskovskiy, Pyanj, Tavildara and Vanj. The arrangements for the liaison office in Taloqan, in northern Afghanistan, had not yet been finalized.

D. Financial aspects

General Assembly resolution 49/240 of 31 March 1995 recognized the costs of UNMOT as expenses of the Organization to be borne by Member States in accordance with Article 17, paragraph 2, of the United Nations Charter. Estimated expenditures from the inception of the mission to 30 June 1996 amounted to $12,367,337 net.[46]

E. Economic and social activities

The United Nations and its programmes and agencies have been involved in relief activities in Tajikistan since the autumn of 1992, when the Department of Humanitarian Affairs of the United Nations Secretariat fielded a mission to assess the country's emergency humanitarian requirements. A representative of the Office of the United Nations High Commissioner for Refugees (UNHCR) was designated coordinator of humanitarian assistance in Tajikistan, and UNHCR began to assist the re-

patriation and integration of more than 800,000 internally displaced persons and refugees. United Nations Consolidated Inter-Agency Appeals were issued by the Department of Humanitarian Affairs in 1993, 1994 and 1995; approximately $64 million was contributed for United Nations humanitarian, relief and development programmes during that period.

[46]A/50/749/Add.1.

Initially, most relief and humanitarian assistance was focused on the southern province of Khatlon, which was most affected by the civil conflict. Subsequently, assistance was gradually retargeted to include other areas of the country. By the end of 1995, the vast majority of internally displaced persons and refugees were successfully resettled and, as a consequence, certain programmes and activities launched by UNHCR were handed over to other agencies. Human rights monitoring, for example, was taken over by OSCE, housing and reconstruction by foreign non-governmental organizations and development activities by the United Nations Development Programme (UNDP). However, the humanitarian situation in the country continues to be a matter of serious concern.

Among other United Nations agencies active in Tajikistan are the United Nations Children's Fund, the World Health Organization and the World Food Programme. Along with UNDP, they have been primarily involved in providing relief, rehabilitation and technical cooperation. The Department of Humanitarian Affairs also sponsored a field coordination unit during 1993-1995 in Dushanbe. In October 1995, Tajikistan became a member of the Food and Agriculture Organization of the United Nations and has become eligible for technical assistance from the United Nations system to develop its agricultural sector. International financial institutions, such as the International Monetary Fund and the World Bank, have also been negotiating large-scale assistance to the country.

Part X
Haiti

Chapter 28

United Nations Mission in Haiti (UNMIH)

Chapter 28

United Nations Mission in Haiti (UNMIH)

A. Background

On 16 December 1990, Mr. Jean-Bertrand Aristide was democratically elected President of Haiti by 67 per cent of Haitian voters. He took office on 7 February 1991. The validity of the election was upheld by the United Nations, the Organization of American States (OAS), and the Caribbean community. It was hoped that the election would put an end to a long period encompassing the dictatorship of François and Jean-Claude Duvalier followed by five years of political instability under five different regimes, and mark the beginning of an era of democracy and economic and social progress. However, on 30 September 1991, President Aristide was overthrown in a *coup d'état*, headed by Lieutenant-General Raoul Cédras, and forced into exile.

Diplomatic efforts

The violent and unconstitutional actions of the Haitian military forces were immediately and strongly condemned by the international community. The Permanent Council of OAS condemned the *coup d'état* and its perpetrators. It demanded adherence to the Constitution and respect for the legitimate Government, the physical safety of the President and the rights of the Haitian people, and called for the reinstatement of the President. United Nations Secretary-General Javier Pérez de Cuéllar also expressed[1] the hope that calm would soon be restored and that the democratic process would be pursued in accordance with the Constitution. The President of the Security Council associated himself with the statement.

Meeting on 2 October 1991, the OAS Ministers for Foreign Affairs heard a statement by President Aristide, and on 3 October they adopted a resolution[2] demanding his immediate reinstatement. The Ministers recommended the diplomatic, economic and financial isolation of the de facto authorities and the suspension of any aid except that provided for strictly humanitarian purposes. They decided to dispatch a mission to Haiti and urged the United Nations to consider the spirit and aims of the resolution. On 4 October, a high-level OAS delegation arrived in Haiti and met with representatives of various groups within the country. The delegation's negotiations with the High Command of the Haitian Armed Forces (FADH) were interrupted on 7 October, when soldiers ordered the delegation members to leave the country.

Meanwhile, on 3 October, President Aristide addressed the United Nations Security Council. The President of the Council made a statement condemning the *coup*, calling for the restoration of the legitimate Government, supporting the efforts of OAS and expressing the hope that the President of Haiti would soon return to his country and resume his functions.[3]

On 7 October, the two Chambers of the Haitian Parliament, under pressure from the military, named an "Acting President", who in turn appointed, on 10 October, a "Prime Minister". The OAS Ministers for Foreign Affairs adopted, on 8 October, a second resolution[4] in which they condemned the decision to replace the President illegally and declared unacceptable any Government that might result from that situation. They urged OAS member States to freeze the financial assets of the Haitian State and to impose a trade embargo on Haiti, except for humanitarian aid. The Ministers called upon the Member States of the United Nations to adopt the same measures. They also decided to constitute, at the request of President Aristide, a civilian mission, known as OEA/DEMOC, to re-establish and strengthen constitutional democracy in Haiti.

On 11 October 1991, the United Nations General Assembly adopted by consensus resolution 46/7, in which it condemned the illegal re-

---

[1]SG/SM/4627. [2]S/23131, annex. [3]S/PV.3011. [4]S/23132, annex.

placement of the constitutional President of Haiti, the use of violence and military coercion and the violation of human rights in Haiti; affirmed as unacceptable any entity resulting from that illegal situation; and demanded the immediate restoration of the legitimate Government of President Aristide, the application of the Constitution and thus the full observance of human rights in Haiti.

The Assembly appealed to Member States to take measures in support of the OAS resolutions and emphasized that, when constitutional order was restored in Haiti, increased cooperation would be necessary to support the country's development efforts in order to strengthen its democratic institutions. The Assembly also requested the United Nations Secretary-General to consider providing the support sought by the OAS Secretary-General in implementing the mandates arising from the OAS resolutions.

Secretary-General Pérez de Cuéllar actively supported the intensive efforts by OAS and its mediator at the time, Mr. Ramírez Ocampo, the former Minister for Foreign Affairs of Colombia, aimed at finding a political solution to the Haitian crisis. This support was continued by the new United Nations Secretary-General, Mr. Boutros Boutros-Ghali. On 15 July 1992, he informed[5] the Security Council that he had accepted the offer of the Secretary-General of OAS, Mr. João Baena Soares, to include United Nations participation in a mission to Haiti. The high-level mission led by the OAS Secretary-General visited Haiti from 18 to 21 August 1992. On 10 September, the Secretary-General informed the Security Council that the Haitian parties did not seem to have come closer together. He also reported that OAS was planning to deploy a first group of observers in Haiti and that it would maintain the economic embargo. He intended to continue cooperating with OAS and stood ready to lend any other assistance.

On 3 November, the Secretary-General reviewed[6] for the General Assembly the efforts made by the international community to resolve the Haitian crisis. He also cited reports of a pattern of gross and widespread human rights abuses during the year since the *coup d'état* in Haiti. As a result of the deteriorating political, economic and humanitarian situation, thousands of Haitians were fleeing their country.

On 24 November 1992, the General Assembly adopted resolution 47/20, in which it again demanded the restoration of the legitimate Government of President Aristide, together with the full application of the National Constitution and the full observance of human rights, and requested

the Secretary-General to take the "necessary measures" in order to assist, in cooperation with OAS, in the solution of the Haitian crisis.

Following the adoption of the resolution, the Secretary-General, on 11 December 1992, appointed[7] Mr. Dante Caputo, the former Minister for Foreign Affairs of Argentina, as his Special Envoy for Haiti. On 13 January 1993, the OAS Secretary-General also appointed Mr. Caputo as his Special Envoy.

The Special Envoy held a series of preliminary consultations between 17 and 22 December 1992 in Washington, D.C., with President Aristide, and at Port-au-Prince, the capital of Haiti, with the Coordinator and members of the Presidential Commission, with the Commander-in-Chief of FADH, Lieutenant-General Raoul Cédras, with the Prime Minister of the de facto Government, Mr. Marc Bazin, and with the Presidents of the two Chambers of the National Assembly of Haiti. Further discussions were held with President Aristide in early January 1993.

On 8 January 1993, President Aristide, in a letter[8] addressed to the Secretary-General, requested, among other things, the following: (a) the deployment by the United Nations and OAS of an international civilian mission to monitor respect for human rights and the elimination of all forms of violence; and (b) the establishment of a process of dialogue among the Haitian parties, under the auspices of the Special Envoy, with a view to reaching agreements for the solution of the political crisis; the designation of a Prime Minister by the President to lead a Government of national concord aimed at the full restoration of democratic order in Haiti; agreements for the rehabilitation of Haitian institutions, including the reform of the judicial system, the professionalization of the armed forces and the separation of the police from the armed forces; international technical assistance for national reconstruction; and a system of guarantees to ensure a lasting solution. An identical letter was addressed to the Secretary-General of OAS.

After further meetings at Port-au-Prince on 16 and 17 January 1993, the Special Envoy received two letters, one from Lieutenant-General Cédras and the other from Mr. Bazin, accepting in principle an international civilian mission and a dialogue among the Haitian parties to resolve the political crisis in the country.

In a letter[9] dated 18 January 1993 to President Aristide, the Secretary-General agreed to

---

[5]S/24340. [6]A/47/599. [7]SG/A/522. [8]A/47/908, annex I. [9]A/47/908, annex II.

United Nations participation in an international civilian mission subject to the approval of the General Assembly and under terms to be agreed jointly with OAS. In the meantime, faced with the announcement by the de facto Government of Haiti that it was proceeding with the holding of elections for a third of the Senate, the Permanent Council of OAS adopted, on 13 January 1993, a declaration repudiating the proposed elections and declaring them to be "illegitimate" and obstructive of the efforts under way by OAS and the United Nations towards restoring the democratic institutional framework in Haiti. Secretary-General Boutros-Ghali supported the OAS declaration; however, his request to the de facto Haitian authorities that the elections be cancelled was not heeded.

MICIVIH

Following the Special Envoy's consultations with the Secretaries-General of the United Nations and of OAS concerning the mandate of the International Civilian Mission in Haiti (MICIVIH) and the modalities of its operations, the joint ideas were presented to and agreed upon by President Aristide. The terms of the agreement regarding the Mission were subsequently incorporated in an exchange of letters between the de facto Prime Minister, Mr. Bazin, and the Special Envoy on 9 February 1993.

Under the agreement, MICIVIH would verify respect for human rights as laid down in the Haitian Constitution and in the international instruments to which Haiti was a party, in particular, the International Covenant on Civil and Political Rights and the American Convention on Human Rights. The Mission would devote special attention to the observance of the rights to life, to the integrity and security of the person, to personal liberty, to freedom of expression and to freedom of association. The Mission would be entitled to receive communications relating to alleged human rights violations, to visit freely any place or establishment, to enjoy entire freedom of movement within Haitian territory, to interview anybody freely and privately, to make recommendations to the authorities and verify their follow-up, to undertake a public information and education campaign on human rights and to use the mass media to the extent useful for the fulfilment of its mandate. It would be understood that the Mission was authorized to resort to other international procedures for the promotion and protection of human rights.

The agreement also provided that once the Mission had been deployed, the Special Envoy would undertake discussions regarding ways and means through which the United Nations and OAS might assist in reinforcing democracy, accelerating economic development and professionalizing national institutions, in particular, the judicial system, the armed forces and the police.

Pending the General Assembly's approval, the Secretary-General dispatched to Haiti on 13 February 1993 an advance team and a survey group to prepare for the deployment of the United Nations component of the Mission. On 14 February, an initial group of 40 observers from OAS arrived in Haiti, where they joined forces with a small team of OAS observers that had been in Port-au-Prince since September 1992.

On 24 March 1993, the Secretary-General recommended[10] to the General Assembly that it establish the United Nations component of the joint mission. The United Nations component would comprise some 200 international staff, including 133 human rights observers. OAS would provide another 133 international observers, plus other required personnel for its component. The Secretary-General also submitted[11] to the Assembly the proposals of three international human rights experts who had visited Haiti from 15 to 22 February 1993, including their recommendations on the deployment of the mission throughout Haiti, the modalities of its operation and its needs in terms of personnel and resources.

On 20 April 1993, the General Assembly adopted, without a vote, its resolution 47/20B authorizing United Nations participation, jointly with OAS, in MICIVIH. The Assembly reiterated the need for an early return of President Aristide to resume his constitutional functions as President and strongly supported the process of political dialogue under the auspices of the Special Envoy. It reiterated that any entity resulting from actions of the de facto regime, including the partial elections to the Parliament in January 1993, was illegitimate. It also considered that any modifications regarding the economic measures recommended by the ad hoc meeting of the OAS Foreign Ministers should be considered according to progress in the observance of human rights and in the solution of the political crisis.

MICIVIH operated under a Head of Mission, appointed jointly by the United Nations and OAS and reporting to the Special Envoy. Its headquarters was established at Port-au-Prince with 14

[10]A/47/908. [11]A/47/908, annex III.

regional offices and sub-offices across the country. Deployment in the provinces began on 5 March 1993. By the end of March, MICIVIH had a team in each of the nine departments of the country.

Oil and arms embargo

In the meantime, the Secretary-General's Special Envoy conducted consultations with the parties concerned aimed at seeking a political solution. The immediate objective was to achieve agreement on three main issues, namely the return of President Aristide to Haiti, the appointment of a Prime Minister to head a Government of national concord and the resolution of the question of amnesty. Other critical issues included technical assistance for the economic and institutional reconstruction of the country, and the nature and duration of the international presence in Haiti, coupled with international guarantees to ensure compliance with the agreements. Despite the mounting international pressure, however, the negotiating process undertaken by Mr. Caputo did not succeed.

On 7 June 1993, the Permanent Representative of Haiti to the United Nations addressed a letter[12] to the President of the Security Council, in which he stated that despite the efforts of the international community, constitutional order had not yet been re-established in Haiti because the de facto authorities continued to obstruct all initiatives. In light of that situation, the letter went on, the Government of Haiti requested the Security Council to make universal and mandatory the sanctions against the de facto authorities adopted at the meeting of Ministers for Foreign Affairs of OAS and recommended in the General Assembly resolutions, giving priority to an embargo on petroleum products and the supply of arms and munitions.

On 16 June, the Security Council, acting under Chapter VII of the Charter of the United Nations, unanimously adopted resolution 841 (1993), by which it decided to impose an oil and arms embargo against Haiti as part of the continuing international effort to restore constitutional rule. The President of the Council, in a statement[13] on behalf of its members, said that the adoption of the resolution was warranted by the unique and exceptional situation in Haiti and should not be regarded as constituting a precedent. The Council decided that the sanctions would enter into force on 23 June 1993 unless the Secretary-General, having regard to the views of the Secretary-General of OAS, reported to the Council that, in the light of the results of negotiations, the measures were no longer warranted. At any time after such reporting, should the de facto authorities in Haiti fail to comply in good faith with their undertakings in those negotiations, the sanctions measures would enter into force immediately.

Resolution 841 obliged States to prevent the sale or supply, by their nationals or from their territories or using their flag vessels or aircraft, of petroleum or petroleum products or arms and related *matériel* including military vehicles, police equipment and their spare parts, to any person or body in Haiti. States were also to prevent any activities by their nationals or in their territories which promoted or were calculated to promote such sale or supply. States were also required to freeze all funds in the name of the Government of Haiti or the de facto authorities there, as well as those funds controlled directly or indirectly by the two wherever located or organized.

B. Agreements for national reconciliation

Governors Island Agreement

On 21 June 1993, the Special Envoy, Mr. Caputo, received a letter from Lieutenant-General Cédras accepting the Special Envoy's earlier invitation to him to initiate a dialogue with President Aristide with a view to resolving the Haitian crisis. On 3 July, after almost a week of talks on Governors Island, New York City, President Aristide and Lieutenant-General Cédras signed an agreement[14]

containing arrangements which the parties felt paved the way to a "satisfactory solution to the Haitian crisis and the beginning of a process of national reconciliation".

Under the Agreement, President Aristide was to appoint a new Commander-in-Chief to replace Lieutenant-General Cédras, who would take early retirement. President Aristide was to return

[12]S/25958. [13]S/PV.3238. [14]A/47/975-S/26063.

to Haiti on 30 October 1993. The parties agreed to a political dialogue, under the auspices of the United Nations and OAS, between representatives of political parties represented in the Parliament, with the participation of representatives of the Presidential Commission. The objectives of the political dialogue were to reach a political truce and promote a social pact to create conditions necessary to ensure a peaceful transition; to establish procedures to enable the Haitian Parliament to resume its normal functioning; to reach an agreement enabling the Parliament to confirm the Prime Minister as speedily as possible; and to reach an agreement permitting the adoption of the laws necessary for ensuring the transition. The parties further agreed that the President would nominate a Prime Minister, to be confirmed by the legally reconstituted Parliament. Following his confirmation and assumption of office, all United Nations and OAS sanctions were to be suspended. Other provisions dealt with issues of amnesty, the creation of a new police force and international cooperation.

The Agreement specifically requested the presence of United Nations personnel in Haiti to assist in modernizing the armed forces and establishing the new police force. The Secretary-General, after consultation with the constitutional Government of Haiti, was to report to the Security Council with his recommendations on that aspect of the implementation of the Agreement. The United Nations and OAS were called upon to verify the fulfilment of all the commitments set out in the Agreement. The Secretary-General entrusted the verification to his Special Envoy and asked him to report regularly to him and to the Secretary-General of OAS.

New York Pact

On 14 July 1993, representatives of political forces and parliamentary blocs, together with the members of the Presidential Commission which represented President Aristide in Haiti, began the inter-Haitian political dialogue under the auspices of the United Nations and OAS. At the conclusion of the talks in New York on 16 July, the parties signed a new document, known as the New York Pact,[15] which provided for a six-month truce "to guarantee a smooth and peaceful transition" in their country. In agreeing to the truce, the parties undertook to promote and guarantee respect for human rights and fundamental freedoms and to refrain from any action that might lead to violence or disrupt the transition to democracy.

They also undertook not to table motions of no-confidence against the new Government of national concord, in so far as it respected the Constitution and the laws of the Republic, or to obstruct the work of the Parliament.

The signatories invited President Aristide to appoint a new Prime Minister as soon as possible, and undertook to ensure that laws necessary for the transition of power were passed on the basis of an emergency procedure. They agreed that the members of Parliament elected as a result of the contested elections of 18 January 1993 would voluntarily refrain from occupying their parliamentary seats until the Conciliation Commission had rendered its verdict on this issue. The United Nations and OAS agreed to make two experts available to help prepare and implement an act establishing the Conciliation Commission.

Suspension of sanctions

On 15 July 1993, the Security Council confirmed[16] its readiness to suspend the sanctions imposed against Haiti under Security Council resolution 841 (1993) immediately after the Prime Minister had been ratified and had assumed his functions. It was agreed that provisions would be made for the automatic termination of such suspension if the parties to the Agreement or any authorities in Haiti failed to comply in good faith with the Agreement. The Council also declared its readiness to terminate the sanctions, upon receipt of a report from the United Nations Secretary-General immediately after the return of President Aristide to Haiti.

On 25 August 1993, the Haitian Parliament ratified the appointment by President Aristide of Mr. Robert Malval as Prime Minister-designate. This led the Security Council, on the Secretary-General's recommendation, to suspend immediately the oil and arms embargo against Haiti as well as the freeze on funds. The Council did so by unanimously adopting resolution 861 (1993) of 27 August in which it also confirmed its readiness to reimpose sanctions if the terms of the Governors Island Agreement were not fully implemented.

Establishment of UNMIH

The Governors Island Agreement included provision for United Nations assistance for modernizing the armed forces of Haiti and establishing a new police force with the presence of United

---

[15]A/47/1000, annex. [16]S/26085.

Nations personnel in these fields. On 25 August, the Secretary-General outlined[17] for the Security Council his plans in this regard. He recommended the dispatch to Haiti of a mission consisting of 567 civilian police monitors, 60 military trainers and a military construction unit with a strength of approximately 500 all ranks for an initial period of six months. The mission would be headed by a Special Representative of the Secretary-General, namely the Special Envoy, Mr. Caputo, who would also oversee the activities of MICIVIH and who would coordinate the activities of the two missions.

Although the Haitian Constitution provided for a police force separate from the armed forces, the responsibilities of FADH included both military and police functions. The Secretary-General said that, pending the creation of a new police force, United Nations civilian police monitors would help the Government in monitoring the activities of those members of FADH involved in carrying out police functions, provide guidance and advice, monitor the conduct of police operations and ensure that legal requirements were fully met.

As to the modernization of the armed forces, the Secretary-General stated that the military training teams would provide training to officers and non-commissioned officers in non-lethal skills in order to prepare them for what would become their primary mission, including disaster relief, search and rescue, and surveillance of borders and coastal waters. The military construction unit would work with the Haitian military in such areas as conversion of certain military facilities to civilian use and renovation of medical facilities.

On 31 August 1993, the Security Council, by its resolution 862 (1993), approved the dispatch of an advance team to prepare for the possible deployment of the proposed United Nations mission to Haiti.

The advance team, headed by Mr. Caputo, travelled to Haiti on 8 September 1993. On the basis of the team's findings, the Secretary-General provided further clarifications[18] to the Council. In analysing the political situation in Haiti, he noted that both sides continued to be divided by deep mistrust and suspicion. The political and social climate in the country continued to be characterized by widespread violations of human rights and by other instances of violence. The Secretary-General shared the view of his Special Envoy that in these circumstances there was an "urgent need to demonstrate through concrete steps the commitment of the international community to the solution of the Haitian crisis". He recommended, therefore, that the Security Council approve the establishment of the United Nations Mission in Haiti (UNMIH).

On 23 September 1993, the Security Council, by its resolution 867 (1993), authorized the establishment and immediate dispatch of UNMIH for a period of six months. Extension of the mandate beyond seventy-five days was made contingent upon a review by the Security Council of substantive progress towards the implementation of political agreements reached. The Council called upon all factions in Haiti to renounce publicly violence as a means of political expression. On 6 October, the Council informed[19] the Secretary-General that they agreed with his intention to appoint Colonel Gregg Pulley (United States) as Commander of UNMIH's military unit and Superintendent Jean-Jacques Lemay (Canada) as Commander of the UNMIH police unit. The Secretary-General also proposed that the military component of UNMIH be comprised of contingents from Argentina, Canada and the United States, and the police component of contingents from Algeria, Austria, Canada, France, Indonesia, Madagascar, the Russian Federation, Senegal, Spain, Switzerland, Tunisia and Venezuela.[20]

C. September 1993–July 1994

In accordance with resolution 867 (1993) and after necessary preparations and consultations, the UNMIH advance team, consisting of 53 military and 51 police personnel, was deployed in Port-au-Prince in the period September–October 1993. However, when the ship *Harlan County*, carrying 220 personnel of the United Nations military contingent arrived in Port-au-Prince on 11 October, armed civilians (known as "attachés") created disturbances in the area of the seaport and prevented the ship from landing. In addition, they

[17]S/26352. [18]S/26480. [19]S/26536. [20]S/26802.

threatened journalists and diplomats waiting to meet the contingent.

The Security Council issued a statement[21] deeply deploring the events of 11 October and reiterating that serious and consistent non-compliance with the Governors Island Agreement would prompt it to reinstate the oil and arms embargo against Haiti. In this context, the Council requested the Secretary-General to report urgently whether the incidents of 11 October constituted such non-compliance by FADH.

Following the departure of the *Harlan County*, the other members of UNMIH, the bulk of MICIVIH staff and non-essential personnel of international agencies left Haiti. Many foreign nationals acted likewise, while Haitians living in the capital attempted to flee to the countryside. The Secretary-General's Special Representative remained at Port-au-Prince until 6 November 1993.

Sanctions reimposed

On 13 October 1993, the Secretary-General called[22] the Council's attention to the "repeatedly observed lack of will on the part of the command of FADH to facilitate the deployment and operation of UNMIH" and to administrative obstacles created to delay the start of the Mission. He also cited incidents demonstrating a lack of will to act against "attachés" who were terrorizing the population through such actions as assassinations, attacks on the offices of the Prime Minister and a general strike against UNMIH. Moreover, police had facilitated and, in some cases, participated in the actions of the armed civilians.

The Secretary-General went on to say that most of the instructions issued by the Government of Haiti to FADH and police had not been carried out. That was a "clear violation of the principle of the subordination of military forces to civilian authority", which was a central feature of the Governors Island Agreement. Incidents had occurred which reflected a lack of will to cooperate fully with the peaceful transition to a democratic society, as well as the "clear and explicit intent to prevent the democratic process, as accepted in that Agreement, from taking its course". The Commander-in-Chief of the armed forces and the police chief and commander of the Port-au-Prince metropolitan area "have failed to fulfil the commitments entered into by General Cédras in his capacity as co-signatory of the Governors Island Agreement". The Secretary-General declared it necessary to terminate the suspension of the oil and

arms embargo and the freeze on funds first imposed by resolution 841 (1993).

The Security Council, by its resolution 873 (1993) of 13 October, decided to reimpose its oil and arms embargo against Haiti and the freeze on funds as of 2359 hours Eastern Standard Time (EST) on 18 October 1993 unless the parties to the Governors Island Agreement and other authorities in Haiti implemented in full the agreement to reinstate the legitimate Government of President Aristide and enable UNMIH to carry out its mandate. The Council said it would also consider additional sanctions if they continued to impede the activities of UNMIH or to refuse to comply with relevant Security Council resolutions and the Governors Island Agreement.

Despite diplomatic efforts to resolve the crisis and mounting international pressure, the military leaders in Haiti continued to defy the Governors Island Agreement. Moreover, on 14 October, the Minister of Justice in the Government of President Aristide, Mr. François-Guy Malary, was assassinated. In a letter[23] dated 15 October 1993, President Aristide requested the Security Council to call on Member States to take the "necessary measures to strengthen the provisions of resolution 873 (1993)".

On 16 October, the Security Council, by its resolution 875 (1993), called upon Member States to ensure the strict implementation of the oil and arms embargo against Haiti, and in particular to halt and inspect ships travelling towards Haiti in order to verify their cargoes and destinations. The Council also confirmed that it was prepared to consider further necessary measures to ensure full compliance with the provisions of relevant Council resolutions.

Reaffirming that, in "these unique and exceptional circumstances", the failure of the military authorities in Haiti to fulfil their obligations under the Governors Island Agreement constituted a threat to peace and security in the region, the Council called on Member States, acting nationally or through regional arrangements and in cooperation with the legitimate Government of Haiti, to use appropriate measures to implement the sanctions called for under resolutions 841 (1993) and 873 (1993).

On 30 October 1993, after the deadline for the return of President Aristide to Haiti had passed, the Security Council condemned[24] the fact that Lieutenant-General Cédras and the Haitian

---

[21]S/26567. [22]S/26573. [23]S/26587. [24]S/26668.

military authorities had not fulfilled their obligations under the Governors Island Agreement, and deplored their fostering and perpetuation of a political and security environment which prevented the return of President Aristide to Haiti. The Secretary-General informed[25] the Council on 26 November 1993 that the Haitian military authorities continued to obstruct the deployment of UNMIH. He concluded that the mandate entrusted to UNMIH could not be implemented until there was a clear and substantial change of attitude on the part of the Haitian military leaders. Notwithstanding that assessment, the Council decided[26] on 10 December 1993 to continue the mandate of UNMIH for the full six-month period, that is until 23 March 1994.

As regards MICIVIH, a small group of administrative personnel remained in Port-au-Prince following the evacuation of the bulk of its personnel in October 1993. The Executive Director of MICIVIH, Mr. Colin Granderson, returned to Port-au-Prince after four weeks of absence. Twenty-two United Nations and OAS observers returned on 26 January 1994, beginning a gradual build-up.

MICIVIH reported an alarming increase in violence in Haiti. There had been an outbreak of violence in Port-au-Prince and surrounding areas, where the number of murders remained at a very high level, with the persistence of grave violations of human rights and, in particular, extrajudicial executions, suspicious deaths and enforced disappearances. There were a number of mutilations and many of those killed were supporters of President Aristide. In certain cases of suspicious death, MICIVIH obtained information leading to the conclusion that the culprits were members of FADH, their auxiliaries or members of the Front révolutionnaire pour l'avancement et le progrès en Haiti (FRAPH). In other cases, testimony pointed to armed civilians and left it unclear whether it was a question of "attachés" or of armed bands acting with the complicity of FADH.

Diplomatic efforts continue

The Secretary-General and his Special Representative, supported by several United Nations Member States ("Friends of the Secretary-General for Haiti"), in consultation with the OAS Secretary-General, continued to work intensively to break the impasse and promote agreement between the parties on measures which would make it possible to resume implementation of the Governors Island Agreement.

An important step forward was taken on 14–16 January 1994, when President Aristide convened a conference in Miami, Florida (United States), to which all the political groups that had signed the New York Pact were invited. At that conference a consensus emerged on a sequence of steps to be taken to break the deadlock. In the course of February 1994, further consultations took place in Washington between leading members of both Houses of the Haitian Parliament, representing all political tendencies in that Parliament. On 19 February, the Secretary-General received a letter from a representative group of those Parliamentarians containing a plan for resolving the crisis. On 3 March 1994, this plan was endorsed in a resolution by the Chamber of Deputies of the Haitian Parliament. The plan[27] as presented to the Secretary-General by its authors was transmitted to the Security Council on 20 February 1994. On that occasion, the Secretary-General stated that he considered it to constitute a significant development.

The plan, which was subsequently set out in detail in a letter received on 23 February 1994, provided for the appointment of a Prime Minister, the departure of the Commander-in-Chief of FADH, a vote on the amnesty law, as well as the adoption, after the installation of the new Government, of a law concerning the establishment of a police force, and the return of President Aristide to Haiti.

On 5 March 1994, the Secretary-General met with President Aristide. During the meeting, the President expressed his opposition to this initiative. He further expressed his position in a 7 March 1994 letter to the Secretary-General. Before appointing a new Prime Minister, President Aristide wished to bring about the departure of the leaders of the *coup d'état*, the adoption of the laws provided for within the framework of the New York Pact and the deployment of UNMIH.

Situation with UNMIH and MICIVIH

As UNMIH's first mandate period neared its end, the Secretary-General saw[28] "no change in the prevailing situation in Haiti that would have allowed the reactivation of UNMIH". In those circumstances, he suggested that the Council might wish to consider authorizing the extension of UNMIH's mandate for a period of three months. In his opinion, that would allow for the possibility

[25]S/26802. [26]S/26864. [27]S/1994/203. [28]S/1994/311.

of reactivating the mission with a minimum of delay, should the implementation of the Governors Island Agreement be resumed.

The Security Council, by its resolution 905 (1994) adopted on 23 March 1994, decided to extend the mandate of UNMIH until 30 June 1994 and requested the Secretary-General to make specific recommendations on the composition of UNMIH and the scope of its activities within the overall personnel levels established by resolution 867 (1993).

On 29 April 1994, the Secretary-General also recommended[29] that the General Assembly extend the mandate and financing of the United Nations component of MICIVIH for one year. In his view, although the Mission had been unable to rectify a distressing situation in Haiti, it had shed light on certain events there and denounced human rights abuses that would not otherwise have been disclosed. President Aristide could only be returned to power, and democracy restored in Haiti, if both sides made "constructive and accepted concessions". The Secretary-General noted that the recent initiative by a group of Haitian Parliamentarians — which had been supported by the United Nations and OAS — had not been endorsed by President Aristide. Meanwhile, unity among the Friends of the Secretary-General for Haiti had waned and Security Council sanctions, reimposed in October 1993, had not been effective.

The Secretary-General said the international community's role had changed from that of mediator between the parties to that of sole agent responsible for finding and implementing a solution to the deadlock. There was a danger that the international community would have too extensive a mission, allowing the parties to shirk their own responsibilities in the negotiating process. Given that negotiations had yielded no significant progress, the Secretary-General recommended that "a more specifically Haitian solution" be found. For this reason, the participants should resume an effective role in this process, and the international community and especially those countries most directly concerned should restore a unified approach in the negotiations. Without positive change, both from the Haitian side and from the international community, it was difficult to determine what additional efforts the United Nations could undertake to resolve the crisis. However, as long as material circumstances would allow, the United Nations must maintain its presence through MICIVIH and ensure the continuity of humanitarian assistance.

The General Assembly, in its resolution 48/27B of 8 July 1994, authorized the extension of the mandate of the United Nations component of MICIVIH for an additional year, and requested the Secretary-General to expedite and strengthen the presence of the Mission in Haiti. At the end of June, MICIVIH had 104 international staff including 70 observers.

Additional sanctions against Haiti

On 6 May 1994, the Security Council adopted resolution 917 (1994), by which it decided to impose a comprehensive set of sanctions against Haiti, which should take effect no later than 2359 hours EST on 21 May, and listed a number of specific conditions for their termination. The Council requested the Secretary-General to report to it no later than 19 May on steps the military had taken to comply with the terms of the resolution. The military authorities in Haiti, however, continued to defy the will of the international community. Moreover, they supported the installation, on 11 May, of Supreme Court Judge Emile Jonassaint as "provisional President".

The Security Council, on 11 May, strongly condemned[30] the attempt to replace the legitimate President of Haiti and reaffirmed the Council members' commitment to the restoration of democracy in Haiti and to the return of President Aristide. On 19 May, the Secretary-General informed[31] the Council that the military authorities had not taken any steps to comply with resolution 917 (1994), and, on the contrary, supported the illegal attempt to replace the legitimate President. The new sanctions against Haiti subsequently took effect as scheduled.

In order to tighten the cordon around the island, the United States deployed two additional navy vessels off Haiti, bringing to eight the number of United States ships working with one Canadian, one Argentine and one Dutch ship. A French vessel was also expected to participate. Steps were also taken on land to enforce the sanctions. At the request of the Dominican Republic, the Secretary-General dispatched a team of technical experts to assess the situation on the Dominican/Haitian border. On the basis of the team's report, on 9 June the Secretary-General communicated his observations and recommendations to the Government of the Dominican Republic.

---

[29]A/48/931. [30]S/PRST/1994/24. [31]S/1994/593.

Tensions in Haiti increase

On 20 June 1994, the Secretary-General reported[32] to the Security Council that no progress had been made towards the implementation of the Governors Island Agreement. On the contrary, tensions in Haiti increased as a result of the installation of an illegitimate government, the growing impact of economic sanctions, the continued repression and the humanitarian crisis. The "provisional President" had announced that he would be organizing elections by the end of 1994 and would leave office in February 1995, after the election of a new President in January 1995. On 11 June, he declared a state of emergency on the grounds that the nation was facing extreme danger and risks of invasion. Despite the electoral timetable, no legislative action was taken to prepare for the legislative elections due in November 1994.

As to human rights, the Secretary-General reported that the situation had deteriorated sharply, with new patterns of repression such as the abduction and rape of family members of political activists. In a growing number of politically related killings, the implication of members of FADH or of FRAPH was established. The humanitarian situation in Haiti also continued to deteriorate in spite of efforts by the United Nations and OAS, non-governmental organizations and bilateral donors.

On 28 June 1994, the Secretary-General told[33] the Security Council that the continued deterioration of the situation in Haiti had substantially changed the circumstances under which UNMIH had been planned. The Council might wish to consider modifying the original mandate. The Secretary-General recommended that the mandate be extended for a period of one month, to allow for consultations on the possible strengthening of UNMIH and its role in overall attempts to find a solution to the Haitian crisis.

The Secretary-General also recalled that in the statement[34] of conclusions adopted at their meeting in New York on 3 June 1994, the Friends of the Secretary-General for Haiti had expressed their determination to promote the full deployment of UNMIH when conditions permitted and envisaged the reconfiguration and strengthening of the Mission. Furthermore, the Ad Hoc Meeting on Haiti of Ministers for Foreign Affairs of OAS had unanimously adopted on 9 June 1994 a resolution which called on all Member States to support measures by the United Nations to strengthen UNMIH in order to assist in the restoration of democracy through the professionalization of the armed forces and the training of a new police, to help maintain essential civil order and protect the personnel of international and other organizations involved in human rights and humanitarian efforts in Haiti.

On 30 June 1994, the Security Council adopted resolution 933 (1994) deciding to extend the mandate of UNMIH until 31 July and requesting the Secretary-General to report to the Council with specific recommendations on the strength, composition, cost and duration of UNMIH, appropriate to its expansion and deployment after the departure of the senior Haitian military leadership.

The situation further deteriorated when, on 11 July 1994, the de facto authorities in Haiti delivered to the Executive Director of MICIVIH in Port-au-Prince a decree of the "provisional President" declaring the international staff of MICIVIH "undesirable" and giving them 48 hours to leave Haitian territory.

Secretary-General Boutros-Ghali and the Acting Secretary-General of OAS issued a joint statement resolutely condemning this illegal action. The Security Council condemned[35] this decision of the de facto authorities stressing that this action further reinforced the Council's determination to bring about a rapid and definitive solution to the crisis. The Secretary-General then informed the General Assembly and the Security Council of his decision, made in consultation with OAS, to evacuate MICIVIH staff from Haiti for security considerations. Both United Nations and OAS personnel of MICIVIH left Haiti on 13 July.

---

[32]S/1994/742. [33]S/1994/765. [34]S/1994/686, annex. [35]S/PRST/1994/32.

D. Multinational force

As requested by Security Council resolution 933 (1994), the Secretary-General, on 15 July 1994, outlined for the Security Council the tasks of a proposed expanded force in Haiti, its strength and concept of operations. He presented to the Council three options for the establishment of such a force. The Secretary-General supported action under Chapter VII of the Charter by a multinational force in order to ensure the return of the legitimate President and to assist the legitimate Government of Haiti in the maintenance of public order. After these goals were achieved, UNMIH, under Chapter VI, would take over from the multinational force.

On 31 July 1994, the Security Council adopted its resolution 940 (1994). By the terms of that resolution, the Council, acting under Chapter VII of the United Nations Charter, authorized Member States to form a multinational force under unified command and control and "to use all necessary means" to facilitate the departure of the military leadership, the prompt return of the legitimately elected President and the restoration of the legitimate Government authorities.

By other terms of the resolution, the Council decided to revise and extend the mandate of UNMIH. An expanded, strengthened UNMIH would assume its full range of functions, and the multinational force would terminate its own mission, when a secure and stable environment had been established and UNMIH had the capability and structure to assume those functions. That determination would be made by the Council, on the basis of recommendations from Member States participating in the multinational force and from the Secretary-General. The Council also approved the establishment of an UNMIH advance team of not more than 60 personnel to monitor the operations of the multinational force. The team would also assess requirements and prepare for the deployment of UNMIH.

The Council extended the mandate of UNMIH for a period of six months and increased its troop level to 6,000. It established the objective of completing UNMIH's mission not later that February 1996. Under its revised mandate, UNMIH would assist in sustaining the secure and stable environment established during the multinational phase and the protection of international personnel and key installations; and in the professionalization of the Haitian armed forces and the creation of a separate police force. It would also assist the legitimate constitutional authorities of Haiti in establishing an environment conducive to the organization of free and fair legislative elections to be called by those authorities, and, when requested by them, monitored by the United Nations, in cooperation with OAS.

Final diplomatic efforts

In August 1994, as a personal initiative aimed at the peaceful implementation of resolution 940 (1994), the Secretary-General dispatched a United Nations official with an exploratory mission in order to consider the possibility of sending to Haiti a high-level delegation which would hold discussions with the military authorities. The military authorities refused to meet with the envoy, and the Secretary-General suspended these efforts unless the Security Council gave him a new mandate or the situation changed. However, he informed the Council that he would continue to seek ways to implement resolution 940 (1994) peacefully. The President of the Security Council, in a statement to correspondents, deplored the rejection by the de facto authorities of the Secretary-General's initiative, and reiterated the Council's condemnation of repression, systematic violence and violations of international humanitarian law in Haiti.

At that point, the President of the United States, Mr. William Clinton, stated that all diplomatic efforts had been exhausted and, in accordance with Security Council resolution 940 (1994), force might be used to remove the military leadership from power in Haiti and ensure the return of the democratic Government of President Aristide. President Clinton stated that more than 20 countries had agreed to join the United States in a multinational force. On 17 September, in a final diplomatic effort, the President of the United States sent to Haiti a high-level mission, headed by former President Jimmy Carter. Faced with imminent invasion and after two days of intensive talks, the Haitian military leaders agreed to resign when a general amnesty would be voted into law by the Haitian Parliament, or by 15 October 1994, whichever was earlier. Under the agreement, the Haitian military and police forces would cooperate with the United States military mission.

Multinational force deployed

On 19 September 1994, in a first phase of the military operation authorized by Security Council resolution 940 (1994), the lead elements of the 28-nation multinational force, spearheaded by United States troops, landed in Haiti without opposition. Upon his arrival in Haiti on the same day, Lieutenant-General Hugh Shelton, the Commander of the force, coordinated the entry of the force with Haiti's military leaders.

The Secretary-General welcomed the fact that conditions had been created for the peaceful implementation of resolution 940 (1994). He also said that an advance group of United Nations military observers would be dispatched to Haiti shortly and that he was considering the early redeployment of MICIVIH. Meanwhile, Mr. Dante Caputo, having cited the changing context of the situation in Haiti, resigned on 19 September 1994 as Special Envoy of the Secretaries-General of the United Nations and OAS for Haiti. The Secretary-General received the resignation with deep regret and expressed to Mr. Caputo his thanks for the courage and devotion he had lent to the discharge of his duties. To succeed Mr. Caputo, the Secretary-General appointed, on 23 September, Mr. Lakhdar Brahimi, former Minister for Foreign Affairs of Algeria, as his Special Representative for Haiti.

On 27 September, the multinational force submitted to the Security Council the first of thirteen reports summarizing operations. The report[36] stated that activities of the force constituted the foundation for establishing the secure and stable environment necessary to restore and maintain democracy in Haiti. There was also evidence that the force was on its way towards establishing the conditions necessary for the full implementation of resolution 940 (1994).

The second report[37] was forwarded to the Security Council on 10 October. It summarized the second and third weeks of operations, during which the overall situation in Haiti was relatively quiet, with some incidents of violence among Haitians. The force continued to search aggressively for and seize weapons caches, to protect public safety and to expand its presence in the countryside. The report stated that substantial progress was made in re-establishing democracy in Haiti; in consequence, the force would be drawn down from its peak of 21,000 troops.

UNMIH advance team arrives in Haiti

The first group of the UNMIH advance team consisting of 12 United Nations military observers from Bangladesh, France, Ireland and New Zealand arrived in Haiti on 23 September 1994. The Chief Military Observer established liaison with the Commander of the multinational force, and the appropriate coordination mechanisms were put in place. The tasks of the team included coordinating with the multinational force in preparation for the full deployment of UNMIH, monitoring the operations of the multinational force, making its good offices available as required and reporting to the Secretary-General on the implementation of resolution 940 (1994).

On 29 September 1994, the Security Council, by its resolution 944 (1994), requested the Secretary-General to ensure the immediate completion of the deployment of the observers and other elements of the sixty-person UNMIH advance team. It also encouraged him, in consultation with the Secretary-General of OAS, to facilitate the immediate return to Haiti of MICIVIH. By other provisions of the resolution, the Council decided to lift the sanctions imposed on Haiti, beginning at 0001 am EST on the day after the return to Haiti of President Aristide.

With the arrival in Port-au-Prince on 30 September of seven additional members of the advance team, including four military observers from Guatemala and Djibouti, and 30 more personnel on 5 October, the team had become fully operational. In addition to the 16 military observers, the advance team comprised 10 military planners from Bangladesh, Canada and the United States; 13 civilian police personnel from Canada and 10 administrative staff personnel. The team was led in the field by the UNMIH Chief of Staff, Colonel William Fulton (Canada), acting under the authority of the Special Representative of the Secretary-General.

The Secretary-General noted[38] that the great majority of the Haitian population welcomed the multinational force, but might be developing unrealistically high expectations of what it would do. He also noted that, in preparation for the transition from the multinational force to UNMIH, the advance team's military component had established a joint working group with the force. The

[36]S/1994/1107, annex. [37]S/1994/1148, annex. [38]S/1994/1180.

transition could only take place when a secure and stable environment had been established, and when UNMIH's strength and structure were adequate for it to assume its functions. The advance team's tasks would expire when the force had completed its mission and when UNMIH had assumed the full range of its functions.

President Aristide reinstated

On 28 September 1994, President Aristide convened an extraordinary session of the Haitian Parliament to consider draft legislation on an amnesty. On 10 October, after the Parliament had passed the amnesty legislation, Lieutenant-General Cédras resigned as Commander-in-Chief of FADH. Other members of the military leadership, Brigadier-General Philippe Biamby and Colonel Michel François, also submitted their resignations. The President of Panama, at the request of President Aristide, agreed to give asylum to Lieutenant-General Cédras and Brigadier-General Biamby. Earlier, Colonel François had gone to the Dominican Republic. The Secretary-General expressed his satisfaction at the resignation of the military leadership in Haiti and hoped that this step would facilitate the return to power of President Aristide and the restoration of democracy in Haiti.

On 15 October 1994, after the departure of the military leadership, President Aristide returned to Haiti and resumed his functions, after three years of enforced exile. The Secretary-General welcomed the long-awaited return of the President and the resumption of the democratic process in Haiti. On the same day, the Security Council, by its resolution 948 (1994), also welcomed the return of President Aristide and, with his return, the lifting of sanctions at 0001 am EST on 16 October.

The Council expressed full support for efforts by President Aristide, democratic leaders in Haiti, and the legitimate organs of the restored Government to bring Haiti out of the crisis and return it to the democratic community of nations. Commending the efforts of all States, organizations and individuals who had contributed to that outcome, the Council recognized in particular the efforts of the multinational force in creating the conditions necessary for the return of democracy in Haiti. It also expressed its support for the deployment of the advance team of UNMIH and urged that cooperation continue between the Secretaries-General of the United Nations and OAS, especially regarding the rapid return to Haiti of MICIVIH.

On 25 October 1994, President Aristide designated Mr. Smarck Michel the new Prime Minister. His appointment was ratified by both Chambers of the Parliament on 4 November and his platform was approved unanimously in the Senate on 6 November and by overwhelming majority in the Chamber of Deputies on 7 November. The new Government took office on 8 November 1994.

From 23 to 29 October, the Secretary-General's Special Representative visited Haiti and had a series of discussions dealing with the situation on the ground, the operation of the multinational force and conditions for the transition from the multinational force to UNMIH. On 15 November, Secretary-General Boutros-Ghali paid a visit to Haiti. He assured President Aristide that the United Nations, in collaboration with OAS, would continue to assist Haiti on the road to national reconciliation, political stability and reconstruction.

Preparations for UNMIH deployment

In the meantime, the advance team of UNMIH reported that the multinational force continued to operate smoothly towards achieving its objectives under resolution 940 (1994), with few incidents and with evident widespread acceptance by the Haitian population. No acts of intimidation or violence against the United Nations or other international presence were reported. In addition to monitoring the operations of the multinational force, the military and police personnel of the advance team were engaged in on-site planning for the transition from the force to UNMIH.

On 21 November, the Secretary-General reported[39] to the Security Council that discussions were under way between the United Nations, the Government of Haiti, the Government of the United States and other interested parties to assure a smooth transition. The issues being addressed included the training of the Haitian police, the timetable for forthcoming legislative elections, and the establishment of a secure and stable environment. The Secretary-General noted that of particular concern was the setting up of an interim Haitian police pending the creation of a National Police.

The head of the UNMIH advance team believed that the strength of the team should be increased in order to further facilitate planning of the Mission, identification of conditions required for the transition and, most important, preparation

[39] S/1994/1322.

for the actual transition. The Secretary-General therefore recommended that the Security Council authorize expansion of the advance team up to 500 members to allow it to be progressively strengthened so that it would be fully prepared to enter the transition period. The Security Council did so on 29 November by resolution 964 (1994). It also welcomed the positive developments in Haiti since the deployment of the multinational force, and the establishment of a joint working group to prepare for the transition by the UNMIH advance team and the force.

MICIVIH returns to Haiti

The core group of MICIVIH returned to Haiti on 22 October 1994 to join the MICIVIH Executive Director, Mr. Granderson, and the staff of the Office of Human Rights, who had arrived on 6 October to evaluate the conditions for a return of MICIVIH. The activities of the Mission resumed on 26 October with the reopening of an office in Port-au-Prince.

In the meantime, the joint United Nations/OAS Working Group on MICIVIH, which had been set up in 1993 when MICIVIH was first sent to Haiti, met to look at the future of the Mission in terms of its redeployment and possible expansion of its mandate. At the meeting on 4 November in Washington, it was decided that MICIVIH would continue to give priority to the monitoring and promotion of respect for human rights in Haiti. As in the past, it would document the human rights situation, make recommendations to the Haitian authorities, implement an information and civic education programme and help to solve problems such as those relating to detentions, medical assistance to victims and the return of displaced persons. It was also decided that MICIVIH would contribute to institution-building.

On 23 November 1994, the Secretary-General proposed[40] to the General Assembly that MICIVIH, while continuing to verify compliance with Haiti's human rights obligations and to promote respect for the rights of all Haitians, should contribute, in so far as possible, to the strengthening of democratic institutions. The broadening of the responsibilities of the Mission would not have any financial implications, for the total number of its staff would remain unchanged.

On 5 December, the General Assembly took note[41] of the Secretary-General's report, in particular his recommendations with regard to MICIVIH's mandate. The Assembly requested the speedy return to Haiti of all members of the Mission "with the task of verifying compliance by Haiti with its human rights obligations, namely, to promote respect for the rights of all Haitians and to contribute to the strengthening of democratic institutions."

Transition date decided

After the arrival of the international force, FADH disintegrated. Politically motivated violence and human rights abuses decreased. The following weeks were marked by further improvement in the overall situation in Haiti. People could move freely throughout the country, the constitutional Government exercised its authority over the whole country and the Provisional Electoral Council was making preparations for legislative and local elections. No serious danger to the existence of the Government could be identified.

On the other hand, the collapse of FADH, the dissolution of the corps of rural police agents (section chiefs) and the lack of a functioning police force created a security void that contributed to a marked increase in banditry and criminality throughout the country. The security situation was very fragile. On 17 January 1995, the Secretary-General listed[42] for the Security Council a number of factors which could lead to future instability. Among them were the disaffection of former FADH members, the probable continued existence of paramilitary networks and the availability of arms; rising frustration at the inability of the justice system to address past human rights violations and current criminality; the delay in translating economic measures and development programmes into concrete improvements in the daily life of the impoverished majority of the population; and the additional tension that might be generated by the forthcoming elections.

Since UNMIH's mandate was expiring on 31 January 1995, the Secretary-General recommended that the Council authorize its extension for a period of six months, to 31 July 1995. He expected that UNMIH would be able to take over from the multinational force on or around 31 March 1995. The Secretary-General further detailed the mandate of the Mission, its rules of engagement, structure, deployment, concept of operations, preparations for the transition and transition timetable. He noted that in the remaining weeks before the handover to UNMIH, the multinational force would continue to work actively with the Government of Haiti to further

---

[40]A/49/689. [41]A/RES/49/27 A. [42]S/1995/46.

improve the security situation. It would continue the disarmament programme even more energetically than before. It would also help the Haitian security forces to investigate every unlawful act and arrest those who, acting individually or in groups, were responsible for many of the crimes in Port-au-Prince and elsewhere. The Secretary-General had already notified[43] the Security Council of his intention to appoint Major-General Joseph Kinzer (United States) as commander of the military component of UNMIH.

In accordance with resolution 940 (1994), the Security Council was to make its determination to terminate the multinational force's mission "taking into account recommendations from the member States of the multinational force, which are based on the assessment of the commander of the multinational force, and from the Secretary-General". On 18 January 1995, the President of the Council received a statement[44] by the member States saying that a secure and stable environment existed in Haiti. They recommended that the Council determine that it was appropriate for UNMIH to begin assuming the full range of its functions. In making this recommendation, they took note of and confirmed the findings of the report[45] of the Commander of the multinational force. The Secretary-General had submitted a report[46] on 17 January 1995.

On 30 January 1995, the Security Council adopted its resolution 975 (1995), in which it determined that a secure and stable environment, appropriate to the deployment of UNMIH, existed in Haiti. The Council authorized the Secretary-General to recruit and deploy military contingents, civilian police and other civilian personnel to allow UNMIH to assume its functions as established in resolutions 867 (1993) and 940 (1994). It also authorized him, working with the commander of the multinational force, to take the necessary steps in order for UNMIH to assume these responsibilities. According to resolution 975, the full transfer of responsibility from the multinational force to UNMIH was to be completed by 31 March 1995. The Council also extended the mandate of UNMIH until 31 July 1995 and authorized the Secretary-General to deploy in Haiti, in accordance with resolution 940, up to 6,000 troops and, as recommended in his report to the Council of 17 January 1995, up to 900 civilian police officers.

E. Transition to UNMIH

As a result of the effective cooperation between the multinational force and UNMIH and thorough preparation work, the transition from the multinational force to UNMIH took place on 31 March 1995, in full compliance with the envisaged timetable. The official ceremony, which was held at the National Palace at Port-au-Prince, was attended, among others, by President Aristide of Haiti, President Clinton of the United States, the President of the Security Council and the Secretary-General.

UNMIH established its headquarters in Port-au-Prince and sub-headquarters in six operational sectors (Cap Haïtien, Gonaïves, Port-au-Prince (2), Jacmel and Les Cayes). Five infantry battalions (including the Quick Reaction Force), support units, a military police battalion, an engineering unit, aviation and logistic elements, a military information support team and a civil affairs unit were deployed in 10 locations (Cap Haïtien, Fort-Liberté, Hinche, Gonaïves, Port-de-Paix, St. Marc, Port-au-Prince, Jacmel, Les Cayes, Jérémie).

Special Forces elements were deployed throughout the country in 25 locations. As at 10 April 1995, the strength of the UNMIH military component stood at 6,017 and the strength of the UNMIH civilian police component (CIVPOL) stood at 791. Chief Superintendent Neil Pouliot (Canada) had been named CIVPOL commander. Approximately two thirds of the military and one third of the civilian police components of UNMIH came from the multinational force. UNMIH also had 122 out of 220 international civilian staff, 175 out of 240 local staff and 12 out of 29 United Nations Volunteers.

UNMIH activities

Following the transition, UNMIH provided security throughout Haiti. The overall situation had continued to be generally stable and secure. There were few cases of violence presumed

---

[43]S/1995/31. [44]S/1995/55, annexes I and II. [45]S/1995/15, annex. [46]S/1995/46.

UNMIH deployment as of November 1995

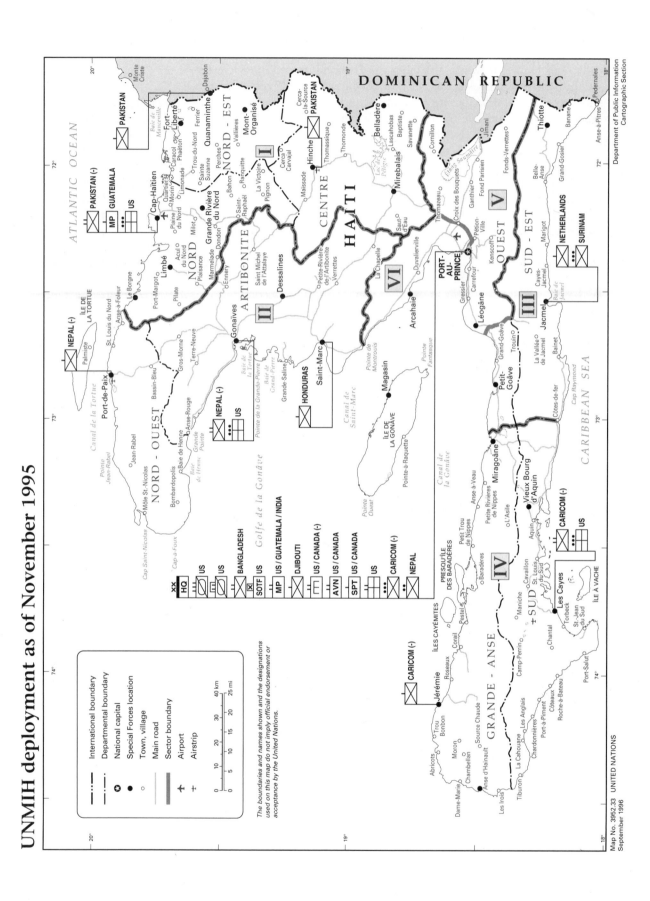

Map No. 3952.33   UNITED NATIONS
September 1996

Department of Public Information
Cartographic Section

The boundaries and names shown and the designations
used on this map do not imply official endorsement or
acceptance by the United Nations.

to be politically motivated and the number of vigilante killings dropped significantly. Common crime also levelled off but remained a primary concern of UNMIH. Humanitarian aid convoys and warehouses continued to be targeted by organized gangs, particularly in the seaport area of the capital and in the north of the country.

In its task of sustaining a secure and stable environment, UNMIH carried out patrols; escorted humanitarian relief convoys; provided back-up to the Haitian authorities in law and order situations; and ensured the security of UNMIH personnel and property. In addition, as the Mission evolved, UNMIH military personnel confronted many unforeseen tasks. For example, they assumed prison guard duties in Cap-Haïtien and Gonaïves for more than a month following riots and disturbances, undertook harbour patrols following the departure of the United States Coast Guard and maintained a presence in the national penitentiary and in some of the Port-au-Prince police stations.

The early deployment of a permanent and effective police force by the Haitian authorities was considered to be central to Haiti's long-term stability. The Interim Public Security Force, consisting of some 3,300 screened and quickly retrained former military personnel as well as 900 other trainees, was gradually being replaced by the new Haitian National Police. It was decided that Haiti would set up a police force of some 5,000 officers. UNMIH's CIVPOL monitored and guided the work of both the Interim Public Security Force and the Haitian National Police, and provided the latter with on-the-job training. CIVPOL had also to undertake such unanticipated tasks as firearm training for the ministerial security force, and security surveys of the facilities of a number of government ministries and of the National Commission for Truth and Justice. CIVPOL also coordinated the delivery of food for prisoners nationwide and helped to provide prison security.

Civil affairs activities undertaken by UNMIH included projects providing assistance to Electricité d'Haïti to improve power supply, security to food convoys, the transportation and security of repatriated Haitian refugees, the development of a disaster response training programme, assistance to the Haitian Government with animal immunization and nutrition management programmes, engineering support for public construction projects and the removal, in collaboration with the municipal authorities, of hundreds of wrecked vehicles littering the streets of Port-au-Prince.

The Special Representative, Mr. Brahimi, and his senior staff met regularly with President Aristide, the Prime Minister and members of the Cabinet, senior government officials, political leaders and members of the general population.

Parliamentary and local elections were scheduled to take place in June 1995. As part of its mandate, UNMIH assisted in maintaining security throughout the election period. In accordance with the division of labour agreed upon by the United Nations and OAS, UNMIH also provided the Haitian Provisional Electoral Council with logistical and financial assistance, while the OAS Electoral Observation Mission (EOM), in cooperation with UNMIH and MICIVIH, organized and led the observation of the elections. In addition, a United Nations Electoral Assistance Team provided technical expertise to the Provisional Electoral Council in such areas as logistical planning and organization of the elections and distribution of electoral materials, budget estimates, preparation of technical documentation, registration of candidates, and polling and counting.

As for MICIVIH, its strength comprised 190 observers (including other substantive staff) and 9 administrative staff (2 OAS, 7 United Nations). Of the observers, 84 were contracted by OAS and 106 by the United Nations, 26 of the latter being United Nations Volunteers. Fifty nationalities were represented. In addition to its headquarters in Port-au-Prince, the Mission maintained nine offices throughout the country. In July 1995, at the request[47] of President Aristide, the Assembly authorized[48] a further extension of MICIVIH's mandate until 7 February 1996.

The Secretary-General reported[49] to the Security Council on 24 July 1995 that UNMIH had made significant progress towards achieving the goals established by the Council. It was hoped that by February 1996 Haiti would have duly elected institutions and that a functioning security system would be in place. Therefore, the Secretary-General recommended that the Council authorize the extension of UNMIH's mandate until the end of February 1996, as envisaged in resolution 940 (1994) establishing the objective of completing UNMIH's mission by that time.

On 31 July 1995, the Security Council commended[50] UNMIH on its successful efforts and decided to extend the mandate of the Mission for a period of seven months. It looked forward to the conclusion of UNMIH's mandate at that time and to the safe, secure and orderly assumption of office by a new, constitutionally elected government.

[47]A/49/926, annex. [48]A/RES/49/27 B. [49]S/1995/614. [50]S/RES/1007 (1995).

Legislative elections

From the outset, the Provisional Electoral Council worked to a very tight schedule, and there were widespread concerns that delays or changes in the calendar might adversely affect the organization of the elections. The Council had to extend the deadline for voter registration three times, from 17 to 30 April, then to 31 May, and again to 3 June 1995. In some areas, registration was still under way as late as one week before polling day. As for candidate registration, the complicated selection system and the large number of applications led to several modifications in the final list of candidates, even after its scheduled printing date of 15 May. This resulted in many errors in the ballots. There were also problems related to the training of polling officers, late decision regarding the counting systems, and financial difficulties.

The municipal and local elections and the first round of the legislative elections were held on 25 June 1995. By comparison with previous elections, voters enjoyed unprecedented security and, despite the traditional lack of interest in such elections, turned out in reasonable numbers. On the whole, election day was peaceful, and the level of violence that some had feared did not materialize. A few incidents did occur, however. A candidate for the Chamber of Deputies was killed and a polling station official in a Port-au-Prince suburb was attacked. Other instances of violence included the burning of electoral material and offices, and demonstrations and threats against electoral officials.

Organizational problems, however, prevented many Haitians from voting. A number of polling stations opened late, did not open at all, or were relocated unannounced. An undetermined number of legitimate candidates were omitted from the ballots, leading in some places to demonstrations and to the cancellation of the vote. A number of ballots and tally sheets reportedly disappeared or were destroyed. Allegations of fraud and some intimidation were levelled, and there were numerous complaints of irregularities.

The Secretary-General of OAS, who was present in Haiti at the time of the elections, issued a statement that day declaring that "from all indications, electors were able to exercise their franchise freely". In a report released by the OAS Secretary-General on 13 July, EOM concluded that the elections had "established a foundation which, although shaky, provides the basis for further positive progress towards the continuing evolution of an increasingly peaceful democracy in Haiti". The Mission expressed the hope that "all of those involved in future elections will profit from the mistakes and problems which arose during the course of this election and will continue to build on the positive aspects in the interests of Haiti and its people".

The elections drew strong criticism from many Haitian political leaders. The Lavalas coalition, which supported President Aristide, considered that mistakes and irregularities had not been directed at any single party and that, consequently, the credibility of the electoral process itself was not affected. Most other political parties held the opposite view, demanding that new elections be held in the constituencies where irregularities had been documented or, in some cases, that the 25 June elections be annulled. The Provisional Electoral Council eventually agreed to complementary elections in some constituencies. Following the publication of preliminary partial election results, however, virtually all non-Lavalas political parties threatened to boycott the complementary elections, as well as second-round elections.

In an effort to encourage a continuation of the political process aimed at bringing Haiti out of crisis, the Special Representative initiated several meetings with the Provisional Electoral Council President and his colleagues, with political leaders and with representatives of foreign Governments and international organizations.

In the wake of the criticism, the President of the Provisional Electoral Council, admitting "serious mistakes", and another member of the Council resigned. They were replaced by presidential decree. These changes did not satisfy most political parties that did not belong to the Lavalas coalition, and virtually all of them decided not to participate in the second round, reruns or complementary elections.

The Security Council reacted[51] with deep concern to the irregularities observed in the first round of elections and urged all parties to the process to make every effort to ensure that such problems were corrected in forthcoming balloting. The Council called upon the Secretaries-General of the United Nations and OAS to continue to render all appropriate assistance to the Haitian electoral process. In pursuance of that resolution, UNMIH, MICIVIH and EOM continued to cooperate closely with the Provisional Electoral Council in the organization of the remaining elections.

On 13 August, complementary legislative and municipal elections were held under peaceful conditions. Thorough preparation and increased security allowed EOM to conclude that there was

[51] S/RES/1007 (1995).

a perceptible improvement in the organization of the elections. However, voter turnout was low, particularly in the Port-au-Prince area.

The second round of the legislative elections and additional reruns took place on 17 September in an atmosphere of tranquillity. The impact of training, better planning and improved security was apparent. According to the Provisional Electoral Council and EOM, voter participation was again rather low (around 30 per cent). While many of the "non-Lavalas" parties boycotted the elections, a substantial number of candidates belonging to them did contest the elections, and five of them were elected. On 8 October 1995, additional run-offs were held in four constituencies and elections were again organized in seven communal sections. These elections also took place without incident.

The polls resulted in a victory for the Lavalas platform, which won a majority in the Senate with 17 of 27 seats and in the Chamber of Deputies with 66 of 83 seats. At the municipal and local levels, the Lavalas platform won 102 mayorships out of 133 and 345 Conseils d'administration de sections communales out of 562. The parties that boycotted the second round of the legislative elections continued to question the results.[52]

November 1995 events

As a result of the more active role played by the Haitian public security forces and of the continued efforts of UNMIH, the security situation in Haiti further improved in September and October 1995. Although the number of popular demonstrations over economic and social issues continued to increase, they were generally peaceful and did not generate any lasting or widespread tensions.

However, the situation deteriorated abruptly in the wake of the attack on 7 November 1995 against two deputies, one of whom was killed

and the other seriously injured. Violent demonstrations erupted in Les Cayes, Département du Sud, to which the two deputies belonged, necessitating the deployment of the Quick Reaction Force and joint Haitian National Police/UNMIH patrols for several days until the situation stabilized. On 11 November, President Aristide called for immediate and total disarmament and accused the international community of complacency in this regard. Agitation quickly spread to other cities. Roadblocks were set up, and demonstrations, acts of arson, looting, weapons searches and vigilante justice occurred in various places throughout Haiti, especially Port-au-Prince, Gonaïves and Cap Haïtien. On 13 November, following a meeting with President Aristide, the Secretary-General's Special Representative appealed to the people of Haiti not to take the law into their own hands, and the police, with the support of UNMIH, slowly re-established control. These incidents, which resulted in at least seven people dead, many more injured and considerable property damage, showed that the security situation was still fragile.

Common crime remained a very serious problem throughout the country, and a major concern for the population. There were also incidents involving theft of property from UNMIH's installations and personnel. Although there was no indication of any organized threat against UNMIH personnel, anti-United Nations slogans appeared on the streets of Port-au-Prince and on some leaflets during the days of renewed tension in mid-November. Earlier, in August 1995, an UNMIH civilian police officer had been shot in his house in Petit Goâve and critically wounded. There were to be other incidents as well. On 17 December, also in Petit Goâve, shots were fired at an UNMIH military vehicle. On 29 January 1996, a civilian police officer was killed in Port-au-Prince in an apparent robbery attempt.

F. December 1995–March 1996

Presidential election

In the following weeks, political activity in Haiti centred around the presidential election. During that period, there was some confusion, including within the Lavalas Movement, stemming from a campaign to have President Aristide

remain in office for three more years, thus making up for the time he had spent in exile. President Aristide, however, made it clear that he would hand over power, as provided for in the Constitution, on 7 February 1996.

[52] S/1995/922.

The election, in which fourteen candidates participated, was held on 17 December 1995. Of the main parties that had boycotted the second round of the legislative elections, only one took part in the contest. In accordance with its mandate, UNMIH provided extensive technical assistance to the Provisional Electoral Council in preparing for the election, as well as the necessary logistical support.

Polling took place in a peaceful environment. There were no major incidents of violence during the run-up to the election, on polling day, or during the counting. While there were minor problems, the Provisional Electoral Council worked with dispatch to solve them. Over 400 international observers, including EOM, a presidential delegation from the United States, a French parliamentary delegation and several NGOs, all concluded that the election had been free, fair and peaceful. The results were announced on 23 December 1995 by the President of the Provisional Electoral Council. Mr. René Préval, President Aristide's Prime Minister in 1991 and the candidate of the ruling Lavalas Movement, won in the first round with 87.9 per cent of the votes. He assumed power on 7 February 1996.

Operation of UNMIH

In the meantime, UNMIH continued to assist in the formation and training of the Haitian national police force. The Interim Public Security Force was abolished by presidential decree on 6 December 1995 following the gradual demobilization of most of its members. By the end of February 1996, the Haitian security forces comprised about 6,000 personnel.

Formal training of the new police force was carried out with the assistance of Canada, France and the United States in the Police Academy, run by the International Criminal Investigative Training Assistance Programme (ICITAP) of the United States. UNMIH worked closely with the Haitian authorities to provide on-the-job training and to give guidance to the new police officers deployed throughout the country and monitor their performance. In addition, three United Nations police officers were assigned to the Criminal Investigation Unit to investigate particularly sensitive murder cases.

UNMIH continued to assist the Government of Haiti in sustaining a secure and stable environment and protecting international personnel. The Mission provided security to humanitarian convoys, airports, seaports, storage locations and United Nations installations. With financial contributions from the Caisse française de développement and the Inter-American Development Bank, UNMIH engineering units rebuilt the bridge in Jacmel that was washed away late in 1994. President Aristide attended the opening of the new bridge on 15 December 1995. Contingents from Canada, the Netherlands and the United States provided the stimulus for small development projects sponsored by their respective Governments, and other UNMIH contingents also contributed to these activities. Overall, some 1,000 small projects, including training courses on disaster relief and prevention, were initiated by UNMIH.

UNMIH also paid special attention to the planning of a smooth and orderly transfer to the Government of Haiti of its responsibilities and functions. The first meeting of the Trilateral Commission, comprising the Government of Haiti, the United Nations and the Friends of the Secretary-General for Haiti (at the time Argentina, Canada, France, the United States and Venezuela), was held in Port-au-Prince on 16 November 1995. The Commission formed joint working groups to deal with all issues pertaining to transition, including disarmament, information, justice, prisons and human rights, presidential security, election security, airports, seaports and coastguards, fire-fighting and urban disorders, and traffic.

At the same time, the Secretary-General, mindful of the need for economy, started to reduce the level of UNMIH personnel. A phased reduction of civilian police was conducted between October 1995 and January 1996, when some 540 personnel left Haiti. At the end of February, a total of approximately 300 French-speaking police officers remained in the country. UNMIH's civilian staff was also significantly decreased. All members of the Electoral Assistance Unit left Haiti during January 1996, following the presidential elections. On the military side, the concept developed for the reduction of the force level envisaged the gradual vacating of outlying areas, starting with the least troublesome operational sectors and culminating in a reduced force in Port-au-Prince and Cap Haïtien. The reduction of the force level was initiated in mid-November 1995. By 29 February 1996, the troop level was down from almost 6,000 to 4,100 combat personnel, deployed in Port-au-Prince and Cap Haïtien.

UNMIH further extended

Since President Aristide's return in October 1994, Haiti had taken a number of steps to strengthen democracy and stability. With the help of UNMIH, local and legislative elections and the presidential election were held in an environment of calm and peace. Power was transferred from one democratically elected President to another in an orderly and constitutional manner. Parliament began to play its assigned role, and measures were taken to improve the functioning of the judiciary.

By all indications, there was no organized threat to the Government of Haiti. However, concern was expressed in many quarters that growing popular discontent could be used by disgruntled groups to foment trouble once President Aristide had handed over power and UNMIH had left the country. Unemployment and underemployment were widespread, services and infrastructure were inadequate or non-existing and there were other economic hardships. The Government of President Préval faced a number of difficult decisions to stimulate economic development and attract domestic and foreign investment.

UNMIH was due to cease all its operations on 29 February 1996. On 14 February, the Secretary-General made an assessment of the situation in Haiti in a report[53] to the Security Council. In the report, he presented his recommendations on the role that the United Nations should continue to play in Haiti to consolidate the gains achieved. The report also took into account a letter[54] dated 9 February 1996 in which President Préval had asked the Secretary-General to "take appropriate steps with a view to bringing about an extension of the mandate of UNMIH so that a gradual withdrawal may take place in the months ahead".

The Secretary-General shared the view expressed by most observers that UNMIH should not cease its activities abruptly on 29 February 1996 but should continue to assist the Government for a few more months. During that time, UNMIH's assets would be gradually withdrawn. The Trilateral Commission also reached the same conclusion. The Secretary-General therefore recommended an extension of the mandate of UNMIH for a period of six months. He also recommended, in the light of the gradual transfer of UNMIH's functions and responsibilities to the Haitian authorities, that the strength of both its military and civilian police components be reduced. Primary responsibility for the maintenance of a stable and secure environment would rest with the Haitian Government. UNMIH would serve mainly as a back-up. It would also continue to focus on training the new civilian Haitian National Police.

In order to achieve UNMIH's objectives, 1,600 infantry personnel, 300 combat support personnel, 300 civilian police, 160 international civilian staff, 18 United Nations Volunteers and 150 local staff would be required. The military component would consist of three infantry battalions, including two incoming reconnaissance companies and a Quick Reaction Force, based on infantry and helicopter assets that would be stationed in Port-au-Prince. The combat support elements would include an engineer company, a transport platoon, an aviation squadron, a field hospital, a military police platoon and headquarters personnel.

On 29 February 1996, acting on the recommendations of the Secretary-General, the Security Council decided[55] to extend the mandate of UNMIH for a final period of four months. It also decided to decrease the level of the military component to no more than 1,200 personnel and the civilian police component to 300 personnel. The Council requested the Secretary-General to take appropriate steps to further reduce UNMIH's strength consistent with the implementation of its mandate, and to initiate planning not later than 1 June 1996 for its complete withdrawal.

In order to bridge the gap between the level of strength of military personnel decided by the Council and the level recommended by the Secretary-General, the Government of Canada decided to make available, entirely at its own expense, 700 additional troops.

G. Composition of UNMIH

In the course of the Mission, UNMIH's military personnel were contributed by the following countries: Antigua and Barbuda, Argentina, Austria, Bahamas, Bangladesh, Barbados, Belize, Canada, Djibouti, France, Guatemala, Guyana, Honduras, India, Ireland, Jamaica, Nepal, Netherlands, New Zealand, Pakistan, Suriname, Trinidad and Tobago, Tunisia and United States. Civilian

---

[53]S/1996/112. [54]S/1996/99. [55]S/RES/1048 (1996).

police monitors were provided by Algeria, Argentina, Austria, Bangladesh, Barbados, Benin, Canada, Djibouti, France, Guinea Bissau, Jordan, Mali, Nepal, Pakistan, Philippines, Russian Federation, Saint Kitts and Nevis, Saint Lucia, Suriname and Togo.

When UNMIH was established in September 1993, it was headed by Mr. Dante Caputo, who served as Special Representative of the Secretary-General and also oversaw the activities of MICIVIH. Mr. Caputo, former Minister for Foreign Affairs of Argentina, had served as Special Envoy of the Secretary-General for Haiti since 11 December 1992. On 13 January 1993, the OAS Secretary-General also appointed Mr. Caputo as his Special Envoy. Following Mr. Caputo's resignation on 19 September 1994, the Secretary-General appointed, on 23 September, Mr. Lakhdar Brahimi, former Minister for Foreign Affairs of Algeria, as his Special Representative. In March 1996, Mr. Enrique ter Horst (Venezuela) succeeded Mr. Brahimi as the Special Representative and Chief of Mission.

In October 1993, the Secretary-General informed the Security Council of his intention to appoint Colonel Gregg Pulley (United States) as Commander of UNMIH's military unit and Superintendent Jean-Jacques Lemay (Canada) as Commander of the UNMIH police unit. However, UNMIH did not deploy at that time. In January 1995, Major-General Joseph Kinzer (United States) was appointed as commander of the military component and Chief Superintendent Neil Pouliot (Canada) was named commander of the civilian police component. In February 1996, Colonel Philippe Balladur (France) succeeded Chief Superintendent Pouliot and, in March, Brigadier-General J.R.P. Daigle (Canada) succeeded Major-General Kinzer.

H. Financial aspects

The costs of the operation were met by the assessed contributions of United Nations Member States and amounted to $336,800,000.[56]

The cost of the operation of the multinational force was borne by the participating member States.

I. Other aspects

Humanitarian assistance

Following the 1991 *coup d'état*, the humanitarian situation in Haiti deteriorated in spite of the efforts of the United Nations and NGOs. In March 1993, the United Nations and OAS launched a consolidated appeal for a humanitarian plan of action designed to respond to the urgent humanitarian needs of the Haitian people. The budget required for the implementation of this plan was estimated at $62.7 million, for the areas of health, nutrition, agriculture and education.

Donors, however, provided only $9.6 million in response to the 1993 humanitarian appeal. Throughout 1994, eight agencies working under the United Nations/OAS umbrella — United Nations Development Programme (UNDP), the Food and Agriculture Organization of the United Nations (FAO), the World Food Programme (WFP), the United Nations High Commissioner for Refugees (UNHCR), the United Nations Children's Fund (UNICEF), the Pan American Health Organization (PAHO)/ World Health Organization (WHO) and the United Nations Educational, Scientific and Cultural Organization (UNESCO) — drew on their core resources to fund the shortfall in donor response to the inter-agency appeal and continued humanitarian assistance programmes in Haiti, despite difficulties created by the de facto authorities and the sanctions regime imposed by the Security Council. United Nations programmes operated under a United Nations Humanitarian Coordinator serving concurrently as Resident Representative of UNDP.

[56]S/1996/416/Add.1/Rev.1.

Working with over 150 Haitian, international and non-governmental organizations, United Nations agencies focused on maintaining health and hospital emergency services, distributing basic drugs and medical supplies, helping control transmissible diseases and maintaining the "cold chain" needed for vaccinations. Food relief was also critical. By the time of the arrival of the multinational force in the country, with United Nations help humanitarian agencies were distributing food to some 940,000 needy Haitians. United Nations agency efforts also sought to prevent the breakdown in farm production and income and to improve water supply and sanitation in areas subject to high public health risks. Bilateral donors also continued to carry out significant humanitarian activities, directly and through NGOs.

In its resolution 873 (1993) of 13 October 1993, the Security Council terminated the suspension of the embargo on petroleum and petroleum products and arms and related *matériel* of all kinds imposed on Haiti by resolution 841 (1993). Within the strict framework of the provisions of the resolution providing for possible exemptions for essential humanitarian needs, the United Nations and OAS invited PAHO to assume responsibility for a fuel management plan to permit the continued functioning of humanitarian activities. This programme, which commenced in January 1994, was managed by a steering committee composed of representatives of the organizations of the United Nations system, donors, NGOs and members of the Government. By mid-September 1994, a total of 1.2 million gallons of diesel fuel and over 206,000 gallons of gasoline had been distributed under the fuel management plan to NGOs and agencies engaged in humanitarian operations.

In view of the uncertainty and potential for violence expected to accompany a military intervention in Haiti, United Nations agencies established a communications network among NGOs and public and private hospitals, made contingency plans for dealing with epidemics and built up decentralized stocks of medicines, health supplies, water supply equipment and food to the maximum degree possible.

In late September 1994, an advance team from the United Nations Department of Humanitarian Affairs arrived in Haiti to strengthen the office of the Humanitarian Coordinator. The team provided liaison between the multinational force and the humanitarian assistance community in Haiti, and led an inter-agency effort to identify post-intervention humanitarian needs. On the basis of its consultations with bilateral donors, and international and Haitian NGOs, the United Nations, OAS and the Government of Haiti prepared an appeal to meet immediate humanitarian needs and to facilitate the transition to reconstruction and development in the country. The appeal, covering the period 1 December 1994 to 31 May 1995, required a total of $93.9 million. Some $51 million was contributed, representing half the needs mentioned in the appeal.

Development activities

The Secretary-General repeatedly stressed the importance of the state of the Haitian economy to the success of the United Nations mission and long-term stability in Haiti. The extreme poverty and high unemployment prevailing in much of the country required sustained international attention. Bearing this in mind, the Secretary-General appointed Mr. Cristián Ossa as his Deputy Special Representative and concurrently UNDP Resident Representative. This marked the first time that the United Nations had linked a peace-keeping mission to development activities in this manner. The linkage was intended to promote closer cooperation between all concerned and facilitate the transition from UNMIH to continuing peace-building activities by the United Nations in Haiti.

The political changes in Haiti created high expectations for swift economic recovery. The Haitian public expected that the return of President Aristide would bring a rapid improvement of their standard of living. This could not happen in a short period of time, and the Government started to be blamed for unemployment and the high cost of living. Suffering from the lack of basic infrastructure, the economy of Haiti was in need of private and public investments. Through dialogue and cooperation between the Government and its development partners, nine priority sectors were identified: agriculture and the environment; energy; governance; justice; infrastructure; private sector development; health; education; and poverty alleviation.

As of 31 August 1995, total financial commitments by multilateral and bilateral donors and creditors for the period October 1994 to the year 2000 reached $1.7 billion. Of this, about $650 million — including balance-of-payments support — was expected to be disbursed before the end of 1995. The commitments of the United Nations system amounted to 37 per cent ($630 million) of total multilateral and bilateral financial resources. Of these resources, about a third (including balance-of-payment support and debt forgiveness) were utilized between October 1994 and the end of 1995, but new commitments were made after August 1995. Thus, external resources available for the next few years continued to be well above US$1 billion.

The United States Agency for International Development was at the forefront of total disbursement following the return of President Aristide. Gradually, financing from the Inter-American Development Bank, the non-conditional resources of the World Bank and the European Union began to play a larger role. Bilateral donors, including Canada, France and Germany, continued to serve as an important source of concessional funding. Other donors, such as Japan, Spain and Switzerland, also became more active in support of development programmes.

Sixteen Latin American and Caribbean countries under the sponsorship of the Latin American Economic System and UNDP met in Port-au-Prince from 22 to 24 November 1995 to negotiate development cooperation projects with the Haitian authorities. This unprecedented effort at horizontal cooperation led to agreement on 22 projects totally financed and 73 projects partially financed by Latin American and Caribbean countries.

The United Nations programmes and specialized agencies present in Haiti — UNDP, including the United Nations Capital Development Fund and the United Nations Volunteers programme, UNICEF, WFP, the United Nations Population Fund, UNHCR, FAO, UNESCO and WHO — took various steps to contribute to the implementation of the emergency economic recovery programme, while paying increasing attention to the developmental aspects of their activities. On 12 December 1995, under the leadership of the Resident Coordinator, these institutions, the International Monetary Fund and the World Bank met to consider joint activities, emerging issues and priorities, their future programmes and interactions, and post-UNMIH activities.

Part XI

Other peace-keeping missions

Chapter 29

United Nations Security Force in West New Guinea (West Irian) (UNSF)/ United Nations Temporary Executive Authority (UNTEA)

Chapter 29

United Nations Security Force (UNSF)/United Nations Temporary Executive Authority (UNTEA)

Background

The territory of West New Guinea (West Irian) had been in the possession of the Netherlands since 1828. When the Netherlands formally recognized the sovereign independence of Indonesia in 1949, the status of West Irian remained unresolved. It was agreed in the Charter of Transfer of Sovereignty — concluded between the Netherlands and Indonesia at The Hague, Netherlands, in November 1949 — that the issue would be postponed for a year, and that "the status quo of the presidency of New Guinea" would be "maintained under the Government of the Netherlands" in the mean time. The ambiguity of the language, however, led the Netherlands to consider itself the sovereign Power in West New Guinea, since this would be a continuation of the "status quo". Indonesia, on the other hand, interpreted the Dutch role there to be strictly administrative, with the implication that West Irian would be incorporated into Indonesia after a year.

The status of the territory was still being disputed when Indonesia brought the matter before the United Nations in 1954.[1] Indonesia claimed that the territory rightfully belonged to it and should be freed from Dutch colonial rule. The Netherlands maintained that the Papuans of West New Guinea were not Indonesians and therefore should be allowed to decide their own future when they were ready to do so.

The future of the territory was discussed at the General Assembly's regular sessions from 1954 to 1957 and at the 1961 session, but no resolutions on it were adopted.

In December 1961, when increasing rancour between the Indonesian and Dutch Governments made the prospect of a negotiated settlement even more elusive, Secretary-General U Thant, who had been appointed Acting Secretary-General following the death of Secretary-General Dag Hammarskjöld, undertook to resolve the dispute through his good offices. Consulting with the Indonesian and Dutch Permanent Representatives to the United Nations, he suggested that informal talks take place between the parties in the presence of former United States Ambassador Ellsworth Bunker, who would act as the Secretary-General's representative. The parties agreed, and talks were begun in early 1962.

A sharpening of tension between the two Governments occurred shortly thereafter, however, when Indonesia landed paratroops in West New Guinea. The Netherlands charged that the landings constituted an act of aggression, but Indonesia refuted this on the grounds that "Indonesians who have entered and who in future will continue to enter West Irian are Indonesian nationals who move into Indonesia's own territory now dominated by the Dutch by force".[2] Secretary-General U Thant urged restraint by both parties but declined a Dutch request to send United Nations observers to the scene, noting that such action could only be considered if both Governments made the request.[3]

Further incidents were reported by the Netherlands during the first months of 1962, and there were intermittent lulls in the progress of Ambassador Bunker's talks. A number of communications from the Netherlands and from Indonesia were circulated as documents of the Security Council in connection with this question.

In one such letter,[4] dated 16 May, the Prime Minister of the Netherlands, stating that Indonesia had landed more parachutists on West New Guinea and had continued its aggressive acts, requested that the Acting Secretary-General make an appeal to Indonesia to remind it of its primary obligations under the United Nations Charter and to refrain from all aggressive acts against the territory and people of West New Guinea. He added that the Netherlands' presence in New Guinea was of a temporary nature and that his Government

[1]A/2694. [2]S/5128. [3]S/5124. [4]S/5123.

was prepared to give its fullest cooperation to the Secretary-General's efforts to find an honest and just solution for the territory on the basis of Article 73 of the Charter — concerning responsibilities of administering Powers towards non-self-governing territories — and General Assembly resolutions on the question of colonialism.

In a reply[5] dated 22 May, Secretary-General U Thant stated that, while he was concerned about developments in the area and had appealed already to the parties to exercise the utmost restraint, he could not accept the suggestion to approach Indonesia with an appeal which would imply that he was taking sides in the controversy. He did, however, keep a close eye on the situation, frequently consulting with the representatives of both countries and appealing to them to resume formal negotiations on the basis of Ambassador Bunker's proposals.

The Acting Secretary-General was at last able to announce, on 31 July 1962, that a preliminary agreement had been reached, and that official negotiations were to take place under his auspices. The final negotiations were held at United Nations Headquarters under the chairmanship of the Secretary-General, with Ambassador Bunker continuing to act as mediator. An agreement was signed at New York by Indonesia and the Netherlands on 15 August 1962. Ratification instruments[6] were exchanged between the two countries on 20 September 1962 and, the next day, the General Assembly took note of the agreement in resolution 1752 (XVII) of the same date, authorizing the Secretary-General to carry out the tasks entrusted to him therein.

The agreement provided for the administration of West New Guinea (West Irian) to be transferred by the Netherlands to a United Nations Temporary Executive Authority (UNTEA), to be headed by a United Nations Administrator who would be acceptable to both parties and who would be appointed by the Secretary-General. Under the Secretary-General's jurisdiction, UNTEA would have full authority after 1 October 1962 to administer the territory, to maintain law and order, to protect the rights of the inhabitants and to ensure uninterrupted, normal services until 1 May 1963, when the administration of the territory was to be transferred to Indonesia.

The agreement also stipulated that the Secretary-General would provide a United Nations Security Force (UNSF) to assist UNTEA with as many troops as the United Nations Administrator deemed necessary. In "related understandings" to the main agreement, it was established that United Nations personnel would observe the implementation of the cease-fire that was to become effective before UNTEA assumed authority. The United Nations was therefore entrusted with a dual peacekeeping role in addition to its administrative responsibilities as the executive authority.

Arranging a cease-fire

To pave the way for the arrival in West Irian of UNTEA and UNSF, a cease-fire between Indonesian and Netherlands forces had to be enforced. The memorandum of understanding concerning the cease-fire — presented on 15 August 1962 in a note[7] to the Acting Secretary-General from the representatives of Indonesia and the Netherlands — requested that the Secretary-General undertake immediately some of the functions outlined in the main agreement, so as to effect a cessation of hostilities as soon as possible. Such action would constitute an "extraordinary measure", because the General Assembly would not be voting on the establishment of UNTEA and UNSF until it convened in late September.

The Secretary-General responded promptly, stating that he was prepared to undertake the responsibilities mentioned in the note. The memorandum on the cessation of hostilities specified that the Secretary-General would assign United Nations personnel to perform certain tasks, including: observing the cease-fire; protecting the security of Dutch and Indonesian forces; restoring the situation in the event of breaches of the cease-fire; assisting in informing Indonesian troops in the jungle of the existence of the cease-fire; and providing a non-military supply line to Indonesian troops.

Although there was no explicit reference to military observers in the memorandum, the Secretary-General selected them to perform these tasks. Furthermore, he agreed to dispatch them without the prior authorization of the General Assembly or the Security Council, a step never before taken by a Secretary-General. Reference was made in the memorandum to UNSF and its law-and-order maintenance role, with the implication that the Secretary-General should address this responsibility with all possible speed.

The Secretary-General appointed Brigadier-General (later Major-General) Indar Jit Rikhye, his Military Adviser, to head the military observer team that was to supervise all arrangements for the cease-fire. Six Member States (Brazil, Ceylon, In-

---

[5] S/5124. [6] A/5170, annex C. [7] A/5170, annex B.

dia, Ireland, Nigeria and Sweden) agreed to provide 21 observers for this purpose. They were drawn from troops of these nations then serving either in the United Nations Emergency Force or the United Nations Operation in the Congo.

The observer force was assembled in West Irian within days of the signing of the agreement at United Nations Headquarters. The observers were informed at that time that the Netherlands military command had proclaimed a cease-fire as of 0001 GMT on 18 August 1962, and had ordered its ground forces to concentrate in the main garrison towns, although air and naval forces continued to patrol the territory. After a visit to Djakarta by General Rikhye, contacts were established with the Indonesian troops in the jungle. In this connection, frequent radio broadcasts on both the Netherlands-owned and Indonesian stations told the troops that hostilities had ceased. Printed pamphlets carrying the cease-fire message were dropped from aeroplanes over the jungle.

Besides supervising the cease-fire, the United Nations observers helped resupply the Indonesian troops with food and medicines and helped them regroup in selected places. The effort was successful owing to the full cooperation of the Indonesian and Netherlands authorities. Aerial support was given by the Thirteenth United States Task Force for the Far East and the Royal Canadian Air Force. Most of the emergency supplies were provided by the Netherlands military command, which also treated any Indonesian troops who were seriously ill. United Nations aircraft landed supplies in four staging areas: Sorong, Fakfak, Kaimana and Merauke.

By 21 September 1962, General Rikhye was able to report that all Indonesian forces in West Irian had been located and concentrated, that resupply had been assured and that over 500 Indonesian political detainees had been repatriated in accordance with the memorandum. The observers' mandate had thus been fulfilled and all actions concerning the cessation of hostilities had been completed without incident.

Establishment of UNSF and UNTEA

With the cessation of hostilities, the next step was to ensure the maintenance of law and order in the territory. In addition to supervising the observer team, General Rikhye had been charged with making preliminary arrangements for the arrival of UNSF.

Article VIII of the Indonesian-Netherlands agreement stipulated the role and purpose of such a force:

> The Secretary-General will provide the UNTEA with such security forces as the United Nations Administrator deems necessary; such forces will primarily supplement existing Papuan (West Irianese) police in the task of maintaining law and order. The Papuan Volunteer Corps, which on the arrival of the United Nations Administrator will cease being part of the Netherlands armed forces, and the Indonesian armed forces in the territory, will be under the authority of, and at the disposal of, the Secretary-General for the same purpose. The United Nations Administrator will, to the extent feasible, use the Papuan (West Irianese) police as a United Nations security force to maintain law and order and, at his discretion, use Indonesian armed forces. The Netherlands armed forces will be repatriated as rapidly as possible and while still in the territory will be under the authority of the UNTEA.[8]

UNSF was thus essentially an internal law and security force — the "police arm" of UNTEA — whose responsibilities would range from ensuring the smooth implementation of UNTEA's administrative mandate to supervising the buildup of a viable, local police force.

In the memorandum of understanding on the cessation of hostilities, it was provided that UNSF would commence its duties as soon as possible after the General Assembly adopted an enabling resolution, but no later than 1 October 1962. In fact, the UNSF Commander arrived in West Irian weeks before the Assembly resolution was passed.

Major-General Said Uddin Khan (Pakistan), appointed by the Secretary-General as Commander of UNSF, arrived in Hollandia on 4 September for preliminary discussions with Netherlands authorities and for a survey of future requirements. Similar efforts had already been exerted to some extent by General Rikhye, who had been charged earlier with making preliminary arrangements for the arrival of UNSF. The two men cooperated closely before and after the establishment of UNSF in West Irian.

[8] A/5170, annex A.

UNSF activities prior to UNTEA

UNSF comprised 1,500 Pakistan troops, made available at the request of the Secretary-General, as were the support units of Canadian and United States aircraft and crews.

By 3 October, an advance party of 340 men of UNSF had arrived in the territory. On 5 October, the balance of the Pakistan contingent took up its positions. Also included in UNSF were some 16 officers and men of the Royal Canadian Air Force, with two aircraft, and a detachment of approximately 60 United States Air Force personnel with an average of three aircraft. These provided troop transport and communications. The Administrator also had under his authority the Papuan Volunteer Corps, the civil police, the Netherlands forces until their repatriation, and Indonesian troops, totalling approximately 1,500.

Establishment of UNTEA

UNSF was created to uphold the authority of UNTEA. Whereas groundwork for the arrival of UNSF troops had been laid in West Irian prior to the General Assembly's recognition of the agreement, it was not until Assembly resolution 1752 (XVII) was adopted that personnel associated with UNTEA were dispatched. This resolution, which would make the United Nations directly responsible for the administration of the western half of New Guinea, was approved by a vote of 89 to none, with 14 abstentions.

In the resolution, the Assembly took note of the agreement between Indonesia and the Netherlands concerning West New Guinea (West Irian), acknowledged the role conferred by it upon the Secretary-General, and authorized him to carry out the tasks entrusted to him in the agreement.

Upon adoption of the resolution, the Secretary-General noted that for the first time in its history the United Nations would have temporary executive authority established by and under the jurisdiction of the Secretary-General over a vast territory. He dispatched his Deputy Chef de Cabinet, Mr. José Rolz-Bennett, as his Representative in West New Guinea (West Irian), where he would make preliminary arrangements for the transfer of administration to UNTEA. Mr. Rolz-Bennett arrived in the territory on 21 September 1962, the date the enabling resolution was passed.

Transfer of administration to UNTEA

Under the agreement, neither Dutch nor Indonesian officials were to hold any of the top administrative positions during the seven-month transition period. In addition, three quarters of the Dutch civil servants of lesser rank had decided to leave the territory before 1 October, thereby creating a vacuum that would have to be filled to prevent a disruption of essential functions and services. In some instances, this was accomplished by promoting Papuan officials to the vacant posts. There was, however, a great shortage of adequately trained Papuans.

Mr. Rolz-Bennett immediately set about assembling an emergency task force to be deployed in key areas of the administration, recruiting international as well as Dutch and Indonesian personnel. The Netherlands Governor of the territory and his senior officials assisted in this effort; measures were also taken by the Netherlands Government to encourage Dutch officials to remain and serve the Temporary Executive Authority. In addition, the Indonesian Government was requested to provide urgently a group of civil servants to fill certain high-priority posts. This request was made with a view to the gradual phasing in of Indonesian officials, whose presence thus facilitated the subsequent transfer of administrative responsibilities to Indonesia. In all, 32 nationalities were represented in UNTEA, among them both Dutch and Indonesian personnel.

The transfer of the administration from the Netherlands to UNTEA took place on 1 October 1962 and, in conformity with article VI of the agreement and its related aide-mémoire, the United Nations flag was raised and flown side by side with the Netherlands flag.

Before his departure from the territory on 28 September, the Netherlands Governor, Mr. Peter Johannis Plateel, appealed to the population to give its support to the United Nations administration. In messages from the Secretary-General and from Mr. Rolz-Bennett (who was designated as Temporary Administrator for approximately six weeks), the population was informed that UNTEA would endeavour to ensure the welfare of the inhabitants. The Temporary Administrator signed an order effective 15 October granting amnesty to all political prisoners sentenced prior to 1 October 1962.

On 1 October, Indonesia and the Netherlands established liaison missions to UNTEA in Hollandia/Kotabaru. An Australian liaison mission replaced one which had formerly served in Hollandia/Kotabaru as an administrative liaison between the authorities of the territory of Papua/New Guinea and West New Guinea, and now provided effective liaison with UNTEA on matters of mutual interest.

The United Nations Administrator, Mr. Djalal Abdoh (Iran), was appointed by the Secretary-General on 22 October 1962, under article IV of the agreement. On 15 November, he arrived in the territory to take up his assignment and Mr. Rolz-Bennett returned to Headquarters the following day.

Activities after the creation of UNTEA

The agreement between the Netherlands and Indonesia entrusted to UNTEA a number of broad powers: to "administer the territory" (article V); to appoint government officials and members of representative councils (articles IX and XXIII); to legislate for the territory, subject to certain qualifications (article XI); and to guarantee civil liberties and property rights (article XXII).

Once the international team that comprised UNTEA was assembled in the capital of the territory, they immediately began to address the vast economic and social problems facing them.

The very nature of the country presented major difficulties. Roads were practically non-existent, with a total length estimated at 900 kilometres. There was no other means of land transportation, which made air transport of all supplies from ports to the hinterland essential. Coupled with the difficulties of physical movement were problems of communication. Telephone systems existed only inside the major towns. UNSF was, however, able to tackle adequately the problems which faced it.

The transfer of authority implied a need to adapt existing institutions from the Dutch pattern to an Indonesian pattern. The first problem was to rebuild the officer and inspection cadres which had almost completely disappeared with the exodus of Dutch officers, and to reinstate a sense of loyalty and discipline in the rank and file, at the same time keeping the police service serving the public. The second problem was to reorient the entire service, substituting the Indonesian language and procedures for those of the Dutch so that there would be no upheaval when UNTEA handed over the reins of government to the Republic of Indonesia.

In accordance with the terms of article VII of the Indonesia-Netherlands agreement, the Papuan Volunteer Corps ceased to be part of the Netherlands armed forces upon the transfer of administration to UNTEA. The Corps, consisting of some 350 officers and men, was concentrated at Manokwari and was not assigned any duties in connection with the maintenance of law and order. As Dutch officers and non-commissioned officers left the area, they were replaced by Indonesian officers. This process was completed on 21 January 1963, when the command of the Corps was formally transferred to an Indonesian officer and the last Dutch officers left the territory.

During the period of UNTEA administration, the Papuan police were generally responsible for the maintenance of law and order in the territory. Before the transfer of administration to UNTEA, all the officers of the police corps were Dutch, there being no qualified Papuans. By the time UNTEA had assumed responsibility for the territory, almost all officers of Dutch nationality had left, having been temporarily replaced by officers from the Philippines who, in turn, were later replaced by Indonesians. By the end of March 1963, the entire corps was officered by Indonesians. However, in accordance with the provisions of article IX of the agreement, the chief of police continued to be an international recruit.

On 1 October 1962, when authority was transferred to UNTEA, the Indonesian troops in the territory consisted of those who had been brought in by parachute during the Dutch-Indonesian conflict and those who had infiltrated the territory. Agreement was reached with the Indonesian authorities to replace a large number of these troops with fresh territorial troops from Indonesia. It was also agreed that the number of Indonesian troops in the territory would not exceed the strength of the Pakistan contingent of UNSF, except with the prior consent of the UNTEA administration.

The withdrawal of the Netherlands naval and land forces from the territory was effected in stages in accordance with a timetable agreed upon by the Temporary Administrator, the Commander of UNSF and the Commander-in-Chief of the Netherlands forces in the territory. By 15 November 1962, this process had been completed without incident.

The situation was generally calm throughout the period of UNTEA. On 15 December 1962, however, two incidents involving the police and a small group of Indonesian troops occurred in Sorong and Doom. One police constable was killed and four wounded. Order was immediately restored by UNSF units while the civil administration continued to perform its normal functions. The area remained quiet for the rest of the temporary administration. In general, the inhabitants of the territory were law-abiding and the task of maintaining peace and security presented no problems. The United Nations Administrator had no occasion to call on the Indonesian armed forces in that connection but only for the purpose of occasional joint patrols with elements of the Pakistan contingent.

With regard to UNTEA's responsibility to uphold the rights of the territory's inhabitants (as outlined in article XXII of the agreement), the Administration ensured the free exercise of those rights by the population, and UNTEA courts acted as their guarantor. One of UNTEA's first concerns was, in fact, the reactivation of the entire judiciary since, with the departure of Netherlands personnel from various judiciary organs, the administration of justice practically came to a standstill. Once UNTEA was established, all the vacant positions in the judicial offices were filled through recruitment of qualified judicial officers from Indonesia.

UNTEA was also responsible for opening and closing the New Guinea Council and for appointing new representatives to the Council, in consultation with the Council's members. On 4 December 1962, the Council members met in the presence of the Administrator and took their new oath of office. The Council's Chairman and all members pledged to support loyally the provisions of the agreement and swore allegiance to UNTEA. As it seemed desirable that members should return to their constituencies in order to explain personally to their constituents the new political situation of the territory, the session was closed on 5 December, after consultation with the Chairman.

During the period of UNTEA's administration, a number of vacancies in the membership of the New Guinea Council occurred because of resignation, departure or absence of members. At the request of the Council's Chairman to fill some of these vacancies, the United Nations Administrator, in conformity with article XXIII, signed appropriate decrees appointing two new members. However, no consultation could take place with representative councils since none existed in the districts from which the two members were appointed.

In addition to the New Guinea Council, there were 11 representative councils, known as regional councils, in the various districts. On 14 February 1963, the Administrator opened the new regional council at Ransiki, Manokwari, elections to which had been held in December 1962.

The United Nations Administrator also toured the territory extensively in conjunction with article X of the agreement, which required that UNTEA widely publicize and explain the terms of the agreement. He took part in all public functions in order to explain personally those parts of the agreement which related to the United Nations presence in the territory and the changes that would take place on 1 May 1963. These efforts supplemented a United Nations information campaign which, with the help of special features, texts, posters and discussion groups, helped prepare the population for the transfer of administration to Indonesia, and informed them regarding the provisions of the agreement on the question of self-determination.

Articles XVII through XXI addressed the issue of self-determination. The relevant clauses of the agreement required that Indonesia make arrangements, with the assistance and participation of the United Nations Representative and his staff, to give the people of the territory the opportunity to exercise freedom of choice. The inhabitants were to make the decision to "remain with Indonesia" or to "sever their ties with Indonesia", under the auspices of a plebiscite to be held no later than 1969.

Day-to-day problems of the territory were addressed and handled smoothly by the civilian administration under UNTEA. In the sphere of public health, UNTEA had to deal with an epidemic of cholera which had begun to spread on the south-west coast of the island shortly after its administration was established. In this, it received valuable assistance from the World Health Organization, which provided a health team and the necessary medical supplies. The administration was able not only to contain the epidemic within a short period but also to declare the whole territory free of cholera. The administration also vigorously pursued plans for establishing hospitals and clinics in various parts of the territory.

In the economic sphere, the administration was mainly concerned with maintaining stability and dealing with a serious unemployment problem. Only 32 of a total of 317 Netherlands officials engaged in public works had been willing to stay on after UNTEA's takeover. Contractors stopped work, and gradually maintenance and repair services came to a halt. Over 3,500 men were idle. In a land where only 300,000 people (a third of the population) were in regular contact with the administration and where skilled labour was at a premium, this was a significant figure. With the cooperation of the Indonesian liaison mission, UNTEA was able to reactivate work on existing projects and draw up plans for similar projects which would be useful for the development of the territory. Forty-five projects were completed by the end of UNTEA, and 32 others were under construction. UNTEA was also able to keep in check the general price level of commodities, most of which had to be imported, and ensure adequate supplies for the population.

All costs incurred by UNTEA during its administration were borne equally by the Netherlands and Indonesia in compliance with article XXIV of the agreement. Consultations between the Secretariat and the representatives of the two Governments regarding the preparation of the UNTEA budget had taken place shortly after the agreement was signed. Later, at Hollandia/Kotabaru, a committee composed of the representatives of the two sides met under the chairmanship of the Deputy Controller of the United Nations and agreed on an UNTEA budget for the period 1 October 1962 to 30 April 1963, which was subsequently approved by the Secretary-General. As the budget committee doubted that UNTEA would be able to collect any revenue, no estimates of income were prepared. The Department of Finance was, however, able to collect a total of 15 million New Guinea florins by the end of the UNTEA period through taxes and customs duties. This was credited to the final budget figure.

On 31 December 1962, the Netherlands flag was replaced by the Indonesian flag, which was raised side by side with the United Nations flag, as contemplated in an aide-mémoire attached to the agreement.

In the last months of 1962 and the beginning of 1963, a number of communications from Papuan leaders and various groups in the territory were addressed to the Secretary-General and the United Nations Administrator requesting that the period of UNTEA administration in West Irian be shortened. On 21 November 1962, a joint declaration by the representatives of the New Guinea Council was transmitted to the Secretary-General asking for the early transfer of the administration to Indonesia. A demonstration to the same effect took place on 15 January 1963, when a petition was presented to the Administrator by 18 political leaders from the area of Hollandia/Kotabaru.

These requests were brought to the attention of the Secretary-General in January 1963 by Mr. Sudjarwo Tjondronegoro, head of the Indonesian Liaison Mission to UNTEA. After consultation with the representative of the Netherlands, the Secretary-General decided that any shortening of UNTEA would not be feasible. However, he sent his Chef de Cabinet, Mr. C. V. Narasimhan, in February 1963, to consult with the United Nations Administrator and the Government of Indonesia, with a view to facilitating the entry of Indonesian officials into the administration of West Irian in order to ensure the continuity and expansion of all essential services. Following these consultations, the Chef de Cabinet announced in Djakarta that the transfer of administration would take place as scheduled on 1 May 1963, and that the replacement of Netherlands officials by Indonesian officials would be accelerated. By the end of March 1963, Indonesian nationals occupied the second highest post in every administrative department in all six divisions in the territory.

The gathering momentum of the phasing in operation was accompanied by an encouraging development in a different sphere. The resumption of diplomatic relations between Indonesia and the Netherlands was announced on 13 March 1963. Thus began a new era in the relationship between the two countries, one which notably helped UNTEA's work as the time approached for the transfer of authority.

In April, the Indonesian Government announced that a Papuan member of the New Guinea Council, Mr. E. J. Bonay, would be installed on 1 May as the first Governor of Irian Barat (the Indonesian name for West Irian). He would be assisted by an Indonesian deputy, and the territory would be administered as a province of the Republic of Indonesia.

The number of Indonesian officials in the Administration towards the end of April reached 1,564, while Papuans and other indigenous people of West Irian occupied 7,625 civil service posts. Only 11 Netherlands officials remained; they were to leave upon the transfer of authority to Indonesia. Stores of goods were procured to ensure adequate supplies for a period after the transfer. Direct negotiations between the Netherlands and Indonesia for the purchase of a number of Dutch interests proceeded smoothly. The economy had been largely stabilized, health and education services were in good order, and all the provisions of the agreement leading up to the transfer of administration fully implemented.

During the last days of April, some 30 Indonesian warships arrived in Biak and Hollandia for the ceremony, as had service squadrons of aircraft of the Indonesian air force. The Pakistan units of UNSF began their withdrawal to Biak, ready for embarkation; the various UNSF garrisons were replaced by incoming Indonesian troops.

Transfer of administration to Indonesia

In accordance with article XII of the agreement, the UNTEA Administrator transferred full administrative control to the representative of the Indonesian Government, Mr. Tjondronegoro, on 1 May 1963. The ceremony was performed in the presence of the Chef de Cabinet as the Secretary-General's personal representative for the occasion, and the Indonesian Foreign Minister. At that time, the United Nations flag was taken down.

Secretary-General's observations

On the completion of UNTEA, the Secretary-General declared[9] that it had been a unique experience, which had once again proved the capacity of the United Nations to undertake a variety of functions, provided that it received adequate support from its Member States. He also announced that, in consultation with Indonesia, he had decided in principle to designate a few United Nations experts, serving at Headquarters and elsewhere, to perform the functions envisaged in article XVII of the agreement, in so far as the article required that the Secretary-General advise, assist and participate in arrangements which were the responsibility of Indonesia for the act of free choice. Those experts would visit West Irian as often as necessary and spend as much time as would enable them to report fully to him, until he appointed a United Nations representative to preside over them as a staff.

Looking to the future, the Secretary-General stated that he was confident that Indonesia would scrupulously observe the terms of the 1962 agreement, and would ensure the exercise by the territory's population of their right to express their wishes as to their future.

In accordance with the Indonesia-Netherlands agreement, the Secretary-General on 1 April 1968 appointed a representative, Mr. Fernando Ortiz-Sanz, to advise, assist and participate in arrangements which were the responsibility of Indonesia for the act of free choice, on retaining or severing ties with Indonesia.

In a report[10] submitted to the Secretary-General, the Government of Indonesia stated that between 14 July and 2 August 1969, the enlarged representative councils (consultative assemblies) of West New Guinea (West Irian), which included 1,026 members, were asked to pronounce themselves, on behalf of the people of the territory, as to whether they wished to remain with Indonesia or sever their ties with it. All those councils chose the first alternative without dissent.

The representative of the Secretary-General reported[11] that within "the limitations imposed by the geographical characteristics of the territory and the general political situation in the area, an act of free choice has taken place in West Irian in accordance with Indonesian practice, in which the representatives of the population have expressed their wish to remain with Indonesia".

Those reports were transmitted by the Secretary-General to the General Assembly, which, by resolution 2504 (XXIV) of 19 November 1969, acknowledged with appreciation the fulfilment by the Secretary-General and his representatives of the task entrusted to them under the 1962 agreement.

[9]A/5501, chapter II.15. [10]A/7723, annex II. [11]A/7723, annex I.

Chapter 30

Representative of the Secretary-General in the Dominican Republic (DOMREP)

Chapter 30

Representative of the Secretary-General in the Dominican Republic (DOMREP)

Background

Towards the end of April 1965, a political crisis developed in the Dominican Republic, resulting in civil strife that had considerable international repercussions. On 24 April, the three-man junta headed by Mr. Donald Reid Cabral was overthrown by a group of young officers and civilians who sought the return to office of former President Juan Bosch, who had been deposed by a military coup in September 1963, and the restoration of the 1963 Constitution.

Mr. Bosch's supporters were opposed by a group of high-ranking officers of the Dominican armed forces, with the result that two rival governments emerged in the Dominican Republic during the first weeks of the civil war. The pro-Bosch forces organized themselves into what was called the "Constitutional Government", headed by Colonel Francisco Caamaño Deñó. The opposing forces established a civilian-military junta which called itself the "Government of National Reconstruction", headed by General Antonio Imbert Barrera.

The military phase of the Dominican crisis took place mainly in Santo Domingo, capital of the country, where heavy fighting broke out between the two contending factions on 25 April 1965.

On 28 April, the United States announced that its troops had been ordered to land in the Dominican Republic. On the following day, the United States representative informed the Security Council of his Government's action and of its call for a meeting of the Council of the Organization of American States (OAS). His letter[1] asserted that the President of the United States had ordered troops ashore in the Dominican Republic in order to protect United States citizens there and escort them to safety. The President had acted, the letter stated, after being informed by the military authorities in the Dominican Republic that lives of United States citizens were in danger, that their safety could no longer be guaranteed, and that the assistance of United States military personnel was required.

On 29 April, the Secretary-General of OAS informed[2] the United Nations Secretary-General that the OAS Council had appealed for the suspension of armed hostilities in the Dominican Republic. On 1 May, the Assistant Secretary-General of OAS informed[3] the Security Council that the Tenth Meeting of Consultation of Ministers for Foreign Affairs of the American Republics had decided on that day to establish a committee, composed of representatives of Argentina, Brazil, Colombia, Guatemala and Panama, and had instructed it to proceed immediately to Santo Domingo to bring about the restoration of peace and normality and to offer its good offices to the contending factions there with a view to achieving a cease-fire and the orderly evacuation of persons.

On 1 May, the Soviet Union requested[4] an urgent meeting of the Security Council to consider the question of the armed intervention by the United States in the internal affairs of the Dominican Republic. The Security Council considered this question at 29 meetings held between 3 May and 26 July 1965.

Security Council action, May 1965

On 6 May, the Assistant Secretary-General of OAS transmitted to the Security Council the text[5] of a resolution by which the Tenth Meeting of Consultation had requested OAS members to make available land, air and naval contingents or police forces for the establishment of an inter-American force, to operate under its authority. The purpose of the force would be to help restore normal conditions in the Dominican Republic, maintain the security of its inhabitants and the inviolability of human rights, and create an atmos-

¹S/6310. ²S/6313. ³S/6364, annex. ⁴S/6316. ⁵S/6333/Rev.1.

phere of peace and conciliation that would allow the functioning of democratic institutions.

On 14 May, Jordan, urging action by the Security Council, submitted, together with Malaysia and the Ivory Coast, a draft resolution whereby the Council would call for a strict cease-fire, invite the Secretary-General to send, as an urgent measure, a representative to the Dominican Republic to report on the situation, and call upon all concerned in the Dominican Republic to cooperate with that representative in carrying out his task.

The three-Power text was unanimously adopted by the Council the same day, as resolution 203 (1965).

Representative's activities

In a report[6] dated 15 May, the Secretary-General informed the Council that he had appointed Mr. José Antonio Mayobre, Executive Secretary of the Economic Commission for Latin America, as his Representative in the Dominican Republic. An advance party, led by Major-General I. J. Rikhye as Military Adviser, had arrived in Santo Domingo earlier that day. The Military Adviser was assisted by two military observers at any one time from three made available from Brazil, Canada and Ecuador.

On 18 May, the Secretary-General informed[7] the Council that his Representative had left for Santo Domingo on 17 May. He had asked Mr. Mayobre to notify formally all the parties concerned of the Council's call for a strict cease-fire and to convey to all those involved in the conflict his most earnest appeal to heed that call so that a propitious climate for finding a solution might be brought about.

On 19 May, the Secretary-General reported[8] that, shortly after his arrival, Mr. Mayobre had met with Colonel Caamaño, President of the "Constitutional Government", and with General Imbert, President of the "Government of National Reconstruction".

Late in the evening of 18 May, Mr. Mayobre had informed the Secretary-General by telephone of heavy fighting in the northern section of the capital and of the numerous casualties caused by it. It had not been possible to persuade General Imbert to agree to a cease-fire, although he had expressed willingness to agree to a suspension of hostilities some time on 19 May to facilitate the work of the Red Cross in searching for the dead and wounded.

Appeal by the Security Council President

At the Council's meeting on 19 May, the Council President made a statement, which was supported by all Council members, requesting the Secretary-General to convey to his Representative the Council's desire that his urgent efforts be devoted to securing an immediate suspension of hostilities so that the Red Cross's work in searching for the dead and wounded might be facilitated.

Communications from OAS

Also on 19 May, OAS transmitted the text[9] of a second report submitted by the Special Committee of the Tenth Meeting of Consultation. The Committee said that efforts to arrange for a meeting between Colonel Caamaño and General Imbert to iron out their differences had proved unsuccessful, and that the Committee had issued an appeal to the parties for strict compliance with the cease-fire agreed upon in the Act of Santo Domingo, signed on 5 May, formalizing a cease-fire achieved earlier through the efforts of the Papal Nuncio in Santo Domingo. The report added that the presence of the United Nations in the Dominican Republic had created a factor which had compromised and interfered with the task of the Committee. It recommended that the Meeting of Consultation agree upon the measures necessary to re-establish peace and normality in the Republic, and that the Security Council be requested to suspend all action until regional procedures had been exhausted.

OAS also transmitted to the Council the text[10] of a resolution adopted by the Meeting of Consultation on 20 May, entrusting the OAS Secretary-General with negotiating a strict cease-fire and with providing his good offices for establishing a climate of peace and reconciliation that would permit democratic institutions to function. The resolution asked him to coordinate his action, in so far as relevant, with that of the Representative of the United Nations Secretary-General.

Further reports by the Secretary-General

The Secretary-General informed[11] the Security Council that his Representative, on the morning of 19 May, had met with representatives of the Dominican Red Cross, the International Red Cross and the Pan American Sanitary Bureau, and

[6]S/6358. [7]S/6365. [8]S/6369. [9]S/6370. [10]S/6372/Rev.1. [11]S/6371.

had suggested that they meet with the leaders of the two factions engaged in the fighting and request a 12-hour suspension of hostilities to remove the dead and wounded from the battle area. On 21 May, the Secretary-General reported[12] on further information from his Representative that, following negotiations with the leaders of the two factions, agreement had been reached for the suspension of hostilities for 24 hours beginning on 21 May, at 1200 hours local time.

Further Security Council action

During a Council meeting of 21 May, the Secretary-General said that his Representative had reported that the cease-fire of 21 May was effective. The Red Cross, which had gone into the battle area early that morning, had been fully engaged in its humanitarian task. In view of the need to evacuate the sick and wounded to less congested hospitals, the Representative was trying to obtain an extension of the truce.

On 22 May, France submitted a draft resolution by which the Council would request that the suspension of hostilities in Santo Domingo be transformed into a permanent cease-fire, and would invite the Secretary-General to report to it on the implementation of the resolution. This was adopted as resolution 205 (1965).

On 25 May, the Council President noted that it appeared that a de facto cessation of hostilities continued to prevail in Santo Domingo and that the Secretary-General had informed him that it was being observed. He therefore suggested that the Council adjourn, on the understanding that it could reconvene if the situation required it.

Further OAS communications

On 2 June, OAS advised[13] the Security Council that the Tenth Meeting of Consultation had appointed an ad hoc committee — composed of representatives of Brazil, El Salvador and the United States — to assist all parties in the Dominican Republic to achieve a climate of peace and to enable democratic institutions to function. It also informed[14] the Council of the arrival in Santo Domingo of the Chairman of the Inter-American Commission on Human Rights in response to requests made by both of the contending Dominican groups.

Security Council consideration, 3–11 June 1965

The question of the Dominican Republic was again considered by the Council at four meetings held between 3 and 11 June. The Council was convened at the request of the Soviet Union to take up two communications from the "Constitutional Government", asking for the dispatch of the United Nations Commission on Human Rights to the Dominican Republic to investigate atrocities allegedly carried out by General Imbert's forces against the civilian population in Santo Domingo.

The question of the scope of the mandate of the Secretary-General's Representative arose during these meetings from suggestions made by France, Jordan and Uruguay to enlarge Mr. Mayobre's staff to enable him to supervise the cease-fire and to investigate complaints of human rights violations. They considered that his mandate was sufficiently wide to cover both tasks. The suggestions were supported by the Soviet Union.

Bolivia, the Ivory Coast, Malaysia, the United Kingdom and the United States, on the other hand, expressed doubt as to the advisability of extending Mr. Mayobre's mandate at that stage. The United States observed, in this connection, that the Inter-American Human Rights Commission, which had been sent to Santo Domingo, was actively investigating human rights violations.

Secretary-General's position

The Secretary-General stated that his Representative's current mandate involved observing and reporting, functions which did not include the actual investigation of complaints and charges about specific incidents, other than those connected with cease-fire violations. Investigative functions would require a directive from the Security Council, a substantially larger staff and increased facilities. Moreover, he could give no assurance that such added responsibility would receive from the contending parties the cooperation necessary to secure effective implementation by his Representative.

The Secretary-General remarked that his Representative was keeping a watchful eye on all aspects of the situation and was reporting what he observed. The size of his staff was under constant

[12]S/6371/Add.1. [13]S/6401. [14]S/6404.

review, and he would be provided with the necessary assistance as the circumstances demanded.

Security Council consideration, 16–21 June 1965

On 16 June, the Secretary-General reported[15] that an exchange of fire had taken place on the morning of 15 June between Colonel Caamaño's forces and troops of the Inter-American Peace Force (IAPF). There was no evidence, however, as to which side had started the firing. By nightfall his Representative had arranged for a cessation of hostilities.

In a later report,[16] the Secretary-General informed the Council that, on 16 June, fighting between the Caamaño forces and IAPF had been renewed along the newly established IAPF positions manned by United States troops. Although the firing had stopped on the evening of 16 June, the situation remained very tense.

This situation was discussed by the Security Council from 16 to 21 June. During these meetings, the Council received from OAS the text[17] of proposals for a political settlement submitted on 18 June by the OAS ad hoc committee to the "National Reconstruction Government" and the "Constitutional Government". The principal points in the OAS proposals were: general elections within six to nine months, under OAS supervision; a general amnesty for all who had participated in the civil strife; surrender of all arms in the hands of civilians to OAS; establishment of a provisional government which would exercise its authority under an institutional act and would call elections; and the convening of a constitutional assembly within six months following assumption of office by the elected government.

On 21 June, the Secretary-General informed the Security Council that he had just received a report from his Representative which stated that the cease-fire had been effective since 16 June.

Secretary-General's report, 16 July 1965

On 16 July, the Secretary-General submitted[18] a report on the situation in the Dominican Republic covering the period from 19 June to 15 July 1965.

Despite a number of isolated incidents, the cease-fire in Santo Domingo had been maintained. The Secretary-General indicated that, as of 26 June, IAPF was composed of 1,700 troops from

six Latin American countries and 12,400 from the United States, of which 1,400 would be withdrawn shortly. He went on to report that the situation outside Santo Domingo — which had been potentially explosive since May, owing mainly to deteriorating economic conditions, to the ineffectiveness of civilian authority and to military and police repression — had become more acute following an abortive uprising by armed civilians at San Francisco de Macorís on 25 June and an attack against a police post at Ramón Santana on 2 July.

The Secretary-General drew attention to repeated complaints of violations of human rights in Santo Domingo as well as in the provinces, involving alleged executions, arbitrary arrests, and cases of missing persons following arrest. He also drew attention to the worsening economic situation. In his Representative's view, an early political solution accompanied by an emergency programme of external financial and technical assistance was essential.

Security Council meetings, July 1965

The Security Council resumed consideration of the question at four meetings held between 20 and 26 July. The Council President ultimately summed up the agreed views of the members of the Council:

- Information received by the Council as well as the Secretary-General's reports showed that, in spite of the Council's resolutions of 14 and 22 May 1965, the cease-fire had been repeatedly violated. Acts of repression against the civilian population and other violations of human rights, as well as data on the deterioration of the economic situation in the Dominican Republic, had been brought to the Council's attention.

- Members of the Council had condemned gross violations of human rights in the Republic, expressed the desire that such violations should cease, and indicated again the need for the strict observance of the cease-fire in accordance with the Council's resolutions.

- The Council members considered it necessary that the Council continue to

[15]S/6447. [16]S/6459. [17]S/6457, annex I. [18]S/6530.

watch the situation closely and that the Secretary-General continue to report on it.

Secretary-General's reports, 22 July 1965–5 January 1966

In a report[19] covering the period between 22 July and 17 August 1965, the Secretary-General informed the Security Council that, except for a few minor incidents, the cease-fire had been maintained. While his Representative continued to receive complaints of alleged cases of arbitrary arrest by forces of the "Government of National Reconstruction", the situation in general had improved. The report referred to negotiations for a political settlement being carried out by the OAS ad hoc committee on the basis of new proposals the committee had submitted to the two contending parties on 9 August 1965.[20]

A proposed Act of Dominican Reconciliation[21] provided that the parties would accept a provisional government presided over by Dr. Hector García Godoy as the sole and sovereign government of the Dominican Republic, and that they would accept a proposed Institutional Act[22] as the constitutional instrument under which the provisional government would exercise its authority. The latter Act also provided for: a proclamation of a general amnesty by the provisional government; the disarmament and incorporation of the "Constitutionalist" zone into the security zone; a procedure for the recovery of arms in the hands of civilians; the reintegration of "Constitutionalist" military personnel who had participated in the conflict; and, finally, a procedure to be followed for the withdrawal of IAPF.

In a report[23] covering the period of 17 August to 2 September 1965, the Secretary-General reported the resignation on 30 August of the members of the "Government of National Reconstruction" headed by General Imbert, and the signing, on 31 August, of an amended text of the Act of Reconciliation by the leaders of the "Constitutional Government". On the same day, the chiefs of the armed forces and the national police had signed a declaration in which they had pledged acceptance of the Act of Reconciliation and the Institutional Act, and support of Dr. García Godoy as provisional President.

On 3 September, Dr. García Godoy was installed as President of the Provisional Government.

On 23 October, the Secretary-General reported[24] to the Security Council that, since the inauguration of the Provisional Government, much progress had been made in efforts to restore normal conditions in the Dominican Republic. Little progress had been made, however, towards the reintegration of "Constitutionalist" military personnel into the regular armed forces, owing mainly to continuing tension between the high command of the Republic's armed forces and "Constitutionalist" officers. The situation had been aggravated by acts of terrorism and violence, and armed clashes between civilians and elements of the police and regular Dominican troops.

In subsequent reports, the Secretary-General informed the Council that the Government had announced that troops of the Dominican armed forces had been ordered to return to their barracks and that law and order in Santo Domingo would be maintained by the national police with the assistance of IAPF. By 25 November, he reported,[25] the situation had improved and the country was returning to normalcy. The bulk of IAPF had been withdrawn from the capital and the national police were gradually assuming responsibility for the maintenance of law and order. There had also been some improvement in the relations between the civilian authorities and the armed forces.

In a report[26] issued on 3 December, the Secretary-General informed the Council that the Provisional Government had promulgated a law calling for national elections to be held on 1 June 1966.

Later in December, the Secretary-General reported on new disturbances. The main disturbance took place on 19 December[27] at Santiago, where former "Constitutionalist" forces and Dominican air force units engaged in heavy fighting that resulted in many casualties, including 25 dead. The Santiago incident was followed by a wave of terrorist activities in Santo Domingo which caused the deaths of eight persons and considerable material damage. The reports indicated that mixed patrols of IAPF, Dominican troops and national police faced a difficult task in maintaining order, as they were continually stoned and shot at by roving civilian groups.

Tension had again subsided by 25 December. On the evening of 3 January 1966, President García Godoy announced that within a few hours an important group of military personnel would leave the country on missions abroad. The Secretary-General concluded his report by stating that, while

[19]S/6615. [20]S/6608. [21]S/6608, annex I. [22]S/6608, annex III. [23]S/6649. [24]S/6822. [25]S/6975. [26]S/6991. [27]S/7032.

Santo Domingo had remained calm since 1 January, the situation there was reported to be tense and unstable.[28]

Secretary-General's observations

The Secretary-General, in the introduction to his annual report[29] on the work of the Organization covering the period from 16 June 1964 to 15 June 1965, discussed the problems and character of the United Nations role in the Dominican Republic situation. He described the task of his Representative there as a "new United Nations mission in the peace-keeping category".

The situation, the Secretary-General wrote, was of unusual complexity and had considerable international repercussions, particularly with regard to the unilateral military involvement of the United States in the initial stage and to the later role of the Inter-American Peace Force. While his Representative's mandate had been a limited one, the effect of his role had been significant, since he had played a major part in bringing about a cessation of hostilities on 21 May 1965, and had supplied information as to the situation both in Santo Domingo and in the interior of the country.

His presence had undoubtedly been a moderating factor in a difficult and dangerous situation, the Secretary-General said, adding that this had been the first time a United Nations peace mission had operated in the same area and dealt with the same matters as an operation of a regional organization, in this instance OAS.

Further, the Secretary-General maintained the view that the developments in the Caribbean should stimulate thought by everyone concerning the character of the regional organizations and the nature of their functions and obligations in relation to the responsibilities of the United Nations under the Charter.

Secretary-General's reports, January–February 1966

In one of eight reports[30] covering developments in the Dominican Republic during January 1966, the Secretary-General informed the Council that, on 6 January 1966, President García Godoy had issued decrees appointing a new Minister of the Armed Forces and new armed services chiefs, and providing for the transfer abroad of several high-ranking military officers, including Commodore Francisco Rivera Caminero, former Minister of the Armed Forces, and Colonel Caamaño Deñó, former "Constitutionalist" leader.

The implementation of these decrees had met with some resistance from the Dominican armed forces, which at one point occupied radio and telecommunications buildings in Santo Domingo. However, by the end of January, 11 high-ranking former "Constitutionalist" officers had left the Dominican Republic to take up diplomatic posts abroad.

In six reports[31] issued during February, the Secretary-General reported to the Security Council several serious incidents and acts of terrorism which occurred in and outside Santo Domingo, beginning 7 February. As a result, economic activity in the city and nearby commercial areas had come to an almost complete standstill. Tension remained high from 12 to 15 February as hostile acts directed against IAPF military police and troops took place in Santo Domingo. A general strike was called off one day after a speech by President García Godoy, broadcast on 16 February, in which he announced orders to put into effect decrees concerning changes and transfers in the Dominican armed forces and ordered all public employees to return to work. The new Minister of the Armed Forces was sworn in on the same day and new chiefs of staff of the army, navy and air force were appointed on 26 February. Also, a new chief of the national police had been appointed by the Provisional Government.

Secretary-General's reports, March–May 1966

In 17 reports[32] issued from March to May 1966, the Secretary-General informed the Security Council that, though fewer in number, acts of terrorism and other disturbances continued to occur in Santo Domingo and in the interior of the country. He stated that the electoral campaign had officially opened on 1 March.

In connection with national elections on 1 June 1966, the Central Electoral Board issued on 15 March a proclamation providing for the election of a President and Vice-President of the Republic, 27 Senators and 74 Deputies for a period of four years beginning 1 July 1966, and for the election, for a period of two years, of 70 mayors and 350 aldermen and their alternates. On 11 May, President García Godoy, in a televised speech, expressed concern over certain signs of pressure exerted by minority groups intent upon disturbing the electoral process. He appealed to all sectors of

---

[28]S/7032/Add.4. [29]A/6001/Add.1. [30]S/7232/Add.4-11. [31]S/7032/Add.12-17. [32]S/7032/Add.18-34.

the population to maintain a peaceful and orderly atmosphere for the elections, and indicated that the problem of the presence of IAPF in the country should be solved before 1 July. On 13 May, the OAS ad hoc committee announced[33] that IAPF personnel would be confined to barracks on election day. This was followed by an announcement on 18 May by President García Godoy of his decision to confine all armed forces to barracks from 19 May until election day. On 29 May, the OAS ad hoc committee indicated, in a press statement, that 41 observers invited by OAS would observe elections in 21 provinces of the Republic and in the National District.[34] The observers would submit a report to the Provisional Government.

At midnight on 30 May, the electoral campaign officially ended. On that day, the Provisional President sent a communication to the Tenth Meeting of Consultation of OAS Foreign Ministers informing it that he had instructed the Dominican representative to OAS to request a meeting of the Tenth Meeting of Consultation to ask for withdrawal of IAPF from Dominican territory.

Election of 1 June 1966

During June and July 1966, the Secretary-General submitted four reports[35] to the Council dealing mainly with the elections on 1 June and related events. According to those reports, the elections had proceeded on schedule in a calm and orderly manner. On 21 June, the final results of elections were announced by the Central Electoral Board. They showed 769,265 votes for Mr. Joaquín Balaguer, 525,230 for Mr. Juan Bosch and 39,535 for Mr. Rafael F. Bonnelly.

Installation of the Government, July 1966

In a report[36] dated 2 July, the Secretary-General informed the Security Council that on 1 July, Mr. Joaquín Balaguer and Mr. Francisco Augusto Lora had been sworn in as President and Vice-President, respectively, of the Dominican Republic by the President of the National Assembly. In his inaugural address, President Balaguer stated that the country was returning to a system of law and that no one would be permitted to live outside legal norms. He set forth a policy of austerity to place the Republic's economic, administrative and financial structure on a sounder footing. His Government would support OAS and would work within it to ensure that national sovereignty would never again be infringed by foreign troops. While his Government intended to act drastically if extremists sought to disturb the peace, it would protect opponents against persecution and would ensure that the symbols of past oppression would disappear for ever from Dominican life.

Phased withdrawal of IAPF

Early in July, a plan for the withdrawal of IAPF in four phases was approved by the OAS ad hoc committee in agreement with the Dominican Government.

On 24 June, the OAS Secretary-General had transmitted to the Security Council the text[37] of a resolution adopted by the Tenth Meeting of Consultation that day. By this resolution, the Meeting of Consultation — noting that the purposes of the Tenth Meeting had been fully achieved inasmuch as popular elections had been held in the Dominican Republic, the results of which had given that nation a constitutional and democratic Government — directed that the withdrawal of IAPF should begin before 1 July 1966 and should be completed within 90 days. It further asked the OAS ad hoc committee, in agreement with the Dominican Government, to give IAPF the necessary instructions concerning the dates for and the manner of effecting the withdrawal.

From 3 August to 21 September 1966, the Secretary-General, on the basis of information received from the office of his Representative in Santo Domingo, submitted a series of reports[38] to the Security Council giving a detailed account of the withdrawal of the United States and the Latin American contingents (Brazil, Costa Rica, El Salvador, Honduras, Nicaragua and Paraguay) of IAPF and of its military equipment. This withdrawal was completed on 21 September 1966.

Withdrawal of the United Nations Mission

In a letter[39] of 13 October addressed to the Secretary-General, the Dominican Republic's Minister for Foreign Affairs expressed the appreciation of his country to the United Nations for its efforts to bring about the restoration of peace and harmony in the Republic, and stated that, in the view of his Government, the objectives of the Security Council's resolution of 14 May 1965 having been achieved, it would be advisable to withdraw

---

[33]S/7032/Add.32. [34]S/7032/Add.34. [35]S/7338/Add.1-3. [36]S/7338/Add.5. [37]S/7379. [38]S/7338/Add.6-15. [39]S/7551.

the United Nations Mission from the Dominican Republic.

In a report[40] issued on 14 October, the Secretary-General informed the Security Council that in the light of the developments which had recently taken place in the Dominican Republic, including the installation on 1 July 1966 of the newly elected Government and the withdrawal of IAPF, he had initiated arrangements for the withdrawal of the Mission in the Dominican Republic, which was expected to be completed shortly.

The withdrawal of the United Nations Mission was completed on 22 October 1966.

[40] S/7552.

Chapter 31

United Nations Good Offices Mission in Afghanistan and Pakistan (UNGOMAP)

Chapter 31
United Nations Good Offices Mission in Afghanistan and Pakistan (UNGOMAP)

A. Introduction

In April 1988, the efforts of the United Nations to end the war in Afghanistan were enhanced when, under its auspices, the Geneva Accords on the Settlement of the Situation Relating to Afghanistan were concluded and a group of military officers was deployed to monitor their implementation. While the mission was considered to be an extension of the exercise of the Secretary-General's good offices which had mediated the negotiations that led to the Geneva Accords, its use of military personnel brought it within the definition of a peace-keeping operation and it functioned in a manner similar to other such operations.

B. Background

On 27 December 1979, Soviet forces entered Afghanistan, in response to a reported request from the Afghan Government for assistance against insurgent movements. More than 100,000 Soviet troops were eventually deployed; they soon became embroiled in a protracted conflict with the factions of the Afghan resistance, or mujahideen.

Security Council debate of the issue in January 1980 failed to produce a resolution. In order to circumvent the deadlock, the matter was referred, under the "Uniting for Peace" procedure (as provided for in General Assembly resolution 377 (V) of 3 November 1950), to an emergency session of the General Assembly, which, by resolution ES-6/2 of 14 January 1980, strongly deplored the armed intervention and called for the "immediate, unconditional and total withdrawal of the foreign troops from Afghanistan".

On 11 February 1981, Secretary-General Kurt Waldheim appointed Mr. Javier Pérez de Cuéllar, then Under-Secretary-General for Special Political Affairs, as his Personal Representative on the Situation Relating to Afghanistan. In visits to the region in April and August 1981, the Under-Secretary-General held extensive discussions with the Governments of Afghanistan and Pakistan to determine the substantive issues to be negotiated in resolving the conflict. The acceptance by the parties of his suggested four-point agenda started the negotiating process which ultimately produced the Geneva Accords.

Geneva negotiations

Upon his assumption of the post of Secretary-General in January 1982, Mr. Pérez de Cuéllar designated Mr. Diego Cordovez, who had succeeded him as Under-Secretary-General for Special Political Affairs, as his Personal Representative. Beginning in June 1982 and over the next six years, Mr. Cordovez acted as intermediary in a series of indirect negotiations between the Governments of Afghanistan and Pakistan at the Palais des Nations in Geneva and in the area.

The conclusion of the Geneva Accords was finally expedited by a growing desire on the part of the Soviet Government to withdraw its forces from Afghanistan. In February 1988, the Soviet Union announced that it would start repatriating its troops in May. The last round of talks ended on 8 April 1988 when Under-Secretary-General Cordovez announced that all the instruments comprising the settlement had been finalized and were open for signature.

The Geneva Accords

The Accords, known formally as the Agreements on the Settlement of the Situation Relating to Afghanistan, consisted of four instruments: a bilateral agreement between the Republic of Afghanistan and the Islamic Republic of Pakistan on the principles of mutual relations, in particular on non-interference and non-intervention; a declaration on international guarantees, signed by the Union of Soviet Socialist Republics and the United States of America; a bilateral agreement between Afghanistan and Pakistan on the voluntary return of refugees; and an agreement on the interrelationships for the settlement of the situation relating to Afghanistan, signed by Afghanistan and Pakistan and witnessed by the Soviet Union and the United States.

This last instrument contained provisions for the timetable and modalities of the withdrawal of Soviet troops from Afghanistan. It also provided for arrangements to assist the parties to ensure the smooth and faithful implementation of the provisions of the instruments of the Accords and to consider alleged violations. Representatives of the Governments of Afghanistan and Pakistan were to meet for this purpose whenever required. The Secretary-General was asked to appoint a Representative to lend his good offices to the parties. The Representative would be assisted in his tasks by a support staff, organized as the United Nations Good Offices Mission in Afghanistan and Pakistan (UNGOMAP), which would investigate and report on any possible violations of the instruments. The mandate of UNGOMAP was derived from the instruments and, accordingly, comprised the monitoring of (1) non-interference and non-intervention by the parties in each other's affairs, (2) the withdrawal of Soviet troops from Afghanistan, and (3) the voluntary return of refugees. The *modus operandi* and logistic support of UNGOMAP were set out in a "Memorandum of Understanding" annexed to the fourth instrument.

UNGOMAP's operations in the field would be directed by a senior military officer designated as Deputy to the Representative. UNGOMAP would be organized into two small headquarters units, one in Kabul and the other in Islamabad, which would each consist of five military officers and a small civilian component. The Deputy Representative would act on behalf of the Representative and would maintain contact with liaison officers designated by each party.

The Memorandum made provision for the deployment of up to 40 additional military officers "whenever considered necessary by the Representative of the Secretary-General or his Deputy". These military officers would be organized into inspection teams to ascertain on the ground any violations of the instruments comprising the settlement. They would all be temporarily redeployed from existing United Nations peace-keeping operations; the nationalities of the observers were subject to approval by the parties.[1]

C. Establishment of UNGOMAP

The Accords were signed by the four countries in Geneva on 14 April 1988. On the same day, the Secretary-General informed[2] the Security Council of the role requested of him in their implementation. He stated his intention to dispatch 50 military observers to the area, subject to the concurrence of the Council.

On 22 April, he submitted a second letter with the texts of the Accords, including the Memorandum. On 25 April, the President of the Council informed the Secretary-General by letter of the Council's provisional agreement to the proposed arrangements. Formal consideration and decision were deferred until later. On 31 October 1988, in resolution 622 (1988), the Security Council confirmed its agreement to the measures envisaged in the letters.[3]

The Secretary-General immediately initiated the creation of UNGOMAP. He retained Mr. Cordovez as his Representative and appointed Major-General Rauli Helminen (Finland) as Deputy to the Representative (Major-General Helminen was succeeded by Colonel Heikki Happonen (Finland) in May 1989). Fifty military officers were

[1] S/19835. [2] S/19834. [3] S/19835, S/19836.

temporarily seconded from the United Nations Truce Supervision Organization, the United Nations Disengagement Observer Force and the United Nations Interim Force in Lebanon. Ten countries contributed to the mission: Austria, Canada, Denmark, Fiji, Finland, Ghana, Ireland, Nepal, Poland and Sweden.

The first elements of an advance party arrived in the Mission area on 25 April 1988. The two headquarters units in Kabul and Islamabad, with the combined total complement of 50 military officers, were operational well in advance of 15 May, when the instruments entered into force.

D. Operations

Monitoring of withdrawal

The strength of the Soviet forces stationed in Afghanistan on 14 May 1988 was declared to be 100,300, all ranks, about two thirds of whom were combat troops. They had already handed over some positions to the armed forces of Afghanistan, but still controlled 18 main garrisons. Soviet forces were present in 17 of the 30 provinces of Afghanistan. At the outset of its operations, UNGOMAP received from military representatives of the Soviet Union in Afghanistan detailed information on the plan and schedule for the withdrawal of the Soviet troops.

This included a map indicating the location of the main garrisons, the routes to be used by the troops as they left Afghanistan, and the crossing points on the Afghan-Soviet border which they would use, namely the towns of Hayratan and Torghundi. Starting on 14 May, UNGOMAP met regularly with the Afghan and Soviet military representatives. At these meetings, the Mission received information on the ongoing withdrawal as well as on any changes made to the original schedule.

UNGOMAP established three permanent outposts on the Afghanistan side: at the border points of Hayratan and Torghundi, and at the Shindand air base which was used for withdrawal by air. Each was normally manned by two officers whose task was to monitor the withdrawal of the Soviet troops.

UNGOMAP's operations also entailed visiting garrisons during or immediately after the departure of Soviet forces. In areas where uncertain security conditions prevented the presence of United Nations observers at the garrisons, the numbers of troops departing were recorded either at the airports of Kabul, Kunduz and Shindand or at the border-crossing points.

First phase

On 15 August 1988, the Soviet military representatives informed UNGOMAP that 10 main garrisons had been evacuated and handed over to the Afghan armed forces; 8 main garrisons remained under Soviet control. The latter were located in Kabul, to the north of Kabul and in north-west Afghanistan.

In accordance with the stipulations of the fourth instrument of the Geneva Accords, slightly over 50 per cent of the Soviet troops had been withdrawn three months after the entry into force of the Accords. A total of 50,183 Soviet troops had been repatriated by land and air. Numbers of fixed-wing aircraft, helicopters and vehicles had also been withdrawn.

Second phase

UNGOMAP had been informed, on 14 May 1988, that the completion of the first phase of the withdrawal in August would be followed by a three-month pause. This would facilitate preparations for the second phase of the withdrawal, which was to be completed by 15 February 1989. Shortly before the withdrawal was due to resume, however, the Soviet representatives announced that it was being postponed in the light of prevailing conditions. They reaffirmed that it would be completed in accordance with the Geneva Accords. Between 15 August 1988 and 1 January 1989, UNGOMAP did not observe any significant withdrawal of Soviet troops.

On 25 January 1989, the Soviet military representatives informed UNGOMAP of the manner in which the final withdrawal of troops would be completed. Over a short period of days in the first half of February, troops would be repatriated both by air and by road in grouped convoys. This duly took place. On 14 February, an UNGOMAP team visited the remaining main garrison in Tashqurghan and confirmed that it had been evacuated on 12 February.

Despite some delays in prior notification of the withdrawal and the need occasionally to limit UNGOMAP's movement for security reasons, the mission concluded that the withdrawal of Soviet troops had been completed in compliance with the fourth instrument of the Geneva Accords. After the completion of the withdrawal, UNGOMAP closed its three outposts at Hayratan and Torghundi and at the Shindand air base.

Monitoring of non-interference and non-intervention

Numerous complaints of alleged violations of the first instrument, on non-interference and non-intervention, were submitted to UNGOMAP from the outset of its mission by both parties. Complaints submitted by Afghanistan included allegations of political activities and propaganda hostile to the Government of Afghanistan taking place in Pakistan, border crossings of men and *matériel* from Pakistan to Afghanistan, cross-border firings, acts of sabotage, rocket attacks on major urban centres, violations of Afghan airspace by Pakistan aircraft, the continued presence in Pakistan of training camps and arms depots for Afghan opposition groups, and direct involvement by Pakistan military personnel inside Afghanistan, as well as restrictions placed on refugees who wished to return to Afghanistan. Complaints lodged by Pakistan included allegations of political activities and propaganda hostile to the Government of Pakistan, bombings and violations of its airspace by Afghan aircraft, acts of sabotage and cross-border firings, including the use of SCUD missiles against Pakistan territory.

Despite the constraints often encountered in the course of its operations, UNGOMAP made every effort to investigate complaints lodged by the two parties and it submitted regular reports to them. However, a number of difficulties unavoidably hampered the effectiveness of the work of UNGOMAP's inspection teams. These included the rough nature of the terrain, the time which lapsed before many of the alleged incidents were reported, and the security conditions prevailing in the area of operation.

Two outposts were established on the Pakistan side in November 1988 — one in Peshawar and one in Quetta — to enhance UNGOMAP's capacity to carry out its investigations promptly. In April 1989, it further strengthened its presence on the Pakistan side of the border by setting up permanent presences at Torkham, Teri Mangal and Chaman.

The fourth instrument of the Geneva Accords had provided that the two parties would hold joint meetings to consider the reports submitted by UNGOMAP. After initial difficulties, the first in a series of joint meetings was held in March 1989. The venue for these meetings alternated between the two UNGOMAP headquarters units in Islamabad and Kabul. The parties were thus able to review their obligations under the Geneva Accords, and UNGOMAP was able to improve its monitoring and investigating procedures.

Implementation of the third instrument: voluntary return of refugees

UNGOMAP maintained close cooperation with the United Nations High Commissioner for Refugees (UNHCR), and it stood ready to discharge its task under the third instrument, the Agreement on the Voluntary Return of Refugees. In particular, it was ready to monitor the situation inside Afghanistan and inform UNHCR of the safety conditions necessary for the return and resettlement of refugees. Up to 5 million refugees were estimated to be living in Pakistan and Iran. However, fighting continued, conditions remained unstable and only a limited number of refugees returned to Afghanistan.

E. Termination of UNGOMAP

The Memorandum of Understanding provided that UNGOMAP's operation would cease two months after the completion of all the time-frames envisaged for the implementation of the instruments. The longest explicit time-frame contained in the instruments was the 18 months provided in

UNGOMAP deployment as of February 1989

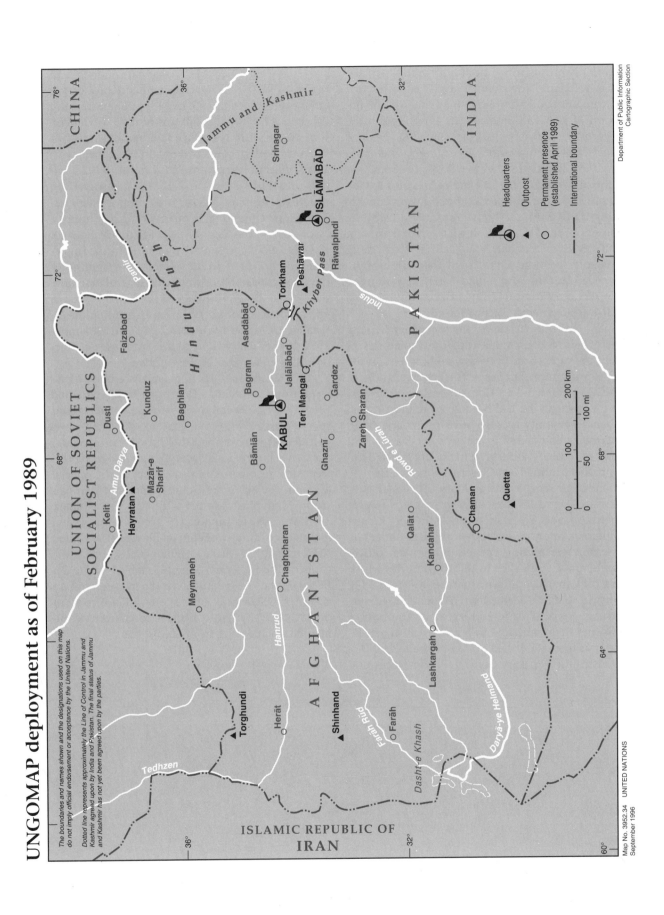

The boundaries and names shown and the designations used on this map
do not imply official endorsement or acceptance by the United Nations.

Dotted line represents approximately the Line of Control in Jammu and
Kashmir agreed upon by India and Pakistan. The final status of Jammu
and Kashmir has not yet been agreed upon by the parties.

CHINA

**UNION OF SOVIET
SOCIALIST REPUBLICS**

Jammu and Kashmir

Srinagar

ISLĀMĀBĀD

Rāwalpindi

INDIA

PAKISTAN

Torkham

Peshāwar

Khyber Pass

Indus

Asadābād

Faizabad

Bagram

Jalālābād

Gardez

Hindu Kush

Kunduz

KABUL

Teri Mangal

Zareh Sharan

Baghlan

Dusti

Kelit

Amu Darya

Hayratan

Mazār-e
Sharif

Bāmiān

Ghaznī

Rowd e Lurah

Qalāt

Kandahar

Chaman

Quetta

Meymaneh

Chaghcharan

Hanrud

Lashkargah

Daryā-ye Helmand

A F G H A N I S T A N

Torghundi

Herāt

Shinhand

Farāh Rūd

Farāh

Dasht-e Khash

Tedhzen

**ISLAMIC REPUBLIC OF
IRAN**

Headquarters
Outpost
Permanent presence
(established April 1989)
International boundary

0   100   200 km
0   50   100 mi

Department of Public Information
Cartographic Section

Map No. 3952.34   UNITED NATIONS
September 1996

665

the third instrument for the arrangements to assist the voluntary return of refugees. The implementation of this instrument did not begin — as Pakistan noted in November 1989 — and the first instrument had an implicit time-frame, so the duration of UNGOMAP's mandate envisaged in the Accords, i.e., 20 months from May 1988, became a matter of interpretation. Accordingly, on 9 January 1990, 20 months after May 1988, the Secretary-General, having consulted the parties and having obtained the concurrence of the countries contributing UNGOMAP's military personnel, sought the consent of the Security Council to an extension of UNGOMAP's mandate, indicating that more needed to be done for the implementation of the Geneva Accords. Two days later, the Council adopted resolution 647 (1990) extending the existing arrangements for two months.[4]

In March 1990, the Secretary-General again held consultations with the signatories of the Geneva Accords but was unable to obtain the consensus necessary for a further extension of UNGOMAP's mandate. Consequently, and in view of the mandate he had been given under General Assembly resolution 44/15 of 1 November 1989 to encourage and facilitate the early realization of a comprehensive political settlement in Afghanistan, he informed the Security Council that he intended to redeploy 10 military officers as military advisers to his Personal Representative in Afghanistan and Pakistan to assist in the further implementation of his responsibilities under the Assembly's resolution. For this purpose one officer was retained from each of the 10 countries which had contributed military observers to UNGOMAP (Austria, Canada, Denmark, Fiji, Finland, Ghana, Ireland, Nepal, Poland and Sweden). The post of Personal Representative in Afghanistan and Pakistan was first established in May 1989 and was held by Assistant Secretary-General Benon Sevan and thereafter by Assistant Secretary-General Sotirios Mousouris.

When UNGOMAP's mandate ended on 15 March 1990, the Secretary-General established the Office of the Secretary-General in Afghanistan and Pakistan (OSGAP). OSGAP was headed by the Personal Representative and was organized into two small headquarters units — one in Islamabad, with a sub-office in Peshawar (closed in July 1992), and one in Kabul — and the Military Advisory Unit, which was responsible for providing military expertise, as required, and maintaining a continued assessment of the security situation in Afghanistan. The Personal Representative assisted in the implementation of the Secretary-General's responsibilities under the resolutions of the General Assembly and served as Coordinator of the United Nations Office for the Coordination of Humanitarian Assistance to Afghanistan (UNOCHA). In December 1994, the Secretary-General discontinued the function of the Personal Representative.[5]

Meanwhile, the General Assembly, by its resolution 48/208 of 23 December 1993, requested the Secretary-General to dispatch a United Nations special mission to Afghanistan to solicit the views of its leaders on how best the United Nations could assist the country in facilitating national *rapprochement* and reconstruction. As Head of the Special Mission, the Secretary-General appointed Ambassador Mahmoud Mestiri (Tunisia). In January 1995, in order to support the special mission and maintain continuity of contact between the United Nations and the various Afghan leaders inside the country, the Secretary-General established the Office of the Secretary-General in Afghanistan (OSGA).[6] OSGA took over the political functions of OSGAP. UNOCHA continues to coordinate humanitarian activities in Afghanistan.

[4]S/21071. [5]A/50/737. [6]A/49/688.

Chapter 32
United Nations Iran-Iraq Military Observer Group (UNIIMOG)

Chapter 32

United Nations Iran-Iraq Military Observer Group (UNIIMOG)

A. Introduction

In August 1988, after almost eight years of war, and following a period of intensive negotiations between the Secretary-General and the two Foreign Ministers, the Islamic Republic of Iran and the Republic of Iraq agreed to a suggestion of the Secretary-General, which combined the coming into force of a cease-fire and the beginning of direct talks between the two Foreign Ministers under the auspices of the Secretary-General. The United Nations Iran-Iraq Military Observer Group (UNIIMOG) was established to verify, confirm and supervise the cessation of hostilities and the withdrawal of all forces to the internationally recognized boundaries without delay. It was deployed in the region several days before the formal commencement of the cease-fire on 20 August 1988.

B. Background

United Nations involvement during the conflict

Attempts by the United Nations to seek an end to the war dated back to 1980, when an outbreak of armed conflict between Iran and Iraq prompted Secretary-General Kurt Waldheim to offer his good offices to work for a peaceful settlement of the conflict. On 23 September 1980, in accordance with Article 99 of the United Nations Charter, he brought to the attention of the Security Council the threat to the maintenance of international peace and security. In resolution 479 of 28 September 1980, the Council, among other things, called upon Iran and Iraq to refrain immediately from any further use of force and to settle their dispute by peaceful means. It had little effect.

On 11 November, Mr. Olof Palme, former Prime Minister of Sweden, was appointed as the Secretary-General's Special Representative to Iran and Iraq and shortly thereafter undertook a mission to the region. Some progress was made over the freeing of merchant shipping caught by the hostilities in the Shatt al-Arab waterway and, in 1981 and 1982, over the exchange of limited numbers of prisoners of war. Yet a settlement remained elusive.

While these efforts stalled over the issues of responsibility for the war and control of the Shatt al-Arab, the United Nations was able to play a role in the issue of the bombing of purely civilian population centres of both countries. Furthermore, missions dispatched by the Secretary-General confirmed the use of chemical weapons and investigated the situation of prisoners of war in both countries.

Military inspection teams

The year 1984 saw the establishment of the first resident United Nations presence in the area. On June 9, Secretary-General Javier Pérez de Cuéllar appealed to both sides to refrain from deliberate military attacks on purely civilian centres of population.[1] When both Iran and Iraq agreed to this, the Secretary-General informed the Security Council of his decision to deploy inspection teams in the region. Their task would be to

[1] S/16611.

investigate alleged attacks on civilian areas. This became known as the truce in the "war of the cities" and lasted for some nine months.

By the end of June, two teams, each composed of three officers seconded from the military personnel of the United Nations Truce Supervision Organization (UNTSO) and one senior official of the United Nations Secretariat, were installed in Baghdad and Tehran. Their presence in the capitals four years later helped to expedite the establishment of UNIIMOG.

In 1986 and 1987, escalation of the war had increasing international repercussions. Attacks on merchant shipping in the Persian Gulf, including repeated strikes against commercial oil tankers, became more frequent. In response, several countries unilaterally dispatched mine-sweeping and escort craft in an attempt to facilitate safe commercial passage through international waters.

In January 1987, the Secretary-General undertook a new diplomatic initiative to reach a settlement. Enlisting the cooperation of all the members of the Council at a meeting in his office on 23 January 1987, he suggested a number of elements for their consideration. On 20 July, after extensive consultations, the Council adopted resolution 598 (1987), which included those elements and the cease-fire which came into effect one year later. The Secretary-General's endeavours benefited from a growing readiness by the five permanent members to work together to seek an end to this long-standing conflict.

Resolution 598 (1987)

In the preamble to resolution 598 (1987), the Council reaffirmed its resolution 582 (1986) (which, among other things, had called for an immediate cease-fire, the withdrawal of all forces to the internationally recognized boundaries without delay and a comprehensive exchange of prisoners of war); expressed its deep concern that the conflict between Iran and Iraq continued unabated with further heavy loss of human life and material destruction; deplored the initiation and continuation of the conflict, the bombing of purely civilian population centres, attacks on neutral shipping or civilian aircraft, the violation of international humanitarian law and other laws of armed conflict, and, in particular, the use of chemical weapons contrary to obligations under the 1925 Geneva Protocol. It expressed its deep concern that further escalation and widening of the conflict might take place, its determination to bring to an end all

military actions between Iran and Iraq, and its conviction that a comprehensive, just, honourable and durable settlement should be achieved between Iran and Iraq. The Council recalled the provisions of the Charter of the United Nations, and in particular the obligation of all Member States to settle their international disputes by peaceful means in such a manner that international peace and security and justice are not endangered. Finally, it determined that there existed a breach of the peace as regards the conflict between Iran and Iraq, and recorded that it was acting under Articles 39 and 40 of the Charter of the United Nations.

In the operative paragraphs, it demanded that, as a first step towards a negotiated settlement, Iran and Iraq observe an immediate cease-fire, discontinue all military actions on land, at sea and in the air, and withdraw all forces to the internationally recognized boundaries without delay; it requested the Secretary-General to dispatch a team of United Nations observers to verify, confirm and supervise the cease-fire and withdrawal and further requested the Secretary-General to make the necessary arrangements in consultation with the parties and to submit a report thereon to the Security Council; it urged that prisoners of war be released and repatriated without delay after the cessation of active hostilities in accordance with the Third Geneva Convention of 12 August 1949; called upon Iran and Iraq to cooperate with the Secretary-General in implementing the resolution and in mediation efforts to achieve a comprehensive, just and honourable settlement, acceptable to both sides, of all outstanding issues, in accordance with the principles contained in the Charter of the United Nations, and upon all other States to refrain from any act which might lead to further escalation and widening of the conflict.

The Council requested the Secretary-General to explore, in consultation with Iran and Iraq, the question of entrusting an impartial body with inquiring into responsibility for the conflict and to report to the Council as soon as possible; to assign a team of experts to study the question of reconstruction; and, in consultation with Iran and Iraq and with other States of the region, to examine measures to enhance the stability of the region. He was asked to keep the Security Council informed on the implementation of the resolution.

Iraq welcomed the resolution and informed the Secretary-General of its readiness to cooperate with him and the Security Council in its implementation. Iran, while not rejecting the resolution, criticized "fundamental defects and incongruities" in it.[2]

In September 1987, the Secretary-General travelled to Tehran and Baghdad, and a period of intense diplomatic activity ensued, with negotiations in the region and at United Nations Headquarters in New York. In October, the Secretary-General tabled the implementation plan of the resolution which he had originally presented to the Council in September. In the spring of 1988, he met repeatedly with representatives of both countries in an attempt to reach accord on the implementation of resolution 598 (1987). In March 1988, the Secretary-General invited both sides to send special emissaries to New York for consultations which took place in April 1988.

Meanwhile, the war continued, with the ever-present risk of a widening of the hostilities. Naval vessels sent by a number of countries to escort merchant shipping in the Persian Gulf were involved in incidents with one or other of the combatants. On 3 July 1988, the *USS Vincennes*, a United States cruiser, mistakenly shot down an Iranian commercial airliner, killing all 290 passengers and crew on board.

Acceptance of resolution 598 (1987)

On 17 July 1988, Iran notified the Secretary-General of its formal acceptance of resolution 598 (1987), expressing the need to save life and to establish justice and regional and international peace and security. The following day, Iraq also reaffirmed its agreement with the principles embodied in the resolution.[3]

Between 26 July and 7 August, the Secretary-General met with the Foreign Minister of Iran nine times and with the Representatives of Iraq six times in talks aimed at bringing about implementation of the resolution. After these intensive efforts, and with the assistance of regional diplomacy, on 6 August the President of Iraq declared his readiness for a cease-fire to be followed by direct talks. In letters dated 8 August 1988, the Secretary-General informed the Permanent Representatives of Iran and Iraq that both Governments had agreed that direct talks between their Foreign Ministers should be held under his auspices, immediately after the establishment of the cease-fire, in order to reach a common understanding of the other provisions of Security Council resolution 598 (1987) and the procedures and timing for their implementation.

Resolution 598 (1987) addressed the need both for verification and supervision of a cease-fire and for mediation to resolve all outstanding issues between the two countries. In pursuance of the latter, on 1 September 1988 the Secretary-General appointed Ambassador Jan Eliasson (Sweden), as his Personal Representative on Issues Pertaining to the Implementation of Security Council Resolution 598 (1987).

Technical mission

With formal agreement to a cease-fire in sight, the Secretary-General sent a technical mission to Iran and Iraq from 25 July to 2 August to work out the modalities for the dispatch of the United Nations observer group. Lieutenant-General Martin Vadset (Norway), Chief of Staff of UNTSO, led the mission, which included a senior political adviser, a civilian logistics expert and four military observers from UNTSO. It was assisted by the small teams which had been stationed in Baghdad and Tehran since 1984. In the course of three working days in Tehran and three in Baghdad, the mission held detailed discussions with the political and military authorities in both capitals about the method of operation of the military observer group called for in resolution 598 (1987), its deployment in each of the two countries, and the cooperation and facilities it would require from both parties.

C. Establishment of UNIIMOG

The information furnished by the technical mission was used in defining the terms of reference and concept of operations of UNIIMOG. On 7 August, the Secretary-General presented to the Security Council a report[4] containing his proposals for the composition and precise mandate of UNIIMOG once a date for the cease-fire had been

2S/19045, S/18993. 3S/20020, S/20023. 4S/20093.

agreed. This was achieved on 8 August, when he announced the agreement of both Iran and Iraq to a cease-fire with effect from 0300 GMT on 20 August; direct talks between the two countries would begin under his auspices on 25 August in Geneva.[5]

UNIIMOG's mandate, in accordance with resolution 598, was "to verify, confirm and supervise the cease-fire and withdrawal". Its terms of reference were set out in the Secretary-General's report of 7 August in the following terms:

(a) to establish with the parties agreed cease-fire lines on the basis of the forward defended localities occupied by the two sides on D-Day but adjusting these, as may be agreed, when the positions of the two sides were judged to be dangerously close to each other;

(b) to monitor compliance with the cease-fire;

(c) to investigate any alleged violations of the cease-fire and restore the situation if a violation took place;

(d) to prevent, through negotiation, any other change in the status quo, pending withdrawal of all forces to the internationally recognized boundaries;

(e) to supervise, verify and confirm the withdrawal of all forces to the internationally recognized boundaries;

(f) thereafter, to monitor the cease-fire on the internationally recognized boundaries, investigate alleged violations and prevent, through negotiation, any other change in the status quo, pending negotiation of a comprehensive settlement;

(g) to obtain the agreement of the parties to other arrangements which, pending negotiation of a comprehensive settlement, could help to reduce tension and build confidence between them, such as the establishment of areas of separation of forces on either side of the international border, limitations on the number and calibre of weapons to be deployed in areas close to the international border, and patrolling by United Nations naval personnel of certain sensitive areas in or near the Shatt al-Arab.[6]

In his report of 7 August, the Secretary-General also drew attention to four essential conditions that had to be met for UNIIMOG to be effective. First, it had to have at all times the full confidence and backing of the Security Council. Secondly, it had to enjoy the full cooperation of the two parties. Thirdly, it had to be able to function as an integrated and efficient military unit.

Fourthly, adequate financial arrangements had to be made to cover its costs.

The Secretary-General further recommended that the guidelines which had been applied to the peace-keeping forces which had been set up since 1973 should be applied *mutatis mutandis* to UNIIMOG. In particular, the Group would be under the command of the United Nations, vested in the Secretary-General, under the authority of the Security Council, which the Secretary-General would keep fully informed. UNIIMOG would act with complete impartiality. It would proceed on the assumption that the parties would take all the necessary steps to comply with the decisions of the Security Council, including giving it the freedom of movement and communication and other facilities that would be necessary for the performance of its tasks. It would be composed of a number of military contingents to be provided by Member States, at the request of the Secretary-General. The contingents would be selected in consultation with the two parties and with the Security Council, bearing in mind the accepted principle of equitable geographical representation.

In its resolution 619 (1988) of 9 August, the Security Council approved the Secretary-General's report and decided to establish UNIIMOG immediately for a period of six months. Major-General Slavko Jovic (Yugoslavia) was appointed to the post of Chief Military Observer and served in this capacity until November 1990. Upon his departure, Brigadier-General S. Anam Khan (Bangladesh) took command of UNIIMOG as Acting Chief Military Observer.

At its peak, the total military strength of UNIIMOG was approximately 400 all ranks, including some 350 military observers. Military observers were contributed by Argentina, Australia, Austria, Bangladesh, Canada, Denmark, Finland, Ghana, Hungary, India, Indonesia, Ireland, Italy, Kenya, Malaysia, New Zealand, Nigeria, Norway, Peru, Poland, Senegal, Sweden, Turkey, Uruguay, Yugoslavia and Zambia. New Zealand operated an air unit, and the Observer Group also included military police provided by Ireland and medical orderlies from Austria. At the beginning of the operation, and pending the establishment of a civilian-operated communications system, a signals unit from Canada ensured the vital communications which UNIIMOG needed. Like other peace-keeping operations, UNIIMOG also in-

[5]S/20095. [6]S/20093.

cluded international and locally recruited civilian staff.

Advance parties

On 10 August 1988, one day after the enabling resolution of the Security Council, the first elements of UNIIMOG's two advance parties arrived in Iran and Iraq. Each group consisted of twelve military observers (nine of whom were temporarily drawn from UNTSO) in addition to team leaders and a civilian component. In the days before the arrival of the main body of military observers, the advance parties established liaison with Iranian and Iraqi authorities and conducted reconnaissance of the forward locations where UNIIMOG would be deployed.

Cease-fire

The cease-fire came into effect at 0300 GMT on 20 August 1988. By that time, 307 military observers and the main elements of the Canadian signals unit were present in Iran and Iraq and 51 patrols were deployed on the first day. These patrols had the double task of establishing the forward defended localities occupied by the two sides when the cease-fire came into effect and of defusing confrontations resulting from actual or alleged breaches of the cease-fire. In some areas there existed disagreement between the two sides over the precise position of the forward defended localities on 20 August 1988, and this became one of the principal causes of tension at certain points on the line.

Deployment

It was originally envisaged that UNIIMOG group headquarters would be divided between Baghdad and Tehran, with its Iran detachment headquarters at Bakhtaran, and the Iraq detachment headquarters alongside group headquarters at Baghdad. To increase efficiency, however, and to release more military observers for patrol duty on the cease-fire lines, group and detachment headquarters were merged into a single UNIIMOG headquarters in Baghdad and another in Tehran.

The Chief Military Observer and his senior staff, known as the "Command Group", spent alternate weeks at each headquarters. An Assistant Chief Military Observer was permanently stationed in each capital and directed UNIIMOG's operations in the country concerned, under the overall command of the Chief Military Observer.

Originally, the military observers were deployed in four sectors on the Iranian side, with sector headquarters at Saqqez, Bakhtaran, Dezful and Ahwaz, and three on the Iraqi side, with sector headquarters at Sulaymaniyah, Ba'qubah and Basra. Each sector controlled a number of team sites, which were located as far forward as possible in order to minimize the time spent by military observers travelling between team site and cease-fire line. The length of the cease-fire line monitored by a team site varied from 70 kilometres in the south to 250 kilometres in the north.

The air wing of UNIIMOG consisted of three fixed-wing aircraft, for communications, observation, and freight and passenger duties. It was envisaged that UNIIMOG would also operate a squadron of United Nations helicopters for observation of no man's land and the cease-fire lines but one of the parties would not agree to that arrangement. As a result, UNIIMOG military observers had to use helicopters provided by the parties themselves and which could therefore fly only behind the respective cease-fire line. This inhibited UNIIMOG's ability to maintain close observation of the cease-fire.

D. Operations

The cease-fire lines, which extended approximately 1,400 kilometres, covered a wide variety of terrain. UNIIMOG's method of patrolling was adapted accordingly. Teams of two or more military observers conducted mobile patrols by vehicle, by helicopter, by boat in the southern marshes, and by mule-back or on foot in the mountains of the north. In winter some patrols used skis. UNIIMOG deployed a daily average of 64 patrols which operated around the clock.

The patrols' primary task was to check that the side to which they were assigned was complying with the cease-fire. They did this through their own regular observation of the forward defended localities and by verifying complaints received from the other side; they also transmitted com-

UNIIMOG deployment as of June 1990

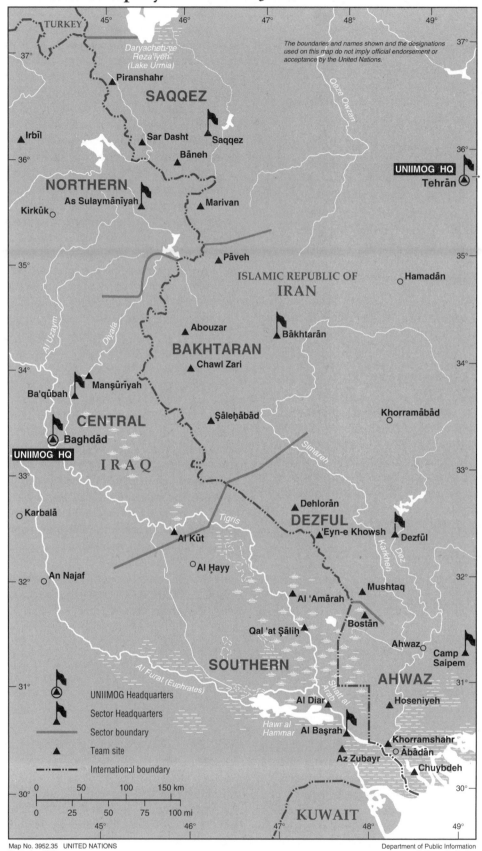

Map No. 3952.35 UNITED NATIONS
September 1996

Department of Public Information
Cartographic Section

plaints to their counterparts on the opposite side of the cease-fire line. Wherever possible, they negotiated a return to the status quo with the commanders on the spot. Where this was not possible, the matter was referred to the relevant sector headquarters so that it could be taken up with the liaison authorities of the side concerned.

In addition to investigating alleged violations, the military observers engaged in such humanitarian and confidence-building measures as the exchange of war dead found on the battlefield.

Military observers from both sides of the cease-fire lines maintained radio communications across no man's land and also met regularly in it.

Relations with the parties

Preliminary agreements concerning the status of UNIIMOG were concluded with the Government of Iraq on 5 November 1988 and with the Government of the Islamic Republic of Iran on 28 March 1989. They embodied the principles of the Charter of the United Nations and of the Convention on the Privileges and Immunities of the United Nations, as well as the experience of previous United Nations peace-keeping operations. They were intended to ensure UNIIMOG's ability to function independently and, in particular, the freedom of movement and communications and other facilities that were necessary for the performance of its tasks.

Both Iran and Iraq established interdepartmental groups to coordinate cooperation with UNIIMOG and both provided liaison officers, as well as the logistic facilities requested of them.

Cease-fire violations

Throughout the mission, UNIIMOG received frequent complaints of alleged cease-fire violations; in the first nine weeks, 1,072 such complaints were recorded, but the number declined steadily as the cease-fire stabilized. All complaints were investigated; of those which have been confirmed, many were minor in nature.

However, more significant violations did occur. On 23–24 August, shortly after the commencement of the cease-fire, several hundred Iranian soldiers were taken prisoner in a serious incident near Eyn-e Khowsh. Another serious violation began on 13 September 1988 when Iran started flooding an area of no man's land in the Khusk region. This created a water obstacle between the forward positions occupied by the two armies, which in this area lay immediately to the east of the internationally recognized border. The area under flooding was the scene of several military confrontations. The flooding ceased to affect Iraqi positions after the withdrawal of Iraqi forces in 1990.

There were also some firing incidents. Other violations included the movement of troops, the establishment of new observation posts or other positions forward of the forward defended localities, and the reinforcement of defensive positions by wiring, mining, improving bunkers and general engineering works. In all such cases, UNIIMOG endeavoured to persuade the side concerned to stop work and restore the status quo.

E. Implementation of mandate

Strength reductions and changes in mandate

The situation in the region worsened significantly following the Iraqi invasion and occupation of Kuwait in August 1990. Although this development complicated the work of UNIIMOG, the Iran-Iraq border remained calm. Despite continuing cease-fire violations of the nature described above, the implementation of UNIIMOG's mandate proceeded overall without major hindrance. By the end of September 1990, the with-

drawal of all forces of both sides to the internationally recognized boundaries had been almost complete, although there were a few locations where, in UNIIMOG's view, the forces of each side remained on the wrong side of the boundaries.

In these circumstances, the Secretary-General recommended[7] that the Security Council extend the mandate of UNIIMOG for a limited period of only two months, instead of six months

[7]S/21803.

as it had done on three previous occasions.[8] This, in his view, would permit UNIIMOG to complete its tasks related to the withdrawal of the forces and would allow time for the parties and the Security Council to judge whether there was a continuing requirement for an impartial third party to monitor the cease-fire.

During that period, UNIIMOG would concentrate on the following tasks: (a) verify, confirm and supervise the remaining stages of the withdrawal; (b) help the parties to resolve any local tensions that might arise, e.g., as a result of differences about the exact line of the border, moves forward, accidental firings, etc.; (c) assist the parties in establishing an area of separation — an area on either side of the border into which each party would agree not to deploy military forces. It was judged that only 60 per cent of UNIIMOG's existing strength would be required to perform those tasks.

Following the adoption of resolution 671 (1990) of 27 September, in which the Security Council concurred with the Secretary-General's recommendations, the strength of UNIIMOG was reduced to 230 all ranks, including 184 military observers. In the course of that reduction, the military observers were redeployed in three sectors on the Iranian side, with sector headquarters at Saqqez, Bakhtaran, and Dezful, and three on the Iraqi side, with sector headquarters at Sulaymaniyah, Mansuriyah and Basra.

In the following two months, both sides continued the process of withdrawal of their forces to the internationally recognized boundaries. Both sides, however, continued to occupy or re-occupied positions in the proposed area of separation. In some cases local tension occurred when the two sides established positions in close proximity to, or even co-located with, each other, but there were no serious incidents. Difficulties also occurred because of the presence of unmarked minefields in areas from which the forces were withdrawing, especially on the Iranian side of the border.

In the meantime, the Secretary-General undertook consultations with the two parties about the future of UNIIMOG after the expiry of the two-month mandate period. The Secretary-General's position was that after the withdrawal of the forces had been completed, UNIIMOG would have a continuing role to play in facilitating the early solution of residual problems arising from the withdrawal and in helping the parties to negotiate and implement agreements on an area of separation and an area of limitation of armaments.

The Secretary-General thought that the mandate should be extended for a longer period than two months and that UNIIMOG could be reduced to 50 to 60 observers on each side.

The parties had divergent views on those issues. The Iraqi side expressed a strong preference for the mandate to be renewed for a full period of six months, with UNIIMOG remaining at its existing strength. The Iranian authorities refused to accept an extension of the mandate for more than two months, although they did not exclude the possibility of a further extension thereafter, and insisted on a reduction to 50 to 60 observers on each side. In these circumstances, the Secretary-General had no choice but to recommend[9] that the Security Council extend the mandate of UNIIMOG for a period of two months, with a strength not exceeding 120 military observers, plus the necessary support personnel. The Council did so on 28 November by adopting resolution 676 (1990).

As agreed with the parties, during that period UNIIMOG was mandated to resolve the remaining problems on the border, to try to arrange an exchange of information between the parties about unmarked minefields, and to help in the negotiation and implementation of an area of separation and, subsequently, an area of limitation of armaments. The reduction in the number of military observers (to 60 on the Iranian side, 56 in Iraq and 3 in the Command Group) necessitated a further reorganization of UNIIMOG's deployment. On each side a small number of observers were deployed at headquarters with approximately 15 military observers in each of the three sectors. All former team sites were closed as permanently manned locations and became forward patrol bases, which were manned as the situation demanded.

Agreements on separation reached

In January 1991, the two parties agreed to convene a technical meeting of military experts to discuss and resolve the questions relating to UNIIMOG's mandate that were still outstanding. The agreement was reached bilaterally, and the meeting itself was organized outside the framework of the Mixed Military Working Group that UNIIMOG had previously been trying to establish. The meeting was attended by the Acting Chief Military Observer of UNIIMOG. The two sides also reached agreements on the question of disputed

[8]S/RES/631 (1989), S/RES/642 (1989), S/RES/651 (1990). [9]S/21960.

positions along the internationally recognized boundaries, an area of separation along those boundaries, and the exchange of information on minefields. These agreements were fully consistent with UNIIMOG's mandate and they provided for UNIIMOG to monitor their implementation within a specified time-frame.

The disputed positions were all to be removed by 22 January 1991, and UNIIMOG was then to verify and confirm the completion of the withdrawal of all forces to the internationally recognized border described in the 1975 Treaty concerning the State Frontier and Neighbourly Relations between Iran and Iraq. The agreements on an area of separation provided for a one kilometre withdrawal on both sides along the entire length of the recognized borders. Its establishment was to take place between 10 and 27 January, with UNIIMOG helping in the implementation.

Due to the outbreak of hostilities in the area in mid-January, however, the implementation of the agreements did not proceed fully according to the schedule. By the end of January, Iran had withdrawn 13 out of 17 disputed positions and Iraq had withdrawn 23 out of 29 such positions. There was little progress made in relation to mine clearing and an area of separation.

Security in Iraq worsens

UNIIMOG's capacity to fulfil the role assigned to it was seriously affected after the adoption of Security Council resolution 678 (1990) on 29 November, authorizing the use of all necessary means by a multinational coalition if Iraq did not withdraw from Kuwait by 15 January 1991. UNIIMOG undertook detailed planning to ensure the security of its personnel without compromising operational efficiency. With the deterioration of the situation in the second week of January 1991, it was decided to thin out both military and civilian staff in Baghdad. Following the Secretary-General's visit to Baghdad on 12–13 January, a decision was taken to relocate UNIIMOG personnel temporarily from Baghdad to the sectors closer to the border. The command group moved to Tehran on 14 January. After the outbreak of hostilities on 16 January 1991, all remaining UNIIMOG staff in Iraq were also moved either to Cyprus or Iran.

Despite these difficulties, the Secretary-General recommended[10] to the Security Council that the mandate of UNIIMOG, set to expire at the end of January 1991, be extended for another month, so that the Group "may fulfil completely its important responsibilities". He stated that the implementation of Security Council resolution 598 (1987) as related to UNIIMOG was very close to completion. To implement what still remained to be done, the role required of the Secretary-General was mainly political, and he intended to recommend how that could be done. On 31 January, the Security Council unanimously adopted resolution 685 (1991), extending the mandate of UNIIMOG to 28 February.

Completion of UNIIMOG's mandate

In the following month, as a result of the continuing hostilities in the Persian Gulf region, UNIIMOG continued to operate in the Iranian part of its area only, but maintained regular contact with the Iraqi authorities through meeting on the border. At the beginning of February some 20 military observers from the Iraqi side whose tours of duty were due to expire, returned home. The balance of the observers who had come from Iraq were temporarily relocated to Cyprus to await a possible return to Iraq when circumstances permitted.

During that period, UNIIMOG continued to assist the parties in the implementation of the January 1991 agreements. On 20 February, the Group reported that the last of the disputed positions along the internationally recognized boundaries had been withdrawn. UNIIMOG thus completed verification and confirmation of the withdrawal of all forces in accordance with resolution 598 (1987). Both sides informed UNIIMOG that they had begun — and, in the case of Iraq, had completed — the establishment of the area of separation, but UNIIMOG was not in a position to verify that. The parties also continued their cooperation with regard to the exchange of information on unmarked minefields.

Reporting to the Security Council on 26 February,[11] the Secretary-General described the general situation along the Iran-Iraq border as very calm. He also reported "with considerable satisfaction" that the forces of the two sides had withdrawn fully to the internationally recognized boundaries, and that the military provisions of resolution 598 (1987) could thus be considered implemented. The remaining tasks under that resolution were essentially political and therefore the Secretary-General recommended to replace UNIIMOG with small civilian offices in Baghdad and Tehran. Accordingly, the Secretary-General

---

[10]S/22148. [11]S/22263.

recommended that the Council take no action to extend the mandate of UNIIMOG.

After the Council had informed[12] the Secretary-General of its concurrence with the proposed arrangements, UNIIMOG completed its mandate on 28 February 1991. At the time of withdrawal, UNIIMOG comprised 96 military observers from the following countries: Austria (1), Bangladesh (1), Canada (4), Denmark (3), Finland (9), Hungary (15), India (11), Ireland (1), Italy (9), Malaysia (10), New Zealand (1), Norway (1), Poland (1), Sweden (7), Turkey (1), Uruguay (9), Yugoslavia (11) and Zambia (1). The Group also included military police provided by Ireland (16) and a medical unit from Austria (2).

The civilian offices were established in February 1991. A few military officers attached to them allowed the United Nations to continue to respond promptly to requests by either Government to investigate and help resolve matters for which military expertise was required. The offices were also important in the Secretary-General's efforts to complete the implementation of resolution 598 (1987).

In December 1991, the Secretary-General commented[13] on the responsibility for the conflict, which was referred to in resolution 598 (1987). He added, however, that no useful purpose would be served in pursuing the matter further. Rather, in the interest of peace, he suggested it would be imperative to move on with the settlement process.

By the end of 1992, the offices in Baghdad and Tehran were phased out, and the Permanent Missions of Iran and Iraq became the channels of communication between those countries and the United Nations for matters related to resolution 598 (1987).

F. Financial aspects

In his report of 7 August 1988, the Secretary-General recommended to the Security Council that the costs of UNIIMOG should be considered as expenses of the Organization to be borne by Members in accordance with Article 17, paragraph 2, of the Charter. He further informed the Council that he intended to recommend to the General Assembly that the assessments to be levied on Member States should be credited to a special account which would be established for this purpose. The General Assembly duly accepted this recommendation in resolution 42/233 adopted on 17 August 1988.

The total cost of UNIIMOG was $177,895,000 (net).

G. Conclusion

UNIIMOG conformed closely to the traditional concept of United Nations peace-keeping. The United Nations military observers were deployed to monitor a cease-fire between two hostile parties, while diplomatic initiatives were pursued to reach a comprehensive settlement. By the time UNIIMOG was terminated, the military aspects of resolution 598 (1987) had been completed; the two sides had withdrawn their forces from lines of confrontation and succeeded in separating them along the internationally recognized border.

[12]S/22280. [13]S/23273.

Chapter 33

United Nations Iraq-Kuwait Observation Mission (UNIKOM)

A. Background
The crisis
Resolution 687 (1991)

B. Establishment of UNIKOM
Resolution 689 (1991)
Establishment of other bodies

C. UNIKOM's activities
UNIKOM carries out its responsibilities
UNIKOM mandate expanded
Situation in the DMZ
Other activities

D. Composition of UNIKOM

E. Financial aspects

Chapter 33

United Nations Iraq-Kuwait Observation Mission (UNIKOM)

A. Background

The crisis

On 2 August 1990, Iraqi armed forces crossed into Kuwaiti territory and invaded that country. On the same day, the Security Council adopted its resolution 660 (1990), condemning the invasion and demanding that Iraq immediately and unconditionally withdraw its forces to the positions they had occupied the previous day. On 6 August, the Council voted to impose mandatory arms and economic sanctions against Iraq, except in respect of medical supplies and, in humanitarian circumstances, foodstuffs. It also established a Sanctions Committee under its authority. It did so in resolution 661 (1990), citing Iraq's failure to comply with the call for troop withdrawal, as well as its usurpation of the authority of the legitimate Government of Kuwait.

In all, over the period between 2 August and 29 November 1990, the Council adopted 12 resolutions in connection with the situation between Iraq and Kuwait, culminating in resolution 678 (1990). That resolution, adopted on 29 November at a meeting at which 13 members of the Security Council were represented by their Foreign Ministers, specified that if Iraq had not fully implemented by 15 January 1991 all of the Council's resolutions relating to the occupation of Kuwait, Member States cooperating with Kuwait's legitimate Government were authorized to use "all necessary means" to compel Iraq to do so and restore international peace and security in the area. These several weeks before the deadline were seen as one final opportunity, a "pause of goodwill", for renewed diplomatic efforts to find a just and peaceful solution to the conflict.

Despite the diplomatic initiatives of a number of Member States and efforts by the Secretary-General, including his meeting with Iraqi President Saddam Hussein in Baghdad on 12-13 January 1991, Iraq continued its occupation of Kuwait. On 15 January 1991, as the deadline neared, the Secretary-General issued an appeal in which he urged Iraq to comply with the relevant Security Council resolutions, beginning with resolution 660 (1990), and thus to "turn the course of events away from catastrophe".

On 16 January 1991, one day after the deadline, the States cooperating with the Government of Kuwait, acting in accordance with the Council's authorization but not under the control of or direction by the United Nations, began offensive military operations. On 27 February, after six weeks of intensive air and ground action, Kuwait City was liberated. The same day, Iraq reported that all of its armed forces had withdrawn from Kuwait. It also within hours informed the Security Council that it had decided to comply fully with Council resolution 660 (1990) and all other Security Council resolutions. Offensive operations were suspended as of midnight (New York time) on 28 February 1991.

On 2 March, the Security Council adopted resolution 686 (1991), demanding that Iraq implement its acceptance of all twelve resolutions and specifying the necessary measures to be undertaken by that country, which would permit a definitive end to hostilities. On 3 March, Iraq informed the Secretary-General and the President of the Security Council that it had agreed to fulfil its obligations under resolution 686.

Resolution 687 (1991)

On 3 April 1991, after more than a month of extensive consultations, the Security Council adopted resolution 687 (1991), setting specific terms for a formal cease-fire to end the conflict. The Council declared that a formal cease-fire between Iraq, Kuwait and the countries cooperating with Kuwait would come into effect after official notification by Iraq of its acceptance of the provisions of the resolution.

On 6 April, Iraq officially notified the Secretary-General and the President of the Security Council that it had no choice but to accept the provisions of resolution 687 (1991). On 11 April, the President of the Security Council, on behalf of its members, formally accepted Iraq's notification. He noted that the conditions established in the resolution had been met and that the formal cease-fire was in effect.

B. Establishment of UNIKOM

Resolution 689 (1991)

By resolution 687 (1991) the Council established, among other things, a demilitarized zone (DMZ) along the boundary between Iraq and Kuwait, to be monitored by a United Nations observer unit, and requested the Secretary-General to submit to the Council for approval a plan for the unit's immediate deployment. The Secretary-General reported[1] back on 5 April 1991, and on 9 April, by its resolution 689 (1991), the Security Council, acting under Chapter VII of the United Nations Charter, approved his plan for the setting up of the United Nations Iraq-Kuwait Observation Mission (UNIKOM). It decided further that the modalities for the Mission should be reviewed every six months, but without requiring in each case a formal decision for its extension. The Council's formal decision would be required only for UNIKOM's termination, thus ensuring the indefinite duration of the Mission, its termination being subject to the concurrence of all the permanent members of the Council.

By acting under Chapter VII, the Council demonstrated that the international community would act decisively should Iraq attempt to attack Kuwait again. To further underline this, all five permanent members of the Security Council, for the first time in a peace-keeping operation, agreed to provide military observers.

The Council gave UNIKOM a mandate to monitor the DMZ and the Khawr 'Abd Allah waterway between Iraq and Kuwait; to deter violations of the boundary through its presence in, and surveillance of, the demilitarized zone; and to observe any hostile action mounted from the territory of one State against the other. The Khawr 'Abd Allah waterway is about 40 kilometres (25 miles) long. The DMZ, which is about 200 kilometres (125 miles) long, extends 10 kilometres (6 miles) into Iraq and 5 kilometres (3 miles) into Kuwait. Except for the oilfields and two towns — Umm Qasr, which became Iraq's only outlet to the sea, and Safwan — the zone is barren and almost uninhabited.

In accordance with its concept of operations, as proposed by the Secretary-General and approved by the Security Council, UNIKOM was to monitor the withdrawal of any armed forces from the DMZ; operate observation posts on the main roads to monitor traffic into and out of the zone; operate observation posts at selected locations in the zone; conduct patrols throughout the zone by land and by air; monitor the Khawr 'Abd Allah from observation posts set up on its shores and from the air; and to carry out investigations.

According to the original mandate, UNIKOM did not have the authority or the capacity to take physical action to prevent the entry of military personnel or equipment into the DMZ. The military observers of UNIKOM are unarmed. Responsibility for the maintenance of law and order in the DMZ rests with the Governments of Iraq and Kuwait which maintain police posts in their respective parts of the zone. Police are allowed only side arms. The number of police deployed in the area as well as the regulation of activities in the DMZ are subject to consultation between the United Nations and the two Governments. Both Governments are required to route all traffic past United Nations observation posts and to notify UNIKOM in advance of sea and air traffic in the DMZ and the Khawr 'Abd Allah.

Establishment of other bodies

In addition to UNIKOM, the United Nations established a number of other bodies in pursuance of resolution 687 (1991):

- The United Nations Special Commission to oversee the destruction, removal or rendering harmless of all Iraq's chemical and biological weapons

[1] S/22454.

and related capabilities and facilities, and its ballistic missiles with a range greater than 150 kilometres. The Commission has also assisted the International Atomic Energy Agency (IAEA) in the destruction, removal, or rendering harmless as appropriate of Iraq's nuclear capabilities.

■ The Iraq-Kuwait Boundary Demarcation Commission to demarcate the international boundary set out in the "Agreed Minutes between the State of Kuwait and the Republic of Iraq regarding the Restoration of Friendly Relations, Recognition and Related Matters", signed by them on 4 October 1963 and registered with the United Nations. The Commission concluded its work and submitted its final report to the Secretary-General on 20 May 1993.

■ The United Nations Compensation Commission to administer the Fund to pay compensation for "any direct loss, damage, including environmental damage and the depletion of natural resources, or injury to foreign Governments, nationals and corporations, as a result of Iraq's unlawful invasion and occupation of Kuwait". The Commission functions under the authority of the Security Council, of which it is a subsidiary organ. The principal organ of the Commission is the Governing Council, composed of the representatives of the current members of the Security Council.

Further to this, in the context of Council resolution 686 (1991), the Secretary-General appointed a senior United Nations official to coordinate the return of property from Iraq to Kuwait.

C. UNIKOM's activities

UNIKOM carries out its responsibilities

The UNIKOM advance party arrived in the area on 13 April 1991. By 6 May, the Mission was fully deployed. UNIKOM then monitored the withdrawal of the armed forces that were still deployed in its assigned zone. That withdrawal having been completed, the DMZ established by the Security Council came into effect at 2000 hours GMT on 9 May, and UNIKOM assumed in full its observation responsibilities.

As of 31 May 1991, the strength of UNIKOM stood at its authorized level of 300 military observers provided by Argentina, Austria, Bangladesh, Canada, China, Denmark, Fiji, Finland, France, Ghana, Greece, Hungary, India, Indonesia, Ireland, Italy, Kenya, Malaysia, Nigeria, Norway, Pakistan, Poland, Romania, Senegal, Singapore, the Soviet Union, Sweden, Thailand, Turkey, the United Kingdom, the United States, Uruguay and Venezuela. In addition, UNIKOM included an engineer unit from Canada (293 all ranks), a helicopter unit from Chile (50), movement control and postal service from Denmark (25), a medical unit from Norway (49) and a logistics unit from Sweden (31).

Initially, to provide essential security during the setting-up phase, UNIKOM included five infantry companies, drawn from the United Nations Peace-keeping Force in Cyprus (UNFICYP) and the United Nations Interim Force in Lebanon (UNIFIL). The infantry came from Austria, Denmark, Fiji, Ghana and Nepal. There was also a logistics company from Sweden. These troops were withdrawn by the end of June 1991.

UNIKOM performed its tasks in accordance with its concept of operations. It enjoyed full freedom of movement throughout the DMZ and observed the zone's length and breadth. It verified that no military personnel and equipment were within the zone and that no military fortifications and installations were maintained in it. For operational purposes, UNIKOM divided the DMZ into three sectors, each having a number of patrol bases, from which the observers patrolled their assigned sectors and manned temporary observation points established in areas of particular activity or where roads and tracks entered the zone. In fact, all movements, including supply runs, were used for observation. UNIKOM patrolled the Khawr 'Abd Allah waterway by helicopter and fixed-wing aircraft. There were also air patrols in the DMZ, especially in the southern sector, where mines and unexploded ordnance limited UNIKOM's ability to carry out ground patrols.

UNIKOM headquarters was initially located south of Kuwait City in a hotel annex made available by the Government of Kuwait. In June 1991, the headquarters moved temporarily to the logistic base at Doha (Kuwait). In November 1991, UNIKOM moved to its permanent headquarters at Umm Qasr on the Iraqi side of the DMZ. The Mission maintains liaison offices in Baghdad and Kuwait City. Since January 1995, the latter is co-located with a logistic base.

From May 1991 to January 1993, UNIKOM observed mainly three types of violations of the DMZ: minor incursions by military personnel on the ground, overflights by military aircraft, and the carrying by policemen of weapons other than side arms.

In January 1993, there was a series of incidents on the newly demarcated boundary between Iraq and Kuwait involving Iraqi intrusions into the Kuwaiti side of the DMZ and unauthorized retrieval of Iraqi property from Kuwaiti territory. The Security Council issued a statement,[2] in which it, *inter alia*, condemned such actions and invited the Secretary-General to explore the possibilities for restoring UNIKOM to its full strength of 300 military observers and to consider in an emergency the need for rapid reinforcement, as well as any other suggestions with a view to enhancing the effectiveness of UNIKOM. At the time of the Council's statement, the strength of UNIKOM stood at approximately 250; some 50 military observers were on standby in their countries.

UNIKOM mandate expanded

In response, the Secretary-General submitted on 18 January a report[3] in which he recalled that UNIKOM had been established as an observation mission. In case of violations, the observers, who were unarmed, reported and made representations, or representations were made at a higher level either in the field or at United Nations Headquarters. Under its original mandate, UNIKOM had neither the authority nor the means to enforce Security Council decisions.

The Secretary-General noted that the January 1993 border incidents had been closely monitored by UNIKOM and reported to United Nations Headquarters. In addition, the Mission made immediate representations to Iraqi personnel on the spot as well as to the Iraqi military authorities. Representations were also made at United Nations Headquarters.

The Secretary-General concluded that UNIKOM had thus performed the function for which it was designed and for which its strength was sufficient. If, however, the Security Council should decide that UNIKOM's present mandate did not permit an adequate response to such violations as had occurred and that UNIKOM should be able to prevent and redress them, then UNIKOM would require a capacity to take physical action. Such action could be taken to prevent or, if that failed, redress: (a) small-scale violations of the DMZ; (b) violations of the boundary between Iraq and Kuwait, for example by civilians or police; and (c) problems that might arise from the presence of Iraqi installations and Iraqi citizens and their assets in the DMZ on the Kuwaiti side of the newly demarcated boundary.

The Secretary-General noted that these tasks could not be performed by unarmed observers. In their place, UNIKOM would have to be provided with infantry in sufficient numbers. He estimated that three infantry battalions would be required, giving UNIKOM a strength of 3,645, including support elements. UNIKOM would be provided with the weapons integral to its infantry battalions, but not authorized to initiate enforcement action. It would use force only in self-defence, which would include resistance to attempts to prevent it by force from discharging its duties.

The Secretary-General emphasized that the recommendation for a reinforced UNIKOM was based on the assumption that the Government of Iraq as well as the Government of Kuwait would cooperate with the restructured Mission. In the absence of such cooperation, it would become impossible for UNIKOM to carry out its functions, in which case the Security Council would need to consider alternative measures.

Subsequently, the Security Council, by its resolution 806 (1993) of 5 February 1993, approved the Secretary-General's report and requested him to plan and execute a phased deployment of the strengthening of UNIKOM. The Council also requested the Secretary-General to report to it on any step he intended to take following an initial deployment.

In his 2 April 1993 report,[4] the Secretary-General informed the Security Council of his intention, in the first phase, to retain the military observers and to reinforce them by one mechanized infantry battalion to be deployed in the

²S/25091. ³S/25123. ⁴S/25514.

northern sector of the DMZ. The Mission's logistic support elements would also be slightly reinforced. On 13 April, the President of the Council informed the Secretary-General that the Council concurred with his recommendations.

In response to the Secretary-General's request, the Government of Bangladesh agreed to contribute a mechanized infantry battalion to UNIKOM. An advance team arrived in the Mission area in mid-November 1993, followed by the remainder of the battalion during the month of December and early January 1994. After a period of training to familiarize it with equipment provided by Kuwait, the battalion became operational on 5 February 1994.

With the addition of the mechanized infantry battalion, UNIKOM's concept of operations was modified. It is now based on a combination of patrol and observation bases, observation points, ground and air patrols, vehicle checkpoints, roadblocks, a force mobile reserve, investigation teams and liaison with the parties at all levels.

The sectors continue to be manned by the military observers, who provide the basis for UNIKOM's patrol, observation, investigation and liaison activities within the DMZ, including the Khawr 'Abd Allah waterway. The main body of the mechanized infantry battalion is located south of Umm Qasr, with a company at Al-Abdaly and a platoon in Sector South. It is tasked to provide reinforcement patrols to sectors, in areas where the situation is sensitive and where an infantry force could be required to prevent incidents. The battalion also provides the force mobile reserve capable of rapid redeployment anywhere within the DMZ to prevent or redress small-scale violations of the DMZ and the boundary. Also, where necessary, it provides security for UNIKOM installations. In the course of 1996, the number of sectors is to be reduced from three to two.

Situation in the DMZ

The overall situation in the DMZ has remained generally calm, although there were periods of tension in November 1993 resulting from the demarcation of the Iraq-Kuwait boundary, and in October 1994 in connection with reports about the deployment of Iraqi troops north of the DMZ.

Otherwise, there were only a limited number of incidents and violations of the DMZ. These involved mainly overflights by military aircraft and the carrying or firing of weapons other than side arms. UNIKOM investigated all ground violations and communicated its findings to the parties. It also investigated all written complaints. In the performance of its functions, UNIKOM has received the cooperation of the Iraqi and Kuwaiti authorities.

Other activities

Throughout the mission, UNIKOM has also maintained contact and provided technical support to other United Nations missions working in Iraq and Kuwait, in particular to the Iraq-Kuwait Boundary Demarcation Commission until its dissolution in May 1993, and to the United Nations office dealing with the return of property from Iraq to Kuwait. UNIKOM has provided movement control in respect of all United Nations aircraft operating in the area. The Mission also provided assistance in connection with the relocation of Iraqi citizens from the Kuwaiti side of the border to Iraq, following the demarcation of the international boundary. This was completed in February 1994.

UNIKOM also continued to act in coordination with the authorities of Iraq and Kuwait in cases of unauthorized border crossings and when responding to requests to facilitate repatriation. The Mission closely cooperated on such matters with the Office of the United Nations High Commissioner for Refugees (UNHCR) and the International Committee of the Red Cross (ICRC). At the request of ICRC, UNIKOM provided the venue and support for meetings of the Technical Subcommittee on Military and Civilian Missing Prisoners of War and Mortal Remains.

Reporting[5] to the Security Council in April 1996, the Secretary-General observed that UNIKOM, through its presence and activities, continued to contribute to the calm that prevailed in the area of operation, and recommended that the Mission be maintained. The Council concurred[6] with this recommendation and decided to review the question by 4 October 1996.

[5]S/1996/225. [6]S/1996/247.

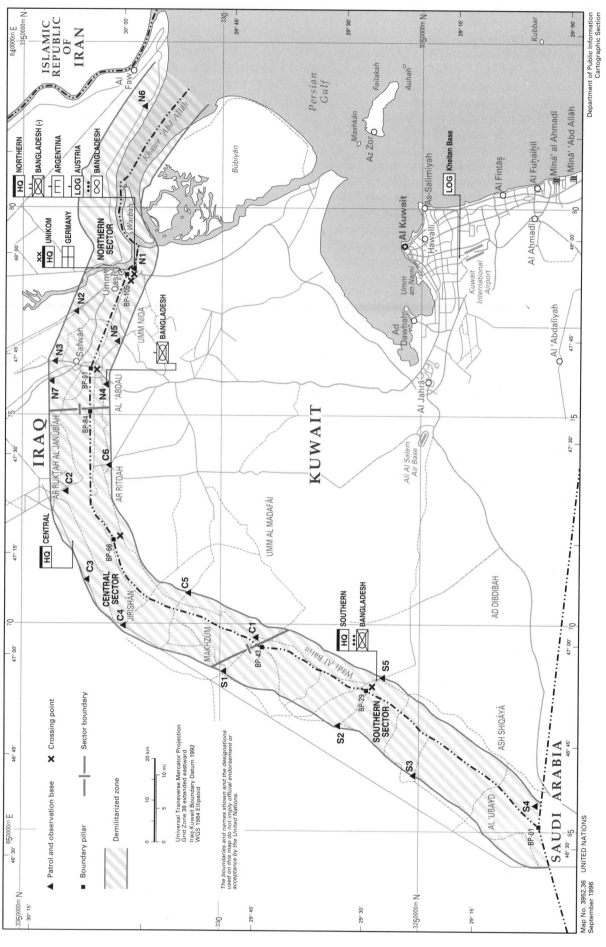

UNIKOM deployment as of April 1996

Legend:

▲ Patrol and observation base
✕ Crossing point
■ Boundary pillar
— Sector boundary
▨ Demilitarized zone

Universal Transverse Mercator Projection
Grid Zone 38 extended eastward
Iraq-Kuwait Boundary Datum 1992
WGS 1984 Ellipsoid

0   5   10   20 km
0   5   10 mi

The boundaries and names shown and the designations used on this map do not imply official endorsement or acceptance by the United Nations.

ISLAMIC REPUBLIC OF IRAN

IRAQ

KUWAIT

SAUDI ARABIA

Persian Gulf

HQ UNIKOM
XX
GERMANY

HQ NORTHERN
BANGLADESH (-)
ARGENTINA
AUSTRIA
BANGLADESH

NORTHERN SECTOR

HQ CENTRAL
CENTRAL SECTOR

HQ SOUTHERN
BANGLADESH
SOUTHERN SECTOR

BANGLADESH

LOG Kheitan Base

Al Kuwait

Al Faw
N6
N1
N2
N3
N5
N4
N7
C2
C6
C3
C4
C5
C1
S1
S2
S3
S4
S5

BP-105
BP-91
BP-84
BP-66
BP-43
BP-29
BP-01

Umm Qasr
Safwān
AL 'ABDALI
UMM NIQA
Warbah
Būbiyān
AR RUKTAH AL JANŪBĪAH
AR RITQAH
JIRISHĀN
MAKHZŪM
Wadi Al Bātin
UMM AL MADAFĀI
AD DIBDIBAH
ASH SHIQĀYĀ
AL 'UBAYD
Ali Al Salem Air Base

Al Jahrā
Ad Dawhah
Umm an Nami
Hawalli
As-Salimiyah
Al Fintās
Al Fuhaihīl
Al Ahmadī
Mina' al Ahmadi
Minā' 'Abd Allāh
Al 'Abdalīyah
Kuwait International Airport

Mashkān
Az Zor
Failakah
Aunah
Kubbar

Khawr 'Abd Allāh

Department of Public Information
Cartographic Section

Map No. 3952.36   UNITED NATIONS
September 1996

D. Composition of UNIKOM

Major-General Günther Greindl (Austria) served as Chief Military Observer of UNIKOM from April 1991 to July 1992. He was succeeded by Major-General Timothy K. Dibuama (Ghana), who served in that capacity from July 1992 to 20 August 1993. The UNIKOM Chief of Staff, Brigadier-General Vigar Aabrek (Norway), then served as Acting Chief Military Observer until December 1993, when Major-General Krishna Narayan Singh Thapa (Nepal) was appointed as Chief Military Observer. In January 1994, his appointment was changed to that of Force Commander to reflect the addition of a mechanized infantry battalion. In December 1995, Major-General Gian Giuseppe Santillo (Italy) succeeded General Thapa as Force Commander.

During the course of the mission, the following States have provided military personnel to UNIKOM: Argentina, Austria, Bangladesh, Canada, China, Denmark, Fiji, Finland, France, Ghana, Greece, Hungary, India, Indonesia, Ireland, Italy, Kenya, Malaysia, Nepal, Nigeria, Norway, Pakistan, Poland, Romania, the Russian Federation, Senegal, Singapore, Sweden, Thailand, Turkey, the United Kingdom, the United States, Uruguay and Venezuela.

Initially, administrative and logistic support was provided by Canada (engineers), Chile (helicopters), Denmark (logistics) and Norway (medical). Chile withdrew its helicopter unit at the end of October 1992; it was replaced by a civilian unit, under contract to UNIKOM, until September 1995 when Bangladesh provided this support. Canada withdrew its engineer unit at the end of March 1993 and the Secretary-General accepted an offer from Argentina to replace it. In January 1996, the Danish logistics unit was replaced by a unit from Austria. The Norwegian medical unit was replaced in November 1993 by a combined medical team composed of 16 members from Bangladesh and 12 members from Austria. The Governments of Austria and Bangladesh withdrew their medical units at the end of February 1995. As a provisional measure, a small medical team was contracted locally until October 1995 when a medical unit was provided by Germany.

Two fixed-wing aircraft operated by civilians were made available at no cost to the United Nations by the Government of Switzerland. This was discontinued in December 1994. UNIKOM's air assets consist of two helicopters and one chartered fixed-wing aircraft.

In the course of 1992, a number of UNIKOM's military observers were temporarily detached to the former Yugoslavia to serve as United Nations military liaison officers. Their number varied, reaching a peak of 50 in March 1992.

Although never reached, the maximum authorized strength of UNIKOM was 3,645 military personnel, including 300 military observers. As of March 1996, the overall strength of UNIKOM was 1,356, including 245 military observers from Argentina, Austria, Bangladesh, Canada, China, Denmark, Fiji, Finland, France, Ghana, Greece, Hungary, India, Indonesia, Ireland, Italy, Kenya, Malaysia, Nigeria, Pakistan, Poland, Romania, Russian Federation, Senegal, Singapore, Sweden, Thailand, Turkey, United Kingdom, United States, Uruguay and Venezuela.

Other military personnel totalled some 900 and included an infantry battalion from Bangladesh, an engineer unit from Argentina, a logistics unit from Austria, a helicopter unit from Bangladesh and a medical unit from Germany. Also serving as of March 1996 were 211 civilian staff, of whom 72 were recruited internationally.

The Secretary-General reported[7] to the Security Council in April 1996 that he had approved a modest streamlining of UNIKOM, reducing the number of military observers by about 50. The operational activities of the Mission would not be affected by the reduction.

[7]S/1996/225.

E. Financial aspects

Effective 1 November 1993, two thirds of the cost of the operation is being paid by the Government of Kuwait. The remainder is met by the assessed contributions of the United Nations Member States.

Estimated expenditures for the period from 9 April 1991 to 30 June 1996 stood at $313,403,233 gross ($303,363,160 net). Cost estimates for the period from 1 July 1996 to 30 June 1997 amount to $57,804,400 gross ($55,467,000 net).[8]

[8]A/50/892.

Appendix
Facts and figures

The data in these charts have been collected by the Department of Public Information from the public record for information purposes only. They do not constitute an official document.

Data are valid as of 31 March 1996 unless otherwise indicated. The term "troops" may include infantry, logistics, engineering, medical, mov-con, staff, etc.

United Nations Truce Supervision Organization (UNTSO)

Authorization:	Security Council resolutions:
	50 (1948) of 29 May 1948
	54 (1948) of 15 July 1948
	73 (1949) of 11 August 1949
	101 (1953) of 24 November 1953
	114 (1956) of 4 June 1956
	236 (1967) of 11 June 1967
	Consensus of 9/10 July 1967 (S/8047)
	Consensus of 19 April 1972 (S/10611)
	339 (1973) of 23 October 1973

Function: Established to assist the Mediator and the Truce Commission in supervising the observance of the truce in Palestine. Since then, UNTSO has performed various tasks entrusted to it by the Security Council, including the supervision of the General Armistice Agreements of 1949 and the observation of the cease-fire in the Suez Canal area and the Golan Heights following the Arab-Israeli war of June 1967. At present, UNTSO assists and cooperates with UNDOF on the Golan Heights in the Israel-Syria sector, and UNIFIL in the Israel-Lebanon sector. UNTSO also has a presence in the Egypt-Israel sector in the Sinai. In addition, UNTSO maintains offices in Beirut and Damascus

Headquarters: Government House, Jerusalem

Duration: 11 June 1948 to date

Strength: Maximum: 572 (1948)
At 31 March 1996: 178 military observers

Fatalities: 12 military observers
17 other military personnel
6 international United Nations staff
3 local staff
38 total (as at 31 March 1996)

Financing: Method of financing: Appropriations through the United Nations regular budget
Expenditures: From inception of mission to 31 December 1995: $463,667,258

Mediators:	Count Folke Bernadotte (Sweden)	May–September 1948
	Ralph J. Bunche (United States) (Acting)	September 1948–August 1949

Chiefs of Staff:	Lieutenant-General Count Thord Bonde (Sweden)	June–July 1948
	Major-General Aage Lundström (Sweden)	July–September 1948
	Lieutenant-General William E. Riley (United States)	September 1948–June 1953
	Major-General Vagn Bennike (Denmark)	June 1953–August 1954
	Lieutenant-General E.L.M. Burns (Canada)	August 1954–November 1956
	Colonel Byron V. Leary (United States) (Acting)	November 1956–March 1958
	Major-General Carl C. von Horn (Sweden)	March 1958–July 1960
	Colonel R. W. Rickert (United States) (Acting)	July–December 1960
	Lieutenant-General Carl C. von Horn (Sweden)	January 1961–May 1963
	Lieutenant-General Odd Bull (Norway)	June 1963–July 1970
	Major-General Ensio Siilasvuo (Finland)	August 1970–October 1973
	Colonel Richard W. Bunworth (Ireland) (Acting)	November 1973–March 1974
	Major-General Bengt Liljestrand (Sweden)	April 1974–August 1975
	Colonel K. D. Howard (Australia) (Acting)	August–December 1975
	Major-General Emmanuel A. Erskine (Ghana)	January 1976–April 1978
	Colonel William Callaghan (Ireland) (Acting)	April 1978–June 1979
	Colonel O. Forsgren (Sweden) (Acting)	June 1979–January 1980
	Major-General Erkki R. Kaira (Finland)	February 1980–February 1981

(continued)

Lieutenant-General Emmanuel A. Erskine (Ghana)	February 1981–May 1986
Lieutenant-General William Callaghan (Ireland)	May 1986–June 1987
Lieutenant-General Martin Vadset (Norway)	June 1987–October 1990
Major-General Hans Christensen (Finland)	October 1990–October 1992
Major-General Krishna Narayan Singh Thapa (Nepal)	October 1992–November 1993
Colonel Joseph Bujold (Canada) (Officer-in-Charge)	December 1993–October 1995
Major-General Rufus Modupe Kupolati (Nigeria)	October 1995 to date

Contributors of military observers

	Duration
Argentina	1967 to date
Australia	1956 to date
Austria	1967 to date
Belgium	1948 to date
Burma	1967–1969
Canada	1954 to date
Chile	1967 to date
China	1990 to date
Denmark	1954 to date
Finland	1967 to date
France	1948 to date
Ireland	1958 to date
Italy	1958 to date
Netherlands	1956 to date
New Zealand	1954 to date
Norway	1956 to date
Russian Federation (Soviet Union before 24 December 1991)	1973 to date
Sweden	1948 to date
Switzerland	1990 to date
United States	1948 to date

Voluntary contributions

	Duration	Contribution
United States	1949–June 1967	Aircraft
Netherlands	June–November 1967	Aircraft
Switzerland	November 1967 to date	Chartered commercial aircraft and crew

In 1988, the Government of Switzerland undertook to make available to all peace-keeping and good-offices missions an emergency air ambulance service for the repatriation of sick and injured personnel, coding equipment and the expenses arising from training personnel for the maintenance and repair of this equipment.

First United Nations Emergency Force (UNEF I)

Authorization:	General Assembly resolutions:
	998 (ES-I) of 4 November 1956
	1000 (ES-I) of 5 November 1956
	1001 (ES-I) of 7 November 1956
	1125 (XI) of 2 February 1957
Function:	Established to secure and supervise the cessation of hostilities, including the withdrawal of the armed forces of France, Israel and the United Kingdom from Egyptian territory, and, after the withdrawal, to serve as a buffer between the Egyptian and Israeli forces. In May 1967, Egypt compels UNEF I to withdraw
Location:	First the Suez Canal sector and the Sinai peninsula. Later along the Armistice Demarcation Line in the Gaza area and the international frontier in the Sinai peninsula (on the Egyptian side)
Headquarters:	Gaza
Duration:	November 1956–June 1967
Strength:	Maximum: 6,073 (February 1957)
	At withdrawal: 3,378 (June 1967)
Fatalities:	106 military personnel
	<u>1</u> local staff
	107 total
Financing:	Method of financing: Assessments in respect of a Special Account
	Expenditures: $214,249,000 (The financial cost was considerably reduced by the absorption by the countries providing contingents of varying amounts of the expenses involved)

Commanders:

Lieutenant-General E.L.M. Burns (Canada)	November 1956–December 1959
Lieutenant-General P. S. Gyani (India)	December 1959–January 1964
Major-General Carlos F. Paiva Chaves (Brazil)	January 1964–August 1964
Colonel Lazar Musicki (Yugoslavia) (Acting)	August 1964–January 1965
Major-General Syseno Sarmento (Brazil)	January 1965–January 1966
Major-General Indar J. Rikhye (India)	January 1966–June 1967

Contributors	Duration	Contribution
Brazil	January 1957–June 1967	Infantry
Canada	November 1956–February 1959	Medical unit
	November 1956–May 1967	Signal, engineer, air transport, maintenance and movement-control units
Colombia	November 1956–October 1958	Infantry
Denmark	November 1956–June 1967	Infantry
Finland	December 1956–December 1957	Infantry
India	November 1956–June 1967	Infantry, and supply, transport and signal units
Indonesia	January 1957–September 1957	Infantry
Norway	November 1956–June 1967	Infantry
	March 1959–June 1967	Medical unit
Sweden	November 1956–June 1967	Infantry
Yugoslavia	November 1956–June 1967	Infantry

Voluntary contributions		
Canada	November 1956	Airlift
Italy	November 1956	Airlift, logistic support
Switzerland	November 1956	Airlift
United States	November 1956	Airlift

Second United Nations Emergency Force (UNEF II)

Authorization:	Security Council resolutions:

340 (1973) of 25 October 1973
341 (1973) of 27 October 1973
346 (1974) of 8 April 1974
362 (1974) of 23 October 1974
368 (1975) of 17 April 1975
371 (1975) of 24 July 1975
378 (1975) of 23 October 1975
396 (1976) of 22 October 1976
416 (1977) of 21 October 1977
438 (1978) of 23 October 1978

Function: Established to supervise the cease-fire between Egyptian and Israeli forces and, following the conclusion of the agreements of 18 January 1974 and 4 September 1975, to supervise the redeployment of Egyptian and Israeli forces and to man and control the buffer zones established under those agreements

Location: Suez Canal sector and later the Sinai peninsula

Headquarters: Ismailia

Duration: 25 October 1973–24 July 1979

Strength: Maximum: 6,973 (February 1974)
At withdrawal: 4,031 (July 1979)

Fatalities: 53 military personnel
<u>2</u> international United Nations staff
55 total

Financing: Method of financing: Assessments in respect of a Special Account
Expenditures: $446,487,000

Commanders: Lieutenant-General Ensio P. H. Siilasvuo (Finland)
Interim Commander, October 1973–November 1973
Commander, November 1973–August 1975

Lieutenant-General Bengt Liljestrand (Sweden)
August 1975–November 1976

Major-General Rais Abin (Indonesia)
December 1976–September 1979

Contributors	Duration	Contribution
Australia	July 1976–October 1979	Air unit (helicopters and personnel)
Austria	October 1973–June 1974	Infantry
Canada	November 1973–October 1979	Logistics: signals, air and service units
Finland	October 1973–August 1979	Infantry
Ghana	January 1974–September 1979	Infantry
Indonesia	December 1973–September 1979	Infantry
Ireland	October 1973–May 1974	Infantry
Nepal	February 1974–September 1974	Infantry
Panama	December 1973–November 1974	Infantry
Peru	November 1973–June 1974	Infantry
Poland	November 1973–January 1980	Logistics: engineering, medical and transport units
Senegal	January 1974–June 1976	Infantry
Sweden	October 1973–April 1980	Infantry

Voluntary contributions

Australia	February 1974	Airlift: Nepalese troops, Calcutta–Cairo
Canada	November 1973	Airlift: Canadian troops
Germany, Federal Republic of	January 1974	Airlift: Ghanaian and Senegalese troops
Japan	February 1974	Cash contribution for airlift of Nepalese troops Kathmandu–Calcutta, and transport of its equipment to UNEF
Norway	October 1973	Airlift: Swedish troops, Sweden–UNEF
Poland	November 1973	Airlift: Polish troops
Sweden	October 1973	Airlift: Swedish troops
Switzerland		Aircraft placed at disposal of UNTSO was available to UNEF as required
United Kingdom	October 1973	Airlift: Austrian, Finnish, Irish and Swedish troops and vehicles, Cyprus–UNEF
Soviet Union	November 1973	Airlift: Austrian troops, Austria–UNEF, Finnish troops and heavy equipment Finland–UNEF
United States	November 1973	Airlift: Irish troops, Ireland–UNEF
	November 1973	Finnish troops, Finland–UNEF
	November 1973	Peruvian troops, Peru–UNEF
	December 1973	Austrian troops, Austria–UNEF
	December 1973	Indonesian troops, Indonesia–UNEF
	December 1973	Panamanian troops, Panama–UNEF
	October 1976	$10 million in goods and services

United Nations Disengagement Observer Force (UNDOF)

Authorization: Security Council resolutions:

350 (1974) of 31 May 1974
363 (1974) of 29 November 1974
369 (1975) of 28 May 1975
381 (1975) of 30 November 1975
390 (1976) of 28 May 1976
398 (1976) of 30 November 1976
408 (1977) of 26 May 1977
420 (1977) of 30 November 1977
429 (1978) of 31 May 1978
441 (1978) of 30 November 1978
449 (1979) of 30 May 1979
456 (1979) of 30 November 1979
470 (1980) of 30 May 1980
481 (1980) of 26 November 1980
485 (1981) of 22 May 1981
493 (1981) of 23 November 1981
506 (1982) of 26 May 1982
524 (1982) of 29 November 1982
531 (1983) of 26 May 1983
543 (1983) of 29 November 1983
551 (1984) of 30 May 1984
557 (1984) of 28 November 1984
563 (1985) of 21 May 1985

576 (1985) of 21 November 1985
584 (1986) of 29 May 1986
590 (1986) of 26 November 1986
596 (1987) of 29 May 1987
603 (1987) of 25 November 1987
613 (1988) of 31 May 1988
624 (1988) of 30 November 1988
633 (1989) of 30 May 1989
645 (1989) of 29 November 1989
655 (1990) of 31 May 1990
679 (1990) of 30 November 1990
695 (1991) of 30 May 1991
722 (1991) of 29 November 1991
756 (1992) of 29 May 1992
790 (1992) of 25 November 1992
830 (1993) of 26 May 1993
887 (1993) of 29 November 1993
921 (1994) of 26 May 1994
962 (1994) of 29 November 1994
996 (1995) of 30 May 1995
1024 (1995) of 28 November 1995
1057 (1996) of 30 May 1996

Function: Established after the 1973 Middle East war to maintain the cease-fire between Israel and Syria, to supervise the disengagement of Israeli and Syrian forces, and to supervise the areas of separation and limitation, as provided in the Agreement on Disengagement of 31 May 1974. Since its establishment, UNDOF has continued to perform its functions effectively with the cooperation of the parties. The situation in the Israeli-Syria sector has remained quiet, and there have been no serious incidents

Location: Syrian Golan Heights

Headquarters: Camp Faouar

Duration: 3 June 1974 to date

Strength: Authorized: 1,450 all ranks

At 31 March 1996:
1,054 all ranks, assisted by approximately 80 military observers of UNTSO's Observer Group Golan; there were also approximately 35 international and 80 locally recruited civilian staff

Fatalities: 35 military personnel
<u>1</u> international United Nations staff
36 total (as at 31 March 1996)

Financing: Method of financing: Assessments in respect of a Special Account originally established for UNEF II
Estimated expenditures: Total expenditures from the inception of UNEF II until liquidation in 1980 and for UNDOF from inception to 31 May 1996 were estimated at $1,089,300,000, of which approximately $446,487,000 represents expenditures for UNEF II and $642,813,000 represents expenditures for UNDOF

Commanders:		
	Brigadier-General Gonzalo Briceño Zevallos (Peru), Interim Commander	June–December 1974
	Colonel Hannes Philipp (Austria), Officer-in-Charge	December 1974–July 1975
	Major-General Hannes Philipp (Austria)	July 1975–April 1979
	Colonel Günther G. Greindl (Austria)	April–November 1979
	Major-General Günther G. Greindl (Austria)	December 1979–February 1981
	Major-General Erkki R. Kaira (Finland)	February 1981–May 1982
	Major-General Carl-Gustaf Stahl (Sweden)	June 1982–May 1985
	Major-General Gustav Hägglund (Finland)	June 1985–May 1986
	Brigadier-General W.A. Douglas Yuill (Canada) (Acting)	June 1986
	Major-General N. Gustaf A. Welin (Sweden)	July 1986–September 1988
	Major-General Adolf Radauer (Austria)	September 1988–September 1991
	Major-General Roman Misztal (Poland)	September 1991–November 1994
	Colonel Jan Kempara (Poland) (Acting)	November 1994–January 1995
	Major-General Johannes C. Kosters (Netherlands)	January 1995 to date

Contributors	Duration	Contribution
Austria	June 1974 to date	Infantry
Canada	June 1974 to date	Logistics
Finland	March 1979–December 1993	Infantry
Iran	August 1975–March 1979	Infantry
Japan	February 1996 to date	Logistics
Peru	June 1974–July 1975	Infantry
Poland	June 1974–December 1993	Logistics
	December 1993 to date	Infantry

United Nations Interim Force in Lebanon (UNIFIL)

Authorization: Security Council resolutions:

425 (1978) of 19 March 1978	583 (1986) of 18 April 1986
426 (1978) of 19 March 1978	586 (1986) of 18 July 1986
427 (1978) of 3 May 1978	594 (1987) of 15 January 1987
434 (1978) of 18 September 1978	599 (1987) of 31 July 1987
444 (1979) of 19 January 1979	609 (1988) of 29 January 1988
450 (1979) of 14 June 1979	617 (1988) of 29 July 1988
459 (1979) of 19 December 1979	630 (1989) of 30 January 1989
474 (1980) of 17 June 1980	639 (1989) of 31 July 1989
483 (1980) of 17 December 1980	648 (1990) of 31 January 1990
488 (1981) of 19 June 1981	659 (1990) of 31 July 1990
498 (1981) of 18 December 1981	684 (1991) of 30 January 1991
501 (1982) of 25 February 1982	701 (1991) of 31 July 1991
511 (1982) of 18 June 1982	734 (1992) of 29 January 1992
519 (1982) of 17 August 1982	768 (1992) of 30 July 1992
523 (1982) of 18 October 1982	803 (1993) of 28 January 1993
529 (1983) of 18 January 1983	852 (1993) of 28 July 1993
536 (1983) of 18 July 1983	895 (1994) of 28 January 1994
538 (1983) of 18 October 1983	938 (1994) of 28 July 1994
549 (1984) of 19 April 1984	974 (1995) of 30 January 1995
555 (1984) of 12 October 1984	1006 (1995) of 28 July 1995
561 (1985) of 17 April 1985	1039 (1996) of 29 January 1996
575 (1985) of 17 October 1985	

Function: Established to confirm the withdrawal of Israeli forces from southern Lebanon, to restore international peace and security and to assist the Government of Lebanon in ensuring the return of its effective authority in the area. UNIFIL has, however, been prevented from fully implementing its mandate. Israel has maintained its occupation of parts of south Lebanon, where the Israeli forces and their local auxiliary continue to be targets of attacks by groups that have proclaimed their resistance to the occupation. UNIFIL does its best to limit the conflict and protect the inhabitants from the fighting. In doing so, it contributes to stability in the area

Location: Southern Lebanon

Headquarters: Naqoura

Duration: 19 March 1978 to date

Strength: Authorized: 7,000 all ranks

At 31 March 1996:
4,568 all ranks, supported by some 58 military observers from UNTSO; there were also approximately 140 international civilian staff and about 190 local staff

Fatalities: 209 military personnel
  1 international United Nations staff
  <u>1</u> local staff
211 total (as at 31 March 1996)

Financing: Method of financing: Assessments in respect of a Special Account
Estimated expenditure: From inception of mission to 31 January 1996: $2,544,800,000 net

Commanders: Lieutenant-General Emmanuel A. Erskine (Ghana)
Interim Commander: March–April 1978
Commander: April 1978–February 1981

Lieutenant-General William Callaghan (Ireland)
February 1981–May 1986

Major-General Gustav Hägglund (Finland)
June 1986–June 1988

Lieutenant-General Lars-Eric Wahlgren (Sweden)
July 1988–February 1993

Major-General Trond Furuhovde (Norway)
February 1993–February 1995

Major-General Stanislaw Franciszek Woniak (Poland)
April 1995 to date

Contributors	Duration	Contribution
Canada	March–October 1978	Signals and movement control units
Fiji	May 1978 to date	Infantry
Finland	November 1982 to date	Infantry
France	March 1978–March 1979	
	May 1982–December 1986	Infantry
	March 1978–December 1986	Logistics: engineering, supply, transport and maintenance units
	December 1986–December 1994	Composite battalion (maintenance and defence company)
	December 1994 to date	Composite unit (maintenance element and defence company)
Ghana	September 1979 to date	Infantry
	September 1979 to date	Integrated headquarters camp command (defence platoon and engineering platoon)
Iran	March 1978–March 1979	Infantry
Ireland	May 1978 to date	Infantry
	October 1978–September 1979	Headquarters camp command (defence platoon and administrative personnel)
	October 1978 to date	Integrated headquarters camp command (administrative personnel)
Italy	July 1979 to date	Air unit: helicopters, ground and air crews
Nepal	April 1978–May 1980	
	June 1981–November 1982	
	January 1985 to date	Infantry
Netherlands	February 1979–October 1985	Infantry
Nigeria	May 1978–February 1983	Infantry
Norway	March 1978 to date	Infantry
	March 1978–July 1979	Logistics: air unit
	March 1978–August 1980	Medical unit
	March 1978 to date	Maintenance company
	March 1978 to date	Movement control unit
Poland	April 1992 to date	Medical unit
	April 1994 to date	Logistics battalion; engineer company
Senegal	April 1978–November 1984	Infantry
Sweden	March–May 1978	Infantry
	August 1980–April 1992	Logistics: medical unit
	December 1986–April 1994	Logistics battalion

In January 1987, a composite mechanized company became operational as the Force Mobile Reserve. In January 1996, its personnel were contributed by Fiji, Finland, Ghana, Ireland, Nepal, Norway and Poland

Voluntary contributions

Australia	June 1978	Arms and ammunition for Fijian contingent
Germany, Federal Republic of	March 1978	Airlift: Norwegian troops
	April 1978	Provided substantial part of vehicles and equipment for Nepalese contingent
Japan	March 1988	Financial
United Kingdom	June 1978	Airlift: Fijian troops
United States	March–June 1978	Airlift: Norwegian, Nepalese, Senegalese and Irish troops
		Airlift: equipment for Fijian troops

The Government of Switzerland makes available to UNIFIL air ambulance service for the repatriation of those wounded or taken ill in the performance of their duties, as and when required

United Nations Observation Group in Lebanon (UNOGIL)

Authorization:	Security Council resolution 128 (1958) of 11 June 1958
Function:	Established to ensure that there was no illegal infiltration of personnel or supply of arms or other *matériel* across the Lebanese borders. After the conflict had been settled, tensions eased and UNOGIL was withdrawn
Location:	Lebanese-Syrian border areas and vicinity of zones held by opposing forces
Headquarters:	Beirut
Duration:	12 June–9 December 1958
Strength:	Maximum: 591 military observers (November 1958) At withdrawal: 375 military observers
Fatalities:	None
Financing:	Method of financing: Appropriations through the United Nations regular budget Expenditures: $3,697,742
Members of Observation Group:	Galo Plaza Lasso (Ecuador), Chairman Rajeshwar Dayal (India), Member Major-General Odd Bull (Norway), Executive member in charge of military observers
Contributors of military observers:	Afghanistan, Argentina, Burma, Canada, Ceylon, Chile, Denmark, Ecuador, Finland, India, Indonesia, Ireland, Italy, Nepal, Netherlands, New Zealand, Norway, Peru, Portugal, Thailand

United Nations Yemen Observation Mission (UNYOM)

Authorization:	Security Council resolution 179 (1963) of 11 June 1963
Function:	Established to observe and certify the implementation of the disengagement agreement between Saudi Arabia and the United Arab Republic
Location:	Yemen
Headquarters:	Sana'a
Duration:	4 July 1963–4 September 1964
Strength:	Maximum: 189 (25 military observers, 114 officers and other ranks of reconnaissance unit (Yugoslavia), 50 officers and other ranks of air unit (Canada)) At withdrawal: 25 military observers and supporting air unit (Canada)
Fatalities:	None
Financing:	Method of financing: Contributions from Saudi Arabia and Egypt in equal parts Expenditures: $1,840,450

Commanders:		
	Lieutenant-General Carl C. von Horn (Sweden)	July–August 1963
	Colonel Branko Pavlovic (Yugoslavia) (Acting)	August–September 1963
	Lieutenant-General P.S. Gyani (India)	September–November 1963

Special Representative of the Secretary-General and Head of Mission:

P. P. Spinelli (Italy)	November 1963–September 1964

Chiefs of Staff:

Colonel Branko Pavlovic (Yugoslavia)	November 1963
Colonel S.C. Sabharwal (India)	November 1963–September 1964

Contributors	Duration	Contribution
Australia	July 1963–November 1963	Military observers
Canada	July 1963–September 1964	Air unit (aircraft and helicopters)
Denmark	July 1963–September 1964	Military observers
Ghana	July 1963–September 1964	Military observers
India	January 1964–September 1964	Military observers
Italy	January 1964–September 1964	Military observers
Netherlands	January 1964–September 1964	Military observers
Norway	July 1963–September 1964	Military observers
Pakistan	January 1964–September 1964	Military observers
Sweden	July 1963–September 1964	Military observers
Yugoslavia	July 1963–November 1963	Reconnaissance unit
	July 1963–September 1964	Military observers

United Nations Military Observer Group in India and Pakistan (UNMOGIP)

Authorization:	Security Council resolutions: 47 (1948) of 21 April 1948 91 (1951) of 30 March 1951 201 (1965) of 6 September 1965
Function:	Established to supervise, in the State of Jammu and Kashmir, the cease-fire between India and Pakistan. Following the 1972 India-Pakistan agreement defining a Line of Control in Kashmir, India took the position that the mandate of UNMOGIP had lapsed. Pakistan, however, did not accept this position. Given that disagreement, the Secretary-General's position has been that UNMOGIP can be terminated only by a decision of the Security Council. In the absence of such a decision, UNMOGIP has been maintained with the same mandate and functions
Location:	The cease-fire line between India and Pakistan in the State of Jammu and Kashmir
Headquarters:	Rawalpindi (November–April) Srinagar (May–October)
Duration:	24 January 1949 to date
Strength:	Maximum: 102 (October 1965) At 31 March 1996: 44 military observers
Fatalities:	1 military observer 5 other military personnel 1 international United Nations staff <u>2</u> local staff 9 total (as at 31 March 1996)
Financing:	Method of financing: Appropriations through the United Nations regular budget Expenditures: From inception of mission to 31 December 1995: $98,399,102

Chief Military Observers:

Brigadier H.H. Angle (Canada)	November 1949–July 1950
Colonel Siegfried Coblentz (United States) (Acting)	July 1950–October 1950
Lieutenant-General R.H. Nimmo (Australia)	October 1950–January 1966
Colonel J.H.J. Gauthier (Canada) (Acting)	January 1966–July 1966
Lieutenant-General Luis Tassara-Gonzalez (Chile)	July 1966–June 1977
Lieutenant-Colonel P. Bergevin (Canada) (Acting)	June 1977–April 1978
Colonel P.P. Pospisil (Canada) (Acting)	April 1978–June 1978
Brigadier-General Stig Waldenstrom (Sweden)	June 1978–June 1982
Brigadier-General Thor Johnsen (Norway)	June 1982–May 1986
Lieutenant-Colonel G. Beltracchi (Italy) (Acting)	May 1986–July 1986
Brigadier-General Alf Hammer (Norway)	August 1986–August 1987
Lieutenant-Colonel G. Beltracchi (Italy) (Acting)	August 1987–September 1987
Brigadier-General James Parker (Ireland)	September 1987–May 1989
Lieutenant-Colonel Mario Fiorese (Italy) (Acting)	May 1989–June 1989
Brigadier-General Jeremiah Enright (Ireland)	June 1989–June 1992
Major-General Ricardo Jorge Galarza-Chans (Uruguay)	June 1992–December 1994
Major-General Alfonso Pessolano (Italy)	December 1994 to date

**Contributors of
military observers:**

Australia	1952–1985	
Belgium	1949 to date	
Canada	1949–1979	
Chile	1950 to date	
Denmark	1950 to date	
Ecuador	1952	
Finland	1963 to date	
Italy	1961 to date	
Mexico	1949	
New Zealand	1952–1977	
Norway	1949–1952	
	1957–1994	
Republic of Korea	1994 to date	
Sweden	1950 to date	
Uruguay	1952 to date	
United States	1949–1954	

Voluntary contributions	**Duration**	**Contribution**
Australia	1975–1978	Aircraft
Canada	1974–1975	Aircraft
Italy	1957–1963	Aircraft
United States	1949–1954	Aircraft

United Nations India-Pakistan Observation Mission (UNIPOM)

Authorization:	Security Council resolution 211 (1965) of 20 September 1965
Function:	Established to supervise the cease-fire along the India-Pakistan border except in the State of Jammu and Kashmir, where UNMOGIP operated, and the withdrawal of all armed personnel to the positions held by them before 5 August 1965. After the withdrawal of the troops by India and Pakistan had been completed on schedule, UNIPOM was terminated
Location:	Along the India-Pakistan border between Kashmir and the Arabian Sea
Headquarters:	Lahore (Pakistan)/Amritsar (India)
Duration:	23 September 1965–22 March 1966
Strength:	Maximum: 96 military observers (October 1965) At withdrawal: 78 military observers
Fatalities:	None
Financing:	Method of financing: Appropriations through the United Nations regular budget Expenditures: $1,713,280
Chief Officer:	Major-General B.F. Macdonald (Canada) September 1965–March 1966
Contributors:	In its initial stage (from UNTSO and UNMOGIP) Australia, Belgium, Canada, Chile, Denmark, Finland, Ireland, Italy, Netherlands, New Zealand, Norway, Sweden September 1965–March 1966 Brazil, Burma, Canada (also air unit, October 1965–March 1966), Ceylon, Ethiopia, Ireland, Nepal, Netherlands, Nigeria, Venezuela

United Nations Peace-keeping Force in Cyprus (UNFICYP)

Authorization: Security Council resolutions:

186 (1964) of 4 March 1964	458 (1979) of 14 December 1979
187 (1964) of 13 March 1964	472 (1980) of 13 June 1980
192 (1964) of 20 June 1964	482 (1980) of 11 December 1980
Consensus of 11 August 1964	486 (1981) of 4 June 1981
194 (1964) of 25 September 1964	495 (1981) of 14 December 1981
198 (1964) of 18 December 1964	510 (1982) of 15 June 1982
201 (1965) of 19 March 1965	526 (1982) of 14 December 1982
206 (1965) of 16 June 1965	534 (1983) of 15 June 1983
219 (1965) of 17 December 1965	541 (1983) of 18 November 1983
220 (1966) of 16 March 1966	544 (1983) of 15 December 1983
222 (1966) of 16 June 1966	553 (1984) of 15 June 1984
231 (1966) of 15 December 1966	559 (1984) of 14 December 1984
238 (1967) of 19 June 1967	565 (1985) of 14 June 1985
244 (1967) of 22 December 1967	578 (1985) of 12 December 1985
247 (1968) of 18 March 1968	585 (1986) of 13 June 1986
254 (1968) of 18 June 1968	593 (1986) of 11 December 1986
261 (1968) of 10 December 1968	597 (1987) of 12 June 1987
266 (1969) of 10 June 1969	604 (1987) of 14 December 1987
274 (1969) of 11 December 1969	614 (1988) of 15 June 1988
281 (1970) of 9 June 1970	625 (1988) of 15 December 1988
291 (1970) of 10 December 1970	634 (1989) of 9 June 1989
293 (1971) of 26 May 1971	646 (1989) of 14 December 1989
305 (1971) of 13 December 1971	657 (1990) of 15 June 1990
315 (1972) of 15 June 1972	680 (1990) of 14 December 1990
324 (1972) of 12 December 1972	697 (1991) of 14 June 1991
334 (1973) of 5 June 1973	723 (1991) of 12 December 1991
343 (1973) of 14 December 1973	759 (1992) of 12 June 1992
349 (1974) of 29 May 1974	789 (1992) of 25 November 1992
364 (1974) of 13 December 1974	796 (1992) of 14 December 1992
370 (1975) of 13 June 1975	831 (1993) of 27 May 1993
383 (1975) of 13 December 1975	839 (1993) of 11 June 1993
391 (1976) of 15 June 1976	889 (1993) of 15 December 1993
401 (1976) of 14 December 1976	927 (1994) of 15 June 1994
410 (1977) of 15 June 1977	969 (1994) of 21 December 1994
422 (1977) of 15 December 1977	1000 (1995) of 23 June 1995
430 (1978) of 16 June 1978	1032 (1995) of 19 December 1995
443 (1978) of 14 December 1978	1062 (1996) of 28 June 1996
451 (1979) of 15 June 1979	

Function: Established to prevent a recurrence of fighting between the Greek Cypriot and Turkish Cypriot communities and to contribute to the maintenance and restoration of law and order and a return to normal conditions. After the hostilities of 1974, UNFICYP's mandate was expanded. Following a de facto cease-fire, which came into effect on 16 August 1974, UNFICYP has supervised the cease-fire and maintained a buffer zone between the lines of the Cyprus National Guard and of the Turkish and Turkish Cypriot forces. In the absence of a political settlement to the Cyprus problem, UNFICYP continues its presence on the island

Location: Cyprus

Headquarters: Nicosia

Duration: 27 March 1964 to date

Strength: Maximum: 6,411 all ranks (June 1964)

At 31 March 1996: 1,165 troops and 35 civilian police; there was also provision for some 370 internationally and locally recruited civilian staff

Fatalities:	161 military personnel
	3 civilian police
	<u>3</u> international United Nations staff members
	167 total (as at 31 March 1996)

Financing: Method of financing: Until 15 June 1993, the costs of UNFICYP were met by the Governments providing contingents, by the Government of Cyprus in accordance with paragraph 19 of the Agreement concerning the Status of the Force, and by voluntary contributions to UNFICYP. By its resolution 47/236 of 14 September 1993, the General Assembly decided that the costs of UNFICYP for the period beginning 16 June 1993 that were not covered by voluntary contributions should be treated as expenses of the Organization to be borne by Member States in accordance with Article 17, paragraph 2, of the Charter of the United Nations. The Assembly further requested the Secretary-General to establish a special account for the Force. Accordingly, the costs since 16 June 1993 have been financed on a basis combining (a) voluntary contributions and (b) contributions assessed on the entire membership of the United Nations Organization in respect of a Special Account

In addition, Greece provides an annual voluntary contribution of $6.5 million while Cyprus pays one third of the force's budget

Expenditures: From inception of mission to 31 December 1995: $816,184,450

Mediators:

| Sakari S. Tuomioja (Finland) | March–September 1964 |
| Galo Plaza Lasso (Ecuador) | September 1964–December 1965 |

Special Representatives of the Secretary-General:

Galo Plaza Lasso (Ecuador)	May–September 1964
Carlos A. Bernardes (Brazil)	September 1964–January 1967
P.P. Spinelli (Italy) (Acting)	January–February 1967
Bibiano F. Osorio-Tafall (Mexico)	February 1967–June 1974
Luis Weckmann-Muñoz (Mexico)	July 1974–October 1975
Javier Pérez de Cuéllar (Peru)	October 1975–December 1977
Rémy Gorgé (Switzerland) (Acting)	December 1977–April 1978
Reynaldo Galindo-Pohl (El Salvador)	May 1978–April 1980
Hugo Juan Gobbi (Argentina)	May 1980–December 1984
James Holger (Chile) (Acting)	January 1985–February 1988
Oscar Camilión (Argentina)	February 1988–March 1993
Joe Clark (Canada)	May 1993–April 1996
Han Sung-Joo (Republic of Korea)	May 1996 to date

Deputy Special Representative of the Secretary-General: Gustave Feissel (United States) April 1993 to date

(Mr. Clark also served as Chief of Mission of UNFICYP. In his absence from Cyprus, the Deputy Special Representative, resident in Cyprus, served as Chief of Mission. Mr. Feissel continues to serve as Deputy Special Representative, Resident in Cyprus, and Chief of Mission of the United Nations Operation in Cyprus.)

Commanders:

Lieutenant-General P.S. Gyani (India)	March–June 1964
General K.S. Thimayya (India)	June 1964–December 1965
Brigadier A.J. Wilson (United Kingdom) (Acting)	December 1965–May 1966
Lieutenant-General I.A.E. Martola (Finland)	May 1966–December 1969
Lieutenant-General Dewan Prem Chand (India)	December 1969–December 1976
Major-General James J. Quinn (Ireland)	December 1976–February 1981
Major-General Günther G. Greindl (Austria)	March 1981–April 1989
Major-General Clive Milner (Canada)	April 1989–April 1992
Major-General Michael F. Minehane (Ireland)	April 1992–July 1994
Brigadier General Ahti T.P. Vartiainen (Finland)	August 1994 to date

Contributors	Duration	Contribution
Argentina	September 1993 to date	Infantry, staff officers
	September 1994 to date	Helicopter unit
Australia	May 1964 to date	Civilian police
Austria	April 1964–July 1977	Civilian police
	May 1964–October 1973	Field hospital and personnel
	October 1973–April 1976	Medical centre
	April 1972 to date	Infantry, staff officers
	August 1993–October 1994	Military observers
Canada	March 1964–July 1993	Infantry
	April 1976–July 1993	Medical centre
	July 1993 to date	Staff officers
Denmark	May 1964–December 1992	Infantry
	May 1964–June 1975	Civilian police
	December 1992–June 1994	Staff officers
Finland	March 1964–October 1977	Infantry
	October 1977 to date	Staff officers
Hungary	August 1993–August 1994	Military observers
	November 1995 to date	Infantry
Ireland	March 1964–October 1973	Infantry
	October 1973 to date	Staff officers
	September 1993–October 1994	Military observers
	October 1993 to date	Civilian police
	March 1994 to date	Camp Command Unit
New Zealand	May 1964–June 1967	Civilian police
Sweden	March 1964–December 1987	Infantry
	January 1988–October 1993	Staff officers
	May 1964–October 1993	Civilian police
United Kingdom	March 1964 to date	Infantry, staff officers
	March 1964–October 1993	Logistic support
	March 1964–September 1994	Air unit
	April 1976–October 1993	Medical centre
	October 1993–September 1994	Supply detachment

Voluntary contributions: Until 15 June 1993, the contributors listed above provided their personnel without cost to the United Nations except in those cases where they requested reimbursement for certain extra and extraordinary expenses

From March 1964 until 15 June 1993, 79 countries, including a number which have contributed troops to the Force, have provided voluntary financial support to UNFICYP totalling some $490.2 million in cash contributions ($474.5 million) and pledges ($15.7 million) as follows: Antigua and Barbuda ($500); Australia ($3,619,879); Austria ($6,190,000); Bahamas ($18,500); Barbados ($8,500); Belgium ($6,518,517); Botswana ($500); Brunei Darussalam ($14,000); Cameroon ($28,853); Cyprus ($11,256,359); Cambodia ($600); Denmark ($6,589,328); France ($517,927); Finland ($1,050,000); Germany ($35,342,346); Ghana ($76,897); Greece ($27,620,311); Guyana ($12,816); Iceland ($196,701); India ($120,000); Indonesia ($15,000); Iran (Islamic Republic of) ($94,500); Iraq ($50,000); Ireland ($50,000); Israel ($26,500); Italy ($11,297,030); Côte d'Ivoire ($60,000); Jamaica ($36,783); Japan ($8,040,000); Jordan ($2,000); Kuwait ($165,000); Lao People's Democratic Republic ($1,500); Lebanon ($5,194); Liberia ($11,821); Libyan Arab Jamahiriya ($50,000); Liechtenstein ($2,000); Luxembourg ($242,246); Malawi ($6,363); Malaysia ($17,500); Malta ($9,622); Mauritania ($4,370); Micronesia (Federated States of) ($300); Morocco ($20,000); Nepal ($2,400); Netherlands ($2,518,425); New Zealand ($71,137); Niger ($2,041); Nigeria ($48,070); Norway ($13,798,275); Oman ($8,000); Pakistan ($77,791); Panama ($2,000); Philippines ($16,443); Portugal ($12,000); Qatar ($21,000); Republic of Korea ($16,000); Sierra Leone ($46,425); Singapore ($9,000); Somalia ($1,000); Spain ($923,237); Sri Lanka ($4,000); Sweden ($8,645,000); Switzerland ($18,882,373); Thailand ($10,500); Togo ($12,209); Trinidad and Tobago ($2,400); Tunisia ($3,000); Turkey ($1,839,253); United Arab Emirates ($30,000); United Kingdom of Great Britain and Northern Ireland ($89,191,363); United Republic of Tanzania ($7,000); United States of America ($234,306,092); Uruguay ($14,000); Venezuela ($72,982); Viet Nam ($4,000); Yugoslavia ($140,000); Zaire ($36,000); Zambia ($45,379); Zimbabwe ($24,918)

Other voluntary contributions:		
	Italy	Airlift
	United States	Airlift

United Nations Operation in the Congo (ONUC)

Authorization:	Security Council resolutions:
	143 (1960) of 14 July 1960
	145 (1960) of 22 July 1960
	146 (1960) of 9 August 1960
	161 (1961) of 21 February 1961
	169 (1961) of 24 November 1961

Function: Initially established to ensure the withdrawal of Belgian forces, to assist the Government in maintaining law and order and to provide technical assistance. The function of ONUC was subsequently modified to include maintaining the territorial integrity and political independence of the Congo, preventing the occurrence of civil war and securing the removal from the Congo of all foreign military, paramilitary and advisory personnel not under the United Nations Command, and all mercenaries

Location: Republic of the Congo (now Zaire)

Headquarters: Leopoldville

Duration: 15 July 1960–30 June 1964

Strength: Maximum (July 1961): 19,828 all ranks
At withdrawal (30 December 1963): 5,871 all ranks

Fatalities: 245 military personnel
<u>5</u> international United Nations staff
250 total

Financing: Method of financing: Assessments in respect of a Special Account
Expenditures: $400,130,793

Special Representatives of the Secretary-General:

Ralph J. Bunche (United States)	July–August 1960
Andrew W. Cordier (United States)	August–September 1960
Rajeshwar Dayal (India)	September 1960–May 1961
Mekki Abbas (Sudan) (Acting)	March–May 1961

Officers-in-Charge:

Sture Linner (Sweden)	May 1961–January 1962
Robert K.A. Gardiner (Ghana)	February 1962–May 1963
Max H. Dorsinville (Haiti)	May 1963–April 1964
Bibiano F. Osorio-Tafall (Mexico)	April–June 1964

Commanders:

Lieutenant-General Carl C. von Horn (Sweden)	July–December 1960
Lieutenant-General Sean MacEoin (Ireland)	January 1961–March 1962
Lieutenant-General Kebbede Guebre (Ethiopia)	April 1962–July 1963
Major-General Christian Kaldager (Norway)	August–December 1963
Major-General Aguiyu Ironsi (Nigeria)	January–June 1964

Contributors:

	Duration	Contribution
Argentina	July 1960–February 1963	Aircraft personnel (air and ground)
Austria	December 1960–August 1963	Aircraft personnel (air and ground), field hospital and personnel, staff personnel
Brazil	July 1960–June 1964	Aircraft personnel (air and ground) staff personnel
Burma	August 1960–June 1964	Staff personnel
Canada	July 1960–June 1964	Aircraft personnel (air and ground), staff personnel, signals
Ceylon	August 1960–April 1962	Staff personnel
Denmark	August 1960–June 1964	Aircraft personnel (air and ground), staff personnel, work-shop control, transport company
Ethiopia	July 1960–June 1964	Infantry, aircraft personnel (air and ground), staff personnel
Ghana	July 1960–September 1963	Infantry, 2 medical units, staff personnel, police companies
Guinea	July 1960–January 1961	Infantry

(continued)

India	July 1960–June 1964	Infantry, aircraft personnel (air and ground), field hospital and personnel, staff personnel, supply unit, signal company, air dispatch team, postal unit
Indonesia	October 1960–April 1964	Infantry
Iran	December 1962–July 1963	Aircraft and air and ground personnel
Ireland	July 1960–May 1964	Infantry, staff personnel
Italy	October 1960–June 1964	Aircraft personnel (air and ground), field hospital, staff personnel
Liberia	July 1960–May 1963	Infantry, movement control, staff personnel
Malaya	October 1960–April 1963	Infantry, staff personnel
Federation of Mali	August 1960–November 1960	Infantry
Morocco	July 1960–January 1961	Infantry, parachute company
Netherlands	August 1960–October 1963	Hygiene teams, staff personnel
Nigeria	November 1960–June 1964	Infantry, police unit, staff personnel
Norway	July 1960–March 1964	Aircraft personnel (air and ground), staff personnel, workshop control
Pakistan	August 1960–May 1964	Ordnance and transport units, staff personnel
Philippines	February 1963–June 1963	Aircraft personnel (air and ground), staff personnel
Sierra Leone	January 1962–March 1963	Infantry
Sudan	August 1960– April–December 1961	Infantry
Sweden	July 1960–May 1964	Infantry, aircraft personnel (air and ground), movement control, engineering personnel, workshop unit, signal detachment, staff personnel
Tunisia	July 1960–May 1963	Infantry
United Arab Republic	August 1960–February 1961	Infantry, parachute battalion
Yugoslavia	July 1960–December 1960	Aircraft personnel (air and ground)

From February 1963 to the end of the United Nations Operation in the Congo, a battalion of the Congolese National Army was incorporated in ONUC

Voluntary contributions:

Country	Duration	Contribution
Canada	Beginning of operation	Airlift of food
Switzerland	Beginning of operation	Airlift of food and other supplies
Soviet Union	Beginning of operation	Airlift of food
United Kingdom	Beginning of operation	Airlift of food and Ghanaian troops
United States	Beginning of operation	Airlift of food supplies and equipment Aircraft Airlift of Ghanaian, Guinean, Moroccan, Swedish and Tunisian troops Sealift of Malayan troops

United Nations Transition Assistance Group (UNTAG)

Authorization:	Security Council resolutions: 435 (1978) of 29 September 1978 632 (1989) of 16 February 1989
Function:	Established to assist the Special Representative of the Secretary-General to ensure the early independence of Namibia through free and fair elections under the supervision and control of the United Nations. UNTAG was also to help the Special Representative to ensure that: all hostile acts were ended; troops were confined to base, and, in the case of the South Africans, ultimately withdrawn from Namibia; all discriminatory laws were repealed, political prisoners were released, Namibian refugees were permitted to return, intimidation of any kind was prevented, law and order were impartially maintained. Independent Namibia joined the United Nations in April 1990
Location:	Namibia and Angola
Headquarters:	Windhoek
Duration:	1 April 1989–21 March 1990
Strength:	Authorized upper limit of military component: 7,500 all ranks Maximum strength of military component (November 1989): 4,493 all ranks Civilian component: 1,500 police and just under 2,000 civilians (including local employees and more than 1,000 additional international personnel who came specifically for the elections)
Fatalities:	11 military personnel 4 civilian police 3 international United Nations staff <u>1</u> local staff 19 total
Financing:	Method of financing: Assessments in respect of a Special Account Expenditures: $368,584,324
Special Representative of the Secretary-General:	Martti Ahtisaari (Finland) July 1978–March 1990
Force Commanders:	Major-General Hannes Philipp (Austria), Commander designate, September 1978–January 1980 Lieutenant-General Dewan Prem Chand (India), Commander designate, January 1980–March 1989; Force Commander, April 1989–March 1990
Police Commissioner:	Assistant Commissioner Stephen Fanning (Ireland): March 1989–March 1990

Contributors:

Australia	Military engineers, electoral supervisors
Austria	Civilian police
Bangladesh	Military observers, civilian police
Barbados	Civilian police
Belgium	Civilian police
Canada	Logistics, civilian police, electoral supervisors
China	Electoral supervisors
Congo	Electoral supervisors
Costa Rica	Electoral supervisors
Czechoslovakia	Military observers
Denmark	Movement control, electoral supervisors
Egypt	Civilian police
Fiji	Civilian police
Finland	Military observers, infantry battalion, electoral supervisors
France	Electoral supervisors
German Democratic Republic	Civilian police, electoral supervisors

(continued)

Germany, Federal Republic of	Civilian police, electoral supervisors, civilian mechanics
Ghana	Civilian police, electoral supervisors
Greece	Electoral supervisors
Guyana	Civilian police
Hungary	Civilian police
India	Military observers, civilian police, electoral supervisors
Indonesia	Civilian police
Ireland	Military observers, civilian police, electoral supervisors
Italy	Helicopter unit
Jamaica	Civilian police
Japan	Electoral supervisors
Kenya	Infantry battalion, military observers, civilian police, electoral supervisors
Malaysia	Infantry battalion, military observers
Netherlands	Civilian police
New Zealand	Civilian police
Nigeria	Civilian police, electoral supervisors
Norway	Civilian police, electoral supervisors
Pakistan	Military observers, civilian police, electoral supervisors
Panama	Military observers
Peru	Military observers
Poland	Logistic battalion, military observers, electoral supervisors
Portugal	Electoral supervisors
Singapore	Civilian police, electoral supervisors
Spain	Light aircraft personnel
Sudan	Military observers
Sweden	Civilian police, electoral supervisors
Switzerland	Civilian medical unit, electoral supervisors
Thailand	Electoral supervisors
Togo	Military observers
Trinidad and Tobago	Electoral supervisors
Tunisia	Civilian police
Soviet Union	Electoral supervisors
United Kingdom	Signals squadron, electoral supervisors
Yugoslavia	Military observers

Voluntary contributions:

Germany, Federal Republic of	Light vehicles, minibuses, mobile workshops, ambulances, spare parts; secondment of technical staff; transportation of civilian police
Greece	Various logistics equipment
Japan	Financial
Switzerland	Three aircraft and crew
United States	Airlift services

United Nations Angola Verification Mission I (UNAVEM I)

Authorization:	Security Council resolution 626 (1988) of 20 December 1988
Function:	Established on 20 December 1988 to verify the redeployment of Cuban troops northwards and their phased and total withdrawal from the territory of Angola in accordance with the timetable agreed between Angola and Cuba. The withdrawal was completed by 25 May 1991 — more than one month before the scheduled date. On 6 June, the Secretary-General reported to the Council that UNAVEM I had carried out, fully and effectively, the mandate entrusted to it
Location:	Angola
Headquarters:	Luanda
Duration:	3 January 1989–30 May 1991
Strength:	Maximum (April–December 1989): 70 military observers At withdrawal (31 May 1991): 61 military observers
Fatalities:	None
Financing:	Method of financing: Assessments in respect of a Special Account Expenditures: $16,404,200 (net)

Chief Military Observer:

Brigadier-General Péricles Ferreira Gomes (Brazil)   December 1988–May 1991

Contributors of military observers (January 1989–May 1991):

Algeria	India
Argentina	Jordan
Brazil	Norway
Congo	Spain
Czechoslovakia	Yugoslavia

United Nations Angola Verification Mission II (UNAVEM II)

Authorization: Security Council resolutions:

696 (1991) of 30 May 1991
747 (1992) of 24 March 1992
785 (1992) of 30 October 1992
793 (1992) of 30 November 1992
804 (1993) of 29 January 1993
823 (1993) of 30 April 1993
834 (1993) of 1 June 1993
851 (1993) of 15 July 1993
864 (1993) of 15 September 1993
890 (1993) of 15 December 1993
903 (1994) of 16 March 1994
922 (1994) of 31 May 1994
932 (1994) of 30 June 1994
945 (1994) of 29 September 1994
952 (1994) of 27 October 1994
966 (1994) of 8 December 1994

Function: Established on 30 May 1991 to verify the arrangements agreed by the Angolan parties for the monitoring of the cease-fire and for the monitoring of the Angolan police during the cease-fire period and to observe and verify the elections in that country, in accordance with the Peace Accords for Angola, signed by the Angolan Government and the União Nacional para a Independência Total de Angola (UNITA). Despite the United Nations verification that the elections — held in September 1992 — had been generally free and fair, their results were contested by UNITA. After renewed fighting in October 1992 between the Government and UNITA forces, UNAVEM II's mandate was adjusted in order to help the two sides reach agreement on modalities for completing the peace process and, at the same time, to broker and help implement cease-fires at the national or local level. Following the signing on 20 November 1994 by the Government of Angola and UNITA of the Lusaka Protocol, UNAVEM II verified the initial stages of the peace agreement. In February 1995, the Security Council set up a new mission — UNAVEM III — to monitor and verify the implementation of the Protocol

Location: Angola

Headquarters: Luanda

Duration: 30 May 1991–8 February 1995

Strength: Authorized May 1991–January 1993:
350 military observers and 126 civilian police. There were also a civilian air unit and a medical unit, as well as some 87 international civilian and 155 local staff. In addition, during the polling, UNAVEM II fielded a total of 400 electoral observers
Authorized January–May 1993:
75 military observers, 30 civilian police and 12 paramedics. These were supported by some 50 international civilian and 70 local staff
Authorized June 1993–October 1994:
50 military observers, 18 civilian police, 11 military medical personnel. There was also provision for 40 international civilian and 75 local staff
Authorized October 1994–February 1995:
350 military observers, 126 civilian police and 14 military medical staff. There was also provision for some 220 international civilian and 145 local staff
At transition to UNAVEM III (31 January 1995):
161 military observers, 107 civilian police and 11 military medical staff

Fatalities: 2 military observers
1 other military personnel
1 civilian police
1 international United Nations staff
5 total

Financing: Method of financing: Assessments in respect of a Special Account
Expenditures: $175,802,600 net

**Special Representatives of the Secretary-General
and Chiefs of Mission:**

Margaret Joan Anstee (United Kingdom)	February 1992–June 1993
Alioune Blondin Beye (Mali)	June 1993–to [see UNAVEM III below

Chief Military Observers:

Brigadier-General Péricles Ferreira Gomes (Brazil)	May 1991–September 1991
Major-General Edward Ushie Unimna (Nigeria)	October 1991–December 1992
Brigadier-General Michael Nyambuya (Zimbabwe)	December 1992–July 1993
Major-General Chris Abutu Garuba (Nigeria)	July 1993–February 1995

Contributors	Duration	Contribution
Algeria	May 1991–January 1993	military observers
Argentina	May 1991–September 1993	military observers, civilian police
	November 1993–February 1995	military observers, civilian police
Brazil	May 1991–February 1995	military observers, civilian police
	October 1991–February 1993	medical unit
	June 1993–February 1995	
Canada	July 1991–May 1993	military observers
Colombia	August 1992–January 1993	civilian police
Congo	May 1991–February 1995	military observers
Czechoslovakia (Slovak Republic from January 1993)	May 1991–February 1995	military observers
Egypt	July 1991–January 1993	military observers
Guinea-Bissau	July 1991–February 1995	military observers
	January 1995–February 1995	civilian police
Hungary	July 1991–February 1995	military observers
	December 1994–February 1995	civilian police
India	May 1991–February 1995	military observers
Ireland	July 1991–September 1993	military observers
	July 1991–January 1993	civilian police
Jordan	May 1991–February 1995	military observers
	December 1994–February 1995	civilian police
Malaysia	July 1991–January 1993	military observers, civilian police
	June 1993–February 1995	military observers
	December 1993–February 1995	civilian police
Morocco	July 1991–January 1993	military observers
	July 1991–February 1995	civilian police
Netherlands	July 1991–February 1995	military observers, civilian police
New Zealand	July 1991–February 1993	military observers
	November 1993–February 1995	
Nigeria	July 1991–February 1995	military observers
	July 1991–January 1993	civilian police
	December 1994–February 1995	
Norway	May 1991–February 1995	military observers
Senegal	July 1991–January 1993	military observers
Singapore	July 1991–January 1993	military observers
Spain	May 1991–November 1993	military observers
Sweden	July 1991–February 1995	military observers
	July 1991–December 1992	civilian police
Yugoslavia	May 1991–February 1993	military observers
Zimbabwe	July 1991–February 1995	military observers, civilian police

Voluntary contributions:
Switzerland   (air ambulance services)

United Nations Angola Verification Mission III (UNAVEM III)

Authorization: Security Council resolutions:

976 (1995) of 8 February 1995
1008 (1995) of 7 August 1995
1045 (1996) of 8 February 1996

Function: Established to assist the Government of Angola and the União Nacional para a Independência Total de Angola (UNITA) in restoring peace and achieving national reconciliation on the basis of the "Accordos de Paz" signed on 31 May 1991, the Lusaka Protocol signed on 20 November 1994, and relevant Security Council resolutions. Among the main features of UNAVEM III's mandate are the following: to provide good offices and meditation to the Angolan parties; to monitor and verify the extension of State administration throughout the country and the process of national reconciliation; to supervise, control and verify the disengagement of forces and to monitor the cease-fire; to verify information received from the Government and UNITA regarding their forces, as well as all troop movements; to assist in the establishment of quartering areas; to verify the withdrawal, quartering and demobilization of UNITA forces; to supervise the collection and storage of UNITA armaments; to verify the movement of Government forces (FAA) to barracks and the completion of the formation of FAA; to verify the free circulation of persons and goods; to verify and monitor the neutrality of the Angolan National Police, the disarming of civilians, the quartering of the rapid reaction police, and security arrangements for UNITA leaders; to coordinate, facilitate and support humanitarian activities directly linked to the peace process, as well as participating in mine-clearance activities; to declare formally that all essential requirements for the holding of the second round of presidential elections have been fulfilled, and to support, verify and monitor the electoral process

Location: Angola

Headquarters: Luanda

Duration: 8 February 1995 to date

Strength: Authorized: 350 military observers, 7,000 troops and military support personnel, 260 civilian police; there is also provision for approximately 420 international civilian staff, 300 locally recruited staff and 75 United Nations Volunteers
At 31 March 1996: 336 military observers, 6,576 troops and military support personnel and 226 civilian police

Fatalities: 11 military personnel
 1 civilian police
12 total (as at 30 April 1996)

Financing: Method of financing: Assessments in respect of a Special Account
Estimated expenditures: From inception to 8 May 1996: $366,523,900 net

**Special Representative
of the Secretary-General:** Alioune Blondin Beye (Mali)   [see UNAVEM II, above] to date

**Force
Commanders:** Major-General Chris Abutu Garuba (Nigeria)   February–September 1995
Major-General Philip Valerio Sibanda (Zimbabwe)   October 1995 to date

**Police
Commissioner:** Chief Superintendent Anwarul Iqbal (Bangladesh)   March 1995 to date

Contributors	Duration	Contribution
Algeria	February 1995 to date	military observers
Argentina	February–November 1995	military observers, civilian police
	October–November 1995	troops

(continued)

Bangladesh	February 1995 to date	military observers
	May 1995 to date	civilian police
	June 1995 to date	troops
Brazil	February 1995 to date	military observers, civilian police
	February 1995 to date	troops
Bulgaria	February 1995 to date	military observers
	March 1995 to date	civilian police
Congo	February 1995 to date	military observers
Egypt	February 1995 to date	military observers
	March 1995 to date	civilian police
Fiji	April 1995 to date	civilian police
France	April 1995 to date	military observers
	August 1995 to date	de-mining instructors
Guinea-Bissau	February 1995 to date	military observers, civilian police
Hungary	February 1995 to date	military observers, civilian police
India	February 1995 to date	military observers
	May 1995 to date	troops, civilian police
Italy	November 1995 to date	de-mining instructors
Jordan	February 1995 to date	military observers, civilian police
Kenya	May 1995 to date	military observers
Malaysia	February 1995 to date	military observers, civilian police
Mali	March 1995 to date	military observers
	May 1995 to date	civilian police
Morocco	February 1995 to date	civilian police
Namibia	November 1995 to date	troops
Netherlands	February 1995 to date	military observers, civilian police
	October 1995 to date	de-mining instructors
New Zealand	February 1995 to date	military observers
	April–May 1995	civilian police
	July 1995 to date	de-mining instructors
Nigeria	February 1995 to date	military observers, civilian police
Norway	February 1995 to date	military observers
Pakistan	March 1995 to date	military observers
	August 1995 to date	de-mining instructors
Poland	February 1995 to date	military observers
Portugal	February 1995 to date	military observers
	March 1995 to date	troops
	June 1995 to date	civilian police
Republic of Korea	October 1995 to date	troops
Romania	May 1995 to date	troops
Russian Federation	February 1995 to date	military observers
	May 1995 to date	troops
Senegal	March 1995 to date	military observers
Slovak Republic	February 1995 to date	military observers
Sweden	February 1995 to date	military observers
	December 1995 to date	civilian police
Ukraine	January 1996 to date	military observers
	February 1996 to date	troops
United Kingdom	May 1995 to date	troops
United Republic of Tanzania	August 1995 to date	civilian police
Uruguay	February 1995 to date	military observers
	May 1995 to date	troops, civilian police
Zambia	March 1995 to date	military observers, civilian police
	July 1995 to date	troops
Zimbabwe	February 1995 to date	military observers, civilian police
	May 1995 to date	troops

Voluntary contributions and trust funds:

Germany (accommodation equipment/disarmament and mobilization support); South Africa (accommodation equipment/disarmament and mobilization support); Switzerland (500,000 Swiss francs for de-mining activities); United Kingdom (accommodation equipment/disarmament and mobilization support); United States (repair of essential bridges)

United Nations Mission for the Referendum in Western Sahara (MINURSO)

Authorization:	Security Council resolutions:
	690 (1990) of 29 April 1991
	907 (1994) of 29 March 1994
	973 (1995) of 13 January 1995
	995 (1995) of 26 May 1995
	1002 (1995) of 30 June 1995
	1017 (1995) of 22 September 1995
	1042 (1996) of 31 January 1996
	1056 (1996) of 29 May 1996

Function: Established in accordance with "the settlement proposals", as accepted by Morocco and the Frente Popular para la Liberación de Saguia el-Hamra y de Río de Oro (Frente POLISARIO) on 30 August 1988, to monitor a cease-fire, verify the reduction of Moroccan troops in the Territory, monitor the confinement of Moroccan and Frente POLISARIO troops to designated locations, ensure the release of all Western Saharan political prisoners or detainees, oversee the exchange of prisoners of war, implement the repatriation programme, identify and register qualified voters, organize and ensure a free referendum and proclaim the results. However, due to the parties' divergent views on some of the key elements of the settlement plan, in particular with regard to the criteria for eligibility to vote, it was not possible to implement the plan in conformity with the repeatedly revised timetable. In its limited deployment, the primary function of MINURSO was restricted to complementing the identification process, verifying the cease-fire and cessation of hostilities, and monitoring local police and ensuring security and order at identification and registration sites. In May 1996, the Security Council suspended the identification process, authorized the withdrawal of the civilian police component, except for a small number of officers to maintain contacts with the authorities on both sides, and decided to reduce the strength of the military component of MINURSO by 20 per cent. It also supported the Secretary-General's intention to maintain a political office in Laayoune, with a liaison office in Tindouf, to maintain a dialogue with the parties and the two neighbouring countries

Location: Western Sahara

Headquarters: Laayoune

Duration: 29 April 1991 to date

Strength: Authorized: Approximately 1,700 military observers and troops, 300 police officers and about 800 to 1,000 civilian personnel
At 31 March 1996: 240 military observers, 48 military support personnel, 64 police officers; there was also provision for approximately 320 international civilian personnel, 90 local civilian staff and 12 observers from the Organization of African Unity

Fatalities:
1 military observer
3 other military personnel
1 civilian police
2 international United Nations staff
7 total (as at 31 March 1996)

Financing: Method of financing: Assessments in respect of a Special Account
Estimated expenditures: From inception to 31 May 1996: $224,813,800 net

Special Representatives of the Secretary-General:

Hector Gros Espiell (Uruguay)	October 1988–January 1990
Johannes Manz (Switzerland)	January 1990–March 1992
Sahabzada Yaqub-Khan (Pakistan)	March 1992–August 1995
Erik Jensen (Malaysia) (Acting)	August 1995 to date

Force Commanders:	Major-General Armand Roy (Canada)	June 1991–April 1992
	Brigadier-General Luis Block Urban (Peru) (Acting)	April–September 1992
	Brigadier-General André Van Baelen (Belgium)	October 1992–March 1996
	Major-General José Eduardo Garcia Léandro (Portugal)	March 1996 to date

Police Commissioners:	Colonel Jürgen Friedrich Reimann (Germany)	June 1993–March 1995
	Colonel Wolf-Dieter Krampe (Germany)	March 1995–August 1995
	Lieutenant-Colonel Jan Walmann (Norway) (Acting)	August 1995–January 1996
	Brigadier-General Walter Fallmann (Austria)	January 1996 to date

Contributors	Duration	Contribution
Argentina	September 1991 to date	military observers
Australia	May 1991–May 1994	military observers
	May 1991–May 1994	signals unit
Austria	September 1991 to date	military observers
	June 1993 to date	civilian police
Bangladesh	September 1991 to date	military observers
Belgium	September 1992–March 1996	military observers
	June 1993–December 1993	civilian police
Canada	May 1991–June 1994	military observers
	May 1991–June 1994	movement control unit
China	September 1991 to date	military observers
Egypt	September 1991 to date	military observers
	April 1995–April 1996	civilian police
El Salvador	January 1995 to date	military observers
Finland	October–November 1991	military observers
France	September 1991 to date	military observers
Germany	June 1993 to date	civilian police
Ghana	September 1991 to date	military observers
	June 1994 to date	troops (clerical unit)
	March 1995–April 1996	civilian police
Greece	September 1991 to date	military observers
Guinea	September 1991 to date	military observers
Honduras	September 1992 to date	military observers
	January–October 1994	movement control unit
Hungary	March 1995 to date	civilian police
Ireland	September 1991 to date	military observers
	May 1995–March 1996	civilian police
Italy	September 1991 to date	military observers
Kenya	September 1991 to date	military observers
Malaysia	September 1991 to date	military observers
	June 1993–July 1995	civilian police
Nigeria	September 1991 to date	military observers
	August 1994–April 1996	civilian police
Norway	July 1994 to date	civilian police
Pakistan	September 1991 to date	military observers
Peru	September 1991–September 1992	military observers
Poland	September 1991 to date	military observers
Portugal	March 1996 to date	military observers
Republic of Korea	August 1994 to date	military observers
	August 1994 to date	medical unit
Russian Federation (Soviet Union before 24 December 1991)	September 1991 to date	military observers
Switzerland	May 1991–August 1994	medical unit
	May 1994–August 1994	military observers
Togo	June 1993 to date	civilian police
Tunisia	September 1991 to date	military observers
United Kingdom	September 1991–December 1993	military observers
United States	September 1991 to date	military observers
Uruguay	April 1994 to date	civilian police
	June 1994 to date	military observers
Venezuela	September 1991 to date	military observers

**Voluntary
contributions:**
Algeria (accommodation premises, office space, fuel, food, water for hygiene facilities, transport and laundry facilities — estimated annual value $2,058,500); Australia (signals unit of 43 military personnel, communications equipment until May 1994); Mauritania (office space — estimated annual value $30,000); Morocco (accommodation premises, office space, fuel, food, water for hygiene facilities, air and land transportation, transport workshop, 21 trucks and personnel — estimated annual value $7,895,700); Frente POLISARIO (accommodation premises, office space, food, water for hygiene facilities, technical personnel and other staff — estimated annual value $390,000); Switzerland (3 aircraft in support of the medical unit, 30 support personnel until June 1994)

United Nations Operation in Somalia I (UNOSOM I)

Authorization:	Security Council resolutions:
	751 (1992) of 24 April 1992
	775 (1992) of 28 August 1992
	794 (1992) of 3 December 1992
Function:	Established to monitor the cease-fire in Mogadishu, the capital of Somalia, and to provide protection and security for United Nations personnel, equipment and supplies at the seaports and airports in Mogadishu and escort deliveries of humanitarian supplies from there to distribution centres in the city and its immediate environs. In August 1992, UNOSOM I's mandate and strength were enlarged to enable it to protect humanitarian convoys and distribution centres throughout Somalia. In December 1992, after the situation in Somalia had further deteriorated, the Security Council authorized Member States to form the Unified Task Force (UNITAF) to establish a safe environment for the delivery of humanitarian assistance. UNITAF worked in coordination with UNOSOM I to secure major population centres and ensure that humanitarian assistance was delivered and distributed
Location:	Somalia
Headquarters:	Mogadishu
Duration:	24 April 1992–26 March 1993
Strength:	Authorized: 50 military observers, 3,500 security personnel and up to 719 logistic support personnel Maximum (28 February 1993): 54 military observers and 893 troops
Fatalities:	8 military personnel
Financing:	Method of financing: Assessments in respect of a Special Account Expenditures: $42,931,700 net

Special Representatives of the Secretary-General:

Mohamed Sahnoun (Algeria)	April 1992–November 1992
Ismat Kittani (Iraq)	November 1992–March 1993
Jonathan T. Howe (United States)	March 1993–[see UNOSOM II below]

Chief Military Observer (subsequently Force Commander):

Brigadier-General Imtiaz Shaheen (Pakistan)	June 1992–March 1993

Contributors	Duration	Contribution
Australia	October 1992–March 1993	troops
Austria	August 1992–March 1993	military observers
Bangladesh	August 1992–March 1993	military observers
Belgium	December 1992–March 1993	troops
Canada	October 1992–March 1993	troops
Czechoslovakia	August 1992–March 1993	military observers
Egypt	August 1992–March 1993	military observers
Fiji	August 1992–March 1993	military observers
Finland	August 1992–March 1993	military observers
Indonesia	August 1992–March 1993	military observers
Jordan	August 1992–March 1993	military observers
Morocco	August 1992–March 1993	military observers
New Zealand	December 1992–March 1993	troops
Norway	December 1992–March 1993	troops
Pakistan	August 1992–March 1992	military observers
	September 1992–March 1993	troops
Zimbabwe	August 1992–March 1993	military observers

Voluntary contributions:

United States   airlift for the emplacement of military personnel
[also see UNOSOM II below]

United Nations Operation in Somalia II (UNOSOM II)

Authorization: Security Council resolutions:

814 (1993) of 26 March 1993
837 (1993) of 6 June 1993
865 (1993) of 22 September 1993
878 (1993) of 28 October 1993
886 (1993) of 18 November 1993
897 (1994) of 4 February 1994
923 (1994) of 31 May 1994
946 (1994) of 30 September 1994
953 (1994 of 31 October 1994
954 (1994) of 4 November 1994

Function: Established to take over from the Unified Task Force (UNITAF). [UNITAF was a multinational force, organized and led by the United States, which, in December 1992, had been authorized by the Security Council to use "all necessary means" to establish a secure environment for humanitarian relief operations in Somalia.] The mandate of UNOSOM II was to take appropriate action, including enforcement measures, to establish throughout Somalia a secure environment for humanitarian assistance. To that end, UNOSOM II was to complete, through disarmament and reconciliation, the task begun by UNITAF for the restoration of peace, stability, law and order. Its main responsibilities included monitoring the cessation of hostilities, preventing resumption of violence, seizing unauthorized small arms, maintaining security at ports, airports and lines of communication required for delivery of humanitarian assistance, continuing mine-clearing, and assisting in repatriation of refugees in Somalia. UNOSOM II was also entrusted with assisting the Somali people in rebuilding their economy and social and political life, re-establishing the country's institutional structure, achieving national political reconciliation, recreating a Somali State based on democratic governance and rehabilitating the country's economy and infrastructure. In February 1994, after several violent incidents and attacks on United Nations soldiers, the Security Council revised UNOSOM II's mandate to exclude the use of coercive methods. UNOSOM II was withdrawn in early March 1995

Location: Somalia

Headquarters: Mogadishu

Duration: 26 March 1993–2 March 1995

Strength: Authorized March 1993–4 February 1994: 28,000 all ranks; there was also provision for approximately 2,800 civilian staff
Authorized 4 February–25 August 1994: 22,000 all ranks
Authorized 25 August 1994–2 March 1995: 15,000 all ranks
Strength at the start of withdrawal (30 November 1994): 14,968 all ranks

Fatalities: 143 military personnel
  3 international United Nations staff
 _1 local staff
147 total

Financing: Method of financing: Assessments in respect of a Special Account
Expenditures: $1,643,485,500 net

**Special Representatives of
the Secretary-General:**

Jonathan T. Howe (United States)	March 1993–February 1994
Lansana Kouyaté (Guinea) (Acting)	February 1994–June 1994
James Victor Gbeho (Ghana)	July 1994–April 1995

**Force
Commanders:**

Lieutenant-General Çevik Bir (Turkey)	April 1993–January 1994
Lieutenant-General Aboo Samah Bin Aboo Bakar (Malaysia)	January 1994–March 1995

Police
Commissioners: Chief Superintendent Mike Murphy (Ireland)   April–June 1994
                Chief Superintendent Selwyn Mettle (Ghana)   June 1994–February 1995

Contributors	Duration	Contribution
Australia	July 1994–February 1995	civilian police
	March 1993–November 1994	troops
Bangladesh	July 1994–February 1995	civilian police
	July 1993–February 1995	troops
Belgium	March 1993–March 1994	troops
Botswana	May 1993–October 1994	troops
Canada	March 1993–May 1994	troops
Egypt	May 1994–February 1995	civilian police
	May 1993–February 1995	troops
France	May 1993–March 1994	troops
Germany	May 1993–March 1994	troops
Ghana	May 1994–February 1995	civilian police
Greece	May 1993–April 1994	troops
India	May 1993–February 1995	troops
Indonesia	May 1994–February 1995	troops
Ireland	May–August 1994	civilian police
	August 1993–January 1995	troops
Italy	May–October 1994	civilian police
	May 1993–March 1994	troops
	June 1994–February 1995	troops
Kuwait	May 1993–March 1994	troops
Malaysia	May–September 1994	civilian police
	July 1993–February 1995	troops
Morocco	May 1993–April 1994	troops
Nepal	October 1993–January 1995	troops
Netherlands	May 1994–February 1995	civilian police
New Zealand	March 1993–June 1994	troops
	July 1994–November 1994	troops
Nigeria	May 1994–February 1995	civilian police
	May 1993–February 1995	troops
Norway	March 1993–March 1994	troops
Pakistan	March 1993–February 1995	troops
Philippines	July 1994–February 1995	civilian police
Republic of Korea	July 1993–March 1994	troops
	May–October 1994	civilian police
	May 1994–February 1995	troops
Romania	June 1993–October 1994	troops
Saudi Arabia	May 1993–March 1994	troops
Sweden	May 1994–September 1994	civilian police
	May 1993–December 1993	troops
Tunisia	May 1993–February 1994	troops
Turkey	May 1993–January 1994	troops
United Arab Emirates	May 1993–March 1994	troops
United States	May 1993–February 1994	troops
Zambia	July 1994–February 1995	civilian police
Zimbabwe	May 1994–February 1995	civilian police
	May 1993–February 1995	troops

**Voluntary contributions
to UNOSOM II:**

UNITAF (operational maps, estimated value $6,000,000)
Voluntary contributions to the Trust Fund for Somalia: Pursuant to Security Council
resolution 794 (1992), the Secretary-General established a fund for the support of UNITAF.
Following the departure of UNITAF, the fund was maintained for receiving contributions
for the maintenance of UNOSOM II forces and for the re-establishment of the Somali
police and judicial and penal systems. After the full and final reimbursement of all
accepted claims from eligible participating Governments in UNITAF, the balance of
individual contributions remaining in the fund was transferred, according to the wishes
of the contributing countries, to the two sub-accounts established for the support of the

Somali police and judicial and penal systems, and for the support of UNOSOM II forces, or returned to the contributor

A. UNITAF: Antigua and Barbuda ($500), Austria ($1,000,000), Brunei Darusalam ($100,000), Denmark ($1,000,000), Finland ($677,295), Iceland ($50,000), Ireland ($115,000), Japan ($100,000,000), Malaysia ($50,000), Philippines ($5,000), Republic of Korea ($2,000,000), Singapore ($25,000)

B. Somali Police and Judiciary: Denmark ($500,000), Finland ($64,410), Iceland ($2,378), Japan ($9,509,899), Malaysia ($4,755), Netherlands ($543,242), Norway ($999,978), Republic of Korea ($90,198), Singapore ($2,377), Sweden ($1,704,918), United Kingdom ($37,273), United States ($8,000,000)

C. UNOSOM II forces: Antigua and Barbuda ($48), Iceland ($2,377), Philippines ($476), Republic of Korea ($100,000)

Voluntary contributions in kind to the Somali police and justice programmes account (total: $43.4 million: Egypt: equipment and personal weapons ($1.8 million) and police training ($0.1 million); Italy: police training ($4.5 million); United States: equipment, vehicles and personal weapons ($25.0 million) and police training ($12.0 million))
[Owing to the prevailing security situation in Somalia, vehicles, equipment and personal weapons donated for the establishment of the Somali police force were withdrawn]
Trust Fund for the Support of Regional and District Councils in Somalia: The Life and Peace Institute (based in Sweden): $778,600

United Nations Operation in Mozambique (ONUMOZ)

Authorization: Security Council resolutions:

           797 (1992) of 16 December 1992
           850 (1993) of 9 July 1993
           879 (1993) of 29 October 1993
           882 (1993) of 5 November 1993
           898 (1994) of 23 February 1994
           916 (1994) of 5 May 1994
           957 (1994) of 15 November 1994

Function: Established to help implement the General Peace Agreement, signed on 4 October 1992 in Rome by the President of the Republic of Mozambique and the President of the Resistência Nacional Moçambicana (RENAMO). The mandate of ONUMOZ was: to facilitate impartially the implementation of the Agreement; to monitor and verify the cease-fire, the separation and concentration of forces, their demobilization and the collection, storage and destruction of weapons; to monitor and verify the complete withdrawal of foreign forces and to provide security in the transport corridors; to monitor and verify the disbanding of private and irregular armed groups; to authorize security arrangements for vital infrastructures; and to provide security for United Nations and other international activities in support of the peace process; to provide technical assistance and monitor the entire electoral process; to coordinate and monitor humanitarian assistance operations, in particular those relating to refugees, internally displaced persons, demobilized military personnel and the affected local population. After successful presidential and legislative elections in October 1994, and the installation of Mozambique's new Parliament and the inauguration of the President of Mozambique in early December, ONUMOZ's mandate formally came to an end at midnight on 9 December 1994. The Mission was formally liquidated at the end of January 1995

Location: Mozambique

Headquarters: Maputo

Duration: 16 December 1992–9 December 1994

Strength: Authorized: 6,625 troops and military support personnel, 354 military observers and 1,144 civilian police; there were also some 355 international staff and 506 local staff; in addition, during the polling, ONUMOZ deployed approximately 900 electoral observers
           Maximum strength of military component (30 November 1993): 6,576 all ranks
           Maximum strength of civilian police component (31 October 1994): 1,087
           At withdrawal (30 November 1994): 3,941 troops and military support personnel, 204 military observers and 918 civilian police

Fatalities: 21 military personnel
            2 civilian police
           <u> 1</u> international United Nations staff
           24 total

Financing: Method of financing: Assessments in respect of a Special Account
           Expenditures: From inception to 15 November 1994: $471,199,200
           In addition, for the liquidation period from 16 November 1994 to 31 March 1995, the General Assembly appropriated $39,053,300

Special Representative of the Secretary-General and Chief of Mission:

           Aldo Ajello (Italy)   October 1992–December 1994

Force Commanders: Major-General Lélio Gonçalves Rodrigues
            da Silva (Brazil)   February 1993–February 1994
           Major-General Mohammad Abdus Salam (Bangladesh) March–December 1994

**Police
Commissioner:**   Brigadier-General Ali Mahmoud (Egypt)   March–December 1994

Contributors	Duration	Contribution
Argentina	April 1993–December 1994	troops
	April 1993–December 1994	military observers
Australia	March–December 1994	civilian police
	August–December 1994	troops
Austria	July–December 1994	civilian police
Bangladesh	January–December 1994	civilian police
	February 1993–December 1994	troops
	February 1993–December 1994	military observers
Bolivia	July–November 1994	civilian police
Botswana	May–December 1994	civilian police
	February 1993–December 1994	troops
	June 1993–December 1994	military observers
Brazil	January–December 1994	civilian police
	February 1993–March 1994	troops
	June–December 1994	
	January 1993–December 1994	military observers
Canada	February 1993–December 1994	military observers
Cape Verde	February 1993–December 1994	military observers
China	July 1993–December 1994	military observers
Czech Republic	June 1993–June 1994	military observers
Egypt	March–December 1994	civilian police
	February 1993–December 1994	military observers
Finland	May–November 1994	civilian police
Ghana	July–December 1994	civilian police
Guinea-Bissau	January–December 1994	civilian police
	February 1993–December 1994	military observers
Guyana	November–December 1994	monitors
Hungary	January–December 1994	civilian police
	February 1993–December 1994	military observers
India	June–December 1994	civilian police
	March 1993–December 1994	troops
	April 1993–April 1994	military observers
	June–December 1994	
Indonesia	June–December 1994	civilian police
Ireland	March–November 1994	civilian police
Italy	January 1993–December 1994	troops
Japan	May 1993–December 1994	troops
Jordan	March–December 1994	civilian police
Malaysia	January–December 1994	civilian police
	January 1993–December 1994	military observers
Nepal	June–December 1994	civilian police
Netherlands	December 1993–December 1994	military observers
New Zealand	March–December 1994	troops
Nigeria	September–December 1994	civilian police
Norway	March–November 1994	civilian police
Pakistan	May–December 1994	civilian police
Portugal	February–December 1994	civilian police
	March 1993–December 1994	troops
	November 1993–December 1994	military observers
Russian Federation	May 1993–December 1994	military observers
Spain	January–December 1994	civilian police
	February 1993–December 1994	military observers
Sri Lanka	May–December 1994	civilian police
Sweden	January–December 1994	civilian police
	January 1993–December 1994	military observers
Switzerland	March–October 1994	civilian police
Togo	July–December 1994	civilian police
United States	March–December 1994	troops
Uruguay	May–December 1994	civilian police
	February 1993–December 1994	troops
	January 1993–December 1994	military observers
Zambia	September–December 1994	civilian police
	February 1993–December 1994	troops
	August 1993–November 1994	military observers

Voluntary contributions:

Italy (1993–1994 — air component: 8 helicopters, 3 fixed-wing aircraft, some 110 personnel [The air component was used by the Italian military forces in the mission area, and all associated costs were borne by the Government of Italy. However, these air resources were available to the United Nations in emergency situations]

Trust Fund for the Implementation of the Peace Process in Mozambique (total: $17,710,806):

Denmark ($500,000), France ($232,143), Italy ($11,447,486), Luxembourg ($42,156), Namibia ($1,000), Netherlands ($988,992), Norway ($107,150), Portugal ($300,000), South Africa ($290,000), Sweden ($367,454), Switzerland ($209,775), United Kingdom ($743,250), United States ($1,000,000), The Commission of the European Communities ($987,600)

Trust Fund for Assistance to Registered Political Parties in Mozambique (total: $3,050,000):

Canada ($163,666), Italy ($1,898,734), The Commission of the European Communities ($1,481,400)

United Nations Observer Mission Uganda-Rwanda (UNOMUR)

Authorization:	Security Council resolutions:
	846 (1993) of 22 June 1993
	872 (1993) of 5 October 1993
	891 (1993) of 20 December 1993
	928 (1994) of 20 June 1994
Function:	Established to monitor the border between Uganda and Rwanda and verify that no military assistance — lethal weapons, ammunition and other material of possible military use — was being provided across it. While the tragic turn of events in Rwanda in April 1994 prevented UNOMUR from fully implementing its mandate, the Observer Mission played a useful role as a confidence-building mechanism in the months following the conclusion of the Arusha Peace Agreement and during UNAMIR's initial efforts to defuse tensions between the Rwandese parties and to facilitate the implementation of that agreement. UNOMUR was officially closed on 21 September 1994
Location:	Ugandan side of the Uganda-Rwanda border
Headquarters:	Kabale, Uganda
Duration:	22 June 1993–21 September 1994
Strength:	Authorized: 81 military observers, supported by international and locally recruited civilian staff Maximum: 81 military observers
Fatalities:	None
Financing:	Method of financing: Assessments in respect of a Special Account Expenditures: From inception to 21 December 1993: $2,298,500 net After 21 December 1993, the costs related to UNOMUR were reflected in the costs of UNAMIR

Chief Military Observer:

Brigadier-General Romeo A. Dallaire (Canada)	June–October 1993
Colonel Ben Matiwaza (Zimbabwe) (Acting)	October 1993–March 1994
Colonel Asrarul Haque (Bangladesh) (Acting)	March–September 1994

Contributors	Duration	Contribution
Bangladesh	June 1993–September 1994	military observers
Botswana	October 1993–September 1994	military observers
Brazil	August 1993–September 1994	military observers
Canada	June–October 1993	military observers
Hungary	June 1993–September 1994	military observers
Netherlands	August 1993–September 1994	military observers
Senegal	September 1993–September 1994	military observers
Slovak Republic	November 1993–August 1994	military observers
Zimbabwe	August 1993–August 1994	military observers

United Nations Assistance Mission for Rwanda (UNAMIR)

Authorization:	Security Council resolutions:

872 (1993) of 5 October 1993
893 (1994) of 6 January 1994
909 (1994) of 5 April 1994
912 (1994) of 21 April 1994
918 (1994) of 17 May 1994
925 (1994) of 8 June 1994
965 (1994) of 30 November 1994
997 (1995) of 9 June 1995
1029 (1995) of 12 December 1995

Function: Originally established to help implement the Arusha Peace Agreement signed by the Rwandese parties on 4 August 1993. UNAMIR's mandate was: to assist in ensuring the security of the capital city of Kigali; monitor the cease-fire agreement, including establishment of an expanded demilitarized zone and demobilization procedures; monitor the security situation during the final period of the transitional Government's mandate leading up to elections; assist with mine-clearance; and assist in the coordination of humanitarian assistance activities in conjunction with relief operations. After renewed fighting in April 1994, the mandate of UNAMIR was adjusted so that it could act as an intermediary between the warring Rwandese parties in an attempt to secure their agreement to a cease-fire; assist in the resumption of humanitarian relief operations to the extent feasible; and monitor developments in Rwanda, including the safety and security of civilians who sought refuge with UNAMIR. After the situation in Rwanda deteriorated further, UNAMIR's mandate was expanded to enable it to contribute to the security and protection of refugees and civilians at risk, through means including the establishment and maintenance of secure humanitarian areas, and the provision of security for relief operations to the degree possible. Following the cease-fire and the installation of the new Government, the tasks of UNAMIR were further adjusted: to ensure stability and security in the north-western and south-western regions of Rwanda; to stabilize and monitor the situation in all regions of Rwanda to encourage the return of the displaced population; to provide security and support for humanitarian assistance operations inside Rwanda; and to promote, through mediation and good offices, national reconciliation in Rwanda. UNAMIR also contributed to the security in Rwanda of personnel of the International Tribunal for Rwanda and of human rights officers, and assisted in the establishment and training of a new, integrated, national police force. In December 1995, the Security Council further adjusted UNAMIR's mandate to focus primarily on facilitating the safe and voluntary return of refugees. UNAMIR's mandate came to an end on 8 March 1996. The withdrawal of the Mission was completed in April

Location: Rwanda

Headquarters: Kigali

Duration: 5 October 1993–8 March 1996

Strength: Authorized 5 October 1993–20 April 1994: 2,548 military personnel, including 2,217 formed troops and 331 military observers, and 60 civilian police; supported by international and locally recruited civilian staff

Authorized 21 April–16 May 1994: 270 military personnel; supported by international and locally recruited civilian staff

Authorized 17 May 1994–8 June 1995: Some 5,500 military personnel, including approximately 5,200 troops and military support personnel and 320 military observers, and 90 civilian police [in February 1995, the authorized strength of the civilian police was increased to 120]; supported by international and locally recruited civilian staff

Authorized 9 June–8 September 1995: 2,330 troops and military support personnel, 320 military observers and 120 civilian police; supported by international and locally recruited civilian staff *(continued)*   Authorized strength, 9 September–11 December 1995: 1,800 troops and military support personnel, 320 military observers and 120 civilian police; supported by international and locally recruited civilian staff

Authorized strength, 12 December 1995–8 March 1996: 1,200 troops and military support personnel and 200 military observers; supported by international and locally recruited civilian staff

Strength at withdrawal (29 February 1996): 1,252 troops and military support personnel, 146 military observers; there were also approximately 160 international and 160 local civilian staff and 56 United Nations Volunteers

Fatalities:

  3 military observers
22 other military personnel
<u> 1</u> civilian police
26 total

Financing:

Method of financing: Assessments in respect of a Special Account
Estimated expenditures: $437,430,100 net
Cost estimate for administrative close down: From 20 April to 30 September 1996: $4,102,000 net

Special Representatives of the Secretary-General and Heads of Mission:

Jacques-Roger Booh-Booh (Cameroon)	November 1993–June 1994
Shaharyar M. Khan (Pakistan)	July 1994–March 1996*

*After the closure of UNAMIR, Mr. Khan continued as the Secretary-General's Special Representative through April 1996

Force Commanders:

Major-General Romeo A. Dallaire (Canada)	October 1993–August 1994
Major-General Guy Tousignant (Canada)	August 1994–December 1995
Brigadier-General Shiva Kumar (India) (Acting)	December 1995–March 1996

Police Commissioners:

Colonel Manfred Bliem (Austria)	December 1993–April 1994
Colonel C.O. Diarra (Mali)	October 1994–January 1996

Contributors	Duration	Contribution
Argentina	November 1994–December 1995	military observers
Australia	August 1994–September 1995	troops
Austria	February–April 1994	civilian police
	December 1993–March 1996	military observers
Bangladesh	February–April 1994	civilian police
	October 1993–November 1994	troops
	April–July 1995	
	November 1993–March 1996	military observers
Belgium	February–April 1994	civilian police
	November 1993–April 1994	troops
Brazil	October 1993–February 1994	troops
	November–December 1993	military observers
Canada	February 1994–February 1996	troops
	December 1993–April 1994	military observers
	June 1994–February 1996	
Chad	May 1995–January 1996	civilian police
	August 1994–October 1995	troops
Congo	August 1994–April 1995	troops
	November 1993–July 1994	military observers
	May 1995–March 1996	
Djibouti	November 1994–January 1996	civilian police
	October–November 1994	military observers
Egypt	January–July 1994	military observers
Ethiopia	August 1994–August 1995	troops
Fiji	October–November 1993	troops
	November 1993–December 1995	military observers
Germany	January–July 1995	civilian police
	September–December 1995	

(continued)

Ghana	September 1994–December 1995	civilian police
	October 1993–March 1996	troops
	December 1993–March 1996	military observers
Guinea	August 1994–March 1996	military observers
Guinea-Bissau	October 1994–December 1995	civilian police
	August 1994–March 1995	troops
	August–November 1994	military observers
	May 1995–March 1996	
Guyana	November 1993–April 1994	civilian police
India	November 1994–March 1996	troops
	November 1994–March 1996	military observers
Jordan	October 1994–January 1996	civilian police
	August–December 1995	military observers
Kenya	August–November 1994	military observers
Malawi	August 1994–March 1996	troops
	March 1994–March 1996	military observers
Mali	February 1994–January 1996	civilian police
	October 1994–January 1996	troops
	December 1993–January 1996	military observers
Netherlands	October 1993–November 1993	troops
	December 1993–April 1994	military observers
Niger	August–December 1995	civilian police
	August 1994–March 1995	troops
Nigeria	September 1994–December 1995	civilian police
	September 1994–March 1996	troops
	January 1993–March 1996	military observers
Pakistan	August 1995–January 1996	military observers
Poland	October–November 1993	troops
	December 1993–June 1995	military observers
Romania	March–April 1994	troops
Russian Federation	January 1994–March 1996	military observers
Senegal	August 1994–March 1996	troops
	November 1993–September 1994	military observers
	April 1995–March 1996	military observers
Slovak Republic	August–November 1994	military observers
Spain	January 1995–March 1995	troops
Switzerland	September–December 1995	civilian police
Togo	February 1994–July 1994	civilian police
	December 1993–July 1994	military observers
Tunisia	November 1993–June 1994	troops
	September 1994–December 1995	
	September 1994–September 1995	military observers
	September–December 1995	civilian police
United Kingdom	August 1994–July 1995	troops
Uruguay	October–November 1993	troops
	December 1993–March 1996	military observers
Zambia	November 1994–January 1996	civilian police
	August 1994–March 1996	troops
	August 1994–March 1996	military observers
Zimbabwe	October 1993–March 1996	military observers

Voluntary contributions: Cash contributions: Namibia ($250,000), Switzerland ($227,273)

Contributions in kind: Belgium (vehicles, field kitchen, ambulances, various equipment for use of infantry company, radios, spare parts, transportation and training (valued at $1,851,500)); Germany (vehicles, field kitchens, vehicle repair workshop (valued at $571,000)); Netherlands (vehicles, generators, kitchen trailers, ambulances, mine detectors, training (valued at $2,942,500)); Republic of Korea (vehicles, containers (valued at $529,300))

Voluntary contributions to the Trust Fund for Rwanda [humanitarian relief and rehabilitation programmes]: Cambodia ($10,000); Denmark ($260,303); Grenada ($1,000); Ireland ($300,000); Mauritius ($5,788); Netherlands ($5,431,997); New Zealand ($263,720); Norway ($727,678); Philippines ($5,000); Saint Kitts and Nevis ($36,000); Singapore ($40,000); Tunisia ($3,044); United Kingdom ($292,726)

United Nations Observer Mission in Liberia (UNOMIL)

Authorization: Security Council resolutions:

866 (1993) of 22 September 1993
911 (1994) of 21 April 1994
950 (1994) of 21 October 1994
972 (1995) of 13 January 1995
985 (1995) of 13 April 1995
1001 (1995) of 30 June 1995
1014 (1995) of 15 September 1995
1020 (1995) of 10 November 1995
1041 (1996) of 29 January 1996
1059 (1996) of 31 May 1996

Function: To supervise and monitor, in cooperation with the Monitoring Group (ECOMOG) of the Economic Community of West African States (ECOWAS), the Cotonou Peace Agreement signed by the Liberian parties on 25 July 1993. In accordance with the Agreement, ECOMOG had primary responsibility for ensuring the implementation of the Agreement's provisions; UNOMIL's role was to monitor the implementation procedures in order to verify their impartial application. Delays in the implementation of the Peace Agreement and resumed fighting among Liberian factions made it impossible to hold elections in February–March 1994, as scheduled. In the following months, a number of supplementary peace agreements, amending and clarifying the Cotonou Agreement, were negotiated. In accordance with the peace agreements, ECOWAS is to continue to play the lead role in the peace process in Liberia, while ECOMOG retains the primary responsibility for assisting in the implementation of the military provisions of the agreements. For its part, UNOMIL is to continue to observe and monitor the implementation of the peace agreements. Its main functions are to exercise its good offices to support the efforts of ECOWAS and the Liberian National Transitional Government to implement the peace agreements; investigate allegations of reported cease-fire violations; recommend measures to prevent their recurrence and report to the Secretary-General accordingly; monitor compliance with the other military provisions of the agreements and verify their impartial application, especially disarming and demobilization of combatants; and assist in the maintenance of assembly sites and in the implementation of a programme for demobilization of combatants. UNOMIL has also been requested to support humanitarian assistance activities; investigate and report to the Secretary-General on violations of human rights; assist local human rights groups in raising voluntary assistance for training and logistic support; observe and verify the election process, including legislative and presidential elections

Location: Liberia

Headquarters: Monrovia

Duration: 22 September 1993 to date

Strength: Authorized 22 September 1993–9 November 1995: 303 military observers, 20 military medical personnel and 45 military engineers; there was also provision for some 89 international civilian and 136 local civilian staff, and 58 United Nations Volunteers
Authorized 10 November 1995 to date: 160 military observers supported by military medical personnel; there was also provision for some 105 international civilian and 550 local civilian staff, and 120 United Nations Volunteers
Maximum (28 February 1994): 374, including 309 military observers and 65 military support personnel, supported by international civilian and local civilian staff
At 31 March 1996: 93, including 86 military observers and 7 military medical personnel, supported by international and local civilian staff

Fatalities: None

Financing: Method of financing: Assessments in respect of a Special Account
Estimated expenditures: From inception of mission to 31 March 1996: $77,981,100* net (*This figure may be revised down.)

**Special Representatives of the
Secretary-General and Heads of Mission:**

Trevor Livingston Gordon-Somers (Jamaica)	November 1992–November 1994
Anthony B. Nyakyi (United Republic of Tanzania)	December 1994 to date

**Chief Military
Observers:**

Major-General Daniel Ishmael Opande (Kenya)	October 1993–May 1995
Major-General Mahmoud Talha (Egypt)	November 1995–May 1996
Colonel David Magomere (Kenya), Acting	June 1996 to date

Contributors	Duration	Contribution
Austria	September 1993–November 1994	military observers
Bangladesh	October 1993 to date	medical staff
	September 1993 to date	military observers
Belgium	September–November 1993	military observers
Brazil	September–November 1993	military observers
China	October 1993 to date	military observers
Congo	September 1993–February 1994	military observers
Czech Republic	December 1993 to date	military observers
Egypt	December 1993 to date	military observers
Guinea-Bissau	September 1993 to date	military observers
Hungary	September 1993–January 1994	military observers
India	February 1994 to date	military observers
Jordan	October 1993 to date	military observers
Kenya	October 1993 to date	military observers
	March–June 1995	military support personnel
Malaysia	September 1993 to date	military observers
Netherlands	November–December 1993	military observers
Pakistan	September 1993 to date	military observers
Poland	September 1993–April 1994	military observers
Russian Federation	September–November 1993	military observers
Slovak Republic	November 1993–November 1994	military observers
Sweden	September–November 1993	military observers
Uruguay	September 1993 to date	military observers

**Voluntary
contributions:**

Voluntary financing authorizations for the Trust Fund for the Implementation of the Cotonou Agreement on Liberia from inception to 31 March 1996 (paid): Denmark ($294,616); Egypt ($10,000); Netherlands ($261,584); Norway ($291,056); United Kingdom ($1,000,000 for humanitarian activities only); and United States ($22,190,400)

United Nations Aouzou Strip Observer Group (UNASOG)

Authorization: Security Council resolution 915 (1994) of 4 May 1994

Function: Established to verify the withdrawal of the Libyan administration and forces from the Aouzou Strip in accordance with the decision of the International Court of Justice. UNASOG accomplished its mandate after both sides — the Republic of Chad and the Libyan Arab Jamahiriya — declared withdrawal to be complete

Location: Aouzou Strip, Republic of Chad

Headquarters: Aouzou Base

Duration: May–June 1994

Strength: 9 military observers and 6 international civilian staff
[the military observers as well as most of the civilian staff were drawn from the United Nations Mission for the Referendum in Western Sahara (MINURSO)]

Fatalities: None

Financing: Method of financing: Appropriations through the United Nations regular budget
Expenditures: $67,471

Chief Military Observer: Colonel Mazlan Bahamuddin (Malaysia)   May–June 1994

Contributors of military observers:
Bangladesh
Ghana
Honduras
Kenya
Malaysia
Nigeria

United Nations Observer Group in Central America (ONUCA)

Authorization:	Security Council resolutions:

644 (1989) of 7 November 1989
650 (1990) of 27 March 1990
653 (1990) of 20 April 1990
654 (1990) of 4 May 1990
656 (1990) of 8 June 1990
675 (1990) of 5 November 1990
691 (1991) of 6 May 1991
719 (1991) of 6 November 1991
730 (1992) of 16 January 1992

Function: Established to verify compliance by the Governments of Costa Rica, El Salvador, Guatemala, Honduras and Nicaragua with their undertakings to cease aid to irregular forces and insurrectionist movements in the region and not to allow their territory to be used for attacks on other States. In addition, ONUCA played a part in the voluntary demobilization of the Nicaraguan Resistance and monitored a cease-fire and the separation of forces agreed by the Nicaraguan parties as part of the demobilization process

Location: Costa Rica, El Salvador, Guatemala, Honduras and Nicaragua

Headquarters: Tegucigalpa, Honduras

Duration: 7 November 1989 to 17 January 1992

Strength: Initial authorization: 260 military observers; crews and support personnel for an air wing and naval unit
Additional authorization: infantry battalion of approximately 800 all ranks
Maximum deployment (May/June 1990): 1,098 military personnel
The mission was supported by a number of international and local civilian staff

Fatalities: None

Financing: Method of financing: Assessments in respect of a Special Account
Expenditures: $88,573,157 (net)

**Personal Representative of the Secretary-General
for the Central American Peace Process:**

Alvaro de Soto (Peru)	September 1989–February 1992

**Chief Military
Observers:**

Major-General Agustín Quesada Gómez (Spain)	November 1989–December 1990
Brigadier-General Lewis MacKenzie (Canada) (Acting)	December 1990–May 1991
Brigadier-General Víctor Suanzes Pardo (Spain)	May 1991–January 1992

Contributors	Duration	Contribution
Argentina	June 1990–January 1992	Naval crew and four fast patrol boats
Brazil	April 1990–January 1992	Military observers
Canada	December 1989–January 1992	Military observers, helicopter unit
Colombia	December 1989–January 1992	Military observers
Ecuador	April 1990–November 1991	Military observers
Germany, Federal Republic of	December 1989–December 1991	Civilian medical personnel, air crew
India	May 1990–January 1992	Military observers
Ireland	December 1989–January 1992	Military observers
Spain	December 1989–January 1992	Military observers
Sweden	May 1990–January 1992	Military observers
Venezuela	December 1989–January 1992	Military observers, logistics unit
	April–July 1990	Infantry battalion

Voluntary contributions:

Germany, Federal Republic of (December 1989–November 1991: rental, equipment and maintenance of a fixed wing aircraft; basic salary of air crew and of civilian medical personnel); Switzerland (air ambulance service)

United Nations Observer Mission in El Salvador (ONUSAL)

Authorization: Security Council resolutions:

693 (1991) of 20 May 1991
729 (1992) of 14 January 1992
784 (1992) of 30 October 1992
791 (1992) of 30 November 1992
832 (1993) of 27 May 1993
888 (1993) of 30 November 1993
920 (1994) of 26 May 1994
961 (1994) of 23 November 1994
991 (1995) of 28 April 1995

Function: Established to verify the implementation of all agreements between the Government of El Salvador and Frente Farabundo Martí para la Liberación Nacional aimed at ending a decade-long civil war. The agreements involved a cease-fire and related measures, reform and reduction of the armed forces, creation of a new police force, reform of the judicial and electoral systems, human rights, land tenure and other economic and social issues. After the armed conflict had been formally brought to an end in December 1992, ONUSAL verified elections which were carried out successfully in March and April 1994. After ONUSAL completed its mandate on 30 April 1995, a small group of United Nations civilian personnel — known as the United Nations Mission in El Salvador (MINUSAL) — remained in El Salvador to provide good offices to the parties, to verify implementation of the outstanding points of the agreements and to provide a continuing flow of accurate and reliable information

Location: El Salvador

Headquarters: San Salvador

Duration: 26 July 1991 to 30 April 1995

Strength: Authorized maximum: 380 military observers; 8 medical officers; and 631 civilian police. Provision was also made for some 140 civilian international staff and 180 local staff
Maximum deployment: 368 military observers (February 1992) and 315 civilian police (May 1992). The Electoral Division was augmented by some 900 electoral observers during the elections

Fatalities: 3 civilian police
2 local staff
5 total

Financing: Method of financing: Assessments in respect of a Special Account
Expenditures: $107,003,650

**Special Representatives of the Secretary-General
and Chiefs of Mission:**

Iqbal Riza (Pakistan)	July 1991–March 1993
Augusto Ramírez-Ocampo (Colombia)	April 1993–March 1994
Enrique ter Horst (Venezuela)	1 April 1994–September 1995*

*Mr. ter Horst continued as Special Representative of the Secretary-General after the termination of ONUSAL's mandate and served as Chief of Mission of MINUSAL until September 1995. He was succeeded by Mr. Ricardo Virgil (Peru) as the Secretary-General's Representative and Director of Mission.

**Chief Military
Observer:** Brigadier-General Víctor Suanzes Pardo (Spain)   January 1992–May 1993

**Police
Commissioners:**

General Homero Vaz Bresque (Uruguay)	March 1992–April 1994
Comisario Principal Alfredo Carballo (Spain)	May 1994–March 1995

Contributors	Duration	Contribution
Argentina	June 1992–November 1994	medical unit
Austria	February 1992–November 1994	civilian police
Brazil	July 1991–April 1995	military observers
	April–May 1992	medical unit
	June 1993–April 1995	civilian police
Canada	July 1991–August 1994	military observers
Chile	April 1992–April 1995	civilian police
Colombia	January 1992–November 1994	military observers
	May 1993–April 1995	civilian police
Ecuador	July 1991–March 1994	military observers
France	July 1991–November 1994	civilian police
Guyana	April 1992–April 1995	civilian police
India	January 1992–April 1994	military observers
Ireland	January 1992–June 1994	military observers
Italy	July 1991–April 1995	civilian police
Mexico	February 1992–April 1995	civilian police
Norway	January–February 1992	military observers
	February 1992–June 1993	civilian police
Spain	July 1991–April 1995	military observers
	July 1991–April 1995	civilian police
Sweden	January 1992–November 1994	military observers
	April 1992–November 1994	civilian police
Venezuela	July 1991–April 1995	military observers

**Voluntary
contributions:**

Switzerland (cash: $70,398)

As at 28 February 1995, voluntary contributions received in the Trust Fund for the Commission on the Truth amounted to $2,309,069

United Nations Advance Mission in Cambodia (UNAMIC)

Authorization:	Security Council resolutions:
	717 (1991) of 16 October 1991
	728 (1992) of 8 January 1992
Function:	Established to assist the four Cambodian parties to maintain their cease-fire during the period prior to the establishment and deployment of the United Nations Transitional Authority in Cambodia, and to initiate mine-awareness training of civilian populations. Later, the mandate was enlarged to include a major training programme for Cambodians in mine-detection and mine-clearance and the mine-clearing of repatriation routes, reception centres and resettlement areas. UNAMIC was absorbed by UNTAC in March 1992
Location:	Cambodia
Headquarters:	Phnom Penh
Duration:	16 October 1991–15 March 1992
Strength:	Initial authorization: 116 military personnel (50 military liaison officers, 20 mine-awareness personnel, 40 military support personnel). There was also provision for approximately 75 international and 75 local civilian support staff.
	Subsequent authorization: 1,090 additional military personnel. Provision was also made for 34 additional civilian staff.
	Maximum deployment: 1,090 (March 1992)
Fatalities:	None
Financing:	[see UNTAC, below]
Chief Liaison Officer:	A.H.S. Ataul Karim (Bangladesh) November 1991–March 1992
Senior Military Liaison Officer:	Brigadier-General Michel Loridon (France) November 1991–March 1992

Contributors	Duration	Contribution
Algeria	November 1991–February 1992	military observers
Argentina	November 1991–February 1992	military observers
Australia	November 1991–February 1992	military observers
Austria	November 1991–February 1992	military observers
Belgium	November 1991–February 1992	military observers
Canada	November 1991–February 1992	military observers
China	November 1991–February 1992	military observers
France	November 1991–February 1992	military observers
	December 1991–February 1992	air unit
Germany	November 1991–February 1992	military observers
Ghana	November 1991–February 1992	military observers
India	November 1991–February 1992	military observers
Indonesia	November 1991–February 1992	military observers
Ireland	November 1991–February 1992	military observers
Malaysia	November 1991–February 1992	military observers

(continued)

New Zealand	November 1991–February 1992	military observers
Pakistan	November 1991–February 1992	military observers
Poland	November 1991–February 1992	military observers
Russian Federation (Soviet Union before 24 December 1991)	November 1991–February 1992	military observers
Senegal	November 1991–February 1992	military observers
Thailand	February 1992	troops
Tunisia	November 1991–February 1992	military observers
United Kingdom	November 1991–February 1992	military observers
United States	November 1991–February 1992	military observers
Uruguay	November 1991–February 1992	military observers

Voluntary contributions: Included in UNTAC; see below.

United Nations Transitional Authority in Cambodia (UNTAC)

Authorization: Security Council resolutions:

745 (1992) of 28 February 1992
860 (1993) of 27 August 1993
880 (1993) of 4 November 1993

Function: Established to ensure the implementation of the Agreements on a Comprehensive Political Settlement of the Cambodia Conflict, signed in Paris on 23 October 1991. Under the Agreements, the Supreme National Council of Cambodia (SNC) was "the unique legitimate body and source of authority in which, throughout the transitional period, the sovereignty, independence and unity of Cambodia are enshrined". SNC, which was made up of the four Cambodian factions, delegated to the United Nations "all powers necessary" to ensure the implementation of the Agreements. The mandate given to UNTAC included aspects relating to human rights, the organization and conduct of free and fair general elections, military arrangements, civil administration, the maintenance of law and order, the repatriation and resettlement of the Cambodian refugees and displaced persons and the rehabilitation of essential Cambodian infrastructure during the transitional period. Upon becoming operational on 15 March 1992, UNTAC absorbed UNAMIC, which had been established immediately after the signing of the Agreements in October 1991. UNTAC's mandate ended in September 1993 with the promulgation of the Constitution for the Kingdom of Cambodia and the formation of the new Government

Location: Cambodia

Headquarters: Phnom Penh

Duration: 28 February 1992–24 September 1993

Strength: Maximum authorized: 15,547 troops, 893 military observers, and 3,500 civilian police. Provision included up to 1,149 international civilian staff, 465 United Nations Volunteers and 4,830 local staff, supplemented by international contractual staff and electoral personnel during the electoral period
Maximum deployment: Military component: 15,991; civilian police component: 3,359 (June 1993). During the electoral period, more than 50,000 Cambodians served as electoral staff and some 900 international polling station officers were seconded from Governments

Fatalities: 41 military
 4 military observers
14 civilian police
 5 international United Nations staff
<u>14</u> local staff
78 total

Financing: Method of financing: Assessments in respect of a Special Account
Expenditures: $1,620,963,300 (UNAMIC and UNTAC combined)

**Special Representative of the Secretary-General
and Chief of Mission:**

Yasushi Akashi (Japan)	January 1992–September 1993

Force Commander: Lieutenant-General John Sanderson (Australia)   March 1992–September 1993

Police Commissioners: Brigadier-General Klaas Roos (Netherlands)   March 1992–August 1993
Deputy Inspector General Shahudul Haque
   (Bangladesh) (Acting)   August–September 1993

Contributors	Contribution
Algeria	civilian police, military observers
Argentina	military observers
Australia	civilian police, troops
Austria	civilian police, troops, military observers
Bangladesh	civilian police, troops, military observers
Belgium	military observers, troops
Brunei Darussalam	civilian police, troops, military observers
Bulgaria	civilian police, troops, military observers
Cameroon	civilian police, military observers
Canada	troops
Chile	troops
China	troops, military observers
Colombia	civilian police
Egypt	civilian police
Fiji	civilian police
France	civilian police, troops, air unit, military observers
Germany	civilian police, troops
Ghana	civilian police, troops, military observers
Hungary	civilian police
India	civilian police, troops, military observers
Indonesia	civilian police, troops, military observers
Ireland	civilian police, troops, military observers
Italy	civilian police
Japan	civilian police, troops, military observers
Jordan	civilian police
Kenya	civilian police
Malaysia	civilian police, troops, military observers
Morocco	civilian police
Namibia	troops
Nepal	civilian police
Netherlands	civilian police, troops
New Zealand	troops, military observers
Nigeria	civilian police
Norway	civilian police
Pakistan	civilian police, troops, military observers
Philippines	civilian police, troops
Poland	troops, military observers
Russian Federation	troops, military observers
Senegal	military observers
Singapore	civilian police, troops
Sweden	civilian police
Thailand	troops
Tunisia	civilian police, troops, military observers
United Kingdom	troops, military observers
United States	troops, military observers
Uruguay	troops, military observers

Voluntary contributions in kind or in services:

Australia	Military support unit
France	Air support unit
Japan	Audio-visual equipment, health kits
Switzerland	Air ambulance services
United States	Ready-to-eat meals

Voluntary contributions in cash:

Japan ($2 million), Australia ($1 million), Netherlands ($2.2 million), Philippines ($100,000), United Kingdom ($1 million), United States of America ($2 million), Luxembourg ($26,054), New Zealand ($25,807), Japan ($1.1 million), Japan — advance ($2 million), private donation ($10,000)

Trust Fund for the Cambodian Peace Process: As at 31 October 1993, $8.7 million had been contributed by Australia, Bangladesh, Barbados, Denmark, Ireland, Italy, Luxembourg, New Zealand, Norway, Senegal, Singapore and Sweden as well as by a private institution

Trust Fund for a Human Rights Education Programme in Cambodia: As at 31 October 1993, a total of $1.6 million had been contributed by Australia, Belgium, Canada, the Netherlands, New Zealand, Sweden, the United Kingdom and the United States

Cambodia Trust Fund: As at 31 October 1993, $2.2 million had been contributed by Australia, Chile, Republic of Korea, the Netherlands, New Zealand and Norway

Trust Fund for the De-Mining Programme in Cambodia: As at 31 October 1993, a total of $713,4000 had been contributed by New Zealand and the United States

United Nations Protection Force (UNPROFOR)
(21 February 1992–31 March 1995)

Authorization:

Security Council resolutions:

743 (1992) of 21 February 1992
749 (1992) of 7 April 1992
758 (1992) of 8 June 1992
761 (1992) of 29 June 1992
762 (1992) of 30 June 1992
764 (1992) of 13 July 1992
769 (1992) of 7 August 1992
776 (1992) of 14 September 1992
779 (1992) of 6 October 1992
781 (1992) of 9 October 1992
786 (1992) of 10 November 1992
795 (1992) of 11 December 1992
807 (1993) of 19 February 1993
815 (1993) of 30 March 1993
819 (1993) of 16 April 1993
824 (1993) of 6 May 1993
836 (1993) of 4 June 1993
838 (1993) of 10 June 1993
842 (1993) of 18 June 1993
844 (1993) of 18 June 1993
847 (1993) of 30 June 1993
869 (1993) of 30 September 1993
870 (1993) of 1 October 1993
871 (1993) of 4 October 1993
900 (1994) of 4 March 1994
908 (1994) of 31 March 1994
914 (1994) of 27 April 1994
947 (1994) of 30 September 1994
982 (1995) of 31 March 1995

Function:

Initially, established in Croatia as an interim arrangement to create the conditions of peace and security required for the negotiation of an overall settlement of the Yugoslav crisis. UNPROFOR's mandate was to ensure that the three "United Nations Protected Areas" (UNPAs) in Croatia were demilitarized and that all persons residing in them were protected from fear of armed attack. In the course of 1992, UNPROFOR's mandate was enlarged to include monitoring functions in certain other areas of Croatia ("pink zones"); to enable the Force to control the entry of civilians into the UNPAs and to perform immigration and customs functions at the UNPA borders at international frontiers; and to include monitoring of the demilitarization of the Prevlaka Peninsula and to ensure control of the Peruca dam, situated in one of the "pink zones". In addition, UNPROFOR monitored implementation of a cease-fire agreement signed by the Croatian Government and local Serb authorities in March 1994 following a flare-up of fighting in January and September 1993. In June 1992, as the conflict intensified and extended to Bosnia and Herzegovina, UNPROFOR's mandate and strength were enlarged in order to ensure the security and functioning of the airport at Sarajevo, and the delivery of humanitarian assistance to that city and its environs. In September 1992, UNPROFOR's mandate was further enlarged to enable it to support efforts by the United Nations High Commissioner for Refugees to deliver humanitarian relief throughout Bosnia and Herzegovina, and to protect convoys of released civilian detainees if the International Committee of the Red Cross so requested. In addition, the Force monitored the "no-fly" zone, banning all military flights in Bosnia and Herzegovina, and the United Nations "safe areas" established by the Security Council around five Bosnian towns and the city of Sarajevo. UNPROFOR was authorized to use force in self-defence in reply to attacks against these areas, and to coordinate with the North Atlantic Treaty Organization (NATO) the use of air power in support of its activities. Similar arrangements were subsequently extended to the territory of Croatia. UNPROFOR also monitored the implementation of a cease-fire agreement signed by the Bosnian Government and Bosnian Croat forces in February 1994. In addition, UNPROFOR monitored cease-fire arrangements negotiated between Bosnian Government and Bosnian Serbs forces, which entered into force on 1 January 1995. In December 1992, UNPROFOR was also deployed in the former Yugoslav Republic of

Macedonia, to monitor and report any developments in its border areas which could undermine confidence and stability in that Republic and threaten its territory. On 31 March 1995, the Security Council decided to restructure UNPROFOR, replacing it with three separate but interlinked peace-keeping operations [see UNPF below]

Location:	Bosnia and Herzegovina, Croatia, the Federal Republic of Yugoslavia (Serbia and Montenegro) and the former Yugoslav Republic of Macedonia
Headquarters:	Initially Sarajevo; later Zagreb
Strength:	Authorized: 44,870 all ranks; there was also provision for almost 1,000 international civilian staff, 1,500 international contractual personnel and more than 3,000 local staff

Maximum (30 September 1994): 39,922, including 38,614 troops, 637 military observers and 671 civilian police
At 31 March 1995: 38,848, including 37,421 troops, 677 military observers and 750 civilian police

Fatalities:

   3 military observers
159 other military personnel
     1 civilian police
     2 international United Nations staff
     2 local staff
167 (total, UNPROFOR until 31 March 1995)

Financing: Method of financing: Assessments in respect of a Special Account
Expenditures: [see UNPF below]

Personal Envoy of the Secretary-General:

Cyrus Vance (United States)	October 1991–April 1993

**Special Representatives of the Secretary-General
and Heads of Mission of UNPROFOR:**

Thorvald Stoltenberg (Norway)	May 1993–December 1994
Yasushi Akashi (Japan)	January 1994–[see UNPF below]

Force Commanders:

Lieutenant-General Satish Nambiar (India)	March 1992–March 1993
Lieutenant-General Lars-Eric Wahlgren (Sweden)	March–June 1993
Lieutenant-General Jean Cot (France)	June 1993–March 1994
General Bertrand de Lapresle (France)	March 1994–February 1995
General Bernard Janvier (France)	March 1995–[see UNPF below]

Police Commissioners:

Chief Superintendent Kjell Johansen (Norway)	1992–1993
Chief Superintendent Mike O'Reilly (Canada)	1993–1994
Chief Superintendent Sven Frederiksen (Denmark)	1994–1995 [See UNPF below]

Contributors	Duration	Contribution
Argentina	April 1992–March 1995	civilian police
	April 1992–March 1995	troops
	April 1992–March 1995	military observers
Australia	April 1992–November 1993	military observers
Bangladesh	April 1992–March 1995	civilian police
	September 1994–March 1995	troops
	April 1992–March 1995	military observers
Belgium	April 1992–March 1995	troops
	April 1992–March 1995	military observers
Brazil	September 1993–March 1995	civilian police
	August 1992–March 1995	military observers
Canada	April 1992–March 1995	civilian police
	April 1992–March 1995	troops
	April 1992–March 1995	military observers

(continued)

Colombia	April 1992–March 1995	civilian police
	April 1992–May 1994	military observers
Czech Republic (Czechoslovakia before 31 December 1992)	April 1992–March 1995	troops
	April 1992–March 1995	military observers
Denmark	April 1992–March 1995	civilian police
	April 1992–March 1995	troops
	April 1992–March 1995	military observers
Egypt	April 1992–July 1994 December 1994–March 1995	civilian police
	April 1992–March 1995	troops
	April 1992–March 1995	military observers
Finland	July 1994–March 1995	civilian police
	April 1992–March 1995	troops
	April 1992–March 1995	military observers
France	April 1992–March 1995	civilian police
	April 1992–March 1995	troops
	April 1992–March 1995	military observers
Ghana	April 1992–March 1995	military observers
India	April 1992–March 1993	military observers
Indonesia	October 1994–March 1995	civilian police
	September 1994–March 1995	troops
	October 1993–March 1995	military observers
Ireland	April 1992–March 1995	civilian police
	April 1992–March 1995	military observers
Jordan	April 1992–March 1995	civilian police
	April 1992–March 1995	troops
	April 1992–March 1995	military observers
Kenya	April 1992–March 1995	civilian police
	April 1992–March 1995	troops
	April 1992–March 1995	military observers
Lithuania	November 1994–March 1995	troops
Luxembourg	April 1992–July 1993	troops
Malaysia	October 1994–March 1995	civilian police
	October 1993–March 1995	troops
	September 1993–March 1995	military observers
Nepal	April 1992–March 1995	civilian police
	April 1992–March 1995	troops
	April 1992–March 1995	military observers
Netherlands	November 1993–March 1995	civilian police
	April 1992–March 1995	troops
	April 1992–March 1995	military observers
New Zealand	September 1994–March 1995	troops
	April 1992–March 1995	military observers
Nigeria	April 1992–March 1995	civilian police
	April 1992–March 1993	troops
	April 1992–March 1995	military observers
Norway	April 1992–March 1995	civilian police
	April 1992–March 1995	troops
	April 1992–March 1995	military observers
Pakistan	October 1994–March 1995	civilian police
	June 1994–March 1995	troops
	September 1993–March 1995	military observers
Poland	April 1992–March 1995	civilian police
	April 1992–March 1995	troops
	April 1992–March 1995	military observers
Portugal	April 1992–March 1995	civilian police
	January 1993–October 1994	troops
	April 1992–March 1995	military observers
Russian Federation	April 1992–March 1995	civilian police
	April 1992–March 1995	troops
	April 1992–March 1995	military observers
Senegal	January–March 1995	civilian police

(continued)

Slovak Republic (Czechoslovakia before 31 December 1992)	April 1992–March 1995	troops
Spain	November 1992–March 1995	troops
	October 1992–March 1995	military observers
Sweden	April 1992–March 1995	civilian police
	April 1992–March 1995	troops
	April 1992–March 1995	military observers
Switzerland	July 1993–March 1995	civilian police
	April 1994–September 1994	troops
	May 1992–March 1995	military observers
Thailand	April 1992	military observers
Tunisia	August 1992–March 1995	civilian police
Turkey	June 1994–March 1995	troops
Ukraine	May 1994–March 1995	civilian police
	August 1992–March 1995	troops
	July 1994–March 1995	military observers
United Kingdom	April 1992–March 1995	troops
	April 1992–March 1995	military observers
United States	November 1992–March 1995	troops
Venezuela	April 1992–November 1994	military observers

Voluntary contributions: [see UNPF below]

United Nations Peace Forces (UNPF)

Authorization: Security Council resolutions:

982 (1995) of 31 March 1995
1031 (1995) of 15 December 1995

Function: On 31 March 1995, the Security Council decided to restructure UNPROFOR, replacing it with three separate but interlinked peace-keeping operations. The Council extended the mandate of UNPROFOR in Bosnia and Herzegovina, established the United Nations Confidence Restoration Operation in Croatia (UNCRO), and decided that UNPROFOR within the former Yugoslav Republic of Macedonia should be known as the United Nations Preventive Deployment Force (UNPREDEP). Their joint theatre headquarters, known as United Nations Peace Forces headquarters (UNPF-HQ), was established in Zagreb, the capital of Croatia. UNPF-HQ was also responsible for liaison with the Government of the Federal Republic of Yugoslavia (Serbia and Montenegro), other concerned Governments and NATO. Each of the three operations was headed by a civilian Chief of Mission and had its own military commander. Overall command and control of the three operations was exercised by the Special Representative of the Secretary-General and the Theatre Force Commander. Eventually, following positive developments in the former Yugoslavia, the termination of the mandates of UNCRO and UNPROFOR and the establishment of two new United Nations missions in Bosnia and Herzegovina and Croatia, this arrangement came to an end on 31 January 1996 and UNPF-HQ was phased out

Location: Bosnia and Herzegovina, Croatia, the Federal Republic of Yugoslavia (Serbia and Montenegro) and the former Yugoslav Republic of Macedonia

Duration: 31 March 1995–31 January 1996

Headquarters: Zagreb

Strength: Authorized strength (UNPROFOR, UNCRO, UNPREDEP and UNPF-HQ): 57,370 all ranks; supported by international and local civilian staff [see UNPROFOR above]

Fatalities (UNPF-HQ):

1 military observer
2 other military personnel
2 civilian police
3 international United Nations staff
1 local staff
9 (total, UNPF-HQ)

Financing: Method of financing: Assessments in respect of a Special Account
Estimated expenditures: From 12 January 1992 to 31 March 1996: $4,616,725,556 net
Includes UNPROFOR (February 1992–March 1995), UNPROFOR (March–December 1995), UNCRO, UNPREDEP and UNPF-HQ

**Special Representative of the Secretary-General
for the former Yugoslavia and Head of Mission:**

Yasushi Akashi (Japan)   March–November 1995*
[*see UNPROFOR above]

**Special Envoy of the Secretary-General
to the former Yugoslavia and in this context to NATO:**

Kofi Annan (Ghana)   November 1995–January 1996

**Theatre Force
Commander:**   General Bernard Janvier (France)   March 1995*–January 1996
[*see UNPROFOR above]

Police Commissioner:	Chief Superintendent Haakan Jufors (Sweden)	August–January 1996

A. Voluntary contributions for the period from 12 January 1992 to 31 December 1995:

Cash contributions: Italy ($2,380,952), Liechtenstein ($7,081), Switzerland ($4,781,589)

Contributions in kind (value indicated in parenthesis):

12 January 1992 to 31 March 1993: Germany (loan: 395 vehicles and trailers ($790,000) and 246 generators (value not yet determined)); Italy (loan: 15 APCs, with full equipment ($5,593,220)); Sweden (donation: two sedans ($42,388)); Switzerland (air ambulance service, Zagreb–Lisbon, July 1992 (value not yet determined) and donation of 40 trucks ($273,000)); United States (donation: operational maps ($1,700,000))

1 April to 30 June 1993: Switzerland (donation: two armoured vehicles ($433,566) and air ambulance service, Zagreb–Dublin, April 1993 (value not yet determined))

1 July 1993 to 31 March 1994: Finland (donation: housing units ($57,000)); United Kingdom (donation: equipment ($90,000))

1 April to 30 September 1994: Germany (loan: 171 APCs ($3,420,000), loan: vehicles and equipment (value not yet determined), loan: vehicles and equipment ($140,526), donation: clothing (value not yet determined)); Netherlands (donation: vehicles ($95,973)); Russian Federation (donation: equipment, vehicles, generators ($80,000)); Switzerland (services ($13,569)); United Kingdom (loan: vehicles and equipment ($4,297,267), donation: vehicles and equipment ($239,553)); NATO (maps (value not yet determined))

1 October 1994 to 31 March 1995: Germany (donation: 50 trucks ($5,000,000))

1 July to 31 December 1995: Germany (donation: 100 APCs ($18,300,000))

B. Voluntary contributions to the reinforcement of UNPF with a rapid reaction capacity for the period from 1 July to 30 November 1995

Voluntary contributions in cash (total: $3,921,721): Austria (value not yet determined), Denmark ($970,000), Finland ($837,914), Greece ($100,000), Ireland ($276,000), Mauritius ($5,000), Monaco ($14,000), Panama ($22,000), Sweden ($1,696,807)
Voluntary contributions in kind: United States: (equipment, services, sealift ($31,874,073))

C. Trust Funds (total: $27,141,088; pledged: $3,283,357)

Trust fund for assistance to the Office of the Special Representative of the Secretary-General for the former Yugoslavia: Japan ($330,000), Sweden ($137,646), private institution ($1,186,791)

Trust fund for de-mining activities: Switzerland ($375,940), Japan ($3,000,060)

Trust fund for the common costs of the Bosnia and Herzegovina command: Austria ($400,000); Belgium ($153,799); Canada ($515,939); Denmark ($449,414); Ireland ($161,234); Italy ($1,363,278); Luxembourg ($288,270), Netherlands ($508,724); Norway ($511,635); Spain ($511,301); Tunisia ($1,989); United Kingdom ($521,972)

Trust fund for the restoration of essential public services in Sarajevo: Austria ($463,392); Belgium ($1,000,000, pledged); Brunei Darussalam ($30,000, pledged); Canada ($356,400); Denmark ($184,075); Dutch Transport Council ($59,043); Indonesia ($30,000); Ireland ($530,802); Italy ($5,735,611); Japan ($1,020,000); Malaysia ($1,050,000); Netherlands ($2,327,864); Norway ($467,978); Pakistan ($50,000, pledged); Portugal ($125,627); Qatar ($690,424); Republic of Korea ($100,000); Spain ($75,000); Sweden ($2,099,737, pledged); United Kingdom ($2,610,500); United States ($896,380, paid, and $103,620, pledged)

United Nations Protection Force (UNPROFOR)
(31 March–20 December 1995)

Authorization:	Security Council resolutions:
	982 (1995) of 31 March 1995 998 (1995) of 16 June 1995 1026 (1995) of 30 November 1995
Function:	After the restructuring of UNPROFOR on 31 March 1995, the Force continued to perform the functions envisaged in Security Council resolutions relevant to the situation in Bosnia and Herzegovina. In November 1995, a United States initiative led to the Peace Agreement initialled and subsequently signed, in December 1995, by the leaders of Bosnia and Herzegovina, Croatia and the Federal Republic of Yugoslavia (Serbia and Montenegro). As requested by the Agreement, the Security Council authorized Member States to establish a NATO-led multinational Implementation Force (IFOR) to help ensure compliance with the provisions of the Agreement. After IFOR took over from UNPROFOR on 20 December 1995, the latter's mandate was terminated
Location:	Bosnia and Herzegovina
Headquarters:	Zagreb
Strength:	Maximum strength (31 August 1995): 30,869, including 30,574 troops, 278 military observers and 17 civilian police At withdrawal: 2,675, including 2,433 troops, 156 military observers and 86 civilian police (31 December 1995)
Fatalities:	31 March 1995–20 December 1995 38 military personnel 1 civilian police 1 local staff 40 total Grand total UNPROFOR (21 February 1992–20 December 1995) 167 (21 February 1992–31 March 1995) [see above] 40 (31 March 1995–20 December 1995) [see above] 207 grand total
Financing:	Method of financing and expenditures: [see UNPF above]
Head of Mission:	Antonio Pedauye (Spain) March–December 1995
Military Commander:	Lieutenant-General Rupert Smith (United Kingdom) March–December 1995
	[From 31 March to 20 December 1995, overall command and control of UNPROFOR was exercised from UNPF Headquarters in Zagreb by the Secretary-General's Special Representatives, Mr. Yasushi Akashi (from 31 March to 31 October 1995) and subsequently Mr. Kofi Annan (from 1 November to 20 December 1995), and the Theatre Force Commander, Lieutenant-General Bernard Janvier (from 31 March to 20 December 1995)]

Contributors	Duration	Contribution
Argentina	April 1995	troops
	April 1995	military observers
	October–December 1995	
Bangladesh	April–May 1995	civilian police
	November–December 1995	
	April–December 1995	troops
	April–December 1995	military observers
Belgium	April–December 1995	troops
	April–December 1995	military observers
Brazil	April–September 1995	civilian police
	April–December 1995	military observers
Canada	April–May 1995	civilian police
	April–December 1995	troops
	April–December 1995	military observers

(continued)

Colombia	April–May 1995	civilian police
Czech Republic	April–December 1995	military observers
Denmark	April–August 1995	civilian police
	December 1995	
	April–December 1995	troops
	April–December 1995	military observers
Egypt	April–July 1995	civilian police
	November–December 1995	
	April–December 1995	troops
	April–December 1995	military observers
Finland	April–December 1995	civilian police
	April–December 1995	military observers
France	April–December 1995	civilian police
	April–December 1995	troops
	April–December 1995	military observers
Germany	August–October 1995	troops
Ghana	April–December 1995	military observers
Indonesia	April 1994–June 1995	civilian police
	August–December 1995	troops
	April–December 1995	military observers
Ireland	April–December 1995	civilian police
	April–December 1995	military observers
Jordan	April–May 1995	civilian police
	November–December 1995	
	April–December 1995	troops
	April–December 1995	military observers
Kenya	April–May 1995	civilian police
	December 1995	
	April–December 1995	military observers
Malaysia	April–May 1995	civilian police
	April–December 1995	troops
	April–June 1995	military observers
Nepal	April–May 1995	civilian police
	April–December 1995	military observers
Netherlands	April–December 1995	civilian police
	April–December 1995	troops
	April–December 1995	military observers
New Zealand	April–December 1995	troops
	April–December 1995	military observers
Nigeria	April–May 1995	civilian police
	April–December 1995	military observers
Norway	April–December 1995	civilian police
	April–December 1995	troops
	April–December 1995	military observers
Pakistan	April–May 1995	civilian police
	April–December 1995	troops
	April–December 1995	military observers
Poland	April–December 1995	civilian police
	April–May 1995	troops
	April–December 1995	military observers
Portugal	April–December 1995	civilian police
	April–December 1995	military observers
Russian Federation	April–December 1995	civilian police
	April–December 1995	troops
	April–December 1995	military observers
Senegal	January–December 1995	civilian police
Spain	April–December 1995	troops
	April–December 1995	military observers
Sweden	April–December 1995	civilian police
	April–December 1995	troops
	April–December 1995	military observers
Switzerland	April–May 1995	civilian police
	April–December 1995	military observers
Tunisia	April–May 1995	civilian police

(continued)

Turkey	April–December 1995	troops
Ukraine	April–December 1995	civilian police
	April–December 1995	troops
	April–December 1995	military observers
United Kingdom	April–December 1995	troops
	April–December 1995	military observers
United States	April–December 1995	troops

Voluntary contributions: [see UNPF above]

United Nations Confidence Restoration Operation in Croatia (UNCRO)

Authorization:	Security Council resolutions: 981 (1995) of 31 March 1995 990 (1995) of 28 April 1995 994 (1995) of 17 May 1995 1025 (1995) of 30 November 1995
Function:	To perform the functions envisaged in the cease-fire agreement of 29 March 1994; facilitate implementation of the economic agreement of 2 December 1994; facilitate implementation of all relevant Security Council resolutions; assist in controlling, by monitoring and reporting, the crossing of military personnel, equipment, supplies and weapons, over the international borders between Croatia and Bosnia and Herzegovina, and Croatia and the Federal Republic of Yugoslavia (Serbia and Montenegro) at the border crossings; facilitate the delivery of international humanitarian assistance to Bosnia and Herzegovina through the territory of Croatia; and monitor the demilitarization of the Prevlaka peninsula. After Croatia's reintegration by force of Western Slavonia and the Krajina region in May and August 1995, the need for United Nations troops in those areas was effectively eliminated. However, in Eastern Slavonia — the last Serb-controlled territory in Croatia — the mandate of UNCRO remained essentially unchanged. The Government of Croatia and the Croatian Serb leadership agreed to resolve the issue of Eastern Slavonia through negotiation. United Nations-sponsored talks concluded with the signing of the Basic Agreement on the Region of Eastern Slavonia, Baranja and Western Sirmium on 12 November. The Agreement provided for the peaceful integration into Croatia of that region and requested the Security Council to establish a transitional administration to govern the region during the transitional period. Following the establishment of the United Nations administration, the mandate of UNCRO was terminated
Location:	Croatia
Headquarters:	Zagreb
Duration:	31 March 1995–15 January 1996
Strength:	Maximum (31 May 1995): 15,522, including 14,663 troops, 328 military observers and 531 civilian police At withdrawal: 3,376, including 3,110 troops, 98 military observers and 168 civilian police
Fatalities:	16 military personnel
Financing:	Method of financing and expenditures: [see UNPF above]
Head of Mission:	Byung Suk Min (Republic of Korea) March 1995–January 1996
Military Commander:	Major-General Eid Kamal Al-Rodan (Jordan) March–December 1995
	[Overall command and control of UNCRO was exercised from UNPF Headquarters in Zagreb by the Secretary-General's Special Representatives, Mr. Yasushi Akashi and subsequently Mr. Kofi Annan, and the Theatre Force Commander, Lieutenant-General Bernard Janvier]

Contributors	Duration	Contribution
Argentina	April 1995–January 1996	troops
	October 1995–January 1996	military observers
Bangladesh	May 1995–January 1996	civilian police
	June 1995–January 1996	troops
	May 1995–January 1996	military observers
Belgium	April 1995–January 1996	troops
	May 1995–January 1996	military observers

The Blue Helmets

(continued)

Brazil	May 1995–January 1996	civilian police
	May 1995–January 1996	military observers
Canada	May–July 1995	civilian police
	April 1995–January 1996	troops
	May 1995–January 1996	military observers
Czech Republic	April 1995–January 1996	troops
	May 1995–January 1996	military observers
Denmark	May 1995–January 1996	civilian police
	April 1995–January 1996	troops
	May 1995–January 1996	military observers
Egypt	May 1995–January 1996	civilian police
	June 1995–January 1996	troops
	May 1995–January 1996	military observers
Estonia	April–November 1995	troops
Finland	May 1995–January 1996	civilian police
	April 1995–January 1996	troops
	May 1995–January 1996	military observers
France	May 1995–January 1996	civilian police
	April 1995–January 1996	troops
	May 1995–January 1996	military observers
Germany	September 1995–January 1996	troops
Ghana	May 1995–January 1996	military observers
Indonesia	May–November 1995	civilian police
	April 1995–January 1996	troops
	May 1995–January 1996	military observers
Ireland	May 1995–January 1996	civilian police
	May 1995–January 1996	military observers
Jordan	May 1995–January 1996	civilian police
	April–December 1995	troops
	May 1995–January 1996	military observers
Kenya	May 1995–January 1996	civilian police
	April 1995–January 1996	troops
	May 1995–January 1996	military observers
Lithuania	April–November 1995	troops
Malaysia	May–September 1995	civilian police
	June 1995–January 1996	troops
	May–June 1995	military observers
Nepal	May–August 1995	civilian police
	April–December 1995	troops
	May 1995–January 1996	military observers
Netherlands	May 1995–January 1996	civilian police
	April 1995–January 1996	troops
	May 1995–January 1996	military observers
New Zealand	June 1995–January 1996	troops
	May 1995–January 1996	military observers
Nigeria	July–December 1995	civilian police
	July 1995–January 1996	military observers
Norway	May 1995–January 1996	civilian police
	April 1995–January 1996	troops
	May 1995–January 1996	military observers
Pakistan	May–November 1995	civilian police
	June 1995–January 1996	troops
	May 1995–January 1996	military observers
Poland	May 1995–January 1996	civilian police
	April 1995–January 1996	troops
	May 1995–January 1996	military observers
Portugal	May 1995–January 1996	civilian police
	May 1995–January 1996	military observers
Russian Federation	May 1995–January 1996	civilian police
	April 1995–January 1996	troops
	May 1995–January 1996	military observers
Senegal	May 1995–January 1996	civilian police
Slovak Republic	April 1995–January 1996	troops

(continued)

Spain	July 1995–January 1996	troops
	May 1995–January 1996	military observers
Sweden	May 1995–January 1996	civilian police
	April 1995–January 1996	troops
	May 1995–January 1996	military observers
Switzerland	July 1995–January 1996	military observers
Tunisia	May–October 1995	civilian police
Turkey	June–October 1995	troops
Ukraine	May 1995–January 1996	civilian police
	April 1995–January 1996	troops
	May 1995–January 1996	military observers
United Kingdom	June 1995–January 1996	troops
	May 1995–January 1996	military observers
United States	April–December 1995	troops

Voluntary contributions: [see UNPF above]

United Nations Preventive Deployment Force (UNPREDEP)

Authorization:	Security Council resolutions:
	983 (1995) of 31 March 1995 1027 (1995) of 30 November 1995 1046 (1996) of 13 February 1996
Function:	To monitor and report any developments in the border areas (with Albania and the Federal Republic of Yugoslavia (Serbia and Montenegro)) which could undermine confidence and stability in the former Yugoslav Republic of Macedonia and threaten its territory
Location:	The former Yugoslav Republic of Macedonia
Headquarters:	Skopje
Duration:	31 March 1995 to date
Strength:	Authorized: 1,050 troops, 35 military observers and 26 civilian police; there is also provision for 76 international staff and 127 locally recruited staff
Fatalities:	None (as at 31 March 1996)
Financing:	Method of financing and expenditures: [see UNPF above] Cost estimate: For the period from 1 January to 30 June 1996: $24,694,800

**Special Representative of the
Secretary-General and Chief of Mission:**

Henryk J. Sokalski (Poland)	February 1996 to date

(Mr. Sokalski served as Chief of Mission beginning in March 1995)

Military Commander:	Brigadier-General Juha Engström (Finland)	March 1995–February 1996
Force Commander:	Brigadier-General Bo Lennart Wranker (Sweden)	March 1996 to date

[From 31 March 1995 to 31 January 1996, overall command and control of UNPREDEP was exercised from UNPF Headquarters in Zagreb by the Secretary-General's Special Representatives, Mr. Yasushi Akashi (from 31 March to 31 October 1995) and subsequently Mr. Kofi Annan (from 1 November 1995 to 31 January 1996), and the Theatre Force Commander, Lieutenant-General Bernard Janvier]

Contributors	Duration	Contribution
Argentina	December 1995 to date	military observers
Bangladesh	May 1995 to date	civilian police
	August 1995 to date	military observers
Belgium	May 1995 to date	military observers
Brazil	May 1995 to date	military observers
Canada	May 1995 to date	military observers
Czech Republic	May 1995 to date	military observers
Denmark	October 1995 to date	civilian police
	April 1995 to date	troops
	May 1995 to date	military observers
Egypt	May–August 1995	civilian police
	August 1995 to date	military observers
Finland	May–June 1995	civilian police
	April 1995 to date	troops
	May 1995 to date	military observers
France	September 1995 to date	civilian police
	May 1995 to date	military observers
Ghana	August 1995 to date	military observers
Indonesia	May–June 1995	civilian police
	July 1995 to date	troops
	May 1995 to date	military observers
Ireland	August 1995 to date	civilian police
	August 1995 to date	military observers
Jordan	June 1995 to date	civilian police
	May 1995 to date	military observers

(continued)

Kenya	June–September 1995	civilian police
	May 1995 to date	military observers
Malaysia	June–September 1995	civilian police
	May–June 1995	military observers
Nepal	June–August 1995	civilian police
	January 1996 to date	military observers
Netherlands	May 1995 to date	civilian police
	August–November 1995	military observers
New Zealand	July 1995 to date	military observers
Nigeria	May–December 1995	civilian police
	May 1995 to date	military observers
Norway	June–October 1995	civilian police
	April 1995 to date	troops
	May 1995 to date	military observers
Pakistan	May–October 1995	civilian police
	May 1995 to date	military observers
Poland	May–October 1995	civilian police
	May 1995 to date	military observers
Portugal	September 1995 to date	civilian police
	August 1995 to date	military observers
Russian Federation	May 1995 to date	civilian police
	October 1995 to date	military observers
Senegal	May–June 1995	civilian police
Spain	May–October 1995	military observers
Sweden	June 1995 to date	civilian police
	April 1995 to date	troops
	May 1995 to date	military observers
Switzerland	May 1995 to date	civilian police
	May–June 1995	
	January 1996 to date	military observers
Ukraine	May 1995 to date	civilian police
	July 1995 to date	military observers
United Kingdom	July 1995 to date	military observers
United States	April 1995 to date	troops

Voluntary contributions: [see UNPF above]

United Nations Mission in Bosnia and Herzegovina (UNMIBH)

Authorization: Security Council resolution 1035 (1995) of 21 December 1995

Function: On 21 December 1995, the Security Council established, for a period of one year, the United Nations International Police Task Force (IPTF) and a United Nations civilian office. This was done in accordance with the Peace Agreement signed by the leaders of Bosnia and Herzegovina, Croatia and the Federal Republic of Yugoslavia (Serbia and Montenegro) on 14 December 1995. The operation has come to be known as the United Nations Mission in Bosnia and Herzegovina (UNMIBH). IPTF tasks include: (a) monitoring, observing and inspecting law enforcement activities and facilities, including associated judicial organizations, structures and proceedings; (b) advising law enforcement personnel and forces; (c) training law enforcement personnel; (d) facilitating, within the IPTF mission of assistance, the parties' law enforcement activities; (e) assessing threats to public order and advising on the capability of law enforcement agencies to deal with such threats; (f) advising government authorities in Bosnia and Herzegovina on the organization of effective civilian law enforcement agencies; and (g) assisting by accompanying the parties' law enforcement personnel as they carry out their responsibilities, as the Task Force deems appropriate. In addition, the Task Force is to consider requests from the parties or law enforcement agencies in Bosnia and Herzegovina for assistance, with priority being given to ensuring the existence of conditions for free and fair elections. The United Nations Coordinator, acting under the Secretary-General's authority, exercises authority over the IPTF Commissioner and coordinates other United Nations activities in Bosnia and Herzegovina relating to humanitarian relief and refugees; de-mining, human rights, elections, and rehabilitation of infrastructure and economic reconstruction. UNMIBH closely cooperates with a NATO-led multinational Implementation Force (IFOR), authorized by the Security Council to help ensure compliance with the provisions of the Peace Agreement, and with the High Representative, appointed by the Peace Implementation Conference and approved by the Security Council, and whose task is to mobilize and coordinate the activities of organizations and agencies involved in civilian aspects of the peace settlement in Bosnia and Herzegovina, and monitor the implementation of that settlement.

Location: Bosnia and Herzegovina

Headquarters: Sarajevo

Duration: December 1995 to date

Strength: Authorized: 1,721 civilian police and 5 military liaison officers; there is also provision for approximately 380 international staff and 900 locally recruited staff
At 30 April 1996: 1,197 civilian police, supported by international and locally recruited civilian staff

Financing: Method of financing: Assessments in respect of a Special Account
Estimated cost: From 1 January to 30 June 1996: $50,794,600 net
Estimated cost: From 1 July 1996 to 30 June 1997: $150,854,700 net
[Cost estimates include the cost of UNMOP, see below]

**Special Representative of the Secretary-General
and Coordinator of United Nations Operations
in Bosnia and Herzegovina:**

Iqbal Riza (Pakistan)   February 1996 to date

Commissioner of IPTF:

Peter FitzGerald (Ireland)   February 1996 to date

Contributors of police personnel	Duration
Argentina	March 1996 to date
Austria	March 1996 to date
Bangladesh	December 1995 to date
Bulgaria	April 1996 to date
Denmark	December 1995 to date
Egypt	December 1995–February 1996
Estonia	April 1996 to date
Fiji	March 1996 to date
Finland	December 1995 to date
France	December 1995 to date
Germany	February 1996 to date
Ghana	March 1996 to date
Greece	February 1996 to date
Hungary	March 1996 to date
India	March 1996 to date
Indonesia	February 1996 to date
Ireland	December 1995 to date
Jordan	December 1995 to date
Kenya	December 1995 to date
Malaysia	March 1996 to date
Nepal	March 1996 to date
Netherlands	December 1995 to date
Norway	December 1995–March 1996
Pakistan	March 1996 to date
Poland	December 1995 to date
Portugal	December 1995 to date
Russian Federation	December 1995 to date
Senegal	December 1995 to date
Spain	February 1996 to date
Sweden	December 1995 to date
Switzerland	February 1996 to date
Tunisia	February 1996 to date
Turkey	March 1996 to date
Ukraine	December 1995 to date
United States	March 1996 to date

United Nations Transitional Administration for Eastern Slavonia, Baranja and Western Sirmium (UNTAES)

Authorization:	Security Council resolutions:
	1037 (1996) of 15 January 1996
	1043 (1996) of 31 January 1996

Function: The 12 November 1995 Basic Agreement on the Region of Eastern Slavonia, Baranja and Western Sirmium provides for the peaceful integration of that region into Croatia. The Agreement requested the Security Council to establish a transitional administration to govern the region during the transitional period of 12 months, which might be extended by up to a further 12 months and to authorize an international force to maintain peace and security during that period and to otherwise assist in the implementation of the Agreement. UNTAES was set up on 15 January 1996 for an initial period of 12 months, with both military and civilian components. The military component is to supervise and facilitate the demilitarization of the Region; monitor the voluntary and safe return of refugees and displaced persons to their home of origin in cooperation with UNHCR; contribute, by its presence, to the maintenance of peace and security in the region; and otherwise assist in implementation of the Basic Agreement. The civilian component is to establish a temporary police force, define its structure and size, develop a training programme and oversee its implementation, and monitor treatment of offenders and the prison system; undertake tasks relating to civil administration and to the functioning of public services; facilitate the return of refugees; organize elections, assist in their conduct, and certify the results. The component has also been requested to undertake other activities relevant to the Basic Agreement, including assistance in the coordination of plans for the development and economic reconstruction of the Region; and monitoring of the parties' compliance with their commitments to respect the highest standards of human rights and fundamental freedoms, promote an atmosphere of confidence among all local residents irrespective of their ethnic origin, monitor and facilitate the de-mining of territory within the Region, and maintain an active public affairs element. UNTAES is also to cooperate with the International Criminal Tribunal for the Former Yugoslavia in performing its mandate. Member States are authorized, acting nationally or through regional organizations, to take all necessary measures, including close air support to defend or help withdraw UNTAES, and that such actions would be based on UNTAES's request and procedures communicated to the United Nations.

Location:	Eastern Slavonia, Baranja and Western Sirmium (Croatia)
Headquarters:	Vukovar
Duration:	January 1996 to date
Strength:	Authorized: 5,000 troops, 100 military observers and 600 civilian police; there is also provision for approximately 480 international civilian staff, 720 locally recruited staff and 100 United Nations Volunteers
	At 30 April 1996: 4,481 troops, 99 military observers and 257 civilian police
Fatalities:	2 military personnel (as at 30 April 1996)
Financing:	Method of financing: Assessments in respect of a Special Account
	Estimated cost: From 1 January to 30 June 1996: $108,151,000 net
	Estimated cost: From 1 July 1996 to 30 June 1997: $275,350,500 net

Transitional Administrator:

	Jacques Paul Klein (United States)	January 1996 to date
Force Commander:	Major-General Jozef Schoups (Belgium)	March 1996 to date
Chief Military Observer:	Brigadier-General Purwadi (Indonesia)	March 1996 to date
Police Commissioner:	Chief Superintendent Haaken Jufors (Sweden)	January 1996 to date

Contributors	Duration	Contribution
Argentina	January 1996 to date	military observers
	March 1996 to date	civilian police
	April 1996 to date	troops
Bangladesh	January 1996 to date	military observers
	January 1996 to date	civilian police
Belgium	January 1996 to date	troops
	January 1996 to date	military observers
Brazil	January 1996 to date	military observers
	January 1996 to date	civilian police
Canada	January–February 1996	troops
	January–February 1996	military observers
Czech Republic	January 1996 to date	troops
	January 1996 to date	military observers
Denmark	January 1996 to date	troops
	January–February 1996	military observers
	January 1996 to date	civilian police
Egypt	January 1996 to date	military observers
	January–February 1996	civilian police
Fiji	April 1996 to date	civilian police
Finland	January–February 1996	troops
	January 1996 to date	military observers
	March 1996 to date	civilian police
France	January–March 1996	military observers
	January–March 1996	civilian police
Ghana	January 1996 to date	military observers
Indonesia	January 1996 to date	troops
	January 1996 to date	military observers
	February 1996 to date	civilian police
Ireland	January 1996 to date	military observers
	January–February 1996	civilian police
Jordan	January 1996 to date	military observers
	January 1996 to date	civilian police
	March 1996 to date	troops
Kenya	January 1996 to date	military observers
	January 1996 to date	civilian police
Nepal	January 1996 to date	military observers
	February 1996 to date	civilian police
Netherlands	January–February 1996	military observers
	January–February 1996	civilian police
New Zealand	January 1996 to date	military observers
Nigeria	January 1996 to date	military observers
	April 1996 to date	civilian police
Norway	January–February 1996	troops
	January 1996 to date	military observers
	January 1996 to date	civilian police
Pakistan	January 1996 to date	military observers
	April 1996 to date	troops
Poland	January 1996 to date	military observers
Portugal	January–February 1996	military observers
	January–March 1996	civilian police
Russian Federation	January 1996 to date	troops
	January 1996 to date	military observers
	January 1996 to date	civilian police
Senegal	January 1996 to date	civilian police
Slovak Republic	January 1996 to date	troops
Sweden	January–February 1996	troops
	January 1996 to date	military observers
	January 1996 to date	civilian police
Switzerland	January 1996 to date	military observers
Tunisia	February 1996 to date	civilian police
Turkey	March 1996 to date	troops
Ukraine	January 1996 to date	troops
	January 1996 to date	military observers
	March 1996 to date	civilian police
United Kingdom	January 1996 to date	military observers

United Nations Mission of Observers in Prevlaka (UNMOP)

Authorization: Security Council resolution 1038 (1996) of 15 January 1996

Function: United Nations military observers have been deployed in the strategically-important Prevlaka peninsula since October 1992, when the Security Council authorized UNPROFOR to assume responsibility for monitoring the demilitarization of that area. Following the restructuring of UNPROFOR in March 1995, those functions were carried out by UNCRO. With the termination of UNCRO's mandate in January 1996, the Council authorized United Nations military observers to continue monitoring the demilitarization of the peninsula for a period of three months, to be extended for an additional three months upon a report by the Secretary-General that an extension would continue to help decrease tension there. United Nations military observers are under the command and direction of a Chief Military Observer, who reports directly to United Nations Headquarters in New York.

Location: Prevlaka peninsula, Croatia

Duration: January 1996 to date

Strength: Authorized: 28 military observers
At 30 April 1996: 28 military observers

Financing: Method of financing: Assessments in respect of a Special Account
Expenditure: Costs related to the operation of UNMOP are included in the cost of UNMIBH [see above]

Chief Military Observer: Colonel Göran Gunnarsson (Sweden)   January 1996 to date

Contributors of military observers   **Duration**

Argentina	January 1996 to date
Bangladesh	January 1996 to date
Belgium	January 1996 to date
Brazil	January 1996 to date
Canada	January 1996 to date
Czech Republic	January 1996 to date
Denmark	January 1996 to date
Egypt	January 1996 to date
Finland	January 1996 to date
France	January 1996 to date
Ghana	January 1996 to date
Indonesia	January 1996 to date
Ireland	January 1996 to date
Jordan	January 1996 to date
Kenya	January 1996 to date
Nepal	January 1996 to date
New Zealand	January 1996 to date
Nigeria	January 1996 to date
Norway	January 1996 to date
Pakistan	January 1996 to date
Poland	January 1996 to date
Portugal	January 1996 to date
Russian Federation	January 1996 to date
Sweden	January 1996 to date
Switzerland	January 1996 to date
Ukraine	January 1996 to date
United Kingdom	January 1996 to date

United Nations Observer Mission in Georgia (UNOMIG)

Authorization: Security Council resolutions:

849 (1993) of 9 July 1993
854 (1993) of 6 August 1993
858 (1993) of 24 August 1993
881 (1993) of 4 November 1993
892 (1993) of 22 December 1993
896 (1994) of 31 January 1994
901 (1994) of 4 March 1994
906 (1994) of 25 March 1994
934 (1994) of 30 June 1994
937 (1994) of 21 July 1994
971 (1995) of 12 January 1995
993 (1995) of 12 May 1995
1036 (1996) of 12 January 1996

Function: Originally established to verify compliance with the 27 July 1993 cease-fire agreement between the Government of Georgia and the Abkhaz authorities in Georgia with special attention to the situation in the city of Sukhumi; to investigate reports of cease-fire violations and to attempt to resolve such incidents with the parties involved; and to report to the Secretary-General on the implementation of its mandate, including, in particular, violations of the cease-fire agreement. After UNOMIG's original mandate had been invalidated by the resumed fighting in Abkhazia in September 1993, the Mission had an interim mandate to maintain contacts with both sides to the conflict and with Russian military contingents, and to monitor and report on the situation, with particular reference to developments relevant to United Nations efforts to promote a comprehensive political settlement. Following the signing, in May 1994, by the Georgian and Abkhaz sides of the Agreement on a Cease-fire and Separation of Forces, UNOMIG's tasks are: to monitor and verify the implementation of the Agreement; to observe the operation of the peace-keeping force of the Commonwealth of Independent States; to verify that troops do not remain in or re-enter the security zone and that heavy military equipment does not remain or is not reintroduced in the security zone or the restricted weapons zone; to monitor the storage areas for heavy military equipment withdrawn from the security zone and restricted weapons zone; to monitor the withdrawal of Georgian troops from the Kodori valley to places beyond the frontiers of Abkhazia; to patrol regularly the Kodori valley; and to investigate reported or alleged violations of the Agreement and attempt to resolve such incidents.

Location: Abkhazia, Georgia

Headquarters: Sukhumi

Duration: 24 August 1993 to date

Strength: Authorized: 136 military observers; there is also provision for 64 international and 75 local civilian staff
At 31 March 1996: 128 military observers, supported by some 50 international and 75 local civilian staff

Fatalities: 2 military observers (as at 31 March 1996)

Financing: Method of financing: Assessments in respect of a Special Account
Estimated expenditures: From inception of mission to 30 June 1996: $30,742,460 net

Special Envoy of the Secretary-General:

Edouard Brunner (Switzerland)   May 1993 to date

Resident Deputy to the Special Envoy and Head of Mission of UNOMIG:

Liviu Bota (Romania)   October 1995 to date

Chief Military Observers:

Brigadier-General John Hvidegaard (Denmark)	August 1993–August 1995
Major-General Per Källström (Sweden)	October 1995 to date

Contributors of military observers

	Duration
Albania	October 1994 to date
Austria	July 1994 to date
Bangladesh	January 1994 to date
Cuba	December 1994 to date
Czech Republic	October 1994 to date
Denmark	September 1993 to date
Egypt	July 1994 to date
France	October 1994 to date
Germany	March 1994 to date
Greece	September 1994 to date
Hungary	January 1994 to date
Indonesia	October 1994 to date
Jordan	July 1994 to date
Pakistan	October 1994 to date
Poland	January 1994 to date
Republic of Korea	October 1994 to date
Russian Federation	October 1994 to date
Sweden	January 1994 to date
Switzerland	January 1994 to date
Turkey	October 1994 to date
United Kingdom	August 1994 to date
United States	November 1994 to date
Uruguay	August 1994 to date

Voluntary and trust fund contributions:

A. Voluntary contributions:

Cash contributions: Switzerland ($327,600)

In-kind contributions pledged: Switzerland (donation one Fokker F-27 aircraft — value not yet determined)

B. Trust funds:

Trust fund in support of the implementation of the Agreement on a Cease-fire and Separation of Forces: Israel ($5,000, pledged)

Trust fund for negotiations to find a comprehensive settlement of the Georgian/Abkhaz conflict: Switzerland ($681,896)

United Nations Mission of Observers in Tajikistan (UNMOT)

Authorization:	Security Council resolutions:

968 (1994) of 16 December 1994
999 (1995) of 16 June 1995
1030 (1995) of 14 December 1995
1061 (1996) of 14 June 1996

Function: Established with a mandate to assist the Joint Commission, composed of representatives of the Tajik Government and of the Tajik opposition, to monitor the implementation of the Agreement on a Temporary Cease-fire and the Cessation of Other Hostile Acts on the Tajik-Afghan Border and within the Country for the Duration of the Talks; to investigate reports of cease-fire violations and to report on them to the United Nations and to the Joint Commission; to provide its good offices as stipulated in the Agreement; to maintain close contact with the parties to the conflict, as well as close liaison with the Mission of the Conference on Security and Cooperation in Europe and with the Collective Peace-keeping Forces of the Commonwealth of Independent States in Tajikistan and with the border forces; to provide support for the efforts of the Secretary-General's Special Envoy; and to provide political liaison and coordination services, which could facilitate expeditious humanitarian assistance by the international community

Location: Tajikistan

Headquarters: Dushanbe

Duration: 16 December 1994 to date

Strength: Authorized: 45 military observers, supported by international and local civilian staff
At 31 March 1996: 45 military observers, supported by 17 international and 26 local civilian staff

Fatalities: 1 military observer (as at 30 April 1996)

Financing: Method of financing: Assessments in respect of a Special Account
Estimated expenditures: From inception of mission to 30 June 1996: $12,367,337 net

Special Envoys of the Secretary-General:

Ismat Kittani (Iraq)   April–December 1993
Ramiro Píriz-Ballón (Uruguay)   December 1993–February 1996

Special Representative of the Secretary-General and Head of Mission: Gerd Merrem (Germany)   May 1996 to date

Heads of Mission of UNMOT: Liviu Bota (Romania)   December 1994–March 1995
[From January 1993 to December 1994, Mr. Bota was head of the United Nations office in Dushanbe]

Darko Silovic (Croatia)March 1995–May 1996
[Mr. Silovic also served as Resident Deputy Special Envoy]

Chief Military Observer: Brigadier-General Hasan Abaza (Jordan)December 1994 to date

[Brigadier-General Abaza arrived in Tajikistan in October 1994 to lead an advance group of United Nations military observers]

Contributors of military observers	Duration
Austria	December 1994 to date
Bangladesh	December 1994 to date
Bulgaria	April 1995 to date
Denmark	December 1994 to date
Hungary	December 1994–October 1995
Jordan	December 1994 to date
Poland	April 1995 to date
Switzerland	April 1995 to date
Ukraine	April 1995 to date
Uruguay	December 1994 to date

Voluntary and trust fund contributions:

A. Voluntary contributions:

Cash contributions: Germany ($717,463)
In-kind contributions: Switzerland (medical supplies valued at $70,537); Tajikistan (office space for UNMOT headquarters and the outstation at Garm)

B. Trust fund:

Trust fund to support the implementation of the Agreement on a Temporary Cease-fire and the Cessation of Other Hostile Acts on the Tajik-Afghan Border and within the Country for the Duration of the Talks: United Kingdom ($54,224); United States (a letter of credit for $28,000)

United Nations Mission in Haiti (UNMIH)

Authorization: Security Council resolutions:

       867 (1993) of 23 September 1993
       905 (1994) of 23 March 1994
       933 (1994) of 30 June 1994
       940 (1994) of 31 July 1994
       964 (1994) of 29 November 1994
       975 (1995) of 30 January 1995
    1007 (1995) of 31 July 1995
    1048 (1996) of 19 February 1996

Function: Originally established to help implement certain provisions of the Governors Island Agreement signed by the Haitian parties on 3 July 1993. In 1993, UNMIH's mandate was to assist in modernizing the armed forces of Haiti and establishing a new police force. However, due to non-cooperation of the Haitian military authorities, UNMIH could not be fully deployed at that time and carry out that mandate. After the restoration, in October 1994, of the Haitian Constitutional Government with the help of a multinational force led by the United States and authorized by the Security Council, UNMIH's mandate was revised to enable the Mission to assist the democratic Government of Haiti in fulfilling its responsibilities in connection with: sustaining a secure and stable environment established during the multinational phase and protecting international personnel and key installations; and the professionalization of the Haitian armed forces and the creation of a separate police force. UNMIH was also to assist the legitimate constitutional authorities of Haiti in establishing an environment conducive to the organization of free and fair legislative elections to be called by those authorities. UNMIH assumed its functions in full on 31 March 1995. Democratic legislative elections were held in summer 1995, despite some logistical difficulties. The Presidential elections were held successfully on 17 December 1995 and the transfer of power to the new President took place on 7 February 1996. Upon receipt of a request by the President of Haiti, UNMIH's mandate was extended until the end of June 1996

Location: Haiti

Headquarters: Port-au-Prince

Duration: 23 September 1993–30 June 1996

Strength: Initial authorization: 567 civilian police and a military construction unit of 700 personnel including 60 military trainers

    Maximum authorization: 6,000 troops and military support personnel, and 900 civilian police; there was also provision for approximately 230 international civilian staff, 200 local staff and 30 United Nations Volunteers

    Maximum deployment: 6,065 troops and military support personnel, and 847 civilian police (30 June 1995)

    Authorization during final period: 1,200 troops and military support personnel, and 300 civilian police; there was also provision for approximately 160 international civilian staff, 180 local staff and 18 United Nations Volunteers

Fatalities: 4 military
2 civilian police
6 total

Financing: Method of financing: Assessments in respect of a Special Account
Estimated expenditures: $336,800,000 net

**Special Envoy of the
Secretary-General:**   Dante Caputo (Argentina)   December 1992–September 1994

(Mr. Caputo also served as Special Envoy of the Secretary General of the Organization of American States. When UNMIH was established, he also became Special Representative of the Secretary-General and Chief of Mission [see below].)

**Special Representatives
of the Secretary-General
and Chiefs of Mission:**   Dante Caputo (Argentina)   September 1993–September 1994
                          Lakhdar Brahimi (Algeria)   September 1994–March 1996
                          Enrique ter Horst (Venezuela)   March 1996 to date

**Commander of the
Military Unit:**   Colonel Gregg Pulley (United States)   October 1993–*
                         *(UNMIH was prevented from deploying at this stage)

Force Commanders: Major-General Joseph Kinzer (United States)   January 1995–March 1996
                         Brigadier-General J.R.P. Daigle (Canada)   March–June 1996

Police Commissioners: Superintendent Jean-Jacques Lemay (Canada)   October 1993–*
                         *(UNMIH was prevented from deploying at this stage)
                         Chief Superintendent Neil Pouliot (Canada)   July 1994–February 1996
                         Colonel Philippe Balladur (France)   February–June 1996

Contributors	Duration	Contribution
Algeria	March 1995–June 1996	civilian police
Antigua and Barbuda	March–August 1995	troops
Argentina	March 1995–January 1996	civilian police
	March–November 1995	troops
Austria	October–November 1994	troops
	March 1995–February 1996	civilian police
Bahamas	March 1995–January 1996	troops
Bangladesh	September 1994–April 1995	military observers
	October 1994–June 1996	troops
	March–November 1995	civilian police
Barbados	March 1995–January 1996	troops
	March–December 1995	civilian police
Belize	May 1995–January 1996	troops
Benin	May 1995–February 1996	civilian police
Canada	October 1994–June 1996	civilian police
	October 1994–June 1996	troops
Djibouti	September 1994–April 1995	military observers
	March 1995–May 1996	troops
	March 1995–June 1996	civilian police
France	September 1994–April 1995	military observers
	October 1994–June 1996	civilian police
	March 1995–June 1996	troops
Guatemala	September 1994–April 1995	military observers
	March 1995–February 1996	troops
Guinea-Bissau	March–June 1995	civilian police
Guyana	March 1995–January 1996	troops
Honduras	March 1995–February 1996	troops
India	March 1995–January 1996	troops
Ireland	September 1994–April 1995	military observers
	March 1995–March 1996	troops
Jamaica	March 1995–January 1996	troops
Jordan	March–November 1995	civilian police
Mali	March 1995–June 1996	civilian police
Nepal	March 1995–February 1996	civilian police
	March 1995–March 1996	troops
Netherlands	December 1994–April 1996	troops
New Zealand	September 1994–April 1995	military observers

(continued)

Pakistan	January–April 1995	military observers
	January 1995–June 1996	troops
	March–November 1995	civilian police
Philippines	March–November 1995	civilian police
Russian Federation	March–June 1996	civilian police
Saint Kitts and Nevis	May 1995–December 1995	civilian police
Saint Lucia	May 1995–December 1995	civilian police
Suriname	March–November 1995	troops
	April–December 1995	civilian police
Togo	March 1995–June 1996	civilian police
Trinidad and Tobago	March 1995–June 1996	troops
Tunisia	December 1994–April 1995	military observers
United States	October 1994–April 1996	troops

A. **Voluntary contributions:**

In-kind contributions received:

1 February–31 July 1995: Canada (compensation for one officer who served as the Civilian Police Commissioner during this mandate period)

1 August 1995–29 February 1996: Canada (compensation for one officer who served as the Civilian Police Commissioner during this mandate period); Netherlands (donation of 20 sea containers); United States (compensation for 149 local staff who served as interpreters)

During the period from February to June 1996, Canada provided to UNMIH on a voluntary basis approximately 700 infantry and support personnel, including a transport platoon, an engineering squadron, a military police platoon and an aviation squadron

B. **Trust funds:**

Trust fund for electoral assistance to Haiti: France ($1,619,047); Japan ($504,000); Luxembourg ($60,000); Norway ($157,006), United States ($9,392,090)

Trust fund to provide goods and services to the international police monitoring programme and other specifically designated purposes in Haiti: Japan ($3,000,000); Luxembourg ($50,501); Republic of Korea ($200,000)

United Nations Security Force in West New Guinea (West Irian) (UNSF)

Authorization:	General Assembly resolution 1752 (XVII) of 21 September 1962
Function:	Established to maintain peace and security in the territory under the United Nations Temporary Executive Authority (UNTEA), established by agreement between Indonesia and the Netherlands. UNSF monitored the cease-fire and helped ensure law and order during the transition period, pending transfer to Indonesia
Location:	West New Guinea (West Irian)
Headquarters:	Hollandia (now Jayaphra)
Duration:	3 October 1962–30 April 1963
Strength:	Maximum: 1,500 infantry personnel and 76 aircraft personnel At withdrawal: 1,500 infantry personnel and 76 aircraft personnel
Fatalities:	None
Financing:	The Governments of Indonesia and the Netherlands paid full costs in equal amounts
Commander:	Major-General Said Uddin Khan (Pakistan)

Contributors (October 1962– April 1963):

Pakistan	Infantry
Canada	Supporting aircraft and crews
United States	Supporting aircraft and crews

From 18 August to 21 September 1962, the Secretary-General's Military Adviser, Brigadier-General Indar Jit Rikhye (India), and a group of 21 military observers assisted in the implementation of the agreement of 15 August 1962 between Indonesia and the Netherlands on cessation of hostilities. The military observers were provided by Brazil, Ceylon, India, Ireland, Nigeria and Sweden.

Mission of the Representative of the Secretary-General in the Dominican Republic (DOMREP)

Authorization: Security Council resolution 203 (1965) of 14 May 1965

Function: Established to observe the situation and to report on breaches of the cease-fire between the two de facto authorities in the Dominican Republic. Following the agreement on a new Government, DOMREP was withdrawn

Location: Dominican Republic

Headquarters: Santo Domingo

Duration: 15 May 1965–22 October 1966

Strength: 2 military observers

Fatalities: None

Financing: Method of financing: Appropriations through the United Nations regular budget
Expenditures: From inception to end of mission: $275,831

Representative of the Secretary-General: José Antonio Mayobre (Venezuela)

Military Adviser: Major-General Indar J. Rikhye (India)

(The Military Adviser was provided with a staff of 2 military observers at any one time. These observers were provided, one each, by Brazil, Canada and Ecuador)

United Nations Good Offices Mission in Afghanistan and Pakistan (UNGOMAP)

Authorization:	Letter of 25 April 1988 from the President of the Security Council addressed to the Secretary-General (S/19836)
	Security Council resolutions:
	622 (1988) of 31 October 1988 647 (1990) of 11 January 1990
Function:	Established to assist the Personal Representative of the Secretary-General to lend his good offices to the parties in ensuring the implementation of the Agreements on the Settlement of the Situation Relating to Afghanistan and in this context to investigate and report possible violations of any of the provisions of the Agreements. When UNGOMAP's mandate ended, the Personal Representative remained in the country and served as Coordinator of the United Nations Office for the Coordination of Humanitarian Assistance to Afghanistan. In December 1994, the Secretary-General discontinued the function of the Personal Representative, creating in its place the Office of the Secretary-General in Afghanistan
Location:	Afghanistan and Pakistan
Headquarters:	Kabul and Islamabad
Duration:	15 May 1988–15 March 1990
Strength:	Maximum (May 1988): 50 military observers UNGOMAP comprised officers temporarily detached from existing operations (UNTSO, UNDOF, UNIFIL) At withdrawal (March 1990): 35 military observers
Fatalities:	None
Financing:	Method of financing: Appropriations from the regular budget of the United Nations Expenditures: From inception until end of mission: $14,029,010

**Representative of the Secretary-General
on the Settlement of the Situation
Relating to Afghanistan:**

Diego Cordovez (Ecuador)	April 1988–January 1990

**Personal Representative of the Secretary-General
in Afghanistan and Pakistan:**

Benon Sevan (Cyprus)	May 1989–August 1992*

[*When UNGOMAP's mandate ended, the Personal Representative served as head of the Office of the Secretary-General in Afghanistan and Pakistan, established on 15 March 1990, as well as Coordinator of the United Nations Office for the Coordination of Humanitarian Assistance to Afghanistan. From August 1992 until December 1994, Mr. Sotirios Mousouris (Greece) served as Personal Representative. In December 1994, the Secretary-General discontinued the function of the Personal Representative, creating in its place the Office of the Secretary-General in Afghanistan.
Mr. Mahmoud Mestiri (Tunisia) served as head of the Special Mission to Afghanistan from February 1994 until May 1996.]

Deputy Representative:	Major-General Rauli Helminen (Finland)	April 1988–May 1989
	Colonel Heikki Happonen (Finland)	May 1989–March 1990
Contributors:	Austria, Canada, Denmark, Fiji, Finland, Ghana, Ireland, Nepal, Poland, Sweden	
Voluntary contribution:	Japan Financial contribution	

United Nations Iran–Iraq Observer Group (UNIIMOG)

Authorization:	Security Council resolutions:

598 (1987) of 20 July 1987
619 (1988) of 9 August 1988
631 (1989) of 8 February 1989
642 (1989) of 29 September 1989
651 (1990) of 29 March 1990
671 (1990) of 27 September 1990
676 (1990) of 28 November 1990
685 (1991) of 31 January 1991

Function: Established to verify, confirm and supervise the cease-fire and the withdrawal of all forces to the internationally recognized boundaries, pending a comprehensive settlement. UNIIMOG was terminated after Iran and Iraq had withdrawn fully their forces to the internationally recognized boundaries. Small civilian offices were established in Tehran and Baghdad to implement the remaining tasks which were essentially political. By the end of 1992, those offices were phased out

Location: Iran and Iraq

Headquarters: Tehran and Baghdad

Duration: 20 August 1988– 28 February 1991

Strength: Strength: 400 military personnel
Strength at withdrawal: 114 (28 February 1991)

Fatalities: 1 military personnel

Financing: Method of financing: Assessments in respect of a Special Account
Operating costs: From inception of mission to 28 February 1991: $177,895,000 net

**Personal Representative
of the Secretary-General:** Jan K. Eliasson (Sweden) September 1988–February 1991

**Chief Military
Observers:** Major-General Slavko Jovic (Yugoslavia) August 1988–November 1990
Brigadier-General S. Anam Khan
 (Bangladesh) (Acting) November 1990–February 1991

Contributors of military observers:

Argentina	August 1988–December 1990
Australia	August 1988–December 1990
Austria	August 1988–February 1991
Bangladesh	August 1988–February 1991
Canada	August 1988–February 1991
Denmark	August 1988–February 1991
Finland	August 1988–February 1991
Ghana	August 1988–December 1990
Hungary	August 1988–February 1991
India	August 1988–February 1991
Indonesia	August 1988–December 1990
Ireland	August 1988–February 1991
Italy	August 1988–February 1991
Kenya	August 1988–December 1990
Malaysia	August 1988–February 1991
New Zealand	August 1988–February 1991
Nigeria	August 1988–December 1990
Norway	August 1988–February 1991
Peru	September 1988–October 1989

(continued)

Poland	August 1988–February 1991
Senegal	August 1988–December 1990
Sweden	August 1988–February 1991
Turkey	August 1988–February 1991
Uruguay	September 1988–February 1991
Yugoslavia	August 1988–February 1991
Zambia	August 1988–February 1991

Other contributions:

Austria	December 1988–February 1991	Medical section
Canada	August–December 1988	Signals unit
Ireland	October 1988–February 1991	Military police unit
New Zealand	October 1988–December 1991	Air unit

Voluntary contributions:

Italy	Airlift: equipment
Japan	Financial
Kuwait	Trucks, vehicle workshop equipment, office, electrical, and communications supplies
Morocco	Financial
New Zealand	Contribution towards preparing and positioning one aircraft in the mission area
Republic of Korea	Forklifts, office equipment
Switzerland	One fixed-wing aircraft
Soviet Union	Airlift: Canadian military personnel

United Nations Iraq-Kuwait Observation Mission (UNIKOM)

Authorization:	Security Council resolutions:
	687 (1991) of 3 April 1991 689 (1991) of 9 April 1991 806 (1993) of 5 February 1993
Function:	Established following the withdrawal of Iraq's forces from the territory of Kuwait. UNIKOM, set up initially as an unarmed observation mission, was to monitor a demilitarized zone (DMZ) along the boundary between Iraq and Kuwait and the Khawr 'Abd Allah waterway, to deter violations of the boundary, and to observe any hostile action mounted from the territory of one State against the other. In February 1993, following a series of incidents on the border, the Security Council decided to increase UNIKOM's strength and to extend its terms of reference to include the capacity to take physical action to prevent violations of the DMZ and of the newly demarcated boundary between Iraq and Kuwait
Location:	Iraq/Kuwait
Headquarters:	Umm Qasr, Iraq
Duration:	9 April 1991 to date
Strength:	Initially authorized: 300 military observers, supported by international and local civilian staff Subsequent authorization: 3,645 all ranks, including 300 military observers, supported by international and local civilian staff Maximum (28 February 1995): 1,187 all ranks, including 254 military observers At 31 March 1996: 1,179, including 244 military observers; there were also approximately 70 international and 140 local civilian personnel
Fatalities:	4 military personnel 1 military observer <u>1</u> international United Nations staff 6 total (as at 30 April 1996)
Financing:	Method of financing: Assessments in respect of a Special Account. Since 1 November 1993, two thirds of the operation's costs are borne by Kuwait. The remainder is met by assessed contributions of Member States Estimated expenditures: From inception of mission to 30 June 1996: $303,363,160 net

Chief Military Observers:	Major-General Günther Greindl (Austria)	April 1991–July 1992
	Major-General Timothy K. Dibuama (Ghana)	July 1992–August 1993
	Brigadier-General Vigar Aabrek (Norway) (Acting)	August–December 1993
	Major-General Krishna Narayan Singh Thapa (Nepal)	December 1993–January 1994*

*In January 1994, General Thapa's appointment was changed to that of the Force Commander to reflect the addition of mechanized infantry battalion

Force Commanders:	Major-General Krishna Narayan Singh Thapa (Nepal)	January 1994–December 1995
	Major-General Gian Giuseppe Santillo (Italy)	December 1995 to date

Contributors	**Duration**	**Contribution**
Argentina	April 1991 to date	military observers
	March 1993 to date	engineer unit
Austria	April 1991 to date	military observers
	November 1993–February 1995	medical team
	January 1996 to date	logistics

(continued)

Bangladesh	April 1991 to date	military observers
	November 1993 to date	troops
	December 1993–February 1995	medical team
	October 1995 to date	helicopter unit
Canada	April 1991 to date	military observers
	April 1991–March 1993	engineer unit
Chile	April 1991–October 1992	helicopter unit
China	April 1991 to date	military observers
Denmark	April 1991 to date	military observers
	April 1991–January 1996	logistics
Fiji	April 1991 to date	military observers
Finland	April 1991 to date	military observers
France	April 1991 to date	military observers
Germany	December 1995 to date	medical unit (civilian)
Ghana	April 1991 to date	military observers
Greece	April 1991 to date	military observers
Hungary	April 1991 to date	military observers
India	April 1991 to date	military observers
Indonesia	April 1991 to date	military observers
Ireland	April 1991 to date	military observers
Italy	April 1991 to date	military observers
Kenya	April 1991 to date	military observers
Malaysia	April 1991 to date	military observers
Nigeria	April 1991 to date	military observers
Norway	April 1991–June 1994	military observers
	April 1991–December 1993	medical unit
Pakistan	April 1991 to date	military observers
Poland	April 1991 to date	military observers
Romania	April 1991 to date	military observers
Russian Federation (Soviet Union before 24 December 1991)	April 1991 to date	military observers
Senegal	May 1991 to date	military observers
Singapore	April 1991 to date	military observers
Sweden	April 1991 to date	military observers
	April–November 1991	logistics
Switzerland	April 1991–December 1994	fixed wing unit
Thailand	April 1991 to date	military observers
Turkey	May 1991 to date	military observers
United Kingdom	April 1991 to date	military observers
United States	April 1991 to date	military observers
Uruguay	April 1991 to date	military observers
Venezuela	April 1991 to date	military observers

[In addition, during the setting-up phase (April–June 1991), UNIKOM included five infantry companies, drawn from UNFICYP and UNIFIL. Those troops were provided by Austria, Denmark, Fiji, Ghana and Nepal. There was also a logistic company from Sweden.]

Voluntary contributions:

Kuwait (two thirds of costs of UNIKOM effective 1 November 1993; vehicles, engineering equipment); Sweden (airlift at the beginning stage of the operation); Switzerland (until December 1994: two fixed-wing aircraft)

Index

A

Aabrek, Vigar, 687
Abaza, Hasan, 596, 606
Abdic, Fikret, 533, 535, 551-552, 559
Abdoh, Djalal, 645
Abidjan, 246
Abin, Rais, 63
Abi-Saab, Georges, 507
Abkhazia. See Georgia situation
Aboo Bakar, Aboo Samah, 317
Abuja, 391-392
Abu Rudais, 67
Abu Suweir, 43
Accra, 387-389, 396
Adabiya, 65
Addis Ababa, 246, 296, 299-300, 306
Aden Protectorate, 121
Adoula, Cyrille, 187-188, 190, 192-195, 198-199
Adriatic Sea, 494; embargo, 540
Afghanistan, 591, 593-594, 596, 600-601, 659-666. See also Pakistan; UNGOMAP; airspace, 664; armed forces, 663; borders: with Pakistan, 664; with USSR, 663; as contributor, 116; Coordinator of the UN Office for the Coordination of Humanitarian Assistance to Afghanistan (UNOCHA), 666; Geneva Accords on the Settlement of the Situation Relating to Afghanistan (1988), 661-663, 666; Agreement on the Voluntary Return of Refugees, 664; Memorandum of Understanding, 662, 664; violations, 662-664; humanitarian assistance, 666; northern, 598; Office of the Secretary-General in Afghanistan and Pakistan (OSGAP), 666; headquarters, 666; Military Advisory Unit, 666; President, 592; resistance (mujahideen), 661; UN Special Mission to Afghanistan, 666; Head, 666; withdrawal of Soviet troops, 661-664
Afgoye, 314
Afmadu, 310
Africa, 171-403. See also Angola; Aouzou Strip; Congo question; Liberia; MINURSO; Mozambique; Namibia; ONUC; ONUMOZ; Organization of African Unity (OAU); Rwanda; Somalia; South Africa; Uganda; UNAMIR; UNASOG; UNAVEM; UNOMIL; UNOMUR; UNOSOM; UNTAG; Western Sahara
Agency for International Development, 636
Agenda for Peace, 5
Ahmed, Rafeeuddin, 450
Ahrens, Geert, 521
Ahtisaari, Martti, 205-206, 227
Ahwaz, 673
Aidid, Mohamed Farah, 287-293, 300, 305-306, 309-311, 313
Ajello, Aldo, 337, 361, 366, 599
Akashi, Yasushi, 455, 480, 489
Akiya bridge, 88-89, 101
Akosombo, 385
Al-Abdaly, 685

Alam, Mujahid, 372
Al-Badr, Imam Mohammed, 121-122
Albania, 564; as contributor, 586
Albanian language, 565
Albertville, 186, 192
Alejandre Sintes, Luis, 443
Algeria, 269, 272, 277, 282; as contributor, 235, 254, 265, 452, 481, 500, 618, 634
Algiers, 269, 276
Al Hijazi, Mohamed Mahmud, 403
Al Hudaydah, 126
Ali Mahdi, Mohamed, 287-290, 306, 309-311, 313
Almaty, 601
Almeling, Jürgen G.H., 372
Al-Rodan, Eid Kamal, 489
Alvor, 233
Amega, Atsu-Koffi, 358
Amman, 30, 120
Amritsar, 139
Andrada, 263
Andulo, 264
Angle, H.H., 136, 142
Angola, 3, 7, 189, 205, 207-208, 217-218, 225, 231-265. See also UNAVEM; amnesty, 263; armed forces, 219; Angolan Armed Forces (FAA), 238-239, 242-243, 248, 252, 256, 259-261, 263-264; FLEC Renovada, 243; Forças Armadas de Libertação de Angola (FALA), 238, 242-243; Forças Armadas Populares de Libertação de Angola (FAPLA), 238, 242; Frente de Libertação do Enclave de Cabinda/Forças Armadas de Cabinda (FLEC/FAC), 243; arms transfers, 246, 258; borders: with Zaire, 264; with Zambia, 235, 264; cease-fires, 238-240, 245-249, 251-253, 255-258, 261, 263; civil war, 246, 256; Cuban troops withdrawal, 208; Brazzaville Protocol (1989), 207, 218; tripartite agreement, 208; detained persons, 238, 242-243, 261; displaced persons, 253, 256, 264; elections, 238-240, 243-244, 249, 255-256; Electoral Law, 244; National Electoral Council (NEC), 243-244; results, 244, 247-248; food supply, 240-242, 253-254, 257-258, 263-264; freedom of movement, 256, 263-264; Frente Nacional de Libertação de Angola (FNLA), 233; Government of Unity and National Reconciliation, 263; humanitarian assistance, 240, 242, 246-250, 253-260, 264-265; first Round-Table Conference of donors, 264; human rights, 260-261, 263; independence, 233, 256; landmines, 243, 256, 261, 264; Central Mine Action Training School, 264; mine clearance, 257-259, 261, 264; Minister for External Relations, 239, 243, 252; missing persons, 243; Movimiento Popular de Libertação de Angola (MPLA), 233, 243-244; National Assembly, 239, 245, 263; national reconciliation, 248-252, 255-256, 258, 264; north, 218; observer States, 238, 247-252, 255, 259, 261; peace process: Lusaka peace talks, 248-250; *Lusaka Protocol*, 251-253, 255-256, 258-261; Joint Commission, 255-256; Peace Accords for Angola (Bicesse Accords), 238-240, 242-249, 251, 255;

F

G

J

K

P

PAHO, 634-635

Pailin, 467

Pakistan, 133-143, 183, 525, 592-596, 601, 659-666. See also Afghanistan; India-Pakistan; UNCIP; UNGOMAP; UNIPOM; UNMOGIP; airspace, 664; borders: with Afghanistan, 664; as contributor, 125, 211, 213-214, 265, 282-283, 292-293, 295, 314, 317, 337, 374, 398, 452, 473, 481, 562, 586, 633-634, 644, 646-647, 683, 687; Minister for Foreign Affairs, 134; President, 139, 142

Pakrac, 550

Pale, 507, 529, 531, 537, 557

Palestine, 13, 17, 19-20, 75. See also Middle East; PLO; UNRWA; armed forces, 92-93, 106; Liberation Army, 27; Palestinian Authority, 14; Palestinian Council, 14; Palestinian people, 14; Palestinians, 13, 24, 90, 93; commandos, 23-24, 27, 54; fedayeen, 24, 35; police, 53; refugees, 22, 27, 51; *camps*, 31; *return*, 22; territorial partition, 13; Truce Commission, 13, 17, 19-21; UN Mediator for Palestine, 13, 358; UN Palestine Commission, 13

Palestine Liberation Organization. See PLO

Palme, Olof, 669

Panama, 409, 625, 651; as contributor, 61-62, 65, 67, 214

Pan American Sanitary Bureau, 652

Paphos, 154, 159

Paraguay, 657

Paris, 100, 302, 560

Parker, James, 143

Pastukhov, Boris, 583

Pataya, 452

Pavlovic, Branko, 125

Peace-building, 5, 8, 635

Peace enforcement. See Enforcement action; Peace-keeping operations, enforcement power

Peace-keeping operations, 3-8, 35, 40, 42, 55, 84, 101, 112; blue berets, 19, 44; blue helmets, 44; command and control, 8-9, 42-44, 60, 75, 137, 154, 177, 294, 452, 541-545, 556, 558, 564-565, 575; consent of parties, 7, 40-41, 54-55, 540, 563; daily subsistence allowance, 19; databases, 7-8; deployment, 5-6, 8; disciplinary action, 43; enforcement power, 19; UNIFIL, 88; UNPROFOR, 515, 520, 524, 528, 536, 563; UNTAES, 554-555; equipment, 3; financing, 4, 7; impartiality, 60; mandates, 3, 7; national uniforms, 19, 44; non-intervention in internal affairs, 84; observer operations, 4; personnel, 3-4. See also Relief personnel; civilian, 3-5; military, 3-4; police, 4; security, 3, 5-8; preventive operation, 538-541; self-defence: ONUC, 178, 180-181; UNAMIR, 350; UNAVEM III, 256; UNFICYP, 154, 156; UNPROFOR, 518, 523, 526, 528-529, 531, 557; statistics, 3-4; UN armband, 19; unarmed status, 19, 30-31; weapons, 6, 60, 74, 101-102

Peacemaking, 5

Pearson, Lester, 35-36, 40

Pédanou, Macaire, 343

Pedauye, Antonio, 489, 560, 562

Pellnäs, Bo, 492

Pérez de Cuéllar, Javier, 153, 203, 239, 270, 288, 411, 420, 425, 450, 455, 488, 613-614, 661, 669

Persian Gulf, 669, 671

Peru, 409; as contributor, 61-62, 65, 67, 74-77, 116, 214, 672

Peruca Dam, 514

Peshawar, 664, 666

Pessolano, Alfonso, 142

Petit Goâve, 631

Petrinja, 550

Philippines, 449-450; as contributor, 318, 481, 634

Phnom Penh, 459, 464, 468, 472-473, 479

Pienaar, Louis, 209

Pink zones. See Croatia

Píriz-Ballón, Ramiro, 594, 596, 599, 605-606

Pitsunda, 584

Plateel, Peter Johannis, 644

Plaza Lasso, Galo, 115, 153

Pleso, 550

PLO, 14, 31, 66, 70, 75, 83, 88-90, 94-97, 99-101. See also Palestine; armed elements, 95, 99; Chairman, 88, 90, 99, 101; commando raids, 83; creation, 54; El Fatah, 54; headquarters, 31; recognition by Israel, 14; troops, 85, 91, 94

Ploce, 554

Poland, 74-76, 78; as contributor, 61-63, 65-67, 70, 74-78, 80, 86-87, 211, 214, 265, 282-283, 374, 452, 473, 481, 500, 562, 586, 606, 663, 666, 672, 678, 683, 687; diplomatic relations, 80

Pol Pot, 449

Port-au-Prince, 614-615, 618-620, 622, 624, 626-633, 636

Port-de-Paix, 627

Port-Francqui, 183, 186

Port Fuad, 26, 50-51

Port Said, 36, 41, 43-45, 50-51

Portugal, 233, 238, 247, 255, 321-323, 328; as contributor, 116, 211, 265, 337, 492, 500

Posavina, 533

Pospisil, P.P., 143

Pouliot, Neil, 627, 634

Prem Chand, Dewan, 153, 210, 214

Préval, René, 632-633

Prevlaka peninsula, 489, 540-541, 554-556. See also Croatia; UNMOP; demilitarization, 491, 514-515, 545, 549, 553, 555-556

Prey Veng, 471

Privileges and immunities, 19, 42, 60, 63, 675

Provost Marshal, 43

Psou river, 575

Pulley, Gregg, 618, 634

Pyanj river, 591, 596-597, 600, 602, 606

Q

Qantara, 26, 65, 67

Qiryat Shemona, 95-96, 100

Quesada Gómez, Agustín, 415, 420-421

Quetta, 664

Quiah, Oscar, 388, 392

Quibaxe, 257

Quinn, J.J., 153

Quneitra, 74, 77; communication relay station, 77; demilitarization, 74; Quneitra-Damascus road, 30, 73

R

Rabah, 65, 67

Rabat, 276

Rabbani, Burhanuddin, 592

U

V

W

Y

Z